CAREERS
2010
6th edition

Devon
County Council

Careers 2010
This sixth edition published in 2009 by Trotman Education,
an imprint of Crimson Publishing, Westminster House, Kew
Road, Richmond, Surrey TW9 2ND.

© Trotman Education 2009

Contributors: Monica Brand, Jennifer Dodd, Rhea Finney,
Ellen Grace, Nicola Houghton, Charlotte Jardine, Cerys Owen,
Elizabeth Rafii-Tabar, Alison Yates and Camilla Zajac.

ISBN: 978–1–906041–47–2

British Library Cataloguing in Publications Data
A catalogue record for this book is available from the British Library

Typeset by RefineCatch Limited, Bungay, Suffolk

Printed and bound in the UK by Ashford Colour Press, Gosport, Hants

CONTENTS

WELCOME TO CAREERS 2010

When you first start choosing your future career it can seem a daunting and complicated process. There are so many different jobs with new ones emerging all the time; how do you begin to search for something that would suit you?

Finding all the information you need to help with your career choices can therefore be difficult – and when you find it, it is not always easy to understand.

We all have different values, interests and ambitions so Careers 2010 lists all of the most important aspects for young people searching for a future career to help make the process of choosing a career path much easier.

Within Careers 2010 you will find brief but detailed entries on hundreds of different jobs, each of which includes entry requirements, advantages and disadvantages, working conditions, your future prospects, a description of the type of person suited to the area of work and a money guide. In addition, there are case studies describing how someone got to where they are today and their personal feelings about their job.

Although you can go straight to the pages on the jobs you're already interested in, to get the most from using Careers 2010 we suggest you first read the opening section, as this will explain more about the content and how to use the publication.

We are confident that Careers 2010 offers a new approach, is interesting and is easy to use. More importantly, however, it will help you to find the answers to the questions that matter to you:

- Which careers will suit me?
- What qualifications will I need?
- How much can I hope to earn?
- What's the future likely to hold?
- Will the studying be worthwhile?

Take a look at the sample job profile overleaf to see how you can use this book to find out exactly what you need to know.

We hope you enjoy using Careers 2010 and wish you all the best with your future career choices.

The Trotman team.

An example job profile

All of the job profiles in Careers 2010 are laid out in the same style with the same sections. This is an example job profile showing you what each section refers to and the information they contain.

Heading/job title

This refers to the title of the job you will find on the page. Some job profiles are very closely linked so they have been merged together so the title will have each job title that is going to be covered in the profile.

What the work involves

These opening bullet points will give you a quick overview of what the job is like.

The type of person suited to this work

Within this category you will find lots of information to help you match your own strengths, weaknesses, likes and dislikes to the individual job.

Sadly it is very common for someone to start a job not knowing everything they'll be expected to do. They may then be confronted with something they find either too hard or not enjoyable; this might mean leaving a job they studied a long time for. To make sure this doesn't happen to you, think carefully about the information provided here and whether it matches your skills, experience and personality.

Working conditions

This section explains where you can expect to work, whether it's outside or inside, in an office or travelling around the country, for the career that interests you. It also tells you the typical working hours you can expect and whether you will be expected to work at weekends, evenings and on shifts. This will give you a good idea of the day to day life you can expect on the job.

Future prospects

This section shows you where you could progress to within a certain career. This may be in terms of climbing the career ladder, or branching into new territory as a career

sector develops and changes. Of course, no one can predict the future of any career sector completely but important changes to the economy, reductions and increases in labour force as well as technological advances will have an impact upon how a sector develops. This information will give you a balanced view of where your future could take you in any given career.

Advantages/disadvantages

It's important that, when choosing a career, you have a well-rounded and honest view of what the work will be like. This section gives you some of the most common good and bad points about a job so that you can decide if a job matches up to your expectations.

REGENERATION MANAGER / ECONOMIC DEVELOPMENT OFFICER

What the work involves

- Many communities in Britain face economic, social or physical disadvantages, with regeneration managers aiming to improve these living environments.

- Areas targeted are dilapidated residential areas where local industries have closed down, areas of low income and high unemployment, and areas with poor access to healthcare and education.

- The specialist areas open to people following this vocation include economic development, planning, surveying, and housing.

- The extent of involvement ranges from the presentation of an idea, to ensuring that the project is completed on time and on budget; the generation of financial support and planning permission; and the gaining of support from local communities.

The type of person

It is necessary to have an interest in the ways in which communities and living environments can be improved when deciding upon whether to become a regeneration manager. Due to this profession involving the implementation or regulation with a variety of people, you will need good communication skills and should be able to influence people towards contributing in a positive way. Regeneration managers often need to be strict with budgets and able to solve problems that may arise; both of which need a strong will and an ability to deliver results in a set amount of time.

Working conditions

Generally, working hours are typical of those for an office job, with the amount of hours worked usually being around 37 a week, with the occasional need to attend residency meeting during the evening or at weekends. Employment with local councils tends to be employee focused, with most offering part-time or job-sharing contracts, alongside flexitime schemes.

Although mostly based in an office, regeneration managers will need to travel to sites that are undergoing the regeneration process in order to meet with residents, clients and agencies.

Future prospects

The government is currently committed to improving community areas through regeneration schemes, making this a very positive vocation to get involved with; especially whilst there is a current shortage of people who have the combination of skills required for this job.

Opportunities are available within the following employers: local authorities and government agencies, regional development agencies and English Partnerships, the government's national regeneration agency. There are also employment possibilities with private consultancies, housing associations and property developers.

Advantages/disadvantages

Both the public and private sector are becoming involved in regeneration projects, with opportunities opening up in senior management roles through the gaining of experience.

This job may become extremely challenging when convincing people that regeneration is positive, especially when they have lived there for a certain amount of years.

Qualifications and courses

All those who wish to enter this profession will require a degree and possibly experience within regeneration. Recommended subjects of relevance are urban studies, housing, and planning, with related subjects including geography, social studies and economics; in addition to these, the Diploma in environmental and land-based studies may of be benefit. In order to get accepted onto one of these degree courses, applicants would usually need at least two A levels/three H grades plus five GCSEs/S grades (A*-C/1-3), including English and maths.

Due to it often being compulsory to hold a degree in order to enter this profession, postgraduate study may be of benefit, with there being a wide range of postgraduate certificates, diplomas and Masters degrees that relate to regeneration.

Prospective entrants to this vocational should aim to gain some relevant work experience or voluntary environmental work in order to improve career and employment prospects.

For those wishing to move into regeneration, areas such as housing, planning, urban design, or surveying are recognised as being of relevance. Alongside this, it is recommended that learning about government policy, the main sources of funding and the planning process in relation to regeneration to strengthen applications.

Money guide

To begin, regeneration managers can expect a salary in the region of £22,000 a year, with this steadily increasing to £40,000 through the gaining of experience. Through a progression to senior management, regeneration managers have the ability to earn around £60,000 a year, depending on their level of responsibility.

Due to there being job opportunities in both the public and private sector, salaries vary widely; it is generally accepted that the private sector offers higher earning possibilities.

Related opportunities

- Chartered Surveyor
- Economic Development Officer
- Local Government Community Development Officer
- Project Manager
- Town Planner

Further information

British Urban Regeneration Association (BURA)
4th Floor, 63-66 Hatton Garden, London EC1N 8LE
Tel: 020 7539 4030
Website: www.bura.org.uk

English Partnerships, Corporate Headquarters
110 Buckingham Palace Road, London SW1 9SA
Tel: 0207 881 1600
Website: www.englishpartnerships.co.uk

Improvement and Development Agency for Local Government
Layden House, 76-86 Turnmill Street, London EC1M 5LG
Tel: 020 7296 6600
Websites: www.idea.gov.uk and www.lgtalent.com

ADMINISTRATION, BUSINESS, OFFICE AND FINANCIAL SERVICES

CRCI: QOF

Entry level

This number corresponds to the Careers 2010 level of qualification you need to start your career in a particular job. For more information about what the entry levels in Careers 2010 mean, see the next column.

Qualifications and courses

This section looks in detail at the most common ways to enter a profession and the qualifications and courses you will need to take. If there are different qualifications available depending on whether you live in England, Scotland, Wales or Northern Ireland, these variations will be listed here too.

As qualifications and courses change often, we would recommend that you use the Further information section addresses to get more advice on which qualifications you will need to give yourself the best chance of entering your chosen careers.

Money guide

For some people one of the most important things they'll consider before undertaking a new course, qualification or a career is 'how much can I expect to earn?'

To help you we have included:

■ the most up-to-date information about pay scales

■ where possible, what you can expect at entry, intermediate and senior levels

■ any regional differences.

Related opportunities

This section gives jobs that are similar in style and the skills they require to the job profile you are looking at. This is to give you lots of options to choose from if you haven't decided which career interests you the most.

You might not have considered or heard of some of these before, so it will help you to broaden out your ideas further.

Further information

Listed here are the contact details of organisations, helplines, websites and other ways to help you continue your research into your chosen job areas.

CLCI/CRCI

CLCI/CRCI (Careers Library Classification Index/ Connexions Resource Centre Index)

These codes show you where you will be able to find additional information about the job title within school, college, university or community-based careers information areas.

The CRCI index has now completely replaced the CLCI index but we have included both to make it easy for you to search for more information about any job profile listed in this book.

Qualifications: what do the entry levels in Careers 2010 mean?

You will see that every job profile in this book has an entry level number assigned to it. This refers to the lowest qualification level that you need to achieve in order to enter the profession. In this book, the levels range from 1 to 8 and each job profile entry level number listed is the lowest one you need in order to gain access to a particular career.

The number shown indicates the level of qualification you are most likely to need:

■ to enter the job and

■ to enter the job and to train while working.

The Qualifications grid

Opposite is a grid which shows what the levels in *Careers 2010* refer to in terms of qualifications that you can take in England, Wales, Northern Ireland and Scotland.

The information from three qualifications frameworks has been incorporated into this table; the National Qualifications Framework (NQF), The Scottish Credit and Qualifications Framework (SCQF) and The Framework for Higher Education Qualifications (FHEQ).

Because the frameworks all have their own levels please be aware that this grid cannot accommodate subtle differences between the frameworks and you should refer directly to the websites below for more information.

The National Qualifications Framework (NQF)

The NQF includes academic and vocational qualifications offered in England, Wales and Northern Ireland up to and including further education level. There are nine levels – from Entry Level up to Level 8.

The Framework for Higher Education Qualifications (FHEQ)

The FHEQ includes higher education qualifications from Certificates of Higher Education through to Doctoral degrees. It applies to qualifications offered in England, Wales and Northern Ireland and includes five levels, each indicated by a letter corresponding with the initial of the main qualification offered at that level.

The Scottish Credit and Qualifications Framework (SCQF)

The SCQF is a 12-level framework including vocational, occupational and academic qualifications offered in Scotland. It covers all levels including further and higher education, from Access through to Doctoral degrees.

Each framework is under continuous review, but information in this book was correct at the time of writing.

For further details and the most up-to date information, refer to the following websites:

NQF: www.qca.org.uk/qualifications
www.qca.org.uk/openquals www.accac.org.uk
www.ccea.org.uk

FHEQ: www.qaa.ac.uk/ academicinfrastructure/fheq

SCQF: www.scqf.org.uk

Key:

Qualifications that are available in England, Wales, Northern Ireland and Scotland.

Qualifications that are available in England, Wales and Northern Ireland.

Qualifications that are available in Scotland

Careers 2010 Level	Rough equivalent framework level	General and academic qualifications	Vocational and occupational qualifications
Entry level	NQF Entry Level Skills for Life at entry level SCQF Access Levels 1–3	**Entry Level Certificate** **SQA Access 1, 2 and 3** **Foundation Standard Grade** **National Certificate**	**National Progression Award (start at SCQF level 2)**
1	NQF Level 1 SCQF Level 4	*GCSE grade D–G* *14–19 Foundation Diploma* *Skills for Life* *Key Skills level 1* **Intermediate 1 General Standard Grade**	NVQ/SVQ Level 1 *BTEC Introductory Certificate/ Diploma* *Level 1Certificate* *OCR Nationals* **National Progression Award**
2	NQF Level 3 SCQF Level 5	*GCSE grade A*–C* *14–19 Higher Diploma* *Skills for Life* *Key Skills level 2* **Intermediate 2** **Credit Standard Grade**	NVQ/SVQ Level 2 *Level 2 Certificate/Diploma* *BTEC First Certificate/Diploma* *Apprenticeship* *BTEC Nationals* *OCR Nationals* **Skillseekers National Progression Award**
3	NQF Level 3 SCQF Level 6	*A level* *Key Skills level 3* *14–19 Advanced Diploma* *Advanced Extension Awards (after June 2009 these will be available in Mathematics only)* *Extended Project* *International Baccalaureate* **Scottish Higher**	NVQ/SVQ Level 3 *A levels in applied subjects* *Level 3 Certificate/Diploma* *BTEC National Award/Certificate/ Diploma* *Advanced Apprenticeship (England)* *BTEC Nationals* *OCR Nationals* **Modern Apprenticeship (Scotland, Wales, Ireland)** **Professional Development Award**
4	NQF Level 4 FHEQ Level C SCQF Level 7	Certificate of Higher Education *Key Skills level 4* **Scottish Advanced Higher** **Higher National Certificate**	NVQs*/SVQ Level 3 *Level 4 Certificate/Diploma* *BTEC Professional Diplomas, Certificates and Awards* **Professional Development Award**
5	NQF Level 5 FHEQ Level I SCQF Levels 8 and 9	Bachelor's degree Diploma of Higher Education *Diploma of Further Education* *Foundation Degree* *Higher National Diploma*	NVQ/SVQ Level 4* Higher National Certificate/Diploma (HNC/HND) *BTEC Professional Diplomas/ Certificates/Awards* *National Diploma in Professional Production Skills* *Level 5 Certificate/Diploma* **Professional Development Award**
6	NQF Level 6 FHEQ Level H SCQF Level 10	Bachelor's degree with Honours Graduate Diploma Graduate Certificate	*NVQs** *Level 6 Certificate/Diploma* *BTEC Advanced Professional Diplomas/Certificates/ Awards* **Professional Development Award**
7	NQF Level 7 FHEQ Level M SCQF Level 11	Master's degree Postgraduate Diploma (PgDip) Postgraduate Certificate (PgCert) Integrated Degree *Diploma in Translation*	NVQ/SVQ Level 5* *Level 7 Diploma/Fellowship* *Level 7 Advanced Professional Certificate* *BTEC Advanced Professional Diplomas/Certificates/Awards* **Professional Development Award**
8	NQF Level 8 FHEQ Level D SCQF Level 12	Doctorate	Specialist awards and diplomas from professional bodies **Professional Development Award**

Notes

* NVQs, SVQs and a small number of related qualifications correspond with NQF Levels 4 and 5 following the original five-level NQF system. The NVQ/SVQ Level 4 corresponds roughly with NQF Levels 4–6 and the NVQ/SVQ Level 5 corresponds roughly with NQF Levels 7–8.

Job Families

The jobs in this book have been divided into job families to make it easy for you to go straight to the right section and find the job you are interested in. At the beginning of each job family section is an introduction to the career sector and a list of all the jobs that will appear in the section. You will also find information on other similar job families and where to find them in the book.

The job families have been grouped in the same way as Connexions group jobs together to make it really easy for you to find the right sector for you.

There are 19 job families in *Careers 2010* which are:

  Administration, Business, Office Work and Financial Services

 Building and Construction

 Catering and Hospitality

 Computers and IT

 Design, Arts and Crafts

 Education and Training

 Engineering, Manufacturing and Production

 Environment, Animals and Plants

 Healthcare

 Languages, Information and Culture

 Legal and Political Services

 Leisure, Sport and Tourism

  Marketing, Advertising, Media, Print and Publishing

 Performing Arts

 Personal and Other Services including Hair and Beauty

 Retail, Sales and Customer Services

 Science, Mathematics and Statistics

 Security and Armed Forces

 Social Work and Counselling Services

 Transport and Logistics

What do the icons mean?

The icons used in this book are the same as those used in the CRCI (Connexions Resources Centre Index) and they will appear at the beginning of each section to make it easy and clear to see exactly which job families are being covered.

Administration, Business, Office Work and Financial Services

To work in this sector you often need to have a great head for numbers and be very good at managing your time effectively. The variety of jobs in this family is huge, so you could work in a large, busy office or you could work for yourself dealing with clients from a host of different professions. Many jobs require you to have an eye for detail as you could be compiling reports and advising organisations on how they could work more effectively or safely or organising other people's time and schedules. In all cases, you should be highly motivated and organised. If you enjoy this responsibility and like the idea of the challenge of keeping a business running like clockwork there are many jobs that would suit you in this sector.

For further information see *Careers Uncovered: E-Commerce* and *Real Life Guide: Business, Administration and Finance*, published by Trotman.

For a full list of jobs in this section turn to page 15.

Building and Construction

The jobs in this sector are very varied; some require a high level of personal fitness, while for others, a creative flair is essential. You may be interested in working on a construction site with a team of people and for this you would need to demonstrate excellent personal safety and be happy to work outside in all weathers. Alternatively, maybe your interest lies in buying and selling property and working in an office is more your sort of thing. All the jobs in the sector require someone with a great eye for detail who is very good at working with others.

If you would like to read further information about this industry and how to go about starting your career please see *Real Life Guide: Construction* and *Real Life Guide: Plumbing* both published by Trotman.

For a full list of jobs in this section turn to page 67.

Catering and Hospitality

Working in this sector, you will meet a wide variety of people and probably need to be a very strong team player. For some of the jobs, you need to be outgoing, confident and sociable and may end up working early mornings or late nights. For other jobs in this sector you need to be very meticulous and a real perfectionist when it comes to standards of cleanliness and tidiness. Workers in the sector thrive on providing an impeccable service and ensuring customers are completely satisfied and are given a wonderful experience whether that be in a restaurant, hotel or bar.

For further information about training for and starting your career in this industry see *Real Life Guide: Catering* and *Real Life Guide: Hospitality & Events Management*, published by Trotman.

For a full list of jobs in this section turn to page 139.

Computers and IT

This sector is still fairly new and so it is expanding all the time, creating new jobs for a whole range of people. You may have a mathematical brain or a real creative ability – or a bit of both! Essentially, you must be passionate about computers to consider working in this sector. You could be working directly with clients and customers, helping them to rectify problems with their computers or you could be researching and developing the latest console for the games market. In all cases you need to keep right up to date with the latest technologies and IT developments as well as people's tastes, interests and hobbies to enjoy working in this sector.

If you want more information about working in this sector see *Real Life Guide: Information & Communications Technology* and *Careers Uncovered: The Internet* both published by Trotman.

For a full list of jobs in this section turn to page 157.

Design, Arts and Crafts

The idea of turning your arts and crafts hobby into a career may be one you like the thought of. Jobs in this sector can involve working in any medium, from textiles to jewellery to metalwork or children's toys. Some jobs may involve you researching current styles and trends and creating your own designs whereas others will involve working to a set brief set out by your customer to create a bespoke product. You may find yourself working for a company but many people in this industry are self-employed working for a range of clients. This means you need to be very organised and have brilliant communication skills to ensure you can give your clients exactly what they want. People working in this industry are extremely passionate about their careers and have a real sense of perfectionism to produce a beautiful finished article.

If you would like more information about training for and getting started in a career in this field see, *Getting Into Art and Design Courses*, *Careers Uncovered: Design* and *Real Life Guide: Creative Industries*, all published by Trotman.

For a full list of jobs in this section turn to page 175.

Education and Training

To work in this sector you need to be motivated and enthusiastic about other people's learning, whether it's adults or children. There are jobs suitable for people with all levels of qualification, but whatever your entry level you will need to be interested in keeping up to date on the latest developments in education and will enjoy working with other people. If you chose to teach, the range of subjects available is huge so whatever your interest - languages, art, sciences, cooking, sports - you can become a teacher in that field. Jobs in this sector require a multitude of skills including: creativity, imagination, numerical skills, good communication and organisational skills and, in some cases, having a lot of patience!

If you would like more help with starting your career in education and training please see the *Careers Uncovered:*

Teaching and *Real Life Guide: Childcare*, all published by Trotman.

For a full list of jobs in this section turn to page 199.

Engineering, Manufacturing and Production

There are a number of highly-skilled jobs available in this job family and workers need to be creative and methodical and combine brilliant technical skill with spatial awareness. Engineers are very well qualified indeed so you should be willing to study hard for good qualifications. Jobs in this sector can take you into a range of different fields, from scientific research to car production to working out at sea; there's something for anyone who has an inquisitive mind and a high level of technical capability. Another attractive element of this industry is that you can work with an enormous variety of different materials. You may be interested in food production but equally your passion could lie in working with aircraft or marine manufacture. People in these professions share the ability to concentrate for long periods of time and work meticulously on a job to finish it to a high standard. Some will also be highly trained with specialist equipment which may sometimes be hazardous to use so a high level of personal safety awareness is vital.

For further information on working in this area see *Real Life Guide: Electrician*, *Real Life Guide: Engineering Technician*, *Real Life Guide: Manufacturing & Product Design* and *Real Life Guide: The Motor Industry*, all published by Trotman.

For a full list of jobs in this section turn to page 219.

Environment, Animals and Plants

Some people working in this sector spend a lot of their time outdoors. This means the jobs are perfect for those of you who don't want to spend every day behind a desk in an office, although this is not to say that you will not need to spend time writing reports and keeping a log of research findings or clients' information. Workers in this sector are passionate about animals or about caring for and maintaining the environment. You will sometimes work in unpredictable settings, especially if you are working outside or have close contact with animals. You should also have brilliant people skills especially if you find yourself responsible for the welfare of someone else's animal. You should be someone who is very observant and interested in the natural world, not just from a welfare point of view but also from an economic one; many jobs in this sector involve using the environment for financial gain but increasingly industry is interested in doing so responsibly.

If you would like more information about jobs in this sector see *Getting Into Veterinary School*, *Real Life Guide: Working Outdoors* and *Real Life Guide: Working with Animals & Wildlife*, all published by Trotman.

For a full list of jobs in this section turn to page 257.

Healthcare

If you are keen to pursue a career in healthcare you must be compassionate and enjoy either caring for people or deciding what treatment they should receive. There is such a wide variety of jobs available in this sector simply because you can specialise in absolutely any aspect of human healthcare. Maybe you're interested in working with athletes or perhaps working with children interests you more. You could be part of the rehabilitation process after an illness or injury or find yourself working as a mental health therapist. Many jobs require a lot of training and you can expect to work in some highly-pressurised and sometimes distressing situations. Workers in healthcare are extremely dedicated and enthusiastic about their careers, which rarely constitute a 9–5 job. You can expect every day to be different and you should relish the challenges working with people of all ages can bring.

For more information about training for and working in healthcare see *Careers Uncovered: Medicine*, *Careers Uncovered: Nursing and Midwifery*, *Careers Uncovered: Psychology*, *Getting Into Medical School*, *Getting Into Dental School*, *Getting Into Physiotherapy Courses*, *Getting Into Psychology Courses* and *Real Life Guide: Care*, all published by Trotman.

For a full list of jobs in this section turn to page 291.

Languages, Information and Culture

If you are really interested in history or perhaps would like to use another language as part of your career, a job in this sector could be right for you. The jobs in this family are quite varied in terms of whether you would work with other people or by yourself. You could find yourself working in a range of different places, from museums to antiques fairs to conferences as an interpreter. Some of the jobs in this family are more unusual and are perfect for those of you who want a fascinating job that allows you to indulge in your passion for historic artefacts and artwork or languages and foreign countries. To excel in this sector you should have an inquisitive mind, be meticulous in your work and enjoy carrying out research. If you are keen to work with languages you should also be willing to travel in order to improve your language and your knowledge of the culture and history.

For a full list of jobs in this section turn to page 347.

Legal and Political Services

Are you interested in justice and fairness for all? Do you relish the opportunity to speak out for what's right and enjoy the challenge of persuading others that everyone needs an equal voice? Maybe you find the law a fascinating subject and you feel you would enjoy a challenging career where the rewards are a good salary and a real sense of achievement when your hard work pays off. If so, a job in this sector could be what you are looking for. Workers in this sector are fiercely passionate about their careers and have more often than not, completed a lot of training and worked hard to establish themselves in this competitive field. You need to be driven and thrive on pressure and tight deadlines; this is a sector for someone who is ambitious and very talented at working tactfully with people.

For more information about training for this sector as well as where to begin job hunting, read *Careers Uncovered: Law* and *Getting Into Law School*, both published by Trotman.

For a full list of jobs in this section turn to page 363.

Leisure, Sport and Tourism

This sector relies on a motivated, up-beat and out-going workforce for its success. You will need to show that you can work very well with other people, providing them with an excellent service when they want to enjoy themselves on holiday or if they are keen to improve their fitness and sporting ability. If you are keen to work with professional sports players or become one yourself you should be very aware of how to keep the body fit while avoiding injury. It's also important that you can keep a level head as you will often be responsible for other people's welfare. You should be warm and friendly but also able to maintain a high level of professionalism at the same time. You should also demonstrate you have patience and tact with people of all ages as well and be clued up on health and safety regulations.

If you would like to read more about getting a job in this area see *Careers Uncovered: Sport and Fitness*, *Careers Uncovered: Travel Industry*, *Real Life Guide: Sport and Active Leisure* and *Real Life Guide: Travel & Tourism*, published by Trotman.

For a full list of jobs in this section turn to page 385.

Marketing, Advertising, Media, Print and Publishing

Do you consider yourself to be a great communicator? Are you interested in working in an exciting and often fast paced environment with passionate, driven and ambitious individuals? If so, a career in this industry could be right for you. People who work in this sector are exceptionally motivated and are willing to put in long hours often on low starting wages because of their love of the job. While you need to be good at preparing your work alone, people who work in this sector tend to be very good at working with others and build up strong professional relationships as part of their job. You should have a great sense of creativity and imagination and be good at putting your ideas on paper, but you will often also need strong business acumen as many of your decisions will be made from an economical point of view as well as a creative one.

If you think this is a career you would like to find out more about why not read: *Careers Uncovered: Journalism*, *Careers Uncovered: The Music Industry*, *Careers Uncovered: Media* and *Real Life Guide: Creative Industries*, published by Trotman.

For a full list of jobs in this section turn to page 405.

Performing Arts

This job family contains a wide range of exciting jobs for those of you who want to work in theatre, music, on screen or behind the scenes. People working in this sector do so because they are passionate and creative and love the arts. Jobs can be scarce, so you will need to demonstrate that you are willing to work very hard but the rewards of being part of a fantastic production can be huge. You won't necessarily be confined to working in one place as your job may take you on tour all over the world. There are also jobs available in this sector for those of you who are more technically minded - sound and lighting engineers also play a vital role in this industry as do people who have trained in fashion and textiles. Make up artists also play a major role in theatre, television and music production.

If you would like to know more about how you can enter the world of performing arts see *Careers Uncovered: The Music Industry, Careers Uncovered: Performing Arts* and *Real Life Guide: Creative Industries*, published by Trotman.

For a full list of jobs in this section turn to page 435.

Personal and Other Services including Hair and Beauty

This is a very wide job family and covers everything from hairdressing and beauty to cleaning to wedding consulting. You can enter this career sector with a host of different skills and qualifications. What all of the jobs have in common is that they provide a particular service that a customer has asked for so you need to be good at listening to others and giving customers exactly what they want – people in this sector have a brilliant way with people. You should also demonstrate creativity and strong practical and technical skill as many of the jobs in this family require you to use specialist equipment, and have knowledge of health and safety.

If this is a sector you would like to know more about, see *Real Life Guide: The Beauty Industry* and *Real Life Guide: Hairdressing*, published by Trotman.

For a full list of jobs in this section turn to page 457.

Retail, Sales and Customer Services

Jobs in this sector are suited to those of you who are very good at communicating with others and are interested in making your customers happy. Maybe you're interested in working with food and want to give your customers high quality, fresh produce. Your interest may lie in fashion retail and you could spend your time providing style advice. You should also be commercially minded and think about how your work relates to the success of the company you work for. Jobs in this sector also involve maintaining standards such as safety and quality to ensure guidelines are met, so a practical outlook can be useful.

For more information about a career in this sector read *Real Life Guide: Retail*, published by Trotman.

For a full list of jobs in this section turn to page 477.

Science, Mathematics and Statistics

Do you have a very mathematical brain? Are you logical in how you approach tasks? Maybe you are fascinated by scientific advances and would like to be involved in future discoveries? People who work in this sector can spend long periods of time carrying out meticulous research. You may find yourself working for a variety of employers, from the health service to a cosmetics company or even a charity. You should be willing to work on your own but also be happy to present your findings in reports to others. People in this sector are very highly skilled individuals who have often been through a lot of training, and possess a questioning and inquisitive mind.

For a full list of jobs in this section turn to page 503.

Security and Armed Forces

Working in the security and armed forces may give you many incredible experiences and opportunities not open to most people. You need to be an excellent team player and in some instances you may find yourself in a potentially dangerous situation. Working in this sector you can expect to spend your day absolutely anywhere! Some roles involve a lot of office work whereas others can involve spending a lot of your time on the road, or even at sea. If you're looking for a job that will be exhilarating but are able to remain calm and professional under pressure this sector could offer you a lot of opportunities.

If you would like to know more about working in this field, see *Real Life Guide: Armed Forces, Real Life Guide: The Police Service* and *Real Life Guide: The Fire Service*, published by Trotman.

For a full list of jobs in this section turn to page 537.

Social Work and Counselling Services

People who work in this sector are dedicated to caring and talking through people's problems and anxieties to improve their general well-being and their future prospects in life. The work requires a lot of patience, an open mind and a friendly and approachable personality. You could be helping people who are distressed and need help and guidance but equally you may be helping people who want to move on to the next stage in their careers or educational choices. Either way, you should be someone who enjoys helping people change their lives for the better. If you are interested in working in this field you need to show that you are compassionate and very good at communicating with people from all walks of life and of all ages. You should also be someone who can maintain a strong sense of professionalism as you could be in a position of trust and you must be very respectful of your clients' privacy.

If this is a career that interests you, you can find more information here: *Real Life Guide: Care*, published by Trotman.

For a full list of jobs in this section turn to page 567.

Transport and Logistics

The jobs in this sector are immensely varied because of the wide range of transport and communication links that exist today to keep our lives running. You could need a high level of technical knowledge in this sector especially for jobs such as a pilot or a train driver. But you could also be great at keeping attention to detail and maintaining schedules if logistics is more where your interest lies. Jobs in transport and logistics require very efficient and practical people to ensure that our infrastructure continues to run smoothly and safely. You may need to cope well under pressurised situations. As you will probably have contact with the general public you should be good with people, and have a calm, professional manner.

If this job family covers jobs that you would like to read about in more detail, see *Real Life Guide: Distribution & Logistics* and *Real Life Guide: Passenger Transport*, published by Trotman.

For a full list of jobs in this section turn to page 593.

Where to go for more help

Below is a brief explanation with some contact details of the main organisations that can help you find out more about the career you are interested in:

England
The Connexions Service
Designed to offer every young person the 'best start in life', the Connexions service is available across England for 13- to 19-year-olds and provides information, advice and guidance on all aspects that affect you. The range of issues covered includes careers, education, training and all life issues such as health, leisure and housing information. The service is managed locally and you should contact your local partnership to see if you can make an appointment to speak to a Connexions Personal Adviser.

For more information:
www.connexions.gov.uk

Connexions Direct
Offering a telephone support service and detailed website, Connexions Direct can help you with information and advice on issues such as your career and learning options, money, health, housing, and relationships with family and friends. It can also let you know about activities you can get involved in.

You can contact Connexions Direct on:
Freephone: 080 800 13 2 19
Text phone: 08000 968 336
Text Message: 07766 4 13 2 19
www.connexions-direct.com

Northern Ireland
If you want advice from a careers adviser you can attend one of the 35 JobCentres and Jobs and Benefits Offices throughout Northern Ireland. Here you will get information on all aspects of work, education and employment issues. Careers Advisers visit schools regularly and you should speak to your careers teacher to arrange a careers interview. If you have left school you should contact your local JobCentre to make an appointment to speak to a Careers Adviser. There are also 27 Careers Service Support Units spread throughout the region offering access to Careers Advisers and resources, and the Careers Service NI website is packed with information.

Tel: 028 9044 1781
www.careersserviceni.com

Scotland
Careers Scotland
Careers Scotland is available to both young people and adults looking for information about careers, education or employment options. If you want to meet a trained adviser you can either visit one of the 100 centres that are available across Scotland or visit the Careers Scotland website.

For more information contact:
Freephone 0845 8 502 502
Textphone: 0141 889 8581
Typetalk: 18001 0845 8502 502
www.careers-scotland.org.uk

Wales
Careers Wales
Offering help both to young people and to adults, Careers Wales provides advice on any issues you have related to careers, work, education or training.

Youth Gateway
In addition to the help and advice Careers Wales has available, they have now introduced Youth Gateway. This is designed specifically for you if you are aged 16–19 and looking for advice about training, employment and education. You will get help from Careers Advisers and Personal Advisers who are working together to make sure you get the help you need.

For further information on both Careers Wales and Youth Gateway see:
www.careerswales.com

Clic
Clic is an information and advice service for young people in Wales. It offers help and guidance on a range of issues from education and employment to relationships, health and housing.

For more information see:
www.cliconline.co.uk

England, Wales and Northern Ireland
learndirect
If you need advice on any aspect of your careers, training or educational options try contacting learndirect. learndirect has trained advisers who can discuss your options over the phone or you can attend one of the many learndirect centres available throughout England, Wales and Northern Ireland. Their help is available to anyone of any age, although it is mainly aimed at adults.

If you want some more information or advice contact:
08000 150 450
www.learndirect.co.uk and www.learndirect-advice.co.uk

Administration, Business, Office Work and Financial Services

To work in this sector you need to have a great head for numbers and be very good at managing your time effectively. Jobs in business and finance can be fast-paced and exciting and workers in all four of these areas are highly motivated and enjoy working in an office environment.

In this section we look at the following jobs:

For similar jobs to this job family please go to the section: *Legal and Political Services* on page 363.

ACCOUNTANT

What the work involves

- Accountancy involves keeping and analysing financial records for companies or individuals, helping them to increase their profits including advising on financial planning and development, tax returns and future costs and budgets.

- You will keep detailed accounts and internal audits and produce regular statements on whether the company's systems are efficient and cost effective.

There are three main areas of work:

Industrial and commercial

- Employed directly by a company, you will provide a range of services and could work for a small local company or a huge multinational.

- You will help to plan the company's development, predicting the costs, benefits and risks.

Private practice

- This involves working for a specialist accountancy firm that offers services to clients.

- Smaller practices usually work for small local businesses. However, accountancy firms can be huge and some companies provide services to multinational corporations.

Public sector

- Working for public bodies like the NHS, universities and local authorities you will offer advice on tax, financial problems, raising money, financial ICT systems and management consultancy.

- Your role will be to help them provide an efficient, quality service that is within the budgets set by the government.

The type of person suited to this work

As you will be making presentations and working with people at all levels, you will need excellent written and verbal communication skills. Much of your work will include confidential reports and financial information, so you will need to be honest and reliable. You will also need to be able to work under pressure and to deadlines and be prepared to study in your own time and to continue to keep up to date with new developments.

An ability with figures and an interest in how businesses work will be essential. You will also have to be able to research and understand complicated financial information, use your skills and knowledge to analyse it, think of solutions to problems and finally produce written reports showing your findings and conclusions.

Working conditions

You could be working in an organisation of any size and will generally be office based, spending a lot of time using ICT, sitting at a desk or meeting clients.

Depending on your role, you might have the opportunity to travel both in this country and abroad, in order to meet your clients. A driving licence could be useful and you might need to be prepared to spend time away from home, sometimes for fairly long periods.

Although you will normally work office hours from Monday to Friday, you may need to work extra hours at busy times, especially during February to March (the end of the financial year).

Future prospects

The growing importance of information technology is having a major impact on the accountancy sector. Access to faster communication systems means more major companies are becoming global, which in turn will have an impact on the numbers required within the accountancy sector. If accountancy is your chosen route, it is recommended you think

very carefully about the area you would like to focus on at an early stage of your career.

In the long term you could choose to become self-employed, offering consultancy services to clients.

Industrial and commercial

There is a high demand for trainees and opportunities throughout the country but, as you would probably be working for a larger organisation, most jobs are in towns and cities. Once you are qualified and experienced you could move into highly paid senior management positions, or you could choose to move to a larger company for promotion.

Private practice

You could work for a small company, offering a personal service to local businesses and individuals or for a huge multinational firm. Job opportunities are good and there is a high demand for qualified people.

Public Sector

The public sector covers a wide range of services, including education, healthcare and social services. Government changes mean that budgets are increasingly held at local level, for example schools and hospitals now manage their own finances. This means that there are increasing opportunities across the country.

If you do well, you can move into high-level management jobs. Many people at the highest levels within the public sector started their careers within accountancy.

Advantages/disadvantages

If you work within the right organisation you can expect to earn extremely high salaries. To achieve this you will need to be very dedicated and able to cope with a lot of responsibility, stress and pressure. Accountancy is a very varied career and there are a lot of opportunities both in this country and abroad. You will be office based and usually need to be prepared to dress formally. You will need to be committed and determined to cope with the training, studying and taking exams whilst you work.

Money guide

Successful accountants can earn very high salaries but a lot will depend on your level, experience and location. The highest salaries are within London and the south-east of England, the lowest are in Northern Ireland, Scotland and the north-east of England.

Private practice

As a graduate starting training you can earn between £18,000 and £25,000 per year depending on where you work and your responsibilities.

Recently qualified graduates earn between £29,000 and £50,000.

When fully qualified, with several years' experience, and perhaps a specialist area of work, salaries can increase to £80,000+.

Public sector

A trainee usually starts on £16,000–£25,000 per year. On completion of training you could earn between £28,000 and £50,000.

Fully qualified senior managers can earn from £50,000–£150,000 per year, while directors could earn £150,000+.

Your salary will depend on the type of organisation you work for, the qualification you have studied, and your location. ACCA qualified accountants typically earn more than those with CAT. Accountants working in London can expect to earn up to 20% more than in other areas.

Related opportunities

- Accounting Technician p19
- Actuary p20
- Auditor p21
- Bank Manager p23
- Financial Adviser p39
- Insurance Broker p42

Further information

Association of Chartered Certified Accountants
29 Lincoln's Inn Fields, London WC2A 3EE
020 7059 5000; www.acca.co.uk; info@accaglobal.com

Qualifications and courses

ENTRY LEVEL 3

Most people start with a degree (usually 2.2 classification or higher). If your degree is in accounting or a related subject you may be exempt from certain papers for some of the professional qualifications.

The minimum entry requirements for a degree are normally 2 A levels/3 H grades and 5 GCSEs/S grades (A–C/1–3), including maths and English, or equivalent; HNC/HND in accounting or a business-related subject followed by a top-up degree may be another route into the profession.

It is possible for school leavers, with a minimum of 4 GCSEs/S grades, including English and maths, to follow a vocational training route. This is normally offered by the Association of Accounting Technicians (AAT) and The Chartered Institute of Management Accountants (CIMA), who offer the Technician route to qualification. There are varied exam requirements, depending on qualifications offered at entry.

Accountants hold a qualification from a recognised accountancy body: Association of Chartered Certified Accountants (ACCA), Institute of Chartered Accountants in England and Wales (ICAEW), Institute of Chartered Accountants in Scotland (ICAS), Institute of Chartered Accountants in Ireland (ICAI), Association of International Accountants (AIA). The Chartered Institute of Management Accountants (CIMA) and the Institute of Financial Accountants (IFA) provide qualifications for management accountants and financial accountants working in industry, commerce or the public sector.

Public sector

Accountants working in the public sector usually hold the Chartered Institute of Public Finance and Accountancy (CIPFA) qualification.

Institute of Chartered Accountants in England and Wales
Chartered Accountants Hall, PO Box 433, London EC2P 2BJ
020 7920 8100; www.icaew.co.uk

Institute of Chartered Accountants of Scotland
CA House, 21 Haymarket Yards, Edinburgh EH12 5BH
0131 347 0100; www.icas.org.uk

Institute of Financial Accountants
Burford House, 44 London Road, Sevenoaks TN13 1AS
01732 458080; www.ifa.org.uk; mail@ifa.org.uk

ACCOUNTANCY

Chelsea

Where it all began...

I studied at Franklin College for my A levels in Business, Finance, Accounts and Mathematics.

After much research into different universities and applying through UCAS, I decided that a degree just wasn't for me - especially as I already knew I wanted to be an accountant.

With this in mind I attended an INS1GHT Day at PricewaterhouseCoopers LLP (PwC) in the Leeds office. The day was really great, and I came away knowing that PwC was the firm for me!

I joined the firm in September 2008 on the HEADstart programme; this is the scheme for school and college leavers like me who have decided that getting straight into work is best for them. The HEADstart programme allows you to train to be an auditor, I am working in Assurance studying my ACCA qualification and should hopefully be a qualified accountant by 2011.

What I do on a day-to-day basis...

One of the big things I love about my job is the variation and meeting and working with different clients.

As a trainee auditor we will attend the client's site just after the year end for the audit. A job will usually last between 1 and 3 weeks, maybe longer for larger jobs. After that it is onto a new client. In our role a lot of our time is spent with the client contacts themselves discussing things and understanding their business and how things work. People always imagine a job like this to be sat at a desk all day typing but this is certainly not the case!

The work we do is always challenging and a lot of understanding is required about what we are testing and the reasons why. This comes with time and practice.

Work life balance...

The work life balance at PwC is good, people are always happy to facilitate your needs when it comes to hobbies and personal interests. Obviously working in a firm like PwC, a couple of hour's overtime is expected when the job requires it.

When college is ongoing it can be challenging having the perfect work–life balance, however studying for a professional qualification is never easy.

The little extras!

Since working for the firm I have really developed my self confidence, working for PwC encourages you to become a more independent person which is very motivating.
I have attended college events and discussed with students and parents who are leaving college what they plan to do next and if they would consider a career in Accountancy.

Attending these events on my own is not something I would have had the confidence to do prior to joining the firm.

There is a great social life at PwC and the work events which are organised by our social clubs are always good fun! I have met some great friends since joining and I look forward to progressing with such a great firm, and getting qualified!

ACCOUNTING TECHNICIAN/ FINANCE CLERK

What the work involves

- Accounting technicians are responsible for financial issues including company expenditure, tax returns and payroll.

- Yourworkwillincludecollectingandanalysinginformation, keeping records and writing reports.

- In a large firm, you will probably work as part of a team and support qualified accountants. In a smaller company, you might cover a wider range of tasks and be responsible for most of the finances.

- Once you are qualified you could specialise in a specific financial area, for example insolvency or tax analysis.

The type of person suited to this work

You will need to be confident with numbers, and have the ability to gather, analyse and record information accurately when under pressure from deadlines.

Good verbal and written communication skills are also essential, as you will often have to explain complicated financial issues to clients in a clear manner.

You must be willing and committed to further study in order to pass your technician exams. You will be expected to continue learning throughout your career, as it is important for accounting technicians to keep up-to-date with changes in financial law.

Good ICT skills are also important, as most of the work is computer based.

Working conditions

You will normally work standard office hours from Monday to Friday, however at busy times you may need to put in extra hours over evenings or weekends.

Most work will be office-based, although you may also travel to meetings with clients within your working day so a driving licence could be useful.

Future prospects

Although the finance industry employs a lot of people, the majority do not hold many professional qualifications. This means there is a skills shortage within the sector, so the higher the qualifications you gain the better your career prospects.

Prospects for promotion are good, and working in a smaller company may also give you the opportunity to take on more responsibility and work at a more senior level earlier in your career. Alternatively, you could choose to become self-employed, or train as a chartered accountant.

Advantages/disadvantages

You will usually be working in a team environment, which means that you will build strong relationships.

The work can be slightly monotonous.

Qualifications and courses

There are no formal academic requirements for entry to the role of an accounting technician, but some GCSEs/S grades (A–C/1–3), including English and maths, are desirable. Employers also welcome mature applicants.

The Association of Accounting Technicians (AAT) and Association of Chartered Certified Accountants (ACCA) award accounting technician qualifications, which are usually studied part time at college or work. These are available at three NVQ/SVQ stages: Level 2 (Foundation), 3 (Intermediate) and 4 (Technician). You may be exempt from some levels with relevant qualifications.

The AAT also offers a diploma for those who are unable to find a work placement whilst they study. This has three stages: Certificate in Accounting (Foundation), Advanced Certificate in Accounting (Intermediate) and Diploma in Accounting (Technician). Technician status is awarded on completion of all three components.

The Certified Accountancy Technician (CAT) qualification, awarded by ACCA, combines a year's practical experience with exams at three levels. With certain qualifications you may receive exemption from some papers.

Both the AAT and CAT allow students to go on and qualify as Chartered Accountants.

Money guide

As a trainee, working towards gaining foundation level qualifications, you can expect to earn £11,000–£19,000 per year. When fully qualified, earnings range from £13,000–£29,000. Once you have gained experience and progressed to a management level, or if you are successfully self-employed, you could earn up to £49,000.

Related opportunities

- Accountant p16
- Pensions Administrator p49
- Bank Cashier/Customer Adviser p22

Further information

Association of Accounting Technicians
140 Aldersgate Street, London EC1A 4HY
0845 863 0800; www.aat.org.uk; aat@aat.org.uk
Association of Chartered Certified Accountants
29 Lincoln's Inn Fields, London WC2A 3EE
020 7059 5000; www.acca.co.uk; info@accaglobal.com

City& Guilds

www.cityandguilds.com/myperfectjob

ACTUARY

What the work involves

- Actuaries calculate financial risk. Using statistics and knowledge of investments, law and business, they make financial predictions to help design products such as insurance and pensions.

- As an actuary you would help set insurance prices based on statistics, probability and risk.

- You would also use your knowledge and skills to help companies make long-term decisions on their investments, insurance and pension funds.

- You might work in insurance, life assurance, pensions, investments or for the government.

The type of person suited to this work

An ability with figures and enjoyment of solving complicated mathematical problems is essential. You should also be able to think clearly and logically, be able to analyse information and data and solve complex financial problems.

You will need to have excellent communication skills for working with other people and explaining complicated financial issues clearly and simply.

Actuaries must pay close attention to detail and you will be working to deadlines and keeping up to date with new developments such as the laws and regulations governing the industry.

You will be expected to dress formally and have excellent ICT skills.

Working conditions

Most of the work is office-based, working normal office hours, but you will also visit clients at their work at times to suit them. This will involve some evening and weekend work and travel, possibly staying away from home. A driving licence and transport could be required.

As a trainee you will have to study in your own time but once you are qualified you could work abroad and might be able to work part time.

Future prospects

Most actuaries work within life assurance companies and numbers in general insurance are increasing rapidly. Although the profession is growing, entry is competitive and you will probably need relevant work experience. Jobs are available throughout the country but most are in Edinburgh, London and the south-east.

As a fully qualified actuary you can work within a specialism or in consultancy, or you could travel as your qualifications will be welcomed all over the world. Within larger companies there are opportunities for promotion to very senior positions.

Advantages/disadvantages

Training after university takes up to 6 years and involves studying whilst working full time. However, actuaries are in demand, there are good promotion prospects and the pay is

Qualifications and courses

Most people enter this career with a degree in maths or a related subject; some entrants have a postgraduate qualification in actuarial science or a professional qualification from the Institute of Actuaries (England and Wales) or the Faculty of Actuaries (Scotland).

Normal entry requirements for a degree course are 2 A levels/3 H grades and 5 GCSEs/S grades (A–C/1–3), or equivalent. For a degree in maths, this will include an A level/H grade in a maths subject.

You could become a trainee actuary after A levels or Scottish Highers. The minimum entry requirements are 2 A levels including a mathematical subject at grade B, or 3 Scottish Highers including maths at grade A.

Trainees are employed by a firm of actuaries, training from 3 to 6 years. To become a Fellow of the Institute or the Faculty of Actuaries, you must be at least 23 years old, have 3 years' work experience, and pass the professional exams.

Trainees with a degree or diploma in actuarial science/ studies may get exemptions from some of the training. Other degrees may give exemption from certain exam papers.

good and UK qualifications are recognised everywhere so you could work abroad.

Money guide

As a graduate trainee you can expect a salary between £23,000 and £28,000 per year. Newly or part qualified staff can expect £40,000–£55,000. Senior staff can earn up to £75,000 and it is possible to earn £100,000+. Salaries vary based on location and specialism, and are expected to be higher in London and the south-east of England.

Related opportunities

- Accountant p16
- Financial Adviser p39
- Stockbroker p64

Further information

Association for Consulting Actuaries (ACA)
St Clement's House, 27–28 Clement's Lane,
London EC4N 7AE
020 3207 9380; www.aca.org.uk

Institute of Actuaries
Staple Inn Hall, High Holborn, London WC1V 7QJ
020 7632 2100; www.actuaries.org.uk;
institute@actuaries.org.uk

Faculty of Actuaries
Maclurin House, 18 Dublin Street, Edinburgh EH1 3PP
0131 240 1300; www.actuaries.org.uk;
faculty@actuaries.org.uk

AUDITOR

What the work involves

- You will be a fully qualified accountant specialising in audit work, exploring all aspects of a business, talking to staff and ensuring that the paperwork and accounts give a true picture of the company's finances.

- Internal auditors work for a company preparing their accounts for external auditors to check.

- All businesses and government departments must be externally audited, by law.

- As an external auditor your work will include creating a detailed report, stating that the accounts are true and accurate and recommending possible improvements to the business.

The type of person suited to this work

You must be happy working with numbers and interpreting statistics and be a thorough, methodical person who pays close attention to detail.

As you will be using your skills and experience to solve financial problems you will need to enjoy researching information and looking into all aspects of a business.

It is important that you have excellent communication skills so that you can present your findings clearly, both verbally and in writing. You should also be able to work effectively as part of a team and with the company you are auditing.

You should be well organised, able to work under pressure, meet deadlines and have excellent ICT skills.

Working conditions

Large companies have internal auditors who prepare their accounts for inspection. External auditors are based temporarily in the firms they are auditing, so they may have to travel and stay away from home. A driving licence and own transport can be useful.

You will do normal office hours but will be working to deadlines and so may have to work evenings and weekends.

Future prospects

There is an increasing demand for qualified auditors. As an internal auditor you could work for a business or government department, or work for yourself, offering consultancy or advice and doing internal audits for companies.

External auditors are employed by accountancy firms or you might work for the National Audit Office (the Accounts Commission in Scotland), auditing central government departments, or the Audit Commission, working with public sector organisations such as local authorities or the NHS.

Advantages/disadvantages

Accountancy training takes about 3 years after university and involves taking exams and studying, often in your own time. Pay is good and external auditors visit other companies and meet new people. There are opportunities for management and consultancy work.

Qualifications and courses

In order to become an auditor, you will need to obtain a professional accountancy qualification (see p16).

Most entrants to this profession are graduates.

Private accountancy firms audit companies in the private sector and some public sector organisations. A chartered accountancy qualification with CIPFA, ACCA, ICAEW, ICAS, ICAI or CIMA is required.

Public sector auditing is usually carried out by national audit bodies such as the Audit Commission, the National Audit Office, Audit Scotland and the Northern Ireland Audit Office. A chartered accountancy qualification with CIPFA, ACCA, ICAEW, ICAS, ICAI or CIMA is required.

The national audit bodies offer graduate training schemes, which allow graduates in any subject to train as auditors and gain a chartered accountancy qualification. The National Audit Office has a 3-year training programme, leading to qualification with the Institute of Chartered Accountants. Minimum entry requirements are a 2.1 Honours degree and 300 UCAS points at A level/H grade or equivalent.

The Audit Commission offers a 4-year training programme including a professional qualification with CIPFA. Minimum entry requirements are a 2.2 Honours degree and 240 UCAS points at A level/H grade or equivalent.

Money guide

As a graduate starting training you could earn £14,000–£25,000 per year. This could rise to £30,000–£45,000 a year when you are qualified. A senior manager can earn between £50,000 and £70,000, up to around £120,000. Salaries can be up to 20% higher in London.

Related opportunities

- Accountant p16
- Actuary p20
- Chartered/Company Secretary p26
- Financial Adviser p39

Further information

Association of Chartered Certified Accountants
29 Lincoln's Inn Fields, London WC2A 3EE
020 7396 5800; www.acca.co.uk; info@accaglobal.com

Chartered Institute of Management Accountants
26 Chapter Street, London SW1P 4NP
020 8849 2251; www.cimaglobal.com;
cima.contact@cimaglobal.com

Institute of Internal Auditors – UK and Ireland Ltd
13 Abbeville Mews, 88 Clapham Park Road, London SW4 7BX
020 7498 0101; www.iia.org.uk; studentsupport@iia.org.uk

Administration, Business, Office Work and Financial Services

CRCI: IE
CLCI: NAD/NAF

BANK CASHIER/ CUSTOMER ADVISER

What the work involves

- Bank cashiers/customer advisers work for banks and building societies, and are the first point of contact for customers with enquiries or complaints.

- You may be working in a branch dealing with customers face to face, or you could be based in a contact centre liaising with them over the phone or by email.

- You will be handling customers' accounts, including the paying in and withdrawing of money using computerised systems.

- You will also be expected to sell the company's products and services, which will involve working to set sales targets.

The type of person suited to this work

You will need excellent customer service skills so that you can process their requests efficiently, and also gain their trust in order to advise them on a range of financial products.

You must be confident working with figures and ICT, and working to targets.

As you will be handling money, you should be trustworthy and able to work accurately, paying close attention to detail.

Since you will be working as part of a team, a helpful and positive attitude coupled with the ability to use your own initiative is valuable.

Working conditions

In a branch you will probably work normal office hours, and Saturdays if the bank is open. Call centres usually offer a 24 hour service, so you should expect to work shifts that include nights and weekends.

Part time and flexible working hours are commonly available.

You should be well presented, and will usually be required to wear a uniform.

Future prospects

Job opportunities in the financial sector are currently depleted due to the economic downturn, with a trend of bank mergers and the closing of high street branches. Despite this, opportunities are still available, especially given the recent trend for re-opening UK call centres as a drive to attract customers.

You could specialise in an area such as mortgages or pensions, or gain further professional qualifications in order to train as a financial adviser or bank manager.

Advantages/disadvantages

Looking after customers and helping to solve their queries can be interesting and rewarding.

Banks offer well-structured training programmes on entry, and you will have a clear route of career progression.

Qualifications and courses

You need a minimum of 4 GCSEs/S grades (A–C/1–3) including English and maths, or equivalent qualifications.

Other useful qualifications include City & Guilds Awards in customer service Levels 1, 2 and 3, City & Guilds Levels 2 and 3 Certificate and Diploma in business and administration, the IFS Level 2 Diploma in Introduction to Financial Services, any BTEC national qualifications in business or personal and business finance, and CCN Level 2 and 3 Awards in introduction to financial services.

Most banks also offer a variety of trainee programmes for A-level or graduate entrants. You will usually need either two A-levels or a higher second class degree in any subject. Competition for places is intense, so some relevant work experience could be helpful.

Training can continue throughout your career via in-house courses.

Because of the economic downturn, entry into this profession is more competitive than ever before.

Money guide

You could expect to earn between £11,500-£14,000 in your first couple of years as a trainee. With several years' experience you could be earning £20,000. Senior customer advisers, especially those who have specialised in a certain financial area, can earn £30,000+.

You may receive bonuses for meeting sales targets, and most employers also offer packages that include cheaper mortgages, pensions, loans and insurance.

Related opportunities

- Financial Adviser p39
- Bank Manager p23
- Accounting Technician/Finance Clerk p19
- Pensions Adviser p50

Further information

IFS School of Finance
IFS House, 4–9 Burgate Lane, Canterbury, Kent CT1 2XJ
01227 818609; www.ifslearning.ac.uk;
customerservice@ifslearning.ac.uk

Financial Services Skills Council (FSSC)
51 Gresham Street, London EC2V 7HQ
0845 257 3772; www.fssc.org.uk; info@fssc.org.uk

www.cityandguilds.com/myperfectjob

BANK MANAGER

What the work involves

- Bank managers are responsible for running branches of either a retail, commercial or corporate bank.

- You will be accountable for staff recruitment, motivation and training, as well as meeting budget and sales targets for products and services.

- You will be required to keep up-to-date with a range of financial products, and market your services to individuals and businesses.

- Attending meetings and preparing reports on branch operations for both staff and head office will also be important tasks.

The type of person suited to this work

Bank managers work with people at all levels, so excellent verbal and written communications skills are essential.

You will be expected to deal with customers on a daily basis, as well as leading and motivating your team, both of which require confidence, organisation, negotiation skills, initiative and the ability to think on your feet.

You should be comfortable working with numbers as you will have to meet budget and sales targets, and calculate profits.

Working conditions

You will usually work normal office hours and occasional Saturdays, in keeping with the opening hours of your bank. If you manage a call centre, you will probably be required to work shifts in order to provide a 24 hour service to customers.

As well as working in an office, you will occasionally travel to visit clients at their business premises, so a driving licence could be useful.

Future prospects

Despite recent bank mergers, the number of management positions has stayed quite stable. As a branch manager, you could progress to become a regional manager, or use your skills and experience to work in the company's head office. You could also specialise in areas such as training, human resources or marketing.

London is one of the leading financial centres of the world and offers the best opportunities for pursing a high-level career. There are also numerous roles located overseas.

Advantages/disadvantages

This challenging, fast-moving industry offers many opportunities in various sectors including telephone and internet banking, and also in various organisations including supermarkets which are now offering banking services.

Within investment and merchant banking you can earn extremely high salaries

You will need to meet challenging targets in an increasingly

Qualifications and courses

ENTRY LEVEL 2

Most entrants to this profession hold a degree or equivalent qualification. If you do start work with only A-levels/H grades or equivalent, you could progress by taking professional qualifications through bodies such as the IFS School of Finance or the Chartered Institute of Bankers in Scotland (CIOBS). NVQs/SVQs at Levels 2, 3 and 4 in providing financial services (banks and building societies) are also available.

From university, you will need at least a 2.2 Honours degree to secure a place on a graduate management training scheme. A relevant subject, such as maths, business studies, economics or accountancy is often preferred. Places are highly sought after, and training usually lasts 18–24 months.

You may also have to take additional qualifications to meet the Financial Services Authority (FSA) requirements to work as a manager.

competitive market which is sensitive to changes in the national and global economy.

Money guide

Graduates on bank management training schemes can expect to make £19,500–£25,000.

With qualifications and experience this increases to £26,000–£43,000. Senior staff, such as area managers, can earn salaries of £50,000–£100,000. Merchant and investment bankers can earn higher salaries still.

You may get bonuses for meeting targets. Additional benefits usually include cheaper mortgages, pensions, loans and insurance.

Related opportunities

- Chartered Accountant p16
- Financial Adviser p39
- Insurance Broker p42

Further information

IFS School of Finance
IFS House, 4–9 Burgate Lane, Canterbury CT1 2XJ
01227 818609; www.ifslearning.ac.uk;
customerservices@ifslearning.ac.uk

Chartered Institute of Bankers in Scotland
Drumsheugh House, 38b Drumsheugh Gardens, Edinburgh EH3 7SW
0131 473 7777; www.charteredbanker.com;
info@charteredbanker.com

City&
Guilds

www.cityandguilds.com/myperfectjob

Administration, Business, Office Work and Financial Services

CRCI: AA
CLCI: CAP

BUSINESS ADVISER

What the work involves

- Business advisers provide independent advice to an array of small and medium-sized businesses or enterprises (SMEs), in order to improve the success of a business.

- You will provide advice on prospective business plans and recommend relevant specialist services and suppliers that could support the venture.

- You may run workshops and seminars that offer basic support and information for new or existing businesses.

- You will need to be informed about more than one area of business, but will often choose to specialise in an area, such as: marketing and public relations (PR), accountancy and taxation, and law.

The type of person suited to this work

You will need to have a good understanding of a variety of business environments and sizes, whilst being able to use this knowledge through offering advice on current business issues, geographical trends and financial help available to support new or failing businesses.

You need to be logical and objective, yet approachable and enthusiastic. You will need the ability to manage a variety of projects whilst consistently meeting tight deadlines.

Working conditions

Hours tend to follow the national average of between 37 and 40 hours a week, working 9–5.30, Monday and Friday. Should there be weekend or evening events to attend then these hours will increase.

You will be mostly office based, with occasional visits to client premises, suppliers' or to networking events. There are also self-employment consultancy opportunities available, which would allow you to work from home.

Future prospects

With approximately 12,000 business advisers in the UK, this is a thriving industry, with opportunities nationwide. Vacancies are posted on enterprise and business support organisations' websites, and in publications, such as IBC's journal, *Business Adviser*.

It is important to gain accreditation, such as the IBC's internationally recognised Certified Management Consultant (CMC) Award, which can be applied for after gaining three years practical experience. Through this, business advisers are eligible to join the national register for business support professionals.

Advantages/disadvantages

Employment as a business adviser allows for a certain amount of autonomy, whilst the using of initiative in an advisery position is often rewarding.

Qualifications and courses

ENTRY LEVEL 5

There are no specific qualifications but advisers must have a successful business history. This can include the gaining experience through running a SME or large business, or having expertise in a key area of business, such as senior management, marketing or finance.

Academic qualifications that would be useful are business-related degree courses and diplomas that include a year in industry. Also, IBC training courses and workshops are helpful as they cover marketing, business advice, counselling and mentoring.

Induction training is available for those working for a business support organisation, which is often followed up by Continuing Professional Development (CPD).

Bodies, such as IBC, Technology Means Business and the Small Firms Enterprise Development Initiative (SFEDI) have begun regulating and accrediting business advisers. Alongside this, the IBC provides professional indemnity insurance, which is important for all those offering their services.

It is important to gain recognised awards, such as the CMC from the IBC, in order to prove to clients that you are a certified adviser with business experience.

Money guide

Business advisers can expect around £20,000 a year.

This will increase to £30,000 through the gaining of experience.

For senior positions, salaries are over £50,000.

Related Opportunities

- Regeneration Manager & Economic Development Officer p57
- Management Consultant p46
- Project Manager p52
- Company Director p30

Further information

Institute of Business Consulting (IBC)
Chartered Management Institute, 4th Floor, 2 Savoy Court, London WC2R 0EZ
020 7497 0580; www.ibconsulting.org.uk

National Federation of Enterprise Agencies (NFEA)
12 Stephenson Court, Fraser Road, Priory Business Park, Bedford MK44 3WJ
01234 831623; www.nfea.com

City&
Guilds

www.cityandguilds.com/myperfectjob

LIVERPOOL BUSINESS SCHOOL

ONLY A FIVE minute walk from the centre of Liverpool you'll find Liverpool Business School (LBS), one of the leading parts of Liverpool John Moores University (LJMU). A modern and dynamic educational establishment, the School is set around tranquil gardens and boasts an award-winning, state-of-the-art learning resource centre. With over 30 years' experience to draw on, this large Business School has over 5,000 students enrolled on undergraduate, postgraduate and professional programmes.

LBS offers a range of degree programmes spanning a number of areas, including: Accounting and Financial Management, General Business and Management, Human Resource Management, Information & Library Management, Marketing, and Public Relations.

At undergraduate level, LBS offers:

- BA Business Studies
- BA Accounting and Finance
- BA Marketing
- BA International Business and Languages
- BA Public Relations and Languages
- BA Business and Economics
- BA Business and Public Relations

LBS has a team of extremely experienced academics who use the latest and most modern student-centred methods of teaching on all courses. The School is continually exploring new ways in which it can improve the employability of its graduates and it places considerable emphasis on the practical nature of its programmes. For example, a number of students were this year able to study for the Chartered Management Institute (CMI) Level 5 Certificate in Management and Leadership alongside their sandwich year placement. Through this initiative the students were able to gain new and invaluable skills, making them more attractive to future employers. One of the students said:

"I am so delighted to be doing the CMI Level 5 Certificate in Management and Leadership as part of my course, it is a unique opportunity that has really put me ahead of the game now in the graduate market.

"I have been given a real chance to gain so many new and practical work skills.

"I know that by the time the placement is finished there will be many things that I achieved to take away with me."

LJMU is a truly international university with over 24,000 students from all over the world. The University has embarked on a major campus redevelopment programme to ensure that LJMU truly is a 21st century university. The £24 million Art & Design Academy - the biggest investment in arts education in the UK today – is the first of our major projects to be completed.

If you want to have a great university experience, graduate with a respected qualification and secure the skills and 'know-how' that will help you climb the professional career ladder, then you should choose Liverpool Business School at LJMU.

For more information about Liverpool Business School contact the BLW Admissions Team on 0151 231 3999 or email: BLWadmissions@ljmu.ac.uk. Alternatively, you can visit the website at www.ljmu.ac.uk/lbs

CHARTERED/COMPANY SECRETARY

What the work involves

- This is a high-level administrative and managerial job.

- You will be in a very senior position advising executives and directors on finance and company law.

- You will be responsible for the legal reports all companies are required to keep, reporting to Companies House and other institutions such as the Stock Exchange.

- You will be responsible for running board meetings and could be responsible for financial planning, accounts, wages, human resources and all administrative and ICT systems.

The type of person suited to this work

You will need excellent communication skills to be able to work with people at all levels. You should be interested in business and have a thorough knowledge of how your organisation works. You will need to understand complicated legal and financial issues and be able to use your knowledge to solve problems, maximise efficiency and advise on ways of improving and developing the company.

You should be highly organised, able to deal efficiently with several tasks at once and pay close attention to detail. You will analyse figures and accounts and work to strict legal guidelines. You will be organising meetings and should be confident making presentations to high-level staff and customers.

Working conditions

Most of your work will be office-based, attending lots of meetings, including working at other sites and outside organisations which could involve some travel and possibly going abroad.

You will normally work office hours but will have a heavy workload and a lot of responsibility, so will require commitment and dedication to work overtime and meet deadlines.

To be successful, a high level of personal and professional integrity is important.

Future prospects

The Companies Act 2006 means that private companies are no longer legally required to have a Company or Chartered Secretary. Despite this change, businesses will still have to meet a range of legal requirements so most will continue to employ a Company Secretary.

An experienced Company Secretary will have opportunities to work in highly paid jobs in a range of organisations, and you could go on to specialise or could become a self-employed consultant.

Advantages/disadvantages

This is a high-level career which is interesting, varied and challenging. You will use a wide range of skills and knowledge, prospects are good and earnings can be high. But you will have

Qualifications and courses

You will probably need a degree, Foundation degree, HNC/HND, or equivalent to enter and train in this career.

At least 1 A level/2 H grades or equivalent are required for entry onto a HNC/HND course, whilst degree courses require 2 A levels/3 H grades and 5 GCSEs/S grades (A–C/1–3) or equivalent.

You will probably need to become a member of the Institute of Chartered Secretaries and Administrators (ICAS), by taking their International Qualifying Scheme. This has four stages: Certificate in Business Practice, Diploma in Business Practice, and the Professional Programme Parts 1 and 2.

To become an associate member (ACIS), you will need at least 3 years' work experience (6 if you have not got a degree).

After at least 5 years (8 if you have not got a degree), and when you are working at a very senior level, you can become a Fellow of the Institute (FCIS).

ICSA offer courses for extra qualifications, which can be done full or part time depending on your job and responsibilities.

to take a lot of responsibility and work long hours and you might have to prepare information for directors if the company is doing badly.

Money guide

Graduates starting out can expect to earn anything between £25,000 and £32,000 per year. With some experience you can earn between £35,000 and £60,000. Very experienced secretaries can earn between £70,000 and £120,000.

Related opportunities

- Accountant p16
- Barrister/Advocate p365
- Company Director p30
- Auditor p21

Further information

Institute of Chartered Secretaries and Administrators
16 Park Crescent, London W1B 1AH;
020 7580 4741; www.icsa.org.uk; info@icsa.co.uk

Institute of Chartered Accountants in England and Wales
Chartered Accountants' Hall (Moorgate Place), PO Box 433, London EC2R 6EA
020 7920 8100; www.icaew.com; library@icaew.com

Council for Administration
18–20 Bromell's Road, London SW4 0BG
020 7627 9876; www.cfa.uk.com; info@cfa.uk.com

CIVIL SERVICE OFFICER (EXECUTIVE AND ADMINISTRATION)

What the work involves

Civil Servant

■ Civil servants provide support to government ministers. They are employed by a variety of departments, such as industry and agriculture, revenue, benefits and pensions, the department that issues driving licences or the central administrative, policy and support services.

Executive Officer

■ A civil service executive officer is the equivalent of a junior manager, with specific activities including the managing of a small team, helping with staff training, advising members of the public and investigating those that are believed to be breaking the law.

Administrative Assistant/Officer

■ Administrative assistants/officers take care of the administration that is required to ensure that government offices are able to operate efficiently.

■ Available positions are usually found in the following areas: working in a minister's private office, working in consumer research and advice, a job involving finance or procurement and working in marketing or public relations.

■ There are also some opportunities in departments such as human resources, neighborhood renewal, social justice and European and international relations.

■ Specific tasks undertaken involve the updating of records on computers, answering public enquiries, replying to incoming letters and helping with statistics and accounts.

The type of person suited to this work

You should have a neutral interest in governmental affairs, and enjoy providing a service to members of the public.

You must be able to work both independently and as part of a team, as much of the work requires liaising with different departments and working on individual assignments with the received data. In addition to this, those wishing to become executive officers or administrative officers should have management and leadership skills, alongside excellent communication abilities.

You will need to understand government and local authority legislation, and to be able to explain it clearly to those who have limited understanding.

Much of the information that you will be come into contact with is of a confidential nature and so you must be appreciative of privacy rules and discreet when processing confidential information for members of the public.

You will often be working to deadlines, so must be calm, prepared and capable throughout these pressurised situations.

Working conditions

Civil servants usually work between 35 and 37 hours a week, Monday to Friday. There are flexitime schemes in place for all government employees, allowing members of staff to occasionally vary their working hours in order to gain extra holiday time through working overtime.

Hours may occasionally increase during busier periods, should this be suitable for individual employees. 20% of employees work part time, and job share is also widely available, with working parents able to work only during school terms.

All of these positions are office based, with some being open to visits from the public that require the services of government

officials. It would occasionally be necessary for executive officers to visit members of the public or organisations.

The dress code tends to be smart/casual, with a relaxed office environment that aims to ensure all employees feel supported in order to reduce stress. 25 days holiday are usually available, and there are even opportunities for career breaks or secondment, which allow for the gaining of experience in a different department for a set amount of time before returning to your permanent position.

Future prospects

The civil service offers a clearly defined promotion structure, with experienced executive officers being able to apply for senior posts after a period of working in their contracted position, gaining experience and building an established reputation in relating departments.

Should employees join the civil service through the Fast Stream entry plan, promotion to more senior posts is often awarded after only three to five years, due to an intense introduction to the scheme.

If an executive officer has at least two years experience and was employed through means other than the Fast Stream service, they are eligible to be nominated as an applicant to the In-service Fast Stream system once they have demonstrated the appropriate skills and abilities.

Through the gaining of experience, civil service administrative assistants can apply for promotion to the role of administrative officer, and once in this position, to executive officer. Executive officers are in a position of junior management and once in this position there are further opportunities for progression.

In all departments of the civil service there is a clear promotional strategy, with it also being possible to cross over into similar departments should the available route of progression not be of interest.

Advantages/disadvantages

The advantages of joining the civil service are the various promotional opportunities on offer, alongside rewarding salaries and the opportunity to help members of the public in a relaxed, yet challenging working environment.

There are many ways in which employees can improve their working experiences through flexitime or even secondment.

The public sector is often viewed as a low paid vocation, with limited budgets sometimes meaning an increased work load when colleagues go on leave or progress to other positions and funds are not available for the replacement of that person.

Money guide

For executive officers, starting salaries are often in the region of £19,000 and £23,000 a year, with those who have gained more experience earning between £24,000 and £28,000. Through gaining knowledge and by highlighting personal skills and capabilities, officers can be promoted to a higher salary of around £38,000 or more, with the possibility of acquiring the bonus of performance-related pay.

Upon appointment, an administrative assistant can expect to earn between £12,500 and £15,000 a year, with this increasing to between £13,500 and £17,200 a year. Once experience has been gained within the sector of employment, experienced administrative officers are able to earn up to £20,000 a year.

It should be noted that those who are based in London are usually paid at a higher rate, although all those employed by the Civil Service benefit from a variety of schemes. Included in this is a pension scheme and even discounts on sports and social facilities or the benefit of a subsidised canteen.

Related opportunities

- Health Records Clerk p311
- Project Manager p52

Further information

Civil Service Fast Stream, Application Helpdesk
Pilgrims Well, 427 London Road, Camberley GU15 3HZ
01276 400333; www.faststream.gov.uk

Government Skills
Cabinet Office, Admiralty Arch, The Mall, London SW1A 2WH
020 7276 1611; www.government-skills.gov.uk

National School of Government
Sunningdale Park, Larch Avenue, Ascot SL5 0QE
01344 634000; www.nationalschool.gov.uk

City&
Guilds

www.cityandguilds.com/myperfectjob

Qualifications and courses

ENTRY 2 LEVEL

For a position as an executive officer it is not necessary to have a degree, although entry requirements tend to vary between departments so you are advised to contact the sector you are interested in directly. Applicants are increasingly being considered on the merits of their competencies and skills, alongside the amount of experience a candidate may have for the particular job being applied for.

In order to gain relevant work experience it is recommended that you view the Civil Service Recruitment Gateway, as you will find opportunities in a variety of departments and agencies, and even the possibility of a day visit to see whether the working environment is of interest.

Upon application, prospective employees will be invited to attend an interview and may even be required to complete a range of tests designed to highlight ability in numeracy, writing, communication and interpersonal skills, along with decision-making and analytical skills.

In order to gain a position as an administrative assistant, it is usually necessary to have at least two GCSEs (A*-C), including English and often maths, or equivalent qualifications. Should you not hold these minimum qualifications, the opportunity to present abilities through a written test is sometimes provided.

For those wishing to apply for a position as an administrative officer it is usually necessary to have at least five GCSEs (A*-C), including English and often maths, or equivalent qualifications. Many applicants wishing to become a civil service administrative officer hold two or more A-levels, or equivalent, or even a degree.

Should prospective applicants not wish to pursue a degree route, the Diploma in business, administration and finance is often recognised as a relevant qualification for this sector. In addition to this, Apprenticeships and Advanced Apprenticeships allow for practical training in a chosen area of work and even provide an income of at least £80 per week - £95 per week from August 2009.

There are also Young Apprenticeships available for 14- to 16-year-olds, which aim to provide vocational opportunities for school leavers, visit: www.apprenticeships.org.uk.

CIVIL SERVICE/LOCAL GOVERNMENT ADMINISTRATOR

What the work involves

- Administrators deal with company paperwork via filing, photocopying and faxing, and also store and update information on computer systems.

- Civil service administrators work for specific national government departments, such as planning or environmental.

- You will be required to deal with members of the public and high-level government staff, as well as carrying out normal administrative duties.

- If you work in local government, you are more likely to work across a range of areas such as leisure, environment and public health.

The type of person suited to this work

You will need excellent organisational skills as you will be responsible for administering numerous important projects at a time. The ability to use your initiative, prioritise your workload, and work autonomously are also essential.

A high level of accuracy and attention to detail is required in order to keep good records and produce clear correspondence.

Since you will be liaising with team members, the public and high level government staff daily, excellent verbal and written communication skills are vital.

You will need to be able to understand complex information, much of which can involve specialist law/medical/financial terminology.

Working conditions

You will probably work normal office hours, and most offices operate a flexitime policy. There are also opportunities for part time work.

Future prospects

The civil service has an established training and development programme for staff, and is keen to reward hard work and effort with promotion or pay increases in keeping with their grading system.

Local government administrators can continue working upward to a senior administrative level, or diversify into a different career. For example, if you became interested in housing policy, you could undertake appropriate training to become a housing officer or similar.

Advantages/disadvantages

Public sector work offers good holidays, flexible working hours and excellent perks.

Qualifications and courses

The majority of entrants have a degree/HND. Degrees in related subjects such as business and management, legal studies, social administration, social policy or politics may give you an advantage.

A civil service Fast Stream scheme is open to all graduates, which allows a more focused and rapid career progression from administrative to management level.

School-leavers with level 2 qualifications can go straight into the civil service, although they will usually begin by working as an office junior and train on the job to become an administrator. 5 GCSEs/S grades (A–C/1–3) are normally required, including English and maths. Equivalent qualifications such as an NVQ/SVQ Level 1 or 2 in administration are accepted.

Some departments will require you to undertake a criminal records bureau check prior to commencing employment.

Even without advanced qualifications there are opportunities to progress into higher level jobs.

In the initial stages of employment and training, work can be repetitive.

Money guide

Local government administrators can start on a salary of £11,500-£18,500. For graduates, a higher starting salary of £15,000-£21,000 is typical.

With experience, you could earn from £20,000 to £30,000 as a local government administrator.

Salaries for civil service administrators are slightly higher, starting between £19,300-£22,300. After four or five years' experience, your salary could rise to £40,000.

In both positions, salaries vary according to department and location. In general, London-based roles pay higher wages.

Related opportunities

- Civil Service Officer p27
- Personal Assistant p51
- Secretary p60

Further information

Civil Service
Most recruitment is via individual departments and agencies; CivilServiceJobs@cabinet-office.x.gsi.gov.uk

Local Government Association (LGA)
Local Government House, Smith Square, London SW1P 3HZ
020 7664 3131; www.lga.gov.uk; info@lga.gov.uk

COMPANY DIRECTOR

What the work involves

- As company director you will have responsibility for every aspect of your business. You will need a thorough knowledge of its products and services and must ensure that it achieves its aims as efficiently as possible.

- You might own the company or head a board of directors. In a large company you will probably lead a team of managers who specialise in specific areas such as sales, finance or product development but you will have overall responsibility.

The type of person suited to this work

The ability to analyse problems, find solutions, make decisions and think through their long-term effects is vital. You will need excellent communication skills to motivate staff and help sell your ideas, products and services to your customers and investors.

You should be highly organised, motivated and prepared to work long hours, be able to prioritise and work to deadlines, supervise others, take advice and respond to changes and developments.

An excellent knowledge and understanding of your business and its markets will be necessary to make your company successful.

Working conditions

You will probably be office-based but attend a lot of meetings with customers, financial and legal advisers, and staff. You should be prepared to work long hours and to travel in this country and abroad.

Although you will probably be advised by a team of experienced and knowledgeable managers, you will make the final decision and must be prepared to take risks and accept consequences.

Future prospects

Once you are at manager level, you can take professional courses to develop your skills and become a member of the Institute of Directors.

If you are successful, there is no limit to what you can achieve.

Advantages/disadvantages

You can get enormous rewards and satisfaction from seeing the company grow and succeed and you could start your own business based on a personal interest or skill.

You will have huge responsibility and need to be dedicated, hard working and able to cope with failure as well as success.

Money guide

Earnings for company directors will vary enormously depending on the size and success of the business. As a trainee manager you may start at around £20,000 a year. With a year or two of experience, this can rise to around £40,000+.

Qualifications and courses

There is no set route to becoming a company director, but you will usually need to acquire experience at senior management level.

You could enter the company at any level and with qualifications and work experience progress up to management-level jobs and then to director.

You could start on a management trainee scheme after taking Level 3 qualifications, but probably after doing a degree. The degree could be in a specialist subject related to the company's business such as engineering, or you could do a business-related degree.

The Chartered Management Institute (CMI) and the Institute of Administrative Management (IAM) offer courses for the professional development of managers, or you may be able to take them through a professional institute related to your business.

Once you have got management experience you could take a Master's degree in Business Administration (MBA).

You may be able to do NVQs/SVQs in Management at Levels 3 and 4 on a management training scheme. Level 5 NVQs/SVQs are available in specialist areas including Operational Management.

You could also study for a Foundation degree in Business Management/Development.

Directors of large private companies can earn between £60,000 and £180,000 – more in London. As director of a large company, you could earn as much as £1,500,000 plus huge bonuses, or as the owner of your own successful company you could become extremely rich.

Related opportunities

- Accountant p16
- Chartered/Company Secretary p26
- Financial Adviser p39
- Management Consultant p46

Further information

Chartered Management Institute
Management House, Cottingham Road, Corby NN17 1TT
01536 204222; www.managers.org.uk;
enquiries@managers.org.uk

Institute of Administrative Management
6 Graphite Square, Vauxhall Walk, London SE11 5EE
020 7091 2600; www.instam.org; info@instam.org

Institute of Directors
116 Pall Mall, London SW1Y 5ED
020 7839 1233; www.iod.com

City&
Guilds

COMPLIANCE OFFICER

What the work involves

- Compliance officers work for financial services organisations, and are responsible for aiding senior management in ensuring that their firm is complying with the rules set by the Financial Services Authority (FSA).

- Alongside this you will investigate complaints from clients that relate to possible breaches of these rules.

- You will explore the ways in which business efficiency can be improved within the FSA rules through the monitoring of sales processes, checking of paperwork and telephone recordings.

The type of person suited to this work

You will need to have an enquiring, analytical mind, enjoy analysing information and be interested in the legal aspects of selling financial products.

It is important that you are an easily approachable person with good communication skills and excellent report writing skills.

The job may be quite demanding and so you should be able to work well under pressure and be capable of working on a variety of projects at one time, whilst remaining organised and informed.

Working conditions

Compliance officers are generally office based, with attendance at meetings being a regular occurrence. They may have to travel around the country, or even overseas for an international company.

Generally, a compliance officer will work in the region of 37 hours a week, 9am to 5pm, Monday to Friday. However, changes to FSA policy may mean that extra hours need to be worked in order to implement changes.

Future prospects

Competition for FSA training posts is high, with only 40 on offer with this particular institution. However, you will be entering one of the fastest growing areas in financial services. There are around 9,000 compliance officers in the UK and many other positions involved with compliance, which highlights that the future is alive with prospects.

As you progress within this role you will have the opportunity to experience greater levels of responsibility and roles within management.

Advantages/disadvantages

There are chances for progression within this vocation and opportunities to work from home as a consultant.

You may feel under pressure at times and will often be asked to explain changes to the financial system in a clear and concise way.

Qualifications and Courses

Typically needed is a legal, accountancy or auditing background with a relevant degree.

Entry requirements for financial degree programmes vary, but are usually a minimum of two A levels/three H grades and five GCSEs/S grades (A*-C/1–3), including maths and English, or equivalent qualifications.

Many employers offer in-house training programmes. Trainees will work under the supervision of an experienced colleague, whilst gaining qualifications through part-time study, including distance learning.

Should you wish to train before entering the workplace, there are a number of professional bodies that offer relevant qualifications. Recommend courses are: The Diploma in Investment Compliance, offered by the Securities & Investment Institute; a Certificate, Diploma or Advanced Diploma in Financial Planning, offered by the Chartered Insurance Institute; The CeFA, offered by the IFS School of Finance.

Compliance qualifications are also available through The International Compliance Association (ICA), in association with the University of Manchester Business School. These vary from introductory courses to programmes designed for those with three years experience in the industry and/or a relevant degree.

Money guide

Although rates of pay vary depending upon geographical location, compliance officers can expect a starting salary in the region of £40,000 a year.

As you gain more experience your salary will increase to around £50,000 a year.

Should you wish to progress further, you can expect to earn over £80,000 a year as a Head of Compliance.

Related opportunities

- Auditor p21
- Financial Adviser p39
- Risk Manager p59

Further information

The Financial Services Authority (FSA)
25 The North Colonnade, London E14 5HS
020 7066 1000; www.fsa.gov.uk

International Compliance Association (ICA)
Wrens Court, 52–54 Victoria Road, Sutton Coldfield, Birmingham B72 1SX
0121 362 7534; www.int-comp.org

Compliance Institute
107 Barkby Road, Leicester LE4 9LG
0116 246 1316; www.complianceinstitute.co.uk

CRCI: IF
CLCI: NAK

CREDIT ANALYST

What the work involves

■ Credit analysts deal with both personal and business credit, assessing the individual circumstances of the application, using statistical and accounting criteria in order to decide the extent of the risk involved when lending.

■ Much of the work involves administration and figure work, due to a need for the analysis of given data and the writing of reports and presentations.

■ To thoroughly assess an application, an analyst must have an understanding of legal, compliance and business issues. For instance, a business application would be considered against economic growth and the country's financial stability.

The type of person suited to this work

You should have an interest in the financial sector and have a general and varied knowledge of the business world. Much of the work deals with statistics and so analysts need computer skills and the ability to work with spreadsheets and specialist statistical software packages.

You need to have good organisational and both verbal and written communication skills so that you can explain concepts to non-specialists.

Working conditions

Daily working hours range from 9am to 5pm or 5.30pm, Monday to Friday. There may be times when they are required to work extra hours. However, there are also opportunities for part-time working.

Generally, credit analysts are based in offices, with much of their work involving computer based activities and the monitoring of the financial markets, with the occasional need to present changes in the market to senior staff.

Future prospects

There are currently more vacancies than applicants, with job opportunities being stable. This vocation holds many avenues for promotion or progression into other areas of banking. Most opportunities are available in London, West Yorkshire, Cardiff and Scottish cities.

Vacancies are published in *The Banker* and *The Economist*. The Institute of Financial Services (IFS) School of Finance, the Chartered Financial Analyst Institute (CFA) and the Institute of Credit Management (ICM) Recruitment Consultancy post vacancies on their websites.

Advantages/disadvantages

There are many opportunities, with routes for promotion and progression being advantageous and salaries being rewarding.

Credit analysts often have to make difficult decisions about awarding or denying credit; this could make it a high pressured job when in a corporate environment.

Qualifications and courses

Credit analysts usually have a degree and enter the profession through a graduate training scheme. Suggested degree courses include economics, business studies, maths and statistics. Also recommended are subjects that include a high level of numerical content, for instance computer science, physics and electronics. Professional qualifications in areas such as accountancy improve career prospects.

In order to be accepted onto one of the above degree courses, prospective students need at least 5 GCSEs/S grades (A*-C/1-3) and 2 A levels/3H grades. However, most degree courses will ask for qualifications above this minimum suggestion.

The larger commercial and investment banks offer career training programmes for mature candidates. There are also some professional bodies that offer relevant qualifications, such as the IFS School of Finance and the ICM.

Credit analysts are expected to take part in Continuing Professional Development (CPD), which involves reading relevant journals and undertaking skills-related courses.

Much of the work involves being office based, using a computer to track market changes and scrutinise statistics.

Money guide

Credit analysts can expect to earn between £22,000 to £25,000 a year when newly appointed, with this rising to between £35,000 and £60,000 a year with experience. Due to the progression opportunities being good in this profession, a senior analyst for a major corporation can expect to earn more than £90,000 a year when part of a senior management team. Additional benefits could include subsidised mortgages, pensions, private healthcare and share option schemes.

Related opportunities

■ Accounting Technician/Finance Clerk p19
■ Bank Manager p23
■ Economist p34
■ Insurance Broker/Underwriter p42

Further information

Chartered Financial Analyst Institute (CFA)
10th Floor, One Canada Square, London E14 5AB
020 7531 0751; www.cfainstitute.org

Financial Services Skills Council (FSSC)
51 Gresham Street, London EC2V 7HQ
0845 257 3772; www.fssc.org.uk

Institute of Financial Services (IFS) School of Finance
IFS House, 4–9 Burgate Lane, Canterbury CT1 2XJ
01227 762600; www.ifslearning.com

DEBT COLLECTOR

What the work involves

- Debt collectors are employed to recover assets for the organisation that is owed the money.

- The debtor is firstly contacted by letter or telephone, they then receive a personal visit should this not work, and are finally contacted by a solicitor if the matter remains unresolved.

- The five areas of specialism include consumer debt collection, commercial debt collection, international collection, legal collection, and debtor tracing.

- Specific activities include helping debtors by arranging payment through instalments and becoming involved with debt collections that have entered the legal system.

The type of person suited to this work

The job of a debt collector can often be challenging and sometimes confrontational, so a person entering this profession needs to be resilient, determined and skilled in all forms of communication. Empathy with the debtor's situation is required at times and is often just as important as assertiveness and the ability to negotiate a suitable solution for both parties.

Debt collectors require commercial awareness and an understanding of consumer and credit law, should they be involved in legal collections. Knowledge of the financial and credit industries, numeracy and IT skills will also be of benefit.

Working conditions

Commercial debt collectors work from 9am until 5pm, Monday to Friday. It may sometimes be necessary to work extra hours, in this case in order to meet monthly collection targets.

In comparison, consumer debt collectors may work from 8am to 9pm, Monday to Saturday. However, these hours are usually part of a flexible shift system.

Most debt collectors will be office based and work in teams; in comparison field agents are often based at home and are self-employed, often visiting debtors' homes or places of work.

Future prospects

You will be entering an ever increasing profession that employs around 10,000 people, with employment opportunities existing throughout the UK.

Due to the UK being a capitalist, consumer society, overdue debt is a constant problem, with this allowing for good opportunities in the future of debt collecting.

This is one of few professions that will benefit from the current economic crisis.

Advantages/disadvantages

The job can often be confrontational and challenging, with consumer debt collectors sometimes working unsociable hours.

Qualifications and courses

ENTRY LEVEL 1

This vocation does not require specific qualifications. However, employers may look for GCSEs (A*-C) in English and maths, and a degree with an element of credit management may aid progression towards a position in management.

There are a variety of vocational courses available, with The Institute of Credit Management (ICM) providing professional qualifications, such as the ICM Diploma in Credit Management. There is also the City & Guilds diploma in debt collection, which is offered by the Credit Services Association (CSA). In addition to this, the CSA offers courses on features of debt collection, and includes information on how to deal with abusive debtors and telephone collection techniques.

Prospective debt collectors could also take part in Credit Management Training courses, with topics including cash collection and DIY legal action. CMT also offer a Level 4 Diploma in Credit Management accredited by NCFE. This awards participants with an MACP (Diploma) as well as membership of the Association of Credit Professionals for the first year.

However, the salary is often rewarding and helping debtors arrange more manageable repayments can often be gratifying.

Money guide

The general starting wage for a debt collector is usually £14,000 a year, with this increasing to £25,000 through the gaining of experience. Through becoming self-employed and establishing a successful business, debt collectors could earn more than £35,000 a year. When working for a company, target related bonuses may be given on top of basic salaries.

Related opportunities

- Bailiff/Enforcement Agent p364
- Debt Counsellor p572
- Financial Adviser p39
- Private Investigator p555

Further information

Credit Management Training Ltd (CMT)
The Old Surgery, Church Street, Cropwell Bishop, Nottingham NG12 3BY
0115 989 9997; www.cmtltd.co.uk

Credit Services Association (CSA)
Wingrove House, Ponteland Road, Newcastle upon Tyne NE5 3AJ
0191 286 5656; www.csa-uk.com

The Institute of Credit Management (ICM)
The Water Mill, Station Road, South Luffenham, LE15 8NB
01780 722900; www.icm.org.uk

ECONOMIST

What the work involves

- Economists play a vital role in a country's financial stability, with the government, financial institutions and major businesses taking heed of their advice.

- Economists research and analyse a variety of mathematical modelling techniques and data, with the information received being used to identify and predict economic changes.

- Many economists work alone, although much of their work will be through consultation with statisticians, civil servants, and marketers.

The type of person suited to this work

The work of an economist takes into account many factors and so it is necessary for them to have an interest in current affairs, politics, social welfare and business, alongside economics. Much of the job centres on the researching and analysing of market trends, so a methodical and accurate, self-reliant nature is essential, as often they are required to advise and report on situations through their own interpretation. Economic information reported in an unambiguous way will be sought; due to this economists must be able to communicate their understanding of a situation in a clear and concise way.

Working conditions

Economists tend to work regular office hours, between 9am and 5.30pm, Monday to Friday. However, some related sectors could require extended hours due to the work topic being unpredictable. For those that work in the Civil Service and similar sectors, flexibility may be allowed in relation to hours worked, with part-time work and job sharing being an option.

Economists are mostly office based, with the occasional need to travel to meet clients or to be present at conferences and seminars, to which they may need to contribute.

Future prospects

This profession holds many exciting opportunities, such as the chance to progress to an economic adviser after only three to four years, based on the ability and drive. Many economists choose to become self-employed or to work abroad with multinational companies after gaining experience and establishing a reputation.

120 new assistant economists are employed by the GES each year through September and February recruitment. The Bank of England also offers opportunities through their three-year Analyst Career Training programme.

Advantages/disadvantages

This job offers fantastic career prospects, with there being opportunities for progression in a short amount of time once training has been completed.

Qualifications and Courses

(ENTRY LEVEL 5)

It is usually necessary to have a 2.i degree in economics or higher. A joint degree with a subject of relevance, such as law, politics, finance, maths, or even a business studies degree with a high economic content, is often acceptable, so long as half the degree content studied was in economics. Postgraduate qualifications in economics could be of benefit to the gaining of certain positions within the industry.

Entry on to an economics degree usually requires at least two A levels, including A level maths and preferably A level economics. Five GCSEs (A*-C), including maths and English are necessary prior to this. Alternative qualifications of a similar nature may be accepted.

On top of academic achievement, knowledge of a foreign language may aid employment prospects, as would relevant work experience. With regard to this, the GES offers work experience placements, as does The Bank of England. These include internships, sponsorships, sandwich placements, gap year placements and vacation work placements.

The salary is highly competitive, when compared to other professions, and the working hours are relatively average.

Tight deadlines, political pressure and the need to juggle different projects can make the job a demanding one.

Money guide

New assistant economists start on a respectable wage of £25,000 a year, with this increasing to approximately £37,000 through the gaining of experience. Once they have progressed to senior level, economists could earn around £50,000 or more, with top economists in finance and consulting having the earning potential of £250,000.

Related opportunities

- Accountant p16
- Actuary p20
- Mathematician p527
- Statistician p534

Further information

Bank of England
Threadneedle Street, London EC2R 8AH
020 7601 4444; www.bankofenglandjobs.co.uk

Government Economic Service (GES)
HM Treasury, 1 Horse Guards Road, London SW1A 2HQ
020 7270 4571/5073; www.ges.gov.uk

Royal Economic Society
School of Economics & Finance, University of St Andrews, KY16 9AL
01334 462479; www.res.org.uk

ENVIRONMENTAL HEALTH PRACTITIONER / OFFICER

What the work involves

- Some environmental health practitioners are responsible for all aspects of environmental health in their local areas, while others specialise in either food safety, housing conditions, workplace health and safety, or environmental conditions.

- Your tasks might include developing public health policies, carrying out inspections in premises such as restaurants, houses and workplaces to identify any hazards and ensure that relevant laws are being followed, and educating and advising the public and businesses.

- You will also carry out investigations of accidents or outbreaks and contaminations.

The type of person suited to this work

You must be interested in finding ways of improving public health, and will need a scientific and logical approach to collect and assess evidence and use it to identify and solve problems. Excellent written and verbal communication skills are vital for explaining regulations clearly and simply to a wide range of people.

You have to be able to handle challenging situations, for example when confronting noisy neighbours. You must be able to enforce the law when necessary.

You need to be comfortable working both alone and as part of a team.

Working conditions

You will be office-based, but spend a lot of time visiting homes and businesses such as restaurants and factories in your local area. Some of the places you visit will be smelly, dirty or potentially dangerous and you will sometimes have to wear protective clothing.

You will probably work a normal working week from Monday to Friday, but you will occasionally need to work evenings and at weekends.

Future prospects

Job opportunities are good as there is a shortage of environmental health practitioners. Most jobs are with local authorities, but you could also work for central government agencies such as the Food Standards Agency, or for environmental protection consultancies, the NHS, holiday companies or the food industry.

With experience, you could progress to higher levels such as senior, principal or chief environmental officer. Self-employment and working abroad are also options.

Advantages/disadvantages

It can be challenging dealing with people who are angry, for example when enforcing regulations.

Qualifications and courses

To become an environmental health officer, you will need a BSc or MSc in environmental science accredited by the Chartered Institute of Environmental Health (CIEH) or the Royal Environmental Health Institute of Scotland (REHIS).

Entry to a first degree normally requires 2 A levels/3 H grades including a science subject, plus 5 GCSEs/S grades (A–C/1–3) including English, maths and science, or equivalent. Entry to the MSc requires a first degree in a relevant science or technology subject accredited by the CIEH or REHIS, or equivalent.

In England and Wales, at least 50% of the training must be with a local authority. Training can be incorporated into a first degree through a sandwich year, and entrants are often part-sponsored by local authorities. Successful completion of all the training requirements leads to the Environmental Health Officers' Registration Board Certificate and graduate membership of the CIEH.

In Scotland, the whole of the training period must be with a local authority, supervised by REHIS. Training may be undertaken during university holidays or after graduation. Successful completion of all the training requirements leads to the REHIS Diploma in Environmental Health.

You will have the satisfaction of protecting the health and safety of people and improving their quality of life.

You may have to face some distressing sights.

Money guide

Starting salaries are around £25,000+ per year for local authority environmental health officers. This can increase to around £37,000 with experience.

Senior staff can earn over £60,000 a year.

Salaries in the private sector vary. Environmental health officers working for private companies may earn more than those in local authorities, but this is not always the case.

Related opportunities

- Food scientist/technologist p518
- Health and Safety Inspector p40
- Health Promotion/Education Specialist p310
- Trading Standards Officer p500

Further information

Chartered Institute of Environmental Health
Chadwick Court, 15 Hatfields, London SE1 8DJ
020 7928 6006; www.cieh.org

Royal Environmental Health Institute of Scotland
3 Manor Place, Edinburgh EH3 7DH
0131 225 6999; www.rehis.org; contact@rehis.com

EQUALITY AND DIVERSITY OFFICER

What the work involves

- You will be promoting equality, ensuring businesses and public organisations do not discriminate on disability, race, gender, sexuality, age or religion.

- You will make sure that services such as education and health are accessible to everyone.

- You will promote positive images of all groups – including disabled people, men and women and those from different ethnic backgrounds.

- You will advise on how to attract job applicants from all sections of the local community and ensure the company is following all the relevant legislation.

The type of person suited to this work

You should feel strongly about equal opportunities for all and be committed to working for change. You should be able to identify problems and find creative solutions. You will need to be sensitive and tactful and good at negotiating and arguing your case.

You will need excellent communication skills and should be confident in making presentations, advising management and delivering training.

You will need to be able to understand all the relevant equal opportunities laws and regulations and be able to apply them to all policies and procedures within the company, and offer advice on any new developments and how to implement them.

For some jobs you may need specialist skills like being able to speak an ethnic minority language.

Working conditions

Much of your time will be office-based doing normal office hours. However, you will probably do quite a bit of evening and weekend work too; organising special events and working with community groups.

You could be visiting businesses and organisations, so a driving licence may be useful.

Future prospects

Opportunities are increasing but competition is strong. Government departments, local authorities and large companies employ specialist equal opportunities advisers. In smaller companies the work is covered by the human resources department.

You could progress into management and will develop specialist knowledge and experience, so you could work for yourself offering a consultancy service to companies who want to ensure they are working within equal opportunities legislation.

Lots of public services are focusing upon delivering services to asylum seekers and immigrants. This means many organisations are employing officers to work specifically with these minority groups.

Qualifications and courses

It is possible to enter this career with qualifications at Levels 2 or 3, but most people have a degree, HND or equivalent, and you will need relevant experience. Degrees and HNDs in education, business administration and law are all relevant to this career.

The most likely route is through experience working in law, human resources, social work or teaching. Many equal opportunities advisers have degrees and are members of the Chartered Institute of Personnel and Development (CIPD).

Relevant postgraduate courses include race relations or disability studies.

The CIPD offer short courses for further study, including Discrimination and the Law, and The Psychology of Diversity. These courses are open to people who are working in a relevant environment.

A number of short courses are run by colleges and training centres. These include Equal Opportunities (Good Practice), Equal Opportunities (Legislation) and Ensuring Equal Opportunities in the Workplace.

Advantages/disadvantages

You will be working for a cause you feel passionately about and could be making a real difference to people.

The work can be stressful – you will be dealing with sensitive issues and may be working with people who do not share your beliefs or want to change.

Money guide

Starting salaries are around £15,000-£20,000 per year. With experience you can expect up to £30,000. Those in senior positions in large companies can earn over £50,000.

Related opportunities

- Human Resources/Personnel Officer p41
- Training Manager p66

Further information

Equality & Human Rights Commission
Arndale House, Arndale Centre, Manchester M4 3AQ
0161 829 8100; www.equalityhumanrights.com;
info@equalityhumanrights.com
(Incorporates Equal Opportunities Commission, Commission for Racial Equality and Disability Rights Commission)

Equality Commission for Northern Ireland
Equality House, 7–9 Shaftesbury Square, Belfast BT2 7DP
028 9050 0600; www.equalityni.org;
information@equalityni.org

ERGONOMIST

What the work involves

- An ergonomist creates designs that aid society, for instance, a chair for comfort and ease or a social environment that accounts for the disabled and the elderly.

- Designs are informed by biomechanics, physiology, psychology, engineering, industrial design, IT.

- Ergonomists consult with other professionals, including design engineers, production engineers, health and safety practitioners, computer specialists and industrial physicians.

The type of person suited to this work

An interest in the human body and mind, and the ways in which designs can aid quality of life, is an important part of this profession. Ergonomists need to be creative, enquiring and observant in order to meet the needs of society, whilst being approachable and communicative when liaising with supporting professions ensuring observations are relevant in contemporary society. In order to create the best designs possible, ergonomists must be resilient and unremitting in their search for a perfect design, whilst being analytical and methodical in their research and conclusions about the needs of society.

Working conditions

The general working hours of an ergonomist are usually 9.00am to 5.00pm, Monday to Friday. However these hours may vary or increase slightly should attendance be required at research projects, or if approaching deadlines require more manpower. It is possible to be self-employed in this line of work, and through this the hours worked may vary further.

Working environments are variable, with offices usually being the primary base, whilst visits to places of work, such as factories, offices or construction sites, or laboratories may be necessary.

Future prospects

By gaining specialist experience with an organisation it is possible to move on to another company by way of progression. Willingness to change geographical location enhances ergonomists' ability to advance within this industry.

Self-employment is a common option for ergonomists, as there is often work with consultancy firms, or they can become a self-employed ergonomic consultant. There are also opportunities in teaching, training, or working abroad.

Advantages/disadvantages

Society's interest in ergonomics is increasing due to a renewed interest in health and safety, and personal welfare through well designed products which aid the body, both psychologically and physiologically.

There may not be as many chances for promotion in this profession as with others, unless you are with a large company.

Qualifications and courses

ENTRY LEVEL 5

Those wishing to enter this profession require a qualification at degree level, with relevant courses being biology, physiology or psychology, as well as computing, industrial design, engineering or physiotherapy. The following specific degrees lead to graduate or associate membership of the Ergonomics society: BSc degree in ergonomics at Loughborough University; BSc degree in psychology with ergonomics, also at Loughborough University; BSc degree in psychology at the University of Hull (associate membership only).

In order to enter degree level education, candidates usually require 3 A levels, or 2 A levels and 2 AS levels, with GCSE maths and English language at grade C or above.

Courses that are involved with ergonomics are becoming increasingly competitive. Due to this, the gaining of relevant work experience is encouraged, as is the gaining of good academic qualifications.

The Ergonomics Society encourages newly qualified ergonomists to take part in their work experience scheme, 'Opening Doors', with many other organisations across the UK offering schemes that are helpful to those entering the profession.

Money guide

Although figures may vary depending upon geographical region and employer, graduates entering the profession can expect to earn between £17,000 and £24,000 a year. This will rise to between £22,000 and £40,000 through the gaining of experience in the professional field. Senior ergonomists who are near the top of their field can expect to earn £40,000–£50,000.

Related opportunities

- Consumer Scientist p513
- Health and Safety Practitioner p40
- Product Designer p195

Further information

The Ergonomics Society
Elms Court, Elms Grove, Loughborough LE11 1RG
01509 234904; www.ergonomics.org.uk,
www.ergonomics4schools.com

Loughborough University (Department of Human Sciences)
Loughborough, LE11 3TU
01509 223013/223036; www.lboro.ac.uk

Ergonomics and Safety Research Institute (ESRI)
Garendon Building, Holywell Park, Loughborough LE11 3TU
01509 22 6900; www.lboro.ac.uk/research/esri

ESTATES OFFICER

What the work involves

- Estates Officers manage, refurbish and uphold land and property that belongs to private landlords, local authorities and organisations involved in land and property owning.

- Specific activities include the management of an organisation's property portfolio, such as ensuring the amount of rent being paid is sufficient, dealing with tenancy agreements/applications, checking that properties are not being maltreated, and organising any necessary building repair or environmental work.

- Letting, buying and management are areas of specialism.

The type of person suited to this work

This job is suitable for someone that is able to communicate well in order to co-ordinate the work of colleagues, and has good negotiating skills when discussing tenancy agreements and the terms of a contract. Organisation is of importance when overseeing a portfolio of properties for a client, with an appreciation for detail being paramount when examining a property, proposed legal documents or finances. It is often necessary to be analytical when dealing with written and numerical information, and the ability to write clear and concise reports and presentations is an important requirement of the job.

Working conditions

Working hours tend to be from 9am to 5pm, Monday to Friday. As with many jobs, extra hours may need to be worked in order to attend committees or meet deadlines, although there are also opportunities for flexitime, job sharing and part-time work. This job is mostly office based, although site visits to portfolio buildings may involve being outside in all weathers, a lot of walking, and the climbing of ladders.

Future prospects

Self-employment or employment with a commercial business may be the most sustainable career path for estate officers, due to local authorities privately contracting work to outside companies. Health authorities, civil service departments, university estates departments, charities and the Office of Government Commerce also provide work opportunities.

Opportunity for promotion is more likely in larger estates businesses and departments, with progression leading to appointment as the head of a unit, a specialist area, or department.

Advantages/disadvantages

This position holds a fair amount of responsibility, with the need to use leadership qualities and organisational skills on a regular basis increasing the chances of promotion.

Qualifications and courses

A degree is not always necessary for this job, although an increasing number of people are gaining a degree or diploma. Entry can often be through apprenticeships, with school leavers generally having at least four GCSEs (A*-C), including English and maths. There are a variety of available apprenticeships in England, with the following website containing information on which would be the most appropriate: www.apprenticeships.org.uk. Similarly, for Careers Scotland www.careers-scotland.org.uk; Careers Wales www.careerswales.com; and Northern Ireland www.delni.gov.uk.

Many estates officers have qualifications as chartered surveyors or surveying technicians, with there being a wide range of entry routes for these professions. A list of relevant qualifications is available on the Asset Skills website at www.assetskills.org.

Although mostly office based, estate officers often have to make visits to buildings within their remit, which may mean having to work outside in all types of weather.

Money guide

When first entering the profession, a junior estates officer can expect to earn between £18,000 and £27,000 a year. Through the gaining of experience and further qualifications, this amount soon rises to around £31,500 a year. Heads of units, specialist areas or departments often have an income of around £43,000 a year.

Related opportunities

- Civil Service Officer p27
- Chartered Surveyor p82
- Facilities Manager p99
- Health Service Manager p312

Further information

The College of Estate Management
Whiteknights, Reading RG6 6AW
0118 921 4696; www.cem.ac.uk

Institute of Revenues Rating and Valuation (IRRV)
41 Doughty Street, London WC1N 2LF
020 7831 3505; www.irrv.org.uk

Royal Institution of Chartered Surveyors (RICS)
Surveyor Court, Westwood Way, Coventry CV4 8JE
0870 333 1600; www.rics.org

City& Guilds

www.cityandguilds.com/myperfectjob

FINANCIAL ADVISER

What the work involves

- Financial advisers offer client consultations on a wide range of financial issues including mortgages, pensions and investments.

- You will also be producing reports and annual summaries for clients to keep them up to date with their financial situation.

- Tied advisers work for a financial institution, like a bank, advising clients on their services.

- Independent advisers sell products and services offered by a range of companies.

The type of person suited to this work

Good communications skills are essential in order to explain complex financial matters simply to your clients.

You will need to enjoy working with numbers, and have the ability to analyse and understand technical financial information.

You should be honest and reliable. This will allow you to gain the trust of your clients and subsequently sell your products.

You must be self-motivated and organised with good ICT skills.

You will also need an understanding of the relevant financial laws, and to keep up with changes in the industry.

Working conditions

You will usually work standard office hours, but you should be prepared to work longer hours at busy times.

Tied advisers usually work some Saturdays, and independent advisers may have to work evenings and weekends to suit their clients.

You will be expected to dress formally, and to visit clients in their homes or offices so a driving licence would be useful.

Jobs are available throughout the UK, but the majority are based within London and the south-east.

Future prospects

The demand for financial advisers is growing as people increasingly take charge of their own pensions and finances.

Financial advisers work in insurance companies, banks and other businesses, and there is also the option of being self-employed.

Promotion prospects are good, and there are opportunities to take additional qualifications and move into management jobs. You could also specialise in a particular area, perhaps training others or marketing products.

Advantages/disadvantages

Pay and prospects are good; you can specialise in specific financial areas, such as savings or pensions, or become self-employed.

Qualifications and courses

ENTRY LEVEL 3

There are no specific entry routes to this career, and requirements depend on the employer. 2 A levels/3 H grades and 5 GCSEs/S grades (A–C/1–3), including English and maths, are usually the minimum sought by employers. Communication and personal skills are also essential.

Trainee financial advisers may be graduates in business-related subjects. They could also have undertaken work-related training at a college, or completed a relevant Apprenticeship course.

Training is done on the job, with additional study undertaken part time or through distance/online learning. This study is regulated by the Financial Services Authority (FSA). Qualified financial advisers usually hold a Financial Planning Certificate (awarded by the Chartered Insurance Institute) or a Certificate for Financial Advisers (awarded by the Institute of Financial Services). In Scotland, the relevant qualifying body is the Chartered Institute of Bankers in Scotland (CIOBS).

The Chartered Insurance Institute, Chartered Institute of Bankers in Scotland and Institute of Financial Services also offer more specialised qualifications, for example the Certificate in mortgage advice and practice.

The job comes with a high level of responsibility, and you will be under pressure to sell products and meet targets.

Money guide

Salaries are often based on performance and meeting targets, so the rates vary between companies. Most financial consultants work either on a fee or commission basis. Starting as a trainee you could earn £19,000–£30,000 per year. Salaries of £35,000–£55,000 are possible if you have a few years' experienced and are meeting targets. For the most successful advisers, a salary of £80,000–£120,000+ is possible.

Related opportunities

- Bank Manager p23
- Business Adviser 24
- Stockbroker p64

Further information

Financial Services Skills Council
51 Gresham Street, London EC2V 7HQ; 0845 257 3772
www.fssc.org.uk; info@fssc.org.uk

IFS School of Finance
IFS House, 4–9 Burgate Lane, Canterbury CT1 2XJ; 01227 818 609; www.ifslearning.ac.uk;
customerservice@ifslearning.ac.uk

Chartered Institute of Bankers in Scotland (CIOBS)
Drumsheugh House, 38b Drumsheugh Gardens, Edinburgh EH3 7SW; 0131 473 7777; www.ciobs.org.uk;
info@ciobs.org.uk

HEALTH AND SAFETY ADVISER

What the work involves

- You will help maintain a safe workplace by developing and implementing health and safety policies and procedures.

- You will inspect premises and ways of working and ensure all relevant laws and regulations are followed.

- The work involves investigating and reporting on accidents and giving specialist advice and training to staff and managers on health and safety issues like fire regulations and dealing with dangerous chemicals.

The type of person suited to this work

You should be able to research a company thoroughly, understand the work and think of ways of improving and ensuring safety.

In industries such as engineering you will need to understand technical processes and be able to explain your findings and recommendations simply and clearly, verbally and in writing.

You should be thorough, methodical and able to understand and apply relevant laws and regulations.

You will also need good ICT and administrative skills and need to be reasonably fit for working safely on large outdoor and industrial sites.

Working conditions

You will be office based but depending on where you work, may have to spend a lot of time visiting factories, oil rigs and building sites. This could mean having to wear protective clothing, working outdoors in all weathers and at heights or in hot, noisy conditions.

You will do normal office hours but many need to be on call at other times in case of emergencies.

Future prospects

The government and European Union are producing more regulations and guidelines to help companies ensure a safe working environment for staff. This means that opportunities for health and safety advisers are increasing as employers need help implementing and monitoring new legislation.

Many health and safety advisers work in engineering, construction and manufacturing; there are also opportunities in other industries or large organisations like hotels, hospitals or government departments or with the Health and Safety Executive.

Advantages/disadvantages

The work can be varied and you could be out and about visiting different sites and meeting people. You will be dealing with important issues that affect people's safety and well-being, so there is a lot of responsibility. You will be instrumental in helping to save people's lives.

Qualifications and courses

Entry to this career normally requires an industry-recognised qualification, which can be a degree, diploma, or equivalent professional qualification. It is possible to gain experience first or alongside taking qualifications, for example at an operational level, such as in a scientific or technical field. Health and safety advisers are normally corporate members of the Institute of Occupational Safety and Health (IOSH).

The main professional qualifications are the newly revised National Diploma awarded by the National Examining Board in Occupational Safety and Health (NEBOSH), and the NVQ/SVQ Level 4 in Occupational Health and Safety Practice.

Entry to the NEBOSH Diploma requires an approved qualification in health and safety accredited at Level 3 or above. Evidence of relevant work experience may also be needed.

Some universities and colleges offer degrees, diplomas and postgraduate courses in occupational health and safety or health and safety management accredited by the Institute of Occupational Safety and Health. With an accredited degree and 3 years' relevant experience you could become a corporate member of IOSH.

Money guide

Starting salaries can range from £20,000 to £24,000 per year. With experience salaries can increase to around £30,000. Salary levels vary according to the sector you work in. In areas such as local government you could earn up to about £35,000 a year, but with experience and working in a high-risk industry such as construction or oil and gas, you could earn over £45,000 a year.

Related opportunities

- Environmental Health Practitioner/Officer p35
- Human Resources/Personnel Officer p41
- Road Safety Officer p622
- Trading Standards Officer p500

Further information

Institute of Occupational Safety & Health
The Grange, Highfield Drive, Wigston LE18 1NN
0116 257 3100; www.iosh.co.uk

Health & Safety Executive
Rose Court, 2 Southwark Bridge, London SE1 9HS
www.hse.gov.uk; hse.infoline@natbrit.com

British Safety Council
70 Chancellors Road, London W6 9RS
020 8741 1231; www.britishsafetycouncil.co.uk;
mail@britsafe.org

HUMAN RESOURCES / PERSONNEL OFFICER

What the work involves

- Human resources officers are responsible for recruiting the right staff for jobs at all levels and helping them get the training and development that they and the company need.

- You will be involved with negotiations between staff and trade unions on issues such as pay and conditions.

- You will also be involved with discipline, complaints and redundancy.

The type of person suited to this work

You will work with people at all levels and will deal with personal information and with staff who could be angry or upset so you will need excellent communication skills.

You should be interested in people and able to solve problems and help with negotiations between staff and managers over issues like pay and conditions.

You may be involved with disciplinary procedures and redundancies which can be very stressful and you will need to be tactful and diplomatic.

You will have to understand and implement employment legislation, may manage a budget and will also need to write clear and accurate reports and be organised and methodical and able to work under pressure.

Working conditions

Much of your work will be office-based, working normal office hours, 9–5.30, Monday to Friday, but you may need to work extra time at busy periods. You will visit the different locations and sites of your organisation so that people get to know and trust you, which could also involve being outdoors or in noisy, dirty places.

You will probably be working as part of a human resources team so you should enjoy working with others.

Future prospects

There are plenty of opportunities as all types of businesses employ HR staff but it's a popular, competitive career so work experience is vital. Many HR officers have a degree but you could work your way up from an administrative role.

You may get more responsibility in a small company but have better prospects in a larger one. You will need to take professional qualifications and could work abroad or become a self-employed consultant.

Advantages/disadvantages

This is a rewarding career if you are interested in people and helping them to develop their skills. You can study for professional qualifications and gain promotion. However, you will be involved in solving disputes between staff and the organisation which can be stressful and you may have to sack staff or make them redundant.

Qualifications and courses

There are no minimum entry requirements for this career, but most human resources officers have a degree or postgraduate qualification. Relevant subjects include business studies, human resource management, management, social administration and psychology.

Employers are likely to ask school leavers for 5 GCSEs/S grades (A–C/1–3), including English and maths, and some A levels/H grades.

Personnel assistants or administrators can take the Chartered Institute of Personnel and Development's Certificate in Personnel Practice (CPP) or Certificate in Recruitment and Selection (CRS), usually part time at college. The CIPD also offers NVQ/SVQ Level 3 in Personnel Support, a work-based equivalent to the CPP. Either route makes you eligible for Associate membership of the CIPD.

With a degree or HND you train on the job, usually taking CIPD professional qualifications. Some degrees and postgraduate qualifications give exemptions from parts of the Professional Development Scheme (PDS). The PDS has four parts: Core Management, People Management and Development, Specialist and Generalist Personnel and Development, and Applied Personnel and Development.

Some companies offer a graduate training scheme.

Money guide

Salaries start at around £22,000–£30,000 per year. Once qualified and with experience, you could earn £30,000–£45,000. Senior staff and HR Managers can earn over £60,000 a year.

Related opportunities

- Recruitment Agency Consultant p56
- School Administrator/Secretary p213
- Training Officer p66
- Work-based Training Instructor p218

Further information

Chartered Institute of Personnel and Development
CIPD House, 151 The Broadway, London SW19 1JQ
020 8612 6200; www.cipd.co.uk

Employment National Training Organisation (ENTO)
Kimberley House, 47 Vaughan Way, Leicester LE1 4SG
0116 251 7979; www.ento.co.uk; info@ento.co.uk

People Management
Personnel Publications, 17–18 Britton Street, London EC1M 5TP
020 7324 2729; www.peoplemanagment.co.uk; editorial@peoplemanagement.co.uk

INSURANCE BROKER/UNDERWRITER

What the work involves

- Insurance brokers will work for clients as opposed to an insurance company, and offer independent advice on the best options to meet their needs. You will also research policies, negotiate deals and sell products.

- Underwriters decide whether or not applications for insurance cover should be accepted, as well as assessing the size of risks to work out premiums.

- For standard risks you will use standard rates. In complicated cases you will use your knowledge and skills to gauge the risks and costs involved to set a price.

The type of person suited to this work

Insurance work involves communicating with people at potentially difficult times, such as after burglary or an accident. This can be stressful and requires a careful balance of sympathy and professionalism

Brokers need excellent verbal and written communication skills in order to obtain information, negotiate deals, sell policies and explain complicated financial issues to clients in simple terms.

Underwriting is a specialist job that requires an in-depth knowledge of risk in order to make predictions from applications. You will need excellent attention to detail, along with extensive knowledge in order to solve complex problems and prepare accurate and detailed reports.

Working conditions

Brokers could work in a high-street location, selling policies to the public, or in an office where customers call for quotes or claims updates. You will spend a lot of time on the phone, visiting customers and sourcing new business.

Underwriters undertake office-based work as well as spending time on site visits in order to meet clients and assess risks in various locations. You may have to investigate dangerous or distressing situations on occasion.

Future prospects

As a broker you could work in a small company, dealing with a wide range of services, or specialise in a specific area within a larger organisation.

Developments such as online insurance have increased job opportunities for people with specialist knowledge.

Underwriters could work in a firm offering a wide range of cover or a specialist organisation. As you progress, you will attract the more difficult and complicated cases which will offer new challenges.

Advantages/disadvantages

The insurance industry offers good career opportunities.

Qualifications and courses

Although there are no formal entry requirements, most organisations prefer at least 2 A levels/3 H grades and 2 GCSEs/S (A-C/1–3), including English and maths for entrance to a junior position such as insurance technician or junior account handler.

Many candidates are graduates in related subjects including accounting, maths, finance, maths, business and economics. Larger companies offer specialised training schemes for graduate entrants.

The Chartered Insurance Institute (CII), the Institute of Financial Services (IFS), and British Insurance Brokers' Association (BIBA) run relevant courses for new entrants to this career. Additional qualifications are offered by the IFS, which are particularly relevant for those seeking to work in financial planning.

Candidates with a criminal record may find it harder to find employment, as recruiters generally look for entrants with a clean background.

Insurance qualifications gained in the UK are respected worldwide. This means you can work in multinational or overseas companies if you would like to pursue a career abroad.

The work can involve a lot of responsibility and stress as you will be dealing with huge sums of money and sometimes major disasters.

Money guide

Trainees brokers start on £14,000-£25,000. This could increase up to £50,000 with 3–5 years' experience. You could earn £100,000+ as a senior broker.

Starting salaries for underwriters range from £18,000 to £20,000, rising to £28,000–£46,000 with 3–5 year's experience. At a senior level, earnings can reach £60,000.

Lloyd's of London underwriters can earn £300,000+.

Related opportunities

- Insurance Loss Adjuster p45
- Financial Adviser p39

Further information

Chartered Insurance Institute
42–48 High Road, London E18 2JP
020 8989 8464; www.cii.co.uk; customer.serv@cii.co.uk

British Insurance Brokers Association
John Stow House, 18 Bevis Marks, London EC3A 7JB
0844 770 0266; www.biba.org.uk; enquiries@biba.org.uk

INSURANCE RISK SURVEYOR

What the work involves

- Insurance surveyors use their in depth technical knowledge to advise insurance companies on the risks of specific requests for insurance cover.

- You will visit sites to collect information by which to assess the level of insurance risk.

- You will prepare reports detailing the risk for each site you are investigating, and recommend ways of reducing this.

- You can work in numerous locations and businesses, from large corporate sites to small residential houses.

The type of person suited to this work

You will be working with other professionals and members of the public, so must be able to communicate with a wide range of people. Excellent written English is also important as you will be writing comprehensive survey reports.

A great deal of work is undertaken on computer, so good ICT skills.

Workloads can be heavy, and dividing time between office-based work and site visits or meetings with clients requires strong organisational and time management skills.

Working conditions

Most of your work is likely to take place in normal office hours, although you may occasionally have to vary your hours to fit in with particular projects and the needs of clients.

Your time will be divided fairly equally between site visits, travelling and office-based tasks. Working from home is also an option. This extensive travelling means a driving licence is required.

When on-site you will need to stick to health and safety regulations such as wearing a hard hat, boots and other protective equipment. You should also be prepared to get dusty, dirty, wet and cold.

Future prospects

Unfortunately, this sector has been affected by the financial crisis so job opportunities are fewer than they were. Nonetheless, you could work for a variety of employers from large insurance companies to smaller specialist firms, both throughout the UK and internationally.

Career progression is usually well defined within each company; as your experience increases you can progress right up to senior surveyor or head of department. You could also become a partner in an insurance surveying firm, or set up your own consultancy.

Advantages/disadvantages

Your work will be varied, and you won't be stuck in an office all day. Jobs are available throughout the UK and overseas, offering the opportunity to work abroad.

Qualifications and courses

The majority of people applying for roles as insurance risk surveyors hold a degree or HND in a relevant subject such as risk management, science, engineering or insurance. The usual entry requirements for a degree are 3 A levels/4 H grades or a relevant BTEC/SQA national award.

Candidates with an unrelated degree can take a postgraduate conversion course. Distance and part time courses are also available for those wishing to work whilst they study.

Even with a relevant degree, it is rare for new graduates to obtain a trainee position without first gaining experience in other areas of the insurance industry. Many people take an underwriting position for 3–5 years before applying for a trainee role as an insurance risk surveyor.

The Chartered Surveyors Training Trust offers work-based training for young people aged 16–24 in London and the south-east of England. Applicants must have a minimum of 4 GCSEs (A–C) or equivalent.

Trainee surveyors are expected to qualify as full Associates in the Chartered Insurance Institute (CII). Flexible study can be undertaken whilst working.

You will occasionally have to work extra hours in order to meet deadlines.

Money guide

Starting salaries for trainee insurance surveyors can range from £18,000 to £21,000.

Qualified surveyors with three years' experience can expect to earn £28,000-£40,000, with some companies offering additional benefits such as a company car, pension scheme and medical insurance.

At a senior level, salaries can reach £65,000+.

Salaries in London are higher than those found elsewhere in the UK.

Related opportunities

- Building Surveyor p75
- Civil/Construction Engineer p83
- Insurance Underwriter p42

Further information

The Institute of Risk Management
6 Lloyd's Avenue, London EC3N 3AX
020 7709 9808; www.airmic.com; enquiries@theirm.org

Lloyd's of London
1 Lime Street, London EC3M 7HA
020 7327 1000; www.lloyds.com; enquiries@lloyds.com

INVESTMENT ANALYST

What the work involves

- The main job of an investment analyst is to inform other professionals, such as stockbrokers, traders and fund managers, about the best and worst investments for making a profit.

- Sell-side analysts assess an individual company's financial output and report this to private investors and unit trust fund managers

- Buy-side analysts research investment opportunities for pension funds, investment banks, and insurance and life assurance companies.

- Activities include analysing the economic stability of various countries, predicting the movement of share prices and taking account of economic implications, such as warfare.

The type of person suited to this work

This job is suitable for someone that has an interest in current affairs, and the impact these have on the financial markets. A certain amount of research is required in order to make informed, accurate decisions on possible financial opportunities, with the presentation of these requiring tenacity and self-belief. The pressured environment and the constant need to be reliable requires someone who can be resilient and trustworthy when calculating risks and forecasting trends. In order to present findings in an effective way, employees need to be good communicators who have initiative and are numerically skilled.

Working conditions

This profession requires employees to work long hours, often starting work before 7am in preparation for the opening of the London Stock Exchange and closure of Far Eastern markets, and working until after 6pm. These hours could change, or even increase, for analysts that need to cover markets operating in different time zones.

Future prospects

There are annual recruitment opportunities for graduates in large companies, with application deadlines usually being in November or December of the year before the graduate programme starts.

Opportunities for promotion are related to individual performance, with seven to eight years of service seeing an analyst progressing to the position of company vice-president; or executive director after ten to fifteen years. Should an individual or team appear to be performing extremely well, there are often competing companies that will poach successful employees.

Advantages/disadvantages

This is an extremely well paid job that allows for progression within a relatively short amount of time.

Qualifications and courses

To enter this profession you usually need at least a 2.1 degree. Subjects that are considered relevant are economics, accountancy, maths and statistics, with a second language being recommended. In order to be accepted on to a desired degree course, most applicants will need at least two A levels and five GCSEs (A*-C).

A relevant postgraduate qualification is also recommended. The internationally recognised Chartered Financial Analyst (CFA) qualification or a Master's in Business Administration (MBA) are recommended. Alongside this, summer internships in the summer of the second year of a degree can help; as many as 60–95% of interns are offered full time employment.

Should you choose not to study for a degree, possible entry routes are as a junior research or administrative support role, which allows for progression to a position as an analyst. Applicants should ensure that they have good A levels and relevant commercial experience.

Due to the fast moving stock market and the handling of vast sums of money, this job can often be highly pressured, yet rewarding.

An extremely high level of concentration is needed.

Money guide

A junior analyst can expect to be paid around £22,000–£40,000 a year. With experience, analysts' income could rise to around £70,000 a year, with a senior analyst (usually a vice president or director), earning around £120,000.

In addition to this, analysts often receive performance-related pay, with there being the possibility of substantial bonuses, low-rate mortgages, medical insurance, and life and pension cover.

Related opportunities

- Credit Analyst p32
- Economist p34
- Stockbroker p64

Further information

Association of Certified International Investment Analysts (ACIIA)
Feldstrasse 80, Buelach, Zurich CH-8180 Switzerland
www.aciia.org

Financial Services Authority (FSA)
25 The North Colonnade, London E14 5HS
020 7066 1000; www.fsa.gov.uk

Securities & Investment Institute (SII)
8 Eastcheap, London EC3M 1AE
020 7645 0600; www.sii.org.uk

LOSS ADJUSTER

What the work involves

■ Loss adjusters are independent specialists who work for insurance companies, investigating and advising on large or complicated claims or where there is a dispute.

■ During your work you will visit premises, check damage and inspect reports from other professionals such as the fire service or police force to assess whether loss resulting from an incident is covered by the insurance policy.

■ On completing your research, you will recommend the size of payments and offer advice to both claimants and providers.

■ You could be investigating numerous claims, including those caused by flood, fire, theft, fraud or accident.

The type of person suited to this work

You will be communicating with distressed claimants on a daily basis, so you will need excellent communication skills in order to be sympathetic whilst maintaining a professional distance.

Part of your job will be resolving disputes between organisations and/or individuals, which will require you to be calm and focused in order to make impartial decisions based on evidence.

You will need excellent written communication skills and numeracy.

You could be dealing with a number of complex cases at once, so good time management and organisational skills are an attribute.

Working conditions

You will usually work normal office hours, although it is not uncommon for adjusters to be called to look at premises in the evening or at weekends in emergency cases.

The majority of work is office-based, but you will have to travel to sites within the local area or overseas to make assessments.

You may be asked to assess the potentially distressing aftermath of situations such as fires, earthquakes, train crashes and robberies, in which case you must be emotionally prepared.

You will be required to wear relevant safety equipment when on site.

Future prospects

Loss adjustment is a highly competitive area of work but opportunities are increasing.

You could work in a large firm, which may allow you to focus on a particular area of interest early on and could create an excellent route of career progression into a management role.

Smaller insurance firms usually hire loss adjusters on a case-by-case basis, so you also have the opportunity of working on

Qualifications and courses

ENTRY LEVEL 3

This career is open to all graduates/HND holders, although qualifications a related subject such as accountancy, insurance studies, law, statistics, surveying, economics or business studies could put you at an advantage.

Postgraduate qualifications are unnecessary and do not usually serve to increase your chances.

You can enter the profession with 2 A-levels/3 Highers but you would have to start lower on the ladder, in a role such as that of a claims handler, and undertake further qualifications whilst you work.

Most qualified loss adjusters become Associate Members of the Chartered Institute of Loss Adjusters (CILA). To take the CILA exams, you need to be an ordinary member of the CILA, have at least two years' work experience in the office of a member company, and have a relevant professional qualification.

To become an ordinary member of the CILA, you need to be over 18 years of age and working for a company or an independent loss adjusting firm.

a freelance basis. With experience, you could set up your own firm.

Advantages/disadvantages

Loss adjusters working for Lloyd's of London, who specialise in major risks, can earn extremely high salaries.

Insurance is a major industry in the UK and overseas, so this career offers plenty of international opportunities.

The work can involve a lot of responsibility and stress, dealing with huge sums of money and sometimes major disasters like plane crashes.

Related opportunities

■ Accountant p16
■ Actuary p20
■ Insurance Broker/Underwriter p42
■ Financial Adviser p39

Further information

Chartered Institute of Loss Adjusters (CILA)
Warwick House, 65/66 Queen Street, London EC4R 1EB
020 7337 9960; www.cila.co.uk; info@cila.co.uk

Association of British Insurers (ABI)
51 Gresham Street, London EC2V 7HQ
020 7600 3333; www.abi.org.uk; info@abi.org.uk

Financial Services Skills Council
51 Gresham Street, London EC2V 7HQ
0845 257 3772; www.fssc.org.uk; info@fssc.org.uk

MANAGEMENT CONSULTANT

What the work involves

- You will work with organisations and companies helping them to develop and improve their efficiency, services, products or staffing.

- This might involve observing and evaluating working practices, researching information, training staff or developing new ways of operating.

- You will need extensive knowledge of the sector you are working within.

- Consultants can work for a private consultancy organisation, be members of a specialised team or be freelance/self-employed.

The type of person suited to this work

You will need to be dynamic, confident and self motivated. You will need to be able to research information, talk to staff and develop a thorough knowledge of an organisation. You will need to be able to identify problems and devise creative solutions and possibly develop training programmes.

You will need excellent communication skills for writing reports, dealing with staff and presenting your findings.

You may have to review budgets and make savings and your decisions might result in redundancies or spending cuts so you will need to have good financial skills and be able to justify your decisions and cope with criticism.

Working conditions

You will spend a lot of time visiting the companies you are advising, so will probably have to travel and spend time away from home.

The work can be pressured and stressful as you will be working to deadlines and taking responsibility for high-level decisions which could have far-reaching consequences.

You could be self-employed, work for a private consultancy service or be part of a team of company improvement specialists.

Future prospects

The consultancy market in this country has grown to become the largest in Europe as many private and government organisations have reduced costs by cutting management staff and employing consultants for specific tasks. There are opportunities in all areas and types of organisation but competition is intense.

To succeed you will need to deliver an excellent service, build a reputation and be able to secure new contracts and work to deadlines.

Advantages/disadvantages

This is a rewarding, varied and interesting career with lots of opportunities. You can earn a lot of money and may be able to travel. However be aware that the work can be stressful and demanding and hours can be long and unpredictable.

Qualifications and courses

Entry to this profession generally requires an Honours degree (minimum 2.1). Any subject is usually acceptable, but if you have a degree in business, management, maths, economics or a related area, this can be an advantage. Typical minimum entry requirements for a degree are 2 A levels/3 H grades and 5 GCSEs/S grades (A–C/1–3).

A postgraduate qualification, such as an MBA (Master's of Business Administration), can be an advantage; entry usually requires a good first degree, and substantial work experience may also be required.

Mature entry may also be possible through relevant work experience in management or a related area. Some entrants have an accountancy qualification with one of the main accountancy firms.

Entrants usually receive training on the job, which may include the chance to study for an employer-sponsored MBA. The Institute of Management Consultancy (IMC) offers professional training courses, including a Diploma in Management Consultancy and the Certified Management Consultant (CMC) award. For the latter, candidates need to be Associate Members of the IMC with appropriate qualifications and at least 3 years' experience as a management consultant.

Money guide

If you are freelance or self-employed you will probably be paid per day and your earnings will depend on your success. An experienced consultant could earn up to about £50,000. Senior consultants can earn over £65,000 and may also receive get commission and bonuses.

Related opportunities

- Company Director p30
- Equal Opportunities Officer p36
- Financial Adviser p39
- Human Resources/Personnel Officer p41

Further information

Chartered Management Institute
Management House, Cottingham Road, Corby NN17 1TT
01536 204222; www.managers.org.uk; enquiries@managers.org.uk

Management Consultancies Association
Institute Management House, 60 Trafalgar Square, London WC2N 5DS
020 7321 3990; www.mca.org.uk

Institute of Business Consulting
4th Floor, 2 Savoy Court, Strand, London WC2R 0EZ
020 7497 0580; www.ibconsulting.org.uk

QUEEN MARY UNIVERSITY OF LONDON - BUSINESS AND MANAGEMENT

Migle Bendziute, Kaunas, Lithuania

Why did you choose Queen Mary University of London School of Business and Management?

Being an overseas student, I had no other way of knowing whether a university is good or bad but checking the rankings online. And the truth is that Queen Mary is a very highly ranked university among all the universities in the UK. What is more, it is part of the University of London, which is a very reputable university, recognised all over the world. It was particularly important to me to be sure that my degree will be accepted anywhere in the world, that is why I chose it.

What transferable skills have you learned?

I was very happy that my university gave me not only theoretical knowledge, but also transferable skills like how to make presentations, how to do research, also team-working, organisational skills, keeping to deadlines – these are the skills that all employers are particularly looking for in candidates.

How did your time at Queen Mary prepare you for life at home (in your country)?

I still live in London and being a student definitely prepares you for life. It teaches you all you need in life – how to manage your time and workload, how to keep to deadlines, how to cope with stress, how to communicate effectively, negotiate, and get everything organised in your life.

How has your course enhanced your career prospects?

The Management course gives you the widest opportunities in your career. You can do or be whatever you want to be. Every sphere in life needs management - education, hospitals, banks, sport and entertainment clubs, retail, etc. You can work for any company or you can start your own business and be your own boss. People turn their career different ways. The best thing is that whatever job you apply for, except very technical professions like medics, the employers just need to know that you have a degree. With such a universal masters degree which covers management, marketing, finance, HR, etc, you can really be whatever you want to be, and you specialise further doing something you find particularly of interest to you. So possibilities are really endless.

What are you hoping for career wise in the next 2-3 years?

I am being really open to all the opportunities that might come my way; therefore I have no answer even to myself where I might be in 3 years time. But I know that in 2-3 years time it is possible to achieve something quite big. I am getting involved in a business that my friend is starting, and perhaps that will be a good start for my career.

Administration, Business, Office Work and Financial Services

CRCI: IA
CLCI: NAB

PAYROLL MANAGER

What the work involves

- Payroll Managers are employed by organisations to arrange and manage employees' salaries.

- You will ensure that each member of staff receives the correct amount on the correct date. When doing this you will take into account laws regarding tax, national insurance, sick pay and maternity/paternity leave.

- Your tasks will include keeping records of hours worked, calculating repayments for salary advances or student loans, calculating pay, pensions and tax deductions.

- As you progress from payroll clerk to payroll supervisor and payroll manager you will gradually take on more responsibilities, such as managing and delegating tasks to a team of payroll clerks, and creating and documenting payroll policies.

The type of person suited to this work

As you will be in contact with many employees and work alongside other payroll staff, you must enjoy working with other people and be able to work in a team.

You should be sensitive in your approach to discussing earnings with employees, and treat their information with confidentiality.

As you will be responsible for maintaining records and large amounts of information you must be organised and methodical in your work.

You will need strong numerical and IT skills as you will be working with figures and working on computerised systems.

You should also be able to multi-task and work to tight deadlines.

Working conditions

From Monday to Friday you will work around 37 hours per week. You may have to work overtime, especially at the end of a financial year which can be a busy time.

You may have the option of working part-time or flexible hours and there may even be opportunities for job-sharing.

You will be largely office-based. You will have a desk from which you will answer the phone, send emails and make calculations. You may have to attend meetings at times.

Future prospects

You will enter this profession as a payroll clerk and after you have gained a few years' experience and qualifications you will be able to progress to payroll supervisor and payroll manager.

These roles will involve more responsibility and managerial tasks such as liaising with HM Revenue and Customs, organising training for other members of payroll staff and being involved in business strategy.

Qualifications and courses

ENTRY LEVEL 2

You will not be required to have any specific qualifications to become a payroll clerk, supervisor or manager. However employers seek candidates who have GSCEs (A-C) in English and maths at least.

You may be an eligible candidate if you have a higher Diploma in business, administration and finance or even NVQs, levels 1 and 2. SQA/BTEC qualifications are also relevant for entry into this profession.

You will train on-the-job as well as taking in-house courses or attend external training courses. Such courses include NVQs in payroll administration, Levels 2 and 3, provided by the Association of Accounting Technicians. The Institute of Payroll Professionals (IPP) provides BTEC Professional Certification in payroll administration or team management.

Advantages/disadvantages

You will be working with a variety of people as you will potentially be working with each employee within an organisation.

At times the administrative nature of your work may become repetitive and monotonous.

Money guide

As a payroll clerk your starting salary can be around £13,000 to £16,500 per year.

In a supervisory position you can earn from £18,000 to £23,000 a year.

If you progress to a role as a payroll manager you can earn £40,000 or more a year.

Related opportunities

- Accounting technician p19
- Finance clerk p39
- Pension administrator p49

Further information

Association of Accounting Technicians (AAT)
140 Aldersgate Street, London EC1A 4HY
0845 863 0800; www.aat.org.uk; info@aat.org.uk

Institute of Payroll Professionals (IPP)
Shelly House, Farmhouse Way,Monkspath, Solihull B90 4EH
0121 712 1000; www.payrollprofession.org ;
info@payrollprofession.org

City&
Guilds

www.cityandguilds.com/myperfectjob

Administration, Business, Office
Work and Financial Services

CRCI: IF
CLCI: NAK

PENSIONS ADMINISTRATOR

What the work involves

- As a pensions administrator you will be responsible for the general management and maintenance of pension schemes and life insurance policies.

- You will answer queries from customers by telephone or email and complete the necessary associated administration. This can include information on policies in general, tax relief entitlement, cash sums on retirement and options for benefit transfer.

- You will undertake a variety of administrative tasks such as calculating pension forecasts, processing pension contributions and keeping up-to-date records.

- When a policy has to be paid out, in case of retirement or a death, you will organise all of the paperwork and arrange the payment of lump sums.

The type of person suited to this work

You should enjoy methodical, detailed work.

You will have strong mathematical and IT skills in order to work out calculations and check databases for information.

As you will be dealing with the public a great deal you should be friendly and polite and be able to explain detailed policies in laymen's terms.

You should have interest in the financial sector and tax regulations and keep up-to-date with economic developments.

As you will be maintaining records and referring back to them frequently you must have excellent organisation skills.

You must be able to multi-task and prioritise your workload.

Working conditions

You will work Monday to Friday, 35 hours a week. At times you may be required to work overtime at weekends or in the evenings. You are likely to be able to work part-time or flexible hours or organise job sharing.

You will be office-based which will have a certain layout and benefits depending on the organisation you work for.

You will have a mainly sedentary working lifestyle, sitting at a desk using computers and answering the telephone.

Future prospects

A good deal of on-the-job assessment and training is required throughout your career, for example pensions companies must assess staff involved in pension schemes due to the Financial Services Authority (FSA) requirements.

With experience and further qualifications you may be promoted to team leader or a management position. There may also be opportunities to move across to pension advice or consultancy where you will provide information and guidance regarding financial planning and employee benefits.

Advantages/disadvantages

Each day you will have to deal with a variety of different queries from customers.

Qualifications and courses

ENTRY 2 LEVEL

The entry requirements for this job can vary widely. The minimum academic requirement employers seek is at least four GCSEs (A*-C) in English and maths.

Initially you will work in various departments and with senior administrators to broaden your understanding of how a pensions organisation functions. You will learn about the organisation's products and services through on-the-job training and programmes run in-house.

You may have to gain professional qualifications as you work. The Pensions Management Institute offers qualifications for administrators involved in occupational pension schemes such as the NVQ in public sector pensions administration and Diploma in Pensions Calculations (DPC). The PMI also provides associateship examinations that cover the whole of pension management and administration. For more information visit the PMI's website.

You can also take one of many qualifications if you are working on personal pension schemes including the Chartered Insurance Institute's (CII) Certificate in financial administration or the PMI's Diploma in member directed pension scheme administration.

Some aspects of your work may be repetitive.

Money guide

As junior administrator you can earn from £14,000 to £18,000 per year.

With experience you can earn from £19,000 to £25,000 per year.

In a senior role or as a team leader you can earn up to £40,000 per year.

Related opportunities

- Accounts/Finance Clerk p19
- Bank/Building Society Cashier p22
- Pensions Adviser/Manager p50
- Insurance Broker/Underwriter p42

Further information

The Chartered Insurance Institute
42–48 High Road, London E18 2JP
020 8989 8464; customer.ser@cii.co.uk; www.cii.co.uk

The Pensions Management Institute
PMI House, 4/10 Artillery Lane, London E1 7LS
020 7247 1452; www.pensions-pmi.org.uk;
enquiries@pensions-pmi.org.uk

City&
Guilds

www.cityandguilds.com/myperfectjob

PENSIONS ADVISER/ MANAGER

What the work involves

- Pension advisers help individuals and organisations to choose, create and manage a pension plan that is most suited to their needs.

- You will work in-house, or as a consultant for businesses and other organisations, to set up and maintain pensions that will suit all employees whilst remaining within budget.

- As you will work with and train a team of pension advisers and administrators you will need to understand and keep up-to-date with the latest changes in financial and tax regulations.

The type of person suited to this work

As you will be working closely with the public you should have excellent communication and interpersonal skills in order to explain complex policies in laymen's terms in a polite, friendly manner.

You should have a genuine interest in answering consumers' financial queries.

You must have strong numerical skills in order to make accurate financial estimates and economic forecasts and IT skills to keep records of current policies and procedures.

You should be able to lead a team as you may manage a group of advisers and administrators. You must have excellent organisational skills and pay attention to detail.

Working conditions

You will work around 40 hours a week, Monday to Friday. You may have to be flexible with your hours to suit clients who need weekend or evening appointments.

You will be mainly office-based but you might occasionally have to travel within the UK to meet with clients and organisations or to liaise with other financial advisers.

Future prospects

As the financial sector is constantly changing and adjusting its regulations, and you must be aware of new developments, you will be subject to training and continuing professional development (CPD).

You may be promoted to senior roles, progress to other advisory roles in financial areas in actuarial firms, with accountants or solicitors for example. You may also be able to become self-employed.

Advantages/disadvantages

Your work will be diverse as you will meet with different customers on a daily basis and tailor your advice to each new client.

Some aspects of your work may be stressful, particularly if you are on performance-related pay.

Qualifications and courses

ENTRY LEVEL 5

You will usually need to have a degree, foundation degree, diploma or at least a HND. Relevant subjects include business, economics and mathematics. However it is possible to become a pension adviser if you gain extensive experience in the industry and professional qualifications.

Usually entrants to this career have previous experience in related industries such as the financial or legal sectors. Entrants with accountancy, actuarial or investment experience and qualifications may find opportunities as pension advisers but will need to take professional qualifications before they can offer advice to the public. These include Chartered Insurance Institute (CII) and PMI qualifications.

Graduate training programmes are provided by some organisations. There are also Apprenticeship and Advanced Apprenticeship opportunities in retail financial services and advising on financial products.

Professional qualifications are necessary for progression. These include CII Certification, the Award and Diploma in Financial Planning, Certificate in Life and Pensions, NVQs in financial advice and service and the IFS School of Finance's Certificate for Financial Advisers. The Pensions Management Institute (PMI) also offers a range of qualifications.

Money guide

In a trainee or graduate role you may have a starting salary of £15,000–£25,000 per year.

With 5 years' experience you can earn up to £30,000 and even £45,000 a year.

If you work in a senior role for a large firm you can earn up to £80,000 per year.

You may also be eligible for performance-related pay and bonuses.

Related opportunities

- Actuary p20
- Accountant (Public/Private Sector) p16
- Financial Adviser p39
- Pensions Administrator p49

Further information

Pension Careers
Unit 6, The Quadrangle, 49 Atalanta Street, London SW6 6TU
020 7565 7900; sales@pensioncareers.co.uk;
www.pensioncareers.co.uk

The Pensions Management Institute
PMI House, 4/10 Artillery Lane, London E1 7LS
020 7247 1452; enquiries@pensions-pmi.org.uk;
www.pensions-pmi.org.uk

PERSONAL ASSISTANT

What the work involves

- Personal Assistants work directly with one or more senior managers, helping them to be as efficient and well organised as possible.

- You will arrange appointments, make travel arrangements and type letters and reports.

- It will be your job to organise efficient administrative systems both paper- and ICT-based.

- You will probably arrange meetings, organise refreshments and take minutes as well as answering phone calls, taking messages and greeting visitors.

The type of person suited to this work

You should be efficient and well organised, be able to deal with several things at once and work to deadlines. You will have to follow instructions but also use your initiative and prioritise your own work. You will need a good knowledge of the company you work for and may have to deal with budgets. Excellent written and verbal communication skills are vital as you will be working with people at all levels and writing minutes and reports.

You may be dealing with confidential information so should be discreet and reliable. You will need excellent ICT skills and to be accurate and pay attention to detail.

Working conditions

You will work in an office, usually doing normal office hours but may have to work longer at times to meet deadlines. You may have to go to other premises for meetings and will be expect to dress fairly formally.

Personal assistants work in all types and sizes of organisations and companies. You could be working in a very small business or a large company with smart, modern offices, or anything in between.

Future prospects

There are opportunities throughout the UK.

Being a PA can be the first step in some very competitive careers such as the media, but these types of jobs will be popular.

With experience you could work for a more senior manager or move into another area of the company, such as marketing.

With language skills you could work abroad, or you could become self employed providing 'virtual' PA services using the internet.

Advantages/disadvantages

The job can be varied and interesting with a lot of responsibility. Opportunities are good and the experience and skills you will develop could lead to other areas. On the other hand, the

Qualifications and courses

There is no set minimum qualification required although employers will look for a good general standard of education and some may expect a bachelor's degree or equivalent. Some GCSEs (A–C) may be advantageous, such as English, and having a business-related BTEC HND or degree could help you find a position with greater responsibilities.

You may find it useful to have NVQ level 2 and/or 3 in Business and Administration, or a secretarial qualification from City & Guilds.

Previous experience is vital and therefore you should be able to demonstrate that you have worked in other administrative or clerical based roles.

You should be computer literate and able to use a variety of office computer software. Extra skills like shorthand, audio typing or a foreign language can also be useful for many jobs.

work can be routine and you will have to meet deadlines and the work can be pressured.

Money guide

Salaries vary according to the size and type of company you work for and you will probably earn more in London and the south-east of England. A starting salary for a Personal Assistant is around £18,000 per year. With experience you could earn around £24,000 – £28,000 per year. A senior Personal Assistant with a lot of experience and responsibility, probably in a large company, could earn £30,000+ per year.

Related opportunities

- Customer Service Assistant/Manager p486
- Public Relations Executive p425
- Receptionist p54
- Secretary p60

Further information

Council for Administration
6 Graphite Square, Vauxhall Walk, London SE11 5EE
020 7091 9620; www.cfa.uk.com; info@cfa.uk.com

Institute of Qualified Professional Secretaries
Suite 464, 24–28 St Leonards Road, Windsor SL4 3BB
0844 8000 182; www.iqps.org; office@iqps.org

www.cityandguilds.com/myperfectjob

PROJECT MANAGER

What the work involves

- Many project managers specialise in a particular area, such as the managing of commercial business improvements.

- In the course of a job, a project manager will liaise with the client, create a timescale, a budget plan that keeps to agreed standards, and choose a capable project team.

- You will need to access specialist software for scheduling, risk analysis, costing and estimating.

The type of person suited to this work

The project manager is relied upon to co-ordinate the operations of his team and solve any problems that may arise. Due to this, it is necessary for people thinking of entering this profession to enjoy team work and have strong people management, communication, and organisational skills. In order to solve any problems which may arise, a project manager must be logical and methodical, especially when under pressure.

In addition to this, the job of a project manager requires good computer skills and an ability to understand complex information and control budgets, whilst working on several other projects.

Working conditions

A certain amount of variation must be allowed for from these hours due to variety in projects. However, generally, hours range from 9am to 5pm, Monday to Friday. Like many jobs, the meeting of deadlines may mean these hours are occasionally increased.

Managers are often office based, with the occasional need to visit sites or clients to check progression. Should a manager be working on a project abroad, it may be necessary to spend prolonged periods of time away from home.

Future prospects

By becoming a project manager you will be joining a growing industry, with The Association for Project Management (APM) having over 15,500 members. Upon entering the profession, most people will make up part of the project support team, progressing to team leader after the gaining of experience, which gradually leads to a position as project manager. There are promotional opportunities to senior management posts from here, although this may mean changing companies, with some managers setting up their own consultancy business.

Advantages/disadvantages

This job allows for variety due to there being many different projects to work on. Although this may cause the employee to

Qualifications and courses

ENTRY LEVEL 5

Although it is not compulsory, it is possible to gain a foundation degree, degree, or postgraduate qualification in project management, with construction or civil engineering often being run in conjunction with this subject. Other helpful subject choices include business, management, ICT, engineering, construction or science.

In order to be accepted onto a degree programme, you will need at least 2 A levels/3H grades and 5 GCSEs/S grades (A*-C/1–3), or equivalent.

For mature applicants, entry is possible through gaining experience within the sector and acquiring knowledge about the area they wish to enter.

feel pressured, the rewards of the completed project may be of greater benefit.

Salaries are very rewarding and the expansion of the industry indicates that this is fast becoming a thriving industry with long term employment prospects.

Money guide

For people entering this profession, the starting salary ranges from around £20,000 to £27,000 a year. This is usually for people that are part of the support team on a project, with salaries rising to £30,000 and £60,000 a year for experienced project managers. For larger and higher profile projects, salaries can rise to more than £75,000 a year, with there often being opportunities for bonuses when a deadline or objective has been met.

Related opportunities

- Civil/Construction Engineer p83
- Business Analyst p158
- Construction Manager p88
- Quality Manager p53
- Risk Manager p59

Further information

Association for Project Management (APM)
150 West Wycombe Road, High Wycombe, HP12 3AE
0845 458 1944; www.apm.org.uk

Chartered Management Institute
Management House, Cottingham Road, Corby NN17 1TT
01536 204222; www.managers.org.uk

Information Systems Examination Board
First Floor, Block D, North Star House, North Star Avenue, Swindon SN2 1FA
01793 417417; www.bcs.org/BCS/Products/Qualifications/ISEB

QUALITY MANAGER

What the work involves

- Quality managers are employed by an organisation to ensure that quality assurance aims are met in relation to products or services; this includes legal compliance levels and customer expectations.

- Practices include monitoring and advising on existing systems in order to consistently improve current standards, and publishing data and reports that inform management.

- Quality managers must ensure that the company they are working for is applying the required level of environmental and health and safety standards.

- Encouraging staff to adhere to new doctrines and legislation is fundamental.

The type of person suited to this work

This job is suited to someone that has an interest in securing and improving standards of quality. In order to do this, it is necessary to have good communication skills in order to influence and persuade others to follow set regulations and uphold required standards. Problems may arise due to complicated legislation and staff lacking interest and so quality managers must be resilient and create ways in which models of quality can be easily understood and adhered to. An organisation's customers must be listened to and so quality managers must be adaptable and approachable.

Working conditions

Normal working hours apply when employed by the government or a bank, although a position in engineering, production or retail could involve shift work. Offices and laboratories are where most are based, although those with experience often become consultants to smaller firms once they have gained enough experience to be self-employed.

It may be necessary to travel to different clients during the working day, or even to stay overnight, should a customer be visiting for a meeting, or should it be necessary to travel overseas.

Future prospects

There are around 25,000 quality managers in the UK, with employment opportunities ranging across business, production, commerce and public sector organisations. Opportunities for progression to managerial and board room levels are ever increasing due to the rising importance of health and safety, and customer expectation.

Quality managers can decide whether to specialise in a particular area or whether to progress to a position of management in other sectors; these include production, health and safety, technical sales, human resources and customer relations.

Advantages/disadvantages

This is an important job, with quality managers being in charge

Qualifications and courses

Although there is no set level of qualification required, the following HND subjects will improve employment opportunities: business/management; production/manufacturing engineering; materials science/technology; printing; textile technology; clothing technology; food science/technology.

The general entry requirements for a HND course are 1 A level and 4 GCSEs grade A*-C or equivalent.

Entry without a degree or HND is often possible when an applicant is moving across from another vocational field involving quality or management. In this instance, the qualifications provided by The Chartered Quality Institute (CQI) would provide the necessary skills for a manager qualified in an area such as accountancy, law, engineering or marketing. These qualifications are the Certificate in Quality (Level 3) and the Diploma in Quality (Level 5). The Chartered Management Institute offers the Diploma in Quality Management (Level 4).

of the levels of service provided to customers and clients. With the importance of this job ever increasing, the work carried out can be rewarding and respected.

Career progression or movement to self-employment is possible. However, quality legislation is constantly updated and so it is important to keep up to date.

Money guide

Quality managers can expect a starting salary in the region of £18,000 - £23,000 per annum, with this increasing after ten to fifteen years to between £25,000 - £43,000 through experience and progression to senior level. Should you make it to a level similar to that of a director, salaries could reach £50,000 - £60,000.

Related opportunities

- Operational Researcher p532
- Project Manager p52
- Quality Control Inspector p246
- Statistician p534

Further information

British Quality Foundation
32–34 Great Peter Street, London SW1P 2QX
020 7654 5000; www.quality-foundation.co.uk

Chartered Management Institute
Management House, Cottingham Road, Corby NN17 1TT
01536 204222; www.managers.org.uk

The Chartered Quality Institute (CQI)
12 Grosvenor Crescent, London SW1X 7EE
020 7245 6722; www.thecqi.org

RECEPTIONIST

What the work involves

General

- As well as greeting visitors and directing them to the right place or arranging for someone to meet them, you will also be answering the telephone and taking messages.

- You might take deliveries, organise tea and coffee for visitors and do general clerical tasks like typing letters and dealing with post.

Hotel

- Your job will be to greet guests, making them feel welcome and at ease, provide them with services during their stay and advise them on the local area.

- Receptionists take bookings and cancellations over the phone and email, giving visitors information about the hotel and its facilities.

- You will take payments, deal with cash, cheques, credit and debit cards.

Medical

- Working in a hospital or surgery you will book appointments for patients, either over the phone or face to face, and will organise the appointments diary, making sure that cancelled appointments are filled.

- You will greet patients when they arrive, direct them to the right place, take messages and answer queries.

- Your job will also include general administrative work, preparing patients' notes and files, dealing with post and typing letters.

The type of person suited to this work

You will create the first impression of your organisation, so it is vital that you should be friendly, welcoming, outgoing and well presented.

You will need to speak clearly and give information in a simple, straightforward way and should be outgoing and able to deal with people who could be angry, upset or frightened, or have very little English.

You will be very busy at times but will have to stay calm and polite even under pressure, making sure that each visitor gets the service they expect.

You should be well organised and efficient, making sure that callers get a prompt service. You should also be able to be discreet when dealing with sensitive or personal information.

You may have to handle cash or other forms of payment, so need to be comfortable dealing with figures.

Working conditions

General

Receptionists work in an office or reception area. You will spend a lot of your time on the telephone, may operate a switchboard and will use computers to find and input information. Reception areas are seen as the face of the organisation so they tend to be very inviting and well presented, but conditions will vary depending on the organisation and its premises.

You will need to dress smartly and may have to wear a uniform. You may work normal office hours but could have to work shifts; there are opportunities for part-time and temporary work.

Hotel

The reception is vital to a hotel as it aims to show the standard of the rest of the accommodation to new guests.

As hotels are open for guests 24/7 you will probably do shift work, including late nights, early mornings and weekend working. Depending on the size and age of the hotel, you may get extra benefits such as access to leisure facilities and meals. You will probably wear a uniform.

Medical

As a medical receptionist you would work in a hospital or GP's surgery dealing with patients who could be angry or upset so the work can be busy and stressful. You may work shifts to cover evenings and weekends and could work part-time. You should be smart and well presented and may have to wear a uniform.

Future prospects

General

Many different types of organisations employ receptionists, so there are varied opportunities in all areas of the country. There can be strong competition though, especially for the more glamorous jobs.

Large companies may have senior receptionists who have more responsibility but promotion might be limited in smaller organisations.

There is no set career structure, although you can gain qualifications whilst you work, and you may have to move into other areas of work to get promotion. Reception work can be a way of starting a career in a very competitive industry.

Hotel

Smaller hotels may not offer much opportunity for promotion, but in larger hotels and chains you could probably take qualifications whilst you work and move into more senior jobs. If you work for an international chain you may get the chance to work abroad.

The tourism industry is growing and there are hotels in all parts of the country so opportunities are good but competition will be strong for some jobs.

Medical

There are hospitals and doctors' surgeries all over the country so there are opportunities everywhere, mainly within the NHS, but entry can be competitive.

You can take specialist qualifications whilst you work and could go on to supervise others or move into other areas of work.

Advantages/disadvantages

This is a great job if you enjoy meeting people and providing a service. The work can be glamorous in a multinational or high-profile company. You could move into other office or customer service work. In a hotel you could be dealing with people tired and stressed from travelling and medical receptionists deal with patients who can be ill, worried or angry. You may have to work shifts and will often work on your own.

Money guide
General

Salaries will depend on the size and type of organisation. Generally, you will earn more in London and the south-east of England, and for shift work. Salaries start at about £10,000–£12,000 per year. With experience this can rise to around £18,000. In a senior position you can expect £24,000+.

Hotel

You may receive benefits such as meals, accommodation and access to facilities. Salaries vary depending on your responsibility and the type and size of hotel. Salaries start at around £11,000 and can rise to around £26,000 with experience. In large hotels you can earn up to £30,000.

Medical

Salaries start at around £13,000 a year, going up to about £16,000 with experience. Senior staff can earn £20,000+.

Related opportunities

- Personal Assistant p51
- Sales Assistant p495
- Secretary p60
- Travel Agency Clerk p403

Qualifications and courses

ENTRY LEVEL 2

There are no minimum entry requirements, although employers are likely to ask for 5 GCSEs/S grades (A–C/1–3), including English and maths or NVQs/SVQs at Levels 1 or 2. Some office work experience and computer skills may also be required.

Some further education and private colleges offer courses in reception work. Specialist training courses are available in, for example, medical or hotel reception work. Entry requirements will vary according to the institution.

Apprenticeships/Skillseekers may be available for candidates aged 16–24.

Further training is usually provided by the employer, and new entrants often work under the supervision of more experienced reception staff. Courses available include NVQs/SVQs in reception Levels 1–2, customer service Levels 2–4, or business and administration Levels 2–4. Again, courses in specialist areas of reception are available.

Further information

Council for Administration
6 Graphite Square, Vauxhall Walk, London
SE11 5EE
020 7091 9620; www.cfa.uk.com; info@cfa.uk.com

London Chamber of Commerce and Industry
33 Queen Street, London EC4R 1AP
020 7248 4444; www.londonchamber.co.uk;
lc@londonchamber.co.uk

Institute of Hospitality
Trinity Court, 34 West Street, Sutton SM1 1SH
020 8661 4900; www.instituteofhospitality.org

Association of Medical Secretaries, Practice Managers, Administrators and Receptionists
Tavistock House North, Tavistock Square,
London WC1H 9LN
020 7387 6005; www.amspar.co.uk; info@amspart.com

City& Guilds

www.cityandguilds.com/myperfectjob

RECRUITMENT AGENCY CONSULTANT

What the work involves

- Working for an agency, you will help companies attract and recruit the right staff for permanent and temporary jobs. To do this effectively you will need to research the company and its staffing needs.

- Your work will include helping people find a job or temporary work to suit their skills and experience.

- You will assess people's skills to help them decide on the type of work they want, and may suggest further training, which could be available through your company.

- You will spend time making contacts with new companies to sell your agency's services.

The type of person suited to this work

You will be selling your agency's services so will need to be enthusiastic and well presented with excellent communication skills and sales ability.

You will probably be working on commission so should be able to keep to tight deadlines and remain calm under pressure.

It is essential that employers continue to use your agency, so you will need persuasive skills to convince them your agency is the best for them. You may need to be persistent if they do not respond after a first approach.

Working conditions

You will probably work Monday to Friday but hours can be long as you may have to speak to clients outside working hours.

You will be based in an office. You will be doing a lot of work over the phone and some agencies are internet based. You may need to visit employer premises, so could need a driving licence. You will probably work in a team and be expected to dress smartly.

Future prospects

Opportunities are good as increasingly people are changing jobs more frequently or working on a contract basis.

You could work for a specialist agency, for example supplying medical staff or legal staff but may need experience within that sector first. Some people work as 'head hunters', actively searching out people for specific high-level jobs such as company director.

If you get good results you could get promotion to management level and go on to start your own agency or you could go into a related area such as human resources.

Advantages/disadvantages

You will meet lots of different people at all levels and will get satisfaction from helping them find the right job or career, and businesses to find the right staff.

Qualifications and courses

You can enter and train in this career with qualifications at Level 2 but people often have Level 3 or 4 qualifications. Entrants come from various backgrounds such as sales, marketing or customer service.

Trainees receive training on the job, and may take courses accredited by the Recruitment and Employment Confederation (REC). The REC's Certificate in Recruitment Practice is designed for those new to the industry or who have no formal training or qualifications. The Diploma in Recruitment Practice is aimed at consultants with a year's experience, or those with A levels, a degree or equivalent. Passing the Diploma makes you eligible for full membership of the REC.

Some consultants take the Chartered Institute of Personnel and Development examinations, for example, the CIPD Certificate in Recruitment and Selection.

Working on commission can be stressful and clients and businesses could be difficult or demanding. This is a very competitive career and your success will depend on your sales ability and communication skills.

Money guide

Consultants often get commission and a small basic salary. They earn their commission when they successfully get new business or place staff. Trainees start on between £15,000 and £20,000 per year. When you are qualified and have experience you can earn up to £25,000. It is possible for the most successful consultants to earn £50,000+. You could earn extra bonuses or commission. You will earn more in London and the south-east of England.

Related opportunities

- Human Resources/Personnel Officer p41
- Marketing Manager p417
- Secretary p60

Further information

Recruitment & Employment Confederation
15 Welbeck Street, London W1G 9XT
020 7009 2100; www.rec.uk.com; info@rec.uk.com

Chartered Institute of Personnel and Development
CIPD House, 151 The Broadway, London SW19 1JQ
020 8612 6200; www.cipd.co.uk

Employment National Training Organisation (ENTO)
4th floor, Kimberley House, 47 Vaughan Way, Leicester LE1 4SG
0116 251 7979; www.ento.co.uk

REGENERATION MANAGER AND ECONOMIC DEVELOPMENT OFFICER

What the work involves

- Regeneration managers aiming to improve living environments in areas such as: dilapidated residential areas where local industries have closed down, areas of low income and high unemployment, and areas with poor access to healthcare and education.

- Specialist fields include economic development, planning, surveying, and housing.

- The extent of involvement ranges from the presentation of an idea, to ensuring that the project is completed on time and on budget and the generation of financial support and planning permission.

The type of person suited to this work

It is necessary to have an interest in the ways in which communities and living environments can be improved when deciding upon whether to become a regeneration manager. Due to this profession involving a lot of negotiation with a variety of people, you will need good communication skills and should be able to influence people towards contributing in a positive way. Regeneration managers often need to be strict with budgets and able to solve problems that may arise; both of which need a strong will and an ability to deliver results in a set amount of time.

Working conditions

Generally, working hours are typical of those for an office job, with the amount of hours worked usually being around 37 a week, with the occasional need to attend a residency meeting during the evening or at weekends. Employment with local councils tends to be employee focused, with most offering part-time or job-sharing contracts, alongside flexitime schemes.

Although mostly based in an office, regeneration managers will need to travel to sites that are undergoing the regeneration process in order to meet with residents, clients and agencies.

Future prospects

The government is currently committed to improving community areas through regeneration schemes, making this a very positive vocation to get involved with; especially whilst there is a current shortage of people who have the combination of skills required for this job.

Opportunities are available within the following employers: local authorities and government agencies, regional development agencies and English Partnerships, the government's national regeneration agency. There are also employment possibilities with private consultancies, housing associations and property developers.

Advantages/disadvantages

Both the public and private sector are becoming involved in regeneration projects, with opportunities opening up in senior management roles through the gaining of experience.

Qualifications and courses:

ENTRY LEVEL 5

All those who wish to enter this profession will require a degree and possibly experience within regeneration. Recommended subjects are urban studies, housing, and planning, with related subjects including geography, social studies and economics. In addition, the Diploma in environmental and land-based studies may of be benefit. To study for a degree, applicants would need at least 2 A levels/3 H grades plus 5 GCSEs/S grades (A*-C/1–3), including English and maths. Postgraduate study may be of benefit.

Prospective entrants should aim to gain some relevant work experience or voluntary environmental work in order to improve career and employment prospects. Areas such as housing, planning, urban design, or surveying are recognised as being of relevance. It is also recommended that you learn about government policy, the main sources of funding and the planning process in relation to regeneration to strengthen applications.

This job may become extremely challenging when convincing people that regeneration is positive, especially when they have lived there for a certain number of years.

Money guide

To begin, regeneration managers can expect a salary in the region of £22,000 a year, with this steadily increasing to £40,000 through the gaining of experience. Through a progression to senior management, regeneration managers have the ability to earn around £60,000 a year, depending on their level of responsibility.

Due to there being job opportunities in both the public and private sector, salaries vary widely; it is generally accepted that the private sector offers higher earning possibilities.

Related opportunities

- Building Conservation Officer p73
- Chartered Surveyor p82
- Project Manager p52
- Town Planner & Town Planning Technician p133

Further information

British Urban Regeneration Association (BURA)
4th Floor, 63–66 Hatton Garden, London EC1N 8LE
020 7539 4030; www.bura.org.uk

English Partnerships, Corporate Headquarters
110 Buckingham Palace Road, London SW1 9SA
0207 881 1600; www.englishpartnerships.co.uk

Improvement and Development Agency for Local Government
Layden House, 76–86 Turnmill Street, London EC1M 5LG
020 7296 6600; www.idea.gov.uk, www.lgtalent.com

REGISTRAR OF BIRTHS, DEATHS, MARRIAGES AND CIVIL PARTNERSHIPS

What the work involves

- Registrars record all births, stillbirths, marriages, civil partnerships and deaths in an area, making sure all details are accurate.

- After a birth, you will interview parents, record the baby's name and date of birth and issue a birth certificate.

- After a death, you will interview relatives before issuing a death certificate and inform the coroner or procurator fiscal if anything seems suspicious.

- You will interview people planning to marry or enter a civil partnership to check they can legally do so, and conduct civil ceremonies.

The type of person suited to this work

As most of the work involves talking and listening to people, you will need good speaking and listening skills. It is also important to judge how people are feeling and be sympathetic if need be, without becoming emotionally involved.

Handling information and attention to detail are vital to be sure that all legal requirements are carried out. You may need patience to explain procedures to people who are unclear about them.

Confidence is important when conducting marriage and civil partnership ceremonies, and good judgement to decide if people are telling the truth. It's important to be flexible to deal with different situations.

Working conditions

You will be based in the registrar's office for your district.

You may travel to some religious marriages to complete the legalities connected with them so a driving licence is useful. You might attend ceremonies within a hotel or other public places.

Computers are becoming increasingly important but good handwriting is often a requirement. You will be sitting down for most of the time.

Future prospects

There are about 1750 registrars in England and Wales and about 500 in Scotland. There are very few vacancies for this kind of work. Part-time work may be possible.

You would usually start as an assistant and be promoted to registrar, but promotion opportunities are limited. You will have opportunities for in-house training and could move into other administration-based careers.

Advantages/disadvantages

The work is varied and no two days are the same and you will meet many different people at their happiest or saddest moments. You will work some weekends and bank holidays

Qualifications and courses

In England and Wales, there are no set entry requirements for this career. A good general standard of education is expected, including English and maths. GCSEs are increasingly preferred and if working in Wales, candidates require GCSE Welsh.

Applicants from certain professions are prohibited from becoming registrars, including doctors, midwives, ministers of religion, funeral directors and anyone working in the life assurance industry.

Register office staff take the Registrar General's Certificate of Competence in Registration Law and Practice.

In Scotland, candidates need 3 GCSEs/S grades (A–C/ 1–3), including English. Assistant registrars must be 18 and registrars must be 21.

Candidates take the examination of the Association of Registrars in Scotland and obtain a Certificate of Proficiency in the Law and Practice of Registration. At least 2 years' experience is required before the certificate can be awarded.

Key Skills are communication, information handling, ICT and working with others. Experience of public speaking and a driving licence may also be useful.

and may be on call at other times. You will probably be well-respected as this is seen as an important community position to hold.

Money guide

You would earn around £17,000–£19,000 per year when starting. £20,000–£30,000 is usual as an experienced superintendent. Up to £45,000 is possible at the most senior levels.

Related opportunities

- Court Administrative Officer p370
- Court Clerk/Sheriff's Clerk p371
- Legal Executive p376
- Secretary (Legal) p60

Further information

General Register Office
Identity and Passport Office, Trafalgar Road, Southport PR8 2HH
www.gro.gov.uk

Association of Registrars of Scotland
Secretary, Registration Area Office, Municipal Buildings, College Street, Dumbarton G82 1NR
01389 738350

Local Government Careers
www.lgcareers.com

RISK MANAGER

What the work involves

- Risk managers ensure organisations are aware of the credit, market, environmental or health risks currently posing a danger to their business.

- A typical investigation of a business may include the implementation of risk control, the explaining of your organisation's risk potential to investors, bankers and clients, and preparing recovery targets after an emergency situation.

- You will liaise with the following professionals: engineers, surveyors, accident liability specialists, internal auditors, accountants, actuaries, financial managers and investment specialists.

The type of person suited to this work

This job would be suited to someone that has a strong interest in the assessing of potential risks in a business environment, particularly the financial sector.

To be successful, you will need strong communication skills in order to be able to explain potential hazards in a diplomatic fashion, whilst ensuring threats are understood and avoided.

You must be able to motivate your colleagues so that they take note of procedures and ensure that these are followed.

This is an important position that requires the thorough investigation of business related risks, and a knowledge of the safety regulations that correlate with the relevant area of industry.

Working conditions

Office working hours usually range from 9 to 5, Monday to Friday, with there being occasional opportunities for part time or flexible working.

It may be necessary to visit potentially dangerous locations, such as construction sites, oil installations and engineering plants. During these visits you may come into contact with chemicals, or work at heights or in dusty and noisy vicinities. Due to this, the work may be physically demanding and the wearing of hard hats, high-visibility jackets and safety boots will be expected.

Future prospects

This is currently a thriving vocation, with there being a shortage of people with risk management skills and an increase in businesses that are recognising the benefit of having a risk manager with skills that can reduce business costs and increase profitability.

There are promotional possibilities to senior positions through the gaining of experience, with opportunities increasing throughout the UK when specialising in a technical field or industry sector.

Advantages/disadvantages

The position of risk manager is a comparatively new position,

Qualifications and courses:

Risk managers are generally expected to hold a degree, with the most popular degree choices generally being risk management, economics, business studies, law, management, insurance or engineering. It is also recommended that relevant experience, such as in insurance, is sought to further enhance career prospects.

General requirements for entry onto a degree course are at least 2 A-levels and 5 GCSEs (A*-C), or equivalent qualifications.

Should those wishing to enter this profession choose not to complete a degree course, positions for school leavers are generally available as insurance technicians, claims handlers or risk assistants. By entering the professional sector through this route, there will be possibilities for progression. However, in order to do this, employers require their employees to study for a professional qualification whilst in employment, such as the IRM Certificate or International Diploma in risk management; both of which can be completed through distance learning.

with the demand for people with the right experience and qualifications barely being met.

There are currently few opportunities for self-employment, with many choosing to follow this route through a career in risk consulting or training.

Money guide

At the start of their career, a risk manager can expect to earn in the region of £21,000 per annum, with this increasing to between £26,000 and £65,000 through the gaining of experience. Salaries at this level are generally higher in London.

Through successful promotion, some risk managers may earn over £100,000 a year, sometimes reaching £300,000 when specialising in the financial sector.

Related opportunities

- Actuary p20
- Chartered Surveyor p82
- Insurance Broker p42
- Insurance Risk Surveyor p43

Further information

Association of Insurance and Risk Managers
6 Lloyd's Avenue, London EC3N 3AX
020 7480 7610; www.airmic.com

Chartered Insurance Institute (CII)
42–48 High Road, South Woodford, London E18 2JP
020 8989 8464; www.insurancecareers.cii.co.uk,
www.cii.co.uk

The Institute of Risk Management (IRM)
6 Lloyd's Avenue, London EC3N 3AX
020 7709 9808; www.theirm.org

SECRETARY

What the work involves

- Secretaries are responsible for organising team diaries, arranging meetings, taking minutes, making travel arrangements, typing letters/reports.

- You will develop administrative systems to keep information organised and easily accessible.

- You will deal with staff and clients at all levels, taking phone calls, answering queries and providing information.

Bilingual

- As well as the above duties, you will use your language skills to translate and write letters, emails and reports.

Farm

- You will help to run the farm, particularly the financial side by keeping accounts, estimating costs, budgeting, doing the staff payroll and researching and applying for government grants.

- You will also be responsible for ensuring that relevant health, safety and environmental regulations are met.

Legal

- Alongside more general secretarial duties, you will use ICT to create and update legal documents, perhaps using dictated audio notes involving specialist legal language.

Medical

- You will work in a GP's surgery or hospital, maintaining patient notes, organising appointments and providing general administrative support to medical workers.

The type of person suited to this work

For all secretarial work you will need to be highly organised and efficient with excellent written and verbal communication skills. Numerical skills are also an asset as you may have to undertake financial tasks. You should also be confident dealing with people at all levels.

You should have excellent keyboard skills, be able to use ICT packages and organise and maintain information systems. You will have to take responsibility, be flexible, use your initiative and be able to work accurately under pressure.

Legal and medical secretaries need particularly good written English for transcribing technical language accurately. You will also have to handle confidential information with discretion.

Working conditions

You will usually be office-based, working normal office hours within a team.

You will use a computer, telephone, fax machine and other office equipment. You will spend a lot of your time sitting, but might have to escort guests around the organisation too.

Bilingual

Bilingual secretaries spend a lot of time at their desk reading and translating documents, talking to people from other countries on the phone, and possibly dealing with the public. In addition, you might get the chance to travel with work.

Farm

Farm secretaries are either based within one farm or work across a number of smaller farms providing a mobile service. A driving licence may be helpful if you are working for several farms.

Legal

You would spend most of your time at a desk, working at a computer, during normal office hours. Sometimes, you might visit other organisations, go to court to deliver documents, attend business meetings and possibly visit police stations. You might be expected to wear formal dress, such as a black suit, especially if you have to attend court.

Medical

You will work in a GP's surgery, hospital or other medical organisation at a desk where you will spend a lot of your time on the phone or typing correspondence on a computer. Work can be busy and stressful and may involve shifts and part time hours. You will probably also have contact with patients.

Future prospects

Secretaries work in all kinds of organisations so there are many employment opportunities, but entry to the most interesting and well-paid jobs is competitive. You can start as a junior secretary and build your career to work with high-flying executives.

Bilingual

A shortage of bilingual secretaries means plenty of opportunities are available, especially if you speak a sought after European language, Japanese or Chinese. The work can be a route into translating or interpreting, or a career like sales or human resources.

Farm

You might work for one farm, several farms, or for the Farm Secretarial Bureau. Recent changes in agriculture have created more secretarial opportunities, as they are needed to keep farms up to date with new laws and financial regulations. You could use your financial skills to take accountancy qualifications, or move into administration or management within the agricultural industry.

Legal

You could work for a firm of solicitors or barristers, a court, or the legal department of large organisations such as banks or local authorities. Prospects are good. You could then go on to train as a legal executive, or progress to do law at university and become a barrister or solicitor.

Medical

You can work in the NHS or private sector, in GPs' surgeries, dentists or hospitals. You can take professional qualifications to become a supervisor or practice manager.

Advantages/disadvantages

The work can give you a good knowledge of a firm or department which you could use to obtain a promotion.

It can be a practical way of using your skills and interests.

There are part-time opportunities.

The work can be routine and you will often be in the background, organising other people's work.

The job can be stressful as it requires balancing a heavy workload and meeting deadlines.

Money guide

Starting salaries range anywhere from £13,000 to £25,000 per year, with London offering the highest wages. With 10 years' secretarial experience, salaries can rise to £40,000. Secretaries with a wealth of experience, working in prestigious law or finance companies, can earn £120,000+.

Generally, popular sectors such as media and charities pay lower salaries than large, corporate businesses.

Legal and medical secretaries can expect to start on a salary of £12,000-£16,000, which can increase up to around £30,000.

Bilingual secretaries will start on between £18,000-£20,000, and can command salaries of £55,000+.

Farm secretaries start on a similar salary to that of legal and medical secretaries, but their upper earning limit tends to be lower at £25,000.

Related opportunities

- Personal Assistant p51
- Receptionist p54

Further information

Institute of Chartered Secretaries and Administrators
16 Park Crescent, London W1B 1AH
020 7580 4741; www.icsa.org.uk; info@icsa.co.uk

Institute of Agricultural Secretaries and Administrators
Stoneleigh Park, Kenilworth, CV8 2LG
024 7669 6592; www.iagsa.co.uk; IAgSA@IAgSA.co.uk

Institute of Legal Secretaries and PAs
20 Portland Square, Bristol BS2 8SJ
0845 643 4974; www.institutelegalsecretaries.com;
info@institutelegalsecretaries.com

Association of Medical Secretaries, Practice Managers, Administrators and Receptionists
Tavistock House North, Tavistock Square, London WC1H 9LN
020 7387 6005; www.amspar.co.uk; info@amspar.co.uk

Qualifications and courses

ENTRY **2** LEVEL

Basic requirements are GCSEs/S grades (A–C/1–3), usually including English and maths, and keyboard and word-processing skills. Other ICT skills and shorthand are useful. School-leavers can start as an office junior and then progress to a secretarial job.

With GCSEs, or equivalent, you can study at college towards a secretarial qualification. These include the Pitman Diploma and Advanced Diploma in secretarial studies, and the OCR Higher Diploma in administrative and secretarial procedures. NVQs/SVQs in administration are also available. With A levels or a degree/HND you could take an intensive secretarial training course aimed specifically at graduates.

Bilingual

Bilingual secretaries must be fluent in at least one foreign language. Entrants often have an A-level/H grade or a degree in languages. Awarding bodies OCR, LCCI, EdExcel, City & Guilds and SQA offer specific qualifications for bilingual secretaries. LCCIEB offers qualifications in French, German and Spanish for business at Levels 1, 2 and 3. The British Computer Society also offers the useful European Computer Driving Licence (ECDL) qualification.

Farm

Specialist training is required to become a farm secretary. A number of agricultural colleges offer courses that are recognised by the Institute of Agricultural Secretaries and Administrators (IAgSA). The National Certificate takes one year, the National Diploma 2 years. Candidates for the Diploma need to be over 18 years of age with 4 GCSEs/S grades (A–C/1–3), including English and maths.

Legal

The Institute of Legal Executives provides training and qualifications for legal secretaries through its ILEX Paralegal Programmes. The Legal Secretarial Certificate at Level 2 and Legal Secretarial Diploma at Level 3 can be studied in the workplace, at college or by distance learning. Qualifications are also available through the Institute of Legal Secretaries and PAs. The Institute offers a diploma for new and experienced legal secretaries, as well as single-subject diplomas.

Medical

The main qualification for medical secretaries is the Advanced Diploma of the Association of Medical Secretaries, Practice Managers and Administrators (AMSPAR). Entry requirements are 4 GCSEs/S grades (A–C/1–3) or the AMSPAR Intermediate Diploma in Medical Reception. To obtain the Advanced Diploma, you will also need to pass RSA/Pitman certificates in two of the following areas: medical shorthand, medical audio transcription, and medical word processing.

City&
Guilds

Organisation Profile

Institute of Legal Executives (ILEX)

Legal secretary

In conjunction with City and Guilds, the Institute of Legal Executives (ILEX) offers an extensive range of qualifications for paralegals, legal secretaries and those in other legal support roles where knowledge of the law is needed. These qualifications can also provide you with the opportunity to transfer to the Legal Executive route to become a qualified lawyer.

Many Legal Executive lawyers started off as legal secretaries, paralegals or legal support staff and have gone on to develop a full career as a lawyer by qualifying through ILEX. However legal secretaries and paralegal/legal support staff enjoy fulfilling careers in their own right. So whatever your ambitions, why not choose the UK's leading qualifications?

If you wish to train as a qualified legal secretary or legal support staff member then we have the qualification for you. Together ILEX and City & Guilds offer the law sector's leading qualifications for legal secretaries and paralegals which are available for study through over 100 approved City & Guilds centres nationwide. Over 20,000 people have chosen these qualifications to advance their career.

Reflecting the National Occupational Standards in Administration, the programmes are now considered a benchmark for those aspiring to or working in a legal environment as secretaries or personal assistants. They offer a flexible route with no entry requirements (although a Grade C or above in English Language GCSE is desirable) and are assessed by task based assignments.

Specially produced course books are available for the City & Guilds/ILEX Diploma in Legal Studies. The qualifications can be used as part of your entry criteria to study as a Legal Executive lawyer with ILEX.

City & Guilds approved centres are available nationwide. To find your nearest centre, simply contact your regional City & Guilds office (details on http://www.cityandguilds.com) or email legalstudies@ilex.org.uk

Legal Secretaries and Paralegals are now eligible to apply to become members of ILEX. The grades and fees for 2010 are as follows:

> Student member – for those wishing to enter the legal profession; those who have no relevant legal qualification; or those with less than three years' work experience of a predominantly legal nature. Annual subscription fees of £50 are payable, plus a one-off initial registration fee of £35.

> Affiliate member – for those with at least one ILEX level 3 unit qualification, or who have completed a relevant legal qualification at level 2, or gained at least three years' work of a predominantly legal nature. Annual subscription fees of £90 are payable, plus a one-off initial registration fee of £35.

For more information on ILEX qualifications or to receive information on your nearest study centre, please call +44 (0)1234 841000 or email info@ilex.org.uk

STOCK MARKET TRADER

What the work involves

- Traders use their knowledge of the market to make the highest possible profit on behalf of investors by buying and selling shares, bonds and other assets.

- There are three types: market traders operate on behalf of clients; sales traders highlight new financial ideas, but take direct orders from clients; and proprietary traders make investments for banks.

- You will deal with large sums of money, so your decisions must be quick and well-informed; due to this, you will need to build strong contacts in order to be successful in this business.

The type of person suited to this work

You should have enthusiasm for the financial sector and enjoy a working environment that is highly performance related.

Alongside this, you will need to be extremely confident and full of informed initiative, whilst having the ability to cope with the constant pressure of trading with large sums of money that belong to other people.

As well as demanding accuracy, skilled analysis and responsibility, the job also requires that you are physically forceful and competitive, an excellent verbal communicator and a team player.

Working conditions

Traders often need to begin work at 7am in order to be informed about developments that have happened in foreign markets overnight and to be ready for the 8am opening of the London Stock Exchange, often not finishing their working day until 5pm.

The highly pressurised trading arena involves the monitoring of markets on a screen, and the making of deals on a phone. This communicative tool has made the environment less noisy, whilst remaining competitive and ruthless.

Future prospects

Given the current financial climate, opportunities for traders are severely limited.

Once in the industry however, there are many opportunities for progression. The gaining of experience and qualifications allows for promotion to an analyst, being put in charge of a team or gaining the responsibility of a new trading desk. These positions often lead to associate, senior associate and director level.

Many traders change career after a few years due to the highly pressurised working environment.

International offices are common with investment banks, bringing an opportunity to work in foreign arenas.

Advantages/disadvantages

This is an exciting and often hugely rewarding job that would

Qualifications and courses:

ENTRY LEVEL 5

You will need at least 2.1 degree or higher, in a subject that has a strong numerical focus to it, such as economics, business studies, accountancy, maths, science or engineering. Minimum requirements for degree courses are often at least 2 A levels and 5 GCSEs (A*-C), including English and maths, or equivalent qualifications.

It is also a good idea to try and gain an internship or financial work experience, alongside the submission of a speculative application, which shows research has been carried out into the industry. Major investment banks offer graduate training schemes.

The Diploma in business, administration and finance may be an alternative route to taking a degree.

never become boring due to the constant changes in the financial market.

The highly pressurised environment can often be stressful and means the professional duration of a stock market trader is generally less than those in another profession.

Money guide

The starting salary of a stock market trader is usually between £25,000 and £40,000 per annum, with this quickly rising to over £100,000 a year through the gaining of experience.

Some traders at the height of their profession can earn more than £200,000 a year. However it must be noted that these are figures for markets in London, and other regions will sometimes pay far less than these top figures.

In addition to these impressive salaries are large bonuses, up to 100 per cent of a salary, non-contributory pensions and mortgage subsidies.

Related opportunities

- Investment Analyst p44
- Risk Manager p59
- Stockbroker p64

Further information

Financial Services Authority (FSA)
25 The North Colonnade, London E14 5HS
020 7066 1000; www.fsa.gov.uk

Financial Services Skills Council (FSSC)
51 Gresham Street, London EC2V 7HQ
0845 257 3772; http://careers.fssc.org.uk, www.fssc.org.uk

London Stock Exchange
10 Paternoster Square, London EC4M 7LS
020 7797 1000; www.londonstockexchange.com

STOCKBROKER

What the work involves

- Companies and the government raise money to fund their work by selling stocks and shares in their business; these are what stockbrokers trade in.

- Stockbrokers work for individuals or companies investing their clients' money to make them a profit by buying and selling stocks and shares.

- You will be advising your clients on investing their money, often dealing with huge amounts.

- You will have to keep up to date with economic trends and predict how a company's stocks and shares are likely to perform.

The type of person suited to this work

To succeed as a stockbroker you must be confident, determined, competitive and outgoing.

You will have to predict trends in a constantly changing market and take risks with huge sums of money so must be decisive and able to work under pressure. You will need to be trustworthy and honest with a good reputation and excellent people skills.

You will need excellent ICT skills and will be expected to work long hours and to dress smartly.

Working conditions

You will be office-based, getting a lot of information from computers and doing much of your work by telephone. Hours are long: you will probably start early and finish late in order to trade on international markets working in different time zones. You will probably have to work over the weekend. Much of your day will be spent in a very busy, tense and pressurised environment.

Future prospects

You could be working for a stockbroking firm which specialises in this work or for other financial institutions such as banks or building societies. Your career will develop by taking on more responsibilities and more important clients.

Competition for jobs is intense so work experience is vital. Economic changes can happen fast so jobs are not always secure.

This is a high pressure job and many stockbrokers finish their careers in their 40s. You could move into other areas within finance or become self-employed as a consultant.

Advantages/disadvantages

The hours are long and the work is very pressurised and stressful.

It is a very competitive job and you will need to be tough and determined to succeed and do well.

The work can be exciting and rewarding and is extremely well paid.

Qualifications and courses

You will normally need at least a 2.1 degree, particularly in such subjects as economics, business studies, maths, physics, accountancy or law. Increasingly, in a very competitive market, possession of a postgraduate qualification such as an MBA (Master of Business Administration) or MSc in subjects such as business or economics, together with another language, will prove very useful.

Typical entry requirements for a degree course are 2 A levels/3 H grades and 5 GCSEs/S grades (A–C/1–3) or equivalent; specific subjects may be required.

Individuals with relevant experience may be able to move into stockbroking from an analyst, research or investment banking role and graduates are allowed to register for the Chartered Financial Analyst (CFA) Institute's exams before starting in stockbroking.

New entrants must be registered by their employer as an 'authorised person' with the Financial Services Authority (FSA). To gain registration, you need to pass an FSA-approved examination, for example the Investment Management Certificate awarded by the UK Society of Investment Professionals, or the Securities and Investment Institute's Certificate in Investment Management.

Many companies have their own, very detailed selection procedures, including psychometric and aptitude testing.

Money guide

You could earn £18,000–£35,000 a year when you first start work and training after university, with a fairly small number of clients.

With experience you could earn between £45,000 and £80,000. After many years of experience and depending on location, some stockbrokers can earn over £150,000. Stockbrokers get bonuses on the trade they do and can earn extremely high salaries.

Related opportunities

- Accountant p16
- Bank Manager p23
- Economist p34
- Financial Adviser p39

Further information

London Stock Exchange
10 Paternoster Square, London EC4M 7LS
020 7797 1000; www.londonstockexchange.com

Securities and Investment Institute
8 Eastcheap, London EC3M 1AE
020 7645 0600; www.sii.org.uk; info@sii.org.uk

Financial Services Authority
25 The North Colonnade, London E14 5HS
020 7066 1000; www.fsa.gov.uk

SWITCHBOARD OPERATOR / TELEPHONIST

What the work involves

- Switchboard operators work at a switchboard, answering calls, connecting callers to the right person and advising them on which department or person they need to speak to.

- You would answer callers' questions about the company, take messages, test phone lines and report faults.

- Some use computer databases to find the numbers of internal staff and connect calls to them.

- You might do other reception duties like meeting and dealing with visitors, taking deliveries and other clerical work.

The type of person suited to this work

Switchboard operators need an excellent telephone manner so you should have good spoken English and be able to speak clearly. You will also need to have good hearing.

Because you will be dealing with the public, you will need good customer service skills, which means staying polite and calm even when you are busy and when dealing with rude or impatient callers.

You should be someone who enjoys working with people in a team and who can work quickly and accurately. You will also need to be able to take messages and remain calm even when you are busy.

Working conditions

Most of your work will be in an office or telephone room, probably with other people. You might be based at a reception desk.

Although you will probably do normal office hours, you may need to be at work to take calls before the company opens. Some switchboards provide a 24-hour service which means working shifts including nights and weekends.

You will probably wear a headset and use computer databases and automated switchboards

Future prospects

Most large or medium-sized companies need people to answer their phones and provide a reception service, so job opportunities are good.

You could work in a call centre where opportunities have increased significantly in recent years. Recent changes in the telecommunications industry have meant more job opportunities as the number of companies providing these services has increased

You could become a senior telephonist receiving training in customer service skills and gaining administrative experience. You could then move into a wide range of jobs working in business administration in offices or with the public.

Qualifications and courses

There are no formal entry requirements for this work, but 5 good GCSEs/S grades (A–C/1–3), including English language and maths, are a distinct advantage. Basic computing skills or an ICT qualification are also useful.

Many colleges offer courses in customer service and call centre techniques at Levels 1–3.

Most training is done on the job. You may be able to work towards an NVQ/SVQ Level 3 in Operating and Maintaining the Performance of Telecommunications Equipment.

ENTRY LEVEL 1

Advantages/disadvantages

On a busy switchboard you will be working under pressure and could be working shifts.

Dealing with the public means staying polite and calm no matter how they speak to you!

You will gain valuable customer service and administration skills to help you progress.

Money guide

As a trainee your starting salary is normally around £12,000 per year. With more experience this rises to £16,000+. Earnings could reach £17,000+ for a senior switchboard operator with experience. Earnings could reach £21,000+ for a senior switchboard operator who has experience and more responsibility, perhaps supervising other staff.

Related opportunities

- Call Centre Operative p485
- Court Administrative Officer p370
- Receptionist p54
- Secretary p60

Further information

Institute of Direct Marketing
1 Park Road, Teddington TW11 0AR
020 8977 5705; www.theidm.com; enquiries@theidm.com

Institute of Customer Service
2 Castle Court, St Peter's Street, Colchester CO1 1EW
01206 571716; www.instituteofcustomerservice.com;
enquiries@icsmail.co.uk

e-skills UK
1 Castle Lane, London SW1E 6DR
0207 963 8920; www.e-skills.com; info@e-skills.com

www.cityandguilds.com/myperfectjob

TRAINING MANAGER

What the work involves

- You will be responsible for making sure your company's staff, from new recruits to experienced managers, have the skills and knowledge they need to make the business as efficient as possible.

- Some of your work will involve looking at how to provide the best training at the lowest cost – from different options such as in-house, distance learning, ICT packages or college courses.

- You will also deliver training yourself or organise other trainers to do this. You will have to write reports and make presentations assessing the value of training.

The type of person suited to this work

You should be interested in people and in helping them to develop and improve their skills. You will need to be able to pass on your knowledge and expertise in a lively, interesting way by designing imaginative and varied training that appeals to everyone.

You will need to be organised and able to plan ahead, meet deadlines and assess the effectiveness of training. To do this you will need excellent ICT skills and an understanding of costs and budgets.

Working conditions

You will usually do normal office hours but may have to work longer at busy times or attend residential, evening or weekend events.

You will be based in an office, probably working as part of a team, but will spend a lot of your time out and about – delivering training, finding training venues, going to meetings and visiting staff in their work places.

You will spend a lot of time in the office using a computer but will oversee and deliver training at a range of venues.

Future prospects

Training managers come from a variety of backgrounds as they often become experts in their own field before moving into training people within the industry, but it is possible to go straight in, possibly as a graduate trainee.

There are opportunities all over the country as all types of organisations have training managers. Developments in new technology and more on the job training have increased the need for staff training. More companies are using consultants to deliver training to their staff so opportunities to become a self-employed consultant are increasing. It is also possible to gain promotion or move into related areas such as personnel.

Advantages/disadvantages

The work can be very varied and you will have the satisfaction of passing on your expertise to help people learn and develop.

Qualifications and courses

There are no formal requirements for entry into this profession, but some employers may require relevant vocational qualifications, such as an NVQ/SVQ Training and Development, or a degree or HND in a subject such as business studies, management, training or personnel.

Training managers are often trained in-house but there are some relevant courses of study. The Chartered Institute of Personnel and Development (CIPD) offers a range of relevant courses, including: the Certificate in Personnel Practice (CPP); Certificate in Training Practice (CTP); and a Professional Development Scheme. The latter consists of 4 modules, completion of which allows the candidate to become a graduate member of the CIPD.

Other relevant NVQs/SVQs include Direct Training and Support at Level 3; Management and Development of Learning Provision, and Training and Development Strategy at Level 5.

Postgraduate qualifications in training and development are also available. Entry usually requires a degree, a relevant professional qualification, or equivalent work experience.

You may need to work hard to motivate staff who are having to do training they are not interested in or do not feel they need.

Money guide

Starting salaries are around £16,000 - £22,000 per year. As an experienced and qualified training officer you can earn £20,000 - £35,000. This could rise to £60,000 a year in some companies for a training manager with responsibility for other staff. Salaries vary, depending on experience and the size of the company.

Related opportunities

- Human Resources/Personnel Officer p41
- Lecturer FE and HE p206
- Teacher Primary and Secondary p212
- Work-based Training Instructor p218

Further information

Chartered Institute of Personnel and Development
CIPD House, 151 The Broadway, London SW19 1JQ
020 8971 9000; www.cipd.co.uk

Employment National Training Organisation (ENTO)
4th floor, Kimberley House, 47 Vaughan Way, Leicester
LE1 4SG
0116 251 7979; www.ento.co.uk; info@ento.co.uk

Lifelong Learning UK (LLUK)
0870 757 7890; www.lifelonglearninguk.org;
enquiries@lluk.org

Building and Construction

Are you interested in working on a construction site with a team of people? Maybe your interest lies in buying and selling property and working in an office is more your sort of thing. All the jobs in the sector require someone with a great eye for detail, creative flair and someone who is very good at working with others.

In this section we look at the following jobs:

For similar jobs to the ones in this section why not have a look at *Engineering, Manufacturing and Production* on page 219.

ARCHITECT

What the work involves

- Architects design new buildings and the spaces around them. They also design changes to existing buildings.

- Your work will include agreeing design briefs with clients, researching development sites, deciding which materials to use for particular buildings and drawing technical plans.

- You will also be responsible for testing new ideas, obtaining planning permission and inspecting building work while it is in progress

- You could specialise in a particular field such as building heritage and conservation, sustainable and environmental design, or project management.

The type of person suited to this work

You must be able to produce creative, detailed designs that meet the needs and wishes of your clients and other people in the community.

You will need excellent verbal communication skills for working with other professionals, such as surveyors, planners and builders, and for presenting your ideas to them and your clients. You also have to be organised and have good research and problem-solving skills.

As you will use computer-aided design (CAD) in your work, ICT skills are also useful.

Working conditions

Although architects are based in offices, you will go out to visit construction-sites and meet clients. You will need to pay attention to health and safety regulations when on-site. A driving licence may be necessary.

You are likely to work regular office hours, although to meet deadlines you may have to do some work at weekends and during the evenings.

Future prospects

Generally, you would start work in a private architect's practice to gain wide experience of the work, but you may also work for other employers, such as local or central government, later on.

Self-employment is common for qualified and experienced architects.

In the long term, your career will be dependent on your experience, ability and competence. If you decide to remain in private work you could progress to associate level and possibly become a partner. Some of the larger architectural practices win international contracts so you could work on projects abroad.

Advantages/disadvantages

There may be problems to overcome when making design decisions. For example, there might be conflicting needs and views to deal with.

Qualifications and courses

Professional architects must have chartered membership of the Royal Institute of British Architects (RIBA) and registration with the Architects Registration Board (ARB). The main route to qualification is via a RIBA/ARB recognised degree. Minimum entry requirements are 2 A levels or 1 A and 2 AS levels, which should be drawn from academic fields of study. In addition you must have passed at least 5 GCSEs. Equivalent qualifications such as a National Certificate/Diploma may be accepted.

Candidates without the usual entry requirements may be able to take a foundation year at a school of architecture to prepare for entry.

Training as an architect takes 7 years. Candidates undertake a 5-year degree programme, divided into three parts. Part 1 takes 3 years and Part 2 takes 2 years. A year is spent working in an architect's office after both Part 1 and Part 2. Candidates then take the Part 3 examination in Professional Practice and Management, leading to chartered membership of RIBA.

If you have passed Part 1, you may be able to join an architectural practice as a part-qualified architect and complete the training over a longer period by part-time study. Part-qualified architects can also work as architectural technicians.

There is personal satisfaction in dealing with these problems and creating designs for buildings that will influence the landscape for many years to come.

Money guide

There are no set pay scales for this work but you can generally earn more if you work in the private sector rather than the public sector. On starting out, with RIBA Part 3 qualifications, you could earn around £28,000–£34,000 per year. Average salaries for experienced architects are from £30,000 to £42,000. Senior architects can earn more than £45,000.

Related opportunities

- Architectural Technician p70
- Architectural Technologist p71
- Construction Manager p88
- Town Planner p133

Further information

Architects Registration Board
8 Weymouth Street, London W1W 5BU
020 7580 5861; www.arb.org.uk

Royal Incorporation of Architects in Scotland
15 Rutland Square, Edinburgh EH1 2BE
0131 229 7545; www.rias.org.uk

Royal Institute of British Architects
66 Portland Place, London W1B 1AD
020 7580 5533; www.architecture.com

FACULTY OF ART, ARCHITECTURE AND DESIGN
University of Lincoln

The Faculty of Art, Architecture and Design houses two Schools:

- The School of Art and Design
- The School of Architecture

The two Schools offer a comprehensive range of visually creative subjects at undergraduate, taught postgraduate and postgraduate research levels.

SCHOOL OF ARCHITECTURE

The **Lincoln School of Architecture**, housed in the award winning Rick Mather designed building on the main Lincoln campus, was originally established in the 1930s in Hull. Today it offers a multidisciplinary 3D design environment, founded on the research and consultancy interests of its staff, having developed an international reputation. The School has benefitted over the years from substantial investment in its facilities which include dedicated design studios, workshops and information technology suites. Modern computer-aided design facilities reinforce the School's progressive and vibrant establishment, preparing students for the creative opportunities of today's world.

Undergraduate courses offered:-

BA (Hons) Architecture RIBA/ARB Part 1 and 2
BA (Hons) Design for Exhibition and Museum
BA (Hons) Interior Design

BA (Hons) Design for Exhibition and Museum shares its first year with BA (Hons) Interior Design, both of which have common links with BA (Hons) Architecture. Design for Exhibition and Museum is a very successful niche course, taking its skill set from disciplines in both Architecture and Design, to allow students to graduate fully equipped to enter into a highly competitive 3D design industry. Interior Design at Lincoln is very much a programme specialising in Interior Architecture or Spatial Architecture, the design of existing space.

For further information on any of these courses, please contact the Faculty of Art, Architecture and Design at aadenquiries@lincoln.ac.uk or telephone 01522 837171.

Web links:-

University website	**www.lincoln.ac.uk/aad**
School of Architecture website	**www.lincoln.ac.uk/lsa**
School of Art and Design website	**www.lsad.co.uk**

UNIVERSITY OF
LINCOLN

ARCHITECTURAL TECHNICIAN

What the work involves

- You will be responsible for liaising between the construction and design teams, making sure everyone is up to date with the latest project developments.

- You will gather and organise all of the technical information which will be required throughout the project.

- You will prepare drawings, plans and specifications using CAD (computer-aided design) software and also by hand.

- This is essentially a support role; you will be providing assistance to the other members of the team including architects, architectural technologists, surveyors and engineers. You will enable them to complete their work as efficiently as possible.

The type of person suited to this work

You need good drawing skills, both hand and computer-aided design (CAD). You will need an ability to visualise in three dimensions.

You must also be able to develop a scientific and technological knowledge of building materials. You will need to understand building regulations and techniques and be able to explain them to others.

You will need to be able to work well alone, as well as having good verbal communication skills for working with other professionals, such as architects, surveyors and engineers.

Your organisational, research and problem-solving skills will need to be excellent.

Working conditions

Architectural technicians are based in offices, but you may visit sites to inspect work in progress. You will need to be aware of health and safety regulations when on-site and will be expected to wear safety clothing. When working on site you will be outdoors in all weathers and may need to climb ladders or scaffolding. You may need a driving licence. You are likely to work normal office hours (9–5, Monday to Friday), although you may have to work late and at weekends on some projects.

Future prospects

An architectural technician may take further CIAT-accredited training to develop their skills and apply to work as an architectural technologist.

You could choose to work in private practice or alternatively within the public sector in an area such as local government, research practices, education or central government. You may need to change employers in order to progress.

There is also the possibility to work freelance or on short contracts.

Advantages/disadvantages

As you will be the main point of contact between contractors

Qualifications and courses

ENTRY LEVEL 5

The most common route into this career is to complete a HNC/HND or a foundation degree in a relevant subject such as architecture or building technology. HND/HNC courses usually require applicants to have at least 1 A level (relevant subjects include physics and maths) as well as a GCSE grade A*–C in your A level subject. You should also have another 3 or 4 GCSEs grade A*–C including maths, English and a science subject.

You can also complete a degree; however most employers will not expect applicants to be graduates.

To become a qualified architectural technician you will need to apply to become an Associate Member (ACIAT) of The Chartered Institute of Architectural Technologists (CIAT). In order to achieve this you must first complete two years of supervised work experience and be assessed against CIAT's professional standards. You can then extend your skills and become a Chartered Member of the Institute (MCIAT).

and clients, when things get heated you will be in the middle of it.

If you work for a larger company you will have the opportunity to work on a range of projects which will keep your job interesting.

Money guide

Technicians can expect a starting salary of between £16,000 and £18,500 per year.

Experienced technicians earn on average £24,000 and project managers may earn over £40,000 a year.

Earnings vary widely depending on location and the individual employer.

If you work as a freelance architectural technician you can expect to earn between £15 and £25 an hour.

Related opportunities

- Architect p68
- Architectural Technologist p71
- Cartographer p79
- Technical Surveyor p130
- Town Planning Technician p133

Further information

ConstructionSkills
Bircham Newton, King's Lynn PE31 6RH
01485 577577; www.cskills.org; www.bconstructive.co.uk

Chartered Institute of Architectural Technologists
397 City Road, London EC1V 1NH
020 7278 2206; www.ciat.org.uk

Chartered Institute of Building
Englemere, Kings Ride, Ascot SL5 7TB
01344 630700

ARCHITECTURAL TECHNOLOGIST

What the work involves

- You will be responsible for ensuring that the architect's design is translated into a functioning building.

- You will be involved right from the start, helping to liaise with the client and the architect and advise them on any issues that might affect the build.

- You will make sure that the more practical elements of the build run smoothly, by ensuring that the right materials are used and that all legal requirements and building regulations are met.

- You will have a leading role within the construction team including developing project briefs, coordinating, negotiating contracts and providing guidance.

The type of person suited to this work

You need good drawing skills, both hand and computer-aided design (CAD). You will need an ability to visualise in three dimensions.

You must also be able to develop a scientific and technological knowledge of building materials. You will need to understand planning regulations and construction law, and be able to explain them to others.

You will need good communication skills for working with other professionals. Your organisational, management, research and problem-solving skills will need to be excellent.

Working conditions

Architectural technologists are based in offices, but you may visit sites to inspect work in progress. You will generally be working 9–5 but you might need to work extra hours to meet deadlines. You will need to be aware of health and safety regulations when on-site and will wear safety clothing. On-site work can be cold and wet or hot and dusty as you will be outdoors in all weathers. You may need a driving licence.

Future prospects

Architectural technologists, with CIAT qualifications and experience, may set up their own practice or work in a partnership with other architectural technologists or architects.

It is also possible to progress within private firms to more senior positions or move to other companies which attract larger and possibly international contracts. Promotion is generally easier within larger firms but you may still need to change employers in order to progress.

Advantages/disadvantages

There may be problems to solve at any time during the architectural process, for example issues with the supply of the right materials.

It is rewarding to make your contribution to the design and construction of buildings that will influence the landscape for many years to come.

Qualifications and courses

The preferred route to becoming an architectural technologist is to complete a degree which has been accredited by the Chartered Institute of Architectural Technologists (CIAT). There are about 29 of these degree programmes and they are listed in CIAT's careers handbook. After this you must complete CIAT's POP record and professional practice interview.

You could alternatively complete an NVQ/SVQ Level 4 in architectural technology or a related industry degree such as architecture, architectural engineering, building services engineering, building/construction, built environment studies, civil and structuring engineering, computer-aided engineering and surveying.

Completion of a HNC/HND in Construction or a foundation degree in Architectural Technology will enable you to become a qualified architectural technician. Once you have had more than 10 years experience and successful completion of CIAT's professional standards assessment you could become an architectural technologist.

You could choose to complete postgraduate study in architectural technology; however this is not a requirement of the profession.

If you can complete relevant work experience this would be extremely beneficial. You can find relevant placements on the CIAT website and in their publications and in other industry publications and websites.

Money guide

Generally salaries are higher in London and the south.

A junior technologist can expect to earn between £15,000 and £22,000 a year.

After three years experience you should be earning between £24,000 and £28,000 a year.

Once you are in a senior position and have been working for 10 years your salary should be somewhere between £35,000 and £42,000 per year.

Related opportunities

- Architect p68
- Architectural Technician p70
- Cartographer p79
- Town Planner p133

Further information

ConstructionSkills
Bircham Newton, King's Lynn PE31 6RH
01485 577577; www.cskills.org; www.bconstructive.co.uk

Chartered Institute of Architectural Technologists
397 City Road, London EC1V 1NH
020 7278 2206; www.ciat.org.uk

CRCI: BA
CLCI: UB

BRICKLAYER

What the work involves

- Bricklayers build and repair external and internal walls.

- As a bricklayer, you will use a range of materials including bricks, stones and mortar to build walls that often include ornamental and decorative effects.

- You will use specialist tools such as trowels to spread mortar and different types of hammers to cut and trim bricks and blocks.

- You will spend a lot of your time outside doing very manual work.

The type of person suited to this work

As the work requires you to move around a lot and lift materials, you must be physically fit. And you must not mind working at heights.

You need to be able to follow plans and work with accuracy and attention to detail, so that the walls you build are structurally perfect and create the right visual effect.

You also need to work in a team with other bricklayers and those in other construction trades and professions.

Working conditions

You will often be working outdoors in all weather conditions. This can mean being cold and wet in the winter and hot and dusty in the summer.

To keep yourself and others safe you will need to observe health and safety regulations, which will include wearing protective clothing.

You are likely to work a normal working week, although weekend work may also be available.

Future prospects

There are currently plenty of opportunities to enter bricklaying. About 30% of the construction workforce is due to retire within the next 10 years and there will be a continuing need to recruit more young people into the industry.

In the long term, you could progress to technical, supervisory and managerial roles. The construction industry has one of the highest percentages of self-employment of any occupational sector and bricklayers are no exception. Many have set up their own businesses, often working on smaller, more local contracts.

Advantages/disadvantages

The work can be physically demanding for some people.

Bricklayers are in demand particularly in the south-east of England.

This is a great career if you like being outdoors, doing practical and creative work.

Qualifications and courses

Apprenticeships/Skillseekers are open to those aged 16–24. Some GCSEs/S grades (A–E/1–5) are normally required, in subjects such as English, maths, science and technology. In England and Wales, a Construction Apprenticeship Scheme allows you to study for NVQ Level 3. Vocational qualifications include: BTEC Introductory Certificate and Diploma in Construction; BTEC First Diploma in Construction; City & Guilds Certificate in Basic Skills (6081). Bricklayers who train on the job can work towards NVQs/SVQs in Trowel Occupations at Levels 1–3 specialising in Bricklaying.

The Construction Industry Training Board (CITB) Construction Award in Bricklaying allows those who have difficulties in gaining work experience to train for an NVQ. You can apply straight to the CITB before or after finding employment or gaining a place on a training scheme.

New Deal offers taster courses and placements with an employer for at least 26 weeks. It may be possible to stay on and study for NVQs/SVQs. To qualify you must be aged 16–24 and unemployed for more than 6 months, or 25 or over and unemployed for 2 years.

Money guide

Salaries for trainees range from £7,000 to £13,000 a year, according to the level of training. Once you have achieved NVQ/SVQ Level 2 qualifications you can expect to earn around £17,000 per year. Experienced and qualified bricklayers can earn £25,000+. Overtime is often available, and on some projects there are bonuses based on outputs, which can lead to higher earnings.

Related opportunities

- Building Technician p76
- Dry Stone Waller p93
- Stonemason p128

Further information

ConstructionSkills
Bircham Newton, King's Lynn PE31 6RH
01485 577577; www.cskills.org; www.bconstructive.co.uk

The Scottish Building Apprenticeship and Training Council (SBATC)
Crichton House, 4 Crichton's Close, Edinburgh EH8 8DT
0131 556 8866; www.sbatc.co.uk

Federation of Master Builders (FMB)
Gordon Fisher House, 14–15 Great James Street, London WC1N 3DP
020 7242 7583; www.fmb.org.uk

City&
Guilds

www.cityandguilds.com/myperfectjob

BUILDING CONSERVATION OFFICER

What the work involves

- Building conservation officers protect and restore buildings of special historical or architectural interest, such as houses, churches, windmills, factories and lighthouses.

- You will be involved in planning the development of listed buildings and sites, recommending buildings for conservation, writing reports on their condition, making schedules and estimates for work required and giving advice to architects, local authorities or planning committees on building conservation.

- You might have to source suppliers or craftspeople who work with specialised or traditional building materials.

The type of person suited to this work

You will be working to restore historical buildings and sites so it is important that you are interested in history, architecture and construction and have an understanding of historical architecture, building methods and techniques.

You will have an eye for architectural detail and be able to sketch designs and plans.

You will also have excellent communication skills as you will need to coordinate the many different aspects involved in the development of one site. You must have excellent verbal and written skills as you may need to give presentations to planning authorities or government agencies to persuade them to follow your advice.

Working conditions

Your work is occasionally office-based, but much takes place outdoors on site. This can be dusty and dirty, working at heights and confined spaces in adverse weather conditions. Protective clothing, including hard hats and safety boots, is necessary as you may be visiting buildings in poor repair.

Travel during the day with the occasional overnight stay may be necessary. Working as consultant may involve travel all over the UK or visiting sites in remote areas so a car and driver's licence are useful. Working hours include regular extra hours but not weekends or shifts.

Future prospects

Positions as historic inspector or conservation office can be found in local authorities, district and county councils.

You may be promoted to senior conservation officer or managerial roles. Promotions are limited in small organisations.

There are many opportunities in national government organisations such as English Heritage, the National Trust, the Victorian Society or the Georgian Group.

As a qualified and experienced professional you can be self employed. With substantial experience and industry contracts

Qualifications and courses

Most entrants are graduates and will probably have studied relevant subjects such planning, building, construction, civil engineering, surveying, architecture, design or history of art. Specific courses in architectural heritage and conservation and building conservation and management are offered by some universities.

Although this is not essential, many graduates nowadays will have a postgraduate qualification as it is quite a specialist area.

Entry with an HND is possible, or alternatively you can enter as a planning technician and as you gain experience and training you can move across to historic buildings inspector or conservation officer roles.

Training is usually provided on the job but employers look for candidates with experience. You could volunteer with the National Trust or a national amenity society to gain some experience.

you can become involved in consultancy work which focuses on advisery and design work.

Advantages/disadvantages

As building conservation officers work to protect and conserve listed buildings, you will gain a great deal of satisfaction from working to ensure the survival of such sites.

Buildings are often in a poor state of repair and building sites may be hazardous.

Money guide

Starting as a trainee or an entry level position you can expect a salary of £18,000–£24,000 depending on your experience. Local authority trainees start on Scale 5 or 6, generally lower than those of historic buildings inspectors employed by central government bodies.

At senior level, with 10–15 years in a role, you can earn £26,000-£40,000.

Related opportunities

- Architect p68
- Building Surveyor p75

Further information

The Institute of Historic Building Conservation
IHBC Business Office, Jubilee House, High Street, Tisbury SP3 6HA
01747 873133; www.ihbc.org.uk

The Society for the Protection of Ancient Buildings
37 Spital Square, London E1 6DY
020 3733 1644; www.spab.org.uk; info@spab.org.uk

ENTRY LEVEL 5

Building and Construction

CRCI: BB
CLCI: UX

BUILDING SERVICES ENGINEER

What the work involves

- Design building services engineers are responsible for each aspect of energy-using building services such as lifts, lighting, heating, air-conditioning, water supply, ventilation and electrical supply.

- You will design and plan services that are efficient, cost effective and sustainable and in the interest of public safety.

- You will also be responsible for organising and supervising the installation and maintenance of these services and you will work with architects and clients to reduce the environmental impact.

- Although the industry is becoming increasingly multidisciplinary, you will probably specialise in mechanical engineering, electrical engineering or public health.

The type of person suited to this work

You should have a good grasp of maths and physics as you will have to plan each stage of a building service system.

You will need good problem-solving skills, and excellent communication and interpersonal skills so that you can work in a team and with those involved in other aspects of a building's design and construction.

You should have an aptitude for design and technical drawing, model making and show proficiency working with computers and computer-aided design (CAD) software.

Working conditions

Your time will be divided between office-based work, such as planning, designing and estimating costs of projects, and spending time on site, coordinating installation or managing existing systems.

You may work on sites such as airports, hospitals, industrial plants, domestic housing, leisure pools, hotels and cinemas. For this you may need specialist skills.

You will usually be expected to work more than the average office hours but not weekends or shifts. Some roles require on-call availability in case of emergencies.

You may have to travel within a day but overnight stays are uncommon.

Future prospects

Opportunities in this field are numerous, with demand for building services engineers usually exceeding supply.

Promotion to a managerial role such as team leader, project manager or department manager is likely, which will involve pay increases. You can then go on to become a company director or partner.

As a chartered engineer you may establish yourself as an independent consultant.

Qualifications and courses

To enter this profession you will need an engineering qualification, such as a Bachelor of Engineering (BEng) degree, that is accredited by the Chartered Institution of Building Services Engineers (CIBSE). This should be in a relevant subject such as electrical, mechanical or building services engineering.

Accredited HNDs or foundation degrees in engineering or technology can be used to progress to full degree courses or trainee posts.

After you graduate you will need to become a chartered engineer (CEng). To do this you can also join the CIBSE or other engineering institutions licensed by the Engineering Council UK (ECUK). To become an incorporated engineer you will need a Master of Engineering (MEng) degree engineer (IEng).

Relevant qualifications are available from Edexcel, ABC Awards and the City & Guilds. NVQs are available in building services engineering technology and project management at Levels 3 and 4.

You can also train as a building services engineering technician and work your way up or apply for an apprenticeship with the Modern Apprenticeship scheme.

Advantages/disadvantages

The profession has been traditionally separated into electrical and mechanical roles, but it is now becoming increasingly multidisciplinary.

This profession depends heavily on the economic climate of the construction industry, so you need to be aware of this, as it will affect your chances of employment.

Money guide

Your starting salaries could range from £17,500 to £24,000.

At senior level your salary can rise to £30,000–£52, 000 and even £70,000.

Your salary will increase with experience rather than qualifications, but if you become a chartered engineer this will influence the level of your pay.

Related opportunities

- Architect p68
- Civil/construction engineer p83

Further information

The Chartered Institution of Building Services Engineers
222 Balham High Road, London SW12 9BS
020 8675 5211; www.cibse.org

The Institution of Engineering and Technology (IET)
Michael Faraday House, Stevenage SG1 2AY
01438 313 311; www.theiet.org

BUILDING SURVEYOR

What the work involves

- Building surveyors work on new building projects, and also suggest ways to improve or enhance existing structures.

- You could work on residential and commercial building projects, and will advise on a number of areas including design, restoration, sustainability and repairs.

- You may also be responsible for ensuring that buildings meet health, safety and access regulations.

The type of person suited to this work

Since the job involves explaining ideas and negotiating with industry professionals and clients, good communication skills are vital. You will produce detailed reports, so a good standard of written English is required.

You will need excellent time management skills and a head for figures to ensure that projects come in on time and within budget.

You will need a logical, analytical and practical approach to work, along with the ability to organise and manage a team.

As much of the work involves computers and electronic equipment, you will need to have good ICT skills.

Working conditions

Working hours are normally 9–5, although longer hours and evening meetings with clients are not uncommon. Most surveyors divide their time equally between office-based work and external client meetings, site visits and surveys. These travel commitments mean it is helpful to have a driving licence and transport.

When on-site you will need to stick to health and safety regulations and be prepared to get muddy, wet and cold.

You may occasionally be called to give evidence in court proceedings concerning a breach of building regulations, which can be stressful.

Future prospects

At the moment prospects are not as good as they once were as the sector has been affected by the financial crisis.

You could work for a variety of employers including surveying practices, construction companies, government departments, mortgage and property companies, both throughout the UK and internationally. Freelance and consultancy work are also a possibility.

With experience, you could become a partner in a company or establish your own firm. You could also specialise in an area that interests you, such as advising on the restoration and improvement of historical or architecturally valuable buildings.

Advantages/disadvantages

Surveying provides a varied career as each day is different and there are a range of areas to work in.

Qualifications and courses

ENTRY LEVEL 5

All building surveyors hold a relevant degree on entrance to the profession. You may study full time at university for a Royal Institution of Chartered Surveyors (RICS) accredited degree in a relevant subject. The Chartered Institute of Building (CIOB), the Association of Building Engineers (ABE), and the British Institute of Facilities Management also offer professional qualifications.

Candidates with a non-accredited degree, or a degree in a non-vocational subject can take a postgraduate conversion course that has been accredited by the RICS.

The Chartered Surveyors Training Trust offers work-based training for young people aged 16–24 in London and the south-east of England. Applicants must have a minimum of 4 GCSEs (A–C) or equivalent.

Graduates who have completed a year in industry as part of their degree have an advantage in the job market.

Many surveyors are self-employed and enjoy the flexibility of working freelance.

Sometimes you will need to work extra hours to meet deadlines, or if you are working towards promotion.

Money guide

Graduate surveyors can expect a salary of £18,000–£20,000, which can rise to £24,000 in London-based roles.

With experience you could earn up to £30,000, and if you became a partner in a firm this could rise to £70,000+.

Some companies offer additional benefits such as a company car, mobile phone and pension scheme.

Related opportunities

- Quantity Surveyor p119
- Rural Property Surveyor p123
- Civil/Construction Engineer p83

Further information

Royal Institution of Chartered Surveyors (RICS)
Surveyor Court, Westwood Way, Coventry CV4 8JE
0870 333 1600; www.rics.org/careers; contactrics@rics.org

Chartered Institute of Building (CIOB)
Englemere, Kings Ride, Ascot SL5 7TB
01344 630700; www.ciob.org.uk; reception@ciob.org.uk

City&
Guilds

www.cityandguilds.com/myperfectjob

Building and Construction

CRCI: BB
CLCI: UD

BUILDING TECHNICIAN

What the work involves

- Building technicians support the work of construction professionals including surveyors and construction managers.

- Your work will vary depending on your employer and each project, but might include planning work schedules, drawing up plans and estimating project costs.

- A building technician is also responsible for buying materials, checking that plans meet building regulations, measuring and preparing construction-sites, and supervising work on-site.

- You will spend a lot of your time on building sites but you will also need to work in an office when drawing up plans and ordering materials.

The type of person suited to this work

You will have to be well-organised to make sure that each construction job is completed properly and on time. Mathematical and ICT skills are important for calculating costs, taking measurements and using computer-aided design.

You must be able to develop knowledge of the technical aspects of construction. You will also need strong communication skills for working with suppliers, site teams and other professionals such as surveyors, engineers and construction managers.

Working conditions

You may work on construction-sites or in an office. Building technicians often divide their time between the two.

You must work safely on-site, by wearing a safety helmet, overalls and boots.

You are likely to work a normal working week, but you may also have to start early, finish late or work at weekends on occasion.

Future prospects

There are about 20,000 building technicians in the UK and currently a shortage of qualified applicants for the steady supply of vacancies.

Building technicians work for employers such as contractors, construction companies, property developers, surveyors' practices and in the public sector.

With experience and further qualifications, you may move up to a higher position such as building/construction manager.

You may also be able to work in countries other than the UK.

Advantages/disadvantages

It can be stressful having to work to deadlines.

The work is interesting because you are likely to carry out many different tasks.

You are an important part of the team that contributes to producing buildings of all kinds.

Qualifications and courses

ENTRY LEVEL 3

Building technicians normally need to train to NVQ/SVQ Levels 3 or 4. It is possible to train as a building technician with an employer as a technician apprentice. Most apprentices start between the ages of 16 and 18, although entry is possible after this. They usually need a minimum of 4 GCSEs/S grades (A–C/1–3), including maths and science or technology, or equivalent.

HNDs in Building Studies or similar subjects can be studied over 2 years full time. Applicants should ideally have a science A level/H grade. Introductory courses to a career at technician level include BTEC National Certificate/Diploma or Scottish Group Award in Construction.

It is possible to enter as a trainee and study part time for a National Certificate or HNC in Building Studies. Trainees may follow the site management education and training scheme, the first line supervisors scheme or NVQs/SVQs in Building Site Supervision/Management.

Many companies run training schemes, day-release study (for HNC and Chartered Institute of Building exams), time spent on building sites, in-house training courses, and the Construction Industry Training Board (CITB) Technician Training Scheme.

Money guide

Starting out you can expect to earn around £14,500 per year. This can rise to £25,000 for building technicians with an increased level of experience. Up to £30,000 is possible for experienced senior building technicians.

Related opportunities

- Architectural Technician p70
- Architectural Technologist p71
- Construction Manager p88
- Technical Surveyor p130

Further information

ConstructionSkills
Bircham Newton, King's Lynn PE31 6RH
01485 577577; www.cskills.net, www.bconstructive.co.uk

Chartered Institute of Building
Englemere, Kings Ride, Ascot SL5 7TB
01344 630700; www.ciob.org.uk

The Institute of Engineering and Technology
Michael Faraday House, Stevenage SG1 2AY
01438 313 311; www.theiet.org; postmaster@theiet.org

City& Guilds

www.cityandguilds.com/myperfectjob

CARPENTER/JOINER

What the work involves

- Carpenters/Joiners make, put in place or repair the wooden parts of buildings.

- You may make and install floorboards, skirting boards, cupboards, partitions, windows and doors.

- You will work with different types of wood and use specialist hand tools such as hammers, chisels and planes, as well as power tools like jigsaws and sanders.

- You will either work in a workshop or on site with other building professionals.

The type of person suited to this work

Most importantly, you will need to have good practical skills and enjoy working with your hands and different tools.

You will be expected to follow plans and work carefully with attention to detail so that the structures you make fit into place correctly. As you will need to take measurements and calculate angles and dimensions, you will have to be good at maths and be accurate.

You will need to be physically fit, because you will have to move around and lift materials.

You must also be able to work in a team with other carpenters and those from the other construction trades and professions.

Working conditions

You may work in a workshop or on construction-sites, or divide your time between the two.

This can be heavy, dangerous and dusty work. You will need to keep to health and safety regulations, which may include wearing protective gear such as safety goggles and a mask. If you suffer from allergies, you could find this work difficult due to the dust.

You are likely to work a normal working week, although weekend work may also be required.

Future prospects

Across the UK, there are currently around 240,000 carpenters/joiners but employers are finding it difficult to recruit well-qualified and experienced carpenters. Many qualified carpenters are self-employed or work as sub-contractors.

With experience, you could move into a related occupation like shopfitting, kitchen fitting or furniture-making, or you may progress to training, technical, supervisory and managerial levels.

Advantages/disadvantages

You may come across problems when carrying out your work and this can be challenging.

You will develop a lot of new skills and knowledge.

You can get a sense of achievement when you see your woodwork in place in a building.

Qualifications and courses

You will normally need 3 to 5 GCSEs/S grades (A–E/1–5), preferably including English, maths, science and technology. Once employed, you can work towards NVQs/SVQs and City & Guilds qualifications, both on the job and at college.

Apprenticeships/Skillseekers opportunities may be available for candidates aged 16–24, and normally take 3 years to complete.

NVQs/SVQs are available in Wood Occupations, Levels 1, 2 and 3 and Wood Machining, Levels 2 and 3.

City & Guilds certificates are available in Basic Carpentry and Joinery Skills (6111); Carpentry and Joinery (5859); Fine Woodwork (5770) and Machine Woodworking (5860).

A Construction Award in Wood Occupations (Carpentry and Joinery Sitework) offered by the Construction Industry Training Board (CITB) allows those who have difficulties in gaining the work experience to train for an NVQ.

New Deal offers taster courses and placements with an employer for at least 26 weeks. It may be possible to stay on and study for NVQs/SVQs. To qualify you must be aged 16–24 and unemployed for more than 6 months, or 25 or over and unemployed for 2 years.

Money guide

Salaries for trainees range between £12,500–£16,000 per year. Qualified carpenters can earn between £17,000–£26,000. Very experienced joiners could have an income of £25,000+. Overtime is often available, and on some projects there are bonuses based on outputs, which can lead to higher earnings.

Related opportunities

- Building Technician p76
- Fence Installer p100
- Labourer/Construction Operative p86
- Window Fitter p138

Further information

Institute of Carpenters
3rd Floor D, Carpenters Hall, 1 Throgmorton Avenue, London ECZN 2BY
020 7256 1700; www.carpenters-institute.org

British Woodworking Federation (BWF)
55 Tufton Street, London SW1P 3QL
0870 458 6939; www.bwf.org.uk

www.cityandguilds.com/myperfectjob

Building and Construction

CRCI: BB
CLCI: OFZ

CARPET FITTER

What the work involves

- Carpet fitters lay new carpets in homes, shops and offices.

- After collecting the carpet, you would clear your work area, take down doors if needed, and remove any existing floor covering.

- You will then use various tools such as knives, staplers, trimmers and stretchers to cut the underlay and carpet to size, stretch and lay it flat, and fix the carpet into place.

- You would do a lot of travelling as part of this job to customers' houses, offices and shops.

The type of person suited to this work

You must have good practical skills for working with tools and carpet materials, and be able to work out simple calculations, such as estimating the amount of carpet you might need for an area and measuring the carpets accurately.

As you will be working on your hands and knees and lifting heavy carpets you will need to be physically fit. Being able to work alone or with one other person all day will also be important. To keep your customers happy you should enjoy meeting and talking to all types of people. You will also have to be trustworthy as you could be working in people's homes, moving their possessions around.

Working conditions

You will work indoors in different locations every day, so a driving licence is often necessary.

You may work a normal working week from Monday to Friday, but you may also need to work outside of normal hours so that you can lay carpets without disrupting the work of shops and businesses, etc.

You will be on your hands and knees, often working in cramped conditions.

Future prospects

There are good prospects for finding work as a trainee carpet fitter because there is a shortage in many areas, and the industry needs more young people to take up the career.

Work is available with carpet retailers, flooring companies or flooring contractors throughout the UK.

With experience, you could set up on your own as a self-employed carpet fitter.

Advantages/disadvantages

Working on floors can make you dusty and dirty, and the work can be physically demanding especially on your knees and back.

A well-laid carpet can transform a room. The ability to use your skills to do this can be very rewarding, especially when the job

Qualifications and courses

There are no formal entry requirements, but it is useful to have GCSEs/S grades (A–E/1–3) in maths, English, design and technology.

Your training will mainly take place on the job with experienced carpet fitters. It is likely to take 2 years or more to become fully proficient.

NVQs/SVQs in Floor Covering at Levels 1, 2 and 3 are available, which you can take while working.

Your employer may also send you on short courses run by the Flooring Industry Training Association (FITA) to learn about all aspects of the work. Courses cover topics such as carpet types, floor presentation, cutting and seaming techniques, estimating and planning and health and safety.

A driving licence is useful, and may be required for some jobs.

Carpet fitters must have a good standard of physical fitness and normal colour vision.

has been tricky, for example when working on an awkward staircase.

Money guide

Starting as a trainee you could earn about £11,500–£12,500 per year. With experience you could earn £15,000–£21,000. Carpet fitters who manage others can earn up to £25,000. Earnings vary among employers and different parts of the country. Salaries in London are higher.

Related opportunities

- Damp Proofer p91
- Floor Layer p101
- Shopfitter p125
- Wall/Floor Tiler p134

Further information

Flooring Industry Training Association
4c St Mary's Place, The Lace Market, Nottingham NG1 1PH
0115 950 6836; www.fita.co.uk

The UK Flooring Academy
Unit 1, Higgs Hill Buildings, Tattenhill Common, Rangemore, Burton upon Trent DE13 9RS
01283 711428; training@uk-flooring-academy.co.uk; www.uk-flooring-academy.co.uk

www.cityandguilds.com/myperfectjob

CARTOGRAPHER

What the work involves

- Cartography involves collecting, evaluating and displaying information gained from a variety of sources, including satellite technology, to create or update maps and navigation charts.

- This is achieved by using artistic, scientific, ICT and technological methods.

- Part of your job will involve travelling around and carrying out surveys.

- You will often use sophisticated information technology for a range of tasks – from collecting to displaying the information.

The type of person suited to this work

You will need a sense of design, ICT, scientific and mathematical skills, and an interest in geography.

It can take months to produce one sheet of a map, so you need to be patient, dedicated and able to concentrate on one piece of work. You also need to work with accuracy and attention to detail so that the map provides the best possible information for the user.

Finally, you need to be willing to keep up with new techniques and experiment with new ways of producing maps. This means you will have to be happy to keep training and developing your skills throughout your career.

Working conditions

You are likely to work normal office hours at a workstation where you will have access to a computer.

Here, you will use graphics software and the different information collected by surveyors or other specialists to produce your maps. You may have some surveying duties.

Future prospects

Most work is available in government departments, such as Ordnance Survey, the Hydrographic Office and the Meteorological Office. You may also work for local authorities, universities, councils, commercial map publishers, oil companies and motoring organisations.

Entry to the work is competitive and you need to keep developing your skills once in the industry.

With experience, you may be able to find work as a freelance cartographer, provide consultancy services or work within higher education as a tutor.

If you are interested in working abroad, there are opportunities to work in cartography all over the world.

Advantages/disadvantages

You can get great satisfaction from producing a map that looks good and is user-friendly. Potentially, a large number of people could use your maps.

Sometimes, you may need to work late so that you can meet deadlines.

Qualifications and courses

The usual entry requirement for a cartographer is a relevant degree. Useful degree subjects include geography, geographical information systems, urban/land studies, surveying and mapping sciences. GCSE/S grade maths is generally needed for entry to these degrees, and an A level/H grade in science or maths may be required for some courses.

It is useful to hold a postgraduate qualification in a relevant subject, for example cartography, geographical information systems or remote sensing. Also useful are art and design technology, maths and computing. Those with additional languages have greater opportunities to work overseas.

Entrants receive on-the-job training in relevant software and techniques. Government departments that employ cartographers have their own training schemes. It is also possible to work towards an NVQ/SVQ Level 4 in Spatial Data Management.

The minimum entry requirements for a cartographic technician are GCSEs/S grades (A–C/1–3), including maths, English and a science. In practice, most entrants have A levels/H grades, and some enter with a National Certificate/Diploma or HNC/D in a relevant area.

It may be possible for people entering as school-leavers to study for a Certificate/Diploma or HNC/D by day-release, whilst training on the job.

The work is varied and combines a variety of subject areas, from design to geography to maths.

Money guide

When starting out you can earn around £15,000–£20,000 per year. With three to five years' experience you can get £20,000–£29,000. It is possible for experienced or senior cartographers to earn up to £45,000. Earnings vary depending on the region, type of employer, your qualifications and experience.

Related opportunities

- Architect p68
- Geographer p520
- Land Surveyor p111
- Town Planner p133

Further information

British Cartographic Society
Wellington TA21 9AT
01823 665775; www.cartography.org.uk

The Survey Association
Northgate Business Centre, 38 Northgate,
Newark-on-Trent NG24 1EZ
01636 642840; office@tsa-uk.org.uk

Association for Geographic Information (AGI)
5, St Helen's Place, London EC3A 6AU
020 7036 0430; www.agi.org.uk

ENTRY LEVEL 3

Building and Construction

CRCI: BC
CLCI: UT

CAVITY WALL INSULATION TECHNICIAN

What the work involves

- Cavity wall insulation technicians insulate the space between the walls of new and existing buildings.

- Your work will include checking that the building is suitable for insulation, drilling holes into the mortar between the bricks, injecting the insulating material into the holes, filling in the holes and checking that air vents are free from blockage.

- You will use a machine and hose to inject the insulation material into the holes and check that the cavity has been filled.

- Your job would involve a lot of travelling to the site you work at, which can include people's homes, offices or building sites.

The type of person suited to this work

You will need practical skills to operate and maintain the drills and machines containing the insulation material. As you will climb ladders and carry tools and equipment you must be physically fit and feel comfortable working at heights.

Ability in maths is useful for calculating the quantities of materials you will need. English is helpful for following written instructions. You must have good communication skills and be able to get on well with people, including your customers.

Working conditions

You will work mainly outdoors, often on ladders or scaffolding. You will use a van to travel from job to job, so you may need a driving licence.

You need to work within health and safety regulations, which includes wearing a mask to prevent you from breathing in fibres, a helmet and ear protectors.

You are likely to work a normal working week, although you may also work at weekends.

Future prospects

According to the National Insulation Association, 9 million UK homes have un-insulated cavity walls. Awareness of the need to reduce fuel consumption and government grants to help with the costs has increased the demand for cavity wall insulators.

Companies, which are often small, employing fewer than ten people are located across the UK.

Many insulators choose to become self-employed once they have enough experience.

Qualifications and courses

There are no minimum entry requirements for this job although GCSEs/S grades (A–E/1–5) in English and maths are useful.

Training follows British Board of Agreement (BBA) and British Standards Institution (BSI) regulations. It involves working with experienced cavity wall insulators as well as attending short classroom courses run by manufacturers and takes 3–6 months to become proficient.

NVQs in Installing Insulation at Levels 1 and 2 and SVQ in Thermal Insulation Engineering at Level 2 are available, which you can take while you are working.

Your employer may also send you on short courses to learn about different kinds of insulation material and safety awareness.

Advantages/disadvantages

Working at heights can be difficult for some people.

It can be satisfying to know that you are making a positive contribution to the environment by helping to reduce the heat loss from buildings.

Money guide

Earnings start at around £11,500–£15,000 per year. £18,000–£22,000 is usual for fully trained cavity wall insulation technicians. £22,000–£25,000+ is possible for senior experienced cavity wall technicians. Earnings vary depending on individual employers and location. Overtime is often available, which can lead to higher earnings. If you are self-employed you may charge a set rate per square metre.

Related opportunities

- Bricklayer p72
- Construction Operative p86
- Painter and Decorator p114
- Scaffolder p124

Further information

National Insulation Association Limited
3 Vimy Court, Vimy Road, Leighton Buzzard LU7 1FG
01525 383313; www.nationalinsulationassociation.org.uk

British Board of Agrément (BBA)
Bucknalls Lane, Garston WD25 9BA
01923 665300; www.bbacerts.co.uk; contact@bba.star.co.uk

City&
Guilds

www.cityandguilds.com/myperfectjob

CEILING FIXER

What the work involves

- As a ceiling fixer you will fit suspended ceilings into new and existing large commercial or public buildings.

- Your work will include fitting a ceiling grid in place and inserting tiles, by using tools such as metal cutters and screwdrivers.

- The ceiling is fitted to the concrete floor of the room above and may hide wiring and systems like air conditioning.

- Because your job requires you to work at heights, you will need to be up to date on safety training.

The type of person suited to this work

As most of your work will be done on ladders you will need to be comfortable working at heights. You will also need to be physically fit to do the necessary climbing, carrying and bending.

You will be expected to understand technical plans and be able to use basic maths skills to work out the amounts of materials needed. You will also have to manage your own time.

It will be important to get on with people as you will work alongside other ceiling fixers and those from other construction trades such as electricians, heating and ventilating fitters, painters and decorators.

Working conditions

You will work indoors in different kinds of buildings in a variety of locations so a driving licence may be useful.

You will need to take safety precautions for yourself and your colleagues and you will be expected to wear protective clothing such as a helmet. You will also have to work to strict procedures while setting up and taking down platforms, and whilst working.

You are likely to work a normal working week, although weekend work may also be available.

This could be dusty work, which might be difficult if you suffer from some allergies.

Future prospects

There is currently a shortage of qualified ceiling fixers in the construction industry.

Work is available with interiors companies and building contractors across the UK.

As well as ceiling fixing, you may work in other related trades such as partition fixing.

With experience, you may progress to a supervisory or managerial position, or perhaps run your own company. Most specialist interiors companies and contractors are owned or run by someone who started out as a tradesperson.

Advantages/disadvantages

Working at heights may be demanding for some people.

Qualifications and courses

No specific qualifications are required, although GCSEs/S grades or a BTEC Introductory Certificate/Diploma in Construction may be useful. Maths, design and technology, science and English are useful subjects.

You will be trained on the job while working towards qualifications. This may also involve going to a college or training centre on day- or block-release.

NVQs/SVQs in Interior Systems (Ceiling Fixing) at Levels 1, 2 and 3 are available.

Apprenticeships/Skillseekers may be available to those aged 16–24.

You can also train by doing a Construction Industry Training Board (CITB) Construction Apprenticeship Scheme in Ceiling Fixing.

The Construction Industry Training Board (CITB) Construction Award in Interior Systems allows those who have difficulties in gaining the work experience to train for an NVQ. You can apply straight to the CITB before or after finding employment or gaining a place on a training scheme.

It is satisfying to see the transformation that takes place when you have worked on fitting a ceiling and hidden away unsightly features such as air conditioning.

Money guide

Trainees generally earn between £7,100 and £13,000 a year. When starting out as a newly qualified ceiling fixer you can expect to earn around £18,000 per year. For those with supervisory responsibility and lots of experience, £25,000–£40,000 is possible. Overtime is often available, and on some projects there are bonuses based on outputs, which can lead to higher earnings.

Related opportunities

- Construction Operative p86
- Painter and Decorator p114
- Plasterer p116
- Roofer p122

Further information

ConstructionSkills
Bircham Newton, King's Lynn PE31 6RH
01485 577577; www.cskills.net, www.bconstructive.co.uk

Association of Interior Specialists (AIS)
Olton Bridge, 245 Warwick Road, Solihull B92 7AH
0121 707 0077; www.ais-interiors.org.uk;
info@ais-interiors.org.uk

City&
Guilds

www.cityandguilds.com/myperfectjob

CHARTERED SURVEYOR

What the work involves

- As a chartered surveyor you will specialise in a particular field of surveying. This can be in building, construction, planning, the environment or quantity surveying.

- You will have a variety of tasks to do such as examining plans, designs and project briefs, taking measurements, recording and analysing data and interpreting it through charts, maps or diagrams.

- You may oversee entire construction projects, where you will ensure that specifications are met, calculate supplies needed, and advise clients on the purchase, sale or development of property or land.

- You will spend time negotiating, advising and explaining designs and construction issues with clients.

The type of person suited to this work

You should have an interest in construction, architecture, landscape and the environment.

As you may be a go-between between construction workers and clients you will need act as a negotiator, have a hands-on approach to problem solving and be able to delegate tasks.

As you may be involved with several large, complex projects at the same time you must be highly organised and methodical in your work and have keen eye for detail.

Working conditions

You will probably work 9 to 5, Monday to Friday. You may have to work longer hours to meet deadlines. You can work part-time.

You will be based in an office but also spend a good deal of time on site.

Depending on the specialised field in which you work, you may have to work in all weathers and wear protective clothing when on site.

You may have to travel for your work purposes, abroad and within the UK. For this a driver's licence is strongly recommended.

Future prospects

You may follow a formal promotion structure to gain senior management roles.

You may choose to become self-employed or to join a private practice.

As a qualified chartered surveyor and member of the RICS you will have to take part in Continuing Professional Development (CPD). For this you must accumulate sixty hours of CPD every three years.

Qualifications and courses

To become a chartered surveyor you must become a member of the Royal Institution of Chartered Surveyors (RICS). For this you will need to have completed a degree course or a postgraduate conversion course that has been accredited by the RICS. In order to take such a degree course you must have five GSCEs (A-C), three A-levels or the relevant BTEC/SQA national awards or the equivalent qualification. After you have completed an RICS-accredited course you will need to gain practical experience before you will be fully qualified as a chartered surveyor.

If you do not have the appropriate A-levels or GCSEs you can take HNC/HND courses or foundation degrees which can then be supplemented by an RICS-accredited degree course.

You can also train on the job as part of the Chartered Surveyors Training Trust scheme. This is available to those aged 16 to 24 who have four GCSEs (A-C) or equivalent.

Advantages/disadvantages

Employers may provide benefits such as a company car and bonuses.

There is significant competition for graduates wishing to gain entry to some areas of chartered surveying.

Money guide

As a graduate your starting salary may be from £15,000 to £22,000 a year.

Average salaries can be £40,000 a year and the high earners can expect £100,000 or more a year.

Related opportunities

- Architect p68
- Estates Officer p38
- Technical Surveyor p130
- Town Planner p133

Further information

The Association of Building Engineers (ABE)
Lutyens House, Billing Brook Road, Weston Favell, Northampton NN3 8NW
0845 126 1058; www.abe.org.uk; building.engineers@abe.org.uk

Chartered Surveyors Training Trust
Downstream Building, 1 London Bridge, London SE1 9BG
020 785 3850; www.cstt.org.uk; cstt@cstt.org.uk

Royal Institution of Chartered Surveyors (ICES)
Dominion House, Sibson Road, Sale M33 7PP
0161 972 3100; www.ices.org.uk; jgray@ices.org.uk

CIVIL/CONSTRUCTION ENGINEER/ CIVIL ENGINEERING TECHNICIAN

What the work involves

Civil engineer (consulting)

■ You will be designing and developing plans for construction projects such as roads, tunnels, bridges, railways, reservoirs, pipelines and major buildings.

■ Your work could span many areas including waste management, coastal development and geotechnical engineering.

Civil engineer (contracting)

■ You will take the consulting civil engineer's designs and make them into a reality at ground level, overseeing and managing the construction project.

■ This will include recruiting a team, sourcing materials, managing budgets and ensuring that the project is completed on time.

Civil engineering technician

■ You will be responsible for providing technical support to the civil engineer, which may include producing costing estimates for a project and helping with recruitment.

■ The role will also include aspects of land and quantity surveying, as well as the production of design drawings.

The type of person suited to this work

Regardless of the area you decide to work in you will need to enjoy finding creative, but workable, solutions to problems.

You will need to be happy and confident when using computers to produce designs, work out costings and undertake research.

You should also be good at maths and science so that you can make accurate calculations and understand the different building materials available to you.

You will also have to be able to think three dimensionally, so that you can visualise and design different buildings and structures.

Written and verbal communication skills are important as you will have to write reports, explain your designs to clients and other professionals, and supervise construction staff.

Your will work as part of a team, so you must be able to communicate with people at all levels including other professionals and clients.

An understanding of environmental building issues, such as the use of energy efficient materials and land protection, is of increasing importance.

Working conditions

Working hours are typically longer than the average working week and can include early morning and evening work onsite. Weekend or shift work is rare for civil engineers, although civil

Qualifications and courses

Entrants to Civil Engineering are usually graduates, although there are opportunities to progress from craft or technical level.

The main route to becoming an engineer is a degree in the relevant branch of engineering, or a closely related subject. The normal minimum entry requirements for an engineering degree are 3 A levels or 5 H grades including maths and a science, usually physics or chemistry. Equivalent qualifications such as BTEC/SQA National qualifications may be accepted.

Candidates who do not have the relevant A-levels or equivalent may gain entry to an engineering degree by taking a 1-year foundation course. Foundation courses are offered by universities and are sometimes taught at local partner colleges.

It is possible to enter engineering after taking GCSEs and progress to technician or professional level by studying part time for an HNC/D or NVQ/SVQ Levels 4 or 5. It is also possible to gain a position as a trainee technician within a company straight after GCSEs, although you will need at least grades A*-C in English, maths and science. There are also BTEC and SQA national certificates or diplomas which will give you the relevant qualifications and which can be studied at any age.

Apprenticeships may be available for candidates aged between 16–24 years.

Professional engineers can be chartered or incorporated members of one of the engineering professional bodies, for example the Institution of Civil Engineers (ICE) or the Chartered Institution of Building Services Engineers (CIBSE). These professional bodies also accredit BEng and MEng degrees.

The usual requirement for chartered status is an accredited MEng degree, or equivalent. For incorporated status, a 3 year accredited BEng or BSc degree or an HND or equivalent, plus an additional period of learning (matching section) is required.

engineering technicians can be required to remain on 24 hour call for some projects.

Your work will involve both being indoors and out onsite. When working onsite you will need to stick to health and safety regulations and be aware of your own and colleagues' safety. You will have to wear safety clothing including a helmet.

You could work in dangerous places including working up ladders or on scaffolding, or in difficult environments.

When you are in your office, you will be based at a workstation where you will use a computer with specialised software and possibly a drawing board. You will attend meetings and speak to clients on the phone or in person.

It is also likely that you will have to work away from home from time to time, including projects abroad, but the extent of this will depend on the size of the company you work for and the type of contracts they attract.

Future prospects

Around 100,000 professional civil engineers work in the UK for a range of employers including health trusts, local authorities, central government, energy suppliers including water, gas, nuclear and electricity companies, contractors, consultancies and transport networks.

Work is available on a variety of projects including the building of new schools, hospitals and the upgrading of public transport networks.

Many UK civil engineering companies also operate globally, increasing the opportunities to work overseas. The range and size of opportunities open to you will depend on the size of the company you work for, and the types of contracts won.

Civil engineering technicians can undertake job-related training and study for more qualifications to become full civil engineers.

There is scope to undertake further study and specialise in areas such as environmental engineering, coastal and marine engineering, geotechnics or tunnelling.

With experience, you can progress into management or possibly associate/partnership positions within UK or international companies, management and chief engineer jobs in public services work, provide training or consultancy services, or choose self-employment.

Advantages/disadvantages

You will play an important part in the design and construction of buildings and structures throughout the world.

Seeing your ideas being built is satisfying.

Having an engineering background and qualifications are keys to entering other non-engineering careers at senior levels.

There is the opportunity to become self-employed, or work overseas.

Work is varied, each day is different and you will be meeting and dealing with a wide range of people.

Sometimes the hours can be long and you may have to juggle a number of projects.

Money guide

Starting salaries for civil engineers, either contracting or consulting, are between £16,000 and £21,000. This will increase to around £24,000 when fully qualified.

With a few years experience, civil engineers can earn between £35,000 and £45,000.

Qualifying as a member or fellow of the Institution of Civil Engineers (ICE) can see salaries for civil engineers rise to £60,000+.

Civil engineering technicians start on about £14,000, and this will rise to £25,000 with a few years' experience. Senior technicians can earn £30,000+, and if you train as a civil engineer then your earning potential increases as above.

Earnings vary among regions and employers. Salaries are generally higher in London and other large cities.

Related opportunities

- Building Surveyor p75
- Insurance Risk Surveyor p43
- Town Planner p133
- Architect p68

Further information

The Engineering Careers Information Service (ECIS)
14 Upton Road, Watford WD18 0JT
01923 238 441; www.enginuity.org.uk,www.semta.org.uk

Engineering Council UK (ECUK)
246 High Holborn, London WC1V 7EX
020 3206 0500; www.engc.org.uk

Institution of Civil Engineers (ICE)
1 Great George Street, London SW1P 3AA
020 7222 7722; www.ice.org.uk; careers@ice.org.uk

Women into Science, Engineering and Construction (WISE)
2nd Floor Weston House, 246 High Holborn, London WC1V 7EX
020 3206 0408; www.wisecampaign.org.uk; info@wisecampaign.org.uk

www.cityandguilds.com/myperfectjob

CONCRETER

What the work involves

- As a concreter you will be preparing appropriate areas for concreting by levelling and compacting the ground for concreting.

- You will ensure that laid concrete is strong and durable.

- You may have to take deliveries of concrete, as well as placing and compacting the concrete, and wrapping it in polythene sheeting in order to cure it.

- You may work for a building contractor or a firm of specialist subcontractors.

The type of person suited to this work

You should have a careful, methodical approach to your work, and as you will be involved with physically placing the concrete you should have good hand skills for laying and finishing concrete.

An aptitude for maths is desirable, as you will be measuring and calculating quantities for materials.

You should also enjoy working outdoors in all weather conditions, as part of a team or on your own.

You must have a good level of fitness as you will be required to work long and at times hard hours.

It is also important that you are someone who is conscious of health and safety requirements, as you may be working on construction sites.

Working conditions

Your work will be site-based largely undertaking manual labour.

You will normally have a working week of 37 hours. This may include working early in the morning and finishing late at night.

You will use traditional hand tools such as picks, shovels, trowels as well as machinery such as cement mixers, drills and rollers.

You will need to wear protective clothing which may be provided by the employer. If you work on a labour-only basis for a contractor all tools and materials will be supplied.

Future prospects

As a concreter you can move into specialised areas of work such as concrete spraying or concrete repair.

With significant experience you can become self-employed.

You can work for building and engineering contractors, local authorities and public organisations.

You can find job opportunities throughout the UK but you can also travel abroad to find work. This job depends on the construction industry so you should be aware of the condition

Qualifications and courses

You can work as a trainee concreter as soon as you leave school and you will learn on the job.

Apprenticeships are still available for young people.

Experienced colleagues will teach trainees but you can also gain qualifications such as NVQs or SVQS from training centres and colleges.

of the industry and any developments that will affect your employment.

Advantages/disadvantages

As you gain experience there may be opportunities to become self-employed or to work abroad on contract.

There is an increased risk of injury as you may be working on construction sites. The cement in concrete can cause burning or inflammation and you should avoid contact with the skin.

Money guide

Your salary will range from £12,500 to £30,000 a year. You may earn more if you set up your own contracting firm.

Related opportunities

- Brick Layer p72
- Construction Operative p86
- Plasterer p116

Further information

The Chartered Institute of Building (CIOB)
Englemore, Kings Ride, Ascot SL5 7TB
01344 630700; www.ciob.org.uk/home

The Concrete Centre
Riverside House, 4 Meadows Business Park, Station Approach, Blackwater, Camberley GU17 9AB
01276 606 800; concretecentre.com;
enquiries@concretecentre.com

Women and Manual Trades (WAMT)
52–54 Featherstone Street, London EC1Y 8RT
020 7251 9192; www.wamt.org; info@wamt.org

www.cityandguilds.com/myperfectjob

CRCI: BB
CLCI: UF

CONSTRUCTION OPERATIVE

What the work involves

- Construction operatives support the work of other construction workers by doing various practical tasks.

- Your work might include tasks such as digging trenches, moving building materials and tools, putting up signs and safety barriers and helping to lay drains.

- You will also be mixing and laying cement.

- The work may also include operating different plant (construction equipment) such as cement mixers, and driving vehicles on the construction-site.

The type of person suited to this work

As the work requires you to lift and carry heavy materials, and be on the move a lot, you must be physically fit. And you must not mind working at great heights or depths.

You need to be able to follow and carry out instructions, and work in a team with other labourers/construction operatives and construction tradespeople and professionals.

Your work will be extremely varied, so you need to be flexible and trustworthy.

Working conditions

You will be working outdoors in all weather conditions, as well as indoors. The work is often dusty and dirty and may be difficult for people suffering from certain allergies.

You will need to pay attention to both your own and colleagues' health and safety. You will be expected to follow the different procedures for each type of work you do, including the wearing of protective clothing.

You may work a normal working week, although evening and weekend work may also be available, and you may need to start early or finish late for some projects.

Future prospects

Building projects, new builds and renovations, can't happen without construction operatives so they are in strong demand when the construction industry is doing well.

You could work for small and large construction companies across the UK.

You may progress to specialist craft careers and supervisory roles. You could also become self-employed.

Advantages/disadvantages

The work can be physically demanding for some people.

This job could be good for you if you enjoy doing something different every day and learning a wide range of skills.

You have an important role to play on-site as without your help the tradespeople will not be able to do their work.

Qualifications and courses

Your training will be given mainly on the job by experienced labourers/construction operatives and tradespeople.

There may be opportunities to work towards NVQs/SVQs at Levels 1 and 2 in Construction and Civil Engineering Services and in Specialised Plant and Machinery Services while you are working.

City & Guilds also offers a certificate in Basic Construction Skills (6051).

You can also train by doing a Construction Industry Training Board (CITB) Construction Apprenticeship Scheme. The Construction Industry Training Board (CITB) Construction Award in Construction Operations allows those who have difficulties in gaining the work experience to train for an NVQ. You can apply straight to the CITB before or after finding employment or gaining a place on a training scheme.

Money guide

As a trainee starting out you can expect to earn around £9,000–£12,000 per year. As a skilled construction operative you could earn £16,000–£18,000. Overtime is often available, and on some projects there are bonuses based on outputs, which can lead to higher earnings. Skilled operatives may be able to earn more than £20,000 on some projects.

Related opportunities

- Bricklayer p72
- Building Technician p76
- Mastic Asphalter p112
- Plasterer p116

Further information

ConstructionSkills
Bircham Newton, King's Lynn PE31 6RH
01485 577577; www.cskills.net, www.bconstructive.co.uk

Federation of Master Builders (FMB)
Gordon Fisher House, 14–15 Great James Street,
London WC1N 3DP
020 7242 7583; www.fmb.org.uk

Women and Manual Trades (WAMT)
52–54 Featherstone Street, London EC1Y 8RT
020 7251 9192; www.wamt.org; info@wamt.org

www.cityandguilds.com/myperfectjob

CONSTRUCTION PLANT OPERATOR

What the work involves

- Construction plant operators operate and maintain different forms of plant (machinery) used for tasks such as moving soil and building materials, flattening the earth and preparing concrete.

- The kinds of plant you may be trained to operate include bulldozers, excavators, diggers, cranes and fork-lift trucks.

- In larger organisations you may be required to specialise in operating one type of plant.

The type of person suited to this work

As you will be handling sometimes large and complex machines you must have good practical skills.

You have to be able to keep your concentration and communicate with your workmates so that you can operate the plant safely.

If you are working on certain types of plant, such as cranes, you need to be comfortable working at heights. It will also be helpful if you have some mechanical knowledge when working with plant in case problems occur.

Working conditions

You will work outdoors in all weathers and in a variety of construction-site locations. Expect to get hot, dusty and dirty in the summer and cold, muddy and wet in the winter.

You will have to stick to health and safety regulations, which will include wearing a protective helmet and boots.

You are likely to work a normal working week from Monday to Friday, but you may also work extra hours at weekends. Some construction firms operate longer hours during the summer months and shorter during the winter. You might have to travel away from home on some contracts.

Future prospects

There is a particular shortage of qualified crane and heavy plant operators, and a demand in general for construction plant operators. Work is available across the UK with plant hire companies and construction companies.

With experience, you may progress to using a wider range of plant, and you may supervise or train plant operators or work as a safety inspector. You may also choose to specialise in operating one type of plant.

With experience and financial backing, it may be possible to start your own construction plant operation or hire business.

Advantages/disadvantages

Working on construction-sites can be noisy, dusty and dirty although you will have safety gear such as ear protectors. Working at heights may be demanding for some people.

Qualifications and courses

ENTRY LEVEL 1

There are no set academic entry requirements, although GCSEs/S grades or equivalent in English, maths and science or technology are useful, along with equivalent vocational qualifications like the Edexcel (BTEC) Introductory Certificate or Diploma in Construction. It is also possible to take NVQs/SVQs at Levels 1 and 2 in Specialised Plant and Machinery Operations and Construction Plant and Equipment Supervision at Level 3.

The minimum age to operate plant is 18, but 17-year-olds may work under supervision while they are training. A full driving licence is sometimes a requirement.

The Construction Plant Competence Scheme (CPCS) card is required to operate most categories of plant. Plant operators aged over 21 with at least 3 years' experience can apply directly for the CPCS Operator Test. New entrants who have completed basic training and passed a health and safety test can obtain the 'red' CPCS card, and convert it to the full 'blue' card on completion of an NVQ/SVQ.

It is a skilled and varied career where you are responsible for some awesome machinery. It can be satisfying to be able to control the machinery efficiently and safely.

Money guide

As a trainee you can expect to earn around £7,100–£13,000 per year. This can rise to £15,000–£20,000 with qualifications and experience. Highly experienced staff can earn more than £25,000. Operators of special types of crane may earn up to £40,000. Overtime is often available, and on some projects there are bonuses based on outputs.

Related opportunities

- Crane Operator p90
- Demolition Operative p92
- Construction Operative p86
- Highways Maintenance/Road Worker p106

Further information

ConstructionSkills
Bircham Newton, King's Lynn PE31 6RH
01485 577577; www.cskills.net; www.bconstructive.co.uk

The Association of Building Engineers
Lutyens House, Billing Brook Road, Weston Favell, Northampton NN3 8NW
0845 126 1058; www.abe.org.uk; building.engineers@abe.org.uk

www.cityandguilds.com/myperfectjob

CRCI: BB
CLCI: UV

CONSTRUCTION SUPERVISOR/ MANAGER

What the work involves

■ Construction supervisors/managers run construction-sites – new builds or maintenance projects.

■ Your duties will include planning the build, preparing the site, arranging for the delivery and storage and checking the quality and costings of building materials and equipment.

■ You will also have the responsibility for overseeing the construction project, making sure everyone is safe on-site, managing construction staff and solving problems when they arise.

■ You will need to report directly to whoever is paying for the work to be done and keep them updated on progress and any problems that may have arisen.

The type of person suited to this work

You have to be able to plan ahead and have good management and problem-solving skills so that projects run smoothly. To ensure that projects run within financial forecasts, numeracy skills are important too.

You will use computer software packages to plan workflow, so IOT skills are useful

You must be able to develop an in-depth knowledge and understanding of all aspects of the construction business.

So that you can supervise the site's workforce and consult with other professionals such as architects and engineers, excellent communication skills are vital

Working conditions

During construction, you will be based on a site and are likely to work from a portable office. You will also work outdoors in all weathers, for example when consulting with the workforce about a problem or making regular safety inspections.

You may work a normal working week, but you may also have to start early, finish late or work at weekends on some projects. As some companies win contracts all over the UK, you may have to work away from home.

Future prospects

Across the UK construction industry, there is a shortage of qualified construction managers and supervisors. There are opportunities across the UK on a wide range of projects including multi-million pound builds. Particular shortages exist in the South and South East of England.

Construction supervisors/managers work for contractors, construction companies, project management companies, surveyors' practices and public services.

With experience, you may be promoted to work as a contract manager on bigger and more prestigious projects.

You may also be able to work on projects in other parts of the world.

Qualifications and courses

The normal entry qualification to be a construction manager is a degree, HND or Foundation degree. Relevant subjects include construction project management, building services and construction management. For entry to a degree, 5 GCSEs/S grades (A–C/1–3) and 2 A levels/3 H grades are normally required. Maths and/or a science may be required.

It may be possible to work your way up from technician level. The NVQ/SVQ Level 3 Site Supervision and Level 4 Site Management are open to anyone with experience in building site supervision and management. Technicians can also study part time towards an HNC or degree.

Recently qualified graduates are likely to continue training on programmes designed for professional and managerial staff. The Chartered Institute of Building (CIOB) runs a Professional Development Programme (PDP) leading to corporate membership of the Institute.

Advantages/disadvantages

It will be great to know that you can begin with an empty piece of land and leave a finished construction behind, a relatively short time later.

When there is a tight deadline to meet and a problem arises, the work can be stressful – particularly as many projects are on large but tightly planned budgets.

Money guide

Salaries for graduate trainees start from £16,000–£23,000 per year. This can quickly rise to £26,000–£37,000 for managers with experience. For managers running the largest projects £40,000+ is possible. Earnings vary depending on geographical location and your particular employer.

Related opportunities

■ Architectural Technician p70
■ Building Surveyor p75
■ Building Technician p76
■ Civil/Construction Engineer p83

Further information

ConstructionSkills
Bircham Newton, King's Lynn PE31 6RH
01485 577577; www.cskills.net, www.bconstructive.co.uk

Chartered Institute of Building
Englemere, Kings Ride, Ascot SL5 7TB
01344 630700; www.ciob.org.uk

City&
Guilds

www.cityandguilds.com/myperfectjob

THE CHARTERED INSTITUTE OF BUILDING (CIOB)

Fancy building a brighter future? Why not think about a career in construction?

If you thought a career in construction was all about hard hats and bricks and mortar, then think again. A career in construction is first and foremost about people and the promotion of the built environment as central to quality of life for everyone everywhere.

The Chartered Institute of Building (CIOB) have over 43,000 members worldwide who all work to contribute to the creation of a modern, progressive and responsible construction industry; able to meet the economic, environmental and social challenges faced in the 21st Century.

> **"Construction is a people industry. We are service providers and it's our job to get the most out of all the professionals and suppliers we are working with in order to realise people's dreams and see buildings come to life. It's inspiring."**
>
> **Simon Matthews, Member of the Chartered Institute of Building (MCIOB).**

The built environment offers diverse career and work opportunities. These can be from thinking about how to utilise the latest technology to create sustainable buildings; how to preserve historic buildings for future generations; planning and implementing reconstruction projects after natural disasters like earthquakes, to planning new roads to help people get from A to B more efficiently.

There are a wide variety of roles within the construction industry including architects, engineers, surveyors, site managers, project managers and planners.

A career in construction is an international passport that can give you the opportunity to work anywhere in the world. It also offers career progression and the chance to influence and really make an impact on social and environmental agendas. So if you think you'd like a career that's diverse, innovative, inspiring and where you can really make a difference to the way in which people live, think seriously about a career in construction.

For 175 years, CIOB members have had a considerable influence on the global skyline and have played leadership roles in creating some of the world's most iconic structures. They left their mark – will you leave yours?

The Chartered Institute of Building (CIOB), Englemere, King's Ride, Ascot, Berkshire, SL5 7TB. Tel: +44 (0) 1344 630700 E-mail: memenquiry@ciob.org.uk Web: www.ciob.org.uk

CRANE OPERATOR

What the work involves

- As a crane operator your job will be to lift and move heavy loads such as building materials, tools and equipment.

- You will be working on construction and engineering sites or around docks and ports.

- You will be helped by an assistant on the ground, who will give directions via signals and radio.

- You may have to control different types of cranes, such as fixed or movable cranes. You may also work in the media or music industries, operating cranes to move heavy camera or sound equipment.

The type of person suited to this work

As a crane operator you will need to have good driving skills, excellent spatial awareness and an aptitude for machinery.

You will also need to be alert and to have the ability to concentrate for long periods of time.

You will need good eyesight and hearing and excellent communication skills.

You will need a good head for heights as you will have to climb up and down to crane cab. For this you will also need to be strong and fit.

As you will be working on construction sites or on other sites you will need to be conscious of health and safety procedures.

Working conditions

You will work an average of 37 hours per week, Monday to Friday, but this can vary as you take on different jobs and overtime. Your working day will depend on daylight hours so may involve early morning starts, late finishes and weekends.

You will be mainly based inside the crane cab, but you will be exposed to varied weather conditions. You will probably be working on construction sites which can be noisy, dirty, dusty and muddy.

You will normally work alone but will be in contact with other construction workers and supervisors on the ground.

Future prospects

As a crane operator you may be employed by building firms, civil engineers, manufacturing plants, port authorities, local authorities and energy utility companies.

You should be able to find work throughout the UK and in most urban development areas.

There are freelance opportunities in the media sector, usually for camera equipment facility houses. You may work on commercials, feature films or on television programmes. This sector may provide the opportunity for travel abroad.

Advantages/disadvantages

Your employment opportunities will fluctuate with the economy

Qualifications and courses

You do not need any specific academic qualifications to be a crane operator.

However, you may have an advantage if you have an understanding of vehicle engineering and have GCSEs in English, maths and technology.

You can also gain vocational qualifications such as the Edexcel Introductory Certificate in construction.

You must be 18 years old at least to operate a crane but you can start to train at 16. You will also need a certain amount of fitness to be able to cope with the physical demands of the job.

Apprenticeships are available to young people. CITB-ConstructionSkills provides guidance on finding and apply for apprenticeships.

If you choose to become a construction crane operator you must register for a Construction Plant Competence Scheme (CPCS) card. This proves to employers that you are a fully competent crane operator. There are two levels: a red card for trainees and a blue/green card for fully trained operators. To gain a blue/green card trainees need to complete 300 hours of operating and NVQs.

but the London 2012 Olympics will create many jobs around the capital.

As you gain experience and training you can learn new techniques to take on roles in the oil industry or marine engineering.

Money guide

You can expect a starting salary from £15,000 a year.

With more experience you may earn £25,000 a year.

If you operate a special type of crane or equipment you can earn up to £50,000.

Related opportunities

- Construction Plant Operator p87
- Demolition Operative p92
- Engineering Construction Technician p83
- Large Goods Vehicle Driver p606

Further information

CITB-ConstructionSkills
Bircham Newton, King's Lynn PE31 6RH
01485 577577; www.ckills.org; call.centre@cskills.org

Construction Industry Council
26 Store Street, London WC1E 7BT
020 7399 7400; www.cic.org.uk

DAMP PROOFER

What the work involves

- You will provide guidance and solutions to those in residential or commercial properties who experience damp problems.

- You also may need to install damp-proof courses to buildings. This is a horizontal layer of water-repellent/proof material that prevents moisture rising from the ground up the walls.

- You will need to be able to install damp-proof courses to old and new buildings. In new buildings this is laid as walls are constructed by the bricklayers.

The type of person suited to this work

As you will be working on buildings or engineering projects, you should have an interest in construction and architecture.

You should have good problem-solving skills and relish new challenges. You should be able to work in a team and cooperate with colleagues and customers.

You need to have a keen eye for detail and have good practical skills to operate drills and specialist machinery such as moisture meters to check damp levels.

You should also have good health and have an understanding of health and safety protocol.

You should be willing to travel.

You will need good written and communication skills to give and follow instructions and guidelines.

Working conditions

You will usually work 38 hours a week, Monday to Friday. You may have to work overtime and this could include evenings and weekends. These hours will vary depending on where you are working, who you are working for and even the weather.

You will have to do a lot of travel to each new site. A driving licence and car would be useful.

Your work will be largely outdoors, so can be affected by the weather.

Future prospects

You can find job opportunities with the 1,500 damp proofing contractors across the UK. You can also find employment in related fields such as timber treatment, waterproofing and pest control.

With experience you will be eligible for promotion to remedial treatment surveyor or supervisory posts. The BWPDA runs its own training courses for surveyors and technicians and with an NVQ/SVQ Level 2 in insulation and remedial maintenance you can apply for occupational assessment under the Construction Skills Certification Scheme (CSCS Card).

You may become self-employed.

Qualifications and courses

ENTRY LEVEL 1

There are no set academic requirements to enter this profession. However GCSE English and maths (grades A-E/1–5) are an advantage as you will need to calculate quantities, make estimates and keep written records.

Currently no colleges provide apprenticeship schemes. Some private companies, involved in Investors in People, may consider apprenticeships.

Young Apprenticeships, Pre-Apprenticeships, Apprenticeships and Advanced Apprenticeships are available in England. Apprenticeship schemes are organised differently in Scotland, Wales and Northern Ireland. You should be aware that pay rates for apprenticeships vary according to area and industry.

You will be trained mainly on the job by experienced damp proofers and damp-proof installer companies may provide special courses on safety awareness.

As a technician you can take short courses at the British Wood Preserving and Damp Proofing Association.

Advantages/disadvantages

As a damp proofer you will have plenty of opportunities to travel around the UK and abroad.

You may have to work in uncomfortable weather conditions and antisocial working hours.

Money guide

Your starting salary may range from £12,000 a year but the average salary of a damp proofer is about £25,000. With specialised skills and training you can earn up to £35,000 or more.

Related opportunities

- Building Technician p76
- Cavity Wall Insulation Technician p80
- Concreter p85
- Thermal Insulation Engineer p132

Further information

British Wood Preserving and Damp Proofing Association (BWPDA) (incorporating the Property Care Association)
1 Gleneagles House, Vernongate, Derby DE1 1UP
01333 225 100; www.bwpda.co.uk

The Institute of Remedial Treatment Surveyors (IRTS)
Essex House, High Street, Chipping Ongar CM5 9EB
0800 915 6363

City&
Guilds

www.cityandguilds.com/myperfectjob

DEMOLITION OPERATIVE

What the work involves

- Demolition operatives demolish or dismantle buildings and structures. You will assess structures and plan for the safest and most efficient way to demolish them.

- You will prepare sites, put up fencing and scaffolding, strip out fittings, and remove, sort and grade reusable materials.

- You will use a variety of tools such as chisels, crowbars and axes for hand demolition of brick and stone and you may also use specialised machinery including pneumatic drills, steel girders, chain saws and even explosives for bigger jobs.

The type of person suited to this work

As you will be involved in the construction industry you should have an interest in building, construction and the environment.

You should have a high level of fitness as your work can be quite physical at times, lifting and carrying, and you should be able to work at heights.

You will also need good manual skills to operate equipment and tools and an aptitude for more delicate tasks such as hand demolition.

You should be willing to work as part of a team and be conscious of practices for your safety and of those around you.

Working conditions

You will normally work 39 hours per week. This will frequently include weekends and overtime.

As you will be working on construction sites you should be willing to work outdoors in dirty, dusty, noisy conditions in all weathers. This will also involve lifting, bending and working at heights.

You will need to wear protective equipment including helmets, boots, gloves and goggles which will be provided by the employer. You may also be required to wear breathing equipment for some jobs.

Future prospects

There are opportunities for demolition operatives on many building and development projects throughout the UK. You can find employment in specialist companies which may be based nationally but many companies are based in urban and traditionally industrial areas of the UK.

You can take courses to become more skilled, such as the demolition supervisors' distance learning course which is a 12 week course that provides progression from demolition operative 1 (labourer), to demolition supervisor.

Advantages/disadvantages

Although it is unusual to be self-employed in this profession, with experience you can set up your own contracting business.

Qualifications and courses

ENTRY LEVEL 1

No formal qualifications are required to be a demolition operative. However GCSEs (A-D) in maths, science subjects and English may be useful.

You can train as an Apprentice. CITB-ConstructionSkills provide 16 week residential courses, for entrants who are 16 and older, where you will have classroom-based lessons alongside practical training sessions on all aspects of demolition work.

You must then train for the Certificate of Competence of Demolition Operation. As you gain experience you will be assessed by the National Federation of Demolition Contractors. After one year's experience you can apply to be assessed as a demolition operative 1 (labourer), after two years, a demolition operative 2, and with three or more years, a demolition operative 3.

To gain a full competence card as a demolition operative you will need an NVQ Level 2 in demolition. Later for further promotion you can gain an NVQ Level 3 in demolition.

You will train on-the-job and take day- or block-release training run by recognised training centres.

At times your work can be strenuous and potentially hazardous if you do not follow safety procedures.

Money guide

Starting salaries range from around £12,000 a year.

As an experienced operative you should earn £18,000 minimum.

As a senior operative you can earn around £20,000.

You may earn significantly more with overtime or for operating plant machinery.

Demolition operatives have nationally recommended minimum rates of pay.

Related opportunities

- Construction Operative p86
- Quarry Worker p247
- Roofer p122
- Scaffolder p124

Further information

CITB-ConstructionSkills
Bircham Newton, King's Lynn PE31 6RH
01485 577577; www.ckills.org; call.centre@cskills.org

National Federation of Demolition Contractors
NFDC Resurgam House, Paradise, Hemel Hempstead HP2 4TF
01442 217144; www.demolition-nfdc.com;
info@demolition-nfdc.com

DRY STONE WALLER

What the work involves

- Dry stone walls are built as boundaries in rural landscapes, and sometimes in gardens and parks. Unlike other walls, they are built without the use of mortar or cement.

- You will build new walls and maintain and rebuild existing walls.

- Preparing foundations, setting up a frame and laying stones, as well as stripping out any existing wall or stones, will be part of the job.

- You will work outside during daylight hours so your job will vary from season to season.

The type of person suited to this work

As the work requires you to move around and lift heavy stones, you must be physically fit and be able to handle the stones safely. Practical skills and a methodical approach to the work are necessary.

An eye for design is useful for creating decorative effects. You may also need to work in a team with other dry stone wallers. You will need to respect the plants, animals and insects that live within, on or around the walls and other parts of your working area so having an interest in conservation and the environment is useful.

Working conditions

Your work will be physically demanding and take place outdoors in most weather conditions. The work may also be dusty and dirty.

You will need to pay attention to health and safety regulations, for example the wearing of protective gear such as boots, strong gloves and safety goggles.

Your working hours are likely to vary according to when the work is available. You may work at weekends.

Future prospects

There are around 600 dry stone wallers working in the UK and numbers are increasing. With a demand for walls on farms, and in parks and gardens, work is available in all rural areas of the UK for skilled dry stone wallers.

Employment is possible with organisations such as National Parks – although most experienced dry stone wallers are self-employed.

You can begin by working for an experienced dry stone waller and gain the necessary skills before working for yourself. Many experienced wallers travel around the UK to complete projects. A few wallers combine this work with traditional bricklaying work.

Advantages/disadvantages

The work can be physically demanding.

It is rewarding to use craft skills to build dry stone walls that are not only functional, but also enhance the landscape and become part of our heritage.

Qualifications and courses

No specific qualifications are required. Many people enter the work after working on a farm and hearing about the work by word of mouth.

You can train with an experienced dry stone waller or do a land-based training course that includes dry stone walling.

Lantra Certificates at Levels 1 and 2 are available in Dry Stone Walling.

The Dry Stone Walling Association of Great Britain (DSWA) runs a National Certification scheme at four levels – Initial, Intermediate, Advanced and Master Craftsman – which is open to anyone, including complete beginners.

Lantra offer an Apprenticeship in Dry Stone Walling (England and Wales). Apprentices work towards NVQ Level 2 in Environmental Conservation, the Lantra Level 2 Certificate in Dry Stone Walling, and Key Skills in Communication and Application of Number. There are no formal entry requirements to an Apprenticeship; commitment to a career in dry stone walling is more important. The Apprenticeship normally takes 12 months.

You also have the chance to be creative when producing decorative effects.

Money guide

The normal starting point for new entrants is around £8,000 per year. For dry stone wallers with some experience £10,500–£14,500 is possible. For very skilled dry stone wallers up to £21,000 is likely. Earnings vary widely across the UK. The rates self-employed dry stone wallers can charge depend a lot on their expertise. They often charge by the metre, and in some areas the demand for this diminishing craft is quite high.

Related opportunities

- Bricklayer p72
- Construction Operative p86
- Stonemason p128
- Thatcher p131

Further information

Dry Stone Walling Association of Great Britain
Westmorland County Showground
Lane Farm, Crooklands, Milnthorpe LA7 7NH
01539 567953; www.dswa.org.uk

Lantra
Lantra House, Stoneleigh Park, Coventry CV8 2LG
0845 707 8007; www.lantra.co.uk

www.cityandguilds.com/myperfectjob

ELECTRICIAN

What the work involves

- Electricians install and inspect the wiring systems in all kinds of buildings (residential and commercial) and mechanical equipment.

- You will follow detailed diagrams and plans when checking and installing new systems. Once installed you will test them to make sure they are safe.

- You may work on quite complex wiring systems, ranging from security circuits and computer networks to traffic lights and other street lighting.

The type of person suited to this work

Normal colour vision is essential. You must also have the practical skills to be able to use tools such as pliers, screwdrivers and drills.

You will need to be physically fit as the work involves bending, stretching, kneeling and generally being active. It can also involve working at heights, so you must be comfortable with this.

You should have the ability to follow wiring diagrams and work within strict safety regulations.

An aptitude in maths and physics is a significant aid.

You may work alone or in a team, but either way you will be talking to customers and explaining electrical problems so good communication skills are an asset.

Working conditions

You may work a normal working week from Monday to Friday, but most electricians work 37–40 hours including evenings and weekend to accommodate the needs of their customers.

Electricians work in a variety of locations from people's homes to offices or building sites. You will almost certainly need a driving licence.

The work can be dusty and dirty.

You will need to keep to health and safety regulations, as otherwise working with electricity can be exceedingly dangerous.

Future prospects

Employment prospects for new trainees are still good, although a halt in construction projects following the financial crash has affected the job market slightly.

Work is available in housing associations, general building companies and public services such as local authorities and health trusts.

With further qualifications and experience, you can progress to approved grade and then technician grade, which will increase your earning potential.

You may hold a supervisory or management position, and owning your own company is also an option.

There are also opportunities to work abroad.

Qualifications and courses

Entry requirements are 4 GCSEs/S grades (A–C/1–3) including English, maths and science subjects. If candidates do not have these qualifications some employers may require the successful completion of an aptitude test.

Most people enter the profession through an Apprenticeship. Applicants need to be aged 16–24. Apprentices work towards three separate qualifications, which are the City & Guilds Certificate in Electrotechnical Technology at Levels 2–3 and an NVQ/SVQ Level 3 in Electrotechnical Services (assessed in the workplace).

Those experienced in other relevant areas such as electronics may also qualify for entrance onto a training course.

Other qualifications on offer include the City & Guilds engineering systems maintenance course, the BTEC National Certificate in Engineering or the NVQ/SVQ in Engineering Maintenance Level 3.

Advantages/disadvantages

You are providing a vital service and it is particularly rewarding to solve problems for people.

Seeing a job through from start to finish is satisfying.

Many electricians are self-employed so you could have increased control over your life/work balance.

Money guide

The Joint Industry Board (JIB) for the Electrical Contracting Industry sets salary rates and travel allowances for apprentices and qualified electricians.

As an apprentice you could start from £10,000. Once qualified, this will rise to between £20,000 and £25,000. Experienced electricians can earn £30,000+. Rates in London are generally higher.

Related opportunities

- Carpenter/Joiner p77
- Plumber p117

Further information

SummitSkills
Vega House, Opal Drive, Fox Milne, Milton Keynes MK15 0DF
01908 303960; www.summitskills.org.uk;
enquiries@summitskills.org.uk

Scottish Electrical Charitable Training Trust (SECTT)
The Walled Garden, Bush Estate, Penicuik EH26 0SE
0131 445 5659; www.sectt.org.uk; admin@sectt.org.uk

City & Guilds

www.cityandguilds.com/myperfectjob

CAREERS IN THE ELECTRICAL CONTRACTING INDUSTRY

Whenever and wherever electrical energy is used, electrical contractors must design, install, maintain and test it. That means electrical contractors, or 'electricians' as they are commonly referred to, have the opportunity of working all over the world and in a wide variety of settings.

Most people tend to think of 'electricians' as the contractors who install a new lighting circuit in the home or perhaps the electric power supply to a new kitchen. Whilst around 40% of all electricians do undertake this type of work, the vast majority actually work in non-domestic settings.

The majority of electrical contractors are employed in industrial and commercial settings. This means designing, installing and maintaining the electrical installations in buildings as diverse as shops, offices, warehouses, factories, hotels, hospitals, churches or farms.

Electrical installations within commercial or industrial settings are generally much more complicated than those in residential settings and require additional skills. Some commercial projects like these are relatively small, whilst others are multi-billion pound construction projects such as the Terminal 5 at Heathrow Airport, Wembley Stadium or the London 2012 Olympic site.

The industry is very fast moving and changing. One reason for this is that the increase in the variety and type of electrical and electronic appliances in a typical home is ten times that of a typical home 50 years ago. Most homes and offices now contain appliances unimagined a few years ago, including computer equipment and networks, fire alarms, security systems, CCTV and even Jacuzzis.

This has resulted in significant changes to wiring regulations, legislation, products and services. Electricians need to keep their theoretical and practical knowledge and skills up to date, as a result.

Another attraction to a career in electrical installation is that it allows contractors to become self-employed if they so choose as a sole trader or as an owner of a large electrical business. However, many contractors prefer to work as direct employees for large firms.

In summary, working as an electrician provides a vast array of opportunities across a variety of settings both home and abroad.

For information on a career in electrical contracting visit www.prospects.ac.uk or careersadvice.direct.gov.uk.

To find out about apprenticeships, visit www.apprenticeships.org.uk. To find out more about electrical qualifications, visit www.cityandguilds.com.

About NICEIC

Established in 1956, NICEIC is the largest and leading voluntary regulatory body for electrical installation matters in the UK. Over 25,000 electrical contractors are registered with NICEIC and have to undergo a vigorous annual assessment. By employing a qualified NICEIC electrician, specifiers of electrical work, from the homeowner to the architect, can ensure that any electrical work carried out in their home is safe and complies with Building Regulations.

To find out more about NICEIC, visit *www.niceic.com*.

ELECTRICIAN

STEVEN BASTIEN NICEIC Approved Contractor

At weekends when I was younger, to earn pocket money I would accompany my electrician uncle on his jobs in London. I was about 14 and I found it interesting working in different types of buildings and areas. The excitement and adventure of going to different places and meeting different people made it enjoyable.

Until the age of 16 I continued working with my uncle at weekends. I learnt how to install new electrical installations and rewire properties. At first, the jobs I did were mainly manual, moving furniture, lifting up carpets and floorboards etc. Sometimes I would get the opportunity to chase out walls to bury cables. I also had to pack away the tools at the end of the day, and make sure none were missing!

As time went on, I realised I really enjoyed electrical work. It made me feel important and made me feel valued. I felt good about myself. I felt I was doing something which was a skilled trade…so becoming an electrician was a straightforward choice. I was advised by my careers adviser and teachers what subjects would be best to study, these subjects were Science, Maths, English, History and Geography.

After leaving school, I studied at College for two years, taking relevant City & Guilds qualifications which I studied very hard to make sure I would pass - which I did with distinction and passes. I then applied to electrical companies for an electrical apprenticeship. I was successful and offered a 5-year JIB Apprenticeship. It was here I gained a vast amount of experience in the electrical field, working in offices, schools, factories and shops. I carried on at college where I continued my studies to gain more qualifications in Electrical Installations.

Three years later I became a Qualified Electrician. I then decided to become even more adventurous by becoming self employed. This gave me the opportunity to work on major building projects throughout the UK. I worked on projects such as Fleet Street working for different newspapers. I even worked on a building which had a helicopter pad on top of it. That was quite exciting! I also worked on the first tower block of Canary Wharf. I worked on Tower Bridge, the NEC in Birmingham, the first Toyota Car Factory in the UK, and many more.

I then started working for local authorities, carrying out maintenance work as well as emergency callouts. Callouts give you a good feeling that you have helped someone.

Recently I have formed my own company - Facelift Electrical Services Ltd and successfully became an NICEIC Domestic Installer. I then become an NICEIC Approved Contractor which involved me taking more qualifications.

I can now say to any young person who would like to become an electrician, that it's a very enjoyable and satisfying career. It's great when you see the beginning of the project and see it through to the end. It's great to know you were part of that project being completed.

For further information visit www.niceic.com or call 0870 013 0382

ESTATE AGENT

What the work involves

■ An estate agent's job is to sell property for their clients, earning a fee for their work

■ This may involve finding suitable properties for people to view and showing them around properties.

■ When a buyer is found, you will help the buyer and seller to agree a price for the property.

The type of person suited to this work

You will need excellent listening and speaking skills so that you can recommend suitable properties to potential buyers. You also have to be good at negotiating so that you can help buyers and sellers to agree prices for properties.

You must be confident dealing with people and prepared to work hard to achieve sales.

As you will be dealing with figures when valuing properties or negotiating prices, you will need numeracy skills and an interest in keeping up to date with what is happening in the housing and property markets.

Working conditions

Some of your time will be spent in the branch office, and the rest of the time you will be visiting properties, so a driving licence is needed.

Estate agency branches are often modern and open-plan with up-to-date equipment. You will spend a lot of your time working at a computer and speaking to your customers on the phone.

This can be very stressful work as you will have sales targets to reach and your earnings will depend on your selling ability.

You are likely to need to work at weekends and evenings (with some time off during the week instead).

Future prospects

Estate agents are located throughout the UK but there tend to be fewer opportunities in a poor housing market.

If you do well and gain experience and qualifications, there are opportunities for promotion – especially in larger estate agencies. For example, you may move from trainee to negotiator, then to senior negotiator and on to branch manager.

Advantages/disadvantages

The work can be stressful if you are finding it hard to meet sales targets, especially if you are working on a commission-only basis in a slowing housing market. However, the financial rewards can be high if the property market is booming.

Money guide

Earnings vary widely depending on region and may be affected by the number of sales you make. Bonuses and commission payments are often added to salaries. Some estate agents work for commission only. New entrants earn about £13,000

Qualifications and courses

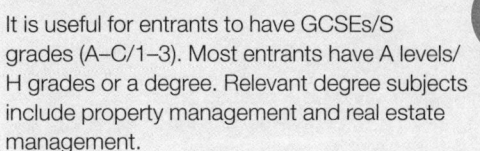

It is useful for entrants to have GCSEs/S grades (A–C/1–3). Most entrants have A levels/ H grades or a degree. Relevant degree subjects include property management and real estate management.

Training can be done on the job. It may involve studying for qualifications such as Technical Awards in Sale of Residential Property and Residential Letting and Property Management through the National Association of Estate Agents (NAEA). Diploma programmes in Residential Estate Agency, Residential Property Letting and Commercial Property Agency are intended for those with around 3 years' experience. Both the Technical Awards and the Diplomas may be studied by distance learning, or part-time at a college.

TTC Training offers an Apprenticeship for young people, leading to NVQ Level 2 or 3 in the Sale of Residential Property. The Apprenticeship also includes The National Association of Estate Agents' (NAEA) Technical Award, and Apprentices gain student membership of the NAEA after three months.

Qualifications are also offered by the Royal Institution of Chartered Surveyors (RICS).

a year. This can rise to £20,000+ for experienced advisers, negotiators and managers. As a partner in a business you could earn around £35,000. Top earners such as area managers could earn up to £40,000+.

Related opportunities

■ Home Inspector/Energy Assessor p107
■ Land Valuer/Auctioneer p110
■ Property Valuer p118
■ Planning and Development Surveyor p115

Further information

Asset Skills (Sector Skills Council in property services, housing, cleaning services and facilities management)
2 The Courtyard, 48 New North Road, Exeter EX4 4EP
01392 423399; www.assetskills.org

National Association of Estate Agents
Arbon House, 6 Tournament Court, Edgehill Drive, Warwick CV34 6LG
01926 496800; www.naea.co.uk

City&
Guilds

www.cityandguilds.com/myperfectjob

FABRICATOR

What the work involves

- Fabricators manufacture, assemble and install structural frames of buildings.

- You will extend and adapt existing buildings or work on manufacturing the entire frame work for new ones. This may include houses, public buildings, swimming pools, airport terminal buildings and caravans.

- Your work will be influenced by architectural demands and advances. The need for thermal performance, speed and versatility in architecture means that traditional forms of construction such as concrete, steel and glass are being replaced with new, more efficient materials.

- You will probably work with a diverse range of materials such as aluminium, PVC foam, timber, natural stone and fibreglass.

The type of person suited to this work

As a fabricator you should have an interest in machinery and the construction industry.

You will be working on site or in a manufacturing plant and as this may include physical labour you should be fit and have good manual skills.

You should also enjoy working as a team and have excellent knowledge and awareness of health and safety practices.

You should be organised and know how to plan ahead.

Working conditions

You will typically work 39 hours per week Monday to Friday. This may vary depending on the project you are working on. You may also be required to do shifts and overtime and work evenings and weekends.

You may work in a variety of locations; outdoors, indoors and at heights. Weather conditions may make this work uncomfortable or delay work.

As a fabricator you may have to operate machinery such as mobile cranes.

Future prospects

As you gain experience you will have the opportunity to specialise in a certain area of fabrication. This could be as an aluminium fabricator (curtain walls, window, frames), a conservatory fabricator (working with timber, aluminium or PVC to erect conservatories) or a window fabricator (working with frame makers and door makers building offsite manufactured rooms that can be assembled onsite).

As you accumulate experience you can progress to higher level positions such as supervisors or you may also choose to become self-employed.

Qualifications and courses

ENTRY
2
LEVEL

There are no specific entry qualifications. However GCSEs or S grades (A-E/1–5) in English and maths are useful. Science and design and technology are required as you will need to have an understanding of calculations, measurements and theory.

CITB-ConstructionSkills may provide apprenticeships. Here you will be assessed on literacy and your ability to work at heights and you will take an aptitude exercise on maths and problem solving.

Young Apprenticeships, Pre-Apprenticeships, Apprenticeships and Advanced Apprenticeships may be available in England. Apprenticeship schemes are organised differently in Scotland, Wales and Northern Ireland. You should be aware that pay rates for apprenticeships vary according to area and industry.

As a construction apprentice you train and gain vocational qualifications on the job. You will learn practical skills under the supervision of skilled fabricators, as well as taking courses at a college or training centre. These may include NVQs/SVQs such as Level 1 in construction and civil engineering services, Level 2 and 3 in fabrication and welding engineering, Level 2 and 3 in carpentry and joinery and Level 4 in construction site management.

Advantages/disadvantages

New and exciting developments and improvements in materials and technology mean that your work is likely to include scope for diversity and creativity.

Your work at times may be physically very demanding.

Money guide

Your starting salary may start around £15,000 a year.

Related opportunities

- Building Technician p76
- Carpenter p77
- Ceiling Fixer p81
- Structural Engineer p129

Further information

The British Woodworking Federation (BWF)
55 Tufton Street, London SW1P 3QL
0870 458 6939; www.bwf.org.uk

CITB-ConstructionSkills
Bircham Newton, King's Lynn PE 31 6RH
www.bwpda.co.uk

National Association of Shopfitters
NAS House, 411 Limpsfield Road, Warlingham CR6 9HA
01883 624961; www.shopfitters.org

FACILITIES MANAGER

What the work involves

- Facilities managers are responsible for the management and administration of premises, including offices, schools and commercial properties.

- You will provide a safe and efficient work environment for staff by implementing procedures to improve facilities, reduce costs and increase productivity.

- Your day to day work will depend on the type of organisation you work for, but will include a broad spectrum of tasks such as coordinating and managing central services, organising mail receipt and despatch, arranging contractors for security, or supervising cleaning and catering.

- You must be able to respond to all problems that arise unexpectedly, and react to them appropriately and efficiently.

The type of person suited to this work

As you will be coordinating many different aspects of an organisation, or many organisations in one location, you need to be highly organised. You should be able to meet deadlines and have strong problem-solving skills.

You will lead a team so you should have excellent negotiation skills and strong written and verbal communication ability.

You should also be aware of environmental issues affecting premises and how budgets are planned and controlled.

As you will be working with a variety of different people you should have good customer service skills.

Working conditions

Your hours will vary depending on the organisation you work for but on average you will work from 9 to 5. You will mainly be office-based, but you will move around a lot to inspect and supervise various projects throughout the location you work in.

You may have a permanent contract or work on a fixed-term contract. At times you may be required to be available at any time in the event of emergencies.

Future prospects

You may begin as an assistant in a particular support field such as IT, HR, finance or purchasing or health and safety and then progress to functional manager, senior manager and director positions.

You can work as a facilities manager in-house or join a facilities management provider or consultancy. This will provide a variety of projects and responsibilities but will not have the same level of stability.

It is recommended that you seek opportunities in different organisations to secure promotion.

Advantages/disadvantages

Prospects for career development can be excellent. If you are hardworking, flexible, and efficient, have commercial acumen and the ability to juggle tight budgets you can progress to higher level general management jobs.

Qualifications and courses

Many entrants to this profession are graduates who have studied property and land-based subjects such as estate management or surveying.

Others gain experience in relevant fields such as construction, building services, engineering or hospitality to acquire skills for facilities management.

You can take vocational courses in facilities management. These include appropriate NVQs/SVQs or professional qualifications from the British Institute of Facilities Management (BIFM). You can also study for a foundation degree (developed by Asset Skills) or an HND in facilities management.

Work experience is recommended and employers will seek candidates with good experience. For graduates year long placements are invaluable.

Entrants to facilities management also come from other areas of employment using relevant skills and experience. Many of these entrants have backgrounds in office management and administration, building services and engineering, customer services and the armed forces.

You may find it difficult to move from an in-house role to a position with a service provider as there is a perceived difference in outlook and experience.

Money guide

Starting salaries may range from around £14,000 to £20,000 per year.

An experienced facilities manager can earn between £25,000 and £35,000 a year.

Senior facilities managers can earn in excess of £40,000.

Related opportunities

- Building Services Engineer p74
- Estates Officer p38
- Health and Safety Adviser p40
- Quality Manager p53

Further information

British Institute of Facilities Management (BIFM)
Number One Building, The Causeway, Bishop's Stortford CM23 2ER
0845 058 1356; www.bifm.org.uk; info@bifm.org.uk

Chartered Management Institute
Management House, Cottingham Road, Corby NN17 1TT
01536 204222; www.managers.org.uk; enquiries@managers.org.uk

www.cityandguilds.com/myperfectjob

FENCE INSTALLER

What the work involves

- Fence installers put up many different kinds of fences in a wide range of locations. For example, they erect motorway barriers, perimeter fencing around prisons and safari parks, as well as fencing for gardens, farms and forests.

- Before putting up a fence, you will measure the area, work out how much fencing you need and prepare the ground.

- As a fence installer, you will work with a range of materials such as wire, wood, concrete or metal.

The type of person suited to this work

You will need to have good practical skills to work with a range of materials, tools and equipment. The job involves working to plans and taking measurements, so you must also be able to work accurately and have basic maths skills.

As you will be working with some heavy materials you will need to be physically fit.

The ability to work in a team with other fence erectors is important. You will also need to understand the use of all types of fencing and related construction materials, and be aware of the environment.

Working conditions

You will work mainly outdoors in a range of locations from people's gardens to construction-sites and motorways. You may need a driving licence and for some projects you will sometimes have to stay away from home.

You will need to work to health and safety regulations, for example the wearing of protective gear such as a safety helmet, gloves and boots.

You are likely to work a normal working week, although weekend work may also be available.

Future prospects

The fencing industry is made up of around 4,000 specialist fencing businesses employing about 25,000 fencing operatives. There are currently plenty of opportunities for skilled fence erectors and the range of work available is as varied as the types of fences needed!

Work is available with fencing companies of all sizes throughout the UK. You may work in the construction, landscape, environmental, forestry and agricultural industries. Some companies specialise in providing soundproofing, while others supply agricultural or roadside fencing.

You may progress to supervisory and managerial levels and, after you have gained enough experience, you could run your own business.

Qualifications and courses

No specific qualifications are required, although GCSEs/S grades (A–E/1–5), in English, maths and technology may be useful. New entrants need to do health and safety training before working on construction-sites.

You will be trained mainly on the job, and you may also attend a college or training centre. You could work towards NVQs/SVQs in Fencing at Levels 2 and 3.

Apprenticeships/Skillseekers are available for candidates aged 16–24.

Lantra awards a card (required by many construction-sites) from a Fencing Industry Skills Scheme (FISS), which is run in partnership with the Construction Skills Certification Scheme (CSCS). The card is provided following attendance on approved health and safety training, passing a health and safety test, and enrolling on an NVQ/SVQ.

Advantages/disadvantages

The work may be physically demanding for some people. Your fencing will help to protect people, buildings, animals and vehicles.

You will develop a range of skills and knowledge on a variety of projects.

You will be outside in all weathers.

Money guide

Starting out as a trainee you could earn between £10,000 and £14,500 per year. Trained and experienced fence installers could earn from £23,000 to £25,000. Up to £40,000 is possible for the highest earners, who may manage a team of workers. Overtime and bonuses based on outputs may be available, which can lead to higher earnings.

Related opportunities

- Building Technician p76
- Carpenter/Joiner p77
- Dry Stone Waller p93
- Labourer/Construction Operative p86

Further information

Fencing Contractors Association
Warren Road, Trellech NP25 4PQ
07000 560722; www.fencingcontractors.org

www.cityandguilds.com/myperfectjob

FLOOR LAYER/FINISHER

What the work involves

- Floor layers fit various rooms and buildings with many different types of flooring, such as vinyl, wood, carpet, tiles, rubber or plastic.

- You will decide on the best material to use for the particular type of floor.

- You will use various tools to prepare the surface, cut the flooring material to size and lay the floor.

- You will work from technical plans and diagrams in order to lay and fit each floor correctly.

The type of person suited to this work

To do this work you will need accurate numerical skills in order to calculate the exact amount of flooring material you will need for each job.

You should be physically fit as you will spend a lot of time lifting and carrying materials, or working on your hands and knees.

You may work alone for some smaller jobs, but you must also be able to work in a team with other construction professionals for larger jobs.

Good planning skills are helpful when organising your workload, and you should be happy meeting and talking to lots of different people.

Working conditions

You will usually work normal Monday to Friday office hours, but you may also need to work through the night or over weekends on some contracts, so that you can lay floors without disrupting the work of shops and businesses.

Most of your work will be spent indoors in a variety of locations including people's homes, hospitals, offices and construction sites, some of which will be dirty and dusty.

This is mobile work, so a driving licence is useful.

Some contracts may involve absence from home overnight or for longer periods of time.

Future prospects

There are good prospects for finding work as a trainee floor layer because there is a shortage of floor layers nationwide.

Once you have qualified, work will be available within small or large flooring companies or contractors across the UK.

You may choose to specialise in using one type of flooring material such as tiles or laminates.

With experience, you can progress to technical, supervisory or managerial posts. Or you could set up on your own as a self-employed floor layer.

Qualifications and courses

No specific qualifications are required, although GCSEs/S grades (A–E/1–5) in maths, design and technology, science and English are useful.

You will be trained on the job while working towards qualifications. This may also involve going to a college or training centre on day- or block-release.

The Construction Industry Training Board (CITB) offers an Apprenticeship Scheme in floor laying. Apprenticeships are available to entrants aged 16–24. The CITB also offers a Construction Award in floor covering.

There are a number of fast-track short courses available from independent providers such as the Flooring Industry Training Association (FITA). NVQs/SVQs in floor covering at Levels 1, 2 and 3 are also available.

Advantages/disadvantages

An attractive and well-laid floor can transform a room. The ability to use your skills and a range of materials to create this effect can give you great job satisfaction.

You will spend a lot of time travelling to and from jobs, and may need to spend time away from home on big flooring projects.

Money guide

Starting rate for trainees is around £12,500 per year. With an NVQ earnings can rise to £14,500+, and as a fully qualified floor layer you could earn about £20,000. Highly skilled, experienced floor layers can earn salaries of up to £30,000.

Earnings vary among employers and in different parts of the country. Salaries in London are higher. Many floor layers are self-employed and earnings will depend on the ability to win contracts.

Related opportunities

- Carpenter/Joiner p77
- Glazier p103
- Plasterer p116
- Roofer p122

Further information

ConstructionSkills
Bircham Newton, King's Lynn PE31 6RH
01485 577577; www.cskills.org

The Flooring Industry Training Association (FITA)
4c St Mary's Place, The Lace Market, Nottingham, NG1 1PH
0115 950 6836; www.fita.co.uk; info@fita.co.uk

www.cityandguilds.com/myperfectjob

THE FLOORING TRADE

Matthew Blackbourn's story:

On the job training has formed a key part of 22 year old Matthew's journey into the flooring trade fitting carpets and other floor coverings in domestic homes. He firmly believes that ensuring you begin your working life with a reputable, established company is vital. Matthew has supplemented the experience he has gained on site with training courses through FITA, after which he applied to become a "Masterfitter" in Carpet via the NICF. Although he has a passion for installation and gets a true buzz from a job well done, Matthew hopes to grow more in to the management side. However, his positive experience of training has also led him to have ambitions to become an instructor and put something back.

For Matthew the future in flooring is bright and full of opportunity.

What the job entails

Working for a small business in the domestic market, means that the range of tasks involved are enormous. "I generally find myself fitting floors during the day and enjoy the diversity of products and skills I have to employ really interesting. I also like working with the public and when we are busy I tend to help out with measures in the evenings. More recently, I have started to get involved with pricing and ordering stock etc."

The commercial sector is of course slightly different with work typically taking place in offices, hospitals and schools. Generally on a bigger scale, some of the contracts involve materials worth many thousands of pounds. Main contractors are often working to tight timescales and obviously floor layers have to enjoy working in a team in what is often essentially a construction environment. As well as a craft and a skill, floor laying is increasing technical and finding the solution to meet the needs of a client (many working on fast track projects) are some of the demands and challenges of the "on site" role.

What you need to succeed

Flexibility, good communication, as well as an obvious natural tendency towards good practical skills, are all qualities required to succeed in the flooring industry. The ability to use your own initiative, as well as work in a team, is often an advantage.

Practical on site experience will always be required, but formal qualifications such as an NVQ level 2 in floor laying are recognised qualifications that can currently be gained through a number of routes including a modern apprenticeship. This can be supplemented with short training courses through organisations such as FITA as both an introduction, as well as a career building strategy.

For further information or advice contact:

The Contract Flooring Association (CFA)
Telephone: 0115 941 1126

The Flooring Industry Training Association (FITA)
Telephone: 0115 950 6836

The National Institute of Carpet & FloorLayers (NICF)
Telephone: 0115 958 3077

GLAZIER

What the work involves

- Glaziers use specialist cutting and fixing tools to cut glass to the correct size and fit it into place.
- You might fit glass into houses, shop fronts, office blocks or roofs.
- You might be working on new buildings or replacing existing or broken glass.
- You will use your knowledge to choose a suitable type of glass for each job.

The type of person suited to this work

You will be measuring and cutting glass accurately so that it fits perfectly into the frame. As you will be using different hand tools a practical ability will be necessary.

You will also need to be physically fit so that you can carry glass and be comfortable working at heights (sometimes extreme heights).

You may work alone for some jobs, such as in people's homes, but you must also be able to work and communicate with other glaziers, especially when working on large jobs with big, heavy panes of glass.

Working conditions

You will work indoors and outdoors in many different locations. A driving licence may be useful.

You will need to work safely and be aware of your own, the public's and your colleagues' safety when carrying, cutting and fixing glass.

You may work normal working hours during the week, but you may also need to work at weekends and during evenings, possibly offering emergency cover for households and businesses when replacing broken glass.

Future prospects

Work is available with glazing and construction companies throughout the UK and the demand for trained glaziers is high. The range of jobs in glazing work is also increasing to include specialist areas, for example automotive glass repair and replacement

After gaining sufficient experience, you may progress to technical or supervisory levels, or you could decide to start your own glazing business. The majority of glaziers are self-employed.

Advantages/disadvantages

Working at extreme heights may be demanding for some. You will get to work in a variety of locations on a wide range of projects. Cutting tools and glass can be dangerous, so you will have to be aware of health and safety regulations. You could be called out at all hours for emergency jobs.

Qualifications and courses

ENTRY 1 LEVEL

There are no set entry requirements, but you may need some GCSEs/S grades (A–C/1–3) or equivalent, vocational qualifications such as a BTEC Introductory Certificate/Diploma in Construction. Maths, English and technology subjects are useful for the parts of the job that involve measurements and calculations, and for theoretical training.

You can train and gain vocational qualifications while you work. You will be taught practical skills and may spend time off-site at a college or training centre.

You are likely to work towards NVQs/SVQs in glass-related subjects. These include Glazing Installation and Maintenance, Automotive Glazing, and Fenestration Installation and Surveying at both Levels 2 and 3.

A scheme is promoted by Glass Training Limited (GTL) called 'Learning for All', whereby companies set up flexible learning programmes, known as 'learning pathways'. In the scheme, NVQs and SVQs can be delivered through distance-learning programmes.

Money guide

The Building and Allied Trades Joint Industrial Council (BATJIC) agrees minimum recommended wage rates annually. Newly qualified glaziers earn round £12,000–£14,000. With experience, glaziers can expect to earn £18,000–£24,000. Those highly skilled, with experience and extra responsibilities, such as emergency call-outs, might achieve up to £40,000.

Related opportunities

- Building Technician p76
- Carpenter/Joiner p77
- Ceiling Fixer p81
- Window Fitter p138

Further information

Proskills UK
Centurion Court, 85b Milton Park, Abingdon OX14 4RY
01235 833844; www.proskills.co.uk

Glass Qualifications Authority
Provincial House, Solly Street, Sheffield S1 4BA
0114 272 0033; www.glassqualificationsauthority.com

Glass and Glazing Federation
44–48 Borough High Street, London SE1 1XB
0870 042 4255; www.ggf.co.uk

City& Guilds

www.cityandguilds.com/myperfectjob

HEATING AND VENTILATING ENGINEER/ GAS FITTER

What the work involves

Heating and ventilating engineer

- Heating and ventilating engineers install equipment such as pipework and boilers for systems including central heating, hot and cold water services and gas supplies in industrial and commercial buildings.

- The systems you will work on are very large, and your work will include cutting, bending and joining pipes that will need to withstand high pressures, so welding is an important part of the work.

- When you have installed a system, you will test it to make sure that everything is working as it should.

Gas service technician

- Your job will be to install, maintain, repair and test gas appliances such as fires, cookers and heating systems.

- Once installed you will test the appliances and give advice.

- You could work in private homes or on business premises.

The type of person suited to this work

Heating and ventilating engineer

You must be a practical person so that you can use the tools and equipment for the job. Understanding and following diagrams is an essential part of the work, so you need a logical, mechanically minded approach to your work. You will also need to be good at maths for making calculations.

It can be physically demanding work, as you will be bending, kneeling and working in tight spaces. You also need a head for heights and a safety-conscious attitude, because you will often be working from ladders and scaffolding.

Teamwork and communication skills are also important when you are installing large systems.

Gas service technician

You will need excellent practical skills and to enjoy using tools and making things work. Some work will involve finding faults - this area needs people who like investigating and working out why things go wrong.

Gas and gas appliances are potentially dangerous, so you should be very thorough and reliable. As you will be working in homes you should have good communication skills to advise customers.

Working conditions

A lot of your time will be spent indoors, but you will also need to work outdoors for part of the work. You may work on building sites, and in buildings such as factories, hospitals and schools. You will need to wear safety gear such as a helmet, goggles and gloves.

You may work a normal working week, but there may be times when you will work different hours, for example to avoid disruption to clients.

You might work weekends and evenings, especially if you provide emergency cover.

Future prospects

Heating and ventilating engineer

There are around 34,000 heating and ventilation engineers within the UK and the heating and ventilating industry has a workforce of about 50,000. There is currently an acute shortage of skilled heating and ventilating engineers.

Once you undertake training and are qualified, work will be available across the UK with specialist heating and ventilation companies, or organisations such as the NHS or local authorities. Many qualified fitters also become self employed, joining up with other engineers to offer sub-contracting services.

There are good prospects for advancement to supervisory roles and it is possible for you to become a heating and ventilating technician. If you take additional qualifications and higher education, progression to professional engineering level is also possible. There are also opportunities to work overseas.

Gas service technician

There is a shortage of gas service technicians. You can work for national or private companies or become self-employed. In larger companies you can progress up to supervisory posts or apply for training posts at local colleges or within private organisations.

Advantages/disadvantages

Working in cramped and awkward spaces can be uncomfortable.

Transforming a building from an empty shell into a warm, comfortable environment can be rewarding.

Career progression opportunities are excellent.

There is demand across the country for work in this area.

Money guide

Heating and ventilating engineer

The Heating and Ventilating Contractors' Association (HVCA) publishes recommended salary rates. Overtime is often available, which can lead to higher earnings.

As a new fitter you could start at around £11,500 per year. As a qualified building services graduate you could earn £21,000–£25,000.

With experience and additional responsibilities, you could earn £35,000– £45,000.

Gas service technician
New apprentices earn around £12,000 per year which, after training, can rise to between £17,000 and £25,000.

The most experienced can earn up to £33,000+. It is also possible to earn extra for overtime and shift work.

Related opportunities

- Mechanical Engineer p240
- Gas Network Engineer p231
- Plumber p117
- Thermal Insulation Engineer p132

Further information

SummitSkills (Sector Skills Council for building services engineering)
Vega House, Opal Drive, Fox Milne, Milton Keynes MK15 0DF
08000 688336; www.summitskills.org.uk

Building Engineering Services Training Ltd
The Mere, Second Floor, Milestone House, Upton Park, Slough SL1 2DQ
01753 531188; www.best-ltd.co.uk

Heating and Ventilating Contractors' Association
Esca House, 34 Palace Court, London W2 4JG
020 7313 4900; www.hvca.org.uk

Building Engineering Services Training Ltd (Scotland)
Unit 4, Bush House, Penicuik EH26 0BB
0131 445 5900; www.best-ltd.co.uk

Council for Registered Gas Installers (CORGI)
1 Elmwood, Chineham Park, Crockford Lane, Basingstoke RG24 8WG
0800 915 0485; www.trustcorgi.com

www.cityandguilds.com/myperfectjob

Qualifications and courses
Heating and ventilating engineer

Most employers train young entrants through Apprenticeships/Skillseekers. 4 GCSEs/S grades (A–C/1–3), including maths, English and science subject may be required for entry to these.

Training for Apprentices/Skillseekers includes attending college on day- or block-release. You will work towards NVQ/SVQ Level 2 in Mechanical Engineering Services: Heating and Ventilation Installation, progressing to NVQ/SVQ Level 3. NVQs/SVQs cover industrial, commercial and domestic installation, and maintenance of components.

The same NVQ qualifications are available to adults, but for entry to these you may be required to be in related work or have relevant experience.

Other training includes: City & Guilds Certificate in Energy Efficiency for Domestic Heating (6084), for domestic fitters; and the Oil Firing Technical Association for the Petroleum Industry's (OFTEC) training scheme for those working with oil-fired equipment.

Gas service technician

At least 4 GCSEs/S grades (A–C/1–3) including English, maths and sometimes science or technology subjects are normally required for entry to this career. Practical subjects such as metalwork and woodwork are useful.

Apprenticeships/Skillseekers are available for people aged 16–24. Apprentices work towards NVQ/SVQ in Domestic Natural Gas Installation and Maintenance, awarded by City & Guilds. Gas service companies also run their own apprenticeship schemes.

Trainees must gain registration with CORGI (Council of Registered Gas Installers). To become registered, trainees need to work towards the NVQ/SVQ in Domestic Natural Gas Installation and Maintenance at Level 2 or 3, or complete equivalent in-house training with a company. Technicians with qualifications or training other than the NVQ/SVQ must complete ACS (Accredited Certification Scheme) assessments.

Gas service technicians have to demonstrate their gas safety competence on a 5-year cycle by successfully completing nationally agreed Accredited Certification Scheme (ACS) assessments.

Building and Construction

CRCI: BB
CLCI: UJ

Building and Construction

CRCI: BB
CLCI: UN

HIGHWAYS MAINTENANCE/ ROAD WORKER

What the work involves

- Road workers' tasks include building new roads, re-routing or widening existing roads, and repairing potholes and cracks in roads.

- You will also have other duties such as putting up warning signs and barriers, controlling the movement of traffic near the work site, laying kerbstones and pavements, and gritting roads in the winter.

- You will work with numerous building materials including concrete, tarmac and paving slabs.

- You will use a range of tools and equipment in your work, including specialised, heavy machinery such as diggers and rollers.

The type of person suited to this work

You must have a good standard of fitness, as the work involves a lot of hard, physical work and requires you to lift and carry heavy materials.

Practical ability with tools such as picks and shovels is useful, as is experience of operating equipment such as cement mixers, diggers and rolling machines.

As much of your work will be undertaken as part of a team of road workers and supervisors, it is important that you can get along with colleagues at all levels, as well as members of the public.

Working conditions

You are likely to work a normal 37 hour working week, although you may also work weekends and evenings to avoid disrupting traffic.

You will need to be aware of the danger of traffic and health and safety for yourself and your colleagues. Onsite, you will wear protective clothing such as a safety helmet, fluorescent jacket and boots.

Future prospects

Road workers may work for local authorities or, as work is increasingly contracted out, for specialist road-building or civil engineering companies.

Work is available across the UK. Some work is short-term or seasonal. You could become self-employed and work on contract basis.

As you develop and gain experience and qualifications, you may go on to lead a small team or become a supervisor.

Advantages/disadvantages

You will be helping to maintain and improve the safety of the roads in your local area, which can be personally rewarding.

You will be outdoors doing physically demanding work in all weathers, so can expect to get hot in the summer and cold in the winter.

Qualifications and courses

ENTRY LEVEL 1

There are no formal entry requirements for this work, but GCSEs/S grades in maths, English and design and technology may be helpful. Personal skills and physical fitness are usually more important than qualifications.

Your training will be given mainly on the job by experienced road workers.

You may be able to work towards NVQs/SVQs in construction and civil engineering services' highway maintenance at Levels 1 and 2, road building at Level 2 and winter maintenance operations at Level 2 whilst you are in employment.

To become a qualified site operative, you need one of the following: a City & Guilds award in streetworks, excavation and reinstatement; an SQA National Award in excavation and reinstatement; or a CABWI award in street works excavation and reinstatement.

If working with plant machinery, you will need to be 18 or over. A driving licence will also be required, and an LGV licence may be needed for some jobs.

Money guide

Trainee road workers start at around £12,000 per year. With experience you could get £15,000–£17,000.

The highest-earning road workers with a lot of experience and relevant qualifications can expect around £19,000+.

You can increase your earnings with overtime and shift work.

Related opportunities

- Concreter p85
- Demolition Operative p92
- Bricklayer p72
- Labourer/Construction Operative p86

Further information

ConstructionSkills
Bircham Newton, King's Lynn PE31 6RH
01485 577577; www.cskills.net, www.bconstructive.co.uk

The Street Works Qualification Register (SWQR)
The Optima Building, 58 Robertson Street, Glasgow G2 8DQ
0845 270 2720; www.swqr.org.uk

City & Guilds

www.cityandguilds.com/myperfectjob

HOME INSPECTOR/ ENERGY ASSESSOR

What the work involves

■ Home inspectors and energy assessors are qualified and accredited to inspect a property and produce a report called a Home Condition Report (HCR) and/or Energy Performance Certificate (EPC).

■ As part of an energy assessment, you will survey the level of energy efficiency at the property.

■ You will then grade the property's energy performance and suggest ways to cut fuel bills.

The type of person suited to this work

Written and verbal communication skills are important, as you will be writing technical reports for both buyers and sellers.

You will need a logical and methodical approach and to be precise and accurate in your work. You also need to be able to use computers and be good at maths, for example when taking measurements.

You need an interest in and knowledge of buildings and building regulations, construction and energy efficiency.

Working conditions

Home inspectors/energy assessors spend some time indoors working in an office, writing reports, but most of their time is spent visiting properties in their local area carrying out inspections.

A driving licence may be necessary.

You may have to work early, late or at weekends to see clients when they are at home.

Future prospects

Demand is set to increase for energy assessors with additional requirements being introduced by the government for private landlords to have an EPC before marketing their property for letting. New builds too now need EPCs.

Employers include property surveying companies, estate agents, construction companies and building service firms. It is difficult to predict long-term prospects in this new job – which will, like estate agency, be dependent on the state of the housing market.

Advantages/disadvantages

You may need to work anti-social hours, to visit working home-sellers who can only be at home for your inspection in the evening or at weekends.

You won't be stuck in an office and you will meet a wide variety of people.

Qualifications and courses

ENTRY **2** LEVEL

Many entrants have A levels/H grades, a degree or vocational qualifications. Relevant degree and vocational subjects include surveying, construction, property management and real estate management.

To work as a Home Inspector you will have to pass the Level 4 Diploma in Home Inspection (DipHI) – awarded by the Awarding Body for the Built Environment (ABBE).

To work as an Energy Assessor there are a range of qualifying Diplomas including the Level 3 Diploma in On Construction Energy Assessment (DipOCEA), Level 3 in Domestic Energy Assessment (DipDEA), Level 3 Diploma in Non Domestic Energy Assessment (DipNDEA) and the Level 4 Diploma in Non Domestic Energy Assessment.

You will also need to be a member of an approved accreditation scheme, have a Criminal Records Bureau check and take out personal indemnity insurance.

Money guide

Starting salaries for newly qualified entrants are between £20,000 and £25,000 per year. Experienced inspectors can earn £30,000–£40,000. Earnings vary widely among regions and employers, and you may improve your salary by changing employer. Salaries are generally higher in London. A top salary of between £40,000 and £50,000 may be possible, depending on the employer and your particular role and responsibilities.

Related opportunities

■ Architectural Technician p70
■ Building Technician p76
■ Estate Agent p97
■ Town Planning Technician p133

Further information

Asset Skills
2 The Courtyard, 48 New North Road, Exeter EX4 4EP
01392 423399; www.assetskills.org

Association of Home Information Pack Providers
55 The Ridgeway, Market Harborough LE16 7HG
0870 950 7739; www.hipassociation.co.uk

Awarding Body for the Built Environment (ABBE)
Room A045, Birmingham City University, Franchise Street, Perry Barr, Birmingham B42 2SU
0121 331 5174; www.abbeqa.co.uk

City& Guilds

www.cityandguilds.com/myperfectjob

HOUSING OFFICER

What the work involves

- You will manage and maintain rented housing, usually for a housing association or local authority.

- Tasks include assessing housing needs in an area and making policies to provide for them, allocating housing to applicants, planning property maintenance and repair.

- You will also need to set rents, and deal with tenants who are behind with their rent as well as resolving neighbourhood disputes and answering tenants' enquiries.

- You will find yourself working with a range of different people which could include vulnerable people or those in particularly bad situations economically.

The type of person suited to this work

As most of your work will involve talking and listening to people, you will need excellent verbal communication skills. You should also be able to work with and relate to a variety of people, including other professionals and tenants.

Maths and numeracy skills are useful for dealing with rental payments, maintenance and repair costs, and budgets.

You will need to keep up to date with a range of housing and tenant welfare issues, and be flexible and able to solve problems as and when they arise.

You will also need to be able to work as part of a team as well as on your own.

Working conditions

Many housing officers are based in an office, but regularly travel to make property inspections, visit tenants or attend meetings. Not all of your tenants will be polite, so expect to deal with some who may be rude and angry.

Some of your work will involve visiting tenants and looking at damage or possibly collecting rents, so a driving licence is required for many posts.

Although you will normally work standard office hours, you could have to do some unsocial hours and weekend work too.

Future prospects

The employment situation is buoyant at the moment, as social housing is a growth area, with organisations taking on a number of new trainees as well as experienced staff. Work is available in towns and cities throughout the UK.

You can increase your chances of employment by doing work experience or voluntary work in housing first.

Most housing officers work for local authorities and housing associations, but you may also work for other employers such as voluntary organisations, property companies, private landlords and housing trusts. You may also be able to

Qualifications and courses

It is possible to enter with GCSEs/S grades (A–C/1–3) and study part time while working. Many people enter with an HNC, Foundation degree, degree or postgraduate qualification in housing studies.

The National Certificate in Housing Studies is often taken before the HNC in Housing. For entry to a Foundation degree in Housing Studies, at least 2 A levels/three H grades are required.

Housing Officers whose degrees do not include a work placement will be expected to gain appropriate industrial experience before they become a member of the Chartered Institute of Housing. The CIH also recognises relevant work experience as a route to Stages 1 and 2 of the Professional Qualification.

specialise in a particular area such as neighbourhood management or welfare benefits.

There are opportunities for promotion from housing officer to roles such as principal housing officer or housing manager.

Advantages/disadvantages

You may need to deal with difficult situations, for example cases of misuse of property or disputes between residents.

The job can be personally rewarding because you are helping to provide people with a good place to live.

Money guide

Starting out you can expect to earn £15,000–£24,000 per year. This can rise to £25,500–£27,000 for experienced housing officers. Up to £38,000 is usual for housing managers. More than £50,000 can be achieved in the most senior posts.

Related opportunities

- Advice Centre/Welfare Adviser p590
- Warden (Accommodation) p589
- Social Worker p585

Further information

Chartered Institute of Housing
Octavia House, Westwood Way, Coventry CV4 8JP
024 768 51700; www.cih.org

Scottish Federation of Housing Associations
38 York Place, Edinburgh EH1 3HU
0131 556 5777; www.sfha.co.uk

City&
Guilds

www.cityandguilds.com/myperfectjob

LAMINATOR

What the work involves

- Laminators work with polymer composite materials to make a variety of products such as hockey sticks, snowboards, canoes, car bodies, yachts and aircraft cabin interiors.

- You will follow a brief for the design of a product, taking into consideration any requirements regarding strength, colour and finish. You will then choose the appropriate material to be pressed, sprayed or poured into a mould, prior to it being shaped into the final product.

- You will work with traditional materials such as wood laminates, fibre glass and resin, and new products such as Kelvar.

The type of person suited to this work

You should have a keen interest in design and technology, engineering and materials science.

You should like practical work and have practical skills to handle tools and use specialist machinery.

You should have initiative, follow a brief and work to a deadline. You should also be interested in, and keep up to date with, technological advancements in laminate materials.

You should like to work in a team.

You need to be reasonably fit and have good vision for monitoring quality and noticing detail.

Working conditions

Your working hours will depend heavily on the project you are working on. Typically it can range from 37–40 hours but will vary according to the rate of your work and deadlines.

You will usually work in an environmentally controlled building. This means that the temperature is controlled and maintained to help resin harden quickly. Air is changed frequently to remove dust and the strong smell of resin.

You will be required to wear full protective clothing.

Future prospects

You may be employed by an engineering consultancy that undertakes installation projects for companies.

With experience and training there are opportunities to be promoted to roles such as technician and senior technician, or to move into design, research or development work for specialist composite laminate manufacturers.

Advantages/disadvantages

You may have the opportunity to work on products that are on the cutting edge of design such as speed boats, formula 1 racing cars and craft for the air force and the military.

Qualifications and courses

ENTRY LEVEL 2

No formal qualifications are required to enter this job. However, some GSCEs/S grades may be required by employers and can be useful, as you will have to have an understanding of design and technology, and calculations.

Some employers will take you on as an apprentice. Apprenticeships usually require four GSCE/S grades (A-C/ 1–3) in maths, science or technology. CITB-ConstructionSkills provides guidance on finding and applying for apprenticeships.

Most of your training will be on the job. However you can also undertake further training at college through courses that focus on the theoretical parts of your job, first aid, and health and safety.

You can also gain a BTEC National Certificate/Diploma in polymer processing and materials technology.

With three years' experience as a laminator, relevant NVQS/SVSs or BTEC certificate or diploma, you may apply to become a member of the Institute of Minerals and Mining.

There is a shortage of laminators, so many employers seek adults with relevant previous experience and will provide further training to technician level following an NVQ/SVQ Level 3 training route.

Your work will frequently be dusty and involve the use of strong industrial chemicals which may be hazardous if handled incorrectly.

Money guide

A salary for an apprentice laminator starts at around £7,000 a year.

As you gain experience and qualifications this may increase to £18,000.

A senior laminator can earn up to £25,000 per year.

Related opportunities

- Marine Craftsperson p237
- Polymer Technologist p245

Further information

Polymer Training Limited (PTL)
Halesfield 7, Telford TF7 4NA
019252 587020; www.polymertraining.co.uk

Institute of Materials, Minerals and Mining
1 Carlton House Terrace, London SW1Y 5DB
020 7451 7300; www.iom3.org

LAND VALUER/AUCTIONEER

What the work involves

- Land and property valuers are specialist surveyors who value and sell property, businesses and land.

- Your job would include valuing and writing a report for use by your client for sale, loan or accounting purposes.

- You will also arrange, market and run live auctions.

The type of person suited to this work

You will need good numeracy skills for valuing and dealing with bids. Communication skills, an ability to concentrate and a high degree of confidence are all important for conducting auctions. You will also need knowledge of the value of local land and properties so you can advise your clients accurately.

Although you will work in a team with other professionals you could also visit clients on an individual basis so you will need good project management skills.

You will have to have an expert knowledge of the particular markets that you are working in and be enthusiastic, with good selling skills.

Working conditions

You will normally work between 37–40 hours a week including evenings and weekends. Many auctions are run at weekends to encourage attendance.

You will spend some of your time outdoors, visiting properties and clients in all weathers. A driving licence is essential and you may have to travel substantial distances. Your indoor work will involve using the computer and phone to do research, arrange meetings, prepare for sales and write reports. You will also liaise with colleagues to organise auctions.

Future prospects

Internet auctions are increasing in popularity for smaller value items but opportunities are stable with most valuers working for estate agents, surveyors and auction houses. With experience you could start your own company or progress to a senior position.

The RICS qualification is recognised worldwide, so you may work anywhere in the world once you are fully qualified.

Advantages/disadvantages

It can be frustrating when it is difficult to get bids for particular items.

This can be a varied career as you are valuing and auctioning various items, and dealing with different people all the time.

Money guide

Salaries vary depending on experience, size of the organisation and location. Some specialists also attract higher salaries than others.

Qualifications and courses

Land or property valuers and auctioneers must be qualified chartered surveyors, who are trained in auctioneering by experience on the job. Chartered surveyors are surveyors who have usually done a degree or postgraduate course that is recognised by the Royal Institution of Chartered Surveyors (RICS), followed by a period of structured practical learning known as the Assessment of Professional Competence.

Auctioneers of other items do not need to be professionally qualified, although you can become a member of the National Association of Valuers and Auctioneers (NAVA) with relevant qualifications and experience.

To qualify as a chartered surveyor specialising in plant and machinery, Units 5 and 6 of the Diploma in Valuation (Plant and Machinery) are required. There is a postgraduate conversion course. For details on the Diploma contact RICS.

Degree courses are available in relevant subject areas such as Real Estate and Property Management.

The Institute of Revenues, Rating and Valuation (IRRV) offers training covering valuation, legal and tax matters.

Details about the NVQ in Valuation at Level 4 can be obtained from The Awarding Body for the Built Environment (ABBE).

While training you can expect around £15,000- £20,000+ per year. With experience this rises to around £30,000.

Average salary at senior level with 10–15 years experience is £40,000+, but will vary considerably with the area and type of work specialisms.

Freelancers can charge according to their experience and contracts.

Related opportunities

- Antiques Dealer p478
- Estate Agent p97
- Technical Surveyor p130

Further information

National Association of Valuers and Auctioneers
Arbon House, 6 Tournament Court, Edgehill Drive,
Warwick CV34 6LG
01926 417 767; www.nava.org.uk

Royal Institution of Chartered Surveyors
Surveyor Court, Westwood Way, Coventry CV4 8JE
0870 333 1600; www.rics.org/careers

Institute of Revenues, Rating and Valuation
41 Doughty Street, London WC1N 2LF
020 7831 3505; www.irrv.org.uk

LAND/GEOMATIC SURVEYOR

What the work involves

- Land/geomatic surveyors collect and analyse information to map the land and/or sea, which is then used when planning construction projects.

- You will use satellite images, GPS, digital mapping and other equipment to produce surveys that record features such as contours, materials below the Earth's surface and man-made objects.

- You will use technical software such as CAD to record and present the data you have gathered. You will also have to interpret data from maps and plans and explain it to clients.

The type of person suited to this work

You will be working with both clients and other professionals on a daily basis, so will need excellent verbal and written communication skills in order to present and explain complex information.

As much of the work involves using technical equipment and producing maps, plans and reports using specialist computer software, you will need to have very strong ICT skills with specific knowledge of geographical information systems (GIS) and AutoCAD.

Working conditions

Working hours are usually 9–5, but weekend or shift work can also be required for certain projects.

You will frequently work away from home, and may even be involved in overseas projects that will require extended absence from family. You will be paid more for overseas work, and most is on a short-term basis although multinational companies offer good long-term opportunities.

Self employment is an option, but finding work is not always easy so most surveyors chose to work in salaried employment.

Future prospects

Prospects are good across the UK as there is a national shortage of land/geomatic surveyors, so demand currently outstrips supply. Most graduates start within a company as a junior surveyor, from which there is a natural progression to surveyor and then on to a team management position. You could alternatively undertake further study and gain a qualification as a chartered surveyor.

You can specialise in a number of interesting areas including offshore engineering and exploration, or cartography.

Advantages/disadvantages

You will have the opportunity to travel throughout the UK and overseas.

You could be playing a key role in land and environmental development.

Qualifications and courses

ENTRY 5 LEVEL

Most entrants have completed a relevant degree such as surveying and mapping science, geography, environmental science, civil engineering, maths or physics. An HND in applied science, land/estate surveying or civil engineering is also accepted, although you would start in a slightly lower position in a company.

If you wish to specialise in a particular area, such as environmental development or offshore engineering, a postgraduate qualification may be helpful in acquiring a job.

Once qualified, many surveyors choose to work towards achieving chartered status and undertake further courses and assessment through bodies such as the Institution of Civil Engineering Surveyors (ICES) and the Royal Institution of Chartered Surveyors (RICS). This usually takes between 4 and 5 years.

Modern apprenticeships in land/geomatics surveying are available at a number of colleges throughout the UK. You will work towards gaining an NVQ.

A considerable amount of time is spent outdoors so be prepared to get cold, wet and muddy.

Overnight or longer absence from home is not unusual.

Money guide

Salaries for newly graduated land surveyors fall between £16,000 and £20,000. If you also hold a qualification in chartered surveying, your starting salary would rise to £35,000–£40,000.

With several years' experience you could earn £40,000-£50,000. At a senior level, either as a manager or a partner, salaries can reach £75,000+.

Salaries are highest in London, or if you work overseas.

Related opportunities

- Rural Property Surveyor p123
- Planning and Development Surveyor p115
- Insurance Risk Surveyor p43
- Town Planner p133

Further information

The Chartered Institution of Water and Environmental Management (CIWEM)
15 John Street, London WC1N 2EB
020 7831 3110; www.ciwem.org

Institution of Civil Engineering Surveyors (ICES)
Dominion House, Sibson Road, Sale M33 7PP
0161 972 3100; www.ices.org.uk; education@ices.org.uk

MASTIC ASPHALTER

What the work involves

- You will work with material called mastic asphalt, a mixture of limestone and bitumen which turns liquid when heated.

- After spreading hot liquid mastic asphalt onto areas such as roofs or floors, it cools into a tough, waterproof surface.

- A lot of the surfaces you will work on will be outside such as parks, car parks and the roofs of buildings.

- You will use various specialised tools and equipment in order to prepare surfaces and apply the mastic asphalt.

The type of person suited to this work

You need to have good practical skills to be able to spread and form the mastic asphalt. Maths skills will be useful too, for calculating the right quantity of mastic asphalt.

It is important to be able to understand plans and instructions and work in a team with other mastic asphalters or people from other construction trades.

As it is an active job you must be physically fit, and you must be happy climbing and working at heights when working on roofs.

Working conditions

You will mainly work outdoors, although some of the work may be under cover.

You will need to stick to health and safety procedures, which include wearing protective gear such as a safety helmet, gloves and boots.

You are likely to work a normal working week, although you may have the opportunity to work at weekends as well.

Future prospects

There is good demand throughout the UK for mastic asphalters.

Most opportunities are with specialist mastic asphalt contractors. Self-employment is also common for skilled mastic asphalters.

Mastic asphalters can work their way up to become a supervisor or trainer in large companies, or set up their own contracting business.

Advantages/disadvantages

Working at heights on roofs, or in cramped conditions when working in tanks or underground spaces, can be demanding for some people.

You will develop a range of skills and work on a variety of surfaces including roofs, floors, bus stations, car parks and pathways.

Money guide

£10,000 per year is average for a trainee starting in this work.

Qualifications and courses

ENTRY 1 LEVEL

To train in this field, it is useful to have some GCSEs/S grades (A–E/1–5) in English, maths, design and technology, or vocational qualifications such as GCSE in Construction and the Built Environment, Scottish Progression Award/Skills for Work Award in Building Crafts, BTEC Introductory, First Diploma or Certificate in Construction, Foundation, Intermediate and Advanced level Construction Awards.

Most training is done on the job whilst attending college to obtain qualifications such as NVQs in Mastic Asphalting at Levels 2 and 3.

Apprenticeships/Skillseekers may be available to those aged 16–24.

You can also train by doing a Construction Industry Training Board (CITB) Construction Apprenticeship Scheme in Mastic Asphalting.

The Construction Industry Training Board (CITB) Construction Award in Mastic Asphalting allows those who have difficulties in gaining the work experience to train for an NVQ. You can apply straight to the CITB before or after finding employment or gaining a place on a training scheme.

Mastic asphalters employed on construction-sites require a Construction Skills Certification Scheme (CSCS) card. This demonstrates that the holder has health and safety training, as well as aiming for competence in a particular occupation (usually requiring an appropriate NVQ/SVQ or equivalent).

With experience you could earn around £22,500. £25,000+ is possible for the highest earners. Overtime is often available, and on some projects there are bonuses based on outputs, which can lead to higher earnings.

Related opportunities

- Building Technician p76
- Floor Layer p101
- Roofer p122
- Thatcher p131

Further information

ConstructionSkills
Bircham Newton, King's Lynn PE31 6RH
01485 577577; www.cskills.net
www.bconstructive.co.uk

Mastic Asphalt Council
PO Box 77, Hastings TN35 4WL
01424 814400; www.masticasphaltcouncil.co.uk

City& Guilds

www.cityandguilds.com/myperfectjob

NAVAL ARCHITECT

What the work involves

■ As a naval architect you will be responsible for the design, construction and repair of marine vessels and offshore structures, including merchant ships, passenger ferries, submarines and offshore drilling platforms.

■ You will coordinate a team of engineers working on a project.

■ You will ensure that the structure you are working on is safe and seaworthy, within budget and to the specifications laid out in the design brief.

■ Your work will depend on the specialism you choose, but you could prepare architectural designs, work with computer or 3D models, source materials or evaluate the safety of the design.

The type of person suited to this work

As you will be working with others and as part of a team you will need to have good written and verbal communication skills.

As you will be coordinating various aspects of a project such as budget, location and facilities you must be organised and efficient in you work.

You must also be able to lead a team and work to a deadline.

You should also have strong IT and numeracy skills and a keen eye for detail.

Working conditions

You will work average office hours, five days a week. However you may have to work extra hours to meet deadlines.

You may be office based while working on design work or visiting construction sites, docks and shipyards within the UK or overseas. Shipyards, docks and marinas can be noisy and dirty. If you are working onboard a craft you may encounter fumes, heat and noise and have to work in all weather conditions. You may be required to wear protective clothing in these areas.

Future prospects

As a naval architect you can become self-employed, work for a company or organisation or work as a design consultant. Organisations such as the Royal Institution of Naval Architects (RINA) provide continuing professional development (CPD) courses which are essential for progression in this job.

You can move up from technical roles to general management roles and then senior roles or directorships. Your career development will depend on the qualifications you have and the specialism you choose to go into.

Advantages/disadvantages

There is a lot of opportunity to work abroad for a ship surveying company, on contract, or you may work on a large scale project abroad.

Qualifications and courses

ENTRY 5 LEVEL

You must be a member of the Royal Institution of Naval Architects (RINA) and register as a chartered engineer (CEng), incorporated engineer (IEng) or engineering technician, with the Engineering Council UK (ECUK). To gain chartered status you must have an accredited/approved MEng or a BEng degree in an engineering subject such as naval architecture, marine technology or engineering, an MA that has been accredited/approved by a professional engineering institution, or appropriate further learning to degree level.

To gain incorporated status, you will need an accredited/approved first degree in technology or a BEng, HNC, HND or foundation degree in engineering or technology, plus appropriate further learning to degree level. It is also possible to register for chartered/incorporated status without the required academic qualifications.

The Defence Engineering and Science Group (DESG) graduate scheme, run by the Ministry of Defence, provides graduates of engineering and science courses with training and the opportunity to do work placements in MOD departments.

Competition for jobs as a naval architect is high.

Money guide

Your starting salary as a naval architect can be from £20,000 to £24,000 per year. With some experience this can increase to £35,000, and with extensive experience you can earn up to £75,000.

Related opportunities

■ Aerospace Engineer p220
■ Electrical Engineer p226
■ Marine Engineer p238
■ Merchant Navy Engineering Officer p611

Further information

Defence Engineering and Science Group (DESG)
Ministry of Defence
01225 449368; www.desg.mod.uk; sit-desgmktman@mod.uk

The Royal Institution of Naval Architects (RINA)
10 Upper Belgrave Street, London SW1X 8BQ
020 7235 4622; www.rina.org; hq@rina.org.uk

UK Resource Centre for Women in Science, Engineering and Technology
Listerhills Park of Science and Commerce, 40–42 Campus Road, Bradford BD7 1HR
01274 436485

PAINTER AND DECORATOR

What the work involves

- Painters and decorators paint and decorate the interior and exterior of people's homes and other new or old buildings.

- They also paint large structures such as bridges.

- Your work will include preparing surfaces by making sure they are clean and smooth, applying primers, undercoats and topcoats of paint, and putting up wall coverings such as wallpaper.

- You will use a range of tools including brushes, rollers and spraying equipment.

The type of person suited to this work

You need to be good with your hands, and particularly skilful and careful when using fine decoration techniques. You will also need an eye for colour and design.

When working on their premises you must be able to get on with your customers. You may also need to work in a team with other painters and decorators, or with those from other construction trades and professions.

As you will need to climb ladders and carry tools and equipment you should be physically fit, and you should not mind working at heights.

You must be able to measure accurately so that you can work out how much paint and other material you will need.

Working conditions

Most of the work is indoors, but some is outdoors. You will regularly work up ladders or on scaffolding. You need to work within health and safety regulations, which might include wearing a mask to prevent you from breathing in paint fumes.

You are likely to work a normal working week, although weekend work may also be available. You may need a driving licence.

Future prospects

There are good employment opportunities for painters and decorators in the UK at the moment.

You can work for painting and decorating companies or building contractors across the UK. Painting and decorating companies may offer a range of work or may specialise in work such as domestic, commercial, new build or industrial.

After you have gained enough experience, you could progress to a supervisory role or go into business for yourself.

Advantages/disadvantages

Working at extreme heights may be difficult for some people.

It can be rewarding to see the improved look of a newly painted building or structure.

There are opportunities to be artistic and use decorative effects.

Qualifications and courses

It is useful to have some GCSEs/S grades (A–E/1–5) in subjects such as maths, design and technology and English. You could also enter with a vocational qualification, such as a BTEC Introductory Certificate/Diploma in Construction.

Construction Apprenticeships offer a training programme leading to NVQ/SVQ Level 3. Apprenticeships are validated by the Construction Industry Training Board (CITB).

Most training is done on the job whilst attending college to obtain qualifications such as NVQs/SVQs in Painting and Decorating (Levels 2/3), CITB Intermediate/Advanced Construction Award in Decorative Occupations, or City & Guilds (6217–03) Level 1 Certificate in Basic Construction Skills (Painting and Decorating). The CITB Construction Award in Painting and Decorating allows those who have difficulties in gaining the work experience to train for an NVQ.

There are several new schemes whereby painters and decorators may apply for a card which proves their skills and qualifications. By 2010, this card will be a prerequisite for employees on construction-sites. All applicants need to have a relevant NVQ/SVQ qualification and to pass a health and safety test.

Money guide

New entrants/trainees can expect to earn between £12,000 and £15,000 per year.

For trained painters and decorators £16,000–£20,000 is possible.

Decorators with specialist skills and supervisory duties can earn £25,000 or more.

Overtime is often available, and on some projects there are bonuses based on outputs.

Related opportunities

- Construction Operative p86
- Plasterer p116
- Signwriter/Signmaker p196
- Wall/Floor Tiler p134

Further information

Painting & Decorating Association
32 Coton Road, Nuneaton CV11 5TW
024 7635 377; www.paintingdecoratingassociation.co.uk

City & Guilds

www.cityandguilds.com/myperfectjob

PLANNING AND DEVELOPMENT SURVEYOR

What the work involves

- Planning and development surveyors develop and manage new building or refurbishment projects.

- You will create proposals and oversee projects from conception through to completion.

- You will be responsible for recruiting team members for each project, as well as liaising with external industry professionals throughout.

- You will also give valuations on properties and developments, advise clients on financing options for their building plans, and prepare their applications for planning permission.

The type of person suited to this work

As you will be managing team members, briefing other professionals and dealing with clients on a daily basis, well-developed communication and negotiation skills are required.

Good numeracy skills, coupled with scientific aptitude, are essential to successfully write proposals and manage financial details within a project. An understanding of legal matters within the building and construction industries is helpful, as is an interest in the environment, architecture, history or preserving the natural landscape.

Working conditions

You may have to work longer than the standard 35 hour week, but weekend and shift work is unusual.

Although there is some day to day travelling involved, overnight stays are also uncommon.

Most jobs are found in cities where there is a high level of commercial activity. You could work for public sector or private companies, which range in size from very small practices up to large multinational firms. Work in the public sector is becoming increasingly flexible, with part time work and career breaks available.

Future prospects

Your career progression should be very straightforward; from graduate trainee, to surveyor, to senior surveyor, and up to associate or partner with several years' experience. If you progress to become an equity partner you will earn a high salary and also get a cut of the company's profits.

If you work in the public sector, you could enhance your career prospects with a Royal Town Planning Institute (RTPI) qualification, or develop a more specialised career in an area of surveying in which you are particularly interested.

Advantages/disadvantages

Work is varied and you have the opportunity to travel within the UK and overseas.

Qualifications and courses

This profession is open to all graduates, although further academic and vocational qualifications from the Royal Institution of Chartered Surveyors (RICS) must be gained before you can qualify as a chartered planning and development surveyor.

Some degree and HND subjects offer exemption from the academic stages of the RICS assessment, and these include surveying, planning, and land/estate/property management. Entry requirements for most degree/HND courses are a minimum of 5 GSCEs (A-C), 3 A levels or the relevant BTEC/SQA national awards (or equivalent).

If your first degree/HND is in a subject completely unrelated to surveying, you will need to take an RICS approved conversion course prior to starting training. Occasionally, larger organisations will employ graduates with unrelated degrees and allow them to undertake a conversion course during their employment.

Although you may need to work extra hours, weekend work is rare.

You will have a lot of responsibility, which can be stressful at times.

Money guide

New graduates can start on salaries of between £18,000 and £23,000, the higher end of which is generally confined to London-based positions.

Fully qualified surveyors can earn upwards of £35,000, with £50,000 being average after a few years' experience.

If you went on to become a partner in a firm, you could be earning £80,000+, with an additional share of profits on top.

Chief executives in the largest, London companies can earn between £350,000 and £800,000.

Related opportunities

- Land/Geomatic Surveyor p111
- Rural Property Surveyor p123
- Civil/Construction Engineer p83
- Town Planner p133

Further information

Royal Institution of Chartered Surveyors (RICS)
Surveyor Court, Westwood Way, Coventry CV4 8JE
0870 333 1600; www.rics.org/careers; contactrics@rics.org

Institution of Civil Engineering Surveyors (ICES)
Dominion House, Sibson Road, Sale M33 7PP
0161 972 3100; www.ices.org.uk; education@ices.org.uk

PLASTERER

What the work involves

- There are three types of plastering that you could do: solid, fibrous or dry lining.

- Solid plastering involves the application of plaster or cement to internal and external walls, ceilings and floors.

- Fibrous plastering involves making ornamental plaster work, such as the kind you see on decorative ceilings.

- Dry lining involves the use of plasterboard to construct walls or partitions and then skimming over the joins with plaster making them ready for decoration.

The type of person suited to this work

To be able to use your tools skilfully, you need to be good with your hands. An ability to use basic maths for calculating the amounts of materials you will need for a particular job is also helpful.

You will need to be able to work in a team with other plasterers, and with those in other construction trades and professions.

You should be physically fit, as the work is very active and can be tiring. It can also be dusty when working with the plaster powder; this may be difficult if you suffer from certain allergies. You will be climbing ladders and possibly scaffolding, so you must not mind working at heights.

Working conditions
Solid/dry lining

Most of the work for solid plasterers and those doing dry lining work is indoors, although you may have to work outdoors if working on exteriors. You will work from ladders and scaffolding.

Fibrous

Most fibrous plasterers work in workshops, although you may also install your work on-site.

All plastering requires an understanding and appreciation of health and safety regulations, which includes wearing protective gear. You may work a normal working week, although you may need to start early or finish late, and weekend work may also be available.

Future prospects

Across the UK there is a shortage of qualified plasterers – and in particular dry lining specialists – who are needed to help finish off new builds getting them ready for decoration. Shortages exist especially in the south and south-east of England.

After you have gained sufficient experience, you could progress to technical, supervisory or managerial roles or become self-employed.

Advantages/disadvantages

Working at heights may be difficult for some people.

Qualifications and courses

To be eligible for an apprenticeship you will need some GCSEs/S grades in subjects such as English, maths, design and technology. Construction Apprenticeships offer a structured training programme leading to NVQ/SVQ Level 3. Apprenticeships are validated by the Construction Industry Training Board (CITB) and last 3 years in England and Wales, and 4 years in Scotland.

Most training is done on the job whilst attending college to obtain qualifications such as NVQs/SVQs in Plastering (Levels 1, 2 and 3), or City & Guilds certificates in Basic Construction Skills – Plastering (6217–04). NVQ Level 3 entitles you to craftsperson status. The CITB Construction Award in Plastering allows those who have difficulties in gaining work experience to train for an NVQ.

Construction Skills Certification Scheme (CSCS) cards are required by plasterers employed on construction-sites to demonstrate that they have health and safety training, are competent in their field or are working towards becoming so.

You will be able to work in a variety of locations, especially as a solid plasterer.

There are opportunities to be creative when producing fibrous plaster work.

Money guide

As a trainee starting out in this work you could earn around £14,000 per year. With a Level 2 qualification this can rise to £16,000+. After qualifying to Level 3 you can expect to earn £18,000–£25,000. Experienced plasterers can earn up to £35,000 or more. Overtime is often available, and on some projects there are bonuses based on outputs.

Related opportunities

- Building Technician p76
- Mastic Asphalter p112
- Wall/Floor Tiler p134

Further information

ConstructionSkills
Bircham Newton, King's Lynn PE31 6RH
01485 577577; www.cskills.net; www.bconstructive.co.uk

Federation of Plastering and Drywall Contractors
1st Floor, 8/9 Ludgate Square, London EC4M 7AS
020 7634 9480; www.fpdc.org

Scottish Building and Trading Council (SBATC)
Crichton House, 4 Crichton's Close, Edinburgh EH8 8DT
0131 556 8866; www.sbatc.co.uk

PLUMBER

What the work involves

- Plumbers install, maintain and repair heating and water systems in various locations including people's homes and construction-sites.

- You will use a range of hand and power tools, such as wrenches, cutters and welding equipment.

- You will also be responsible for routine check ups on things like boilers.

- When you have completed a job, you will need to test the system to make sure that everything is working properly.

The type of person suited to this work

You must have good practical skills to be able to use the various tools. You have to be able to work carefully, measuring accurately and following plans and instructions correctly so that systems work properly and safely. Problem-solving skills are important for finding faults.

You need to be physically fit for bending, kneeling and working in tight spaces. You may also need to be comfortable working at heights, for example when working on drainpipes.

You are likely to work alone for some jobs, for example when in people's homes, and you must be able to deal directly with customers. You also need to be able to work in a team when you are working on larger jobs.

Working conditions

You will work both indoors and outdoors, possibly within confined spaces and at heights. As you will travel to a variety of locations, a driving licence and own transport will be useful. You may work a normal working week but, if your organisation offers a 24/7 call-out service, you may also need to work at weekends and be available all times of the day.

Future prospects

Once qualified, work is available across the UK.

With additional training and CORGI registration, you could move into gas central heating installation and repair. You could also move into related career areas such as heating and ventilation, refrigeration or air conditioning.

With experience, you may progress to technical, supervisory, training or managerial positions or set up your own plumbing business.

Advantages/disadvantages

You could be called out at all times of night and day, to deal with plumbing emergencies, which can be difficult for those with family commitments.

Being able to solve a difficult problem and make a customer happy can be very rewarding.

Money guide

The Joint Industry Board for Plumbing Mechanical Engineering

Qualifications and courses

To train as a plumber, either on the job or via an Apprenticeship/Skillseekers, you will normally need 3–4 GCSEs/S grades (A–C/1–3) preferably including English, maths, and science and technology. Equivalent qualifications, such as an Intermediate 2 in Construction and the Built Environment, SGA Intermediate in Construction or BTEC First in Construction may also be accepted. Entrants for apprenticeships or training schemes will need to pass a selection test and have their colour vision tested.

Trainees can work towards a City & Guilds (6089) NVQ Levels 2 and 3 in Mechanical Engineering Services: Plumbing (Domestic), City & Guilds (6129) Technical Certificates: Levels 2 and 3 Plumbing Studies. Most training is done on the job whilst attending college.

The British Plumbing Employers Council (BPEC) provides a range of assessments, covering domestic gas safety and appliances, oil-fired appliances and water regulations.

CORGI registration and possession of a CORGI ID card is a legal requirement for anyone installing or repairing gas fittings or appliances.

Services (JIBPMES) agrees wage rates. Overtime is often available, which can lead to higher earnings.

You can start at around £6,000–£7,500 per year as a first-year apprentice.

This can rise to £15,000–£17,000 in the final year of training. When qualified you could get £17,500–£21,000.

With experience you could expect anything between £20,000 and £30,000.

Earnings for self-employed plumbers can be much higher. Top earners can get £35,000–£40,000 or more. Salaries are highest in London and the south-east of England.

Related opportunities

- Construction Operative p86
- Gas Network Engineer p231
- Heating and Ventilating Engineer p104
- Refrigeration Engineer p121

Further information

SummitSkills
Vega House, Opal Drive, Fox Milne, Milton Keynes MK15 0DF
08000 688336; www.summitskills.org.uk

Institute of Plumbing and Heating Engineering
64 Station Lane, Hornchurch RM12 6NB
01708 472791; www.plumbers.org.uk

City&
Guilds

www.cityandguilds.com/myperfectjob

PROPERTY VALUER

What the work involves

- As a property valuer you will assess the value of property (buildings, land or personal items) for a client and give them advice on how the property may be sold, loaned, taxed, acquired by a company or made part of a compensation claim.

- You will assess new commercial and industrial property and reassess existing property that has been altered and improved.

- You will provide reports on your valuations which may be important if property becomes part of legal negotiations or insurance claims.

- You may have to run live auctions where you will sell items that you have valued, or you may pass them to a specialist.

The type of person suited to this work

You should have a keen interest in property valuation law and taxes.

You must have strong numerical skills to make accurate calculations, such as working out taxes or analysing accounts.

As you may be hired by a company on a freelance basis, you must be organised and able to work on your own initiative.

You need to have excellent written and verbal communication skills in order to communicate with clients, employers and government bodies and contact those in the locality as you assess a particular property.

Working conditions

You will work about 35–40 hours per week, Monday to Friday. You may have to work weekends depending on the project or your employer.

You will be mainly office-based but will frequently have to visit and inspect properties or meet clients.

As you may need to travel locally to visit clients or inspect properties you may need a driving licence.

Future prospects

There are many opportunities in the UK. You may work for an estate agent in order to value property that is being sold, rented or mortgaged. You may find opportunities in the Valuation Agency assessing property for local authorities and government departments.

Valuers are also needed by HM Revenue and Customs (HMRC) where you will value property and land that must be taxed when it is sold or bought.

Qualifications and courses

There are no formal qualifications required to become a property valuer but entrants are usually graduates or hold at least HND or HNC qualifications. Entry requirements vary depending on the employer.

If you become a property valuer you should become a member of a professional body such as the Royal Institution of Chartered Surveyors (RICS) or the Institute of Revenues, Rating and Valuation (IRRV). You will find a full list of accredited degree and diploma courses on the RICS website.

You can take an accredited postgraduate degree or diploma course in an auctioneering/valuation subject. Please see the Royal Institution of Chartered Surveyors for a full list. You may have to combine these courses with work experience and further professional qualifications.

Advantages/disadvantages

Usually you will combine your role as a valuer with other roles such as estate management, surveying and even auctioning.

Property and land valuations may become part of compensation claims which could take a long time to sort out.

Money guide

Your starting salary can be from £18,000 to £21,000 a year.

With experience this can increase to £27,000 to £36,000.

You can find salaries of £42,000 each year.

Related opportunities

- Land Valuer/Auctioneer p110
- Estate Agent p97
- Loss Adjuster p45
- Insurance Risk Surveyor p43

Further information

The Institute of Revenues Rating and Valuation (IRRV)
41 Doughty Street, London WC1N 2LF
0207 831 3505; www.irrv.net

National Association of Valuers and Auctioneers
Arbon House, 6 Tournament Court, Edgehill Drive, Warwick CV34 6LG
01926 417 774; www.nava.org.uk; member@nava.org.uk

Royal Institution of Chartered Surveyors (RICS)
Surveyor Court, Westwood Way, Coventry CV4 8JE
www.rics.org; contactrics@rics.org

QUANTITY SURVEYOR

What the work involves

- Quantity surveyors are responsible for calculating costs, issuing contracts, keeping projects to time and within budget, managing subcontractors and arranging payments for work.
- You will need a good understanding of building regulations to ensure that projects meet the required standards of quality and safety.
- You could work on a wide variety of projects from residential developments to hospitals or sports stadiums.

The type of person suited to this work

You must have a high level of numeracy and the ability to manage financial projects as you will be responsible for all the financial details of projects. Good negotiation skills are also important, as you must agree contracts and prices with workers and contractors.

Excellent verbal and written communication skills are vital for leading and motivating the onsite team, liaising with clients and subcontractors, and producing accurate and detailed progress reports.

Finally, a good understanding of business and legal matters in relation to the building and construction industry is needed, since you will be responsible for ensuring that all projects meet current regulations and standards.

Working conditions

Working hours are slightly longer than average and will include early starts, late evenings and weekend work.

You will usually be office-based, although it is not uncommon for the office to be in the form of a temporary hut onsite. Travel to client meetings and other projects is also expected.

Self-employment is possible, and many companies use freelance quantity surveyors on projects. There is also the opportunity to travel overseas.

Future prospects

Your opportunities are likely to lie within local authority or government departments, private practices, building contractors, property companies or commercial organisations both in the UK and abroad.

With experience, you can undertake a more comprehensive project management role and have the satisfaction of taking a job through from conception to completion. There is also a natural progression from quantity surveying to commercial management.

Advantages/disadvantages

Working on numerous projects and with a range of people makes the job varied.

Qualifications and courses

Most employers look for candidates who have a degree, particularly in quantity surveying or a related subject such as maths or physics. If your degree subject is completely unrelated, you will need to take a postgraduate conversion course that is recognised by the Royal Institution of Chartered Surveyors (RICS).

An HND in a related subject such as building/construction, civil engineering or urban and land studies is also valued by employers and may gain you employment as a technical surveyor, from which you can study for more qualifications to become a full quantity surveyor. A range of RICS recognised part time and distance learning courses are available.

Entry without a degree or HND is sometimes possible, although unusual. You would have to work your way up through the industry, undertaking relevant courses and gaining qualifications as you go.

Once you are in employment, you will need to become a member of the RICS and this is achieved through attaining both an approved degree in quantity surveying, and also completing the Assessment of Professional Competence (APC) which requires at least two years' practical, work-based experience.

There are good opportunities for career progression and specialisation.

Hours are longer than average, with occasional weekend work.

Money guide

Starting salaries for quantity surveyors can range from £17,000 to £25,000, whether in private practice or working for local government. If you have gained chartered status, you can expect a considerably higher starting salary.

At a senior level salaries reach £45,000, but can be considerably more for those in partner positions in private firms.

If you undertake shift work or are required to travel extensively, allowances are often paid on top of your basic salary.

Related opportunities

- Building Surveyor p75
- Insurance Risk Surveyor p43
- Civil/Construction Engineer p83
- Town Planner p133

Further information

ConstructionSkills
Bircham Newton, King's Lynn PE31 6RH
01485 577577; www.cskills.net; www.bconstructive.co.uk

Royal Institution of Chartered Surveyors (RICS)
Surveyor Court, Westwood Way, Coventry CV4 8JE
0870 333 1600; www.rics.org; contact@rics.org

BALFOUR BEATTY CONSTRUCTION

Jayne Blyth

After completing my A Levels, I was offered the job as Trainee Quantity Surveyor with Balfour Beatty Construction. This involves studying a part time degree on a 'day release' basis whilst performing my day role for the remainder of the week.

I chose to study at Salford University on the BSc (Hons) Quantity Surveying course lasting 5 years because it is an RICS accredited university. The advantage of studying part time is that I can apply the theory based learning from university into day-to-day practice in my working day. The experience gained within my role at work has also proved to be beneficial when completing course works.

Working as a Contractor's Quantity Surveyor means I spend most of my time on site, which gives me a varied and interesting day. My current roles include, site measures, tender enquires, valuing subcontractors work, negotiating final accounts, payments and orders. I have been involved in numerous initiatives including; the construction of a multi storey car park, shopping centre, student accommodation and a primary school all of which have given me a valuable perspective on site functions.

Combining work and a degree gives many challenges leaving little spare time, however the experience gained over the 5 years whilst studying for a degree will be invaluable to my further career prospects.

For further information please contact Tony Ellender, Training Manager on:
0161 972 7500 (Switchboard)
0161 972 7567 (DD)
0161 972 7502 (Fax)
tony.ellender@bbcl.co.uk
www.bbcl.co.uk

Balfour Beatty Construction Northern Limited | Cavendish House | Cross Street | Sale | Manchester | M33 7BU

REFRIGERATION ENGINEER/ TECHNICIAN

What the work involves

- Your work as a refrigeration engineer will involve the design, installation and repair of refrigeration equipment and air conditioning systems.

- Refrigeration engineers aim to create and maintain comfortable working/living environments in offices and homes, that are both energy-efficient and safe.

- Your work in commercial buildings and factories will be to provide refrigeration systems that keep food at the correct, safe temperature.

- You will be called out to undertake repairs and maintenance, estimate costs of construction and installation projects, carry out inspections on existing equipment, and give advice on adjustments and improvements.

The type of person suited to this work

It is important that you like hands-on work and have a practical approach to problem-solving.

You should be interested in the building services industry and keep up to date with relevant developments in legislation and technology.

Written and spoken communication skills are important as you will be in contact with clients and planning projects.

You should have an aptitude for maths and physics and have strong technical skills.

Working conditions

You will normally work around 37 hours a week and how this is spread over a week may vary. However you may have to work longer hours during the summer which is peak time for refrigeration engineers.

You will be office-based to plan visits to sites and organise jobs, but you will also visit various locations such as offices, shopping centres or factories to complete practical jobs such as maintenance, repair and installation.

You may also work in refrigeration transport, on specially adapted vehicles such as trucks, aircraft and fishing vessels or in vehicle workshops.

On certain visits you may have to wear protective clothing or equipment.

Future prospects

As you gain experience in the field you will find opportunities for progression to roles as supervisors and managers.

To improve your skills you may take further qualifications such as NVQs in Building Services Engineering at Levels 3 and 4 in refrigeration and air conditioning specific topics. Such courses also act as a stepping stone to the Chartered Institution of Building Services Engineers (CIBSE).

Qualifications and courses

Entry to this profession is usually through apprenticeship. To qualify for an apprenticeship you are likely to need four GCSEs (A-C) in core subjects such as English and maths and relevant subjects such as physics, design and technology. You will learn on the job over a period of three to four years.

While on your apprenticeship you can gain NVQs, Levels 2 and 3, in Mechanical Engineering Services and Refrigeration and Air Conditioning, and in health and safety procedures at colleges or training centre. Arrangements for apprenticeships are different in Scotland, Wales and Northern Ireland.

You can also gain further qualifications such HNCs/HNDs in Refrigeration and Air Conditioning, the BTEC national certificate or diploma, and foundation degrees in Building Services Engineering.

You can add further experience with further qualifications and work towards becoming an incorporated or chartered engineer.

Advantages/disadvantages

There are opportunities to work abroad as UK qualifications are internationally respected.

You may also be required to do overtime work and to be on call overnight and on weekends.

Money guide

Starting salaries are around £14,000 to £18,000 a year.

This can increase from around £20,000 to £30,000 with experience, qualifications.

A high earning refrigeration engineer can earn up to £50,000 per year.

Related opportunities

- Electrical Engineer p226
- Electrician p94
- Civil Engineering Technician p83

Further information

Institute of Refrigeration (IOR)
Kelvin House, 76 Mill Lane, Carshalton SM5 2JR
020 8647 7033; www.ior.org.uk

City& Guilds

www.cityandguilds.com/myperfectjob

ROOFER

What the work involves

- Roofers remove old roofs and replace them, cover new roofs and repair existing ones.

- You will have a choice of roofing materials to work with, such as tiles, slates, felt, mastic asphalt or sheet materials.

- You will use specialised tools for each type of roofing material that you work with.

- Roofers may specialise in flat or pitched roofs (sloping roofs) or work on both.

The type of person suited to this work

You need to have good practical skills to be able to use the tools and equipment.

You must also be physically fit so that you can climb ladders and scaffolding, and carry roofing materials. You must be comfortable working at heights.

It is important to be able to understand plans and instructions. You also need to be able to work in a team with other roofers and those from other construction trades and professions.

Good verbal communication skills will help you to be able to talk to your colleagues and your customers. It will also be useful if you have a pride in your work and enjoy being outdoors.

Working conditions

You will be working outdoors on roofs in various locations from people's homes to historic cathedrals and construction-sites. The work can be dusty and dirty, and you will be outdoors in all weathers.

As you will be working up ladders, on scaffolding or on the roof itself, you will need to pay close attention to all health and safety procedures, which includes wearing protective gear such as a safety helmet and boots.

You are likely to work a normal working week, although extra work may also be available at weekends.

Future prospects

There is a good demand for qualified roofers across the UK at the moment. Work is available within roofing companies, contractors, local authorities, roofing material suppliers and other public organisations. Self-employment is common.

You can decide to specialise in using one type of roofing material (such as slate) or you can train to become skilled in using several types.

You may work your way up to technical, supervisory and managerial levels. After you have gained enough experience, you could start your own roofing company.

Advantages/disadvantages

Working at heights may be difficult for some people.

It is satisfying to produce a lasting structure that is functional and looks good.

Qualifications and courses

To train as a roofer it is useful to have some GCSEs/S grades (A–E/1–5) or a vocational qualification. Maths, English, craft, design and technology are all relevant subjects.

Construction Apprenticeships offer a structured training programme leading to NVQ/SVQ Level 3. Apprenticeships are validated by the Construction Industry Training Board (CITB) and last 3 years in England and Wales, and 4 years in Scotland.

Most training is done on the job whilst attending college to obtain qualifications such as NVQs/SVQs in Roofing Occupations and City & Guilds Certificates. The CITB Construction Award in Roofing allows those who have difficulties in gaining the work experience to train for an NVQ.

Many employers on construction-sites require workers to have a Construction Skills Certification Scheme (CSCS) card. This demonstrates that the holder has health and safety training.

You could get to work on some impressive projects such as fitting the roof on a new football stadium.

You will gain an understanding of other construction work, such as joinery.

Money guide

The Building and Allied Trades Joint Industrial Council (BATJIC) agrees minimum wage rates annually. Trainee salaries are about £13,000 per year. After NVQ/SVQ qualifications this rises to around £15,000. As a trained roofer with qualifications you can earn £16,500–£22,000. £26,000+ is possible for very experienced roofers.

Overtime is often available, and on some projects there are bonuses based on outputs, which can lead to higher earnings.

Related opportunities

- Building Technician p76
- Construction Operative p86
- Scaffolder p124
- Thatcher p131

Further information

ConstructionSkills
Bircham Newton, King's Lynn PE31 6RH; 01485 577577; www.cskills.net, www.bconstructive.co.uk

The Institute of Roofing
Roofing House, 31 Worship Street, London EC2A 2DX; 020 7448 3194; www.instituteofroofing.co.uk

RURAL PROPERTY SURVEYOR

Building and Construction

CRCI: BC
CLCI: UM

What the work involves

- Rural property surveyors are concerned with the development of the countryside. They give advice to rural landowners about how to manage their assets in the form of land, buildings and livestock. They also value and auction rural property.

- You may manage rural estates, in which tasks include organising staff, overseeing finances, marketing properties and advising on farming grants and subsidies.

- You could also be involved in a variety of environmental projects.

The type of person suited to this work

You should have good communication skills, as you will be called upon to negotiate with people at all levels and from a range of sectors.

An analytical mind and sound writing ability is needed in order to understand and explain complex statistical information verbally and in reports.

A good understanding of rural and agricultural issues, including knowledge of crops and breeds of animal, is essential in order to assess their economic viability with accuracy.

Problem-solving and forward planning skills are also essential to keep on top of the heavy and varied workload.

Working conditions

Because you are dealing with agricultural clients, the work is not 9–5. You will find that early morning and weekend work is common as you need to adapt around factors such as harvests and other rural events. You can also expect to work longer hours than in many roles; about 45 per week is average.

The majority of the work is outdoors. If you are office-based, it will be in rural market towns or villages.

You may work across a large area, so should be prepared to drive and travel regularly.

Future prospects

As a rural surveyor, your career path is narrow but progression can occur very quickly whether you are employed by a small or large company, in the public or private sector.

In larger companies, there may be the opportunity to specialise in areas such as agriculture or renewable energy use in the countryside. By contrast, a smaller company could give you a greater range of projects which will build broader experience.

With 10–15 years of experience, you could become a partner in a firm.

Advantages/disadvantages

You will be based in peaceful rural locations.

You will be instrumental in developing the future of the countryside and rural industries.

Qualifications and courses

This sector is open to all graduates, although a degree or HND in a related subject such as agriculture, forestry, estate management or land management is particularly useful. Most degree/HND courses require qualifications of 5 GSCEs (A-C), 3 A levels or relevant BTEC/SQA national awards (or equivalent qualifications). Degree courses accredited by the Royal Institution of Chartered Surveyors (RICS) will reduce the length of time you will have to spend in professional training by a year.

If your first degree was in an unrelated subject, the College of Estate Management offers a postgraduate conversion course that can be studied by distance learning.

Once qualified, you will need to complete the Assessment of Professional Competence (APC) which is undertaken during your first 2 years of employment.

Hours can be long and you should expect to regularly work early mornings and weekends.

Salaries in this sector are lower than those of other types of surveyor.

Money guide

Average earnings for new graduates are between £16,000 and £20,000. After a few years, your salary will rise to £30,000-£40,000.

Compared with other surveying roles, rural property salaries are fairly low and the opportunity to earn in excess of £50,000 is rare.

Additional benefits such as a company car or health insurance are sometimes offered by employers, and subsidised accommodation may be available for surveyors managing a farm or estate.

Related opportunities

- Land/Geomatic Surveyor p111
- Building Surveyor p75
- Land Valuer/Auctioneer p110
- Civil/Construction Engineer p83

Further information

Agricultural Development and Advisery Service (ADAS)
Woodthorne, Wergs Road, Wolverhampton WV6 8TQ
0845 766 0085; www.adas.co.uk

Department for Environment, Food and Rural Affairs (DEFRA)
Eastbury House, 30–34 Albert Embankment, London SE1 7TL
0845 933 5577; www.defra.gov.uk; helpline@defra.gsi.gov.uk

Royal Agricultural College
Stroud Road, Cirencester GL7 6JS
01285 652531; www.rac.ac.uk; admissions@rac.ac.uk

SCAFFOLDER

What the work involves

- Scaffolders put up scaffolding so that new constructions, or the maintenance of existing buildings and structures such as bridges, can take place.

- You will put together metal tubes, fittings and wooden or metal platforms to create the scaffolding.

- You will use tools such as swivel spanners and spirit levels in your work.

- You may also put up spectator stands, stages and rigging for outdoor concerts and events.

The type of person suited to this work

Safety is the main priority in scaffolding. You need to make sure that it is safe for the people who will be working on it, passers-by, workmates and yourself. For this reason, you have to be able to keep your concentration, have good practical skills, be well organised and be able to follow instructions and take measurements accurately.

You must be physically fit so that you can lift and carry equipment up and down ladders and, of course, you must be happy working at heights.

You also need to be able to work as part of a team of scaffolders.

Working conditions

You will be working mainly outdoors in most weather conditions, often at great heights.

You will need to wear protective equipment such as a helmet, boots and a safety harness.

You may work a normal working week from Monday to Friday, although you may need to start work early or finish late. Extra hours at weekends may also be available.

Future prospects

There is a good demand for scaffolders across the UK and opportunities with specialist scaffolding firms and building contractors as well as oil and power companies.

You may progress from basic to advanced scaffolder, and then on to supervisory and managerial positions. Some experienced scaffolders set up their own businesses.

You may also work offshore or in other countries.

Advantages/disadvantages

This can be physically challenging work and working at heights can be demanding for some people.

You will get to work in a variety of locations and you may have the chance to put up scaffolding for major sports and music events, or for film sets.

Money guide

Starting as an apprentice or trainee you can expect to earn £12,500–£13,000 per year.

Qualifications and courses

There are no set entry requirements to train as a scaffolder, but it may be useful to have some GCSEs/S grades (A–E/1–5) or a vocational qualification such as the BTEC Introductory Certificate or Diploma in Construction.

Training is normally provided on the job with part-time attendance at college or training centres to get qualifications.

The Apprenticeship/Skillseekers scheme is a 2-year programme that combines learning on the job with 11 weeks spent on residential training. This leads to an NVQ/SVQ Accessing Operations and Rigging – Scaffolding Level 2 and the Construction Industry Scaffolders Record Scheme (CISRS) Basic Card.

Trainees can, after at least 6 months' scaffolding experience, do the Scaffolding Basic Part 1 course, followed by Part 2, and then go on to the NVQ/SVQ Accessing Operations and Rigging – Scaffolding Level 2. The CISRS operates a card system for operatives, aiming to ensure that they are properly trained and sufficiently experienced to work safely and correctly.

The Construction Industry Training Board (CITB) Construction Award in Scaffolding allows those who have difficulties in gaining the work experience to train for an NVQ. You can apply straight to the CITB before or after finding employment or gaining a place on a training scheme.

With qualifications you could get £16,000–£23,500. Very experienced scaffolders can earn £25,000 or more. Overtime is often available, and on some projects there are bonuses based on outputs, which can lead to higher earnings.

Related opportunities

- Building Technician p76
- Construction Operative p86
- Roofer p122

Further information

ConstructionSkills
Bircham Newton, King's Lynn PE31 6RH
01485 577577; www.cskills.net, www.bconstructive.co.uk

National Access and Scaffolding Confederation
Carthusian Court, 12 Carthusian Street, London EC1M 6EZ
020 7397 8120; www.nasc.org.uk

www.cityandguilds.com/myperfectjob

SHOPFITTER

What the work involves

- As a shopfitter you will create and install the interiors and exteriors of commercial buildings such as shops, banks, offices, restaurants and hotels.

- You may be working from designs made by an architect or designer, or you may have to research and prepare your own design drawings.

- You will prepare, assemble and finish joinery and metalwork according to the design, before bringing each part together and assembling them on site.

- You will probably specialise in a particular area . These include a metal fabricator, cutting and shaping metal components; a wood machinist, using specialist machinery to cut precise parts for joiners.

The type of person suited to this work

As you will be working in a workshop or on site you should have a keen interest in practical work and have good hand skills.

You should also be interested in design and construction.

You should have an eye for detail and a high level of concentration.

You should have a certain level of fitness as you will be required to work long and at times hard hours.

As you will be taking measurements and making calculations frequently you should have good spatial awareness and an aptitude for maths.

Working conditions

You will normally work around 40 hours per week. Your work may be in an office, a workshop, a machine shop or a paint shop. You may have to travel to work onsite and this may involve working away from home at times. You can often do overtime work.

You may have to work irregular hours, overnight or at weekends to accommodate clients – work may need to be done during the night when premises are closed.

Onsite work may be dusty, dirty and noisy and usually involves physical work such as lifting and bending.

Future prospects

When you have been trained and qualified and have gained experience you may choose to set up your own business.

Advantages/disadvantages

This is a diverse profession because as a shopfitter your work will change according to the project that you are working on. This could include working with a variety of materials such as

Qualifications and courses

You can enter this profession as a trainee in a specific area such as shopfitting joiner, wood machinist or metal fabricator.

There are no formal academic qualifications required but some employers may seek candidates with GCSEs/S grades (A-D/1–4) in English, maths and a science subject. GSCEs in art, design and technology may also be useful.

Normally you will begin as an apprentice with a shopfitting company. This will lead to NVQs/SVQs in Shopfitting Levels 2, 3 and 4 which will include training on site work, bench work and site management respectively or equivalent qualifications. You can take an apprenticeship in Shopfitting as with the CITB-ConstructionSkills' Construction Apprenticeship Scheme.

As you gain experience you can apply for membership of the National Association of Shopfitters which provides training to increase your skills.

wood, glass, aluminium and plastic and you may also be working with many other professionals involved in construction such as engineers, architects, electricians and plumbers.

Your work can be hard and hours long.

Money guide

Your starting salary may be around £9,000 a year.

As a qualified shopfitter you may earn £18,000 a year and as an experienced shopfitter around £23,000 or more.

Related opportunities

- Builder's Merchant p480
- Carpenter/Joiner p77
- Furniture Manufacturing Operative p230

Further information

CITB-ConstructionSkills
Bircham Newton, King's Lynn PE31 6RH
01485 577577; www.ckills.org;
call.centre@cskills.org

National Association of Shopfitters
NAS House, 411 Limpsfield Road, Warlingham CR6 6HA
01883 624961; www.shopfitters.org

www.cityandguilds.com/myperfectjob

Building and Construction

CRCI: BB
CLCI: UD

SITE MANAGER/ CLERK OF WORKS

What the work involves

- As a site manager/clerk of works you will be responsible for supervising all the onsite aspects of a construction contract.

- You must ensure that good standards are maintained and that work is carried out efficiently and on time.

- You will inspect and monitor materials, procedures and work so that the client is guaranteed quality and value for money.

- You will also act as a superintendent, advising contractors about aspects of work and solving problems as they arise.

The type of person suited to this work

You should have an interest in construction.

You need to be responsible, organised and honest as you may be in control of projects involving large teams of workers and a variety of materials.

You should enjoy working outdoors and in all weather conditions.

You need to be physically fit and have a head for heights.

You should have excellent communication skills, be able to lead a team and to establish appropriate working relationships with contractor's staff.

You will need a keen eye for detail and to be thorough and vigilant in maintaining quality standards of work and material.

Working conditions

You will usually work around 40 hours a week, Monday to Friday. However you will frequently have to work at the weekend and during the evening depending on deadlines.

You will be based in a site office which will usually be a temporary structure. You will have to spend much of your time outdoors in all weather conditions.

When you are inspecting a site you may have to wear protective clothing such as hard hats and work boots.

You may have to climb ladders and scaffolding or in tunnel construction, work underground.

Future prospects

As an experienced clerk of works you must take Continuing Professional Development. This is so that you can keep up-to-date with advances in areas such as new materials, practices, law and regulations, and health and safety issues.

Clerks of works can move up to roles in site management or other management roles in the construction industry.

You may have the opportunity to become self-employed and to work abroad.

Qualifications and courses

ENTRY 1 LEVEL

There are no set qualifications to become a clerk of works/site manager. However experience in a relevant industry is necessary such as construction or civil engineering. It is not normally something you can begin as soon as you leave school.

As well as experience you may need certain construction and civil engineering qualifications. This might include City & Guilds qualifications, NVQs Level 2 or 3, BTEC/SQA national award, a BTEC higher national award or a foundation or honours degree.

When you are working you can gain NVQs in Site Inspection at Levels 3 and 4. As you accumulate qualifications you can achieve levels of membership of the Institute of Clerks of Works Student, Licentiate and Member; although this is not essential it is increasingly sought by employers. To enter each level of membership you will need to have a relevant qualification, a report of your professional history and a materials identification test.

Graduates may be taken on by companies as apprentices where they will learn on the job.

Advantages/disadvantages

You can choose to specialise in particular areas such as building, civil engineering or mechanical and electrical installations.

On-site inspection may be dusty, dirty and noisy.

Money guide

Your starting salary may be at around £20,000 a year.

With experience as a clerk of works you can earn over £25,000 a year and senior clerks may earn more than £35,000.

Related opportunities

- Building Surveyor p75
- Civil Engineering Technician p83
- Construction Supervisor/Manager p88
- Quality Control Inspector p246

Further information

Chartered Institute of Building
Englemere, Kings Ride, Ascot, Berkshire SL5 7TB
01344 63700; reception@ciob.org.uk; www.ciob.org.uk

The Institute of Clerks of Works (ICW)
Equinox, 28 Commerce Road, Lynch Wood,
Peterborough, PE2 6LR
01733 405160; info@icwgb.org.uk; www.icwgb.org.uk

City& Guilds

www.cityandguilds.com/myperfectjob

STEEPLEJACK

What the work involves

- Steeplejacks work on high structures including power station chimneys, cooling towers, oil refineries, factories and church spires.

- Your work on these structures will include climbing to high places with your tools to complete routine maintenance and repairing jobs or renovation projects.

- You will plan each job carefully. To ensure a safe and accessible working environment you will put in ladders, specialist scaffolding or industrial rope access (abseiling), work platforms (cradles) and bosun's seat (harness) and fall arrest devices.

- You will be working on both historic buildings and modern constructions, in urban and rural areas.

The type of person suited to this work

You should be organised as you will have to plan each project so that you know which safety equipment to use and which tools are required when you reach your elevated working area.

You absolutely must have a good head for heights to do this job and it is equally important that you can work in small or confined spaces (chimneys).

You will enjoy working outdoors in all weather conditions.

You will have good hand skills for installing rigging and using tools.

You will be very conscious of, and committed to, health and safety procedures.

Working conditions

Your working hours and shifts can vary and you may have to work during the evenings and weekends.

Your work will be physically demanding as it will involve rigging, climbing, carrying ladders and tools and working with your hands.

You will need to wear protective clothing and headgear.

You may have to work on industrial chimneys which can be extremely dusty, requiring respiratory equipment.

Future prospects

As a steeplejack you will probably work for construction firms that specialise in steeplejacking. These tend to be based in London, Middlesbrough, Manchester, Nottingham, Bristol, Cardiff, Edinburgh and Glasgow, and are likely to seek local employees.

With experience you will be eligible for promotion to roles as supervisors and managers within a firm. With significant experience you can become self-employed, although this is not common.

You may be able to travel and increasingly you can find work abroad.

Qualifications and courses

There are no formal entry qualifications for this job but you will find it useful to have GCSEs (A-C) in maths, English, science and CDT for calculations, measurements and theory work.

Young entrants can train on the job with an employer or as an apprentice with an approved apprenticeship scheme. The Atlas Training Group and Construction Industry Training Board (CITB) provide such opportunities. You will take aptitude tests in maths and problem solving and will be assessed for literacy and ability to work at heights.

There are usually 12 places each year for apprentice steeplejacks on this course. You will be sponsored by an employer and spend six months (over two/three years) at the residential National Construction College where you can gain NVQs in accessing and rigging, Levels 2 and 3, Key Skills Level 1 and various other CITB courses such as Health and Safety, Working at Heights certification and First Aid Certification.

If you are training with an employer you can also gain NVQs in Construction in accessing and rigging and steeplejacking, Levels 2 and 3, at approved colleges and training centres.

Advantages/disadvantages

Currently in the UK there are there are between 800 and 1,000 steeplejacks. As a qualified steeplejack you may find work easily and there are plenty of opportunities in this area.

Your work may be hampered by weather conditions for example high winds may prevent access to structures and delay completion of projects.

Money guide

Your starting salary can be from around £15,000 a year. As an experienced steeplejack you may earn around £22,000 a year. If you become a senior engineer you can earn over £28,000 a year.

Related opportunities

- Bricklayer p72
- Scaffolder p124
- Stonemason p128

Further information

The Association of Technical Lighting and Access Specialists
4c St Mary's Place, The Lace Market, Nottingham, NG1 1PH
0115 955 8818; nfo@atlas-1.org.uk; www.atlas-1.org.uk

City&
Guilds

www.cityandguilds.com/myperfectjob

STONEMASON

What the work involves

- Stonemasons cut and shape stone and fix it to buildings. Some work on new buildings, but many work on restoring and repairing old ones.

- There are three types of stonemason. Banker masons cut, shape and carve the stone, fixer masons assemble and fix stones into place and monumental masons make things such as plaques and headstones.

- You will use traditional hand tools, modern power tools and cutting machines.

- While the work is very manual and strenuous it is also very creative.

The type of person suited to this work

Banker mason

As a banker mason, you have to be good with your hands to cut, shape and carve stone accurately. You also need artistic skills for producing decorative finishes.

Fixer mason

You must be physically fit so that you can lift the stones, although you will use special equipment to lift heavy stones And as a fixer mason, you must not mind working at heights.

Monumental mason

In this sector, you will be working closely with the funeral industry so you need to be sensitive to what people require and have a good eye for design. It is also useful to be interested in architecture and history, as much of the work involves restoring old buildings.

Working conditions

Banker and monumental masons mainly work in a workshop, while fixer masons work on-site, often at heights. Both types of mason work can be dusty and noisy and unsuitable for people who have dust allergies. You will need to follow health and safety procedures, including wearing protective clothing such as a mask, a helmet and boots.

You are likely to work a normal working week, although extra work at weekends may also be available.

Future prospects

There is good demand for stonemasons in the UK.

You can choose to work for stonemasonry companies and larger building contractors. If you work for a small stonemasonry company you are likely to have to do both banking and fixing work

After training you can decide to specialise in new building or restoration work. You can also specialise as a memorial mason, making and carving gravestones.

Qualifications and courses

Training is provided on the job with part-time attendance at college or training centres to gain relevant NVQs/SVQs. Apprenticeships/Skillseekers may be available for those aged 16–24.

NVQs/SVQs at Levels 2 and 3 are available in relevant subjects (e.g. Architectural Stonemasonry, Carving, Heritage Skills), as well as City & Guilds Certificates. There is also a City & Guilds Diploma in Advanced Stonemasonry and the new NVQ/SVQ Level 3 in Heritage Skills. The Construction Industry Training Board (CITB) Construction Award in Stonemasonry allows those who have difficulties in gaining work experience to train for an NVQ.

Many employers on construction-sites require workers to have a Construction Skills Certification Scheme (CSCS) card. This demonstrates that the holder has health and safety training, as well as aiming for or competence in a particular occupation.

Advantages/disadvantages

Working at heights and the physical side of the work may be demanding for some people.

You may have the opportunity to work on impressive restoration projects such as those on cathedrals.

It can make you proud to produce work on a building that will be admired for many years.

Money guide

As a new entrant you could earn between £8,000 and £13,500 per year. When trained and with some experience you could get £18,000–£22,500. Senior and experienced stonemasons can achieve up to £30,000. Overtime is often available, and on some projects there are bonuses based on outputs.

Related opportunities

- Bricklayer p72
- Building Technician p76
- Dry Stone Waller p93
- Roofer p122

Further information

National Heritage Training Group
Carthusian Court, 12 Carthusian Street, London EC1M 6EZ
01159 217562; www.nhtg.org.uk

Stone Federation Great Britain
Channel Business Centre, Ingles Manor, Castle Hill Avenue, Folkestone T20 2RD
01303 856123; www.stone-federationgb.org.uk

City&
Guilds

www.cityandguilds.com/myperfectjob

STRUCTURAL ENGINEER

What the work involves

- Structural engineers design structures that are strong, durable and able to withstand the high pressure they are placed under.

- You will work with architects on the design and construction of a variety of structures including bridges, tunnels, domestic houses, office blocks or sports stadia.

- Among other tasks you will calculate the loads and stresses of a structure, analyse potential problems and test digital models to examine how they will endure influences such as wind, gravity and earth tremors.

- You will investigate soil conditions, visit construction sites, and undertake projects that involve demolition or repair of a structure.

The type of person suited to this work

You should be interested in the construction industry.

You should have an aptitude for problem-solving and analytical thinking.

You should also have strong skills in maths, physics and IT.

You must have a keen eye for detail and accomplish your work efficiently and with utmost accuracy.

You will need to be good at technical drawing and have 3D concept skills.

You must be able to work in a team as well as being able to work with other professionals from across the construction industry.

Working conditions

You will work a total of approximately 40 hours a week, Monday to Fridays. At times you might have to work on the weekend.

You will work both in an office and out on site. This can be in all weather conditions and you will have to wear protective clothing such as hard hats.

You will frequently have to travel from site to site and a driving licence may be useful for this.

Future prospects

Many employers provide training schemes for new structural engineers which allow you to work towards the specific core objectives necessary for you to achieve professional status, during your work placement.

You may follow a formal progression structure within an engineering organisation.

You can become self-employed although chartered status is necessary if you want to start up your own business.

Advantages/disadvantages

Despite the recent decline in the construction industry, many

Qualifications and courses

ENTRY LEVEL 5

Structural engineers normally have a degree in engineering or a highly numerate science degree. This could be a three-year BEng degree in structural engineering, civil engineering or general engineering and when you have completed this course you can directly become an incorporated engineer. To gain status as a chartered engineer you will need further academic qualifications.

To become a chartered engineer you will need a four year MEng degree in structural engineering, civil engineering or general engineering, accredited by the Engineering Council UK (ECUK). When you have qualified you will work alongside engineers as you train.

A Higher National Diploma in construction, civil engineering or other engineering subject must be combined with further studies before you acquire chartered or incorporated engineer status.

If you take a course that is not accredited you can go on to take an accredited postgraduate degree. A specialist Masters programme in structural engineering will allow you to increase your depth of knowledge in the discipline.

Apprenticeships may be available at technician level which will allow you to train on the job and take courses to gain qualifications and achieve incorporated and chartered status.

construction projects are planned in London and the South East.

Money guide

A typical starting salary is around £22,000.

With several years' experience this can rise to £36,000 and in a senior role of structural engineering you can earn in the region of £50,000.

Related opportunities

- Architect p68
- Civil Engineer p83
- Quantity Surveyor p119
- Technical Surveyor p130

Further information

Association for Consultancy and Engineering (ACE)
Alliance House, 12 Caxton Street, London SW1H 0QL
020 7222 6557; consult@acenet.co.uk; www.acenet.co.uk

CITB-ConstructionSkills
Bircham Newton, King's Lynn, Norfolk, PE31 6RH
01485 577577; call.centre@cskills.org; www.ckills.org

The Institution of Structural Engineers (IStructE)
11 Upper Belgrave Street, London, SW1X 8BH.
020 7235 4535; www.istructe.org.uk

TECHNICAL SURVEYOR

What the work involves

- Technical surveyors work alongside chartered surveyors, providing hands-on support across the full range of surveying specialisms including building, land, rural and quantity.

- You will be expected to carry out a range of administrative tasks associated with each project, such as putting together contracts and writing reports.

- You will also be using complex computer programmes and technical equipment both onsite and in the office in order to create reports and survey drawings, and to assess various aspects of each project.

The type of person suited to this work

You will be working closely with other professionals and clients at all levels, so the ability to communicate confidently and clearly both verbally and in written documents is vital.

Because you will be dealing with very specific technical issues in each project, you will need to have an accurate and methodical approach to work, good numerical skills and the ability to think on your feet.

You will need a good level of IT literacy, and confidence in using the wide range of sophisticated equipment required for the job.

Knowledge of business, law and health and safety related regulations is also desirable.

Working conditions

Working hours usually follow those of a normal office job, but you will occasionally be called to work early mornings, evenings and at weekends during busy times or for certain site visits.

Most of the work is office-based, but you will also spend time working onsite and outdoors. This means you must be prepared to get cold, wet, muddy and dusty, and wear appropriate safety equipment at all times.

You will be carrying out a lot of complex technical tasks which require excellent concentration and can be quite tiring.

Future prospects

You could work with central or local government, large construction firms, smaller surveying companies or even financial businesses, and art and antiques auction houses.

You could progress to become a consultant, a partner in a firm or even move into related sectors such as town planning or chartered surveying with the right qualifications. Self-employment is also an option.

Advantages/disadvantages

You will be providing invaluable support on a number of important projects, so should have job satisfaction.

There is the opportunity to become self-employed, or work overseas.

Qualifications and courses

Entry to this profession is usually with a degree or diploma, preferably one that is accredited by the Royal Institution of Chartered Surveyors (RICS). For a degree course, the usual qualifications needed are 3 A levels/4 H grades or a relevant BTEC/SQA National award.

To become a chartered member of RICS, you then need to complete the 2 year Assessment of Professional Competence (APC), consisting of structured practical training and experience. Candidates with a non-accredited degree, or a degree in a non-vocational subject can take a postgraduate conversion course, followed by the APC.

The Chartered Surveyors Training Trust offers work-based training for young people aged 16–24 in London and the south-east of England. Applicants must have a minimum of 4 GCSEs (A–C) or equivalent.

Once you have qualified as a technical surveyor, further training is possible in the form of NVQs through which you could specialise in an area such as construction or the built environment.

Earning potential is not as high as some other roles in surveying.

Hours can be long and unpredictable at busy times.

Money guide

Starting salaries range from £17,000 to £21,000 per year. With experience, this will rise to £24,000-£30,000. Becoming a partner in a firm can see earnings increase to £50,000+. Salaries are generally higher in London.

Related opportunities

- Quantity Surveyor p119
- Chartered Surveyor p82
- Construction Manager p88
- Civil/Construction Engineer p83

Further information

Chartered Surveyors Training Trust (CSTT)
New Broad Street House, 35 New Broad Street, London EC2M 1NH
020 7194 7952; www.cstt.org.uk; cstt@cstt.org.uk

Royal Institution of Chartered Surveyors (RICS)
Surveyor Court, Westwood Way, Coventry CV4 8JE
0870 333 1600; www.rics.org/careers;
contactrics@rics.org

Association of Building Engineers (ABE)
Lutyens House, Billing Brook Road, Weston Favell NN3 8NW
0845 126 1058; www.abe.org.uk;
building.engineers@abe.org.uk

THATCHER

What the work involves

■ Thatching is the covering of roofs with plant stems such as water reed, combed wheat reed and long straw.

■ Your tasks will include removing old thatched roofs and replacing them, thatching new roofs and repairing or re-thatching existing thatched roofs.

■ Your work will include using many different tools, including mallets, hooks, needles, knives and shears.

■ As thatchers work outside all year round, your hours will differ depending on the season.

The type of person suited to this work

You need to have good practical skills to be able to use the specialised tools and equipment, and to develop an expertise in the craft. You must also be physically fit so that you can climb ladders and scaffolding, carrying thatching materials. You will need to be comfortable working at heights.

It is important to be able to measure roofs accurately so you can work out the required amount of thatching material. Communication skills are necessary for talking to customers and planning officers. You will also need to be interested in learning a traditional rural craft.

Working conditions

You will work outdoors on roofs in rural locations in most weather conditions. The work can be dusty, which can be difficult if you suffer from certain allergies.

You will need to pay close attention to health and safety procedures when working on roofs.

Your working hours are likely to vary according to when the work is available. You may work at weekends and this can be seasonal work, meaning you will be busiest during the spring and summer months when the weather is best.

Future prospects

There are about 1000 thatchers in the UK and, as about a half of all thatched buildings are protected and need to be re-roofed every 15–20 years, there is a steady demand for thatching work. However, there is fierce competition for training vacancies and some thatchers have another job to supplement their income. Not all areas of the UK have thatched buildings so you may have to relocate to find work.

It can take a number of years to become highly skilled. Many thatchers become self-employed once they are fully trained.

Advantages/disadvantages

Working at heights may be demanding for some people and potentially dangerous.

It is rewarding to work in an ancient craft and create thatched roofs that are both functional and decorative.

Qualifications and courses

ENTRY 1 LEVEL

There are no set entry requirements for this work. It may help to have GCSEs/S grades (A–E/1–5) in English, maths and ICT, which are useful for running small businesses.

The Countryside Agency has a New Entrants' Training Scheme aimed at candidates aged 16–25 working in rural areas. Candidates must have worked in the industry for at least six months. The scheme takes 2 years and leads to NVQ/SVQ Level 2 in Thatching. An optional third year leading to NVQ/SVQ Level 3 is available, which places greater emphasis on the skills of thatching, covering the detailing and decorative effects.

The Construction Industry Training Board (CITB) Construction Award in Thatching allows those who have difficulties in gaining the work experience to train for an NVQ.

This may be difficult work if you suffer from certain allergies.

You may need a second job to supplement your earnings from thatching.

Money guide

Earnings vary from county to county and among different employers. These salaries are guidelines only. As a trainee you can earn around £14,000 a year. An experienced thatcher can earn £17,000–£23,000. £35,000 or more is possible for very experienced thatchers able to negotiate their own contracts.

Related opportunities

■ Dry Stone Waller p93
■ Mastic Asphalter p112
■ Roofer p122
■ Stonemason p128

Further information

Lantra
Lantra House, Stoneleigh Park, Coventry CV8 2LG
0845 707 80007; www.lantra.co.uk

National Heritage Training Group
Carthusian Court, 12 Carthusian Street, London EC1M 6EZ
01159 217562; www.nhtg.org.uk

Thatching Advisery Services
The Old Stables, Redenham Park Farm, Redenham, Andover SP11 9AQ
01264 773820; www.thatchingadviseryservices.co.uk

www.cityandguilds.com/myperfectjob

CRCI: N
CLCI: SAW

THERMAL INSULATION ENGINEER

What the work involves

- You will use various types of insulation to either prevent heat loss or keep heat out within different types of products and equipment, such as boilers, pipe-work, refrigeration or air conditioning.

- The types of insulation you will use will be dependent on the actual project but could involve silicate or foam.

- You will measure, cut and shape insulating materials to fit around pipes, boilers and duct work.

- Once the item is insulated, you will cover it using sheet metal or another cladding material.

The type of person suited to this work

Some of the materials you will be exposed to will have the potential to be dangerous, so you will have to be aware of your own safety and that of others.

Much of the work involves strenuous lifting, balancing and some climbing up scaffolding, so you will have to be physically fit.

The ability to work in a team and get on with other people will be important as you will often work alongside other professionals from the construction and engineering industries.

You should be able to understand instructions, have a practical approach to your work and enjoy using manual skills.

Working conditions

You could be working indoors or outside at heights, in places that are cramped or difficult to access.

You may be exposed to harmful substances and be working in dusty and dirty environments, so you will wear protective clothing, like goggles and sometimes a face mask.

You will normally work a standard 38-hour week, but overtime and evening or weekend working might be required.

You will probably need to travel around the country to different sites and projects.

Future prospects

The energy conservation industry is expanding and there is a growth in demand for qualified thermal insulation engineers to work on a wide range of engineering and construction projects. With training and experience your main opportunities will be within building, building service engineering or specialised energy conservation companies.

Within the larger companies it might be possible to progress into supervisory posts and work abroad can be available.

Advantages/disadvantages

You will be working alongside people from different industries.

The skills needed to be able to start and finish a job will be varied.

Qualifications and courses

Although no formal qualifications are required, employers usually require GCSEs/S grades in English, maths, science and an engineering or construction subject.

It is possible to enter this career from an Apprenticeship/Skillseekers opportunity if you are aged 16–24.

You will have to pass an entry test after which you will undertake on-the-job and off-the-job training at college. Your employer could use a training programme provided by the Insulation and Environmental Training Agency (IETA).

It is also helpful if you can evidence some practical work experience when applying.

NVQs/SVQs in Thermal Insulation Engineering are available in relevant subjects at Levels 2–3.

You may need to stay away from home – this could be difficult if you have family commitments.

Opportunities are good and overseas work may be possible.

Money guide

Whilst training, your earnings will range from £9,000–£16,000 a year. With qualifications this rises to between £17,000 and £21,000. Senior thermal insulation engineers can earn up to £30,000. Expenses may be paid when you need to live away from your home base during a project.

Related opportunities

- Damp Proofer p91
- Gas Network Engineer p231
- Heating and Ventilating Engineer p104
- Plumber p117

Further information

Insulation and Environmental Training Agency
Tica House, Allington Way, Yarm Road Business Park
Darlington, Co Durham DL1 4QB
01325 466704; www.tica-acad.co.uk

Thermal Insulation Contractors Association
TICA House, Allington Way, Yarm Road Business Park,
Darlington, County Durham. DL1 4QB
01325 466704; www.tica-acad.co.uk

City&
Guilds

www.cityandguilds.com/myperfectjob

TOWN PLANNER/ PLANNING TECHNICIAN

What the work involves

Town planner

- You will manage and develop urban or rural areas to best serve the population, by deciding on the best use of land, taking into account commercial and social needs, alongside environmental and heritage considerations.

Town planning technician

- You will support the work of town planners.

- Your tasks are likely to be varied and may include carrying out surveys, mapping, recording information, analysing and presenting reports, and providing advice on planning permission.

The type of person suited to this work

As you will be meeting other professionals and members of the public, as well as producing comprehensive written reports, you should have excellent communication skills.

You will need to be organised with good research, problem-solving and analytical skills, as you will be investigating the potential effects of different proposals for land use.

Specialist skills required include competency in graphic design, desktop publishing and familiarity with computer-aided design (CAD), geographical information systems (GIS) and cartography.

Working conditions

You are likely to work regular office hours, although you may sometimes need to attend meetings in the evening.

Most town planners are based in offices but often go out on site visits, or to attend meetings. A driving licence may be necessary.

Future prospects

Town planning is a growing profession, but there is still a demand for more qualified planners in the UK and overseas.

Most employers are local authorities and planning consultancies, but opportunities also exist within central government, construction companies and environmental organisations. With experience, you may be promoted to senior or chief town planner, or move sideways into related careers such as recreation management, market research or property development.

Advantages/disadvantages

There is personal satisfaction in dealing with public problems, and helping to improve the environment in which people live and work.

Qualifications and courses

Town planning technician

There are no set qualifications for a career as a town planning technician, but at least 5 GCSEs/S grades (A-C/1–3) including English and maths, are usually required. Many entrants also have A levels/Highers or other Level 3 qualifications. Planning technicians are trained on the job and may also undertake part-time study. To achieve Technical Membership of the Royal Town Planning Institute (RTPI), you need a recognised qualification at NVQ Level 3 or higher and 2 years' work experience.

Town planner

A qualification accredited by the RTPI is necessary. This could take the form of a first degree or a postgraduate qualification. The normal minimum entry grades for a planning degree are 2 A levels/3 Highers. Some institutions also offer a 12 month fast track course. For entry to a postgraduate course, a related degree in subjects such as geography, architecture, or statistics is required. Following completion of an accredited qualification, plus 2 years' relevant work experience, you can apply for full membership of the RTPI.

You may find the need to compromise on planning initiatives frustrating. Dealing with angry or upset members of the public can be difficult.

Money guide

The starting salary for a trainee town planning technician can range from £14,000 to £16,000, and can reach around £20,000 when qualified. Technicians with considerable experience can earn up to £32,000.

Newly graduated town planners could earn between £18,000 and £25,000. This will rise to £35,000 with a few years' experience. Principal planners or heads of a team can earn £30,000-£40,000. If you progress to become a chief planning officer, head of department or company director then your salary could reach £50,000 to £80,000.

Related opportunities

- Land Surveyor p111
- Planning and Development Surveyor p115

Further information

Royal Town Planning Institute (RTPI)
41 Botolph Lane, London EC3R 8DL
020 7929 9494; www.rtpi.org.uk

Royal Town Planning Institute in Scotland
57 Melville Street, Edinburgh EH3 7HL
0131 226 1959; www.scotland.rtpi.org.uk

WALL/FLOOR TILER

What the work involves

- Wall and floor tilers fit tiles in various locations, from bathrooms and kitchens to hospitals and swimming pools.

- The tiles you work with may range from small mosaic tiles to large heavy-duty tiles.

- You will plan the work by making sure you have enough tiles of the right type. You will then use various tools to prepare the surface, cut tiles, apply adhesive, fix the tiles in the correct position and grout them.

- Mathematical ability is very important as you will be required to measure and calculate the number of tiles for any given job

The type of person suited to this work

You must be able to plan your work and use your mathematical skills to work out the number of tiles you will need for a particular job. You have to work carefully and accurately when cutting and placing tiles. It is important to match colours and patterns, so a flair for design is useful.

You need to be physically fit for carrying the materials, and for working on your hands and knees.

You may work alone for some jobs but you must also be able to work in a team when you are working on larger jobs.

Working conditions

You will work mainly indoors in a variety of locations, including people's homes, offices, factories and construction-sites. A driving licence may be useful.

You may work a normal working week, but you may also need to work evenings or weekends so that you can tile walls and floors without disrupting businesses.

As you will use special cutting tools and adhesives, you will need to be aware of health and safety procedures.

Future prospects

Due to the increased demand across all of the construction industry there is currently a lot of work available for skilled tilers.

Work is available with specialist tiling companies and building contractors, or you may choose to become self-employed, providing services to individuals or sub-contracting to organisations.

It is possible to specialise in using one type of tiling, for example flooring tiles, mosaic work or bathrooms.

With experience, you may progress to technical, supervisory or managerial positions.

Advantages/disadvantages

You will be on your hands and knees, sometimes working in dusty, dirty or cramped conditions.

The work is varied and you can achieve spectacular results using coloured and textured tiles to decorate walls and floors.

Qualifications and courses

ENTRY LEVEL 1

No specific qualifications are required, although GCSEs/S grades (A–E/1–5) may be useful in subjects like maths, technology or English. Similar subjects may be needed to be eligible for an Apprenticeship or equivalent vocational qualifications like the Edexcel Introductory Certificate or Diploma in Construction.

You will be trained on the job while working towards qualifications. This may also involve going to a college or training centre on day- or block-release.

NVQs/SVQs in Wall and Floor Tiling at Levels 2 and 3 are available.

Apprenticeships/Skillseekers may be available to those aged 16–24. In Scotland, applicants for a construction apprenticeship need to take a selection test.

You can also train by doing a Construction Industry Training Board (CITB) Construction Apprenticeship Scheme in Wall and Floor Tiling.

The Construction Industry Training Board (CITB) Construction Award in Wall and Floor Tiling allows those who have difficulties in gaining the work experience to train for an NVQ. You can apply straight to the CITB before or after finding employment or gaining a place on a training scheme.

Money guide

Salaries start between £12,000 and £16,000 per year while training. This can rise to £18,000–£24,000 for skilled tilers. With experience this rises to £25,000+. £40,000 is possible for the highest earners. Overtime is often available, and on some projects there are bonuses based on outputs, which can lead to higher earnings.

Related opportunities

- Building Technician p76
- Carpet Fitter p78
- Floor Layer p101
- Construction Operative p86

Further information

ConstructionSkills
Bircham Newton, King's Lynn, Norfolk PE31 6RH
01485 577577; www.cskills.net; www.bconstructive.co.uk; construction careers site

The Tile Association
Forum Court, 83 Copers Cope Road, Beckenham, Kent, BR3 1NR
020 8663 0946 www.tiles.org.uk

City & Guilds

www.cityandguilds.com/myperfectjob

WASTEWATER TREATMENT PLANT OPERATOR

What the work involves

- Water treatment plant operators monitor wastewater as it goes through various treatment processes which remove harmful substances. They ensure that treated water is returned to the water cycle and that wastewater is removed and destroyed as appropriate.

- You will be responsible for the operation and maintenance of the plant, ensuring that septic tanks, filters and screens are disinfected, checking water samples, and adding treatment micro-organisms and chemicals to the water when necessary.

- You will conduct tests on samples, take readings from monitors and adjust treatment equipment as necessary.

- You will work with a team composed of a supervisor, senior technicians, engineers and a manager.

The type of person suited to this work

You should have a keen interest in the environment, science and technology.

You should also have good communication skills as you will have to work in a team.

You must be committed to health and safety regulations.

You must be organised and methodical as you will be testing samples to ensure that harmful substances are removed from the water cycle.

You also need to be happy to work with new technology which you will use on a daily basis.

You will be required to have a certain level of fitness as you may be doing practical strenuous work at times, such as cleaning and maintenance.

Working conditions

You will work approximately 37 hours a week. Overtime may be possible but part time work is rare. You will probably have to work shifts as water treatment plants operate 24 hours a day. You may have to join a call-out rota to cover nights and weekends.

You will be based indoors in control rooms but some of your work will involve being outside in all weather conditions. You may also have to carry out work at heights or in confined spaces.

Protective clothing is provided. This may include breathing apparatus, and should be worn to prevent contact with harmful substances.

A driving licence may be required.

Future prospects

As you progress you will be promoted to supervisory roles and from there to roles as an inspector, a superintendent or a plant manager. You may also choose to move into a related area such as treatment plant design.

Qualifications and courses

There are no formal academic qualifications required to become a wastewater treatment plant operator. However some companies seek employees with a minimum of four GCSEs/S grade (A-E/1–5) in maths, English and a science or technology subject.

You can train as an apprentice or apply for a government-funded training programme in wastewater treatment plant operating. Throughout these programmes you will be trained on the job and take courses at a college or training centre.

You can also take a course at the City & Guilds to improve your skills, including the level 2 Certificate for Water Sector Competent Operators.

An important qualification for a wastewater treatment plant operator is the NVQ in Operating a Process Plant (Water), Level 2. You can also gain an NVQ in Utilities Control Centre Operations, Level 2, and SVQs in Controlling Water Operations, Level 3, and Water Industry Operations, Level 3.

You can also take a Higher National Certificate, Diploma or degree which will allow you to move to higher positions.

Advantages/disadvantages

You may find opportunities to increase wages by taking extra shifts, going on stand-by and doing overtime.

Your working environment in the plant may be smelly and wet.

Money guide

Your salary as a trainee can start at around £10,500 a year.

With experience you can earn from £17,000 to £20,000.

Related opportunities

- Brewery worker p225
- Oil/gas drilling engineer p243
- Water network operative p137

Further information

Energy and Utility Skills Limited
Friars Gate, 1011 Stratford Road, Shirley, Solihull, B90 4BN
enquiries@euskills.co.uk; www.euskills.co.uk

City & Guilds
1 Giltspur Street, London, EC1A 9DD
enquiry@cityandguilds.com; www.cityandguilds.com

Water UK
1 Queen Anne's Gate, London, SW1H 9BT
020 7344 1844 www.water.org.uk

A career in the environment and why IEMA membership is important

Gillian Gibson FIEMA, Cenv

When I was at college the only environmental courses were the ones concerned with ecology. I am very fond of wildlife, but have no interest in studying it. What did excite me was human biology- the workings of the human body, and the influence of drugs on it, as well toxicological influences, so I studied Applied Biology, specialising in pharmacology and microbiology.

My first jobs were in pharmaceutical research, before moving to teaching. Whilst teaching I made changes to what was taught, and brought environmental matters into the courses. How can we understand our existence in an environment if we don't understand our interaction with it?

I took a Master's degree in Environmental Monitoring and Assessment, which I really enjoyed, and which enabled me to have a greater depth of understanding of those things which I felt to be important, and about which we were beginning to know more. However, the more we knew, the worse things seemed. Not least the effect on humans from the environment which we had created for ourselves from thoughtless technological expansion (that is to say, the consequences of our actions were not given due consideration).

I moved from teaching full time, (though I still lecture at various universities) into environmental management and auditing, but the health question never got left behind, and I spent a couple of years working for a health authority. With the advent of IPPC with its need for evaluation of health effects, the twin tracks of my career finally met a common output. I spent several very happy years consulting for the various Primary Care Trusts in the North West, evaluating all those thick files for the potential effects on health, and liaising with the Environment Agency on the best way forwards at the permitting stage. Although those heady days are over, I am still involved with Health Impact Assessment (HIA) at the planning stages, evaluating the effects on health of proposed developments. This uses my auditing skills, and my technological understanding of air emissions, contaminated land, etc.

In addition to the consulting, I run courses in environmental awareness, auditing, EMS implementation, the business impact of climate change, amongst others.

I have been a member of IEMA since its inception, having come in through the Auditor route, as a member of the old EARA. This membership is important to me: I am a member of the North West Steering Group, (I think we can deliver a number of events for the local membership, from social networking through to knowledge exchange, as well as representing member's views at a national level) Professional Standards Committee, (maintaining standards, as a teacher, is dear to my heart) national council (trying to ensure that members' needs are always paramount) as well as being a full member and Chartered Environmentalist assessor. Why? Because I want to ensure that the role of the environmentalist within the business world is taken seriously, sits centrally in the organisation, is recognised by government as someone who speaks ethically and altruistically, and is respected within the wider community. IEMA is helping to 'professionalise' the profession.

WATER/SEWERAGE NETWORK OPERATIVE

Building and Construction

CRCI: BB
CLCI: UN

What the work involves

■ Water/sewerage network operatives lay, maintain and repair the pipework that carries drinking water, waste water and sewage.

■ Your tasks might include digging trenches in roads and relaying them afterwards, putting up barriers and warning signs, laying pipes, repairing leaks, clearing blockages and installing water meters.

■ You will use a range of tools such as welding equipment to join pipes together.

■ You will also use machinery such as mechanical diggers.

The type of person suited to this work

You must have good practical skills and be mechanically minded so that you can use tools, equipment and machinery effectively. Working on-site can be dangerous, so a responsible attitude is essential. You will have to follow plans and instructions accurately, so that systems are installed correctly and safely.

You need to be physically fit for bending, kneeling and carrying materials and equipment.

You must be able to deal directly with members of the public, who might be upset that their water services are disrupted. You must also be able to work in a team with other water/sewerage network operatives. A driving licence may be required.

Working conditions

You will work outdoors in all weather conditions. The work can be dusty, dirty and wet, as well as smelly.

You will need to follow strict health, safety and hygiene regulations, which may include wearing breathing apparatus, a safety helmet, boots and gloves.

You may work normal working hours or shifts, but the particular hours you work will vary according to the needs of the job and the hours of daylight available. You may also be called out at weekends and at all times of the day and night to do emergency repairs.

Future prospects

There is currently quite a lot of work available for water/sewerage network operatives because the privatised water companies, who manage water supply and sewerage disposal, are investing money in developing their systems.

Work is available across the UK with water companies and construction firms.

With experience, you may be promoted to a team leader or supervisor post.

Some operatives move into related areas such as water distribution inspection work.

Qualifications and courses

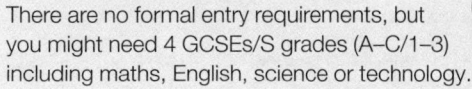

There are no formal entry requirements, but you might need 4 GCSEs/S grades (A–C/1–3) including maths, English, science or technology.

Relevant experience, for example in site maintenance work, is useful. Registration in an appropriate safety passport scheme could be required by many employers to be able to work on-site.

Entrants are trained on the job, and may work towards vocational qualifications. An NVQ/SVQ Level 2 is available in Water Distribution. CABWI offers a range of relevant NVQs, including Distribution Control Level 2, Operating Process Plant (Water) Level 2, Leakage Control Level 3 and Maintaining Water Supply Level 3.

Apprenticeships/Skillseekers may be available for people aged 16–24. The scheme starts with basic preliminary training, with apprentices usually working towards NVQs/SVQs at Level 2 in subjects such as customer care, water distribution, construction and technical drawing.

Advantages/disadvantages

The work can be physically demanding for some people, and it can get smelly if you are working on sewerage systems.

It can be satisfying to know that you are helping to provide people with an essential service.

Money guide

As a trainee you can earn around £9,000–£13,000 a year. This can rise to £14,000–£16,000+ for fully trained operatives with one year's experience. With additional experience earnings can increase to £20,000 or more. Earnings vary depending on your employer and which part of the country you work in.

Related opportunities

■ Construction Plant Operator p87
■ Construction Operative p86
■ Gas Network Engineer p231
■ Plumber p117

Further information

Energy and Utility Skills
Friars Gate Two, 1011 Stratford Road, Solihull, B90 4BN
0845 077 9922; www.euskills.co.uk

Water UK
1 Queen Anne's Gate, London, SW1H 9BT
020 7344 1844; www.water.org.uk

www.cityandguilds.com/myperfectjob

WINDOW INSTALLER

What the work involves

- Window fitters install windows and doors into new and existing buildings.

- You will use hand and power tools to take out any old windows and fit new ones. You will work with materials such as wood and plastic, as well as glass.

- Once you have fixed a new window into the surrounding brickwork, you will need to give it a weatherproof seal.

The type of person suited to this work

You will need good practical hand skills for using tools and as you will be lifting and carrying windows you will need to be physically fit. Also, as you will be using ladders, you will need to have a head for heights, and be aware of your own safety and that of those around you.

You must be able to measure accurately so that the window frames fit properly.

You may work on your own for some jobs, but you will often work with one other window fitter or in a small team, so you must be able to work with others. You should also be able to get on with customers, because you will spend a lot of time on their premises,

Working conditions

You will work indoors and outdoors in a variety of locations, and you will be working in most weather conditions. A driving licence may be useful or required.

You will need to pay attention to health and safety when working with glass and be happy clearing up after your work has finished.

You are likely to work normal working hours during the week, but overtime may be available at weekends.

Future prospects

Work is available with window and conservatory fitting companies of all sizes throughout the UK. Increasing awareness of energy issues, and the need for all houses to have an energy assessment before sale, has increased demand for more energy efficient replacement windows.

Conservatories are also growing in popularity in the UK.

After gaining sufficient experience, you may progress to team leader or supervisory positions. You could also run your own window-fitting business. There are also openings within the sales and marketing sides of the industry.

Advantages/disadvantages

Lifting and carrying windows and working at heights may be difficult for some people.

You will get to travel to many different locations in your job.

Qualifications and courses

There are no formal entry requirements, but you may need some GCSEs/S grades, or equivalent vocational qualifications such as a Foundation GNVQ/GSVQ Level 1. Maths, English and design and technology subjects are useful.

Apprenticeship/Skillseekers may be available for people aged 16–24. Applicants normally need GCSEs/S grades (A–E/1–5), or an equivalent qualification such as Intermediate GNVQ or First Diploma.

Initial training is provided by employers and covers removing and fitting window frames, health and safety, customer relations and relevant paperwork. Entrants then work with experienced window installers before being allowed to work alone.

You can gain vocational qualifications while you work. You will be taught practical skills and may spend time off-site at a college or training centre. You may work towards NVQs/SVQs in Fenestration Installation at Level 2, Fenestration Installation and Surveying at Level 3, and Glazing Installation and Maintenance at Levels 2–3.

It is satisfying to make customers happy by improving the appearance, value and function of their buildings by installing new windows.

Money guide

Whilst training you will earn around £12,500 a year. Once trained, you can expect an average salary of around £14,000–£18,000. £20,000–£26,000 is likely to be earned by a competent installer. Earnings will depend on where you work and the size of the organisation.

Related opportunities

- Carpenter/Joiner p77
- Carpet Fitter p78
- Ceiling Fixer p81
- Glazier p103

Further information

Proskills UK
Centurion Court, 85b Milton Park, Abingdon, OX14 4RY
01235 833844; www.proskills.co.uk

Glass and Glazing Federation
44–48 Borough High Street, London, SE1 1XB
0870 042 4255; www.ggf.co.uk

City&
Guilds

www.cityandguilds.com/myperfectjob

Catering and Hospitality

Working in this sector, you will meet a wide variety of people and probably need to be a very strong team player. Workers in the sector thrive on providing an impeccable service and ensuring customers are completely satisfied and are given a wonderful experience whether that is in a restaurant, hotel or bar.

In this section we look at the following jobs:

For similar jobs to the ones in this section why not have a look at *Leisure, Sport and Tourism* starting on page 385 and *Retail Sales and Customer Services* from page 477.

BAR MANAGER/LICENSEE/ PUBLICAN

What the work involves

- Your duties will include the recruitment, training and management of staff. You will also deal with the accounts, stock replenishment, maintaining links with suppliers and business development.

- You will need to keep up-to-date with any changes to licensing laws and other legal requirements such as health and safety or fire safety regulations, and ensure that your customers and staff adhere to them.

- In addition, you will demonstrate a high level of customer service to ensure client satisfaction.

The type of person suited to this work

It is essential to have excellent communication skills and to enjoy meeting and speaking to people of all ages. A confident, professional attitude is needed to deal with customer or supplier problems.

Being physically fit and able to stay on your feet all day is helpful. You should be practical, flexible and good at multi-tasking.

Good numeracy skills are expected as you will be managing cash on a daily basis. Finally, you should keep up to date with legal requirements, and enforce those that affect you.

Working conditions

Although pubs, clubs and bars can remain open for 24 hours a day, most only extend their hours at weekends or for special events.

You will work long hours in an environment which can be busy, noisy and hot. You will be required to stand for lengthy periods and lift and carry heavy items such as barrels.

You may have to deal with demanding or difficult customers who are intoxicated. Changes to smoking legislation have resulted in the need to provide outside facilities, where problems may occur.

Future prospects

A publican can own, lease or become a tenant of their premises. You can be a manager on behalf of a brewery or different premises like high street chains, family establishments, café bars or themed pubs and restaurants across the country.

With experience, you could progress to a larger establishment or even manage a bar overseas.

Advantages/disadvantages

The hours will be long and irregular, which might affect your personal life.

You will have to deal with drunk customers, who may be difficult or aggressive, on a fairly regular basis.

Qualifications and courses

No formal entry qualifications are required for this work and there are various routes into the profession.

You can start work as a bar person from the age of 18, and work up to a supervisory or management position. NVQs/SVQs are available in bar service (Level 2), on-licensed premises supervision (Level 3) and on-licensed premises management (Level 4). You could study for an HNC/HND, foundation degree or degree in a related subject such as hospitality management with licensed retail.

In England and Wales new entrants to on-licensed premises can take the Professional Barperson's Qualification of the British Institute of Innkeeping Awarding Body (BIIAB). The Award in Beer and Cellar Quality is also available.

For people wishing to progress to management, the National Certificate in licensed retailing and the National Certificate for personal licence holders are available. In Scotland, the BIIAB offers the Scottish Licensee's Certificate for on-licensed and all other premises and the Scottish Licensee's Certificate (off-sale).

Money guide

Earnings vary according to the location, type and size of the premises you work in.

The average starting salary for a trainee manager is £14,000–£15,000, but with experience this can increase to between £22,000 and £30,000.

If you work within a very successful and large establishment, it is possible to earn up to £50,000.

Related opportunities

- Brewer p225
- Catering/Restaurant Manager/Maître d'hôtel p141
- Hotel Manager p149
- Waiting Staff p154

Further information

British Institute of Innkeeping
Wessex House, 80 Park House, Camberley GU15 3PT
01276 684449; www.biiab.org

British Beer and Pub Association
Market Towers, 1 Nine Elms Lane, London SW8 5NQ
020 7627 9191; www.beerandpub.com

Scottish Licensed Trade Association
10 Walker Street, Edinburgh EH13 7LA
0131 225 5169; www.slta.co.uk

City& Guilds

www.cityandguilds.com/myperfectjob

CATERING/RESTAURANT MANAGER/ MAÎTRE D'HÔTEL

What the work involves

- You will manage, train and employ staff in a kitchen or restaurant. A maître d'hôtel is specifically responsible for running a hotel restaurant.

- Part of your work will involve planning menus, checking stocks of food and drink and ordering fresh supplies when needed. You will be expected to carry out paperwork, and will have to manage budgets and organise staff rotas.

- You will be responsible for the health and safety of both your staff and customers.

The type of person suited to this work

You will be dealing with kitchen staff, suppliers and other business professionals, so you should be confident and have excellent communication skills. It is essential to provide good customer care at all times.

As you will be involved with preparing food for the public you will be required to follow and keep up-to-date with health and safety laws. You will also need a good knowledge of food.

Good management skils, including an understanding of the different roles undertaken by your staff, is essential. Exceptional organisational abilities are also necessary.

You will also need good numeracy skills as you will be managing a budget and working out stock quantities.

Working conditions

Much of your time will be spent in your kitchen or restaurant, which can get very hot and busy. You might be using cutting tools and knives and be on your feet for long periods.

Expect to wear a uniform or protective clothing and regularly work unsociable hours. It is important to follow high standards of food safety and hygiene.

It is possible to work as a catering manager in the Armed Forces, in which case you may find yourself working in challenging environments, anywhere in the world, in a variety of climates.

Future prospects

The sector offers a wide range of career opportunities and quick progression. However, it will help your career if you work in increasingly bigger and well-known premises.

In some parts of the UK – the major cities and south-east of England – where there are lots of restaurants, there are management skill shortages. This means that if you do well your future prospects are very positive.

Advantages/disadvantages

The job can provide the chance to work creatively with food.

You may live on-site.

This can be a very busy job where you will be doing several tasks at the same time.

Qualifications and courses

ENTRY LEVEL 2

You can start in a job as a kitchen assistant, waiter/waitress, chef or cook and work your way up. People working in the industry can take NVQs/ SVQs, for example hospitality supervision Level 3 or hospitality management Level 4.

The Institute of Hospitality (formerly the Hotel and Catering International Management Association) offers a selection of courses for staff in specific roles.

If aged 16–24, you could also undertake an Apprenticeship in hospitality.

Many hotels and hotel chains offer training schemes. It may be possible to join a scheme with A levels/H grades or equivalent, but the usual requirement is a degree or HND/ C in a relevant subject (for example hospitality management, hospitality and catering, hotel management, international hospitality management). Minimum requirements for degree entry are usually 5 GCSEs/S grades (A–C/1–3) and 2 A levels or 3 H grades. Postgraduate courses are also available.

A second language may also be helpful.

Hours are long and will involve unsociable hours including weekend or evening work.

Money guide

Salary rates vary depending on the type and size of restaurant, location and level of responsibility. Salaries tend to be higher in London and large cities.

Trainee starting salaries are £16,000–£20,000. With experience, and in a large restaurant, this can rise to £30,000–£40,000.

A senior manager in the most successful premises can earn £35,000–£70,000.

Related opportunities

- Food Safety Officer p147
- Events and Exhibition Organiserr p389
- Kitchen Supervisor p153

Further information

People 1st
2nd Floor, 38 Market Square, Uxbridge UB8 1LH; 01895 817 000; www.people1st.co.uk

Institute of Hospitality
Trinity Court, 34 West Street, Sutton SM1 1SH
020 8661 4900; www.instituteofhospitality.org

City& Guilds

www.cityandguilds.com/myperfectjob

CELLAR TECHNICIAN

What the work involves

- You will set up and maintain the systems that provide alcoholic and soft drinks in pubs, hotels and other sites.

- Visiting a range of locations, you will install equipment and deal with emergencies or problems.

- You will undertake regular maintenance checks to make sure that everything works properly and train the staff on how to operate it.

- You might work from home or be based within a brewery.

The type of person suited to this work

Because of the technical nature of the work, you will need good practical skills and the confidence to work and operate different systems quickly and efficiently. As you will be handling heavy equipment, a good level of physical fitness is helpful. The ability to speak to lots of different people is useful, as is a confidence in your ability to do the job well.

You will need to be sociable and friendly and be willing to do lots of driving from site to site. As you will be providing a service on behalf of your company for lots of different licensed premises you will need to have excellent customer care skills.

Working conditions

You will spend lots of time driving from site to site. Some of your work will be attending emergency call-outs which could include evenings and weekends that might affect your personal life. The extended pub opening hours might mean this includes 24-hour call-out duties.

You will work in dark, cramped conditions using specialist tools and equipment.

Future prospects

Because of the steady growth in hospitality venues and the need for branded drinks, the number of jobs is expected to grow steadily. Many applicants come from the licensed trade who have watched the job and become interested. It is therefore useful to have pub experience or relevant qualifications before applying.

With experience you can apply for senior/managerial posts or move into other areas of the licensed or food and drink sector.

Advantages/disadvantages

This job combines meeting and training people and lots of practical work.

You will have to travel from your base to customers over a geographical area.

Qualifications and courses

There are no minimum entry requirements for this job, though some employers prefer candidates with a good general education, particularly with GCSEs in maths, science or technology subjects.

The following qualifications are also useful: NVQ/SVQ Levels 2 or 3, City & Guilds or BTEC First or National awards. Some employers in particular may prefer electrical or electronic engineering.

Employers provide training that covers areas such as health and safety, customer care, refrigeration, checking systems and working with equipment.

You could work towards the NVQ/SVQ Levels 2 and 3 Drinks Dispense Systems (Installation and Maintenance).

The British Institute of Innkeeping (BII) offers a Level 2 award in Cellar Service Installation.

You may work in uncomfortable conditions, for example when fitting a new dispensing system in a cellar.

Money guide

The starting salary is normally around £11,500 per year.

With experience this can increase to £20,000+. When fully qualified you could get up to £25,000. You may also be paid overtime for emergency call-out duties or for working in the evenings or at weekends.

Related opportunities

- Bar Manager/Licensee/Publican p140
- Brewery Worker/Technician p225
- Plumber p117

Further information

British Soft Drinks Association
20–22 Stukeley Street, London, WC2B 5LR
020 7430 0356; www.britishsoftdrinks.com

People 1st
2nd Floor, 38 Market Square, Uxbridge, UB8 1LH
0870 060 2550; www.people1st.co.uk

Scottish Licensed Trade Association
10 Walker Street, Edinburgh, EH13 7LA
0131 225 5169, www.slta.co.uk

City & Guilds

www.cityandguilds.com/myperfectjob

CHEF/SOUS CHEF

What the work involves

- Chefs and sous chefs work in restaurants, cafés, bars, cruise ships and catering firms. Some also work for specialist food companies, helping to create new products.

- You will coordinate kitchen activities and supervise the preparation of food by your team of kitchen staff.

- Sous chefs are second in command of the kitchen. They will be required to recruit and train kitchen staff.

- Planning new menus and dishes, checking stocks of food and drink and dealing with suppliers are also included in the sous chef role.

The type of person suited to this work

Kitchens can be hot and hectic environments, therefore it is essential to have the ability to remain calm under pressure.

Good team working, communication and multi-tasking skills are important to ensure the smooth running of the operation. As you are responsible for the health and safety of everyone in your kitchen, you must also be vigilant at all times.

You should have excellent cooking skills, be very creative and have a passion for food. It is also helpful if you want to try out new things and set trends. Good numeracy skills are also required to measure ingredients, and in order to manage budgets and stock levels.

Working conditions

Most of your work will be within a kitchen, which will be hot, busy and noisy. You will be required to use equipment and cutting tools that can be dangerous if not used correctly.

As you will be preparing food you will be expected to wear protective clothing and pay attention to health and hygiene. Hours are unsociable and include evenings and weekends. Part-time work can be found however you will normally work about 40 hours a week in a shift pattern, which might affect your personal life.

Future prospects

In many areas of the UK there is a shortage of chefs, due to an increasing number of establishments opening and a lack of chefs with the required skills and qualifications.

Starting as a commis chef you will help in different sections of the kitchen. With experience, you can progress to sous chef where you act as deputy to the chef and manage a section of your own.

Gaining significant experience may allow you to open your own business or even become a lecturer.

Advantages/disadvantages

Preparing high-quality food is very rewarding and will be a memorable event for your customers.

Qualifications and courses

No academic qualifications are required to enter this profession. Most training is on-the-job and you will be taught by an experienced chef whilst you work in the kitchen. It is possible to work your way up with enough kitchen experience

You can study for NVQs/SVQs (Levels 2–3) in food preparation and cooking, and it can be helpful to gain a food hygiene certificate whilst working towards becoming a chef.

Further qualifications are also available, including Foundation HNCs in professional cookery or professional patisserie which require NVQ/SVQ Level 3 or a National Certificate in catering, or HNDs in culinary art, patisserie, food service or kitchen and larder work. Scotland has a variety of qualifications available.

You will have the opportunity to combine creativity with practical skills.

This type of work requires you to work long hours including weekends and evenings.

You will be working on your feet for much of the time in a hot and busy environment.

Money guide

Salaries vary according to the type of employer and geographic area. Where there are chef shortages, salaries are higher.

Salaries start at £12,000 per year for a junior commis chef, rising to £18,000 as a chef de partie and £25,000 as a sous chef.

Executive chefs can earn £50,000+. However, your earnings will be based on your experience, reputation, and size and type of premises.

Related opportunities

- Catering/Restaurant Manager/Maître d'hôtel p141
- Food Safety Officer p147
- Kitchen Assistant/Porter p152
- Kitchen Supervisor/Manager p153

Further information

Institute of Hospitality
Trinity Court, 34 West Street, Sutton SM1 1SH
020 8661 4900; www.hcima.co.uk

People 1st
2nd Floor, 38 Market Square, Uxbridge UB8 1LH
0870 060 2550; www.people1st.co.uk

City&
Guilds

www.cityandguilds.com/myperfectjob

HARVEY NICHOLS

WHY JOIN US?

Our Reputation

Harvey Nichols has a reputation for providing the very best in fashion, food and beauty, leading the way in luxury retail.

Working with the Best

If you would like to work with the best luxury brands in the world and work with knowledgeable managers and sales advisors then this is the place to be.

Grow and Develop

If you would like to grow and develop your career, Harvey Nichols provides the opportunity for you to increase your knowledge, competence and earnings potential through our 'Steps to Success' programme.

We also have competencies in place in other areas of the business such as Buying, Merchandising and some of our Support areas which support you in developing your skills and knowledge if you're not on the shop floor.

Working in our hospitality division will give you the opportunity to gain a nationally recognised qualification.

By progressing through these programmes you will also increase your salary.

Working for a company with stores and restaurants across the UK and franchise stores overseas there are many opportunities to advance your career. We always advertise internally first.

We take development seriously and all staff have regular reviews during their probation period and everyone has an annual review resulting in a personal development plan.

We Care What You Think

Each store has a staff council who meet once a month. The council is updated on changes in the business and are encouraged to voice their opinions.

We encourage our employees to put forward their ideas and suggestions for improving our business through our Suggestion Scheme. We actively reward the ones that we use.

We Recognise Success

We hold monthly breakfasts to recognise our people who have lived our Vision and Values where we present all winners with their reward prize.

We also award prizes quarterly for the best cross sellers in store and for people who have used their language abilities to participate in our Store Ambassador Scheme.

If you're looking to start your career with a leading Fashion and Hospitality business, visit www.harveynicholscareers.com

THE
HARVEY NICHOLS
CHEF APPRENTICESHIP

Nourish your ambition

Harvey Nichols is a leading international lifestyle store, renowned for its luxury brands and destination restaurants. The restaurants are located on the top floor of the Harvey Nichols stores situated in Knightsbridge, Bristol, Dublin, Manchester, Edinburgh and Leeds. Harvey Nichols also has two stand alone restaurants located in London; OXO Tower and Prism.

Harvey Nichols provides excellent training and support, using work and college based training at Thomas Danby College*, Leeds, to give you the best start in your chosen career. You will be mentored by our senior chefs, all at the top of their profession and many of whom have risen through the ranks in our kitchens.
Using all our resources you will be trained in all aspects of the kitchen including:
choosing and buying the best ingredients, craft kitchen skills including pastry and butchery, food safety, health and safety, customer service, food and wine matching, menu writing and nutrition.

An opportunity to...

Achieve a nationally recognised qualification within the industry and participate in local/national chef competitions.

Undertake a three week overseas restaurant work placement, organised through our partnership colleges.

A promise of...

*   Development, support and a clearly defined career path.
*   Dedicated block periods out of the work place for technical and theoretical development within a college environment.
*   Salaried commis chef role while part of the Apprentice Scheme.
*   A guaranteed chef's position upon successful completion of the programme.

"Through enrolling in the Harvey Nichols Chef Apprentice Scheme I have had the opportunity to learn about a variety of foods both British and international, meet a number of suppliers and travel to Europe. My highlight was going to Italy and experiencing how different kitchens operate and learning from their methods and techniques. The scheme has made me more independent and increased my confidence in dealing with people and the training I have received in the kitchens has allowed me to determine which direction I would like to take my cooking in."

Seraiah Richards, Demi Chef, OXO Tower Brasserie, London
Harvey Nichols Chef Apprentice Scheme 2005 – 2007

"It is an approach that clearly works. The apprentices have all developed brilliantly in the short time they have been with us."

Richard Walton Allen, Executive Chef, Fourth Floor Café, Leeds

*About Thomas Danby College
Faculty of Catering, Hospitality, Food Manufacture and ICT
Recognised by the industry both in the UK and abroad, and recently awarded as a Centre of Vocational Excellence for Food Technology, Thomas Danby College is highly respected for providing acclaimed staff. They offer state of the art facilities with first class training rooms and working environments.

To apply for this exciting opportunity or for further career information, visit www.harveynicholscareers.com

Catering and Hospitality

CRCI: C
CLCI: IB

CONCIERGE

What the work involves

■ Concierges work as part of the front of house team in a hotel, apartment block or corporate organisation.

■ You will be responsible for greeting guests, assisting with their baggage, answering questions, giving advice or directions, and generally making them feel as comfortable as possible.

■ If you work in a hotel you must keep up-to-date on events and functions in the hotel, and may be asked to book tickets and organise travel for guests.

■ You may manage a team of other concierges, reception or door staff. Some organisations may require you to undertake extra services such as shopping and pet walking/sitting.

The type of person suited to this work

As you will be the first port of call for guests and visitors to the establishment you work for you should enjoy meeting new people and working in a busy environment.

You must be polite, friendly, helpful and informative at all times.

You should have an interest in the catering and hospitality industry.

You need to have a practical approach to problem solving and be able to remain calm.

As you will be entrusted with important errands and messages you must be responsible and reliable.

You should also have a certain level of strength and fitness to carry bags and work long shifts.

Working conditions

You will work 40 hours a week on average. This will mainly be shifts of 12 hours and will include working at night, early mornings and weekends.

You may have a desk or an office, where you will use the telephone or computer, but you will spend the majority of your time on your feet in the reception area meeting and helping guests, or running errands within the establishment or around the local area on behalf of guests.

You may be required to lift heavy bags.

Usually your employer will provide you with a uniform.

Future prospects

Establishments may have formal progression routes and this may consist of moving up from a position as a porter to deputy head concierge, head concierge and then up again to front office management positions.

You may also transfer to another discipline within hospitality and even set up your own business.

You may travel abroad as there are international opportunities within certain establishments, such as hotels.

Qualifications and courses

ENTRY LEVEL 1

You do not need to have any academic qualifications to be a concierge. You will have an advantage if you have a basic ability in at least one foreign language.

To enter this profession you will usually start in a front of house role such as porter or receptionist and with experience you can progress to the role of concierge. Some establishments may provide a formal in-house training programme. Apprenticeship training schemes in hospitality may also be available.

You will learn and train as you work. This may include gaining knowledge of the establishment's policies for organising and setting up conferences, and techniques in waiting and room service.

Work experience in catering or hospitality will allow you to familiarise yourself with the daily responsibilities of a concierge.

Advantages/disadvantages

You will meet new people each day and will be responsible for a wide variety of guests or visitors and their requirements.

You may have to work long and unsociable hours.

Money guide

Your starting salary as a concierge can be from £12,000 a year.

As you gain experience over the years you can earn around £20,000 a year.

If you reach the position of head concierge of a four-five star establishment you could earn up to £25,000 or more.

Related opportunities

■ Butler p154
■ Customer Service Manager p486
■ Personal Assistant p51
■ Receptionist p54

Further information

Institute of Hospitality
Trinity Court, 34 West Street, Sutton, Surrey SM1 1SH
020 8661 4900; www.instituteofhospitality.org

People 1st
2nd Floor, Armstrong House, 38 Market Square, Uxbridge, UB8 1LH
01895 817000; www.people1st.co.uk

City& Guilds

www.cityandguilds.com/myperfectjob

FOOD SAFETY OFFICER

What the work involves

- You will advise those working in catering/food premises by providing information on healthy eating and the presentation, preparation and storage of food for public consumption.

- Your role will be to investigate outbreaks of food-related illnesses and implement hazard warnings.

- Some of your work will include liaising with colleagues across the country and specialists in disease control and microbiology.

- If you work for a food business you will provide training and advice to other employees.

The type of person suited to this work

You should have an interest in both food and science. This job involves helping people to put into place safe ways to prepare, produce, store and package food. To do this, you will need a high level of knowledge about environmental health.

You will also need a good understanding of law and be confident – especially if you have to shut down a business. You should enjoy doing lots of different jobs at once and be flexible and happy to travel.

Some of your work might involve giving presentations to audiences that range from school children to company managers, so you should be happy talking to people of differing ages and backgrounds.

Working conditions

Although you will have an office, most of your time will involve visiting people in their workplaces or homes following up complaints and giving advice.

This could involve seeing things which could be smelly and unpleasant. You will spend time driving and will wear protective clothing such as masks, hair protection and boots. You might have to work evenings and weekends.

Future prospects

Due to the rise in mass manufacturing of food, take-aways and fast food outlets, the need for food safety officers has remained steady.

Outside of Scotland, most food safety officers begin as environmental health officers and specialise later. In Scotland, inspection and food hygiene is undertaken by registered food safety officers.

With experience you can progress to senior positions within food safety or return to other areas of environmental health or enter self-employment/consultancy.

Advantages/disadvantages

This job offers flexibility, variety, challenge and some travelling.

You might be responsible for closing down businesses.

Qualifications and courses

To become a food safety officer outside Scotland, you will need to train as an environmental health officer.

Candidates need a BSc or MSc in environmental science accredited by the Chartered Institute of Environmental Health (CIEH) or the Royal Environmental Health Institute of Scotland (REHIS). Entry to a first degree normally requires 2 A levels/3 H grades including a science subject, plus 5 GCSEs/S grades (A–C/1–3) including English, maths and science. Entry to the MSc requires a first degree in a relevant science or technology subject accredited by the CIEH or REHIS, or equivalent. Before qualifying as an environmental health officer, graduates must undertake a minimum of 48 weeks' practical training.

In England and Wales, at least 50% of the training must be with a local authority. Training can be incorporated into a first degree through a sandwich year, and entrants are often part-sponsored by local authorities.

Food safety officers working in Scotland must meet the requirements of the Scottish Food Safety Officers' Registration Board. Candidates for the Higher Certificates in Food Premises Inspection and Food Standards Inspection must have a minimum of an HND in food science or food technology.

Money guide

Future earnings depend on the size and type of organisation worked for, for some small companies it's £20,000–£25,000 per year. Within local authorities salaries range from £24,000–£31,000+ per year. Senior positions range from £35,000–£65,000 (for those with extensive experience and responsibility). If you are self-employed, daily rates range from £250 to £460 per day.

Related opportunities

- Environmental Health Practitioner/Officer p35
- Health and Safety Adviser p40
- Meat Hygiene Inspector p491

Further information

Chartered Institute of Environmental Health
Chadwick Court, 15 Hatfields, London, SE1 8DJ
020 7928 6006; www.ehocareers.org

Royal Environmental Health Institute of Scotland
3 Manor Place, Edinburgh, EH3 7DH
0131 225 6999, www.rehis.org

City&
Guilds

www.cityandguilds.com/myperfectjob

HOTEL/ACCOMMODATION ROOM ATTENDANT

What the work involves

- You will clean, tidy and prepare guest rooms to a high standard using cleaning materials and equipment. This could include cleaning bathroom and toilet areas and other parts of the hotel.

- Work involves stocking up levels of supplies as they are used and keeping records of any items of lost property left in rooms.

- Using a trolley or cart, you will move supplies of linen, towels and other items around the hotel.

- You will also check for maintenance problems or damage to hotel property.

The type of person suited to this work

Because much of the work involves cleaning areas of the site and moving supplies around, you will need a good level of physical fitness. You will also need to be well organised, enthusiastic and able to work quickly to get all your tasks completed on time. Although you will need good individual skills, team-working skills are also helpful.

You must have a polite and friendly manner, because you will meet hotel guests. In order to keep up standards of cleanliness for guests, you must have a good eye for detail. As you will be cleaning areas around guests' personal belongings, you should be very honest and trustworthy.

Working conditions

This is physical work so expect to be on your feet for much of the time, using cleaning equipment and pushing a cart with your equipment from room to room.

You will be working with cleaning fluids and other cleaning equipment on a daily basis, which could affect those with skin problems.

You will probably work shifts and it is sometimes possible to live in.

Future prospects

There are around 48,000 hotels in the UK employing 280,000 people. However, these figures do not include the other options in this area such as bed and breakfasts or leisure facilities. Larger employers provide staff with good training and development support. The number of top level hotels is increasing, and is expected to grow further as we get nearer to the London Olympics in 2012.

You could also work abroad, for an international hotel or in a resort. With experience, you could go on to work as an accommodation manager or housekeeper.

Advantages/disadvantages

In some jobs, you can live on-site and have some meals provided.

Qualifications and courses

There are no minimum entry requirements for this job. Some companies prefer to employ people aged over 18.

Employers provide on-the-job training when you first start work, usually under the supervision of a more experienced member of staff. This could include aspects such as safe lifting methods and furniture and carpet cleaning.

It may be useful to gain an NVQ/SVQ Level 2 in Housekeeping or Levels 1 and 2 in Cleaning Support Services.

You could undertake Apprenticeships/Skillseekers to enter this area of work.

To progess into accommodation manager or staff supervisor work, you could gain an NVQ/SVQ Level 3 in Hospitality Supervision.

There are opportunities to gain seasonal and holiday work. This type of job is also available on a part-time basis.

On the days when lots of guests are arriving and leaving this is very busy work.

Money guide

Earnings vary according to employer and location and may be based on hourly rates from the minimum rate up to £7–£8 per hour, which might include your room and meals. This can rise to between £10,000 and £12,000 per year with experience and training. Guests often leave tips for room attendants, which you may share with other staff or be allowed to keep yourself.

Related opportunities

- Cleaner p463
- Hotel Manager p149
- Hotel Porter p150
- Housekeeper p151

Further information

Institute of Hospitality
Trinity Court, 34 West Street, Sutton, Surrey, SM1 1SH
020 8661 4900; www.hcima.co.uk

People 1st
2nd Floor, Armstrong House, 38 Market Square, Uxbridge, UB8 1LH
01895 817000; www.people1st.co.uk

www.cityandguilds.com/myperfectjob

HOTEL MANAGER

What the work involves

- You will manage the services and staff of your hotel making sure that it is a successful business and gains new customers to make a profit.

- As the manager, you will be responsible for checking that the buildings and grounds of your hotel meet health and safety and other standards.

- Your work could also involve promoting and developing the hotel to increase numbers of customers.

- You could work in all types of hotel from a small private one up to large national or international chain.

The type of person suited to this work

As you will manage budgets and cash flow, you will need a good level of numeracy and the confidence to handle large quantities of money. Communication skills are very important as you will be organising staff and dealing with guests. You will be working in a sociable, busy environment so you will need to enjoy meeting lots of different people.

You should be well organised and able to work to targets. Strong customer care and good business skills are essential and because the working hours can be long, you will need to be flexible.

A knowledge of tourism is useful.

Working conditions

This work involves working long hours that include evenings and weekends. You might spend some of your evenings living-in so you can be on-site in case of emergencies. You are also likely to work shifts.

Some members of the public can be rude and aggresive so you will need to maintain a calm professional manner at all times.

You will also need to have a smart appearance at all times and might have to wear a uniform.

Future prospects

Hospitality is a developing sector and there are about 48,000 hotels of all kinds throughout the UK employing over 280,000 people. After a difficult period the hotel sector is showing signs of growth which should continue up until 2012. There is currently a strong demand for hotel management staff.

With experience, you could work overseas or progress from hotel management into other areas of a company such as human resources, finance and IT.

Advantages/disadvantages

Live-in accommodation within the hotel is offered with some jobs.

There are opportunities to travel and work overseas.

You can progress to be a manager of a large hotel relatively quickly.

Qualifications and courses

ENTRY LEVEL 2

No specific academic qualifications are required, as it is possible to enter the industry at a lower level and work your way up. You can study part time towards NVQ/SVQ Level 1 and 2 in Catering and Hospitality and Level 3 Supervisory Management.

Apprentices undertake on-the-job training and work towards NVQ/SVQ Level 1 and 2 in Catering and Hospitality and Level 3 Supervisory Management.

It is possible to join with previous hotel experience and through attending fast-track training schemes. Knowledge of a second language can be useful.

The Institute of Hospitality (formerly the Hotel and Catering International Management Association) offers a selection of courses for staff in specific roles.

Many entrants to this profession have a degree, HNC/D or postgraduate qualification, and enter as management trainees. Relevant degree subjects include Hospitality Management and Hotel and Catering Management.

Money guide

Salaries will depend on the size, reputation and location of the hotel in which you work. London and the south-east of England pay the highest.

As an assistant trainee manager you could earn £12,000–£15,000 per year. As trainee manager you could earn £14,000–£18,000 per year.

An experienced manager could earn anything from £20,000 to £50,000 with salaries of £100,000+ possible for the largest London hotels.

Related opportunities

- Bar Manager/Licensee/Publican p140
- Catering/Restaurant Manager p141
- Holiday Centre Worker/Manager p392
- Housekeeper p151

Further information

Institute of Hospitality
Trinity Court, 34 West Street, Sutton, Surrey, SM1 1SH
020 8661 4900; www.hcima.co.uk

Springboard UK
3 Denmark Street, London, WC2H 8LP
020 7497 8654; www.springboarduk.org.uk

City&
Guilds

www.cityandguilds.com/myperfectjob

HOTEL PORTER

What the work involves

- As a porter, you will greet hotel guests, answer the phone, take reservations and deal with general enquiries.

- You will also be responsible for moving guests' luggage to and from rooms.

- If you work as a night porter, you will look after the security and safety of the hotel site.

- As a head porter in a large hotel, you will be responsible for a team of porters that will include night, conference and kitchen porters.

The type of person suited to this work

As you will be working with hotel guests, you will need good customer-care skills and a smart appearance. Good communication skills and an ability to work as part of a busy team are also important.

Because you will be required to undertake duties as and when required, you will need a flexible and enthusiastic attitude. Being responsible for the security of the hotel site and guests' belongings means that you must be aware of security issues and be honest and reliable. As the work regularly includes lifting and carrying, you will need a good level of physical fitness. The ability to drive is useful.

Working conditions

This work can be physically demanding as you will spend a lot of time on your feet. Even though you will be doing a lot of physical work, you will need to keep up a smart appearance and may have to wear a uniform.

You could work shifts or standard hours. You may live in and possibly be on call. If you work as a night porter you will work throughout the evening which can affect your personal life.

Future prospects

There are many opportunities to work as a porter in hotels all over the country. You could also gain part-time or seasonal portering work to suit you. You could also work in portering roles abroad.

Smaller hotels tend to employ one porter so you would need to move to larger hotels if you want to progress, so being mobile can be helpful. In larger companies, you could work towards a job as a head porter or a reception-based role.

Advantages/disadvantages

In some hotels, you would be able to live in on-site.

This job can fit educational commitments by offering seasonal opportunties.

This is a job which provides the opportunity to meet many different people.

Some hotels prefer to employ mature individuals.

Qualifications and courses

There are no minimum entry requirements for this job although some employers prefer individuals with a good general education.

Communication skills and confidence with numbers are useful.

A driving licence and experience of driving a car can be helpful. Some employers prefer individuals to be over 18 years of age as you may be required to serve alcohol.

Many hotels will provide training to new staff, whether or not they have previous experience. This is usually gained over a few weeks or longer, under the supervision of a more experienced member of staff.

It is possible to gain qualifications whilst working, including the NCFE Level 2 Certificate in Customer Service for Hospitality, NVQs Level 1 and 2 in Front Office, or SVQ Level 1 in Porter Service.

You could undertake an Apprenticeship/Skillseekers to enter this area of work.

With experience, it is possible to progress to working as Head Porter.

Money guide

Salary levels vary according to the type of hotel you work for and geographic location. When starting you can earn around £11,000 per year.

This can rise to £12,000–£15,000 with experience. Head Porters in large hotels could earn up to £22,000. You can also earn more through tips from guests.

Related opportunities

- Concierge p146
- Hotel/Accommodation Room Attendant p148
- Housekeeper p151
- Receptionist p54

Further information

Institute of Hospitality
Trinity Court, 34 West Street, Sutton, Surrey, SM1 1SH
020 8661 4900; www.hcima.co.uk

People 1st
2nd Floor, 38 Market Square, Uxbridge, UB8 1LH
0870 060 2550, www.people1st.co.uk

Caterer.com
Holden House, 57 Rathbone Place, London, W1T 1JU
020 7572 4290; Sales@Caterer.com; www.caterer.com

City&
Guilds

www.cityandguilds.com/myperfectjob

HOUSEKEEPER

What the work involves

- Working in hotels, conference centres and other sites you will be responsible for a high standard of cleanliness and hygiene at all times in areas such as bedrooms and meeting rooms.

- You will manage a housekeeping budget and oversee staff salaries.

- You will also manage a team of room attendants and other housekeeping staff. This includes organising work rotas and allocating staff duties.

- You may carry out staff training in the safe use of equipment and company standards.

The type of person suited to this work

As you will be managing a team of staff, you will need strong management skills. You will be responsible for making sure that housekeeping staff work to a high standard, so good verbal communication skills are also important.

You will need to be confident in things such as explaining working procedures or training new staff. Good business sense and an ability to manage budgets are useful.

Working conditions

You will be on your feet for much of the time as this job involves a wide range of tasks. You will use a range of cleaning chemicals and equipment that could cause problems if you have skin problems. Although you will have an office, during your work you will visit many parts of the hotel. You might be expected to live in and work unsociable hours.

Future prospects

This is a key role within the hotel sector but is often overlooked. There is some scope for developing a career in management in this area but opportunities do not come up often and you will have to work your way from junior or deputy housekeeper to senior housekeeper. In larger hotels, you could go on to a role in head office, in areas such as human resources or training.

International companies could provide the opportunity to work overseas. With enough experience, you could go on to own and run a hotel.

Advantages/disadvantages

There is a lack of promotional opportunities as people stay in their jobs for many years.

You will have to work some unsociable hours, which could affect your personal life.

Some larger hotel and leisure companies provide leisure and restaurant discounts to staff.

Qualifications and courses

ENTRY LEVEL 1

It is possible to enter this career without academic qualifications. Many people work their way up from a job as a room attendant.

Good communication and organisation skills are important for this type of work.

Training usually takes place on the job. Candidates can work towards NVQs/SVQs or can study for qualifications through The Institute of Hospitality, including Leisure and Tourism (Level 3), the Diploma in Management for Hospitality, Leisure and Tourism (Level 4) or the Certificate in Management for Hospitality.

Some people enter Housekeeping as trainees, otherwise A levels/H grades or HNCs/HNDs in Hospitality may be required.

Apprenticeships/Skillseekers placements may be available for those aged 16–24.

Money guide

A salary starting at £11,000 per year is usual for a junior housekeeper. This can rise to £14,500–£18,000 with experience. As housekeeper in a small hotel, you could get up to £28,000. Salaries up to £40,000 are possible for head housekeepers working in the largest London-based hotels.

Related opportunities

- Cleaner p463
- Hotel/Accommodation Room Attendant p148
- Hotel Manager p149
- Hotel Porter p150

Further information

People 1st
2nd Floor, 38 Market Square, Uxbridge, UB8 1LH
0870 060 2550; www.people1st.co.uk

Institute of Hospitality
Trinity Court, 34 West Street, Sutton, Surrey, SM1 1SH
020 8661 4900; www.hcima.co.uk

Springboard UK
3 Denmark Street, London, WC2H 8LP
020 7497 8654; www.springboarduk.org.uk

City& Guilds

www.cityandguilds.com/myperfectjob

KITCHEN ASSISTANT/ PORTER

What the work involves

- Kitchen assistants/porters prepare food, clean, wash-up equipment and undertake general kitchen duties for hotels, restaurants and other sites.

- You will prepare meals for customers quickly and to a high standard. You will also prepare the kitchen before cooking and clean it afterwards.

- You will be required to move heavy equipment and might have to transport material by car.

- You might also assist the chef to plan menus and check food and drink stock levels.

The type of person suited to this work

Kitchens can be hot and hectic environments, therefore it is essential to have good team working, communication and multi-tasking skills to ensure the smooth running of the operation.

You should have the ability to remain calm under pressure as well as good time-keeping skills, stamina, flexibility and enthusiasm.

A good knowledge of food safety, health and hygiene are important for this work, as you will be preparing food for customers and will have to keep the kitchen areas clean. You should also have a high standard of personal cleanliness and a tidy appearance.

Working conditions

The majority of kitchen jobs are part-time and split shifts are common. You will work unsociable hours and on weekends.

You will carry out most or all of your work in kitchens, which can be noisy, hot and crowded. You will spend a lot of time on your feet undertaking a range of tasks, sometimes using potentially dangerous kitchen equipment.

You will work to a high standard of hygiene, and will be required to wear protective clothing and, in some cases, a company uniform.

Future prospects

There are about 400,000 kitchen assistants in the UK and demand is high for people with the right attitude and practical skills. You could work in a wide range of food preparation organisations and settings, however a larger company might facilitate career progression or movement to different departments.

With experience, you could work as an assistant chef and then, with further experience or qualifications, go on to be a head chef.

Advantages/disadvantages

Some employers provide subsidised accommodation and free meals.

There are many options to gain this type of work on a part-time, flexible basis.

Qualifications and courses

There are no minimum qualifications. Previous catering or kitchen experience and the basic food hygiene certificate can be useful. Employers normally provide training in basic cookery techniques, food hygiene and manual lifting and handling. This is usually with the support of a more experienced member of staff.

You could undertake Apprenticeships/Skillseekers opportunities in this area of work.

You may also receive on-the-job training, which can lead to qualifications such as NVQ/SVQ Level 1 in Hospitality or NVQ/SVQ Level 2 in Food Processing.

You can take general catering courses, which include NVQ/SVQ Levels 1 and 2 in Food Preparation and Cooking or Food and Drink Service. You can also take a City & Guilds certificate in Food Preparation before you start work, or whilst in work. In Scotland the SQA National Qualification in Health and Food Technology is available.

You will be required to work long shifts at unsociable times, such as evenings and weekends.

This work can be physically demanding.

Money guide

Earnings vary according to the size, reputation and location of your employer.

You could be required to work part-time, from 10 hours up to 25 hours a week, in which case your salary will be pro rata.

Annual salaries for working a 40 hour week range from the national minimum wage of £9,500 for those with limited or no experience, to £16,000 per year.

Related opportunities

- Chef/Sous Chef p143
- Kitchen Supervisor p153
- Housekeeper p151
- Waiter/Waitress p154

Further information

Institute of Hospitality
Trinity Court, 34 West Street, Sutton SM1 1SH
020 8661 4900; www.hcima.co.uk

People 1st
2nd Floor, 38 Market Square, Uxbridge UB8 1LH
0870 060 2550; www.people1st.co.uk

City&
Guilds

www.cityandguilds.com/myperfectjob

KITCHEN SUPERVISOR/ MANAGER

What the work involves

- Kitchen supervisors are experienced, trained chefs who supervise the running of a professional kitchen.

- You will hire, train and manage a team of chefs and other kitchen staff.

- You will plan menus, order ingredients, oversee food preparation, presentation and quality control and contact suppliers to place orders and negotiate prices.

- You will work closely with chefs, suppliers, catering companies and other clients to produce high quality food within budget and for a profit. You will also be responsible for upholding the highest health and safety standards, ensuring that the kitchen, and all kitchen equipment, is in good condition.

The type of person suited to this work

As you will be fully immersed in the food industry you should be passionate about cooking and all aspects of food preparation.

You should have excellent verbal and written communication skills as you will have to delegate tasks to a team of chefs, resolve disputes, negotiate prices, keep records of accounts and stay in control of a hectic work environment.

You should have a certain level of fitness to keep up with, and maintain amongst your team, a high-energy environment. You must adhere to and impose very strict health and safety procedures and standards of hygiene.

Working conditions

You will work an average of 40 hours per week, including shift work, split shifts and overtime. This can include weekends and holidays. Hours may be more regular in industrial catering.

Your working environment will be hot and cramped and very busy. You will be required to wear overalls, an apron and hat to ensure that food is not contaminated.

You will be standing for most of the time, and may lift heavy items.

You may have a small office in which to carry out paperwork and other tasks.

Future prospects

As a kitchen supervisor you may progress to a larger kitchen, be promoted to general manager or into head office management posts. These promotions may involve greater responsibility and more staff.

You may wish to take further training opportunities such as management qualifications.

You may become self employed if you set up an independent or franchise restaurant.

Qualifications and courses

To become a kitchen supervisor you will need to have significant experience as a fully trained chef.

To become a chef you will usually begin in a training role as a commis chef or kitchen assistant. These positions do not require any academic qualifications but relevant qualifications, such as a GCSE in food technology, may be helpful.

Many employers seek candidates with previous experience or NVQs, Level 1 or 2 in catering.

You can take a BTEC Introductory or First Certificate/ Diploma in Hospitality to increase your skills.

HNCs/HNDs, degrees or postgraduate qualifications in hospitality or catering will help you to learn about the industry and may even provide work placements where you will learn on the job.

Advantages/disadvantages

Working with a team in a fast-paced kitchen can be exciting.

Your hours may be long, stressful and very tiring.

Money guide

You may have management tasks as a chef de partie and earn from £14,000 to £23,000 a year.

In a supervising or management role in a kitchen you can earn between £18,000 and £25,000 a year.

With experience you can earn from £25,000 to over £45,000 as a professional kitchen manager.

Related opportunities

- Bar Manager p140
- Catering Manager p141
- Chef p143
- Hotel Manager p149

Further information

Institute of Hospitality
Trinity Court, 34 West Street, Sutton, Surrey, SM1 1SH
020 8661 4900; www.instituteofhospitality.org

People 1st
2nd Floor, Armstrong House, 38 Market Square, Uxbridge, UB8 1LH
01895 817000; www.people1st.co.uk

www.cityandguilds.com/myperfectjob

WAITING STAFF

What the work involves

Waiter/waitress

- You will take food orders from customers and provide meals, through table or counter service.

- You will provide accurate bills for meals and take payment from customers. Before and during your shift you will probably have to keep the eating area clean and prepare tables for customers.

Butler

- You will work in a private household where you will be responsible for arranging travel and security, providing and serving food and welcoming visitors.

- You will usually work within a wealthy household, including those of famous celebrities or royalty.

Sommelier

- You will be responsible for the provision of wines or other alcoholic beverages such as spirits.

- You will be expected to attend tastings and to design a wine list or cocktail menu.

- It is important to understand how beverages complement food in order to aid customer selection. You will need to serve beverages correctly at the expected temperature.

The type of person suited to this work

Waiter/waitress

As you will be working with the public, you should possess a polite attitude, a neat appearance and good customer service skills.

You may have to explain parts of the menu to customers, so an interest in food and drink is useful.

You will need a good memory and communication skills to take food orders correctly from customers and pass them on to kitchen staff. You should be happy to work as part of a team.

The ability to work with numbers and deal with cash is important. You must work to a high standard of health and hygiene at all times.

Butler

In addition to the above skills, you should be very well presented, honest and reliable. Your employers will expect you to be dedicated, loyal and completely trustworthy as you will be responsible for their day-to-day security and their home when the family is away.

Sommelier

It is essential to be enthusiastic about wines and have an interest in food. You should understand tasting notes and demonstrate a thorough knowledge of wines and beverages from all over the world.

Working conditions

Waiter/waitress

This role includes shift work and you will have to work unsociable hours, including evenings and weekends.

It is essential to have lots of energy for this role as you will be on your feet for most of the time, carrying heavy plates and dishes.

Most waiting staff service a number of tables at once and have to remember different customer requests. It is important to have the ability to remain calm in the face of customer complaints.

You will be required to wear a uniform and may be exposed to a hot, noisy kitchen environment. You will be expected to work to a high standard of cleanliness at all times

Butler

You will probably work within luxurious surroundings in the UK or abroad and will normally live in and have your own quarters.

You may be required to stay in and care for the home whilst your employer is away, and you may also escort them overseas and travel extensively.

Sommelier

You will probably wear a uniform and work shifts, including weekends and evenings until the early hours of the morning.

You will spend most of your time front of house and should be energetic and have high hygiene standards.

You may have the opportunity to travel domestically and internationally to attend tastings.

Future prospects

Waiter/waitress

The hospitality industry is growing in the UK, with further expansion predicted. As a result there is a strong demand for waiting staff with good customer service skills and experience in the UK and overseas.

With experience, you could become junior or head waiter. Larger employers such as hotel chains increasingly provide formal training and support for staff, and may allow inter-departmental movements.

Butler

Opportunities to become a butler are increasing. You are more likely to get a job if you are willing to be flexible and take on other responsibilities, such as those of a personal assistant, or provide some childcare services. Many catering firms provide butler services and there is demand from contract caterers, hotels and financial institutions.

Many of the jobs are overseas and the most successful butlers are willing to travel.

Sommelier

There are a growing number of opportunities to work in a variety of outlets in the UK and abroad. An increasing number of women are entering the profession.

With experience it is possible to progress to a higher managerial position in the hospitality industry or start your own business in the wine sector.

Advantages/disadvantages
Waiter/waitress

Catering staff are often provided with uniforms, free meals and on-site accomodation.

The role can be physically draining.

Butler

Your job could include lots of travelling and the opportunity to live in the luxurious homes of the rich and famous.

This job can affect your personal life as it is difficult to be off duty.

Sommelier

You may have the opportunity to travel within the UK and abroad.

Working long and unsociable hours can affect your personal life.

Money guide
Waiter/waitress

Salaries will depend on the location, size and reputation of your employer. Starting out you can expect around £10,000 per year. With experience this rises to £14,000.

If you become a section head, or sommelier, this will increase to £19,000–£25,000+.

In most jobs you would receive tips from customers in addition to your salary.

Butler

Your salary will depend on your experience and your employer. Starting salaries are around £15,000 per year and this can increase to between £20,000 and £45,000 with experience. The most successful can achieve £75,000.

In addition, you will be provided with free accommodation and meals.

Sommelier

Salaries will depend on the location, size and reputation of the organisation you work for. Starting out you can expect around £13,000 per year, with experience this rises to £30,000.

A head sommelier could earn £40,000+

Earnings can be increased with tips and bonuses. Live-in accommodation and free meals may also be provided.

Related opportunities

- Cruise Ship Purser/Steward p601
- Housekeeper p151
- Kitchen Assistant/Porter p152
- Kitchen Supervisor/Manager p153

Qualifications and courses
Waiter/waitress

ENTRY LEVEL 1

No minimum qualifications are required to enter this profession. However key skills in communication and numeracy are important.

It is possible to gain NVQs/SVQs Levels 1 & 2 in catering and hospitality. You could also work on a part-time basis towards NVQs/SVQs in food and drink service Level 1 & 2. Further on in your career, you could study for an NVQ/SVQ in food and drink service or hospitality supervision at Level 3.

Higher profile employers may require staff with experience in specialist areas such as fine dining and silver service. Some employers would train you in these areas and The Academy of Food and Wine Service provides short courses.

Butler

No formal qualifications are required to enter this profession, however hospitality experience is essential. Qualifications in general hospitality and catering, such as BTEC Awards, are well regarded.

It is possible to attain a City & Guilds Level 2 Diploma for butlers as well as NVQs in food and drink service at Level 2 and hospitality supervision at Level 3.

Some large institutions such as hotel chains provide formal training.

You will probably need a driving licence and a second language may be useful.

Sommelier

There are no minimum qualifications but you must be 18 years or over to serve alcohol. Bar or restaurant experience is also useful.

It is possible to gain knowledge certificates with the Wine & Spirit Education Trust (WSET) from the Level 1 Foundation Certificate in wines to a Level 5 Honours Diploma.

NVQs/SVQs are also available in food and drink service.

Further information

Institute of Hospitality
Trinity Court, 34 West Street, Sutton SM1 1SH
020 8661 4900; www.hcima.co.uk

Springboard UK
3 Denmark Street, London WC2H 8LP
020 7497 8654; www.springboarduk.org.uk

Wine & Spirit Education Trust (WSET)
International Wine & Spirit Centre
39–45 Bermondsey Street, London SE1 3XF
020 7089 3800; www.wset.co.uk

City& Guilds

www.cityandguilds.com/myperfectjob

Catering and Hospitality

CRCI: C
CLCI: IC

Computers and IT

This sector is still fairly new and so it is expanding all the time, creating new jobs for a whole range of people. You may have a mathematical brain or a real creative ability – or a bit of both! Essentially, you must be passionate about computers to consider working in this sector. You need to keep right up to date with the latest technologies and IT developments as well as people's tastes, interests and hobbies to enjoy working in this industry.

In this section we look at the following jobs:

For similar jobs to the ones found in this section have a look at *Administration, Business, Office Work and Financial Services* on page 15 and *Retail Sales and Customer Services* starting on page 477.

Computers and IT

CRCI: D
CLCI: CAV

BUSINESS ANALYST

What the work involves

- You will meet with your clients to find out how their businesses work and what they want to achieve with ICT.

- Making suggestions about the types of technology that could be used to improve clients' profitability and efficiency will also be part of your job.

- It will be your responsibility to produce a brief for the project to assist colleagues, such as software developers, in designing the best systems solution.

- You may also train staff to use the new system.

The type of person suited to this work

Your understanding of how businesses work is the key to being a successful business analyst – you will be aware of the need to balance costs with solutions.

You will also need to be a good negotiator, able to influence managers who may not understand how the new solutions or products you are suggesting can benefit their businesses.

Excellent communication skills are crucial because you will need to put across your ideas in meetings and in written reports.

You will also need a strong knowledge of what is available in the technology market and how it works in order to develop project briefs

Working conditions

You will spend time at your office base, meeting and working with other members of the project team. It is likely that your job will also involve travelling to meet clients at all stages of the project and you may be away from home for several days at a time.

Although your hours will be usually Monday to Friday, when projects are near to completion you will need to work some evenings and during weekends.

Future prospects

Employers include specialist ICT consultants, software houses and computer companies.

There is a growing market for ICT analysts with the right combination of skills and talents. Analysts with e-commerce technology skills and experience are in particular demand, due to the continued growth of internet use in business.

Progression is possible into senior analyst jobs and on to project management or consultancy work.

Advantages/disadvantages

You can get a real sense of satisfaction from producing successful solutions that transform a business.

There often has to be a trade-off between the solution you would like to recommend and the limitations put down by your client who has a tight budget.

Qualifications and courses

ENTRY 4 LEVEL

You may need a degree, Foundation degree or HNC/D in a relevant subject, for example e-business/commerce, accountancy, business or computer science to enter this job.

A sponsored degree from e-skills – information technology management for business – is available. This is focused on learning through project work in compact teams with external mentors from sponsoring organisations such as BT, CA, Ford, Fujitsu, Hewlett Packard, IBM, Morgan Stanley and Norwich Union.

The normal minimum entry requirements for degrees are 2 A levels/3 H grades and 5 GCSEs/S grades (A–C/1–3), and for Foundation degrees or HNC/Ds, 1 A level/2 H grades and 3 GCSEs/S grades (A–C/1–3). Maths may be a required subject.

Another funded route that may be on offer in your area is the Higher Apprenticeship in IT. This leads to a full Honours degree in addition to vocational, technical and Key Skills qualifications and work experience.

The new 14–19 Diploma in IT is available at Levels 1–3 and focuses on competencies relevant to IT professional work. Level 3 is equivalent to A levels.

Money guide

£18,000–£25,000 per year is usual for starting salaries. This can rise to £25,000–£45,000 with experience. Senior business analysts can earn £60,000 or more. Additional benefits may include profit sharing, performance-related pay and a car.

Related opportunities

- Internet/Web Professional p167
- Software Developer/Programmer p170
- Systems Analyst p171
- Technical Sales Specialist p172

Further information

British Computer Society
North Star House, North Star Avenue, Swindon, Wiltshire, SN2 1FA
01793 417424; www.bcs.org

Institute for the Management of Information Systems
5 Kingfisher House, New Mill Road, Orpington, Kent, BR5 3QG
0700 002 3456; www.imis.org.uk

e-skills UK (Sector Skills Council for information technology, telecommunications and contact centres)
1 Castle Lane, London, SW1E 6DR
020 7963 8920; www.e-skills.com

COMPUTER ENGINEER / SCIENTIST

What the work involves

- Working as an expert, you will be developing the solutions and products for tomorrow's computer industry.

- You may work as a researcher in industry or in an academic institution.

- You may be working as a hardware research engineer or a programming specialist developing fifth-generation artificial intelligence languages.

- You will use facts, data measurements, tools and methodologies to research and build solutions in a logical manner.

The type of person suited to this work

You will need technical, practical and creative ability. It will be useful if you write your own programs or have built your own computer system.

You should be an excellent problem-solver, able to use information to find solutions. You will need to be able to anticipate problems and work out ways to prevent them.

You must have enough patience to be able to produce accurate work when your deadline is close and your tests are not going well.

Your teamwork and communication skills should be strong as you will be working with a project team. At higher levels you will be giving presentations or lectures.

Working conditions

You may be based in a laboratory, a research and development unit, or a workshop.

At project management level you may travel nationally and internationally to meetings and conferences. You will work a 37- to 40-hour week but you will need to be flexible and put in extra hours at key times.

Future prospects

There is a strong demand for computer scientists in many sectors, including academia, government research, computer manufacturing, software development and electronics and telecommunications.

There is a particularly strong need for talented computer engineers or scientists who are both technical and creative.

You will start work as a junior member of a project team. With experience you could move into lecturing or project management.

Advantages/disadvantages

Your team's work could make the headlines. New products and cutting-edge research, such as the building of world-class supercomputers, are of international interest.

Qualifications and courses

The usual entry qualification is a degree or a Master's in a relevant subject, for example computer science, artificial intelligence or electronic engineering. Some employers will expect a doctorate.

The normal minimum entry requirements for degrees are 2 A levels/3 H grades and 5 GCSEs/S grades (A–C/1–3). Required subjects usually include maths and physics.

Should you have no formal qualifications, there may be the opportunity of an Apprenticeship in IT within your area. Otherwise Access courses are generally available if you wish to progress to a degree.

Training programmes are on offer for graduate entrants from any discipline. Engineers must ensure their technical knowledge is always up to date by completing the Continuing Professional Development course.

Computer engineers can gain professional engineering qualifications. To become an incorporated engineer you will need an engineering degree (BEng) plus experience and a professional review. To become a chartered engineer you will need a Master's degree in engineering (MEng), plus experience and a professional review.

The new 14–19 Diploma in IT is available at Levels 1–3 and focuses on competencies relevant to IT professional work. Level 3 is equivalent to 3.5 A levels.

Solutions to problems do not happen quickly. It can be really frustrating to retest hundreds of times and still not get the result you are looking for.

Money guide

Starting salaries are usually from £18,000 to £25,000 per year. With experience you can expect to get between £25,000 and £35,000. At senior levels you can earn between £40,000 and £60,000+.

Related opportunities

- Computer Hardware Engineer p161
- Software Developer/Programmer p170

Further information

British Computer Society
North Star House, North Star Avenue, Swindon SN2 1FA
01793 417424; www.bcs.org

e-skills UK
1 Castle Lane, London, SW1E 6DR
020 7963 8920; www.e-skills.com

City&
Guilds

www.cityandguilds.com/myperfectjob

COMPUTER GAMES DESIGNER

What the work involves

- Using storyboards and flowcharts, you will present your ideas for a new computer game to a panel for acceptance or rejection.

- If it is accepted you will manage all aspects of the playing experience, from scripts to programming and from animation to sound effects and music.

- You will work with a team of specialists, such as programmers and graphic artists, to produce a prototype.

- Once a computer games play-tester has picked out any flaws and if the panel think it is a winner, it will go into full development by your team.

The type of person suited to this work

To be a top-class computer games designer you will need creativity and an ability to see how ideas could work together. You will also have a passion for and knowledge of the computer games market.

Your ideas need to be technically viable and cost-effective, so you will need a broad understanding of computers and games consoles, multimedia and the internet.

You will need to be a team player to work with specialists such as graphic designers to make sure that their part of the project fits in with your vision of the final version of the game.

Working conditions

You will be mainly based in an office or studio working with other members of the games project team.

Although your hours will be usually Monday to Friday, when there is a deadline for your game you will need to work some evenings and weekends.

Future prospects

Employers are specialised companies producing games for PCs or games consoles such as the Xbox or PS2. This is a growth area as the computer games industry is a profitable global business.

It is a popular career choice so entry is competitive. You will need to be talented and may need to get experience in games programming or testing first.

There may be opportunities to work abroad. Progression is possible into management or consultancy work.

Advantages/disadvantages

Games designers say it is enjoyable creating entertainment for a living. It is a young business and the rewards can be high. It can be tough when a game does not sell or has poor reviews. It is stressful producing a game for a timed release such as the Christmas market.

Qualifications and courses

The computer games industry generally requires relevant experience. Many employers will ask for a degree, Foundation degree or HND plus a portfolio of game projects or design.

Useful degree subjects include computer games technology, computer arts, or computer animation. At least 2 A levels/3 H grades or equivalent may be required or preferred for entry to related degrees.

A funded route that may be on offer in your area is the Higher Apprenticeship in IT. This leads to a full Honours degree in addition to vocational, technical and Key Skills qualifications and work experience.

If you are aged 16–24 you could enter IT work directly through an Apprenticeship/Skillseekers and work for the qualifications needed for higher-level IT work.

Training programmes are on offer for graduate entrants from any discipline.

The new 14–19 Diploma in IT is available at Levels 1–3 and focuses on competencies relevant to IT professional work. Level 3 is equivalent to 3.5 A levels.

Money guide

£12,000–£25,000 per year is usual for starting/training salaries in this area of work. This can then rise to £28,000–£35,000 with more experience. £35,000–£55,000 is possible for senior games designers to earn. Additional benefits usually include profit sharing and performance-related pay or a bonus.

Related opportunities

- Interactive Media Designer p166
- Internet/Web Professional p167
- Software Developer/Programmer p170
- Website Designer p174

Further information

British Computer Society
North Star House, North Star Avenue, Swindon, Wiltshire, SN2 1FA
01793 417424; www.bcs.org

Institute of IT Training
Westwood House, Westwood Business Park, Coventry, CV4 8HS
0845 006 8858; www.iitt.org.uk

City&
Guilds

www.cityandguilds.com/myperfectjob

COMPUTER HARDWARE ENGINEER

What the work involves

- You will be responsible for installing and repairing computer hardware – the computer itself rather than the applications or software.

- To find out more about the fault you will use a set of diagnostic CDs.

- When repairing a fault or upgrading a machine you will open up the computer and use tools to install upgrades or replace faulty parts.

- You may specialise in installing new computer systems and training the people who use them.

The type of person suited to this work

You will need both technical and practical ability. Building your own computer system and repairing friends' machines is something you will probably already be doing in your spare time.

You should be a good problem-solver. You will need to be able to identify what is wrong and put it right quickly as your customer may be losing money while you do the repair.

Your verbal and listening skills should be strong because you will have to find out what is wrong and then explain what needs repairing to the computer user who may have no technical knowledge.

Often working on your own you will also need to be reliable and able to work unsupervised.

Working conditions

You may be based in a workshop, or be repairing hardware for one firm, but many technicians travel to customers' premises or homes. You may need to drive a vehicle to each job and cover a large area of the UK. You will work a 37- to 40-hour week, but as businesses need major work to be done on evenings and weekends you will have to work shifts or be on a call-out rota.

Future prospects

Computer hardware technicians are employed by computer manufacturers, computer service firms and by a range of large organisations such as banks, hospitals and universities.

This is a stable area of work because computers need regular repairs or upgrades to improve performance or capacity.

Promotion could be to team leader or supervisor and then on to senior engineer. Self-employment as a freelance/consultant engineer is possible.

Advantages/disadvantages

There is lots of variety as few problems are the same. It is rewarding to get a computer up and running again. Your customer may have a service agreement requiring you to put the problem right in a fixed period of time, which can be stressful.

Qualifications and courses

ENTRY LEVEL 2

A degree, Foundation degree or HND/C is sometimes required to work as a computer hardware technician, but previous experience in other areas can be just as important.

Useful degree subjects include computer systems engineering or electronic engineering.

The normal minimum entry requirements for degrees are 2 A levels/3 H grades and 5 GCSEs/S grades (A–C/1–3). For technical degrees, maths, technology or a science subject may be required.

If you are aged 16–24 you could enter computer engineering work directly through Apprenticeships/Skillseekers and work for the qualifications needed for higher-level work. You will need a driving licence to work for the majority of employers.

Training programmes are on offer for graduate entrants from any discipline. Engineers must ensure their technical knowledge is always up to date by completing the Continuing Professional Development course.

The new 14–19 Diploma in IT is available at Levels 1–3 and focuses on competencies relevant to IT professional work. Level 3 is equivalent to 3.5 A levels.

Money guide

When you begin work as a computer hardware technician you can expect your starting/trainee salaries to be from £13,500 to £18,000 per year. This could then increase once you have experience to around £19,000–£25,000. Salaries can rise to between £35,000 and £40,000 at supervisory level. Additional benefits may include a car.

Related opportunities

- Computer Engineer/Scientist p159
- Computer Technical Support Person p164
- Software Developer/Programmer p170
- Telecommunications Technician p173

Further information

e-skills UK (Sector Skills Council for information technology, telecommunications and contact centres)
1 Castle Lane, London, SW1E 6DR
020 7963 8920; www.e-skills.com

Engineering Careers Information Service
SEMTA House, 14 Upton Road, Watford, Hertfordshire, WD18 0JT
0800 282167; www.enginuity.org.uk

Institute of IT Training
Westwood House. Westwood Business Park, Coventry, CV4 8HS
0845 006 8858; www.iitt.org.uk

COMPUTER HELPDESK ADVISER

What the work involves

■ You will answer telephone calls or emails from computer users who are having technical problems.

■ You will ask the customer to take certain actions to try to correct the fault.

■ You will log the query and give the customer a job number.

■ If the problem is too complex to sort out by phone or email you may arrange for a technician to repair faulty hardware or arrange delivery of a replacement software disk.

The type of person suited to this work

You should have lots of tact and patience. When people are impatient or angry they will think they have checked the basics, for example the wiring, but the problem may be caused by user error.

Your verbal and listening skills need to be good to be able to guide a customer to take the action they need to put a problem right.

You will need to enjoy a challenge as well as be able to think quickly and logically. To solve a problem you may have to move from idea to idea and approach it from different directions.

You will need to be keen to learn and keep up to date with your employer's new products.

Working conditions

You will be sitting in front of a screen wearing a headset to talk to customers. You may be based in a call centre with lots of activity and background noise.

Employers usually give frequent breaks from the screen for advisers to make the job less stressful.

You will work 37–40 hours a week usually in shifts often including weekend and evening work.

Future prospects

The main employers are computer hardware and software manufacturers and internet service providers who offer support to their customers.

Support work has grown rapidly in recent years, but helpdesks are sometimes sourced outside the UK by employers looking for lower costs.

This is a job with a high turnover as it is often used as a stepping stone to move into the competitive software industry.

Promotion to supervisory and management work is possible.

Advantages/disadvantages

You will get useful training in computers and software. It is rewarding to resolve a problem. Your work will be very closely monitored by managers. The job can be stressful because

Qualifications and courses

ENTRY 2 LEVEL

It may be possible to enter as a trainee or apprentice with GCSEs/S grades, including English, maths, science and IT. It is also possible to enter with an Applied A level or BTEC National qualification in IT or Computing.

Many people enter this career with no formal qualifications but with relevant computer knowledge and good customer service experience. However, employers generally prefer you to have a qualification such as a degree, HNC/HND in computing, BTEC National Diploma or C&G in IT Practitioners. A degree would be an advantage in entering a training scheme as a specialist.

You could also study for a Higher Apprenticeship in IT. This leads to a full Honours degree in addition to vocational, technical and Key Skills qualifications and work experience.

The Help Desk Institute offers recognised qualifications for people working in the sector. The Customer Support Specialist qualification is aimed at new entrants; the Help Desk Analyst qualification is for people with at least 9 months' experience; Service Desk Manager is available to people with 3–5 years' experience.

The new 14–19 Diploma in IT is available at Levels 1–3 and focuses on competencies relevant to IT professional work. Level 3 is equivalent to 3.5 A levels.

customers can be angry and frustrated by the time they ring you.

Money guide

When you start in this profession you can expect to be on £13,000–£16,000 as a starting/trainee salary. This can rise to £18,000–£23,000 once you have gained more experience in the industry. £30,000 and above is possible at supervisory level.

Related opportunities

■ Computer Technical Support Person p164
■ Database Operator p165
■ Computer Operator p163
■ Technical Sales Specialist p172

Further information

British Computer Society
North Star House, North Star Avenue, Swindon, Wiltshire, SN2 1FA
01793 417424; www.bcs.org

Institute of IT Training
Westwood House, Westwood Business Park, Coventry, CV4 8HS
0845 006 8858; www.iitt.org.uk

City& Guilds

www.cityandguilds.com/myperfectjob

COMPUTER OPERATOR

What the work involves

- ICT or computer operators work for organisations that operate a multi-user computer system to store, manage and present their data.

- Your main responsibility will be starting up, running, backing up data, closing down and cleaning your employer's multi-user computer system.

- You will be updating and running database programmes and tasks prepared by programmers or database managers.

- Routine recording and reporting of any errors you spot to your manager or ICT specialist will also be your responsibility.

The type of person suited to this work

Attention to detail and a responsible attitude are vital in this job. The data you enter needs to be accurate and if you do not spot errors they may lead to costly problems and delays.

Routine tasks such as backing up data, cleaning the equipment and putting the data in using a keyboard are central to this job, so you will need good keyboard skills and be practical and methodical.

You will also need to be good with figures as most databases have lots of data in number format.

The computer system you will be dealing with is complex and you will need to be keen to understand how both the hardware and software operate.

Working conditions

You will be working in an office, possibly in the same room as a noisy computer server. For long periods you will sit at your workstation. You will have to be aware of health concerns such as eye strain and your sitting position.

You will probably work office hours, Monday to Friday. You may have to work shifts.

Future prospects

Computer Operators work for large organisations using large multi-user databases. Examples include banks, retailers, universities, hospitals and government departments.

Job opportunities are decreasing. ICT systems are now usually networked and data put in by authorised computer users with support from a specialist database or network manager.

With experience and training, you may be able to gain promotion to technical support, database or network management.

Advantages/disadvantages

With extra study you can train up to database or network management level. This job is starting to disappear as content management programs become more user-friendly and more employees at all levels input data as one of their work tasks.

Qualifications and courses

You do not need specific entry qualifications for this job, but GCSEs/S grades (A–C/1–3) in such subjects as maths, English and IT are an advantage. Employers may prefer Customer Service skills.

Useful qualifications include BTEC National Awards in computer- and business-related subjects.

The Help Desk Institute (HDI) offers recognised qualifications for people with or without experience working in the sector.

If you are aged 16–24 you could enter IT work through an Apprenticeship/Skillseeker route. You would then work towards NVQs/SVQs Levels 2 or 3 in information technology.

Trainee computer operators can start as an Apprentice and develop skills as they work. The British Computer Society (BCS) offer professional qualifications for those who wish to improve their existing skills

Training is usually provided by employers on the job.

The new 14–19 Diploma in IT is available at Levels 1–3 and focuses on competencies relevant to IT professional work. Level 3 is equivalent to 3.5 A levels.

Money guide

Starting salaries are around £14,000–£18,000 per year as a Computer Operator. Once trained as an operator and with experience, you could earn around £25,000+. At managerial level an operator can earn between £30,000 and £50,000.

Related opportunities

- Computer Technical Support Person p164
- Database Operator p165
- Network Manager p169
- Secretary p60

Further information

British Computer Society
North Star House, North Star Avenue, Swindon, Wiltshire, SN2 1FA
01793 417424; www.bcs.org

e-skills UK
1 Castle Lane, London, SW1E 6DR
020 7963 8920; www.e-skills.com

Institute for the Management of Information Systems
5 Kingfisher House, New Mill Road, Orpington, Kent, BR5 3QG
0700 002 3456; www.imis.org.uk

City& Guilds

www.cityandguilds.com/myperfectjob

ENTRY
1
LEVEL

Computers and IT

CRCI: D
CLCI: CAV

Computers and IT

CRCI: D
CLCI: CAV

COMPUTER TECHNICAL SUPPORT PERSON

What the work involves

■ You will work for an organisation which has lots of ICT equipment, offering specialist technical support to its computer users.

■ You may install new systems and upgrades and train staff in their use.

■ Initially, you may try to resolve the problem by telephone or email, only going out to the user's workstation if necessary.

■ You will try to fix the problem but if the hardware is under guarantee you will call out the manufacturer's service engineer.

The type of person suited to this work

You should be interested in knowing how technology works. You may have tried building or upgrading a PC. You will need to be both technical and practical to resolve hardware or software problems.

You will also need to be a good communicator – able to explain technical stuff to users who may not be clear about what it means.

You need to cope well with stress and deadlines. You will be under pressure to get the problem sorted in the shortest possible time so that staff can get back to work. A keenness to keep learning and stay up to date is vital – you will be expected to be the expert.

Working conditions

You will probably be based in an office with a technical workshop attached.

Your employer may have several sites you need to travel between, sometimes in different parts of the UK.

You may have to work shifts to cover your employer's hours of operation, which may be 24/7, or to install or repair equipment outside office hours.

Future prospects

The main employers of computer support technicians are large organisations such as banks, retail chains, hospitals, airlines and universities, who are dependent on their large computer networks to be functional during working hours.

This is a growth area of work with increasing numbers of organisations becoming dependent on ICT to operate efficiently.

With experience, promotion could be to network manager/administrator or on to network development.

Advantages/disadvantages

If you take advantage of the training on offer, this broad-based job can be a stepping stone to jobs at a higher level in the ICT industry.

By the time you arrive at a colleague's workstation you will be under pressure to sort out their problem quickly.

Qualifications and courses

The majority of technical support staff are expected to have a degree with relevant work experience. Access courses are available for those with no qualifications or an alternative option is for those with little IT experience or more than 1 year's work experience to obtain qualifications from The Help Desk Institute (HDI).

It is possible for school-leavers to enter this work as trainees or via an Apprenticeship/Skillseekers.

Acceptable entry qualifications include BTEC National Diploma in IT, SQA National Certificate in IT or BSC Information Technology Management for Business. Some candidates enter with a degree or HNC/D in computing, computer science or a related subject.

Entrants are trained on the job, and may work towards further qualifications.

Some IT companies offer certification courses in their own products. The CompTIA (Computing Technology Industry Association) A+ Certificate is recognised by the industry as an entry-level qualification.

The new 14–19 Diploma in IT is available at Levels 1–3 and focuses on competencies relevant to IT professional work. Level 3 is equivalent to 3.5 A levels.

Money guide

£13,500–£17,000 per year is usual for starting/trainee salaries. This can rise to £18,000–£23,000 with experience. £40,000+ is possible at supervisory level. Additional benefits may include a car.

Related opportunities

■ Computer Hardware Engineer p161
■ Computer Helpdesk Adviser p162
■ Network Manager p169
■ Technical Sales Specialist p172

Further information

British Computer Society
North Star House, North Star Avenue, Swindon, Wiltshire, SN2 1FA
01793 417424; www.bcs.org

e-skills UK (Sector Skills Council for information technology, telecommunications and contact centres)
1 Castle Lane, London, SW1E 6DR
020 7963 8920; www.e-skills.com

Institute of IT Training
Westwood House, Westwood Business Park, Coventry, CV4 8HS
0845 006 8858; www.iitt.org.uk

DATABASE OPERATOR

What the work involves

- If lots of information needs to be stored with the capacity to search and access specific parts of the data, a database will be used. For example, a hospital uses a database to manage information about its patients.

- You would be responsible for making sure that your databases are accurate, accessible and secure.

- To keep the data secure you will issue staff with passwords, train users and back up the contents regularly.

- You may be responsible for setting up a new database.

The type of person suited to this work

Databases operate to give people the information they require to do their jobs, so you will need strong communication skills. You will be offering support to staff using the database and preparing reports and guidelines for managers and staff.

You should be a good negotiator. To train users to input or access a new or modified database you will need to be able to convince them the changes will benefit them.

To set up or develop a database you will need to be very technical with a high level of programming knowledge. You will also need to be a good listener, able to find out what the database users want the new design to achieve.

Working conditions

You will be based mainly in your own office although in some cases the work can be carried out away from the office base using laptops and broadband wireless technology.

Your employer may have several sites you need to travel between, sometimes in different parts of the UK.

You may have to be on-call to deal with problems outside your normal working hours.

Future prospects

The main employers of database managers are large organisations, such as banks and retailers. You could also work for a specialist ICT firm providing a complete database service to customers.

This is a growth area because increasing numbers of businesses are developing databases for their websites to allow customers to look at information about their goods online and then go on to buy them.

With experience, promotion could be to network development or into consultancy work.

Advantages/disadvantages

If you are methodical and analytical, you will enjoy the complex job of writing a new database. It can be frustrating when database users cause problems by not keeping their information up to date or leaving vital parts out.

Qualifications and courses

The usual entry qualification for this work is a degree, Foundation degree or HNC/D in a relevant subject, for example computer science, software development, operational research, e-commerce technology or maths. Other qualifications may be acceptable, such as BTEC National Diplomas and NVQs/SVQs.

The normal minimum entry requirements for degrees are 2 A levels/3 H grades and 5 GCSEs/S grades (A–C/1–3), and for Foundation degrees or HNC/Ds, 1 A level/2 H grades and 3 GCSEs/S grades (A–C/1–3). For technical degrees, maths/science may be required.

A funded route that may be on offer in your area is the Higher Apprenticeship in IT. This leads to a full Honours degree in addition to vocational, technical and Key Skills qualifications and work experience.

Entry without a degree may be possible if you have got significant programming experience and knowledge. Training programmes are on offer for graduate entrants from any discipline including the Graduate Professional Development Award (GPDA). Database managers may also take manufacturers' courses in particular operating systems/packages.

The new 14–19 Diploma in IT is available at Levels 1–3 and focuses on competencies relevant to IT professional work. Level 3 is equivalent to 3.5 A levels.

Money guide

£13,000–£25,000 per year is usual for starting salaries as a database operator. This can rise to £27,000–£35,000 once you have gained some experience. £50,000 and above is possible at supervisory level.

Related opportunities

- Computer Operator p163
- IT Trainer p168
- Network Manager p169
- Software Developer/Programmer p170

Further information

British Computer Society
North Star House, North Star Avenue, Swindon, Wiltshire, SN2 1FA
01793 417424; www.bcs.org

e-skills UK (Sector Skills Council for information technology, telecommunications and contact centres)
1 Castle Lane, London, SW1E 6DR
020 7963 8920; www.e-skills.com

Institute for the Management of Information Systems
5 Kingfisher House, New Mill Road, Orpington, Kent, BR5 3QG
0700 002 3456; www.imis.org.uk

Computers and IT

CRCI: D
CLCI: CAV

INTERACTIVE MEDIA DESIGNER

What the work involves

- You will help clients look at how they can use multimedia to improve their marketing, information or learning resources.

- You will work out the right medium to use, for example an interactive website or a virtual reality training program.

- Meeting to agree a solution, you will develop a brief and then create prototypes or simulations to show the customer your ideas.

- Your role will also involve planning, coordinating and overseeing the whole project as well as testing, integrating and, if needed, installing at the customer's site.

The type of person suited to this work

Your creative skills need to be outstanding for this job. Every project will be different and you will need the vision to be able to think about what a client wants to achieve with a multimedia project and then develop ideas to produce a solution.

You need to be good at working in a team and motivating others to achieve tight deadlines. This job is never done alone – you will be working with both artistic and technical colleagues, all trying to put your vision into practice.

You should have excellent presentation and communication skills, as you may need to bid against other designers to win contracts for new projects.

Working conditions

You will spend time working in an office at your workstation, but you will also be working with your project team and meeting customers.

You may have to travel regularly to clients, to meet and present your solutions to them.

Although your hours will be usually Monday to Friday, when you are preparing a bid or projects are near to completion you will need to put in extra hours.

Future prospects

Employers include specialist multimedia consultancies, internet service providers, e-learning specialists, software houses and hardware manufacturers.

Interactive media is a growth industry and designers who have an understanding of both the technical and creative sides of the industry are currently in demand.

Once experienced you could move into self-employment, or work on a contract or consultancy basis. You could also move into management or training.

Qualifications and courses

Entry is often by means of a degree, Foundation degree or HNC/D in a relevant subject.

The normal minimum entry requirements for degrees are 2 A levels/3 H grades and 5 GCSEs/S grades (A–C/1–3), and for Foundation degrees or HNC/Ds, 1 A level/two H grades and three GCSEs/S grades (A–C/1–3). For technical degrees, mathematics/science may be required.

A funded route, which may be on offer in your area, is the Higher Apprenticeship in IT. This leads to a full Honours degree in addition to vocational, technical and Key Skills qualifications and work experience.

Entry without a degree, Foundation degree or HNC/D usually requires practical experience in the field and a portfolio of relevant samples.

Training programmes are on offer for graduate entrants from any discipline including the Graduate Professional Development Award (GPDA). This offers training and accreditation to IT professionals working in the industry.

The new 14–19 Diploma in IT is available at Levels 1–3 and focuses on competencies relevant to IT professional work. Level 3 is equivalent to 0.5 A levels.

Advantages/disadvantages

This job uses cutting-edge technology and is a young, vibrant industry to work in. The pace of development means you will never be able to stand still. You will have to keep up to date and keep learning to stay on top of the game.

Money guide

£17,000–£25,000 per year is usual for starting salaries. The average salary for an experienced interactive media designer is £30,000+, more in London. Highly experienced, you could earn £50,000+. The more skills and experience you have to offer, the more you can earn.

Related opportunities

- Computer Engineer/Scientist p159
- Internet/Web Professional p167
- Software Developer/Programmer p170
- Website Designer p174

Further information

e-skills UK (Sector Skills Council for information technology, telecommunications and contact centres)
1 Castle Lane, London, SW1E 6DR
020 7963 8920; www.e-skills.com

British Interactive Multimedia Association
Briarlea House, Southend Road, Billericay, CM11 2PR
020 7436 8250; www.bima.co.uk

INTERNET/WEB PROFESSIONAL

What the work involves

- You may work in or supervise a team of staff who design, program and maintain the various pages that make up an Internet site.

- In a small company, you may be the programmer, designer and master/manager of the site.

- You may write content or develop a content management program for authorised staff to contribute material.

The type of person suited to this work

You should be the kind of person who always carefully checks their work. You will need to set up secure data entry checking systems and regularly test them for faults. If your shopping site's database is matching the wrong prices to the wrong goods, you will need to spot them and sort it out quickly.

You may have set up your own website or have helped maintain one for a group you belong to. Creative skills are important but you will have to make sure you do not make it difficult for customers to find the information they want. Strong communication skills are vital – you will be required to lead a project team at senior level.

Working conditions

You will be mainly office-based, using a computer to manage the site. You may have to move around your company's site to train, meet with managers and discuss site improvements. You will work a 37- to 40-hour week, normally Monday to Friday, but if you are working to maintain and support a 24/7 shopping site you will work shifts as part of a team to cover all hours.

Future prospects

Websites are big business, with growing numbers of organisations using them to share information, market themselves, sell goods or services and advertise jobs.

Employers of web professionals include web-based retailers, travel companies, the multimedia industry, local and central government and financial companies.

Promotion could be to project management level. A talented web professional could move into freelance or website development consultancy work.

Advantages/disadvantages

If you have got the right skills, this is an expanding market with high rewards on offer.

Being responsible for the internet window of your company can be stressful.

Money guide

£18,000–£22,000 per year is usual for starting salaries as an internet or web professional. This can rise to around £35,000

Qualifications and courses

The usual entry qualification for this work is a degree, Foundation degree or HNC/D in a relevant subject, such as e-business/commerce, e-systems design and technology, three-dimensional design, graphic design, computer science or other related areas.

A new sponsored degree from e-skills, information technology management for business, is available. This is focused on learning through project work in compact teams with external mentors from sponsoring organisations.

The normal minimum entry requirements for degrees are 2 A levels/3 H grades and 5 GCSEs/S grades (A–C/1–3), and for Foundation degrees or HNC/Ds 1 A level/2 H grades and 3 GCSEs/S grades (A–C/1–3).

Another funded route that may be on offer in your area is the Higher Apprenticeship in IT. This leads to a full Honours degree in addition to vocational, technical and Key Skills qualifications and work experience.

Training programmes are on offer for graduate entrants from any discipline, including the Graduate Professional Development Award (GPDA). This offers training and accreditation to IT professionals working in the industry. It includes e-skills, internet services delivery and industrial management and practice.

The new 14–19 Diploma in IT is available at Levels 1–3 and focuses on competencies relevant to IT professional work. Level 3 is equivalent to 3.5 A levels.

with experience. £40,000+ is possible for senior web managers with additional responsibilities. £50,000+ is achievable for project managers.

Related opportunities

- Database Operator p165
- Interactive Media Designer p166
- Network Manager p169
- Software Developer/Programmer p170

Further information

British Computer Society
North Star House, North Star Avenue, Swindon SN2 1FA; 01793 417424; www.bcs.org

e-skills UK
1 Castle Lane, London SW1E 6DR; 020 7963 8920; www.e-skills.com

British Interactive Multimedia Association
Briarlea House, Southend Road, Billericay CM11 2PR; 020 7436 8250; www.bima.co.uk

IT TRAINER

What the work involves

- IT trainers give people user skills, for example in applications such as Word, Excel or desktop-publishing packages but you may also train in advanced computer skills such as programming languages.

- Planning courses, preparing learning materials and setting up the computers ready for a session will all be involved.

- You will do presentations and network some materials. You will walk around the room to support individuals in your group.

- Evaluating what has been learned and changing future learning materials as required will also be part of your job.

The type of person suited to this work

The constant release of new ICT products guarantees a future for trainers but only if you are keen to stay up to date. You will need lots of self-discipline to do research and prepare learning materials.

As e-learning and virtual classroom technology expands, more learners are being taught over the internet. Therefore, you will need to be up to date with e-learning tools, technologies and processes.

This job is about helping others to learn. Whether you train face to face or by virtual technology, you will need strong interpersonal and communication skills. All learners are sensitive to criticism and need to be motivated and encouraged.

Working conditions

You may be based in a modern office training room or you may travel to clients' premises to train their staff on-site.

Although your hours will be usually Monday to Friday, you will have to prepare learning materials and keep up to date by working some evenings and weekends.

Future prospects

Employers such as hardware and software manufacturers, ICT consultancies, training organisations and colleges employ ICT trainers. There is a strong demand for trainers and there are currently over 60,000 ICT trainers in the UK.

This job is rarely a first job. Most trainers have gained experience in other areas of computing first.

Experienced ICT trainers can move into self-employment as consultants. Promotion into supervisory or management roles may be possible.

Advantages/disadvantages

You can get a real feeling of achievement when your learners succeed in understanding a difficult subject. This job can be

Qualifications and courses

To work as an IT trainer you need to first gain the relevant skills and experience in IT yourself.

Although no set qualifications are required, it may be an advantage to have a degree, Foundation degree or HNC/D in a relevant subject, for example computer science, e-business/commerce or software engineering.

The normal minimum entry requirements for degrees are 2 A levels/3 H grades and 5 GCSEs/S grades (A–C/1–3), and for Foundation degrees or HNC/Ds, 1 A level/2 H grades and 3 GCSEs/S grades (A–C/1–3).

You could enter this job without a degree if you have got significant experience and training in IT.

The Institute of IT Training is the certification awarding body for a range of courses in e-learning training skills offered by the Training Foundation.

You can qualify as an assessor by taking the Assessors Award. This would be needed to assess learners working towards NVQs/SVQs.

The new 14–19 Diploma in IT is available at Levels 1–3 and focuses on competencies relevant to IT professional work. Level 3 is equivalent to 3.5 A levels.

badly affected when the economy is depressed as training is often the first thing businesses cut back on in difficult times.

Money guide

Starting salaries are usually £16,000–£19,000 per year. With experience, you could earn £23,000–£28,000+. At senior levels, with management responsibilities, it is possible to earn £35,000+. Self-employed trainers work for set fees either per day or per training course and can earn over £30,000.

Related opportunities

- Business Analyst p158
- Network Manager p169
- Teacher p212
- Training Officer p66

Further information

Institute of IT Training
Westwood House, Westwood Business Park, Coventry, CV4 8HS
0845 006 8858; www.iitt.org.uk

British Computer Society
North Star House, North Star Avenue, Swindon, Wiltshire, SN2 1FA
01793 417424; www.bcs.org

NETWORK MANAGER

Computers and IT

CRCi: D
CLCi: CAV

What the work involves

- You will be responsible for a network of computers and any linked equipment such as printers. This could be in just one building or extending across different sites.

- Managing access to and the security of your network, you will put in place and monitor firewalls, password systems and antivirus software.

- You will support any network users experiencing problems and track down and fix the problem.

- In large organisations you may be responsible for a team of computer technicians.

The type of person suited to this work

Your communication and interpersonal skills need to be top-notch for this job. You will be dealing with computer users with little technical knowledge and you will need to be able to clearly explain any actions they may need to take to get back onto the network.

You should have technical ability as well as determination. You may develop and write software programs for your network and need to be determined and logical to work out how to sort out any problems.

Network solutions are developing very quickly so you will need to be prepared to carry on learning to keep up your expert status.

Working conditions

You will be mainly office-based, using a computer to manage the system. You may need to work in the same room as a noisy mainframe server.

You may have to move around your company's site to attend meetings, train staff and resolve problems.

You will work a 37- to 40-hour week, normally Monday to Friday, but may need to work outside these hours to install systems or be on call.

Future prospects

Most organisations use networks to enable their staff to work together, communicate and share information and resources from their own workstations. Employers of network managers include industry, retailers, schools and universities, hospitals, local and central government and financial companies.

Promotion could be into the job of senior network manager. A talented network manager could also move into freelance or network design consultancy work.

Advantages/disadvantages

You will feel valued – a key person in your company – because communication and the sharing of information are central to the effective running of any organisation. The network you are responsible for is so crucial that when it goes wrong users and managers will put you under lots of pressure to sort out the problem as soon as it happens.

Qualifications and courses

ENTRY LEVEL 4

The usual entry qualification for this work is a degree, Foundation degree or HNC/D in a relevant subject, for example control and network computing, software engineering, artificial intelligence or computer science. The normal minimum entry requirements for degrees are 2 A levels/3 H grades and 5 GCSEs/S grades (A–C/1–3), and for Foundation degrees or HNC/Ds, 1 A level/2 H grades and 3 GCSEs/S grades (A–C/1–3). For technical degrees, maths/science may be required.

A funded route that may be on offer in your area is the Higher Apprenticeship in IT. This leads to a full Honours degree in addition to vocational, technical and Key Skills qualifications and work experience.

Training programmes on offer to graduates from any discipline include the Graduate Professional Development Award (GPDA). This offers training and accreditation to IT professionals working in the industry. It includes e-skills, internet services delivery and industrial management and practice.

The new 14–19 Diploma in IT is available at Levels 1–3 and focuses on competencies relevant to IT professional work. Level 3 is equivalent to 3.5 A levels.

Money guide

Starting salaries are usually from about £24,000 to £30,000 per year as a network manager. With experience you could earn from £33,000 to £47,000. Senior network managers can earn £55,000+. Additional benefits may include profit sharing or performance-related pay.

Related opportunities

- Computer Hardware Engineer p161
- Computer Operator p163
- Computer Technical Support Person p164
- Database Operator p165

Further information

British Computer Society
North Star House, North Star Avenue, Swindon SN2 1FA;
01793 417424; www.bcs.org

e-skills UK
1 Castle Lane, London SW1E 6DR
020 7963 8920; www.e-skills.com

Institute for the Management of Information Systems
5 Kingfisher House, New Mill Road, Orpington BR5 3QG
0700 002 3456; www.imis.org.uk

City&
Guilds

www.cityandguilds.com/myperfectjob

SOFTWARE DEVELOPER/ PROGRAMMER

What the work involves

- Multimedia, in ICT, means a system that combines a number of different formats, such as text, data, graphics, sound, images and animation.

- You will be part of a team working together to build a multimedia project such as a website or interactive program.

- You will use specific languages such as HTML, Lingo and Java, and use tools for multimedia applications such as FrontPage, Visual Tools and Illustrator.

- You will test and sort out any technical bugs in your program.

The type of person suited to this work

Knowledge of specific multimedia programming languages is essential, as is a broad understanding of how multimedia works. If you are planning to go on a course to learn these skills, you will need to be a logical and analytical thinker.

Your communication and team-working skills will also need to be as good as your technical ability, because you will be working alongside other professionals, such as graphic designers, sound engineers and scriptwriters.

If you are creative – able to write scripts or to visualise how screens should look – as well as technical, you will be able to set your sights on project management.

Working conditions

You will be mainly working in a software development laboratory or office at your workstation, but you will also be working with your project team.

Although your hours will be usually Monday to Friday, when projects are near to completion you will need to work some evenings and weekends.

Future prospects

Employers include specialist multimedia product development consultancies, internet service providers, website development firms, software houses and e-learning specialist companies. Multimedia is one of the growth industries of the decade.

If you are creative as well as technical, you will be able to progress up to project management level. You could also move into self-employment, or work on a contract or consultancy basis.

Advantages/disadvantages

You will get a buzz from using your skills to make a project come alive.

This is a young industry, developing at a rapid pace, so you will need to keep up to date with technological change.

If you are creative as well as technical, rewards are high.

Qualifications and courses

Entry is usually by means of a degree, Foundation degree or HNC/D in a relevant subject, for example multimedia technology, software engineering or computer science, or a degree with modules in computer graphics or Hypertext and Java programming.

The normal minimum entry requirements for degrees are 2 A levels/3 H grades and 5 GCSEs/S grades (A–C/1–3), and for Foundation degrees or HNC/Ds, 1 A level/2 H grades and 3 GCSEs/S grades (A–C/1–3). For technical degrees, maths/science may be required.

A funded route that may be on offer in your area is the Higher Apprenticeship in IT. This leads to a full Honours degree in addition to vocational, technical and Key Skills qualifications and work experience.

Entry without a degree, Foundation degree or HNC/D is unusual unless you have substantial experience in programming work and experience of designing or programming websites using new media. A strong portfolio will be required.

Training programmes are on offer for graduate entrants from any discipline, including the Graduate Professional Development Award (GPDA). This offers training and accreditation to IT professionals working in the industry.

The new 14–19 Diploma in IT is available at Levels 1–3 and focuses on competencies relevant to IT professional work. Level 3 is equivalent to 3.5 A levels.

Money guide

£19,000–£25,000 per year is usual for starting salaries. Some companies may offer less. £28,000–£35,000 is possible with experience. Senior multimedia programmers can earn £45,000.

Additional benefits may include profit sharing, performance-related pay and a car.

Related opportunities

- Internet/Web Professional p167
- Interactive Media Designer p166
- Website Designer p174

Further information

e-skills UK (Sector Skills Council for information technology, telecommunications and contact centres)
1 Castle Lane, London, SW1E 6DR
020 7963 8920; www.e-skills.com

British Interactive Multimedia Association
Briarlea House, Southend Road, Billericay, CM11 2PR
020 7436 8250; www.bima.co.uk

SYSTEMS ANALYST

What the work involves

- You may work with a business analyst to prepare a brief of what your client wants a computer system to do and you will be responsible for translating this brief into recommendations.

- To determine the system needed you will use performance monitoring or sizing tools. You will then design, cost and recommend suitable hardware/software solutions.

- If purpose-built software is needed, you may write it or brief a programmer on your team.

- You will go on to install and test the configuration you have developed.

The type of person suited to this work

An excellent all-round knowledge of ICT, including hardware and software, is vital. You will also have to be keen on learning, as new ICT products continue to be developed and produced at a rapid pace and you will be expected to be the technical expert.

Your teamwork and communication skills will need to be good as you will be working with business clients and colleagues such as business analysts and programmers to produce the best value system as a team.

To make systems that work well and enhance profitability and efficiency for your customer, you will also need to be a problem-solver who understands how businesses work.

Working conditions

You will be mainly based in an office, working with other members of the project team. You will have to travel to clients at all stages of the project and may be away for several days when installing and testing the new system.

Although your hours will be usually Monday to Friday, when projects are near to completion you will need to work some evenings and weekends.

Future prospects

Employers include software and systems houses, ICT consultants and large organisations. This is an expanding job area especially for systems analysts who have a business understanding as well as a broad technical knowledge.

You could move from this broad-based job to specialise either in offering ICT solutions for business, or a technical area such as software or website development.

Progression is possible into project management or consultancy work.

Advantages/disadvantages

It is rewarding to put together hardware and software to create a unique solution designed for your customer. Clients tend to

Qualifications and courses

A degree, Foundation degree or HND/C is usually required. Useful degree subjects include computing or e-systems design and technology. A level/H grade maths may be required or preferred for these degrees.

A new sponsored degree from e-skills, information technology management for business, is available. This is focused on learning through project work in compact teams with external mentors from sponsoring organisations.

Another funded route that may be on offer in your area is the Higher Apprenticeship in IT. This leads to a full Honours degree in addition to vocational, technical and Key Skills qualifications and work experience.

Late entry is often possible for those who have developed computer skills working in other fields.

Training programmes are on offer for graduate entrants from any discipline including the Graduate Professional Development Award (GPDA).

A new 14–19 Diploma in IT is available at Levels 1–3, focusing on competencies relevant to IT professional work. Level 3 is equivalent to 3.5 A levels.

set very stressful, demanding briefs to deliver the right solution both at the lowest cost and in the shortest time possible.

Money guide

Starting/training salaries are usually from £20,000 to £28,000 per year. With experience, you could earn from £30,000 to £48,000. Successful systems analysts can earn £50,000+. With management responsibilities £80,000 is possible in the south-east of England. Additional benefits may include profit sharing, performance-related pay and a car.

Related opportunities

- Business Analyst p158
- Database Operator p165
- Network Manager p169
- Software Developer/Programmer p170

Further information

e-skills UK
1 Castle Lane, London SW1E 6DR
020 7963 8920; www.e-skills.com

Institute for the Management of Information Systems
5 Kingfisher House, New Mill Road, Orpington BR5 3QG
0700 002 3456; www.imis.org.uk

Institute of IT Training
Westwood House, Westwood Business Park, Coventry CV4 8HS
0845 006 8858; www.iitt.org.uk

Computers and IT

CRCI: D
CLCI: CAV

TECHNICAL SALES SPECIALIST

What the work involves

- You will talk to customers interested in your product, finding out what they are looking for, explaining how it works, and hopefully selling it to them.

- This may mean that you have to have the technical ability to change and adapt products to suit the need of your client.

- Once you have clinched the deal you will take payment and arrange delivery dates.

The type of person suited to this work

You should be a people person who is interested in technology. You will also need good communication skills as you will be dealing with customers face to face and on the telephone.

You must be able to clearly explain technical jargon to customers who may have no technical knowledge. Equally, you will need to understand all the technical specifications of your products as some of your customers will be experts.

It is a competitive market so you will need to be good at selling, persuading and building customer loyalty. You will also need to be up to date with all the products out there so that you know what you are up against.

Working conditions

You may be based in an office, dealing with customers by phone or email, or in a retail outlet, selling direct.

If you specialise in selling to retail chains or organisations, you will spend lots of time driving and in meetings.

Your hours will depend on your customers. Your employer may operate a shift system to deal with queries and sales from early until late, seven days a week.

Future prospects

Employers include large ICT companies producing and retailing products such as mobile phones, computer hardware and software. Large specialist ICT retailers also employ technical sales staff.

The demand for new ICT products continues to grow but new competitors are always entering the market. Strong areas of demand include secure wireless broadband and mobile working.

You may be able to gain promotion to a supervisory or sales management role.

Advantages/disadvantages

If you close a deal at a good price or sell extras such as a service contract, you may be paid a bonus. Selling can be very stressful, with high sales targets to achieve. It is frustrating if you have spent lots of time with a customer without it resulting in a purchase.

Qualifications and courses

You will usually need a degree, Foundation degree or HNC/D in a computer-related subject to enter this job.

The normal minimum entry requirements for degrees are 2 A levels/3 H grades and 5 GCSEs/S grades (A–C/1–3), and for Foundation degrees or HNC/Ds, 1 A level/2 H grades and 3 GCSEs/S grades (A–C/1–3). Maths may be a required subject.

A funded route that may be on offer in your area is the Higher Apprenticeship in IT. This leads to a full Honours degree in addition to vocational, technical and Key Skills qualifications and work experience.

Some people move into sales from a technical job in design or production.

A thorough understanding of the products to be sold is essential, and may be more important than formal qualifications.

You will normally need to hold a driving licence for this job.

Initial training is usually intense as you will need to gain a thorough technical knowledge of your employer's products and their preferred communication style.

The new 14–19 Diploma in IT is available at Levels 1–3 and focuses on competencies relevant to IT professional work. Level 3 is equivalent to 3.5 A levels.

Money guide

£20,000 per year is usual for starting salaries. This could rise to £25,000–£38,000 with experience. Sales managers can earn more than £50,000. Additional benefits may include profit sharing, performance-related pay and a car.

Related opportunities

- Business Analyst p158
- Computer Helpdesk Adviser p162
- IT Trainer p168
- Sales Assistant p495

Further information

British Computer Society
North Star House, North Star Avenue, Swindon SN2 1FA;
01793 417424; www.bcs.org

e-skills UK
1 Castle Lane, London SW1E 6DR
020 7963 8920; www.e-skills.com

Institute of Sales & Marketing Management
Harrier Court, Lower Woodside LU1 4DQ
01582 840001; www.ismm.co.uk

TELECOMMUNICATIONS TECHNICIAN

What the work involves

■ Telecommunications technicians install, test and repair networking and communications technology and systems across a range of applications, including mobile phones, telephones, satellite and radio networks, and aerials.

■ Your day to day tasks will vary but you may be assembling, installing and testing telecommunications equipment; laying copper and fibre optic wire in the street or other sites; setting up or repairing networks.

■ You may also be involved in designing or consulting on plans for telecommunications systems.

The type of person suited to this work

You should be interested in maths, IT, electronics and communications.

As you will be working in a team and explaining technical terms to customers you should have good communication and customer service skills. You should also have good writing skills to write up reports and produce statistics.

As you may be installing systems and laying wires which may involve heavy lifting and carrying, digging or using ladders you should be fit and have a good head for heights.

Working conditions

You will work from 9 to 5, Monday to Friday. You may be required to work shifts which may include evenings, weekends or to be available on-call. Overtime may be necessary to complete projects or meet deadlines.

You may be based in a factory workshop or in a control centre from where you will travel to complete projects which may be in homes, offices or outdoors.

Future prospects

To progress as a telecommunications technician you can apply to become a professionally recognised engineering technician (EngTech) or ICT technician (ICTTech).

With experience and qualifications you may be promoted to senior technician or supervisor. With further experience, qualifications and skills you can apply for incorporated and chartered engineer status.

You can become self-employed, or work on a contract basis.

There are numerous opportunities to work abroad.

Advantages/disadvantages

You may be in a diverse working environment as new and exciting developments in technology are occurring rapidly.

You may have to work outdoors in uncomfortable weather conditions.

Qualifications and courses

You can enter this profession as an apprentice, where you will be supervised by a qualified telecommunications technician. Apprenticeships usually last for two years. You will also gain NVQs/SVQs, Levels 2, 3 and 4 in IT or Telecoms at local colleges.

The IT and Telecoms Professionals Apprenticeship requires that candidates have four GSCES (A*-C) which must include English, science or technology, or a BTEC first diploma in a relevant subject.

You can also take a vocational course such as a BTEC national certificate or diploma, HNC, HND or a foundation degree in a relevant subject such as telecommunications, technology, electronics or computing, and then apply for trainee technician positions.

You may also find the Diploma in information technology useful for this field.

Depending on the company you work for, continuing in-service training may be available. This can be combined with specific manufacturers' courses and vendor qualifications such as the networking qualifications offered by CISCO and Microsoft.

Money guide

Your starting salary will begin around £12,000 a year. With experience and qualifications you can earn up to £32,000 a year. The most experienced technicians can earn in the region of £40,000 a year.

Related opportunities

■ Computer Hardware Engineer p161
■ Electrical Engineer p226
■ Network Manager p169

Further information

The Institute of Telecoms Professionals (ITP)
Sunbury TE, Green Street, Sunbury-on-Thames, Middlesex, TW16 6QJ
01932 788861; enquiries@theitp.org; www.theitp.org

The Institution of Engineering and Technology (IET)
Michael Faraday House, Six Hills Way, Stevenage, Hertfordshire, SG1 2AY
01438 313311; postmaster@theiet.org; www.theiet.org

**City&
Guilds**

www.cityandguilds.com/myperfectjob

WEBSITE DESIGNER

What the work involves

- You will find out what a customer needs to achieve with a new or updated website and what the budget is.

- You may need to do a presentation in competition with other developers to win the contract.

- You will have regular review meetings to try out web ideas and pages you have developed, and test for bugs.

The type of person suited to this work

Creativity is central to this job. You will need to listen to what the client wants to achieve and then turn your vision into a unique, working website.

As sites increasingly use a complex mixture of text, graphics, data, music and interactive functions, your technical skills are as important as your creativity.

Your communication and presentation skills need to be excellent to take your client with you from winning the contract to launching the site.

You will be working as part of a team, especially if developing a complex web project, so you will need to be a team player.

Working conditions

You will need to travel to meet clients on a regular basis. At certain key times in the project, such as building the specification and launch of the site, you may be away from home for long periods.

You will be working on a computer with internet access to develop your client's site. You will probably work remotely, at home or in an office base.

You will work a 37- to 40-hour week, normally Monday to Friday, but as deadlines loom you will have to put in extra hours.

Future prospects

Website development is expanding. There are growing numbers of even quite small businesses using the web to share information, market themselves, sell goods or services or advertise jobs.

Work is competitive for website consultants who often have to bid for projects against other website developers. You need to be talented to stay in the business.

Promotion could be to project management level. Website developers can specialise in the growing interactive or multimedia business.

Advantages/disadvantages

If you create a top-class site, not only will it generate more business for your client, it will also build your future success. It is stressful; you cannot ever do a poor job. Consultants say that 70% of new business comes from recommendations from existing clients.

Qualifications and courses

The usual entry qualification for this work is a degree, Foundation degree or HNC/D in a relevant subject, for example e-commerce technologies, e-systems design and technology, multimedia design or graphic design. A new sponsored degree from e-skills, information technology management for business, is available.

Another funded route that may be on offer in your area is the Higher Apprenticeship in IT. This leads to a full Honours degree in addition to vocational, technical and Key Skills qualifications and work experience. You can also start an Apprenticeship at a lower level and build up the qualifications you need for higher-level work.

If you have not got a degree but have lots of experience and training, for example in interactive programming languages, and a strong portfolio of web-design work, you should be able to enter this field.

Training programmes are on offer for graduate entrants from any discipline including the Graduate Professional Development Award (GPDA). This offers training and accreditation to IT professionals working in the industry.

The new 14–19 Diploma in IT is available at Levels 1, 2 and 3 focuses on competencies relevant to IT professional work. Level 3 is equivalent to 3.5 A levels.

Money guide

£18,000–£25,000 per year is usual for starting salaries. With experience this can rise to £30,000 or more. Senior web developers with specialist skills can earn up to £50,000. £60,000+ is possible for successful consultants.

Related opportunities

- Business Analyst p158
- Internet/Web Professional p167
- Interactive Media Designer p166
- Software Developer/Programmer p170

Further information

British Computer Society
North Star House, North Star Avenue, Swindon SN2 1FA
01793 417424; www.bcs.org

British Interactive Multimedia Association
Briarlea House, Southend Road, Billericay CM11 2PR
020 7436 8250; www.bima.co.uk

e-skills UK
1 Castle Lane, London SW1E 6DR
020 7963 8920; www.e-skills.com

www.cityandguilds.com/myperfectjob

Design, Arts and Crafts

The idea of turning your arts and crafts hobby into a career may be one you like the thought of. Jobs in this sector can involve working in any medium, from textiles to jewellery to metalwork or children's toys. You may find yourself working for a company but many people in this industry are self-employed working for a range of clients. This means you need to be very organised and have brilliant communication skills to ensure you can give your clients exactly what they want.

In this section we look at the following jobs:

For similar jobs to these have a look at these sections: *Marketing, Advertising, Media, Print and Publishing* on page 405 and *Performing Arts* starting on page 435.

ANIMATOR

What the work involves

- You will create animations by developing cartoons, drawings, images on computer-assisted drawing (CAD) programmes or 3D forms and figures into a continuous story.

- You may also plan speech and music soundtracks for animated films.

- Working in fine detail, you will ensure that the animation works as smoothly and convincingly as possible.

- Animators produce creative and commercial work for use by TV companies, in computer games, advertising and films.

The type of person suited to this work

You will need strong creative flair and imagination to develop new ideas for animated stories and characters.

You must have excellent computer skills: able to work with design packages. Although computerised animation is increasing in popularity, the ability to draw forms and figures and to model is still important.

Problem-solving skills are important in a job where you may need to adapt to technical challenges. An ability to work in a team with others, contributing equally while working patiently towards the finished product, is also an important attribute for an animator.

Working conditions

Your working environment will depend on the type of animation you do. In some jobs, you will work with tools to hand-create images or forms in different materials. You could be on your feet (using your hands) all day: bending, lifting and shaping models.

Many new animation jobs involve work with specialist CAD packages at a PC console – sometimes with colleagues. Most of your work will be done during normal office hours except when projects have tight deadlines!

Future prospects

This is a competitive area to enter. Although there are some opportunities for traditional drawing-based animators, the growth area is within computer-generated areas. WAP technology, the popularity of computer games and TV work have contributed more opportunities.

Once within the industry, contracts are usually short-term, but it is possible to move from working as a key animator, to an animation director role. At senior levels, you would have more creative input and be less directly involved with the technical side. With experience, you could set up as a freelance animator or start your own company.

Advantages/disadvantages

This type of work can be highly satisfying, providing opportunities to develop your own creative ideas and style.

Qualifications and courses

Entry usually requires an HND, Foundation degree or degree in animation, art and design, or a related area; a relevant postgraduate qualification can be an asset. A portfolio of relevant work is also normally required.

Entry to the profession without a degree/HND may be possible, in which case a good portfolio is essential.

Gaining unpaid experience as a general or animation assistant for a company is a good way to build up relevant skills.

With experience, you could work towards an NVQ/SVQ Level 3 in Animation Assistance; Skillset vocational courses for the industry are also available in Design for the Moving Image at Levels 2, 3 and 4.

In more commercial jobs, you would need to produce work under pressure to meet a client's requirements.

Animation is rising in popularity amongst the public. Many animated films are highly successful at the box office.

Money guide

BECTU, the union for broadcasting, film, theatre, entertainment, leisure, interactive media and allied sectors, sets minimum wage guidelines for the industry, but animators negotiate their own rates and may receive more depending on the project. A new animator can expect to earn £17,000–£25,000 a year. An experienced animator could earn £23,000–£35,000 a year. Senior animators can expect to earn £40,000+ a year. Contact BECTU for details of current freelance salaries.

Related opportunities

- Cartoonist p177
- Fine Artist p183
- Graphic Designer p186
- Photographer/Photographic Stylist p421

Further information

Skillset (Sector Skills Council for the audiovisual industries)
Focus Point, 21 Caledonian Road, London N1 9GB
08080 300900; www.skillset.org/animation

Guild of British Animation
26 Noel Street, London W1T 9PV
020 7434 2651

Broadcasting Entertainment Cinematograph and Theatre Union
373–377 Clapham Road, London SW9 9BT
020 7346 0900; www.bectu.org.uk

CARTOONIST

What the work involves

- You will plan and draw original cartoons and captions. These can be single images, whole cartoon strips or entire books.

- You will promote and market your work, for example by sending out samples to newspapers and advertising through the internet.

- Cartoonists create images for greetings cards, adverts, book illustrations, magazines, newspapers and websites.

- A small number of cartoonists are employed to run regular cartoon features in newspapers or other media. but most maintain a 'web comic' of their work.

The type of person suited to this work

You will need a streak of imaginative humour and strong creative flair to come up with new ideas – sometimes, on a day-by-day basis. Cartoon ideas often draw on situation humour or arise in quick response to headline news.

Even if you use a software art package, good drawing skills are very important. You may have to work to deadlines – creating cartoons for a variety of clients – so need to be well organised, with good business management skills. A good standard of numeracy is useful if you are self-employed.

You must also be able to adapt your drawing style to different projects. As you will be sending out examples of your work to potential employers, you will need to be able to deal with rejection.

Working conditions

Most professional cartoonists work on a freelance basis, either in a studio or from home. This can be isolating as many work alone. Much of your time will be spent at a drawing board or a PC console where you will either sit or stand using the materials required.

Sometimes you may need to attend meetings with clients or potential employers, which could involve travelling long distances.

Future prospects

Most cartoonists work on a freelance basis for a number of employers at the same time. Because it can be difficult to make a living initially, most cartoonists do related work such as design, art teaching and illustration. Some work as animators for companies that develop games and other ICT resources.

It has become usual to develop and promote your own work with the use of home computer design software and the internet. Many cartoonists maintain webcomics – strips and archives of their past work which are freely accessible. Very few webcomic artists receive financial reward. If numerous surfers access their webcomic pages, internet advertisers may pay cartoonists to promote their goods alongside.

Qualifications and courses

ENTRY LEVEL 4

A strong portfolio and relevant experience are usually more important than formal qualifications.

Most entrants have an HNC/D or degree in an art and design subject.

There are a small number of cartooning qualifications available through distance learning courses, including a Cartoon Diploma course. These can help you develop your cartooning skills and provide feedback on your work.

In England, Wales and Northern Ireland, many students take a 1-year Foundation course as preparation for entry to an art and design degree course. 5 GCSEs (A–C) and a relevant A level are usually required.

In Scotland the first year of an Art and Design degree course equates to the Foundation year.

Advantages/disadvantages

Because cartoonists are usually paid for individual pieces of work, they have little job security especially at the start of their careers.

You would have the satisfaction of creating original work and seeing it in print.

Money guide

Salaries vary widely. It is possible to earn higher levels of pay by doing commercial work for greetings cards and adverts. Cartoonists starting out in full-time employment can expect to earn around £15,000–£20,000 per year. If you become established, well known, and are in demand for your work, you could earn up to £50,000. Cartoonists are usually paid on a freelance, one-off basis. Cartoonists creating work to illustrate books can earn royalties from sales.

Related opportunities

- Animator p176
- Fine Artist p183
- Graphic Designer p186
- Signwriter/Signmaker p196

Further information

Arts Council of England
2 Pear Tree Court, London, EC1R 0DS
0845 300 6200; www.artscouncil.org.uk

Scottish Arts Council
12 Manor Place, Edinburgh, EH3 7DD
0131 226 6051; www.scottisharts.org.uk

ccskills – Creative and Cultural Skills
4th Floor, Lafone House, The Leathermarket, Weston St, London, SE1 3HN
020 7015 1800; www.ccskills.org.uk

Design, Arts and Crafts

CRCI: E
CLCI: ED

COSTUME DESIGNER

What the work involves

- Costume designers work from both original ideas and background research in order to design, buy or hire the clothes and accessories worn by the cast in films, plays and TV dramas.

- You will decide which fabrics and materials to use. You could also be involved with making or overseeing costume production.

- You will be responsible for organising fittings and ensuring that costumes are delivered on time and within budget. Depending on the size of the production, you may also manage a team of costume professionals.

The type of person suited to this work

It is essential to have a strong creative flair and the imagination to develop original designs. Having the skills to draw designs by hand and to use specialist CAD software when required are also very important.

You should also be detail driven and demonstrate a passion for costume history, fashion and the arts.

These abilities should be balanced with good communication skills to aid leadership and self-promotion.

Organisational skills are important to ensure that projects are carried out on time, within budget and as requested. As deadlines can be tight, you should also have the ability to work well under pressure.

Working conditions

Hours are long and irregular, including evenings and weekends.

It is possible to work for production companies, however most costume designers are freelancers.

You will normally work within a studio using drawing tables, computers, cutting tables and sewing machines. This can be dusty and the cutting required can be dangerous.

As some of the work could involve intricate beading and embroidery, good eyesight and manual dexterity are required.

It is likely that you will be standing for long periods of time, and may carry out some heavy lifting.

Future prospects

The contribution of design towards the UK economy is very important and the significance of this intensely competitive sector continues to grow.

Costume designer vacancies are rarely advertised and most work is centred in major cities like London and Manchester. It is essential for costume designers to have a strong portfolio and to build up good contacts to stimulate positive word of mouth.

The UK industry has an excellent international reputation offering progression to work overseas if desired.

Qualifications and courses

Most people have a foundation degree, degree, or postgraduate diploma in a related subject such as art, fashion or performing arts.

A City & Guilds qualification is also available in design and craft – theatre costume at levels 2 and 3. There are some formal training schemes, such as the BBC Design Trainee Scheme in costume design and you can study wardrobe assistance at FT2 - Film and Television Freelance Training.

Advantages/disadvantages

The creation of original work and seeing your ideas being used in a decorative manner is satisfying.

Working as a freelancer can result in greater flexibility

Meeting tight deadlines can result in high stress levels

As competition is fierce, it can be difficult to build up the reputation and contacts necessary to succeed in this profession

Money guide

Industry salaries vary depending on type of employer and geographical location.

New entrants to the profession can expect to earn about £18,000 per year, rising to £30,000–£40,000 per annum with experience.

The most experienced costume designers can earn £40,000+ per year.

Freelancers can expect to earn about £800 per week.

Related opportunities

- Fashion Designer p181
- Display Designer/Window Dresser p180
- Knitting/Sewing Machinist p232
- Tailor/Dressmaker p250

Further information

Costume Society of Great Britain
28 Eburne Road, London N7 6AU
www.costumesociety.org.uk

Department for Culture, Media and Sport
2–4 Cockspur Street, London SW1Y 5DH
020 7211 6000; www.culture.gov.uk

Design Council
34 Bow Street, London WC2E 7DL
020 7420 5200; www.designcouncil.org.uk

www.cityandguilds.com/myperfectjob

TEXTILE TECHNOLOGIST

Sourcing new fabrics to use in innovative fashion garments

The Work

Every item of clothing you see, on the high street or the catwalk, is the result of a whole team of people's work. One of these people is a textile technologist.

Textile technologists are concerned with the scientific makeup of fabrics and sourcing new fabrics that they can introduce to the existing market. They usually work in-house for clothing companies, where they are required to work closely with the buying, marketing, sales and design teams.

A textile technologist's role can be very varied as they need to spend time both sourcing and testing materials. When sourcing new fabrics, a textile technologist may have to travel both within the UK and overseas. They would need to develop strong working relationships with suppliers to secure the best deal. It is important for a textile technologist to source new and innovative fabrics so their company can stay ahead of the competition.

The other aspect of a textile technologist's role is to be involved in testing the fabrics they have sourced. This usually takes place in a dedicated testing laboratory within the company. They would conduct quality control tests, for example to see how crease resistant a material is. Technologists in this area would also experiment with the dyeing and production process to ensure the best possible result is achieved.

The Skills

- Knowledge of textile fabrics and production processes
- Specialist fabric testing knowledge
- Ability to lead a team and prioritise workloads
- Excellent communication and organisation skills
- Creativity and the ability to be resourceful
- An interest in solving problems and experimenting with new ideas

Ways In

A degree in a relevant subject area, such as textile technology, textile science, physics, maths or manufacturing engineering, is usually required for a career in this area. It is important to select a course which offers the technical skills needed to succeed, such as materials testing and experience of production processes

The Money

The starting salary for a textile technologist is usually around £21,000 a year. This will increase to around between £25,000 and £35,000 a year with experience. A research and development textile technologist or those with management duties may earn up to £45,000 a year.

Find out about fashion's hidden careers at
www.canucutit.co.uk
www.skillfast-uk.org/justthejob

DISPLAY DESIGNER/ WINDOW DRESSER

What the work involves

- You will plan and design eye-catching window or shop front displays for shops, businesses and other organisations.

- You will work closely with clients to make sure that your designs meet their requirements.

- First identifying materials and props for a window display, you will design an arrangement to create a striking theme or effect.

- You may also provide advice and information to other shop branches or organisations on successful display design.

The type of person suited to this work

As the job involves a lot of hands-on design work, you will need strong creative flair. Your ideas will need to be balanced with those of your client. Planning displays that succeed in attracting customers and visitors requires a strong awareness of what interests people. As your work will often be used to promote services or products, you need to have an interest in business.

The ability to work with a wide range of people is also important. You may have to manage project budgets so you will need to be numerate. Physical stamina is helpful, as putting displays together can be tiring.

Some displays, such as fashion shop windows, require designers who are very aware of trends.

Working conditions

Normally, you will be working indoors with different hand tools, materials, fabrics and the products to be displayed in the window or display. The work can often be pressured due to strict deadlines.

The job can involve a great deal of physical activity and manual work. You will do lots of lifting and be on your feet for long periods, which can be very tiring.

You may have to work late especially in the build-up to holiday seasons such as Christmas.

Future prospects

This is an area of work which is looking for talented new entrants. There are a range of opportunities, for example working for specialist display consultancy firms, large retailers, museums, theme parks and other visitor attractions. You will probably start as a junior and progress to a more senior position. You could also go on to teach or lecture in design-related subjects.

With experience, some display designers set up their own businesses or provide consultancy support to other organisations.

Qualifications and courses

There are no minimum qualifications for this type of work. However, many entrants will have done an accredited course.

Many different courses are available. Degree courses in Visual Merchandising usually require 2 A levels/H grades and 5 GCSEs/S grades (A–C/1–3). Foundation degrees typically require 1 A level/H grade and 5 GCSEs/S grades (A–C/1–3). Other courses include City & Guilds Level 2 award in Visual Merchandising, the Fashion Retail Academy Diploma in Fashion Retail at Levels 1 and 2 and various British Display Society certificates and diplomas.

A portfolio of art and design work is usually required. Experience in display and the retail or exhibition sector can also be helpful.

It is possible to gain NVQs/SVQs in Visual Merchandising Levels 2–4 and Design Level 3.

You could also undertake Apprenticeships/Skillseekers opportunities.

Advantages/disadvantages

This type of work can be pressured due to tight deadlines. You will have the satisfaction of seeing very visible results from your work. Many people will enjoy your displays and give you positive feedback. You could get the chance to work with animatronics or other special effects.

Money guide

Junior display staff entering the profession can earn around £15,000 per year. Earnings can rise to £20,000–£30,000 with experience. £45,000+ is possible for top designers at the most senior levels.

Related opportunities

- Buyer (Retail) p482
- Interior Designer p189
- Model Maker p192
- Store Manager p499

Further information

British Display Society
12 Cliff Avenue, Chalkwell, Leigh-on-Sea, Essex, SS9 1HF
020 8856 2030; www.britishdisplaysociety.co.uk

Design Council
34 Bow Street, London, WC2E 7DL
020 7420 5200; www.designcouncil.org.uk

FASHION DESIGNER/ MILLINER

CRCI: E
CLCI: EJ

What the work involves

- Using your design sense and knowledge of textiles and other materials you will develop clothing, shoes and accessories. This could include articles such as footwear, babywear or sports clothes. A milliner specialises in creating headwear such as hats, fascinators etc.

- You will specialise in one of the three main sectors namely; haute couture, ready-to-wear or high street.

- You will be responsible for analysing trends in fabrics, colours and shapes.

- As well as creating initial designs by hand and with computer aided design (CAD), you may also oversee the manufacture of these items.

The type of person suited to this work

It is essential to have a strong creative flair and the imagination to develop original designs.

Having the skills to draw designs by hand and to use specialist CAD software when required are also very important. You should also have technical skills, such as pattern cutting and a good eye for design, colour and detail.

These abilities should be balanced with good business sense and the competency to see a project through.

You should have excellent communication, negotiation and organisational skills to ensure that projects are carried out on time, within budget and as requested.

Working conditions

This can be very stressful work, especially during the lead up to shows. Expect to work very long hours and to change ideas up until the last minute.

You will work alone, or in a small team, within a studio with large cutting tables and sewing machines. The environment can be dusty and the cutting required can be dangerous.

You will also spend some of your time visiting textile producers and clients at their premises, which may be overseas. This job offers the opportunity to meet many different people.

Future prospects

The contribution of design towards the UK economy is very important and the significance of this intensely competitive sector continues to grow.

Most designers work in and around the fashion hub of London, for independent labels, clothes manufacturers, and in-house for retail brands. Due to the rise of online shopping, an increasing number are choosing self-employment, either immediately after graduation or after gaining work experience.

The UK industry has an excellent international reputation, offering progression to work overseas if desired.

Qualifications and courses

ENTRY LEVEL 3

Entry to this profession is rare without an HNC/HND, foundation degree or degree in art or design. A postgraduate degree, such as an MA in fashion, will enable students from other academic backgrounds to show their commitment to working in the industry.

Most entrants are young, and have a diverse portfolio that encompasses the breadth of their design capabilities.

It is essential to gain some experience in the industry, even if unpaid, to demonstrate your commitment and passion. Some graduates gain experience with Italian, French or American designers before aiming to break into the UK market.

Advantages/disadvantages

The creation of original work and seeing your ideas in the public eye is satisfying.

You will have the opportunity to meet interesting people of different nationalities.

Meeting tight deadlines in the lead up to shows can result in stress.

There may be a lot of travel involved, which can disrupt your personal life.

Money guide

Earnings vary according to type of employer and location. Your salary will be determined by your success and the most famous designers earn huge amounts. However, those starting out can expect to earn around £15,000–£22,000 per year, rising to an average of £30,000–£40,000 with five years' experience. At senior level you could earn up to £60,000.

Related opportunities

- Display Designer/Window Dresser p180
- Illustrator p188
- Interior Designer p189
- Model Maker p192

Further information

Design Council
34 Bow Street. London WC2E 7DL
020 7420 5200; www.designcouncil.org.uk

City&
Guilds

www.cityandguilds.com/myperfectjob

FASHION DESIGNER

Creating new and innovative garment designs for the fashion industry

The Work

Fashion designers have an exciting and demanding career in a competitive industry. There are a wide range of career opportunities from designing catwalk collections to creating wearable garments for the high street. They will usually specialise in either men's, women's or children's wear.

A fashion designer's role is varied and can involve travel both within the UK and overseas to meet customers or suppliers and to attend trade shows. It is important for them to develop excellent working relationships with suppliers and marketing teams to ensure their garments make it to production.

Fashion designers will usually spend time collecting ideas and researching trends, these will then form part of their design specification. They also have to take into consideration the 'look' of the company they are working for so that the new designs sit well alongside existing collections.

The next stage of the process is to produce the design ideas. This can be done by hand or using a computer programme. A fashion designer is responsible for turning these sketches into pattern pieces, which can then form the sample garment. It is likely that these prototype garments would be studied by a garment technologist, pattern cutter and sample machinist to check that the garment can be effectively manufactured.

The Skills

- A creative eye for colour and shape
- Technical skills in sewing and pattern making
- The ability to draw designs and communicate these effectively
- An interest in past and future fashion trends
- Excellent communication and people skills

Ways In

A degree in a relevant subject, such as fashion design, is usually preferred for a career in this area. Many courses are available but it is important to choose one which offers the technical skills needed to succeed in this area, such as pattern cutting and garment construction.

Work experience in the industry is also important when applying for a job; some courses offer a work placement as part of the course. If this is not an option then work experience placements can be arranged in the holidays.

The Money

When starting out, a fashion designer may be paid between £12,000 and £14,000 a year. This will increase to around £22,000 a year with experience. Top, experienced designers could earn over £60,000 a year.

Find out more about a career in fashion design at
www.canucutit.co.uk
www.skillfast-uk.org/justthejob

FINE ARTIST

What the work involves

■ Fine artists work with various media such as oil paints, charcoal or stone, to create two-dimensional pieces of various sizes. Sculptors create three-dimensional pieces and use materials like clay, bronze, stone and metal.

■ You will be responsible for promoting your work to sponsors, galleries and other organisations, by networking or issuing publicity material.

■ You may organise solo or joint exhibitions in a variety of venues to showcase your work. Some residencies are available in institutes like schools and prisons.

The type of person suited to this work

As you will be creating original works of art, you will need strong artistic and technical skills, well-developed powers of observation and vivid imagination.

Self-belief and motivation are important, as it takes perseverance and application to turn an original idea into a finished piece of artwork. Sculptors will also require a high level of physical fitness and manual dexterity.

Many artists are self-employed, necessitating good business sense and organisational skills.

Good communication skills will help you to convince galleries to show and sell your work. An ability to network and make contacts in the art world is also useful.

Working conditions

You will work on pieces in a studio, research your work on location, or teach workshops at a residency. The majority of your time will be spent alone, which can be isolating for some people.

Many artistic materials are dusty, oily or may stain and, even wearing overalls, you can expect to get dirty.

You may have to work with solvents and other chemicals, which can adversely affect those with sensitive skin, allergies or respiratory problems.

Sculptors will work with dangerous tools such as knives, chisels and welding equipment.

Future prospects

This job demands confidence and persistence as few artists and sculptors earn their full living from art alone. Many earn additional income by working in related areas including arts education, community development and art galleries.

There is a range of networks supporting developing artists. It is possible to sell work through a number of galleries, shops, workshop co-operatives, studios and increasingly the internet. Larger cities or tourist hotspots with more of these venues do provide more opportunities to sell artwork.

Qualifications and courses

Most artists have formal qualifications such as a degree in fine art, or an HNC/HND or degree in art and design. Postgraduate qualifications in fine art are also available. Sculptors usually have a fine art degree with a specialisation in sculpture. Entry requirements vary. Some institutions require A-levels/H grades in relevant subjects, while others accept students on the strength of their portfolio.

It is possible to gain NVQ/SVQs in the following subjects: arts development and teaching (Levels 3 and 4) and visual and applied arts practice Level 4.

For sculptors, training usually occurs on the job under the supervision of an experienced professional

Advantages/disadvantages

You will have the pleasure of seeing customers enjoy and appreciate your work.

Your work will be personally fulfilling.

It can be an isolated way of life and may not always lead to recognition.

There can be hard times as it can be difficult to earn a living as an artist or sculptor.

Money guide

It is possible to earn a regular income from your work, but this is more likely with experience.

Many artists have another job to provide a more stable source of income. Some teach part-time, while others may work on a commission basis on community projects.

New artists can expect to earn about £19,000 a year, rising to £30,000 with 10 years' experience.

Sculptors can earn £26,000 per year for a residency.

Related opportunities

■ Animator p176
■ Cartoonist p177
■ Graphic Designer p186
■ Illustrator p188

Further information

Arts Council of England
2 Pear Tree Court, London EC1R 0DS
0845 300 6200; www.artscouncil.org.uk

Scottish Arts Council
12 Manor Place, Edinburgh EH3 7DD
0131 226 6051; www.scottisharts.org.uk

Department for Culture, Media and Sport
2–4 Cockspur Street, London SW1Y 5DH
020 7211 6200; www.culture.gov.uk

Design, Arts and Crafts

CRCI: E
CLCI: ED

ENTRY LEVEL 3

GEMMOLOGIST

What the work involves

- Gemmologists work with diamonds, gems, precious stones and other ornamental materials.

- You will identify such materials and examine their quality. This may involve assessing or grading the cut of the stone, or identifying flaws or imitations (stones that are made of synthetic or artificial materials).

- You are likely to work for a jewellery house where you will be involved in making evaluations for customers and clients, and buying and selling stones.

- You may also be employed by an insurance company where you will make appraisals for those who wish to insure their jewellery.

The type of person suited to this work

It is important that you have an interest in rocks, gems and crystals, design, the earth sciences and geology.

You should also have a keen eye for detail as you will have to look for the slightest qualities to make valuations and identify stones.

As your work will mainly be hands-on you should be good with your hands and have good eyesight and memory.

You should be trustworthy and happy to work in high-security environments.

Working conditions

Your working hours will depend on the type of organisation that you work for. Retail jewellers work around 40 hours a week, including weekends.

You could work in an office, laboratory, workshop or studio. If you become involved in mining or travelling to gem markets you may have to work in remote and uncomfortable conditions.

You will use specialist equipment such as lenses, refractometers, spectroscopes and microscopes to examine gemstones.

Due to the nature of your work, you will have to adhere to strict security protocol, including locked doors, barred windows, armed guards, CCTV surveillance and alarm systems.

Future prospects

After you have finished your training and gained qualifications and experience, you may move up to senior management positions.

You may find opportunities in wholesale organisations, retail operations such as jewellery houses, and insurance companies.

There may be opportunities to work abroad.

With significant experience and good contacts you may become self-employed or work as a consultant or setting up your own business as a jewellery maker or designer.

Qualifications and courses

ENTRY LEVEL 5

There are no set entry requirements for this profession, however many entrants are graduates of relevant subjects such as art, craft, earth sciences, geology, sciences, physics in particular, and technology.

If you have a qualification in a geological subject, and experience in a relevant field such as diamond mining, you may be able to train as a gemmologist. Other qualifications that may help you to enter this profession include a degree in a geoscience subject such as geology, geophysics or geochemistry or the BTEC National Diploma in gemmology (Birmingham City University).

You are likely to train on-the-job and study for qualifications on a part time basis. This may take one to four years. The Gemmological Association (GEM-A) offers qualifications (in conjunction with Kingston University) which combine theoretical and practical work.

Jewellery courses and qualifications are available in many institutions throughout the UK.

Advantages/disadvantages

As a self-employed gemmologist your work may involve travel to mines, markets and international gem-selling centres such as Africa, Russia, Australia, Thailand, Brazil or Madagascar.

As you may be working with valuable materials you may have to work in restricted, high security environments.

Money guide

Starting salaries for gemmologists are around £12,000 a year.

As an experienced gemmologist you can earn between £25,000 and £35,000 a year.

You can earn more than £50,000 a year in a senior position.

Related opportunities

- Gold/Silversmith/Engraver p185
- Jeweller p489
- Materials Scientist p526

Further information

British Jewellers Association
Federation House, 10 Vyse Street, Hockley,
Birmingham, B18 6LT
info@bja.org.uk; www.bja.org.uk

The Gemmological Association (GEM-A)
27 Greville Street, London, EC1N 8TN
020 7407 3334; info@gem-a.com; www.gem-a.info

Jewellery and Allied Industries Training Council (JAITC)
Federation House, 10 Vyse Street, Hockley,
Birmingham, B18 6LT
0121 237 1109; www.jaitc.org.uk

GOLD/SILVERSMITH/ ENGRAVER

What the work involves

- Gold/silversmiths create large and small items such as boxes, figures, picture frames and clocks in gold and silver.

- Engravers will create and insert or engrave images, words or patterns onto stone, glass, metal or wood.

- You will be required to work with your hands and use specialist equipment.

- You may create objects commissioned by jewellers or individual clients, or develop your own craft pieces to sell through galleries and craft shops.

The type of person suited to this work

This job demands tremendous dexterity and conscientiousness. A technical and creative approach is useful to help you to plan a piece and decide on the amount of material needed.

An artistic flair is essential in this type of work, as is the ability to see a project through from start to finish. You will need considerable patience to undertake delicate and sometimes repetitive work with specialist materials and equipment.

If you run your own business you will need a confident and determined approach so that you can promote yourself and your products. Financial and business skills are also needed.

Working conditions

You will probably work in a workshop or studio – either with other craftspeople or on your own. You may work in a shop and will have meetings with customers to discuss pieces of work.

You will use specialist tools for heating, cutting, bending and shaping the metals, which can be dangerous if used incorrectly. You will therefore need to wear eye, face, hand and possibly ear protection for some jobs.

If you work on stone, engraving headstones with machine tools for example, there can be some heavy lifting involved.

Future prospects

This is a competitive area due to the high cost of silver and gold, and the limited demand for glass and metal engraving.

However, stone engravers are sought by stone masonry firms, which are doing less hand-carving than before.

You could work for a specialist company or a shop. With experience and funding, you could set up your own studio/ shop to sell individual pieces.

Advantages/disadvantages

This type of work provides the intense satisfaction of creating attractive and lasting objects.

If you are self-employed, you will have the opportunity to indulge your creativity.

Qualifications and courses

No formal educational qualifications are required to become a gold/silversmith or engraver, but GCSE grades in art and design or design and technology are useful. A variety of formal qualifications are available, from City & Guilds certificates to postgraduate courses.

For those interested in the creative side of engraving, there are degree courses in metalwork, jewellery making and silversmithing. Entry requirements usually include a portfolio of work, an art and design foundation course and/ or a BTEC National Diploma in a relevant subject.

The National Association of Goldsmiths have created a range of courses, designed to complement a traineeship. Many of these can be undertaken by distance learning.

Training is usually done on the job, working with an experienced goldsmith, silversmith or engraver. There is no age limit for entry to training.

Because you will be working with expensive materials, there is very little room for mistakes.

Working with materials such as glass and metal can be challenging and time-consuming.

Money guide

Many goldsmiths/silversmiths work on a part-time basis either for themselves or for jewellers.

As a guide you could start out as a full-time employed designer earning £12,000+ per year, rising to £20,000–£25,000.

Engravers should expect to earn £10,000 – £14,000 to begin with. This can rise to £16,000 to £20,000 with experience. Top earners can expect to earn £30,000.

Related opportunities

- Jewellery Designer p190
- Model maker p192

Further information

British Jewellers' Association
Federation House, 10 Vyse Street, Birmingham B18 6LT
0121 237 1110; www.bja.org.uk

Crafts Council
44a Pentonville Road, London N1 9BY
0207 806 2500; www.craftscouncil.org.uk

Institute of Professional Goldsmiths
PO Box 668, Rickmansworth WD3 0EQ
www.ipgold.org.uk

www.cityandguilds.com/myperfectjob

Design, Arts and Crafts

CRCI: E
CLCI: EG

GRAPHIC DESIGNER

What the work involves

- Graphic designers produce original images and designs for use in published or other materials, such as leaflets, brochures, websites, logos and stationery. Most work is now done on computer, although manual techniques are also occasionally used.

- You will need a thorough understanding of clients' needs in order to develop appropriate designs for specific projects.

- You will be responsible for producing time and budget schedules, and ensuring that they are adhered to.

The type of person suited to this work

It is essential to have a strong creative flair, the imagination to develop original designs and a good eye for layout. Having the skills to draw designs by hand and to use industry-specific graphics or multimedia software packages is also important

You should also have good communication skills, including the confidence to present ideas to colleagues and clients.

It is likely you will work in a fast-paced environment with tight deadlines and will need to be a good multi-tasker, who works well under pressure.

Organisational skills are essential to ensure that projects are carried out on time, within budget and as requested.

Working conditions

Most of your work will take place at a computer and drawing board within a studio. However, you may undertake external research in order to gain inspiration for a project and you will also be required to attend client meetings to present your ideas.

The majority of graphic designers work 37 hours a week, from Monday–Friday. You will be expected to work supplementary hours in order to meet deadlines. Part-time work is available and many designers become freelancers having gained significant experience.

Future prospects

In the UK there are about 40,000 businesses in this growing sector, with over half being in London and the South East. The diversity of graphic design qualifications available has resulted in increased competition for positions.

There is the possibility to work for a range of clients in an agency or in-house for a large organisation such as a bank. Junior designers can progress to senior and eventually a director role. With experience there are many freelance opportunities.

Qualifications and courses

Although it is not a pre-requisite, the majority of graphic designers have a degree or diploma in a related subject like graphic design, or art. For a degree you should have 2 A levels including an art related subject and 5 GCSEs (A-C).

It is essential to have a diverse portfolio that encompasses the breadth of your design capabilities. In the absence of formal qualifications, a keen interest in the sector and an exceptional portfolio may help to secure a trainee post.

Advantages/disadvantages

You will have the opportunity to be creative and hone your business skills simultaneously.

The creation of original work and seeing your ideas being used in the public eye is satisfying.

Competition is becoming increasingly fierce, as the number of available qualifications in this field rises.

Meeting tight deadlines can result in high stress levels.

Money guide

Earnings vary according to the type of employer and geographical location. Large organisations tend to offer higher salaries.

A junior designer can expect to earn from £11,000–£18,000 a year. This may rise to £25,000 with experience.

A creative director can earn £65,000+.

It is possible for a highly regarded freelancer to amass up to £40 per hour.

Related opportunities

- Advertising Art Director p407
- Animator p176
- Cartoonist p177
- Illustrator p188

Further information

Department for Culture, Media and Sport
2–4 Cockspur Street, London SW1Y 5DH
020 7211 6000; www.culture.gov.uk

Design and Art Direction
9 Graphite Square, Vauxhall Walk, London SE11 5EE
020 7840 1111; www.dandad.org

Design Council
34 Bow Street, London WC2E 7DL
020 7420 5200; www.designcouncil.org.uk

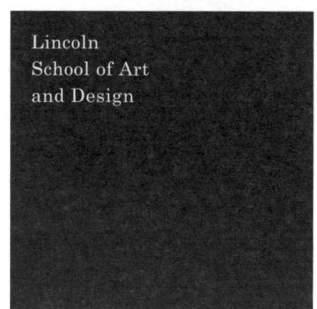

SCHOOL OF ART AND DESIGN
University of Lincoln

The **Lincoln School of Art and Design**, at the University of Lincoln, founded in the 1860s, provides a range of exciting, popular and well-regarded courses in Art and Design disciplines, taught by experienced and committed staff in various sites across the historic part of the city. Many of the courses are vocational in nature, with strong industry links, and with regular field trips, both nationally and internationally, students are often able to exhibit their work outside of Lincoln, such as in London, Milan and Shanghai. Our students are also regular winners of international awards such as D&AD, MPA Roses Student Creativity, New Designers and Brahm SH.

Undergraduate courses offered:-

BA (Hons) Animation

BA (Hons) Conservation and Restoration

BA (Hons) Contemporary Lens Media (Photography and Moving Image)

BA (Hons) Creative Advertising

BA (Hons) Fashion Studies

BA (Hons) Fine Art

BA (Hons) Graphic Design

BA (Hons) Illustration

BA (Hons) Interactive Design (Web design, moving graphics, sound)

BA (Hons) Jewellery and Object (new for 2010)

BA (Hons) Product Design (3D design)

For further information on any of these courses, please contact the Faculty of Art, Architecture and Design at aadenquiries@lincoln.ac.uk or telephone 01522 837171, or visit the School Blog at www.lsad.co.uk

Web links:-

University website	www.lincoln.ac.uk/aad
School of Art and Design website	www.lsad.co.uk
School of Architecture website	www.lincoln.ac.uk/lsa

UNIVERSITY OF
LINCOLN

ILLUSTRATOR/ TECHNICAL ILLUSTRATOR

What the work involves

- You will create original illustrations for published material such as books, magazines and greetings cards. You may also create images for TV and the internet.

- You will work with specialist design software, pen and ink and other media to develop strong designs.

- Your work will include attending client meetings, agreeing payments and contracts, and working to fulfil specific clients' requirements.

- Technical illustrators design accurate graphics or illustrations to accompany and clarify often complex technical information in product and systems manuals, training information, presentations and technical websites.

The type of person suited to this work

You will need strong design skills, a creative flair and imagination for illustration work.

Technical illustration necessitates high attention to detail and strong technical drawing skills to plan and create accurate images.

You should also be able to work well with computer design software.

Sharing ideas and working around another person's vision or 'brief' demands good communication skills.

As many illustrators/technical illustrators work on a self-employed basis, you will need the confidence to promote your services as well as good business and financial sense.

You will require a good knowledge of legal issues in order to protect your copyright and licence rights.

Working conditions

You are likely to work in a shared studio or at your own premises. Technical illustrators occasionally work in offices, and some illustrators are employed in publishing or design houses, but freelancing is increasing.

You will probably use paints and adhesives which may cause respiratory problems or skin allergies for susceptible people.

Future prospects

The internet and email have made it easier for illustrators to promote themselves and find work, and it is now possible to gain work from clients based overseas.

Some people choose to specialise in competitive areas such as medical, botanical or technical illustration.

To subsidise their income, some illustrators also teach, lecture or work in other related areas. A small number write and illustrate their own books. Others supplement their salary by selling illustrations and paintings through galleries.

Qualifications and courses

ENTRY LEVEL 3

Most professional illustrators have an HNC/HND, foundation degree or degree in art and design related subjects such as graphic design, fine art and fashion. A strong portfolio is essential, and an excellent portfolio can be a substitute for academic qualifications.

Technical illustrators are required to demonstrate a good knowledge of science and/or technology depending on your desired specialisation.

Training is provided on the job, and can lead to specialisation in such areas as technical illustration or medical illustration.

The Association of Illustrators (AOI) offer practical advice to illustrators and run training seminars on business and computer related subjects.

Advantages/disadvantages

This type of work provides the satisfaction of seeing your work in print and often in the public domain.

Working on a freelance, job-by-job basis can be an insecure way to make a living. Generally, illustrators have a second job to support them during quiet periods.

Money guide

Salaries vary according to employers and individual projects. Projects can range from one image to a series of illustrations. Illustrators may be paid per project, by the hour or by the day. Hourly pay is around £35.

Income for employed new entrants is around £14,000–£18,000 per year. Experienced illustrators could earn £20,000–£30,000. With 10 years' experience, the best known can earn in excess of £40,000 per year.

Related opportunities

- Fine Artist p183
- Cartoonist p177
- Graphic Designer p186
- Medical Illustrator p191

Further information

Association of Illustrators
2nd Floor, Back Building, 150 Curtain Road, London EC2A 3AT
020 7613 4328; www.theaoi.com

Institute of Scientific and Technical Communicators
(ISTC) Airport House, Purley Way, Croydon, CR0 0XZ
020 8253 4506; www.istc.org.uk

INTERIOR DESIGNER

What the work involves

- Interior designers create specific, co-ordinated styles for homes, commercial spaces and other buildings.

- You will be required to assess spaces, produce detailed designs, increasingly using computer-aided design (CAD) software, and choose suitable materials for the project, which may include upholstery, wallpaper, furniture and decorative objects

- You will need to get a good understanding the client's needs, and also negotiate fees with them.

- You will provide supervision to ensure that the project is completed accurately and is in accordance with the budget and schedule.

The type of person suited to this work

It is essential to have a strong creative flair and the imagination to develop original designs. Having the skills to draw designs by hand and to use specialist CAD software when required are also very important.

You will be required to keep up-to-date with changes in design and architecture, and to understand building regulations.

These abilities should be balanced with good business sense and the competency to see a project through.

You should also have good communication, negotiation and organisational skills to ensure that projects are carried out on time, within budget and as requested.

Working conditions

The main employers in this sector are design and architectural firms. However many designers are self-employed and part-time work is possible.

Many client meetings occur in the evenings and at weekends. You could be working on several contracts at the same time and tight deadlines can result in stress and may necessitate extra working hours.

Your work will be divided between meeting clients in their own premises and working in your studio, or other work space.

Smart dress is expected and protective clothing may be required on-site.

Future prospects

The contribution of design towards the UK economy is very important and the significance of this intensely competitive sector continues to grow.

Although many interior designers work for design and architectural companies, some are freelance and many choose self-employment, either immediately after graduation or after gaining work experience.

Gaining significant experience can result in progression to a partner role in a consultancy.

The UK industry has an excellent international reputation offering progression to work overseas if desired.

Qualifications and courses

ENTRY LEVEL 3

Entry to this profession is rare without an HNC/HND, foundation degree or degree in art or design; 5 GCSEs (A–C) and 2 relevant A levels are usually required.

In the absence of formal qualifications, an exceptional portfolio may secure a trainee post within a design or architectural firm.

A City & Guilds qualification is also available in interior design and CAD skills.

Advantages/disadvantages

The creation of original work and seeing your ideas being used in a practical or decorative way is satisfying.

Working as a freelance designer can result in greater flexibility.

You will have to adapt your ideas to fit the client's requirements.

Money guide

Junior interior designers can expect to earn between £22,000 and £26,000 per year.

Senior designers can earn £30,000+ per year, while directors can earn up to £75,000 per year.

In contrast, earnings for self-employed designers can be very low, particularly at the beginning. Freelancers typically earn from £18 per hour upwards.

Related opportunities

- Display Designer/Window Dresser p180
- Illustrator p188
- Model Maker p192

Further information

British Interior Design Association
Units 109–111 The Chambers, Chelsea Harbour,
London SW10 0XF
020 7349 0800; www.bida.org

Design Council
34 Bow Street, London WC2E 7DL
020 7420 5200; www.designcouncil.org.uk

The Society for Professional Designers
5 Bermondsey Exchange, 175–181 Bermondsey Street,
London SE1 3UW
020 7357 8088; www.csd.org.uk

City&
Guilds

www.cityandguilds.com/myperfectjob

JEWELLERY DESIGNER

What the work involves

- Jewellery designers are involved in each aspect of the production of decorative pieces of jewellery, made of gold, silver, precious metals and stones.

- You will research the design and the function of a piece; its symbolism, the materials used, the cost, the potential buyer and even current trends.

- You will prepare detailed drawings which you or a craftworker will construct using traditional crafting methods or using high-tech machinery. A design may be for a one-off piece or part of a range of pieces.

- You will undertake tasks such as stone cutting and setting, model-making, mounting, engraving, enamelling, welding, chain-making, cleaning and polishing.

The type of person suited to this work

You should have a strong interest in art, design and craftwork. As your sales may be influenced by the current design marketplace you should keep up-to-date with jewellery fashion and design trends.

You must have a keen eye for detail and patience as you will be working with small scales and intricate and delicate designs.

You will need to be organised and self-motivated as you will probably be working on a variety of projects at the same time.

You should also be able to visualise two-dimensional designs as three-dimensional objects.

Working conditions

If you are employed by a company you will usually work 39 hours a week, Monday to Friday, including late night or weekend work when deadlines are approaching.

You can also work on a freelance basis or become self-employed. If you are self-employed you are likely to work on commission and produce designs specifically tailored to the client's requirements.

You may work in a studio which can be bright and airy or in a large workshop, which may be noisy and dusty. You must wear protective clothing.

Future prospects

As you gain experience and build up a good reputation you may be able to become self-employed. To stay ahead in the industry you should attend trade fairs and exhibitions.

As an employed goldsmith or silversmith you may be able to progress to management positions or retail positions such as international buyer.

Advantages/disadvantages

You may be able to work from your own designs and see your creations become popular pieces.

Qualifications and courses

There are no academic requirements in order to become a jewellery designer. However many courses and programmes are available which may help you to develop your skills.

You can take GCSEs in art and design or design technology which will help you to gain entry to this profession or to higher level courses. These include HNDs, foundation degrees or degrees in art and design or craft making such as goldsmithing, silversmithing, and jewellery design. It may be possible to move across from another relevant subject such as fashion design, textile design, fine art, or applied arts if you build up a suitable portfolio.

If you are interested in gold and silver craftwork specifically you may benefit from a BTEC National Certificate or Diploma course in Design Crafts which are available at some colleges.

However, qualifications are not as important as craft skills. Work placements can help you to accumulate experience of the jewellery industry and build up a network of contacts which will help you to develop skills and find buyers and sellers for your work.

Without further education you may need to take an apprenticeship or receive on-the-job training.

As a self-employed jewellery designer you may find that without the right support system in areas such as promotion, marketing and sales it can be difficult to become established.

Money guide

As a graduate your salary can start at around £15,000 but this can increase to £25,000 or more with experience.

Your salary will depend greatly on factors such as whether or not you are self-employed, experienced and have enough success to gain a reputation within the industry.

Related opportunities

- Gold/Silversmith/Engraver p185
- Fashion Designer/Milliner p181
- Product Designer p195

Further information

The British Jewellers Association
Federation House, 10 Vyse Street, Birmingham, B18 6LT
info@bja.org.uk; www.bja.org.uk

Crafts Council
44a Pentonville Road, Islington, London, N1 9BY
0207 806 2500; education@craftscouncil.org.uk;
www.craftscouncil.org.uk

City&
Guilds

www.cityandguilds.com/myperfectjob

MEDICAL ILLUSTRATOR

What the work involves

- Medical illustrators create annotated or labelled images to provide visual information to professionals and trainees working in medical care, research and education.

- You may also work as a medical photographer and video producer (digital technician), or combine all these functions in one role.

- You will have to record images of patients and develop graphics for health/medical publications such as information leaflets and websites. You could work in wards, operating theatres, pathology labs, mortuaries and clinical exam centres.

Qualifications and courses

2010 will see the inauguration of a national register for medical illustrators. Qualified clinical illustrators will be required to register with the Health Professions Council (HPC) and will need to have a degree or postgraduate degree in clinical photography.

The Medical Artists' Educational Trust postgraduate diploma in medical art is available in Manchester and London. Entrants require a degree and a relevant portfolio. Completion results in membership of the trust.

Medical illustrators usually enter the profession as trainees and learn on the job while working towards a medical illustration qualification.

The type of person suited to this work

Good visual sense and attention to detail is very important.

You should have excellent technical skills to work with equipment such as videos and cameras, and will have to work creatively yet accurately with computer design packages.

As you will have to record images of patients, a sensitive, tactful and ethical approach is very important.

Also required is the ability to communicate with all sorts of people, some of whom could be very ill. You must be able to cope with upsetting situations and sights, for example, if visiting someone who is terminal, or if working in a mortuary or operating theatre.

Working conditions

You may be based within a group of hospitals and other centres and have to travel regularly between these. During the day you will visit theatres, wards, training centres and mortuaries – all of which could involve distressing sights and intense odours. You may have to be on call at night to photograph emergency operations.

Using a computer and software design packages, you will work within an office or studio to prepare and produce images and visual information. You may also have to record laboratory results.

Future prospects

Whilst this is a relatively small and quite competitive area of work, there is a steady need for accurate medical visual information.

Gaining a range of technical skills and experience rather than specialising in one area could open more opportunities.

After training, it is possible to progress within one organisation to head of department or you could go on to provide freelance services for medical establishments or medical and scientific publications.

Advantages/disadvantages

This job gives the satisfaction of providing valuable visual information to help medical professionals and their patients.

You may have the opportunity to freelance, which offers flexibility.

You will work with sick and sometimes distressed patients and may have to deal with upsetting sights.

You may have to be on call at night in order to photograph emergency operations.

Money guide

£18,000 per year is usual for starting salaries.

With experience, senior medical illustrators can earn around £30,000+.

Up to £50,000 is possible for a head of department in a university teaching hospital.

Medical illustrators in large universities could be employed on a number of pay scales covering technicians, medical laboratory officers, or sterile services technicians. Check with the universities for more details.

Related opportunities

- Fine Artist p183
- Graphic Designer p186
- Illustrator p188
- Photographer p421

Further information

Association of Illustrators
2nd Floor, Back Building, 150 Curtain Road,
London, EC2A 3AT
020 7613 4328; www.theaoi.com

Health Professions Council (HPC)
Park House, 184 Kennington Park Road, London SE11 4BU
020 7582 0866; www.hpc-uk.org

Institute of Medical Illustrators
29 Arboretum Street, Nottingham NG1 4JA
01216 272336; www.imi.org.uk

Design, Arts and Crafts

CRCI: E
CLCI: ED

MODEL MAKER

What the work involves

- Working with materials such as fibreglass, resin, wood and rubber you will create three-dimensional images or models.

- You will construct detailed and accurate models of buildings and other architectural sites. Also, you might make figures for museums, TV or film companies.

- You will work with clients to develop their ideas into a convincing and practical model, deciding which materials to use.

- Finally, you will plan models using technical drawings or computer software

The type of person suited to this work

You will need a strong creative flair and imagination to visualise and develop models. Producing detailed models out of fragile materials demands tremendous patience. You will also need good technical skills. In addition, you should have a logical approach, in order to plan and create accurate work.

The tasks will demand great attention to detail. Good eyesight is important in this role. A feel for and interest in design will enable you to create well-planned models.

You will also need a basic knowledge of maths and the ability to understand technical drawings. The capacity to work effectively with computer design packages is increasingly important in this area of work.

Working conditions

Your work will be carried out in a studio, where you will wear protective clothing to suit the materials and tools you are using. This could include eye, ear and skin protection. Sometimes you may be based in an office, planning models with specialist design software.

As this job involves a great deal of close eye-work, it may not be suitable for those with even slight visual impairment.

Model makers work with chemicals, which can affect people with skin or respiratory conditions.

Future prospects

Most model makers work within London and the south-east of England. Whilst this is quite a small area of work, there are a number of career routes and demand is stable.

You could focus on architectural model making and work for a large architectural practice. Other organisations requiring model makers include museums, creating historical models for display purposes. However, most model makers work on a freelance basis and are paid on a contract-by-contract basis.

Model makers also create the props and figures in all kinds of films including animations, adverts and TV programmes, which offer other job opportunities.

Qualifications and courses

There are no formal entry requirements for this job. However, most entrants complete a model-making course and a portfolio of work is usually required.

The ability to work with your hands, using specialist tools, is required.

There are a wide variety of courses available, from a City & Guilds Level 2 Progression Award in Applying Engineering Principles to degrees in 3-dimensional design. Entry requirements vary, but entry is very competitive and most institutions will expect at least some GCSEs/S grades in subjects such as maths, design and technology, and physics.

Entry via an Apprenticeship/Skillseekers programme may be possible.

Advantages/disadvantages

This job can provide the satisfaction of using your creativity and developing original work. You may need to create highly detailed work to fairly limited deadlines, which can be stressful.

Money guide

Starting salaries begin at around £13,000–£17,000 per year as a model maker. With experience this rises to around £22,500-£30,000. At senior level with many years of experience you could earn up to £45,000.

Related opportunities

- Fine Artist p183
- Graphic Designer p186
- Signwriter/Signmaker p196
- Toymaker/Designer p198

Further information

Design Council
34 Bow Street, London, WC2E 7DL
020 7420 5200; www.designcouncil.org.uk

Crafts Council
44a Pentonville Road, Islington, London, N1 9BY
0207 806 2500; www.craftscouncil.org.uk

ccskills – Creative and Cultural Skills
4th Floor, Lafone House, The Leathermarket, Weston St, London, SE1 3HN
020 7015 1800; www.ccskills.org.uk

MUSICAL INSTRUMENT MAKER/ REPAIRER/PIANO TUNER

What the work involves

- You will repair and service musical instruments such as pianos, flutes and violins. This can involve replacing worn-down or broken parts or checking for the cause of specific faults.

- Your work will include meeting customers and dealing with repair requests or commissions for new instruments.

- Piano tuners check the condition and tonic range of different types of pianos by undertaking assessments using specialist equipment. This could range from fine tuning to obtain 'concert pitch', to significant maintenance work.

The type of person suited to this work

A passion for music and a practical understanding of how musical instruments function is essential. They are complex objects so you will need a good eye for detail and a patient approach. In addition, piano tuners should have a good ear for sound.

Strong technical skills will enable you to design, create or repair instruments. You will need to be dextrous and confident in working with your hands and in using materials such as wood and glue.

Good verbal communication skills and the ability to work with people is also important for customer care.

Working conditions

You will work with a range of specialised tools in the workshop of a specialist company or from home if self-employed.

With larger instruments, such as pianos, organs or timpani, you will need to visit private homes and other locations (such as concert halls, theatres or music studios) to do repairs on-site. A driving licence and your own transport will be helpful.

The work requires strong manual handling skills. Some of the specialist materials used in the work could affect people with skin or respiratory conditions.

Future prospects

This is a specialised area of work, but these services are required by educational music departments, major orchestras, opera houses and theatres, rehearsal studios, retailers, individual musicians and others.

Some musical instrument makers/repairers specialise in a specific area such as early musical instruments or classical guitars or make more unusual instruments to customer requests.

Many people are self-employed in this area and some music shops will publicise local repairers, instrument makers and tuners, rather than employing their own.

Qualifications and courses

Musical instrument maker/ repairer

Applicants should have GCSEs/S grades in relevant subjects, such as design and technology, plus a professional qualification. These range from City & Guilds certificates to degrees.

Specific vocational qualifications are available in music technology, musical instrument making, and musical instrument technology and repair. Some courses allow specialisation in certain types of instruments such as strings or woodwind.

It is useful to be able to play a musical instrument.

Piano tuner

Piano-tuning courses are available. The Royal National College for the Blind runs the VIEW National Diploma for piano tuners. Students learn about the tuning and repair of pianos as well as the practicalities of running a small business.

Advantages/disadvantages

Many musical instrument repairers/makers/piano tuners freelance and work on a project-by-project basis, which can create some job insecurity.

If you enjoy making or listening to music, this career has excellent fringe benefits as you could work for some of the best musical talents in the UK.

Money guide

In some parts of the country there is not sufficient work for full-time employment so earnings will depend on your location, the local music scene and your specialism.

You could earn £16,000–£20,000 per year once trained. The most experienced people can earn up to £40,000.

Related opportunities

- Musician p446
- Music Teacher p209
- Art Therapist/Drama Therapist/Music Therapist p296
- Model Maker p192

Further information

Crafts Council
44a Pentonville Road, London N1 9BY
0207 806 2500; www.craftscouncil.org.uk

Institute of Musical Instrument Technology
Northfield House, 11 Kendal Avenue South, Croydon CR2 0QR
www.imit.org.uk

Pianoforte Tuners' Association
PO Box 1312, Lightwater, Woking GU18 5UB
0845 602 8796; www.pianotuner.org.uk

Design, Arts and Crafts

CRCI: NJ
CLCI: SAB

PICTURE FRAMER

What the work involves

- You will plan and create attractive and protective surrounds or frames for prints, paintings, photographs and three-dimensional objects.

- Working with specialist equipment and materials you will create strong, high-quality frames.

- Helping customers choose the most suitable style and size of frame will be part of your job, as will advising them on the most practical and appropriate method of framing and glazing the artwork.

- If you work on a self-employed basis you will need to promote your services to potential customers.

The type of person suited to this work

Framing services are used to protect valued or valuable works of art, so an interest in art is essential. You will also need good customer service skills. Technical skills and the ability to work safely with potentially dangerous equipment are highly important. You should be able to carry out a range of framing techniques.

Paying attention to detail and taking a pride in your work will ensure that you produce high-quality frames. You will need to be able to work under pressure as short deadlines can be a part of this job. You should also be commercially aware. If self-employed, you will require business, financial and marketing skills to be successful.

Working conditions

You could work in a shop or workshop. When working in the shop you will have to deal with customers who can sometimes be rude or confrontational, if dissatisfied. Workshops can be noisy and busy.

Picture framers generally work 37 hours a week, with overtime during busy periods. Some picture framers work on a part-time basis.

Picture framers work with potentially dangerous equipment such as specialist cutting machinery so you will need to be aware of health and safety requirements.

Future prospects

As there are fewer than 10,000 picture-framing businesses across all of the UK, opportunities for new entrants can be limited.

Many picture framers set up their own studios or shops and often sell works of art and artists' materials as well as providing framing services. Others work solely in framing and are employed in larger workshops – mass-producing framed prints and mirrors. With experience and additional training in conservation techniques and materials, some framers progress into art and furniture restoration work.

Qualifications and courses

ENTRY LEVEL 1

There are no formal educational requirements. However, an interest and experience in woodwork or metalwork would be useful. Some GCSEs/S grades (A–E/1–5) can also be an advantage; relevant subjects include art and design and craft, design and technology.

Training is usually done on the job. Some specialist training courses are also available.

Picture framers are able to work towards the Fine Art Trade Guild Commended Framer (GCF) qualification, which involves both practical and written assessments. In order to work with high-value items, framers need to be trained to conservation standards.

Advantages/disadvantages

This job provides the satisfaction of creating enduring and high-quality items. This is precise, careful work that demands a lot of patience.

You will sometimes have to take responsibility for highly valuable works of art whilst they are in your care.

Money guide

Your salary will depend on where you work and your employment situation. As a trainee picture framer you could earn around £11,000 per year. This rises to £15,000 with experience. If working in a workshop or specialist shop in a management role you could earn £20,000–£26,000. Earnings for self-employed framers vary depending on location and expertise.

Related opportunities

- Antiques Dealer p478
- Conservator/Restorer p353
- Gold/Silversmith/Engraver p185
- Model Maker p192

Further information

Fine Art Trade Guild
16–18 Empress Place, London, SW6 1TT
020 7381 6616; www.fineart.co.uk

Institute of Conservation (Icon)
3rd floor, Downstream Building, 1 London Bridge, London, SE1 9BG
020 7785 3807; www.icon.org.uk

City&
Guilds

www.cityandguilds.com/myperfectjob

PRODUCT DESIGNER

What the work involves

- Product designers create products and improve the aesthetic appeal, functionality or cost efficiency of existing offerings. These could be day-to-day consumer products like tables, or specialist medical, scientific or telecommunications equipment. You will use both traditional drawing techniques, as well as specialist computer software.

- You will need a thorough understanding of clients' needs and consumer behaviour in order to develop appropriate designs for specific projects.

- You will be responsible for producing time and budget schedules, and ensuring that they are adhered to.

The type of person suited to this work

This job marries creativity with technical expertise.

You will be expected to use your imagination to develop original designs, so you should have a good eye for aesthetics and the skills to draw designs by hand and to use specialist software packages.

It is important to have good practical and technical knowledge, and to understand the functionality of different materials and production methods.

You should also have good communication skills and an understanding of clients' needs, consumer behaviour, product selection and usage.

Problem-solving and organisational skills are essential to ensure that projects are carried out on time, within budget and as requested.

Working conditions

The majority of product designers work 37 hours a week, from Monday–Friday. You will be expected to work supplementary hours in order to meet deadlines. Part-time work is available and many designers become freelancers having gained significant experience.

Most of your work will take place in a bright, clean studio or office. However, you will undertake some experiments and material testing in lab conditions, using some dangerous cutting and construction tools. In addition you may have to visit external production factories, which may be dusty and noisy.

Future prospects

Product designers work in a variety of manufacturing settings in the UK. Employment is available all over the UK, with most work in manufacturing firms and design companies, which produce material for a variety of sectors.

Competition to attain an entry level job is stiff; however there is a shortage of experienced product designers with a high level of technical expertise. Experienced designers may have the opportunity to work abroad.

Qualifications and courses

ENTRY LEVEL 3

Entry to this profession is rare without an HNC/HND or degree in product design, industrial design or a related subject. Degree courses usually last 3 or 4 years and some include a sandwich year, during which an industrial placement is undertaken. Entry requirements are usually 2 A levels and 5 GCSEs. For an HND, you should have an A-level in an art and design related subject.

A postgraduate or Masters qualification may be particularly useful in specific sectors and with certain European clients.

It is helpful to attain experience before entering this profession as it highlights commitment to the industry. This can be achieved by means of an industrial placement, freelance work or design competitions.

Advantages/disadvantages

You will have the opportunity to be creative and use your technical skills simultaneously.

The creation of original work and seeing your ideas being used in the public eye is satisfying.

Competition for entry level jobs is fierce.

Meeting tight deadlines can result in high stress levels

Money guide

Earnings vary according to the type of employer and geographical location. Large organisations tend to offer higher salaries.

Newly qualified product designers can expect to earn from £17,000–£20,000 per year. This may rise to £25,000 to £35,000 with experience. Senior product designers can earn £45,000+ and the most skilled and experienced can achieve £50,000+. However, most industrial/product designers will earn more than those within three-dimensional design.

Related opportunities

- Manufacturing Engineer p236
- Toolmaker p253
- Toymaker/Designer p198

Further information

The Society for Professional Designers
5 Bermondsey Exchange, 175–181 Bermondsey Street, London SE1 3UW
020 7357 8088; www.csd.org.uk

City&
Guilds

www.cityandguilds.com/myperfectjob

Design, Arts and Crafts

CRCI: E
CLCI: EG

SIGNWRITER/SIGNMAKER

Design, Arts and Crafts

CRCI: E
CLCI: ED

What the work involves

- You will design, plan and produce signs with graphic images, lettering and logos to publicise companies, attract customers and draw attention to specific locations.

- You will work closely with customers to develop appropriate, attractive designs that match their requirements.

- You could work with any number of different materials; from plastics to glass to sketching as well as using Computer Aided Design (CAD).

- Signwriters/signmakers work for a range of companies and organisations, producing signs for shop fronts, roadsides, hospitals, vehicles and even boats!

The type of person suited to this work

As you will be creating signs to attract, interest or warn people, you will need strong graphic design skills. A creative flair and good drawing skills are also important. You will need a good understanding of the materials you work with and good practical and manual skills.

You will need to pay attention to detail and have a logical approach to ensure that your signs are well produced and precise. Technical skills will allow you to work with a range of equipment. ICT skills are increasingly important in this area. Good written and verbal communication skills will help you to meet clients' requirements accurately and avoid expensive errors.

Working conditions

You could work within a studio or manufacturing site, which can get messy and noisy. You may attend meetings with customers. Much of your time will be spent drafting signs at a computer using special software.

You may work with large or small-scale specialist equipment, with printing inks and chemical finishes, which can affect people with skin or respiratory conditions.

Sometimes, you will make site visits to ensure that your signs will be highly visible.

Future prospects

This is a fairly competitive area; however, the demand for high-quality signs from a range of organisations means that there are many opportunities. You could work in the more commercial side of signwriting, within a specialist company on the design or manufacturing side. Or you could work within the more creative, hand-crafted side of the industry.

Some signwriters go into set design for theatre. With experience, you could start your own business – perhaps specialising in pub or restaurant signs.

Qualifications and courses

ENTRY LEVEL 1

There are no formal educational requirements, but relevant vocational qualifications can be useful. NVQs/SVQs are available in Signmaking.

Training is usually done on the job.

Many employers offer Apprenticeships/Skillseekers for people aged 16–24. Applicants normally require 4 GCSEs/S grades (A–D/1–4), including maths, English language, a science and an art and design subject, or other evidence of aptitude and achievement.

It is also possible to take a full- or part-time course in signwriting and signmaking. Or you can specialise in this area after taking a general Art and Design course.

Advantages/disadvantages

This kind of work can provide some opportunities to work creatively and use your imagination to help customers, for example when designing a company logo. You may travel to visit a range of locations, to take measurements or photographs. You can work abroad as a signwriter.

Money guide

Trainees are most likely to start at around £7,500–£9,000. With experience, signwriters can earn £17,000–£24,000 per year. With management responsibilities you could earn up to £30,000. Self-employed signwriters will earn more.

Related opportunities

- Cartoonist p177
- Fine Artist p183
- Gold/Silversmith/Engraver p185
- Graphic Designer p186

Further information

British Sign and Graphics Association
5 Orton Enterprise Centre, Bakewell Road, Peterborough, Cambridgeshire, PE2 6XU
01733 230033; www.bsga.co.uk

ccskills – Creative and Cultural Skills
4th Floor, Lafone House, The Leathermarket, Weston St, London, SE1 3HN
020 7015 1800; www.ccskills.org.uk

The Faversham House Group Ltd
Faversham House, 232a Addington Road, South Croydon, Surrey, CR2 8LE
020 8651 7100; www.fhgmedia.com

City&
Guilds

www.cityandguilds.com/myperfectjob

STAGE/SET DESIGNER

What the work involves

- Stage/set designers are responsible for the visual elements of a theatre (stage designer), TV or film production (set designer) including sets, locations and possibly props and costumes.

- From background research, you will be required to create original ideas which accurately reflect the relevant style and historical period of the piece.

- Working closely with the production team, you will oversee the development and installation of the sets and ensure that everything is delivered on time and within budget.

The type of person suited to this work

It is essential to have a strong creative flair and a good eye for design. Having the skills to use specialist CAD software, to draw designs by hand and to create scale models when required is also very important.

You should be detail driven and demonstrate a passion for history, culture and the performing arts.

These abilities should be balanced with good communication skills to aid leadership and self-promotion.

Organisational skills are important to ensure that projects are carried out on time, within budget and as requested. As deadlines can be tight, you should also have the ability to work well under pressure.

Working conditions

Designers either work directly for the production company or freelance. Working hours are long and unsociable and travel may be involved. You will be expected to work supplementary hours in order to meet deadlines.

Your work will be divided between being in a studio designing and building models of the sets, and consequent supervision or involvement in their creation. Normally this happens behind the scenes in theatres, television studios or purpose-built warehouses.

You will work on large pieces, which necessitate the use of ladders and scaffolding.

Future prospects

Stage designers work for theatres and opera houses and may have the opportunity to oversee a travelling production. There is fierce competition for entry level positions.

Set designers can work for the BBC or one of the 1,500 production firms in the country.

Part-time work is difficult to find and although there are many freelancers in the industry, work can be sporadic.

Advantages/disadvantages

The creation of original work and seeing your ideas being used in the public eye and in high profile productions is satisfying.

Qualifications and courses

ENTRY LEVEL 3

It is possible to enter the industry as a craft assistant in a design studio and work your way up. However, most people have an HND, a degree, or postgraduate diploma or degree in theatre design or a related art and design subject.

For a degree you should have 2 A levels, a BTEC national diploma in a relevant subject and 5 GCSEs (A-C). For an HNC you are normally required to have one A-level.

FT2 – Film & Television Freelance Training offers a full-time Design First course. This would help you to become an art department assistant, although places are limited.

It is helpful to attain experience before entering this highly competitive profession as it highlights commitment to the industry. This can be achieved by means of an unpaid placement, freelance work, involvement in student productions or design competitions.

Working as a freelancer can result in greater flexibility.

Competition for entry level jobs is fierce and a strong portfolio and good networking skills are important.

Meeting tight deadlines can result in high stress levels.

Money guide

Newly qualified assistant designers in a theatre can expect to earn about £15,500 per year. This may rise to £20,000 for a resident head designer position and those with the most experience can earn about £40,000.

Many designers are freelancers. Their earnings will be dependent on individual ability and contract sizes. According to the Broadcasting Entertainment Cinematographic and Theatre Union (BECTU) the current minimum rate for a freelance art assistant is £280.

Related opportunities

- Costume Designer p178
- Interior Designer p189
- Model Maker p192
- Production Assistant/Runner p424

Further information

Design Council
34 Bow Street, London WC2E 7DL
020 7420 5200; www.designcouncil.org.uk

The Society of British Theatre Designers
4th Floor, 55 Farringdon Road, London EC1M 3JB
020 7242 9200; www.theatredesign.org.uk

City&
Guilds

www.cityandguilds.com/myperfectjob

Design, Arts and Crafts

CRCI: E
CLCI: ET

TOYMAKER/DESIGNER

What the work involves

- You will design, plan, test and create toys for babies, children and even adults!

- As a traditional toymaker, you could use early designs to make traditional toys by hand, such as doll's houses and rocking horses.

- You will spend time promoting your work and design services to clients and customers. Your work could be sold in shops or at craft fairs and toy fairs.

The type of person suited to this work

As you will be developing original ideas, you will need a strong creative flair. Practical design skills and an active imagination will help you create long-lasting and functional toys from your designs. A genuine interest in how individuals respond to toys will help you design appealing items that sell well.

If creating objects by hand, as many toymakers do, you will need good manual handling skills and an understanding of the materials you work with.

If self-employed, you will also need good business and financial skills and the confidence to promote your work.

Working conditions

Most toymakers/designers spend a lot of time in a workshop, planning and developing their products. Here you will use your tools, equipment and different materials. Some of them can be dangerous so you will need to be aware of health and safety regulations and of the need to wear protective clothing and masks.

If employed as a toy designer by a toy production company, you may work purely with computer design software and create, rather than construct, your designs.

Future prospects

Public interest in traditional toys and games is growing. You could work on a self-employed basis, making and designing toys. Some toymakers/designers own shops where they sell unusual and traditional toys as well as their own handmade toys. A growing number sell their products at craft fairs, on the internet or by mail order. With rising concerns for the environment, you may have to ensure your materials are from sustainable sources and ecofriendly.

A small number of toymakers also restore antique toys. There is steady demand for innovative toys in high street shops and you will always have an emerging potential market for new products!

Advantages/disadvantages

This work provides the enjoyment of creating fun, attractive objects.

Qualifications and courses

There are no formal entry requirements, but many entrants have a background in art and design, and HND or degree qualifications can be an advantage. Relevant subjects include art and design, graphic or three-dimensional design, creative arts and craft and model making.

In England, Wales and Northern Ireland many students take a 1-year Foundation course as preparation for entry to an art and design degree; 5 GCSEs (A–C) and a relevant A level are also usually required. In Scotland the first year of a degree equates to the Foundation year.

There are various courses available, such as Foundation degrees in 3-dimensional design and creative arts, and degrees in craft studies. Institutes sometimes have links with toy manufacturers, which can provide a useful first step into the industry. Degree entry requirements are usually 2 A levels/3 H grades or equivalent.

It can take time to build up a business, if working on a self-employed basis.

If self-employed you will need both creative and business skills to succeed.

Money guide

Starting salaries for toy designers working for toy manufacturers range from £9,000–£16,000 per year. With experience and working in a large company this can increase to £23,000–£35,000. As a top designer you could get up to £45,000. Traditional toymakers are usually self-employed and salaries will depend on the success of the business.

Related opportunities

- Animator p176
- Carpenter/Joiner p77
- Model Maker p192
- Picture Framer p194

Further information

British Toymakers Guild
124 Walcot Street, Bath BA1 5BG
01225 442440; www.toymakersguild.co.uk

Design Council
34 Bow Street, London WC2E 7DL
020 7420 5200; www.designcouncil.org.uk

Crafts Council
44a Pentonville Road, London N1 9BY
0207 806 2500; www.craftscouncil.org.uk

City&
Guilds

www.cityandguilds.com/myperfectjob

Education and Training

To work in this sector you need to be motivated and enthusiastic about other people's learning, whether it's adults or children. If you chose to teach, the range of subjects available is huge so whatever your interest – languages, art, sciences, cooking, sports – you can become a teacher in that field. Jobs in this sector require a multitude of skills including: creativity, imagination, numerical skills, good communication and organisational skills and, in some cases, having a lot of patience!

The following jobs are covered in this section:

Education and Training

CRCI: F
CLCI: KEG

COMMUNITY EDUCATION OFFICER

What the work involves

- Community education officers provide all members of the community with information on, and access to, educational and developmental programmes.

- You will identify the needs and interests of the community, and sensitively and creatively organise a variety of suitable activities and courses to improve learning, career and personal development opportunities.

- You will plan projects and outreach programmes, liaise with community and local authority groups, and recruit and train staff. At a senior level your job will involve policy development and negotiating funding.

- You may work in areas of social deprivation or high unemployment, or with certain disadvantaged groups such as ethnic minorities or the homeless.

The type of person suited to this work

You should have a genuine interest in helping people and charitable work.

As you will be liaising with communities and official government and voluntary bodies you must be able to communicate with a variety of different people and situations, both casual and formal, whilst maintaining a professional approach.

You should be a good listener and have a practical, optimistic approach to problem solving.

You will need to show initiative in your approach to your work but you will also require patience as many projects are long-term developments rather than quick-fix solutions.

Working conditions

You will probably work flexible hours as many posts are short-term contracts because their existence is heavily dependent on funding which can be difficult as many projects are long-term programmes. There is plenty of opportunity for part time work and flexible hours but these may involve working during the evening and at weekends.

You will have an office based in a community centre, a local authority or a college, from which you will travel to the surrounding region.

Future prospects

You will receive formal training once you have secured a post consisting of short courses that will develop skills or examine new issues such as health development or training.

You may find that postgraduate MA programmes in community studies and education are beneficial to your progress. NVQs and diploma qualifications in relevant subjects such as youth and community work will boost your opportunities for progression.

Qualifications and courses

ENTRY LEVEL 5

You can gain entry to this profession as a graduate, a Diplomate or with a HND/foundation degree. A qualification in a relevant subject such as community education, sociology, social sciences or educational studies may give you an advantage.

Normally employers seek candidates who have combined their qualification with voluntary community experience.

If you accumulate significant experience but have no qualifications it may be possible for you to achieve a post in the voluntary sector involving recreational activities for example. However, it is likely that you will be required to have academic qualifications to secure a senior level role. Some undergraduate and postgraduate courses provide part time or distance learning and many employers will support you while you are studying.

You can gain experience when you are a student to learn about the sector and decide if it is an area you would like to work in. Information and advice about voluntary work is available from local volunteer bureaux, student volunteer centres and the YouthNetUK online volunteer service.

Advantages/disadvantages

You will provide communities and their members the educational opportunities they require for personal or career growth which can be highly rewarding.

Your work may be frustrating at times as certain aspects such as the establishment of courses and programmes will depend on the availability of funding.

Money guide

If you work for the public sector you will earn around £20,000 to £23,000 on average. This may be lower if you work in the voluntary sector. With experience and qualifications you can progress to a senior post where may earn in the region of £30,000 to £35,000.

Related opportunities

- Social Worker p585
- Volunteer Organiser p588
- Youth and Community Worker p591

Further information

Workers' Educational Association (WEA)
Corporate Services, 3rd Floor, 70 Clifton Street,
London, EC2A 4HB
020 7426 3450; national@wea.org.uk; www.wea.org.uk

City&
Guilds

www.cityandguilds.com/myperfectjob

DANCE TEACHER

What the work involves

- Planning dance lessons for pupils which adhere to a syllabus or curriculum set out by a school or in order to gain a dance qualification

- Helping your pupils to develop their fitness and agility and ensuring that they do so safely without causing injury to themselves or others

- Entering pupils into examinations

- Choreographing dance routines, choosing music and costumes

The type of person suited to this work

You need to have a high level of fitness and stamina and be able to demonstrate complicated dance moves and positions to your pupils. You should also be very enthusiastic about music and the performing arts in general and possess good rhythm and balance. As a teacher of any subject it is imperative that your communication skills are impeccable but for dance teachers this is especially important because you need to ensure that everyone in your class is dancing safely and not likely to injure themselves or others. Creativity and self-discipline are very important traits to possess as well.

Working conditions

If you are employed in the state school sector you will be working during the school day, however it is likely that you will run classes after school in the early evening as well. This is certainly true of the private sector.

If you are a freelance teacher you can expect to need to travel as you will work at a variety of different venues; from schools and colleges to theatres and community centres.

Future prospects

As a dance teacher you can progress to becoming self-employed and even to running your own dance school. There are also other performing arts sectors you could branch into such as choreography. For experienced dance teachers there is the possibility to branch into community work as a dance therapist working with people from all walks of life.

Advantages/disadvantages

You will always be active as part of your job so you will stay fit and healthy and will not be stuck behind a desk all day.

Your work will often be fun as it is a very creative and expressive art form.

You may injure yourself from constantly dancing and this could jeopardise how much you could work.

Qualifications and courses

To become a dance teacher you would typically have a degree in a dance related subject or a HND or foundation degree.

There are also many vocational qualifications in dance available at specific dance and performing arts institutions.

If you want to go on to teach in a state school you will need to obtain Qualified Teacher Status (QTS). This can be achieved by doing a PGCE after your degree or some degrees in dance subjects hold QTS status themselves. Working as a dance teacher in the private sector requires being accredited by the Council of Dance Education and Training.

It might become stressful preparing for a big performance especially if you are working with children who can be unpredictable.

Money guide

Starting salaries as a dance teacher can vary widely and this will also be influenced by whether you work in a state or private school. Typically, starting salaries in the state sector are £19,000. This can progress to around £30,000 with experience and lots of responsibility.

If you run your own private dance school you could earn £50,000 and more.

Related opportunities

- Choreographer p438
- Dancer p441
- Music teacher p209
- Primary and Secondary Teacher p212

Further information

Council for Dance Education Training
Old Brewer's Yard, 17–19 Neal Street, Covent Garden, London, WC2H 9UY
020 7240 5703; www.cdet.org.uk

Imperial Society for Teachers of Dancing
22/26 Paul Street, London, EC2A 4QE
020 7377 1577; www.istd.org

National Dance Teachers Association
NDTA, PO Box 4099, Lichfield, WS13 6WX
01543 308618; www.ndta.org.uk

CRCI: F
CLCI: FAB

Education and Training

EARLY YEARS SPECIALIST/ NURSERY WORKER

What the work involves

- Within a nursery or private home, early years specialists/nursery workers look after young children, from newborn babies up to the age of eight, ensuring they are safe and comfortable.

- Much of your work will involve feeding, changing, dressing and bathing babies, and helping older children to develop in areas such as language, art, practical skills and music.

- You will plan the day to include play, exercise, meals and rest, to keep children healthy and mentally stimulated.

The type of person suited to this work

It is essential to enjoy caring for young people and to be outgoing, with a friendly manner towards children and adults alike. You also need to be patient and tolerant to deal with different types of behaviour.

Planning activities needs imagination and creativity, and it is helpful to be good at art, practical tasks and singing.

You will need to be flexible, enjoy team working and be comfortable working with many different types of people from all cultures and backgrounds.

Working conditions

The majority of nursery workers work 40 hours a week, however hours can vary depending on parents' requirements. Most of your work will be indoors in a nursery, school, hospital or private home. You may 'live in' if you are a nanny in a private home.

If you have to travel locally with children in your care, a driving licence is useful.

The work involves bending, lifting and playing with children so you need to be physically fit.

Future prospects

Nursery workers work in nurseries, schools and hospitals, and as nannies in private homes.

With the large rise in working mothers, there is high demand for qualified childcare staff throughout the UK. Sometimes, there are opportunities to travel, particularly in private work.

You can start to train straight from school or after gaining experience in other types of work.

Promotion prospects are limited. You could take further training to enter paediatric nursing or primary school teaching.

Advantages/disadvantages

The work is varied and rewarding.

As well as children, you will have the opportunity to work with adults.

Qualifications and courses

ENTRY LEVEL 1

Academic qualifications are not necessary to work as a nursery worker, although a good general standard of education is an advantage.

There is a framework of nationally accredited nursery worker qualifications in England and Wales. Typical qualifications include CACHE Level 3 Diploma in child care and education; BTEC National Diploma in children's care, learning and development and NVQ/SVQ Level 3 in children's care, learning and development.

In Scotland, registration of nursery workers has been introduced. Early years practitioners with qualifications such as SVQ Level 3 or an HNC can register with the Scottish Social Services Council (SSSC). Support workers, qualified to SVQ Level 2 or equivalent, can register from October 2008.

Supervised practical training forms an important part of all courses.

All applicants must pass a Criminal Records Bureau check before working with young people.

The hours can be long, particularly in nanny work, and you may have to work shifts and weekends.

Money guide

Expect to start on around £9,000–£11,500 per year. You can earn £14,000–£17,000 with experience.

Salaries can rise to rise to £30,000+ for a senior post. £23,000+ a year, with accommodation and food, is possible for a nanny working in a private home.

Related opportunities

- Childminder p569
- Children's Nurse p298
- Healthcare Assistant p576
- Teaching/Learning Support Assistant p217

Further information

CACHE
Beaufort House, Grosvenor Road, St Albans, AL1 3AW
01727 818616; www.cache.org.uk

Care Commission
Compass House, 11 Riverside Drive, Dundee, DD1 4DY
0845 6030890, www.carecommission.com

City& Guilds

www.cityandguilds.com/myperfectjob

EDUCATION AND CHILDCARE INSPECTOR

What the work involves

- You will use your extensive experience gained from working in schools, colleges, nurseries or youth service settings (normally at management level), to undertake inspections.

- You might inspect early years learning, or focus on secondary education and preparation for work. Inspections cover special schools and out-of-school learning units.

- Although inspectors work within a team of 2–3, you will spend some of your time alone.

- During the visit, you will contribute to the inspection report, which is then made available for everyone to read on the internet.

The type of person suited to this work

Inspectors need to know about the types of organisation that they inspect very well, so they know what things to look out for. You should enjoy meeting people of all ages and backgrounds, and know how to put them at their ease. You will need to explain to very young children what you are doing in ways that are easy to understand.

You should be confident and happy to stand by your decisions, which can be difficult if the organisation you have inspected is not doing well.

Finally, you should be happy writing reports, using a laptop and speaking to large groups of people explaining what you have found out.

Working conditions

As you will be visiting organisations all over the country, you should be happy to spend periods away from home.

Most of the work takes place in classrooms or offices where you will speak to head teachers, pupils, parents, governors and the other professionals linked to the organisation.

Future prospects

Recently, the way in which inspections are undertaken has changed, resulting in them now lasting a few days rather than the 2–3 weeks that they previously took. As a result, fewer inspectors are needed. If you are interested in this type of work, any future openings are likely to be on a part-time basis.

Inspectors are now recruited by private companies, so you should approach them for information on their recruitment schemes.

Advantages/disadvantages

This job offers you the chance to use your experience to make sure that the correct quality is in place.

It offers the opportunity to visit different organisations around the country.

Qualifications and courses

Team and registered inspectors in England and Wales, and Inspectors in Scotland, must be qualified teachers.

Qualified Teacher Status (QTS) is gained through Initial Teacher Training (ITT). The two main routes are a first degree followed by a Postgraduate Certificate in Education (PGCE) or a first degree (BEd/BA/BSc) leading to QTS.

Registered inspectors in England and Wales must be experienced Team Inspectors. Inspectors in Scotland must have 5 years' teaching experience, including experience in a senior position.

Lay inspectors are members of the team who have not had paid teaching experience. Non-teaching experience in the education sector and/or management experience is useful. In Scotland, inspection teams also include practising teachers and lecturers.

Training for inspectors is provided by the Office for Standards in Education (Ofsted) in England, Estyn in Wales, HM Inspectorate of Education in Scotland, and the Department of Education for Northern Ireland.

There is rarely any follow-up in the role of inspector as you are unlikely to repeat an inspection of the same institution or home.

Money guide

Inspectors generally earn the same as advisers employed by local authorities. Pay varies, depending on the level of work. Childcare inspectors are usually employed by private organisations, salaries vary but as a guide starting salaries are around £25,000. HMIs can earn £48,500–£62,000 per year for full-time employment, with pro rata for part time.

Related opportunities

- Education Officer p204
- FE lecturer/HE lecturer p206
- Primary and Secondary Teacher p212
- Work-based Training Instructor p218

Further information

Ofsted (Office for Standards in Education)
www.ofsted.gov.uk

HM Inspectorate of Education in Scotland
01506 600 200; www.hmie.gov.uk

City & Guilds

www.cityandguilds.com/myperfectjob

EDUCATION OFFICER

What the work involves

- Education officers prepare educational materials and resources for visits of school students to galleries, museums or other organisations.

- A museum education officer is responsible for designing and delivering the museum's educational programme to primary and secondary schools.

- An environmental education officer is responsible for raising awareness of environmental issues, promoting sustainability and conservation and teaching a wide range of age groups about the natural world.

- It will be your responsibility to increase public awareness about new exhibitions and events, and to update the educational sections of your website by producing lesson materials and careers information.

The type of person suited to this work

As an education officer, you will need self-confidence and an ability to talk to young people in a way that will interest and excite them. You must be bright, interesting, humorous, have lots of patience and a willingness to listen.

You will always be busy, so you will need good organisational abilities, as well as excellent written and verbal communication skills. An understanding of ICT and confidence in handling budgets will also be useful.

Working conditions

Your time will be spent in an office or lecture room, on the exhibition floor of a museum or gallery, or visiting local schools where you will represent your organisation. You might wear a uniform or protective clothing.

Depending on your organisation, you might spend some of your time outdoors in all weathers, for example at a zoo or community farm. You might do some evening work, especially if you work with community groups.

Future prospects

Entry to this profession is very competitive, but there is a steady increase in the number of educational jobs available in organisations.

Alongside traditional exhibits, learning through demonstrations, videos, talks and other presentations is being introduced by education officers as interactive experiences increase in popularity.

Advantages/disadvantages

This offers an opportunity to be involved in teaching without being in the classroom.

You will contribute to making a visit to your organisation a more memorable one for everyone.

You will be juggling lots of different tasks at once.

Qualifications and courses

To work as an education officer in a museum or gallery, a degree or HND is required. Useful degree subjects include history, archaeology, anthropology, museum studies, cultural studies, history of art and education. Museums favour certain degree subjects that are particular to their collection e.g. history of art for the Burrell Collection in Glasgow.

An environmental education officer will require a degree in a biological or environmental science degree eg ecology or zoology. It is also possible to enter this position with an HND in a related area such as countryside management.

Qualifications and/or experience in teaching or community education are useful, and may be required. Relevant work experience is essential in order to secure a paid position.

Postgraduate qualifications are available in relevant subjects such as museum studies and heritage management. Entry to these courses requires a degree in any subject, and, normally, some related work experience. A Postgraduate Certificate in Education (PGCE) is useful for museum education officers working with school children, as it demonstrates a good understanding of the requirements of the national curriculum.

You may have to work evenings, which may affect your personal life.

Money guide

Museum education officers working in large prestigious museums or educational adventure establishments in full-time positions can earn £19,000–£23,000 per year. With substantial experience this rises to £30,000–£35,000. Environmental education officers can expect to earn £15,000–£19,000 to begin with. This rises to £22,000–£30,000 at senior level. Education assistants who work alongside education officers can earn £16,000–£21,000.

Related opportunities

- Arts Administrator p351
- Learning Mentor p208
- Museum Assistant p361

Further information

GEM – Group for Education in Museums
Primrose House, 93 Gillingham Road, Gillingham, ME7 4EP
01634 853424;www.gem.org.uk

City&
Guilds

www.cityandguilds.com/myperfectjob

EDUCATION WELFARE OFFICER

What the work involves

- You will work with young people who are not attending school, and their families, to support them back into education.

- Often, you will help explore alternatives to school. If things do not work out, you may have to prosecute parents of children who are not attending school.

- You will help families get all the benefits they are entitled to, such as free school meals, clothing or transport.

- As a link between families and schools, you will try to improve existing relationships – writing reports, attending meetings and case conferences.

The type of person suited to this work

As there can be many reasons for poor attendance at school, such as fear of bullying, caring responsibilities at home or difficulty in coping with school work, it is important to be open-minded and to listen impartially to school staff and parents. You will also need to be strong enough to prosecute a family if it becomes necessary.

You must enjoy working with young people and see the value in education, because you may have to convince parents who do not share your views of its importance.

You will also have to keep up to date with relevant legislation and you must be able to work on your own and as part of a team.

Working conditions

You will have an office base, but most of your time will be spent visiting young people and their families at home or looking for young people in the local area, so a driving licence is useful.

You may go to other agencies' offices to attend meetings and case conferences.

Families may view your interventions as interfering rather than assisting; you must always consider your personal safety.

Future prospects

There are about 4000 education welfare officers in England, Wales and Northern Ireland. In Scotland, they are called attendance officers. Education welfare officers tend to be people with a considerable amount of life and work experience.

There is a promotion structure within local authorities and you can become a specialist, for example dealing only with primary school pupils. With further training, you can do similar work in care and social services.

Advantages/disadvantages

You will have the satisfaction of helping people – sometimes quite profoundly.

You may have to work in the evenings to find parents at home.

Qualifications and courses

There are a number of routes into this profession. Candidates generally have relevant work experience, for example in special education, counselling or youth work.

Some entrants are already qualified with degree-level qualifications in areas such as social work or teaching. Degree courses usually require a minimum of 2 A levels/3 H grades and 5 GCSEs/S grades (A–C/1–3), including English and maths. In Northern Ireland, 3 A levels/5 H grades are required for social work degrees.

Entry requirements are flexible but a good standard of general education to A level/H grade is preferred. It is also possible to get a job and study for qualifications through in-service training.

A number of additional skills and aptitudes are valuable for entry to this work, for example skills in advising/counselling work or caring for people, high-level skills in communication, decision-making, ICT and information handling, as well as working with others.

Some people may be abusive and you may find yourself in stressful situations.

Money guide

You will earn around £21,000 per year on entry. With experience you could earn £24,000–£30,000. For a head of service salaries are up to £50,000+.

Related opportunities

- Careers Adviser p568
- Probation Officer p580
- Social Worker p585
- Youth and Community Worker p591

Further information

General Social Care Council
Goldings House, 2 Hays Lane, London, SE1 2HB
020 7397 5100; www.gscc.org.uk

Northern Ireland Social Care Council
7th Floor, Millennium House, 19–25 Great Victoria Street, Belfast, BT2 7AQ
028 9041 7600; www.niscc.info

Scottish Social Services Council
Compass House, 1 Riverside Drive, Dundee, DD1 4NY
01382 207101; www.sssc.uk.com

City&
Guilds

www.cityandguilds.com/myperfectjob

ENTRY 3 LEVEL

Education and Training

CRCI: V
CLCI: KEB

FURTHER EDUCATION LECTURER/ HIGHER EDUCATION LECTURER

What the work involves

Lecturer in further education (FE)

- You will teach students aged 16+, on vocational (work-based) or academic (general) courses at a further education college, the information and skills needed to achieve their qualifications.

- As well as teaching your main subject you will also be a pastoral tutor helping students with their personal development and career planning.

- You will also arrange work placements with local companies, visit students to monitor and assess their progress, act as a student mentor and meet your colleagues to develop courses.

Lecturer in higher education (HE)

- As a higher education lecturer you will teach undergraduate or postgraduate students at a university or franchised college.

- As well as delivering lectures you will take tutorials, act as a consultant for individual research projects and run seminars on topics related to the department's research interests.

- To maintain your professional knowledge you will also carry out research in your specialist area, submit papers for publication in academic journals and periodicals.

The type of person suited to this work

Lecturers need to be patient and interested in helping people of all ages to learn and increase their knowledge by developing their ability, skills and interests. It is also important to be comfortable talking to large groups of students.

If you choose to lecture in HE, you are likely to have already done research work and completed a thesis. You must be very interested in your subject and how facts support hypotheses and theories. To be able to help your students learn you will also need to enjoy debating and arguing different ideas and concepts.

FE lecturers often have extensive practical experience of their specialist area before entering the profession.

Working conditions

Most of your time will be teaching in either lecture theatres, classrooms, labs or workshops. For some practical subjects you might spend some of your time outdoors.

When not teaching you will be office-based, using a computer for research, writing papers, storing data, reports and analyses, and recording students' progress, etc.

Although you are likely to work mostly during the day you will also work at night and occasional weekends. Depending on your institution, you will mostly work term time although FE conditions are changing to all year round.

Future prospects

There are around 500 colleges and universities across the UK with over 4 million students aged 16+. Around 39% of jobs are held by women. In a bid to increase national competitiveness, the government is promoting lifelong learning as an important requirement for all individuals. Both universitiies and FE colleges are being expected to talk to employers to make sure their courses meet the needs of companies as well as individuals.

All of this means that lecturers are playing a vital role in helping to increase the skills levels of the country.

There are a number of progression routes open to both type of lecturer.

For FE lecturers there are opportunities to enter other areas of teaching including HE, financial work, quality improvement and human resources. In addition, you could also look to take more senior positions within your current or another college.

As an HE lecturer, some of your options will depend on the size and financial status of your institution. There is evidence to show that taking a career break can be a disadvantage as this can reduce your ability to do the research work which is so important if you are to build your reputation. Sabbaticals, however, are considered to be positive as they will enable you to spend time doing research. HE lecturers can apply for promotion within their own or other institutions, undertake consultancy, enter the media or do public speaking. You could also find part-time work providing advisery or training services or start your own business.

Advantages/disadvantages

You will be working in an area that has great importance to the government.

You are a professional teacher, but in a less-structured, formal environment than a school.

In HE, it can be hard to follow up your own research interests when you have to set up and help run demonstrations or tutorials for undergraduates, while marking essays and assignments.

In FE, you could teach students of all ages with many different reasons for studying.

Money guide

Most full-time FE lecturers start their career within the range of £16,000–£22,000 per year. With several years experience or promotion to senior level this rises to £32,000+. Those employed on part-time or sessional basis earn £16–£25+ per hour.

HE lecturers are paid more, with starting salaries after a PhD ranging between £25,000 and £42,000. At senior lecturer level, salaries can be between £38,000 and £55,000. Salaries for both jobs are dependent on the research of your department, links with local businesses and the size and status of your university/college.

Related opportunities
- Personal Adviser – Connexions p579
- Primary and Secondary Teacher p212
- Work-based Training Instructor p218

Further information

Lifelong Learning UK
5th floor, St Andrew's House, 18–20 St Andrew Street, London, EC4A 3AY
0870 757 7890; www.lifelonglearninguk.org

Association of University Teachers
Egmont House, 25–31 Tavistock Place, London, WC1H 9UT
020 7670 9700; www.aut.org.uk

NATFHE (University and College Lecturers' Union)
27 Britannia Street, London, WC1X 9JP
020 7837 3636; www.natfhe.org.uk

www.cityandguilds.com/myperfectjob

Qualifications and courses

Lecturer in further education

All new lecturers in FE must have Qualified Teacher, Learning and Skills (QTLS) status.

The minimum qualification you will need to work as a full lecturer is the Level 5 Diploma in Teaching in the Lifelong Learning Sector, which leads to QTL status. The Diploma is roughly equivalent to the PGCE/CertEd in Further or Post-Compulsory Education, and many institutions will continue to use the old qualification names, referenced against the new Diploma.

You will generally need an NQF Level 4–6 qualification for entry to a Diploma or CertEd programme, and a degree for entry to a PGCE. You will normally also need at least a Level 3 qualification in the subject you wish to teach.

In Scotland, further education lecturers can take a Further Education Teaching Qualification (TQFE) through an approved university. Entrants must be in employment for a minimum of 120 hours during the course and must hold an HNC, HND, relevant professional qualification, or a degree.

In Scotland, further education lecturers can take a Further Education Teaching Qualification (TQFE) at certain universities, or a Professional Development Award in further education teaching. Both types of qualification are normally studied part time, while in the post.

Lecturer in higher education

HE lecturers need a 1st or 2.1 Honours degree and a postgraduate qualification. A PhD is normally required, but a Master's may be acceptable, and candidates working towards a PhD may be considered.

For posts in academic subjects, a record of research and publication is required. Teaching experience whilst working towards a PhD is also valuable. Lecturers in vocational subjects should have several years of relevant work experience.

Opportunities to study for a postgraduate qualification followed by a fellowship or lecturing post can arise for research assistants.

Lecturers normally receive further training from their employer institution. The Higher Education Academy accredits in-service programmes for lecturers.

Education and Training

CRCI: F
CLCI: FAB

Education and Training

CRCI: F
CLCI: FAB

LEARNING MENTOR

What the work involves

- You will support different people whilst they are learning.

- Working on a one-to-one basis, you will listen to their difficulties, offer solutions and suggest different ways to approach problems.

- You will help everybody you work with to succeed, enjoy their learning experience and want to keep trying.

- You will also work with the teachers and parents of the student you are focusing on.

The type of person suited to this work

To be a good learning mentor, you will need to have experience of the subject you mentor, along with an understanding of different styles of studying. You should enjoy helping and listening to people and have good communication skills. You should be patient and willing to listen.

The best mentors are those who can be a critical friend and know the benefits of learning and can explain them to the people you will work with.

It will also help if you have had first-hand experience of the issues yourself, probably whilst you were learning as this will help you to appreciate the difficulties people face.

Working conditions

You can work on a part- or full-time basis with people at school, home or sometimes at a college, university or training centre. You might be employed on a term-time only basis or all year round. Some of your work might involve weekends and evenings – this will depend on the organisation you work for. You will meet in a quiet confidential area where you will examine workbooks and essays, talk over any issues and give help.

Future prospects

Mentoring is one way to help students who might otherwise drop out or may not achieve their qualifications. At every level of learning, mentors have been proved to be key workers and operate alongside other teaching professionals.

The government initiative 'Excellence in Cities' requires every participating secondary school to employ at least one mentor. The role has been so successful that Ofsted reported that '95% of all surveyed schools' showed that mentoring had played a positive contribution to the school's development.

Advantages/disadvantages

This job involves lots of different roles – friend, confidence builder and motivator.

Results have shown how important this job can be in helping learners to succeed.

You will be working with students without being a teacher.

Qualifications and courses

There are no formal entry requirements for this career. However, most entrants have a degree, HND or equivalent vocational qualification.

Relevant degree subjects include social sciences, psychology and National Curriculum subjects, particularly English and maths.

Experience of working with young people is required, and experience in a related area such as social work, counselling or teaching is useful.

Experience on a voluntary mentoring scheme is also useful.

Newly-appointed learning mentors take part in a 5-day national initial training programme provided by the DCSF. The Mentoring and Befriending Foundation also provides training opportunities.

It may be possible to work towards a Foundation degree or NVQ/SVQ Level 3 or 4 in Learning, Development and Support Services. The Level 4 NVQ/SVQ is normally required to become a learning mentor coordinator.

All candidates are required to undergo a Criminal Records Bureau check.

Money guide

Within schools, salaries for newly appointed mentors range between £15,000 and £19,000 per year. With experience, you can expect this to increase to £23,000, and as a senior mentor up to £40,000.

Other organisations may pay more. For example, mentoring a company's chief executive or operations manager, means your pay could reach £50+ per hour.

Related opportunities

- Careers Adviser p568
- Personal Adviser – Connexions p579
- Special Educational Needs Teacher p215
- Youth and Community Worker p591

Further information

Mentoring and Befriending Foundation
1st floor, Charles House, Albert Street, Eccles, Manchester M30 0PW
0161 787 8600; www.mandbf.org.uk

Learning Mentors
www.standards.dfes.gov.uk/learningmentors

City& Guilds

www.cityandguilds.com/myperfectjob

MUSIC TEACHER

What the work involves

- Music teachers are either classroom teachers in primary or secondary schools where they help pupils to develop vocal, instrumental skills and performance technique; or private or visiting teachers, giving instrumental, theory or voice tuition.

- You will be teaching an appreciation of musical theory and composition, musical development and different composers' works.

- You will be expected to plan lessons, organise groups such as orchestras, and you may have to prepare students for external exams.

The type of person suited to this work

You should be patient, have a caring attitude towards others and an interest in drawing out and developing individuals' potential in learning about music.

Excellent communication skills are important, as is firmness and commitment, imagination and creativity.

You have to be well organised, flexible and able to change plans and the sequence of lessons to accommodate unexpected events.

It is important to be comfortable in maintaining discipline and be confident when speaking to large groups of young people and other professionals.

Working conditions

Music teachers work indoors in all kinds of settings within public and private sector schools and learning centres, and in their own or pupils' homes as tutors.

Classroom teachers will usually work 8:45 to 15:45, with some evening and weekend work required for tuition, rehearsals and concerts.

It is likely that you will work evenings and weekends, and part time work is common. Private music teachers should expect to carry out some travelling and you may be expected to lift and carry heavy musical instruments.

Future prospects

Although budgets have meant that some schools have been forced to increase class sizes and have therefore recruited additional teaching assistants, there is now more money coming to schools and additional teachers are being recruited. Music teaching has suffered, but more music teachers are predicted to be needed.

Many private teachers combine this work with composing or performing, and career breaks are common.

Advantages/disadvantages

Teaching is a rewarding profession in which you can witness a student's progression.

Qualifications and courses

Music teachers working in state schools must have Qualified Teacher Status (QTS). There are two main routes to QTS: a first degree, such as a music degree, followed by a Postgraduate Certificate in Education (PGCE) qualifies candidates to teach; a BEd degree such as music with primary teacher training combines a degree and QTS training.

In addition, music teachers must be able to demonstrate a good standard of musicianship, usually grade 7/8 from an Associated Board on a first instrument and grade 6 on a second.

Graduate diploma courses offered by conservatoires are equivalent to degrees but would need to be followed by a 1 year PGCE.

If you are not teaching in state schools then entry routes can vary.

There are no set qualifications for private music teachers; however it is essential that you have excellent music competence and knowledge of your instrument. The Incorporated Society of Musicians (ISM) offers a diploma, which can be related to the instrument you wish. Rockschool offers a music educator course, which will help to demonstrate your commitment to the teaching and learning process.

You will be kept very busy with preparation, classes, marking and assessing, analysing coursework, communicating with examining bodies, meetings and ordering materials.

Money guide

Starting salaries for classroom teachers are £20,000–£24,000. With experience this can rise to £29,000–£33,000. With Advanced Skills Status teachers can earn £34,000–£59,000. For private teachers the Musicians' Union recommends a rate of £25.40 an hour. Generally, wages are between £20 and £30 per hour depending on reputation, experience and location.

Related opportunities

- Education and Childcare Inspector p203
- FE Lecturer/HE Lecturer p206
- Teaching/Learning Support Assistant p217

Further information

Incorporated Society of Musicians (ISM)
10 Stratford Place, London, W1C 1AA
020 7629 4413; www.ism.org

Musicians' Union
33 Palfrey Place, London, SW8 1PE
020 7840 5504; www.musiciansunion.org.uk

Rockschool Ltd
Evergreen House, 2–4 King Street, Twickenham, Middlesex, TW1 3RZ
0845 460 4747; www.rockschool.co.uk

Education and Training

ENTRY LEVEL 4

CRCI: F
CLCI: FAB/GAD

NVQ/SVQ ASSESSOR

What the work involves

- NVQ/SVQ assessors work alongside trainees to ascertain their current knowledge, and from this formulate a plan for their development.

- You will offer feedback on their progress as they gain experience and take their NVQ/SVQ qualifications.

- You will observe how trainees do different tasks and measure their achievements against the standards for the qualification.

- You will also read through each trainee's portfolio of evidence, checking that tasks are undertaken.

The type of person suited to this work

It is essential to demonstrate an interest in other people and a commitment to helping them to progress.

You will need to motivate and encourage all kinds of individuals – some of whom will not have enjoyed school and find training difficult.

Excellent communication skills are important for the amount of speaking, questioning, listening and reporting that is involved.

In addition you should be organised and able to interpret the different standards in ways that are helpful to those who are learning. You should also have an interest in the area you are assessing.

Working conditions

You will have access to an office where you will use a computer to update learner records and check portfolios. You will also spend lots of time travelling to meet employers and trainees at their places of work.

Depending on your specialist area you could have very early starts (for example assessing bakers at work) or late finishes (assessing car finishers working nights).

It is necessary to keep up-to-date with the changes and developments in your occupational area.

Future prospects

The government is currently encouraging learning through work-based qualifications and school/college leavers now have more opportunities to pursue Apprenticeships, National Traineeships or Skillseekers.

There is currently a national shortage of skilled professionals in this area, and there will be increasing need for NVQ/SVQ assessors in the future. This may result in more firms and organisations having a team of specialists who train other employees in their particular area of expertise e.g. health and safety.

Advantages/disadvantages

This work involves being at the centre of improving the skills levels of the workforce.

You will spend lots of your time meeting, speaking to and getting to know other people.

Qualifications and courses

It is necessary to have between 2 and 4 years' occupational experience in the subject or work area to be assessed. For this reason it is not possible for school or college leavers to enter this area straight away. Many training practitioners choose to work towards NVQ/SVQ assessor qualifications.

It is necessary to have an assessor qualification, either A1 (assesses candidates using a range of methods) or A2 (assesses candidates' performance through observation), which are carried out whilst you are working and take 6 months to complete. To obtain the qualification, you need to build up a portfolio of evidence from your work with NVQ/SVQ candidates.

Some courses only accept candidates who have been nominated by their employer and have extensive experience in the specialist area and a level two qualification (or higher) in the area.

Qualified assessors can carry out further training to work as NVQ/SVQ verifiers. Verifier qualifications are V1 (conduct internal quality assurance of assessment process) or V2 (conduct external quality assurance of assessment process).

Depending on your specialist area, you may have to work unsociable hours in order to assess candidates in their workplace.

It can be challenging to motivate and encourage candidates who do not enjoy learning to achieve an academic qualification.

Money guide

Average starting salaries are between £14,000 and £20,000.

More experienced assessors can expect to earn up to £25,000 per year which can increase beyond £35,000 for the most senior positions.

It is also possible to do this work on a freelance basis. Rates start at £225 or more per day.

Related opportunities

- Driving Examiner/Driving Instructor p603
- Human Resources/Personnel Officer p41
- FE Lecturer/HE Lecturer p206
- Training Manager p66

Further information

Qualifications and Curriculum Authority
83 Piccadilly, London, W1J 8QA
020 7509 5555; www.qca.org.uk; info@qca.org.uk

City&
Guilds

www.cityandguilds.com/myperfectjob

PLAY WORKER/ HOSPITAL PLAY SPECIALIST

What the work involves

- Play workers and hospital play specialists are responsible for ensuring that children between the ages of 5 and 15 play in a safe environment.

- Your will encourage children and young people to learn through play by giving them the freedom to explore and get to know themselves.

- Hospital play specialists use play to entertain children and help them to deal with their experiences in hospital. This includes using play to prepare them for treatments and diverting their attention from unpleasant procedures. You may work with severely disabled children.

The type of person suited to this work

Imagination and creativity are needed to do this job well. It is essential that you like being with children of all ages, understand what they like to do and recognise how they change as they develop.

You should be positive and patient with lots of energy and stamina. As the safety of the children will be your responsibility, you will need high levels of concentration and to stay alert at all times.

A hospital play specialist needs to be sympathetic to the needs and issues of each child, have some understanding of medical conditions, and must be able to cope with distressing situations.

Working conditions

As many opportunities operate after school or during holidays you will normally work in the early evening, at weekends and in school holidays. Many jobs are seasonal and most are part time.

Play specialists work in children's hospitals, children's wards and outpatients' clinics. You may take children on trips or visit them in their homes, so you may need a driving licence.

Future prospects

This area of work is rising in importance and is part of the National Childcare Strategy, which recognises the significance of giving young people opportunities to improve their lives through education, sport and leisure.

With the increased number of working parents, the need for out-of-school carers has grown.

There is currently an increase in the number of hospital play specialist posts available nationally. Most opportunities are with NHS hospitals but you could also work in hospices or community paediatric teams.

Qualifications and courses

No formal qualifications are required to become a play specialist, but all candidates are subject to a Criminal Records Bureau (CRB) police check.

Relevant courses include the CACHE Certificate in playwork and NCFE Certificate in playwork, both at Level 2, and the CACHE Certificate and Diploma in child care and education. NVQs/SVQs are available.

To become a qualified hospital play specialist, you must be 20 or over and will need the Edexcel BTEC Professional Development Diploma in specialised play for sick children and young people, approved by the Hospital Play Staff Education Trust (HPSET). Applicants must have an appropriate qualification in a subject such as childcare, nursery nursing, drama or music therapy, occupational therapy, teaching or social work, and at least 3 years' recent experience of working with children in a group setting.

For those students not working in a hospital setting, a 200-hour practical experience placement will be undertaken as part of the programme.

Advantages/disadvantages

Helping children who are ill to enjoy themselves can be extremely rewarding.

Hospital play specialists may have to deal with sad and distressing situations.

Money guide

As most play workers are employed on a part time or seasonal basis, pay rates are lower than in some similar types of work. Starting salaries are £11,500–£15,000 per year. With experience or promotion, salaries can increase to £20,000+. As a senior manager, it is possible to achieve salaries up to £35,000. Newly qualified hospital play specialists earn around £17,000–£20,000 per year, rising to £20,000–£26,000 with experience. Team managers can earn up to £32,000.

Related opportunities

- Childminder p569
- Youth and Community Worker p591

Further information

CACHE
Beaufort House, Grosvenor Road, St Albans, AL1 3AW
01727 818616; www.cache.org.uk

www.cityandguilds.com/myperfectjob

Education and Training

CRCI: F/JG
CLCI: J/KEB

PRIMARY AND SECONDARY TEACHER

Education and Training

CRCl: F
CLCl: FAB

What the work involves

Teacher: primary school

- Primary school teachers prepare materials and resources for structured play and social development work within early years classes.

- Responding to the National Curriculum, you will teach young children reading, writing and number work, following frameworks for literacy and numeracy.

Teacher: secondary school

- Secondary school teachers teach pupils the requirements of the National Curriculum, following the standards laid down by the Department for Children, Schools and Families.

- Your work will involve assessing progress, forward planning, acting as a form tutor, and encouraging personal development, good behavioural patterns and social awareness amongst students.

The type of person suited to this work

You need patience and a caring attitude towards others, excellent communication skills, firmness and commitment, fitness and stamina, imagination and creativity.

You have to be well organised and flexible. You must be able to recognise and praise efforts and achievements, however small.

You should be comfortable in maintaining discipline and be confident when speaking to large groups of young people.

Working conditions

You must be prepared to travel, as there are school trips, visits to students on work placements and overseas visits for modern foreign language and PE teachers.

There are opportunities for promotion within your own or another school, initially to department head, and later up to management level. You may have to move schools to take up your next post.

Future prospects

At present, there are shortages of maths, physics and chemistry teachers. It is also hard to recruit modern foreign language and design technology teachers in some parts of the country.

Although budgets have meant that some schools have been forced to increase class sizes and have therefore recruited additional teaching assistants, there is now more money coming to schools and additional teachers are being recruited.

Advantages/disadvantages

Teaching is a rewarding profession in which you can witness a student's progression.

You will be kept very busy undertaking a range of duties which include preparation, taking classes, marking and assessing and analysing coursework.

Qualifications and courses

Teaching in primary and secondary schools is a graduate profession with two main entry routes.

You can take a BEd, BA or BSc degree leading to QTS over 3 or 4 years of full time study. QTS is awarded subject to passing skills tests in numeracy, literacy and information and communications technology. Shortened degrees are available for candidates with previous study at higher education level (eg HND or DipHE) and for candidates who are qualified to teach overseas.

There are also employment-based routes to QTS for people who wish to qualify while working in a school. The Graduate Teacher Programme, for people with a degree, takes between 3 months and 1 year. The Registered Teacher Programme, for people with an HND, foundation degree or equivalent, normally takes 2 years. You can do a BA or BSc degree in another subject and then a PGCE at university or college. School-centred Initial Teacher Training offers the option of PGCE study based in and run by schools. PGCE candidates must pass the skills tests to obtain Qualified Teacher Status.

Newly qualified teachers must complete an induction period and register with the General Teaching Council.

Work starts the moment you enter the building and continues until you leave, but it does mean that you value your holidays.

Money guide

In England, Wales and Northern Ireland, primary level salaries begin at £20,627 per year and rise to £30,148 – more if working in London. In Scotland, they are £19,440–£31,008. With promotion, in all areas salaries can be in excess of £33,444.

Newly qualified teachers (NQTs) start at £20,627 in England and Wales, or £24,168+ if they work in inner London.

With experience and passing through different thresholds, this can rise to £30,148–£35,121.

Related opportunities

- Education and Childcare Inspector p203
- FE Lecturer/HE Lecturer p206
- Teaching Assistant/Learning Support Assistant p217
- Work-based Training Instructor p218

Further information

General Teaching Council Scotland (GTCS)
Clerwwod House, 96 Clermiston Road, Edinburgh, EH12 6UT
0131 314 6000; www.gtcs.org.uk

Training and Development Agency for Schools
Portland House, Stag Place, London, SW1E 5TT
020 7925 3700; www.tda.gov.uk

City&
Guilds

www.cityandguilds.com/myperfectjob

SCHOOL ADMINISTRATOR/ SECRETARY

What the work involves

- Working on reception or in the school office school administrators/secretaries are responsible for greeting visitors and answering telephone calls.

- You will develop administrative systems (both paper- and ICT-based) to keep information organised and easily accessible.

- In some schools you might also collect money for lunch and school trips, and could be in charge of the sick room.

The type of person suited to this work

You will be required to be highly organised and efficient with excellent written and verbal communication skills. You should be confident dealing with people at all levels, including teachers, students and their guardians, and may have to work with people who are ill, angry or upset.

You should have excellent keyboard skills, be able to use ICT packages and organise and maintain information systems.

You will have to take responsibility, prioritise your workload, be flexible and use your initiative. You should also be able to work calmly under pressure, meet deadlines and handle confidential information.

Working conditions

You will usually be office-based, doing normal school hours (08.45–15.45). You will use a range of office equipment, including computers, photocopiers, telephones, fax machines.

School offices are open to visitors and pupils and can be very busy. On a reception desk, you will be responsible for greeting visitors and showing them to their meeting room or contacting colleagues.

Lots of school secretaries work part time and do not work at all during the school holidays.

Future prospects

In the UK, there are about 55,000 administrators employed in nursery, primary and secondary schools. There are job opportunities in all areas of the country, although jobs can be competitive as the accompanying hours and holidays are appealing.

Much of the work is part time and there are not usually many opportunities for promotion, but you could go on to become a teaching assistant.

Advantages/disadvantages

If you have family commitments there are part-time opportunities. The hours and holiday allowances are attractive.

Qualifications and courses

There are no formal entry requirements but you will need a good standard of maths and English. Adult entry is common and many entrants have several years of office experience.

You will need keyboard and word-processing skills and probably office experience. Other ICT skills and shorthand are also useful. Training is mostly on the job and some schools will require you to carry out external training.

It is possible to study for the national certificate in educational administration at the School of Educational Administration (SEA). This course has been accredited by the Qualifications & Curriculum Authority and can be undertaken in 2 years by distance learning. They also offer a 2 month introductory course that covers principal areas of educational administration.

In addition an NVQ in business and administration at Levels 1 to 4 is available, and City & Guilds offer an award or certificate at Level 2 or Diploma at Level 3 in support work in schools.

The work can be routine and repetitive when you start, with not much variation.

Money guide

On average you could earn £10,000–£15,000 if you are working full time in a state school. This could rise to around £20,000+ if you are working in a large secondary school and have additional responsibility or staff to manage. The most experienced people in this profession can expect to earn up to £40,000. Salaries in private schools vary a lot.

Related opportunities

- Arts Administrator p351
- Personal Assistant p51
- Receptionist p54

Further information

School of Educational Administration (SEA)
Earlstrees Court, Earlstrees Road, Corby, Northamptonshire, NN17 4HH
01536 399 007; www.admin.org.uk

www.cityandguilds.com/myperfectjob

Education and Training

CRCI: F
CLCI: CAM/CAT

SCHOOL BUSINESS MANAGER/ BURSAR

What the work involves

- You will be responsible for the financial planning and accounts of a school or college.

- The term 'bursar' is common in independent schools; in the state sector you might also be called a school business manager or finance manager.

- Your role will include the staff pay, some recruitment and managing contracts such as cleaning and maintenance companies. You will also have to keep all the school premises insurance documents up to date.

- In independent schools, you will also set fees and distribute bursaries, scholarships and awards.

The type of person suited to this work

It will be helpful if you have worked with different people, as you will deal with the head teacher and senior staff, other professionals (auditors, company managers, etc), parents and students! You need a polite yet firm approach and excellent communication skills.

You will need a head for figures and be happy using computers and financial software. There will always be lots of jobs needing your attention so you should be a good organiser and enjoy keeping busy.

Working conditions

Normally, you will work in an office sitting at a desk. Here, you will have access to a computer and spend lots of time talkng to people – both in or outside of your organisation.

You will attend lots of meetings with the headteacher and other professional staff – sometimes staying late to give reports to your school's governing body.

You may also need to work during the evenings and in school holidays.

Future prospects

Most bursars progress to the job after working in either a private financial organisation, after being an accountant or occasionally after working their way up from within a school/ college.

With experience, bursars can move to larger organisations or return to the private sector. It is also possible to work in British schools overseas.

Posts are advertised in local and national level publications such as the Times Educational Supplement. Jobs are also posted on the National Bursars Association (NBA) website.

Advantages/disadvantages

You will have lots of opportunity to use your own initiative.

You will meet people of all ages and from different backgrounds.

Qualifications and courses

Most entrants have experience in related fields, and many hold a degree or professional qualification. Management experience in education, accountancy or personnel is of value.

Qualifications such as NVQ Level 3 or 4 in Administration or Management, or SVQ Level 3 or 4 Business Administration or Management, may be an advantage

For people already in posts, the National College for School Leadership offers a Bursar Development Scheme. The Certificate of School Business Management is aimed at newly-appointed bursars or those in school administration posts, and the Diploma of School Business Management is intended for experienced bursars/ business managers.

The Independent Schools' Bursars Association offers training for those working in independent schools.

The National Bursars Association (NBA) Registration Scheme is also aimed at experienced bursars. The scheme can be completed in 1 year and leads to a postgraduate-level qualification. The NBA also offers the Institute of Administrative Management (IAM) Diploma by distance learning. Postgraduate courses in subjects such as education business management are available.

Money guide

The salary range for bursars differs greatly depending on where you work and the size and type of institution you work in. The average starting salary in a state school or college is £20,000–£27,000 per year, rising to £50,000+ with experience.

In the independent sector, salaries are higher and it is possible to earn between £60,000 and £100,000.

Related opportunities

- Accountant p16
- Accounting Technician p19
- Financial Adviser p39

Further information

National Bursars Association
Top Floor Offices, 140 Wood Street, Rugby, CV21 2SP
01788 573300; www.nba.org.uk

Independent Schools' Bursars Association
Units 11–12 Manor Farm, Cliddesden, Basingstoke, RG25 2BJ
01256 330369; www.isba.uk.com

City& Guilds

www.cityandguilds.com/myperfectjob

SPECIAL EDUCATIONAL NEEDS TEACHER

What the work involves

- Teachers for special educational needs help children with disabilities, learning difficulties or emotional or behavioural problems to achieve their best.

- You make also work with exceptionally gifted children.

- Working with educational psychologists, social workers, other teachers and learning support workers, you will assess each child's individual needs and draw up an Individual Education Plan.

- In each of these teaching jobs, you will accompany students on visits and trips, help them understand the world around them, and teach life skills to give them greater independence.

The type of person suited to this work

As you will be dealing with challenging behaviour it is essential to have high levels of patience and perseverance to solve communication problems with pupils. You should be observant and must be able to recognise and praise efforts and achievements, however small.

It is important to have a caring attitude towards others, excellent communication skills and a commitment to drawing out and developing individuals' potential in learning. You have to be well organised, flexible and able to change plans and the sequence of lessons to accommodate unexpected events.

Working conditions

SEN teachers are required all over the UK and may be based in one school or work in teams covering a number of institutions. It is possible to obtain part-time work if you are registered with your local authority (LA) but freelance or self-employment is less common.

You will work 39 weeks a year in school. Hours are usually 9am-4pm Monday to Friday and you will be required to work additional hours in order to create lesson plans and attend meetings.

Future prospects

There are over 150,000 SEN teachers working in the UK. Most work in mainstream schools, whilst others work in special schools like hospital schools, pupil referral units, youth custody centres and community homes. At present there is a shortage of skilled candidates.

SEN teachers working in a mainstream school may have the opportunity to be promoted to Special Education Needs Co-ordinator (SENCO). There is also the possibility of becoming a special needs assessor in a local education authority.

Advantages/disadvantages

Helping children with disabilities, learning difficulties or emotional or behavioural problems and knowing that you helped them to progress is extremely rewarding.

Qualifications and courses

ENTRY LEVEL 4

It is generally necessary to have 2 years' teaching experience in a mainstream school before training to become a teacher for pupils with special educational needs. In addition in England and Wales it is necessary to have qualified teaching status (QTS) or a teaching qualification (TQ) in Scotland. In order to obtain these you should have a Postgraduate Certificate in Education (PGCE), a Bachelor of Education (BEd), or a BA or BSc with QTS.

You must have a relevant qualification within 3 years if you are teaching children with visual, hearing or multi-sensory impairments.

Postgraduate qualifications are available in subjects such as special educational needs, specific learning difficulties (dyslexia), and visual impairment. Courses can usually be studied part time or by distance learning.

Qualified teachers of hearing impaired pupils require CACDP Stage 1 in sign language, or equivalent. Qualified teachers of visually impaired pupils must be proficient in Braille.

You will be kept very busy with duties including preparation, classes, marking and assessing, analysing coursework, communicating with examining bodies, meetings and ordering materials.

Money guide

Special Educational Needs (SEN) teachers' starting salaries depend on the employer, location, level of qualifications and responsibilities. Those living in London and the South East of England will receive additional allowances.

Salaries start at £19,500 per year and rise incrementally to £28,500. With experience you can earn between £31,000 and £33,000. With added responsibility and additional points, you can achieve up to £37,000.

Related opportunities

- Education and Childcare Inspector p203
- FE Lecturer/HE Lecturer p206
- Work-based Training Instructor p218

Further information

National Association for Special Educational Needs
4/5 Amber Business Village, Amber Close, Amington, Tamworth, Staffordshire, B77 4RP
01827 311500; www.nasen.org.uk

www.cityandguilds.com/myperfectjob

Education and Training

CRCI: F
CLCI: FAB

TEACHER OF ENGLISH TO SPEAKERS OF OTHER LANGUAGES

What the work involves

- You may be based in the UK or overseas and will teach English to students who are not native speakers. As a term (TESOL) Teachers of English to speakers of other languages, is only used when the students are in the UK. Teaching English as a Foreign Language (TEFL) is used if you are teaching students abroad.

- You will teach students of every age who want to learn to speak English, for educational, cultural or business reasons.

- It is your responsibility to demonstrate your passion for the English language as well as inspiring and encouraging your students.

The type of person suited to this work

You should be patient, have a caring attitude towards others and an interest in drawing out and developing individuals' potential in learning. Excellent communication skills are important, as is firmness and commitment, imagination and creativity.

You have to be well organised, and flexible. You must be able to recognise and praise efforts and achievements. You should be comfortable in maintaining discipline and be confident when speaking to large groups of young people and other professionals.

Working conditions

If you teach English as a foreign language, you may work in this country or abroad, teaching in community and learning centres, commercial and industrial settings. Hours vary according to the employer, however evening and weekend work is normal in this profession.

Future prospects

There is always a need for EFL teachers to cope with the high demand of people who wish to learn English. At present, there are many TESOL jobs available but competition is fierce for full-time positions. Most EFL teachers are employed overseas on temporary contracts. They spend the academic year, from September to June, working overseas and return to teach in the UK peak summer season during July and August. Some contracts include flights, accommodation and extra bonuses.

Advantages/disadvantages

Time is short – there is preparation, classes, marking and assessing, analysing coursework, communicating with examining bodies, meetings and ordering materials.

Work starts the moment you enter the building and continues until you leave, but it does mean that you value your holidays.

Qualifications and courses

ENTRY LEVEL 4

There are no set entry requirements for this work, but some employers prefer a degree. Useful subjects are English, linguistics, modern foreign languages and education. Courses include:

CELTA (Cambridge Certificate in English Language Teaching to Adults) and CELTYL (Cambridge Certificate in English Language teaching to Young Learners). Two A levels/Advanced Highers or equivalents are required and candidates should be over 18. An Extension Certificate is available for holders of CELTA who wish to gain CELTYL. TESOL has the same entry requirements as CELTA.

Higher-level courses are also available for people with a Certificate qualification and TEFL/TESOL experience: DELTA (Cambridge Diploma in English Language Teaching to Adults) and the Trinity Licentiate Diploma. Experienced teachers with a degree and/or TESOL qualification can also study for a Master's in TESOL.

If candidates wish to teach in a state school, a teaching qualification must be held (degree or PGCE).

Teaching is a rewarding profession in which you can witness a student's progression and know that you played a major role in helping them to master the English language.

Money guide

If you work within the UK you can earn approximately £13,000–£20,000 per year, but short-term contracts are usual and opportunities are often seasonal. Senior positions attract salaries of between £22,000 and £30,000. Top earners can expect a maximum of £36,000, which is likely to entail management duties. If you work outside the UK, your salary is likely to be much lower.

Related opportunities

- Education and Childcare Inspector p203
- FE Lecturer/HE Lecturer p206
- Teaching/Learning Support Assistant p217

Further information

Cambridge ESOL
1 Hills Road, Cambridge, CB1 2EU
01223 553355; www.cambridgeesol.org

City & Guilds

www.cityandguilds.com/myperfectjob

TEACHING ASSISTANT/ LEARNING SUPPORT ASSISTANT

What the work involves

- Teaching/classroom assistants help pupils to learn by supporting the teacher and, sometimes, by describing the work in a more visual way or reading questions aloud.

- You may be required to plan and deliver parts of a lesson for the main teacher, working together to make the best use of time and resources.

- Some teaching/classroom assistants will offer one-to-one support to students with learning difficulties or disabilities.

The type of person suited to this work

In this work, you need to like children to help them make the most of their time in school.

You will need lots of patience and possess the ability to stay calm, as all pupils have their off-days when they are noisy or upset. Sometimes, you will work with students who need extra help so you should have an interest in young people who have special needs.

Working conditions

Many learning support assistants work in mainstream schools, but some are employed in independent schools, in residential institutions for students with special needs or specialist colleges.

You will normally work between 8.30am and 4.30pm, although you might have to attend meetings after this and sometimes at weekends.

Future prospects

Recent changes to teachers' workload have involved freeing them from some administrative tasks so they have more classroom time. This has increased the need for teaching assistants working across the UK.

Often, teaching assistants train to become teachers themselves, and there are Initial Teacher Training courses especially for teaching assistants. Special needs learning assistants may specialise in helping young people with a particular disability.

Advantages/disadvantages

This can be a very rewarding job, as you will witness students' educational development and growth. You might help students take steps towards independent living.

You will be very busy, so you may have to snatch meetings with colleagues to share information.

Qualifications and courses

Previous relevant experience, for example in nursery nursing, is an advantage. Candidates need to be at least 18.

Level 2 pre-entry certificates for teaching assistants are offered by CACHE, NCFE, Edexcel (BTEC) and ABC. CACHE, NCFE and Edexcel (BTEC) also offer a Level 3 Certificate, aimed at experienced teaching assistants.

Teaching/classroom assistants are trained on the job. Local authorities in England and Wales may provide additional training.

People already working as teaching or classroom assistants can work towards NVQ Level 2 and 3 in teaching assistants or SVQ Level 2 and 3 in classroom assistants. There are also NVQs/SVQs in early years care and education. Teaching assistants in England can work towards Higher Level Teaching Assistant (HLTA) status

A number of colleges and universities offer foundation degrees for teaching assistants and learning support assistants. Anyone who will be working with children must undergo a CRB police check.

Money guide

Pay levels are set by local authorities or sometimes by school governors, so the rate can vary across regions. The rate for a HLTA is set by the local authority. The starting salary for this profession is normally between £12,000 and £16,000 per year. With experience, if you become a unit manager or work with young people with severe difficulties, you could earn up to £21,000.

Related opportunities

- Childminder p569
- Play Worker/Hospital Play Specialist p211
- Primary and Secondary Teacher p212

Further information

Training and Development Agency for Schools
151 Buckingham Palace Road, London, SW1W 9SZ
0845 6000 991; www.tda.gov.uk

CACHE
Beaufort House, Grosvenor Road, St Albans, AL1 3AW
01727 818616; www.cache.org.uk

www.cityandguilds.com/myperfectjob

Education and Training

CRCI: F
CLCI:

WORK-BASED TRAINING INSTRUCTOR

What the work involves

■ Work-based training instructors work alongside employees, who are carrying out work-based training in their workplace or in a training centre, teaching them and developing their skills.

■ You will be required to liaise closely with the employer's training or human resources manager in order to ascertain the type of training needed and organisational aspects.

■ It is likely that you will specialise in an area such as IT, management, personal development, customer service or craft.

The type of person suited to this work

It is essential to demonstrate a real interest in other people and a commitment to helping them to learn and progress.

This is not a fixed area of work – the need for new skills arises all the time, particularly in ICT – so you must be interested in new technology, efficiency and cost-effectiveness.

Excellent communication skills are important for the large amount of speaking, questioning, listening and reporting that are involved.

Working conditions

You will have access to an office where you will use a computer to prepare lessons and update learner records. However, you will also spend lots of time travelling to meet employers and learners at their places of work.

It is necessary to keep up-to-date with the changes and developments in your occupational area.

Future prospects

The arrival of new technologies and different ways of working means that there is a continual need to help businesses and industry develop the right people to carry out new work tasks.

All companies today are expected to develop their workforces and the government is currently encouraging learning through work-based qualifications, and school/college leavers now have more opportunities to pursue Apprenticeships, National Traineeships or Skillseekers. Training is important and there will be increasing need for instructors in the future.

Advantages/disadvantages

This work involves being at the centre of improving the skills levels of the workforce.

Depending on your specialist area, you may have to work unsociable hours in order to train employees in their workplace.

Qualifications and courses

You can work towards relevant qualifications whilst in employment, including the Chartered Institute of Personnel and Development (CIPD) Certificate in Training Practice (CTP) and NVQs/SVQs in learning and development at Levels 3, 4 and 5. The CTP is equivalent to NVQ/SVQ Level 3, and has no formal entry requirements.

The higher level NVQs/SVQs and the CIPD Professional Development Scheme are appropriate for people in training manager posts.

Postgraduate qualifications are available in subjects such as education and training management, training and development, mentoring and coaching. These programmes can usually be studied part time or by distance learning, and entry requirements are a degree or equivalent professional qualification.

Training practitioners can also work towards gaining NVQ/SVQ assessor qualifications. Entry requirements are at least 2 years' occupational experience in the subject or work area to be assessed.

It can be challenging to motivate and encourage trainees who do not enjoy learning to achieve an academic qualification.

Money guide

Salaries vary depending on the type and size of employer and location. There is the potential to earn larger salaries if the specialised skill you teach is in high demand. Starting salaries for work-based learning instructors are about £16,000 a year. With experience this can rise to £18,000–£25,000. Top earners can expect £26,000 a year.

Related opportunities

■ Human Resources/Personnel Officer p41
■ Lecturer Further Education and Higher Education p206
■ Training Manager p66

Further information

Chartered Institute of Personnel and Development
CIPD House, 151 The Broadway, London, SW19 1JQ

www.cityandguilds.com/myperfectjob

Engineering, Manufacturing and Production

There are a number of highly skilled jobs available in this job family and workers need to be creative and methodical and combine brilliant technical skill with spatial awareness. You may be interested in food production but equally your passion could lie in working with aircraft or marine manufacture. People in these professions share the ability to concentrate for long periods of time and work meticulously on a job to finish it to a high standard. Some will also be highly trained with specialist equipment which may sometimes be hazardous to use so a high level of personal safety awareness is vital.

This section looks at the following jobs:

AEROSPACE ENGINEER

What the work involves

- Aerospace engineers research, design and manufacture space vehicles, satellites, missiles and aircraft.

- You can specialise in mechanical, electrical or electronics engineering, and within these areas you can focus on airframes, hydraulics, materials and structures, or engines.

- Your work might involve research, design and manufacture, or experimenting with new materials.

- You may also undertake flight test programmes, and maintain and improve fleets of aircraft all over the world.

The type of person suited to this work

You should have a logical mind and be good at problem solving. You should also be good at maths, and be able to produce good drawings and diagrams, as well as being able to interpret them well.

Your verbal and written communication skills should also be good, as you'll need to communicate ideas effectively. Teamworking skills are essential, but you must also be able to take on responsibility and work independently.

You'll be expected to keep up to date with new technology and developments in the industry, and for some roles you need to have normal colour vision.

Working conditions

It's usual to work 37–40 hours a week, but this depends a lot on project deadlines and what's currently taking place: hours can be longer. You might have to work evenings and weekends, as work often fits around timetables for aircraft testing.

Work usually takes place in clean quiet laboratories, but visits to production areas are essential and these areas are usually dirty and noisy.

Visits to airfields also take place, where you might be required to inspect and test the functions of the aircraft.

Future prospects

There are good opportunities for promotion in aerospace engineering. The skills you will require will make you suitable for higher positions even in other branches of engineering, and many aerospace engineers move into management positions or research roles as their career progresses.

Some aerospace engineers work independently as consultants, and others find work abroad for foreign governments or aircraft construction companies.

Advantages/disadvantages

You may have to work long hours, evenings and weekends. Stress levels can also be high if you're trying to meet deadlines.

Qualifications and courses

Most entrants are graduates, and many have studied Aeronautical Engineering as a degree. BEng degrees last 3 years, MEng last four, and both are offered at many universities in the UK.

It is possible to enter at a lower level by beginning to train for a craft or technician job straight from school. Apprenticeship schemes usually require good GCSE grades in English, Maths, and Science. Some schemes will require A Levels in Science subjects.

Entry to Employment (e2e) schemes can help prepare you if you're not quite ready for an apprenticeship. Young Apprenticeships are available if you're between 14–16 years old.

Following a HND/HCD after further training with an employer will enable you to register with the ECUK (Engineering Council).

As an aerospace engineer, you will be expected to attend continuing professional development courses (CPDs). This development might include classes, seminars, and workshops.

The starting salary is relatively high, and you can work your way up to a good wage with time and experience.

Money guide

Starting salaries for graduates tend to range from £20,000 to £25,000 per year.

Depending on your professional status, you can work your way up to £40,000 per year as an experienced engineer.

Senior engineers might earn over £50,000.

Related opportunities

- Mechanical Engineer p240
- Electrical Engineer p226

Further information

The Engineering and Technology Board
2nd Floor, Weston House, 246 High Holborn, WC1V 7EX
020 3206 0400; www.etechb.co.uk

The Institution of Engineering and Technology (IET)
Michael Faraday House, Six Hills Way, Stevenage,
Hertfordshire SG1 2AY.
01438 313311; www.theiet.org

Royal Aeronautical Society (RAeS)
4 Hamilton Place, London W1J 7BQ.
020 7670 4325/6; www.aerosociety.com

City&
Guilds

www.cityandguilds.com/myperfectjob

ASSEMBLER

What the work involves

- You will work on an assembly line within a large or small factory or workshop, or at a bench. You could work on products within sectors as diverse as: engineering, furniture production, soft-furnishings, domestic electrical equipment, vehicles, electrical circuit boards and more.

Assembly line

- You will help to produce products or components as they arrive at your work area. Sometimes they may not stop, but keep moving along a belt or route in the factory.

- As the line needs to keep going at a set speed, you will be required to work at the same pace as everyone else.

Bench

- Using hand tools, and in some cases simple machinery, you will carry out specific assembly tasks or create a finished product.

The type of person suited to this work

You will need to have practical skills and enjoy making or repairing items.

In order to construct your product or components you will have to follow diagrams and instructions and be able to work quickly and precisely.

You will need to be able to get on with people and be responsible and hard working.

As it can be repetitive work you must be able to do the same task many times a day.

Working conditions
Assembly line

You can expect to be in a large factory type of environment – in some sectors this could be noisy, dirty and busy and in others, such as the electronics industry, it would be clean and dust-free.

Some assembly lines require 24/7 production; if so, you will normally work a shift pattern.

Bench

You will be sitting or standing using the tools and machinery positioned around you. If you need to use a soldering iron for assembly it can be hot work and may cause fumes.

Part-time work is possible.

Future prospects

The largest employers of assemblers are the electrical, electronic and information technology industries.

As machines are increasingly replacing some of the assembly work that used to be done by people, jobs are reducing and will continue to do so. However there is still demand for assemblers to work on assembling products that are too intricate to be done by machine, or for assembling very small batches of goods.

With experience, you may be able to progress into other areas of manufacturing such as quality control, or go on to train as an engineering craft worker.

Qualifications and courses

There are no formal entry requirements for this work. Key Skills, GCSEs/S grades in English, maths and practical subjects or vocational qualifications in engineering/manufacturing can be useful.

Apprenticeships/Skillseekers may be available to enter this area of work.

ENTRY LEVEL 1

Advantages/disadvantages

You will need to concentrate and work quickly for long periods of the day whilst doing repetitive work.

You could be working in a dirty and noisy environment.

The number of vacancies will continue to drop as more machines replace people.

This type of work is available on a part-time basis, which is attractive to people with families wanting to supplement their income.

Money guide

Starting salaries for assemblers are on average £10,000–£12,000 per year. For experienced assemblers salaries can range from £12,000 to £17,000. Very skilled and experienced assemblers in certain parts of the industry, such as automotive assembly, can earn £20,000+. Productivity bonuses are commonly used as an incentive and will increase salaries.

Related opportunities

- Food Processing Operative p229
- Mechanical Engineer p240
- Welder p255

Further information

Engineering Council UK
10 Maltravers Street, London WC2R 3ER
020 7240 7891; www.engc.org.uk

Semta
14 Upton Road, Watford WD18 0JT
01923 238441; www.semta.org.uk

Proskills UK
Centurion Court, 85B Milton Park, Abingdon OX14 4RY
01235 833844; www.proskills.co.uk

City&
Guilds

www.cityandguilds.com/myperfectjob

Engineering, Manufacturing and Production

CRCI: NJ
CLCI: SAB

BLACKSMITH

What the work involves
Artist blacksmith
- You will produce architectural and decorative pieces such as gates, garden features and furniture.
- You may create specially commissioned pieces such as a large sculpture or a stairway for a building project.

Industrial blacksmith
- You will produce functional objects for use by companies such as fire escapes, security screens or specialist tools.
- You may specialise in an area such as agricultural engineering, security or the mining industries.

The type of person suited to this work
As you will mostly work alone, you should enjoy your own company and be able to use your initiative.

Much of your time will be spent on your feet using different hand tools, often near to the forge which will be very hot.

Although you will be wearing protective clothing you will need to be very responsible as the tools and materials that you will be working with can be dangerous.

Having a creative and artistic flair will help you to use your materials imaginatively.

Working conditions
To be able to work with the different metals you will be using different hand and bench tools and a forge. This will result in conditions that can be noisy, dirty and sometimes cramped.

You will spend much of the time on your feet working with your tools. This is physically demanding work, so you will need to be fit.

You will wear protective clothing such as gloves, ear protectors and goggles.

You may need to travel to meet customers or to install pieces of work 'on-site'.

Future prospects
Most blacksmiths are sole traders, working for themselves. Those who work within a company might progress to supervisory or managerial posts.

If you are self-employed, future success will rely on your ability to gain orders. You will need to build your reputation based on the quality and creativity of your work.

Advantages/disadvantages
Much of the work is done alone in a forge or workshop. This can be isolating.

The work is tiring, hot and dirty, but when you have created what a customer requires it can be satisfying too.

Qualifications and course
ENTRY LEVEL 2

Training can be by an apprenticeship or college course. Some courses may require specific GCSEs/S grades and forgework experience. HNDs and degrees in creative aspects of blacksmithing are available. Two A levels/3 H grades and 5 GCSEs/S grades(A–C/1–3) are required for degree entry.

The National Crafts Training Programme combines on-the-job training with periods of block-release study at the college, and lasts from 2 to 3 years.

Industrial blacksmiths can train through an Apprenticeship/Skillseekers in engineering, which combines NVQ/SVQs in fabrication and welding with on-the-job blacksmith training.

If you are involved in a creative project such as a commissioned sculpture, it can be very rewarding.

If self-employed your long-term future could be uncertain.

Money guide
There are currently no agreed minimum rates for apprentice blacksmiths so salaries can vary widely. Starting salaries generally range from £11,000 to £16,000 a year. Once training has been completed you could earn £25,000+ a year depending on regional differences.

Related opportunities
- Farrier p268
- Sheet Metal Worker p249
- Welder p255

Further information
British Artist Blacksmiths Association
60 Buchanan Street, Balfron, Glasgow, G63 0TW
01360 440830; www.baba.org.uk

National Association of Farriers, Blacksmiths and Agricultural Engineers
The Forge, Avenue B, 10th Street, Stoneleigh Park, Coventry CV8 2LG
024 7669 6595; www.nafbae.org

Worshipful Company of Blacksmiths
48 Upwood Road, London, SE12 8AN
020 8318 9684; www.blacksmithscompany.org.uk

City&Guilds

www.cityandguilds.com/myperfectjob

CAD DRAUGHTSPERSON

What the work involves

- You will produce the drawings and instructions that will enable others to create structures, equipment or components.

- Using a CAD workstation you will draw up technical drawings for components or sections of a structure or piece of equipment.

- Depending on the specialism of the company you work for, you may design part of a structure as large as a factory or bridge, or a component as small as an electronic circuit.

The type of person suited to this work

You will have to be patient and accurate, and have a good understanding of different engineering processes.

Much of your time you will be working at your computer but you will also have to visit and instruct other staff and talk to supervisors. This means you should be happy working with people of all levels, and be confident and articulate.

Although an art ability is not necessary, an interest in technical drawing, ICT, maths and science is.

You will be creating the drawings and instructions that will aid production so you will look for creative solutions to problems. You will design using manual or computerised equipment, so you should be happy using both styles.

Working conditions

Most of your work will be done sitting in front of your computer or drawing board in an office or design area.

You will work office hours but you may need to work overtime when deadlines are close.

Sometimes you will visit the shop floor or factory area where the product you are designing is being made – which could be noisy, hot and dirty.

Future prospects

A wide range of employers recruit CAD draughtspeople, including aeronautical, civil, electrical, mechanical and marine engineering companies, central and local government and the public utilities such as water and electricity supply.

Due to the recent advancements in CAD work, there is currently a shortage of draughtspeople across the country.

You can progress on to senior, supervisory and team-leader work with experience and training.

There are opportunities to work abroad.

Advantages/disadvantages

As much of your work involves using your drawing board or computer, your eyes could get tired and strained.

Currently there is a shortage of skilled CAD draughtspeople.

Qualifications and courses

You can enter this job as a trainee technician with an employer, through an Apprenticeship/Skillseekers scheme. Most entrants are aged 16–19, but entry is possible up to the age of 24. Applicants require four 4 GCSEs/S grades (A–C/1–3) or equivalent including maths and science or technology.

Alternatively, you can take relevant pre-entry qualifications such as a BTEC First Certificate in Engineering or First Diploma in Manufacturing Engineering, National Certificate/Diploma in Manufacturing Engineering, or a City & Guilds Level 2 award in CAD, and gain entry at technician level

Qualifications that can be obtained through on-the-job training include NVQs/SVQs at Level 3, BTEC National Certificates or Diplomas, an SQA National Certificate Group Award or a City & Guilds certificate.

If you want to progress you can move to supervisor level within your own company or elsewhere.

With experience, it may be possible to do this work on a freelance basis, being contracted by smaller companies who do not employ their own draughtsperson.

Money guide

Earnings will be affected by the type of industry you work in and your location.

General starting salaries are around £15,000–£20,000 per year.

With experience, and working in one of the higher paying industries, you can earn up to £30,000.

At senior level you can earn more than £40,000.

Related opportunities

- Architectural Technician p70
- Architectural Technologist p71
- Graphic Designer p186

Further information

Engineering Careers Information Service
SEMTA House, 14 Upton Road, Watford, WD18 0JT
0800 282167; www.enginuity.org.uk

Chartered Institute of Architectural Technologists
397 City Road, London, EC1V 1NH
020 7278 2206; www.ciat.org.uk

City& Guilds

www.cityandguilds.com/myperfectjob

Engineering, Manufacturing and Production

CRCI: GH
CLCI: RAX

CHEMICAL ENGINEER

What the work involves

- Chemical engineers are responsible for devising low-cost, safe and environmentally friendly methods by which to transform raw materials into products such as fuel, pharmaceuticals, plastics and toiletries.

- You will be involved with the operational control of the manufacturing plant, working with colleagues to ensure production levels are maximised, and designing and maintaining equipment.

- You will also have to undertake research and analysis into the running of the plant and the quality of its products.

The type of person suited to this work

You will need to have good oral and written communication skills in order to brief colleagues and compile useful and extensive reports from research you have undertaken. This includes good project management skills.

In keeping with this, an analytical mind and ability to problem solve are helpful when designing and testing products or equipment in the plant itself.

You will also need to be creative, in order to come up with cost-effective products and solutions to problems.

An aptitude and interest in chemistry is also recommended, as is a good understanding of engineering and mathematics.

Working conditions

Working hours are normally fairly standard from Monday to Friday although you may have to work extra hours on occasion, particularly if you are developing a new product, and this can include evenings and weekends.

You will usually work in a plant, laboratory or research establishment so conditions can vary from peaceful, sterile labs to noisier factory floors.

You may need to wear appropriate safety equipment for certain aspects of the job.

Future prospects

There is currently a shortage of chemical engineers, so career prospects are good. It is a dynamic industry so you will have the opportunity to undertake continuing professional development in order to boost your skills and knowledge.

Because of this, opportunities for progression and promotion are great and you could obtain a position in senior management relatively quickly. Self-employment or moving into consultancy are also common options.

Larger companies may also provide opportunities to work overseas.

Advantages/disadvantages

A current shortage of chemical engineers means that prospects are good and career progression rapid.

Qualifications and courses

ENTRY LEVEL 5

This career is open to all graduates with a degree in physical or applied sciences, and engineering. Specific subjects such as chemistry, chemical engineering, applied chemistry and polymer science may improve your chances further. HNDs in similar subjects are also considered although you may have to start as a technician and work up to the position of chemical engineer as you gain further qualifications. You will need a minimum of 5 GCSEs/Highers (A-C/1–3) including English, maths and science, and 2 A-levels/Highers in order to gain a place on an engineering or related degree/HND course.

Your degree or HND must be IChemE accredited by the Engineering Council UK (ECUK) if you want to qualify as a chartered (CEng) chemical engineer. Qualifying will add considerable scope to your career potential.

Entry without a degree or HND is uncommon, although an Advanced Apprenticeship in engineering could lead to a role as an engineering technician or enable you to take a relevant degree.

You will gain further qualifications and skills as you develop in your career, so it shouldn't get boring.

You will rarely have to work away from home, and there are opportunities to become self-employed.

Working in a sterile lab environment, or a noisy factory, can be off-putting.

Money guide

Typical starting salaries range from £20,000 to £30,000. With experience and gaining a more senior role in the company, you can expect to earn £45,000–£50,000. If you achieve chartered status, you could earn £70,000+.

Related opportunities

- Environmental Engineer p228
- Mechanical Engineer p240
- Manufacturing/Production Engineer p236

Further information

The Career Engineer
Beaumont House, Kensington Village, Avonmore Road, London, W14 8TS
0845 241 4022; www.thecareerengineer.com

SEMTA
14 Upton Road, Watford, WD18 0JT
01923 238 441; www.semta.org.uk

British Chemical Engineering Contractors Association
1 Regent Street, London, SW1Y 4NR; 020 7839 6514
www.bceca.org.uk; ecoles@bceca.org.uk

City & Guilds

CRAFT TECHNICAL BREWER/ BREWERY WORKER

What the work involves

Craft technical brewer

- Your job will be to manage the production of beers and lagers in a brewery. You will also manage the brewery workers.

- In a large brewery you may have responsibility for one part of the brewing process such as mixing the ingredients, fermentation or quality control. In a small brewery you may manage the whole process.

- You will be responsible for checking the consistency and quality of the beer or lager, keeping records, and the ordering of stock and raw materials. You may also develop new beers.

Brewery worker

- You could be involved in the whole process, or just one aspect. You will operate computerised machinery and monitor the quality and temperature of the beer.

The type of person suited to this work

Craft technical brewer

You will need to be scientific, with an enquiring mind and a particular interest in biochemistry. Both a practical ability and an interest in engineering are useful. As you will be managing the people working in the brewery, excellent management and communication skills are needed.

Brewery worker

You will need to be practical, physically fit and able to be on your feet for long periods at a time. Good communication and team-working skills are important.

Working conditions

The process of brewing involves working in a hot, steamy, noisy and often smelly environment. The brewery will need to operate 24/7, so expect to work on average 39 hours a week on shifts, including evenings and weekends. You will have to wear overalls, a mask, boots and ear protection.

Future prospects

Craft technical brewer

With experience, you could progress to positions such as senior/head brewer, or enter self employment running your own specialised microbrewery.

Brewery worker

With experience you could progress into supervisory levels or transfer to other breweries for promotion. If you obtain degree-level qualifications you could apply for technical brewer positions.

Qualifications and courses

ENTRY LEVEL 2

Craft technical brewer

Entrants need a degree in brewing/distilling, a pure or applied science such as biological science, microbiology, chemistry, chemical/mechanical engineering or food science/technology. Trainee brewers must achieve the professional qualifications of the Institute of Brewing and Distilling.

Brewery worker

There are no specific entry qualifications for this career, but GCSEs/S grades in English and maths are helpful. Brewery workers are trained on the job, and may work towards NVQs/SVQs in Food and Drink Manufacturing Operations at Levels 1 and 2. The Institute of Brewing and Distilling offers courses.

Advantages/disadvantages

Due to automation and low staff turnover, competition for vacancies can be high. The work includes lots of different aspects that include science, production, engineering, retail and distribution.

Working in a brewery can be smelly, hot and physically demanding. You can feel a strong sense of satisfaction in being involved in producing a high-quality product.

Money guide

Craft technical brewer

As a new entrant you can expect to earn on average £18,000 per year, rising with experience to £28,000. Middle managers on average earn £30,000–£40,000. Head brewers and production directors of large breweries can earn from £45,000 to £60,000+.

Brewery worker

Starting salaries are around £14,000 rising to £22,000 with experience. With promotion, £26,000–£35,000 is possible.

Related opportunities

- Biotechnologist p508
- Cellar Technician p142

Further information

Institute of Brewing and Distilling
33 Clarges Street, London, W1J 7EE
020 7499 8144; www.ibd.org.uk

City& Guilds

www.cityandguilds.com/myperfectjob

Engineering, Manufacturing and Production

CRCI: NJ
CLCI: SAB

ELECTRICAL ENGINEER

What the work involves

- Electrical engineers research, design and develop a range of electrical equipment.

- You will be making, testing and servicing all types of electrical equipment and machinery, and as such will be involved in projects from conception to completion.

- You will usually work on projects with a team of professionals, such as contractors and engineers from other specialisms.

- You will also be liaising with clients and contractors about the development of each project, which will include preparing reports and giving presentations.

The type of person suited to this work

You should have excellent mathematical ability and a very analytical mind in order to successfully design and develop complicated new electrical systems. A logical approach to problem solving is also beneficial.

You will need good communication skills, both verbal and written, for working alongside team members and clients. This will include explaining and talking through projects, as well as compiling written reports and leading presentations.

You must have normal colour vision and natural manual dexterity.

Working conditions

Although electrical engineers usually work within the normal working week, you may find that you will need to work additional or unsociable hours in order to solve problems and meet project deadlines.

Your time will be divided between office-based and onsite work, and you can expect to travel on a daily basis so a driving licence is useful.

Conditions onsite can often be dirty, cramped and potentially hazardous, so you should be prepared to get your hands dirty and wear safety equipment.

Future prospects

There are no set pathways of career progression for electrical engineers, and many decide to stay in a purely engineering role for the duration of their working life.

Alternatively, there are possibilities of going into project management, becoming a consultant, or taking on a more managerial role within a company.

Advantages/disadvantages

Your work will be undertaken at a mixture of indoor and outdoor locations, so you won't be stuck in the office on a daily basis.

You will play an instrumental role in developing new and increasingly safe electrical equipment for a variety of important functions.

Qualifications and courses

ENTRY LEVEL 5

Most employers require a relevant degree in a subject such as electrical or electronic engineering. Other subjects that are favoured include mechanical and production engineering, physics and applied physics, or computing and software engineering.

You can also enter with an HND in a relevant subject such as general engineering, mechatronic engineering, applied physics or computing and IT. Some employers do prefer graduates however, so supplementing your HND with work experience is highly recommended.

Apprenticeships are occasionally available to candidates following completion of A-levels/Highers, through which companies sponsor candidates through their full or part-time degree programme.

To become a professional engineer, you will need to take a masters degree to gain incorporated (IEng) or chartered (CEng) status. This can be taken straight after a degree or HND, or after a few years working as an electrical engineer.

Gaining relevant work experience, or undertaking a sandwich year, is viewed favourably by potential employers.

Hours can be long and unpredictable, especially when nearing completion of a project.

Money guide

The starting salary for an electrical engineer can range from £17,000–£25,000. With 10–15 years' experience, your salary could rise to £40,000+.

Within engineering, salaries vary greatly according to location (London usually yields the highest wages) and the size of the company that you work for. Some companies also offer excellent benefit packages and bonus schemes in addition to a basic wage.

Related opportunities

- Telecommunications Engineer p251
- Mechanical Engineer p240
- Engineering Technician p83
- Electrician p94

Further information

The Institution of Engineering and Technology
Michael Faraday House, Stevenage, Hertfordshire, SG1 2AY
01438 313 311; www.theiet.org; postmaster@theiet.org

City& Guilds

www.cityandguilds.com/myperfectjob

ELECTRICITY DISTRIBUTION WORKER

What the work involves

- Electrical distribution workers are responsible for installing, checking and maintaining all machinery and equipment that supplies electricity to commercial and residential properties.

- You will be working on the overhead lines, masts, and underground cables that run from power stations and connect all the electricity networks together.

- You could work as a cable jointer who mainly works on the underground cables, an overhead line worker, or an electrical fitter who installs, tests and repairs equipment in the regional electricity substations.

- You will be working on a variety of projects from small scale domestic problems to regional electrical concerns.

The type of person suited to this work

You will need to be practical and good with your hands as you will be using a variety of tools and undertaking fiddly tasks.

You should be reasonably fit with a head for heights, as some jobs may require lifting and carrying heavy equipment or working high above the ground.

You must have normal colour vision and pay meticulous attention to detail.

Since you will be working with live electricity, you must be aware of your own safety and that of others around you. You may need to wear protective equipment at times.

Working conditions

Although you will usually work an average 37 hours a week, these may well be over shift patterns including evening and weekends. You should also expect to work overtime on occasion in order to complete projects on time.

The work can be physically demanding as you will be bending and carrying large cables and equipment.

You may work outdoors in damp and muddy trenches, and can expect to be carrying out tasks in cramped conditions from time to time.

Future prospects

As an electricity distribution worker, you will have various options open to you as you progress in your career. You may go on to become a supervisor or manager and be responsible for a team of workers. Alternatively, you could move into another related craft job within the industry.

Your career prospects could be improved further by studying for additional qualifications as you work, such as an NVQ Level 4 or BTEC National Certificate in electrical engineering, or even starting on a related degree course.

Qualifications and courses

Most people start in this career as an apprentice. Although there are no qualifications stipulated to become an apprentice, most employers look for at least 4 GCSEs/S grades (A-C/1–3) including English, maths and a related subject such as science, design and technology or engineering. Apprenticeships are open to those aged 16–24 and could last up to 4 years. You will undertake a mixture of on-the-job practical training and college based study.

An HND in a relevant subject may also prove beneficial.

On completion of your training, you could work towards becoming a registered engineering technician which will increase your earning potential. You could work towards an NVQ Level 2 or 3 in electricity system technology engineering, or a Technical Certificate from BTEC or City & Guilds.

Advantages/disadvantages

You will be on site for the majority of your time so won't be cooped up in an office.

Possibilities for career progression or diversification are good.

Although you may have to work irregular hours, nights away from home are uncommon.

Conditions can be unpleasant, due to weather or space constraints.

Money guide

Starting salaries for an apprentice are around £8,000, and will rise to around £18,000 near the completion of training. With experience, your salary could increase to between £19,000 and £25,000. As a senior electricity distribution worker, especially if you become a team supervisor or manager, you could earn £30,000+.

Related opportunities

- Gas Network Engineer p231
- Electrician p94
- Electrical Engineer p226

Further information

Engineering Council UK (ECUK)
246 High Holborn, London, WC1V 7EX
020 3206 0500; www.engc.org.uk

The Institution of Engineering and Technology
Michael Faraday House, Stevenage, SG1 2AY
01438 313 311; www.theiet.org; postmaster@theiet.org

City&Guilds

www.cityandguilds.com/myperfectjob

Engineering, Manufacturing and Production

CRCI: GE
CLCI: RAK/ROK

ENVIRONMENTAL ENGINEER

Engineering, Manufacturing and Production

CRCI: TD/BB
CLCI: U/Q

What the work involves

■ Environmental engineers work on projects concerning waste management, land reclamation and pollution control, and liaise with a variety of clients from local authorities to private property developers.

■ You will visit and assess numerous sites in relation to their environmental impact, and will have to explain your findings to clients via presentations and reports.

■ You may also have to communicate the environmental issues of a project or site to the general public, green groups and regulatory authorities.

The type of person suited to this work

You should have excellent mathematical ability and a very analytical mind in order to successfully carry out complicated procedures and calculations to assess sites and projects.

A swift and logical approach to problem solving is also beneficial when dealing with often unforeseen environmental complications.

You will need good communication skills, both verbal and written, for working alongside team members and clients.

Good negotiation skills are also helpful as you may need to reach compromises over projects with local government officials, residents or clients.

Working conditions

You will usually work about 39 hours from Monday to Friday, although it is not uncommon to work additional or unsociable hours should problems occur or if deadlines need to be met on a project.

Your time will be divided between office-based and onsite work, so you can expect to travel on a daily basis. Because of this, a driving licence is essential.

You will work in all weather conditions onsite, so should be prepared to get cold and muddy. You will also have to adhere to site safety regulations and wear relevant protective clothing.

Future prospects

As environmental concerns become an increasingly important aspect of construction projects across the globe, there are good prospects and opportunities within this field for career progression.

With experience, you could move into consultancy and set up your own firm. Alternatively, you could specialise in an area such as treatment of industrial waste, or provision of drinking water in developing countries.

You could work in a small company, or in much larger multinational firms. There are also numerous opportunities to work on projects abroad.

Advantages/disadvantages

You will be responsible for minimising the environmental impact of building projects and protecting the well-being of the natural surroundings, which will be rewarding.

Qualifications and courses

ENTRY LEVEL **5**

Most employers require a degree in a relevant subject such as civil or environmental engineering. You may be considered if you have studied another engineering subject, or something related such as physics, applied physics or maths. You can also enter with an HND in a relevant subject such as general engineering, civil engineering, environmental engineering, applied physics or computing and IT. Some employers do prefer graduates, however, so supplementing your HND with work experience is highly recommended.

Apprenticeships are occasionally available to candidates following completion of A levels/Highers, by which companies sponsor candidates through their full or part-time degree programme.

To become a professional engineer, you will need to take a Master's degree to gain incorporated (IEng) or chartered (CEng) status. This can be taken straight after a degree or HND, or after a few years working as an environmental engineer.

Working on potentially controversial developments could lead to confrontation with local residents or clients.

There are excellent opportunities to work overseas, or set up your own company.

Money guide

The starting salary for an environmental engineer can range from £18,000 to £24,000. With a few years' experience, your salary could rise to £30,000–£40,000. Senior environmental engineers can earn £60,000+.

Related opportunities

■ Environmental Health Officer p35
■ Marine Engineer p238
■ Mechanical Engineer p240

Further information

Environmental Careers
The Chartered Institution of Water and Environmental Management (CIWEM), 15 John Street, London, SC1N 2EB
020 7831 3110; www.ciwen.org

Engineering Council UK (ECUK)
246 High Holborn, London, WC1V 7EX
020 3206 0500; www.engc.org.uk

The Career Engineer
Beaumont House, Kensington Village, Avonmore Road, London, W14 8TS
0845 241 4022; www.thecareerengineer.com

City&
Guilds

www.cityandguilds.com/myperfectjob

FOOD PROCESSING OPERATIVE

What the work involves

- Food processing operatives can be involved in one of many areas of food processing. These include freezing, canning, baking, drying, cooking, chilling, pasteurising, or a combination of several of these processes.

- Since much of the work above is carried out by machines, you may be involved in operating the machinery, and you might also be expected to carry out basic maintenance on it.

- You might be involved in the production of the food, for example placing different components of foodstuffs in containers.

- Packaging and labeling are other tasks that you might be required to carry out.

The type of person suited to this work

It's helpful if you have an interest in food and food processing.

You should be good at working in a team, and be able to respond quickly to problems that may arise. You need to be able to stay alert and perceptive at all times, even if tasks are mundane or boring. Good ability to concentrate and observe what's going on around you will really help with this.

Good literacy and numeracy skills are also essential, and you'll need to be able to follow instructions easily, both written and spoken. A thorough understanding of health and safety requirements is also an advantage.

Working conditions

You will be working in a factory environment most of the time. This will involve standing in a production line, as well as bending and lifting.

Temperature in the factory varies according to the processes taking place, and could be very warm or quite chilly.

You'll almost certainly be required to wear special clothing, such as overalls and hats, and a high level of personal hygiene is essential.

You can expect to work 37 to 40 hours a week, usually on a shift system which may include weekends. Overtime is often available.

Future prospects

Progression within the food and drink industry is relatively common, and if committed you stand a good chance of moving up in your company or moving to others.

You can progress to supervisory and management positions quite quickly. Most managers in this sector started out as a food processing operative or something similar.

Advantages/disadvantages

The working environment may not always be pleasant: it can be very hot or very cold. Work may be mundane at times, and the salary isn't very high.

Qualifications and Courses

Working as a food processing operative doesn't generally require any formal qualifications. Some employers will ask for basic levels of literacy and numeracy.

If you want to progress into a supervisory role, you might need a few GCSEs.

Apprenticeships are sometimes available.

Some companies will require you to be 18 or over.

Once you've got the job, training usually happens as you work. Practical skills will be taught, as well as general health and safety, and food safety.

If you decide you'd like to, you can improve your skills by taking an NVQ or SVQ (Level 1–4) in Food and Drink Manufacturing Operations.

With time, you can work towards progressing to a management role or supervisory position. At an operative level, you can choose to move to different areas of food production, such as baking, freezing or brewing.

There are usually plenty of jobs available in this sector, and prospects for promotion are good. If you work your way up, jobs become more interesting and better paid.

Money guide

Salaries start at about £11,500 per year, but some apprentices might earn less.

This can rise to £15,000 per year as you gain experience.

Supervisors and managers can earn £18,000 upwards.

Related opportunities

- Brewery Worker p225
- Meat Process Worker p239

Further information

Food and Drink Federation (FDF),
6 Catherine Street, London, WC2B 5JJ
020 7836 2460; www.fdf.org.uk

Improve Ltd
Ground Floor, Providence House, 2 Innovation Close, Heslington, York, YO10 5ZF.
0845 644 0448; www.improveltd.co.uk

Scottish Food and Drink Federation
4A Torpichen Street, Edinburgh, EH3 8JQ
0131 229 9415; www.sdf.org.uk

City & Guilds

www.cityandguilds.com/myperfectjob

Engineering, Manufacturing and Production

CRCI: NC
CLCI: SAC

CRC : NL
CLCI : SAJ

Engineering, Manufacturing and Production

FURNITURE MANUFACTURER

What the work involves

- Furniture manufacturers construct pieces of furniture, either using machinery or by hand.

- This involves cutting and shaping individual parts of each piece, then assembling them to make a finished item.

- You may then have to smooth and finish items, getting them ready for sale.

- Once you've done the above, you'll usually be asked to add handles and hinges, and sometimes to upholster the furniture too.

The type of person suited to this work

You must be practical and good with your hands. You should also have excellent eyesight and full colour vision. Hand-to-eye coordination is a must.

Your physical strength should be reasonably good, as you'll need to lift and carry things.

You must be able to take orders, and to work under supervision, as well as being good at team work.

Some jobs will require artistic ability, and all will need you to be accurate, careful, and above all patient.

Tasks may become repetitive, but you need to be able to stay focused all the time.

Working conditions

You'll be working in a factory, so the environment may be noisy. Most jobs require you to stand in a production line all day, and the air may be dusty and smell strongly of the products used to treat finished furniture. Protective clothing is usually worn, including ear protectors and face masks for many jobs. Many jobs involve standing for long periods, lifting heavy weights, and bending.

It's normal to work a 39 hour week, but overtime is sometimes necessary if the factory has a delivery deadline, or during seasonal peaks.

Future prospects

Promotion is a possibility, and many manufacturers move into more senior roles within companies, managing projects and gaining responsibility.

Others choose to specialise in specific areas of furniture manufacture, for example furniture restoration, craft cabinet making, or even furniture design.

Some furniture manufacturers choose to teach their craft, or set up their own business.

Advantages/disadvantages

If you're interested in your craft and willing to put a little time in, a career in furniture manufacture can really grow, and so can your salary.

Qualifications and courses

Most employers don't require any specific qualifications, but some ask for GCSEs.

Apprenticeships are available for training, and can help to give your career focus. Those on offer include Young Apprenticeships, Pre-Apprenticeships, Apprenticeships, and Advanced Apprenticeships.

Once you're in, training usually occurs on the job. Some people who are new to the industry choose to follow a part-time course in college to enrich their skills and gain a relevant and useful qualification. This could be a City & Guilds Certificate in Manufacturing Furniture, or one of many NVQ qualifications including Production of Furniture and Furnishings, Making and Installing Furniture, Making and Repairing Hand-Crafted Furniture and Furnishings, and Making and Installing Production Furniture. There is also a City & Guilds qualification available in Furniture Crafts.

This job can be satisfying if you enjoy building and making things and are good at DIY.

Working on constructing the same item over and over again can get repetitive.

Money guide

Most operatives start on a salary of around £12,000 per year.

Once you've gained some experience, this might increase to about £15,000 per year.

If you become highly skilled, you can expect to earn £20,000 upwards.

Related opportunities

- Carpenter p77
- Joiner p77
- Shopfitter p125

Further information

Association of Master Upholsterers and Soft Furnishers
102A Commercial Street, Newport, South Wales, NP20 1LU
01633 215454; www.upholsterers.co.uk

British Furniture Manufacturers Association (BFM)
Wycombe House, 9 Ambersham Hill, High Wycombe, HP13 6NR
01494 523021; www.bfm.org.uk

FFINTO
67 Wollaton Road, Beeston, Nottingham, NG9 2NG.
0115 9221200; www.ffinto.org

City& Guilds

www.cityandguilds.com/myperfectjob

GAS NETWORK ENGINEER

Engineering, Manufacturing and Production

CRCI: GI
CLCI: ROB

What the work involves

- Gas is transported from its supply points (called beaches) to domestic and industrial customers by a network of pipes and meters that it will be your responsibility to maintain.

- To gain access to pipework you will probably need to dig a hole in a road, garden or pavement.

- You will be responsible for the safety of yourself and others when carrying out work. This will include putting up warning signs, barriers and traffic control if needed.

- You may have to deal with emergency gas leaks.

The type of person suited to this work

You will normally work in a small team, so you should enjoy working with and be able to get on with people. Before you start work you might have to knock on customers' doors informing them of who you are, so being polite and courteous are also important skills.

This can be a physically demanding job. You will be using digging and excavating tools and pipe-laying equipment. To make sure you do the job correctly you will have to understand and follow technical instructions and drawings.

When the job is complete, you will have to make sure the finished surface is safe and as good as it was when you started, so you should be tidy and efficient.

Working conditions

You will be working in a team outdoors in all weathers. You will normally work a 37–40 hour week, overtime and weekend work will be expected on a rota basis.

You will be using equipment which can be physically demanding and you will get dirty. As this can be dangerous work you will wear protective clothing such as high-visibility and fireproof clothing, steel toe-capped boots and head gear.

Future prospects

The National Grid coordinates and monitors the gas distribution network in the UK. There are four gas distribution companies; National Grid Distribution, Wales and West Utilities, Northern Gas Networks and Scotia Gas Networks (operating in the south of England as Southern Gas and in Scotland as Scotland Gas Networks). There is currently a national shortage of gas distribution workers, particularly in cities and industrial areas.

With experience and training, you could progress to a technician, supervisory or management position where you would be responsible for a number of teams.

Advantages/disadvantages

Being outside in all weathers can be a positive or negative depending on the time of year!

You might get verbal abuse from angry customers complaining about holes in their road.

Qualifications and courses

You will normally start as a trainee or an apprentice.

There are no formal qualifications required, however, employers look for good GCSEs/S grades in maths, science, English and a practical technical subject.

It's also useful to have some experience in engineering or building work. A lot of adults are recruited through this route.

You can also enter through an Advanced Apprenticeship with the National Grid. You will need 4 GCSEs/S grades (A–C/1–4) including maths and English.

Once employed you can work towards NVQ Gas Appliances Installation and Maintenance at Level 2 and Gas Network Engineering at Level 3, or SVQ Domestic Natural Gas Installation and Maintenance at Levels 2 and 3. Once you have completed an NVQ/SVQ Level 3 it is possible to apply for HND/degree or higher level NVQ/SVQs.

Having a clean driving licence is increasingly important.

It can be satisfying to know that you are helping members of the community receive power for their homes and businesses.

Money guide

Whilst training, workers can earn from £9,000 to £15,000 per year.

Upon qualification and with experience this rises to between £17,000 and £25,000.

As a team leader or with more responsibility you can expect your salary to increase to £25,000–£30,000+.

Related opportunities

- Construction Operative p86
- Construction Plant Operator p87
- Plumber p117
- Water/Sewerage Network Operative p137

Further information

Northern Gas Networks
1100 Century Way, Colton, Leeds, LS15 8TU
0113 397 5300; www.northerngasnetworks.co.uk

Scotland Gas Networks
Inchcolm House, 11 West Shore Road, Edinburgh, Scotland, EH5 1RH
0131 559 6000; www.scotiagasnetworks.co.uk

City&
Guilds

www.cityandguilds.com/myperfectjob

KNITTING/SEWING MACHINIST

What the work involves

- Clothing machinists are responsible for both stitching together pre-cut pieces of fabric and creating finished garments from scratch. They also finish garments with extra embroidery, fastenings and other trimmings.

- You will have to complete a number of garments within a strict timeframe, working to deadlines.

- You may create an entire garment from start to finish, or be responsible for a certain stage of the overall process.

- You could make a wide variety of garments, including jumpers, trousers, bags and wedding dresses, and work with a number of materials from silk and wool through to leather.

The type of person suited to this work

You will need to be very practical and good with your hands in order to operate the machinery and complete frequently fiddly tasks.

Accuracy, a good eye for detail and excellent eyesight are also valuable so that you can pick out any irregularity in stitching or fabric colours.

Because you will be completing garments according to demand, you will be working within strict timescales so must be able to produce high quality results at speed.

Finally, enjoyment of craft and a creative flair is advantageous, especially if you are producing more individual designs.

Working conditions

Most machinists are factory based, and work normal hours during a regular Monday to Friday week.

Because of peak periods of demand in the industry, overtime and part-time work are common. Some employers also operate a shift system which could create irregular hours.

You will probably work as part of a team, but will be responsible for meeting your own targets so will mainly be working autonomously.

The work can be repetitive and strenuous on the eyes, and working in a factory environment is noisy.

You may have to wear protective equipment.

Future prospects

You could be employed by a large company, producing items for well known high street brands, or a smaller boutique enterprise.

Skilled machinists can go on to become sample machinists, producing prototype garments for fashion designers.

Alternatively, with experience you could build a career in production management, or set up your own garment design and manufacturing business.

Qualifications and courses

There are no formal academic qualifications to enter the profession as either a knitwear or sewing machinist, but employers do usually look for some sewing experience. Because of this, you may have to complete a practical test at an interview. It might also be useful to have samples of your work available for employers to assess. Apprenticeship opportunities may be available to those aged 16–24.

As you progress in the job, you will probably be required to undertake additional training as you will need to master increasingly complicated techniques. This may not include taking professional qualifications, although options such as NVQ Level 2 in manufacturing sewn products, or NVQ Level 2 knitting and crochet are available.

There are also various other courses, ranging from full time, part time, short courses and distance learning.

Advantages/disadvantages

You will be working in a creative role, making garments that are both beautiful and functional.

With experience, you can set up on your own as a clothes designer and manufacturer.

If you work on a particular task for long periods of time, the work can be slightly monotonous.

Money guide

Starting salaries can range between £10,000 for basic entry level roles, up to £13,000 for those with some proven experience and ability. With experience, this can rise to £16,000.

Salaries depend greatly on the employer. It is also possible to earn more if you undertake overtime, gain more qualifications in order to diversify into additional areas such as pattern cutting and alterations, or if you set up your own clothing business.

Related opportunities

- Fashion designer p181
- Machinist p235
- Tailor/dressmaker p250

Further information

Drapers
Greater London House, Hampstead Road, London, NW1 7EJ
020 7728 5000; www.drapersonline.com

www.cityandguilds.com/myperfectjob

LAND-BASED ENGINEER

What the work involves

- Land-based engineers design, develop, test and modify agricultural and horticultural equipment in order to ensure that these industries stay up-to-date.

- You will need to carry out extensive research into the needs of those using the equipment you are producing, as well as assessing and limiting the environmental impact of your projects.

- You will also be called upon to compile reports and undertake presentations on your work, as well as offering expert advice to clients and other professionals.

The type of person suited to this work

You will need to have great ingenuity in order to find solutions to problems, or design new equipment to aid agricultural and horticultural processes.

Alongside this, you will need excellent communication skills in order to understand the needs of your clients and translate them into designs and instructions for your team.

Good ICT skills, problem-solving abilities and a flexible approach to work are also essential in order to cope with the various demands that differing projects will make of you.

Working conditions

You will usually work hours within the normal working week, although occasional overtime may be necessary to complete projects to deadline.

Although you will be office-based for the majority of the time, there will be some onsite and field work so that you can assess projects and carry out tests on equipment.

Because of the onsite work, you may find that you have to work outdoors in unpredictable weather in conditions that are cold, wet and muddy.

You will also need to wear relevant safety equipment whilst onsite.

Future prospects

There are opportunities for land-based engineers to work all over the world, undertaking a variety of projects from food production in the UK to creating effective water supplies in areas of the developing world.

You could work in a large multinational organisation, or a smaller company. Larger firms offer greater scope for career progression, and you could soon be managing your own projects and moving up the career ladder. Smaller firms offer less opportunity for progression, so you may have to move to another company in order to develop in your field.

Advantages/disadvantages

You will be working towards developing and preserving the landscape and rural life for future generations.

Qualifications and courses

This career is open to all graduates with a degree in engineering. Specific subjects such as agricultural engineering, environmental engineering, ergonomics or mechanical engineering may improve your chances further. HNDs in similar subjects are also considered for entry level positions, and employers may be willing to support further study to take you to degree level. You will need a minimum of 5 GCSEs/Highers (A-C/1–3) including English, maths and science, and 2 A-levels/ Highers in order to gain a place on an engineering or related degree/HND course.

Your degree or HND must be accredited by the Institution of Agricultural Engineers (IAgrE), or a similar licensed body of the Engineering Council UK (ECUK) if you would like to progress to qualifying as a chartered (CEng) or incorporated (IEng) engineer. Qualifying in either will add considerable scope to your career potential.

Each day will present new problems and challenges, so the work will always be interesting and stimulating.

You will be working with a variety of people from many professional sectors and areas of the community.

On average, you will earn less than engineers in other industries.

Money guide

Salaries for graduates typically range from £18,000-£24,000. Once you have gained experience and qualified as a chartered or incorporated engineer, your salary could rise to between £35,000 and £55,000. Additional allowances and benefits are usually given for overseas work.

Related opportunities

- Agricultural Scientist p258
- Environmental Engineer p228
- Land Surveyor p111
- Product Designer p195

Further information

British Agricultural and Garden Machinery Association
Entrance B Level 1, Salamander Quay West, Park Lane, Harefield, UB9 6NZ
0870 205 2834; www.bagma.com; info@bagma.com

Engineering Council UK (ECUK)
246 High Holborn, London, WC1V 7EX
020 3206 0500; www.engc.org.uk

www.cityandguilds.com/myperfectjob

ENTRY LEVEL 5

Engineering, Manufacturing and Production

CRCI: GB
CLCI: RAD/RAX

LOCKSMITH

What the work involves

- You will sell, install and maintain the locks of houses, cars and businesses for your customers.

- You will use specialist machinery to cut replacement keys for locks.

- Advising on, repairing and installing security and closed-circuit television systems may be part of your job.

- You may also provide a 24-hour call-out service for those who have lost keys or locked themselves out of their home, car or business.

The type of person suited to this work

If you have ever been locked out of your home or a car you will know how distressing it can be. As a locksmith you will have to be calm and patient – reassuring your customers whilst providing a prompt and reliable service. Good communication skills are important in this job.

Your customers and employer will also expect you to be totally trustworthy and honest.

To do this job you will have to enjoy using your hands, different tools and equipment. You should enjoy practical tasks and be able to offer solutions to security problems. Carpentry or general engineering skills are also helpful.

A driving licence may be required.

Working conditions

If you work in a shop you will probably have a 37–40-hour Monday–Saturday week. Self-employment is possible.

If you, or your employer, offer a 24 hour call-out service, you could be working at all times of day or night. This can be difficult if you have family commitments.

Where you work will depend on your customers and could include working outdoors in all weathers.

You may work mainly from a van that holds your tools, and do lots of driving.

Future prospects

As worries about home and business security have increased, the demand for more secure locks and security systems to be fitted by qualified locksmiths has grown too. Currently there are around 2000 qualified locksmiths in the UK.

Employers include independent small locksmiths, larger national companies offering a 24-hour call-out emergency service, specialist security companies, DIY hardware stores and shoe repairers which offer a key-cutting service.

Progression for locksmiths is mainly achieved by becoming self-employed and building up a profitable business. It is also possible to progress into more specialist areas of work such as safe engineering.

Qualifications and courses

There are no formal educational requirements, but most applicants will be required to hold GCSE/S grades in English, mathematics and preferably a practical subject like craft or technology.

Some locksmiths offer apprenticeship opportunities – contact local locksmiths to see if they require new staff or trainees. You might be able to gain an Apprenticeship/ Skillseeker opportunity if you are aged 16–24.

The Master Locksmiths Association (MLA) offers a General Locksmithing Course at their training centres.

To apply you will have to be a member of the British Locksmithing Institute (BLI). Individuals can apply for student membership of the BLI without any prior experience, and then study for 3 years to be become an Advanced Student; further examinations are available after this.

NVQs/SVQs are available in Providing Security or Emergency and Alarm Systems.

Advantages/disadvantages

This can be a varied job. You will never know what your next job will be, or where you will have to go.

Meeting the public can be interesting and knowing you've helped people can be rewarding.

Working all hours of the day and night can be difficult and call-outs to replace locks after burglaries can be distressing.

Money guide

As a trainee you can expect to earn around £13,000 per year. With experience this can increase to £15,000–£30,000. Many locksmiths choose to become self-employed. Earnings will then depend on individual charges and company success. Earnings will be affected by regional differences; more can be expected in the larger cities as 24-hour call-outs will be more common.

Related opportunities

- Carpenter/Joiner p77
- Glazier p103

Further information

Master Locksmiths Association
5D Great Central Way, Woodford Halse, Daventry, Northamptonshire, NN11 3PZ
01327 262255; www.locksmiths.co.uk

City& Guilds

www.cityandguilds.com/myperfectjob

MACHINIST

What the work involves

- Engineering machinists make engineered parts from various materials, such as metals or heavy and lightweight plastics.

- You could be making parts for a variety of products, from domestic appliances and machines to wind turbines and aeroplane engines.

- You will be using a range of machinery, including grinding and cutting machines, drills and presses. Increasingly, computer numerically controlled (CNC) machinery is being used which combines some of the manufacturing processes.

- You will need to interpret complicated engineering drawings in order to assess which materials, tools and machines to use to produce each part.

The type of person suited to this work

You will need to have good eyesight, excellent co-ordination and sound practical ability in order to operate machinery safely and accurately.

Good mathematical skills and the ability to read complicated engineering drawings and interpret them into a 3D part are essential.

You should have good communication skills as you will mainly be working in a team environment.

A good level of physical fitness is also beneficial as the job involves lifting heavy materials and standing or bending over machinery for the majority of the day.

Working conditions

Working hours are usually around 38 per week, Monday to Friday, although you will usually start early in the morning and finish early in the afternoon.

Some larger companies operate 24 hour production, and in this case you would be required to work shifts which could include evenings and weekends. Conditions in factories and workshops are usually fairly pleasant, although can be noisy at times.

Because you are operating machinery you will also need to wear appropriate safety equipment at all times.

Future prospects

There are jobs available for machinists all over the country, although the majority are found in larger cities and within general mechanical engineering companies.

With experience, you could be promoted to become team leader or supervisor, and if you gain further qualifications you could go on to specialise in areas such as design.

As there is currently a shortage of machinists in the engineering sector, job prospects are good.

Qualifications and courses

Entry into this career is usually between the ages of 16–18 via an Advanced Apprenticeship in engineering. Most employers require candidates for apprenticeships to have at least 4 GCSEs/S grades (A-C/1–3) including English, maths, a science subject, and either technology/engineering or a related subject.

As an apprentice, you will undertake several months of learning skills and studying away from the workplace in order to build up your skill level. You will then spend 2–3 years working for a company whilst also attending college and studying towards an NVQ Level 3 or higher in engineering production.

Entry for older candidates is possible, although they must be able to demonstrate some relevant experience and skills. Some employers will also be willing to support you in working towards gaining an NVQ Level 3 qualification.

Advantages/disadvantages

Jobs are available throughout the UK and there is little travelling involved, so you will rarely be absent from home for any period of time.

It is a physically demanding job, with large amounts of time spent standing or bending over machinery and lifting heavy materials and equipment.

You may have to work unsociable hours due to early starts or unpredictable shift patterns.

Money guide

The starting salary for an apprentice machinist will be between £6,000 and £8,000. Once you have qualified, your salary should rise to around £16,000–£18,000. With several years' experience, and as you move into a more senior position within a company, your salary could increase to £25,000+.

Related opportunities

- Engineering Technician p83
- Motor Vehicle Technician p241
- Sheet Metal Worker p249
- Toolmaker p253

Further information

SEMTA
14 Upton Road, Watford, WD18 0JT
01923 238441; www.semta.org.uk

City&
Guilds

www.cityandguilds.com/myperfectjob

Engineering, Manufacturing and Production

CRCI: GF
CLCI: R

MANUFACTURING/PRODUCTION ENGINEER

What the work involves

- Manufacturing engineers design, implement and maintain manufacturing processes.

- You will be consulting with other professionals, such as design engineers, in order to produce high quality products efficiently and with minimum cost.

- You could work in a variety of industries, including food and drink, fashion, and pharmaceuticals.

- You could work across a project from design and research to after-sales care, and as such you will be using a variety of manufacturing equipment and computer systems on a daily basis.

The type of person suited to this work

You should be able to work as part of a team with a variety of people, as you will be liaising with other professionals on a daily basis to discuss product ideas and manufacturing solutions.

You should be good at analysing and solving problems in order to understand and stay ahead of potential manufacturing issues. The ability to prioritise your workload is also beneficial.

Strong numerical skills are essential.

Working conditions

You will usually work 37 hours per week, but this often includes evening and weekend work. Extra or unsociable hours can be expected when a new production process is being tested, or if the company you are working for operates a shift system.

You will divide your time between office-based work, meetings and time spent on the shop floor/in the factory. When on the shop floor, you may have to wear relevant safety equipment or protective clothing.

Future prospects

You could work in a variety of manufacturing sectors, building diverse experience that will help you move across industries and sectors within manufacturing, taking up managerial or marketing roles.

Alternatively, you could specialise in a certain area (such as pharmaceuticals or clothing) and move into production management or consultancy, drawing upon your unique knowledge and experience to motivate and advise others.

There are also numerous short-term contracts available for manufacturing engineers, which would allow you to become self-employed.

Advantages/disadvantages

Manufacturing engineers enjoy one of the most creative roles in the engineering sector, with great input into product design and final function.

If you work in a large company, there may well be opportunities to travel in the course of your employment.

Qualifications and courses

ENTRY LEVEL 5

The most common entry route is taking a relevant degree in an engineering subject. For entry onto a degree course, you will need 3 A-levels/ Highers (including maths and physics) and 5 GCSEs/S grades (A–C/1–3).

HNDs in similar subjects are also considered by employers, but you will have to start in a lower position and undertake further training and study towards degree level qualifications whilst you work.

Apprenticeships for those aged 16–24, or Young Apprenticeships for those aged 14–16, are available in which you work towards a technician level position. From here you will need to take further qualifications to become a manufacturing engineer. You will need at least 3 GCSEs/ S grades (A–C/1–3) to be eligible for an apprenticeship. As an apprentice, you will train on-the-job and also gain qualifications through college-based study. You will study towards an NVQ Level 2 or 3 in Engineering Production.

You may work evenings and weekends on a regular basis, although absence from home overnight is rare.

Money guide

The average graduate starting salaries on completion of initial training range from £20,000 to £24,000. With 5–10 years' experience, you could earn up to £37,000. Senior manufacturing engineers can expect to earn £45,000+.

Related opportunities

- Chemical Engineer p224
- Electrical Engineer p226
- Mechanical Engineer p240
- Textile Operative p252

Further information

Institution of Mechanical Engineers (IMechE)
1 Birdcage Walk, London, SW1H 9JJ
020 7222 7899; www.imeche.org.uk;
enquiries@imeche.org.uk

The Sector Skills Council for Science, Engineering and Manufacturing Technologies (SEMTA)
14 Upton Road, Watford, WD18 0JT
01923 238 441; www.semta.org.uk

The Institution of Engineering and Technology
Michael Faraday House, Stevenage, SG1 2AY
01438 313 311; www.theiet.org; postmaster@theiet.org

City& Guilds

www.cityandguilds.com/myperfectjob

MARINE CRAFTSPERSON

What the work involves

- A marine craftsperson takes part in the building and repair of many different kinds of ships and boats.

- Repairers and shipbuilders work with big vessels such as ferries, dredgers, tugs, submarines, tankers and warships.

- Boat builders work with smaller boats, like wooden dinghies, sailing boats, narrow boats and powerboats.

- Both crafts require you to work from a design to create the ship or boat. This has usually been created on a computer, and you work at marking and cutting out shapes, welding, and cutting and bending steel and other materials.

The type of person suited to this work

You should be a good team worker, and a good communicator.

A practical, logical and problem-solving mindset is essential, as you'll not only be required to interpret drawings and plans but will also need to solve problems on the job quickly and intelligently.

You should also be good with numbers, and have good eyesight and good physical fitness.

Working conditions

Marine craftspeople tend to work a normal 37 hour week, but overtime is usually available. Some urgent repair jobs may take place overnight and during weekends, but this is relatively rare.

Working conditions

Working at heights is normal, and you will probably spend the majority of your time indoors.

Future prospects

As you gain experience, it may be possible to progress to a position such as supervisor or inspector. You could also work towards becoming workshop manager.

Another option is to use your experience to become self-employed in areas such as boat building and repair.

Some people choose to gain further qualifications and become a marine engineering technician.

Advantages/disadvantages

If you have an interest in practical work and building things, and in ships and maritime matters, then this job can be really enjoyable. It can be really satisfying to create something you're passionate about.

The grubby working conditions might not sit well with everybody, so if you want to work in a clean and tidy environment your skills may be better suited elsewhere.

Qualifications and courses

ENTRY LEVEL 2

Many employers ask for GCSEs in English, Maths and a science or related subject. Sometimes employers will ask for further qualifications, or even set an aptitude test.

It's normal to train on the job, usually through an apprenticeship. Apprenticeships are open to entrants aged 16–24, and Young Apprenticeships for those aged 14–16.

You can take an engineering-related vocational course at college, such as an NVQ or BTEC, which will enable you to apply for an Advanced Apprenticeship.

You can undertake a mixture of on-the-job and classroom-based training, which most employers will be willing to fund. Training usually starts with health and safety regulations and an induction course, followed by basic skills including selecting materials, interpreting drawings, how to use relevant tools and developing skills.

Possible boat-building qualifications you can take include NVQs in Boat Production and Support Services, Boat Building and Maintenance, and a City and Guilds Certificate in Boat Building, Maintenance and Support.

You could also take a specialist degree in leisure boat design and construction.

Money guide

As an apprentice at the age of 18, you'll probably earn about £8,000 a year. Once you're qualified, the average salary is about £20,000 a year. Experienced marine craftspeople who have worked their way up may earn about £30,000 a year.

Related opportunities

- Engineering Construction Technician p83
- Marine Engineer p238
- Marine Engineering Technician p238
- Merchant Navy Engineering Officer p611

Further information

British Marine Federation
Marine House, Thorpe Lea Road, Egham, TW20 8BF
01784 473377; www.britishmarine.co.uk

The Institute of Marine Engineering, Science and Technology (IMarEST)
80 Coleman Street, London, EC2R 5BJ
020 7382 2600; www.imarest.org

SEMTA
14 Upton Road, Watford, W18 0JT
0800 282 167; www.semta.org.uk

www.cityandguilds.com/myperfectjob

Engineering, Manufacturing and Production

CRCI: GG
CLCI: RAC

MARINE ENGINEER

What the work involves

- Marine engineers design, construct and maintain ships' seafaring equipment, as well as developing and preserving offshore systems.

- You could work in a shipbuilding company, on board ships and submarines, in marine surveying, in an oil company, or in the leisure industry.

- You will work across a range of engineering disciplines, including electrical, construction and mechanical.

- You will work closely with naval officers, architects, other professionals and team members.

The type of person suited to this work

You will need excellent communication skills, both verbal and written, in order to manage and lead your team as well as liaising with other professionals and clients.

Excellent maths and IT skills are essential, as is an ability to solve problems under pressure. Prioritising your workload through careful planning and project management is also a skill you will need to develop.

You should be good at working within a team, especially as you may have to live and work with colleagues in confined areas when undertaking projects on boats, submarines, or out at sea.

Working conditions

You could work anywhere from an office to a boatyard, or even on a submarine, and many jobs involve a combination of office-based and onsite work.

If you are working on projects on a ship or offshore installations, living accommodation can be tight and you will probably need to spend time away from home.

The job involves climbing and lifting equipment so you will need to be physically fit.

Future prospects

Prospects are good for marine engineers. You could work for a variety of companies, from small shipping businesses, to leisure cruise liners, through to joining the Royal Navy.

When you have gained skills and experience, you could go on to specialise in project management or marine research, or even work as a consultant.

There are plentiful opportunities to work abroad.

Advantages/disadvantages

There are a huge variety of employment options available to you, from conservation projects to defence systems.

You will work in numerous diverse areas, and with many different people, so the work will always be interesting and fresh.

You may be working in cramped, uncomfortable conditions for long periods of time. This includes living and working with colleagues 24 hours a day on certain projects.

Qualifications and courses

You can enter this career with a relevant degree in a subject such as marine engineering, marine technology, offshore engineering or naval engineering. Entry to a degree course usually requires at least 5 GCSEs/Highers (A–C/1–3) and 3 A-levels, including a maths and science subject.

You can also enter the industry with an HND in a relevant subject such as general or marine engineering, or marine technology. Entry requirements for an HND course are usually 1 A level or a BTEC National Certificate in a relevant subject.

You could undertake an Apprenticeship as a marine engineering technician and work towards becoming a marine engineer via this route, undertaking additional training and qualifications on the job.

The Merchant Navy Training Board offers a number of training and sponsorship schemes for entrants at GCSE, A-level, undergraduate or graduate stages of their education. Undergraduate and graduate applicants must have degrees in a scientific subject.

The Royal Navy accepts applications for engineering officers from candidates in their final year of university

Money guide

As a graduate marine engineer, you could expect to earn around £21,000. With a few years' experience, this can rise to £35,000. Experienced and highly skilled marine engineers can expect to earn £50,000+. Some companies also offer excellent benefit packages and bonus schemes in addition to a basic salary.

Related opportunities

- Electrical Engineer p226
- Environmental Engineer p228
- Marine Craftsperson p237
- Mechanical Engineer p240

Further information

Institute of Marine Engineering Science & Technology (IMarEST)
80 Coleman Street, London, EC2R 5BJ
020 7382 2600; www.imarest.org

Merchant Navy Training Board
Carthusian Court, 12 Carthusian Street, London, EC1M 6EZ
www.mntb.org.uk; enquiry@mntb.org.uk

Engineering Council UK (ECUK)
246 High Holborn, London, WC1V 7EX
020 3206 0500; www.engc.org.uk

www.cityandguilds.com/myperfectjob

MEAT PROCESS WORKER

What the work involves

Abattoir operative

- You will be part of the process that slaughters animals for food.

- After the animals have been humanely killed, you will remove the skins, internal organs and inedible parts of the dead animal – separating the edible meat from the waste.

Meat manufacturing operative

- You will work as part of the manufacturing process that produces meat products.

- You may weigh, wrap and label meat products.

- If working in a specialist chicken plant you may use machinery to kill and prepare poultry.

The type of person suited to this work

This can be distressing and smelly work, so you should be aware of what the job involves and be prepared to cope with blood and mess.

As you will have to do lots of lifting, carrying and operating machinery, you will need to be physically fit and able to be on your feet for long periods at a time.

You should have a responsible attitude as you may use dangerous knives, cutting tools and machinery. You also need to be aware of your personal cleanliness as you are part of a food production process.

Working conditions

Refrigerated areas are cold and all areas need frequent cleaning and so may be wet. You will be expected to wear protective clothing, including footwear, hairnets and warm clothing if needed.

You will normally do a 40-hour week, although shift and part-time work are possible.

Future prospects

Abattoir operative

With experience you could apply for senior internal positions or look to move to related areas such as butchery, retail, food marketing or preparation. Quality control, health and safety consultancy or self-employment are also possible.

Meat manufacturing operative

With experience you could apply for supervisory, quality control and management jobs or move into related areas of work such as butchery, food preparation or retail.

With the right experience, qualifications and training you may be able to progress into work on the meat inspection teams employed by the Meat Hygiene Service (MHS) – part of the Food Standards Agency.

Qualifications and courses

There are no formal entry qualifications for these jobs. However, GCSEs/S grades in English and maths are useful, particularly if you want to move up to supervisory, inspection or technical level. You could work towards NVQs/SVQs at Levels 1–3 in Meat and Poultry Processing or Meat and Poultry Plant Operations and then onto an NVQ/SVQ at Level 4 in Meat Processing Management. The Meat Training Council offers other courses.

To work as a slaughterman/woman, you must be aged 18 or over, and be licensed with the Department for the Environment, Food and Rural Affairs (DEFRA).

Advantages/disadvantages

This can be cold, smelly and dirty work.

You will be part of a team and often there is a good working atmosphere within a production team.

Many employers welcome mature entrants.

The job can be repetitive and monotonous.

Money guide

Abattoir operative

The minimum salary for trained adults is around £11,500 per year, rising to £20,000 with experience. Experienced abattoir workers with supervisory duties may earn up to £25,000.

Meat manufacturing operative

The starting salary is usually about £11,000 per year. Experienced meat manufacturing operatives earn up to £18,000 per year.

Related opportunities

- Butcher p481
- Kitchen Assistant/Porter p152
- Meat Hygiene Inspector p491

Further information

Meat Training Council
PO Box 141, Winterhill House, Snowdon Drive, Milton Keynes, MK6 1YY
01908 231062; www.meattraining.org.uk

City& Guilds

www.cityandguilds.com/myperfectjob

Engineering, Manufacturing and Production

CRCI: NC
CLCI: SAC

MECHANICAL ENGINEER

What the work involves

- Mechanical engineers design, develop and maintain the moveable parts of all equipment, ranging from those in small household appliances up to large machinery or vehicles.

- You will probably work on a project from conception to completion, so will be involved with all aspects from design and development through to final manufacture.

- You could work in a number of industries, including manufacturing, construction, sport, medicine or transport.

- You will also have to manage budgets, resources and people on each project.

The type of person suited to this work

You will need an exceptionally high level of scientific knowledge and technical ability in order to design mechanisms and solve practical problems as they occur in the development process.

Good communications skills, both verbal and written, are essential for dealing with colleagues, other professionals and clients on a daily basis. You will also be required to produce detailed reports and occasional presentations.

Excellent organisational skills and the ability to work under pressure are a must, as are good IT skills including knowledge of computer-aided design (CAD).

Working conditions

You will usually be required to work longer hours than those of the average working week, but evening or weekend work is rare.

You will be based mainly in an office although you will also spend a good amount of time on site, whether in a factory, workshop, hospital or other building. Despite this travel, overnight absence from home is uncommon.

You will need to wear a smart suit or similar whilst in the office, but appropriate safety equipment when on site.

Future prospects

Job opportunities for mechanical engineers are found throughout the UK, particularly in larger towns and cities. With experience, you could become self-employed and undertake freelance work which will give you greater flexibility over your work/life balance.

Alternatively, you could go on to increasingly senior engineering posts, or even set up your own consultancy.

Some engineers choose to move into a more business-orientated role within their company such as sales, marketing or HR.

There are also excellent opportunities for working abroad.

Qualifications and courses

Most employers require a good degree in a relevant subject such as mechanical, nuclear, aeronautical, civil or computer-aided engineering. You can enter the industry with an HND in a relevant subject such as general engineering, civil or environmental engineering, applied physics, or computing and IT but you may be employed at a lower, technician level.

To become a professional engineer, you will need to take a Master's degree to gain incorporated (IEng) or chartered (CEng) status. This can be taken straight after a degree or HND, or following a few years working as an electrical engineer.

Advantages/disadvantages

It is exciting to be at the forefront of creating new products and solving solutions to mechanical problems across numerous industries.

You will be working on a variety of projects and meeting a range of people, so the work is rarely boring.

There are excellent opportunities for career development, including the option of working overseas.

You may have to work long hours to meet project deadlines.

Money guide

Starting salaries for mechanical engineers can range from £19,000–£28,000, although the average is around £22,000.

With 10 years' experience, your salary could increase to £40,000–£55,000+.

Within engineering, salaries vary greatly according to location (London usually yields the highest wages) and the size of the company that you work for. Some companies also offer excellent benefit packages and bonus schemes in addition to a basic salary.

Related opportunities

- Clinical/Biomedical Engineer p300
- Electrical Engineer p226
- Environmental Engineer p228
- Marine Engineer p238

Further information

Engineering Council UK (ECUK)
246 High Holborn, London, WC1V 7EX
020 3206 0500; www.engc.org.uk

Institution of Mechanical Engineers (IMechE)
1 Birdcage Walk, London, SW1H 9JJ
020 7222 7899; www.imeche.org; enquiries@imeche.org

City&
Guilds

www.cityandguilds.com/myperfectjob

MOTOR VEHICLE TECHNICIAN

What the work involves

- Motor vehicle technicians are responsible for the maintenance and repair of all vehicles, including cars, motorbikes, lorries and coaches.

- You will need to carry out routine jobs such as servicing, as well as identifying technical problems, and advising customers as to which repairs are necessary and the costs involved.

- You will work on a variety of different mechanical and electrical systems and use a range of tools and equipment.

The type of person suited to this work

You will need an excellent technical and mechanical knowledge of most motor vehicles, on which you can build when in employment.

You will be working in a team and with the general public, so will need excellent communication skills in order to get along with colleagues and advise customers.

Full colour vision, a good level of fitness, and the ability to think quickly and work methodically are all essential.

You will also need good ICT skills in order to understand and fix the computerised equipment in vehicles.

Working conditions

You will usually work 40 hours per week, just above the national average. Regular working hours are usual, but shift work, weekend work and overtime are not uncommon.

If you specialise in repairing broken down vehicles, you may have to travel to their location at any time of day or night.

You will usually work in a garage, which can be noisy at times and very cold in winter.

You will need to wear overalls and other safety equipment to protect you and your clothes whilst you work.

Future prospects

Being a motor vehicle technician provides good career opportunities as demand is relatively high all over the UK. This means, you could work in a large city or a small village, for a large company or a tiny independent garage.

Within a larger organisation, you could progress to a senior or supervisory level as a technician, or alternatively move into a management or training role.

There is also the option of setting up your own repair business, although the initial costs of hiring and equipping premises can be expensive.

Advantages/disadvantages

There is demand for technicians throughout the UK, so you should be able to find a job in the location of your choice.

Qualifications and courses

ENTRY 2 LEVEL

Although you do not need any formal qualifications to begin training as a motor vehicle technician, most employers (especially the larger companies) prefer you to have at least 4 GCSEs/S grades (A-C/1–3) including English, maths and a science.

There are several ways to enter the industry at a trainee level. You could undertake an Apprenticeship and learn on-the-job whilst gaining qualifications at college. Alternatively, some larger employers have dedicated training facilities for their employees at which you can learn the skills you need.

You could also undertake a course at college, which will provide both theoretical and practical training towards a relevant qualification. Many colleges will also have links to local employers which could be a route into work experience or employment. Relevant courses include NVQ Levels 2 and 3 in vehicle maintenance and repair, motorcycle maintenance and repair, vehicle fitting and auto electrical. City & Guilds also offer useful courses in vehicle maintenance and automotive vehicle servicing and repair. BTEC National Certificates and Diplomas are also available in vehicle technology.

Hours are generally fairly regular, and you won't need to be away from home overnight.

You may have to work in cold, damp or cramped conditions which can be unpleasant.

Money guide

As a trainee motor vehicle technician, you could expect to start on around £11,000. As you gain experience and qualifications, this will rise to £16,000–£18,000. With 5–10 years' experience and even some specialised skills, you could earn £23,000+. Garage owners and self-employed technicians can earn considerably more.

Related opportunities

- Electrician p94
- Highways Maintenance/Road Worker p106
- Sheet Metal Worker p249
- Welder p255

Further information

GoSkills
Concorde House, Trinity Park, Solihull, B37 7UQ
0121 635 5520; www.goskills.org; info@goskills.org

The Institute of the Motor Industry (IMI)
Fanshaws, Brickendon, Hertford, SG13 8PQ
01992 511 521; www.motor.org.uk; imi@motor.org.uk

City & Guilds

www.cityandguilds.com/myperfectjob

Engineering, Manufacturing and Production

CRCI: GJ
CLCI: RAE

NUCLEAR ENGINEER

What the work involves

- Nuclear engineers work mainly in the large-scale production of nuclear energy, although they can be involved in smaller industrial or medicinal projects.

- You could alternatively work in developing effective nuclear waste management systems.

- You could also lecture and train other people on the subject of nuclear power.

The type of person suited to this work

You will need excellent communication skills, both verbal and written, in order to manage and lead your team as well as liaising with other professionals and clients. You should also enjoy working as part of a team.

You should possess an analytical mind and a logical approach to problem solving. Excellent maths and ICT skills are also essential.

Because you will be working with nuclear hazards, you must be able to take responsibility for your own safety and that of your colleagues.

Working conditions

You will usually work a normal 37 hour week, although you may be required to put in additional hours as project deadlines approach. If you work in a nuclear power station, your hours will usually adhere to a 7-day shift system.

The majority of the work will be indoors, either in a power plant, laboratory, office or factory.

You may have to work in hot, cramped conditions and will have to wear protective clothing in certain situations. As you will be working with radioactive substances, you will also need regular medical check-ups.

Future prospects

Prospects are good for nuclear engineers, especially given the government's new drive to increase nuclear power production in the forthcoming years.

The majority of nuclear engineers work in large power plants and companies, although you could work in medical research or in the field of nuclear waste disposal. With continued study and increasing experience, you can move into more senior positions within any company and discipline.

Once you have built a good reputation, you could work as a freelance consultant.

Advantages/disadvantages

Nuclear power is a growing industry, so employment opportunities will increase accordingly.

You have the opportunity to work freelance after building significant experience, so you can achieve a suitable work/life balance for yourself.

Qualifications and courses

ENTRY 5 LEVEL

The most common entry qualifications are BEng and MEng degrees in mechanical, electrical or control system engineering. You could also enter with a related degree such as maths, physics or science. Entry to a degree course usually requires at least 5 GCSEs/Highers (A-C/1–3) and 3 A-levels, including a maths and science subject.

You can also enter the industry with an HND in a relevant subject such as general engineering, civil engineering, maths or physics. Entry requirements for an HND course are usually 1 A-level or a BTEC National Certificate in a relevant subject.

Graduate apprenticeships may also be available, which bring together study at a degree or postgraduate level with work-based learning.

The Nuclear Institute (NI) and The Institution of Engineering and Technology (IET) have schemes for candidates aged over 35 who would like to become incorporated or chartered engineers, or engineering technicians, but who do not have the relevant qualifications.

You will be working in an environmentally controversial industry, which has the potential to upset friends and family.

Money guide

As a newly qualified graduate nuclear engineer, you could expect to earn around £24,000.

With 5–10 years' experience, coupled with professional association membership, you should earn between £35,000 and £45,000. As a senior chartered engineer, you could earn £55,000+.

Some companies also offer excellent benefit packages and bonus schemes.

Related opportunities

- Aerospace Engineer p220
- Chemical Engineer p224
- Electrical Engineer p226
- Mechanical Engineer p240

Further information

The Nuclear Industry Association (NIA)
Carlton House, 22a St James's Square, London, SW1Y 4JH
020 7766 6640; www.niauk.org; info@niauk.org

The Sector Skills Council for Science, Engineering and Manufacturing Technologies (SEMTA)
14 Upton Road, Watford, WD18 0JT
0845 643 9001; www.semta.org.uk

City& Guilds

www.cityandguilds.com/myperfectjob

OIL/GAS DRILLING ENGINEER

What the work involves

- Drilling engineers plan, schedule and supervise the drilling process behind creating oil and gas wells.

- You will be involved in the drilling project from the initial planning and design of the well, through to its completion and eventual closure.

- You could be working on land, or on sites out at sea, depending on where the oil or gas reserves are situated.

- You may also have to undertake certain administrative tasks, such as drawing up contracts and planning and managing the budget of each project.

The type of person suited to this work

You will need excellent communication and interpersonal skills, as you will be working in a team environment and will need to build strong relationships with other professionals and clients. Because you will be leading your team, you will also need to be driven and motivational.

You should have a high level of numeracy and comprehensive ICT skills, as well as good scientific understanding of related fields such as geology, chemistry, physics and maths.

Working conditions

The work is both mentally and physically demanding, especially in the early years when you could be working 12 hour shifts on off-shore oil rigs. Conditions are noisy, wet, cold and inhospitable at times.

Living standards on the rigs are good, with excellent sports and social facilities.

You could be working anywhere in the world for long periods of time, which brings exciting travel prospects but can be difficult for family life.

Opportunities for office-based work increase once you have gained a few years' experience in the field.

Future prospects

The career of a drilling engineer can move quickly over a short period of time, and within a few years you could find yourself in control of projects worth up to £10 million.

Typically you will need to spend 2–4 years working on projects all over the world, and then you can settle into a steadier, office-based design role.

You could progress to a management position within an oil company, or undertake independent consultancy work.

Advantages/disadvantages

Travelling around the world and working closely with colleagues on the rigs can prove to be exciting, rewarding and challenging.

The harder you work the faster your career will progress and the better your opportunities will become.

Qualifications and courses

ENTRY LEVEL 5

This career is open to all graduates with a degree in engineering. Specific subjects such as petroleum engineering, mineral engineering, mechanical engineering or structural engineering may improve your chances further. Employers may also consider candidates with a degree in geology or natural science.

Most entrants to graduate training programmes for the larger oil companies will have gained a high 2:1 classification in their subject, and MEng degrees are preferred. A postgraduate MSc qualification in offshore or petroleum engineering may also increase your chances of employment.

You will need a minimum of 5 GCSEs/Highers (A-C/1–3) including English, maths and science, and 3 A-levels/ Highers in order to gain a place on an engineering or related degree course. Entry with an HND alone is not possible.

Evidence of pre-entry work experience is not essential, but is viewed favourably by employers. As much of the work takes place overseas, a basic knowledge of another language is also desirable.

Oil drilling in particular operates in some of the most dangerous and hostile areas of the world, so your safety could be threatened on a daily basis.

Money guide

Salaries for graduates typically range from £26,000–£33,000, with the larger salaries coming from the big oil companies. After 15 years as a drilling engineer, you could be earning £50,000–£75,000+.

It is worth remembering that salaries are performance based, and the location of your projects will influence the amount you are paid. Most companies give additional benefits or allowances for overseas work.

Related opportunities

- Mechanical Engineer p240
- Engineering Technician p83
- Environmental Engineer p228

Further information

Oil Careers
Westhill Business Centre, Arnhall Business Park, Westhill, Aberdeenshire, AB32 6UF
0870 870 4564; www.oilcareers.com; uk@oilcareers.com

City& Guilds

www.cityandguilds.com/myperfectjob

Engineering, Manufacturing and Production

CRCI: GI
CLCI: ROB

PAPER MANUFACTURER/ TECHNOLOGIST

What the work involves

- Paper manufacturers work with the equipment and systems that turn wood pulp and other materials into many different kinds of paper.

- Your role can vary greatly depending on which sector you decide to work for within the paper mill.

- You might be operating the machine that breaks down the raw materials, managing what's going on inside, adding chemicals, checking consistency, or adjusting the controls.

- You could also be managing the steam system that dries the paper, controlling it in reels, or overseeing the packaging process.

The type of person suited to this work

If you'd like to be a paper manufacturer or technologist, you need to be good with your hands, and good at team working and communication with others.

Being able to act on your own initiative is important, and you should have an accurate and methodical mindset.

Following plans and diagrams is a big part of the job, so you should be confident in this, and the ability to work with chemicals is also important.

Working conditions

This kind of work usually takes place in shifts. You could be working daytimes, evenings, nights or weekends depending on your company, and it may well be a combination of them all.

It's normal for your working hours to add up to 38–40 per week, and overtime is usually available and often encouraged.

You'll be working on the factory floor most of the time, in the control room. This is so that you can monitor the processes being carried out by the machines you're looking after.

Future prospects

There are opportunities for progression within the industry. With experience you can apply for positions at technician and supervisor level, which can turn into engineering roles.

If you choose to you can also move around in the industry, changing to a career in management or sales, for example.

Roles and jobs such as these might require additional qualification which you may be able to pursue.

Qualifications and courses

ENTRY LEVEL 2

Most employers don't ask for any formal qualifications, but having GCSEs in English, Maths and Science will help. You can start straight from school, working your way up and training on the job as an apprentice. If you'd rather enter at a higher level, you might want to consider taking a HNC or HND in something like engineering.

Once you're in you'll probably train on the job. Practical training may well be combined with study towards gaining an NVQ in a subject like Engineering or Combined Working Practices. There are also courses in paper technology that many people choose to follow.

Advantages/disadvantages

Opportunities to progress are good in this job, and even if you come straight from school and work on the factory floor, you could move up to sales or management relatively quickly: keep this in mind.

The work may be a little mundane to start with.

Money guide

Trainees earn around £12,000 a year, but this can be boosted with overtime.

This can increase to £22,000.

Related opportunities

- Chemical Engineer p224
- Production Engineer p236
- Textile Operative p252

Further information

Confederation of Paper Industries,
1 Rivenhall Road, Swindon, SN5 7BD
01793 889600; www.paper.org.uk

The Paper Industry Technical Association (PITA),
5 Frecheville Court, Bury, Lancashire, BL9 0UF
0161 764 5858; www.pita.co.uk

Proskills UK,
Centurion Court, 85b Milton Park, Abingdon, OX14 4RY
01235 432032; www.proskills.co.uk

City&
Guilds

www.cityandguilds.com/myperfectjob

POLYMER TECHNOLOGIST

What the work involves

- Polymer technologists use polymer materials, such as plastics, rubber, adhesives, resins and fibres, to manufacture products.

- You will use these materials to make a wide range of products, including toys, casings for mobile phones, medical devices, tyres, wetsuits and hoses.

- You might also use composite polymer materials in place of traditional materials such as metal in e.g. the manufacture of car bodies or aircraft wings.

- You will be responsible for developing the moulds used to form materials during manufacture. This is job that requires specialist skills as a minor flaw could ruin an entire product.

The type of person suited to this work

You should have a strong interest in materials science, chemicals and engineering and a good understanding of manufacturing processes and construction methods.

You should also be interested in design and technology and be familiar with computer aided design.

You will need to be able to analyse projects or problems that arise and have strong numeracy skills.

As you will be part of a team, or leading a team you will need strong communication skills.

You should also be able to take initiative and find a solution when you are confronted with a problem.

Working conditions

You will work between 35 to 40 hours per week, Monday to Friday. It may be necessary for you to work overtime to meet deadlines. Overtime and weekends will increase your pay accordingly.

Your time may be divided between the office, the laboratory and the factory. This may involve travel.

You will wear protective clothing at times.

Future prospects

Polymer science is a growing industry; there are many opportunities for promotion.

You could work for a variety of companies, including manufacturers of medical equipment, toy companies, or aerospace engineering firms.

You could choose to specialise in a specific area such as vehicle manufacturing, aviation or medical equipment.

Advantages/disadvantages

You won't be stuck in an office all day, and may have the opportunity to travel locally and abroad as part of your work.

Hours can be long and unsociable at times.

Qualifications and courses

ENTRY LEVEL 5

Most entrants to this profession have a first degree in a related subject. This could be polymer science, materials engineering, or materials science. However the minimum entry is a BTEC Higher National Diploma/Certificate in polymer processing, manufacturing engineering and materials technology. For entry into a degree course in a related subject you will need at least five GSCE A*-C and two or three A-levels including chemistry, maths or physics.

Vocational qualifications may be helpful and there is a new Diploma in manufacturing and product design which may help you gain entry into this job.

Postgraduate courses in materials engineering or polymer technology may be available after you have taken a first degree in engineering or science. Graduates may also apply for programmes in companies where they will be trained as a full-time employee. Work placements may also be available for those on sandwich courses.

For those without the required scientific or engineering background some universities provide one year foundation courses in preparation for degree courses.

Those with relevant experience are welcomed into the industry and part time study towards a HND is possible.

Money guide

A starting salary for a polymer technologist is around £14,000.

The average salary is between £22,000 and £26,500 but this can rise to £39,000.

Related opportunities

- Aerospace Engineer p220
- Chemical Engineer p224
- Manufacturing Production Engineer p236
- Materials Scientist p526

Further information

British Plastics Federation
5–6 Bath Place, Rivington Street, London EC2A 3JE
020 7457 5000; www.bpf.co.uk ; reception@bpf.co.uk

The Institute of Materials, Minerals and Mining
1 Carlton House Terrace, London SW1 5DB
020 7451 7300; www.iom3.org

The Polymer Innovation Network
1 Carlton House Terrace, London SW1Y 5DB
020 7451 7404; www.polymerinnovate.com

Engineering, Manufacturing and Production

CRCI: NI
CLCI: SAN

QUALITY CONTROL INSPECTOR

What the work involves

- Quality control inspectors work in a variety of industries such as engineering, food, pharmaceuticals and clothing, where manufacturing procedures must be monitored to ensure that products meet specified standards.

- You will test products as they go through each stage of production by observing, measuring, and weighing samples, and comparing results against specified requirements.

- You will also work to ensure that quality and safety standards are maintained by checking and testing materials sourced from external suppliers.

- You will write reports on the testing that you carry out and help to come up with solutions to any problems or inconsistencies that arise.

The type of person suited to this work

As you will be regularly inspecting products and manufacturing processes you must be highly organised, methodical and have a keen eye for a detail.

You will be responsible, thorough and be able to solve problems efficiently.

You will have an aptitude for communicating with others and for advising and compelling people to improve standards. You will have good written skills for writing up reports on testing methods and results.

You should also have an interest in the science and technology of the industry that you are monitoring.

You should have a strong interest in health and safety issues and procedures.

Working conditions

You will work 35 to 40 hours per week, this will often include shift work, weekends and nights.

You could work in a laboratory or an office. You will also frequently visit factory floors or warehouses to monitor production processes or meet with staff.

These factories may be clean and bright or noisy and dirty.

Protective clothing is required in laboratories and may be required on factory or warehouse visits.

Future prospects

You can also gain NVQs/SVQs in Business Improvement Techniques at Levels 2, 3, and 4.

In Scotland you can work towards Professional Development Awards in Quality.

When you have some experience you may progress to roles as a team leader, supervisory roles, quality management roles or move across to technical sales or production management.

Qualifications and courses

Most entrants to this profession have prior experience in a relevant industry; you may have started your career in a production role, for example.

Employers usually seek applicants with four GSCEs/S grades (A-C/1–3) which should include maths, English and a science subject.

As a Quality Control Inspector you will specialise in a particular sector such as aerospace or pharmaceuticals. For this you may require A levels/H grades, a BTEC/SQA national qualification, an HNC/HND or a degree in science or technology.

Apprenticeships may be available in areas such as engineering, food and drink processing. You will be able to learn on the job and possibly take courses at a college or training centre to further your skills.

With experience as a Quality Control Inspector you can take courses to increase your skills, including the City & Guilds Certificate in Quality Assurance and the Chartered Quality Institute's (CQI) Certificate in Quality. The latter allows you to apply for associate membership of the CQI.

Advantages/disadvantages

There may be opportunities for travel and work abroad as a Quality Control Inspector.

You may become self-employed.

Due to developments in technology companies are increasingly using advanced equipment to monitor standards.

Money guide

Salaries for this job can start at £20,000 per year. When you have gained some experience this can rise to £24,000. As you gain responsibility you can earn from £30,000 to £35,000 depending on the industry in which you are working. If you work as a freelance high-technology quality control inspector specialist, you can earn between £40,000 and £60,000.

Related opportunities

- Laboratory Technician p524
- Quality Manager p53
- Trading Standards Officer p500

Further information

Chartered Quality Institute
12 Grosvenor Crescent, London SW1X 7EE
020 7245 6722; www.thecqi.org; info@thecqi.org

SEMTA
14 Upton Road, Watford WD18 0JT
0845 643 9001; www.semta.org.uk

QUARRY WORKER/ ENGINEER

What the work involves

- Quarrying involves opencast mining to extract various minerals from the ground.

- You could work in a variety of roles including: plant and process operators working on the crushers, grading and screening plant; plant maintenance workers; shotfirers, working mostly with the explosives; drilling holes for exploration or explosives.

- You may be a technician working in the laboratories undertaking quality control and sampling excavated minerals.

The type of person suited to this work

Quarry worker

Much of your work will involve being physically active, so you should be very fit and healthy. You will probably work in a team so getting along with others will be an important requirement.

Quarry engineer

You will also need to understand technical drawings and plans. You should be able to work in a team, with good communication skills.

Working conditions

The working conditions will be dusty, noisy and dangerous. The sites are often in the country so travelling could be involved. Your working hours may be worked in shifts and could include weekends and evenings.

Quarry worker

You will be working outside in all weathers. You will be expected to wear protective clothing such as hard hats, gloves and ear protection.

Quarry engineer

Work has moved from being mostly on-site to a more office-based function.

Future prospects

Quarry worker

If you are working as an operative, driver, mechanic or fitter it is possible to train to be a driller or shotfirer. With experience, you may be promoted to a supervisory post or you could work abroad. You could also take additional qualifications and apply for technician level work.

Quarry engineer

The industry has a strong professional development system in place which is supported by the Institute of Quarrying (IOQ). This ranges from student to fellowship levels. Ongoing study is recommended. There are good opportunites to work abroad

Qualifications and courses

ENTRY 1 LEVEL

There are no formal educational requirements for general quarry work, but the majority of employers seek 5 GCSEs/S grades (A–C/1–3). There are NVQ/SVQ Level 1–2 opportunities. Courses are also provided by EPIC (the training organisation and awarding body for the extractive and mineral processing industries). The ability to drive or willingness to attain LGV status would prove useful.

To become a quarry engineer a degree, Foundation degree or HND in a relevant subject is required. Degree courses are available. Entrants will normally gain professional accreditation with the Institute of Quarrying or the Institute of Materials, Minerals and Mining.

and many engineers have found undertaking a period abroad has added to their progression opportunities.

Advantages/disadvantages

The industry has an excellent training and development structure in place for staff of all levels. There are good employment opportunities at all levels. If you have a good aptitude and undertake training you will be able to advance to supervisory or management work.

Money guide

All earnings will be dependent upon additional payments such as overtime, bonuses and shift pay.

Quarry worker

Unskilled starting salaries are around £12,500 a year. At craft level and with experience this rises to £15,000–£20,000.

Quarry engineer

Upon graduation salaries are around £19,500–£24,000. With experience you can earn £25,000–£35,000. The most senior can earn £40,000+ a year.

Related opportunities

- Construction Operative p86
- Demolition Operative p92

Further information

Institute of Quarrying
7 Regent Street, Nottingham NG1 5BS; 0115 945 3880; www.quarrying.org

City& Guilds

www.cityandguilds.com/myperfectjob

Engineering, Manufacturing and Production

CRCI: G
CLCI: R

RAILWAY FITTER/ ELECTRICIAN

Engineering, Manufacturing and Production

CRCI GE
CLCI: RAB/RAK

What the work involves

- A mechanical fitter will maintain and service the traction and rolling stock, plant, machinery and passenger coaches. You could also repair station equipment such as customer lifts and hoisting equipment.

- If you are an electrical fitter, you will work alongside mechanical fitters and other engineers, specialising in the electrical side of the maintenance and servicing work. You will work on the traction and rolling stock, plant machinery and passenger coaches.

- You might be a multi-skilled fitter in which case you will have a combination of both of the sets of skills held by mechanical and electrical specialists – and you will be able to work in either aspect.

The type of person suited to this work

You should enjoy working with your hands, diagnosing faults and working out solutions. You will be comfortable using different hand tools and equipment and enjoy working in a team alongside other fitters.

Physically fitness is important as you will be on your feet, working at your bench or directly within the various railway stock.

You should be happy to follow verbal and written instructions, be able to read and understand technical drawings and diagrams and have a responsible attitude to health and safety.

Working conditions

Much of your work will take place within heated workshops or depots. Depending on your work you might have to visit jobs which are outdoors, for example near to railway sidings or within a station. On these occasions it might be cold and dark. As many of the work places are in remote or difficult areas to access, having your own transport is often essential.

You will have to wear protective clothing and be happy working in cramped places, using lots of bending and lifting.

Your normal working week will be 37 hours worked in shifts that cover early, late, evening and weekend working.

Future prospects

There are a number of specialist maintenance companies carrying out work for operating companies and engineering companies making new traction units and carriages.

There are well-developed promotional and in-service training programmes which help fitters to progress to supervisor, technician, team leader and, finally, management level.

Qualifications and courses

ENTRY LEVEL 2

It is sometimes possible to start as a trainee straight from school, but a better route of entry is through an Apprenticeship/Skillseekers scheme. Entry requirements are usually 3–5 GCSEs/S grades (A–C/1–3) including English, maths, science and technology. You will also need to pass a medical exam and an aptitude test may be set.

NVQs/SVQs in Rail Transport Engineering: Maintenance (Traction and Rolling Stock) or (Plant) at Levels 2 and 3 are available.

An ability to drive, with access to personal transport, is often required

Advantages/disadvantages

The rail industry is beginning to expand – so there will be an increasing need for new recruits.

The training and career routes are well developed.

Due to the range of jobs within the railway industry it is possible to move sideways into other related job areas.

Money guide

During an Apprenticeship you will receive around £9,500–£13,000 per year. With experience and qualifications you can get £14,000–£22,000. Very skilled and experienced railway fitters can earn £30,000+ per year.

Overtime and free or reduced rail travel are also common.

Related opportunities

- Mechanical Engineer p240
- Rail Track Maintenance Operative p619
- Rail Signalling Technician p618
- Train Driver p626

Further information

Network Rail
40 Melton Street, London, NW1 2EE
020 7557 8000; www.networkrail.co.uk

Careers in Rail
www.careersinrail.org

GoSkills (Sector Skills Council for passenger transport)
Concorde House, Trinity Park, Solihull, B37 7UQ
0121 635 5520; www.goskills.org

City&
Guilds

www.cityandguilds.com/myperfectjob

SHEET METAL WORKER

What the work involves

- Sheet metal workers produce parts for a number of important items ranging from vehicles and aeroplanes, through to electrical equipment and common domestic appliances.

- You will be using complex engineering drawings as a guide to marking out and cutting each piece.

- You will also be operating a variety of machines including hand-powered tools, cutting and pressing devices, and increasingly also computer numerically controlled (CNC) devices.

The type of person suited to this work

You should have good communication skills as you will be working as part of a team so building good relationships with colleagues is important.

Good numerical skills and the ability to interpret complicated technical drawings are essential for making accurate calculations and creating precise parts.

You should have a good level of fitness as you will be expected to lift large items and operate heavy machinery. Good eyesight and excellent practical skills are also required in order to use tools and equipment safely.

Finally, you should have good ICT skills as computer-operated machinery is increasingly used in this role.

Working conditions

You will usually work standard hours during the week, although shift work and overtime is also common. If you are producing bespoke items for a customer to a tight deadline, you may be required to work overnight on occasion.

Work is usually undertaken in a factory or workshop. You will spend the majority of your time at a bench so will be bending over for most of your day. The work also involves lifting, and spending hours on your feet. You will be required to wear appropriate safety equipment at all times.

Future prospects

Prospects are good for sheet metal workers. Once your initial training is completed, you could go on to work towards qualifying as an engineering technician. Alternatively, you could become supervisor/manager of an engineering workshop which provides increased responsibility and salary. Because of demand, opportunities are available on small and large projects both in the UK and overseas.

Advantages/disadvantages

You will be working with a variety of materials and tools, which will enable you to build specialist understanding and knowledge quickly.

Working hours usually fall within the week, so you will rarely be called in to work over weekends.

Qualifications and courses

You will need to have at least 5 GCSEs/S grades (A*-C/1–3), including maths, English and a science subject (or equivalent qualifications).

Apprenticeships opportunities may be available to those aged 16–24. If you are aged 14–16, you could begin your training through a Young Apprenticeship.

The Engineering Construction Industry Training Board (ECITB) offers a fast-track advanced Apprenticeship under the National Apprenticeship Scheme for Engineering Construction (NASEC).

You can study at college for qualifications such as City & Guilds awards or a BTEC in relevant subjects. You could also undertake a Diploma in engineering, construction, or manufacturing and product design.

If you are looking to enter this profession as an adult, then training is available through the National Skills Development Scheme (NSDS). No qualifications or previous experience is required for this programme, but you should already be working in a job that is related to that of a sheet metal worker.

Money guide

As a trainee sheet metal worker, you could earn between £8,000 and £11,000. Once fully qualified, this will rise to around £14,000. With between 3–5 years of experience, you could expect to earn between £20,000 and £23,000. Highly skilled sheet metal workers who are fully competent with using computer-controlled equipment can earn up to £27,000.

Related opportunities

- Assembler p221
- Blacksmith p222
- Welder p255

Further information

Engineering Construction Industry Training Board
Blue Court, Church Lane, Kings Langley, WD4 8JP
01923 260000; www.ecitb.org.uk; ECITB@ecitb.org.uk

SEMTA
14 Upton Road, Watford, WD18 0JT
01923 238441; www.semta.org.uk

City & Guilds

www.cityandguilds.com/myperfectjob

Engineering, Manufacturing and Production

CRCI: NE
CLCI: SAM

TAILOR/DRESSMAKER

Engineering, Manufacturing and Production

CRCI NB
CLCI: SAH

What the work involves

- Tailors and dressmakers can design and make made-to-measure, bespoke items of clothing.

- Tailors usually make structured items such as suits, jackets and coats. Dressmakers can make a range of clothing, from day dresses and casual trousers to ballgowns and wedding dresses.

- You will be working with numerous materials, including silk, linen, cotton and polyester, and will also use equipment such as sewing machines, scissors, tape-measures and pins.

The type of person suited to this work

Since you will be dealing with a range of people, including clients and suppliers, you will need to have excellent interpersonal and verbal communication skills.

You must be highly creative, with an excellent eye for colour and knowledge of the diverse properties of different kinds of fabric.

Understanding how different cuts, styles and colours flatter various shapes and figures is important for customer satisfaction, as is maintaining a smart/fashionable appearance.

Working conditions

You can expect to work 37–40 hours a week. Saturday and weekend work is common as that is when most of your clients will be available for meetings and fittings.

You could be situated in a workshop, small factory or work from home if you are self-employed.

A reasonable level of physical fitness and flexibility is required, as you will be bending and kneeling when measuring customers and fitting clothes. You may also need to lift and carry heavy rolls of fabric.

A lot of the work is very detailed, so you will need a high level of accuracy and good eyesight.

Future prospects

You could work for a small or large company, and create high fashion or more classic pieces. You can also opt to be self-employed.

In larger companies, you may be promoted to a supervisory position, and there may also be the opportunity to diversify into pattern cutting or design.

There are opportunities to travel and work overseas, especially if you are involved in fashion and haute couture tailoring or dressmaking.

Advantages/disadvantages

You will be undertaking very creative work with lots of scope to use both your talent and imagination on a daily basis.

Qualifications and courses

ENTRY LEVEL 2

The main route into tailoring or dressmaking is straight from school. No experience is necessary as all training is provided on the job by more experienced colleagues. A demonstrable aptitude for design, sewing and art is usually sought be employers, as are GCSEs/S grades in English and maths.

If you are specifically looking to train as a prestigious Savile Row tailor, you could join the Bespoke Tailoring Apprenticeship programme run by Newham College. It lasts four years and teaches you all you need to know to become a top tailor, including pattern cutting, garment construction and sewing by both machine and hand.

A number of courses are available on a full or part time basis, or via distance learning, including: BTEC awards, certificates and diplomas in textiles, fashion, art and design, and ABC Level 3 Diplomas in production or handcraft tailoring.

Fashion is a fast-paced, interesting and potentially lucrative industry to be working in.

Money guide

The average starting salary for both tailors and dressmakers ranges from £10,000 to £13,000. With 3–5 years' experience, your salary could rise to £14,000–£18,000. Senior tailors or dressmakers, especially those located on Savile Row or who work in high fashion, could earn £40,000+.

Related opportunities

- Fashion Designer p181
- Knitting/Sewing Machinist p232
- Textile Operative p252

Further information

Newham College of Further Education
East Ham Campus, High Street South, London, E6 6ER
020 8257 4000; www.newham.ac.uk;
ExternalEnquiries@newham.ac.uk

ABC Awards
Robins Wood House, 1 Robins Wood Road, Aspley, Nottingham, NG8 3NH
0115 854 1616; www.abcawards.co.uk;
enquiries@abcawards.co.uk

City& Guilds

www.cityandguilds.com/myperfectjob

TELECOMMUNICATIONS ENGINEER

What the work involves

- Telecommunications engineers are responsible for designing, testing and overseeing the installation of all telecommunications equipment and facilities.

- You could work across a variety of engineering fields, including electronics and construction, providing technical guidance and offering solutions to other professionals and clients.

- You will be responsible for the management of telecommunications projects, which includes planning budgets, recruiting a team and implementing onsite safety.

- You will also produce written reports and verbal presentations in order to keep both your team and your clients up-to-date on how each project is progressing.

The type of person suited to this work

Good communication skills are essential for managing and briefing your team, as well as negotiating with clients and explaining complex technical information to them in a clear and simple manner.

You should have an analytical mind and be excellent at problem-solving. The ability to work efficiently under pressure and organise your workload effectively is also essential.

Working conditions

You will usually work a normal week of about 37 hours from Monday to Friday. Occasionally additional hours may be required, particularly as you progress to more senior positions.

Your working hours may be fairly flexible and you will not always be office-based, as the industry is seeking to promote working from home and part-time opportunities.

You will need to spend time onsite, checking and overseeing the installation of telecommunications equipment. In these instances, you may find yourself working outdoors or in cramped conditions. You will usually be required to wear appropriate safety equipment as well.

Future prospects

As the telecommunications industry is continually expanding and improving, job prospects for engineers in this sector are good.

Working in this fast-paced industry will require you to undertake further training throughout the course of your career in order to stay up-to-date with new products, techniques and developments.

As you progress, you could study to achieve professional status as a chartered engineer (CEng) which will improve your earning potential. If you work within a company, you could move into increasingly senior positions as your experience grows.

Qualifications and courses

ENTRY LEVEL 5

Most employers require a relevant degree in a related subject such as telecommunications, electronic engineering, computer science, physics or maths.

It is possible to enter with an HND in a relevant engineering subject, but you will only be able to take a role at technician level. From there, you can supplement your on-the-job experience with further qualifications in order to achieve a relevant degree.

Many employers also look for candidates who have a postgraduate qualification such as a MEng or suitable MSc. A PhD could also help you enter the industry at a more senior level than that of a graduate trainee.

Once in employment, you may want to pursue further study to qualify as a Chartered (CEng) or Incorporated engineer (IEng). This will improve your long term career prospects.

Advantages/disadvantages

Hours are generally regular, and there are increasing opportunities to work from home or undertake part-time hours.

In such a rapidly changing industry, you will be learning continually as you progress so the job will not become monotonous.

You will have to spend time on site which may involve working in cold, muddy conditions, at heights, or in cramped and uncomfortable surroundings.

Money guide

Starting salaries for graduate trainee telecommunications engineers range from £18,000 to £22,000. After 5–7 years, this can rise to £30,000–£40,000. If you reach a senior level and gained chartered status, you can expect to earn £50,000+.

Some companies also offer excellent benefit packages and bonus schemes in addition to a basic salary.

Related opportunities

- Electrical Engineer p226
- Engineering Technician p83
- Electrician p94

Further information

The Institution of Engineering and Technology
Michael Faraday House, Stevenage, SG1 2AY
01438 313 311; www.theiet.org; postmaster@theiet.org

City & Guilds

Engineering, Manufacturing and Production

CRCI: GI   CLCI: R

TEXTILE OPERATIVE

What the work involves

- Textile operatives manufacture carpets, prepare the yarns of fibres to be woven or knitted (which may involve carding and combing or chemical processing), spin yarn on a machine, or even make fabric on a loom.

- You will carry out basic maintenance on your machinery, make sure you have a supply of raw materials and keep your work area clean and tidy in accordance with health and safety regulations.

- You may also work on finishing processes such as dying or waterproofing fabrics.

The type of person suited to this work

You will need to be practical in order to operate the machinery skilfully and responsibly. In keeping with this, you should have good concentration as you will be doing repetitive tasks for long periods of time.

Manual dexterity and good spatial awareness, coupled with excellent eyesight and in the majority of cases full colour vision, are also requirements for carrying out tasks such as spinning or weaving textiles.

A reasonable level of personal fitness, an understanding of and adherence to work place health and safety rules, and enjoyment of working in a team are also attributes.

Working conditions

Although you will work an average 37–40 hours per week, you will usually be doing shift work which is likely to involve early mornings or later evenings. Overtime and part-time work is also available.

You will usually work in a textile factory, which should be light and well-ventilated, although the machines can be noisy and you will have to wear relevant safety equipment at all times.

It can be physically tiring, as you will spend the majority of your time standing over your machine or walking between the various pieces of equipment you are using.

Future prospects

The opportunities for textile operatives are good, as there has been increasing demand for textile production in recent years so a larger number of people are gaining employment at entry level and progressing more quickly to supervisory or managerial positions.

If you gain experience in using a variety of machines and performing a range of tasks, you will find your prospects improve accordingly.

You could also choose to move into quality control or sales once you have gained a full knowledge of the textile industry.

Advantages/disadvantages

You will be putting your practical skills to good use creating a range of textiles for various purposes.

Qualifications and courses

ENTRY LEVEL 1

Although there are no specific entry requirements for this position, there are several courses available that would build valuable understanding of the industry and what the role would involve. Courses include GCSE art and design (including a textiles module), Edexcel BTEC introductory certificate/diploma in art, design and media, Edexcel Level 1 BTEC first certificate in art and design. The Textile Centre of Excellence also offer a Technical Certificate in textiles that provides a flexible, distance learning programme.

Once qualified, the Textile Institute (TI) offers a range of qualifications for professional development from Licentiate to Fellow level. Alternatively, ABC offers a variety of courses in sewing, manufacturing and textiles, as do City & Guilds at Levels 1–3.

The work can become monotonous.

Hours can involve unsociable shift work in the early morning or evening.

Money guide

Starting salaries for new entrants range from £10,000 to £12,500. With a couple of years experience and increasingly diverse skills, you could earn between £13,000 and £17,000.

Once you have become a multi-skilled senior operative you could earn up to £20,000.

If you work shifts, or undertake overtime, earnings could be higher. Piecework payments (rewarded for high production volume) can also boost earnings.

Related opportunities

- Knitting/Sewing Machinist p232
- Tailor/Dressmaker p250

Further information

The Textile Institute (TI)
1st Floor, St James's Buildings, Oxford Street, Manchester, M1 6FQ
0161 237 1188; www.textileinstitute.org; tiihq@textileinst.org.uk

Society of Dyers and Colourists
PO Box 244, Perkin House, 82 Grattan Road, Bradford, BD1 2JB
01274 725138; www.sdc.org.uk

City & Guilds

www.cityandguilds.com/myperfectjob

TOOLMAKER

What the work involves

- Toolmakers make specialist tools and devices that are used to cut, shape, mould and form various materials for use in the production of all items from domestic appliances to aeroplanes.

- You will work with a range of materials, including metals and plastics.

- You will also be using complex engineering drawings as a guide to marking out and cutting each piece.

- You will be operating a variety of machinery including drills, grinding and miling machines, cutting and pressing devices, and increasingly also computer numerically controlled (CNC) equipment.

The type of person suited to this work

Good hand-to-eye co-ordination and a keen eye for detail will be beneficial when operating machinery, and to check the quality of the tools produced. Because you will be making extremely precise devices, it is essential to be able to spot any faults or errors before the tools are despatched to customers.

Good numerical skills and the ability to interpret complicated technical drawings are essential for making accurate calculations and creating precise parts.

Finally, you should have good ICT skills as computer-operated machinery is increasingly used in this role.

Working conditions

You will usually work 39 hours per week from Monday to Friday, although some larger companies operate shift patterns so evening and weekend work may be necessary.

Work is usually undertaken in a toolroom within a factory or workshop. This means that you will be working in a fairly quiet environment, away from the main factory machinery. You will normally stand for the duration of your working day, which can be tiring.

You will be required to wear appropriate safety equipment at all times.

Future prospects

Prospects for toolmakers are good, and there are employment opportunities in most parts of the UK.

After gaining 5–10 years' experience as a toolmaker, you could move into a supervisory role within a company, overseeing production within a toolroom or workshop. This could then lead into a management position.

You could also undertake further qualifications in order to work towards employment as an engineering technician, which could in turn lead to undertaking a degree course in order to become an engineer of some kind.

Advantages/disadvantages

You will be making tools which are vital for the construction of

Qualifications and courses

You will need to have at least 5 GCSEs/S grades (A*-C/1–3) or equivalent, including maths, English and a science subject.

Most people start on the Advanced Apprenticeship in engineering scheme on completion of school or college. Most apprentices spend several months learning their initial skills off site at a training centre. They will then spend two or three years working within their company whilst also attending college.

If you have difficulty finding an apprenticeship, there is also the option of taking an NVQ that is related to engineering. Once you have this qualification, it may be easier to find a company willing to take you on.

There are opportunities to study through Young Apprenticeship schemes whilst still at school.

Entry opportunities for adults are limited unless you have significant previous experience, as companies generally just train up existing employees when necessary.

important equipment ranging from aeroplanes to washing machines.

You will be using both your practical skills and your mental abilities daily.

The work can be physically exhausting, as you will spend the majority of your day on your feet.

Money guide

Starting salaries for toolmakers range from £15,500 to £17,000. With a few years' experience, you could expect to earn around £25,000. Highly skilled toolmakers, who are fully competent with using computer-controlled equipment, can earn up to £35,000.

Related opportunities

- Motor Vehicle Technician p241
- Sheet Metal Worker p249
- Welder p255

Further information

Science, Engineering and Manufacturing Technologies Alliance (SEMTA)
14 Upton Road, Watford, WD18 0JT
01923 238441; www.semta.org.uk

Engineering Council UK (ECUK)
246 High Holborn, London, WC1V 7EX
020 3206 0500; www.engc.org.uk

www.cityandguilds.com/myperfectjob

Engineering, Manufacturing and Production

CRCI: GF
CLCI: R

VEHICLE MAINTENANCE PATROLLER

What the work involves

- Vehicle maintenance patrollers travel to motorists who have broken down in order to diagnose the problem with the vehicle and fix it if possible. If repair isn't possible, you will need to tow the vehicle to the nearest garage.

- You will be responding to urgent calls from a central control centre, and may need to reassure worried or shaken motorists.

- You will be driving a van or truck, and operating a range of electronic equipment alongside general tools and car parts.

The type of person suited to this work

You will need excellent communication skills in order to explain to motorists what is wrong with their vehicle and what can be done to fix it. You may be required to reassure people who are distressed or upset following an accident.

The ability to think quickly when assessing vehicles at the roadside is necessary.

You should be good with your hands as you will be operating various tools and machines and undertaking fiddly jobs from time to time.

Working conditions

An average working week comprises 39 hours, usually worked on a shift system including evening and weekend work. You may also be required to remain on standby on occasion.

Since the majority of work is undertaken on the road, a driving licence is essential. Depending on the vehicle you drive, you may also need an additional HGV or LGV licence. You will be working on the roadside in all conditions, including hazardous weather such as snow and fog, so must wear relevant safety equipment at all times.

Future prospects

Vehicle maintenance patrollers enjoy a variety of employment options. You could work for a large, well known national organisation such as the Royal Automobile Club (RAC) or the Automobile Association (AA), or for a smaller garage providing a localised breakdown service.

With experience you may progress to a supervisory role in a larger organisation, in which you will oversee and develop the performance of a number of breakdown engineers across a region.

In larger organisations, you could also move into a managerial or senior administrative position.

Advantages/disadvantages

You will be providing a valuable and well appreciated service to people every day.

Qualifications and courses

Vehicle maintenance patrollers are qualified vehicle technicians, and as such must hold NVQ Levels 1 and 2 in motor vehicle maintenance and repair along with having a minimum of 3 years' relevant experience in motor vehicle repair.

Employers require you to have a clean driving licence, and may also ask you to undertake a driving assessment and aptitude test. A full medical assessment will be carried out

NVQs are available in roadside assistance and recovery, which encompass all aspects of the job including assessing the vehicle and carrying out minor repairs at the roadside.

Some of the larger organisations offer induction programmes that allow new entrants to train on the job and learn skills such as customer service techniques, alongside building their technical knowledge. They may also support study for relevant NVQs.

There is great job satisfaction in being able to repair a vehicle at the roadside and send a happy customer on their way.

You will spend long periods of time on your own, which can get boring and lonely.

Money guide

The starting salary for a qualified vehicle breakdown engineer is around £25,000. With 3–5 years' experience, you could expect this to rise to £30,000–£33,000. Senior engineers, including those working in supervisory positions within larger companies, can earn up to £40,000.

Related opportunities

- Assembler p221
- Engineering Construction Technician p83
- Motor Vehicle Technician p241

Further information

The Automobile Association (AA)
Member Administration, Contact Centre, Lambert House, Stockport Road, Cheadle, SK8 2DY
0870 600 0371; www.theaa.com

Royal Automobile Club (RAC)
8 Surrey Street, Norwich, NR1 3NG
01922 727 313; www.rac.co.uk/careers/

Institute of Vehicle Recovery (IVR)
Top Floor, Bignell House, Horton Road, West Drayton, UB7 8EJ
01895 436 426; www.theivr.com; mail@theIVR.com

City&
Guilds

www.cityandguilds.com/myperfectjob

WELDER

What the work involves

- Welders work with metals and heavy duty plastics, which they join together using heat to form plates, pipes and other items.

- You could use a number of welding techniques that are either classed as manual, semi-automatic or fully mechanised. You will most likely specialise in one of these areas as opposed to working across all three.

- You may have to work from technical drawings, using them as a guide by which to weld components together.

The type of person suited to this work

You will need good hand-to-eye co-ordination, coupled with manual dexterity, to successfully operate your tools and machinery.

You should be willing to work responsibly within strict health and safety guidelines, and to look out for the safety of others in your team. This will prove especially important when you are called upon to work unsupervised.

An interest in craft, design or technology is also helpful.

Working conditions

Hours are usually 37 per week, and often operate on a shift pattern. Opportunities for overtime work are common.

You could find yourself working in almost any location, from standard factory or workshop roles to onsite jobs which could be outdoors or even under the sea. This means you may have to work in confined spaces which can be uncomfortable.

You will also need to wear safety equipment, including protective goggles to shield your eyes from UV light and sparks, and also fire retardant aprons and gloves.

Future prospects

There are excellent employment opportunities for welders throughout the UK, although the majority are found in fairly industrial areas.

Employers are mostly small and medium-sized firms, although some larger companies do also employ welders. There is also the option to be self-employed.

As you gain experience within a company, you could move into a supervisory role. Alternatively, you could undertake further qualifications in order to specialise in a particular area of welding, or work towards a career as an engineer.

Advantages/disadvantages

Practical work, where you can see the result of your efforts, is extremely rewarding.

Career prospects are good, with opportunities throughout the UK.

Qualifications and courses

There are three paths into a career as a welder. Most common is undertaking an Apprenticeship or Advanced Apprenticeship after school. Most apprentices spend several months learning their initial skills off site at a training centre. For a further 2 or 3 years, they will work within their company whilst also attending college, prior to qualifying as a welder.

Alternatively, you can take related NVQs or BTEC Certificates and Diplomas at college in order to gain knowledge prior to entering the industry. Relevant qualifications include NVQ Level 2 in fabrication and welding engineering, NVQ Level 3 in welding (pipework) and welding (plate), the Welder Approval Certificate which is the industry-recognised qualification, a BTEC in manufacturing engineering, or completing Vocationally Related Qualifications (VRQs) in welding at Levels 1, 2 and 3.

Finally, you could start in a more general role within a company and work towards becoming a welder over time.

Most employers expect you to have least 5 GCSEs/S grades (A*-C/1–3) or equivalent, including maths, English and a science subject.

You will be operating machinery that is potentially dangerous.

Money guide

Trainee or apprentice welders can start at about £8,000, rising to £13,000 as they gain qualifications. Once qualified, you could earn around £22,000.

With experience and increased levels of skill you could earn £40,000 and above, especially if you work on specialised projects or overseas.

Salaries and additional benefits vary according both to the region you are working in, and the company you are employed by.

Related opportunities

- Blacksmith p222
- Engineering Construction Technician p83
- Sheet Metal Worker p249
- Toolmaker p253

Further information

Engineering Construction Industry Training Board (ECITB)
Blue Court, Church Lane, Kings Langley, WD4 8JP
01923 260 000; www.ecitb.org.uk; ecitb@ecitb.org.uk

The Welding Institute (TWI)
Granta Park, Great Abington, Cambridge, CB21 6AL
01223 899 000; www.twi.co.uk; twi@twi.co.uk

Engineering, Manufacturing and Production

CRCI: GF
CLCI: RON

Environment, Animals and Plants

Jobs in this sector are perfect for those of you who don't want to spend every day behind a desk in an office, although this is not to say that you will not need to spend time writing reports and keeping a log of research findings or clients' information. Workers in this sector are passionate about animals or about caring for and maintaining the environment. You should also have brilliant people skills especially if you find yourself responsible for the welfare of someone else's animal. You should be someone who is very observant and interested in the natural world, not just from a welfare point of view but also from an economic one; many jobs in this sector involve using the environment for financial gain but increasingly industry is interested in doing so responsibly.

We look at the following jobs in this section:

For similar jobs to the ones in this section turn to *Leisure, Sport and Tourism* starting on page 385.

AGRICULTURAL SCIENTIST

What the work involves

- Agricultural scientists use biology, biochemistry and chemistry to research and develop more efficient ways to breed and manage livestock and/or increase plant or crop production. Employers include private chemical or agricultural companies and national or local government.

- Your work might include teaching and informing farmers or other growers about the results of your research on aspects like fertilisers, using chemicals, animal genetics or fungicides.

Agronomist

- Agronomists specialise in improving the quality of soil to raise the quality and productivity of crops.

- Your areas of expertise would include irrigation, drainage, plant breeding, soil classification, soil fertility and weed control.

The type of person suited to this work

You will need an interest in and in-depth knowledge of the environment and science, particularly biology and chemistry. More importantly however, will be how you use your science background in your work. You will spend a lot of time communicating and listening to growers' problems before researching solutions within the laboratory or in the field to meet their needs.

You should be able to handle lots of complex problems and be patient and organised in the way you approach them, as some of your work will take a long time to develop.

This job requires you to work both alone and as part of a team, so you should be happy to work with people from different backgrounds and have excellent communication skills.

Working conditions

Depending on the area of your research or work you could be indoors within a laboratory, outdoors on farms and nurseries or a combination of both. You are likely to work with hazardous equipment, so protective clothing will be provided.

If you suffer from allergies related to animals, pollen or dust this work could be difficult for you. Some jobs will also require good colour vision.

You might have to travel, so a driving licence could be useful.

Future prospects

General research opportunities are reducing but some areas like genetic engineering are increasing. Although small, the main openings for applicants continue to be as consultants within manufacturing companies which produce animal feed, chemicals, fertilisers and seeds, research organisations and national or local government offices. Recently there have been openings within international organisations such as the United

Qualifications and courses

The normal entry is by a Foundation degree, HND or degree in a relevant discipline such as agriculture/agricultural science, biochemistry or a horticultural, biological or related subject. Some jobs will also require a higher degree or postgraduate qualification in a specialist area like seed production or agricultural development.

To enter a degree you will need A levels/H grades including science subjects and GCSEs/S grades including English, maths and science subjects.

Nations to help to develop Third World economies by improving their food production and farming ability.

With experience you could lecture or teach within universities, colleges or schools and there are opportunities to work abroad.

As a lot of this work involves selling and communicating to different people, sales-related work for the production companies is also possible.

Advantages/disadvantages

This job offers the opportunity to combine scientific research with practical work.

Some jobs are in decline.

It is a great career if you love plants, animals or the land.

Money guide

Pay will depend on the location and type of employer. Some private companies and most public organisations have structured pay scales in place.

Generally new graduates can expect between £18,000 and £25,000 per year.

This can rise to around £30,000–£40,000 with experience.

People in senior positions such as department heads, can earn £60,000+.

Related opportunities

- Botanist p509
- Chemist p510
- Ecologist p515
- Laboratory Technician p524

Further information

Lantra
Lantra House, Stoneleigh Park, Coventry, CV8 2LG
024 7669 6996; www.lantra.co.uk

Institute of Biology
9 Red Lion Court, London, EC4A 3EF
020 7936 5900; www.iob.org

ANIMAL BEHAVIOURIST

What the work involves

- Animal behaviourists advise owners whose pets have developed inappropriate and dangerous behaviour.

- Although working with all domestic animals, you would probably focus on dogs, cats and horses. Typical problems include aggressive behaviour, soiling or destructiveness. You will also aid owners in achieving general control over their pets.

- You could be connected to a veterinary practice, work in kennels, catteries and welfare societies or be freelance.

The type of person suited to this work

You will need a strong interest in animals, their care and welfare. As this job also involves working with the owner, you will have to be able to communicate with people too! Whilst dealing with the owner you should be able to maintain a certain level of tact. Working with animals can be messy and smelly work, so you must be prepared to get dirty.

You will also need to have lots of patience and the ability to remain calm. You should be good at science, especially biology and have a certain degree of business acumen along with the ability to keep records and accounts.

Working conditions

This work takes place in clinics and clients' homes and so a driving licence would be extremely helpful. You could be indoors or outside in all weathers.

Some jobs will involve evening and weekend work, especially if you visit your clients and animals in their own homes. Most Animal Behaviourists are self-employed and therefore set their own hours.

The work can be dusty, dirty and physically demanding, so you will need to be fit and active. This profession can be difficult for those who suffer from allergies.

Future prospects

Although demand across the canine and equine areas has increased due to television programmes and press coverage there are still very limited career opportunities for this job. Some of the larger animal welfare charities are starting to employ staff with these skills, however most are self-employed and running their own practices. To be successful you will need to build up a client list and have good business skills. Other options include lecturing and writing papers on animal behaviour.

Advantages/disadvantages

You will be working with animals, perhaps helping them to have a better quality of life.

Pet owners can be more difficult than their pets!

This job offers the opportunity for self-employment.

Qualifications and courses

ENTRY 6 LEVEL

Membership of the Certificated Clinical Animal Behaviourists (CCAB) which is administered by the Association for the Study of Animal Behaviour (ASAB) requires a degree or postgraduate qualification in a biological or behavioural science.

The Association of Pet Behaviour Counsellors (APBC) also requires the acquisition of a degree for membership.

Typical entry requirements consist of 2 A levels (which should include biology and/or another science subject) and 5 GCSEs grade A*-C. These GCSEs should include English and maths.

In order to gain entry to a Postgraduate course, applicants will normally require a first degree in a relevant subject, such as animal science, biology, psychology veterinary science or zoology.

It can be difficult to build up a client list, which will affect your income.

Money guide

Many working in this area are self-employed, average fees are around £20–£50 for each consultation.

Once qualified, you can expect a salary of around £15,000 per year. Depending on experience you could expect to earn between £25,000–£35,000 a year. The highest paid animal behaviourists may exceed this amount.

It is unusual for an animal behaviourist to make a full time living from this industry. Many supplement their income by lecturing or writing articles.

Related opportunities

- Animal Physiotherapist p260
- Dog Trainer/Handler p264
- Kennel Worker p276
- Veterinary Surgeon p288
- Zookeeper p290

Further information

Association of Pet Behaviour Counsellors
PO Box 46, Worcester WR8 9YS; 01386 751151;
www.apbc.org.uk; info@apbc.org.uk

ASAB Membership Secretary
School of Psychology, University of St Andrews, St Mary's College, South Street, St Andrews, KY16 9JP
www.asab.nottingham.ac.uk ; susan.healy@st-andrews.ac.uk

City& Guilds

www.cityandguilds.com/myperfectjob

Environment, Animals and Plants

CRCI: HC
CLCI: WAL

ANIMAL PHYSIOTHERAPIST

What the work involves

- Animals suffer from joint and muscular pain in the same way that humans do. As a result animal physiotherapy has become a regular part of animal care.

- You would be used by many domestic pet owners and even more so by horse owners.

- Techniques you will use may include soft tissue mobilisation, ultrasound (including long-wave), neuromuscular stimulation, joint mobilisation, magnetic field therapy, hydrotherapy and massage.

The type of person suited to this work

This job involves working with the owner so you will have to be able to communicate with people too!

Working with animals can be messy and smelly, so you must be prepared to get dirty. You should expect the work to be occasionally distressing, especially if the animal is injured or has died.

You will need to have good dexterity and be physically fit. You should have experience of working with animals and the ability to match treatments with problems.

Working conditions

You will be working in clinics, clients' homes, farmyards and/or stables. You could be indoors or outside in all weathers.

A driving licence is essential for some posts and you will normally wear protective clothing. This job will probably involve some heavy lifting and you will need to be physically fit.

Some assignments will involve evening and weekend work, especially if you visit your clients and animals in their own homes. As most animal physiotherapists are self-employed, working hours must be flexible to suit the client.

Future prospects

This profession is extremely competitive and employs very small numbers. Work experience will improve your chances of employment.

Some of the larger animal welfare charities and veterinary surgeries employ animal physiotherapists; however most are self-employed running their own practices. To be successful you will need to build up a client list and have good business skills. There is not a structured career path in place.

With experience you could work as a lecturer or consultant.

Advantages/disadvantages

You will be working with animals, perhaps helping them to have a better quality of life.

Pet owners can be more difficult than their pets!

There is the opportunity for self-employment.

Some heavy lifting will be required.

Some aspects of the job may be messy and smelly.

Qualifications and courses

ENTRY LEVEL 5

To qualify as a chartered animal physiotherapist, you can complete a degree in human physiotherapy. You will need the highest level A levels/H grades in maths and science for entry. Upon completion of the degree you then can choose to either spend a further two years (at least) gaining work experience with a practising chartered animal physiotherapist, or study part time for the PG Dip or MSc in veterinary physiotherapy with the Royal Veterinary College.

Alternatively, you can choose to complete an animal physiotherapy course, such as a certificate in animal physiotherapy offered by the National Association of Veterinary Physiotherapists (NAVP). Entry requires a suitable first degree such as equine sciences; veterinary nurses with four years experience are also considered. This programme lasts two years.

The College of Animal Physiotherapy also offers a diploma in animal physiotherapy. This course lasts one to two years part time. If you successfully complete this course you will be accepted to the International Association of Animal Therapists.

Money guide

Many working in this area are self-employed, average fees are around £35 to £70 for each consultation of one hour.

The average starting salary is about £18,500 per year, this can increase to around £20,000 to £25,000 with experience. As a senior animal physiotherapist or consultant you could earn up to £65,000 a year.

Related opportunities

- Animal Behaviourist p259
- Masseur p319
- Physiotherapist p334
- Veterinary Surgeon p288

Further information

Association of Chartered Physiotherapists in Animal Therapy
Morland House, Salters Lane, Winchester, SO22 5LP
01962 844390; www.acpat.org

National Association of Veterinary Physiotherapists
43 Heath Avenue, Rode Heath, Stoke-on-Trent, ST7 3RY
01270 876115; www.navp.org.uk

The College of Animal Physiotherapy
Tyringham Hall, Cuddington, Aylesbury, HP18 0AP
01844 290512; www.tcap.co.uk

City&
Guilds

www.cityandguilds.com/myperfectjob

ARBORICULTURAL WORKER/ TREE SURGEON

What the work involves

- You will carry out all kinds of work on the trees in private and public gardens, parks, roadsides and on paths.

- You will also be responsible for planting new trees and shrubs, taking direction from a landscaper or garden designer.

- Using chainsaws, hand tools, ropes, ladders and other specialised climbing equipment, you will use your practical skills and knowledge of trees to make them safe, help them grow or increase the light available for other species.

The type of person suited to this work

You will need to have practical skills and be happy using potentially dangerous machinery and tools. You will also have to be interested in trees and want to learn about them and the problems that can occur with them.

This job involves lots of physically demanding work, including lifting, bending, cutting and climbing so you will need to be strong and agile. You would need to understand and observe health and safety rules and be happy working in a team or on your own. As you will be dealing with customers and explaining what work needs to be done, you will need excellent communication skills.

Working conditions

This is a real outdoor job, summer and winter. You will be out in all weathers, hanging from ropes and using dangerous tools like a chainsaw.

If you suffer from an allergy to pollen and dust, or vertigo, this work would be difficult for you. You will have to wear protective clothing and be very safety conscious.

In the summer your working hours might be long, and they would be shorter in the winter

Future prospects

As with other areas of garden design and improvement, there are reasonable opportunities in town and country. Around 2000 people are employed within local authorities and 10,000 work for the private employers whose focus is on tree care.

If you choose to take further qualifications you could enter senior or managerial positions, but this might involve moving to larger organisations.

Advantages/disadvantages

The work can be hazardous so you have to obey safety regulations.

You will be outside working in all weathers.

Qualifications and courses

Entry into this profession is through a combination of on-the-job work experience and qualifications. Some employers require a degree. There are NVQs/SVQs available in Forestry and Arboriculture at Levels 1 and 2, which include workplace assessment.

The National Trust can help in organising work experience placements. The Woodland Trust and the British Trust for Conservation Volunteers (BTCV) provide opportunities for volunteer experience.

Degrees are available in arboriculture but a degree in a related horticultural subject may be accepted.

There are short part-time and full-time courses available at land-based colleges of further education in chainsaw use, maintenance of equipment, health and safety and climbing techniques. Tree surgeons must obtain a Competency Certificate from the National Proficiency Training Council or Scottish Skills Testing Service before working on their own or with machinery.

The Royal Horticultural Society (RHS) also offers short courses leading to Arboricultural Association certificates. Lantra-accredited apprenticeships are also available.

You could do very long hours in the summer and shorter hours in the winter, which may affect your earnings.

Money guide

Salaries will depend on whether you are working for a contractor or are self-employed. You will probably earn more in the south-east of England. Starting salaries are around £12,000–£16,000 per year. This rises to around £18,000 with experience. The most experienced can earn between £20,000 and £30,000.

Related opportunities

- Countryside Ranger p262
- Forestry Worker/Officer p270
- Gardener/Garden Designer p272
- Horticultural/Garden Centre Worker/Manager p275

Further information

Lantra
Lantra House, Stoneleigh Park, Kenilworth, CV8 2LG
024 7669 6996; www.lantra.co.uk

City& Guilds

www.cityandguilds.com/myperfectjob

Environment, Animals and Plants

CRCI: HB
CLCI: WAF

COUNTRYSIDE RANGER

What the work involves

- By patrolling the countryside throughout the year you will monitor the success and progress of the plants, animals, fencing and buildings in your care.

- You will be responsible for the safety and enjoyment of any visitors, answer their queries and help them get the most from their visit.

- You will keep a record of any work that is carried out, along with inspections, accidents and incidents.

The type of person suited to this work

You will need to enjoy being outdoors and have a strong interest in wildlife and the countryside.

To ensure the future of your area you will need to provide information to the public which could include talking to potential funding organisations or local politicians. You will therefore have to be confident speaking in public and have excellent written and spoken communication skills. You might have to write reports and sometimes undertake research.

To find work you may have to start with some voluntary or community-based work, so it's important that you are keen and willing.

Working conditions

Most of your work will be outdoors, driving or walking around your area. You will be working in all weathers and despite protective clothing you will be, at times, cold and wet or hot and dusty. This is physically demanding work and is likely to involve walking over difficult terrain.

You are likely to work longer hours during the spring and summer, especially if there are animals or plants that require protection.

This work can be difficult if you suffer from pollen or dust allergies.

Future prospects

Once employed within the industry it is likely that you will need to move from employer to employer in order to progress.

Many jobs are offered on temporary contracts or on a seasonal basis.

After gaining experience, it is possible to enter lecturing, consultancy or research work. You could also progress to the role of officer or a more managerial position, which would be more office based. You might choose to move to leisure management, agriculture or horticulture work.

Advantages/disadvantages

You will spend a lot of time in the open air combining your interest in the countryside with work!

You could be working in remote areas.

It is a very competitive area to enter so unpaid experience can be vital.

Qualifications and courses

There are no set entry qualifications, but GCSEs/S grades or higher-level qualifications in science and geography may be required.

Relevant courses include NVQs/SVQs at Levels 2 and 3 in Environmental Conservation and BTEC/SQA National Certificates and Diplomas in Countryside and Forestry, Conservation, Countryside Skills or Countryside Management. You will require 1 A level and relevant work experience to gain entry to these.

Some people become countryside rangers after doing a relevant degree or HND, although most training for rangers is done on the job.

Courses for professional development are provided by Lantra National Training Organisation. NVQs/SVQs may be available for people working in the industry.

A driving licence is essential. These jobs are not normally suitable for school leavers as employers prefer applicants aged 21 or over.

Money guide

These figures are only approximate and may vary depending on location and employer.

Initial salaries are between £9,000 and £13,000 per year. With experience this can rise to around £20,000 a year. The most senior Countryside Rangers can earn over £25,000 per year. You may also be given additional payments if you are required to work unusual hours.

Related opportunities

- Environmental Conservation Officer p265
- Farm Manager p266
- Forestry Worker/Officer p270
- Gamekeeper p271

Further information

Lantra
Lantra House, Stoneleigh Park, Coventry, CV8 2LG
0845 707 8007; www.lantra.co.uk

British Trust for Conservation Volunteers (BTCV)
Sedum House, Mallard Way, Potteric Carr, Doncaster, DN4 8DB
01302 388888; www.btcv.org.uk

Countryside Agency
John Dower House, Crescent Place, Cheltenham, GL50 3RA
01242 521381; www.countryside.gov.uk

www.cityandguilds.com/myperfectjob

DOG GROOMER

What the work involves

- Working from home, in a grooming salon, pet shop or veterinary practice you will bath, groom, trim, clip nails and clean the teeth of your clients' dogs.

- You may also be required to check for fleas, ticks or sore areas of skin and sometimes provide treatment for these.

- You will also provide advice to the owners on grooming and diet.

The type of person suited to this work

To work in this area you will have to love dogs and want to work with them for hours at a time. This industry also involves working with people, so you will need excellent communication skills and be very enthusiastic.

Working with animals requires great patience and understanding. You should have excellent hand-eye co-ordination and attention to detail. You will need to have the confidence to handle the larger and more nervous dogs.

As you could be on your feet for a lot of the day you will have to be physically fit. If you suffer from allergies this work could be difficult for you.

Working conditions

You will be working indoors in a private home, shop, veterinary practice or grooming room and will be on your feet for a great deal of the day. You will be required to lift the dogs, so a certain level of fitness is needed.

You may be expected to wear an apron whilst shampooing and gloves when applying treatments for parasites or skin conditions. You might need to travel between locations so a driving licence would be beneficial. The working week is usually around 35 hours from Monday to Saturday.

Future prospects

Demand for dog grooming has increased recently. However, there may not be sufficient work yet for full-time employment for all. This work can be seasonal as during the winter months many owners choose to keep their dogs' coats longer than in the summer. In larger groomers you may progress to senior groomer, supervisor or manager. There is the possibility of self-employment. There is also the option of teaching or lecturing or even moving into other industries involving animal care.

Advantages/disadvantages

If you really are a dog enthusiast, this might be your idea of heaven.

Qualifications and courses

There are no formal educational requirements, although some employers prefer applicants with GCSEs grade A*-C. There are numerous courses in dog grooming available, these include: NVQ/SVQ Levels 1–3 or BTEC National Qualifications in Animal Care; the City & Guilds Dog Grooming certificate; the Animal Care College offers several qualifications including a course in dog grooming (theory). Other programmes available include the National Small Animal Care Certificate and a course on The Anatomy and Physiology of Cats and Dogs at Level 2.

Apprenticeship/Skillseekers available for those aged 16–24.

Your employer might be in a remote location so personal transport could be essential.

Dog owners can be as difficult as their dogs.

Some jobs can be part time or seasonal.

There is the possibility of self-employment.

Money guide

Salaries may vary depending on employer and location.

Rates are around £2,000 to £5,000 per year if you work part time. A full time entry level salary is around £8,000, which can rise to £12,000 or more with experience. Once very experienced or at management level this can increase to over £15,000 per year. Self-employed groomers charge a fixed rate and earn around £20 to £50 per hour.

Related opportunities

- Dog Trainer/Handler p264
- Kennel Worker p276
- RSPCA/SSPCA Inspector p282

Further information

The Animal Care College
Ascot House, High Street, Ascot, SL5 7HG
01344 628269; www.animalcarecollege.co.uk

The Pet Care Trust
Unit A, Bedford Business Centre, 170 Mile Road, Bedford, MK42 9TW
01234 273933; www.petcare.org.uk

City& Guilds

www.cityandguilds.com/myperfectjob

Environment, Animals and Plants

CRCI: HC
CLCI: WAM

DOG TRAINER/HANDLER

What the work involves

Dog trainer

- You could support security staff, the police force or animal charities like the Guide Dogs for the Blind. Your work will be divided between training the dogs and their human carers.

- You might run one-to-one and group classes on obedience training for dogs.

Dog handler

- Working as a team, you will search buildings, vehicles and open spaces for such things as people, illegal drugs, firearms or evidence. You may protect property including private property or military establishments.

- You might attend large-scale disturbances to control crowds or search for casualties at disaster scenes.

The type of person suited to this work

You may need to house and care for your dog from puppyhood right to the time it retires 7–10 years later. You will require a stable home environment.

Most police dog work involves attending incidents, so you will need to be able to stay calm in an emergency. You will need to be patient, self-confident, alert and observant.

Dog trainer

You will need to be patient and a good teacher. You will need to have a good imagination to make classes fun and also be physically fit.

Working conditions

If you work with domestic owners you will probably be self-employed and work from a community setting like a village hall.

Dogs are used in dangerous situations and so you will be at risk of injury.

Future prospects

The main employers are the police, armed forces and customs and excise. Some other organisations employ a few dog handlers, for example the fire service, security companies and search and rescue services.

This job is fiercely competitive as many handlers stay in the job for life.

There is also the option of self-employment or lecturing on dog training courses.

Advantages/disadvantages

There is the possibility of self-employment.

You may at some point be bitten or scratched.

Qualifications and courses

Dog handler

Dog handling is usually a second career. Employers such as HM Customs and Excise, the RAF, the police, the army and the fire service expect you to start your career in mainstream work first before applying for dog handling work.

There is an ASET Level 2 National Award in Security Dog Handling and an NVQ/SVQ Level 1–3 in Animal Care. There is a legal requirement for security guards, including dog handlers, to have a Security Industry Authority (SIA) licence.

Dog trainer

After working as a handler you can then apply to become a trainer. Some organisations require three GCSEs/S grades (A*–C/1–3) or equivalent, including English language. A full driving licence is often required. A training course usually needs to be passed.

You will form a strong bond with your dog.

It is really rewarding when the dog you have trained catches a criminal, or finds dangerous drugs or explosives.

Money guide

Domestic dog trainers earn around £15,000 a year. Police dog trainers make about £21,000 which can rise to £30,000 with experience. If you are self-employed your earnings will depend on your success.

On average dog handlers earn between £15,000–£25,000 a year depending on experience. Extra allowances are paid when the dog lives with and is cared for by you.

Related opportunities

- Animal Behaviourist p259
- Racehorse Trainer p281
- Police Officer p551
- RSPCA Inspector p282

Further information

Police recruitment information
0845 608 3000; www.policecouldyou.co.uk

Armed Forces Careers RAF
22 Unthank Road, Norwich, NR2 1AH
01603 614616; www.rafcareers.com

Association of Pet Dog Trainers (APDT)
PO Box 17, Kempsford, GL7 4WZ
01285 810811; www.apdt.co.uk

City&
Guilds

www.cityandguilds.com/myperfectjob

ENVIRONMENTAL CONSERVATION MANAGER/OFFICER

What the work involves

- Environmental conservation officers/managers preserve and protect important wildlife areas, including nature reserves and sites of special scientific interest (SSSIs).

- You will achieve this through methods such as raising awareness of the issues that affect the natural environment, monitoring species to see which require protection, and gathering evidence of pollution.

- You will advise authorities and communities on the effect developments will have on the natural environment.

- Managers are responsible for the hiring, training and supervising staff. You will also be in charge of the way budgets are spent.

The type of person suited to this work

In order to pursue this career you must have an interest in and a passion for environmental conservation.

You should have strong observational skills. You will also need to be physically fit. You should be capable of conducting research, have strong communication and negotiation skills, both in person and on paper and the ability to speak in public.

You might have to be involved in enforcing environmental laws and so you will have to be able to remain calm and logical.

Working conditions

You will spend some of your time in an office environment and the rest working outdoors.

Working hours will vary depending on the season, but the average is about 40 hours a week. This is not a 9–5 job and working weekends, evenings and bank holidays is common.

You might be required to travel between sites and so a driving licence may be useful. As an officer you may be provided with protective clothing.

Future prospects

Officers may progress into a managerial position, for example countryside manager or senior officer. In order to gain this kind of promotion you will need to gather qualifications and experience. However, promotion opportunities can be hard to come by and so you may need to change employers in order to progress.

You may also be able to specialise in an area of conservation which could increase your employment potential.

Advantages/disadvantages

You will have to work outside in all weather.

This job has many elements to it and so every day will be different.

Qualifications and courses

ENTRY LEVEL 3

Most environmental conservation manager/officers have completed a degree; however it is possible to enter this profession with a HND, foundation degree, A levels or equivalent. It is important to remember that this is an extremely competitive industry and so a postgraduate qualification would be beneficial.

Subjects such as environmental science, biological sciences (e.g. zoology), environmental conservation, countryside management and earth sciences (e.g. geography) would all be relevant.

Generally degree programmes require applicants to have achieved at least two A levels and five GCSEs grades A*-C or equivalent. Entry requirements do vary so it is important to check with the individual institution.

You will also have to demonstrate your commitment to this career, which you can do by completing work experience placements within conservation groups or wildlife trusts.

An alternative route into this industry is to start as a ranger or warden, gather experience and then apply for an environmental conservation officer. There are Apprenticeships available for this particular career.

You will have to enforce environmental legislation which might place you in heated situations.

Money guide

These figures will vary depending on location, employer and sector. Your salary will increase as you gain responsibility. The average starting salary for an environmental conservation officer is between £19,500 and £21,500 per year. With experience this can increase to between £24,000 and £32,000. Those who excel in the field can earn up to £36,000 a year.

Related opportunities

- Countryside Ranger p262
- Landscaper/Landscape Manager p278
- Landscape Architect/Designer p277

Further information

BTCV, Head Office
Sedum House, Mallard Way, Potteric Carr,
Doncaster, DN4 8DB
01302 388 883; information@btcv.org.uk; www.btcv.org.uk

City& Guilds

www.cityandguilds.com/myperfectjob

FARM MANAGER

What the work involves

- You will be responsible for the overall running of a farm. This includes making the decisions about which crops to grow or livestock to raise.

- You will supervise the work of your staff, keep up to date with farming developments and oversee the economic side of the business.

- You will have to communicate with government officials, farming suppliers and feed merchants and your customers who could be major supermarkets or small local shops.

- You will keep farm records up to date such as the budget and where crops and livestock are sold to and bought from.

The type of person suited to this work

You should have a passion for science, the environment and business, combined with a strong understanding of farming and a desire to learn.

You will also need an appreciation of health and safety and the ability to recruit, develop and retain your staff, as well as run the business of the farm.

You should be capable of motivating staff, be computer literate and work well when under pressure.

Working conditions

Farm managers tend to work long hours, with particular times of year being exceptionally busy, for example harvest or lambing season. This job involves early mornings.

Managers will spend a lot of their time doing accounts and making sure the farm is operating profitably, but will also need to muck in with general farm work during busy periods. On smaller farms this may be a regular occurrence. The outdoors work will involve heavy lifting and will be dirty, smelly and/or dusty.

Future prospects

Competition for jobs is intense and career progression is likely to involve moving from one part of the country to another. With substantial experience and qualifications it is possible to progress into other related areas of agriculture, such as plant breeding, crop protection, plant trials or genetics. These opportunities are available within private companies or academic/research organisations. Training or research opportunities are also possible. There could be the chance to work abroad.

Advantages/disadvantages

You will spend a lot of time in the open air caring for living and growing things.

At some times of the year your social life may be restricted.

Qualifications and courses

There are no formal entry requirements but most that enter this area do so with an HND, degree or other higher level qualification. Courses are available in agriculture, agricultural science, land and property management, and agricultural engineering. A levels/H grades or their equivalent, often including a science subject will be required. Postgraduate courses are also available which will require a relevant degree or HNC/D and experience.

It is possible to enter with an NVQ/SVQ in Agriculture Crop Production or Livestock Production Level 3, Agriculture (Livestock Management) Level 4 or Agricultural and Commercial Horticulture (Crop Management) Level 4. Candidates should also have previous experience of farm work, and most degree-level courses include sandwich placements for this purpose. A driving licence is essential.

You will get to combine business acumen and an understanding of nature.

Your future can depend on things outside of your control such as bird flu or foot and mouth disease.

Money guide

Average salaries are around £16,500. With experience this can increase to between £24,000 and £30,000. Managing a large farm, once enough experience has been gathered, may increase this to over £50,000. Some jobs include rent-free accommodation and a vehicle. There is a set minimum wage, decided upon by the Agricultural Wages Boards for England and Wales, Scotland and Northern Ireland.

Related opportunities

- Parks Officer p279
- Fish Farmer p269
- Forestry Worker/Officer p270
- Horticultural/Garden Centre Manager p275
- Farmhand p267

Further information

Lantra
Lantra House, Stoneleigh Park, Coventry, CV8 2LG
0845 707 8007; www.lantra.co.uk

National Federation of Young Farmers' Clubs (NFYFC)
YFC Centre, 10th Street, Stoneleigh Park, Coventry, CV8 2LG
024 7685 7200; www.nfyfc.org.uk

City&
Guilds

www.cityandguilds.com/myperfectjob

FARMHAND

What the work involves

- You will undertake the practical duties on a farm, working with crops, livestock or both.
- You will be responsible for planting, harvesting and storing the crop.
- You may also be responsible for the general care of some livestock such as cows, sheep, poultry and pigs. This may involve feeding, administering medication, milking cows, mucking out and helping with birthing.

The type of person suited to this work

You must enjoy being outdoors in the countryside, working in all weathers. As you will be caring for animals or getting things to grow you should have an interest in the environment. If you are allergic to pollen or animals this work will be very difficult for you.

You will have to be fit and active, able to be on your feet all day and prepared to work very long hours, especially during the summer months. If your animals become ill, you will have to be prepared to be with them and administer drugs when needed.

Working conditions

This job involves a lot of time outdoors, so you will be out in the wind and the rain, summer and winter. Farming is not a 9–5 job and is very physical work. It can also be dangerous, as a lot of the equipment is hazardous.

Most farmworkers work around 39 hours a week and at particular times of the year such as harvest or lambing season this may increase. Those working with agricultural machinery will be provided with ear protection. Working on non-organic farms may involve using chemicals.

Future prospects

The kinds of farming opportunities available will vary depending on the part of the country where you live. The eastern side of the UK has mainly arable farming, whilst the west concentrates on livestock. Experienced workers with training can become managers without having to buy their own farms but opportunities are scarce and promotion unlikely unless you work on a very large farm.

There may be the opportunity to work abroad.

Advantages/disadvantages

You will spend a lot of time in the open air caring for living and growing things.

At some times of the year your social life may be restricted.

You could be alone for long periods of the day.

Qualifications and courses

Formal qualifications are not normally needed but relevant work experience is useful. You may also be given the opportunity to train on the job, whilst attending college part time. You could work towards an NVQ in a number of subjects such as Agricultural (level 1), Mixed Farming (Levels 2 and 3) and Agricultural Crop Production (Levels 2 and 3).

A driving licence is normally required. CITB or NPTC accredited tractor driving, chainsaw use and pesticide use courses are also recommended.

Apprenticeships/Skillseekers may be available for those aged 16–24.

Your future can depend on things outside of your control such as bird flu or foot and mouth disease.

You might have to stay up through the night to care for animals that are ill or giving birth.

Money guide

At the age of 16 a farmhand can earn £11,000, increasing to £12,100–£14,300 with training and qualifications. A supervisor should earn at least £15,200. These figures may be lower in Northern Ireland.

Some jobs include accommodation with free or subsidised rent or a lodgings allowance and there is the possibility of overtime which would increase earnings.

There is a set minimum wage, decided upon by the Agricultural Wages Boards for England and Wales, Scotland and Northern Ireland.

Related opportunities

- Farm Manager p266
- Gamekeeper p271
- Shepherd/Shepherdess p283
- Stockman/Stockwoman p285
- Zookeeper p290

Further information

Lantra
Lantra House, Stoneleigh Park, Coventry, CV8 2LG
0845 707 8007; www.lantra.co.uk

National Federation of Young Farmers' Clubs (NFYFC)
YFC Centre, 10th Street, Stoneleigh Park, Coventry, CV8 2LG
024 7685 7200; www.nfyfc.org.uk

City&
Guilds

www.cityandguilds.com/myperfectjob

Environment, Animals and Plants

CRCI: HA
CLCI: WAD/WAB

FARRIER

What the work involves

- Farriers shoe, trim and care for the feet of horses.

- You could work from a blacksmith's forge or a mobile workshop and go to the horses in a converted vehicle.

- As well as the skills of removing and fitting new shoes, you will have to keep up to date with new practices and know about horse anatomy, illnesses and how the two are linked.

- You would often work in partnership with vets to treat leg and joint problems.

The type of person suited to this work

You should enjoy being around horses and have the right temperament to handle them. As you are providing a service you will need to get on with your customers and deliver high-quality care to them and their horses.

You will have to enjoy being outdoors working in all weathers, often in a muddy environment. This work is both practical and physical, so you will need to be strong and able to do manual work using lots of hand tools.

Working conditions

Your days will involve driving to each customer, working with the horses and returning to your forge to prepare shoes and collect materials. In the summer months your hours will be long, especially when more people are riding their horses. This can be hot, tiring work, especially if fitting shoes to a difficult horse.

Future prospects

Riding is a very popular activity and there are stables all round the country. There are about 2900 farriers who are mostly self-employed. There are always more young people interested in entering the profession than vacancies, resulting in high competition for each apprenticeship. On average 80–100 apprentices are recruited annually.

Some farriers supplement their earnings by undertaking blacksmithing whilst they build up their farriery client list.

Advantages/disadvantages

You should enjoy being around horses.

It's a satisfying skill to have; using your hands.

The work is physically demanding and can result in back injuries.

This is a great job if you want to work with horses without riding.

Money guide

The Farriers Registration Council sets minimum wages. When starting you can expect a salary of around £8,500 per year.

Qualifications and courses

Younger trainee farriers are required to take a 4-year Advanced Apprenticeship with an FRC Approved Training Farrier (ATF). They must be at least 16 years old, have 4 GCSEs/S grades (A–C/1–3), including English language, and hold a Forging Certificate. Candidates should contact the Farrier Training Agency (FTA) for information regarding the FRC Approved Training Farrier list and colleges running approved block-release courses.

Applicants will need 4 GCSEs/S grades (A–C/1–3) or equivalent including English language, NVQ Level 2, Key Skills Level 2 in communication and application of number, or to pass an entrance exam.

They will then complete an apprenticeship while working for the approved training farrier; this takes 4 years and 2 months. An NVQ/SVQ is available at Level 3 and the course combines on-the-job training with periods at a college.

By law farriers must be registered with the Farriers' Registration Council and have passed the diploma of the Worshipful Company of Farriers (DipWCF) in order to practise.

A driving licence is required.

Once qualified, earnings range from £10,000 to £20,000, depending on success and the number of customers. Some experienced and popular farriers can earn over £35,000.

Related opportunities

- Animal Behaviourist p259
- Blacksmith p222
- Farm Manager p266
- Racehorse Trainer p281

Further information

Farriery Training Agency
Sefton House, Adam Court, Newark Road, Peterborough, PE1 5PP
01733 319911; www.farrier-reg.gov.uk

Worshipful Company of Farriers
19 Queen Street, Chipperfield, Kings Langley, Hertfordshire, WD4 9BT
01923 260747; www.wcf.org.uk

City&
Guilds

FISH FARMER

What the work involves

- As a fish farmer you will raise fish from small (juvenile) fry until they reach saleable size. The most common fish to raise are salmon and trout.

- You will feed, check for disease and protect them from predators. You will finally net the catch and pack them for market.

- Some farms specialise in producing the breeding stock: the fingerlings (the tiny fish that other farmers bring to saleable size).

- Some shellfish farms in coastal locations also produce oysters, scallops and mussels.

The type of person suited to this work

You will need to be a practical type with the ability to learn a lot about fish and be happy to get wet and dirty. Much of this work is scientific in approach, so you should have good observational skills, to be able to identify anything that might affect the quality and success of the fish in your care.

You will need to be patient, hard working and persevere if things are tough. This work is difficult and long-term security is not guaranteed.

If you become a manager, in addition to your practical ability, you will also have to have good business and administrative skills.

Working conditions

Working with fish is the same as any animal-based work, which means they need care and attention 24/7. You are likely to work on a rota basis with 2 days off every week and work very long hours including early mornings, late evenings and weekends. You will be outdoors in damp, cold conditions having to cope with all types of weather. Some of the work will be unpleasant and will involve the sight of blood.

Future prospects

With the problems related with sea fish stocks, fish farming is becoming quite important as a source of fish. There are plans to farm other kinds of fish such as turbot and cod.

Like other farming enterprises, fish farms are vulnerable to price fluctuations, so predicting the future is risky. Around 7500 people are employed in the industry, most of whom are based in Scotland. Of these, half are managers mainly with a scientific background.

There are 300 trout farms located in Scotland, southern and central England and north Yorkshire.

Advantages/disadvantages

You will spend a lot of time in the open air.

You may spend a lot of time working on your own.

There are only limited areas where the work is available.

This work can affect your social life.

Qualifications and courses

ENTRY LEVEL 1

Applicants do not necessarily require formal educational qualifications, but fish-related qualifications and previous related work experience are useful.

A BTEC First Diploma in Fish Husbandry is available to those with 4 GCSE/S grades (A–C/1–3); students can then progress to the National Diploma in Fish Management or the Scottish group Award in Fishery Studies.

BTEC and SQA Higher National qualifications can be taken in Fish Farm Management, Aquaculture or Fishery Studies.

Training can be done on the job with attendance at short courses. Entrants may work towards NVQs/SVQs at Levels 2 and 3 in Fish Husbandry, or may study by distance learning for the Institute of Fisheries Management Diploma.

Degrees in aquaculture/fisheries studies, biology, marine and freshwater biology are available.

In Scotland, entry is available through Skillseekers.

Fish farming is a risky business as fish can be very affected by disease

Money guide

Fish farm worker

Starting out you can expect to earn around £10,000-£14,000. per year. Average earnings for those with experience are between £12,000 and £20,000.

Manager

Experienced managers can expect up to £40,000.

Related opportunities

- Countryside Ranger p262
- Farm Manager p266
- Fisherman/Woman/Skipper p284

Further information

Institute of Fisheries Management
22 Rushworth Avenue, West Bridgford, Nottingham, NG2 7LF
0115 982 2317, www.ifm.org.uk

British Trout Association
The Rural Centre, West Mains, Ingliston, EH28 8NZ
0131 472 4080; www.britishtrout.co.uk

City&
Guilds

www.cityandguilds.com/myperfectjob

Environment, Animals and Plants

CRCI: HA
CLCI: WAG

FORESTRY WORKER/OFFICER

What the work involves

Forestry worker

■ Work would include planting trees, felling trees, managing weeds and undergrowth, maintaining fencing and carrying out tree surgery.

■ In addition, you would use hand and power tools, drive vehicles and repair any broken fences or pathways.

Forestry officer

■ You would plan and manage the annual programme of your forest. This would include organising the clearing of areas, planting and felling trees, and overseeing the general maintenance.

The type of person suited to this work

This can be dangerous work as you will be using heavy machinery and hand tools. It is important that you can follow instructions, enjoy being outdoors and want to work with nature.

Forestry officer

You will have to be an excellent organiser and administrator as you will be planning jobs months in advance. You will need both technical skills and theoretical knowledge of forests and wildlife.

Working conditions

Forestry worker

You will probably work a standard Monday–Friday week with overtime and weekend work during the busier summer months. You will have to be aware of health and safety legislation as this can be dangerous work, using potentially hazardous tools.

Forestry officer

Much of your time will be spent outdoors but you will also work indoors planning and creating jobs for your staff to follow. You are likely to do a lot of travelling, whilst you check the different areas under your responsibility.

Future prospects

The range of employers open to you includes the Forestry Commission, private landowners and estates, local authorities and large companies. Career progression is likely to involve moving, as promotion is rare within all but the largest employers. Many contracts are short term so you need to have a flexible approach to employment opportunities. With significant experience, self-employment as a consultant or trainer is possible.

Advantages/disadvantages

As in all jobs with plants, you are often at the mercy of the weather.

Some jobs are in remote areas.

Qualifications and courses

Forestry worker

There are no formal entry requirements but at least 2 GCSE/S grades (A–C/1–3) or a forestry qualification would be an advantage. These include: NVQs/SVQs in Forestry (Establishment and Harvesting) Level 2 and Treework (Forestry Establishment or Forestry Harvesting) Level 3; BTEC/SQA in Forestry and Arboriculture and Countryside Management (Woodland Management).

The National Proficiency Tests Council (NPTC), the Scottish Skills Testing Service (SSTS) and Lantra award competence certificates in skills such as operating chainsaws and carrying out chemical spraying.

Forestry officer

Entry is with a Foundation degree, HND, degree or postgraduate qualification in forestry. For entry to a degree, 2 A levels/3 H grades, normally including maths or a science, and 3 GCSEs/S grades (A–C/1–3) are required. At least 1 A level/H grade or equivalent is required for entry to an HND or Foundation degree.

Money guide

Forestry worker

You are likely to earn around £12,200 per year when starting out. This rises to around £17,000 with experience. Some employers also provide subsidised accommodation.

Forestry officer

Forestry Commission salaries for officers start at £19,800 per year, with experience it can rise to £30,000.

Related opportunities

■ Countryside Ranger p262
■ Gardener/Garden Designer p272
■ Rural Surveyor p123

Further information

Forestry Commission
Silvan House, 231 Corstorphine Road, Edinburgh, EH12 7AT
0845 367 3787; www.forestry.gov.uk

Institute of Chartered Foresters
7a St Colme Street, Edinburgh, EH3 6AA
0131 225 2705; www.charteredforesters.org

City&
Guilds

www.cityandguilds.com/myperfectjob

GAMEKEEPER

What the work involves

- As a gamekeeper you would work on a large country estate, where shooting for sport is part of the estate business.

- You will be responsible for providing birds and other animals such as deer or hares for the clients to shoot, or possibly fish to catch.

- This is usually achieved by raising pheasants and other game birds and releasing them into the wild once they are mature enough.

- You will control predators by shooting and trapping (rats, foxes and crows are some of the birds' principal enemies).

The type of person suited to this work

You must have an unsentimental approach to wildlife as this job involves the killing of animals for sport. To enable the clients to get the most from their day of sport you will have to be a good communicator and able to offer advice about using their guns and how to be successful.

You will have to be physically fit with lots of stamina and happy to work on your own for long periods of time. This is a varied job with lots of responsibility – your success will be measured by the enjoyment of the clients.

Working conditions

You will be outdoors in all weathers all through the year. Your hours will be flexible and will involve weekend working and late/early starts. You will spend long periods of time on your own, doing lots of walking checking the estate and the progress of the game.

As you will be handling and using guns, traps and poisons, you will have to be confident using them and very aware of your own safety and that of others.

This work will be difficult for those who suffer from allergies to animals, pollen or dust.

Future prospects

Most of this work is within remote parts of the country or on large country estates. This work is in decline as trends have changed resulting in many gamekeepers being expected to combine this work with other estate jobs, such as maintenance and general forestry/conservation duties.

If you are able to find work there is a formal promotion path in place which most have followed, from trainee gamekeeper to underkeeper, up to beatkeeper and then finally head keeper.

Advantages/disadvantages

This job combines outdoor physical work with lots of practical skills.

Qualifications and courses

ENTRY LEVEL 1

No formal qualifications are needed for this role. However, 2/3 GCSEs/S grades (A–E/1–5) may be an advantage. Voluntary or relevant work experience is very useful.

Training is generally on the job, but there are some courses available to applicants who wish to progress.

City & Guilds offer the National and Advanced National Certificate in Environmental Conservation (Countryside Management); National Certificate in Gamekeeping Level 2 and the Certificate in Land-based Studies Level 1.

NVQs/SVQs are available in Gamekeeping and Wildlife Management at Levels 2 and 3. A BTEC National Award is available in Gamekeeping.

An HNC is available in Gamekeeping and Wildlife Management. Candidates would need practical experience and/or the National Award in Gamekeeping.

Foundation degrees are available in Countryside and Environment (Gamekeeping) at several colleges. These generally require a National Diploma or 2 or more A levels for entry. Apprenticeships/Skillseekers may be available for those aged 16–24.

You will be on your own a lot.

You might be provided with a house.

The industry is in decline and jobs are difficult to find.

Money guide

Starting salaries for new entrants are around £11,000 per year. Single-hand gamekeepers earn between £13,000 and £18,500. Head gamekeepers can expect up to £21,500.

Related opportunities

- Countryside Ranger p262
- Farm Manager p266
- Farrier p268
- Forestry Worker/Officer p270

Further information

British Association for Shooting and Conservation
Marford Mill, Rossett, Wrexham, Clwyd, LL12 0HL
01244 573 000; www.basc.org.uk

Game Conservancy Trust
Fordingbridge, Hampshire, SP6 1EF
01425 652381; www.gct.org.uk

City&
Guilds

www.cityandguilds.com/myperfectjob

GARDENER/ GARDEN DESIGNER

What the work involves

Gardener

- Gardeners work in a wide range of settings from large gardens such as those in stately homes and National Trust properties to small urban parks and private gardens.

Garden designer

- You would advise clients on how to improve the look and planting of their garden. You would present your ideas as a series of plans and drawings and you would probably supervise a landscape contractor to turn your design into reality.

The type of person suited to this work

You will need to be physically fit and confident in using hand tools. Depending on your employer, you will probably spend periods driving to different locations.

You will need to be a creative person who can picture how a piece of bare or neglected ground can be transformed into something beautiful.

Drawing and ICT skills will be useful as is extensive knowledge of plants and the environments they need to grow well.

Working conditions

Gardeners will mostly be working outdoors. There will be quite a lot of physical work lifting large pots and bags of peat and digging and clearing beds.

Garden designers will spend as much time in a studio designing and researching designs. You will spend some time outdoors overseeing the practical tasks.

Future prospects

Gardener

Many gardeners are self-employed offering services to both the public and private sectors. With experience, you could move on to supervisor or manager jobs, especially if you get some further qualifications.

Garden designer

Half of all designers work in private practice, which can be small businesses providing services to the public and private sectors. Some specialise in certain types of design such as planting, landscaping, etc. Some designers choose to be self-employed offering services to private home owners who may contract in other professionals as needed.

Advantages/disadvantages

Designers can mix creative, practical and outdoor work.

Your work will depend on the weather.

Qualifications and courses

Gardener

There are no set requirements for entry to this career. GCSEs/S grades (A–C/1–3) would be useful. Courses are available to those who wish to progress, these include: a BTEC, NVQs/SVQs. The Royal Horticultural Society (RHS) have a general examination, which allows entry onto the Advanced National Certificate in Horticulture.

ENTRY 1 LEVEL

Garden designer

Although there are no formal requirements for this job, a design-orientated qualification is an advantage. Many garden design courses are offered at land-based colleges and some art colleges too. Courses include NVQs/SVQs. Degrees in garden design and related subjects are also available. The Society of Garden Designers offers registered membership.

You may work in beautiful places (or create them if you are a designer).

Some contracts can be seasonal.

Money guide

Gardener

Gardeners start at around £10,000–£12,000 per year. With experience this can rise to £20,000+.

Garden designer

As a guide, trainee rates start at between £10,000 and £20,000 per year. Designers' pay will depend entirely on how well they can market themselves and generate work; many are self-employed and charge around £30–£60 per hour.

Related opportunities

- Groundsperson/Greenkeeper p274
- Horticultural/Garden Centre Worker/Manager p275
- Landscape Architect/Manager p277

Further information

Royal Horticultural Society
Education Department, Wisley, Woking, GU23 6QB
www.rhs.org.uk

City&
Guilds

www.cityandguilds.com/myperfectjob

GROOM/STABLE HAND/ STUD HAND

Environment, Animals and Plants

CRCI: HC/MB
CLCI: WAM

What the work involves
Groom/stable hand

■ You would be responsible for the health and welfare of the horses in your care. You would groom, feed, muck out and tack up.

■ You could be based within a riding school, competition or livery yard, racing stable or veterinary hospital. You may have the opportunity to ride and even compete.

Stud hand

■ This is a specialised area of work, you will be working with stallions, brood mares and young stock.

■ You will use your understanding and knowledge of breeding lines to help owners breed a foal that meets their requirements.

The type of person suited to this work

As well as having lots of patience and the right temperament to be with the horses, you will need communication and team-working skills to work with your colleagues, owners and stable visitors.

Most of your work will be outdoors undertaking hard physical, dirty work. You will have to be happy to get your hands dirty by mucking out, grooming and cleaning tack. The hours are long and the pay can be low!

Working conditions

You will spend most of your time outdoors lifting heavy bags of feed, hay and bedding. You will carry tack, clean up the yard or ride. In the summer the work can be hot, dusty and smelly. In the winter it is cold, wet and muddy.

You will wear protective clothing and, as this work can be dangerous you must be aware of your own and others' safety. Horses can kick and bite.

You can expect to work 24/7 especially if you live-in including some holidays and weekends.

Future prospects
Groom/stable hand

With experience it is possible to specialise. Competition grooms (show-jumping, dressage and eventing) are in demand. Gaining your HGV driving licence can increase opportunities. Most grooms progress to more successful yards that compete internationally or keep more expensive and quality horses.

Stud hand

Interest in breeding quality British horses and ponies has increased due to European competition. Stud work is therefore rising in importance and those with skills are in demand.

Qualifications and courses
Groom/stable hand

Full-time courses include BTEC National Diploma in Horse Care or Equine Studies and NVQ in Equine Studies; NVQ/SVQ Levels 1–3 in Horse Care and Horse Care Management, the British Horse Society (BHS) stage 1–4 exams; and the Association of British Riding Schools (ABRS) certificates and diplomas. A driving licence is useful.

Stud hand

There are no formal entry requirements. Some knowledge of stable work and horse care is expected. Candidates under the age of 19 may enter as a trainee stud hand and work towards an NVQ Level 2. Training is free and starts with a residential course at a Centre, then continues in the workplace. Some people choose to enter as a working pupil; this option is especially popular within competition yards.

Advantages/disadvantages

You really need to be a horse lover. If you are you will put up with the disadvantages!

Pay can be low and stables can be in remote locations.

Injury risks are high in all horse activities and this could affect your long-term career security.

Looking after horses is not a 9 to 5 job.

Money guide

The horse industry has a reputation for low salaries and long hours. As a starting salary you can expect to be on the minimum wage up to around £10,500 per year. This can rise to between £15,000 and £16,000 for the most experienced. As head groom you can expect £20,000 or more. If you live-in, free or supplemented board and lodging is common.

Related opportunities

■ Dog Groomer p263
■ Farrier p268

Further information

British Horse Society
Stoneleigh Deer Park, Coventry, CV8 2XZ
0844 848 1666; www.bhs.org.uk

City& Guilds

www.cityandguilds.com/myperfectjob

GROUNDSPERSON/ GREENKEEPER

What the work involves

- Your main role will be to prepare and maintain the grounds used for different sports. Although you might work on synthetic surfaces for games like tennis and hockey, most of the time you will be working with grass.

- You will cut, treat, weed and prepare the surface before each game, match or event.

The type of person suited to this work

Both of these jobs require people who can combine specialist horticultural knowledge with an understanding of the different sports and what the competitors of each sport require.

As well as the horticultural side, you will also have to be prepared to do a range of other jobs from putting up nets, to preparing seating and applying fertilisers. You will need lots of stamina and be willing to work unsocial hours.

Working conditions

You will have to work flexible hours including evenings and weekends. You will need to be fit, strong and active with a strong eye for detail. If you suffer from an allergy to pollen this work might be difficult for you.

You will spend a lot of your time outdoors working in all weathers, although when repairing and maintaining the equipment you will probably be in a workshop. You will need to wear protective clothing.

Future prospects

The range of potential places for you to work is increasing and demand for staff is growing. You could work in a professional sports club, local authority education or sports and leisure department, hotel, university or college.

With additional qualifications and experience you could apply for promotion to head ground staff positions or become an area manager looking after a large number of sites.

Some of this work may be seasonal and part time, so you may need additional work to supplement your earnings.

Advantages/disadvantages

This job offers the opportunity for your work to be seen by thousands of people!

It offers non-sportspeople a chance to get involved with sport.

At lower levels of sport you might get the opportunity to play your favourite sport having prepared the ground first!

Qualifications and courses

There are no set qualifications required for this role. Training generally takes place on the job, but it is possible to study relevant courses on a day-release basis to gain qualifications. Some of these could be NVQs at Level 1 in Horticulture; Levels 2–4 in Amenity Horticulture (Sports Turf Management); Levels 2–3 in Greenkeeping and Sports Turf Management.

Higher level courses are available including Foundation degrees in sports turf and golf course management. There are also degrees in sports turf science and management. Entry requirements are 2 A levels/3 H grades and 5 GCSEs/S grades (A–C/1–3).

The Institute of Groundsmanship (IOG) offers three levels of courses covering practical greenkeeping, scientific principles of groundsmanship, and grounds management. The British and International Golf Greenkeepers Association (BIGGA) offers various training courses. It also operates a Master Greenkeeper Certificate Scheme which recognises qualifications, skills and experience in golf course management.

Money guide

A trainee groundsperson will start at around £10,500. Unskilled staff can expect £14,190-£17,340. Skilled staff can expect £17,715–£21,640. A head groundsperson earns £21,640–£30,000. Staff who are responsible for the major sporting venues can receive higher salaries.

Related opportunities

- Gardener/Garden Designer p272
- Horticultural/Garden Centre Worker/Manager p275
- Lifeguard p393
- Forestry Worker/Officer p270

Further information

Institute of Groundsmanship
28 Stratford Office Village, Walker Avenue, Wolverton Mill East, Milton Keynes, MK12 5TW
01908 312511; www.iog.org

British International Golf Greenkeepers Association
BIGGA House, Alne, York, YO61 1UF
01347 833800; www.bigga.org.uk

www.cityandguilds.com/myperfectjob

HORTICULTURAL/ GARDEN CENTRE WORKER/MANAGER

What the work involves

Horticultural worker

- You will look after the plants, check for disease, feed, water, prune and spray them.

- To produce new stock, you will plant out cuttings and seedlings. You will also pot-up and pack plants ready for despatch.

Horticultural manager

- As manager you will supervise, train and recruit staff as well as looking after the day-to-day running of the organisation.

- You make decisions about which plants to grow. You will also manage the budgets and make sure deliveries are despatched on time.

Garden centre worker/manager

- You will maintain outdoor display areas and give advice to customers.

- You will look after the stock, water and feed the plants, make sure the public spaces are safe, unload deliveries and spend time on the tills.

The type of person suited to this work

Much of your day will involve lifting, carrying and working with the plants, so you will need lots of stamina and have to be physically fit. You will also do lots of bending.

Some of your time will be spent indoors. However, you will be outdoors for much of the time working in all weathers, doing dirty and dusty work. These jobs could be difficult if you suffer from allergies to pollen or dust.

Working conditions

Garden centre

You will spend time outdoors sometimes in wet and windy conditions. Some garden centres have jobs where you are indoors in the sales area for some of the time, and if you are a manager you will have an office.

Horticultural manager/worker

You will generally do a 40-hour Monday–Friday week, with additional hours at busy times.

Future prospects

Horticultural jobs are available within major plant producers, national parks, public gardens and local and national garden shops/nurseries.

Advantages/disadvantages

There is a good mix of practical and managerial work.

These jobs combine lots of skills and can be very rewarding.

Qualifications and courses

Horticultural worker

There are no formal entry requirements for horticultural work, but GCSEs/S grades (A–C/1–3) in science subjects. There are a number of vocational qualifications that could be useful, including a BTEC and NVQ/SVQs. City & Guilds offer the Horticultural Skills test and the National/Advanced National Certificate in Horticulture Levels 2 and 3. There are also Foundation Degrees and Degrees covering Horticulture, Retail Horticulture and Amenity Horticulture.

Horticultural manager

In addition to those courses above you could gain: NVQs/SVQs in Management or Supervisory Management and an HND/BSc in Horticulture with Business Management. The Royal Botanical Gardens at Kew offer International Diploma courses in Botanic Garden Management.

Garden centre worker/manager

To work within a garden centre, qualifications in both horticulture and customer service are an advantage. NVQs/SVQs in Customer Service Levels 1 to 3 may be taken.

This is an expanding market with lots of opportunities.

Money guide

Starting salaries for trainee workers is around £10,000 per year. With experience this rises to around £20,000. Overtime pay might be available.

Horticultural manager

Starting salaries are around £16,000 per year rising to £21,000 for graduates. Qualified and experienced managers can earn between £22,000 and £40,000.

Related opportunities

- Gardener/Garden Designer p272
- Groundsperson/Greenkeeper p274
- Tree Surgeon p261

Further information

Institute of Horticulture
14–15 Belgrave Square, London, SW1X 8PS
020 7245 6943; www.horticulture.org.uk

City & Guilds

www.cityandguilds.com/myperfectjob

ENTRY LEVEL 1

Environment, Animals and Plants

CRCI: HB
CLCI: WAD

KENNEL WORKER

Environment, Animals and Plants

CRCI: HC
CLCI: WAM

What the work involves

- There are lots of types of kennels including: boarding, pet sanctuary, breeding and quarantine kennels for dogs brought from overseas.

- As well as cleaning the kennels, you will feed, exercise and check on the dogs' (and sometimes cats') health.

- You might need to complete some administration work including answering the phones, taking payments and keeping records when medicine is administered or if any behavioural problems are displayed.

- In a pet sanctuary you might be required to show prospective owners around and answer any questions they have on animal care.

The type of person suited to this work

You will need to enjoy spending time outdoors and not mind getting dirty. Some of the animals you will be working with might have behavioural problems or nervous dispositions and so you will need to be calm and patient.

You will require a good level of fitness as you will spend a large part of the day being active.

You should have strong communication skills and the ability to work well alone or as part of a team.

A good knowledge of small pet care is vital.

Working conditions

This is physically demanding work involving walking dogs and cleaning the kennels. You may work shifts and your hours will probably include evenings, weekends and public holidays.

Many animals will be frightened and confused so they could be aggressive, you will therefore have to be aware of your own and others' safety. There is a strong possibility you may be bitten or scratched at some point.

You will spend a lot of time outdoors in all weathers and the work can be smelly, dirty and noisy.

Future prospects

There are approximately 3500 kennels, but with recent changes in quarantine laws numbers employed within this job have reduced. However, you could work for national charitable organisations like the RSPCA, Guide Dogs for the Blind Association or a private breeder. The Army and Police recruit service and civilian kennel staff.

In a larger kennel there may be the opportunity to progress to the position of supervisor or manager. You might at some point wish to open your own kennel.

Advantages/disadvantages

This is not a 9–5 and the unusual hours may affect your social or family life.

There is the possibility of being attacked by an animal.

Qualifications and courses

ENTRY LEVEL 1

There are no formal educational requirements although some employers will favour candidates with GCSEs grade A*-C in English and/or maths. NVQ/SVQ Levels 1–3, BTEC National Qualifications in Animal Care and the City & Guilds Advanced National Certificate in Animal Care may be useful.

The Animal Care College also offers training programmes which may prove helpful. The Guide Dogs for the Blind Association can provide work experience for applicants aged over 18. They also require a full UK driving licence for all Puppy Walkers. Hearing Dogs for the Deaf also recruit volunteer puppy socialisers from people who have experience of looking after young dogs and have an approved home.

Apprenticeship/Skillseekers available for those aged 16–24.

Lantra have developed several Apprenticeship/Skillseekers schemes for those aged 16–24. Training takes place on the job and is given by the manager or an experienced staff member.

There is an opportunity to become self-employed by opening your own kennel.

Money guide

Pay will depend on the nature of your employer, however most start at levels around £8,000. If you are working for a private kennels £12,000–£15,000 is likely. For animal charities and larger organisations you may get more. The RSPCA offers a minimum of £10,500 to its kennel workers (animal care assistants). You may be provided with accommodation and extra pay could be offered for overtime.

Related opportunities

- Dog Groomer p263
- Dog Trainer/Handler p264
- RSPCA/SSPCA Inspector p282
- Veterinary Nurse p287
- Zookeeper p290

Further information

Guide Dogs for the Blind Association
Burghfield Common, Reading, RG7 3YG
0118 983 5555; www.guidedogs.org.uk

The Animal Care College
Ascot House, High Street, Ascot, SL5 7HG
01344 636436; www.animalcarecollege.co.uk

City & Guilds

www.cityandguilds.com/myperfectjob

LANDSCAPE ARCHITECT/ DESIGNER

What the work involves

- You will design or develop a new or existing outside space. You will then make a plan, saying what plantings should be included, and calculate the cost.

- You would then see the project through to completion by supervising the work on-site.

- Although you will understand garden design you will also have an understanding of civil engineering, horticulture and planning law.

- You could work on projects aimed to regenerate towns and cities and developments to help combat climate change.

The type of person suited to this work

You will have to enjoy being outdoors and want to make a difference to the environment. You will be interested in making, building and constructing hard landscaping but will appreciate and understand the impact that different plants can have. You should be physically strong and able to use machinery and hand tools. You must be creative, artistic and have strong computer skills. You will need to be happy in the open in both the summer and the winter and be prepared to spend time away from home on some jobs. You should have solid communication and negotiation skills.

Working conditions

Landscape Architects spend a lot of time in the design studio sitting at a computer and drawing board or attending meetings on-site at clients' premises. You could spend about a quarter of your time at the project site, supervising operations. Some of your time will also be spent on the phone dealing with contractors and suppliers. Site work will involve being outdoors in all weather. Average hours are about 37 per week Monday to Friday. You may spend some time away from home.

Future prospects

Due to the impact of home improvement programmes, designing and developing gardens is now a popular and growing business. However, it can be a competitive area so many choose self-employment.

Organisations who recruit landscape staff include local authorities, botanical gardens, large private estates, the National Trust, English Heritage, building contractors and landscape design houses.

If you choose to become self-employed your success will depend upon finding customers, the quality of your work and how quickly you can build your reputation.

Advantages/disadvantages

There is a good mix of practical hands-on work with planning, design and meeting people.

You will get satisfaction from knowing your work will have an impact on future generations.

Qualifications and courses

You will need a degree in landscape architecture or a degree in any subject with a relevant postgraduate qualification. In order to gain entry to a degree course you will usually need at least 2 A levels and 5 GCSEs grade A*-C, or a Diploma in an environmental and land-based subject. In order to gain access to a postgraduate course you will usually need to complete an honours degree in a relevant subject.

Entrants who have completed a course accredited by the Landscape Institute (LI) can work towards chartered membership of the LI through the Professional Practice Examination.

Courses are also available at land-based colleges of further education, who offer a range of HND/HNC/BTEC National qualifications in relevant subjects.

You could get wet, cold, hot and dusty.

You will not be able to do this work if you suffer from pollen or dust allergies.

Money guide

Salaries vary depending on location and employer.

Starting salaries for assistants in local government are around £20,000 per year.

Salaries for the more experienced could range from between £24,000 to £30,000 a year.

When working as a principal landscape architect in local government this figure could increase to about £38,500 per year.

If you work in private practice these figures could increase substantially.

Related opportunities

- Town Planner p133
- Architect p68
- Ecologist p515
- Landscaper/Landscape Manager p278

Further information

Landscape Institute (LI)
33 Great Portland Street, London, W1W 8QG
020 7299 4500; www.landscapeinstitute.org

Landscape Design Trust (LDT)
Bank Chambers, 1 London Road, Redhill, RH1 1LY
01737 779257; www.landscape.co.uk

City&
Guilds

www.cityandguilds.com/myperfectjob

LANDSCAPER/ LANDSCAPE MANAGER

What the work involves

Landscaper

- You will do the practical work of turning a landscape architect's plan into the finished thing.

- You will operate machinery, carry out planting schemes, put up fences, create ponds, lay paths, construct decking and make terraces.

Landscape manager

- You will use your specialist knowledge to advise others on the development and maintenance of a wide range of landscapes such as historic gardens, motorway verges and public parks.

- Duties include deciding where to place features like footpaths and play areas, overseeing the people contracted to carry out work and completing reports and budget management.

The type of person suited to this work

You will have to enjoy being outdoors and want to make a difference to the environment. You will be interested in making, building and constructing hard landscaping but will appreciate and understand the impact that different plants can have. You will need to be physically strong and able to use machinery and hand tools.

An understanding of the laws surrounding the environment and the countryside is essential.

Working conditions

Landscaper

You will be outdoors in all weathers creating the design and working on landscape maintenance. There is a lot of physical labour involved such as heavy lifting, operating machinery and digging. You will need to wear protective clothing.

Landscape manager

You will work in an office for a lot of your time, but you will also go out for meetings to check and supervise work on-site. On average you will work 37 hours a week, though overtime may be required. You may need to spend time away from home.

Future prospects

The types of organisations who recruit landscape staff are local authorities, botanical gardens, large private estates, the National Trust, English Heritage, building contractors and landscape design houses.

Landscape Managers in government can follow a structured career path, in other organisations you may find yourself moving companies in order to progress. Self-employment is also an option.

Qualifications and courses

Landscaper

There are no required qualifications but relevant GCSEs/S grades, National Proficiency Tests Council (NPTC) certificates, BTEC and RHS certificates/ diplomas are useful. NVQ/SVQs are available. Apprenticeships/Skillseekers may be available for those aged 16–24. A driving licence is often required.

Landscape manager

Although there are no set qualifications needed this is still an extremely competitive industry. A HNC/HND, degree or postgraduate qualification in a relevant subject would prove valuable. The Landscape Institute has accredited some degree courses.

Advantages/disadvantages

You will get satisfaction from knowing your work will have an impact on future generations.

You could get wet, cold, hot and dusty.

You will not be able to do this work if you suffer from pollen or dust allergies.

Money guide

Landscaper

Starting rates are generally between £12,000 and £16,000 per year and range from £19,000 to £20,500 for those with experience. Senior Landscapers with additional responsibilities can get up to £45,000.

Landscape manager

The starting salary would be around £20,000 and this can rise to between £24,000 and £38,500 with experience. Rates for those who are self-employed will depend on their personal success. Work may be seasonal.

Related opportunities

- Forestry Worker/Officer p270
- Groundsperson/Greenkeeper p274
- Landscape Architect/Designer p277

Further information

Landscape Institute
33 Great Portland Street, London, W1W 8QG
020 7299 4500; www.landscapeinstitute.org

City&
Guilds

www.cityandguilds.com/myperfectjob

PARKS OFFICER

What the work involves

- You will supervise the gardeners and horticulturists who maintain and look after local parks, sports and recreation centres, gardens and public places.

- As well as planning new planting schemes you will organise staffing rotas and plan annual work programmes.

- You will be responsible for the recruitment and monitoring of your team, and budget control.

- You will have to liaise with your employer, which is normally local government, and other department colleagues.

The type of person suited to this work

To do this work you will have to be very organised, be able to plan ahead and manage people. You will need to use your technical and practical horticultural skills, have an understanding of budgets and an ability to meet and negotiate with those who work in different departments. You will also combine outdoor practical work with indoor planning and administration. You should have a good understanding of plants and how to present outside spaces so they look good all year round.

To do this job you will need to be physically fit. If you suffer from asthma, pollen-based allergies or some skin conditions this work might be difficult for you.

Working conditions

You will normally work for a local authority who often adopt a flexible Monday–Friday system of attendance. At busier times, particularly in the spring and summer you may do extra hours.

You will be provided with protective clothing and will have to ensure health and safety rules are followed by your teams. Some of your work will be indoors at a computer in an office where you will spend time ordering plants and materials.

Future prospects

Most parks officers are employed by a local or county council. A small number are employed by companies who win park management contracts.

It is likely that you will start your career as a gardener or horticulturist and then progress to parks officer once you have gained sufficient experience. Additional management training may be required.

You might have to move for career progression. Some move into department or divisional management within local/county authorities.

Advantages/disadvantages

This is a mixture of indoor and outdoor work, using lots of different skills.

Qualifications and courses

ENTRY 1 LEVEL

No formal qualifications are required for this work although GCSEs/S grades at A–E/1–5 are helpful. Employers also look for practical skills.

Many parks officers begin as gardeners/horticulturists. NVQs/SVQs in Amenity Horticulture at Level 1–2 are available and are useful qualifications to take at the early stages of your career.

Land-based colleges offer a range of horticulture qualifications which will be useful, including the Royal Horticultural Society (RHS) General Examination, City & Guilds Advanced National Certificate in Horticulture (ANCH), BTEC and SQA National qualifications.

Once you are employed as a parks officer, NVQs/SVQs in Amenity Horticulture and training skills are available at Levels 3–4.

You will use your experience and knowledge to make a difference in your community.

You might have to wait for opportunities to become available or be willing to move.

Money guide

As a parks officer your earnings will depend on the size of your employing authority and the number of sites you are responsible for.

If you work for a local authority you will normally receive around £17,000–£18,000 per year. With experience you could earn up to £25,000. At senior level you could earn £40,000+.

Related opportunities

- Countryside Ranger p262
- Groundsperson/Greenkeeper p274
- Horticultural/Garden Centre Worker/Manager p275
- Tree Surgeon p261

Further information

Local Government Careers
www.lgcareers.com

Institute of Leisure and Amenity Management
ILAM House, Lower Basildon, Reading, Berkshire, RG8 9NE
01491 874800; www.ilam.co.uk

Convention of Scottish Local Authorities
Roseberry House, 9 Haymarket Terrace, Edinburgh, EH12 5XZ
0131 474 9200, www.cosla.gov.uk

City& Guilds

www.cityandguilds.com/myperfectjob

POULTRY WORKER

What the work involves

- Poultry workers are involved in the production of chickens, ducks, turkeys and geese for human consumption or breeding.

- Your job will be to keep the animals healthy and productive. This means feeding, watering and providing basic healthcare.

- In mechanised operations, you will keep a check on the machinery controlling their water, feed and environment.

- You will have to keep the houses and cages clean using high-pressure cleaning equipment.

The type of person suited to this work

Much of this work is repetitive, so it will suit you if you like doing the same things every day. You will be around birds, looking after their welfare and making sure they grow well. Because of worries about diseases such as avian flu you will also have to keep a check for signs of illness.

You will have to be happy handling the birds, which can be dirty work. Some birds may bite so you must be aware of your own safety.

You will need to be free of asthma and other allergies.

Working conditions

Most poultry operations are based in large purpose-designed buildings where the temperature and humidity are closely controlled. Expect there to be a lot of dust and unpleasant smells as many poultry are kept in confined areas. You will wear protective clothing and footwear and the work includes lots of bending over. You might have to do shift work.

If you work for a meat producer you will not be able to be squeamish.

Future prospects

There is a steady source of employment in this industry. Most jobs are located in the rural parts of the country. With experience you could become a unit manager.

There are more free-range and small-scale operations now, but these tend to be smaller so career progression will be more limited. Some producers breed more exotic birds such as quail and guinea fowl. There are still a lot of large poultry operations in the UK where birds are raised on a factory scale.

Advantages/disadvantages

You may spend a lot of time working on your own.

This can be noisy, dusty and smelly work.

You will be responsible for the health and welfare of the birds in your care.

Recent avian flu scares have affected the need for additional levels of hygiene and cleanliness

Qualifications and courses

There are no minimum entry requirements for this job although experience of agriculture would be helpful. Some GCSEs/S grades can be an advantage for career progression.

The Scottish Agricultural College (SAC) runs a specialist HNC in Poultry Production and there is a BTEC National Award in Agricultural Production (Poultry). Another useful qualification to have to gain a job in this sector is the National Certificate and the Advanced National Certificate run by the National Proficiency Test Council (NPTC) in Agriculture.

NVQs are available at a variety of levels including Level 1 Agriculture, Levels 2 and 3, Livestock Production (in which Poultry is incorporated) and at all three levels, Animal Care.

Apprenticeships/Skillseekers opportunities might be available if you are aged 16–24. It is possible to take full- and part-time poultry husbandry courses at local land-based colleges, although applicants are usually required to be in relevant employment. There are also independent training providers such as Progressive Poultry Training, who offer short courses to those employed in the industry.

Money guide

It is the Agricultural Wages Board that sets the minimum wage for starting work in this area. Rates of pay will vary depending on where in the country you are based and on your employer. Poultry workers receive about £12,000–£15,000 per year once they reach craftworker level.

This rises to around £16,000–£18,000 with experience.

Overtime payments may be available

Related opportunities

- Farmhand p267
- Fish Farmer p269
- Gamekeeper p271

Further information

Lantra
Lantra House, Stoneleigh Park, Kenilworth, CV8 2LG
024 7669 6996, www.lantra.co.uk

National Farmers' Union (NFU)
Agriculture House, Stoneleigh Park, Stoneleigh, Warwickshire, CV8 2TZ.
024 7685 8500; www.nfuonline.com

City&
Guilds

www.cityandguilds.com/myperfectjob

RACEHORSE TRAINER

What the work involves

- Trainers usually own or lease their stables and train horses for owners as well as owning horses themselves. Most trainers start as jockeys or assistant trainers and progress to running their own yard.

- You will have to ready the horses for races by increasing their stamina, technique and fitness. In order to do this you will have to create training regimes.

- To be successful you will work closely with all of those in your team including other professionals like vets and farriers.

The type of person suited to this work

You should have a strong interest in horse racing, a flair for business and an inherent talent for training horses. You will need the ability to communicate well and be a strong leader and manager of people.

You will have to love being around and caring for horses and have lots of patience and the right temperament to work with them.

You will need to enjoy working outside, in all weathers as this is where most of your duties will take place. You should be the kind of person who doesn't mind getting their hands dirty. You will require a certain level of fitness.

Working conditions

Much of your work will take place outdoors. In the summer months it may be hot, smelly and dusty, whereas in winter it could be cold, wet and muddy. You will also spend some time in an office environment. When riding you will wear a hard hat and a body protector. Horses can be unpredictable and so there is a certain level of risk involved. The hours are long and may include weekends. There will also be some travel involved if you are required to attend race meetings.

Future prospects

There are around 500 licensed trainers in the UK. Before you are granted a licence the Jockey Club expects several years' experience as an assistant trainer. Your success will then depend on attracting and retaining the owners of good quality horses, and lots of luck! You will need to build up a strong client base in order to progress. Owning your own successful yard may allow you to take on staff to complete some of the more mundane tasks.

Advantages/disadvantages

You really need to be a horse lover. If you are you will put up with the disadvantages!

This can be an extremely lucrative profession.

Injury risks are high in all horse activities. This could affect your long-term career security.

Qualifications and courses

ENTRY LEVEL 3

Racehorse trainers need to be licensed with the Jockey Club. There are three types of licence: a Combined Jump and Flat Licence, a Jump Only Licence and a Flat Only Licence. All candidates for a trainer's licence must hold an NVQ Level 3 in Racehorse Care and Management and should attend three one-week modules: Racehorse Management; Business Skills for Racehorse Trainers; and Staff Management.

Trainers must have spent at least 2 years in an assistant trainer position, previous experience in a racing yard or as a jockey is desirable. Some people choose to enter as a working pupil; this option is especially popular within competition yards.

Looking after horses is not a 9 to 5 job and the hours may affect your social or family life.

Money guide

As you are likely to be self-employed your earnings will depend on the size and success of your yard.

As a guide, a trainer can earn anything from £15,000 per year to over £50,000 if they are very experienced and have a good record of winning.

You will decide on your own fees and these will be dependent on a variety of factors including costs and the market rates.

Related opportunities

- Groom/Stable Hand/Stud Hand p273
- Farm Manager p266
- Farrier p268
- Shepherd/Shepherdess p283

Further information

Association of British Riding Schools
Queen's Chambers, 38–40 Queen Street, Penzance, TR18 4BH
01736 369440; www.abrs-info.org

British Horse Society
Stoneleigh Deer Park, Kenilworth, CV8 2XZ
0844 848 1666; www.bhs.org.uk

British Racing School
Snailwell Road, Newmarket, CB8 7NU
01638 665103; www.brs.org.uk

City&
Guilds

www.cityandguilds.com/myperfectjob

RSPCA/SSPCA INSPECTOR

What the work involves

Animal inspector

- You will work for an animal protection organisation or local authority offering a 24/7 service. You will undertake rescue work, but you will also visit and advise pet and animal owners.

- Other duties also include managing staff from the other public services at rescues, taking cases to court, checking conditions within animal auction houses and kennels.

Animal collector

- You will be on-call and have to be able to move quickly to rescue animals at risk, possibly from a dangerous location. This involves working alongside vets and other emergency services.

The type of person suited to this work

You will find yourself in situations that could be potentially dangerous, so you will have to be aware of your own, the public's and the animals' health and safety. Some work will be distressing, especially if you have to carry out euthanasia.

Although you will often work on your own, you may well work within a team, especially in rescue situations. You will need excellent communication skills with the ability to remain calm in a crisis.

Working conditions

Each day will be different; you could be in a factory, private house, animal establishment or outdoors up to your waist in water.

You will spend a lot of your time travelling around your area driving a van. You will probably have to work shifts including evenings and weekends.

Animals can bite and kick, especially when they are frightened, so you will have to use your skills to make sure they remain safe and that you do not put yourself at risk. You will not be able to do this work if you suffer from animal or dust-based allergies.

Future prospects

This type of work is very competitive and applicants outnumber vacancies.

Animal inspector

Inspectors can be promoted to chief inspectors and could then lead a regional team. Once qualified you can be posted anywhere in the UK.

Animal collector

With experience you can apply for related work, such as an inspector's job. You can also move into other related jobs such as local authority dog and animal warden, kennel and cattery work.

Qualifications and courses

ENTRY LEVEL 1

Animal inspector

You will need a full driving licence and experience of working with animals. GCSEs/S grades including English and a science subject are required. Physical fitness is as important as academic qualifications; you have to be able to swim 50m fully clothed. The RSPCA has its own 6-month training course including animal welfare legislation, basic veterinary training, rescue situation techniques, interview and communication techniques, animal handling and public speaking.

Animal collector

There are no formal qualifications required for this work, but GCSEs/S grades in English and science would be helpful. You need to have held a driving licence for at least 3 years and have previous experience of working with animals. The RSPCA provides on-the-job training and certificates in animal rescue techniques and providing euthanasia.

Advantages/disadvantages

You will have the satisfaction of rescuing animals that are being abused and mistreated.

Some people will be abusive and you may come across dangerous situations.

It is rewarding to know you have made a difference to the quality of animals' lives and given them a chance to be re-homed.

Money guide

Salaries will depend on the size of the employer. Starting salaries as a trainee Animal Inspector are around £15,750 per year. Fully-trained inspectors are paid from £20,0000 to £27,000 per year. Chief inspectors can earn up to £30,000 a year.

Related opportunities

- Dog Trainer/Handler p264
- Kennel Worker p276
- Trading Standards Officer p500
- Veterinary Nurse p287

Further information

Royal Society for the Prevention of Cruelty to Animals
Wilberforce Way, Southwater, Horsham, RH13 9RS
0870 333 5999; www.rspca.org.uk

Scottish Society for the Prevention of Cruelty to Animals
Braehead Mains, 603 Queensferry Road, Edinburgh, EH4 6AE
0131 339 0222; www.scottishspca.org

City& Guilds

www.cityandguilds.com/myperfectjob

SHEPHERD/SHEPHERDESS

What the work involves

- Working mainly in remote locations, you will care for a flock of sheep.

- You will be responsible for the health and safety of the animals, feed them, administer injections, clean their fleeces and make sure they remain disease free.

- You will also be responsible for keeping a record of breeding cycles as you will need to know when to arrange mating or artificial insemination. You may assist with the birthing process and look after the animals through pregnancy.

- You might also complete general tasks such as driving the tractor or maintaining the farm.

The type of person suited to this work

You must enjoy being outdoors in the countryside, working in all weathers. As you will be caring for animals, you should have an interest in the environment. If you are allergic to pollen or animals this work will be very difficult for you.

You will have to be fit and active, able to be on your feet all day and prepared to work very long hours, especially during the summer months. If your animals become ill, you will have to be prepared to be with them and administer drugs when needed. You cannot be squeamish as you may need to help with the lambing process.

Working conditions

This job involves a lot of time outdoors, so you will be out in the wind and the rain, summer and winter. The work will be dirty and smelly. Shepherding is not a 9–5 job and is very physical work. You may have to work long hours including evenings, weekends and bank holidays, particularly in lambing season. Some of your duties may involve using potentially dangerous equipment such as tractors.

Future prospects

The overall number of people employed across UK farms has dropped during the last decade to just under 300,000. This fall is due to international competition and falling prices. Fewer shepherds are now being employed and those who do find employment can expect to do general farm work duties as well. Pure shepherding jobs are generally within the most remote areas of the country and on the larger estates. Self-employment is possible as a contract shepherd caring for several flocks.

Advantages/disadvantages

You will spend a lot of time in the open air.

At some times of the year your social life may be restricted.

Your future can depend on things outside of your control such as foot and mouth disease.

Qualifications and courses

ENTRY LEVEL 1

Formal qualifications are not normally needed, but an interest or work experience in animal-based work is useful. Some employers also allow you to attend college whilst working using a day-release system.

There are short courses available covering specialist areas such as shearing and lambing at land-based colleges and further education centres across the UK. These short courses do not generally have entry requirements and most of them charge a fee for attendance.

Other courses such as those run by Edexcel (BTEC) in Agriculture and the City & Guilds NPTC National Certificates in Agriculture may also prove useful. There are generally no set entry requirements for these courses.

You might have to stay up through the night to care for animals that are ill or giving birth.

Money guide

All earnings will depend on the size and success of the farm and its location.

Many starting salaries are at the minimum wage levels. With experience this can increase from £11,000 to £13,730. The most experienced staff achieve over £20,000.

Some jobs include accommodation with subsidised rent. At busy times you may get overtime payments which can make a significant addition to pay.

Related opportunities

- Farm Manager p266
- Farmhand p267
- Gamekeeper p271
- Stockman/Stockwoman p285
- Zookeeper p290

Further information

Lantra (Sector Skills Council for the environmental and land-based industries)
Lantra House, Stoneleigh Park, Coventry, CV8 2LG
0845 707 8007; www.lantra.co.uk

Farming and Countryside Education
The National Agricultural Centre, Stoneleigh Park, Coventry, CV8 2LZ
024 7685 8261; www.face-online.org.uk

City & Guilds

www.cityandguilds.com/myperfectjob

Environment, Animals and Plants

CRCI: HA
CLCI: WAM

SKIPPER/ FISHERMAN/WOMAN

What the work involves

- You will spend anything from a few days to several weeks at sea.

- You will drop the nets, wind them in, sort the catch and then box it up. If your vessel has the facility you might help to process fish on board by gutting and filleting.

- You might keep watch, steer the ship and use winching gear. Duties may also include vessel maintenance and cooking.

- As a Skipper you will be in charge of the vessel, including health and safety, navigation, paperwork, crew management and management of business arrangements.

The type of person suited to this work

This work is very practical, physically demanding and can involve being away from home for periods of time.

As you will be at sea in dangerous and treacherous conditions, experiencing all types of weather, you should be able to cope with whatever you come up against but remain positive and focused.

Working conditions

This is a very tough outdoor job. You will be out in the wind and the rain, summer and winter getting wet and cold.

Fishing is the most dangerous industry in the UK, with big machinery and rough seas producing a combination of risks which must be treated with great caution. You will have to work long hours at sea, often for substantial periods away from home and conditions below deck may be basic and cramped. There could also be a great deal of heavy lifting and carrying involved.

Future prospects

There are two job progression routes. The first is from deckhand to ship's mate and then skipper. The other is to begin as an engineer watch-keeper and progress to second engineer, then chief engineer.

Jobs are located around the coasts of Scotland, the south-west and eastern England. Many are part of family-owned businesses which have been in existence for generations, making it difficult to find work. Some are seasonal meaning long-term security can be difficult.

Self-employment is a possibility.

Advantages/disadvantages

You will spend a lot of time onboard your boat at sea working as part of a small team.

Qualifications and courses

ENTRY LEVEL 1

New entrants must take the Marine Coastguard Agency approved basic Safety Training course. This programme consists of four one-day courses in sea survival, first aid, fire fighting and basic health and safety.

Most people enter through one of 15 Catching Sector Group Training Associations (GTAs) in the UK. The Seafish Industry Training Division also provides new entrant training programmes. Apprenticeships/Skillseekers opportunities might be available for those aged 16–24.

Skippers have to take the Marine Coastguard Agency certificates which cover different levels of competence, before they can take charge of a fishing vessel.

Open Learning Modules are available allowing fishermen, from deckhands to skippers, to develop their skills and knowledge on board rather than in the classroom.

Due to periods at sea, your social and family life may be difficult. Jobs are limited to certain locations in the UK.

Money guide

Earnings from fishing can be very variable, as pay often includes a share of the profit, which often depends on weather conditions. New entrants can expect to receive around £10,000 per year as a starting salary. With experience this can rise to up to £25,000.

Skippers are generally self-employed so their earnings will depend on the success of their team and good weather. Some very experienced skippers can earn between £40,000 and £100,000 a year.

Related opportunities

- Coastguard p540
- Fish Farmer p269
- Merchant Navy p609

Further information

Maritime and Coastguard Agency (MCA)
Seafarer Training and Certification Branch, Spring Place, 105 Commercial Road, Southampton, SO15 1EG
023 8032 9231; www.mcga.gov.uk

Scottish Fishermen's Federation
24 Rubislaw Terrace, Aberdeen, AB10 1XE
01224 646944; www.sff.co.uk

City& Guilds

STOCKMAN/STOCKWOMAN

What the work involves

- You will undertake the practical duties on a farm, caring for livestock, such as pigs, poultry, cattle and/or sheep, and possibly crops as well.

- You will be required to keep track of animals' breeding cycle in order to know when mating or artificial insemination should take place. You will also be responsible for caring for the animals through pregnancy and the birthing process.

- You may also complete general tasks such as farm maintenance.

The type of person suited to this work

You must enjoy being outdoors in the countryside, working in all weathers. As you will be caring for animals you should have an interest in the environment. If you are allergic to pollen or animals this work will be very difficult for you.

You will have to be fit and active, able to be on your feet all day and prepared to work very long hours, especially during the summer months. If your animals become ill, you will have to be prepared to be with them and administer drugs when needed.

Working conditions

This job involves a lot of time outdoors; you will be out in the wind and the rain, summer and winter. Farming is not a 9–5 job and is very physical work, you may be expected to work weekends, evenings and public holidays as animals need constant care. You can expect to work around 39 hours a week and at particular times of the year this may increase. A lot of the work you will be doing is smelly and dirty. Animals can be unpredictable and at times dangerous.

Future prospects

The main concentration of livestock farming is in the west of the UK. Experienced Stockmen/Stockwomen with training can become supervisors or unit managers without having to buy their own farms. However opportunities are scarce and promotion unlikely unless you work on a very large farm. In order to progress you can complete diplomas or degree courses. There is the opportunity to set up your own business as a farmer or farm contractor.

There are opportunities for Stockmen/Stockwomen to work abroad.

Advantages/disadvantages

You will spend a lot of time in the open air caring for living things.

At some times of the year your social life may be restricted.

You will usually be given free accommodation or subsidised rent.

Your future can depend on things outside of your control such as bird flu or foot and mouth disease.

Qualifications and courses

ENTRY LEVEL 1

Formal qualifications are not normally needed but relevant work experience is useful. It might be a good idea to do some casual work at weekends and evenings while still at school. Apprenticeships/Skillseekers may be available for those aged 16–24. The pay for these apprenticeships will vary depending on location and employer.

Qualifications in agriculture could be useful. Qualifications for livestock farming include a BTEC National Certificate or Diploma in Agriculture (Livestock) and Animal Management (Care), BTEC National Awards in Agricultural Production, NVQs at level 1 in Agriculture, levels 2 and 3 in Livestock Production and levels 1 to 3 in Animal Care, SQA National Course in Livestock Production and the National Proficiency Test Council (NPTC) National and Advanced National Certificate in Agriculture.

Money guide

These figures will vary depending on location and employer.

A stockman/stockwoman in their first year should earn at least £6,976 increasing to £13,730 with qualifications and experience. Once fully qualified and with extra supervisory responsibilities this may increase to over £20,000.

Some jobs include accommodation with subsidised rent and the possibility of overtime. The accommodation is generally an estate house or farm cottage.

Related opportunities

- Farmhand p267
- Gamekeeper p271
- Shepherd/Shepherdess p283
- Zookeeper p290

Further information

Lantra
Lantra House, Stoneleigh Park, Coventry, CV8 2LG
0845 707 8007; www.lantra.co.uk

Department for Environment, Food and Rural Affairs
Nobel House, 17 Smith Square, London, SW1P 3JR
08459 335577; www.defra.gov.uk

National Federation of Young Farmers' Clubs (NFYFC)
YFC Centre, 10th Street, Stoneleigh Park, Coventry, CV8 2LG
024 7685 7200; www.nfyfc.org.uk

City& Guilds

www.cityandguilds.com/myperfectjob

Environment, Animals and Plants

CRCI: HA
CLCI: WAM

TAXIDERMIST

What the work involves

- As a taxidermist you would make lifelike representations of animals, birds and fishes using the skin of a dead creature.

- You could spend time observing the animal in its natural environment taking photographs or drawing them.

- You would skin and cure the skin to preserve it, while keeping as much of the original colour and texture as possible.

- The body of the animal is then modelled by using a range of rather sculptural techniques, sewing and gluing pieces into place and then stretching the finished skin over the model.

The type of person suited to this work

This is very time-consuming work, which requires an understanding and appreciation of wildlife. You will have to be good with your hands, be patient and have an eye for colour and detail.

You will have good observation skills, but you will not be able to be squeamish as it can involve working on animals who have been in accidents. This can be lonely work, so you will need to like your own company.

Working conditions

You could work in your own home, within the conservation department of a museum or at a workshop. If you are working from home you will be able to do flexible hours to suit; however, if you choose to work for an employer you will probably do 37 hours, Monday–Friday.

You will use different hand tools and materials from real animal products like teeth and claws, to man-made products.

Future prospects

This is a very small profession and there are only a handful of professional taxidermists. Many people do this as a hobby rather than for employment.

You could work for a national or local museum or a national taxidermy company. If you work within a museum you might also do other conservation work with biological specimens. It is likely that you would have to move into managerial jobs to get promotion.

In recent years there has been a slight growth as opportunities abroad – particularly in the US and Africa – have become available.

Advantages/disadvantages

This combines using your artistic and practical ability with your understanding of animal anatomy.

The general public can learn a lot about species by looking at your work.

Qualifications and courses

ENTRY LEVEL 2

There are no set qualifications for this work, but at least 3 GCSEs/S grades including English, maths, art, biology and/or a technical subject or equivalent are normally needed for entry to a junior museum post in taxidermy.

Lengthy on-the-job training, by watching an experienced taxidermist, is required. Some commercial taxidermy firms may offer apprenticeships which are generally over 3–5 years.

Courses in subjects such as animal anatomy, biology, natural sciences or specimen conservation would prove useful for this work, as would good knowledge of wildlife.

If you want to be a professional taxidermist you need to register with the Department for the Environment, Food and Rural Affairs (DEFRA) and follow their strict guidelines for the collection of specimens.

The Guild of Taxidermists runs seminars and demonstrations suitable for those with some taxidermy experience. Independent taxidermists also occasionally offer short and residential courses for varying fees.

There is a 2-year Master's course in conservation offered by the Royal College of Art/Victoria and Albert Museum which specialises in natural history. Essential entry requirements are a good knowledge of natural history along with a degree in a relevant subject, such as conservation or natural sciences.

Money guide

Those who are self-employed can expect a low income that may need to be supplemented with additional part-time work. As a trainee you could expect to get around £12,000 per year. If you are employed by a museum, earnings are generally between £15,000 and £28,000. Higher salaries around £50,000 are available for senior managers.

Related opportunities

- Archaeologist p349
- Embalmer p467

Further information

Guild of Taxidermists
c/o Glasgow Museums Resource Centre, 200 Woodhead Road, South Nitshill, Glasgow, G53 7NN
0141 267 9445; www.taxidermy.org.uk

Department for Environment, Food and Rural Affairs (DEFRA)
Nobel House, 7 Smith Square, London, SW1P 3JR
020 7238 6000; www.defra.gov.uk

VETERINARY NURSE

What the work involves

- Veterinary nurses assist vets in their work by helping to treat animals suffering from disease and injury.

- As well as carrying out simple treatments such as dressings and nail trimming, you will give injections, prepare and help in the theatre and sterilise the instruments after use.

- You might also work in reception giving an initial assessment of animals, order drugs and arrange future appointments.

- Most nurses also undertake the day-to-day care of animals recovering from treatment within veterinary hospitals.

The type of person suited to this work

You will have to be passionate about animals and want to help them. To do this, you will need to learn about different diseases and treatment. Although lots of animals get better, some of this work will be sad and distressing. This means you will have to work in a practical and unsentimental way.

As much of your work will also involve working with the animals' owners, you will need to be sympathetic and have excellent communication skills to explain what is happening in the treatment.

If you do not like the sight of blood, or suffer from an animal-based allergy, this job will be difficult for you.

Working conditions

Although there are still lots of general practices that deal with small animals (dogs, cats, rabbits, etc), many more are becoming specialist centres as animal hospitals or large animal practices (cows, horses, sheep), and some are working with just horses or zoo animals. Your working conditions will depend on the type of practice you work in. You are likely to have to do emergency out-of-hours cover during evenings and weekends.

Future prospects

Due to the rise in the number of specialist practices and more organisations like the Blue Cross and RSPCA employing veterinary nurses, job opportunities are improving. If you are really keen and jobs are difficult where you live, you could try starting as a veterinary receptionist and wait for a vacancy to come up in your practice or you could gain experience with a local animal charity. 75% of all staff are female.

With experience you could progress to be a practice manager or head nurse, or move into related areas like research or work for a drugs firm.

Advantages/disadvantages

You will get to help sick animals which will rely on you for their care.

It is an interesting job with lots of variety.

Qualifications and courses

ENTRY LEVEL 3

You can follow a Veterinary Nursing training scheme recognised by the Royal College of Veterinary Surgeons (RCVS). This is available as an Apprenticeship/Skillseekers if you are aged 17–24. In Scotland, Lantra-accredited apprenticeships are available.

The scheme lasts 2 years, and consists of practical training and attendance at college. It leads to NVQs/SVQs at Levels 2 and 3 and, following 2 years' approved employment, the RCVS Certificate of Veterinary Nursing.

Entry requirements are 5 GCSEs/S grades (A–C/1–3) including English language and 2 science or maths subjects. Trainees must be at least 17. For those without these qualifications, an alternative route may be through a National Qualification in Animal Nursing Assistant, Animal Management, or the NPTC Veterinary Care Assistant National Certificate.

Candidates without the minimum qualifications can take a pre-veterinary nursing course before proceeding to the Veterinary Nursing scheme.

You can do a 3- or 4-year degree course in Veterinary Nursing, which includes the full RCVS training. A level/H grade biology is normally required. Equivalent qualifications such as National Diploma in science may also be accepted.

It can be stressful and distressing.

You may have to work irregular hours which will affect your social life.

Money guide

New entrants can expect to earn about £10,500–£12,000 per year.

With experience this rises to around £14,000–£18,000.

Head nurses generally earn £19,000–£25,000, depending on the size and type of their practice.

Related opportunities

- Dog Trainer/Handler p264
- RSPCA/SSPCA Inspector p282
- Veterinary Surgeon p288
- Zookeeper p290

Further information

British Veterinary Nursing Association
Suite 11, Shenval House, South Road, Harlow, Essex, CM20 2BD
01279 408644; www.bvna.org.uk

City&
Guilds

www.cityandguilds.com/myperfectjob

CRCI: HC
CLCI: WAM

Environment, Animals and Plants

VETERINARY SURGEON

What the work involves

- A vet treats animals that are suffering because of disease or injury. They administer vaccinations, prescribe drugs and deliver newborn animals. They also advise owners on caring for their animals.

- You might carry out surgical operations and be involved in the inspection of livestock and meat.

- Some vets work in local practices and others become specialists carrying out complex surgery on a certain part of the anatomy or become an expert for a particular animal.

The type of person suited to this work

You will need to be able to learn large amounts of complex scientific information and apply it to treating animals.

Some of your work will be sad or distressing, so you will have to work in a practical and unsentimental way. Vets have to put animals first, which includes putting them down when they are too sick or old to treat. You must have good communication skills to talk to the owners.

Working with large animals is physically demanding work, so you will need to be fit. If you dislike the sight of blood or suffer from animal allergies this job will not suit you.

Working conditions

Your working conditions will depend on the type of practice that employs you. In small-animal practice you will spend a lot of time in the surgery. Working with farm livestock and horses, you will be out on the road visiting your patients. Some of this work will be unpleasant or smelly and involve travelling long distances to get to the animals. Some of your work may be dangerous as animals can be unpredictable. You will work long hours and be on call to cover emergencies.

Future prospects

There are around 20,000 registered vets in the UK. The majority of these work in private practice.

Once you are qualified, finding a first job is not too difficult. You will normally join an established practice and would hope eventually to become a partner (effectively part-owner) of a practice. This would probably involve buying your way in.

Some vets work for the government or for firms researching and producing animal pharmaceuticals.

Advantages/disadvantages

The training is long and very competitive to enter.

It can be a very stressful but rewarding job, with lots of responsibility.

In this career you will never stop learning – more experience will make you a better vet.

Qualifications and courses

ENTRY LEVEL 6

Vets must obtain a degree in veterinary science/veterinary medicine approved by the Royal College of Veterinary Surgeons (RCVS). Normal minimum entry requirements are 3 A levels at grades AAB including chemistry and one or two from biology, physics and maths. A good range of GCSE/S grades (A*–A/1) are required.

Degree courses usually last five years but courses may include an optional additional year in which students gain an Honours degree in a related science subject. All courses include the 38 weeks of practical experience required by RCVS.

Before being able to work as a veterinary surgeon, you must register with the Royal College of Veterinary Surgeons (RCVS).

You will have to deal with the death of some of the animals you treat, including times when you put them down.

Money guide

Salaries are dependent on the type of practice you work in and its location. The figures below are a rough guide.

Newly qualified vets earn around £31,000 per year. This might also include a car and free accommodation.

With 5–10 years' experience, this rises to £40,800+ (including rewards).

A senior partner can expect to earn up to £100,000.

Related opportunities

- Animal Behaviourist p259
- Doctor p315
- Farm Manager p266
- Veterinary Nurse p287

Further information

Royal College of Veterinary Surgeons
Belgravia House, 62–64 Horseferry Road, London, SW1P 2AF
020 7222 2001; www.rcvs.org.uk

British Veterinary Association
7 Mansfield Street, London, W1G 9NQ
020 7636 6541; www.bva.co.uk

City& Guilds

www.cityandguilds.com/myperfectjob

WATER BAILIFF/KEEPER

What the work involves

- Water bailiffs work outdoors, maintaining lakes or rivers and everything that lives in them, for the purpose of legitimate recreational use.

- You'll confront two main problems in your work; breaches of the law and ecological problems.

- You will basically be a gamekeeper for water. Water bailiffs have the same powers of search and arrest as police officers. You would mostly be looking out for poachers and lawbreakers, and you'll be granted a warrant by the Environment Agency.

The type of person suited to this work

Ideally, you should be a friendly yet firm person, able to deal with members of the public effectively and politely, sometimes in difficult disciplinary situations.

An interest in the environment and working outdoors is really useful, as is knowledge of waterways. You need to be aware of the main environmental threats, and understand the basics of how ecosystems maintain themselves, and know about fish diseases and biology.

You also need to know about fishery law, not only in the UK (although this is most useful), but also at EU level. Be aware that it may even be different at local level, for example if you live in Scotland.

Working conditions

You will spend the majority of your time outside, patrolling areas either in a car, by boat or on foot.

You will usually work 37–39 hours per week, which will involve night shifts and weekends. Part time or seasonal work is also available.

The work is physical and tiring. You may have to pursue offenders across rough terrain on foot, and could find yourself wading through cold rivers and ponds. For this reason, you will probably spend your days in waterproofs, wellies, and even lifejackets.

Future prospects

Once you're working for the Environment Agency, many possibilities arise. You will have the opportunity to become a team leader within the agency, and this may lead to promotion and managerial opportunities.

Another option would be to move into related areas of work, such as fish farming or gamekeeping. Once you have a little experience in the area it will be possible to choose what interests you most, and in which direction you want your career to progress.

Advantages/disadvantages

This can be a really satisfying and exciting job, and if you're the kind of person who loves being outside and finds the idea of

Qualifications and courses

ENTRY 2 LEVEL

In England and Wales, there are no set requirements for those wishing to become water bailiffs. In Scotland, there is a training module that you need to pass, set by the Institute of Fisheries Management. In Northern Ireland, you need at least 5 GCSEs at C grade or above, and these have to include English and Maths.

Medical examinations usually need to be passed, and many people work their way into the industry by working unpaid for angling clubs to begin with.

This is a popular second career, and if you want to get into the field then any experience you can gain in gamekeeping, security work, police work, or farm work will be advantageous.

The Scottish IFM offers a course in Fisheries Management. You can choose between a one-year certificate or a two-year diploma, covering all aspects of working with fish and pondlife. You can also follow an NVQ in Fisheries Management if you choose to do so.

a desk job a nightmare, you'll probably thoroughly enjoy it. It's good if you like your own company, and that of the great outdoors.

It can be lonely, and conditions can be hard if you're not naturally a country person. You need to be prepared for all weather conditions, and work can be cold, wet, and tiring.

Money guide

Salaries vary, and can range from around £14,500 to £25,000 upwards per year.

Related opportunities

- Countryside Ranger p262
- Forestry Worker/Officer p270
- Fish Farmer p269
- Gamekeeper p271

Further information

Environment Agency
Rio House, Waterside Drive, Aztec West, Almondsbury, Bristol, BS32 4UD
08708 506506; www.environment-agency.gov.uk

Institute of Fisheries Management (IFM)
22 Rushworth Avenue, West Bridgford, Nottingham, NG2 7LF
0115 982 2317; www.ifm.org.uk

City& Guilds

www.cityandguilds.com/myperfectjob

ZOOKEEPER

Environment, Animals and Plants

CRCI: HC
CLCI: WAM

What the work involves

- You could work in a safari, wildlife or birdlife park where you would care for and treat the animals.

- You will feed the animals, look for signs of disease or injury and clean out the cages of the animals in your care.

- As zoos have changed, now placing more importance on conservation and education, some of your work could involve talking to visitors.

- You will keep records of feeding, health and behaviour and check the safety of the animals and visitors.

The type of person suited to this work

As with every job working with animals, you will have to be patient and like handling and being around them. Some of this work is physically demanding so you will have to be fit and active. Some animals you will work with could be dangerous, so you will have to respect them and be aware of your own and others' safety.

Working conditions

Your working conditions will depend on the type of animal park and the animals in your care. However, as animals require 24/7 care, you will work 5–6 days a week, normally on a shift system including early mornings, late evenings, weekends and bank holidays, especially during the busiest periods.

You will be doing physically demanding and dirty work so you will be provided with protective clothing. If you suffer from allergies this work will be difficult for you.

Some centres close for parts of the year which means your work could be seasonal.

Future prospects

There are 350 zoos and animal parks throughout the UK employing around 3000 people. Expect to move for work or promotion. Jobs can be very competitive meaning work experience is highly recommended. Many zoos offer a volunteer work experience scheme: contact your local park for details.

The work might be part time or seasonal so you may need to have additional work to supplement your earnings.

Advantages/disadvantages

This can be difficult work to enter and progress in.

The rewards can be small.

You will be working with the most unusual or exotic animals. The role of zoos as centres of breeding and supporting conservation has increased recently, so you could undertake important work.

Qualifications and courses

No specific qualifications are required although an interest in biology or natural sciences is useful. GCSEs/S grades (A–C/1–3), especially in English and science subjects, will be useful.

Previous experience of zoo work is useful, through a volunteer programme or holiday job.

General animal care and management courses available include City & Guilds Advanced Certificate in Animal Care, NVQs/SVQs in Animal Care Level 2, BTEC First Diploma and National Diploma in Animal Care, Foundation degree or BSc Honours degree in animal management.

The National Extension College runs an Animal Management course in conjunction with recognised zoological bodies including the Association of British Wild Animal Keepers (ABWAK).

Sparsholt College in Hampshire offers a Foundation degree in Zoo Resource Management for people in relevant employment.

Apprenticeships/Skillseekers opportunities may be available if you are aged 16–24.

Money guide

Pay will depend on the location and type of animal park. Many jobs include free or subsidised accommodation. As a guide salaries are likely to be £13,000 a year at trainee level. With experience, this can rise to £15,000–£16,000. Senior keepers can earn up to £25,000.

Related opportunities

- Dog Trainer/Handler p264
- RSPCA/SSPCA Inspector p282
- Veterinary Nurse p287
- Veterinary Surgeon p288

Further information

Association of British Wild Animal Keepers
Chessington Zoo, Leatherhead Road, Surrey, KT9 2NE
01372 731555; www.abwak.co.uk

Federation of Zoological Gardens of Great Britain & Ireland
Zoological Gardens, Regents Park, London, NW1 4RY
020 7586 0230; www.zoofederation.org.uk

City & Guilds

www.cityandguilds.com/myperfectjob

Healthcare

If you are keen to pursue a career in healthcare you must be compassionate and enjoy either caring for people or deciding what treatment they should receive. There is such a wide variety of jobs available in this sector simply because you can specialise in absolutely any aspect of human healthcare. Many jobs require a lot of training and you can expect to work in some highly pressurised and sometimes distressing situations. Workers in healthcare are extremely dedicated and enthusiastic about their careers, which rarely constitute a 9–5 job.

We look at the following jobs in this section:

For similar jobs to the ones in this section turn to *Science, Mathematics and Statistics* on page 503 and *Social Care and Counselling Services* on page 567.

ACUPUNCTURIST

What the work involves

- Acupuncturists work from ancient Chinese holistic guidelines. They treat medical illnesses and imbalances of energy by inserting very fine needles into identified pressure points on the human body.

- You will need to talk to patients about their problems, taking plenty of notes, in order to explore their lifestyle and emotional state, and then assess all of these factors to determine a suitable treatment.

- In addition you may carry out procedures such as burning herbs on needles, and passing small electric currents through them.

The type of person suited to this work

You must be very personable, with excellent communication skills in order to elicit trust and personal information from your patients, as well as being able to explain the techniques you are using to them.

Being comfortable with close and physical contact is also important when examining and treating your patients.

You will need an analytical mind in order to understand each patient's problem and formulate a beneficial course of treatment.

As you will probably be running your own business, you will need excellent business acumen in order to successfully take on aspects such as marketing, accounting, and administrative tasks.

Working conditions

Hours vary and tend to fit around the needs of clients. This usually involves evening and weekend work.

You could work from your own rented treatment room, from home, in your patients' homes, or in hospices, health clinics and addiction treatment centres. As you may work across a number of locations, a driving licence is really useful.

You'll usually be working on your feet, standing and bending a lot.

Conditions have to be clean and sterile, and there are strict health and safety guidelines to adhere to.

Future prospects

If you are self-employed, the success of your career depends on your reputation and marketing skills. If you build up a strong client base there are plenty of opportunities for expansion and even setting up your own health clinic.

Many practising acupuncturists choose to teach their subject, or carry out research and write articles for books and magazines.

You could work abroad, although qualifications for practice vary from country to country.

Qualifications and courses

ENTRY LEVEL 2

Careers in acupuncture usually begin with a course in the subject, and this can vary from three-year part time courses to full-time degrees that can last up to four years. Most of the institutions that offer these courses require at least 5 GCSEs and 2 or 3 A levels. Science subjects are useful.

Courses vary between institutions, but generally cover topics such as anatomy and physiology, techniques and acupuncture points, ethical issues, clinical experience, and advice on setting up a practice. Some courses are even available at postgraduate and doctorate levels.

Advantages/disadvantages

This can be a really rewarding career, especially if you like being with people and enjoy helping them.

You'll be working in a nice clean environment.

You may hear distressing stories and have insight into some upsetting personal lives, so need to be able to leave work at work.

Money guide

Earnings in acupuncture depend a lot on your situation, marketing ability, and experience.

As a newly-qualified acupuncturist starting up your own practice, you'll probably earn around £12,500 per year.

Once you've started to build up clients and gain experience, you can expect something like £18,000–£20,000 a year.

If you grow your business into a large established practice, your earnings may rise to about £40,000 a year.

Related opportunities

- Chiropractor p299
- Counsellor p571
- Homeopath p314

Further information

The Acupuncture Society
27 Cavendish Drive, Edgware HA8 7NR
0773 4668 402; www.acupuncturesociety.org.uk

The British Acupuncture Accreditation Board (BAAB)
63 Jeddo Road, London, W12 9HQ
020 8735 0466; www.baab.co.uk

British Acupuncture Council (BAcC)
63 Jeddo Road, London, W12 9HQ
020 8735 0400; www.acupuncture.org.uk

ADULT NURSE

What the work involves

- Adult nurses assess the needs of each patient in order to plan a care programme for them.

- You will observe how they progress on this treatment plan, and modify it as necessary as they improve or otherwise.

- You will also give patients practical care such as administering medicines and injections, changing dressings, and checking blood pressure.

- You could work in a variety of positions, including a community or occupational nurse, or as a healthcare assistant.

The type of person suited to this work

You will be working with patients from all sectors of the community who will have a wide range of problems, so it is essential to remain non-judgemental and sympathetic.

You will need excellent communication skills in order to interact with patients, explaining care plans and illnesses, and also calming those who are angry or distressed.

You will also need to be very practical, with good manual dexterity for undertaking precision jobs such as taking blood, and also helping patients with everyday things like washing and cooking.

Working conditions

You will usually work 37.5 hours per week, although overtime hours are available. If you are working in a hospital, these hours will encompass night and weekend shifts.

You could work in a number of locations, including hospitals, GP surgeries, prisons, hospices and in patients' homes. If you are required to travel around in the local community on a daily basis, a driving licence may be useful. Adult nurses in hospitals work in specific wards, such as intensive care or accident and emergency.

Future prospects

There is currently a shortage of trained adult nurses, so employment prospects are very good.

The majority of job opportunities lie within the NHS, although other employers include private hospitals, the armed forces, hospices and nursing homes, and the prison service.

With experience and additional qualifications, you could specialise in a subject of interest to you such as neurology or cardiology, and go on to become a nurse consultant.

UK nursing qualifications are recognised across the globe, so there are also opportunities to work abroad.

Advantages/disadvantages

Working with a wide range of people, helping them to get better or become more independent, is both rewarding and enjoyable.

Qualifications and courses

ENTRY LEVEL 5

All nurses must hold a degree or diploma in nursing that has been recognised by the Nursing and Midwifery Council (NMC). Degree courses usually require at least 3 A levels or equivalent, alongside 5 GCSEs/S grades (A-C/1–3) including English, maths and a science subject. Entry for a diploma is slightly lower at just 5 good GCSEs or equivalent. If you do not have any formal qualifications, Access courses are available in health and social care, and these will give you the experience and qualifications necessary to apply for a degree or diploma course.

Graduates with a relevant degree in biology or another health-related subject may apply for an accelerated programme, which on average lasts about 2 years.

It is also possible to join a nurse cadet Apprenticeship if you are aged between 16 and 18. These usually last 2 years and will provide you with an NVQ Level 3 or Access course pass, from which you can apply for a place on an accredited degree programme.

There are opportunities to work flexible hours or part time. Career breaks are common and the NHS runs specialist courses to get nurses who have had a break back up to speed quickly.

You may have to deal with distressed, angry or violent patients.

Money guide

As a newly qualified nurse, you can expect to earn around £17,600. With experience and additional responsibility, such as becoming a sister or charge nurse, your salary can increase to between £24,600 and £29,000.

If you specialise in a particular area and undertake the training to become a nurse consultant, you could earn up to £52,000.

Related opportunities

- Learning Disabilities Nurse p318
- Mental Health Nurse p321
- Health Visitor p313
- Hospital Doctor p315

Further information

The Nursing and Midwifery Council (NMC)
23 Portland Place, London, W1B 1PZ
020 7637 7181; www.nmc-uk.org; periodics@nmc-uk.org

Royal College of Nursing (RCN)
20 Cavendish Square, London, W1G 0RN
020 7409 3333; www.rcn.org.uk

NHS Careers
PO Box 2311, Bristol, BS2 2ZX
0845 606 0655; www.nhscareers.nhs.uk

Healthcare

CRCI: JI
CLCI: JAD

ANAESTHETIST

What the work involves

- Anaesthetists are doctors who have undergone further training in anaesthesia.

- You will prepare and administer drugs to make patients unconscious and pain free during surgery, you will monitor them during the procedure and bring them back to consciousness afterwards. You will also give local anaesthesia to specific areas of the body.

- You will also give pain relief after surgery, to seriously ill patients or during procedures such as childbirth.

- Anaesthetists also work in intensive care, resuscitation and pain management.

The type of person suited to this work

Anaesthetists need excellent communication skills to care for patients, listening to them and reassuring them about the procedures they are having. You should also be able to work well in a team with other medical staff and be able to both give and follow instructions.

You should be able to stay calm in an emergency and make decisions under pressure. You will need to be able to use complicated equipment and administer powerful drugs safely and accurately.

Finally, you must be prepared to undergo a long programme of education and training in order to gain the in-depth knowledge and skills necessary to become an anaesthetist.

Working conditions

Anaesthetists work in operating theatres, wards, clinics and accident and emergency departments within hospitals.

You will work directly with patients and as part of a medical team and will handle potentially dangerous drugs and equipment.

You will work shifts and be on an on-call rota, which includes working at nights, at weekends and on bank holidays.

Future prospects

There are opportunities throughout the UK, mainly within the NHS but also in private hospitals and clinics. Promotion to consultant posts is very competitive. Anaesthetists may work in sub-specialities such as paediatrics, obstetrics, cardiac surgery, resuscitation or intensive care.

Once fully qualified, you will probably be expected to teach and examine students and trainees and to carry out research. With experience you could move into teaching and research within medical schools.

Advantages/disadvantages

Being responsible for the safety of patients in your care and dealing with emergency situations means that this is a very demanding job.

Qualifications and courses

The initial training is the same as that required to become a hospital doctor (see p 315); candidates must complete a medical degree recognised by the General Medical Council (GMC). This requires very high A level/H grade results, including chemistry and other science subjects. Competition for a medical school place is very high.

After completing a medical degree, candidates must undergo specialist postgraduate training for around 7 years in anaesthesia, intensive care medicine and pain management while working under supervision. After completing the training programme, trainees receive a Certificate of Completion of Training (CCT) and become eligible to have their names added to the General Medical Council's register.

It is rewarding to be able to help patients through surgery and other medical procedures by giving them pain relief.

Money guide

Salary levels in the NHS may vary in different locations, the figures below are a guide.

Junior hospital doctors usually earn a supplement on top of their basic salary. Most earn £33,285 in their first year of training and £41,285 in their second year. A doctor training as a specialist could earn between £44,000 and £69,000.

Consultants can earn from £74,000 upwards.

Some senior consultants can earn up to £176,000.

Earnings are often more through private practice work.

Related opportunities

- General Practitioner p308
- Hospital Doctor p315
- Pathologist p329
- Psychiatrist p338

Further information

NHS Careers
0845 60 60 655; www.nhscareers.nhs.uk

British Medical Association
BMA House, Tavistock Square, London, WC1H 9JP
020 7387 4499; www.bma.org.uk

Association of Anaesthetists of Great Britain and Ireland
21 Portland Place, London, W1B 1PY
020 7631 1650; www.aagbi.org; info@aagbi.org

The Royal College of Anaesthetists
Churchill House, 35 Red Lion Square, London, WC1R 4SG
020 7092 1500; info@rcoa.ac.uk

AROMATHERAPIST

What the work involves

- Aromatherapists use essential oils to improve the health and well-being of clients.

- You'll be required to look into the medical history of all your clients, discussing their lifestyle, diet, exercise, allergies and stress levels.

- Using information gathered, you'll decide on blends and mixes of oils appropriate for the needs of the client.

- You will administer oils to the skin by massage, provide instructions for aftercare, and maintain records of each of your clients.

The type of person suited to this work

You must be very personable, with excellent communication skills in order to elicit trust and personal information from your patients, as well as being able to explain the techniques you are using to them.

Being comfortable with close and physical contact is also important when examining and treating your patients.

You will need an analytical mind in order to understand each patient's problem and formulate a beneficial course of treatment.

As you will probably be running your own business, you will need excellent business acumen in order to successfully take on aspects such as marketing, accounting, and administrative tasks.

Working conditions

Aromatherapists tend to be self-employed, and so working conditions vary. You could rent a treatment room in a health clinic, gym or leisure centre, work from home, or travel to patients' homes to provide treatment.

Hours depend on individual schedules and the needs and demands of clients. You should expect to work evenings and weekends. Part-time hours are a possibility.

Rooms and workspaces must be clean and quiet, and most aromatherapists tend to wear white clothes.

You will be bending, stretching, and spending most of the day on your feet.

Future prospects

Success in aromatherapy depends on effective business skills. If you build a strong client base and market your business well, your practice will grow into a successful business.

You could train in another relevant practice such as homeopathy, reflexology, or counselling, which could attract more clients.

If you like the idea of working abroad, you can even take your skills overseas. Just make sure the country you choose recognises your qualifications.

Qualifications and courses

ENTRY LEVEL 2

Professional aromatherapy training courses are the standard method of entry in to the profession, and you usually have to be 18 or over to enrol on one. If you can get some experience in a related profession like massage beforehand, this will help your application.

The General Regulatory Council for Complementary Therapies have devised national occupational standards for aromatherapy (NOS). Some courses will not qualify you for practice, so be sure that the course you choose is certified by the Aromatherapy Council.

Most courses include modules on anatomy, physiology, pathology, therapeutic relationships, along with both the theory and practice of aromatherapy. You'll also cover the practicalities of being a practising aromatherapist, from legal and ethical issues to business studies and understanding practice.

Advantages/disadvantages

This can be a really rewarding career, especially if you like being with people and enjoy helping them.

You'll be working in a nice clean environment.

There is a lot to remember in aromatherapy, so it requires a calm and intelligent person to remember all the chemicals and administer them carefully.

Money guide

Whilst the process of building up the practice is taking place, salary can be quite low – between £5,000 and £10,000 a year. This should increase to about £18,000 to £20,000 a year once you've gained some experience. Once you have a well-established practice, your annual income can range between £25,000 and £30,000.

Related opportunities

- Acupuncturist p292
- Beauty Therapist p459
- Homeopath p314

Further information

Institute for Complementary and Natural Medicine (ICNM)
Can-Mezzanine, 32–36 Loman Street, London, SE1 0EH
020 7922 7980; www.i-c-m.org.uk

The General Regulatory Council for Complementary Therapists (GRCCT)
Office 6, Slington House, Rankine Road,
Basingstoke, RG24 8PH
0870 3144031; www.grcct.org

Healthcare

CRCI: JA
CLCI: JOD

ART/DRAMA/MUSIC THERAPIST

What the work involves

- Therapists use all kinds of art to help clients who may have difficulty in expressing themselves through the medium of words.

- You may work closely with people suffering from mental health problems, emotional problems, or those with drug and alcohol addiction, helping them to recover. People with speech and language difficulties also benefit from art therapy.

- You will create a safe environment where patients feel free to express themselves and their feelings and move on positively.

The type of person suited to this work

If you want to work with people with emotional and psychological difficulties, you need to be a calm, caring, understanding and trustworthy person.

You will need a lot of patience, excellent communication skills, and a very sensitive nature.

These skills need to be combined with strong artistic ability: you have to be a creative thinker prepared to take on the responsibility of helping clients who may be in a great deal of emotional pain. An interest in all forms of art is also essential.

If you plan on starting your own business, you'll need good marketing and accounting skills.

Working conditions

These depend on who you choose to work for. If being employed by the NHS appeals to you, hours are likely to be 37.5 per week, with weekends free.

If you work in private practice, your hours will vary and will probably include evenings and weekends.

If you're an art therapist, you'll probably have to travel around to give therapy, so a driving licence is really useful. You could work in hospitals, prisons, clinics and community centres.

Surroundings for therapy must always be warm, light and comfortable, so you can expect this to be your working environment.

Future prospects

If you work for yourself, you can grow and expand your business by building up a solid client base and making good contacts.

If you choose to work for the NHS, you could be promoted to management positions, becoming a specialist, head of profession, or consultant.

You might decide you'd like to specialise within a particular area, such as mental health of palliative care. Alternatively, you could combine art therapy with another complementary treatment such as psychotherapy.

Qualifications and courses

Most people who choose to go into Art Therapy have a first degree in art and design or a related subject but all have taken a Master's degree in the subject. Make sure you enrol on one that has been approved by the Health Professions Council. You must be at least 23 at time of entry. To apply for a Master's, you will need a strong portfolio, and at least a year's experience in working in health, education or social care. Institutions sometimes consider graduates from other disciplines, notably psychology and teaching.

Master's degree courses last two years full-time, or four years part-time. Many areas are covered, including psychodynamics, psychopathology of art, contemporary art therapy and practice skills.

You will have to have art therapy yourself as part of training, and will also be expected to spend 120 days on clinical placement during the course.

Advantages/disadvantages

If you have both a love of art and a desire to help people this will prove a very rewarding career. Opportunities for progression are good, and experiences can be enriching and very fulfilling; there will never be a boring day at work.

You will have to deal with people who are in pain or mentally unstable, which can be extremely upsetting.

Money guide

In the beginning, you will earn about £24,000 a year working for the NHS, probably less through setting up your own practice. As you gain experience this figure will rise to about £38,000 a year. If you get into a management or supervisory role, you can earn around £45,000 a year.

Related opportunities

- Clinical Psychologist p570
- Counsellor p571
- Learning Disability Nurse p318

Further information

The British Association of Art Therapists (BAAT)
24–27 White Lion Street, London, N1 9PD
020 7686 4216; www.baat.org

Health Professions Council (HPC)
Park House, 184 Kennington Park Road, London, SE11 4BU
020 7582 0866; www.hpc-uk.org

NHS Careers
PO Box 2311, Bristol, BS2 2ZX
0845 606 0655; www.nhscareers.nhs.uk

AUDIOLOGIST

What the work involves

■ Audiologists examine patients to identify and assess hearing and balance disorders.

■ As an audiologist, you will use specialist equipment to test patients and assess their problems and needs.

■ You will also fit hearing aids and give treatment and advice to patients on how to improve and manage their conditions.

■ Audiologists usually work in one of four main areas: paediatrics, adult assessment and rehabilitation, special needs groups, and research and development.

The type of person suited to this work

As an audiologist you will need to speak clearly and be easily understood by people who are lip reading. You will need to be a caring person with excellent communication skills to deal sensitively with patients of all ages and backgrounds, listening to them and explaining the tests and procedures you are doing. You should also be flexible and able to work as part of a team.

You will need to be practical to operate specialist equipment and take a logical, scientific approach to your work and be able to assess patients' needs and conditions correctly, keep accurate records and provide solutions and practical help.

Working conditions

Most audiologists work as part of a hospital team but you could also be based in a clinic or visit patients in their homes or in care homes or schools. You could also be involved in teaching and research work in a university.

You will probably work Monday to Friday but could have to be on call and cover shifts including nights, weekends and bank holidays.

Future prospects

Audiology is a rapidly developing area of healthcare, there is a shortage of qualified staff so job prospects are good.

There are opportunities within the NHS throughout the UK. There are also jobs available in research and in private hospitals.

You could specialise in one area such as paediatrics or adult rehabilitation.

Within the NHS you could progress to higher grades, where you will have more responsibility including managing and training others.

Advantages/disadvantages

Working face to face with patients can be challenging.

Qualifications and courses

The professional qualification for audiologists is a 4-year BSc degree in audiology. The entry requirements for an audiology degree are 3 A levels/5 H grades or equivalent including at least 1 science subject, maths or psychology.

You will spend the first 2 years of the course at university. During year 3, you will work in a placement in an audiology setting. The final year will be spent back at university learning about more advanced aspects of audiology.

It is also possible to enter this profession with a degree in another appropriate subject and a Master's in audiology. Relevant degree subject areas include medical sciences, life sciences, physical sciences, or mathematical/applied sciences. The best entry route into the MSc is as an NHS regionally funded trainee.

It is satisfying to use your knowledge and skills to improve people's hearing and balance conditions. A National Study of Hearing showed that about 16% of the population have a significant hearing loss, so work in this field is important.

Money guide

The NHS sets rates for audiologists. There are extra payments available, for example if you work in London.

Trainees start on NHS band 5: £20,225–£26,123 per year. Once qualified this rises to band 7: £29,091–£38,352.

Senior posts have a salary range at bands 8–9 of £37,106–£93,098.

Related opportunities

■ Occupational Therapist/Occupational Therapy Support p323
■ Physiotherapist p334
■ Rehabilitation Worker (Visually Impaired) p583
■ Speech and Language Therapist p341

Further information

NHS Careers
0845 60 60 655; www.nhscareers.nhs.uk

British Academy of Audiology
PO Box 346, Resources for Associations, Association House, South Park Road, Macclesfield, Cheshire, SK11 6SH
01625 504066; www.baaudiology.org; admin@baaudiology.org

British Society of Audiology
80 Brighton Road, Reading, Berks, RG6 1PS
01189 660622; www.thebsa.org.uk; bsa@thebsa.org.uk

Healthcare

CRCI: JF
CLCI: JOB

CHILDREN'S NURSE

Healthcare

CRCI: JI
CLCI: JAD

What the work involves

- Children's nurses work specifically with babies and young people up to the age of 18.

- You will also be working closely with the parents and family of your patients, providing support, education and advice on treatment and care plans.

- You will take medical histories from children and their families, devise a care plan for them with the help of other medical professionals, and record their treatment procedures and outcomes in detailed records.

- You will also have to carry out procedures such as checking blood pressure, taking temperatures, dressing wounds and taking blood samples.

The type of person suited to this work

You will need to be a very warm, approachable person in order to gain the trust of young patients and their families, who will be understandably concerned about each child. At the same time, you must be highly professional and authoritative at times in order to handle difficult children.

You should be a patient teacher, as you will need to demonstrate treatment techniques to both your patients and their parents or carers. You will also need to motivate them to continue treatment at home.

Working conditions

On average, you will work 37.5 hours per week and this will usually include early morning, evening, night and weekend work as part of a shift-based rota. Part time and flexible hours are commonly available.

You could work in children's wards within NHS hospitals, in specialist hospitals, hospices and GP surgeries. You may also work in various locations throughout the community such as visiting patients at home, or in care homes and schools.

You will usually be required to wear a uniform and suitable sterile clothing for certain procedures, such as gloves and an apron.

Future prospects

As you gain experience, you can undertake further training and specialise in a certain area such as neurological or cardiovascular conditions in children. You could eventually become a nurse consultant.

Alternatively, you could apply for team leadership roles such as sister, or move into general NHS management.

Advantages/disadvantages

Working with children, helping them to get better, managing their treatment and easing their suffering, is extremely rewarding.

Qualifications and courses

All nurses must hold a degree or diploma in nursing that has been recognised by the Nursing and Midwifery Council (NMC). Degree courses usually require qualifications of at least 3 A levels or equivalent, alongside 5 GCSEs/S grades (A-C/1–3) including English, maths and a science subject. Entry for a diploma is slightly lower at just 5 good GCSEs or equivalent, as above.

If you do not have any formal qualifications, Access courses are available in health and social care, and these will give you the experience and qualifications necessary to apply for a degree or diploma course.

Graduates with a relevant degree in biology or another health-related subject may apply for an accelerated programme, which on average lasts about 2 years.

It is also possible to join a nurse cadet Apprenticeship if you are aged 16–18. These usually last 2 years and will provide you with an NVQ Level 3 or Access course pass, from which you can apply for a place on an accredited degree programme.

There are plenty of opportunities to work part time in order to fit your job around your own family commitments.

It can be upsetting to deal with distressed children.

Money guide

Starting salaries for newly qualified children's nurses are around £19,000. As you gain experience, this will increase to between £24,000 and £32,000. With increasing seniority, you could earn around £40,000. Nurse consultants can earn as much as £60,000.

Related opportunities

- Adult Nurse p293
- Learning Disabilities Nurse p318
- Speech and Language Therapist p341
- Occupational Therapist p323

Further information

The Nursing and Midwifery Council (NMC)
23 Portland Place, London, W1B 1PZ
020 7637 7181; www.nmc-uk.org; periodics@nmc-uk.org

Royal College of Nursing (RCN)
20 Cavendish Square, London, W1G 0RN
020 7409 3333; www.rcn.org.uk

NHS Careers
PO Box 2311, Bristol, BS2 2ZX
0845 606 0655; www.nhscareers.nhs.uk

CHIROPRACTOR

What the work involves

- Chiropractors work with joints, bones and muscles, using hands and other physical tools, as opposed to drugs, in order to treat patients.

- You could treat a variety of ailments, including back and neck problems, joint stiffness, postural and muscular complaints, headaches and sports injuries.

- Techniques include massage, movement, and applying ice or heat to troublesome areas.

- You will also need to carry out full patient examinations, listen to their concerns and complaints, and record detailed notes of each consultation.

The type of person suited to this work

You should have exceptional communication skills, as you will need to listen to patients carefully in order to understand their complaint, and explain the techniques you are using to them simply.

You will need to be professional and approachable in order to inspire confidence and trust in your patients.

Good organisation and commercial awareness are essential if you are to run your own successful business.

Working conditions

Working hours are usually the standard 9 to 5 from Monday to Friday, although some flexibility may be required to suit the needs of clients. Many clinics and practitioners are increasingly offering early morning, evening, and weekend appointments.

Most chiropractors work either in a specialist clinic, a doctor's surgery, at home or at the houses of their clients. This means you could be working alongside other chiropractors or healthcare professionals, or alone.

It is a physically demanding job, so you will have to ensure your own fitness levels remain high in order to avoid work-related injuries.

Future prospects

The chiropractic profession is gaining medical credibility and growing rapidly, so there are increasing opportunities within the sector but also an increasing number of graduates competing for clients.

Most chiropractors are self-employed or work in private practice. A few are employed by the NHS.

Numerous options are open to you as you gain experience. You could choose to specialise in a specific area, such as children or sports injuries, you could set up your own practice, or you could teach.

Advantages/disadvantages

Each day you will be meeting new people and relieving their physical aches and ailments, which gives great job satisfaction.

Qualifications and courses

ENTRY LEVEL 5

In order to practise as a chiropractor, you must complete a degree course that has been recognised by the General Chiropractic Council (GCC). You must be 18 years old to start training, and entry requirements are at least 3 A-levels/Highers or equivalent, including biology or another related subject. For candidates who do not meet these requirements, year-long preliminary courses are available as an entry route to the full degree.

More mature applicants, looking to move into chiropractic as a second career, are considered for degree courses without the usual entry qualifications providing they have relevant experience or knowledge of science.

You must undergo an Advanced Criminal Records Bureau check prior to acceptance on a course, as you will be working with children and vulnerable adults.

Being self-employed can be extremely stressful. Your earnings are dependent on the number of clients you attract, which can vary greatly from month to month. You will also have to do your own administration, including filling out complicated tax forms.

Money guide

Newly-qualified chiropractors may earn up to £20,000, although if you are self-employed this figure could vary depending on your initial success in attracting clients.

With experience and once you have built a good reputation, your salary could rise to £40,000.

Once you are in a senior position, either as a partner or running your own practice, you could earn £70,000+.

Related opportunities

- Osteopath p327
- Physiotherapist p334
- Massage Therapist p319

Further information

General Chiropractic Council (GCC)
44 Wicklow Street, London, WC1X 9HL
020 7713 5155; www.gcc-uk.org; enquiries@gcc-uk.org

British Chiropractic Association (BCA)
59 Castle Street, Reading, RG1 7SN
0118 950 5950; www.chiropractic-uk.co.uk;
enquiries@chiropractic-uk.co.uk

City& Guilds

www.cityandguilds.com/myperfectjob

Healthcare

CRCI: JB
CLCI: JOD

CLINICAL/BIOMEDICAL ENGINEER

What the work involves

- Clinical engineers design and maintain medical equipment such as scanners, x-ray machines, pacemakers, heart rate and blood pressure monitors, equipment for surgery, and instruments used in medical research.

- You would work on testing equipment, and collaborate with hospital staff installing and teaching them how to use the equipment.

- All kinds of engineers, from physicists to computer scientists, work on many different parts of the process.

The type of person suited to this work

If you're looking to go into this field, you need to have a natural interest in both electronic and mechanical engineering, and in health and medical issues.

Along with this interest, you'll need to be skilled in engineering and have in-depth knowledge of your subject.

You should be good at problem solving, and be used to keeping up to date with developments in the science and medical research world.

Working conditions

You could work in a hospital or laboratory, depending on the nature of the work. Those working in hospitals might have to work on-call, and are often on standby duty; laboratory hours tend to be more fixed.

The usual working hours for clinical engineers are Monday to Friday, and you would normally be working 37.5 hours a week.

A driving licence is useful, as this job often involves a lot of travel, whether between different hospitals or even overseas: this is relatively common in this industry.

Future prospects

There are good opportunities for progression and promotion for clinical and biomedical engineers.

With the right experience, you can move into management and senior management jobs, and if you're working for the NHS you could be promoted to consultant level. If you don't want to stay with the NHS, you can look for jobs with medical equipment manufacturers.

Advantages/disadvantages

This career requires real skill and education, and it can be a really rewarding experience building up this knowledge, studying for your degree, and putting it into practice.

You're helping people by building and maintaining medical equipment, and doing a job that's really worthwhile.

Qualifications and courses

ENTRY LEVEL 5

You will need either a first class or 2.1 degree in a subject such as mechanical, electronic or electrical engineering. A degree in physical or engineering science may be acceptable, as might a degree related to medicine. Most degree course providers require entrants to have at least 3 A levels or equivalent, including maths and physics.

Mature students without relevant qualifications may be considered if they have significant work experience in this area. An Access course is also a way in for mature students.

Once employed, you will probably start training in a large teaching hospital. Graduate recruitment schemes are available, most of which last 4 years with the final two spent specialising in a particular area. Upon finishing the first 2 years of the course, you're awarded a Postgraduate Diploma, then after at least 4 years in a training post you can apply to be a member of the Health Professions Council.

You can also consider working towards chartered engineer status.

It can be stressful at times, and working in a hospital environment won't suit everybody.

Money guide

Starting salaries are usually around £23,000 a year for an NHS trainee.

If you become a state registered clinical scientist with the NHS, this will probably increase to something between £28,000 and £36,000.

If you work your way up to a senior position, you'll be on the same wage as consultants, and might be earning anything between £36,000 and £88,000.

Related opportunities

- Biotechnologist p508
- Clinical Scientist p512
- Medical Physicist p320

Further information

Association of Clinical Scientists
c/o The Association for Clinical Biochemistry,
130–132 Tooley Street, London, SE1 2TU
020 7940 8960; www.assclinsci.org

Clinical Scientist Recruitment Centre
239 Thorpe Park, Peterborough, PE3 6JU
0871 433 3070; www.nhsclinicalscientists.info

CRITICAL CARE SCIENTIST

What the work involves

- Critical care scientists support other medical staff caring for critically ill patients by maintaining and operating life-support equipment in intensive care units.

- As a critical care scientist, your work will include setting up equipment, taking readings and checking the equipment is working correctly.

- You will work closely with patients and their relatives.

- You will also need to keep detailed reports of all your work.

The type of person suited to this work

You will need maturity and excellent communication skills to work with patients and their relatives at a time of intense stress, and be able to explain things simply and clearly. You will need to be practical with good technical skills to operate complex equipment and will need to be able to concentrate and pay attention to details for long periods of time as patients' lives will depend on your skills. You will need to be able to work as part of a team, follow instructions accurately, take responsibility and be able to remain calm and work quickly under pressure.

Working conditions

Critical care scientists mainly work as part of a team in the intensive care unit of a hospital using specialist equipment and machinery.

You will need to work to strict health and safety regulations ensuring that infections and diseases are safely contained.

You will need to work shifts on a rota basis, which includes nights, weekends and bank holidays.

Future prospects

This is a small but growing profession with opportunities within the NHS throughout the country. Job prospects are good as there is a shortage of applicants for job vacancies.

You may progress your career by applying for higher grades. The higher grade posts involve more responsibility for managing and training others.

Many critical care technologists are involved in research and teaching, as well as in practice.

Advantages/disadvantages

Working under pressure in emergency situations is emotionally and physically demanding.

It is extremely rewarding to help patients recover.

You will have a varied working day, be using your technical skills and have contact with patients.

Qualifications and courses

There are no formal entry requirements, but most hospitals expect a good general education and may prefer 4 GCSEs/S grades (A–C/1–3). Critical care technology is moving towards becoming a degree-entry career.

Many candidates enter with higher qualifications, for example A levels, Advanced Highers or a BTEC National qualification in science subjects or electronics.

Degrees in life sciences, science, maths or electronics are a good grounding for this type of work. A degree in physiological measurement is available.

Trainee technicians follow a 2-year training programme based in a hospital with day-release to a local college. Qualifications include a BTEC National Certificate in Science: Medical Physics and Physiological Measurement or NVQ/SVQ Level 3 in Medical Physics and Physiological Measurement.

Apprenticeships/Skillseekers may be available to those between the ages of 16 and 24.

Money guide

The NHS sets pay rates for critical care technologists (on the sterile services technician pay scale).

Critical care scientist trainees earn up to £17,257 per year. Once qualified and with experience this rises to £25,829.

Specialists can earn up to £33,436.

As a team manager you could get £36,719.

There are extra payments available, for example if you work in London.

Related opportunities

- Audiologist p297
- Medical Physicist p320
- Sterile Services Technician p343
- Operating Department Practitioner p324

Further information

Skills for Health
2nd floor, Goldsmiths House, Broad Plain, Bristol, BS2 0JP
0117 922 1155; www.skillsforhealth.org.uk;
office@skillsforhealth.org.uk

NHS Careers
0845 60 60 655; www.nhscareers.nhs.uk

Society of Critical Care Technologists
6 South Bar, Banbury, Oxfordshire, OX16 9AA
023 8079 6123; www.criticalcaretech.org.uk

Healthcare

CRCI: JF
CLCI: JOB

DENTAL HYGIENIST/ THERAPIST

Healthcare

CRCI: JC
CLCI: JAF

What the work involves

- Dental hygienists and therapists are predominantly concerned with oral hygiene, teaching patients how to look after their teeth and gums in order to prevent decay and disease.

- You will carry out a variety of dental processes, including scaling and polishing teeth, putting in or replacing fillings, taking impressions and X-rays, and applying protective coatings to teeth to prevent decay.

- You will be using a range of dental instruments, including scraping devices and drills.

The type of person suited to this work

You will need to have excellent communication skills as the majority of your time will be spent dealing with patients of all ages, advising them on oral care and explaining useful techniques.

You will need to combine good scientific knowledge with a personable approach to your work in order to motivate patients and convince them to stick to new dental routines.

You will need good eyesight and precise manual skills so that you can carry out close dental work with delicate instruments.

Working conditions

You will usually work a 37 hour week from Monday to Friday, although occasional evening and Saturday morning work may be required according to practice opening hours. Part-time work is available.

Dental hygienists and therapists are most commonly based in practices and surgeries, but you could also be employed by the Community Dental Service (CDS) in which case you can expect to travel to see patients in various locations such as schools, residential homes or community centres.

You will have to wear a white coat or tunic and appropriate safety equipment.

Future prospects

There is currently a shortage of hygienists and therapists, so employment opportunities are plentiful and prospects good.

Although the majority of hygienists and therapists work in dental surgeries, you could also work for the CDS, in a hospital, or for the Defence Dental Agency (DDA) who provide dental treatment for the British Armed Forces all over the globe.

You could become self-employed and work across several practices, undertaking part-time hours in each.

Money guide

Recent graduates can expect to earn between £20,000 and £26,000 in their first few years as a hygienist or therapist.

Qualifications and courses

You will need to register with the General Dental Council (GDC) prior to working as a dental hygienist or therapist. To do this, you will need to pass a qualification that is approved by them, such as a Diploma in dental hygiene, a combined Diploma in dental hygiene and therapy, or an approved degree. Entry requirements for the Diploma/degree courses are at least 5 GCSEs/S grades (A-C/1–3) or equivalent, including English, maths and a science related subject, plus 2 A-levels. Some dental schools may accept a GDC recognised qualification in dental nursing in place of A-levels.

Since you will be working with both children and vulnerable adults in the course of your career as a hygienist or therapist, you will also need to have a Criminal Records Bureau check prior to commencing any course.

Once you have gained 3–5 years' experience, you could earn from £24,000-£38,000.

If you work in private practice and have considerable experience and a good reputation, you could earn up to £45,000.

Advantages/disadvantages

You will be working with a variety of people on a daily basis which creates diversity in the working day. Knowing you are improving their dental hygiene and comfort is also rewarding.

You may come across nervous or anxious patients who may be difficult to reassure and calm down.

Related opportunities

- Dentist p305
- Dental Technician p304
- Orthodontist p326

Further information

British Society of Dental Hygiene & Therapy (BSDHT)
3 Kestrel Court, Waterwells Business Park, Waterwells Drive, Quedgeley, GL2 2AT
0870 243 0752; www.bsdht.org.uk; enquiries@bsdht.org.uk

British Dental Association (BDA)
64 Wimpole Street, London, W1G 8YS
020 7935 0875; www.bda.org; enquiries@bda.org

NHS Careers
PO Box 2311, Bristol, BS2 2ZX
0845 6060 655; www.nhscareers.nhs.uk

City& Guilds

www.cityandguilds.com/myperfectjob

DENTAL NURSE

What the work involves

- Dental nurses assist dentists in all aspects of clinical life and patient treatment.

- You will be expected to prepare the surgery each day and for each patient, ensuring that all instruments are to hand and sterilised ready for use.

- You will also assist in dental procedures by holding suction devices in the patient's mouth, ensuring that they are comfortable throughout their treatment, and giving patients pre- and post-operative advice.

- You may also take responsibility for the day to day running of the surgery, including maintaining stock and ordering equipment, and undertaking some administrative duties.

The type of person suited to this work

You should have excellent interpersonal skills as you will be dealing with patients on a daily basis, many of whom may be anxious about forthcoming treatment and in need of kindness and reassurance.

Good eye-sight and manual dexterity are helpful when aiding in procedures, as is a calm approach to jobs and the ability to react quickly and calmly to unforeseen situations.

As you will be working closely with a dentist and other colleagues, you will need to enjoy being part of a team environment.

Good time management and organisational skills are necessary in order to fulfil the range of duties you will be expected to undertake.

Working conditions

You will usually work from 8am to 5:30pm Monday to Friday, and some evening or weekend work may be required. Part-time work is often available.

If you work in a hospital, you may be asked to remain on-call over weekends and provide emergency cover at any time of day or night.

Dental nurses are also employed by the salaried primary care dental service (SPCDS) to work in local communities, assisting with patient care in various locations such as mobile clinics, schools and residential homes.

You will have to wear a uniform, and relevant safety equipment such as surgical gloves and a face mask.

Future prospects

Once qualified, you could continue your studies in order to gain further qualifications that will allow you to take on additional responsibilities such as sedation of patients and radiography.

Another option is to train to become a specialist orthodontic dental nurse, or a dental hygienist.

Some dental nurses also move into teaching roles and train student nurses.

Qualifications and courses

ENTRY LEVEL 2

Although there are no set qualifications needed to become a student dental nurse, recent legislation from the General Dental Council (GDC) stipulates that entrants need to study for recognised qualifications. Many of these courses require GCSEs/S grades (A-C/1–3) in English, maths and a science subject for entry.

Qualifications recognised by the GDC are the Certificate of Higher Education in dental nursing, the City & Guilds Level 3 Award in dental nursing, the SQA Level 3 in dental nursing, the National Examining Board for Dental Nurses (NEBDN) National Certificate examination, or a Certificate of Proficiency in dental nursing from a recognised dental hospital.

The Armed Forces also offer several routes into dental nursing.

Advantages/disadvantages

You will be working in pleasant, clean environments helping to treat patients and maintain a high standard of dental care across the UK.

Hours are usually standard and regular, with the opportunity to work part-time for a better work/life balance.

Money guide

These salaries are based on those found in the NHS, and they may vary according to your employer and the location in which you work.

Student dental nurses can start on a salary of between £15,000 and £17,750.

Once qualified, you could expect to earn between £17,000 and £21,000.

If you reach a more senior position, such as team leader or nurse specialist, your earnings could rise to £26,000-£33,000.

Related opportunities

- Dentist p305
- Dental Hygienist/Therapist p302
- Nurse p293
- Healthcare Assistant p576

Further information

British Association of Dental Nurses (BADN)
PO Box 4, Room 200, Hillhouse International Business Centre, Thornton-Cleveleys, FY5 4QD
01253 338 360; www.badn.org.uk; admin@badn.org.uk

General Dental Council (GDC)
37 Wimpole Street, London, W1G 8DQ
020 7887 3800; www.gdc-uk.org ; CAIT@gdc-uk.org

City& Guilds

www.cityandguilds.com/myperfectjob

Healthcare

CRCI: JC
CLCI: JAF/JAD

DENTAL TECHNICIAN

What the work involves

- Dental technicians make and repair dental accessories such as braces, crowns and false teeth. You could work across all three areas, or specialise in just one.

- You will follow detailed prescriptions, written by a doctor or dentist, in order to create individual, patient-specific appliances.

- You will use a variety of materials for crafting each device, including gold, steel, porcelain and plastic.

- You will also use numerous technical instruments in order to accurately carve, mould or wire each accessory.

The type of person suited to this work

You will be producing extremely delicate, precise devices so you will need excellent manual dexterity, good eye-sight and full colour vision.

It helps to have some artistic ability so that you can make items such as false teeth and crowns look at natural and aesthetically pleasing as possible.

You will need to be able to concentrate on a task for lengthy periods of time, and maintain a high level of accuracy throughout.

You should also be comfortable understanding and interpreting complex technical instructions in order to create them as 3D devices.

Working conditions

You should expect to work between 37–40 hours per week. Hours usually fall on weekdays but if you work in a hospital dental unit you may have to work evenings and weekends to cover emergency clinics.

You will be working in a laboratory, either within a hospital, dental practice, or independent commercial facility.

You will be expected to wear protective clothing and safety equipment when undertaking certain tasks.

Future prospects

Dental technicians usually work for commercial laboratories that produce equipment for a number of different practitioners in an area. These range in size from smaller businesses to large companies.

Other employers include hospital dental units, the Royal Army Dental Corps (RADC), the RAF, and the Royal Navy. There is also the option to be self-employed, although this is relatively uncommon.

Within larger companies, prospects for promotion are good.

Advantages/disadvantages

You will have job satisfaction in knowing you are producing high quality dental devices to improve a patient's dental health or appearance.

Qualifications and courses

You will need to register with the General Dental Council (GDC) prior to working as a dental technician, and to do this you need to pass a qualification that is recognised by them. These include the BTEC National Diploma, a foundation degree, or a BSc (Hons) degree in dental technology.

Entry requirements for the BTEC National Diploma are at least 4 GCSEs/S grades (A-C/1–3) or equivalent, including English, maths and a science related subject. For a foundation degree in dental technology, you will need 4 GCSEs/S grades (A-C/1–3) or equivalent, and an A-level. Entry requirements for a BSc (Hons) course are 5 GCSEs/ S grades (A-C/1–3) or equivalent, and 2 A-levels including a science related subject.

You can work as a trainee in a laboratory or hospital whilst you study to obtain a relevant qualification that will enable you to register as a practising dental technician.

The Armed Forces recruit dental technicians, but you will need to be fully qualified at the time of applying, and be under 29 years of age.

Later entrance for older applicants is common in this profession, and you will need to obtain the same qualifications as those of recent school leavers.

It is not the most sociable job in the world. Although you will be working in a laboratory with other professionals, you will be responsible for you own projects and have no patient contact.

Money guide

As a newly-qualified dental technician, you could expect to earn in the region of £20,000-£26,000.

With experience you could earn up to £30,000, and if you specialise in a particular area this could increase further to between £33,000 and £35,000.

As a senior technician, you could earn around £40,000.

Related opportunities

- Dentist p305
- Dental Hygienist/Therapist p302
- Dental Nurse p303
- Orthodontist p326

Further information

The British Institute of Dental and Surgical Technologists
4 Thompson Green, Shipley, West Yorkshire, BD17 7PR
0845 644 3726; www.bidst.org

www.cityandguilds.com/myperfectjob

DENTIST

What the work involves

- Dentists are trained to recognise, diagnose and treat all problems that affect the teeth, gums and mouth.

- You will examine teeth and carry out appropriate treatments, such as fitting or replacing fillings, scraping away plaque, polishing and removing teeth, as well as educating patients about good oral habits in order to prevent disease or decay.

- You will also need to keep detailed dental records for each patient, alongside managing your staff and, if you are a practice manager, looking after the practice budget.

The type of person suited to this work

You will need to have excellent communication skills in order to inspire your team and build good relationships with your patients, who will represent all ages, sectors and backgrounds.

You should also be compassionate and sympathetic, as you will encounter patients who are nervous or anxious about their treatment and you will need to be able to soothe and reassure them.

You will need good eye-sight, concentration and manual dexterity to successfully carry out complicated and delicate procedures.

If you intend to run your own practice, you will also need good business acumen.

Working conditions

If you work in a dental surgery, you should have regular Monday to Friday hours, and may even enjoy some flexibility within this framework.

Dentists who work in hospitals will usually work longer hours, including weekends, and will have to adhere to an on-call rota.

You could work across the community, travelling to provide treatment in locations such as schools and retirement homes.

You will need to wear protective, hygienic clothing such as a white coat and surgical gloves when dealing with patients.

Future prospects

Most dentists are self-employed, working in general practice across the UK. Some work for the NHS, and some take on a mixture of private and NHS patients. A recent surge in dental graduates has increased competition in this sector. There is still demand for graduates across the UK, but this is mostly within the NHS which is viewed by some as a less lucrative career move than private practice.

You could undertake further training to specialise in a field such as orthodontics or maxillofacial surgery.

Advantages/disadvantages

The majority of dentists are self-employed and work in the private sector, so you have a good amount of control over the hours you work and the patients you see.

Qualifications and courses

There are 14 dental schools that offer degrees approved by the British Dental Association (BDA) with the standard degree programme lasting 5 years. You will need at least 3 good A-levels/Highers or equivalent qualifications, including chemistry and biology. GCSE/S grade results may also be taken into account, and at least 8 passes (A-C/1–3) are required for consideration.

If you have good A level results, but not in the required subjects for entrance onto the degree course, you can apply for a 6 year programme that includes an initial 30 week course that will get you up to speed in chemistry, physics and biology.

If you have already completed a degree in another subject it is possible to take an accelerated degree lasting only 4 years. To qualify for entry, you will need to have achieved at least a 2.1 in your first degree, and have relevant qualifications in biology and chemistry.

There are excellent opportunities for rapid career progression or further training if you want to specialise in a specific area.

You will mainly be undertaking routine check-ups and very standard procedures, so work can feel monotonous at times.

Money guide

Salaries for recently graduated, trainee dentists in general practice start at around £28,000. If you start your career in the NHS, your salary will be slightly lower at about £26,000.

Experienced dentists in general practice can earn £80,000+, especially if they run their own surgery.

If you reach consultant level in a hospital, your salary could exceed £95,000.

Related opportunities

- Orthodontist p326
- Dental Hygienist/Therapist p302
- Dental Nurse p303
- Dental Technician p304

Further information

British Dental Association (BDA)
64 Wimpole Street, London, W1G 8YS
020 7935 0875; www.bda.org; enquiries@bda.org

The General Dental Council
37 Wimpole Street, London, W1G 8DQ
0845 222 4141; www.gdc-uk.org; CAIT@gdc-uk.org

NHS Careers
PO Box 2311, Bristol, BS2 2ZX
0845 606 0655; www.nhscareers.nhs.uk

ENTRY LEVEL 6

Healthcare

CRCI: JC
CLCI: JAF

DIETITIAN

What the work involves

- Dietitians use their scientific knowledge of food to provide information and advice about diet and nutrition.

- As a dietitian, you will give advice to a broad range of people, such as hospital patients, caterers, sports professionals and the general public.

- You will help people improve their health and prevent disease by making changes in their diet.

- Dietitians prevent and treat food-related disorders, illnesses and diseases. Some work in industry developing food products and others in the media.

The type of person suited to this work

Dietitians need to be able to develop expert knowledge of the science of nutrition and how the body works. They must also have excellent communication skills to be able to give practical information and advice to a range of people from school children to food manufacturers.

If you are working with patients, you will need to be caring, supportive and non-judgemental, and able to understand the needs and issues of individual patients. You should also be able to motivate people so that they can follow your advice and make the changes that you recommend.

Working conditions

You may work in a range of locations such as hospitals, laboratories, offices and sports centres.

You are likely to work a normal working week from Monday to Friday, although in hospitals you may be called in to work at weekends and on bank holidays.

In most jobs you will be working directly with patients who can be ill, distressed or reluctant to take your advice.

Future prospects

The British Dietetic Association (BDA) has over 5000 members, and the profession is growing. There are opportunities across the UK and abroad but jobs can be competitive.

A lot of dietitians work in the NHS, but there are also many opportunities in areas like sports nutrition, the food and pharmaceutical industries, scientific research, education and journalism. You could become self-employed working as a consultant or seeing private clients.

In the NHS, you could go on to specialise in areas such as cancer care, or with particular groups such as children or the elderly. You could also move into management.

Advantages/disadvantages

People may be unable or unwilling to take on your advice, which can frustrating.

Qualifications and courses

To become a dietitian, an approved degree or postgraduate qualification (PgDip/MSc) in dietetics or human nutrition and dietetics is required. You must then register with the Health Professions Council in order to practise in the NHS. You will need 2–3 A levels/3 H grades including chemistry and another science and 3 GCSEs/S grades (A–C/1–3) including English and maths, or equivalent, for entry to a degree in dietetics.

Entry requirements for a postgraduate diploma are typically an Honours degree in a science subject with an acceptable level of biochemistry and human physiology, along with a good command of spoken and written English.

Mature applicants can complete an Access course in science to be accepted into a degree programme.

Some institutions expect applicants to have visited a dietetic department before applying for a place.

It is rewarding to see improvements in people when they put into practice the information and advice you have given them.

Money guide

Starting salary for an NHS dietitian is around £20,225, rising to £26,123 per year.

Salaries for senior grade dietitians can be £29,091–£38,352.

A district chief dietitian can earn up to £45,000 and a consultant £50,000+.

There are higher grades for chief members of staff, or for work outside the NHS. There are also additional payments available, for example if you work in London.

Related opportunities

- Health Visitor p313
- Health Promotion/Education Specialist p310
- Sport and Exercise Scientist p342
- Food Scientist/Technologist p518

Further information

Skills for Health
2nd floor, Goldsmiths House, Broad Plain, Bristol, BS2 0JP
0117 922 1155; www.skillsforhealth.org.uk;
office@skillsforhealth.org.uk

NHS Careers
0845 60 60 655; www.nhscareers.nhs.uk

British Dietetic Association
5th Floor Charles House, 148–9 Great Charles Street, Queensway, Birmingham, B3 3HT
0121 200 8080; www.bda.uk.com; info@bda.uk.com

DISPENSING OPTICIAN

What the work involves

- Dispensing opticians use prescriptions from optometrists to supply and fit glasses.

- The work includes measuring the patient's face to ensure the glasses will fit and advising on lenses and frame styles to suit them and their prescription.

- The optician checks the finished glasses meet the original specifications and supplies them to the patient and will also do repairs.

- Some dispensing opticians take further training to supply and fit contact lenses.

The type of person suited to this work

You will need to be able to develop the scientific knowledge needed to interpret prescriptions.

You will need good communication skills to listen and talk to patients of all ages and backgrounds when advising them, and to work well in a team with other staff such as optometrists. Manual skills are important for taking measurements and for adjusting and repairing glasses.

If you run your own opticians business, you will also need sales and business skills.

Working conditions

Most dispensing opticians work in high-street opticians. Some run their own practices so have to deal with the financial and management challenges of being self-employed.

You may work 35–40 hours a week from Monday to Friday, but will probably have to work on Saturdays as well (with some time off during the week instead).

Future prospects

This is a growing field with most dispensing opticians working for high-street companies. There is also some work available in hospitals.

With experience, you may specialise, for example in supplying and fitting contact lenses or low vision aids.

You may also be promoted into a management position within a high-street optical chain. With experience, some opticians choose to run their own practices. Success in this depends on a good choice of location and strong business skills.

Advantages/disadvantages

It can be stressful having to meet sales targets in some opticians.

If you enjoy combining scientific knowledge with working with the public, this job could be good for you.

Money guide

Salary levels vary enormously and are usually higher for opticians with management responsibility for an outlet within an optical chain.

Qualifications and courses

ENTRY LEVEL 2

In order to practise as a dispensing optician, you must be registered with the General Optical Council (GOC). To qualify for full registration, you must complete an appropriate training course, pass the Professional Qualifying Examinations of the Association of British Dispensing Opticians (ABDO), and undergo a pre-registration year working under the supervision of a qualified optician.

There are a number of training routes available. It is possible to study full time before starting work. You could take a 3-year degree course in optical management, ophthalmic dispensing, or a related area. Alternatively, 2-year diploma courses or Foundation degrees in ophthalmic dispensing are available. Typical entry requirements for a degree or Foundation degree are 2 A levels/3 H grades, normally including relevant science subjects, and 5 GCSEs/S grades (A–C/1–3) including English, or equivalent. For a diploma, you will normally need at least 5 GCSEs/S grades (A–C/1–3) including English, maths and a science, or equivalent.

It is also possible to start work as a trainee with a qualified optometrist and work towards part-time qualifications. ABDO offers a 3-year distance learning course and certain colleges offer a 3-year day-release programme for those in suitable employment. Typical entry requirements are 5 GCSEs/S grades (A–C/1–3) including English, maths and a science, or equivalent. ABDO runs a series of Access courses for those lacking these qualifications.

ABDO also offers a Continuing Education and Training (CET) scheme for qualified opticians.

Starting salaries are around £16,000 per year which can rise to around £40,000 per year.

Some dispensing opticians can earn up to £80,000.

Related opportunities

- Optometrist p325
- Pharmacist p330

Further information

NHS Careers
0845 60 60 655; www.nhscareers.nhs.uk

Association of British Dispensing Opticians
199 Gloucester Terrace, London, W2 6LD
0207 298 5100; www.abdo.org.uk; general@abdo.org.uk

General Optical Council
41 Harley Street, London, W1G 8DJ
020 7580 3898; www.optical.org; goc@optical.org

City & Guilds

www.cityandguilds.com/myperfectjob

Healthcare

CRCI: JJ
CLCI: JAL

GENERAL PRACTITIONER

What the work involves

- General Practitioners (GPs) diagnose various health problems, physical or emotional, within their local community.

- You will be talking to and examining patients in order to find out what is wrong with them, and then deciding on how to treat them. This could include giving them advice, prescribing medicine or referring patients to a specialist doctor.

- You may occasionally have to perform minor surgery such as removing moles or warts.

- You are responsible for educating your patients about how to live a healthy lifestyle and prevent illness.

The type of person suited to this work

You will need to have excellent communication skills in order to gain the trust of your patients and build good relationships with them. You should be able to put them at their ease quickly whilst maintaining a professional attitude.

You must have excellent scientific and medical knowledge in order to assess problems quickly and reach a suitable diagnosis, all within the time limit of a 15 minute appointment.

You should have an enquiring mind as you will need to continually update your knowledge and learn about new techniques and medicines in order to keep up-to-date in this fast moving discipline.

Working conditions

You will usually work normal hours from Monday to Friday, although increasingly surgeries are offering evening and weekend appointments which you may have to cover on a rota basis.

GPs are practice-based in small or large surgeries within cities, towns and rural areas.

You may also have to spend some time on call, visiting patients at home at any hour of the day or night.

GPs have to adhere to time and budget constraints, which can make the work stressful and demanding.

Future prospects

As a general practitioner you will be able work anywhere in the UK, in a larger practice with healthcare professionals from a number of disciplines, or a smaller surgery.

As the healthcare system evolves, there is opportunity for GPs to becoming increasingly involved in directing how health is promoted in their local community.

You could undertake work for the NHS, enjoy the freedom of self-employment, or opt for a combination of the two.

Advantages/disadvantages

The training period prior to qualifying as a GP takes, on average, 10 years.

Qualifications and courses

To become a GP you must first take an undergraduate degree in medicine with the standard programme lasting 5 years. You will need at least 3 good A-levels/Highers or equivalent, including chemistry and biology. Most medical schools also require applicants to sit the UK Clinical Aptitude Test (UKCAT).

If you do not have science A-levels, some universities offer a 6 year programme that includes an initial 'pre-medical' 30 week course that will get you up to speed. If you already have a 2.1 degree in another subject, some medical schools offer an accelerated degree in medicine lasting only 4 years.

On completion of your degree, you will then undertake 2 years on a Foundation programme of work-based training, which includes placements in a number of specialist areas such as surgery, paediatrics and general medicine. You must then complete a further 3 years' training in hospital and practice environments before qualifying for a place on the GP register.

Dealing with a number of patients with varying complaints each day can be stressful, but helping them to recover is rewarding.

Money guide

During your Foundation years in a hospital, you could expect to earn about £21,000, plus additional extras for working longer hours or nights. Once you are in training as a GP, this should rise to between £29,000 and £45,000 depending on your experience level.

Qualified, salaried GPs can earn between £50,000 and £80,000. If you are self-employed this could rise to £80,000–£120,000.

Related opportunities

- Hospital Doctor p315
- Surgeon p344
- Pharmacist p330

Further information

Royal College of General Practitioners
14 Princes Gate, London, SW7 1PU
0845 456 4041; www.rcgp.org.uk; careers@rcgp.org.uk

British Medical Association (BMA)
BMA House, Tavistock Square, London, WC1H 9JP
020 7387 4499; www.bma.org.uk

General Medical Council (GMC)
Regent's Place, 350 Euston Road, London, NW1 3JN
0845 357 3456; www.gmc-uk.org;

City&
Guilds

www.cityandguilds.com/myperfectjob

GP PRACTICE MANAGER

What the work involves

- Practice managers run local doctors' surgeries and health centres.

- As a practice manager, you will be responsible for managing finances, resources and staff.

- Your work may include duties such as managing reception and clerical staff, organising patients' records, controlling the stock of equipment and supplies, monitoring budgets, planning new services and arranging work rotas for staff.

- You may have responsibility for more than one practice.

The type of person suited to this work

Practice managers have a range of management skills. You will need to be able to lead and motivate staff, supervise and organise their work, solve problems as they arise, make decisions and manage financial information and budgets. ICT skills are also useful.

You must also have a responsible attitude, because you will be dealing with confidential patient information. Good communication skills are important for working with doctors, nurses, other staff and patients.

Good business sense and a commitment to delivering a high level of healthcare to patients in the local community are also essential, as well as decision-making and planning skills.

Working conditions

You are likely to be based in an office within a surgery or health centre, but you may work in more than one practice, so a driving licence is useful.

You will work normal working hours from Monday to Friday, though you may need to work longer hours if you are busy.

General practices and clinics can be very busy working environments with many different activities demanding your attention.

Future prospects

There are employment opportunities for practice managers in NHS surgeries and health centres throughout the UK.

With experience you may progress to more senior posts, for example running a larger practice. It may also be possible to move into other areas of health service management, such as in hospitals or health authority offices.

Alternatively, you could use your skills to progress into management careers outside of healthcare.

Advantages/disadvantages

This is a high level, responsible job so can be stressful and demanding.

Qualifications and courses

There are no formal requirements for entry to this career, but experience as an administrator or manager in a health or social care setting is essential, which means that most new entrants are in their mid-to-late twenties or older. Qualifications in management or a related area can also be an advantage.

People in posts as practice managers or assistant practice managers can work towards the main professional qualification in this field, the Association of Medical Secretaries, Practice Managers, Administrators and Receptionists (AMSPAR) Diploma in Primary Care Management.

Candidates for the Diploma must be educated to Level 3 (A level/H grade, National Certificate/Diploma or equivalent). Candidates should normally have 2 years' relevant experience.

It is satisfying to be able to run a practice effectively and efficiently, to provide a good working environment for staff, and to give good service to patients in the local community.

Money guide

Salary levels in the NHS are set each year; those below are a guide only.

The starting salary for managers of a small practice is around £21,000–£28,000 per year.

Managers in a group practice can earn up to £33,000 and senior practice managers can earn £70,000 depending on size and location of the practice.

There are extra payments available, for example if you work in London.

Related opportunities

- Accountant p16
- Company Secretary p26
- Health Service Manager p312
- Human Resources Officer/Manager p41

Further information

NHS Careers
0845 60 60 655; www.nhscareers.nhs.uk

Association of Medical Secretaries, Practice Managers, Administrators and Receptionists
Tavistock House North, Tavistock Square, London, WC1H 9LN
020 7387 6005; www.amspar.co.uk

Institute of Healthcare Management
18–21 Morley Street, London, SE1 7QZ
020 7620 1030; www.ihm.org.uk; enquiries@ihm.org.uk

Healthcare

CRCI: JE
CLCI: CAL

HEALTH PROMOTION / EDUCATION SPECIALIST

What the work involves

- Health promotion/education specialists aim to promote public health.

- You could work with organisations such as schools or directly with individuals, groups or communities or could be developing community policies.

- Your work might include advising individuals on how to make lifestyle changes such as taking more exercise or giving up smoking, encouraging organisations like workplaces, schools and hospitals to improve diets and promote health, and developing partnerships with communities to improve public health.

- You could also be responsible for putting together materials to promote healthy living and working with the press and the media.

The type of person suited to this work

As a health promotion/education specialist you will need to be able to encourage and motivate individuals and communities. Good communication and negotiation skills are important for working with people from school children to community members and policy makers.

You should be able to research information, write clear reports and think of imaginative ways to encourage people and organisations to make changes. You will need to be understanding, supportive and non-judgemental and able to relate to the needs and problems of a wide range of people, communities and cultures. You will also have to have good organisational skills to run and manage projects.

Working conditions

You may work in a range of locations such as health centres, local authority buildings, hospitals, workplaces and fitness centres.

You are likely to have a normal working week from Monday to Friday. Some employers offer flexible working schemes.

The job often involves travel to and attendance at meetings, for example at local schools or community groups.

Future prospects

There are around 2000 health promotion specialists in the UK and public health is a priority for the government. Jobs can be very competitive though and you will probably need to do work experience.

Most health promotion/education specialists work for the NHS, health promotion agencies, local authorities, or in social and community settings. You can progress to management roles or go into research and lecturing in health promotion.

Advantages/disadvantages

Changing people's habits can be difficult and take a long time.

Seeing improvements in public health when people put into practice the information and advice you have provided is very rewarding.

Qualifications and courses

Entrants to this field need a degree. This can be in any discipline, but courses in health promotion, health studies, public health, social science, environmental health or related subjects provide an advantage. Entry requirements for degrees are usually a minimum of 2 A levels/3 H grades. More senior posts generally require a postgraduate diploma or MSc in Health Promotion.

It may be possible to train on the job for recognised qualifications. The Open University offers certificates in Health Promotion and Promoting Public Health: Skills, Perspectives and Practice. Some colleges run a Health Studies Access Course, which gives candidates the entry requirements needed to study in higher education.

It is possible to enter the profession through related fields. It is advisable to undertake relevant voluntary work in order to gain experience.

The Society of Health Education and Health Promotion Specialists (SHEPS) maintains a voluntary register for specialists in this field, and recommends degree and postgraduate courses to its members.

This job can provide the chance to work with many different people.

Money guide

Pay varies among employers.

In the NHS starting salaries when qualified are £19,683–£31,779 per year.

More experienced and senior staff can earn up to £38,000 and managers £60,000+.

With some employers, there may be extra payments available, for example if you work in London.

Related opportunities

- Dietitian p306
- Environmental Health Practitioner/Officer p35
- Health and Safety Inspector p40
- Youth and Community Worker p591

Further information

Faculty of Public Health
4 St Andrews Place, London, NW1 4LB
020 7935 0243; www.fphm.org.uk; enquiries@fph.org.uk

NHS Careers
0845 60 60 655; www.nhscareers.nhs.uk

Society of Health Education and Health Promotion Specialists
School of Health and Policy Studies, UCE, Birmingham, B42 2SU
0121 331 5511; www.hj-web.co.uk/sheps

HEALTH RECORDS CLERK

What the work involves

■ Health administrators and records clerks are responsible for preparing and maintaining records of patients' medical notes, including details about the medicines they take and any other care needs.

■ You will be collating, organising and archiving relevant notes and documents in each patient's file, and also ensuring that they are easily accessible for other healthcare professionals.

■ You will be working with both paper documents and electronic records, which will include using equipment such as computers, photocopiers and scanners.

■ You will also undertake other administrative duties, such as making and rearranging patients' appointments, sorting incoming correspondence and covering reception from time to time.

The type of person suited to this work

You will be working within a team of healthcare professionals as well as dealing with patient enquiries, so you should be personable and have excellent communication skills.

You will need a good level of numeracy and ICT skills as much of the work involves handling numerical information and working with various computer programs. As you will be dealing with a variety of tasks each day, you will need to have good organisational skills and be able to prioritise your workload.

You will be working with confidential information so must be discreet at all times.

Working conditions

You will usually work a 37 hour week from Monday to Friday, although occasionally some jobs require employees to work shifts. Part-time opportunities are common.

As you will be moving and transporting large, heavy piles of paper files around the hospital or practice, you will need to be reasonably strong and fit.

The majority of the work is office-based, although you may need to courier documents to various departments within your building. You will be expected to look fairly smart, although a business suit is unnecessary.

Future prospects

Although the NHS is the biggest employer of administrative staff, there are also opportunities in smaller GP surgeries, private hospitals and voluntary organisations.

Increasingly, the NHS is providing a more structured career path for administrators. This means you could progress to a supervisory or managerial role within your department, move sideways to work in another branch or hospital, or move into supporting a specialist area such as neurology or gastroenterology.

Qualifications and courses

ENTRY 2 LEVEL

For entrance into employment as a health authority administrator or health records clerk, most employers require candidates to have at least 5 GCSEs/S grades (A-C/1–3) or equivalent, including English and maths.

You could take the society, health and development Diploma for added understanding of the industry prior to starting employment, as an additional qualification.

Apprenticeships may also be available for candidates aged 16–24. These are regulated and monitored by Skills for Health and Skills for Care.

If you have administrative experience, employers usually look more favourably on your application.

As you will be working with children and vulnerable adults, you will need to get clearance from a Criminal Records Bureau (CRB) check prior to commencing employment.

Advantages/disadvantages

You will be providing an essential service to both patients and other healthcare professionals by ensuring the smooth running of behind the scenes operations.

You can expect to have a heavy workload at times.

Hours are regular and there is plenty of opportunity for part-time work which fits in around family commitments.

Money guide

The starting salary for a health authority administrator or health records clerk usually starts from £12,000–£14,000. As you gain experience over a few years, this should rise to between £15,000 and £18,000. If you move into a more senior supervisory or management position, you can expect to earn up to £30,000.

Salaries do vary according to your employer and where you work in the UK. Some employers offer additional benefits such as a pension scheme.

Related opportunities

■ Nurse p293
■ Pharmacy Technician p332
■ Health Visitor p313

Further information

Institute of Health Record and Information Management
744A Manchester Road, Castleton, Rochdale, OL11 3AQ
01706 868 481; www.ihrim.co.uk; ihrim@zen.co.uk

City&
Guilds

www.cityandguilds.com/myperfectjob

Healthcare

CRCI: JE
CLCI: CAL

HEALTH SERVICE MANAGER

What the work involves

- Health service managers are responsible for the delivery of healthcare services, e.g. you may run a hospital or be responsible for managing a section of the hospital, such as surgery or medicine.

- You could work in a specialist role such as human resources or financial management, or you might oversee the delivery of services in a whole regional health authority.

- Your tasks might include managing staff, organising day-to-day work, setting budgets and allocating resources.

The type of person suited to this work

You will need to be able to plan delivery of services, organise work, solve problems as they arise, analyse financial information and plan projects.

Good verbal and written communication skills are important for working with colleagues at all levels and for report writing.

You should be committed to delivering a high level of healthcare to patients and able to take responsibility and make difficult decisions.

Working conditions

You are likely to be based in an office, but you may need to travel to meetings, so a driving licence is useful.

You will work normal working hours from Monday to Friday, but will probably have to work longer hours and may have to be on call in the evenings and at weekends on a rota basis.

This role often involves managing people, which can be very demanding.

Future prospects

There are opportunities for health service managers all over the UK, mainly within the NHS. The NHS Graduate Scheme recruits graduates to intensive training schemes in General Management, Human Resources and Finance. Competition for entry to these schemes is fierce. There are also jobs available in private hospitals and with the Armed Forces.

With experience, you can progress to more senior posts. You will usually need higher management or specialist qualifications to gain promotion and will probably have to move area.

Experienced health service managers can go on to become consultants or use their skills to enter other management careers outside of healthcare.

Advantages/disadvantages

You will have to deal with a variety of tasks at once, so the work can be pressured and demanding.

It is rewarding to know that you are playing an important role in delivering a high level of care to patients.

You will gain valuable skills and the NHS offers a range of career options.

Qualifications and courses

ENTRY LEVEL 4

It is possible to join the NHS at an administrative level and progress into management. Entry at this level is usually with at least 4 or 5 GCSEs/S grades (A–C/1–3) or equivalent. Many health service managers enter the profession from other roles in the NHS having gained sufficient experience and qualifications. Others gain managerial experience elsewhere before moving into the NHS.

You can apply for a place on one of the NHS graduate management training schemes. Entry requires a 2.2 degree in any discipline or a postgraduate qualification. The General Management Training Scheme in England and the NHS Scotland Management Training Scheme last for 2 years and lead to a Master's in Healthcare Leadership and Management. The Financial Management Training Scheme lasts up to 40 months and leads to a professional accountancy qualification with the Chartered Institute of Management Accountants (CIMA) or the Chartered Institute of Public Finance and Accountancy (CIPFA). The Human Resources Management Training Scheme lasts 2 years and leads to a Postgraduate Diploma in Human Resources and graduate membership of the Chartered Institute of Personnel and Development (CIPD).

Money guide

The starting salary for a health service manager is around £20,000 per year.

Salaries for experienced managers vary according the type of job and level of responsibility, ranging from around £35,000 to £70,000+.

Chief executives can earn £120,000+.

Related opportunities

- Accountant (Public Sector) p16
- GP Practice Manager p309
- Human Resources Officer/Manager p41
- Records Manager p350

Further information

NHS Careers
0845 60 60 655; www.nhscareers.nhs.uk

Institute of Healthcare Management
18–21 Morley Street, London, SE1 7QZ
020 7620 1030; www.ihm.org.uk; enquiries@ihm.org.uk

NHS Graduate Management Training Scheme
www.futureleaders.nhs.uk

City&
Guilds

www.cityandguilds.com/myperfectjob

HEALTH VISITOR

What the work involves

- Health visitors are vital members of the healthcare profession, working with people from all ages, backgrounds and cultures in various settings such as residential homes, schools, GP surgeries and village halls.

- You will provide advice on all sorts of issues ranging from problems in children's sleep or feeding patterns, to postnatal depression, bereavement, or relationship problems.

- You will also be involved in organising community events designed to promote health and wellbeing.

The type of person suited to this work

You will be working closely with patients and within a team of healthcare professionals, so you will need excellent communication skills.

You must be trustworthy, understanding, reassuring and professional in order to inspire confidence in your patients and allow them to share their problems and concerns with you openly. You should also be able to motivate them to make important lifestyle changes on occasion.

You must be able to prioritise a heavy workload, and maintain discretion when dealing with confidential information.

Working conditions

You will usually work a 37 hour week from Monday to Friday, and flexible hours or part-time work are often available. You will work in a variety of locations, including schools, GP surgeries, health centres and residential homes. Because this will require a good deal of travelling within the local area, a driving licence is usually required.

You will encounter patients who are extremely difficult or distressed at times, which can be stressful and upsetting.

Future prospects

All health visitors work for the NHS, and they can be based in larger areas such as cities and towns, or work across villages and rural communities.

Career progression could take the form of managing a team of health visitors, moving into a role as a consultant nurse, specialising in a particular area of nursing, education or research, or even taking up a position in general management within the NHS.

Advantages/disadvantages

You will be offering healthcare advice and treatment across the community, including to those who may otherwise not be able to reach a doctor or hospital very easily such as the elderly.

There are opportunities to work part-time or on a job share basis, which would allow you to work around other commitments.

You may have to deal with difficult, potentially threatening patients, which can be frightening and upsetting.

Qualifications and courses

All health visitors must be registered nurses or midwives. To become a nurse or midwife, you must complete either a degree or diploma in nursing that is recognised by the Nursing and Midwifery Council (NMC). Generally, you will need 5 GCSEs/S grades (A-C/1–3) or equivalent, and 2 A-levels. The degree course lasts 3 or 4 years. Entry requirements for a diploma course are slightly lower at 5 GCSEs/S grades (A-C/1–3) or equivalent. Full time diploma courses last 3 years.

It may also be possible to undertake an apprenticeship or similar training scheme. Those available are Young Apprenticeships (for candidates aged 14–16), Apprenticeships and Advanced Apprenticeships (for entrants aged 16–24). Most apprenticeships last 2 years, during which you will gain an NVQ Level 3 in nursing. This would give you the qualifications necessary to study for a full diploma course. Access courses are also available to those without the necessary entry requirements.

Once you have completed your training as a nurse, you will need to undertake a further degree-level course in public health nursing. These last 1 year full time, or are available as a 2 year part-time option.

Money guide

The starting salary for a newly qualified health visitor is usually around £22,000.

Once you have gained a few years' experience, this will rise to £25,000–£30,000.

Senior health visitors, who have supervisory or managerial duties across a team, can earn around £36,000.

Related opportunities

- Occupational Therapist p323
- Nurse p293
- Paramedic p328
- Midwife p322

Further information

Nursing and Midwifery Council (NMC)
23 Portland Place, London, W1B 1PZ
020 7637 7181; www.nmc-uk.org; advice@nmc-uk.org

Royal College of Nursing (RCN)
20 Cavendish Square, London, W1G 0RN
020 7409 3333; www.rcn.org.uk

City&
Guilds

www.cityandguilds.com/myperfectjob

ENTRY LEVEL 5

Healthcare

CRCI: JI
CLCI: JAD

HOMEOPATH

What the work involves

- Homeopaths use highly dilute doses of natural remedies to treat patients for a variety of ailments ranging from simple headaches to complicated emotional issues, addiction and disease.

- You will need to take into account not only patients' physical symptoms, but also their psychological and emotional state, as well as their lifestyle.

- You will be working with a variety of patients of all ages, backgrounds and cultures.

- You could undertake general cases, or specialise in areas such as fertility and drug addiction.

The type of person suited to this work

You will need excellent communication and listening skills in order to quickly build a rapport with patients and encourage them to discuss their problems and concerns honestly.

As you will need to build your own practice and find clients from scratch, you must have good business acumen, confidence and motivation.

You should also be well-organised and methodical, as you will need to undertake your own administration and keep detailed, informative patient notes.

Working conditions

You will be self-employed and reliant on your clients, so will find that you mainly work at evenings and weekends (especially when newly qualified) in order to fit around their lifestyles.

You could work in a clinic with other healthcare professionals, in an alternative therapy centre, in your own home, or you could travel to see patients in their houses.

Patient appointments can take anywhere between 45 minutes and an hour and a half, so the work is mentally and emotionally draining. Because of this, most homeopaths only work part-time.

Future prospects

Alternative therapy has increased in popularity in recent years. This means that there are more people willing to explore it as a means of treatment, but also that there are an increasing number of practising homeopaths. Competition for clients, especially in the early years, can be great.

The majority of homeopaths are self-employed, although there are opportunities in independent surgeries, private hospitals, and in one of the 5 homeopathic NHS hospitals in the UK. With experience you could use your knowledge to teach in a university or college, or write related books and articles.

Advantages/disadvantages

Spending time talking to patients about their concerns and alleviating their ailments is extremely rewarding.

Qualifications and courses

ENTRY LEVEL 5

Although it is not yet compulsory to hold any qualifications in order to practise homeopathy, it is unlikely that you will attract many patients if you are not registered with one of the UK regulatory bodies, the most well known of which is the Society of Homeopaths.

In order to register, you will need to complete an accredited degree or diploma which leads to the qualification of Licentiate in Homeopathy. Entry requirements for a diploma will usually require 5 GCSEs/S grades (A-C/1–3) or equivalent, and a degree will need at least 2 A-levels in addition to good GCSEs. Degree courses can be taken full time over 3 years, or part time over 4.

Qualified healthcare professionals can undertake shorter accredited courses in homeopathy at various universities, each of which is regulated by the Faculty of Homeopathy.

If you are self-employed, overheads such as renting clinic space and buying remedies and other equipment will eat into your earnings.

You must be commercially aware in order to successfully market your business, and be prepared to do your own complicated tax forms.

Money guide

Most homeopaths charge their patients directly by appointment. They usually ask between £35 and £65 per hour. A newly qualified homeopath who is just starting to build a reputation and attract clients could earn between £6,000 and £10,000.

With a few years' experience, this could rise to £25,000. At the highest end of the profession, you could earn up to £60,000.

Related opportunities

- Acupuncturist p292
- Chiropractor p299
- Osteopath p327
- Aromatherapist p295

Further information

The Society of Homeopaths (SOH)
11 Brookfield, Duncan Close, Moulton Park, Northampton, NN3 6WL
0845 450 6611; www.homeopathy-soh.org; Info@Homeopathy-Soh.Org

British Homeopathic Association
Hahnemann House, 29 Park Street West, Luton, LU1 3BE
0870 444 3950; www.trusthomeopathy.org; info@britishhomeopathic.org

Alliance of Registered Homeopaths (ARH)
Millbrook, Millbrook Hill, Nutley, TN22 3PJ
01825 714 506; www.a-r-h.org; info@a-r-h.org

HOSPITAL DOCTOR

What the work involves

- Hospital doctors work in either NHS or private establishments, diagnosing illnesses, treating patients and monitoring their care.

- You may treat patients yourself or, having assessed them, refer them to their GP or another healthcare professional.

- You will work in one of over 60 specialisms, which include cardiology, general medicine, paediatrics, orthopaedics and psychiatry.

- You will also be required to carry out surgical operations within your specialism, for example fitting a pacemaker if you are in cardiology. You may also be responsible for teaching medical students.

The type of person suited to this work

You must have excellent communication skills as you will be dealing with both patients and other healthcare professionals on a daily basis.

When handling patients, you should be empathetic, non-judgemental, professional and down to earth.

You should be good at working under pressure, making sensible decisions and solving problems whilst thinking on your feet.

You will need a good academic understanding of science and medicine so that you can apply this knowledge to patients to accurately and effectively solve their complaints.

Working conditions

Generally you can expect to work longer hours than in most other professions, although new guidelines prohibit doctors from working more than a 48 hour week. You will usually work on a shift pattern of days and nights, and will need to be on call on occasion.

You will be working in a consulting room, on the wards and in operating theatres. Conditions are usually quiet and clean, although things can get very fast paced during times of emergency.

You will also be required to attend numerous meetings and conferences across the UK, Europe, and perhaps the world.

Future prospects

Once you have completed your 2 year foundation period as a junior doctor, you can choose to follow a specialist subject such as gastroenterology or geriatric medicine. You will then follow a training programme in your specialism in order to pass the necessary exams to become a consultant.

Increasingly, senior level hospital doctors undertake managerial responsibilities, alongside teaching and mentoring work with students or junior doctors.

Qualifications and courses

ENTRY LEVEL 5

All entrants to become a hospital doctor need to hold a degree in Medicine, earning the qualification of a Bachelor of Medicine and Surgery. Courses normally last five years and you will need at least 3 A-levels including chemistry and biology, along with good GCSEs/S grades (A-C/1–3) or equivalent, including English, maths and science to gain entry.

If you don't have the relevant A levels, some universities offer a 6 year medical degree, the first year of which consists of a 30 week course designed to get you up to speed. Graduates from another discipline could also apply for a 4 year, fast-track medical degree programme.

Once you have gained your first degree, you will need to complete a 2 year foundation programme within a hospital, where you will gain on-the-job experience of a number of specialist fields. On completion of this, you can begin training as a hospital doctor in your chosen area.

Advantages/disadvantages

You will be responsible for finding out what is wrong with people, helping them get better, and making them comfortable throughout their illness, which is very rewarding.

Hours can be long and unpredictable, so it can be difficult to get a satisfactory work life balance.

Continuous developments in medicine and medical technology mean that you will be continually learning and developing throughout your career.

Money guide

Starting salaries for junior doctors in their foundation years range from £20,700 to £25,800. Once you are in speciality training, you will earn between £29,000 and £44,000, depending on which stage you have reached.

Five years after your graduation from university, you can expect to be earning about £48,000. Once you reach consultant level, you could earn between £70,000 and £95,000.

Related opportunities

- Surgeon p344
- General Practitioner p308
- Nurse p293
- Pharmacist p330

Further information

British Medical Association (BMA)
BMA House, Tavistock Square, London, WC1H 9JP
020 7387 4499; www.bma.org.uk

NHS Careers
PO Box 2311, Bristol, BS2 2ZX
0845 606 0655; www.nhscareers.nhs.uk

Healthcare

CRCI: JH
CLCI: JAB

HOSPITAL PORTER

What the work involves

- Hospital porters transport patients, equipment and other items to where they need to go within the hospital.

- One of your main tasks would be to move frail and ill patients between departments and wards, while keeping them safe and comfortable.

- You will transport patients using wheelchairs and trolleys.

- You may also have a variety of other tasks such as delivering mail and moving medical equipment and supplies.

The type of person suited to this work

Hospital porters need to be responsible and reliable with a positive attitude to make sure that people and equipment are transported to the correct part of the hospital on time. You will need to learn special techniques for lifting and handling patients and equipment, and should be able to follow instructions and work well as part of a team.

Patients may be distressed or in pain so you must be caring and sympathetic and be able to reassure them and keep them comfortable.

Physical fitness is important, because you will walk long distances during your shift and you will have to lift and move patients and equipment.

Working conditions

You will work with patients and other staff, mainly indoors, although you may need to travel to other hospital sites to make deliveries.

You will need to pay attention to health and safety when lifting and handling people and equipment.

Porters usually wear a uniform and often need to work shifts, which includes working nights, weekends and bank holidays.

Future prospects

Most jobs are within NHS hospitals, although there are also posts within private hospitals. There are opportunities throughout the country but they can be competitive in some areas.

With experience you could become a supervisor and then take management qualifications for promotion to head porter or porter manager. You could also do further training to move into related careers, such as healthcare assistant or ambulance work.

Qualifications and courses

There are no formal entry requirements for this job, but applicants must be literate and have good all-round communication skills.

There is no set minimum age, but most applicants are at least 18 years old, and there are good opportunities for mature entrants.

Candidates usually have to pass a medical examination, and may be required to take a physical fitness test.

Experience of volunteer hospital portering work, or of paid or voluntary work in another area of healthcare or another job that involves contact with the public, can be useful.

A driving licence may be required.

Advantages/disadvantages

The work can be physically demanding and stressful at times.

You will meet people and the job is active and busy.

It is satisfying to play a vital role within a hospital; without porters a hospital would not be able to function.

Money guide

The NHS sets national pay rates for hospital porters.

Earnings start at around £12,517–£13,253 per year.

With experience this can rise to around £15,950. Team leaders can get up to £17,732.

Extra payments are available, for example for working extra hours.

Related opportunities

- Hotel/Accommodation Room Attendant p148
- Hotel Porter p150
- Paramedic p328
- Sterile Services Technician p343

Further information

Skills for Health
2nd floor, Goldsmiths House, Broad Plain, Bristol, BS2 0JP
0117 922 1155; www.skillsforhealth.org.uk;
office@skillsforhealth.org.uk

NHS Careers
0845 60 60 655; www.nhscareers.nhs.uk

City&
Guilds

www.cityandguilds.com/myperfectjob

IMMUNOLOGIST

What the work involves

- Immunologists work with the body's immune system. They study functions and use the knowledge gained to treat and control illness and disease.

- You might work on developing vaccines against diseases such as HIV or meningitis.

- You could also find yourself studying the causes of allergies and looking at ways to stop the human body rejecting transplanted organs.

The type of person suited to this work

If you're thinking of becoming an immunologist, you naturally need to be interested in medicine and healthcare, and the way the body works.

You should have a logical, scientific mind and be good at solving problems, as well as being good at biology and science subjects in general.

You may spend years researching one area or topic, and so will need to be patient and enjoy in-depth research work.

You'll often have to work in teams, so should enjoy this but equally be able to use your initiative and work independently. If you choose to lecture, your communication skills need to be excellent.

Working conditions

Working hours will vary depending on your employer, but will generally fall into the average 9–5 Monday to Friday pattern. During busy periods you may be required to work overtime.

Work tends to take place in a laboratory environment, often in sterile conditions. You'll probably be required to wear appropriate clothing, and this often includes a white coat, face mask and rubber gloves. If you choose to lecture, the environment will be very different, and you'll spend most of your time in classrooms and lecture theatres.

Future prospects

Once you're a researcher, you can work your way towards a promotion to lecturer, then senior lecturer and so forth, up to professor and head of department.

If you follow the NHS pathway, the career progression structure is very clear. You basically work your way up the grades, from A to B to C.

Other options to consider include scientific writing and publishing, or working on drugs trials and quality assurance. You could also progress to sales, finance and management positions within the biotechnology industry.

Advantages/disadvantages

This is a skilled profession, and training and progression can be really rewarding, especially in such an interesting job. There's also the added advantage that you'll be helping people.

Qualifications and courses

All immunologists hold a relevant degree in immunology or a related science subject such as medical microbiology, biomedical science, or genetics. Most institutions require at least 5 good GCSEs and 2 A Levels (including biology) for entrance.

You'll need at least a 2.1 degree and a postgraduate qualification is required for many NHS positions. You can also enter the profession through working in a pathology laboratory straight from school (ie after A-levels), but this route is less common.

You can enter this profession as a mature student, and there are Access courses available which can help those who are out of practice at education prepare for a degree.

Once you're in the industry, there is plenty of training on offer. Many employers train you in house, and with the NHS you can apply for a post as a Grade A Clinical Scientist Trainee. Some programmes lead to a Masters degree, and contribute to the requirements for membership of professional bodies.

The job can be stressful and demanding, and the work is by no means easy.

Money guide

As a new graduate in an NHS training post, you'll probably earn around £19,000 to £25,000. Once you gain experience, this can increase to about £31,000 a year. If you work your way up to a senior position, you may earn up to £74,000 a year.

Related opportunities

- Doctor p315
- Clinical Scientist p512
- Bacteriologist p530
- Biomedical Scientist p507

Further information

Association of Clinical Scientists in Immunology
130–132 Tooley Street, London, SE1 2TU
020 7940 8960; www.acsi.org.uk

British Society for Immunology
Vintage House, 37 Albert Embankment, London, SE1 7TL
020 3031 9800; www.immunology.org

Grade A Clinical Scientists Recruitment Centre
239 Thorpe Park, Peterborough, PE3 6JY
0871 4333070; www.nhsclinicalscientists.info

Healthcare

CRCI: TD
CLCI: QOD

LEARNING DISABILITIES NURSE

What the work involves

- Learning disabilities nurses work with people with learning disabilities in order to teach them new skills and support them in becoming as independent as possible.

- You will be assessing patients and devising suitable care plans for them, as well as supporting their families or carers by helping them implement development strategies, and arranging for them to take a break from their responsibilities when necessary.

- You will work in a range of locations, including people's houses, care homes and schools.

The type of person suited to this work

You will need excellent communication skills in order to develop a good relationship with patients and colleagues alike. You will also need to be a good, and patient, teacher in order to successfully help your patients learn new skills.

You should be compassionate and empathetic so that you can understand your patients' feelings and frustrations, whilst maintaining a professional attitude so that you can distance yourself from your work at the end of the day.

You will need both physical and mental stamina in order to support your patients fully.

Working conditions

You will usually work 37 hours a week, and these will commonly include evening, night and weekend work. Part-time work and flexible hours are frequently available.

As you will be working in the community, you will spend time travelling to and from patients' homes, schools, clinics and residential homes. Because of this, a driving licence may be required. You may also accompany and support clients as they undertake everyday tasks such as going to the shops or the gym, booking a holiday, travelling on public transport or even going to work.

Future prospects

Most learning disabilities nurses are employed by the NHS, although there are also opportunities in the private sector and with local authority healthcare teams.

You may undertake further training that could allow you to specialise in an area that particularly interests you, such as education or cognitive disability.

You could go on to become a team leader, supervisor, or even a nurse consultant. Alternatively, you could move into research or teaching.

Advantages/disadvantages

You will be providing a life enhancing service for a number of people in your local community.

Qualifications and courses

ENTRY LEVEL 5

All learning disabilities nurses must undertake a degree or diploma recognised by the Nursing and Midwifery Council (NMC). Degree courses last 3 or 4 years and you will need 5 GCSEs/S grades (A-C/1–3) or equivalent, and 2 A-levels to gain entry. Entry requirements for a diploma course are slightly lower at 5 GCSEs/S grades (A-C/1–3) or equivalent. Full time diploma courses last 3 years.

It may also be possible to undertake an apprenticeship or similar training scheme. Those available are Young Apprenticeships (for candidates aged 14–16), Apprenticeships and Advanced Apprenticeships (for entrants aged 16–24). Most apprenticeships last 2 years, during which you will gain an NVQ Level 3 in nursing.

Access courses are available to those without the necessary entry requirements, as is the Nurse Cadet scheme which is a 2 year training programme that is sufficient qualification for entry onto a degree or diploma course.

There are good opportunities for career development or diversification, as well as the option of flexible working hours to suit your lifestyle and personal commitments.

You may encounter difficult or abusive patients, which can be distressing and unpleasant.

Money guide

The starting salary for a newly qualified learning disabilities nurse is between £18,000 and £20,000. With a few years' experience, this could rise to £25,000–£35,000. If you specialise or become a nurse consultant, you could earn up to £60,000.

Salaries do vary according on your employer and where you work in the UK. Some employers offer additional benefits such as a pension scheme.

Related opportunities

- Nurse p293
- Health Visitor p313
- Occupational Therapist p323

Further information

NHS Careers
PO Box 2311, Bristol, BS2 2ZX
0845 606 0655; www.nhscareers.nhs.uk

Nursing and Midwifery Council (NMC)
23 Portland Place, London, W1B 1PZ
020 7637 7181; www.nmc-uk.org; advice@nmc-uk.org

MASSEUR

What the work involves

- A masseur uses massage as a therapy to relieve clients of pain or stress.

- As a masseur, you're trained in techniques and movements that have proven therapeutic effects and aid the healing process.

- Some practitioners specialise in specific areas of the body, whilst others work on the entire body.

- Many practitioners are self-employed and either work from home or run their own salons.

The type of person suited to this work

You will need to be good with people, and have a reassuring friendly manner.

You will need to be able to explain what you're doing clearly, and have to be able to respond to your client effectively and calmly. You should be very comfortable with close physical contact, and have good manual dexterity.

You should have excellent concentration skills, as the work demands great physical and mental energy.

You will need good organisational skills, as you may well end up running your own business. This will also require confidence and good business acumen.

Working conditions

If you work in a beauty clinic, you will usually do a 40 hour week, whilst self-employed masseurs can opt for fewer hours. Either way, you will have to work around your clients' lifestyles, which means working evenings and weekends.

You could work in hospitals, beauty salons, health spas, care homes, leisure centres, and clients' homes. You could also work from home, or even set up your own clinic.

Treatment rooms should be (and usually are) clean, warm and peaceful. You may often play calming music or use aromatherapy oils to add to the experience.

Future prospects

Once you've gained some experience, you can think about setting up your own practice, provided you have the business sense to do so.

You might also decide you'd like to learn about a similar profession such as reflexology or aromatherapy so that you can offer your clients a wider range of services. You could even teach massage, if you're prepared to study for a teaching qualification.

Advantages/disadvantages

If you like working with and helping people you should really enjoy this work. It's a good opportunity to use your skills to help others, and you can really see the results.

The job can be tiring, and you need to be physically fit to do a good job and enjoy it properly.

Qualifications and courses

There are no set requirements to enter this profession, but many authorities recommend you should have at least five good GCSEs to enrol on a course.

The course you choose will need to be recognised by the General Council for Massage Therapy, and include beauty therapy, Swedish massage, holistic massage, and anatomy and physiology. Awarding bodies include ITEC and VTCT.

Once you start training, you'll not only cover massage itself, but also first aid, health and safety, employment law, and assessing clients.

You could begin on the path to massage by following an apprenticeship in beauty therapy. If you already have experience of work in health and beauty, you can enter this field as a second career: many people choose to do this.

Once you're fully qualified you can choose to become a member of a professional body and register with the General Council for Massage Therapy. This will keep you up to date with developments in the field, and you may receive additional training. You can also expand your repertoire by studying related areas of massage such as sports therapy.

Money guide

When you start out, you'll probably be earning about £10,000.

This can rise to £15,000 with experience.

If you work your way up to specialist and work in a private practice, you could earn over £40,000 a year.

Related opportunities

- Acupuncturist p292
- Aromatherapist p295
- Physiotherapist p334

Further information

Complementary and Natural Healthcare Council (CNHC)
83 Victoria street, London, SW1H 0HW
020 3178 2195; www.cnhc.org.uk

General Council for Massage Therapy (GCMT),
27 Old Gloucester Street, London, WC1N 3XX
0870 850 4452; www.gcmt.org.uk

ITEC
2nd Floor, Chiswick Gate, 598–608 Chiswick High Road, London, W4 5RT
020 8994 4141; www.itecworld.co.uk

City & Guilds

www.cityandguilds.com/myperfectjob

Healthcare

CRCI: JA
CLCI: JOD

MEDICAL PHYSICIST

What the work involves

- Medical physicists have expert knowledge of the techniques and equipment used to diagnose and treat disease.

- You would deal with X-ray diagnosis, radiography, ultrasound, infrared and radio-frequency radiation, and measurements of pressure and temperature in the body.

- This is a very varied career. You might design, develop and maintain equipment, and advise medical staff on its use.

- Your role may also involve patient contact, explaining procedures or supervising the doses of radiation for treatment.

The type of person suited to this work

Medical physicists need to have a strong interest in science and want to use their skills and knowledge to solve problems and improve the diagnosis and treatment of disease.

You should have research skills, be able to work accurately and take responsibility for decisions which will have a direct effect on patients. You will need good communication skills to explain complex procedures clearly and simply to patients, and to work as part of a team. You must also be prepared to keep up with the latest developments and continue to learn new skills.

Working conditions

Most medical physicists work in hospitals and laboratories and some have contact with patients on wards or in clinics.

You will need to work safely with the equipment and chemicals in the laboratory, some of which can be hazardous.

You are likely to work a normal working week from Monday to Friday, but may have to work outside normal hours and may have to travel to conferences.

Future prospects

The number of medical physicists is increasing although trainee posts are competitive and you may have to relocate for some specialist roles. Most jobs are in the larger NHS hospitals throughout the UK. There are also some opportunities in the medical equipment industry, private hospitals and medical research institutes.

Within the NHS there is a recognised career path and you could even reach consultant level. Employment in the private sector is less structured.

Advantages/disadvantages

Some parts of the work may be routine at times.

You will be playing an important role in the overall healthcare of the patients, because you will be contributing to the diagnosis and treatment of their diseases.

Qualifications and courses

ENTRY LEVEL 4

Candidates will need a 1st or 2.1 degree in a physical science or engineering subject, such as physics, medical physics, electrical engineering, medical engineering, or computer engineering. Entry to a relevant degree course requires at least 2 A levels/3 H grades, plus 5 GCSEs/S grades (A–C/1–3), including English and maths, or equivalent qualifications. In practice, 3 A levels/4 H grades may be required. It is almost essential for medical physicists to have physics and maths at A level/H grade, or equivalent qualifications.

An MSc, PhD or industrial experience may also be useful.

Candidates go into the profession as Grade A trainees. The training programme lasts 2 years, and includes study for an MSc in medical physics. Successful completion of Grade A training also leads to the Diploma of the Institute of Physics and Engineering in Medicine (IPEM). Candidates may then apply for a Grade B post.

Grade B medical physicists undertake 2 years of training in a specialist field. On completion, they are eligible for registration with the Health Professional Council to work in the NHS. Grade B also leads to Corporate Membership of the IPEM.

Money guide

As a trainee you could expect a salary between £24,000 and £32,600 per year.

With several years' experience and with training, you could earn around £38,000 per year.

Senior posts can have a salary of around £50,000–£80,000+.

Rates in the private sector are similar.

Related opportunities

- Hospital Doctor p315
- Radiographer p339
- Radiologist p340
- Physicist p533

Further information

Skills for Health
2nd floor, Goldsmiths House, Broad Plain, Bristol, BS2 0JP
0117 922 1155; www.skillsforhealth.org.uk;
office@skillsforhealth.org.uk

NHS Careers
0845 60 60 655; www.nhscareers.nhs.uk

Institute of Physics and Engineering in Medicine
Fairmount House, 230 Tadcaster Road, York, YO24 1ES
01904 610821; www.ipem.ac.uk; office@ipem.ac.uk

Become instantly more attractive

What is WorldSkills?

WorldSkills is the biggest international skills competition in the world and it represents the ultimate in excellence in vocational training.

Every two years, hundreds of highly skilled young people from across the world come together to compete against each other and test their knowledge and ability in a wide variety of trades and specialisms.

Competitions take place in over 40 skill categories ranging from mechatronics and web design to floristry and jewellery, plumbing and bricklaying to hairdressing and confectionery.

Participants battle against the clock, and in front of a live audience, to tackle challenges that would be frequently found in the workplace.

Who can take part?

To get to WorldSkills, UK Skills run over 60 vocational skills competitions across the UK. Medal ceremonies celebrate the success of competitors as well as the support of their tutors, colleges, training providers and employers. National winners of WorldSkills UK competitions then have the chance to compete to represent the UK at WorldSkills.

In the UK, competitions are open to all ages, however, at WorldSkills competitors must be 22 years old or under and either a student, trainee or employee.

Competitors at WorldSkills represent the best of the best and are drawn currently from 51 countries covering every corner of the globe – from Belgium and Ireland to Brazil and Venezuela, Tunisia and South Africa to Saudi Arabia and New Zealand.

Taking part in WorldSkills represents a unique and invaluable learning experience for all competitors. Many go on to excel in their chosen careers.

WorldSkills London 2011

In May 2006, the UK won the bid to host the 41st WorldSkills Competition in London in October 2011. Beating off fierce competition, the UK bid team, of which City & Guilds was a member, vowed to host the most exciting, interactive and inspiring skills competition that the world has ever seen.

The four day event will be held at ExCeL exhibition and conference centre in London's docklands. Reaching up to 250,000 people, visitors to the event will be encouraged to 'have a go' and try the trades of their choice with lots of experts on hand, including our premier sponsor City & Guilds, to offer advice on future career options and opportunities.

For more information please visit: worldskillslondon2011.com

WorldSkills 2007 Japan

In November 2007 the UK WorldSkills team travelled to Japan to compete in the gruelling four day event.

Watched by over 200,000 spectators the team competed hard in 21 different skill categories and won a fantastic four medals and nine medallions of excellence.

Managed by UK Skills, a not-for-profit organisation which champions skills and learning for work, the 22-strong team of highly talented young people were ranked 11th in the world overall and 4th in Europe. This improved the UK's position in the team league table by one place from 2005.

Medal winner

Gary Tuddenham is 22 years old and lives in Longtown, North Cumbria. He successfully completed an NVQ at Levels 2 and 3 in Fine Furniture Making at Carlisle and Kendal College and now works at Edward Barnsley Workshop. At WorldSkills 2007 Gary won a Gold Medal in the Cabinet Making competition.

"WorldSkills is vast, the sheer size of it is amazing and the standards are really high. You have to train and practice again and again. The more you practice the more your performance improves.

Once I calmed down I treated WorldSkills like every other competition I'd done. All the training I'd put in meant I was able to maintain good concentration throughout the competition. I made a silly mistake at one point, but by keeping calm and controlled I was able to see what I'd done and correct it – something perhaps I'd have missed if I hadn't been so prepared.

WorldSkills helps you develop personally and professionally. It has given me confidence and skills which I'd never have achieved without competing but I've still got a long way to go in my career and I'll continue to learn and grow at work. I want to be the best I can and maybe run my own business one day."

So what would Gary say to anyone thinking about taking part in WorldSkills?

"Get involved. It is the best thing you could ever, ever do."

Government backing

"WorldSkills is about raising the status and the standards of vocational education. For our team to have achieved such great results in Japan 2007 proves we have skills in this country at world class levels. The team is helping to break down the snobbery around skills training – there is nothing second best about good skills-based careers. I hope that young people seeing what has been achieved in Japan will feel inspired to take up skills they can excel at professionally. I want many more to rise to the challenge themselves for the next competition in Canada in 2009 and again in 2011 when London will be hosting WorldSkills – and when we can show we can be the best!"

John Denham, **Former Secretary of State**

City & Guilds

City & Guilds is the UK's leading body dedicated to vocational learning. It offers over 500 qualifications in 28 different industry areas so that learners can gain the skills and knowledge they need to fulfil their career ambitions.

In operation for the last 130 years, 20 million people in the UK have City & Guilds qualifications and the organisation awards a further 1.5 million qualifications to learners every year.

City & Guilds qualifications are offered through 8500 centres in approximately 100 countries worldwide, so learners are never too far from a place where they can gain the skills they need.

City & Guilds qualifications are valued by employers because they are developed in conjunction with key industry bodies – so they are always relevant and up to date. Many leading businesses and organisations, such as Honda, Tesco and the London Underground, work with City & Guilds to train and develop their staff.

For more information about WorldSkills and the work of City & Guilds visit our website www.cityandguilds.com

City & Guilds
1 Giltspur Street
London EC1A 9DD
Tel: 020 7294 2468

THE HAPPINESS INDEX

What is the Happiness Index?

The City & Guilds Happiness Index provides a snapshot of how happy and fulfilled British workers are in their jobs. 2,000 people across 20 different professions were surveyed to measure how happy they were at work. The Index highlights the key contributors to happiness and how these factors change over time.

The Happiness Index

The results of the survey reveal that financial rewards are not enough to guarantee job satisfaction. An overwhelming 95% of workers questioned agreed that having an interest in what you do for a living is the number one factor for ensuring on-the-job happiness. Happiness levels stay the same regardless of the size of workers' pay cheques.

The happiest workers are beauty therapists, with one in three of all those surveyed registering a happiness level of 10 out of 10.

The happiest professions

Position	Profession
1	Beauty Therapists
2	Hairdressers
2	Armed Forces
4	Catering / Chefs
5	Retails Staff
6	Teachers
6	Marketing / PR
6	Accountants
9	Secretaries/Receptionists
9	Plumbers
9	Engineers
9	Architects
13	Journalists
13	Mechanics / Automotive
13	Human Resources
16	Call Centre
17	IT Specialists
17	Nurses
17	Banker / Finance
17	Builders/Construction

The best and the worst

The UK's happiest worker profile
- Female
- Beauty Therapist
- Over 60 years old
- From north-east England

The UK's unhappiest worker profile
- Male
- Builder
- 40–49 years old
- From Northern Ireland

Loyalty and satisfaction

The Happiness Index provides a unique insight into why workers in the UK choose to stay with their employer:

57% remain with their current employer because they have a strong interest in what they do for a living

56% stay as a result of good relationships with work colleagues

48% appreciate the work / life balance they have achieved in their present job

Reasons to be cheerful

The Happiness Index reveals the essential keys to job satisfaction:
- Having a keen interest in what you do
- Undertaking hands-on / vocational work
- Feeling appreciated for what you do

A happy professional

Beauty Therapist Naomi Watts is set for a positive future career despite the fact that she has only been working in the beauty industry for a short time. Originally from Durham, 23-year-old Naomi relocated to East Bolton in order to study for a City & Guilds Levels 2 and 3 in Beauty Therapy, and since gaining her qualifications she has gone from strength to strength. She works as a Beauty Therapist at the popular Relax and Glow beauty clinic in Cleadon and has even won a Gold Award at the WorldSkills competition.

"I'm really happy in my job because I love meeting new people who come from all walks of life, which I get to do every day. I also get job satisfaction from the idea that what I do for a living makes a difference. I can help some people change their lives by building up their confidence and self-esteem, so I feel like I'm making a valuable contribution."

City & Guilds

City & Guilds is the UK's leading body dedicated to vocational learning. It offers over 500 qualifications in 28 different industry areas so that learners can gain the skills and knowledge they need to fulfil their career ambitions.

In operation for the last 130 years, 20 million people in the UK have City & Guilds qualifications and the organisation awards a further 1.5 million qualifications to learners every year.

City & Guilds qualifications are offered through 8500 centres in approximately 100 countries worldwide, so learners are never too far from a place where they can gain the skills they need.

City & Guilds qualifications are valued by employers because they are developed in conjunction with key industry bodies – so they are always relevant and up to date. Many leading businesses and organisations, such as Honda, Tesco and the London Underground, work with City & Guilds to train and develop their staff.

For more information about the Happiness Index and the work of City & Guilds visit our website www.cityandguilds.com

City & Guilds
1 Giltspur Street
London EC1A 9DD
Tel: 020 7294 2468

DIPLOMAS

What are Diplomas?

Diplomas are a new type of qualification that aim to provide young people with a unique combination of academic and vocational skills. They have been developed to improve the employability of 14 to 19 year olds by:

- Providing training in the specific workplace skills that employers are looking for
- Focusing on key general skills such as numeracy, literacy, communication and IT
- Providing preparation for the world of work through relevant placements and team projects
- Delivering a new and different way of learning that offers a route into both higher education and employment

AQA and City & Guilds – working together

AQA – the UK's main provider of GCSEs and A levels – and City & Guilds – the UK's leading body dedicated to vocational learning – have joined together to develop and deliver the new range of Diplomas.

Their combination of experience and expertise in both academic and vocational qualifications guarantees that the Diplomas offer the very best in general education as well as specific workplace skills.

Together they are committed to delivering the highest quality qualifications and providing full support to ensure that Diplomas provide a successful route to both work and higher education.

Subjects available

Launched in September 2008 the first four Diplomas focus on:
- Construction and the built environment
- Creative and media
- Engineering
- Information Technology

Construction and the Built Environment

Exploring the fabric and significance of the built environment, this Diploma provides learners with the underpinning knowledge and basic skills needed in a wide range of industry areas. From architecture and surveying to painting and decorating, the Construction and the Built Environment Diploma provides an understanding of how this key sector works from the inside out.

Creative and Media

Focusing on knowledge, skills and creativity, this Diploma enables learners to experience the wide variety of career paths encompassed by the media and creative arts. From graphic design and advertising to creative writing and computer games, the Diploma allows learners to bring their ideas to life through making, doing and performing, whilst also encouraging critical thinking and good communication skills.

Engineering

Introducing learners to the fascinating world of engineering, this Diploma covers key principles and explores significant aspects of the role of an engineer including research, design, product development, manufacturing and production. It will captivate the imagination of all potential engineers and provide an understanding of how their future role could contribute positively to the world around them.

IT

Exploring the knowledge and abilities needed to succeed in the IT and Telecommunications sectors, this Diploma transforms technology-related education for young people. By allowing learners to experience key functions such as project management, IT support, website development and the design of new business solutions, the IT Diploma provides a realistic reflection of the blend of business, technical and interpersonal skills required by today's successful IT specialists.

A range of benefits

As well as combining academic and vocational learning, Diplomas also help students to develop both general and specific knowledge and skills. Every Diploma includes:

- Functional skills – the practical skills in English, mathematics and ICT that have been identified as vital to enable young people to succeed
- Additional and specialised learning (ASL) – the opportunity for students to specialise in particular areas and take up complementary studies. This can include options such as languages, music or science which relate to individuals' needs, interests, hopes and ambition
- Projects – specific tasks which are designed to support each student's individual progression and development

City & Guilds

City & Guilds is the UK's leading body dedicated to vocational learning. It offers over 500 qualifications in 28 different industry areas so that learners can gain the skills and knowledge they need to fulfil their career ambitions.

In operation for the last 130 years, 20 million people in the UK have City & Guilds qualifications and the organisation awards a further 1.5 million qualifications to learners every year.

City & Guilds qualifications are offered through 8500 centres in approximately 100 countries worldwide, so learners are never too far from a place where they can gain the skills they need.

City & Guilds qualifications are valued by employers because they are developed in conjunction with key industry bodies – so they are always relevant and up to date. Many leading businesses and organisations, such as Honda, Tesco and the London Underground, work with City & Guilds to train and develop their staff.

For more information about Diplomas and the work of City & Guilds visit our website www.cityandguilds.com

City & Guilds
1 Giltspur Street
London EC1A 9DD
Tel: 020 7294 2468

Become instantly more attractive

City&
Guilds

1NQUISITIVE?

Career Insights and Opportunities 2010

Got an enquiring mind and a keen interest in business? Then discover how much a professional services powerhouse can offer you. If you also have a strong team ethic and plenty of drive, you could soon be making the most of all your potential on one of our programmes.

- Our HEADstart Programmes in Tax and Assurance are designed for school and college leavers and career changers.

- Our Flying Start Degree at Newcastle University, which combines study with paid work placements, will help you qualify as a Chartered Accountant faster.

- Our 1NSIGHT Day gives you loads of information about what we do and where we do it so you can work out which of our career options interests you most.

If you're as curious as we expect you to be, you'll want to find out more.

pwc.com/uk/careers/

Text: PwC to 85792 to visit our website on your mobile

(Texts charged at your standard network rate.)

THE TIMES TOP 100 GRADUATE EMPLOYERS — EMPLOYER OF THE YEAR

**HEADstart Programmes
Flying Start Degree
1NSIGHT Days**

Requirements:
From 280 UCAS tariff or equivalent depending on entry route.

We value diversity in our people.

PRICE**W**ATERHOUSE**C**OOPERS

Recession-proof your career prospects

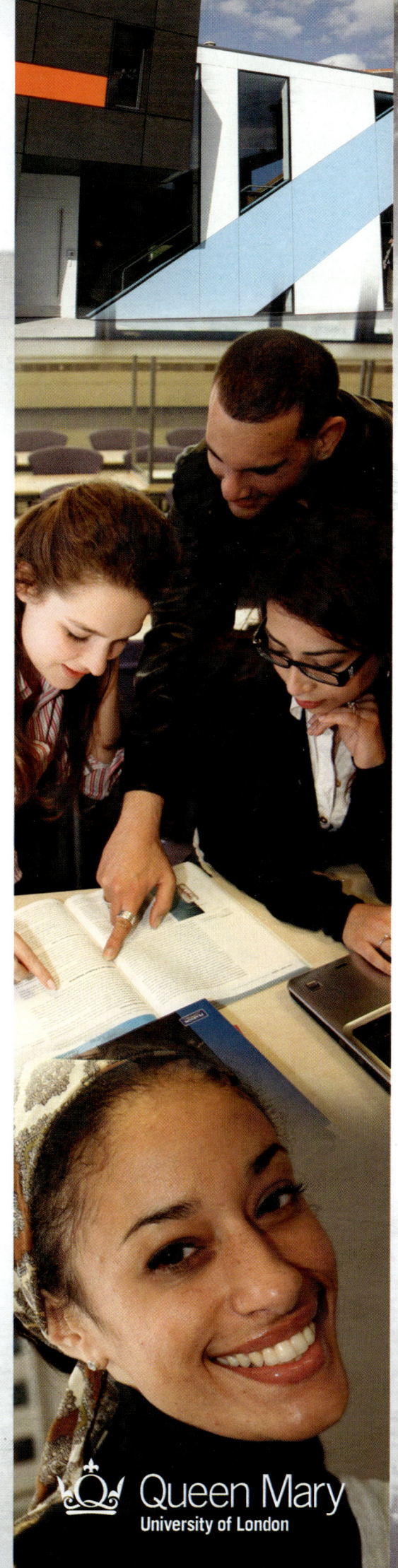

As a graduate, one of your options, rather than looking for work is to consider gaining a competitive advantage by specialising (i.e. studying management). In just one year you can gain a University of London Masters degree in a management science programme.

The School of Business and Management at Queen Mary University of London delivers high quality research activity and represents an exciting expansion in business and management education within the University of London. Queen Mary was ranked in the top fifteen research Universities in the UK. This emphasis on quality is also central to our pedagogy and teaching. The School's success derives from its strategy of taking a highly innovative inter-disciplinary approach to the study of management and business, to its unique focus on the relationship between business and society, and to its commitment to international partnership and global citizenship.

The School of Business and Management is offering six full-time programmes at Masters level for the academic year commencing September 2010. These are

- **MSc Management and Organisational Innovation**
- **MSc International Human Resource Management and Employment Relations**
- **MSc International Financial Management**
- **MSc Marketing**
- **MSc Global Business**
- **MSc Corporate Social Responsibility, Governance and Ethics**

Business and Management graduates are qualified for a whole range of career areas, including finance, the City, journalism and public sector management. Our graduates have gone into a wide range of management, marketing, accounting and finance positions in both the public and private sectors, including charities and the arts. Many of our graduates go on to start their own companies or use their knowledge in family businesses (especially international students).

Other popular areas of employment include: advertising, teaching, banking (some of our graduates work for Standard Chartered and HSBC), and recruitment (HR). Many students go on from studying Business and Management to qualify as accountants. Some have gone into the retail industry, working for major organisations such as Tesco and Marks & Spencer. Students from overseas have gone back home to work for companies such as Bank of Nigeria, Reuters and Unilever.

Come and visit us in person to find out more.

Contact
Geraldine Marks
Postgraduate Admissions Secretary
School of Business and Management
Queen Mary, University of London
London E1 4NS
Tel: +44 (0)20 7882 7470
email: sbm-postgrad@qmul.ac.uk
www.busman.qmul.ac.uk

Queen Mary
University of London

Make the **right choice**

Considering a career in flooring?

A job within the flooring industry is a trade to be proud of and often very lucrative. Whether it be fitting floors in residential or commercial environments, the opportunities for individuals with good practical skills and an eye for detail are endless.

Whilst school leavers should, wherever possible, gain their skills from formal programmes like apprenticeships, they can also choose to supplement this through organisations such as FITA, the Flooring Industry Training Association, www.fita.co.uk, who offer practical training courses to suit all levels of experience, from real beginners just getting started in the industry to upskilling courses aimed towards the more seasoned professional.

The Contract Flooring Association (CFA) and the National Institute of Carpet and Floorlayers (NICF) offer guidance on all aspects of floor fitting to companies and individuals. For more information on the world of flooring from the leading trade associations representing the commercial and domestic markets visit their websites at www.cfa.org.uk and www.nicfltd.org.uk.

Whatever path you choose, from laying that perfect floor to estimating, planning and even self employment, with experience and skills the future is bright in flooring!

For further information or advice contact:

The Contract Flooring Association (CFA)
Telephone 0115 941 1126

The Flooring Industry Training Association (FITA)
Telephone: 0115 950 6836

The National Institute of Carpet & Floorlayers (NICF)
Telephone: 0115 958 3077

CONTRACT FLOORING ASSOCIATION
cfa

fita
THE FLOORING INDUSTRY
TRAINING ASSOCIATION

N I C F
National Institute of Carpet & Floorlayers

Choose a bright future with a career in the environment

If you want a career that makes a real difference, why not consider working in one of the many areas of the environmental industry, the sector supported by the Institute of Environmental Management & Assessment (IEMA)?

With Student membership at just £20 per year and Graduate membership starting at £40 per year, it is easy to get your career off to a great start with IEMA.

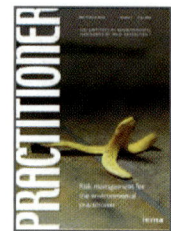

Quote code TCG-10 when applying to receive a FREE IEMA Practitioner best-practice guide worth £15!!!

(please note that the edition of the Practitioner sent to new members may differ from that pictured)

For information on training, jobs, publications and the benefits of membership, simply visit

The premier membership body for environmental professionals

www.iema.net

Tel: +44 (0)1522 540069   Fax: +44 (0)1522 540090   E-mail: info@iema.net

HARVEY NICHOLS
CHEF APPRENTICE SCHEME

The Harvey Nichols Chef Apprentice Scheme is aimed at ambitious people with a genuine passion for food who are driven towards a career that promotes creativity, flair and personal growth. Work and train in a busy and prestigious environment alongside a talented team of chefs across a multi-site restaurant operation in eight exclusive dining destinations.

To apply for this exciting opportunity or for further career information, visit www.harveynicholscareers.com

HARVEY NICHOLS

Got an eye for fashion?

Get the skills to make it happen.

It takes technical skills in pattern-cutting, garment making, production and marketing to bring an idea to life.

Find out about fashion's hidden careers at
www.canucutit.co.uk
www.skillfast-uk.org/justthejob

The Sector Skills Council
for fashion and textiles

skillfast-uk

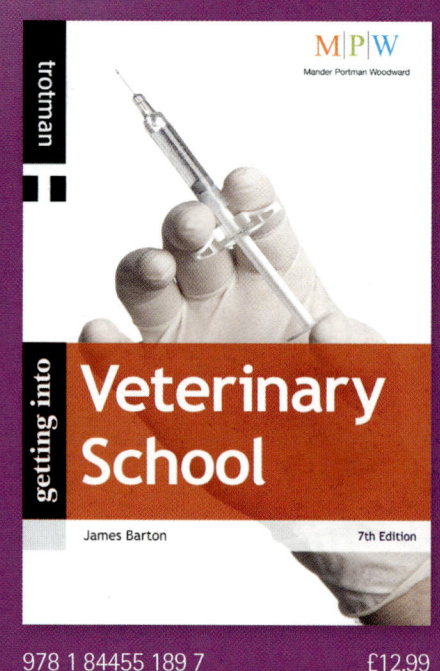

Institute of Legal Executives

Your best route to becoming a lawyer

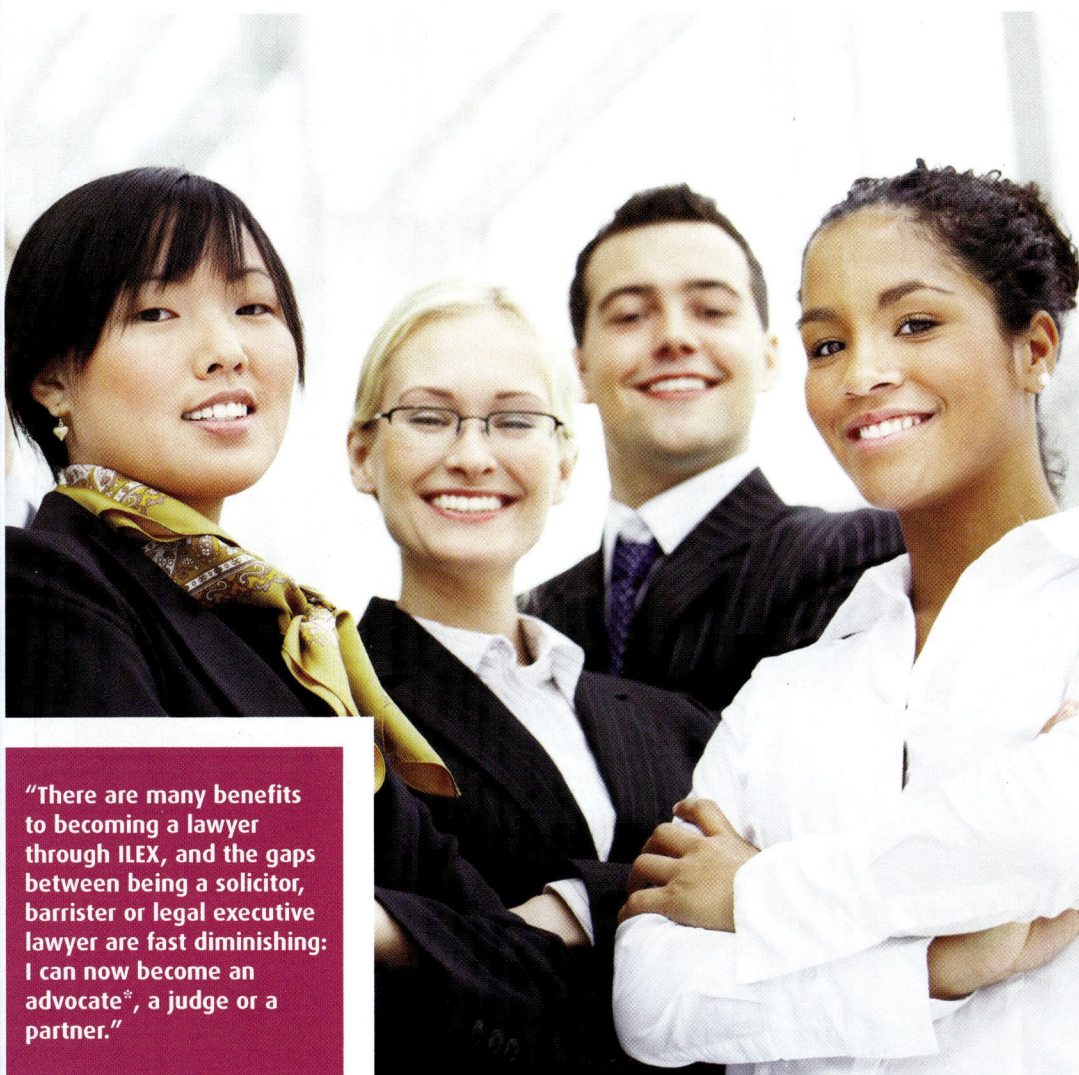

"There are many benefits to becoming a lawyer through ILEX, and the gaps between being a solicitor, barrister or legal executive lawyer are fast diminishing: I can now become an advocate*, a judge or a partner."

The academic requirement for Graduate Members is comprised of two stages of formal training: 10 units of study to achieve the Level 3 Professional Diploma in Law and Practice (set at 'A' level standard), followed by six units of study to achieve the Level 6 Professional Higher Diploma in Law and Practice (set at degree-level standard).

If you already hold a qualifying law degee you just need to study two ILEX Level 6 practice units (one of which must have been studied as part of your law degree), and the ILEX Level 6 Client Care Skills qualification to complete your academic studies.

If you hold the Legal Practice Course (LPC) or the Bar Vocational Course (BVC) you do not have to take the ILEX qualifications, and can immediately apply to become a Member of ILEX and use the designatory letters "M.Inst.L.Ex". Exemption fees will be payable in addition to your ILEX Membership fees.

As well as the relevant academic qualifications, you also need to have a minimum of five years' employment experience in legal work, including at least two consecutive years' experience which falls after successful completion of your ILEX Level 6 studies. Then you can be a qualified lawyer with ILEX* and use the designatory letters "F.Inst.L.Ex.". With further training*, you can go on to become a Legal Executive Advocate and represent your clients in court.

Applicants must satisfy the Council of ILEX as to fitness for admission.

*Careers*inPassengerTransport.org

Get careers moving with
CareersInPassengerTransport.org

Find out about

- the types of jobs available in passenger transport
- the people who work in the sector
- potential career development and progression

Developed by *GoSkills*, the sector skills council for passenger transport, *www.CareersInPassengerTransport.org* provides the latest information on working in the sector, including an in-depth suite of job profiles and access to a range of case studies. The site will enable you to see the wide variety of roles and opportunities offered by this interesting and diverse sector.

GoSkills
Moving skills forward

adventure

If you're the kind of person who can't stand looking at a lifetime of nine to fives then we have **just the job for you**

Just the job for you....

Working for Maersk means you're working for one of the world's largest shipping fleets. And it's definitely not 9 to 5. On our Cadet Training Scheme, you'll learn about practical seamanship, and also study for an internationally recognised qualification at a nautical college.

You'll see the world, and get paid for it — we'll even fund your studies. For more information on these exciting opportunities please visit our website, www.seacareers.co.uk or contact the recruitment team at GBRMMSREC@maersk.com

For information on training opportunities go to
www.seacareers.co.uk

MENTAL HEALTH NURSE

What the work involves

- Mental health nurses care for people with mental health problems both in hospitals and within the wider community, helping patients come to terms with their problems by listening to them as they talk through their illness and anxieties, and helping them overcome these limitations.

- You will also work with a patient's friends and family where possible to create a stable and proactive network around the individual, and also to provide support to those closest to him/her.

- You could encounter patients with problems including stress-related conditions, eating disorders, drug and alcohol dependency, and personality disorders.

The type of person suited to this work

You will need excellent communication skills in order to develop a good relationship with patients and their families, and other healthcare professionals. You must be extremely observant and attentive in order to spot any minor changes in a patient's condition and manage them before they trigger undesirable results.

You should be non-judgemental and empathetic in order to understand your patients' feelings and frustrations, but maintain a professional attitude.

Working conditions

You will usually work 37 hours a week, and these will commonly include evening, night and weekend work. Part-time work and flexible hours are frequently available. You could work in a hospital, in the community, or undertake a mixture of both.

If you work across the community, you will travel to a variety of places including patients' houses, hostels, day centres and drug dependency units. Because of this necessity to move between locations, a driving licence may be required.

Future prospects

Most mental health nurses are employed by the NHS, although there are also opportunities in the private sector and in local social services teams.

You may undertake further training that could allow you to specialise in an area that particularly interests you, such as drug abuse.

You could go on to become a team leader, supervisor, nurse consultant, or even into a general NHS management position. Alternatively, you could move into research or teaching.

Advantages/disadvantages

You will be providing a life enhancing service for a number of people in your local community.

Qualifications and courses

All mental health nurses must undertake a degree or diploma recognised by the Nursing and Midwifery Council (NMC). The degree course lasts 3 or 4 years and you will need 5 GCSEs/S grades (A-C/1–3) or equivalent, and 2 A-levels to gain entry. Entry requirements for a diploma course are slightly lower at 5 GCSEs/S grades (A-C/1–3) or equivalent. Full time diploma courses last 3 years.

It may also be possible to undertake an apprenticeship or similar training scheme. Those available are Young Apprenticeships (for candidates aged 14–16), Apprenticeships and Advanced Apprenticeships (for entrants aged 16–24). Most apprenticeships last 2 years, during which you will gain an NVQ Level 3 in nursing.

Access courses are available to those without the necessary entry requirements, as is the Nurse Cadet scheme which is a 2 year training programme that is sufficient qualification for entry onto a degree or diploma course.

After gaining a few years' experience, you should have the option of flexible working hours that will suit your lifestyle and personal commitments.

You may encounter difficult or abusive patients, which can be distressing and unpleasant.

Money guide

The starting salary for a newly qualified mental health nurse is between £18,000 and £20,000.

With a few years' experience, this could rise to £25,000-£35,000.

If you specialise or become a nurse consultant, you could earn up to £60,000.

Salaries do vary according on your employer and where you work in the UK. Some employers offer additional benefits such as a pension scheme.

Related opportunities

- Learning Disabilities Nurse p318
- Adult Nurse p293
- Health Visitor p313
- Occupational Therapist p323

Further information

NHS Careers
PO Box 2311, Bristol, BS2 2ZX
0845 606 0655; www.nhscareers.nhs.uk

Royal College of Nursing (RCN)
20 Cavendish Square, London, W1G 0RN
020 7409 3333; www.rcn.org.uk

ENTRY LEVEL 5

Healthcare

CRCI: JI
CLCI: JAD

Healthcare

CRCI: JI
CLCI: JAD

MIDWIFE

What the work involves

- Midwives help and support women and their partners from early pregnancy, through the antenatal period, during the labour and birth, and also for up to a month after the baby has been born.

- You will be responsible for monitoring your patient throughout her pregnancy, providing advice and support on issues ranging from nutrition, through to methods of childbirth, and breastfeeding.

- You may deliver babies, or assist in the birthing process.

- You will also be responsible for identifying high risk pregnancies and arranging specialist care and provisions where necessary.

The type of person suited to this work

You will need excellent communication skills in order to develop a good relationship with patients, their partners, and other healthcare professionals. You should be kind and caring in order to inspire trust and confidence from the women under your guidance.

As childbirth is strenuous, messy and unpredictable, you should be able to stay calm in pressurised situations, think on your feet, and have good mental and physical stamina.

You will also need to be accurate and meticulous in your work, as keeping detailed and up-to-date patient notes is vital.

Working conditions

You will usually work 37 hours a week, and these will commonly include evening, night and weekend work. You may also be on-call at times. Part-time work and flexible hours are frequently available.

You could be based in the maternity unit of a hospital or in a birth centre. Midwives are also increasingly affiliated with GP surgeries and other health centres.

You will probably spend a good amount of time travelling from your place of work to the houses of your patients, so a driving licence could be helpful.

Future prospects

Most midwives are employed by the NHS, although there are also opportunities in the private sector and in GPs' surgeries or local health centres.

You may undertake further training that could allow you to specialise in an area that particularly interests you, or to move into a related profession such as neonatal nursing.

Other opportunities include undertaking research, or training and teaching student midwives.

Advantages/disadvantages

Supporting women and families through pregnancy and childbirth is both rewarding and fulfilling.

Qualifications and courses

ENTRY 5 LEVEL

All midwives must undertake a relevant qualification that is recognised by the Nursing and Midwifery Council (NMC). There are a number of courses and routes available.

You could take a full time, 3 year degree courses in midwifery. These are available at universities throughout the UK and entry requirements vary. Generally, you will need 5 GCSEs/S grades (A-C/1–3) or equivalent, and 2 A-levels. The degree course lasts 3 or 4 years.

It may also be possible to undertake an apprenticeship or similar training scheme. Those available are Young Apprenticeships (for candidates aged 14–16), Apprenticeships and Advanced Apprenticeships (for entrants aged 16–24). Most apprenticeships last 2 years, during which you will gain an NVQ Level 3 in nursing. This will give you the qualifications necessary to study for a full diploma course.

Foundation degrees lasting 2 years are available for those who do not have the relevant qualifications to move straight into a midwifery degree. Once this has been completed they can move onto the full degree course.

For qualified nurses who are looking to move into midwifery, an 18-month fast track course is available.

Problems with pregnancy and labour do occur and can be upsetting and difficult to come to terms with.

Money guide

The starting salary for a newly qualified midwife is between £19,000 and £21,000. With a few years' experience, this could rise to £26,000–£37,000. If you specialise or become a consultant midwife, you could earn up to £65,000.

Salaries do vary according on your employer and where you work in the UK. Some employers offer additional benefits such as a pension scheme.

Related opportunities

- Adult Nurse p293
- Children's Nurse p298
- Health Visitor p313
- Occupational Therapist p323

Further information

The Royal College of Midwives
15 Mansfield Street, London, W1G 9NH
020 7312 3535; www.rcm.org.uk

Nursing and Midwifery Council (NMC)
23 Portland Place, London, W1B 1PZ
020 7637 7181; www.nmc-uk.org; advice@nmc-uk.org

OCCUPATIONAL THERAPIST

What the work involves

- Occupational therapists help people overcome physical, psychological or social problems arising from illness or disability.

- You could see patients with problems stemming from conditions such as multiple sclerosis or Parkinson's, those with physical and mental disabilities or issues, and those who are affected by drug and alcohol use.

- You will help patients with everyday tasks such as washing, cooking and even going to work. Your care will focus on what patients can achieve, rather than on their disabilities.

- Your job will include writing treatment plans, giving advice on practical issues such as disability equipment, teaching coping strategies and using activities to stimulate your patients.

The type of person suited to this work

You must have excellent interpersonal skills as you will need to inspire trust and confidence in patients with a range of problems, including some who are difficult, anxious or unpredictable. You will need to be patient, caring, and sensitive to your patients' needs, concerns and expectations.

You should have both mental and physical stamina as you will need to provide hands-on support to patients as well as coping with their emotional issues.

You should be a natural problem-solver with a flexible and creative approach to your work. The ability to motivate your patients and other professionals is also essential.

Working conditions

Most occupational therapists work a normal working week from Monday to Friday, although you may have to work evenings and weekends to provide a 24 hour community service.

You may work in a variety of locations, such as hospitals, people's own homes, residential homes, prisons and workplaces. A driving licence may be useful since you will need to travel between these locations during the day.

Working with clients can be emotionally demanding and physically tiring.

Future prospects

Demand for occupational therapists is high, but you may still find that there is competition for jobs in certain areas.

You could be employed by the NHS, private hospitals, local authorities, charities or voluntary agencies. There are also opportunities to work abroad.

With experience, you could move into a more clinical position or take up a research post. Alternatively you could progress to a managerial role within the NHS, or opt to teach within your field.

Qualifications and courses

ENTRY LEVEL 5

To become an occupational therapist, you need a degree or postgraduate diploma in occupational therapy approved by the Health Professions Council (HPC). You must also be registered with the HPC in order to practise in the NHS.

For entry to a degree course, you will normally need at least 2 A levels/3 H grades including a science, preferably biology, human biology or psychology and 5 GCSEs/S grades (A–C/1–3), or equivalent.

A degree in occupational therapy normally takes 3 years. An accelerated 2-year diploma programme is available for graduates in other subjects who have experience in health or social care.

In-service courses are available for those employed as occupational therapy support workers or technical instructors. Courses are studied part time on a day-release basis and lead to professional qualification as an occupational therapist.

Before you can register with the HPC and start work as a qualified occupational therapist, you must undergo a Criminal Records Bureau (CRB) background check.

Advantages/disadvantages

It is very rewarding to be able to help people to overcome difficulties and achieve their goals.

You could specialise in a variety of areas such as rehabilitation, learning disability or paediatrics.

The work can be emotionally and mentally demanding.

Money guide

Starting salaries for newly qualified occupation therapists are usually around £20,000. With 3–5 years' experience, this can rise to about £28,000. If you move into a more senior role, perhaps encompassing supervisory or managerial responsibilities, your earnings could increase to between £32,000 and £38,000.

Related opportunities

- Health Visitor p313
- Learning Disabilities Nurse p318
- Mental Health Nurse p321

Further information

British Association/College of Occupational Therapists
106–114 Borough High Street; Southwark; London; SE1 1LB
020 7357 6480; www.cot.org.uk; careers@cot.co.uk

NHS Careers
PO Box 2311, Bristol, BS2 2ZX
0845 606 0655; www.nhscareers.nhs.uk

Healthcare

CRCI: JG
CLCI: JAR

OPERATING DEPARTMENT PRACTITIONER

What the work involves

■ Operating department practitioners work alongside surgeons, anaesthetists and other staff before, during and after operations.

■ As well as playing a vital role in the preparation of the operating theatre, you will be involved with assessing and monitoring the well-being of patients before, during and after surgery.

■ Your role will include preparing equipment and drugs, transferring patients to operating theatres and passing instruments and dressings to surgeons during operations.

■ It will be your responsibility to ensure that all medical equipment is accounted for during surgery.

The type of person suited to this work

Operating department practitioners need the scientific knowledge and practical skills to prepare specialist equipment and drugs. You will be helping with operations so cannot be squeamish.

It is important to pay close attention when monitoring patients because their lives depend on it. You must be able to react quickly and accurately if the patient experiences any complications.

You will talk and listen to patients before and after operations, so must be caring and sensitive. You will also need good communication skills to follow instructions and work well as part of a team with other medical staff.

Working conditions

You will mainly work in operating theatres, anaesthetic areas and recovery rooms in hospitals.

You will need to follow hygiene procedures closely and wear a sterile gown and gloves during operations and be able to stand for long periods.

You will usually work shifts which may include working at nights, at weekends and on bank holidays. You may also have stand-by or on-call duties.

Future prospects

This is a growing area of work and there is a shortage of trained operating department practitioners, so job prospects are excellent. Most employment is available with the NHS throughout the UK and there are also opportunities in private hospitals.

You could progress into higher grade posts which involve more responsibility for managing and training others. There are also opportunities to enter research or teaching.

Qualifications and courses

Entry into this work requires a Diploma of Higher Education (DipHE) in Operating Department Practice approved by the Health Professions Council (HPC). Courses are available throughout the UK and generally last 2 years. The normal minimum entry requirements are 5 GCSEs/S grades (A–C/1–3) preferably in English, maths and/or a science based subject or equivalent, but some institutions may require AS levels or A levels/H grades.

The minimum age for entry is 18, and adult entry is common. Access courses may be taken prior to diploma programmes.

Entrants often have experience of other types of hospital work, for example as a healthcare assistant, and apply to become operating department practitioners later.

Advantages/disadvantages

The work can be stressful at times and it's important not to be squeamish as you will see some unpleasant things.

It is rewarding to be part of a team improving people's health and saving lives.

You could work in a range of areas, such as resuscitation, intensive care or day surgery.

Money guide

Starting salaries for qualified staff with the NHS are around £17,000–£20,261 per year.

With experience you can earn up to £32,600 per year.

Related opportunities

■ Paramedic p328
■ Critical Care Scientist p301
■ Sterile Services Technician p343

Further information

Skills for Health
2nd floor, Goldsmiths House, Broad Plain, Bristol, BS2 0JP
0117 922 1155; www.skillsforhealth.org.uk;
office@skillsforhealth.org.uk

NHS Careers
0845 60 60 655; www.nhscareers.nhs.uk

College of Operating Department Practitioners
197–199 City Road, London, EC1V 1JN
0870 746 0984; www.aodp.org; office@codp.org.uk

OPTOMETRIST

What the work involves

- Optometrists examine patients' eyes for disease or abnormalities, and carry out sight tests.

- Your work will include using instruments to look into the eye, using various tests to check how well a patient can see, asking the patient questions about any problems, and placing lenses in front of the eye to work out a patient's prescription.

- You may also supply and fit glasses or contact lenses.

- Optometrists working in hospitals often deal with the more complex eye conditions.

The type of person suited to this work

You will need to be able to pay close attention to detail and apply your scientific knowledge and skills in order to examine eyes accurately and diagnose problems correctly.

Manual skills are important for using instruments, handling lenses and fitting contact lenses.

You must also be able to listen and talk to patients of all ages when examining them and explaining procedures. You will need good communication skills to work as part of a team with other staff, such as dispensing opticians.

Working conditions

Optometrists work in high-street opticians and hospitals, in examination rooms which usually have no natural light and often have to be quite dark.

You will probably have a normal working week from Monday to Friday, but may need to work on Saturdays as well.

Future prospects

Job prospects are good but vary throughout the UK. You may work for a chain of opticians, an independent practice, or a hospital. You could also do related work with lens manufacturers.

With experience, you may specialise, for example in children's vision, low vision or contact lenses. You may choose to run your own practice. There are opportunities to move into research and university teaching.

Advantages/disadvantages

The work can be routine and repetitive at times.

If you enjoy combining scientific knowledge with working with the public, this job could be good for you.

Working closely with patients can be demanding.

Money guide

Optometrists in private practice start on around £17,000 per year and can earn up to around £36,000 with experience, but salaries can be a lot higher.

Qualifications and courses

The only route into optometry is through professional qualifications.

The Professional Qualification Examination of the General Optical Council (GOC) is in two parts.

Part 1 of the Professional Qualifying Examination involves gaining a degree.

Accredited degrees are offered at several universities. Entry requirements may vary according to the institution. Candidates are normally expected to have 5 GCSEs/S grades (A–C/1–3), including English language, maths and physics or double award science, and 3 A levels/5 H grades including at least 2 from biology, maths, physics and chemistry, or equivalent.

After graduation, new entrants must follow a pre-registration year of supervised clinical experience. Part 2 of the Professional Qualifying Examination is taken during the training year. After qualification, trainees are eligible to register with the GOC and as Members of the College of Optometrists.

There are many advanced courses that allow qualified optometrists to specialise in other areas. Courses can include paediatric vision, vision therapy and sports vision.

Qualified and experienced optometrists can earn up to £40,000 in NHS hospitals.

Consultants can earn up to £75,000 in NHS hospitals and more in the private sector.

Related opportunities

- Dentist p305
- Dispensing Optician p307
- Hospital Doctor p315
- Physiotherapist p334

Further information

General Optical Council
41 Harley Street, London, W1G 8DJ
020 7580 3898; www.optical.org; goc@optical.org

College of Optometrists
41–42 Craven Street, London, WC2N 5NG
020 7839 6000; www.college-optometrists.org;
optometry@college-optometrists.org

www.cityandguilds.com/myperfectjob

Healthcare

CRCI: JJ
CLCI: JAL

ORTHODONTIST

What the work involves

- Orthodontists are concerned with the growth of teeth and jaws, specifically correcting irregularities or abnormalities in either area.

- You will be responsible for rectifying cosmetic and physical problems in your patients, resulting in a considerable improvement in their quality of life.

- The most common procedures that you will carry out involve fitting and maintaining fixed or removable braces, and extraction of teeth. You may occasionally have to carry out jaw surgery.

- You will also need to examine the mouths and teeth or your patients, take x-rays and impressions, and keep detailed medical records of their treatment.

The type of person suited to this work

You will need to have excellent communication skills in order to gain the trust of your patients and build good relationships with them.

You will be working with and possibly managing other professionals, so you should also enjoy working in a team environment and motivating those around you.

Good eyesight and manual dexterity are essential for undertaking fiddly tasks such as fitting and tightening braces or performing jaw surgery. The ability to maintain your concentration during occasionally lengthy procedures is also important.

Working conditions

If you work in private practice you can generally expect to do normal office hours, although some orthodontists choose to work evenings and weekends to suit their patients' lifestyles. Those working in hospitals must be more flexible, occasionally undertaking emergency shifts and being on-call.

You will have to wear a white coat or tunic, along with surgical gloves and a mask when working on patients in order to maintain high levels of hygiene and safety.

Future prospects

There is a constant demand for orthodontists in both the private and public sector, so career prospects are good.

Jobs can be found across the UK in both large cities and smaller towns. You could work in the NHS or as a self-employed professional.

There are opportunities in order to specialise in certain areas of orthodontics, such as adult cosmetic dentistry or children's corrective orthodontics.

Advantages/disadvantages

The majority of orthodontists are self-employed and work in the private sector, which gives you greater control over your working hours and salary.

Qualifications and courses

(ENTRY LEVEL 7)

All orthodontists must first qualify as a dentist. The standard degree programme lasts 5 years and you will need at least 3 good A-levels/Highers or equivalent qualifications, including chemistry and biology. GCSE/S grade results may also be taken into account, and at least 8 passes (A-C/1–3) are required for consideration.

If you have good A level results, but not in the required subjects for entrance onto the degree course, you can apply for a 6 year programme that includes an initial 30 week course that will get you up to speed.

Once you have qualified as a dentist, you will need to gain 2 years of clinical experience before applying for a place on an orthodontic course. Orthodontic training combines academic study with hands-on training in a hospital, and lasts 3 years full time. You will then sit the Membership in Orthodontics (MOrth) exam to qualify as an orthodontist.

If you are looking to progress to become a hospital consultant, you will need to undertake a further 2 years' training and pass the Intercollegiate Specialty Fellowship Examination.

You will be correcting physically obvious imperfections in your patient's teeth and jawline, and seeing the subsequent improvements in their health and happiness will be rewarding.

A lot of your patients are likely to be children, who may well be anxious and frightened of many procedures which can be upsetting.

Money guide

Generally, salaries start at around £28,000-£30,000. Working in a specialist private practice, you could earn £40,000+. If you run your own practice, you could earn in excess of £150,000.

Related opportunities

- Dentist p305
- Dental Hygienist/Therapist p302
- Dental Technician p304
- Surgeon p344

Further information

British Orthodontics Society
12 Bridlewell Place, London, EC4V 6AP
020 7353 8680; www.bos.org.uk

British Dental Association (BDA)
64 Wimpole Street, London, W1G 8YS
020 7935 0875; www.bda.org; enquiries@bda.org

NHS Careers
PO Box 2311, Bristol, BS2 2ZX
0845 606 0655; www.nhscareers.nhs.uk

OSTEOPATH

What the work involves

- Osteopaths work on the musculo-skeletal system of their patients, rectifying problems with all areas of the body including the circulatory, gastro-intestinal and nervous systems.

- You will focus on understanding each patient's problem through talking to them, observing their movements and carrying out physical examinations.

- You will then rectify the problem using a serious of manipulative techniques on the muscles and bones of your patient, such as stretching the muscles, mobilising the joints and realigning bones.

The type of person suited to this work

You will need a highly developed sense of touch and strong observational skills in order to identify points of slight weakness or pain in your patients. Logic and problem-solving abilities will also help you diagnose correctly and treat the problem creatively where necessary.

You will need excellent communication skills so you can develop a good relationship with patients in order to inspire their trust and confidence.

As the majority of osteopaths are self-employed, you will need to have confidence and good business acumen in order to successfully set up, market and manage your business.

The work can be very physical, so you should also have a good level of fitness.

Working conditions

As a self-employed osteopath, you have complete control over the hours you work. Most professionals offer evening and weekend appointments as well as those during the day, as these tend to be more convenient for patients.

You could practise in a variety of locations including leisure centres, therapy centres, private clinics, hospitals and even your own home.

Future prospects

As awareness of osteopathy grows, there is increasing demand for qualified and registered professionals, so career opportunities are correspondingly positive. Most osteopaths are self-employed, and usually start out by working as an associate in a practice to establish a reputation and solid client base. After a few years, many then go on to set up their own practice.

You could also choose to specialise in an area of particular interest to you, such as treating sports injuries or problems resulting from childbirth.

Advantages/disadvantages

You will be providing a highly effective, natural alternative to drugs and surgery for your patients.

Qualifications and courses

All osteopaths must be registered with the General Osteopathic Council (GOsC) before they are legally allowed to practise. In order to register, you must hold a recognised qualification in osteopathy. Most recognised courses are at degree level. Each takes 4 years when studied full time, and 5 on a part time basis. For entry onto these courses, most of the universities require at least 5 GCSEs/S grades (A-C/1–3) or equivalent and a minimum of 2 A-levels, with chemistry or biology preferred.

Many people train in osteopathy as a second career. If you have relevant experience in healthcare or hold medical-related qualifications prior to commencing your degree, you may be exempt from parts of the course. Short courses are available for fully qualified healthcare professionals.

You will work with a variety of people and encounter a wide range of new complaints and challenges on a daily basis.

Self-employment can be stressful as your income is not predictable and you have to handle all your own marketing, accounts and expenses.

Money guide

As the majority of osteopaths are self-employed and work varying hours, it is difficult to predict an exact level of earnings at any stage. Generally, most charge between £25 and £50 for a 30–45 minute session.

Newly qualified osteopaths can expect to earn from £10,000–£20,000 in their first couple of years. With experience, you could see this increase to around £30,000.

If you run your own practice, your salary could rise to £35,000–£50,000 and above.

Related opportunities

- Chiropractor p299
- Physiotherapist p334
- Acupuncturist p292
- Homeopath p314

Further information

General Osteopathic Council (GOsC)
176 Tower Bridge Road, London, SE1 3LU
020 7357 6655; www.osteopathy.org.uk;
contactus@osteopathy.org.uk

British Osteopathic Association
3 Park Terrace, Manor Road, Luton, LU1 3HN
01582 488455; www.osteopathy.org; boa@osteopathy.org

The British School of Osteopathy
275 Borough High Street, London, SE1 1JE
020 7089 5316; www.bso.ac.uk

Healthcare

CRCI: JB
CLCI: JOD

PARAMEDIC

What the work involves

- Paramedics provide a rapid response to 999 calls reporting medical emergencies.

- You will be the first healthcare professional to reach a patient and as such must assess their condition and administer immediate treatment.

- You will need to resuscitate and stabilise patients using a variety of methods and equipment, including life support techniques, oxygen, drugs and occasionally performing minor operations such as tracheotomies.

- You will also have to make notes of all the treatments administered so you can brief hospital staff.

The type of person suited to this work

You must have good communication skills and a caring disposition to successfully soothe and comfort patients.

You should be mature, responsible and non-judgemental so that you can relate to people from a wide range of ages, backgrounds and cultures.

You must be able to keep your head in a crisis, as you will be making life and death decisions on a fairly regular basis.

A good level of physical fitness is required for lifting and carrying both patients and equipment. Mental stamina is also essential for coping with occasionally horrific and frightening circumstances.

Working conditions

You will work 37.5 hours a week on rotational shifts. This means you will work nights, weekends and on public holidays regularly. Part-time work is commonly available.

You will either work for a local ambulance service or be based at a hospital, but you will travel to a range of locations in response to emergency calls. You should be prepared to undertake treatment of patients in unfamiliar and potentially distracting surroundings.

Because you will be responsible for full or shared driving responsibilities of your vehicle, you need a full, clean driving licence.

Future prospects

Career prospects for paramedics are good. Once you have completed your training and gained 3–5 years' experience you could be promoted to a team leader.

Further promotion can take you into management posts within the ambulance service, although you will need to supplement your work experience with further relevant qualifications to achieve this level.

You could also move into related careers such as nursing or occupational therapy.

Advantages/disadvantages

Providing rapid response in emergency situations means that you really will be responsible for saving lives on a weekly basis.

Qualifications and courses

All paramedics must be registered with the Health Professions Council (HPC). There are two approved routes you can follow. You could apply to an ambulance service trust for a role as a student paramedic, and they will put you through an approved course. This training is provided on a full or part time basis and takes between 2 and 5 years to complete. Most ambulance services require at least 5 GCSEs/S grades (A-C/1–3) or equivalent including English and maths.

An alternative option is to apply for an approved degree or diploma in paramedic science which can be a 2 year higher education diploma or foundation degree, a 3 year full time degree course, or a 4 year full time course, including a paid sandwich year. Entry requirements are usually at least 1 A-level or equivalent. For a full degree, most universities require 2/3 A-levels, including a science subject.

You will also need to pass a Criminal Records Bureau check, fitness test, and medical assessment.

You could find yourself confronted with very difficult patients; those who are frightened, angry, or under the influence of drugs and alcohol may be violent and hostile to treatment.

You will have to work unsociable hours fairly regularly.

Money guide

Salaries for student paramedics range from £17,000 to £20,000. Once qualified, this should rise to around £22,000. With a few years' experience, you could earn £26,000-£28,000.

If you have undertaken the relevant training to take on responsibilities at a senior level, you could earn £30,000-£36,000.

Related opportunities

- Hospital Doctor p315
- Adult Nurse p293
- Midwife p322
- Occupational Therapist p323

Further information

British Paramedic Association
28 Wilfred Street, Derby, DE23 8GF
01332 746356; www.britishparamedic.org

The Ambulance Service Network
c/o The NHS Confederation, 29 Bressenden Place, London, SW1E 5DD
020 7074 3200; www.nhsconfed.org/networks/ambulanceservice

NHS Careers
PO Box 2311, Bristol, BS2 2ZX
0845 606 0655; www.nhscareers.nhs.uk

PATHOLOGIST

What the work involves

- Pathologists are doctors who have undergone further training to specialise in pathology.

- As a pathologist you will detect and diagnose diseases and help to identify sources of disease and reduce the risk of it spreading further.

- You could work in one of many branches including haematology (studying diseases of the blood), histopathology (studying tissue samples removed for diagnosis, and determining cause of death by performing post mortems) and immunology (studying diseases and conditions of the immune system).

- You will spend a lot of time in a laboratory, but will also work directly with patients.

The type of person suited to this work

To be a pathologist you should be able to use your medical knowledge and training to diagnose patients' conditions accurately. You must have problem-solving skills and pay close attention to detail when carrying out laboratory assessments.

You need to be caring and interested in patients, with excellent communication skills to be able to listen to them carefully and explain their conditions and treatments in a clear, simple way. You should be able to make decisions and work well as part of a team with other medical staff such as doctors and biomedical scientists.

Becoming a pathologist involves a long programme of education and training in order to gain the in-depth knowledge and skills necessary.

Working conditions

You will normally work within a hospital as part of a medical team working both in a laboratory and with patients. You will need to work safely in the laboratory and wear protective clothing such as a lab coat and gloves.

Hours can be long and you will probably work shifts and be on an on-call rota, which includes working at nights, at weekends and on bank holidays.

Future prospects

Most pathologists work within the NHS throughout the UK. There are also opportunities in industry, working for private companies.

You may decide to specialise further in particular areas of the work such as forensic pathology or transfusion medicine. You may also move into academic work, carrying out research or teaching students.

Qualifications and courses

As for hospital doctors (see p 315), candidates complete a medical degree recognised by the General Medical Council (GMC).

Following a medical degree and the 2-year Foundation programme, pathologists begin specialist training, which can last from 5–8 years.

On completion of the training, pathologists are awarded the Certificate of Completion of Specialist Training (CCST), which enables them to work as consultants.

There are also similar careers in pathology for clinical and biomedical scientists, but they do not treat patients.

Advantages/disadvantages

The work can be emotionally demanding because it includes dealing with patients who have life-threatening conditions.

Your work can be vital in finding an accurate and early diagnosis for patients, which can help to save lives.

Money guide

Salary levels in the NHS have a national rate, but this can also vary in some areas.

Most junior doctors and senior house officers earn around £33,000 in their first year of training, rising to £41,0000 in the second. Doctors on specialist training can earn up to £69,000.

Specialists with experience can earn up to £78,000.

Consultants earn from £74,000 and with additional payments and merits it is possible for consultants to earn anything up to £170,000.

Related opportunities

- Anaesthetist p294
- Psychiatrist p338
- Radiologist p340

Further information

Skills for Health
2nd floor, Goldsmiths House, Broad Plain, Bristol, BS2 0JP
0117 922 1155; www.skillsforhealth.org.uk;
office@skillsforhealth.org.uk

NHS Careers
0845 60 60 655; www.nhscareers.nhs.uk

Royal College of Pathologists
2 Carlton House Terrace, London, SW1Y 5AF
020 7451 6700; www.rcpath.org; info@rcpath.org

Healthcare

CRCI: JH
CLCI: JAB

PHARMACIST

What the work involves

- Pharmacists work in one of three areas: hospital, community or industry.

- Hospital pharmacists are responsible for buying, manufacturing, dispensing and supplying medicines to in and out-patients. You will ensure that patients receive the most appropriate treatment in the correct dosage.

- Community pharmacists work in high-street pharmacies both in large cities and small rural villages. You will supply medicines over the counter, make up doctors' prescriptions, and advise people on general health-related queries.

- Industrial pharmacists work for pharmaceutical companies. You will be discovering, developing, manufacturing, testing and marketing new drugs.

The type of person suited to this work

You should be a strong communicator, as you will be advising patients on choosing medications and clearly explaining how to administer them. You will also need to be comfortable working in a team with other pharmacy staff or healthcare professionals.

You will need in depth medical knowledge as well as problem solving skills in order to prepare medications for patients and advise them on what to take for minor ailments.

Accuracy and attention to detail are essential when selecting, preparing, measuring and labelling medicines.

Working conditions

Hours will depend on where you work. Community and industrial pharmacists will usually work 39 hours per week from Monday to Friday, although Saturday work is increasing in order to meet patients' requirements. Hospital pharmacists may need to work shifts in order to provide a 24 hour service. There are opportunities to work part time.

You could be working in a shop, hospital or laboratory, and may occasionally be required to travel in order to provide a service to nursing homes and community health centres/clinics.

Future prospects

Opportunities for pharmacists are good as there is currently a shortage, particularly in hospitals.

You will be able to choose from a range of working environments including community shops and large hospitals.

As you gain experience, you could choose to combine your work with other responsibilities such as teaching. You could also go on to write about pharmaceutical matters.

Advantages/disadvantages

You will be working with a range of patients and colleagues, so your work will be varied and rewarding.

You can choose to work in a more relaxed retail environment, in the bustle of a hospital, or in a professional industrial setting.

Qualifications and courses

ENTRY LEVEL 5

All candidates who wish to become pharmacists need to hold a degree in pharmacy in order to gain the necessary M.Pharm qualification. Throughout the UK, there are 25 schools of pharmacy at which you can study for a degree that has been approved by the Royal Pharmaceutical Society of Great Britain (RPSGB).

The degree course lasts 4 years, and most universities require at least 3 A-levels or equivalent, including chemistry and biology, along with at least 5 GCSEs/S grades (A-C/1–3) including English, maths and science.

It is not possible to start work as a pharmacist with just an HND qualification. You could, however, gain employment as a pharmacy technician to gain experience whilst you study for a degree level qualification.

Prior to registration as a pharmacist, entrants have to complete a year in industry, where they will work as either a community, hospital or industrial pharmacist and gain experience. You will then have to pass the RPSGB's registration examination prior to becoming a fully qualified, registered pharmacist.

You may have to work evenings and weekends in order to provide a good level of service to patients and healthcare professionals.

Money guide

Starting salaries for pharmacists range from £24,000 - £26,000. With 5–10 years' experience, you could expect to earn up to £38,000 if you are working in industry, and £35,000 for community and hospital based roles.

If you reach a very senior level, you could expect to earn over £55,000 in a community position, and £70,000+ if you are working in industry or within a hospital.

Related opportunities

- Pharmacologist p331
- Biochemist p506
- Pharmacy Technician p332
- Hospital Doctor p315

Further information

Royal Pharmaceutical Society of Great Britain (RPSGB)
1 Lambeth High Street, London, SE1 7JN
020 7735 9141; www.rpsgb.org.uk; enquiries@rpsgb.org.uk

The Association of the British Pharmaceutical Industry
12 Whitehall, London, SW1A 2DY
0870 890 4333; www.abpi.org.uk

NHS Careers
PO Box 2311, Bristol, BS2 2ZX
0845 606 0655; www.nhscareers.nhs.uk

PHARMACOLOGIST

What the work involves

- Pharmacologists study the effect of drugs on the body. Their work includes discovering, researching, developing and testing new drugs and medicines.

- You will study the actions of drugs via computer simulations, or in biological tests in cells and tissues, or in animals and human volunteers.

- You could specialise in a number of areas, including neuropharmacology or clinical pharmacology.

The type of person suited to this work

You should be a strong communicator with the ability to both work within a team, and also lead and motivate your colleagues in order to drive projects.

You will need excellent analytical skills as you will be gathering and interpreting complex information, and since the majority of equipment used to undertake experiments is computer-based it is essential to have good ICT skills.

You should be adaptable and creative in order to develop and modify experiments by which to successfully understand the effectiveness of a wide variety of drugs.

Working conditions

You will usual work from 9 to 5 during the week, but occasionally may have to work evenings and weekends in order to monitor the more complex experiments.

You will be working in a laboratory environment, usually within a university, government or commercial research centre, or a pharmaceutical company. This means that the environment is generally clean and quiet, and you may be required to wear protective clothing when undertaking certain experiments.

Future prospects

Although the industry is competitive, once you have gained a position as a pharmacologist the opportunities for career progression are good. You could work within a university, undertaking research and gaining a PhD, and then perhaps moving into a position as a lecturer. Within commercial laboratories, experience will lead to increased responsibility and subsequently managerial opportunities.

There are many opportunities to work abroad, particularly in Europe and the United States.

Advantages/disadvantages

It is a competitive industry so gaining an entry level position is difficult. Once you are in though, prospects are excellent and career progression rapid.

You will be working towards developing new drugs that will enhance thousands of people's quality of life across the globe.

Qualifications and courses

ENTRY LEVEL 5

Because the work is incredibly scientific, most entrants to pharmacology have a relevant degree in a subject such as pharmacology, biomedical sciences, biochemistry, molecular and cell biology, chemistry or biology.

Most universities require 3 A-levels or equivalent, including chemistry and biology, for entrance onto a degree course. At least 5 GCSEs/S grades (A-C/1–3) or equivalent, are also required.

It is possible to enter this career with a relevant HND, but this is uncommon and you would have to start in a lower position and gain qualifications as you work. Entry requirements for an HND are usually 5 GCSEs/S grades (A-C/1–3) or equivalent, including English, maths and science.

Because competition is so fierce in this industry, many new entrants hold a postgraduate qualification as well as an undergraduate degree. These include research courses in related subjects such as pharmacology. Undertaking a PhD also gives candidates essential lab experience, which is viewed favourably by employers.

Pre-entry work experience within a pharmaceutical company is also desirable as it demonstrates your enthusiasm and commitment.

You will have to experiment on animals, which may be upsetting.

Money guide

Starting salaries range from £21,000 for pre-doctoral roles, to £26,000 for those with a PhD. After approximately 10–15 years' experience, you can expect to earn anything from £30,000 to £100,000 depending upon your employer and where you work in the world.

Commercial salaries tend to be higher than those offered by academic institutions, and holding a PhD will generally increase your earning potential by 25%.

Related opportunities

- Pharmacist p330
- Biochemist p506
- Toxicologist p535

Further information

British Pharmacology Society
16 Angel Gate, City Road, London, EC1V 2PT
020 7239 0171; www.bps.ac.uk; pt@bps.ac.uk

Association of the British Pharmaceutical Industry (ABPI)
12 Whitehall, London, SW1A 2DY
0870 890 4333; www.abpi.org.uk

Healthcare

CRCI: JK
CLCI: JAG/QOB

PHARMACY TECHNICIAN

What the work involves

- Pharmacy technicians work under the supervision of a qualified pharmacist, helping to prepare, supply and dispense medications, whilst also advising on how to take them.

- You will also be responsible for monitoring stocks of medicines, checking expiry dates and reordering supplies as necessary.

- You could work in a retail environment as a community pharmacy technician, within a hospital, or in a commercial pharmaceutical lab.

- You will be working with a variety of healthcare professionals, including pharmacists, doctors and nurses, and could also have a good amount of contact with patients.

The type of person suited to this work

You will need to be a strong communicator, as you will be advising patients on choosing medications and explaining how to administer them clearly. You will also need to be comfortable working in a team with other pharmacy staff or healthcare professionals.

You should be good with figures and calculations, and also be extremely accurate in order to ensure that you are making and labelling medications correctly, and also keeping detailed records of each patient's medication needs.

You must be able to be mature and tactful when dealing with patients who will present a variety of unusual complaints, and always remain non-judgmental.

Working conditions

Hours will depend on where you work. Community pharmacy technicians usually work 39 hours a week from Monday to Saturday. Industry and hospital technicians work a 37 hour week, but may be required to cover evening and weekend shifts on occasion.

You could be working in a shop, hospital or laboratory, and may occasionally be required to travel in order to provide a service to nursing homes or community health centres and clinics.

When working in a hospital or industrial laboratory, you may be required to wear sterile clothing such as gloves and a gown.

Future prospects

You could work in a community context, within a small local pharmacy or a larger well-known chain. Alternatively, you could be in an NHS or private hospital, or based in a prison or working for the Armed Forces.

If you work in a hospital, you could move into a specialised, supervisory role after gaining a few years' experience. Additionally, many clinical pharmacy technicians in hospitals are now more involved with patients, undertaking ward rounds and other such duties.

Qualifications and courses

Although there are no specific entry requirements to become a pharmacy technician, most employers ask for 5 GCSEs/S grades (A-C/1-3) or equivalent, including English, maths and at least one science subject.

Training is vocational so you will start in a trainee post within either a community pharmacy or a hospital, working under the supervision of a qualified pharmacist whilst also studying for an NVQ Level 3 in pharmacy services.

Apprenticeships and Advanced Apprenticeships may be available for those aged 16–24. Entry requirements are usually at least 4 GCSEs/S grades (A-C/1-3) or equivalent, including English, maths, and a related science subject.

Once you have gained your qualifications and experience as a pharmacy technician, you can register with the Royal Pharmaceutical Society of Great Britain.

Advantages/disadvantages

You will be working with a range of patients and colleagues, so your work will be varied and rewarding.

You can choose to work in a more relaxed retail environment, in the bustle of a hospital, or in a professional industrial setting.

You may have to work evenings and weekends in order to provide a good level of service to patients and healthcare professionals.

Money guide

Starting salaries for trainee pharmacy technicians are usually around £17,000.

With 5–10 years' experience, and having gained a more senior position, you could earn between £20,500 and £26,000.

If you become a team manager within the NHS, your salary could reach £38,000.

Many employers also offer additional benefits such as a pension scheme.

Related opportunities

- Pharmacist p330
- Sterile Services Technician p343
- Health Records Clerk p311

Further information

Royal Pharmaceutical Society of Great Britain (RPSGB)
1 Lambeth High Street, London, SE1 7JN
020 7735 9141; www.rpsgb.org.uk; enquiries@rpsgb.org.uk

The Association of Pharmacy Technicians UK (APTUK)
4th Floor 1 Mabledon Place, London, WC1H 9AJ
020 7551 1551; www.aptuk.org; website@aptuk.org

PHLEBOTOMIST

What the work involves

- Phlebotomists are specialist medical laboratory assistants who collect blood samples for analysis to help diagnose diseases.

- They take blood samples from patients as painlessly as possible, label them and make sure they are taken promptly and safely to a laboratory for examination.

- Some phlebotomists combine this work with the various other duties of a medical laboratory assistant within laboratories, such as sterilising equipment and maintaining laboratory stocks.

- Your work may involve visiting patients in their homes.

The type of person suited to this work

Phlebotomists need to be practical and good with their hands to take blood without harming the patient or disturbing nursing care. You will also have to work accurately and pay attention to detail to ensure that samples are taken and labelled correctly and not contaminated during collection, as this could affect results.

It is important that you are able to communicate well with a range of people from children to the elderly. Some people are scared of having their blood taken, so you need to be able to reassure them.

You will also need good communication skills to work well in a team with colleagues, such as other medical laboratory assistants and biomedical scientists (who analyse the blood samples that you collect).

Working conditions

You will carry out your work in hospital wards, out-patient departments and in the community. You will also spend time working in laboratories.

You will need to pay close attention to health and safety to prevent infection, and will wear a uniform and protective clothing such as gloves.

You are likely to work a normal working day during the week, but you may also need to work at weekends.

Future prospects

Most employment is available in NHS hospitals throughout the UK. There is also similar work available in the blood transfusion services, government research departments and university laboratories.

The demand for phlebotomists varies locally, so contact your local hospital for more information.

Although there is no route for phlebotomists to progress to a career as a biomedical scientist, you may be encouraged to gain the qualifications that you need to train as a biomedical scientist. You may also train to enter other areas of healthcare, such as nursing.

Qualifications and courses

There are no formal entry requirements for this job, but 4 or more GCSEs/S grades (A–C/1–3), English, maths and science, or equivalent, may be an advantage, and are essential for more advanced work.

Training is usually done entirely on the job. After training, you may be awarded a Certificate of Competence, which will allow you to work without close supervision throughout the hospital. You will be trained to National Occupational Standards.

Phlebotomists may be able to work towards related qualifications, such as NVQ/SVQ Medical Assistance Level 2 or City & Guilds Level 2 in Medical Assistance. The National Association of Phlebotomists offers short training courses and workshops.

Advantages/disadvantages

Some of your patients will be scared of blood and needles which can be stressful.

It can be rewarding to work with patients and pay a vital role in helping to diagnose illnesses.

Money guide

The NHS sets national pay rates for phlebotomists each year; those listed below are a guide only.

Salaries start at £12,900 per year and generally go up to £16,000.

Seniors can earn £17,300–£20,800. Managers can get up to £32,600.

There are also extra payments available if you work in London.

Related opportunities

- Biomedical Scientist/Medical Laboratory Assistant p507
- Immunologist p317
- Laboratory Technician p524

Further information

Skills for Health
2nd floor, Goldsmiths House, Broad Plain, Bristol, BS2 0JP
0117 922 1155; www.skillsforhealth.org.uk;
office@skillsforhealth.org.uk

NHS Careers
0845 60 60 655; www.nhscareers.nhs.uk

National Association of Phlebotomists
12 Coldbath Square, London, EC1R 5HL
020 7833 8784; www.phlebotomy.org;
phlebotomy@btinternet.com

Healthcare

CRCI: JF
CLCI: JAX

PHYSIOTHERAPIST

What the work involves

- Physiotherapists treat patients with problems affecting their muscles, bones, heart, circulation and lungs that have been caused by accident, illness or aging.

- You will assess patients, then decide on an appropriate course of treatment for them. This could include exercise, movement, hydrotherapy, massage or manipulation.

- Sports physiotherapists use the same techniques as those above, but focus solely on treating sports-related injuries.

The type of person suited to this work

You must have excellent communication skills as you will be dealing with both patients and other healthcare professionals on a daily basis. When treating patients, you will need to be able to listen to their concerns, explain the best course of treatment, and motivate them to persevere with their programme.

You will need to have a practical, logical mind in order to think around problems and solve unusual complaints in a creative way.

You must be physically fit, as much of the work can be strenuous and involve a good deal of hands-on contact and muscle manipulation.

Working conditions

You will generally work a 37 hour week, although you should expect to work evenings and weekends to fit in with your clients' lifestyles.

You could be employed by the NHS, private practices and health centres, residential homes, or sports centres and specialist clinics. A good number of physiotherapists opt for self-employment and work in a mixture of locations.

You will need to wear practical clothes, and certain employers may require you to wear a uniform.

Future prospects

60% of physiotherapists are employed by the NHS, although this number is significantly lower for those who have specialised in sports physiotherapy. There are opportunities with numerous other employers such as health clinics and sports centres, and you can be self-employed.

You could go on to specialise in an area such as orthopaedics or geriatric care, or pursue more senior positions. The NHS now offers consultant-level posts for experienced physiotherapists.

Advantages/disadvantages

You will have a great deal of contact with patients and other healthcare professionals so the job is varied and rewarding.

Qualifications and courses

ENTRY LEVEL 5

All physiotherapists must hold a degree that has been recognised by the Health Professions Council (HPC). Most degrees last for 3 or 4 years when studied full time, and part time courses are also available.

Entry requirements vary according to the university, but you will usually need 3 A-levels (A-C) or equivalent, including biology or similar. You will also need at least 5 GCSEs/S grades (A-C/1–3) or equivalent, including English, maths and science.

You may also be considered for a university place if you hold a BTEC National Diploma/Certificate in science, applied science, or health sciences, a Diploma in society, health and development, or an NVQ Level 3 in a related subject.

Graduates with a related science degree could opt for a 2 year fast-track degree programme, and Access courses are available for entry onto a degree programme for candidates without the relevant science qualifications.

It is recommended to get work experience prior to applying for your degree, as universities look very favourably on this.

If you opt for self-employment, you have control over your working hours and the patients you decide to take on.

It is physically demanding work, and working with injured or ill people can also prove emotionally draining.

Money guide

Starting salaries for newly qualified physiotherapists depend on your employer, or whether you are self-employed, but generally fall around £20,000. With a few years' experience, you could earn up to £32,000, and at a senior level you could look to earn around £38,000.

Consultant physiotherapists in the NHS earn £45,000+, and those who have specialised in sports physiotherapy can earn up to £53,500.

Related opportunities

- Chiropractor p299
- Osteopath p327
- Acupuncturist p292
- Hospital Doctor p315

Further information

The Chartered Society of Physiotherapy (CSP)
14 Bedford Row, London, WC1R 4ED
www.csp.org.uk

NHS Careers
PO Box 2311, Bristol, BS2 2ZX
0845 606 0655; www.nhscareers.nhs.uk

PODIATRIST

What the work involves

- Podiatrists (also commonly known as chiropodists) are healthcare practitioners responsible for assessing, diagnosing and treating problems relating to the lower limb.

- The work involves musculoskeletal assessment and orthotic provision (using medical braces to correct deformities), administering local anaesthetics to enable pain free specialist foot treatment, wound care, neurological assessment, skin, nail and bone surgery, care planning and health promotion.

- You will treat a variety of people including those with disabilities and long-term illnesses, children and people with sports related injuries.

The type of person suited to this work

Podiatrists need to be caring and understanding. You will be talking and listening to patients of all ages and with a wide range of problems, and who could be distressed or in pain. You should be able to reassure them and explain their treatment clearly and simply. You will also need good communication skills to be an effective part of a healthcare team. You should be able to apply your skills and knowledge to diagnose and solve problems.

You should be good with your hands as you will be using a range of equipment and techniques.

Working conditions

Podiatrists can work in many different settings. This could be in a retirement home, on the sports field or even working closely with the police if you decide to follow forensic podiatry. It will undoubtedly involve working closely with other medical professionals such as GPs and physiotherapists. Podiatry offers excellent employment flexibility with the opportunity to work in the NHS, private practice, commerce, leisure, education and occupational health to name but a few. All of the work requires a combination of technical knowledge, specialist practical skills, and great interpersonal skills.

Future prospects

Job prospects are good. Around 85% of students are employed within the first year after graduating.

After you have qualified as a podiatrist there are a range of job opportunities that you may wish to consider.

You may choose to specialise in one area of podiatry such as diabetes, biomechanics (musculoskeletal disorders), forensic podiatry, working with children or surgery. You could also go on to teach and do research in a university or move into management.

Advantages/disadvantages

The idea of working with other people's feet may not appeal instantly, but podiatrists generally get great satisfaction from their work.

Qualifications and courses

To work as a podiatrist in the NHS, you need to have passed a BSc (Hons) degree in podiatry (lasting 3 or 4 years) approved by the Health Professions Council (HPC). You must be registered with the HPC in order to practise.

You will need 300 tariff points to gain entry to a podiatry degree. You are generally required to have a minimum of 2–3 A-levels/4 Highers, one of which should be science, preferably biology, based. Entrants must pass a police background check, and are medically screened.

You will have to deal with people who may be badly injured or very ill and who are distressed and in pain.

Money guide

Salary levels in the NHS may be subject to change and additional allowances may also be available for those living in or near London.

A new graduate in podiatry would have a starting salary of approximately 21k in the NHS but the earning potential could be in excess of 100k depending on which career path you choose.

Starting salaries for chiropody assistants in the NHS are £14,800–£17,700 per year. With a relevant NVQ and some experience this rises to £21,000.

Related opportunities

- General Practitioner p308
- Occupational Therapist p323
- Physiotherapist p334
- Prosthetist p337

Further information

Society of Chiropodists and Podiatrists
1 Fellmonger's Path, Tower Bridge Road, London SE1 3LY
020 7234 8620; www.feetforlife.org

Skills for Health
2nd floor, Goldsmiths House, Broad Plain, Bristol BS2 0JP
0117 922 1155; www.skillsforhealth.org.uk;
office@skillsforhealth.org.uk

NHS Careers
PO Box 2311, Bristol BS2 2ZX
0845 606 0655; www.nhscareers.nhs.uk

Healthcare

CRCI: JG
CLCI: JAT

PODIATRIST

Joe Parker's story:

After graduating from his BSC (Hons) in Podiatry, Joe started out as a community podiatrist working in a local health centre dealing with people from the local community who have a range of foot disorders and complaints. He did this for three years before being moved on to a promoted post where he specialises in children's foot health, working in different health centres and hospitals.

What the job entails

"Working with children is a specialist area which covers a variety of foot and gait (walking) complaints. I get referrals from Health Visitors, GP's, Physiotherapists and other Podiatrists. My referrals include children with ingrown toe nails, verrucae, curly toes but mostly I get children who have flat feet, in-toeing gait or other unusual walking/development problems. I also go out to schools and give Health Promotion talks to pupils on foot health."

A bad day in the office for Joe

"When a child comes into the clinic with a really sore toe and it's so sore that they don't want you to even touch it. Most children don't like getting an injection so won't let you give them a local anaesthetic and it can take you a long time to try and persuade them that you will be able to make them feel better. The parents can put pressure on you also as they know how sore it has been and know that it has become infected."

What makes Joe good at his job

"You need to be very patient and sympathetic towards the children to make them feel relaxed with you to allow you to assess and treat them. Good communication skills are vital to be able to decipher what is wrong. Problem solving skills help you to be able to come up with a management plan that suits you, the patient and the parents."

What Joe personally gets out of it

"It is really rewarding working with children, when that crying child with the sore toe comes back to you smiling as the pain has gone and their foot is better, it makes it all worthwhile. Also working as part of a team with the Health Visitors, GP's, Physiotherapist etc is interesting as you are all working together to help your patient.

No two days are the same in this job, there is always something different to do i.e. one day you could be treating ingrowing toenails, the next you are giving exercises to help correct a child with an in toeing gait, you could also be in the lab making specialist insoles to fit into someone's shoes, then going off to give a talk to children in a primary school – there is never a dull moment!".

www.feetforlife.org

The Society of Chiropodists and Podiatrists
1 Fellmongers Path, Tower Bridge Road, London SE1 3LY

PROSTHETIST/ORTHOTIST

What the work involves

Prosthetist

- Prosthetists design and fit artificial limbs for patients who have lost a limb, have a deformity or who were born without a limb.

- Work will include taking a cast of the area where the artificial replacement limb will fit and modelling it so that it will be safe and comfortable for the patient. You will also fit and adjust the replacement limb and teach the patient how to use it.

Orthotist

- Orthotists provide surgical appliances such as braces, collars, splints and special footwear for patients.

- Work will include assessing the patient's problem, designing, fitting and adjusting the orthosis, and helping the patient to use it.

The type of person suited to this work

Prosthetists and orthotists need a high level of technical knowledge and aptitude in areas such as biomechanics and movement.

You must be good with your hands to take measurements, design devices and do fittings and make adjustments. You must be good at using technical skills to solve problems and be able to work accurately because each device must be made perfectly to fit each individual patient.

You also need excellent communication skills for working with patients. You have to be caring, patient, tactful and able to reassure and encourage patients and explain procedures to them. You need to be able to work well as part of a team that includes doctors, nurses, physiotherapists and occupational therapists.

Working conditions

Prosthetists and orthotists work in locations such as hospitals, clinics and centres for people with disabilities. You will also spend some time in workshops where the prostheses and orthoses are made.

You will generally work normal hours from Monday to Friday, although you may have to work late at busy times. A driving licence is useful if you are working in a number of different locations

Future prospects

With a shortage of prosthetists and orthotists, job prospects are generally excellent in most areas of the UK. Most prosthetists and orthotists work within the NHS but there are also opportunities in private practice and with commercial companies that make devices for NHS hospitals.

With experience, you may specialise in a particular area of the work such as upper or lower limb prosthetics or spinal orthotics; you could also move into management or carry out research and teaching.

Qualifications and courses

Training to become a prosthetist and orthotist takes 4 years, leading to a BSc (Honours) degree. Entry requirements are usually 240 tariff points including A levels in biology and maths or another science, plus 5 GCSEs/S Grades (A–C/1–3). Equivalent qualifications may be acceptable.

Graduates can either specialise in one area or practise both specialities but must register with the Health Professions Council before being allowed to practise.

There are also many opportunities to work all over the world. Prosthetic and orthotic work is especially important in parts of the world where development programmes are working with communities affected by war.

Advantages/disadvantages

Working with ill and injured patients who are upset and in pain can be emotionally demanding.

It is satisfying to be able to see the positive effects that the artificial limbs and surgical appliances have on people's lives. For example, you can help people to move around more easily or relieve them from discomfort.

Money guide

There is no set salary scale for NHS prosthetists and orthotists, but salaries tend to be similar to those in commercial companies.

The starting salary for prosthetists and orthotists is around £20,000 per year.

Experienced prosthetists and orthotists can earn up to £40,000.

Some seniors in the NHS can get up to £60,000.

Earnings are generally higher in London. There may also be higher earnings for those with management responsibilities.

Related opportunities

- Medical Physicist p320
- Occupational Therapist p323
- Physiotherapist p334

Further information

Skills for Health
2nd floor, Goldsmiths House, Broad Plain, Bristol, BS2 0JP
0117 922 1155; www.skillsforhealth.org.uk;
office@skillsforhealth.org.uk

NHS Careers
0845 60 60 655; www.nhscareers.nhs.uk

British Association of Prosthetists and Orthotists
Sir James Clark Building, Abbey Mill Business Centre,
Paisley, PA1 1TJ
0845 166 8490; www.bapo.com

Healthcare

CRCI: JF
CLCI: JOL

PSYCHIATRIST

What the work involves

- Psychiatrists are doctors who have undergone further training in psychiatry.

- As a psychiatrist, you will diagnose mental health problems by talking to patients and carrying out tests. You will then decide on a course of treatment which could include prescribing drugs and talking to patients to help them deal with their problems.

- You will treat people with a range of mental health problems. These include depression, schizophrenia, eating disorders, anxieties, phobias, drug and alcohol abuse, and post-traumatic stress disorder.

- You will probably specialise in one area such as child and adolescent psychiatry, forensic psychiatry or learning disabilities.

The type of person suited to this work

As a psychiatrist you need to be patient and caring. You will need excellent communication skills to listen carefully to people who might be confused or withdrawn. You will help them talk through and come to terms with their problems or illness and should be able to explain their conditions and treatment in a clear, simple way. You will work with relatives and carers, and as part of a team with other medical staff such as psychiatric nurses and occupational therapists.

You will need to be prepared to undergo a long programme of education and training in order to gain the in-depth knowledge and skills necessary to become a psychiatrist.

Working conditions

You could work in a range of locations, including hospitals, people's own homes, schools, residential homes and prisons.

You are likely to work shifts and be on an on-call rota, which includes working at nights, at weekends and on bank holidays.

Working closely with patients can be emotionally demanding. You will work as part of a team of healthcare professionals.

Future prospects

Most psychiatrists work within the NHS throughout the UK. There is also a small amount of work available in private hospitals, care homes and rehabilitation centres. The armed forces also employ psychiatrists.

There are six specialist areas of psychiatry that you may work in: adult psychiatry; child and adolescent psychiatry; forensic psychiatry; psychiatry of learning disability; old age psychiatry; and psychotherapy.

Entry to psychotherapy is competitive, but there is currently a shortage of psychiatrists in other specialities.

You could move into academic work, either carrying out research or teaching medical students.

Qualifications and courses

To become a psychiatrist you need to qualify as a doctor first. You will therefore need to complete a medical degree recognised by the General Medical Council (GMC).

After graduating, candidates undertake a 2-year foundation programme before applying for specialist training in psychiatry.

Training as a specialist registrar takes up to a further 6 years, spent training in general adult and old age psychiatry and gaining experience of other specialisms. This leads to the Certificate of Completion of Specialist Training (CCST), and eligibility for entry on the GMC's Specialist Register. It then becomes possible to apply for work as a consultant.

Advantages/disadvantages

Your patients could be confused or aggressive with a range of difficult problems so the work can be demanding.

It is rewarding to be able to make a difference to people's lives by helping them to regain their self-respect and happiness.

Money guide

Salary levels in the NHS have a national rate, but this can also vary in some areas.

Most junior doctors and senior house officers earn around £33,285 in their first year of training, rising to £41,285 in the second. Doctors on specialist training can earn up to £69,000.

Specialists with experience can earn up to £80,000.

Consultants earn from £71,000 and with additional payments and merits it is possible for consultants to earn anything up to £176,000.

Extra earnings may be available through private practice work.

Related opportunities

- Hospital Doctor p315
- Psychologist p570
- General Practitioner p308

Further information

NHS Careers
0845 60 60 655; www.nhscareers.nhs.uk

British Medical Association
BMA House, Tavistock Square, London, WC1H 9JP
020 7387 4499; www.bma.org.uk

Royal College of Psychiatrists
17 Belgrave Square, London, SW1X 8PG
020 7235 2351; www.rcpsych.ac.uk; rcpsych@rcpsych.ac.uk

RADIOGRAPHER

What the work involves

- There are two types of radiographer: diagnostic and therapeutic.

- Diagnostic radiographers produce images of organs, limbs and other parts of the body that are used to diagnose injury and disease. You may use a variety of methods such as X-ray, computed tomography (CT) scanning and ultrasound.

- Therapeutic radiographers treat patients, mostly those who have cancer, by delivering controlled doses of radiation. You will usually be involved in every aspect of the treatment, including pre-treatment preparation, planning, the delivery of the radiation and follow-up care of patients.

The type of person suited to this work

You will work with a range of patients from children to the elderly. You need to be caring and able to focus on each patient's needs. You must be able to listen and talk to patients and reassure them when carrying out diagnostic tests or treatments.

An ability to assess and treat patients' conditions accurately is vital, so you have to be able to concentrate and pay attention to detail. You should also be interested in science and technology and be confident when operating sophisticated computerised equipment.

Working conditions

You will work mainly in hospitals, in departments such as radiography, accident and emergency, or oncology (study of tumours).

Working with radiation is potentially dangerous, but you will be trained in how to work safely.

You may have a normal working week from Monday to Friday, but might have to work shifts on a rota basis, particularly if you are a diagnostic radiographer. This may include working at nights, at weekends and on bank holidays.

Future prospects

Although this is a growing area, there is a shortage of radiographers, so employment prospects are excellent. Most employment is available with the NHS throughout the UK. There is also work available in private hospitals and clinics and in industry. When you first qualify as a diagnostic radiographer, you will probably spend a lot of your time working in the accident and emergency department.

Promotion prospects in radiography are excellent. Diagnostic radiographers can move into specialist areas such as MRI, ultrasound or nuclear medicine. Therapeutic radiographers may specialise in areas such as treatment planning or treatment review.

Qualifications and courses

Radiographers must be registered with the Health Professions Council to be able to work in the NHS. Candidates who complete a degree approved by the Health Professions Council or Society of Radiographers are eligible for registration.

Degree courses are available in diagnostic and therapeutic radiography. Typical minimum entry requirements are 2 A levels/3–4 H grades including at least 1 science subject plus 5 GCSEs/S grades (A–C/1–3) including maths, English and science subjects. Most degree courses accept mature candidates and encourage qualifications other than A levels, including science-based Access courses.

Those with a relevant first degree may qualify as a therapeutic radiographer by studying for a postgraduate pre-registration qualification. Specialist postgraduate courses allow graduates to specialise in subjects such as ultrasound, computed tomography (CT) scanning, magnetic resonance imaging (MRI) or research.

Radiographers could move into management, teaching or research. There are also good opportunities to work abroad.

Advantages/disadvantages

The work can be challenging when working with patients who are frightened or distressed, particularly in therapeutic radiography.

It is extremely fulfilling to be able to use your knowledge and skills to diagnose or treat patients' conditions.

Money guide

£20,000–£26,000 per year is the starting salary for NHS radiographers. Senior grade and supervisory radiographers earn from £24,000–£38,000. Consultants can earn £60,000+.

There are also higher grades for radiography teachers and chief members of staff. And there are extra payments available, for example if you work in London.

Related opportunities

- Medical Physicist p320
- Critical Care Scientist p301
- Radiologist p340

Further information

Society of Radiographers
207 Providence Square, Mill Street, London, SE1 2EW
020 7740 7200; www.sor.org; ifno@sor.org

Radiography Careers
www.radiographycareers.co.uk

Healthcare

CRCI: JF
CLCI: JAP

RADIOLOGIST

What the work involves

- Radiologists are doctors who have undergone further training in radiology.

- As a radiologist, you will diagnose patients' diseases by using information gained from images such as X-rays, and computed tomography (CT) or magnetic resonance imaging (MRI) scans.

- Radiologists increasingly perform interventional procedures such as biopsies, using image guidance.

- You will also play an important role in identifying sources of disease and reducing the possible risks of it spreading further.

The type of person suited to this work

As a radiologist, you need to care about patients, and you must be able to explain things to them simply and clearly so that they understand their health conditions and any treatments they may need. You will also need good communication skills to work well as part of a team with other medical staff.

Scientific and technical knowledge and an ability to diagnose patients' conditions accurately are also necessary. You will need good eyesight and excellent attention to detail for interpreting images and practical skills for caring for patients and operating equipment.

Radiologists undergo a long programme of education and training in order to gain the in-depth knowledge and skills necessary.

Working conditions

You will work within a hospital, mainly in the radiology department.

Scientific and technical knowledge and an ability to diagnose patients' conditions accurately are also necessary. You will need good eyesight and excellent attention to detail for interpreting images and practical skills for caring for patients and operating equipment.

Radiologists undergo a long programme of education and training in order to gain the in-depth knowledge and skills necessary.

Future prospects

Career prospects are excellent due to an international shortage of radiologists. Most radiologists work within the NHS throughout the UK. There is also some work available in private hospitals.

You may decide to specialise further in particular areas of the work, or you could move into management. You may also move into academic work, either carrying out research or teaching medical students.

Advantages/disadvantages

The work can be emotionally demanding because you will be dealing with patients who may have life-threatening conditions.

Qualifications and courses

ENTRY LEVEL 4

Entry to radiology is initially the same as for hospital doctors (see p 315). To enter, candidates complete a medical degree recognised by the General Medical Council (GMC).

Candidates require at least 2 years' post-qualifying experience to enter training as a radiologist, but in practice, competition for training positions is very intense, and many new entrants have more than 3 years' clinical experience and a postgraduate qualification. New entrants must enrol as Members of the Royal College of Radiologists.

Specialist training as a radiologist takes at least 5 years, and leads to the Certificate of Completion of Specialist Training (CCST). At least 4 years of the training are spent in clinical posts, and 6 months' research in any aspect of diagnostic imaging is also included. Trainees must pass all 3 parts of the Fellowship of the Royal College of Radiologists (FRCR) examination.

The Royal College of Radiologists operates a Continuing Professional Development scheme for qualified radiologists to update their knowledge and skills.

Your work can be vital in finding an accurate and early diagnosis for patients, which can help to save lives.

Money guide

The salary for senior house officers with 5 years' experience could be up to £70,000 per year.

Specialists and consultants can earn from £75,000 to £150,000+.

Salary levels in the NHS have a national rate, but this can vary in some areas. Extra earnings may be available through private practice work.

Related opportunities

- Anaesthetist p294
- Hospital Doctor p315
- Psychiatrist p338
- Radiographer p339

Further information

NHS Careers
0845 60 60 655; www.nhscareers.nhs.uk

British Medical Association
BMA House, Tavistock Square, London, WC1H 9JP
020 7387 4499; www.bma.org.uk

Royal College of Radiologists
38 Portland Place, London, W1B 1JQ
020 7636 4432; www.rcr.ac.uk; enquiries@rcr.ac.uk

SPEECH/LANGUAGE THERAPIST

What the work involves

- Speech and language therapists work with patients who have problems speaking, chewing or swallowing.

- You will be responsible for assessing patients, and prescribing a suitable course of treatment.

- You will work with a range of patients including children who need help in developing their speech, people with a speech defect such as a stammer, and those who have trouble eating because of an accident or illness.

- You will also work with each patient's family, partner or carer in order to show them how to support your patient at home.

The type of person suited to this work

You will need excellent communication skills in order to develop a good relationship with patients and colleagues alike. You will also need to be a patient teacher in order to successfully help your patients learn new skills to overcome their problems.

You should be mature and non-judgmental in your approach to patients as you will be dealing with people of varying ages, backgrounds and cultures.

You will work both on your own and within a wider team of healthcare professionals, so you must have plenty of initiative couple with a good approach to working within a team.

Working conditions

Speech and language therapists usually work 37.5 hours per week from Monday to Friday. Evening, weekend or shift work is rare. There are plenty of opportunities to work part time.

You could work in one or several of a variety of locations, including hospitals, schools, residential homes, health centres, young offenders' institutions and in patients' houses. Since local travel in the community is required, it is useful to have a driving licence.

Future prospects

There is a current shortage of registered speech and language therapists, so job opportunities outweigh the number of candidates.

Most therapists are employed by the NHS and work throughout their local community. Others work for social services, local education authorities, charities and schools. There is a growing trend amongst therapists to be self-employed and treat patients privately. You could progress to more senior supervisory positions, specialise in an area that particularly interests you, or move into research.

Advantages/disadvantages

Speech and language therapists are in great demand, so you will have a greater choice of job opportunities open to you than in some other health-related professions.

Qualifications and courses

All speech and language therapists are registered with the Health Professions Council (HPC). In order to qualify for registration, you must complete an HPC approved training programme.

These take the form of either a 3 year degree or a 2 year Diploma in society, health and development. For entrance onto a degree course you will need 3 A-levels or equivalent, and 5 GCSEs/S grades (A-C/1–3) including English, science and maths. The Diploma entry criteria are 5 GCSEs/S grades (A-C/1–3) or equivalent, including English, science and maths.

There are also foundation courses available for those who do not have the relevant qualifications to go straight onto a degree programme, and accelerated 2 year degree courses for students who already have a health-related degree. All courses comprise of a balance between academic study and on-the-job training.

Because you will be working with children and vulnerable adults, you will need to undergo a Criminal Records Bureau check and medical screening.

Working closely with patients and seeing them improve under your care and guidance is rewarding.

You may have to work with difficult patients in unfavourable conditions on occasion, such as young offenders' institutions or prisons.

Money guide

As a newly qualified speech and language therapist, you could expect to earn around £20,000. This usually rises quite quickly to £24,000, and, as you gain experience, up to £33,000. Senior therapists can earn up to £43,000, and if you take on significant supervisory and management responsibilities as well you could expect £50,000+.

Related opportunities

- Occupational Therapist p323
- Learning Disabilities Nurse p318
- Health Visitor p313

Further information

Royal College of Speech and Language Therapists (RCSLT)
2 White Hart Yard, London, SE1 1NX
020 7378 1200; www.rcslt.org; info@rcslt.org

NHS Careers
PO Box 2311, Bristol BS2 2ZX
0845 606 0655; www.nhscareers.nhs.uk

CRCI: JG
CLCI: JAS

Healthcare

ENTRY LEVEL 5

SPORTS AND EXERCISE SCIENTIST

What the work involves

- Sports scientists work either with athletes to help build their performance or with people who need or wish to improve their health. Clients may also be recovering from illness or injury.

- As a sport or exercise scientist, you require a lot of scientific knowledge, including an understanding of biology, biomechanics, and physiology.

- You also need to have an understanding of psychology, as you may have to assess the mental state of some athletes, and you'll also spend time on performance analysis (usually done with video footage).

- You'll spend some time outside, and also conduct research.

The type of person suited to this work

If you want to be a sports or exercise scientist, above all you need to be a good communicator. Your work will centre around building relationships with people, and you have to be good at listening and aware of your client's needs. It's essential that you're a good team player too.

Aside from this, you need to have a clear writing style to communicate findings, and be good at research and problem solving. You should be good with numbers and statistics, well organised, accurate, and good with computers.

It helps if you have an interest in sport and the sciences.

Working conditions

You'll usually work in leisure and sports centres and gyms, usually for 38 hours a week. If you're a sports scientist, some clients may require you outside regular working hours, and part-time work is also available.

You'll also spend a lot of time outdoors, and probably travel too. For this reason, a driving licence is an advantage.

Future prospects

Although there's no specific career path for this job, progression is possible. Building a list of contacts is important, and with the right experience you may be able to work your way up to helping people who play sport at an international level.

You could also teach, or, if you're an exercise scientist you might be able to move into a specific area such as cardiology. You could also work for a local healthcare trust.

Advantages/disadvantages

This job is really rewarding for those who are interested in exercise and science, and like to be out and about being active rather than sitting still. You have to use your brain and your body, and the job is unlikely to become boring as you'll be working with so many different people.

Qualifications and courses

Most entrants to this profession have a degree in sports science, but it's also fine if you take a degree in psychology or any kind of physical education. You surprisingly don't actually need to be very good at sport yourself, although it does help.

To follow a degree in sports science, you usually need five good GCSEs and three A Levels. Some of these should be in sciences, especially Biology. There's also the option of following an access course before taking a degree, or doing a postgraduate degree in sports science after an initial science degree.

Once you have a relevant degree, you can seek accreditation through BASES, which can help improve job prospects. You can even be a member while you're still a student as there's a special category for student membership.

Continuing Professional Development (CPD) and keeping your skills up to date is really important, and there are plenty of opportunities to do this with BASES.

It can be tiring, and you need quite specialist knowledge that has to be constantly maintained.

Money guide

Newly qualified, you'll probably earn around £18,000 a year.

As you gain experience, this may rise to about £35,000.

If you work with top athletes, you might earn about £60,000 a year.

Related opportunities

- Health and Fitness Instructor p390
- Leisure Centre Manager p392
- Sports Coach p397
- Sports Development Officer p398

Further information

British Association of Sport and Exercise Sciences (BASES)
Leeds Metropolitan University, Carnegie Faculty of Sport and Education, Fairfax Hall, Headingley Campus, Beckett Park, Leeds, LS6 3QS.
0113 283 6162; www.bases.org.uk

English Institute of Sport (EIS)
4th Floor, Byrom House, 21 Quay Street, Manchester, M3 3JD.
0870 759 0400; www.eis2win.co.uk

SkillsActive
Castlewood House, 77–91 New Oxford Street, London, WC1A 1PX.
020 7632 2000; www.skillsactive.com/careers

STERILE SERVICES TECHNICIAN

What the work involves

- Sterile Services Technicians work as part of a team responsible for helping to prevent infections spreading by making sure that hospital equipment is sterile.

- Your work will involve collecting and cleaning a range of instruments from things like syringes to larger pieces of equipment.

- Some things will have to be dismantled and examined through a microscope before being sterilised and then reassembled and tested afterwards.

- You will work to national standards, operating highly technical machines, and must keep accurate records of your work.

The type of person suited to this work

You will need to be good with your hands to operate complex equipment and must be able to work accurately, pay attention to detail and follow instructions and set procedures carefully.

Sterile Services Technicians should be very careful about hygiene and interested in keeping hospitals and equipment clean and safe for patients and staff. You will work in a team so will need good communication skills. You should also be well organised and able to keep clear, detailed records.

You will be collecting and dismantling machinery so will need to be fit.

Working conditions

You will work in a hospital as part of team and will also have contact with doctors, nurses and other staff. Based in the sterile services department, you will collect equipment from all parts of the hospital and this will involve lifting and pushing trolleys.

You will have to wear protective clothing and may have to work shifts.

Future prospects

Most jobs are in NHS hospitals throughout the UK, but you could also work in a private hospital. Opportunities are good, as there is a shortage of applicants for vacancies.

With experience, you could get promotion to senior technician or supervisor. You could then take professional qualifications and become a Sterile Services Manager. As a manager you could move in to management in other areas of the NHS.

Qualifications and courses

There are no set minimum qualifications to begin work in this position. However, employers will expect you to have a good general standard of education, to have strong reading skills and neat handwriting (for labelling materials and equipment clearly and correctly).

Some employers may prefer you to have 5 GCSEs (A–C). Qualifications such as a BTEC National Certificate or Diploma in Applied Science could also be an advantage.

Whilst on the job, you may be encouraged to train for an ASET Level 2 Certificate in Control of Infection and Contamination, or an NCFE Level 2 Certificate in Infection Control.

Advantages/disadvantages

The work can be routine and physically demanding.

You will be making a vital contribution to controlling the spread of potentially deadly infections.

Money guide

Starting salaries are from £12,900–£16,000 per year.

As an assistant manager you can expect to earn £20,000–£28,000.

Related opportunities

- Hospital Porter p316
- Biomedical Scientist/Medical Laboratory Assistant p507
- Operating Department Practitioner p324

Further information

Skills for Health
2nd floor, Goldsmiths House, Broad Plain, Bristol, BS2 0JP
0117 922 1155; www.skillsforhealth.org.uk,
office@skillsforhealth.org.uk

NHS Careers
0845 60 60 655; www.nhscareers.nhs.uk

Institute of Decontamination Sciences
Chesterfield Royal Hospital NHS Foundation Trust, Calow,
Chesterfield, S44 5BL
01246 513069; www.idsc-uk.co.uk;
idsc.admin@googlemail.com

Healthcare

CRCI: JG
CLCI: JAN

SURGEON

What the work involves

- Surgeons work in hospitals, operating on patients in order to remove, isolate or prevent the spread of disease, treat injury, and fix other complaints.

- You will also be responsible for diagnosing problems, taking case histories, talking patients through surgical procedures and advising them on post-operative care.

- You will specialise in operating on specific conditions or diseases relating to a particular system of the body, such as neurological, gastrointestinal or cardiovascular.

- You will see patients on ward rounds and in outpatient clinics, as well as undertaking administrative work, such as updating patient records.

The type of person suited to this work

You will need excellent communication skills in order to develop a good relationship with patients and colleagues alike. You will be required to direct your team through complex surgical procedures in the operating theatre, as well as explaining them to patients in simple terms.

You should have excellent manual and technical skills in order to operate with precision and confidence. As you will be working under immense pressure whilst in theatre, you should also be able to think quickly and clearly when solving problems.

You must be prepared to break news to patients and relatives on occasion, which requires sensitivity and diplomacy.

Working conditions

Most surgeons work extremely long hours which often include nights and weekends. Most of your work will take place in hospitals, working with other health professionals, including other surgeons, nurses, anaesthetists and GPs. You could work in the NHS or in private hospitals, although the majority of surgeons divide their time between the two.

The work is mentally and physically exhausting, as you will need to concentrate for hours at a time and spend a lot of time on your feet.

Future prospects

There are many opportunities to work abroad, particularly in conjunction with specialist charities operating in developing countries.

You will continue to train and learn new skills throughout your career as technology and techniques develop, change and improve. Once you have qualified as a surgeon, you can become a consultant and work within the NHS or in private practice, both of which are lucrative options.

Advantages/disadvantages

You will be personally responsible for transforming and saving a number of lives throughout your career. Jobs don't really get much more rewarding than that.

Qualifications and courses

ENTRY LEVEL 5

Before commencing training as a surgeon you will need to study for a degree in medicine. Most medical degrees take 5 years; entrants require at least 3 A-levels in subjects including chemistry and biology, and 5 GCSEs/S grades (A-C/1–3) or equivalent.

If you do not have science related A-levels, you could undertake a 6 year degree programme that includes a preliminary 30 week course to get you up to speed. A 4 year fast-track degree course is available to those who already hold a degree.

On completion of a medical degree, you will need to undertake a 2 year, hospital based foundation programme of general training. At the end of this, you can choose to specialise in surgery. You will then undertake a further 6 years of training in order to pass your surgical exams and qualify for entry onto the General Medical Council specialist register as a surgeon.

The training period is extremely long, often in excess of 12 years, so you have to be extremely dedicated.

You will work long hours and unpredictable hours, which can have an adverse effect on your personal life.

Money guide

Once you have completed your medical degree, you can expect to earn around £20,000 during your foundation years. As you start on speciality surgical training, this will increase to around £29,000, and should increase to around £45,000 during the 6 year period.

Once you have qualified and become a consultant, you can earn £70,000+. Senior consultants' salaries reach in excess of £170,000.

Related opportunities

- Hospital Doctor p315
- General Practitioner p308
- Dentist p305

Further information

The Royal College of Surgeons of England
35–43 Lincoln's Inn Fields, London, WC2A 3PE
020 7405 3474; www.rcseng.ac.uk

British Medical Association (BMA)
BMA House, Tavistock Square, London, WC1H 9JP
www.bma.org.uk

NHS Careers
PO Box 2311, Bristol, BS2 2ZX
0845 606 0655; www.nhscareers.nhs.uk

TRICHOLOGIST

What the work involves

- Trichologists diagnose and treat diseases and disorders of the scalp and hair such as hair loss, hair breakage and dandruff.

- As a trichologist, your role will include talking to the patient about their medical history, health and diet and closely examining the patient's hair and scalp.

- You will give advice and recommend any necessary treatment, such as creams or shampoos.

- You may also refer patients on to other healthcare professionals if appropriate.

The type of person suited to this work

Trichologists need good communication skills to talk to patients about their concerns and explain their condition and any treatments they may need. You should be sympathetic and tactful and able to reassure patients, put them at their ease and listen carefully to their concerns.

You will need to apply your scientific knowledge and experience to your work, have a methodical approach and pay attention to detail so that you can assess patients' conditions accurately and plan appropriate treatment.

Working conditions

Most trichologists work in clinics, but those who are involved in research and teaching work in universities and colleges, or in pharmaceutical and cosmetics companies.

You may have normal working hours from Monday to Friday, but if you work in private practice you will probably need to work in the evenings, or occasionally at weekends, to treat people at times that suit them.

The work involves close contact and hands-on treatment of patients.

Future prospects

Most trichologists are self-employed and run their own clinics, usually working on their own. Dermatologists are doctors who have trained in trichology and are usually employed in hospitals.

Trichologists may also go on to work as lecturers in colleges or universities, often in hair and beauty departments.

There are also a small number of opportunities to work in research in pharmaceutical and cosmetics companies.

Advantages/disadvantages

Working with patients can be challenging and stressful.

It is rewarding to be able to use your knowledge to treat patients successfully.

Money guide

Most trichologists are self-employed and charge clients by the session. Earnings vary widely, depending on how much you

Qualifications and courses

The main route into trichology and entry to the register of qualified members of The Institute of Trichologists is by successful completion of the Institute's 2-year training course in trichology (there are limited exceptions to this, for example for doctors (dermatologists) and graduates of HND trichology courses at selected colleges).

Entrants are often mature, though there is no set minimum age. There are no set minimum entry requirements, but the course is academic and scientific in nature and the progress of students is closely monitored.

Successful completion of the Institute's course makes you eligible for admission as an Associate Member of the Institute (AIT). Progression to full membership (MIT) is available upon further study and a minimum of 2 years' professional practice as a trichologist.

To become a doctor (dermatologist), candidates complete a medical degree recognised by the General Medical Council (GMC) as outlined in the doctor entry (see p315).

charge and how many clients you see. How much you earn can depend on which area of the country you are working in.

Earnings for newly self-employed practitioners may start from about £12,000–£14,000 a year. Experienced practitioners may earn up to £40,000.

For NHS (doctor) dermatologists, you must complete a medical degree, and the salary for these posts is outlined in the hospital doctor information page.

Extra earnings may be available through private practice work.

Related opportunities

- Hospital Doctor p315
- Hairdresser/Barber p469
- Dietitian p306

Further information

Skills for Health
2nd floor, Goldsmiths House, Broad Plain, Bristol, BS2 0JP
0117 922 1155; www.skillsforhealth.org.uk;
office@skillsforhealth.org.uk

NHS Careers
0845 60 60 655; www.nhscareers.nhs.uk

Institute of Trichologists
24 Langroyd Road, London, SW17 7PL
0870 607 0602, www.trichologists.org.uk,
admin@trichologists.org.uk

Healthcare

CRCI: JI
CLCI: JAD

Languages, Information and Culture

The jobs in this family are quite varied in terms of whether you would work with other people or by yourself. You could find yourself working in a range of different places, from museums to antiques fairs to conferences as an interpreter. Some of the jobs in this family are more unusual and are perfect for those of you who want a fascinating job that allows you to indulge in your passion for historic artefacts and artwork or languages and foreign countries. To excel in this sector you should have an inquisitive mind, be meticulous in your work and enjoy carrying out research.

The following jobs are covered in this section:

For similar jobs to the ones in this section please see *Design, Arts and Crafts* on page 175 and *Marketing, Advertising, Media, Print and Publishing* on page 405.

ANTHROPOLOGIST

What the work involves

- You will study and research the behaviour and beliefs of people and social groups.

- You will investigate specific issues and areas that make up part of everyday culture in the UK and other parts of the world.

- You will apply specialist knowledge and research skills to find out about differences between human cultures.

- Anthropologists undertake their research around a wide range of areas such as archaeology, the arts, the environment, biology and religion.

The type of person suited to this work

Whatever job you do as an anthropologist, you will need a strong interest in people and a respectful, flexible attitude to other people's beliefs and customs. You should also enjoy meeting new people and going into different social situations.

Good communication skills are also very important. Strong research skills and an organised approach are useful. ICT skills and a good level of numeracy are also helpful. You will need an observant approach with an interest in a wide range of subjects.

Working conditions

For research-based work, you may need to visit and stay in different areas. Spending time in other places means that anthropology is not generally a 9–5 office-based job. The work can involve travel in the UK and overseas. Some physical or biological anthropologists work in laboratories analysing and researching samples.

Future prospects

You could gain employment as a researcher on specific projects. Many anthropologists progress within academia by undertaking research and teaching around their specialist interests. You could also work for government bodies and charities. There are some opportunities to work overseas.

Anthropologists also apply their research skills and training to their work in other areas such as social care, teaching and the health service.

Advantages/disadvantages

This job can provide opportunities to develop and research theories about people and cultures. Anthropology can also provide the chance to meet a variety of people and visit different places.

Field research can be physically demanding and spending time away can be difficult if you have family commitments.

Money guide

Anthropologists work in a wide range of sectors, so salaries vary widely.

Qualifications and courses

Entry to this area is usually gained with degree-level or postgraduate training or qualifications. Voluntary or paid work experience can be useful.

There are limited opportunities to gain qualifications in this area before degree level. Sociology A levels and GCSEs cover some aspects of anthropology. For biological anthropology, an A level in biology may be useful.

Access and degree courses in this area cover subjects such as social anthropology and physical/biological anthropology. Anthropology can also be studied as part of a combined Honours degree with subjects such as social anthropology or psychology.

It is also possible to study for a Master's or other postgraduate degree in anthropology following a first degree in any subject.

The Association of Social Anthropologists runs seminars and conferences, and has information on bursaries and awards for anthropology students. Some universities such as Wolverhampton and Brighton have Centres for Learning and Teaching which run courses on sociology, anthropology and politics, although these are aimed at applicants with some knowledge of the subject.

Professionals using their anthropology training in another area are likely to have gained a qualification or degree in another subject.

Researchers in this area are often required to have a relevant postgraduate qualification or the equivalent practical experience.

Starting salaries for graduates are around £21,000+ per year, rising to £26,000 for research assistants/researchers, depending on experience. £24,000–£30,000 per year is usual for lecturers. £28,000–£50,000 is the range for senior lecturers.

Related opportunities

- Archaeologist p349
- Historian p355
- Archivist/Records Manager p350

Further information

Royal Anthropological Institute of Great Britain and Ireland (RAI)
50 Fitzroy Street, London, W1T 5BT
020 7387 0455; www.therai.org.uk

Higher Education Academy Subject Network for Sociology, Anthropology and Politics (C-SAP)
The University of Birmingham, Edgbaston, Birmingham, B15 2TT
0121 414 7919; www.c-sap.bham.ac.uk

ARCHAEOLOGIST

What the work involves

- Using your specialist knowledge and skills you will investigate and record physical evidence of the past and develop public understanding of history.

- You will provide practical support on archaeological excavations or 'digs', which may include undertaking basic digging work, project-managing an excavation or researching evidence found on-sites.

- You could manage and oversee historic buildings and monuments.

- You may provide information and advice on how to protect and maintain historical sites.

The type of person suited to this work

You will need a strong interest in history and how people lived in the past. For practical work you will need a patient and careful approach. You should also be observant with an eye for detail. A good level of physical fitness and manual dexterity will be needed when working on digs and handling objects.

The ability to work as part of a team is useful. In more senior jobs, you will need to explain your work to others so communication skills are important. Writing skills will help you to be able to write up reports and keep detailed records. ICT skills are also useful.

Working conditions

Archaeologists often work on-sites or digs that are outdoors. Varying weather conditions and the nature of the work make this job physically demanding.

You will need good manual handling skills and a conscientious approach when working with historical artefacts.

Some archaeologists are based in offices within government bodies, heritage organisations and museums.

Future prospects

Whatever route you follow, this is a very competitive area in which to develop a career. You will need to gain practical experience on a voluntary or paid basis. With further experience you could project-manage site excavations or work as a researcher analysing excavation findings.

Some archaeologists work for heritage organisations to help preserve the historic monuments and buildings. Others go into teaching or follow an academic career.

Advantages/disadvantages

It is likely that you will need to move around different geographical areas to gain practical experience.

There are opportunities to work overseas.

Archaeologists with a good level of experience in a specialist area can go on to work as consultants.

Qualifications and courses

Most professional archaeologists have a degree or postgraduate qualification.

Degree entry usually requires 5 GCSEs/S grades (A–C/1–3) or equivalent, with a good mix of arts and sciences. High grades in 3 A levels/4 H grades are often needed. There are no specific subject requirements at A level/H grade. NVQs Level 3 and 4 are available in archaeological practice.

Archaeology can be studied as a single Honours degree or in combination with another degree subject. A small number of HNCs, HNDs, Foundation degrees and DipHEs are available in archaeology.

Entry to postgraduate courses requires a good first degree.

Voluntary experience on digs is very useful. The key professional bodies can provide details of holiday work experience opportunities. The Archaeology Training Forum (ATF; a consortium of professional bodies involved in archaeology) develop and offer short courses in Continuing Professional Development, including the programme at Oxford University Department of Continuing Education, and others at the Institute of Archaeology and Antiquity at Birmingham University, the Ironbridge Institute and the School of Archaeology and Ancient History at Leicester University.

Money guide

£14,300–£15,500 per year is usual for starting salaries.

With experience and some supervisory responsibilities this can rise to around £20,000.

Project managers can expect a salary of around £30,000.

Related opportunities

- Archivist p350
- Conservator/Restorer p353
- FE Lecturer/HE Lecturer p206
- Librarian p358

Further information

Creative and Cultural Skills
4th Floor, Lafone House, London, SE1 3HN
020 7015 1847; www.ccskills.org.uk

Institute of Field Archaeologists
PO Box 227, University of Reading, Reading, RG6 6AB
0118 378 6446; www.archaeologists.net

Council for British Archaeology
St Mary's House, 66 Bootham, York, YO30 7BZ
01904 671417; www.britarch.ac.uk

Languages, Information and Culture

CRCI: K
CLCI: FAH

ARCHIVIST/ RECORDS MANAGER

What the work involves

Archivist

- You will manage and organise stored sets archives, including records such as documents, maps, films and other items. Many archivists deal with information enquiries and advise on the availability of records. You will ensure that archives are maintained in an appropriate way. You may also conserve documents and prepare them for storage.

Records manager

- You will be responsible for organising records and information and advising your organisation as to which should be classified, stored or destroyed. You could be dealing with paper based or electronic records.

The type of person suited to this work

Both records managers and archivists manage information so a well-organised and methodical approach is essential. They need strong analytical and IT skills.

Archivists will need an interest in preserving historical records. You may provide information and advice to members of the public so strong communication skills are useful.

Working conditions

Record/archive centres can be modern and spacious, but if based in older buildings, space may be limited.

Accessing records from cramped storage rooms or high shelves can be physically demanding. This job may not suit people with dust allergies.

In archivist roles dealing with enquiries from visitors, the working environment can be very busy.

Future prospects

Archivist

Public records offices, private companies and other organisations need skilled information professionals. With experience, you could progress from an assistant archivist role into senior management.

Records manager

Records managers may need to change employers in order to progress. Consultancy work is an option.

Advantages/disadvantages

Archivist

This job allows you to preserve and protect historical documents.

Employers often offer short-term contracts which can create job instability.

Qualifications and courses

Archivist

Entrants to this profession need a 2.1 Honours degree followed by a postgraduate qualification in archives and records management or archival studies. The Society of Archivists recognises postgraduate courses in archives and records management/archival studies at certain UK universities.

Work experience is an advantage in gaining a place on a postgraduate course, and the Society of Archivists provides information about placements.

Records manager

You will normally require both an honours degree and a postgraduate qualification in records management or in archives and records management. To gain entry to a postgraduate course you will normally need at least a second class honours degree. Relevant experience is an important requirement.

If you do not have a degree you can enter this career as a records assistant, in some cases promotion to records manager might be possible but many employers will require a postgraduate qualification.

Records manager

You may have to change employers in order to progress.

You will constantly be learning as computer software and legislation are always changing.

Money guide

£17,000–£24,000 is typical for starting salaries (before gaining a professional qualification).When qualified and with some experience you could earn around £27,000. As a senior archivist it is possible to earn £60,000. Records managers receive a starting salary of about £23,000, with experience this can increase to £26,680-£40,000. With enough experience and within a large enough team you could earn over £70,000.

Related opportunities

- Archaeologist p349
- Librarian p358

Further information

Society of Archivists
Prioryfield House, 20 Canon Street, Taunton, TA1 1SW
01823 327030; www.archives.org.uk

City& Guilds

www.cityandguilds.com/myperfectjob

ARTS ADMINISTRATOR

What the work involves

- You will support the development and operation of activities and events in areas such as visual arts, drama and music.

- You will undertake a range of administrative tasks including coordinating facilities and office management. You may be responsible for managing funding applications and budgets.

- Your job could also involve arts marketing activities such as writing press releases.

- Arts administrators are employed within galleries, arts centres, community arts groups and one-off arts projects.

The type of person suited to this work

Enthusiasm for the arts is essential for this role. You will need a committed approach and to be able to take the initiative. A good range of administrative, office and ICT skills are also essential. You will be able to communicate well in person and in writing. Because it is likely that you will have to manage project budgets, numeracy skills are also useful.

As you will coordinate a number of activities at once, you will need a well-organised approach. You should enjoy working with a range of people including artists and members of the public. You should be able to work independently and as part of a team. A flexible outlook is useful.

Working conditions

Working hours can vary but it is likely that you will need to work some evenings and weekends to attend events.

Working environments vary according to employer. You may be based in a spacious office or have to work in more cramped conditions.

Within roles that have an arts development aspect, you will be required to travel between locations to attend meetings and make contacts.

Future prospects

As with many aspects of arts management, this is a competitive area to get into. Developing expertise in a specific area such as community arts or theatre can be helpful. With experience, you could progress from an assistant administrator role into a more senior job.

With higher levels of experience, you could provide freelance support to arts groups and projects. You could specialise in a particular area such as arts marketing and management.

Advantages/disadvantages

This job provides the satisfaction of working in the arts.

Many roles are available on a part-time or project basis which can create job insecurity.

You may have to move geographic areas to gain work.

Qualifications and courses

There are no specific entry requirements, but most arts administrators have a degree in an arts subject or business studies.

At degree level, arts management can be studied on its own, or in combination with related subject such as events management and heritage management. There are no particular subject requirements for entry to these degrees.

Postgraduate courses in arts administration/arts management are available. A degree and/or relevant work experience is required for entry to these programmes.

NVQs are available in Cultural Venue Operations and Support at Level 2 and Cultural Venue Administration or Cultural Heritage Operations at Level 3, Cultural Heritage at Level 4 and Cultural Heritage Management at Level 5.

Some entrants to this profession take the Institute of Chartered Secretaries and Administrators (ICSA) professional examinations. Candidates without formal qualifications can take the Certificate in Business Practice and then progress to the Diploma and Professional Programme. Degrees, professional and vocational qualifications give exemption from some parts of the qualifying programme.

Experience in the arts, in administration or business, and ICT skills can be an advantage.

Money guide

Salary levels vary according to the type of organisation you work for.

£13,000 per year is a normal starting salary for an assistant or trainee. When qualified this rises to £15,500. This can rise to £25,000+ with experience. Senior managers may earn between £25,000 and £60,000. Salaries are higher in London and in other large cities.

Related opportunities

- Museum Assistant p361
- Personal Assistant p51
- Museum/Art Gallery Curator p359

Further information

Arts Council of England
2 Pear Tree Court, London, EC1R 0DS
0845 300 6200, www.artscouncil.org.uk

Scottish Arts Council
12 Manor Place, Edinburgh, EH3 7DD
0845 603 6000; www.scottisharts.org.uk

www.cityandguilds.com/myperfectjob

Languages, Information and Culture

CRCI: K
CLCI: E

AUCTIONEER

What the work involves

- Auctioneers sell items at auctions, getting the best market price possible for the items they're selling.

- It's your responsibility to make sure the item sells for the best price, both by selling well on the day and by organising and publicising sales in advance.

- You'll be inspecting and valuing items and coming to price agreements with the sellers, making sure that reserves set are appropriate

- On auction days, you'll run through the items on sale, observe customers, and take bids. You may specialise in a particular area, and could be working on anything from antiques and property to livestock and motors.

The type of person suited to this work

You will need to be good with people and communicate well, so that you can interact with customers and successfully sell goods. In addition, you should be outgoing and confident, with excellent knowledge of what you're selling.

You should have excellent observational skills and a good attention to detail, as valuing objects is also a big part of the job. For this reason you also need to be able to think on your feet, and work well under pressure.

You must have shrewd business sense and a good head for figures, as much of your day will revolve around numbers.

Working conditions

You'll usually be working in an auction house, or an office or auction room within. Normal working hours are 9–5.30 Monday to Saturday, but be prepared to carry out viewings and valuations during evenings and weekends.

A driving licence is useful as travel may be necessary, for example if you're selling the contents of a large house clearing.

You may also sell livestock and motors outdoors.

Future prospects

Career development relies on building up a list of contacts, and working towards moving to larger more prestigious auction houses.

You may want to become self-employed, or work towards a management position or partnership.

You may also have the chance to travel, as some auction houses have offices abroad.

Advantages/disadvantages

This work is stimulating and challenging, and especially rewarding if you choose to work with items or goods you have a genuine interest in.

Every day will be different, and you will constantly be interacting and communicating with people.

Qualifications and courses

There are no set entry requirements, but most employers prefer candidates with good communication skills and sound GCSE results . You can enter the profession by working as a salesroom assistant and progressing to the position of auctioneer. If you want to go into property auctioning, you could start out by gaining experience in valuation work. Some employers will be willing to take you on as a trainee.

The Royal Institution of Chartered Surveyors accredit some degree courses in property and valuation. You can also follow a foundation degree in auctioneering and valuation, or the arts market (offered at Wolverhampton and Kingston universities), or property and rural auctioneering as offered by Cumbria University. Sotheby's also offer an MA degree in Arts Business.

Another option is to study for a degree in a subject related to fine arts, for example history of art. For entry onto these courses, you will need good GCSEs and at least two A-levels.

Once you're in, training will mostly take place on the job, and you'll be shadowing experienced auctioneers most of the time. They'll expect you to study in your own time in order to understand in depth the areas that their auction house specialises in.

It can be tiring work, and much of the day will be spent on your feet. As the person leading an auction, you have to be 100% alert all the time.

Money guide

Starting salaries for trainees are about £15,000 a year.

As you gain experience, this may rise to about £30,000–£40,000 a year.

If you become a business partner, you might earn over £60,000.

Related opportunities

- Antiques Dealer p478
- Chartered Surveyor p82
- Estate Agent p97
- Rural Surveyor p123

Further information

Livestock Auctioneers' Association Limited (LAA)
Cobblethwaite, Wreay, Carlisle, Cumbria, CA4 0RZ.
01697 475433; www.laa.co.uk

National Association of Valuers and Auctioneers (NAVA),
6 Tournament Court, Edgehill Drive, Warwick, CV34 6LG.
01926 417774; www.nava.org.uk

National Federation of Property Professionals (NFoPP),
Arbon House, 6 Tournament Court, Edgehill Drive,
Warwick, CV34 6LG.
01926 496800; www.nfopp.co.uk

CONSERVATOR/RESTORER

What the work involves

■ You will manage the preservation of historical objects and artworks, applying your specialist knowledge of subjects such as textiles and furniture.

■ You may undertake conservation work, treating objects to protect them against wear and tear, or restore objects to as close to their original state as possible.

■ Your job may involve managing freelance restorers/ conservators.

■ As well as objects in museums and galleries, restoration/conservation officers manage the care of historic houses and stately homes.

The type of person suited to this work

The role of preserving and protecting valuable collections or buildings requires a good knowledge of conservation and restoration issues. In some jobs, you will undertake conservation/restoration work yourself so you will need excellent practical skills and good attention to detail.

In other jobs you will manage other professionals to do the work, so communication skills are essential. These skills will also be useful when advising colleagues and providing information at public events. Writing skills are also helpful and ICT skills are increasingly important. The ability to work as part of a team is essential.

Working conditions

Your work is likely to involve handling and treating fragile objects, so good practical skills are important.

You may have to work with specialist materials and equipment, which can affect people with skin conditions.

In most jobs, you will spend much of your time assessing and researching collections. You will also attend meetings with colleagues.

Future prospects

Restoration/conservation officers work in museums, galleries and historic houses, often with alternative job titles such as Collections Manager or Curator. Many will have worked as craft conservators/restorers or have gained extensive experience in caring for collections.

Having geographic mobility will help you to gain work. With experience, you could progress into managing a historic house or into a senior management role in a museum or gallery.

Advantages/disadvantages

This type of work offers the chance to protect and care for valuable historical collections.

Most galleries/museums employ only one person in this type of role, so you may have to move around to develop your career in this area.

Qualifications and courses

Entry is usually by degree or postgraduate qualification, though candidates with relevant craft qualifications and experience may be eligible.

Degrees and Foundation degrees are available in various restoration and conservation areas such as furniture and buildings. For Foundation degrees, work experience or a range of GCSEs are usually required. For degree entry, a Foundation degree or HND or 2 A levels/3 H grades (including chemistry) are normally required.

For postgraduate courses a relevant degree, such as science, fine art or art history, is usually required.

Voluntary experience is useful, and can be gained through the National Association of Decorative and Fine Arts Societies (NADFAS) volunteer scheme.

Restorers/Conservation Officers can work towards NVQs/ SVQs in Cultural Heritage Operations (Level 3), Cultural Heritage (Level 4) and Cultural Heritage Management (Level 5).

Money guide

Salaries vary according to your employer.

New entrants may start at £16,000–£21,000 per year.

This can rise to £20,000–£30,000 with experience.

£35,000+ is possible at senior levels.

Your salary will depend on the high quality of your work and it may be easier to get work in London and the larger cities.

Related opportunities

■ Archaeologist p349
■ Architect p68
■ Archivist/Records Manager p350
■ Museum/Art Gallery Curator p359

Further information

Creative and Cultural Skills
4th Floor, Lafone House, London, SE1 3HN
020 7015 1847; www.ccskills.org.uk

National Association of Decorative and Fine Arts Societies
NADFAS House, 8 Guilford Street, London, WC1N 1DA
020 7430 0730; www.nadfas.org.uk

Institute of Conservation (Icon)
3rd floor, Downstream Building, 1 London Bridge, London, SE1 9BG
020 7785 3807, www.icon.org.uk

Languages, Information and Culture

CRCI: K
CLCI: FAE

GENEALOGIST

What the work involves

■ You will organise and plan research into the history or ancestry of individual families (genealogy) and write reports from your findings.

■ You will work with a range of historical information such as newspapers and directories to trace specific facts about family histories.

■ Your work could also involve liaising with or supervising the work of researchers.

■ Meeting with clients and keeping them updated with your research would also be part of your job.

The type of person suited to this work

As you will be investigating family history, a strong enthusiasm for historical research is essential. You will also need excellent research skills and the ability to understand detailed information. ICT skills will help you work with specialist research and information management software. You will also need writing skills to produce reports.

You should enjoy meeting a range of people. You will also need a good knowledge of historical resources and subject areas. An organised, thorough approach to your work is important. Working with unique historical documents demands good manual handling skills.

Working conditions

Most genealogists are self-employed and work from home or from offices. However, they spend a lot of their time in public records offices or in other sites, undertaking research. The job can involve some travel, for example to public records offices or archive collections.

You will spend a lot of time reading and assessing detailed information.

Future prospects

Genealogy is usually followed as an interest rather than as a profession. The number of opportunities for work in this area is very small so there is a lot of competition.

Most genealogists work on a self-employed basis whilst a small number work for specialist research companies. They develop specialist knowledge on a specific subject or geographical area. Genealogists often undertake additional work such as teaching genealogy.

Advantages/disadvantages

There are very few job opportunities. Most genealogists have additional employment.

The work is often project-based, which creates some job insecurity.

This work gives the satisfaction of providing people with information about their family history.

Qualifications and courses

There are no formal qualifications needed to be a professional genealogist. However, a good basic education along with a sound knowledge of social and local history sources are necessary. Knowledge of palaeography (the study of ancient writing and scripts) and Latin are also essential.

Direct entry to this profession is not usual. Entrants normally have qualifications and experience in a related field such as archive administration, librarianship or historical research.

A degree in history provides a useful first step, while University Campus Suffolk has a degree in Family and Community History. Blackpool and the Fylde College runs a Foundation degree in History and Heritage Management Studies, which covers genealogy.

The Society of Genealogists provides short courses in genealogy and palaeography both for beginners and for those already working in the field. The Institute of Heraldic and Genealogical Studies provides qualifications for genealogists, including a certificate, higher certificate and diploma in genealogy. People who complete these qualifications may be able to progress to Licenciateship of the Institute.

Money guide

Freelance genealogists are usually paid at an hourly rate which can range from £16 to £35.

For more complex projects, genealogists may charge a total fee. This can range from £35 to £100 depending on the amount of work involved.

Genealogists with a postgraduate qualification can expect to earn £26,500–£35,000 per year.

Very experienced/senior genealogists can earn £50,000+.

Related opportunities

■ Archivist/Records Manager p350
■ Library Assistant p358
■ Registrar of Births, Deaths, Marriages and Civil Partnerships p58
■ Private Investigator p555

Further information

Creative and Cultural Skills
4th Floor, Lafone House, London, SE1 3HN
020 7015 1847; www.ccskills.org.uk

Society of Genealogists
14 Charterhouse Buildings, Goswell Road, London, EC1M 7BA
020 7251 8799; www.sog.org.uk

Institute of Heraldic and Genealogical Studies
79–82 Northgate, Canterbury, Kent, CT1 1BA
01227 768664; www.ihgs.ac.uk

HISTORIAN

What the work involves

- You will undertake historical research using ICT and paper-based information and other resources to broaden public and academic understanding of the past.

- You may teach and lecture on specific historical subjects. You could also write articles for professional journals and other publications.

- Heritage organisations sometimes employ historians.

- Professional historians usually specialise in a specific area of history such as women's history, the history of science or industrial history.

The type of person suited to this work

For any job in this area, you will need a strong enthusiasm for history. You should also have a good knowledge of your specialist subjects. The ability to work with ICT and paper-based resources is also important. Good attention to detail will ensure that you undertake accurate research.

As you may need to explain complex issues to others, good verbal communication skills are important. Writing skills will help you write up research and articles. Historians need to consider a wide range of theories, so an open-minded approach is important. You should also be well organised to manage and plan your research.

Working conditions

You will undertake some of your work in libraries and archive centres. This will involve reading and assessing information. Some historical researchers are based in public records offices.

Historians in an academic role spend time lecturing and teaching students.

Undertaking historical research on a self-employed basis can create some job insecurity.

Future prospects

As a professional historian you could go into historical research or follow an academic career path. Many historians combine both roles and write, teach and research on their specialist area of interest. Others combine historical research with other related areas such as genealogy.

A small number of historians are employed by heritage organisations to provide expert advice and support.

Advantages/disadvantages

This type of work provides the satisfaction of undertaking original research and finding out about the past.

Qualifications and courses

An MA in history or historical archaeology is usually required for work as an archival or historical researcher.

Entry requirements for postgraduate degrees are a first degree in history. Entry requirements for first degrees are generally 3 A levels/5 H Grades including history (A–C).

For a position in a university faculty, a PhD is usually required.

Training courses in historical research are available through the Institute of Historical Research, the Society of Genealogists and the Institute of Heraldic and Genealogical Studies.

It takes time to get established as a specialist on a specific historical period or subject either in research, writing or academic work.

Money guide

Earnings vary according to your job.

Historical researchers usually charge by the hour; rates vary from £16 to £50.

Starting salaries for academic posts range from £21,000 to £27,000 per year.

With experience this rises to around £38,000.

At senior academic levels, this could increase to £35,000–£50,000.

Related opportunities

- Archaeologist p349
- Archivist/Records Manager p350
- Genealogist p354
- Museum/Art Gallery Curator p359

Further information

Institute of Historical Research
University of London, Senate House, Malet Street, London, WC1E 7HU
020 7862 8740; www.history.ac.uk

Royal Historical Society
University College London, Gower Street, London, WC1E 6BT
020 7387 7532; www.rhs.ac.uk

Creative and Cultural Skills
4th Floor, Lafone House, London, SE1 3HN
020 7015 1847; www.ccskills.org.uk

Languages, Information and Culture

CRCI: K
CLCI: FAG

INFORMATION SCIENTIST

What the work involves

- You will develop, manage and coordinate information systems in a range of organisations and companies.

- You will utilise information systems and resources to locate and provide information in response to enquiries. You may work with ICT or paper-based information.

- You could work in a range of sectors, including law, education and business.

- Information scientists are employed in a variety of job roles and work as information analysts, information officers, information managers and librarians.

The type of person suited to this work

Managing and working with information requires a range of skills. You should be able to work with different forms of information such as databases, the internet and paper resources. You may provide information for members of the public or staff within an organisation so strong communication skills are important. An interest in customer care is useful.

You will need writing skills for some roles and ICT skills are increasingly important. Managing information demands an organised, methodical approach. A good level of numeracy can be useful. You will need a resourceful approach when undertaking detailed research.

Working conditions

Information scientists work in offices, resource centres, libraries and other sites.

You may be based in a public centre and work face to face with members of the public or staff within your organisation. You may also deal with information enquiries over the phone and through email.

Future prospects

Information science is a very broad area. You could begin in an assistant or junior information job. With experience, you could progress to working in an information management role.

Some information scientists with experience in a specialist area work on a consultancy basis. Some specialise in undertaking research whilst others organise new information systems. There are also opportunities to work abroad on a short-term or longer-term basis. you will need to attend meetings with colleagues and managers.

Advantages/disadvantages

Depending on the sector you work in, this job can be very fast paced.

Information science skills are transferable to a wide range of job areas, allowing you to develop a career in areas that interest you such as the public sector or business.

Money guide

£17,000–£22,000 per year is usual for starting salaries.

Qualifications and courses

Most professional information scientists are graduates.

The fastest route to professional qualification is via a first degree in subjects such as information management, information studies and information and library studies, which are accredited by the Chartered Institute of Library and Information Professionals (CILIP).

An alternative route to professional qualification is via a degree in any subject, followed by a CILIP-approved postgraduate qualification. Experience of information-related work is advantageous, and may be a requirement for some postgraduate courses. Graduate training opportunities are available for people who wish to pursue a career in this area, and need to gain relevant experience before studying for a postgraduate qualification. Details are available through CILIP.

It is also possible to become a qualified information scientist from a library/information assistant post. CILIP offers a Certification scheme for people with 5 years' experience of information work, or 2 years' experience plus relevant work-based training.

Entrants through both the educational and certification routes may have the opportunity to work towards Chartered membership of CILIP. Candidates for Chartership must have completed an approved period of professional experience.

When qualified you can get up to £27,500.

With experience this rises to £40,000.

£65,000+ is possible at senior levels in large commercial organisations.

Information consultants can earn around £400–£500 a day.

Related opportunities

- Archivist/Records Manager p350
- Library Assistant p358
- Museum/Art Gallery Curator p359
- Researcher (media) p428

Further information

Chartered Institute of Library and Information Professionals
7 Ridgemount Street, London, WC1E 7AE
020 7255 0500; www.cilip.org.uk

Aslib, The Association for Information Management
Holywell Centre, 1 Phipp Street, London, EC2A 4PS
020 7613 3031; ww.aslib.com

Arts and Humanities Research Council (AHRC)
AHRC, Whitefriars, Lewins Mead, Bristol, BS1 2AE
0117 987 6500; enquiries@ahrc.ac.uk; www.ahrc.ac.uk

INTERPRETER

What the work involves

- Interpreters convert words spoken in one language into conversation or speech in another language.

- Using your knowledge of foreign languages, you will enable speakers of different languages to communicate with each other.

- You may interpret while a person speaks or make notes and then interpret their statements.

- Interpreters provide services for international political conferences, court hearings, business meetings and public services.

The type of person suited to this work

As an interpreter you will need a strong grasp of at least one and preferably two foreign languages. An understanding of the culture of the languages you are working in is important. You will also need to be able to listen well and speak clearly.

A confident approach is useful when interpreting in conferences and courts. You will interpret on areas such as business and law, so you will need a good knowledge of a range of subjects and of current affairs. You may have to interpret confidential information so a discreet approach is important. A good memory is useful. This type of work requires a good standard of health.

Working conditions

Intepreters have to concentrate continuously for long periods, which can be physically demanding.

The nature of the job demands the ability to travel to different geographic locations at fairly short notice, either abroad or within the UK.

Interpreters work in a range of environments, including high-profile conferences and formal meetings.

Future prospects

This area of work is very competitive with a limited number of full-time opportunities. A small number of interpreters work for international or European agencies. Others are employed by local governments and interpret in courts, hospitals and police stations.

You may choose to work within community organisations, helping people gain access to public services. Many interpreters work on a freelance basis for organisations or individuals.

Advantages/disadvantages

This type of work provides the opportunity to travel and live abroad.

Due to tight schedules and high levels of travel, this can be a pressured job.

Freelance interpreters often need to take on additional work to support themselves.

Qualifications and courses

Most interpreters have a degree in languages or in translation and interpreting, or a combined degree in languages with a subject such as business, law or engineering. For modern language degrees, a modern language A level/H grade is normally required.

Fluency in two languages including English is usually required to work as an interpreter.

The Chartered Institute of Linguists (IoL) offers vocational qualifications in a wide range of languages, including the Certificate in Bilingual Skills (equivalent to A Level/H grade), the Diploma in Public Service Interpreting at NQF Level 6, and the Diploma in Translation at Level 7. Examinations are open entry, but candidates are expected to have achieved the required level of competence before sitting an exam.

CILT, the National Centre for Languages, has developed National Occupational Standards for professional linguists. The Standards form the basis of NVQ/SVQ units, which may be awarded individually or may lead to NVQ/SVQ Level 4 or 5 in Public Service Interpreting.

Qualified interpreters can work towards membership of the IoL or Institute of Translation and Interpreting. These professional bodies provide further training and development opportunities.

Money guide

Newly qualified interpreters can expect a salary of around £20,000 per year.

This can rise to £35,000 with experience and £60,000 at senior levels.

Working freelance, you could charge between £275 and £700 per day.

Related opportunities

- Importer/Exporter p605
- Secretary p60
- Teacher of English to Speakers of Other Languages p216
- Translator p362

Further information

CILT – The National Centre for Languages
20 Bedfordbury, London, WC2N 4LB
020 7379 5101; www.cilt.org.uk

Chartered Institute of Linguists
Saxon House, 48 Southwark Street, London, SE1 1UN
020 7940 3100; www.iol.org.uk

Institute of Translation and Interpreting
Fortuna House, South Fifth Street, Milton Keynes, MK9 2EU
01908 325250; www.iti.org.uk

Languages, Information and Culture

CRCI: K
CLCI: FAL

LIBRARIAN/ LIBRARY ASSISTANT

What the work involves

Librarian

- You will manage collections of books, newspapers and documents and ICT resources in libraries and information services to make them available to visitors.

- You may choose new resources to suit the library or information service you work in. You will also help visitors look for information and use ICT and other resources.

Library assistant

- You will organise and reshelve books and other resources. You may also work on the library counter to help visitors with enquiries and check books in and out of the library. You might deal with petty cash, catalogue new library resources and maintain databases.

The type of person suited to this work

You should enjoy helping people with enquiries and customer care skills are essential. You will also need good research skills and the ability to use resources to locate information. The ability to work with ICT software, the internet and databases as well as explaining these to others is important.

Librarians will need management skills, as well as the ability to work as part of a team. Financial skills will help you manage budgets. You will need an organised approach to your work.

Working conditions

You are likely to work face to face with members of the public or staff within an organisation. Working on a counter, dealing with information enquiries, and lifting and carrying books can all be physically demanding. Library work can be pressured, as you will need to locate and provide information to meet specific requests.

Regular weekend or evening work may be part of your job. It is possible to do this job on a part-time basis.

Future prospects

Librarians could progress to a senior level, meaning they would manage a branch library or department. Some librarians move into information management roles within public services or private companies.

Library assistants are employed in library and information services in businesses, community library services and government. Larger organisations provide opportunities to progress into senior roles and take on additional responsibilities.

Advantages/disadvantages

You will be able to exercise your creativity by thinking up ways to promote the library and its resources.

You may need to move geographic locations to develop your career.

Qualifications and courses

The fastest route to becoming a qualified librarian is via a degree accredited by the Chartered Institute of Library and Information Professionals (CILIP). The usual entry requirements are two A levels/three H grades (any subjects), but people with experience as library assistants are often admitted to the degree courses with vocational qualifications.

An alternative route is via a degree in another subject followed by a CILIP-accredited postgraduate qualification. Prior experience of library or information work is advantageous, and is a requirement for some postgraduate courses.

Library assistants are often expected to have at least five GCSEs/S grades A*–C/1–3 or the equivalent, usually including English. Some assistant posts may require A levels/H grades.

It is also possible for people working as library assistants to qualify as librarians through a scheme like the one CILIP offers. Senior library assistants can study for a librarianship qualification (degree or postgraduate qualification) accredited by CILIP.

This type of work provides the satisfaction of helping people access information and other services.

Money guide

Salaries vary according to the sector in which you are employed, but CILIP recommends the following minimum salaries. Starting salaries range from £19,000 to £23,000. At chartered librarian level, you could earn up to £28,000. A senior academic librarian can earn up to £40,000, and a head of service £47,000+. Most library assistants start on £15,000, with experience this can increase to £18,000. Senior assistants earn over £20,000.

Related opportunities

- Arts Administrator p351
- Information Scientist p356
- Archivist/Records Manager p350

Further information

Chartered Institute of Library and Information Professionals (CILIP)
7 Ridgemount Street, London, WC1E 7AE
020 7255 0500; www.cilip.org.uk

City& Guilds

www.cityandguilds.com/myperfectjob

MUSEUM/ART GALLERY CURATOR

What the work involves

- You will manage and maintain collections of artworks, historical objects or documents. Curators usually have specialist knowledge of a specific historical or cultural field such as women's history, textiles or archaeology.

- You will write and research on the collections in your care.

- You might organise ways in which you can gain funding for your museum/gallery. You will also organise exhibit loans with other museums/galleries.

- You will work with other museum/gallery staff to plan exhibitions using items and information from your collection. You may also give talks to members of the public at special events.

The type of person suited to this work

You will need a good knowledge of history and of your specialist area. You will also need to be able to communicate this information to other staff and to members of the public. You may speak at educational events, so enthusiasm for your subject is essential. You will need good written communication skills for writing reports. ICT skills are increasingly important in this area, for example when managing collection information through specialist databases.

Working conditions

Curators generally work 37 hours a week, however these hours may be extended for special exhibitions and private showings. This job will probably involve weekend or evening work. You may have to be on call to respond to emergencies at the gallery/museum. Working environments also vary depending on the size and how busy a gallery/museum is. There may be some heavy lifting and carrying involved when exhibits need to be moved.

Future prospects

Museum/gallery work is a competitive area in which to develop a career and offers a variety of interesting roles. You could work your way up in some larger organisations, but often you will need to move employers in order to move up the career ladder.

From working as an assistant curator, you could progress into a curator's role. From here you could move on to work as a senior curator or go into managing museums/galleries or historic buildings.

Advantages/disadvantages

This job provides the satisfaction of working closely with works of art and historical objects, some of which can be very valuable.

You will help create exhibitions and then watch the public enjoy them.

Gaining necessary funding may be difficult.

Qualifications and courses

ENTRY 6 LEVEL

Entrants should normally have a relevant degree and/or a postgraduate qualification in museum, gallery or heritage studies. Voluntary experience in a museum, gallery or other heritage site is also important.

A wide range of degree subjects are relevant to museum work. Some degrees include modules/placements specifically relevant to museum studies. Some specialised degrees such as museum and gallery studies, art gallery and heritage management are available. Most degree programmes expect candidates to have achieved two A levels and five GCSEs grade A*-C (or equivalent).

NVQs/SVQs offer an alternative route for people with relevant work experience. NVQs/SVQs are available at Levels 3, 4 and 5 in Cultural Heritage Operations, Cultural Heritage and Cultural Heritage Management.

People working in museums can also work towards Associateship of the Museums Association. This qualification is available to people in all areas of museum work, and takes two years.

Most entrants to this career begin as an assistant or junior curator.

Graduate training programmes are available.

Money guide

These figures are only approximate and may vary depending on location, sector and employer. The Museums Association publishes salary guidelines each year.

Starting salaries are generally between £15,500 and £23,000 a year. This can increase to between £23,000 and £30,000 a year with experience. If you reach the level of senior curator you could earn over £30,000.

Related opportunities

- Archaeologist p349
- Exhibition Organiser p389
- Arts Administrator p351
- Museum/Art Gallery Technician p360
- Museum/Art Gallery Visitor Services Assistant p361

Further information

Museums Association
24 Calvin Street, London, E1 6NW
020 7426 6970; www.museumsassociation.org

City&Guilds

www.cityandguilds.com/myperfectjob

MUSEUM/ART GALLERY TECHNICIAN

What the work involves

- You will help prepare gallery and museum spaces for temporary exhibitions and collection displays.

- Your work will involve installing audio-visual equipment, such as lighting to suit specific exhibitions. You will also transport objects and artworks to and from exhibition spaces.

- You will provide general technical support to the museums/gallery team as required.

- You might be responsible for maintaining files, mending and cleaning exhibitions and labelling and storing specimens.

The type of person suited to this work

You will need a good range of technical skills to meet the varied practical demands of a museum/gallery environment. As well as providing support for setting up new exhibitions, you will have to deal with practical problems as they arise. The ability to handle fragile or valuable objects and artworks carefully is also useful. You will need a good knowledge of building security and maintenance. You may also be responsible for the fire safety of the gallery/museum. You will be a good team player and have a strong interest in helping people get the most out of their visits to galleries and museums.

Working conditions

Although you may spend some of the time within an office environment a great deal of it will be spent around the museum/gallery. Generally technicians work about 36 hours a week; however you may have to be on call to respond to emergencies at the gallery/museum. You might also have to work longer hours when setting up or dismantling exhibitions. You may have to work some weekends, evenings and bank holidays. You could be required to wear a uniform and/or name badge.

Future prospects

Whilst museum/gallery work is a competitive area in which to develop a career, it offers a variety of interesting roles. You could work your way up in some larger organisations, but often you will need to move employers in order to move up the career ladder.

It is possible to progress to working as a senior or head technician. In larger organisations, you could manage a team of technicians.

Advantages/disadvantages

This job provides the satisfaction of working closely with works of art and historical objects, some of which can be very valuable.

This is a competitive area of work, so you may have to change jobs to receive promotion.

You may have to work some unsociable hours which could disrupt your social or family life.

Qualifications and courses

Technical knowledge, experience of working with the public and an interest in museums/galleries are more important than formal qualifications for this role. Specific craft skills such as carpentry can be useful. For some roles, people with knowledge of art and artistic techniques may be preferred.

A good general education is usually required and some museums/galleries require five GCSEs/S grades A*–C/1–3. Some other museums/galleries might ask for a degree in a relevant subject. Appropriate degree courses include heritage management, museum and gallery studies, history, museums and heritage and arts and cultural management. English and history may also prove relevant. In order to gain entry to a degree course you will usually require two A levels and five GCSEs grades A*-C.

Postgraduate degrees in museum studies are available.

You may be able to gain NVQs/SVQs in Heritage Care and Visitor Services at Level 2 and Cultural Heritage Operations at Level 3 whilst working.

Relevant work experience would be extremely useful.

If you will be working with children you will need to pass a Criminal Records Bureau check.

Money guide

These figures are only approximate and may vary depending on location and employer. Larger galleries and museums may pay their technicians a higher rate.

Starting salaries for technicians are generally around £13,000 a year.

You can expect to earn between £15,000 and £17,000 per year once you have gained some experience.

Senior technicians, with added responsibilities, can make over £20,000 per year.

Related opportunities

- Archaeologist p349
- Art Exhibition Organiser p389
- Art Restorer p353
- Museum/Art Gallery Curator p359
- Museum/Art Gallery Assistant p361

Further information

Creative and Cultural Skills
4th Floor, Lafone House, London, SE1 3HN
020 7015 1847; www.ccskills.org.uk

Museums Association
24 Calvin Street, London, E1 6NW
020 7426 6910; www.museumsassociation.org

Association of Independent Museums (AIM)
4 Clayhall Road, Gosport, Hampshire, PO12 2BY
02392 587751; www.museums.co.uk

MUSEUM/ART GALLERY VISITOR SERVICES ASSISTANT

What the work involves

- You will work face to face with visitors to galleries and museums, deal with enquiries and provide information. You will therefore need to keep up to date with information on the material showcased in the museum/gallery.

- Your role will also involve attending and watching over the security of exhibitions and displays.

- You will help set up and dismantle exhibitions. You may also be responsible for museum/gallery security and fire safety.

- You may conduct tours and/or work in the museum/gallery shop.

The type of person suited to this work

You should enjoy meeting and helping people, because you will deal with members of the public on a regular basis. You will need a patient and friendly approach when responding to enquiries and protecting fragile exhibition pieces from over-enthusiastic visitors! You will need a good understanding of fire and security issues. Manual handling skills are useful for setting up and taking down exhibitions. As you may deal with money in a museum or gallery shop, cash-handling skills are useful. You should also be able to work well as part of a team.

Working conditions

You will work around 36 hours a week, this will probably include some weekends, evenings and bank holidays. Generally this job takes place indoors; however there are some open-air museums. You will have to spend a lot of your time on your feet when undertaking security at exhibitions, which can be physically demanding. You might be required to wear a uniform and/or name badge.

Future prospects

Whilst museum/gallery work is a competitive area in which to develop a career, it offers a variety of interesting roles. You could work your way up in some larger organisations, but often you will need to move employers in order to move up the career ladder.

With experience, you could go on to work as a senior attendant/assistant, managing a team of attendants/assistants.

Advantages/disadvantages

This job provides the satisfaction of working closely with works of art and historical objects, some of which can be very valuable.

Because of the public nature of assistant roles, this can be a sociable job.

This is a competitive area of work, so you may have to change jobs to receive promotion.

Qualifications and courses

ENTRY LEVEL 1

Experience of working with the public and an interest in museums/galleries are more important than formal qualifications for this role. A good general education is usually required and some museums/galleries require five GCSEs/S grades A*–C/1–3.

Some other museums/galleries might ask for a degree in a relevant subject. Appropriate degree courses include heritage management, museum and gallery studies, history, museums and heritage and arts and cultural management.

English and history may also prove relevant. In order to gain entry to a degree course you will usually require two A levels and five GCSEs grades A*-C, although universities vary in their requirements and so it is best to check with the individual institution.

Postgraduate degrees in museum studies are available.

You may be able to gain NVQs/SVQs in Heritage Care and Visitor Services at Level 2 and Cultural Heritage Operations at Level 3 whilst working.

Relevant work experience would be extremely useful, either within a museum/gallery or working with the general public.

If you will be working with children you will need to pass a Criminal Records Bureau check.

Money guide

Starting salaries are generally between £11,000 and £13,000 per year. With experience or progression to a senior assistant/attendant role you could earn somewhere between £15,000 and £16,000 a year. It is possible to achieve a salary of over £19,000 per year.

These figures are only a guide, as actual rates of pay may vary, depending on the employer and where people live.

Related opportunities

- Art Exhibition Organiser p389
- Museum/Art Gallery Curator p359
- Museum/Art Gallery Technician p360

Further information

Museums Association
24 Calvin Street, London, E1 6NW
020 7426 6910; www.museumsassociation.org

Association of Independent Museums (AIM)
4 Clayhall Road, Gosport, Hampshire; PO12 2BY
02392 587751; www.museums.co.uk

Languages, Information and Culture

CRCI: K
CLCI: FAE

TRANSLATOR

What the work involves

■ You will convert written text from one language to another. You will ensure that your translation matches the tone and style of the original text and has a high standard of grammar.

■ You will translate documents such as letters, reports, leaflets and brochures.

■ Your work will also involve meetings with employers to agree projects.

■ Translators provide services to specialist translation agencies, private companies, local government bodies and international organisations.

The type of person suited to this work

Translators must work to a high standard of accuracy, so attention to detail is important. The ability to write in your chosen languages in a range of styles is essential. You should also be able to understand and translate complex documents. ICT skills are very useful. Your verbal communication skills will help you to discuss and agree projects with employers.

Discretion is important as you may translate confidential information. Being well organised will help you to meet project deadlines. You will need a confident approach to work on a freelance basis and promote your services. Numeracy skills are also useful.

Working conditions

Translators are usually based in offices at home, if self-employed, or in companies.

You may attend meetings with employers and colleagues.

This type of work involves close working at a computer and the use of resources such as dictionaries and technical reference books.

Future prospects

As a translator you could work for a variety of employers, translating medical, technical, legal and other documents. This is a competitive area, but the increase in internet-based business and the communication needs of organisations offers some interesting opportunities. Many translators work on a freelance basis.

There are opportunities to work for private companies and international organisations on a permanent basis, in the UK or abroad.

Advantages/disadvantages

This area of work can provide opportunities to travel and work abroad.

Working on a self-employed project-by-project basis can create some job instability.

Translation can be very demanding due to short deadlines and the constant demand for accuracy.

Qualifications and courses

Most translators have a relevant degree. These include degrees in one or more foreign languages (preferably applied), a foreign language combined with a specialist subject such as business, law, engineering, computer studies, Asian or European studies, or translation or interpreting.

For modern language degrees, a modern language A level/H grade is normally required.

Postgraduate courses in translation are available, and usually require a degree in a modern language. The Chartered Institute of Linguists (IoL) offers vocational qualifications in a wide range of languages, including the Certificate in Bilingual Skills (equivalent to A Level/H grade) the Diploma in Public Service Interpreting at NQF Level 6, and the Diploma in Translation at Level 7. Examinations are open entry, but candidates are expected to have achieved the required level of competence before sitting an exam.

Fluency in two or more languages is required to work as a translator.

Qualified translators can work towards membership of the IoL or Institute of Translation and Interpreting. These professional bodies provide further training and development opportunities.

Money guide

Translators may be paid between £75 and £180 per 1000 words, depending on the language they are translating.

Translators employed by business, for example in technical translation, can earn £18,000 per year as a starting salary.

This can increase to £25,000–£50,000 with experience.

Related opportunities

■ Interpreter p357
■ Secretary p60
■ Importer/Exporter p605
■ Teacher of English to Speakers of Other Languages p216

Further information

CILT – The National Centre for Languages
20 Bedfordbury, London, WC2N 4LB
020 7379 5101; www.cilt.org.uk

Chartered Institute of Linguists
Saxon House, 48 Southwark Street, London, SE1 1UN
020 7940 3100; www.iol.org.uk

Institute of Translation and Interpreting
Fortuna House, South Fifth Street, Milton Keynes, MK9 2EU
01908 325250, www.iti.org.uk

Legal and Political Services

If you find the law a fascinating subject and you feel you would enjoy a challenging career where the rewards are a good salary and a real sense of achievement when your hard work pays off, a job in this sector could be what you are looking for. Workers in this sector are fiercely passionate about their careers and have more often than not, completed a lot of training and worked hard to establish themselves in this competitive field. You need to be driven and thrive on pressure and tight deadlines; this is a sector for someone who is ambitious and very talented at working tactfully with people.

In this section we cover the following jobs:

BAILIFF/ENFORCEMENT AGENT

What the work involves

- Court bailiffs deliver legal documents such as court summonses to people who owe money and might also take steps to get the money paid.

- Certificated/private bailiffs visit people in debt to recover the money they owe, arranging for removal of their property where necessary.

- In Scotland, officers of court deliver legal documents to people who owe money and take all the legal steps required to get the money paid.

- You might also give advice on how to pay debts.

The type of person suited to this work

As there are strict legal procedures connected with recovering debt, you will need to be sure you are completely up to date with legislation to conduct you work correctly and within legal guidelines.

The work will bring you into contact with many different people, so it's important that you are able to deal with all members of the public.

You may need to be assertive to deal with people's resistance and be persistent to get the job done. Being tactful and able to cope with people under stress are also important.

Working conditions

You will spend a lot of time travelling and so will need a clean driving licence. Although you will be based in an office, you might have to visit people's homes in the evenings and early mornings to make sure that someone is there.

If you have to remove furniture in payment of debt, you could have to do a lot of heavy lifting, so you will need to be physically fit.

Future prospects

In England and Wales, court bailiffs generally work for the county courts and private bailiffs with magistrates' court orders.

In Scotland, officers of court are called sheriff officers in the sheriff court and messengers-at-arms in the Court of Session.

There are few openings for this kind of work and you are unlikely to start straight from school.

Promotion prospects are limited. You could progress into other types of work, for example security.

Advantages/disadvantages

The work is varied and no two days will be the same.

You will not spend all your time in one place.

You will meet many different people, some of whom may be difficult to deal with and threatening.

The hours can be long and unsocial.

Qualifications and courses

Employers prefer candidates to have 4 GCSEs/S grades (A–C/1–3), including English and maths. Applicants must be aged between 21 and 62 but mature candidates, without a criminal record or debt, are often preferred because their life experience may help them deal with difficult situations.

To become a certificated bailiff, candidates need to obtain a Bailiff's General Certificate. This is issued by a circuit judge. The necessary legal knowledge can be gained by taking the examinations of the Certificated Bailiffs' Association.

To be commissioned as a sheriff officer, candidates need to pass the examinations of the Society of Messengers-at-Arms and Sheriff Officers. The minimum age to be commissioned is 20 but training, which normally takes 3 years, can begin earlier.

A clean current driving licence is useful.

A bond up to the value of £10,000, plus two references will be required for insurance purposes.

Money guide

Starting salaries are around £14,000–£15,000 per year. Some firms offer less - and only part-time opportunities.

This rises to £20,000–£25,000 with experience.

A top rate of £30,000 per year is possible for the very capable and highly experienced.

Private firms may pay you a basic salary plus some form of commission – or, commission only.

In Scotland you could start at around £17,000; with experience you could get £26,000–£28,000.

Related opportunities

- Police Officer p551
- Police Support Worker p552
- Security Officer/Manager p562
- Door Supervisor/Bouncer p544

Further information

Enforcement Services Association
Park House, 10 Park Street, Bristol BS1 5HX
0117 907 4771; www.ensas.org.uk

Society of Messengers-at-Arms and Sheriff Officers
11 Alva Street, Edinburgh, EH2 4PH
0131 225 9110; www.smaso.org

Association of Civil Enforcement Agencies (ACEA)
513 Bradford Road, Batley, West Yorkshire WF17 8LL
01924 350 090; www.acea.org.uk; info@acea.org.uk

BARRISTER/ADVOCATE

What the work involves

- Barristers/Advocates give legal advice to solicitors and other professionals and act for clients in certain cases in the high courts.

- You will research information and past cases before giving advice to solicitors and advise them on whether a case should come to court.

- In court, you will examine witnesses and present the case for the prosecution or the defence.

- You will also act for clients at tribunals or enquiries if asked to act by a solicitor.

The type of person suited to this work

You will need to research large amounts of information before giving legal advice so the ability to handle information is essential. You will need to be able to think logically to work out what's important in the case and apply the law to it.

You will need to be confident to speak in court and convince a jury with your arguments, and think quickly when questioning witnesses or defendants. Good writing and speaking skills are needed to prepare your case. Keeping an open mind is important and you must be able to gain people's confidence.

Working conditions

Barristers usually work in offices called 'chambers', and advocates in groups known as 'stables' in the Advocates' Library in Edinburgh.

If you specialise in criminal law, you will spend more time in court than civil law specialists would. As you will travel widely, a driving licence is useful.

Future prospects

Most barristers/advocates are self-employed and it can take around 5 years to establish a practice and become known. After 10–15 years' experience you can apply to 'take silk' to become a Queen's Counsel. This is essential if you want to become a judge in the higher courts. Some people work in central or local government where there is a clear promotion structure.

Advantages/disadvantages

The work is varied and you will get satisfaction when you win a case.

Some cases may put you under pressure, particularly if they attract media attention.

You will sometimes work long hours to meet deadlines.

Money guide

During pupillage, £11,000–£18,500 per year.

Earnings between £25,000 and £56,000 are normal in the Crown Prosecution Service in England and Wales.

Qualifications and courses

England and Wales

ENTRY LEVEL 5

You will need either an approved law degree or another degree (minimum 2.2 for both) followed by a postgraduate law conversion course, known as the Common Professional Examination, or a Postgraduate Diploma in Law.

For the vocational stage, you must become a member of one of the 4 Inns of Court and undertake the Bar Vocational Course. You must also complete two 6-month pupillages working in Chambers.

Training for the 'bar' continues for 3 years, working in one of the Inns of Court.

Scotland

You will need either an Honours degree in Scottish Law from a Scottish University (minimum 2.2); an Ordinary degree in Scottish Law from a Scottish University with an Honours degree from a UK university (minimum 2.2); or a Scottish Ordinary degree with distinction. You must also undertake a 1-year full-time postgraduate Diploma in Legal Practice at a Scottish university.

For the vocational stage, you will need to work for 12–21 months in a solicitor's office and 'devilling' to a member of the bar for 9 and a half months, before taking the entry examinations of the Faculty of Advocates.

Advocates will normally practise as a solicitor for 10 years, prior to acting as an advocate.

As an Advocate in Scotland you may start at around £11,000; moving up to £24,000–£56,000 in the Procurator Fiscal Service.

The majority of barristers in England and Scotland are self-employed. Earnings can be up to £250,000, sometimes more, depending on experience, location and reputation.

Related opportunities

- Barrister/Advocate's Clerk p367
- Crown Prosecutor/Procurator Fiscal p374
- Paralegal p380
- Solicitor/Notary Public p384

Further information

The Bar Council
289–293 High Holborn, London WC1V 7HZ
020 7242 0082; www.barcouncil.org.uk

The Faculty of Advocates
Parliament House, Edinburgh EH1 1RF
0131 226 5071; www.advocates.org.uk

Skills for Justice
9–11 Riverside Court, Don Road, Sheffield S9 2TJ
0114 261 1499; www.skillsforjustice.com

Legal and Political Services

CRCI: L
CLCI: LAB

LJMU LAW SCHOOL

The School of Law at Liverpool John Moores University (LJMU) offers a broad portfolio of undergraduate, postgraduate and professional programmes in law, legal practice and criminal justice.

The following degree programmes are available within the School of Law:

LLB (Hons) Law
LLB (Hons) Law and Criminal Justice
BA Single Honours Criminal Justice
BSc Single Honours Forensic Psychology and Criminal Justice
Graduate Diploma in Law (GDL)
LLM International Business & Commercial Law
Legal Practice Course (LPC)
LLM in Legal Practice
MA Criminal Justice
MRes Business and Law

Graduate skills development and work-related learning are embedded in all of our programmes, helping you gain the essential skills and experience demanded by today's employers. The School of Law has invested significantly in staff development, with an emphasis on enhancing the status and quality of teaching and learning. School staff are also engaged in a wide range of law and criminal justice research, and the School hosts the Centre for Criminal Justice.

Lectures are delivered at the John Foster Building and Modular Building within the Mount Pleasant Campus. These buildings boast a range of modern facilities, including 'Hi-Tech' lecture and seminar rooms, a moot room, reading rooms, and a fully equipped IT Suite. The John Foster Building is an 19th Century Listed building and, along with the award-winning Aldham Robarts Learning Resource Centre, is built around an enclosed garden with lawns and benches offering a peaceful retreat in between study.

Student Lawyers at LJMU have done very well over the years in National Mooting Competitions, Client Interviewing, Mediation and National Negotiation Competitions. The teams won the 2007 English Speaking Union – Essex Court Chambers National Mooting Competition and 2008 National Negotiation Championship, reaching the final of the 2009 Client Interviewing and Mediation Competitions.

Additionally, the Student Law Society is a vibrant organisation of law students supporting law students. The Society organises a wide variety of events, such as meet and greets with local legal professionals, public speaking courses and mooting competitions, alongside their social events.

Liverpool John Moores University (LJMU) is a truly international university with over 24,000 students from all over the world. The University has embarked on a major campus redevelopment programme to ensure that LJMU truly is a 21st century university. The £24 million Art & Design Academy - the biggest investment in arts education in the UK today – is the first of our major projects to be completed.

If you want to have a great university experience, graduate with a respected qualification and secure the skills and 'know-how' that will help you climb the professional career ladder, then you should choose the School of Law at LJMU.

For more information about the LJMU School of Law contact the BLW Admissions Team on 0151 231 3999 or email: BLWadmissions@ljmu.ac.uk. Alternatively, you can visit the website at www.ljmu.ac.uk/lbs

BARRISTER'S/ADVOCATE'S CLERK

What the work involves

- Clerks manage the day-to-day work for a group of barristers (England and Wales) or advocates (Scotland).

- An important task will be liaising with solicitors to encourage them to give work to your business.

- You will estimate how much work is involved in a case to see how much time it will take, allocate cases to barristers/advocates and negotiate fees.

- When you first enter this career, you will prepare accounts, do filing and photocopying, and answer the phone.

The type of person suited to this work

As your work will involve meeting people and talking to them, you will need excellent speaking skills. Good writing skills are useful for writing letters and preparing notes and reports. Being good with figures is essential when negotiating fees and preparing accounts.

You will need to be businesslike and have good negotiating skills to bring in work, and confidence to deal with solicitors, court officials and clients.

Your work will involve handling confidential information, which means discretion and tact are necessary. It is also important to be a good team worker and flexible in your approach to work.

Working conditions

You will work mainly indoors in an office, probably using computers and spending a lot of time on the telephone. However, you may travel in connection with your work so a driving licence is useful.

As you will also be meeting other professionals, you will have to be smartly dressed at all times.

Most of your work will be Monday to Friday during standard office hours with evenings and weekends during busy periods.

Future prospects

Competition is fierce for entry to this profession.

Barristers are based in offices known as 'chambers' with one clerk serving more than one barrister. Advocates work in groups known as 'stables' in the Advocates' Library in Edinburgh.

You would start as a junior clerk and progress to clerk with experience. Training will be ongoing throughout your career. With experience you could train for another legal profession or move into general administrative work.

Advantages/disadvantages

Your work will be interesting and varied.

You will have a lot of responsibility.

Qualifications and courses

In England and Wales, barristers' clerks usually require a minimum of 4 GCSEs/S grades (A–C/1–3), including maths and English. A levels are an advantage. In Scotland (for the Advocate's clerk post) applicants will be at a distinct advantage if they offer H grades.

Candidates may join the Institute of Barristers' Clerks (IBC). After completing an appropriate BTEC course and 5 years' service in Chambers, a student can apply for qualified membership of the IBC. IBC provide training courses, such as the BTEC Advanced Award in Chambers Administration, Level 3 for junior clerks with approximately 3 years of experience.

In Scotland, advocates' clerks are usually employed from age 17–18 or after several years' legal experience and require a minimum of an H grade in English, and evidence of computer literacy and numeracy. Most training is on the job but candidates are encouraged to take courses organised by Faculty Services Ltd.

You might have to work long hours and stay late in the evenings to meet deadlines.

With extra training you can progress into other legal careers.

Money guide

Salaries start at around £12,500, increasing to £16,800 per year. With experience, clerks can earn between £30,000 and £50,000. Senior clerks with a high level of responsibility, in busy chambers, can earn up to £100,000. With further experience, self-employment might be an option where you could earn around £25,000 to £33,000.

In Scotland you can earn between £24,000 and £28,000. As a senior, you can earn up to £45,000.

Related opportunities

- Barrister/Advocate p365
- Court Administrative Officer p370
- Paralegal p380

Further information

Institute of Barristers' Clerks
289–293 High Holborn, London WC1 7HZ
020 7831 7144; www.barristerclerks.com

Skills for Justice
9–11 Riverside Court, Don Road, Sheffield S9 2TJ
0114 261 1499; www.skillsforjustice.com

The Bar Council
289–293 High Holborn, London WC1V 7HZ
020 7242 0082; www.barcouncil.org.uk

Legal and Political Services

CRCI: L
CLCI: LAG

CONSTITUENCY AGENT/ POLITICAL RESEARCHER

What the work involves

Constituency agent

- Your job will be to organise the running of the constituency for your political party, including election campaigns. You will arrange meetings, coordinate PR and marketing, and deal with enquiries. As secretary to the local office, your duties will include managing local membership, fundraising and organising volunteers.

Political researcher

- You will research information on political subjects and provide your employer with a coherent briefing of your conclusions. Your duties may include helping to create political speeches, finding sources of expertise on a specific issue and monitoring parliamentary reports.

The type of person suited to this work

You will need a solid understanding of the political system, along with a genuine interest and love of politics. It is important to have strong political opinions whilst understanding that sometimes you must look at the bigger picture.

Key skills for constituency agents are communication, information handling, IT, managing money, management and supervisory skills and working with others.

Key skills for political researchers include tact, IT, resourcefulness, debating abilities, research skills, resilience, communication, articulation and analytical abilities.

Working conditions

Constituency agent

Most of your work will be based in the party office which will be open to the public. However, you will be expected to do lots of travelling both locally and nationally, so a driving licence and car will be useful. You could work evenings, weekends or during the day. Hours could increase during national or local events like elections.

Political researcher

You will be working in an office, normally 9–5 although some longer hours might be required to meet specific deadlines. You may need to travel.

Future prospects

Constituency agent

Your prospects could depend on the size of the party you support. Later, you could become a local councillor or Member of Parliament.

Political researcher

This is an excellent starting point for a career in politics. Progression may include becoming an MP. You could take on extra responsibilities and move between public affairs firms in order to achieve promotion.

Qualifications and courses

There are no set entry requirements, although many employers expect candidates to have a 2:1 level degree or above. The degree subject is not that important, however degrees in politics, industrial relations, social policy, economics, marketing, public relations or journalism may prove valuable.

Experience of working for the party or organisation on a voluntary basis is very useful, some employers will place experience above academic qualifications. Most agents are members of the party they work for with significant voluntary experience. Experience in other areas is also useful, for exampl involvement with a trade union or employer's organisation, holding office in a students' union or parent teacher association, or campaign work for a charity group. In general, candidates must be at least 20 years of age.

Advantages/disadvantages

You will get a good deal of job satisfaction as your work will be making a difference.

You may find this career stressful, particularly when you have to meet project deadlines or when there are elections.

Money guide

Constituency agent

You could expect to earn around £16,000 per year as a starting salary. This can rise to between £28,000 and £35,000 a year, depending on experience and level of responsibility.

Political researcher

Starting salaries begin at about £16,000 a year. This can increase to £20,000 after a year. After two or three years, in a senior position you could earn up to £24,000 per year.

Related opportunities

- Researcher (Media) p428
- Politician p383
- Welfare Rights Officer/Worker p590

Further information

Association of Professional Political Consultants, c/o Precise Public Affairs
The Registry, Royal Mint Court, London EC3N 4QN
www.appc.org.uk

The Chartered Institute of Public Relations (CIPR) Government Affairs Group
32 St James's Square, London SW1Y 4JR
020 7766 3333; www.cipr.co.uk

CORONER

What the work involves

- You will investigate sudden and suspicious deaths in England and Wales, and decide whether or not an inquest and/or post-mortem are required.

- Coroners preside at inquests and make decisions on whether or not further action is required.

- You will need to work with police and medical services in order to decide whether a person died of natural causes or not and keep detailed records of all proceedings.

- Once you have completed your investigations you must provide families or the relevant authorities with your report.

The type of person suited to this work

Preparing cases involves looking at statements and reports so you need to be able to read and analyse a lot of information. You might need to check points of law and ask for more information, so you must pay attention to detail.

Much of your work will be talking to people, and writing reports, so you need to have excellent speaking, listening and writing skills. Being confident to speak in court and argue logically are important.

You must be organised, able to meet deadlines and handle distressing situations calmly.

Working conditions

You will be based in an office but will spend time in court, at crime scenes and in hospitals. You will usually work normal office hours, however you will need to be available at all times when you are on call.

Although most of your work will be indoors, you will spend time outdoors at scenes of crime and accidents.

Most coroners work part time and spend the rest of their time in private legal practice.

Future prospects

Coroners are appointed and paid for by local councils, but hold office under the crown.

Although at the moment there is no promotion route, the Coroners and Justice Bill has proposed that there be posts such as Senior Coroner and Chief Coroner in the future.

Advantages/disadvantages

The work is varied, carries responsibility and can be satisfying.

You will have contact with many different types of people, some of whom may be difficult to deal with.

There will be a lot of administration and paperwork.

You will be on an on-call rota for evenings, weekends and bank holidays.

Qualifications and courses

ENTRY LEVEL 7

Candidates usually start as deputy or assistant deputy coroners and must be qualified lawyers or legally qualified medical practitioners with at least five years' experience.

In order to qualify as a doctor you must complete an undergraduate course which leads to a degree in medicine. To do this you will need three A levels (with high grades) and good GCSEs grade A*-C (or equivalent). A levels in chemistry and biology are usually required. Entry requirements will differ between universities and so it is best to check with the individual institution.

To train as a lawyer you must complete a qualifying law degree, an undergraduate degree followed by a law conversion course, a senior status law degree or complete exams to become part of the Fellowship of the Institute of Legal Executives (ILEX). To be accepted onto a law degree you will usually require two or three A levels and five GCSEs grade A*-C (or equivalent).

Aldermen and councillors of local authorities are not eligible for appointment as coroners in their counties or districts until six months after the end of their service.

Money guide

Coroners receive an agreed fee, and as a guide, if you work full time as a deputy coroner, you can earn around £25,000 per year.

As a full-time coroner you can expect between £68,000 and £96,500 a year depending on how large the population is that you cover.

Part-time coroners are paid in proportion to the amount of cases they complete; salaries generally vary between £9,600 and £49,000 per year.

Related opportunities

- Barrister/Advocate p365
- Hospital Doctor p315
- Judge/Sheriff p375
- Solicitor/Notary Public p384

Further information

The Coroners' Society of England and Wales
HM Coroner's Court, The Cotton Exchange, Old Hall Street, Liverpool L3 9UF
0151 233 4708; www.coronersociety.org.uk

Ministry of Justice
102 Petty France, London SW1H 9AJ, United Kingdom
www.justice.gov.uk; 020 3334 3555

Department for Constitutional Affairs
Selborne House, 54 Victoria Street, London SW1E 6QW, United Kingdom
020 7210 8500; www.dca.gov.uk

Legal and Political Services

CRCI: L
CLCI: LAZ

COURT ADMINISTRATIVE OFFICER

What the work involves

- You will organise all the papers and information for a court hearing so that everything is ready for the judge or magistrate when the hearing starts.

- Booking dates, times and courtrooms for court hearings will be part of your job and you will prepare the timetable for each day.

- You will make sure everyone arriving at court knows where to go and receives the relevant paperwork.

- After the hearings, you will carry out court orders, for example endorsing driving licences, writing adoption orders or collecting fines.

The type of person suited to this work

As you will be responsible for making sure that court hearings run smoothly and everything is ready on time, it is important to be methodical and pay attention to detail.

As many different people come to court, you need to be polite and helpful so that you can put them at ease and explain things clearly.

If you are working in a finance section, you need to be able to work with figures to deal with fines and costs. You should also have good IT skills.

Working conditions

Most of your time will be spent indoors in courtrooms and offices in the court. You will be working around 37 hours a week, however overtime may be necessary if there is a hearing in the evening or on the weekend.

You will sit at a desk in an office for the majority of your day. Part-time work is often possible. Some of the people coming to court may be aggressive. You may have to travel to different courts, so a driving licence is useful.

Future prospects

Court administrative officers in England and Wales are employed by the Magistrates' Courts and move through promotion grades. In Scotland they are often known as court officers and are employed by the Scottish Court Service. Most training is on the job. You may have to move courts to widen your experience. You could move into similar work in the legal field such as legal executive roles or into general administrative work. Promotion to senior administration roles is possible.

Advantages/disadvantages

The work is varied and no two days will be the same.

You will meet and work with many different people.

Some people could be aggressive and threatening, which you could find frightening.

You may have to start early or work late at busy times.

Qualifications and courses

Qualification requirements vary within different regions, but a good general education is required, with two to five GCSEs/S grades, including maths and English, depending on the type of court and location. Some areas require administrative, typing, office or computing experience with others also requiring a minimum of one year of relevant office-based experience.

Applicants without formal qualifications may be able to sit an aptitude test or could be considered based solely on relevant administrative experience. New recruits tend to hold A levels/H grades and will usually need five GCSEs/S grades A*–C/1–3 or equivalent qualifications.

On-the-job qualifications are offered through locally based short courses. NVQ/SVQ Level 2 Administration may be available. Many officers start as Administrative Assistants.

Many people who work as court administrative officers are already completing articles or undertaking other legal training.

Money guide

These figures are only approximate as salaries could vary depending on your employer and location.

Salaries for court administrative officers could start at around £12,000 per year.

With experience, you could earn somewhere between £14,000 and £17,000 a year.

If you progress to become a senior clerk or team leader you could earn over £20,000 per year.

Related opportunities

- Civil Service/Local Government Administrator p29
- Barrister/Advocate's Clerk p367
- Court Usher/Officer/Macer p373
- Receptionist p54
- Court Clerk/Sheriff's Clerk p371

Further information

Her Majesty's Courts Service (HMCS)
Customer Service Unit, 5th Floor, Clive House, Petty France, London SW1H 9EX
020 7189 2000 and 0845 456 8770;
www.hmcourts-service.gov.uk

Scottish Court Service (SCS)
Hayweight House, 23 Lauriston Street, Edinburgh EH3 9DQ
0131 229 9200; www.scotcourts.gov.uk

City&
Guilds

www.cityandguilds.com/myperfectjob

COURT CLERK/ SHERIFF'S CLERK

What the work involves

Court clerk (England and Wales)

- Court clerks are qualified solicitors or barristers with responsibility for advising magistrates in magistrates' courts.

- You will use your legal knowledge to advise magistrates on points of law, procedures, penalties and other issues.

Sheriff's clerk (Scotland)

- Sheriff's clerks carry out a range of duties which will vary according to the size of court and their experience.

- You may advise on points of law and procedures in any court (civil or criminal), or you may have a more general administrative role.

The type of person suited to this work

As you will be expected to advise on a wide range of issues, it is important to have an interest in law and enjoy dealing with large amounts of information.

You will deal with many different people so it's important to be tolerant and remain detached from emotionally demanding cases. You will need to be discreet to deal with confidential information and remain impartial.

Court clerks must be organised to deal with a number of tasks whilst being able to think logically and communicate well.

Working conditions

You will normally have an office in one court building. You will generally be working Monday to Fridays but your working hours may, at times, be irregular due to complex cases. Some courts also open as early as 8.00am. There may be some call for weekend work. You might travel around different courts so a driving licence is useful. You may use computers in your work.

Future prospects

There's a career structure for court clerks in the HM Court Service and you could become a justices' clerk or a justices' chief executive. In England and Wales, court clerks are increasingly known as judicial advisers.

In Scotland, sheriff's clerks are employed by the Scottish Court Service. Small rural courts may have only one clerk, while a court in a big city will have several. There is a clear promotion structure within the Scottish Court Service.

Advantages/disadvantages

The work is varied and no two days will be the same.

You might have to work unsocial hours at times which may impact on your home or social life.

You might find it hard not to be the decision-maker.

Qualifications and courses

Court clerk (England and Wales)

Candidates must be either barristers or solicitors, or have successfully completed the examinations for one of these professions.

Barristers need an approved law degree or a non-law degree followed by the Common Professional Examination (CPE), Postgraduate Diploma (PgDL) in Law. They then complete a Bar Vocational Course followed by two 6-month 'pupillages' with an experienced barrister. In Scotland, advocates need a law degree followed by the Diploma in Legal Practice and 21 months' experience with a solicitor and nine months' 'devilling' experience.

Solicitors need an approved law degree or a non-law degree followed by the CPE PgDL. They can also qualify through ILEX. They must then take a Legal Practice Course followed by two years' training with a solicitor.

Sheriff's clerk (Scotland)

There are no minimum entry requirements but a good standard of education is expected. Fast-track entry is sometimes available to those with a degree. The normal route is a law degree followed by the Diploma in Legal Practice and two years' training with a solicitor.

Clerks then follow training programmes organised by their courts.

Money guide

You can expect around £19,000 to £24,000 per year on entry as a court clerk. With experience you can earn up to £28,000+.

Sheriffs' clerks can expect to earn about £24,000 per year on entry, rising to between £28,000 and £35,000 a year with experience and seniority.

Related opportunities

- Barrister/Advocate p365
- Barrister/Advocate's Clerk p367
- Legal Executive p376
- Solicitor/Notary Public p384

Further information

Her Majesty's Courts Service
5th Floor, Clive House, Petty France, London SW1H 9HD
020 7189 2000; www.hmcourts-service.gov.uk

Scottish Court Service
Hayweight House, 23 Lauriston Street, Edinburgh EH3 9DQ
0131 229 9200; www.scotcourts.gov.uk

www.cityandguilds.com/myperfectjob

Legal and Political Services

CRCi: L
CLCi: LAG

COURT REPORTER/ VERBATIM REPORTER

What the work involves

- As a court reporter, also known as a verbatim reporter, your job could involve attending court hearings, listening and reporting what is said.

- Using a stenotype machine, or sometimes other recording equipment, you will write down everything a witness says, but you may edit other speakers to correct the grammar.

- Mostly you will work on your own, but in complex cases where lawyers may want a daily transcript of proceedings, you will work in a team of three on a rota basis.

- You may also record proceedings within other legal meetings such as industrial tribunals.

The type of person suited to this work

You must be able to concentrate for a long time and listen carefully to what is said. Good attention to detail is essential to ensure your record is accurate. You will need fast typing skills, good grammar and punctuation, and a clear speaking voice so you can read back what you have written.

If you do not catch what is said or get behind, it's important to have the confidence to stop proceedings or ask for something to be repeated.

You need to be able to work on your own and in a team, depending on whether you are taking the complete record or working a rota.

Working conditions

You will operate a steno machine, a machine with a keyboard layout which enables whole words and phrases to be typed at one stroke. You may also use other equipment.

You may have to travel to different courts, so a driving licence is useful.

Future prospects

You could attend criminal cases in the crown courts, or civil cases in the high courts. You will also be present at other events, including industrial tribunals, public enquiries and in Parliament to record proceedings for Hansard. Some reporters also provide the media industry with captions and subtitles.

Most court reporters are self-employed and there is no defined promotion ladder. Others work for companies contracted to service courts. This is a small but growing profession with a shortage of trained staff.

Advantages/disadvantages

You will have contact with a wide range of people.

You will have to concentrate for long periods so the work is demanding.

Qualifications and courses

Candidates are usually required to have 3–5 GCSEs/S grades (A–C/1–3), including English. Thorough knowledge of English language, grammar and punctuation is required.

Maturity and work experience is an advantage.

Applicants need to have qualifications in using shorthand machines. For real-time court reporting you will be expected to have shorthand at 160–200 words per minute.

Courses are available through the BIVR on both a full-time and a distance-learning basis. Courses are not available in Scotland as all training is done on the job with a mentor.

It is possible after training and 3 years' experience to become a member of the BIVR by taking an examination. Qualified members of the BIVR with Deaf Awareness training can become accredited Speech to Text (STT) Reporters. In Scotland, court reporters are usually trained on the job.

Training for real-time reporting takes approximately 2 years.

You might have to work in the evenings at very short notice to complete reports for the next day.

Money guide

Starting salaries are around £15,000 per year. You could earn £24,000 as an experienced real-time reporter, i.e. working in a team of three. In Scotland you could earn up to £19,500. You can expect a daily rate of around £175–£195 if you work freelance. Real-time reporters working freelance can earn £300+ a day.

Related opportunities

- Court Administrative Officer p370
- Court Clerk/Sheriff's Clerk p371
- Paralegal p380

Further information

British Institute of Verbatim Reporters
73 Alicia Gardens, Kenton, Harrow, Middx HA3 8JD
020 8907 8249; www.bivr.org.uk

Sorene Court Reporting & Training Services
73 Alicia Gardens, Kenton, Harrow HA3 8JD
020 8907 8249; www.sorene.co.uk;
marysorene@ntlworld.com

COURT USHER/OFFICER/ MACER

What the work involves

- Court ushers make sure that everything in the courtroom is ready for court proceedings to begin, for example that all papers are ready, glasses and water are on tables and fire exits are clear.

- When people arrive at court, you will meet them and direct them to the right courtroom.

- In court, you will tell people to stand when the judge comes in, call witnesses and administer the right oath to witnesses.

- In Scotland, you will be known as a court officer in the sheriff court and a macer in the supreme courts.

The type of person suited to this work

As courtrooms must be properly prepared with everything ready at the beginning of the day, court ushers need to be thorough in their work and pay attention to detail. They need to be organised and methodical.

All kinds of people come to court, some of whom may be nervous, and it is important to have good speaking skills to explain what is happening and put people at ease. You will also need to be confident to call witnesses and sound in control in court.

It is important to stay calm at all times and be impartial to deal with people from both sides of a case.

Working conditions

Most of your work will be in a courtroom but you might also have an office in the courthouse. In certain jury cases, you may have to stay away from home overnight and you will have to be smartly dressed at all times.

You might have to travel between courts, so a driving licence is useful.

Future prospects

There are not many jobs for court ushers and getting in can be competitive in some areas of the UK. Most people have experience of other work first, for example within the police or armed services.

You can be promoted to senior and supervisory grades. You could also progress into other administrative jobs within the legal profession or outside.

Overall, promotion prospects can be difficult due to the competitive nature of the career.

Qualifications and courses

ENTRY LEVEL 2

Whilst no formal qualifications are required, a minimum of at least 4 GCSEs/S grades (A–C/1–3), or the equivalent, including English, is strongly recommended. Training is conducted on the job, as well as through short courses.

The stated minimum age is 21 (16 in Scotland), but most courts prefer to recruit mature people under the age of 63 (60 in Scotland).

A background in the police or armed forces can be an advantage. A driving licence may be required.

Advantages/disadvantages

The job will be varied and no two days will be the same.

You might have to stay late or start early if proceedings overrun.

You will meet many different people.

Some people may be difficult to deal with.

Money guide

As a starting salary in England and Wales, you can expect to earn between £12,299 and £14,908 per year.

This rises to around £17,500 with experience.

Around £12,000–£13,750 is usual as a macer in Scotland.

Overtime payments for late nights or early starts are often paid.

Related opportunities

- Civil Service/Local Government Administrator p29
- Court Clerk/Sherrif's Clerk p371
- Court Administrative Officer p370
- Receptionist p54

Further information

Her Majesty's Courts Service (HMCS)
5th Floor, Clive House, Petty France, London SW1H 9HD
020 7210 8500; www.hmcourts-service.gov.uk

Scottish Court Service
Hayweight House, 23 Lauriston Street, Edinburgh EH3 9DQ
0131 229 9200; www.scotcourts.gov.uk

Skills for Justice
9–11 Riverside Court, Don Road, Sheffield S9 2TJ
0114 261 1499; www.skillsforjustice.com

Legal and Political Services

CRCI: L
CLCI: LAG

CROWN PROSECUTOR/ PROCURATOR FISCAL

What the work involves

Crown prosecutor

- You will look at reports from the police and other agencies and decide whether or not crimes in England and Wales should be prosecuted. You will take statements from witnesses before a trial and examine witnesses in court, guiding them through their evidence. You will then sum up the case for the prosecution.

Procurator fiscal

- You will carry out similar duties to crown prosecutors in England and Wales, based on the Scottish legal system. In Scotland, sudden and suspicious deaths are investigated by the Procurator Fiscal Service.

The type of person suited to this work

Preparing cases involves looking at statements and reports so you need to be able to read and analyse a lot of information. You must be able to spot gaps and pay attention to detail.

As much of your work will be talking to people and writing reports, you must have excellent listening and writing skills. Being confident to speak in court and argue logically are also important.

Working conditions

You will be based in an office but will spend time in court. Although most of your work will be indoors, you might spend time outdoors at scenes of crime and accidents.

Future prospects

Crown prosecutor

There is a clear promotion structure within the service but very few top senior posts. Competition for jobs in the CPS is very keen.

Procurator fiscal

Candidates apply to join the Procurator Fiscal Service through the Crown Office. Applicants start as deputes, working under guidance of senior colleagues and gradually taking more responsibility. After a few years, they can apply to become procurator fiscals but promotion is not automatic.

Crown prosecutors and procurators fiscal can transfer into other areas of law such as private practice.

Advantages/disadvantages

The work is varied, carries responsibility and can be satisfying.

You will have contact with many different types of people, some of whom may be difficult to deal with.

Qualifications and courses

Crown prosecutor

You must be either a solicitor admitted in England and Wales with a full current practising certificate, or a barrister called to the English Bar who has completed pupillage. The Crown Prosecution Service offers a few 2-year training contracts to solicitors who have completed their Legal Practice course, and 1-year pupillages to barristers who have completed their BVC.

Administrative Officers or caseworkers with at least 12 months' qualifying service with the CPS can apply for the Law Scholarship Scheme and Legal Trainee Scheme.

Procurator fiscal

Candidates are solicitors qualified in the Scottish legal system. An LLB degree in Scottish law (or 3 years of pre-diploma training and a pass in the Law Society of Scotland's exams) is required, followed by a Diploma in Legal Practice and 2 years working as a trainee solicitor. The Procurator Fiscal Service offers a few 2-year traineeships, the final stage in qualifying as a solicitor.

You will be on an on-call rota for evenings, weekends and bank holidays.

Money guide

Crown prosecutor

Crown prosecutors start at £29,000 per year. As a Senior Crown Prosecutor you could earn around £48,000–55,000.

Procurator fiscal

As a procurator fiscal you can earn around £28,000 a year after 2 years as a trainee. You could expect to earn around £40,000–£47,000 with more experience, rising to around £58,000 at the top level.

Related opportunities

- Barrister/Advocate p365
- Solicitor/Notary Public p384
- Paralegal p380

Further information

Crown Prosecution Service
50 Ludgate Hill, London EC4M 7EX
020 7796 8000; www.cps.gov.uk

Crown Office Scotland
25 Chambers Street, Edinburgh EH1 1LA
0131 226 2626; www.crownoffice.gov.uk

Legal and Political Services

CRCI: L
CLCI: LAG

JUDGE/SHERIFF

What the work involves

- Judges (sheriffs in Scotland) preside over courts and make judgements on what should happen based on the evidence from both sides.

- You will listen to all the evidence and decide on procedures, including whether a piece of evidence can be used, and keep order in court.

- In jury cases, you will instruct and advise the jury on the strength of the evidence before the jury leaves court to consider the verdict.

- You will decide on penalties in criminal courts and on settlements in civil cases.

The type of person suited to this work

As judges make the final decisions in any court case, it is important to be able to grasp facts quickly and analyse the evidence to help make your decision. Judges must think logically and not become emotionally involved.

You will need to have good speaking skills to explain things to the jury and to consult with other legal professionals, and good listening skills to pay careful attention to the evidence. You will also need to have confidence to speak in public.

It is important to have the confidence to make difficult decisions and stick by them. Discretion is needed to deal with confidential information.

Working conditions

You will spend much of your time in court but will also have an office with support staff to help you. You will travel between courts and may have to spend time away from home.

You will dress smartly at all times and wear robes in court. Courts are also very formal and have traditions which you must observe.

Future prospects

There are very few openings for judges and sheriffs, which means entry is competitive, and they have normally followed a long career in law as a barrister/advocate.

Most judges work in one type of court, such as a Crown Court or Court of Appeal. Senior positions, such as Lord Chief Justice and Master of the Rolls, are made on the recommendation of the Prime Minister.

In Scotland, most sheriffs work in sheriff courts. A few with experience become supreme court judges in the High Court of Justiciary or the Court of Session.

Advantages/disadvantages

The work is varied and no two days will be the same.

It's a very responsible job.

Qualifications and courses

ENTRY LEVEL 5

Candidates are almost always qualified barristers or advocates who have 5–7 years' experience and have progressed to working as a deputy district judge or a recorder. District or circuit judges are usually appointed after 10–15 years' court experience. Judges are appointed by The Lord Chancellor.

After 10–15 years' experience, barristers may apply to become a Queen's Counsel and may eventually become a High Court judge or a Court of Session judge in Scotland.

Judicial office holders must retire on their 70th birthday.

Sheriffs are required to be qualified advocates (members of the Scottish Bar) of 10 years' experience.

You will meet many different people and hear some cases which will have a high media interest or involve upsetting or distressing evidence.

Some courts work into the evenings.

Money guide

Salaries can vary according to region, but start at around £99,500–£168,000 per year as a senior district judge.

You could earn £127,000 as a circuit judge.

Sherrifs earn around £120,800 per year.

Around £167,000 + is possible as a High Court judge.

Around £237,300 a year is the salary as Lord Chief Justice, the highest legal position in the land.

Related opportunities

- Barrister/Advocate p365
- Crown Prosecutor/Procurator Fiscal p374
- Legal Executive p376
- Solicitor/Notary Public p384

Further information

Judicial Communications Office
Office of the Lord Chief Justice, 11.07 Thomas More Building, Royal Courts of Justice, Strand, London WC2A 2LL
www.judiciary.gov.uk

Judicial Appointments Commission
11 Tothill Street, London SW1H 9LJ
020 7210 1453; www.judicialappointments.gov.uk

Skills for Justice
9–11 Riverside Court, Don Road, Sheffield S9 2TJ
0114 261 1499; www.skillsforjustice.com

Legal and Political Services

CRCI: L
CLCI: LAF

LEGAL EXECUTIVE

What the work involves

- Legal executives work with solicitors, preparing complex cases for them and dealing with straightforward cases yourself.

- You will interview clients, asking questions to help you give them legal advice and explain legal points to them clearly. You will write letters on their behalf, checking points of law and paying close attention to detail.

- In certain cases, you may represent clients in court or at tribunals.

The type of person suited to this work

As much of the work involves talking and listening to all sorts of people, you need very good speaking and listening skills. Excellent writing skills are important for producing letters and taking statements.

Clients will give you confidential information so it is important to be discreet and tactful. You will also need patience as legal points can be difficult to grasp.

When preparing cases, you will be handling large amounts of information, which means it is useful to be a thorough, well-organised worker.

Working conditions

You will be based in an office but you may attend court. You will be sitting down for most of the time but will stand when speaking in court. You will be expected to dress smartly.

You may have to travel to visit clients or legal libraries, so a driving licence is useful.

Excellent communication skills will be important because you will need to get along with your clients, colleagues and other professionals.

Future prospects

Most work for solicitors in private practice, but there are jobs in local and central government and industry. Legal executives usually specialise in one area, for example property or business law.

You can train to qualify as a legal executive advocate, which allows you to follow a case right through to court.

This is a very competitive career, and the majority of entrants are now graduates.

Advantages/disadvantages

This is a very competitive area to enter.

You will have the chance to work in a legal environment while studying part time and earn a good salary.

You may have to work under pressure to meet deadlines and possibly work evenings and weekends.

Qualifications and courses

ENTRY LEVEL 3

The normal minimum requirements are 4 GCSEs/S grades (A–C/1–3) in academic subjects, including English. City & Guilds/ILEX Paralegal Programmes Level 2 Certificate in Vocational Paralegal Studies is a suitable alternative to GCSEs for older candidates.

Students may begin their training with the Institute of Legal Executives' certificate in Law and Practice Level 3, which requires 4 GCSEs/S grades (A–C/1–3) including English language or literature, or equivalent (including the C&G/ILEX Level 2 Vocational Paralegal Studies Certificate). Trainees then take the Level 3 Professional Diploma in Law and Practice.

Trainees then progress to the Higher Diploma in Law. Full training at Levels 3 and 4 takes 3–4 years (while working full time) and leads to ILEX Membership. ILEX qualifications can also be taken as part of a Modern legal Apprenticeship scheme.

Some qualifications may provide exemption from some academic parts of the ILEX qualifications. People with relevant experience can also apply to have their experience approved by ILEX.

In Scotland, staff are known as paralegals or solicitors' assistants. Generally 4 GCSEs/S grades (A–C/1–3) including English and maths, followed by office experience, are required.

Money guide

Starting salaries for trainee legal executives are around £12,000, rising to nearly £20,000 with experience. Once you have passed ILEX exams you can earn £21,000–£26,500, depending on where you work. Legal executives with a bit more experience can earn around £30,000. Senior ILEX Fellows can earn over £45,000.

Related opportunities

- Civil Service/Local Government p29
- Barrister/Advocate's Clerk p367
- Court Clerk/Sheriff's Clerk p371
- Solicitor/Notary Public p384

Further information

Institute of Legal Executives
Kempston Manor, Kempston, Bedford MK42 7AB
01234 841000; www.ilex.org.uk

Law Society of Northern Ireland
40 Linenhall Street, Belfast BT2 8BA
028 90 231614; www.lawsoc-ni.org

Law Society of England and Wales
The Law Society's Hall, Chancery Lane, London WC2A 1PL
0870 606 2555; www.lawsociety.org.uk

Institute of Legal Executives (ILEX)

Legal Executive Lawyers

The term lawyer is not technically limited to just solicitors and barristers. It means someone qualified and experienced in the law. Legal executives are qualified lawyers in England and Wales who do similar work to solicitors, but specialise in one area of law.

The Institute of Legal Executives (ILEX) offers an exceptionally cost-effective and accessible route to becoming a lawyer. ILEX study fees cost between £3,500 to £5000 (depending on where the qualifications are studied), which compares exceptionally well to the rising costs of University: Students are now leaving Uni with average debts of up to £20,000–30,000 (NUS figures). To become a solicitor or barrister there are post-Uni cots, for example the Bar Vocational Course (BVC) costs from £8,000 to £11,000, and becoming a solicitor costs between £6,000 to £10,000 with a law degree, plus another £3,000 to £7,000 for those without a law degree. Training Contracts and Pupillages are very hard to secure and are currently mandatory. These are not required for the Legal Executive route to becoming a lawyer. As such, becoming a Legal Executive Lawyer is viewed as an increasingly appealing alternative to becoming a solicitor or barrister, and exemptions are available from ILEX for those with legal qualifications.

There have been a number of recent changes that put Legal Executive lawyers on a more level footing with Barristers and Solicitors:

- Under the Legal Services Act 2007, Legal Executive lawyers are 'authorised persons' undertaking 'reserved legal activities', alongside solicitors and barristers.

- Legal Executive lawyers are now able to become partners or managers in Legal Disciplinary Practices (firms of different lawyers with 25% non-lawyer managers).

- Looking ahead, when the relevant sections of the 2007 Act come into force, Legal Executive lawyers will be able to become partners or managers in Alternative Business Structures (firms with external ownership and investment) and set up their own practices.

- Legal Executive lawyers are now eligible to apply for prescribed Judicial posts and become Chairs of Tribunals.

- After taking an additional course, Legal Executive lawyers can undertake Advocacy and represent their clients in court.

- Legal Executive lawyers are Commissioners of Oaths; give advice on compromise agreements; and are able to instruct barristers directly without going through a solicitor.

- Legal Executive lawyers must adhere to a code of conduct and, like solicitors, are required to continue training throughout their careers in order to keep themselves abreast of the latest developments in the law.

Routes to ILEX Qualification:

ILEX students usually 'earn whilst they learn' and so take home a salary (usually from £14,000 to £20,000 per year when still qualifying), by working in a law firm whilst studying. Study takes one or two nights a week for the typical four years it takes to do all the ILEX qualifications required, either via a local college or distance learning. On average ILEX students earn around £65,000 during this time.

The ILEX qualifications are set and assessed at Level 3 (equivalent to 4 'A' level) and Level 6 (honours degree level). There is also five years' of work experience required in a legal environment before yopu can become a fully qualified Legal executive lawyer. Once qualified, you and your family can attend the ILEX graduation day complete with mortarboard cap and gown.

Organisation Profile

The ILEX route to becoming a lawyer is open to all, though it is recommended that at least 4 GCSEs are held. It is also ideal for those with degrees in law and non-law subject, and those with a BVC or LPC.

For those already holding a qualifying law degree awarded within the last seven years, ILEX offers a Graduate 'Fast-Track' Diploma. This just requires completing two ILEX level 6 practice units (one of which must relate to the subject areas studied within the law degree), and the ILEX level 6 Client Care Skills unit to complete academic studies. After five years' relevant work experience (at least two of which must be after completion of the ILEX fast-track qualification) you will be eligible to apply to become a qualified Legal Executive lawyer. This route costs approximately £1,700 to complete.

Non-qualifying law degrees or degrees that have sufficient legal content will be assessed on a subject by subject basis. A full syllabus transcript must be provided with the application to ILEX so that the contents of the qualification can be mapped against the appropriate ILEX unit. If no exemptions are granted, then applicants need to study the two stages of ILEX academic courses (the ILEX Level 3 Professional Diploma in Law and Practice and the ILEX Level 6 Professional Higher Diploma in Law and Practice qualifications) and this usually takes four years of part-time study. However, because the studies are usually through evening classes or by distance learning, this route has the advantage that trainee Legal Executive lawyers can earn a salary whilst qualifying. They must still undertake five years' relevant work experience (again, at least two of which must be after completion of the ILEX academic qualifications) to become a qualified Legal Executive lawyer.

Salaries

Salaries will vary according to location and chosen specialist area of law, but starting salaries are approximately £14,000 a year. Fully qualified Legal Executives can then expect to earn around £35,000 on average across England and Wales, with more being offered for Legal Executives in major cities such as London, where salaries can reach as high as £95,000.

Institute of Legal Executives

Tel: 01234 841000
Email: info@ilex.org.uk
www.ilexcareers.org.uk

Institute of Legal Executives (ILEX), Kempston Manor, Kempston, Bedford, MK42 7AB.

LICENSED CONVEYANCER

What the work involves

- Licensed conveyancers deal with the legal side of buying and selling houses, flats, business premises and other property.

- You will draw up the legal documents, known as contracts, that buyers and sellers exchange to make a sale legal.

- You will deal with enquiries from clients, explaining legal phrases in contracts in simple language.

- Other work includes liaising with lawyers and estate agents involved in the sale and researching details in the contract.

The type of person suited to this work

Dealing with people is a big part of the job, requiring good communication skills. Being a good team worker is useful to liaise with others involved in a contract.

As legal contracts must be completely accurate, you will need to be very thorough in your work and pay close attention to detail. It is important to be able to handle large amounts of information when drawing up contracts.

You will be dealing with several properties at the same time, which will need good organisation and being able to do several jobs at once. You will need to be able to meet deadlines.

Working conditions

Most of your work will be office-based. You will normally work Monday to Friday office hours, but may be required to work some late evenings or Saturday mornings to meet your clients. Your job may be salaried or commission only.

Future prospects

Conveyancing is a very small profession with under 1000 licensed conveyancers in England and Wales, and very few qualified conveyancers in Scotland. Job opportunities are mainly with legal practices. You could become self-employed and run your own business.

Training is ongoing to ensure you keep up to date with developments in property law. You could progress into other legal professions or the property world.

Advantages/disadvantages

The work is varied and you will meet different people.

You will get satisfaction when clients get their dream home.

There may be stress when you are trying to meet deadlines or clients feel things are moving too slowly.

Some people may be difficult.

Money guide

As a trainee licensed conveyancer, you could earn around £16,000 per year. Salaries for qualified conveyancers start at around £18,500–£23,500.

Qualifications and courses

England and Wales

Candidates must pass the Council for Licensed Conveyancers (CLC) training and exams. To begin the training they must be 21 years old and have 4 GCSEs including English. An A level in law is useful. Many applicants will hold a law degree or might have undertaken the Institute of Legal Executives (ILEX) course.

They must have at least 2 years' practical training with a 'qualified employer' and pass the Council of Licensed Conveyancers (CLC) examination, which is taken by over half of all students as a correspondence course, and is also offered at some colleges on a part-time basis.

After passing the course, candidates apply for a limited licence. After a further 3 consecutive years you can apply for a full licence.

Scotland

Qualified conveyancers generally require a degree in law from a Scottish university or a Diploma/Certificate in legal studies which lasts at least 2 years.

They then undertake a training contract of at least 1 year with an independent qualified conveyancer. After 6 months of training, trainees are required to attend a Professional Competence Course, which comprises 36 hours of core requirements and 18 hours of electives. Attendance at the course is an integral part of the traineeship.

Candidates for law degrees usually need 5 GCSEs/S grades (A–C/1–3) and 3 A levels/H grades. Alternatively, some universities require applicants to take the National Admissions Test for Law (LNAT).

This rises to £26,500–£38,000 after gaining further experience.

Related opportunities

- Barrister/Advocate p365
- Estate Agent p97
- Surveyor/Surveying Technician p130

Further information

Council for Licensed Conveyancers
16 Glebe Road, Chelmsford, Essex CM1 1QG
01245 349599; www.conveyancer.org.uk

Law Society of Scotland
26 Drumsheugh Gardens, Edinburgh EH3 7YR
0131 226 7411; www.lawscot.org.uk

The Institute of Legal Executives (ILEX)
Kempston Manor, Kempston, Bedfordshire MK42 7AB
01234 845718; www.ilex.org.uk

ENTRY LEVEL 3

Legal and Political Services

CRCI: L
CLCI: LAZ

PARALEGAL

What the work involves

- A paralegal is somebody who is not a qualified lawyer, but whose job involves dealing with a lot of legal issues and law.

- You may have legal training or experience, and will work in a law firm or similar organisation.

- Your duties will be varied, but will probably involve legal research and drafting documents, as well as other administrative tasks.

- You'll also interview witnesses and clients, and appear in court, often acting on behalf of lawyers. You might specialise in a specific area of law.

The type of person suited to this work

You should have a natural interest in law and current affairs, and be discreet in your work, as you may frequently be dealing with confidential information.

Attention to detail is essential, as is a good command of English, and the ability to communicate well with everybody, from the lawyers you'll be working with to all of their clients.

You should also be patient, understanding, tactful and sympathetic, and be able to work well under pressure.

Organisational skills are essential, as is computer literacy, excellent concentration and a good memory. You also need to be able to understand and absorb large quantities of information.

Working conditions

You'll probably be working in an office for about 37 hours a week. However, some of these will be spent visiting clients, which means that a driving licence is useful.

You may spend time in police stations and court, occasionally out of office hours. You may be required to work weekends and bank holidays, if necessary.

Some trained paralegals work freelance.

Future prospects

Future prospects for a paralegal are good. You can use the knowledge you gain on the job to develop your legal career. Since you often have similar responsibilities to a solicitor, it really does look good on your CV.

With experience, you can take on additional responsibilities and move up within the firm. You may choose to move on to freelance work.

If you have the necessary qualifications, you can become a solicitor or barrister, and even work your way up to partner.

Advantages/disadvantages

Working as a paralegal is stimulating and rewarding, especially if you have an interest in or study law.

Qualifications and courses

You don't need any specific qualifications to become a paralegal, and can start work straight from school. However, most employers prefer you to have some relevant qualifications, for example good GCSEs or a BTEC or SQA in law or legal studies.

You may have completed a legal secretary apprenticeship, or have a foundation degree in law. Some employers ask for a HND or degree in law, and others even request the LPC (Legal Practice Course) postgraduate qualification.

Becoming a paralegal is a popular option with those who graduated in law but don't have a training contract to become a solicitor.

Training usually takes place on the job, and you'll be supervised by experienced lawyers. Employers may well encourage you to follow courses in legal training; these are widely available. These might include a HND, BTEC or City & Guilds qualification in law or legal studies.

It can really give your law career a nudge in the right direction, and is a great option if, for example, you're training to be a solicitor and want to take a gap year or year out.

Occasionally tasks may be a little mundane, and meeting with clients can be stressful.

Money guide

As a paralegal who is starting out, you may earn £14,000 to £25,000 a year.

This can grow with experience to £25,000 to £40,000 a year.

As a senior paralegal you might be earning over £70,000 a year.

Related opportunities

- Court Administrative Officer p370
- Legal Executive p376
- Legal Secretary p60

Further information

Institute of Paralegals
2nd Floor, Berkeley Square House, Berkeley Square, Mayfair, London W1J 6BD
020 7887 1420; www.instituteofparalegals.org

Institute of Legal Executives (ILEX)
Kempston Manor, Kempston, Bedfordshire MK42 7AB
01234 845718; www.ilex.org.uk

The National Association of Licensed Paralegals
73 Shenley Road, London SE5 8NE
020 7252 7545; www.nationalparalegals.com

Institute of Legal Executives (ILEX)

Paralegal

The Institute of Legal Executives (ILEX) offers an extensive range of qualifications aimed at enhancing the career prospects of paralegals.

In conjunction with City and Guilds, ILEX also offers a specific range of qualifications aimed at those seeking a career as a paralegal and those working in other legal support roles where knowledge of the law is needed. If you don't already hold a law degree, these qualifications can also provide you with the opportunity to transfer to the Legal Executive route to become a qualified lawyer.

Together ILEX and City & Guilds offer the law sector's leading qualifications for legal secretaries and paralegals. Over 20,000 people have chosen these qualifications to advance their careers. They are available for study through over 100 approved City & Guilds centres nationwide.

Specially produced course books are available, and the City & Guilds/ILEX Level 2 Certificate/Diploma in Legal Studies can be used as part of your entry criteria to study as a Legal Executive with ILEX.

Legal Secretaries and Paralegals are also now eligible to apply to become members of ILEX. The grades and fees for 2010 are as follows:

Student member – for those wishing to enter the legal profession; those who have no relevant legal qualification; or those with less than three years' work experience of a predominantly legal nature. Annual subscription fees of £50 are payable, plus a one-off initial registration fee of £35.

Affiliate member – for those with at least one ILEX level 3 unit qualification, or who have completed a relevant legal qualification at level 2, or gained at least three years' work of a predominantly legal nature. Annual subscription fees of £90 are payable, plus a one-off initial registration fee of £35.

To find your nearest centre, simply contact your regional City & Guilds office (details on http://www.cityandguilds.com) or email legalstudies@ilex.org.uk

For more information on ILEX qualifications or to receive information on your nearest study centre, please call +44 (0)1234 841000 or email info@ilex.org.uk

PATENT AGENT/EXAMINER

What the work involves

Patent agent

- You will advise clients on the law of intellectual property.

- The work involves checking that an invention is a new one and not one which already exists.

- After checking, you will prepare specifications for the Patent Office, carrying out any negotiations required and representing the client before the patent examiner.

Examiner

- You will examine patent applications submitted by patent agents for new inventions, trademarks or a design.

- The work involves carrying out a search to check that each application is a new invention.

- You will carry out a detailed examination of the application to ensure it is clear and meets legal requirements.

The type of person suited to this work

You will need a thorough knowledge of applying intellectual property to inventions and the laws regarding this sector. You will need to be good at researching and handling information to check all work thoroughly.

You will need good speaking and listening skills. You will be required to explain legal points to people in simple language.

Good organisation is important to deal with several jobs at once and you will need to be able to make decisions.

Working conditions

Most of your work would be based in an office although patent agents do some travelling in the UK, for which a driving licence is useful, and may travel abroad.

A lot of the work involves using computers to research and write reports. Most of your work will be during office hours, Monday to Friday.

Future prospects

There are around 1750 registered agents in the UK. Around 80% of these work in private practices, mostly in the larger towns and cities. Around 20% work with industrial companies or local government agencies.

Patent examiners are civil servants, mostly based in the Patent Office in Newport with a few working in London. The civil service has a formal promotion structure leading to senior patent examiner.

Advantages/disadvantages

The work is varied, responsible and intellectually demanding.

Qualifications and courses

Patent agent

All patent agents need a scientific or technical background. Students usually need 5 GCSEs/S grades (A–C/1–3) including English and maths, and at least 2 A levels/H grades.

Patent agents receive specialist training in intellectual property law. Qualified solicitors with experience of working in an intellectual property department or those training to become patent agents and similar professions may apply to join the Chartered Institute of Patent Agents (CIPA).

A high level of skill in the English language is required, and a knowledge of other languages, particularly French and/or German, is an advantage.

Admission to the Register of Patent Agents and the Register of Trade Mark Agents requires a training period and the passing of examinations. It usually takes 4–5 years to qualify.

The Certificate in IP Law, offered by several universities as a short course (typically 1–3 months) gives exemption from all the Foundation Papers of the CIPA examinations.

Examiner

Candidates normally require a good Honours degree in science, maths, engineering or technology. An equivalent professional qualification or corporate membership of a relevant major professional institution may be accepted. Candidates must also meet the civil service's nationality and residency requirements.

You will get satisfaction from helping new inventions become recognised and being involved at an early stage of the job.

Money guide

As a trainee you could earn around £21,500, rising to £27,500 per year with experience. Technical assistants can expect £28,000, and to progress to £48,000. Once qualified you could get £52,000–£72,000. With 5 years' experience this rises to £68,000, reaching £95,000+ for senior partners in private practices.

Related opportunities

- Barrister/Advocate's Clerk p367
- Legal Executive p376
- Solicitor/Notary Public p384

Further information

Chartered Institute of Patent Agents
95 Chancery Lane, London WC2A 1DT
020 7405 9450; www.cipa.org.uk

The UK Patent Office
Concept House, Cardiff Road, Newport NP10 8QQ
0845 950 0505; www.patent.gov.uk

POLITICIAN

What the work involves

■ MPs represent the people in their local constituencies in Parliament, usually as a member of a political party.

■ You will hold 'surgeries' in your local constituency and deal with issues raised by local people at local and national level. MEPs (members of the European parliament) deal with European legislation.

■ In Parliament, you will join committees, attend meetings and take part in debates. You will also vote on new policies or laws.

■ You may specialise in a particular area, and may hold office in the government or for the Opposition.

The type of person suited to this work

You should be passionate about politics and have strong social beliefs, along with a desire to represent the people of your constituency.

Key skills include: communication, decision making, information handling, supervisory and management skills.

A pleasant manner and the ability to gain people's confidence are also important.

You will be expected to keep up to date with party policies and legislation, which requires being able to deal with large amounts of information quickly and thoroughly.

Working conditions

Your time will be split between your local constituency and Parliament/Scottish Parliament/Welsh Assembly.

MEPs spend one week a month in Strasbourg and much of their remaining time in Brussels.

Politicians tend to work very long hours when parliament is sitting. From the end of July to the beginning of October parliament breaks, so that politicians can spend time in their constituencies. This is an extremely demanding job, with a great deal of responsibility.

There is a lot of travel involved both at home and overseas.

Future prospects

Your job in any parliament will depend on being re-elected, which means it is important to have another career option to fall back on.

Although most MPs represent the local people in their constituencies, they are also involved in the government of their country. You could be offered a post in a ministry, which may lead to appointment as a minister in a particular area. In exceptional circumstances, you could become the leader of your party and the Prime Minister.

Advantages/disadvantages

The work is varied and challenging, and no two days will be the same.

Qualifications and courses

Any British citizen may stand for election as long as they are over 18 years old. There are no formal minimum educational requirements but many MPs are graduates or hold other professional qualifications. Qualifications in business, law or economics are particularly useful.

It is essential to be actively involved in a political party and experience in areas such as trade union work is helpful.

In Scotland and Wales there are regional members as well as constituency members.

There is a series of selection interviews before candidates can be 'adopted' by their party and their local constituency to stand for election. Candidates must then carry out a successful electoral campaign and be elected by the votes of the local people.

Those disqualified from election are undischarged bankrupts, prisoners of more than one year, members of the House of Lords and people holding offices listed in the House of Commons Disqualification Act 1975.

You will get satisfaction, particularly if your party is in power, but also frustration when votes do not go your way.

You will need plenty of stamina to handle the long hours and the job can be pressurised.

Money guide

Basic salary for an MP in the House of Commons is £64,766. Additional allowances are also available for things like travel and communications. Salaries depend on the types of responsibilities. You could earn £144,520 as a cabinet minister. You could earn around £197,689 a year as Prime Minister.

MEPs are paid the same salaries as national MPs in their own countries.

Related opportunities

■ Constituency Agent/Political Researcher p368
■ Public Relations Officer p425
■ Trade Union Official p587
■ Welfare Rights Officer/Worker p590

Further information

House of Commons Information Office
House of Commons, Westminster, London SW1A 0AA
020 7219 4272; www.parliament.uk

Scottish Parliament
Public Information Services, Edinburgh EH99 1SP
0845 278 1999; www.scottish.parliament.uk

National Assembly for Wales
Cardiff Bay, Cardiff CF99 1NA
0845 010 5500; www.wales.gov.uk

Legal and Political Services

CRCI: L
CLCI: COB

SOLICITOR/NOTARY PUBLIC

What the work involves

Solicitor

■ A major part of your job will be giving clients advice on legal matters, making a will or setting up a business. You will also carry out legal work on their behalf.

■ In certain circumstances you may represent clients in court, or you may have to instruct a barrister or advocate to act for your client.

Notary public

■ Your main job will be to certify deeds and other documents so that they will be accepted by judicial and public authorities anywhere in the world as authentic and legally binding. Notaries public are generally solicitors who combine this function with other legal work.

The type of person suited to this work

You must be able to examine and analyse vast amounts of information and pay close attention to detail.

When dealing with clients, you will need to be discreet to deal with confidential information. It is important to remain impartial.

Working conditions

Most of your work is indoors in an office. You might spend time in court. You might have to visit clients at home or other places, for example a police station or prison.

Future prospects

There is keen competition for every traineeship vacancy, but there are good prospects for qualified solicitors in private practice, local and central government and industry. You will usually specialise in one area of law.

Advantages/disadvantages

The work is varied and no two days will be the same.

You might have to work long hours, including evenings, weekends and even bank holidays.

Some people may be difficult and unpleasant.

Money guide

As a trainee, you can expect to earn a minimum of £21,450 per year in England; in Scotland you start at £19,500 for the first year rising to £22,500 in the second. Pay increases to £30,000–£55,000 once you are qualified and have experience. Up to £150,000+ is possible as an experienced senior partner of a legal practice, depending on the size and location of the practice. Notaries public are paid set fees for work on individual cases, reflecting the responsibilities of their professional role.

Qualifications and courses

England and Wales

Candidates with either an approved law degree, or a non-law degree followed by the Common Professional Examination (CPE), the Postgraduate Diploma in Law (PgDL) or the Senior Status Law degree.

Candidates without a degree can take examinations to become Members or Fellows of the Institute of Legal Executives (ILEX). A Legal Practice Course (LPC) must be completed followed by 2 years of training with a solicitor.

Scotland

Candidates need either an approved Scottish Law degree, or a good non-law degree followed by a 2-year graduate law degree. Entry is usually with 5 H grades (A–B) including English. Candidates can take 3 years' pre-diploma training and pass the Law Society of Scotland exams.

Entrants must complete a 26-week Diploma in Legal Practice followed by a 2-year training contract with a practising solicitor in Scotland.

Northern Ireland

Solicitors must complete an apprenticeship programme of 2–4 years, depending on the academic route taken.

Notary public

In England and Wales qualified solicitors can take a Postgraduate Diploma in Notarial Practice and be approved by the Master of the Faculties to act within a specific area.

In Scotland solicitors can apply to be enrolled as notaries on qualifying as solicitors.

Related opportunities

■ Barrister/Advocate p365
■ Crown Prosecutor/Procurator Fiscal p374
■ Legal Executive p376

Further information

Law Society of Northern Ireland
Law Society House, 98 Victoria Street, Belfast BT1 3JZ
028 9023 1614; www.lawsoc-ni.org

Law Society of Scotland
26 Drumsheugh Gardens, Edinburgh EH3 7YR
0131 226 7411; www.lawscot.org.uk

Law Society of England and Wales
The Law Society's Hall, Chancery Lane, London WC2A 1PL
0870 606 2555; www.lawsociety.org.uk

Leisure, Sport and Tourism

This sector relies on a motivated, up-beat and out-going workforce for its success. You will need to show that you can work very well with other people, providing them with an excellent service when they want to enjoy themselves on holiday or if they are keen to improve their fitness and sporting ability. If you are keen to work with professional sports players or become one yourself you should be very aware of how to keep the body fit while avoiding injury. You should be warm and friendly but also able to maintain a high level of professionalism at the same time. You should also demonstrate you have patience and tact with people of all ages as well and be clued up on health and safety regulations.

In this section we look at the following jobs:

- Bookmaker p386
- Croupier p387
- Entertainments Manager p388
- Events and Exhibition Organiser p389
- Fitness Instructor/Personal Trainer p390
- Holiday Representative p391
- Leisure Centre Assistant/ Manager p392
- Lifeguard p393
- Nightclub Manager p394

- Outdoor Pursuits Instructor p395
- Projectionist p396
- Sports Coach p397
- Sports Development Officer p398
- Sports Professional p399
- Theme Park Assistant/ Manager p400
- Tour Guide/Manager p401
- Tourist Information Centre Assistant p402

- Travel Agency Sales Consultant p403

For similar jobs to the ones in this section turn to *Catering and Hospitality* on page 139.

BOOKMAKER

What the work involves

- Bookmakers take bets from punters (clients) on the outcomes of sporting events and contests, and issue betting cards.
- As a licensed bookmaker you will be running a betting shop, or your own or employer's 'bookie's pitch' at different racing events all over the country.
- Working out the betting odds for every race entrant and communicating with other bookies via the internet or by 'tic-tac' semaphore at racing events.
- Writing up and adjusting the changing odds for each track event on a display board.

The type of person suited to this work

You need to be alert to gather vital information about race entrants' recent performance ratings and handicaps.

The odds you offer will be influenced by those of competing bookmakers, and you need to make rapid adjustments as the odds shorten just before 'off'.

Confidence and good verbal and negotiating skills are vital.

Working conditions

As a bookie setting up pitch on racecourses, you cover large distances to attend all major sporting events.

Much of your work is outdoors – perhaps standing on a stepladder for visibility.

Bookmakers who work only in betting shops may find the environment restricting, especially at times when punters become agitated and excited. You may have to handle difficult, even menacing, punters who have lost their stake.

Future prospects

Some bookies only do a short stint on a mobile pitch before moving into a more settled job, such as working for the national Tote (Horserace Totaliser Board), as a betting shop manager, or as a games host in a social club or holiday camp.

Successful bookmakers often prefer to move into self-employment and many experienced bookies work well beyond normal retirement age.

Advantages/disadvantages

Bookmakers are involved with betting and gambling – with people taking risks. You have to be calm and collected.

The lifestyle is not an easy one, especially if you have to follow all the racing action to make a living.

Some people find the long hours (past 6.30pm in winter and up to 9.30pm in summer) difficult.

Money guide

Starting as a trainee you could earn £13,300, rising to

Qualifications and courses

There are no formal entry requirements for bookmakers, although the large betting shop chains may ask for 3 GCSEs/S grades (A–C/1–3), including English, ICT and maths. You may have to take a basic maths test at interview, focusing on the calculation of percentages, odds and payments.

Some entrants – particularly to trainee management positions – have a degree, HND or Foundation degree. Business or mathematical subjects can be useful.

A high level of numeracy and excellent knowledge of betting opportunities and basic computer skills are all essential for this work.

Experience of customer service and reliability with handling money is an advantage. Betting shop employees may have opportunities to work towards NVQs/SVQs at Levels 2 and 3 in Customer Service or in Licensed Bookmaking.

Training is provided on the job, and covers areas such as calculating betting odds and payouts, administration, customer service, business skills, managing staff, betting laws and company policies. Large companies may provide training in their own training centres.

By law, you have to be 18 to work in a betting office and you have to be at least 20 to start as a manager.

£16,000 per year. Betting shop cashiers start on a lower wage of around £10,500.

Bookmakers managing small betting shops earn between £15,000 and £25,000+ in their own shop, or, up to £30,000 in an outlet of a major employer.

Earnings of bookies on race courses fluctuate with racing conditions, the number of entrants and punters, and the number of events in the calendar

Related opportunities

- Accounting Technician p19
- Betting Shop Cashier p386
- Croupier p387

Further information

Gambling Commission
Victoria Square House, Victoria Square, Birmingham B2 4BP
0121 230 6666; www.gamblingcommission.gov.uk

Association of British Bookmakers Ltd
Regency House, 1–4 Warwick Street, London W1B 5LT
020 7434 2111; www.abb.uk.com

National Association of Bookmakers
PO Box 2442, East Molesey, Surrey KT8 2WE
01884 841859, www.nab-bookmakers.co.uk

CROUPIER

What the work involves

- Croupiers are responsible for setting up gaming tables, preparing packs of cards and selling gaming tokens to casino-goers.

- Greeting customers, inviting them to join games of roulette, black jack or baccarat and explaining the rules if necessary.

- Spinning the roulette or money wheel, shuffling and dealing cards, shaking mini dice cages and encouraging players to place their bets.

- Announcing and paying out wins and collecting in lost bets.

The type of person suited to this work

You should have an engaging personality, and possess the ability to make customers feel happy and relaxed, so good interpersonal skills are key. Appearance is highly important in casino work. You must be smartly dressed in evening clothes, clean and manicured, with immaculately groomed hair.

There may be difficult moments, when people are emotional, distressed, even angered by losing, so you must be confident, firm and assertive if necessary.

Although you must be aged 18 to enter the gaming industry, most casino-operating companies encourage early entry.

Being able to speak an additional language is an asset.

Working conditions

Casinos open 7 days a week and on all the usual holidays from 2pm to 6am, so staff work shifts, from 2pm–10pm and from 10pm–6am.

On cruise liners, croupiers spend up to 12 months on board, with about 6 weeks' vacation. Casinos close when in port, so you do get some time ashore in exotic locations!

Casinos are well-appointed venues, and you mix mainly with a smartly dressed clientele.

Future prospects

The number of casinos across Britain is increasing, so prospects are good. Furthermore, gambling has become better regulated in recent years, and employers really value good staff.

Significant numbers of croupiers are needed to fill jobs on cruise liners, and this can be a favourite choice for experienced croupiers seeking management-level experience. Many certificated gaming staff from Britain now work abroad, particularly in the USA.

Advantages/disadvantages

If you are quick and ambitious, you can make rapid progress from croupier to casino manager.

Standing for hours and concentrating on running the games without error, while talking to customers, can be tiring.

Qualifications and courses

All casino staff are vetted for a clean criminal record by the Gambling Commission which sets strict controls across the gaming industry. Unless you hold their Red Licence, you will be barred from the work.

You have to be 18 years old, but there are no specific entry requirements. Prospective employers may set you tests at interview.

Most major casino operators run training schemes for entrants, both in-house and externally. To gain a BTEC Advanced Diploma in Casino Operations, entrants may attend a 12-week course available at Blackpool and the Fylde College.

As a croupier of 2-years' experience, with additional training you can progress to supervise a number of gaming tables. Floor managers have additional security responsibilities in counting, checking and locking away all the money taken by close of business.

You can progress to become an inspector and, finally, manager of a casino.

Croupiers who have 2 years' or more experience or who enter the work with a BSc (Hons) in Business Economics and Gambling Studies may fast-track to management responsibilities.

Casino-goers drink alcohol, which exacerbates the emotional tension during gaming. Arguments often break out which you must be able to handle according to the rules and regulations governing gaming.

Money guide

Starting salaries are £12,500 per year for trainee croupiers. After two years, experienced croupiers can earn £18,500–£22,500, but salaries are higher abroad.

Casino inspectors earn between £24,000 and £29,000, casino managers – slightly more.

Pay scales for casino staff on cruise liners are similar, but meals and accommodation are free and salaries are often boosted by tips. Salaries in London are higher.

Related opportunities

- Entertainments Manager p388

Further information

British Casino Association
38 Grosvenor Gardens, London SW1W 0EB
020 7730 1055; www.britishcasinoassociation.org.uk/careers

www.cityandguilds.com/myperfectjob

Leisure, Sport and Tourism

CRCI: MA
CLCI: GAK

ENTERTAINMENTS MANAGER

What the work involves

- Entertainment managers take responsibility for the schedule of visiting entertainers to a venue, achieving a balance of activities that engage the age, gender, and cultural interests of the audience.

- You will plan, organise, advertise and oversee the running of a full calendar of social events.

- You will contact acts and agents, and negotiate the best possible prices with them. When the events listing is finalised, you will be promoting the programme on a weekly and daily basis.

- You will also be responsible for costing out the entertainment plan to see if the social budget will cover the proposals.

The type of person suited to this work

Entertainments managers are people who enjoy life, can think on their feet and can make audiences cry with laughter, if need be. They are skilled communicators, who also make good use of ICT.

This job requires high-level skills in problem solving.

Your organisation depends on you to find reliable acts – often, to a new formula. You have to make quick appraisals to drive home a deal. You need persuasive powers, imagination and considerable personal initiative.

Working conditions

Your job might be a permanent post in a grand hotel based in a popular resort, on a cruise liner, or with a large company that frequently entertains important clients.

Entertainments managers work invisibly in an office during daylight hours, emerging only after 6pm to manage the flow of evening entertainment, introducing the artists and ad-libbing between acts.

There is seasonal work for entertainments managers in all the major holiday centres.

Future prospects

Corporate hospitality is used to create a good relationship between client and service provider. As entertainments manager, you have a job with considerable responsibility.

As the travel and tourism industry is still growing at a fast rate, there will be increasing need for entertainment to fill evenings for holidaymakers. Memorable evenings – being entertained by stand-up comics or flamenco dancers – encourage them to rebook with the same cruise line, hotel or tour company.

Advantages/disadvantages

You will meet and mix with some interesting and entertaining artists.

Almost every evening, weekend and public holiday, you have to work hard and stay focused while others are enjoying themselves and relaxing.

Qualifications and courses

There are no formal entry requirements for this career, and relevant experience can be more important than qualifications.

Useful courses at further and higher education level include hospitality management, leisure management, events management, management and travel and tourism.

You could enter with a degree, HND or Foundation degree in a subject such as hospitality, leisure management, business studies, marketing or events management. The minimum entry requirements for a degree are 2 A levels/3 H grades and 5 GCSEs/S grades (A–C/1–3) or equivalent, and for an HND or Foundation degree, 1 A level/2 H grades and 4 GCSEs/S grades (A–C/1–3).

People working in the industry can work towards NVQs/ SVQs in Cultural Venue Operations at Level 2, Cultural Venue Administration at Level 3 or Arts Development and Teaching at Level 3.

NCFE offers Certificates at Level 2 in Event Planning and in Event Management at Level 3.

Pressure can build if an act does not show up, so you might occasionally need to fill a gap and prevent the audience from getting irritable.

Money guide

Generally, travel and recreation work is not well paid.

Entertainment trainee managers can expect to earn £12,000, but between £18,000 and £20,000 per year, with experience.

If you hold this post with a large international company, pay and prospects could be much higher, so your earnings might be nearer to £25,000–£35,000.

Related opportunities

- Croupier p387
- Holiday Representative p391
- Theme Park Assistant/Manager p400

Further information

People 1st
2nd floor, Armstrong House, 38 Market Square, Uxbridge, Middlesex UB8 1LH
0870 060 2550; www.people1st.co.uk

NCFE national awarding body
Citygate, St James' Boulevard, Newcastle upon Tyne NE1 4JE
0191 239 8000; www.ncfe.org.uk

www.cityandguilds.com/myperfectjob

EVENTS AND EXHIBITION ORGANISER

What the work involves

- As an events and exhibition organiser, you'll be planning and organising events of varying sizes and ensuring that they run to plan on the day.

- You could find yourself organising anything from conferences, seminars and meetings to parties, ceremonies, weddings or even the 2012 Olympics!

- Your role will depend on the event itself, but you might be researching, planning, marketing the event, setting the budget, and sorting out all of the little details that go into planning an event.

- Hours can be late and involve working at weekends – but you may get to attend a free party or two!

The type of person suited to this work

You need to be incredibly well organised.

Work can be tough and stressful, so you need energy and stamina: you should relish taking on a heavy workload, not crumple beneath it.

You should be a team player who is really good at communicating with others.

You need to be creative and have a good imagination, but also have a business mind. Your project management and problem solving skills should be top notch, and you must be able to market, sell and negotiate.

Working conditions

You will be extremely busy and rushing to and from various locations.

You'll usually work office hours, although additional hours are common when events require extra last minute work

Your time will be divided between the office, events venues, and client meetings. You may well have to travel away from home, sometimes abroad.

You'll be working both indoors and outdoors, and may find yourself in hotels, museums, castles, showgrounds. . . the list is endless.

Future prospects

By starting off in roles such as assistant events organiser, you're paving the way and can aim towards positions like event organiser or manager. From this level you can progress to event director, or even start up your own company.

It is often necessary to move company more than once to progress in this industry.

Advantages/disadvantages

This is an exciting job, and the sense of achievement when an event you've planned is a success is a great feeling.

Planning an event can be stressful, and you may have to work

Qualifications and courses

There are no set entry requirements for this profession, but many entrants have degrees and postgraduate qualifications. There are relevant courses offered by over 50 higher education institutions in areas such as events management, conference and exhibition management, and hospitality management. Other relevant courses include marketing, tourism, and business. A diploma in Hospitality is also available.

For entry to one of these courses, you will need five good GCSEs and two A Levels.

The NCFE Certificate in Events Management is also relevant, and is good if you want to work at a supervisory level or if you're already in the industry and want to move forwards.

The best advantage you can have when you're looking to enter the industry is probably gaining as much experience as you can of organising events. Try to help with organising charity events, local festivals or anything similar. It'll also give you an idea of whether the job suits you.

Once you're in the industry, there is lots of training available. Courses cover everything from planning techniques and marketing to crowd safety.

flat out to meet deadlines and make your event a success, sacrificing your evenings and weekends in the process.

Money guide

As you start out, you might earn between £15,000 to £18,000 a year.

With experience this can grow to £20,000 to £40,000 a year.

As an event manager you might earn around £60,000, or even more at the most senior levels.

Related opportunities

- Catering/Restaurant Manager p141
- Entertainment Manager p388

Further information

Association for Conferences and Events,
Riverside House, High Street, Huntingdon,
Cambridgeshire PE18 6SG
01480 457595; www.aceinternational.org

Association of British Professional Conference Organisers
Association House, South Park Road, Macclesfield, Cheshire
SK11 6SH
01625 267883; www.abpco.org

City&
Guilds

www.cityandguilds.com/myperfectjob

Leisure, Sport and Tourism

CRCI: O
CLCI: GAZ

FITNESS INSTRUCTOR/ PERSONAL TRAINER

CRCI: MB
CLCI: GAG

Leisure, Sport and Tourism

What the work involves

- Fitness instructors/personal trainers teach people how to exercise in a safe and effective manner, whilst also helping them work towards personal fitness targets.

- You could provide a one-on-one service to your clients, direct and choreograph group fitness activities and classes, or undertake a mixture of the two.

- You could work in a health club, community gym, leisure centre, or a private gym.

- Other duties may include writing individual training programmes for clients, showing them exercise techniques and how to use equipment, and offering advice and guidance on nutrition and other lifestyle related issues.

The type of person suited to this work

You will need excellent interpersonal skills so that you can attract new business opportunities, chat to clients and advise them on fitness and dietary requirements, and build good relationships with other team members.

You must be very enthusiastic about training and fitness in order to motivate your clients and persuade them to persevere with exercise.

You should look smart and fit yourself, so as to promote a good image to existing and potential clients.

You must be innovative in your approach to keeping fit, thinking up new routines for classes, or creating diversity in one-on-one clients' training programmes so people remain enthused and interested in their activities.

Working conditions

Fitness instructors work longer hours than most other professionals, between 38 and 40 hours per week, and these often include early mornings, evenings and weekends to suit the needs of their clients.

Most instructors work on a part time basis, and are affiliated to one or a number of gyms in their local area.

Most instructors wear a uniform of sorts, consisting of matching polo shirt and jogging bottoms.

Future prospects

As society has become increasingly aware of health and fitness issues, the demand for fitness instructors has grown. This trend is set to continue for the foreseeable future, so employment prospects are good.

In certain areas, and in popular high street gyms, competition for jobs can be tough.

With experience, you could move into roles such as fitness manager or sports facility manager. Alternatively, you could build your own fitness consultancy.

Qualifications and courses

No formal academic qualifications are required to work as a fitness instructor or personal trainer, but you do need an industry recognised qualification in order to be placed on the Register of Exercise Professionals (REPs).

Qualifications that are approved by REPs include NVQ Level 2 or above in a subject such as instructing exercise and fitness. For entrance onto an NVQ course, you will usually need 4 GCSEs/S grades (A-C/1–3) or equivalent, including English, maths and a science subject.

Other approved qualifications include degrees in sports science/studies or movement studies, and an HNC/HND in fitness, health and exercise. For entrance onto a degree course, you will need at least 2 A-levels or equivalent (including biology), and 5 GCSEs (A-C) or equivalent. HNC/HND courses require 1 A-level and 5 GCSEs (A-C) or equivalent.

Apprenticeships may also be available for entrants aged 16–24.

Advantages/disadvantages

You will play an active role in enhancing many people's lives by introducing them to exercise and ensuring they continue with it. You will see tangible results of your efforts and guidance as people become fitter and slimmer during the course of your work with them.

You will have to work unsociable hours.

Money guide

On average, fitness instructors and personal trainers who are new to the industry earn about £12,000. As you build a reputation and client base over a few years, this should increase to anywhere between £14,000 and £25,000. Highly successful personal trainers, fitness managers and exercise specialists can earn £30,000+.

Related opportunities

- Sports Coach p397
- Outdoor Pursuits Instructor p395

Further information

Register of Exercise Professionals (REPs)
3rd Floor 8–10 Crown Hill, Croydon CR0 1RZ
020 8686 6464; www.exerciseregister.org

City&Guilds

www.cityandguilds.com/myperfectjob

HOLIDAY REPRESENTATIVE

What the work involves

- Holiday representatives meet holidaymakers at airports and other terminals, helping them to locate their luggage and directing them towards the transport that will take them to their accommodation.

- You will be responsible for checking all the details of each passenger's transport and accommodation to ensure everything is in place for their stay.

- You will inform customers of important information, including local bus routes, recommended restaurants and sites of interest. You will also sell excursion tickets.

- You may also be expected to accompany tourists on expeditions, and provide them with holiday entertainment.

The type of person suited to this work

You will need to look smart and have a pleasant, approachable attitude so that customers are comfortable speaking to you.

You will need to be sociable and also very patient, as you will be dealing with customers 24 hours a day for the duration of the holiday season.

You should also have a methodical approach to your work and excellent organisational skills as you will be co-ordinating lots of details for numerous people at one time.

Fluency in the language of the country in which you are working is also an asset.

Working conditions

Working hours vary from day to day, but are usually long and unpredictable. Most reps only have one day off a week, and even then they will be on call in case of a customer emergency.

The work is seasonal, although there are opportunities all year round including beach holidays over the summer months and ski work during winter.

You could work indoors or outdoors.

You will usually have to wear a uniform.

Future prospects

Although there are many vacancies for holiday representatives each year, competition is tough as it is a very popular job.

You could work for a large international travel company or a smaller, more specialist firm. Most opportunities are overseas, although there are a few jobs available in the UK.

With experience, you could move into a supervisory or managerial position. Some representatives also branch out into another area of travel and tourism, such as hotel management or working on a tourist board.

Advantages/disadvantages

You will have plenty of opportunities to work abroad in a number of diverse and exciting areas.

Qualifications and courses

Academic qualifications are not essential, as most employers place higher value on good experience in a customer service role. Having said that, holding GCSEs (A-C) or equivalent, in subjects such as English, maths, geography and a foreign language can be very useful in an increasingly competitive market.

There are professional courses available that offer related qualifications. These include: Level 2 Certificates in travel and tourism (resort representatives), travel and tourism communication skills, and resort representation; BTEC Intermediate Diploma Level 2 in overseas resort operations; Level 3 Certificate in travel and tourism, or travel and tourism communication skills. AS/A-levels and other qualifications are also available in relevant subjects.

Certain organisations may require their staff to have specialist knowledge in an area such as archaeology, wine growing or history, in which case a relevant academic qualification or recognised accreditation would be essential.

If you are looking to work with children, you will need at least 6 months practical experience and you must pass a Criminal Records Bureau check.

You will be dealing with a range of people from all ages and backgrounds on a daily basis, making the work diverse and challenging.

You will have to work long hours which can make the job both physically and mentally exhausting.

Money guide

Starting salaries for holiday representatives are usually around £6000 per year (£500 per month), with accommodation provided. With experience, representatives can obtain salaries of between £10,000 and £14,000.

If you move into a supervisory or managerial role, your earnings could increase to £18,000+.

Related opportunities

- Hotel Manager p149
- Travel Agency Sales Consultant p403
- Tour Guide/Manager p401
- Air Cabin Crew p594

Further information

Career in Travel
Fusion 2, Parkway, Solent Business Park, Whitley, Fareham PO15 7AB
www.careerintravel.co.uk; RepHelp@careerintravel.co.uk

City& Guilds

www.cityandguilds.com/myperfectjob

Leisure, Sport and Tourism

CRCI: MC
CLCI: GAX

LEISURE CENTRE ASSISTANT/MANAGER

What the work involves

Assistant

- Helping to run sports and exercise sessions in the leisure centre, setting out any equipment necessary, and demonstrating the safe use of equipment to members.

- Working on the reception desk issuing tickets and tokens, taking bookings, answering enquiries and doing other tasks specified by your line manager.

Manager

- Overseeing and managing the day-to-day work of all the staff running the leisure centre, including recruiting staff and dealing with member queries.

- Meeting with the company or council reps responsible for the leisure centre to discuss budgets, sources of funding and marketing issues, and for planning new activities and developments.

The type of person suited to this work

You will need common sense and a responsible attitude towards others. If you are keen to progress to managerial level, you will need some examples of situations where you have taken a lead role. Excellent interpersonal skills are essential, as you should be friendly and helpful. As you will be working within or leading a team, you must have the ability to communicate and mix well.

Working conditions

Most of your time will be spent indoors – at the poolside, in a sports hall, in the weights room, at reception or in the office. You should expect to work unsociable hours – early starts or late finishes.

In leisure centres, often it is assistants who have to hose down pool sides, showers and changing rooms and do other cleaning tasks on a rota basis.

Future prospects

Currently, interest in sport and leisure centres is booming and this trend looks set to continue.

New government legislation may try to counter the growing problem of obesity across Britain, and leisure centres will be working more intensely with school-age children, possibly planning and overseeing exercise programmes to promote individuals' health and fitness.

Advantages/disadvantages

Most leisure centre staff are very relaxed and, normally, there is a good working atmosphere.

Earnings can be low, unless you start on the trainee management route.

Qualifications and courses

Assistant

Although there are no formal entry requirements, many leisure development organisations prefer applicants with a good standard of education, including GCSE/S grades in maths, English and a science.

Training is often given on the job, although a number of courses are offered through the Institute of Leisure and Amenity Management (ILAM) and the Institute of Sport and Recreation Management (ISRM). Normally, assistants try for an instructor or coach award in their preferred sport or activity and are expected to gain a Lifeguard's Certificate and take on pool duties. The more technically minded can study towards NVQs/SVQs in Operating Equipment and Facilities.

Manager

To gain valuable work experience, some aspiring managers work part time in leisure centres while taking full-time courses such as a GCSE/S grade, an A level in leisure and recreation, or a BTEC National or SQA National in Sports Studies. Trainee managers will work towards Level 3 and 4 qualifications (NVQ/SVQ, HND or degree) in Sports and Leisure Studies, or Sport and Recreation.

Money guide

For trainee leisure centre assistants, pay starts at around £11,000 per year rising to £15,500 with qualifications and experience. A trainee manager will start at around £17,000, rising quickly to over £18,000. When qualified, salaries rise to £22,500–£26,000.

£35,000+ is possible at the top end of the scale.

Related opportunities

- Fitness Instructor p390
- Lifeguard p393
- Outdoor Pursuits Instructor p395
- Sports Development Officer p398

Further information

ISRM – Institute of Sport and Recreation Management
Sir John Beckwith Centre for Sport, Loughborough University, Loughborough, Leicestershire LE11 3TU
01509 226474; www.isrm.co.uk

City& Guilds

www.cityandguilds.com/myperfectjob

LIFEGUARD

What the work involves

- Lifeguards are responsible for overseeing, patrolling and monitoring the water and weather conditions where people are swimming, surfing or boating, displaying warning flags if necessary.

- Keeping watch on stretches of shoreline, observing all activities to reduce the risk of tragic accidents occurring; taking rapid action to alert the public to danger.

- Monitoring the safety of swimmers in public swimming pools.

- Rescuing people at risk from drowning, towing them to safety, assisting them ashore, carrying out mouth-to-mouth – sometimes CPR (cardiopulmonary resuscitation).

The type of person suited to this work

You must be fit and active, with an interest in watersports – canoeing, sailing, swimming, or surfing. You should also have a full understanding of the level of danger in all watersport activities.

You should be confident in water and a strong swimmer (able to cover 400 metres of a pool in less than 8 minutes). The ability to work within a team is also essential.

You must be assertive in order to take command and manage dangerous incidents using loud verbal directives.

Working conditions

You will either work on the beach or poolside. Either way, you will need to cover early morning and later shifts as part of your hours in order to provide a full emergency service to water users.

You must keep alert and vigilant at all times as when emergency strikes, you have to be ready to act in seconds – not minutes.

Future prospects

Interest in watersports has grown dramatically and so lifeguards, or sports trainers with lifeguard proficiency qualifications, are in great demand.

Swimming pools are always busy with club trainees, learners and keep-fit enthusiasts. Attendants working at a poolside must have a lifeguard certificate and over 32,000 are issued by the national governing body for lifeguarding (the RLSS) each year. There is increasing work for qualified lifeguards at all water sport facilities.

Advantages/disadvantages

You have to work without distraction, surrounded by people enjoying leisure time.

There can be periods of boredom that you have to work through, maintaining vigilance. Accidents can happen at any time.

Qualifications and courses

Lifeguard training, for the National Pool Lifeguard Qualification of the Royal Life Saving Society, is for those over 16. It is mandatory to take the 7th edition 1st revision NPLQ. Training is over 6 days and covers 2 assessed units: The Principles of Lifesaving and Swimming Pool Supervision, and The Application of Supervision and Rescue in a Swimming Pool.

NPLQ training can only take place in a centre approved by the Institute of Qualified Lifeguards (over 1900 pools in Britain now have IQL). Entrants can receive a copy of IQL's training handbook, The Lifeguard, directly from Lifesavers.

All lifeguards need to hold a valid First Aid Worker Certificate.

Lifeguard qualifications must be renewed every 2 years.

Ocean/beach lifeguards can take additional, intensive courses covering practical ocean rescue skills involving the use of boards and tubes. You must be 18 years or over to train as a Beach/Ocean lifeguard. The NaRS Beach Lifeguard award covers sea-rescue, professional management skills, practical lifeguarding and managing beaches.

Although you can gain a glowing tan while keeping watch, there are dangers of overexposure to sunlight.

Money guide

Pay levels vary, depending on employer and patrol times involved.

Many qualified ocean/beach lifeguards work as voluntary Beach Rescue Lifeguards for the RNLI (Royal National Lifeboat Institute) which helps to arrange training.

Starting salaries are around the full-time equivalent of £12,000 per year. With experience, pay can rise to £16,000+. Some lifeguards work for local authorities on a part-time basis when rates of pay can vary from £6 to £9 per hour.

Related opportunities

- Leisure Centre Assistant/Manager p392
- Outdoor Pursuits Instructor p395
- Sports Coach p397
- Fitness Instructor/Personal Trainer p390

Further information

Royal Life Saving Society UK
River House, Broom, Warwickshire B50 4HN
01789 773994; www.lifesavers.org.uk

Saltwater Training
23 Grenville Road, Padstow, Cornwall PL28 8EX
01841 533076; www.saltwatertraining.com

Leisure, Sport and Tourism

CRCI: MB
CLCI: GAG

NIGHTCLUB MANAGER

What the work involves

- Nightclub managers take responsibility for the smooth running of a late evening entertainment venue which offers music and is licensed to sell alcohol and food.

- Helping to hire and train staff to operate the club's techno-equipment – sound system, DVD and lighting – to run the bar and wait at tables, to look after the premises and trouble-shoot within the club and on the door.

- Drawing up future nightly listings, booking and paying artists and DJs to perform in the nightclub.

The type of person suited to this work

You must appear open and attentive, with an alert but calm appearance, demonstrating that you are watchful and aware. You have to be high profile throughout the opening hours and be available to defuse issues before they start. You also have to get on well with accountants, licensing authorities, environmental health inspectors and fire officers, suppliers and performers.

You need to be able to maintain a nightclub with a fun and stimulating atmosphere, where people have no concerns about coming in for a good time.

Working conditions

You will lead and direct a support team of nightclub workers. This means putting in longer hours than most. You may be on-site from early afternoon until after 2.30am – even 4.00am or later at weekends.

The dim lighting, high-volume sounds and stuffy atmosphere, together with the late nights, can harm your health over time.

It is essential to be of good appearance, dressed extremely smartly. Never appear without looking sharp because it is you that sets the style code for the club.

Future prospects

There are various styles of nightclub meeting the needs of quite different club-goers – especially in large cities. You could manage a dance clubs aimed at a young clientele, or a more sophisticated late night venue.

There is a constant turnover of nightclub staff, including managers, so there will be plenty of job opportunities in different kinds of nightclubs for the foreseeable future.

Some managers move to work abroad in resorts, or on cruise liners, and there is similar work in holiday centres across Britain.

Advantages/disadvantages

Being in a nightclub, evening after evening until the early hours, has an appeal for some people. However, the majority who leave manager positions say the work pattern was their main reason for going.

You rub shoulders with many interesting and well-known people; this is certainly not a dull job if you enjoy socialising.

Qualifications and courses

There are no formal educational qualifications which are essential to starting work as a nightclub manager, but employers do look for a number of qualities and skills.

Problem solving is an important skill in nightclub work.

You should be able to demonstrate high levels of the other Key Skills, for example an ability with numbers is useful for budget management. Good verbal and written communication skills are also helpful, as is being confident, a good organiser, and having a knowledge of health and safety.

Being a manager means leading the team of nightclub workers, so any qualifications you can gain in human resource management are useful.

Accountancy or amenity management qualifications are useful: Edexcel offers NVQs/SVQs for Accounting Technicians at Levels 2 and 3, and NCFE offers a Certificate at Level 2 in Event Planning and 3 in Events Management.

There can be a good ambience in the club, between customers and staff, but creating that magic atmosphere is largely down to you.

Money guide

Nightclub managers may start at around £22,000+ per year.

With experience this can rise to £26,500. You may receive bonuses from the owning leisure organisation if your club does well.

In London and other cities, pay may be higher, possibly rising to £32,000 – even, over £40,000 – for those with the qualities and skills sought by owners of more exclusive nightclubs.

Related opportunities

- Entertainments Manager p388
- Croupier p387
- Door Supervisor/Bouncer p544
- Public Relations Executive p425

Further information

Edexcel
Customer Service, One90, High Holborn, London WC1V 7BH
0870 240 9800; www.edexcel.org.uk

NCFE national awarding body
Citygate, St James' Boulevard, Newcastle upon Tyne NE1 4JE
0191 239 8000; www.ncfe.org.uk

City&
Guilds

www.cityandguilds.com/myperfectjob

OUTDOOR PURSUITS INSTRUCTOR

What the work involves

- Outdoor pursuits instructors lead groups of people through a range of challenging activities, designed to help them bond, have fun, learn more about themselves and develop new skills.

- You will work with people of all ages and backgrounds, including those with disabilities, children with special needs, adult recreation groups, and business professionals.

- You will be responsible for guiding these groups though a range of activities

- You will also be responsible for checking safety equipment, ensuring that group members are comfortable with each activity, and giving practical demonstrations.

The type of person suited to this work

You should have strong leadership skills as you will be required to persuade a group of people who have never met you before to undertake activities that are frightening and push them out of their comfort zone.

You must have an excellent level of physical fitness, alongside good eyesight and hearing.

You must be responsible and maintain continual awareness of the safety of both yourself and those around you.

You should have good communication skills and a personable manner to explain activities clearly.

Working conditions

Hours are generally long and irregular, usually falling over evenings and weekends, including bank holidays. Much of the work is seasonal. Part time hours are commonly available.

Many outdoor pursuits centres are located in the countryside, so a driving licence may be useful in order to travel to and from work with ease. Holding a licence for a passenger carrying vehicle (PCV) may also be helpful.

You should expect to be working outdoors in all weather conditions. Long treks may also involve spending evenings away from the centre, camping in a tent.

Future prospects

Although the outdoor leisure industry is growing, there is still a lot of competition for jobs.

Most opportunities are in independently run activity centres, or those owned by local authorities and charities. There are also jobs available with expedition companies who organise overseas excursions.

Many instructors specialise in a particular discipline, such as canoeing or abseiling, and work freelance across several activity centres.

Qualifications and courses

No formal academic qualifications are required to work as an outdoor pursuits instructor, but employers usually expect applicants to hold 2 or more relevant proficiency or coaching awards in their chosen sporting field. These qualifications should be recognised by the national governing body for the sport, and include courses such as Sports Leaders UK Basic Expedition Leadership Award (BEL), British Canoe Union Level 1 Coach, and the Mountain Leaders Training UK Single Pitch Award. Full-time college courses and degrees are also available that provide relevant qualifications.

As well as holding suitable qualifications, candidates are also expected to be able to demonstrate a history of leading and taking responsibility for others.

You will need to be 18 years old before you can work as an instructor. You will also need to undergo a Criminal Records Bureau check as you will be working with children and vulnerable adults from time to time.

Advantages/disadvantages

You will be helping people to break down boundaries and overcome fear, which will increase their self-reliance and self-confidence.

You will be working with a wide range of people, from all backgrounds and ages, which will give great diversity to your working day.

You will have to work unsociable hours.

Money guide

As an outdoor pursuits instructor, you could expect to earn between £8,000 and £11,000 as a starting salary. As your experience grows, this should increase to around £12,000–£18,000. Once you have reached the level of a more senior instructor, perhaps also developing specialist skills, you could earn £25,000+.

Related opportunities

- Sports Coach p397
- Sports Development Officer p398

Further information

Institute for Outdoor Learning (IOL)
Warwick Mill Business Centre, Warwick Bridge, Carlisle, Cumbria CA4 8RR
01228 564 580; www.outdoor-learning.org

British Activity Holiday Association (BAHA)
The Hollies, Oak Bank Lane, Hoole Village, Chester CH2 4ER
01244 301 342; www.baha.org.uk; info@baha.org.uk

Leisure, Sport and Tourism

CRCI: MB
CLCI: GAG

PROJECTIONIST

What the work involves

- Projectionists work in cinemas and are responsible for operating film screening equipment, ensuring that everything runs smoothly throughout the feature.

- You will also be required to monitor other technical equipment in the cinema, including lighting, heating and ventilation systems, electrical and gas supplies, and ensuring that all fire alarms and extinguishers are in good working order.

- You may work with traditional 20-minute reels of film, or modern digital versions that are stored on a hard drive.

- You will be expected to check that the sound on each film is operating properly, and that it is the right volume.

The type of person suited to this work

You should enjoy working on your own, and watching films, as the majority of your time will be spent alone, operating machinery in the projection room.

You will need good ICT skills in order to use increasingly complicated film screening technology and equipment.

Be alert and observant so you can pick up on problems quickly, and also have the practical skills and knowledge to solve these issues effectively and under pressure.

You should be able to observe the strict timings given on schedules to ensure each film runs according to plan.

Working conditions

You will work 5 days a week, but hours are generally long and irregular as most cinemas screen films from the afternoon up until late in the evening. Shift work and overtime are common.

You will spend most of your time in a projection room. Most of these do not have windows, but in modern cinemas they are usually air-conditioned. You will be working alone in the projection room for the majority of your shift.

Future prospects

The rise of new multiplex cinemas across the UK has created an excess of jobs for projectionists. Demand currently outstrips supply, so prospects are good.

Opportunities can be found in large cinema chains, or in smaller and often more specialist independent theatres. Most cinemas are located in city or town centres.

In larger organisations, you could be promoted to senior projectionist or an administrative role. Small independent cinemas offer scope for experienced staff to become more involved with the running of the business.

Advantages/disadvantages

If you love cinema, you will enjoy being able to watch films for free.

Qualifications and courses

ENTRY LEVEL 1

There are no academic qualifications required to undertake work as a projectionist, but you are usually expected to be at least 18 years of age in order to legally be able to watch all of the films offered by a cinema.

Many employers also look for candidates who have some knowledge or experience or working with electronic or sound equipment. This could be gained by working as an assistant projectionist for a few months.

There are also short and part-time courses available which could give you the experience needed to go straight into employment as a projectionist. Providers include The National Film and Television School, and The Moving Image Society (BKSTS).

All employers look for candidates who can demonstrate a real enthusiasm for the moving image. Joining a film club or taking a part-time job in a cinema can give you essential career-related knowledge in this respect.

Apprenticeships may be available to entrants aged 16–24.

You will have the opportunity to work for a number of employers, ranging from large multiplexes screening major blockbusters, to small independent cinemas who may specialise in art-house or international films.

You will be working alone for the majority of the time and your hours will be unsociable, including evenings and weekends.

Money guide

Starting salaries for cinema projectionists tend to be around £12,000.

With a few years' experience, this could rise to about £15,000.

In larger cinemas, if you reach the position of a senior projectionist, you could earn up to £25,000.

Related opportunities

- Lighting Technician p444

Further information

The Moving Image Society (BKSTS)
Pinewood Studios, Iver Heath, Buckinghamshire SL0 0NH
01753 656 656; www.bksts.com; info@bksts.com

The National Film and Television School (NFTS)
The Registry, Beaconsfield Studios, Station Road, Beaconsfield HP9 1LG
01494 671 234; www.nftsfilm-tv.ac.uk; info@nfts.co.uk

The British Film Institute (BFI)
21 Stephen Street, London W1T 1LN
020 7255 1444; www.bfi.org.uk

SPORTS COACH

What the work involves

- Sports coaches provide specialist support, motivation and knowledge to athletes in order to help them attain their best performances and achieve personal goals.

- As a competitive coach, you could work with a variety of levels of athlete, ranging from children's football or netball teams, through to professional and even world class sports professionals.

- At a non-competitive level, you will focus on providing fun and accessible exercise sessions for participants with a range of abilities and fitness levels.

- You will usually coach one specific sport.

The type of person suited to this work

You will need excellent communications skills. You will also need to have good motivational abilities in order to inspire and encourage sports players to push themselves.

You will need an in depth knowledge of your chosen sport, and a good understanding of nutrition and physiology is also very useful.

It is also essential that you understand a variety of training methods and principles so that you can provide an informed and beneficial service to your clients. Patience and determination are also vital qualities.

Working conditions

You will usually work early mornings, evenings and weekends, as that is when the majority of your athletes will be available.

If you are working in a seasonal sport such as cricket or football, you may have to supplement your income with another job during the quiet months.

You will spend hours on your feet, and may also have to undertake activity in order to demonstrate methods and principles to athletes.

Future prospects

The vast majority of sports coaches working in the UK do so on a voluntary or part time basis. Competition for full time positions is fierce, although opportunities may increase in the run up to the 2012 Olympics.

Career prospects will depend on the level of success you achieve in your work. If you gain credibility, it may be possible to move into a sports-related development or management position.

You could be self-employed, work for a local authority, or in a school, gym or professional sports club.

Advantages/disadvantages

You will be teaching the sport you love to a range of people, and developing their interest in it.

You may have the opportunity to work with incredibly talented athletes.

Qualifications and courses

ENTRY LEVEL 4

All sports coaches must hold a qualification that has been accredited by the National Governing Body (NGB) of their chosen discipline. You can start working towards recognised qualifications at the age of 16, but must be 18 or over to work as an independent coach.

Accredited courses are available directly from the NGB, or you can undertake a college or university course. NGB qualifications are equivalent to studying for NVQs Level 1–4, and no academic qualifications are required. They are usually studied on a part time basis.

Relevant courses at college/university include: BTEC national certificate/diploma in sports coaching or leisure studies, entry requirements are 4 GCSEs (A-E) or equivalent; BTEC HNC/HND in leisure studies, requires 1 A-level and 4 GCSEs (A-C) or equivalent; foundation degree in sports coaching, entry requirements vary; degrees in sports science/studies, coaching, and physical education, usually require 2 A-levels and 5 GCSEs (A-C) or equivalent, including English and maths.

An Apprenticeship in active leisure and learning is also available for people aged 16–24.

Some employers may require a first aid certificate, and if you intend to work with children you must first obtain Criminal Records Bureau clearance.

You will have to spend long periods of time standing outside in all weather conditions.

Money guide

As a newly qualified coach working for an employer, you could earn between £15,000 and £25,000. Experienced coaches who work for a NGB or professional association can earn between £30,000 and £35,000.

If you work at the highest level of your sport, such as coaching premiership football players, you could earn £100,000+.

Related opportunities

- Fitness Instructor/Personal Trainer p390
- Outdoor Pursuits Instructor p395
- Professional Sportsplayer p399

Further information

Sports Coach UK
114 Cardigan Road, Headingley, Leeds LS6 3BJ
0113 274 4802; www.sportscoachuk.org;
coaching@sportscoachuk.org

SkillsActive
Castlewood House, 77–91 New Oxford Street,
London WC1A 1PX
020 7632 2000; www.skillsactive.com

Leisure, Sport and Tourism

CRCI: MB
CLCI: GAG

SPORTS DEVELOPMENT OFFICER

What the work involves

- Sports development officers are responsible for ensuring that sports and related activities are available to people of all ages and abilities.

- You will be promoting the benefits of exercise and encouraging people to live a healthy lifestyle by devising simple but effective strategies that increase participation in sport.

- You will work within the local community, liaising with schools, gyms and social clubs, and also have involvement with larger agencies such as sports national governing bodies (NGBs).

- You may work closely with groups who are usually excluded from sports-related activity, such as disadvantaged youths, prisoners, and disabled people.

The type of person suited to this work

You will need a positive attitude, coupled with a commitment to sport, that will help you to persuade local community members and service providers to back your initiatives.

You will need excellent verbal and written communication skills in order to illustrate your objectives to other professionals. This includes strong persuasive and negotiating skills.

Good ICT and administrative ability will be essential for creating reports, producing material to support your ideas, and keeping accurate records.

You will also need to be confident and present an authoritative presence.

Working conditions

You will usually work a 36 hour week within normal office hours. Flexible hours and overtime are often available.

It is not unusual to have to work additional hours during evenings and weekends, attending meetings or networking events.

You will work in an office environment, and also spend time at local schools, clubs and community venues. Since a good deal of travelling is required each day, a driving licence can be helpful.

Future prospects

The pending 2012 Olympics are set to increase demand for sports development officers across the UK as increasing amounts of people are looking for ways to become involved with sport.

You will most likely be working for either a local authority, county sports partnership, or NGB. A few opportunities are available in specialist sports colleges.

Career progression for sport-specific development officers is fairly limited; you could be promoted to the role of sports development manager, or become more involved with other community initiatives.

Qualifications and courses

ENTRY LEVEL 5

Although there are currently no specific academic requirements, new entrants to the profession are usually graduates, which means that your chances of finding employment without a degree are minimal. It may be possible to enter the industry without a degree if you have extensive previous experience in sports or sports coaching.

Relevant first degree subjects include sports science/studies, physical education, recreation/leisure management, and health and exercise sciences. Most university require candidates to have 2 A-levels or equivalent, on in a related subject such as biology, and 5 GCSEs (A-C) or equivalent, including English, maths and a science. Some employers will also accept entrants with relevant BTEC or HNC/HND qualifications in sport, sports science, leisure management, sports development or another related subject.

Apprenticeships in active leisure and learning are available to entrants aged 16–24.

Advantages/disadvantages

You will play an active role in enhancing many people's quality of life by providing them with access to sport in their local area. You will be liaising with a variety of people on a daily basis, which should make the work dynamic and interesting.

You will need a resilient approach to your work, as suggestions and plans will often be knocked back or fall through.

Money guide

The starting salary for a newly qualified sports development officer is usually between £15,000 and £17,000. With a few years' experience, your wages could rise to about £24,000. If you reach a management position, you could earn £35,000–£40,000.

Related opportunities

- Sports Coach p397
- Fitness Instructor/Personal Trainer p390
- Outdoor Pursuits Instructor p395

Further information

The Institute of Sport and Recreation Management (ISRM)
Sir John Beckwith Centre for Sport, Loughborough University, Loughborough LE11 3TU
01509 226 474; www.isrm.co.uk; info@isrm.co.uk

Sports Leaders UK
23–25 Linford Forum, Rockingham Drive, Linford Wood, Milton Keynes MK14 6LY
01908 689 180; www.sportsleaders.org

SPORTS PROFESSIONAL

What the work involves

- Sportsplayers are paid professionals who compete across the globe in their chosen sport, often in front of an audience.

- You could compete individually in sports such as boxing, swimming, golf and athletics, or alternatively with a team in sports like football, hockey, cricket and rugby.

- You will need to spend a great deal of time training in order to maintain a high standard of general fitness, alongside honing your skills in your chosen sport.

- You may also be required to attend social events, give interviews, and promote the companies that provide you with sponsorship.

The type of person suited to this work

First and foremost, you will need to have an outstanding natural ability for your chosen sport.

From this, you must have the necessary commitment and self-discipline to maintain a continuous training schedule and strict eating regime.

You will need to have a highly competitive nature, but also a polite and pleasant manner in order to get on with team members, fellow players, and coaches.

As well as being physically fit, you must be mentally stable so that you can cope with both the pressure of competition, and defeat and disappointment at times.

Working conditions

Competitions and matches usually fall on weekends, although qualifying rounds may take place during the week.

You will usually need to travel to reach competitions, which may involve overnight absence from home. If you are competing at an international level, you could be away for weeks at a time.

You will need to train most days, and if you are supplementing your professional sports income with a regular job, this will mean working out either early in the morning or in the evening.

Future prospects

Most professional sportsplayers are spotted at an early age by a talent scout or coach. From this point, they build up skills and a reputation through competitions.

Unfortunately, the majority of professionals cannot earn a living playing their chosen sport alone, so you may have to supplement your income with full or part time work.

Sports professionals rarely continue to compete once they have reached their mid-30s, but there are plenty of opportunities to work as a coach or manager, commentator, or even earn money as a TV personality.

Advantages/disadvantages

Pursuing your dream as a professional sportsplayer will not feel like work.

Qualifications and courses

You do not need any academic qualifications for most sports. The only exception to this rule is found in golf, in which the Professional Golfers' Association requires player to have 4 GCSEs/S grades (A–C/1–3) or equivalent.

It can be beneficial to your performance as a sports professional to undertake some relevant education. Knowledge in areas such as anatomy, psychology and nutrition gained through GCSE/A-level study or equivalent is worth gaining.

Across the UK, there are opportunities for gaining additional help and support if you are a promising young athlete. In England, the Talented Athlete Scholarship Scheme (TASS) awards funding of up to £3000 for sports training. Scotland and Wales also provide similar assistance to young sports stars; their bodies are The Athlete Support Scheme and Elite Cymru respectively.

Apprenticeships are also available to young people, although only those who genuinely have the potential to reach the top of their sport are considered.

The hard work and dedication you put in should be repaid in the form of sporting achievements and acclaim.

One bad injury could ruin your career at a very early stage.

Money guide

If you start your professional career as an apprentice, you will earn about £6,000. You may also receive accommodation and food allowances.

Once you are established as a professional, competing in and winning competitions regularly, you should earn £20,000+.

Highly successful sports professionals working in well-supported sports, such as tennis and football, can earn anything from £100,000 to £5,000,000 and beyond.

Related opportunities

- Sports Coach p397
- Fitness Instructor/Personal Trainer p390
- Outdoor Pursuits Instructor p395

Further information

Talented Athlete Scholarship Scheme (TASS)
City Sports Centre, off Northumberland Road, Northumbria University, Newcastle-upon-Tyne NE1 8ST
0191 243 7356; www.tass.gov.uk; info@tass.gov.uk

SkillsActive
Castlewood House, 77–91 New Oxford Street, London WC1A 1PX
020 7632 2000; www.skillsactive.com

Leisure, Sport and Tourism

CRCI: MB
CLCI: GAG

THEME PARK ASSISTANT/MANAGER

What the work involves

Assistant

- You will work as part of a team, greeting customers, checking ticket holders' ages and heights, and operating and supervising rides.

- You must always observe safety rules, and keep a close eye on the environment surrounding rides you work at, ensuring there are no hazards.

Manager

- You will need to oversee all the different operations within a theme park, ensure the smooth running of all amusements, the catering operations, the maintenance and surveillance of the park.

- You will be responsible for recruiting and training staff, managing the budget of the park, and handling any problems that arise.

The type of person suited to this work

Theme park workers should be happy relating to the public, wanting them to have an exciting and memorable experience, but also being aware of and concerned for their safety.

Except for the managers and a few experienced assistants, this is seasonal work, carried out by people who move around the country between casual work opportunities. Because of the potential hazards for the public at theme parks, workers must be trustworthy and dependable, with good practical and mechanical skills, able to follow instructions carefully and safely.

Working conditions

Theme parks are open 7 days a week, and on bank holidays, so you work shifts and get a full day off each week. Assistants are also required to carry out repairs and maintenance on machines each morning and evening.

The manager must inspect the whole site before opening time, taking responsibility for seeing all the necessary safety checks have been done, and that the rides and other facilities are fully staffed.

Future prospects

There is always a high turnover of staff in theme parks, but a core of workers stay on, benefiting from training and increased responsibility which allows them to gain certificates as evidence of their skills.

There is more work in Europe for trained, experienced theme park workers. It helps if you speak their language.

Advantages/disadvantages

Managers, with qualifications and experience in the leisure and entertainment industry, can move between employment areas more easily.

Qualifications and courses

Assistant

You have to be 18 to start work in a theme park. No formal qualifications are needed, but if your aim is to become a supervisor or manager then it is best to have some GCSEs/S grades in maths, English, ICT and, possibly, DT and sports education. There are work-based qualifications available: there are NVQs/SVQs in Mechanical Ride Operations at Level 2, and you receive health and safety training from day one. NVQs/SVQs in customer care, catering and sales could also be relevant.

Manager

With experience and qualifications, you can progress to team leader and then gain promotion to managerial jobs, taking the ISPAL (Institue of Sport, Parks and Leisure) Certificates and Diploma.

Large parks, such as Alton Towers, need several specialist managers to plan and oversee all the catering, site cleaning and waste management, the ride operations, financial arrangements and marketing.

This is a specialised line of entertainment and leisure work and might not prove to be a stepping stone to other areas.

Money guide

Assistant

You might expect to get around £9,000 per year when starting out. With experience, this could rise to over £15,000. There might be a few benefits for employees, such as paid overtime, free health insurance and a cash bonus at the season's close.

Manager

Managers can earn £22,000–£24,500 per year.

Related opportunities

- Entertainments Manager p388
- Leisure Centre Assitant/Manager p392

Further information

EQ
Suite E229, Dean Clough, Halifax, West Yorkshire HX3 5AX
01422 381618; www.thinkeq.org.uk

City&
Guilds

www.cityandguilds.com/myperfectjob

TOUR GUIDE/MANAGER

What the work involves

- Tour guides are responsible for meeting and greeting parties of people who are taking a holiday, trip, cultural visit or tour together.

- You will accompany the sightseers on their journey and inform them of the historical/environmental/cultural interests of the area they are visiting. You will also assist them if they encounter problems or difficulties.

- Tour managers are responsible for putting together proposals for day trips and excursions in order to attract holidaymakers to the company.

- You will visit destinations to assess their potential as a tour venue, and may also assist tour guides with the delivery of the trip itself.

The type of person suited to this work

Tour guides and managers both need excellent communication skills in order to convey enthusiasm and interest for venues to both customers and potential clients.

You will need good stamina in order to keep up a high level of energy and interest throughout tours.

You will also need to have excellent customer relation skills in order to soothe any disgruntled holiday-makers and reach amicable solutions to problems.

Tour managers should also be methodical in order to put together logistically plausible, suitably detailed plans for excursions.

Working conditions

You may work long hours, and when out on a tour you will be on call for customers 24 hours a day should they need anything.

You could work for a large international company, or a small independent tour provider, but either way your focus will be on promoting the company image and following their tour policies carefully.

You will be expected to wear a uniform when on duty, which usually includes a shirt and tie.

Future prospects

The travel and tourism industry is in a period of expansion, so job prospects for tour guides are good.

You could work in a large international company that runs tours throughout the UK and overseas, or a smaller provider that focuses on specific tourist areas in the UK such as Bath or London.

Competition for work as a tour manager is tough, but if you have built up good skills and knowledge as a tour guide first, you will be in a good position for promotion.

Advantages/disadvantages

You will be dealing with a variety of people of all ages and

Qualifications and courses

Most tour guides and managers are aged 18 or over. Although no formal academic qualifications are required, some GCSEs (A-C) or equivalent may be useful, particularly in subjects such as English and maths.

Fluency in another language may well be an asset if you intend to work abroad, or for taking groups of foreign tourists around UK sites.

Tour guides can study towards a number of useful professional qualifications, which include NVQ Level 2 and Level 3 in travel and tourism. The Institute of Tourist Guiding also accredits additional training courses at 3 levels: Level 2 covers flexible route commentary, interpretation and presentation; Level 3 (the 'Green Badge') covers a greater level of heritage interpretation; Level 4 (the 'Blue Badge') is the highest qualification available.

Professional courses for tour managers include full-time HND and degree courses in travel and tourism management, City & Guilds HLQ Level 4 in travel and tourism, and a range of related NCFE certificates.

backgrounds on a daily basis, educating them about areas in which you have an interest.

It can get monotonous as you will be repeating the same spiel over and over again for weeks, months, and even years.

Money guide

Tour guides can expect to start on around £10,000, and with experience this could rise to up to £25,000.

Tour managers generally start on about £16,000, and with experience this rises to around £20,000.

Particularly experienced or specialised tour managers can earn up to £28,000.

Related opportunities

- Tourist Information Centre Assistant p402
- Travel Agency Sales Consultant p403
- Holiday Representative p391

Further information

Institute of Travel and Tourism (ITT)
PO Box 217, Ware SG12 8WY
0844 4995 653; www.itt.co.uk; enquiries@itt.co.uk

International Association of Tour Managers Limited
397 Walworth Road, London SE17 2AW
020 7703 9154; www.iatm.co.uk; iatm@iatm.co.uk

www.cityandguilds.com/myperfectjob

Leisure, Sport and Tourism

CRCI: MC
CLCI: GAX

TOURIST INFORMATION CENTRE ASSISTANT

What the work involves

■ You will be answering questions face to face, over the phone or via the internet, from adults, tourists from Britain and overseas, business people, local young people and researchers.

■ Working in a team in a centre, you will provide information, make bookings and reservations, locate places and businesses, and inform people about forthcoming shows and events in the local area.

■ From a counter in the centre, you will issue leaflets and sell maps, postcards and items of interest from the local area and region.

The type of person suited to this work

You need to have an interest in local matters and in promoting your local area. Good, up-to-date knowledge about places of interest is useful.

A methodical approach to researching difficult questions to dig out answers is an asset in this work.

Other useful attributes are having customer-service experience, the ability to research information using the internet, and verbal communication skills.

Most TIC assistants jobshare and enjoy teamworking, when they can back each other up by answering the phone or fetching leaflets if another assistant is busy at the counter.

Working conditions

Usually, tourist information centres are modern, bright spaces that make pleasant work surroundings.

There is quite a lot of standing at the counter and moving to and from storage areas with piles of information leaflets and stock items.

You may spend some hours sitting at a computer, researching routes, or B&B facilities in distant locations. Although local TICs hold local and some regional information, you often have to find out facts about distant areas for travellers or people relocating.

Future prospects

Since there is a slow turnover of jobs in this industry, it can prove extremely difficult to move from being a casual part-time worker into a permanent full-time job in a Tourist Information Centre.

Although every centre has to have an experienced, permanent manager, smaller centres may only have two paid employees. Large centres, in big cities, can have the equivalent of seven or eight full-time employees, some working a jobshare on a part-time basis.

Advantages/disadvantages

There are busy and slack times at the counter in TICs.

Much of the work may be done over the phone and not face to face.

Qualifications and courses

No formal educational qualifications are required to work as a TIC assistant. In this type of work, it is personal qualities that are usually more important.

Listening acutely and speaking clearly are essential skills, and it is very helpful if assistants can use ICT to research information and respond to enquirers via the internet.

Applicants who have got GCSEs/S grades (A–C/1–3) may be at an advantage. A number of TICs are close to international airports or in popular destinations for overseas visitors. In these centres it is valuable if one or more TIC assistants have modern language skills to help newly-arrived tourists, business travellers and foreign visitors. British Sign Language will also be an advantage.

Working as an assistant, you can be assessed for NVQs/SVQs in Tourist Information in the workplace, and many employees within TICs work towards these awards.

There are also the part-time HLQ Level 4 or BTEC or SQA HNC qualifications in Leisure and Tourism which might be useful for career progression to become a TIC manager. However, it is possible to move into supervisory and managerial positions simply with experience in the work.

Today, TICs may be contacted via the internet from anywhere in the world.

You will play an important role in promoting both the local region and its economy.

Money guide

TIC staff mainly work part time, but for full-time equivalent starting salaries are around £10,500 per year.

With experience, this can rise to £18,000.

You can earn up to £23,000 as full-time manager of a city TIC.

Related opportunities

■ Travel Agency Sales Consultant p403
■ Holiday Representative p391

Further information

VisitBritain
Thames Tower, Black's Road, London W6 9EL
020 8846 9000; www.tourismtrade.org.uk

VisitScotland
Fairways Business Park
Deer Park Avenue, Livingston EH5 48AF
0131 624 9840; www.visitscotland.com

City&
Guilds

www.cityandguilds.com/myperfectjob

TRAVEL AGENCY SALES CONSULTANT

What the work involves

- You will be selling holiday packages to the public and trying to meet your company's sales targets.

- Putting together individual holidays for an independent customer or for an organisation that seeks travel, accommodation and entertainment arrangements that are distinct from the travel company's normal holiday packages.

- Contacting airline, ferry and rail sales operatives to arrange transport, and then making reservations for accommodation, meals, hire cars and entertainment with hotels, restaurants, car rental companies and box offices, whether in this country or abroad.

The type of person suited to this work

You will need excellent administrative and research skills to quickly track down, assemble and book all the component parts needed for each customer's ideal journey or holiday.

You must have excellent listening and questioning skills in order to find the right holiday package for each individual customer.

If you are friendly, communicative and methodical, with excellent ICT skills, you will suit both your customers' and your employers' needs. It helps if you have a real interest in exploring new places yourself.

Working conditions

You work indoors, in a modern retail outlet, mainly at a desk or behind a counter.

There are numerous details to check over the phone and tickets, booking confirmations and insurance notes to post out to customers. Almost all the work is done at a computer screen, except for scanning through brochures for holiday deals and consulting transport timetables.

The agency can be very busy at lunchtimes, near to closing time and on Saturdays, before holiday periods. Many sales consultants work part time and there may be only two or three workers in the agency.

Future prospects

With growing interest in travel and holidays abroad, the travel industry now enjoys the highest turnover and numbers of employees of all major business sectors.

There are over 7000 travel agencies in Britain, so there are plenty of opportunities to advance to a managerial position, or even to start your own independent holiday company offering special-interest holidays.

You can move sideways into another area of tourism work, such as holiday repping or working as a tour guide, to see more of the world.

Advantages/disadvantages

A real perk in this work is that you do get some free or discounted holidays.

Qualifications and courses

Although no formal educational qualifications are needed, it's helpful to have a good standard of education with GCSEs/S grades (A–C/1–3) in English and maths as a minimum. Skills in geography and ICT are also sought.

Young people aged 16–24 can train in travel agency work through an Apprenticeship/Skillseekers training. You can start with very few GCSEs/S grades, taking work-based NVQs/SVQs Levels 2 and 3 in Travel Services. Some of the study is part time at a Further Education college.

Full-time A level and National Diploma/SQA courses in Travel and Tourism also make an excellent starting point for this work.

There are some full-time management courses offered by TTC Training for those who want to progress to travel agency manager.

The travel industry offers its own examinations – the ABTA Travel Agents Certificate. ABTA Primary and Advanced Examinations take place in March, June and December.

There can be long periods sitting at the computer, answering emails, checking flight and booking details, and waiting 'on hold' to confirm bookings, which can be boring.

Money guide

Starting pay for a sales consultant is around £11,000 per year. Employed apprentices will get less.

With experience and some NVQs/SVQs you can earn up to £15,000.

Senior consultants receive salaries of around £20,000.

Although this is a low paying area of work, employees at every level benefit from discounts.

Related opportunities

- Tour Guide/Manager p401
- Holiday Representative p391
- Tourist Information Centre Assistant p402
- Events and Exhibitions Organiser p389

Further information

Association of British Travel Agents Limited (ABTA)
68–71 Newman Street, London W1T 3AH
020 7637 2444; www.abta.com

Institute of Travel and Tourism (ITT)
PO Box 217, Ware SG12 8WY
0844 499 5653; www.itt.co.uk; enquiries@itt.co.uk

City&
Guilds

www.cityandguilds.com/myperfectjob

Marketing, Advertising, Media, Print and Publishing

Do you consider yourself to be a great communicator? Are you interested in working in an exciting and often fast-paced environment with passionate, driven and ambitious individuals? If so, a career in this industry could be right for you. People who work in this sector are exceptionally motivated and are willing to put in long hours often on low starting wages because of their love of the job. You should have a great sense of creativity and imagination and be good at putting your ideas on paper, but you will often also need strong business acumen as many of your decisions will be made from an economic point of view as well as a creative one.

In this section we look at the following jobs:

For similar jobs to the ones in this section turn to *Design, Arts and Crafts* on page 175 and *Performing Arts* on page 435.

ADVERTISING ACCOUNT EXECUTIVE

What the work involves

- You will plan and develop strategies for campaigns to suit different clients' requirements, working for advertising, PR or media agencies.

- Project-managing several client briefs at the same time, you will be making sure that all the campaigns run smoothly, are within budget and run to schedule.

- Your work will involve liaising between clients and the agency staff, such as designers and budget planners.

- Identifying, approaching and engaging potential clients will also be important.

The type of person suited to this work

Because much of your work involves discussions with clients and agency staff, you will need to be flexible, with good communication skills. Being good with record-keeping and having a well-organised approach are essential because you will be running a number of campaigns at the same time.

You will need a strong creative flair and a resourceful attitude. A key ability will be to manage clients' campaigns within budget.

You will need to be confident and enjoy negotiating. Being a strong team player with a flexible and enthusiastic attitude is valuable.

Working conditions

You will work mostly in an office, spending a lot of time at your computer, when not attending campaign planning meetings and speaking on the phone. It is almost certain that at times you will have to work under pressure to complete projects within limited time-scales.

It will be possible to work normal office hours in the quieter periods, but during busy times you will have to work late if required.

Future prospects

Due to the popularity of this sector, competition for jobs is tough and there can be 15 graduate applicants – all with media-related qualifications – for every person employed in the industry. You will need to have particular skills or work experience that make you stand out. Even with a job in the advertising industry it can be difficult to progress due to a lack of higher-level opportunities. Consult the IPA's online magazine Campaign for opportunities. The majority of agencies have fewer than 100 employees.

However, if you are unable to find advertising work, the skills you will gain through your training will be relevant to the related industries of marketing, market research, business or retail and commerce.

Advantages/disadvantages

The job is fast-paced, with hectic periods of work which you will need to log. There are opportunities to meet and work with a

Qualifications and courses

There are no minimum educational requirements, but entry into advertising is very competitive and most entrants are graduates. A degree or Higher National Diploma (HND) is often required by large agencies, while smaller agencies also look for relevant work experience.

A range of related courses are available at universities and colleges at HND, Foundation degree, Honours degree and postgraduate levels. Subjects include advertising, marketing, English, communications or advertising/marketing combined with another subject; a sandwich course can be particularly useful.

Training tends to be done on the job. Staff may enrol on an Institute of Practitioners in Advertising (IPA) course if their employer is a member. Some staff may be required to study towards Communications Advertising and Marketing Education Foundation (CAM) qualifications.

wide range of people. It is a very competitive career to enter, so you will have to be very determined. It can be rewarding when your clients' campaigns are successful.

Money guide

Salaries vary according to employer and geographical location, although London agencies tend to pay the highest. Starting as a graduate you can expect to earn £18,000–£24,000 a year. £30,000–£50,000 can be expected at senior levels, with the most successful earning £65,000+. In some jobs you can earn commission in addition to your salary.

Related opportunities

- Advertising Art Director p407
- Advertising Media Planner p409
- Marketing Manager/Assistant/Executive p417
- Market Researcher p416

Further information

Advertising Association
7th Floor North, Artillery House, 11–19 Artillery Row, London SW1P 1RT
020 7340 1100; www.adassoc.org.uk

Communication, Advertising and Marketing Education (CAM) Foundation
Moor Hall, Cookham, Maidenhead, Berkshire SL6 9QH
01628 427120; www.camfoundation.com

Institute of Practitioners in Advertising
44 Belgrave Square, London SW1X 8QS
020 7235 7020; www.ipa.co.uk

ADVERTISING ART DIRECTOR

What the work involves

- You will design and create effective brand styles and images, with immediate impact, for advertising campaigns to suit clients' requirements.

- Working with specialist software, you will develop new designs, often at short notice, to convey the required mood or tone of a particular campaign.

- Working closely with colleagues, especially copywriters and reprographic specialists, you will make sure your ideas come together.

- You may also be involved in selecting photographers and other professionals to create additional visuals for use in a campaign.

The type of person suited to this work

You will need visual design skills and creative strengths, but also the know-how and skills to develop commercial ideas. The capacity to understand and adapt to a client's requirements is also important.

As you will be using software to create new designs, you will need to have up-to-date computer skills. However, the ability to get ideas across with pen and paper is also important.

Much of your time will be spent working as part of a team, so you will need excellent communication and people skills. You may have to deal with your ideas being rejected or changed so a flexible yet confident attitude is essential.

Finally, it is important to be able to work to exacting standards, paying close attention to detail.

Working conditions

Most of your tasks will be office-based, sometimes in a studio; you will be seated for long periods at a workstation using a number of computers, and may often be on the phone. The majority of your work will be done in normal office hours. However, you will be under a lot of pressure to complete jobs in the lead-up to contract deadlines and at these times will be expected to work late. Your job will involve attending meetings and visiting your clients which could involve travel and overnight stays.

Future prospects

This is a highly competitive area of work to enter. There are currently around 1000 office-based advertising agencies across the UK, over half of which are in London. Although newer agencies exist in some of the larger cities (Manchester, Bristol and Newcastle), the numbers of creative art directors employed are still low.

With experience – and some successful campaigns in your portfolio – you could move up to work as a senior art director. Some established art directors go on to work on a freelance basis.

Qualifications and courses

While there are no specific entry requirements, most art directors are usually graphic designers trained to HND, degree or postgraduate level. Courses combining elements of graphic design and advertising are particularly useful.

Students generally require at least 2 A levels/3 H grades and 5 GCSEs/S Grades (A–C/1–3) to get a place on a degree course. Foundation courses are also available.

Advertising or marketing and other relevant postgraduate degrees may improve chances of entry in a very competitive industry.

D&AD runs workshops in which participants develop skills and build up a portfolio of work. See www.dandad.org for details.

Advantages/disadvantages

This job is rewarding as it offers creative, design-conscious individuals the chance to influence the images of major companies and their brands. As there is a constant need to develop new ideas, the job can be high-pressured – even stressful at times. It is a very competitive area to enter with more creative graduates wanting work than available vacancies. These tend to appear in MediaGuardian or Campaign – the IPA's online magazine (see Further information).

Money guide

Salaries vary according to employer and geographical location. The highest earnings are normally with London-based agencies. Starting salaries at junior art director level are around £18,000–£25,000 per year. With experience and success this can rise to £35,000–£70,000. At senior and very senior levels you could earn £50,000–£150,000. A very few progress to Creative Arts Director and have salaries of around £300,000.

Related opportunities

- Advertising Account Executive p406
- Advertising Media Planner p409
- Copywriter p414
- Graphic Designer p186

Further information

Communication, Advertising and Marketing Education (CAM) Foundation
Moor Hall, Cookham, Maidenhead, Berkshire SL6 9QH
01628 427120; www.camfoundation.com

Design and Art Directors Association (D&AD)
9 Graphite Square, London SE11 5EE
020 7840 1111; www.dandad.org

Institute of Practitioners in Advertising
44 Belgrave Square, London SW1X 8QS
020 7235 7020; www.ipa.co.uk

Marketing, Advertising, Media, Print and Publishing

CRCI: O
CLCI: OD

ADVERTISING MEDIA BUYER

What the work involves

- Advertising media buyers research, identify and negotiate the purchase of media space (e.g. advertising time on television or radio).

- Working for an advertising agency, you will work from a brief laid out by your clients, taking into consideration target audiences, media events and activities, schedules and budgetary constraints.

- You will present proposals, advise creative teams, estimate costs and profits, and monitor and keep records of the progress of your media campaigns.

- You will make media contacts and liaise with other media companies in order to get the best deal and most exposure on behalf of your client.

The type of person suited to this work

You should have a keen interest in media, marketing and advertising and constantly thinking of new creative ways to approach your work.

As you will need to have a good understanding of your target audiences and markets you should also be interested in the reasons why people purchase certain products or use certain media channels.

You must have good communication skills as you will have to make presentations, draw up proposals and correspond with contacts on a regular basis.

You should have strong organisational skills and be able to work under pressure and within tight deadlines.

You will need to have initiative, drive and be able to work in a team.

Working conditions

You will work around 40 hours a week, Monday to Friday. You may have to work longer hours to meet deadlines. Part-time work or flexible hours may be possible.

You will be mainly office-based although as you gain more experience you will spend more time meeting with clients, making presentations and discussing proposals.

You may have to travel away from home; this could include overnight stays.

The majority of your correspondence with media owners and companies is conducted on the phone, by email or by socialising.

Future prospects

You will usually progress to a permanent position after one year in a junior role. Your promotions will depend largely on personal performance and successful campaigns.

You may have to move between agencies in order to progress.

You can take postgraduate qualifications to increase your knowledge about specific aspects of your job such as business or marketing.

Qualifications and courses

Most entrants to this profession are graduates of degree or diploma programmes. Relevant subjects include marketing, media studies, statistics and business management.

Entrance is possible without a higher level qualification, but will depend on experience and skills.

Post-graduate courses are not needed for entry-level positions.

Building up a portfolio of work experience through work placements or on a voluntary basis, will greatly increase your chances of getting your first job. This will help you to develop skills and afford practical experience in media buying, negotiation, and sales.

After three to five years you may gradually take on more account management and responsibilities or you may take a position in data management or account planning.

Advantages/disadvantages

Advances and changes in the media industry mean that you will find new and exciting opportunities to work with multimedia technologies.

This is a highly competitive industry and your work may involve long and stressful hours.

Money guide

As a junior advertising media buyer your starting salary may be from around £15,000 to £20,000 a year.

After you have gained three or four years' experience you can expect to earn around £25,000 to £45,000 a year.

At a senior level you may reach £60,000 a year, but this can vary greatly.

Related opportunities

- Advertising Account Executive p406
- Marketing Manager/Assistant/Executive p417
- Market Researcher p416
- Public Relations Executive p425

Further information

The Account Planning Group (APG)
16 Creighton Avenue, London N10 1NU
020 8444 3692; mail@apg.org.uk; www.apg.org.uk

The Advertising Association
7th Floor North, 11–19 Artillery House, London SW1P 1RT
020 7340 1100; aa@adassoc.org.uk; www.adassoc.org.uk

The Institute of Practitioners in Advertising (IPA)
44 Belgrave Square, London SW1 X8QS
020 7235 7020; www.ipa.co.uk

ADVERTISING MEDIA PLANNER

What the work involves

- You will research public opinion and interest in a client's product or service to develop new advertising and media campaigns.

- Market research, positive and negative, will form a starting point from which you will plan and develop new advertising strategies for your clients.

- You will need to be very clear when interpreting your clients' intentions.

- The work will require close cooperation with your clients and your creative team in order to create strong and successful advertising.

The type of person suited to this work

As you will be developing fresh advertising ideas, you will need to have creative ideas that meet the clients' requirements.

To understand and make use of a range of facts and figures in support of your work, you will need an ability to interpret and analyse trends in data.

As you will have to make presentations to your clients and colleagues at progress meetings, excellent verbal and written communication skills will be essential. Being self-motivated and confident is also important.

Good business skills are helpful and you will need to use clear verbal reasoning when stating your point of view: an air of self-possession – even assertiveness – can be an asset at times, tempered by a sense of humour and a flexible approach to working.

Working conditions

Most of your work will be undertaken in an office or at clients' premises. You will be expected to dress formally and be well presented at all times. Although you will work mainly in normal office hours, you can expect to work overtime and at weekends during busy periods.

You will have to travel to attend meetings on a regular basis, perhaps staying overnight.

Future prospects

The majority of job opportunities in advertising are based in London although the number of companies in other large cities is growing. Despite this, there are still only around 21,000 people working within the sector of advertising and media, making entry highly competitive. Realistically, account planning makes up only a very small part of the overall advertising/media sector.

If employed by one of the few larger companies – with over 300 employees – it is occasionally possible to work abroad in areas such as Europe. With experience, you could work on a freelance basis or move into market research, design or management.

Qualifications and courses

Although there are no minimum educational requirements to becoming an advertising media planner, competition is high and most entrants will have a degree. It is rare to get into the profession with less than an HND. Smaller agencies also tend to require relevant work experience, and a sandwich course can be a particular advantage.

Useful Key Skills include application of number, communication and people skills.

Training tends to be done on the job. New account planners may train with the Account Planning Group and Market Research Society, or work towards NVQ/SVQ Levels 3 or 4 in Advertising and Public Relations. You may enrol on a course run by the Institute of Practitioners in Advertising (IPA) if your employer is a member, or take qualifications with the Communications Advertising and Marketing Education Foundation (CAM).

Advantages/disadvantages

This type of work can provide the opportunity to work for high-profile companies with a Europe-wide or global reach. You will have to develop new ideas, often at relatively short notice. This is a very competitive career and only the most determined will succeed. Besides reflecting positive opinion you will sometimes have to pass negative information to clients about how their products are currently viewed.

Money guide

Starting salaries range from £18,000 to £23,000 per year. Experienced advertising media planners can earn between £30,000 and £50,000. At the most senior level £70,000+ is possible. Some employers provide bonuses if you develop successful campaigns or gain new business. The highest salaries are in London.

Related opportunities

- Advertising Account Executive p406
- Market Researcher p416
- Marketing Manager/Assistant/Executive p417
- Researcher (Media) p428

Further information

Communication, Advertising and Marketing Education (CAM) Foundation
Moor Hall, Cookham, Maidenhead, Berkshire SL6 9QH
01628 427120; www.camfoundation.com

Account Planning Group
16 Creighton Avenue, London N10 1NU
020 8444 3692; www.apg.org.uk

Institute of Practitioners in Advertising
44 Belgrave Square, London SW1X 8QS
020 7235 7020; www.ipa.co.uk

AGENT/LITERARY AGENT

What the work involves

■ Agents represent and promote artists and creatives in the film, television, radio, theatre, music and publishing sectors. They can also play a similar role for sporting professionals.

■ You will be expected to work proactively to enhance your client's career by securing work and negotiating to ensure that the client attains the best work at the highest fee.

■ Literary agents are responsible for assessing the quality and commercial potential of manuscripts submitted by authors.

■ You will also have to develop publication and rights agreements with publishers and TV, radio and film producers on their behalf.

The type of person suited to this work

As you will be acting as the link between your client and the world they work in, you will need excellent communication skills. The ability to develop good contacts and a name for reliability is essential. It is also important to develop good working relationships with clients.

You should have a good head for business and an assertive approach will be helpful when it comes to agreeing contracts on behalf of clients.

You should have a good knowledge of the law and how it applies to your client's sector, as they will rely on you for professional advice in this area.

Working conditions

Agents are office-based and can be self-employed or work for agencies.

Although, theoretically, they could work anywhere, most agents are based near London. Literary agents can also be found in Edinburgh, which is an important centre for the UK publishing industry.

Travel is common and you should expect to work 30–40 hours a week, including evening and weekends, as some of your work will involve attending performances and social events to network and raise the profile of your clients.

Future prospects

This is a diverse and extremely competitive area. Agencies are constantly being set up but few stand the test of time. However publishers increasingly prefer to respond to new publication ideas through agents.

Your success will be determined partly by the standard of the clients you represent but, also, by the quality of the advice you can provide to them.

With sufficient experience you may have the opportunity to work abroad in entertainment and publishing hubs such as New York.

Qualifications and courses

Enthusiasm, good industry knowledge and the ability to make good contacts take precedence over qualifications.

It is possible to commence in an administrative position in an agency and work your way up to this position.

Agencies usually require experience and qualifications from a related area such as sales, business, music, performing arts or publishing. Many entrants have a degree in a related subject, including business, music or literature.

Contract law knowledge and a second language may be useful in the negotiation of rights deals.

Most literary agents have substantial work experience and/or qualifications in publishing.

A degree or postgraduate qualification in publishing can be an advantage for initial entry into the profession of literary agent.

Advantages/disadvantages

You will have the satisfaction of supporting new artists and helping them to succeed.

As you will earn your income from commissions, you will be under pressure to identify and promote new artists.

Unsociable hours and extensive travelling can affect your personal life.

Money guide

Salaries vary widely according to the nature of the agent, the number of artists they work with and the success they have in their field.

Literary agents are paid commission which is usually between 10% and 25% of authors' earnings. New entrants can expect to earn £15,000 in a large agency, progressing to £30,000 with experience. Top agents with prestigious clients can earn £100,000+.

Related opportunities

■ Marketing Manager/Assistant/Executive p417
■ Public Relations Executive p425
■ Publisher/Commissioning Editor p426

Further information

Association of Authors' Agents
14 Vernon Street, London W14 0RJ
www.agentsassoc.co.uk

The Agents' Association (Great Britain)
54 Keyes House, Dolphin Square, London SW1V 3NA
020 7834 0515; www.agents-uk.com

AUTHOR/SCRIPTWRITER

What the work involves

- Authors write the text for books, magazines, ICT resources and more. This can involve developing initial ideas to create a complete piece, or simply rewriting sections.

- Scriptwriters create text for TV, film, radio and theatre productions.

- As part of the work, you will undertake research using resources such as the internet and libraries.

- Authors often specialise in a particular subject area such as technical writing, science, medicine, cookery, travel or education. A small number of authors write and publish creative works of fiction, poetry or drama.

The type of person suited to this work

It is essential to have an excellent command of the English language and the ability to write with your audience in mind. Having a good imagination and a creative approach is important.

As you will be explaining project ideas to publishers and producers/directors, you will need strong communication skills. However you should also be able to cope with working alone for much of the time.

Many authors work on a self-employed basis, so business awareness and numeracy are very helpful.

You will also need to be able to handle rejections from publishers.

Working conditions

The majority of authors and scriptwriters are self-employed and work from home. Most of your time will be spent researching and writing, whilst sitting at a computer for long periods.

It may be necessary to juggle deadlines with other part-time employment taken on to supplement income. Most authors/scriptwriters are employed on a project-by-project basis, so the work provides very little job security.

Most of your work will be undertaken alone, which can be isolating.

Future prospects

Making a living as a professional can be challenging, and it takes time to develop your writing expertise and specialist areas.

Having an established network of contacts helps.

A variety of support groups, writers' groups and courses exist to help people develop their writing skills. There are opportunities to write and share your work in amateur dramatic groups and writers' circles, some of which publish work on the internet.

At present, short dramas for radio broadcast are actively sought.

Qualifications and courses

Authors/scriptwriters are not required to have any specific qualifications, although many are graduates. It may be useful to have a degree in English, journalism, media studies or performing arts.

There are a variety of English and creative writing courses available. These range from degree and postgraduate courses to evening classes designed to improve a writer's technique. Above all it is essential to have a good command of the English language, also imagination and originality.

This is a fiercely competitive profession and few authors progress to attain mass-market appeal and a high level of commercial success. For this reason it is often necessary to obtain a second job in order to supplement income.

It is important to be proactive and establish a good network of contacts to aid self-promotion.

Arts Council grants may be available to new authors for work in literature and drama. It is necessary to request such a grant in the form of a written proposal.

Advantages/disadvantages

This type of work can provide the satisfaction of being creative and seeing your work in print and in the public domain.

Not all authors succeed in publishing their work and you may need to take on other types of work to make a living.

Money guide

Earnings vary widely depending on the nature of the writing project, your experience, and your popularity as a writer. Publishers may give a one-off payment for a piece of work or will pay you royalties (a percentage of the sales income of the book). Salaries can be £15,000–£30,000 for authors employed in a commercial environment. You may have a higher income if you are well known and your work is popular.

Related opportunities

- Copywriter p414
- Journalist p415
- Publisher/Commissioning Editor p426
- Technical Author p429

Further information

BBC Writersroom
Grafton House, 379–381 Euston Road, London NW1 3AU
www.bbc.co.uk/writersroom

Society of Authors
84 Drayton Gardens, London SW10 9SB
020 7373 6642; www.societyofauthors.org

Marketing, Advertising, Media, Print and Publishing

CRCI: PB/D
CLCI: FAC

CAMERA PERSON (TV/FILM CAMERA OPERATOR)

What the work involves

- Camera operators use digital, electronic and film cameras to capture images for use in films, television programmes or other broadcasts.

- You will work closely with a director or director of photography and will be helped by a 'grip' (a camera assistant) and other crew members such as pullers, clappers, sound engineers and lighting technicians.

- You will understand the technical and creative aspects of filming, including how to work with a script or list of shots, planning shots and shooting images.

- You will have an in-depth knowledge of the equipment you work with, how best to use it, maintain and repair it.

The type of person suited to this work

You must be interested in photography and camera technology. You should also be interested in video, film and TV production.

You will be required to have a certain amount of physical fitness as your work may involve carrying heavy equipment for long periods of time.

As you will be working in a creative environment you will need to have a good imagination and at times an abstract approach to problem solving.

Working conditions

Your working hours will vary greatly. You may be required to work early mornings, late nights and on the weekend. Shooting may be long and run over planned schedules.

You may be based in a studio or work on location, both of which may include travel abroad.

You work may be affected by weather, for example some shoots may be cut short, or extended, if they depend on natural light.

You may have to work with cameras on cranes, scaffolding, in moving vehicles or in venues such as concert halls, theatres and sports grounds.

Future prospects

Skillset and regional screen agencies run schemes for those who have some experience and wish to work on a freelance basis within the industry.

Camera operators usually learn most of their skills on the job. However, constantly changing technology means that continuing professional development (CPD) is also essential. Regular training in health and safety is also essential.

Advantages/disadvantages

You may work on a variety of exciting projects, including big-budget films or breaking-news programmes.

Qualifications and courses

To be a TV/film camera operator you do not need any specific academic qualifications. GCSEs (A*-C) in English, maths, science or other relevant subjects may be useful.

You will start as a trainee, runner or camera operator's assistant. You will learn mainly on the job and you might also undertake a short training course.

In practice you will find that technical knowledge, practical skills, experience and contacts are as important as qualifications. However the majority of camera operators have higher-level qualifications. Such courses include HNDs, HNCs, foundation degrees and degrees in film and TV production and photography.

Large companies, such as the BBC, offer work experience placements that will provide you with the opportunity to work with camera equipment or in a set-up studio for example. Camera equipment hire companies or television production companies may also take on work experience candidates.

Film and Television Freelance Training (FT2) offers a technical training scheme which you can use to train as a camera assistant.

City & Guilds offer a Diploma in media techniques or Certificate for audiovisual industries induction. The BTEC National Diploma/Certificate in media production may help you improve your skills.

Working on location may be dangerous at times, especially if it involves shooting footage for news broadcasts.

Money guide

A starting salary for a trained camera operator is around £13,800. With experience this can increase to £22,000 and £32,000.

As a camera person you are likely to work on a freelance basis or on fixed term contracts and your rate of pay will vary according to each production you work on.

Related opportunities

- Lighting technician p444
- TV, Film and Radio Director p431

Further information

BBC Training and Development
35 Marylebone High Street, London W1U 4PX
0370 010 0264; training@bbc.co.uk; www.bbctraining.com

FT2 – Film and Television Freelance Training
3rd Floor, 18–20 Southwark Street, London SE1 1TJ
020 7407 0344; www.ft2.org.uk

COPY EDITOR/ SUB-EDITOR/ PROOFREADER

What the work involves

- Copy editors prepare manuscripts for publication by checking for grammatical errors, spelling mistakes and inconsistencies in style.

- You will also be responsible for checking the legality of the text.

- Sub-editors are copy editors who work in newspapers and magazines. They may also create headlines and introductory paragraphs and manipulate text to fit a word count.

- Proofreaders carry out the final quality checks on texts before they go to the production team for publication. They utilise a recognised set of symbols and normally mark changes on a hard copy, but sometimes make alterations on screen using specialist software.

The type of person suited to this work

As you will be responsible for preparing texts for publication, you will pay great attention to detail and take pride in your work. An excellent knowledge of the English language and strong writing skills are expected.

Patience and a methodical approach to your work are also helpful.

If you are working in-house for a publishing or other company, you will need good team-working skills. In addition you will need to be able to deal tactfully with people, for example when explaining changes to authors' manuscripts.

The ability to manage budgets is useful, as is the ability to work to tight deadlines and cope with pressure.

Working conditions

Most copy editors work within offices or are self-employed and work from home. Many publishing companies are based around London and Edinburgh. You will spend your time attending meetings with authors, designers, printers, illustrators and colleagues, which may involve some travelling and overnight stays.

At the busiest times you may have to work late to meet copy or production deadlines, but mostly you will work normal working hours.

Future prospects

This is a very competitive area and many copy editors start off in an administrative or related role and work their way up. Sub-editors may commence as general reporters.

It may be necessary for in-house copy editors to change their job frequently to aid career progression. With experience you could become a project manager or commission or manage publications.

Increasingly, copy editors work on a freelance basis for a number of employers.

Qualifications and courses

Candidates may be taken on as editorial assistants or trainees to gain experience. Building a portfolio of work and experience is important.

Although there are no set formal entry qualifications for this career, most copy editors are graduates. Relevant degree subjects include English and humanities, and degrees in publishing are also available.

To work in specialist areas of publishing, a degree in a relevant discipline is an advantage; for example a science degree may be preferred by scientific publishers. It is also possible to study for a postgraduate qualification in publishing (PgDip or MA).

The Society for Editors and Proofreaders (SfEP) and the Publishing Training Centre offer introductory and advanced training courses on topics such as copy editing and grammar skills. The National Council for the Training of Journalists (NCTJ) also offers an introductory sub-editing qualification.

Advantages/disadvantages

The work provides the satisfaction of shaping and improving the style and tone of manuscripts.

You will meet and work with many different types of people.

As you will be making sure a publication goes into production on time, this can be a high-pressured job.

Money guide

Earnings vary according to employer and geographic location. Starting salaries are between £16,000 and £22,000 per year. Salaries for experienced editors employed in-house vary between £23,000 and £30,000. The most senior can earn up to £60,000.

Freelance rates vary between £20 and £35 an hour, with higher rates for more complex project management editorial work.

Related opportunities

- Copywriter p414
- Publisher/Commissioning Editor p426
- Journalist p415

Further information

Society for Editors and Proofreaders
Erico House, 93–99 Upper Richmond Road, Putney, London SW15 2TG
020 8785 5617; www.sfep.org.uk

National Union of Journalists (NUJ)
Headland House, 308–312 Gray's Inn Road, London WC1X 8DP
020 7278 7916; www.nuj.org.uk

Marketing, Advertising, Media, Print and Publishing

CRCI: PD
CLCI: FAD

COPYWRITER

What the work involves

- Copywriters create informative, well-constructed text (or 'copy') on a wide range of subjects, from a range of perspectives and for a variety of audiences.

- Advertising copywriters produce text for TV, film, radio, press and internet advertisements.

- You will create copy for websites, company magazines/publications, direct mail, brochures and product information guides.

- Design companies, sales promotion organisations and other companies employ copywriters to write text that promotes their services or products and helps to increase sales.

The type of person suited to this work

As you will be writing copy for a range of uses, you will require excellent writing skills, a strong creative flair and a good imagination. The ability to describe a subject concisely can also be important.

In discussing innovative ideas with your colleagues and clients, you will make valuable use of your strengths in verbal and written communication skills.

You will have to be flexible and willing to alter what you think are good ideas to meet clients' requirements.

It is essential to have good organisational skills, to be able to work well under pressure and to meet tight deadlines.

Working conditions

Many copywriters work on a freelance basis for a number of employers. In-house copywriters will work 9am-5pm from Monday to Friday, within an office or studio environment.

You will spend long periods of time sitting typing, which can be tiring. You will also be expected to attend client meetings, which may involve overnight travel. You will have to work long hours to meet project deadlines, which can be stressful.

Advertising copywriters normally work with an art director, who creates the visual aspect of the campaign.

Future prospects

There are interesting opportunities available, particularly in the website domain, as an increasing number of organisations require innovative copy for service and product promotion.

Competition is fierce but with good contacts, a strong writing style and knowledge of your market, it is possible to make a living in this area.

With experience, some copywriters become freelancers or set up agencies in partnership with other 'creatives'. Other copywriters go on to work in related areas such as public relations and publishing.

Advantages/disadvantages

This job provides the satisfaction of seeing your work in print and in the public domain.

Qualifications and courses

There are no formal entry requirements to be a copywriter, but most entrants have a degree or HND. Relevant subjects include advertising or design, or disciplines such as English, journalism, communications or media. A postgraduate qualification in copywriting or creative advertising, such as the West Hertfordshire College PG Diploma in copywriting, can be useful for graduates without a relevant background.

Students generally require at least 2 A-levels/3 H grades and 5 GCSEs/S Grades (A–C/1–3) to get a place on a degree course. Foundation courses are also available.

You will require determination to enter the profession and you will probably need to complete several unpaid work experience placements as a copywriter before being taken on. The most common entry route involves producing a high-quality portfolio ('book') and showing this to agencies.

Entry-level jobs are seldom advertised and there are currently no graduate training schemes into the creative side of advertising.

You will be working alongside imaginative colleagues, which can be stimulating.

Copywriting can be stressful because of the need to produce new ideas to tight deadlines.

There may be some job instability if working on a self-employed basis.

Money guide

Earnings vary according to employer and project. Self-employed copywriters may charge hourly rates, by the day, or for individual projects. Starting salaries outside London are around £14,000 per year. London-based, you could start on £18,000. With 3–5 years' experience, and when employed by individual companies, you could earn between £32,000 and £40,000. Senior level salaries can range between £45,000 and £200,000+.

Related opportunities

- Author/Scriptwriter p411
- Journalist p415
- Technical Author p429

Further information

Institute of Copywriting
Overbrook Business Centre, Poolbridge Road, Blackford, Wedmore, Somerset BS28 4PA
0800 781 1715; www.inst.org/copy

Institute of Practitioners in Advertising
44 Belgrave Square, London SW1X 8QS
020 7235 7020; www.ipa.co.uk

JOURNALIST

What the work involves

- Journalists research and write stories on subjects such as current affairs, business, health and culture. Broadcast journalists also digitally present these features on radio, television or the internet.

- These stories can immediately become live news articles or features for local and national newspapers, magazines, TV, radio and online broadcasts.

- You will be planning, writing and editing articles in keeping with a house style, usually to very short deadlines.

The type of person suited to this work

As you will be producing articles on a regular basis you will need to thrive on working under pressure.

Strong ICT, written and verbal communication skills are essential for this job and broadcast journalists should have a clear and professional voice.

You should be a highly organised multi-tasker with a good instinct for a potential story and the ability to undertake research through interviews and contacts. You will be expected to research difficult stories and meet hostile people which can be stressful.

Working conditions

Your work will be dictated by the story you are following. You could visit a range of locations in the working day, often at short notice as news stories unfold.

Overnight travel is often part of this job when chasing a story or undertaking research. You will have to work long, sometimes irregular hours in order to meet publication deadlines. Whilst you may be part of a wider team, you could work alone for much of the time, or in the company of a photographer.

Future prospects

This is a highly competitive area to enter and approximately a third of all journalists work freelance. Many full-time journalists started work as freelancers to establish their reputations.

Most jobs are within London and the south-east of England, although opportunities do arise in regional or local newspapers and other local/national media (radio and television).

It is possible to cross over from newspaper/magazine journalism into broadcast journalism as a reporter or presenter. There may be opportunities to work abroad.

Advantages/disadvantages

You will create features that could be read, heard or seen by thousands of people – often beyond the UK.

This profession offers exciting, varied work.

Due to short deadlines, you will have to regularly produce work under pressure.

Qualifications and courses

The most common route is with pre-entry qualifications. The National Council for the Training of Journalists (NCTJ) accredits HND, foundation degree and degree courses. You could also do a degree in another subject, followed by a 1-year postgraduate course accredited by the NCTJ.

A fast-track postgraduate course lasting 18–20 weeks is available at some colleges. New entrants who have completed a pre-entry course will then complete an 18-month training period with their employer.

Direct entry candidates need a minimum of 5 GCSEs/S grades (A–C/1–3) including English.

Candidates entering into journalism without a relevant qualification will often be required to study for professional qualifications. Newspapers often ask trainees to study toward the National Certificate of the National Council for the Training of Journalists. Magazines tend to have their own training courses accredited by the Periodicals Training Council. NVQs/SVQs are also available.

Broadcast journalism is fiercely competitive and entrants should have a strong showreel and work experience in student or community media.

You might have to get information or photographs to support sad and distressing stories, which could make you unpopular.

Money guide

Salaries start at £10,000–£15,000 per year at trainee level on a local newspaper. Broadcast journalists can expect to earn £15,000 to begin with and around £17,000 is usual if starting at a magazine. Experienced journalists can earn £22,000–£45,000. The most successful and well-known journalists can earn in excess of £100,000.

Related opportunities

- Author/Scriptwriter p411
- Copywriter p414
- Magazine/Newspaper Editor p420
- Researcher (Media) p428

Further information

National Council for the Training of Journalists
The New Granary, Station Road, Newport, Saffron Walden, Essex CB11 3PL
01799 544014; www.nctj.com

Broadcast Journalism Training Council
18 Millers Close, Rippingale, Lincolnshire PE10 0TH
01778 440025; www.bjtc.org.uk

National Union of Journalists
308–312 Gray's Inn Road, London WC1X 8DP
020 7278 7916; www.nuj.org.uk

Marketing, Advertising, Media, Print and Publishing

CRCI: PB
CLCI: FAC

MARKET RESEARCHER

What the work involves

- You will undertake research to obtain people's opinions on specific products, services or issues and then analyse the results.

- Developing surveys to analyse public opinion on a wide range of subjects or issues will be part of your job.

- You may also interview small groups of people, known as focus groups or panels, to assess in more detail their views on a specific topic.

- You will compile the results of your research in the form of detailed reports or summary analyses to be used by your clients, businesses and other organisations.

The type of person suited to this work

This job is all about people and their opinions, so verbal communication skills are essential. You will also need strong writing skills to create surveys, plan interviews and write reports.

You will need to understand exactly what your client wants to know and think up ways to get this information. A logical and deductive approach to your work is important.

Also, as you will be working with facts and figures and a lot of paperwork you will need to be well organised. Confidence in working with numbers will be useful in helping you to perform statistical analyses. Being aware of the marketplace and what sells is also important.

Working conditions

Market researchers work from offices and attend meetings, presentations and interviews. You could work in a specialist market research agency or department within a larger organisation. Some market researchers work freelance.

The job can involve frequent daily and overnight travel.

This can be a pressured role as you will be required to produce detailed information at short notice. It can be difficult working with the public if they do not want to help you.

Future prospects

The market research industry is worth over £1 billion a year. As well as businesses, many other organisations increasingly depend on market researchers to provide up-to-the-minute facts and figures concerning public opinion on everything from train services to trainers!

After gaining experience as a market research interviewer you can move up to research executive, and then progress to senior research executive. With sufficient experience you could enter a senior management role or set up your own agency.

Advantages/disadvantages

You will work on a variety of projects and meet many different types of people, which can be very interesting. You will have to work antisocial hours (at weekends or evenings) on a regular

Qualifications and courses

There are no set qualifications for this role. Employers tend to look for an outgoing personality and enthusiasm for the job, rather than academic qualifications. However, most new entrants are graduates.

Training will usually be in-house. This generally comprises a 2- or 3-day intensive course, which may award a certificate.

NVQs/SVQs are available in Customer Service at Levels 2 and 3 and Marketing Research (Interviewing) at Level 1. These may be useful and some companies may support further study.

The Market Research Society (MRS) awards an Introductory Certificate in Market and Social Research. This can be upgraded to an Advanced Certificate. The MRS also offers a Market Research Society Diploma and, if this is successfully completed, the candidate will be eligible for full membership of the Market Research Society.

MA courses are available in social and market research or in marketing management specialising in market research. Candidates would need to hold a first degree.

basis. The public may not want to speak to you and getting the information needed may be difficult.

Money guide

Starting salaries for interviewers range from £17,000 to £22,000 per year. With 3–5 years' experience this can rise to £26,000-£35,000. Agencies pay £10–£15 per hour. A very experienced market researcher could earn between £40,000 and £80,000.

Related opportunities

- Advertising Media Planner p409
- Marketing Manager/Assistant/Executive p417
- Researcher (Media) p428
- Statistician p534

Further information

Market Research Society
15 Northburgh Street, London EC1V 0JR
020 7490 4911; www.mrs.org.uk

ESOMAR
(World Association for Opinion and Marketing Research Professionals)
Eurocenter 2, 11th floor, Barbara Strozzilaan 384, 1083 HN Amsterdam, The Netherlands
+31 20 664 2141; www.esomar.org

International Marketing Research Information (IMRI)
IMRI Ltd, PO Box 7742, Loughborough LE12 8WG
01509 891 216; www.imriresearch.com

MARKETING MANAGER/ ASSISTANT/EXECUTIVE

What the work involves

Marketing assistant/executive

- Marketing assistants/executives co-ordinate activities and events to promote or raise awareness of a particular product or service through advertising, branding, direct marketing, poster and leaflet campaigns, public relations, website promotions, developing newsletters and setting up special events.

- Your work will involve liaising with designers, media contacts and venue managers.

- You may also be responsible for planning events and overseeing budgets.

Marketing manager

- You will create marketing campaigns to promote and increase sales of specific products or services as well as managing the image, known as the branding, of specific products.

- You will also be responsible for post-campaign evaluations and assessing past marketing strategies. Information generated from these activities will help you to develop angles for future campaigns.

- You will also be responsible for business development and finding ways to put new leads into action

- You will be expected to manage marketing assistants/ executives and additional members of staff.

The type of person suited to this work

As marketing is all about getting a message across to people, you will need to be well-presented with a professional appearance as well as strong written and verbal communication skills.

Having an understanding of consumer behaviour and a strong sense of what sells, and why, will help you to be successful in this profession.

Good multi-tasking, organisational and financial skills are also important to ensure that projects are delivered on time and within budget.

High levels of ICT skills are invaluable for these roles, as you will be using specialist software that will interface with the programs used by designers and printers

You should be an assertive, confident and sociable person who enjoys meeting and working with different people.

There will be a heavy focus on promoting yourself and your clients and so you should feel comfortable attending public meetings and different social events such as those at the Chamber of Commerce.

Working conditions

Marketing assistant/executive

Most of your time will be spent in an office, working about 37 hours a week from 9am-6pm from Monday to Friday.

You may have to travel to meet clients, make presentations, attend trade exhibitions and launches. There is a possibility that you will have to stay at events overnight, which could be difficult if you have family commitments.

Some executives undertake part or all of their work from home, however this largely depends on the size of their employer and the sector that they operate in.

Marketing manager

As your work will involve overseeing marketing campaigns you will travel extensively to meet clients and communicate with other professionals (designers, printers, the press, venue/conference managers).

The remainder of your time will be spent in the office, where you will work 37 hours a week, Monday to Friday.

You will spend most of your time working at a computer and communicating with clients on the telephone.

This can be very stressful work, especially during the lead up to a new campaign launch, when you will usually be required to work extra hours, possibly even weekends. In some areas of marketing international travel may be required.

Future prospects

Marketing assistant/executive

Many organisations and companies that are aiming to sell products or services employ marketing executives to promote them. You will have the opportunity to work in a variety of sectors, such as finance, manufacturing or not-for-profit, or you could work in a specialist marketing agency for a variety of clients. Positions are available nationwide but there are more opportunities in major cities.

Most graduates enter marketing as assistants or executives and then progress to either marketing management or into related work offering more challenges, such as export marketing. This role includes international travel and the opportunity to widen your career experience. Others opt for self-employment.

Marketing manager

As a marketing manager your main progression routes will be: to move to other organisations that will offer increased career challenges and higher-profile contracts; to become self-employed or to aim for promotion to a marketing director post. It is possible to work for companies that are based overseas, or have offices abroad, if you want international experience.

Marketing, Advertising, Media, Print and Publishing

CRCI: O
CLCI: OB

Advantages/disadvantages

If you are successful, you will have the satisfaction of increasing people's use of services and levels of product sales, as well as raising company profits.

You may have the opportunity to work on high-profile campaigns, which will be visible in the public domain.

This type of work can be very fast-paced and stressful, particularly around the time of a new campaign launch. You may be required to travel to attend meetings, trade exhibitions and launches, which could be detrimental to your personal life.

Money guide

Salaries will depend on where you work, and the size and type of your organisation. Generally salaries tend to be higher in the financial and professional services arena as opposed to those in the not-for-profit or agency sector. In terms of location, salaries are higher in the south-east of England and major cities such as London and Manchester. It is possible to increase your earnings by commission or bonuses.

Marketing assistant/executive

Starting salaries for new graduates as a marketing assistant/executive range from £18,000–£25,000 per year.

This rises to £30,000–£40,000 with experience and additional management responsibilities.

Marketing managers with extensive experience can expect to earn £75,00 at director level and this may rise to as much as £105,000 dependent on sector.

Related opportunities

- Advertising Account Executive p406
- Copywriter p414
- Importer/Exporter p605
- Public Relations Executive p425

Further information

Chartered Institute of Marketing
Moor Hall, Cookham, Maidenhead, Berkshire SL6 9QH
01628 427120; www.cim.co.uk

Communication, Advertising and Marketing Education (CAM) Foundation
Moor Hall, Cookham, Maidenhead, Berkshire SL6 9QH
01628 427120; www.camfoundation.com

The Institute of Direct Marketing (IDM)
1 Park Road, Teddington, Middlesex TW11 0AR
020 8977 5705; www.theidm.com

The Institute of Sales and Marketing Management (ISMM)
Harrier Court, Lower Woodside, Luton, Bedfordshire LU1 4DQ
01582 840 001; www.ismm.co.uk

Qualifications and courses
Marketing assistant/executive

Employers tend to look for candidates with HNDs and degrees, although it is possible to enter the profession through relevant work experience and on the strength of your personal qualities.

A BTEC National Certificate/Diploma, in business (marketing) is available.

HNDs and foundation degrees are available in business and marketing. There are numerous degree courses in marketing, and in marketing combined with another subject such as economics, accounting or a foreign language. Other useful degree subjects include business, maths and computing.

The Chartered Institute of Marketing (CIM) offers qualifications to enable school-leavers and graduates of different disciplines to enter the profession. There are no formal entry requirements for the Introductory Certificate; 2 A-levels are required for the Professional Certificate; a degree or equivalent is required for the Professional Diploma.

The Communication, Advertising and Marketing Foundation also offer a qualification, the Advanced Diploma in communication studies. It is aimed at candidates with a degree, but if you have more than 2 years' experience in the industry, you will be considered.

Marketing manager

Entry may be via a degree or work experience and professional qualifications.

Graduates can go straight into marketing on a graduate trainee scheme. The Chartered Institute of Marketing offers qualifications at four levels.

The Introductory Certificate in Marketing requires no previous experience. Applicants need to be over 17 years old. The Professional Certificate in Marketing requires 2 A-levels or equivalent and candidates must be aged over 18. The Professional Diploma in Marketing requires a CIM Certificate, a degree or 3 years' work experience (one of which should be at managerial level).

For the postgraduate Diploma, the Advanced Certificate, a marketing degree or 6 years' marketing management experience is required.

Many employers prefer candidates to have a degree and those which include work placements will be looked upon favourably.

Graduates can take a 1 year postgraduate course in marketing or management studies.

The Communications, Advertising and Marketing Foundation (CAM) offers an Advanced Diploma in communication studies aimed at graduates.

NVQs/SVQs in marketing communications at Level 2 and marketing products and services at Levels 3 and 4 are available for people working in marketing.

MODEL

What the work involves

- Depending on the contracts agreed by your model agency, you could be involved in different types of modelling, such as fashion, photographic or demonstration work.

- You could work in a studio, on location outdoors, at fashion shows or at events such as car shows or conventions.

- It is necessary to build a good portfolio of your work and establish a good reputation within the industry

- Your job will be to show off new clothing or products to their best advantage in order to help potential customers visualise them being worn or in use.

The type of person suited to this work

This is a very competitive area to find work. You will have to be determined and prepared to deal with disappointment if contracts do not come your way.

Most fashion model agencies have set physical requirements that you will have to meet before you are accepted onto their books.

There is also scope for models with one particularly good feature, such as hands, feet, eyes or hair, to model specific items.

During your work you will meet a mix of people from many backgrounds, so you will have to be confident and have good communication skills.

Working conditions

The places you will work will depend on the type of modelling that you do and the nature of the contracts you are offered. You might work indoors within a studio, which can be hot and can involve many hours to get the correct shot, or you could be on location doing catalogue work. You might also work at large events, or helping to launch a new product.

You will be on your feet for long periods at a time and will always have to look your best, even if you have been travelling from one country to another.

Future prospects

Only the most successful models are always in work. Most are self-employed and have to take up temporary or part-time work when necessary.

To build your reputation, you will have to create a portfolio of work using photos from previous contracts. As you win new contracts, the quality of your portfolio should improve and more agencies will take you on.

Whilst top models are very famous and can be rich, there are hundreds more who struggle to find work and pay their bills. Most models have to finish their career in their early 30s.

Advantages/disadvantages

Only a few models get the top contracts.

Qualifications and courses

There are no formal entry qualifications, but an excellent appearance and personality are beneficial.

A portfolio of photographs is normally required for modelling agencies.

Female models should be at least five feet eight inches (1.72m) tall and around 34–24–34 inches (86–61–86cm). Male models should be at least six feet (1.83m) tall. However, some photographic models are required to be smaller or larger than the usual sizes, depending on employer requirements.

There are modelling courses which focus on diet, health and figure correction, deportment, fashion coordination, grooming, catwalk turns and movements, photographic modelling techniques and how to work with agents. There are also fashion-related courses which include business aspects.

Any young person under 16 years of age and carrying out modelling work is required to be licensed by the local Education and Welfare Authority.

You could get to see other parts of the world.

You will be standing for long periods while always having to look your best.

It can be also boring and hard work.

Money guide

You will probably be self-employed so your earnings will depend on your success in finding regular, well-paid work. Most agencies keep 20% of earnings as commission.

You can expect to start on around £10,000–£17,000 per year, rising to 40,000 - £60,000+ a year for the most successful.

Related opportunities

- Beauty Consultant p458
- Beauty Therapist p459
- Fashion Designer p181
- Wardrobe Assistant p455

Further information

Alba Model Information
PO Box 588, Southport PR8 9BR
0871 717 7170; www.albamodel.info

Association of Model Agents (AMA)
122 Brompton Road, London SW3 1JD
020 7584 6466

London College of Fashion
20 John Prince's Steet, London W1G 0BJ
0207 514 7400; www.fashion.arts.ac.uk

Marketing, Advertising, Media, Print and Publishing

CRCI: O
CLCI: OT

NEWSPAPER/MAGAZINE EDITOR

What the work involves

- Newspaper/magazine editors are responsible for the coordination of each aspect of a publication.

- You will understand the readership of the publication and include informative, newsworthy articles, entertaining features and high quality images.

- You will work with the editorial, design and advertising departments, as well as journalists, printers and publishers.

- Tasks include editing and proofreading articles and features, assigning journalists to cover stories, commissioning freelance writers for features, meeting with photographers, and conducting interviews.

The type of person suited to this work

You should be able to demonstrate excellent writing skills and a creative flair.

You must have a strong interest in current affairs.

You will have a practical approach to problem solving and remain calm in a crisis situation. You need to show initiative, persistence and decisiveness.

You must pay attention to detail, be meticulous in your organisation and time management and be able to work to a deadline. You must also have excellent communication skills to be able to delegate tasks and persuade others to meet deadlines.

Working conditions

You will probably work around 40 hours a week, which may include early morning starts, working into the night and even working at the weekend to cover a breaking story. Some large newspapers may offer shift work.

You will be almost entirely office-based which may be noisy and busy at times but you may at times be required to meet with other editors, journalists or photographers outside of the office.

Future prospects

Journalism is a very competitive industry to break into. Work experience, published articles and evidence of commitment to journalism are as important as qualifications.

The typical route to becoming a newspaper/magazine editor is to begin in a junior role as a journalist and work your way up through the editorial department until you are in charge of the content of the magazine or newspaper.

You may also move across and work in PR, press offices or on a freelance basis.

Advantages/disadvantages

Your work will be diverse and stimulating as it will involve ever-changing content and working with various people involved with the production of the publication.

Qualifications and courses

Most entrants to this profession are graduates. It is not essential that you take a degree in journalism; in fact a degree in any subject is usually accepted. Some relevant degrees include English, history and politics. However specialist publications may require you to have taken a specific degree.

Postgraduate qualifications in journalism can help you to gain entry to this profession. The National Council for the Training of Journalists (NCTJ) provides many accredited postgraduate courses in newspaper journalism.

Experience is essential if you want to be a newspaper/magazine editor. Building up a strong portfolio by writing for student publications or local newspapers will help you gain a journalism position. From there you can build up experience and contacts and may progress to an editorial role.

You will be mainly trained on the job as you work alongside other journalists and those in senior positions. Some national papers provide a formal graduate trainee scheme. In an entry-level role you can work towards NVQs in Newspaper Journalism and from there gain the National Certificate Examination that is accredited by the NCTJ.

You may work in a highly stressful environment, working long, tiring and unsociable hours.

Money guide

Your starting salary as a newspaper editor can be around £14,000 per year if you work for a small local paper. Large regional or national papers will start around £18,000.

This can increase to around £22,000 to £40,000 per year with experience.

Senior editors with ten years' experience or more can earn around £50,000 or more per year depending on the publication.

Related opportunities

- Copy editor/Sub-editor/Proofreader p413
- Journalist p415
- Publisher/Commissioning Editor p426

Further information

National Council for the Training of Journalists (NCTJ)
The New Granary, Station Road, Newport, Saffron Walden, Essex CB11 3PI
01799 544014; info@nctj.com; www.nctj.com

Newspaper Society
8th Floor, St Andrew's House, 18–20 St Andrew Street, London EC4A 3AY
020 7632 7400; ns@newspapersoc.org.uk; www.newspapersoc.org.uk

PHOTOGRAPHER/ PHOTOGRAPHIC STYLIST

What the work involves

- Photographers create photographic images using technical lighting and equipment. Using your eye for design and knowledge of photographic techniques you will create images for a specific brief.

- Photographic stylists help the photographer to design the look of the photograph.

- Many photographers work with digital enhancing techniques to modify and improve, or add interest and illusions to the images they produce.

The type of person suited to this work

You will need a strong visual sense and an eye for what makes a good picture. You will need the technical knowledge and skills to get the most from lighting, studio set-ups and, of course, camera equipment. The use of editing software means that ICT skills are increasingly important.

Strong communication skills and a flexible attitude come in useful when discussing projects with clients, or putting nervous subjects at ease.

To work on a freelance basis, business skills and self-confidence are essential.

Working conditions

You will either be studio- or location-based. In a studio you could work with still-life and portraiture. Lighting equipment can be heavy and the work can be physically tiring as you will be on your feet for long periods.

If you work outdoors you could record images for advertising and photo-journalism. This may require patience if the weather or light conditions are not correct for your shot.

Commercial photography is completed to tight deadlines, which can be stressful.

Future prospects

In order to gain the essential skills and an understanding of your specialist type of photography, you could work as a photographer's assistant. Nowadays, positions are even more limited as digital photography has reduced the work of professionals.

With experience you could progress into freelance work or specialise in a particular area such as press, medical or food photography.

Advantages/disadvantages

You will have the satisfaction of using your creativity and technical skills to create original images, which may end up in the public eye.

It takes time in this competitive industry to develop contacts, so if you work on a freelance basis you may need a second job to support yourself.

Qualifications and courses

ENTRY LEVEL 3

There is no set route from training to employment in this sector. Applicants will need a strong portfolio of work comprising between 10 and 15 shots.

Candidates wishing to pursue careers as police, medical or press photographers will need 5 GCSEs/S grades (A–C/1–3) including English and maths. One A-level/ Advanced Higher and relevant work experience may be required. It is necessary for medical photographers to have a degree or postgraduate certificate in clinical photography.

A variety of college courses are available. City & Guilds offer awards in photography at Level 1, 2 and 3. They also offer photo imaging Level 4. NVQ/SVQ photography is available at Levels 2–4 and photo imaging and photo processing at Levels 2–4. BTEC National Certificates and Diplomas are available in art and design (photography). HNC/HND, foundation degree and degree courses are available in photography. There are GCSE and AS/A2 qualifications in art and design (photography).

The British Institute of Photography's professional qualifying exam requires an HND or a degree.

Apprenticeships/Skillseekers opportunities may be available for those aged 16–24.

Money guide

As a trainee assistant photographer you can expect to earn about £12,000 per year. This rises to £16,000–£20,000 with experience. £60,000+ is possible at senior levels.

Earnings will vary if you are self-employed or freelance. You are likely to earn between £150 and £600 per day. You may have periods of inactivity and many people have a second job in an area such as teaching to supplement their income.

Related opportunities

- Camera Person p412
- Graphic Designer p186
- Illustrator p188

Further information

Association of Photographers
81 Leonard Street, London EC2A 4QS
020 7739 6669; www.the-aop.org

City& Guilds

www.cityandguilds.com/myperfectjob

PRINTER

What the work involves

Machine printer

- Machine printers oversee the production of printed items on machines of various sizes for products such as newspapers, posters, book etc. You will set up the printing press correctly for the specific job. This includes ensuring that the appropriate plates, paper and inks have been selected.

- You will trial the print run, check for errors and ensure that the quality is up to standard.

Screen printer

- Screen printers create visual images by organising and operating hand- or power-driven screen printing machines which print graphics onto fabrics and paper by forcing ink through a delicate mesh overlay of the stencil design.

- You will be required to prepare the stencils, inks and print processes.

Bookbinder

- Bookbinders are responsible for transforming the printed material into the finished product. Nowadays the majority of bookbinding is a machine orientated process, which involves stitching, stapling, collating, cutting, binding and coating.

Print production planner

- Print production planners are responsible for workflow in the printing firm and ensuring that the efficiency is maximised by checking orders, creating schedules, allocating work, supervising and quality control. This is similar to the traffic controller role in an advertising agency.

The type of person suited to this work

Printing requires good teamwork and communication skills.

It is usual that your work will involve computers and other types of machinery and equipment so you will need good practical skills and an understanding of ICT.

It is important to have normal colour vision, good hand-to-eye co-ordination and a high level of physical fitness.

You should have a meticulous eye for detail, and you will need to demonstrate art and design skills to convince customers that you can make aesthetically pleasing finished products, from CD covers to pages of pure text or full-colour brochures.

As print runs do not always go smoothly you will need to be adept at problem-solving, have a long concentration span and the ability to work under pressure. Furthermore you should be flexible as some print companies run 24 hour operations and you may have to work shifts at night and at the weekends.

Print production managers should also have good multi-tasking skills, a good head for numbers and the ability to influence people.

Working conditions

In smaller print companies you will normally work office hours, that is 9am to 5pm, but during busy periods you could do additional hours in order to ensure that projects are completed on time. Larger companies tend to run 24 hour operations and you will be expected to work shifts and weekends. Overtime is largely available. Bookbinders may also have the opportunity to work part-time.

Your working environment will depend on your role and the size of the firm. Printshops can be dirty and noisy when machines are functioning. Hazardous chemicals are used in finishes and to wash inks from the press but usually there is good ventilation to cope with the resulting fumes.

You will be required to adhere to health and safety regulations at all times and use protective gear such as, overalls, boots, gloves and ear protectors.

It is necessary to have a good level of physical fitness as you will be standing for long periods of time. Upper body strength is also important as you may be required to carry out some heavy lifting.

Print production planners will work in an office but will also carry out work on the production floor and may have to travel to attend meetings with clients.

Future prospects

The printing, packaging and design industry is the UK's sixth largest manufacturing sector. 316,000 people are employed in over 15,000 companies mostly around London, south-east England, Bristol, Leeds and Glasgow.

At present in the UK there are about 12,000 print companies, which employ about 160,000 people. There are about 30,000 machine printers and bookbinders and 15,000 print production planners.

The majority of the industry comprises small, family-owned enterprises. The industry is sensitive to wider economic issues, such as cheaper rates from foreign print companies, increasing use of electronic resources and seasonal order variations

Opportunities will depend on your skills and the size and type of your company. Although printers cover all the stages of production, the job of folding machine operator (at the finishing end of the process) is becoming a skills shortage area.

With experience and additional design skills, you could work for a specialist press production company, a design or reprographic house or general printers. To run a printing business takes a high-level of business skills, including accounting and sales.

Advantages/disadvantages

This job combines creative and artistic skills with technical and computer aided design.

There are good entry opportunities for some printing jobs such as specialist print finishers, which have become skills shortage areas.

Due to the nature of the industry, you might have to move to other parts of the country for promotion.

Many companies now produce high quality publications in-house, so printers need to work with large volumes or specialist niche markets to make a profit.

Money guide

Salaries are dependent on the size and location of your employer.

Machine printer

New entrants can expect to earn £15,000. More experienced machine printers can amass £45,000 including shift allowances and bonuses and the highest salaries in this profession are £60,000.

Screen printer

Screen printers can expect to start on £16,000, rising to £24,000 with experience. Top earners can amass £36,000.

Bookbinder

Bookbinders can expect to earn a starting salary of £16,000, rising to £28,000, including shift bonuses, with experience. Those with extensive experience and who lead a team can earn up to £30,000.

Print production planner

New entrants can expect to earn £16,000. With experience, print production planners can amass £30,000 and senior planners can earn £35,000.

Related opportunities

- CAD Draughtsman p223
- Publisher/Commissioning Editor p426
- Quality Control Inspector p246
- Signwriter/Signmaker p196

Further information

British Printing Industries Federation
Farringdon Point, 29/35 Farringdon Road, London EC1M 3JF
0870 240 4085; www.britishprint.com

Institute of Paper, Printing and Publishing
Runnymede Malthouse off Hummer Road, Egham,
Surrey TW20 9BD
0870 330 8625; www.ip3.org.uk

Scottish Print Employers Federation
48 Palmerston Place, Edinburgh, Scotland EH12 5DE
0131 220 4353; www.spef.org.uk

www.cityandguilds.com/myperfectjob

Qualifications and courses

ENTRY LEVEL 1

Although there are no set entry requirements for this career, GCSEs/S grades (A–C/1–3) in English, maths, science and computer studies are an advantage.

Many people enter these professions by means of an apprenticeship. Apprenticeships/Skillseekers may be available for candidates aged 16–24.

In addition you can study a relevant college course prior to entry.

Machine printer

There are several NVQs available in machine printing, mechanised print finishing and binding, digital print production, and envelope manufacture at levels 2 and 3, and handbinding and carton manufacture at level 3.

Machine printers may specialise in a specific printing process and may move into a supervisory role.

Screen printer

It is possible to attain City & Guilds Certificates in printing and graphic communications at levels 2 and 3, an NVQ in screenprinting at levels 2 and 3, an ABC Level 3 Award in printmaking skills, screen printing, and screen printing skills. You could also carry out an ABC Level 3 Double Award in printmaking, an ABC Level 3 Certificate in graphic printmaking and an ABC Level 3 Diploma in print media. Much training takes place on the job with experienced colleagues and many companies provide in-house training schemes.

The Digital and Screenprinting Association, and specialist schools such as London College of Communication, also run courses in this area.

Bookbinder

It is possible to commence this career at any age and craft bookbinding is often a second career path. NVQs are available in mechanised print finishing and binding at levels 2 and 3 and handbinding at level 3.

Print production planner

This job requires maturity and practical industry experience. It is possible to commence as a machine printer and work your way up to this position.

Many print production planners have a degree or diploma in a related subject such as print management or publishing, For a degree, entry requirements are usually 2 A levels and 5 GCSEs. For an HND, you should have one A level or a BTEC national diploma in a related subject. You can study for an NVQ in print administration at level 3, which includes modules on health and safety.

The British Printing Industries Federation (BPIF) offers a 12 month distance learning certificate in print management, which is aimed at first-time managers.

Marketing, Advertising, Media, Print and Publishing

CRCI: PD
CLCI: SAR

PRODUCTION ASSISTANT/RUNNER (TV, FILM AND RADIO)

What the work involves

Production assistant

- Production assistants provide support to the producer and director to help ensure that productions run smoothly and to schedule.

- You will manage a range of key administrative activities, such as organising scripts and filming updates, booking hotels and hiring equipment. You may also be responsible for managing budgets for productions.

Runner

- You will provide a wide range of practical help and support to all members of the production team.

- As well as some administrative work, you will pass messages on and carry equipment and scripts between offices and sets – often, with no prior notice.

The type of person suited to this work

It is essential to be enthusiastic, possess a willingness to learn and a passion for your chosen medium. You should have an interest in learning about all areas of the field and be well versed in recent trends in the industry. You should also enjoy problem-solving and have the ability to work well under pressure and to adhere to strict deadlines.

Working conditions

There are no standard hours in this profession as they vary depending on production size and type. This role requires a great deal of flexibility as during production hours can be long and unpredictable and include evenings and weekends. Many employees are freelancers, shift work is common and you may be required to be on call at all times.

Future prospects

Most opportunities are in London and south-east England, where over half of the TV and film industries are based.

This profession is fast-paced and there is fierce competition for entry level positions. Any relevant work experience, will help to secure a position. There are many freelancers in this sector. This usually involves working on several projects simultaneously, and balancing bursts of assignments with quiet periods of inactivity.

Advantages/disadvantages

This is a fast-moving and varied industry with exciting opportunities. These entry level positions are demanding and unglamorous.

Money guide

Earnings in this sector vary greatly according to role, media area, employer and project. Many people are employed on a freelance or contract basis.

Qualifications and courses

Production assistant

No formal qualifications are required for this role but entry is highly competitive, and many entrants have qualifications ranging from A-levels/H grades up to degrees. Understanding of the production process is very important and relevant previous experience is advantageous. Many production staff begin as runners and work their way up.

As there are many unadvertised vacancies in this field, it is important to be proactive and network to aid self-promotion.

In a bid to create a formal entry path and provide industry-specific education, the UK Film Council and Skillset have joined forces to open a number of specialist training academies and offer advice on professional development.

Runner

There are no formal entry requirements for this role and it is often a key starting point into the TV and film industry. However it may be advantageous to have a degree in a TV/film production or media related subject and an understanding of the production process. Enthusiasm is essential and it would be beneficial to have gained work experience, even if unpaid.

Production assistant

Starting salaries range between £15,000 and £22,000 per year; with experience you could earn £30,000 per year. Working freelance you could expect around £520 per week.

Runner

New entrants can expect to earn £10,000–£14,000 per year. This can rise to £20,000 with experience.

Related opportunities

- Camera Person p412
- Special Effects Technician (TV, Film and Theatre) p451

Further information

Broadcasting Entertainment Cinematograph and Theatre Union
373–377 Clapham Road, London SW9 9BT
020 7346 0900; www.bectu.org.uk

Skillset (Sector Skills Council for the Audiovisual Industries)
Focus Point, 21 Caledonian Road, London N1 9GB
020 7713 9800; www.skillset.org

PUBLIC RELATIONS EXECUTIVE

What the work involves

- You will manage the image and reputation of organisations by writing publicity materials, studying and advising clients and responding to enquiries or complaints.

- It will be important that you develop and maintain positive working relationships with the local, national and relevant trade press and TV news reporters.

- Public relations (PR) executives work in public relations or communications departments in large organisations and PR companies. Some work on a freelance basis.

The type of person suited to this work

PR is all about maintaining a positive image, so you will need a confident approach and a well-presented appearance. You will be a strong communicator and enjoy liaising with a wide range of people. Written communication and research skills are essential, so good ICT skills are highly important.

You will need to be able to cope with pressure. You should also have a flexible approach in a job where you will manage several projects at once. Financial management skills are also useful.

Working conditions

Most of your work will be within an office where you will have a workstation with computer, access to office equipment and your phone. You will have meetings with clients, colleagues or other professionals. Although you will work normal office hours, longer hours are common in this job, particularly in busy periods.

On a regular basis, you will need to travel to attend meetings, special events and presentations. Working for global companies or high-profile charities may mean some overseas travel.

Future prospects

PR is a growing industry. However, competition in this area is strong, with often hundreds of well-qualified applicants for one post. The normal progression route within PR is to work as a PR assistant and then as an account executive, followed by a move into a senior role.

It is possible to work abroad either within an existing organisation or by moving to one based overseas or with offices abroad. With experience, some PR professionals set up their own companies or work freelance for other organisations.

Advantages/disadvantages

There can be opportunities to take part in high-profile campaigns. This job can be pressured due to the speed of information releases and the range of activities you will have to juggle. If working for a high-profile organisation, you may have to be on call to respond to unexpected situations or emergencies.

Qualifications and courses

ENTRY LEVEL 4

Most entrants to this profession are graduates. Degrees are available in relevant subjects, such as public relations and marketing. There is also a Foundation degree in business (public relations).

Entry is highly competitive and a postgraduate qualification and previous work experience are an advantage.

Employers provide training, and some have graduate training schemes.

The Chartered Institute of Public Relations (CIPR) offers professional qualifications. Entry requirements for the CIPR Advanced Certificate are a first degree or 2 years' experience and 5 GCSEs/S grades (A–C/1–3), including English language.

The Public Relations Consultants Association offers a Diploma in Public Relations Consultancy Management. A degree or 2 years' experience in a senior role is required.

The Communication, Advertising and Marketing Foundation (CAM) offers qualifications. The Advanced Certificate requires a degree or relevant experience and 5 GCSEs/S grades (A–C/1–3), including English and maths or equivalent. For the Higher Diploma, experience and a good educational background are required.

Money guide

Starting salaries are usually around £14,000–£25,000 per year. This rises to £22,000–£36,000 with experience. £40,000–£100,000 is possible as a senior manager/director in a large company. The type of organisation you work for will affect your earnings. The voluntary and charity sector tend to pay less than public or government organisations.

Related opportunities

- Advertising Account Executive p406
- Advertising Media Planner p409
- Journalist p415

Further information

Chartered Institute of Public Relations
CIPR Public Relations Centre, 32 St James's Square, London SW1Y 4JR
020 7766 3333; www.ipr.org.uk

Communication, Advertising and Marketing Education (CAM) Foundation
Moor Hall, Cookham, Maidenhead, Berkshire SL6 9QH
01628 427120; www.camfoundation.com

International Public Relations Association (IPRA)
1 Dunley Hill Court, Ranmore Common, Dorking, Surrey RH5 6SX
01483 280 130; www.ipra.org

Marketing, Advertising, Media, Print and Publishing

CRCI: O
CLCI: OG

PUBLISHER/ COMMISSIONING EDITOR

What the work involves

- Publishers/commissioning editors plan and manage ranges or lists of books, magazines or ICT resources produced by their department or company. This could include researching consumers' needs and identifying gaps in the company's list of publications.

- You will develop ideas for new publications and respond to proposals from authors. You will also oversee the entire process of developing new publications from an original idea to completed manuscript.

- Responsible for keeping individual projects to budget, you will ensure that items are produced on time.

- You may also be responsible for developing marketing strategies to increase publication sales.

The type of person suited to this work

You will need a strong interest in producing books and publications that have extensive commercial appeal.

As you will liaise closely with authors and colleagues, you should enjoy meeting and working with a variety of people. You will also need strong written and verbal communication skills and the ability to encourage people to complete tasks to deadlines. You must be well organised and able to plan ahead.

Working conditions

Most of your work will involve attending meetings or working at a computer within the office of a company or organisation.

You will be expected to liaise with authors, colleagues, designers, ICT specialists and printers either face to face, by email or on the phone.

Although your working week will comprise normal office hours, you can expect to work late at times in order to meet strict publication deadlines or to attend evening events. Business trips, including overnight stays, are a possibility and you could travel abroad.

Future prospects

This is a competitive profession to enter. The main employers are publishing houses, specialist business, professional and educational companies.

Sales and marketing experience can facilitate entrance to this sector. It is possible to set up your own publishing company, although the market is well covered and profit margins narrow.

Currently, the area of greatest expansion is that offered by the internet and digital publishing.

Advantages/disadvantages

You will meet and work with an interesting cross-section of people.

You will be responsible for creating strategies to increase sales of publications, which can be stressful.

Qualifications and courses

The majority of new entrants to this industry have gained a degree. Relevant experience can be very helpful, although some publishing companies do advertise for trainees with no experience necessary.

A relevant postgraduate qualification, such as an MA or MSc in Publishing is not essential but is certainly advantageous given the competition for places.

As this is a senior role, it is unlikely that a new graduate would enter the publishing trade as a publisher/ commissioning editor. Most entrants start as an editorial assistant before being promoted to an editor position and then going on to secure a publisher/commissioning editor role.

Specialist training centres such as the Publishing Training Centre provide short courses on different areas of publishing and organisations such as Women in Publishing can provide advice and support to women entering the field.

Entry into the industry is highly competitive and it is important to learn as much as possible about publishing from trade magazines or people in the industry before applying. Experience of writing or editing at a non-professional level can be useful.

Developing new publications can be a lengthy process and requires patience.

Money guide

Salaries can vary depending on the size and type of employer. Commission and productivity bonuses can be paid, so the more books that are sold, the higher potential earnings can be. Starting salaries in editorial roles can be around £18,000–£28,000 per year (depending on the role). With experience you could earn up to £35,000.

Senior managers and directors of a large publishing company can earn between £48,000 and £80,000.

Related opportunities

- Copy Editor/Sub-editor/Proofreader p413
- Copywriter p414
- Literary Agent p410
- Newspaper/Magazine Editor p420

Further information

Publishers Association
29b Montague Street, London WC1B 5BW
020 7691 9191; www.publishers.org.uk

Publishing Training Centre at Book House
45 East Hill, Wandsworth, London SW18 2QZ
020 8874 2718; www.train4publishing.co.uk

RECORDING INDUSTRY PRODUCER

What the work involves

- Recording industry producers are employed by the Artists and Repertoire (A&R) department of a recording company to work with artists to produce successful music tracks or demos.

- You will discuss ideas with artists and their management, plan new projects, listen to existing tracks and identify areas for improvement.

- You will be involved in the organisation of each stage of the recording process, including rehearsal time, recruitment of sound engineers, booking studio time, directing the artists, and suggesting alterations that will produce the desired sound.

The type of person suited to this work

You must have excellent communication skills to give instructions to others, persuade people to try your ideas and to build up a good network of contacts.

As you will have to spend long hours in the studio you should have a good ear for music, high stamina, self discipline and patience.

You should also have good planning skills to work out budgets, organise time scales for recording studios and estimate production and post-production costs.

Working conditions

You will work long, irregular hours. This may include working late into the night and at the weekends. Your work may not always be constant and you may have to find other methods of earning money.

You may have to travel within the UK and abroad.

Future prospects

You will probably progress to a production position after several years of working in assistant sound engineer and engineer roles.

At first, you will approach A&R departments with your services until you establish your reputation, usually by producing music that is commercially successful.

Advantages/disadvantages

You may have the opportunity to work with a diverse range of artists and to be a part of the creative process of making music.

Prolonged exposure to loud music may damage your hearing.

Qualifications and courses

There are no specific qualifications required to become a recording industry producer, although formal music training of some kind is recommended. Work experience and voluntary work for a studio and record companies are vital.

Courses that may help you develop skills and experience include foundation degrees and degrees in music production, music technology, music practice and music industry management, the BTEC National Diploma in music technology, Level 3, or the HNC/HND in music production, Level 5 or diplomas in creative and media subjects.

Short music courses are available for young professionals beginning in the music industry such as the BPI seminar, 'Music, It's the Business'.

The Music Producers' Guild (MPG) have created a Knowledge Band and Members' Directory to encourage debate and facilitate future recording industry producers' networking within the industry. The MPG, in association with the Association of Professional Recording Services (APRS), has set up the Joint Audio Media Education Services (JAMES) to allow new entrants to learn from experienced professionals.

Money guide

You can expect a starting salary of around £15,000 per year. With experience and constant work you can earn from £30,000 a year. The top recording industry producers can earn over £100,000 and considerably more.

You may be paid 'on spec' if you work with an unsigned band. This means that you will be paid if and when the artist is successful.

Usually you will be paid a flat fee, but this will also include an agreed percentage of the sales income. This can be minimal or thousands of pounds.

Related opportunities

- DJ p442
- Sound Engineer p450

Further information

BPI British Recorded Music Industry
Riverside Building, County Hall, Westminster Bridge Road, London SE1 7JA
020 7803 1300; www.bpi.co.uk

Music Producers Guild UK Ltd
4 Wheelwrights Corner, Crossack Square, Nailsworth, Gloucestershire GL6 0DB
020 3239 7606; www.mpg.org.uk

Marketing, Advertising, Media, Print and Publishing

CRCI: PA
CLCI: GAL

RESEARCHER (MEDIA)

What the work involves

- Researchers develop TV and radio programmes and documentary films by gathering and checking information on specific subjects, people or places.

- You will use the internet and phone, conduct face-to-face interviews and visit different locations to do your research.

- It will be your job to research guests and programme contributors as well as to find relevant images, film clips and music. You could also write and edit programme scripts.

- You will brief the production team on the specific subjects covered by your research in preparation for filming.

The type of person suited to this work

The ability to find accurate, relevant information quickly is central to this role. To do this you will need a creative flair and the ability to think big to develop programme ideas. A flexible approach will help you balance varied tasks and unsociable hours.

Strength in written and verbal communication will enable you to work as part of a production team and to get the most from your research. Tight deadlines require the ability to work well under pressure. You will also need to be well organised to be able to manage your work. As you will be responsible for gaining permission to access and make use of information, you will need a clear understanding of the law.

Working conditions

Media researchers are based in offices or studios to undertake their desk research. They also spend time on research trips to locations in the UK or overseas.

The work usually needs to be completed to strict deadlines which can create a pressured, but fast-moving and interesting working environment.

It is likely that you would have to work at weekends and in the evenings on a regular basis.

Future prospects

Whilst this is a competitive area to get into, researchers are employed in many areas of the media including radio, production companies, television and film companies. Researchers normally provide the information for factual rather than drama-based productions; this can limit the volume of work available.

With experience, you could progress into a role as an assistant producer and then on to working as a producer/programme director.

Qualifications and courses

ENTRY LEVEL 4

Graduates are preferred, and subjects such as legal studies, history, journalism and media studies are useful. Relevant work experience and evidence of research skills can be accepted in some cases.

Work experience is very important.

IT skills and a driving licence are essential.

Many researchers have experience in other areas of the industry or journalism. A good knowledge of current affairs and media practice can be an advantage.

Many researchers work freelance, getting paid on a contract-by-contract basis.

Others specialise in areas such as documentaries on wildlife, architecture, social history, travel, while others concentrate on picture research.

Advantages/disadvantages

You will have to work long and often unsociable hours, which can affect family and personal life.

This is a varied job in a fast-moving industry. You could get the opportunity to travel to a range of places.

Money guide

Trainee starting salaries are around £15,000–£19,000 per year. £22,000–£26,000 is possible with experience. Specialists could earn up to £50,000. Freelance researchers can earn from £180 to £450 a day, depending on experience and employer.

Related opportunities

- Historian p355
- Journalist p415
- Market Researcher p416
- Records Manager p350

Further information

Skillset (Sector Skills Council for the audiovisual industries)
Prospect House, 80–110 New Oxford Street,
London WC1A 1HB
08080 300900; www.skillset.org

Film and Television Freelance Training (FT2)
3rd Floor, 18–20 Southwark Street, London SE1 1TJ
020 7407 0344; www.ft2.org.uk

Research Centre for Television and Interactivity
227 West George Street, Glasgow G2 2ND
0141 568 7113; www.researchcentre.co.uk

TECHNICAL AUTHOR/ MEDICAL WRITER

What the work involves

- Technical authors/medical writers interpret technical information and communicate it in written language, which the intended audience can understand.

- You will create content, commission images, organise and design the layout of the document.

- Technical authors work in various sectors from medicine and defence to business and finance.

- You should be an expert in your specialist sector, but your audience may be novices as well as specialists. For example you may write mass market instructions for a mobile phone, or a medical writer may create a report on clinical trial results for the medical community.

The type of person suited to this work

It is essential to have an excellent command of English and the ability to write concisely and convincingly, with your audience in mind. You should also be detail driven and have a good eye for design.

Having a passion for your specialist sector and an inquiring mind is a necessity. The ability to solve problems, multi-task and to work to deadlines is also important.

Good communication and team working skills are required as you will have to work closely with technical colleagues, such as doctors, as well as liaising with suppliers including printers and translators.

Working conditions

The majority of work will take place at a computer within normal office hours. However supplementary hours may be required in order to meet tight deadlines, and you may have to undertake travel to meet clients.

Having gained experience, many people decide to start up their own business or go freelance, specifically as the pay is more attractive.

Future prospects

At present there are 5,000 to 10,000 technical authors working in the UK in a variety of sectors. There are jobs all over the nation, but more in England than elsewhere. In addition more positions are available in technological clusters e.g. defence in the South West.

It is helpful to establish a network of useful contacts, and mature entry is common as being an expert in your chosen sector is a necessity.

Advantages/disadvantages

This type of work can provide the satisfaction of seeing your completed work in print and sometimes in the public domain.

This profession is likely to be particularly sensitive to the effects of the recession as many technical authors may lose their positions to developers and new software.

Qualifications and courses

It is possible to enter this profession without an HND or degree but a demonstration of extensive specialist knowledge will be required.

Many entrants have a degree or qualification in English, journalism or media studies. Others have qualifications in the area that they wish to specialise in, for example engineering or computer science. Minimum degree entry requirements are usually 2 A-levels and 5 GCSEs

Most training takes place on the job and many technical authors choose to study for a specialist qualification whilst working. Sheffield Hallam University has a master in technical writing qualification aimed at experienced professionals, which takes 3 years to complete via distance learning. In addition the University of Portsmouth offer a one-year MA in technical communications, and other related degrees are available at institutes throughout the UK.

It is common for adults to enter this profession as it necessitates expert knowledge. There is the possibility to study for an open-learning course in the communication of technical information at the Institute of Scientific and Technical Communicators (ISTC), which may be beneficial for mature entrants.

Money guide

Earnings vary widely depending on the technical writer's specialist sector and the size of the employer. However software and telecommunications currently offer particularly attractive salaries.

New entrants can expect to earn about £18,000 per year, with experience this can rise to £30,000.

Top earners in senior roles with extensive experience can amass £50,000+ per year.

Related opportunities

- Copy Editor/Sub-editor/Proofreader p413
- Copywriter p414
- Journalist p415
- Publisher/Commissioning Editor p426

Further information

British Association of Communicators in Business
Suite GA2, Oak House, Woodlands Business Park,
Linford Wood, Milton Keynes MK14 6EY
www.cib.uk.com

Institute of Scientific and Technical Communicators (ISTC)
PO Box 522, Peterborough PE2 5WX
01733 390 141; www.istc.org.uk

E-Skills UK
1 Castle Lane, London SW1E 6DR
020 7963 8920; www. .e-skills.com/careers

Marketing, Advertising, Media, Print and Publishing

CRCI: PB
CLCI: FAC

TV FLOOR MANAGER/ FILM ASSISTANT DIRECTOR

What the work involves

- TV floor managers/film assistant directors are responsible for the coordination of many aspects of the filming process.

- You will ensure that all sets, props and technical equipment are working, in place and set up correctly.

- In situations where the director is away from the set (in the gallery or a broadcast vehicle) you will wear headphones to relay instructions from the director to the crew, actors or audience members.

- You will make sure that everyone involved in the production process knows what to do so that everything runs according to schedule.

The type of person suited to this work

You must be passionate about the media industry, TV and film production in particular.

You should be very organised and able to work under pressure and to a tight schedule.

As you will be working with a variety of people from directors to the most junior crew members, you will need to have good communication skills to create an efficient working environment.

You must have an understanding of the technical and creative aspects of production to ensure that you can deal with problems encountered during the filming or recording stage.

Working conditions

Hours are likely to be long and irregular, including early starts, late nights and weekend work. If you work on feature films, six day weeks are common.

You will probably work on a freelance basis, which may involve periods of unemployment between jobs.

You will spend most of your time at work on your feet.

You may have to work outdoors in all weather conditions.

You may have to travel within the UK or abroad, at short notice for varying periods of time.

Future prospects

You may find opportunities to move up to positions as first director and eventually producer or director.

You may also find that you move across into other aspects of the industry such as production or broadcasting.

As you will be working on a freelance basis most of the time you will depend on having a good portfolio of work behind you, having an excellent reputation and making good contacts within the industry to guarantee work.

Qualifications and courses

ENTRY LEVEL 2

There are no set academic qualifications needed to become a TV floor manager or film assistant director. It may be useful to have GCSEs (A*-C) and A-levels in subjects such as maths, English or theatre and drama studies.

Degrees or HNDs in relevant subjects such as media studies, drama, photography, film and television may also be an advantage.

Other qualifications that may help include the BTEC First Diploma or National Certificates in media and media production, City & Guilds Level 3 Diploma in media techniques.

Screen Academies and Media Academies, run by Skillset, offer film and television training which will include working towards vocational qualifications. BBC and Channel 4 run similar schemes. See websites for further information.

The most essential requirement for entry to this job is to gain practical work experience. Before you can become a floor manager you will probably start as a runner, production assistant, or have had a technical role. Employers will seek candidates with a proven commitment to the job and the industry.

Advantages/disadvantages

Your work may involve a diverse range of projects including creative, practical and technical tasks.

You working hours may be long, stressful and unsociable.

Money guide

Your starting salary, in a junior role such as third assistant director, may be around £16,000 a year. As you are promoted to positions as second assistant director you can earn around £25,000 and with experience this can rise to £29,000 a year. First assistant directors can earn in the region of £35,000.

Related opportunities

- Camera Person p412
- Production Assistant/Runner (TV, Film and Radio) p424
- TV, Film and Radio Director p431

Further information

National Film and Television School (NFTS)
Beaconsfield Studios, Station Road, Beaconsfield, Buckinghamshire HP9 1LG
01494 671234; info@nfts.co.uk; www.nftsfilm-tv.ac.uk/

Skillset
Focus Point, 21 Caledonian Road, London N1 9GB
0808 300 900; info@skillset.org; www.skillset.org

TV, FILM AND RADIO DIRECTOR

What the work involves

- Directors manage the process of creating films, radio and TV programmes. This involves both commissioning each project and overseeing the work and schedules of the entire production team.

- You will define the presentation and style of films and productions by making decisions about content, scripting, camera work, editing and acting.

- You will also be required to handle any problems with presenters, actors or production staff, as well as editing the final 'cut' of the show you have directed.

The type of person suited to this work

Working in these competitive sectors can be very demanding and stressful. You should be confident and able to react quickly and calmly to any crises that may arise.

Good verbal communication, interpersonal and team working skills are important, especially as on some jobs you could be away from home on location for weeks at a time. In addition you should have good organisational skills to ensure that projects are carried out on time and within budget.

Working conditions

A good level of physical stamina and fitness is required as this job involves lengthy days spent standing up and carrying, lifting and erecting heavy equipment.

In TV and film you will work on set and on location and will have to cope with changeable outdoor conditions. You will also be expected to be flexible and work at night and at weekends, both during and post-production.

Future prospects

In the UK there are around 110,000 people working in TV and radio, many of whom are freelancers.

Recent financial unrest has resulted in a slow-down in the TV industry with fewer new productions scheduled. The British film industry is coping well, but obtaining finance backing to develop larger productions will get harder.

Entry to the industry is very competitive and excellent technical skills are expected from all applicants.

Advantages/disadvantages

This type of work provides the satisfaction of seeing the results of your work in the public sphere. This is a fast-moving and varied industry with exciting opportunities.

Increasingly, directors are employed on a freelance or short-term contract basis which can lead to job instability.

Contrary to popular belief, this is not glamorous work!

Qualifications and courses

There are no specific entry requirements, but most entrants will have a drama or media-related degree or postgraduate qualification.

It is possible to take media, film and television studies at GCSE, BTEC National Diploma, A-level, HND, degree and postgraduate level at institutions all over the UK.

Entry requirements are usually 2 A-levels and 5 GCSEs. For an HND, you should have an A-level in an art and design related subject.

Practical work experience is essential and most budding directors create a 'showreel' of self-funded projects to promote their work.

Some organisations, such as BBC Talent, offer work experience placements upon submission of new ideas, which can often lead to full-time employment.

In a bid to create a formal entry path and provide industry-specific education, the UK Film Council and Skillset have joined forces to open a number of specialist training academies and offer advice on professional development.

Funding and training courses are available from organisations such as The UK Film Council.

Money guide

Earnings in this sector vary greatly according to media, location, employer and project. New entrants can expect to earn about £20,000 per year. This may rise to £40,000 with experience. The most successful directors can earn anything up to £200,000.

Many directors are employed on a freelance or contract basis. Rates vary between roles and media area, but are usually paid on a daily basis.

Related opportunities

- Artistic Director p437
- Production Assistant/Runner (TV, Film and Radio) p424
- TV, Film and Radio Producer p433

Further information

BBC Recruitment
PO Box 48305, London, W12 6YE
www.bbc.co.uk/jobs

Skillset (Sector Skills Council for the Audiovisual Industries)
Focus Point, 21 Caledonian Road, London N1 9GB
020 7713 9800; www.skillset.org

Marketing, Advertising, Media, Print and Publishing

CRCI: PA/Q
CLCI: GAL/GAB

TV, FILM AND RADIO EDITOR

What the work involves

- Editors play a key role in the post-production process by assembling the final product from captured footage and additional sound and graphics. They are also responsible for storing the footage.

- You will fulfil a brief and liaise closely with the director.

- You will create the flow and pace of a production by using specialist ICT editing equipment to put shots together in a smooth sequence.

- You will ensure the continuity and order of these productions, which may include TV and radio programmes, films, music and corporate videos, and advertisements.

The type of person suited to this work

It is essential to be creative and to have a passion for your chosen medium. You should have a high attention to detail, an inordinate amount of patience and the ability to identify good storytelling techniques.

You will be expected to be well-versed in the latest technological advances in the field, as well as possessing advanced IT skills and the willingness to try new techniques.

Working conditions

In this profession hours vary depending on workload but are typically 9am-5pm, from Monday to Friday. However it should be noted that your personal life may be affected by long and unpredictable hours, which are common in order to meet tight deadlines.

The majority of the work takes place at a computer in an editing suite, and may be carried out alone or with a director. Larger projects may require the assistance of a sound effects editor, music editor as well as assistant editors.

Future prospects

At present there are about 11,000 people working in post-production roles in the UK. This profession is fast-paced and there is fierce competition for entry level positions.

The majority of roles are based in London in post-production companies, independent production firms, broadcasters, and companies in the film and computer software sectors.

Having gained experience, many editors choose to go freelance. This involves working on several projects simultaneously and balancing bursts of assignments with quiet periods of inactivity.

Advantages/disadvantages

This type of work provides the satisfaction of seeing the results of your work in the public domain.

Qualifications and courses

There are no specific entry requirements, but the majority of entrants will commence as runners or assistants in order to gain experience. Practical work experience is essential and most budding editors create a diverse 'showreel' to promote their work.

Some editors have a degree or postgraduate qualification in film, IT or a media-related subject. Entry requirements are usually 2 A-levels and 5 GCSEs. For an HND, you should have an A-level in a related subject.

It is possible to take an NVQ in electronic and film post-production editing at level 2 and editing at levels 3 and 4.

In a bid to create a formal entry path and provide industry-specific education, the UK Film Council and Skillset have joined forces to open a number of specialist training academies and offer advice on professional development.

Entry level training courses are offered by the BBC as well as independent organisations like FT2, Cyfle, Production Guild, Scottish Screen and Screen Yorkshire.

This is a fast-moving and varied industry with exciting opportunities.

Increasingly, editors are employed on a freelance or short-term contract basis which can lead to job instability.

Money guide

Earnings in this sector vary greatly according to employer and project. New entrants can expect to earn £15,000–£25,000, rising to £30,000 with experience. The most experienced producers can earn up to £70,000

The majority of editors are employed on a freelance or contract basis. The Broadcasting Entertainment Cinematographic and Theatrical Union (BECTU) provide a benchmark for current rates.

Related opportunities

- Camera Person p412
- Researcher (Media) p428
- Special Effects Technician (TV, Film and Theatre) p451

Further information

Broadcasting Entertainment Cinematograph and Theatre Union
373–377 Clapham Road, London SW9 9BT
020 7346 0900; www.bectu.org.uk

Skillset (Sector Skills Council for the Audiovisual Industries)
Focus Point, 21 Caledonian Road, London N1 9GB
020 7713 9800; www.skillset.org

TV, FILM AND RADIO PRODUCER

What the work involves

- A producer originates ideas, employs pivotal team members, has creative input, gets involved in casting decisions and script editing, and generally oversees the complete production.

- You will be the lead person in TV, film and radio production. They all have a detailed knowledge of the industry, coupled with sound business skills.

- Many producers also play a financial role, approaching initial backers, securing rights and managing the budget throughout production.

- You may also be expected to oversee the final editing process, as well as marketing and distribution plans.

The type of person suited to this work

It is essential to have a strong creative flair and a passion for your chosen medium. A well-rounded knowledge of your sector, spanning technical, creative and commercial aspects is also required.

Excellent communication skills are important and you should have the ability to provide inspiration and motivation for team members. An enjoyment of problem-solving and the ability to work well under pressure will be helpful.

You should also have a good head for figures, and solid negotiation, multi-tasking and organisational skills to ensure that projects are carried out on time, within budget and as requested.

Working conditions

Producers work in a variety of environments including offices, studios and external filming locations.

This role requires a great deal of flexibility, as during production hours can be long and erratic, and travel is often required to assess venues and attend meetings.

Future prospects

At present there are 18,000 TV and film producers in the UK and vacancies tend to be centred in major cities such as London, Manchester and Glasgow.

The main employers are well-known broadcasters such as the BBC, TV and film production firms and production and facilities houses.

Entry to the industry is very competitive and establishing good contacts is essential as many jobs are never advertised and awarded based on the reputation of the producer.

Advantages/disadvantages

This type of work provides the satisfaction of seeing the results of your work in the public domain.

Qualifications and courses

There are no specific entry requirements, but producers need extensive industry experience and most will have worked their way up the ladder. In TV and film, many people start as a runner, which gives them contacts, a well-rounded view of the industry and invaluable knowledge.

Many entrants will have a media-related degree or postgraduate qualification.

It is possible to take media, film and television studies at GCSE, BTEC National Diploma, A-level, HND, degree and postgraduate level at institutions all over the UK.

Entry requirements for degrees are usually 2 A-levels and 5 GCSEs. For an HND, you should have an A-level in an art and design related subject.

In a bid to create a formal entry path and provide industry-specific education, the UK Film Council and Skillset have joined forces to open a number of specialist training academies and offer advice on professional development.

This is a fast-moving and varied industry which can provide exciting opportunities.

Increasingly, producers are employed on a freelance or short-term contract basis which can lead to job instability.

Although you will work with many celebrities, this is not glamorous work.

Money guide

Earnings in this sector vary greatly according to media, role, employer and project.

New entrants can expect to earn between £15,000–£25,000, rising to £30,000 with experience. The most experienced producers can earn up to £70,000.

Almost half of producers in the industry are freelancers and can earn from £900 to £1300 a week for a 16-week slot.

Related opportunities

- Camera Person p412
- Production Assistant/Runner (TV, Film and Radio) p424
- TV Floor Manager/Film Assistant Director p430
- Researcher (Media) p428

Further information

BBC Recruitment
PO Box 48305, London W12 6YE
www.bbc.co.uk/jobs

UK Film Council
10 Little Portland Street, London W1W 7JG
020 7861 7861; www.ukfilmcouncil.org.uk

Performing Arts

This job family contains a wide range of exciting jobs for those of you who want to work in theatre, music, on screen or behind the scenes. People working in this sector do so because they are passionate and creative and love the Arts. Jobs can be scarce, so you will need to demonstrate that you are willing to work very hard but the rewards of being part of a fantastic production can be huge. There are also jobs available in this sector for those of you who are more technically minded - sound and lighting engineers also play a vital role in this industry as do people who have trained in fashion and textiles.

In this section we look at the following jobs:

- Actor/Actress p436
- Artistic Director p437
- Choreographer p438
- Composer/Songwriter p439
- Conductor p440
- Dancer p441
- Disc Jockey p442
- Entertainer p443
- Lighting Technician p444
- Make-up Artist p445

- Musician p446
- Props Maker/Assistant p447
- Roadie p448
- Singer p449
- Sound Engineer and Technician p450
- Special Effects Technician p451
- Stage Manager p452
- Stunt Performer p453

- Theatre Producer / Production Assistant p454
- Wardrobe Assistant p455

For similar jobs to the ones in this section turn to *Design, Arts and Crafts* on page 175 and *Marketing, Advertising, Media, Print and Publishing* on page 405.

ACTOR / ACTRESS

What the work involves

- Actors/actresses perform in front of audiences and this can sometimes include dancing and singing as part of the role.

- There are opportunities for acting parts in dramatic plays, comedies or musicals on stage or on TV.

- Actors/actresses need to have lots of stamina, as rehearsals can be long and hard in order to get things right before the show opens.

- Work is rarely permanent or regular and a lot of time may be spent looking for jobs and attending auditions.

The type of person suited to this work

Acting is a very competitive area so you should be truly dedicated to this career path. You will need lots of stamina and a good level of fitness.

There will be many times when you will be rejected at auditions mainly because you are just not the right face for the part, and so you will need to be able to cope with this and keep trying.

It is a tough, demanding career to enter and to stay in, but once you get regular work it can be very satisfying.

Working conditions

You will work mainly indoors, in theatres, halls and sometimes studios.

Sometimes summer productions are performed in open-air theatres, arenas or stately homes and castles.

You could have to travel to different venues for your performances where you might spend time waiting for your part in the performance.

Future prospects

Prospects for success as an actor depend on talent, hard work and a bit of luck.

Some actors go on to work as writers or directors, while others train to teach drama in schools and colleges.

Advantages/disadvantages

The long travelling hours to get to performance venues and then waiting to perform could be boring.

This area of work is very competitive.

It is not all glamour and money, but can be great fun.

Money guide

Basic rates of pay depend on experience and reputation; outside London you could earn up to £12,000 per year with regular employment, rising to around £14,000.

An actor working in a London West End theatre could expect around £15,500 per year for a once-per-night performance,

Qualifications and courses

Although there are no specific requirements to enter this profession, it is very competitive and almost all actors have formal training.

You can take an acting course (usually a Diploma/Professional Diploma) at a drama school. Courses last between 1 and 3 years. Entry is by audition and interview, and A levels/H grades or the equivalent are often required.

The National Council for Drama Training (NCDT) accredits full-time vocational drama school courses and degrees. Graduates of NCDT-accredited courses who are legally entitled to work in the UK are eligible for Equity membership. Part-time courses and more academic degrees in, for example, drama or theatre studies, are not accredited.

You can do a degree in acting (or a related subject like drama or performing arts). Acting degrees are offered by drama schools and by universities. Entry requirements vary, but always include an audition and interview, as well as A levels/H grades or the equivalent.

Some courses may specify 5 GCSEs/S grades (A–C/1–3) and some may require 2 A levels/3 H grades or a BTEC Diploma in Performing Arts.

and £19,000 for twice-nightly performances. Continuous employment is unusual.

As you become recognised as an actor, your income could be much more than this, but it may take many years.

It is important to join Equity, the union for the world of entertainment – as this can help you negotiate fair rates of pay, terms and conditions. Union-negotiated pay scales are on the Equity website.

Related opportunities

- Dancer p441
- Artistic Director p437
- Entertainer p443
- Stage Manager p452

Further information

National Council for Drama Training
1–7 Woburn Walk, London WC1H 0JJ
020 7387 3650; www.ncdt.co.uk

Creative & Cultural Skills (Sector Skills Council for advertising, crafts, cultural heritage, the arts and music)
11 Southwark Street, London SE1 1RQ
020 7089 5866; www.ccskills.org.uk

Equity
Guild House, Upper St Martin's Lane, London WC2H 9EG
020 7379 6000; www.equity.org.uk

ARTISTIC DIRECTOR

What the work involves

- Artistic directors have control over the artistic interpretation of plays, ballets, operas and other performances.

- You will be responsible for coordinating all the creative elements of each production, including set and costume design, stylistic presentation, the interpretive work of artists, and any musical or choreographic sequences.

- You will liaise with a number of other professionals on a daily basis, including producers, musical directors, technicians, theatre managers, financial backers, performing artists and writers.

- You will select each production, oversee casting, and appear at performances and press events to help generate publicity around each show.

The type of person suited to this work

You will need fantastic artistic and creative vision, that you are able to express both verbally and in written documents. You will also need to have the courage and tenacity to make your vision a reality and present it to an audience.

You must be an excellent leader with the ability to inspire and motivate others. Being able to negotiate with writers, actors and other professionals is an asset.

You should have an in depth knowledge of the theatre, including productions past and present, theatrical trends, and the history of the industry.

Working conditions

Hours can be irregular and you will be employed on a freelance basis through which contracts can be short. Longer fixed-term contracts are available, but they usually only last 3–5 years.

You will be mainly working in theatres and other performance venues. Although the final production may take place on a large stage, you could spend a great deal of time directing scenes from small, offsite rehearsal rooms.

You will mainly work indoors, although certain venues will require you to work outdoors in occasionally inhospitable conditions.

Future prospects

Competition in the theatrical industry is fierce, so you will need talent, dedication, good qualifications and experience.

Since the majority of theatrical work takes place in London you can expect to work there at some period in your career. The city is a base for most freelance directors, although there are opportunities in regional theatres.

As an experienced and admired artistic director, you could set up your own theatre company through which you can stage your performances. Other directors move from theatre into film or television work.

Qualifications and courses

Most artistic directors hold a relevant degree in English, creative/performing arts, drama or theatre studies on entry to the industry. HNDs and foundation degrees in creative/performing arts or drama/theatre studies are available and may also be useful qualifications to hold prior to entering the theatre. If you are looking to move into the industry after completing your first degree, Birkbeck College, RADA and Mountview offer postgraduate courses in theatre direction.

Of equal importance to professional qualifications are practical skills, acquired through work experience and involvement in school, college or university productions. Since few theatre companies offer in-house training, gaining this practical experience prior to applying for positions is vital.

The Arts Council England runs assistant director schemes for new entrants to the profession, and a few theatres and regional arts councils also offer training bursaries for candidates with exceptional potential.

Advantages/disadvantages

Your creative ability will be the driving force behind the production of visually and technically beautiful or unusual performances.

The industry is extremely competitive so you may have to spend long periods of time working for free or at a minimal wage in order to build enough experience to work as an artistic director.

Money guide

Theatre directors who are working regularly can earn around £19,000. Reaching the level of artistic director should increase your salary to about £23,000. Well-established artistic directors who have built up a good reputation and are in demand across the industry can earn £40,000+.

Related opportunities

- Theatre Producer/Production Assistant p454
- Stage Manager p452
- Actor/Actress p436

Further information

The Directors Guild Trust and the Directors Guild of Great Britain
4 Windmill Street, London W1T 2HZ
020 7580 9131; www.dggb.org; info@dggb.org

Arts Council England
14 Great Peter Street, London SW1P 3NQ
0845 300 6200; www.artscouncil.org.uk

Performing Arts

CRCI: Q
CLCI: GAB

CHOREOGRAPHER

What the work involves

- As a choreographer, you will create, design and develop new dance movements for productions such as ballets, opera and musicals.

- Creating a dance means planning the way dancers move around the set to create beautiful and exciting routines which interpret the music.

- You will be on your feet a lot of the day and have to deal with many performers with different levels of expertise.

- Choreographers work closely with performance artists, musical directors, ballet dance teachers and trainers.

The type of person suited to this work

You will need to have a keen, lively interest in music and movement, and a very well-developed sense of rhythm and timing.

To develop new ballets, dances and shorter dance routines requires an excellent knowledge of past and present pieces, complete understanding of how the body works and of possible movements within dance and the creative imagination to interpret the significance of events and mood changes through physical expression.

Choreographers have responsibility for developing and teaching complicated movements and routines. You will need a good memory, clear communication skills, patience and an ability to get on well with others.

Working conditions

Your work will be mainly indoors in dance studios, theatres, TV or film studios.

Your initial contacts are likely to be producers, directors and musical conductors. Some choreographers work directly with modern composers, interpreting their music.

As production plans progress, you will start working directly with the performers and a repetiteur who plays rehearsal music.

Future prospects

Jobs and opportunities can be limited as this is a highly competitive area of work, where experience counts.

It is possible to find opportunities outside the mainstream ballet areas, for example in modern dance companies and developing international venues.

Opera and musicals are becoming reinvigorated through audience demand and both performance areas require choreographers to interpret dance music and contextual pieces as dance routines.

Advantages/disadvantages

Many hours are spent traveling to different venues – even overseas.

Qualifications and courses

There are no formal entry qualifications for this career. GCSEs/S grades and AS/A levels/H grades are available in dance, and some institutions offer a BTEC National Diploma in Performing Arts.

Most choreographers have experience as dance performers prior to becoming choreographers.

Choreography can be studied as an option on some full-time vocational dance courses accredited by the Council for Dance Education and Training, as part of a degree course in dance or as a postgraduate course.

Work experience alongside an experienced practitioner offers a good introduction to choreography and will certainly be taken into account if applying for a dance or choreography-related course.

Seeing your finished routine beautifully performed will boost your morale.

Enthusiastic reviews will help your career progression.

It will be hard going, and you will need patience and enthusiasm to get the best from dancers.

Money guide

Equity recommends a minimum daily sum of up to £113.

You could earn round £12,500 per year if you have just finished at a dance college, or completed a degree or other college courses.

Your salary will reach £20,000 if you have moved into choreography as an experienced dancer.

Experienced, well-known choreographers can earn £50,000, but good salaries will depend on your skills and experience.

Related opportunities

- Dancer p441
- Artistic Director p437
- Make-up Artist p445
- Special Effects Technician p451

Further information

Council for Dance Education and Training
Toynbee Hall, 28 Commercial Street, London E1 6LS
020 7247 4030; www.cdet.org.uk

Dance UK (includes British Association of Choreographers)
Battersea Arts Centre, Lavender Hill, London SW11 5TF
020 7228 4990; www.danceuk.org

Creative and Cultural Skills (Sector Skills Council for advertising, crafts, cultural heritage, the arts and music)
11 Southwark Street, London SE1 1RQ
020 7089 5866; www.ccskills.org.uk

Performing Arts

CRCI: Q
CLCI: G

COMPOSER/SONGWRITER

What the work involves

- Composers and songwriters create original music for a variety of uses.

- You could use a variety of tools and instruments when composing or writing, from a pen and paper to advanced computer software programmes.

- You may also perform your compositions and songs, although this is most common for composers who are just starting out and those writing for individuals or small groups.

The type of person suited to this work

You will need to have outstanding musical or lyrical talents. You will need dedication, determination and self-discipline as the music industry is extremely tough and knock-backs will be frequent.

You should have a flexible attitude to your work and be willing to take on a range of commissions and assignments in order to build up your experience and reputation.

Working conditions

Composers and songwriters (the former in particular) can expect to work long and unsociable hours writing, rehearsing and performing their work.

Since most musical events take place over evenings and weekends (when most of the working population is free to attend) you can expect to regularly work during these times.

You may have to travel in order to see publishers, musicians or artists who will be performing your work, as well as going to rehearsals and performances.

Most composers and songwriters have other jobs in order to fund themselves whilst they establish a name in the music industry.

Future prospects

The music industry is highly competitive, so it can take a long time to gain any recognition for your work. This makes composing a challenging profession to choose and you will need to be extremely resilient.

Most composers or songwriters are self-employed, although opportunities are available with theatrical companies, music publishers and universities.

You could gain great critical acclaim and commercial success, although the majority of composers' and songwriters' work stems from smaller commissions within the media, including writing for television, film and radio.

Advantages/disadvantages

You will be working in a job that you are passionate about,

Qualifications and courses

Useful qualifications include GCSE and A-levels in music, BTEC National Diplomas in music practice or popular music, and relevant degree courses. For entry onto a BTEC National Diploma you will need 4 GCSEs (A-C) or equivalent. Degree courses usually require 5 GCSEs (A-C) and at least 2 A-levels, preferably with one in music or a related subject, and most usually prefer candidates to have reached grade 8 in an instrument as classified by the ABRSM.

A wide variety of postgraduate courses is also available. If you are looking to break into the world of classical composition, you are strongly advised to attain a postgraduate qualification.

It is possible, but extremely rare, to achieve success without having undertaken some of the relevant qualifications to this industry.

which will be immensely satisfying. If you gain recognition the personal and financial rewards can be excellent.

The industry is highly competitive and chances of success are relatively slim.

Money guide

It is very hard to gauge salaries in this industry as so many composers and songwriters are freelance. If you are commissioned by a large company or orchestra, as a composer you can expect to earn around £500-£1000 for each minute of music you create. Songwriters could earn around £300 per minute. For title music, jingles and commercials, both composers and songwriters can earn about £350 per minute.

You could also be entitled to royalties from your work.

Related opportunities

- Musician p446
- Singer p449
- Conductor p440

Further information

Arts Council England
14 Great Peter Street, London SW1P 3NQ
020 7580 3869; www.bmic.co.uk; info@bmic.co.uk

The British Academy of Songwriters, Composers and Authors (BASCA)
26 Berners Street, London W1T 3LR
020 7636 2929; www.basca.org.uk

British Music Information Centre (Bmic)
1st Floor British Music House, 26 Berners Street, London W1T 3LR
0845 300 6200; www.artscouncil.org.uk

Performing Arts

CRCI: Q
CLCI: GAD

CONDUCTOR

What the work involves

- Music conductors work with musicians and singers to help shape their performance and make sure each musical piece is performed the way it should be.

- You'll be responsible for preparing musical scores for the performance, and taking decisions about how each musical piece should sound.

- You need to understand the role of each performer, and make sure every musician knows which part to play and does so correctly.

- You may work with a wide variety of musicians, both amateur and professional, and these may include choirs and choruses, music students, youth groups and professional artists.

The type of person suited to this work

An interest in music is essential. You should also have good knowledge of music, and be able to play an instrument, preferably the piano.

Good communication skills are vital, as is the ability to work flexibly and with lots of different creative people.

You should also have the command of an additional European language.

Working conditions

Working hours for conductors are varied, and you must be prepared to work whenever and wherever the opportunity arises. Hours include evenings and weekends for both rehearsals and performances.

You will divide your time between working in rehearsal rooms, concert halls, churches, theatres, opera houses and other venues.

A driving licence is useful, as travel is often involved.

It's common to spend a lot of time away from home in venues of a varying standard.

Future prospects

Succeeding in conducting is all about building up your reputation. Once you've proved yourself you can make a name for yourself and start to conduct bigger and better orchestras.

Advantages/disadvantages

If you're musical and want a balance between working independently and working with people, this job may really suit you.

Work can be difficult to come by and there isn't much job security initially.

Qualifications and courses

ENTRY LEVEL 5

Most conductors have a degree in music. Most universities require at least five GCSEs and two A-levels, as well as the ability to play an instrument to Grade 7 or 8.

Following completion of a degree, it is usual to undertake a postgraduate course in conducting at music college. Whilst you're doing this, it's a good idea to try and get some work experience as a deputy or assistant conductor.

Most conductors speak at least two European languages. The most useful are English, German, French and Italian.

It's a good idea to attend the seminars run by the Association of British Orchestras: they run many intended specifically for those interested in conducting.

Working as a repetiteur in opera is also a good idea, as you can watch and learn from excellent and experienced conductors.

If you achieve good marks in your conducting studies, keep your eye out for the scholarships offered by organisations like the Royal Opera House.

Even once you're a qualified conductor, there's always more to learn. Almost all conductors spend their own time studying music theory and constantly keeping up to date with what's going on.

Money guide

Conductors tend to be paid per concert. In the beginning this may be about £380 per concert, and it is likely to increase to about £1000 once you gain experience.

The best conductors can earn about £5000 per concert.

Related opportunities

- Musician p446
- Composer p439
- Music Teacher p209

Further information

Association of British Orchestras, 20 Rupert Street
London W1D 6DF
020 7287 0333; www.abo.org.uk

Incorporated Society of Musicians (ISM)
10 Stratford Place, London W1C 1AA.
020 7629 4413; www.ism.org

The International Artist Managers' Association (IAMA),
23 Garrick Street, Covent Garden, London WC2E 9BN.
020 7379 7336; www.iamaworld.com

DANCER

What the work involves

- Dancing is an exhilarating but physically demanding career. You need a keen interest in dance and may have attended lessons from an early age.

- Dancers at every level of the profession spend long hours in classes – exercising, practising routines, working with choreographers and other dancers. Some dancers now do fitness training alongside dance, to reduce the risk of injury.

- You will find work in theatres, cabaret clubs, cruise ships or video/TV studios, in performances as diverse as ballet, stage musicals, jazz and contemporary dance.

The type of person suited to this work

Anyone entering this area of work must love dancing and be very talented to succeed. Dancers must be dedicated to improving technique through daily practice – sometimes, for as long as 10 hours each day.

To be a successful dancer, you need a good sense of rhythm and timing. Being creative and imaginative with routines and choreography is desirable.

It is important that you can cope with setbacks and remain positive and focused.

Working conditions

Most of your rehearsals and performances will take place indoors in studios, schools, theatres or other venues.

While training, most dancers work closely with others in small or larger groups for long hours each day, so it is important that you get on well with all kinds of people. Also, you need patience to handle the strains of working within the same competitive group for a long time.

Future prospects

Your future prospects as a dancer will largely depend on talent, hard work and luck; competition is always strong. Only a few individuals become top performance artists in solo roles.

Dancers with dance companies can progress from chorus to solo parts, but this is dependent on the skills and dedication of the individual dancer. Although dancing is a career for younger people, dance teachers can continue long after they are no longer professional performers, and many leave dancing to set up private dance schools.

Advantages/disadvantages

Dance can be a fantastically rewarding career.

Your career as a top soloist can be finished by the age of 30.

Getting paid work can sometimes be difficult.

You will need to stay fit and healthy: injuries can necessitate a complete career change.

Qualifications and courses

You can do a vocational dance performance course at a specialist school such as the Royal Academy of Dance. These courses (Diploma, National Diploma or degree) are usually 3 years in duration. Entry is by audition, interview and a medical, and 5 GCSEs/S grades (A–C/1–3) are usually required.

For ballet, there are also physical requirements, including height requirements and body proportions.

The Council for Dance Education and Training accredits full-time courses at vocational dance schools.

You can do a degree in dance at a university or college of higher education. A levels/H grades or the equivalent are usually required, and candidates attend an audition.

Some courses offer a teacher-training element. The Royal Academy of Dance and Imperial Society of Teachers of Dancing offer specialist teacher training programmes.

The British Ballet Organisation and the British Theatre Dance Association also offer dance and teacher training qualifications.

Money guide

Salaries for dancers depend on length, type and location of the job. Most dancers are members of the British Actors Equity Association which negotiates performers' salaries and sets a minimum of £336 per week, rising to £360 for experienced dancers. Some dancers are self-employed and set their own rates per contract. Starting full-time employment with a recognised dance company, you should earn £23,000 per year. As a soloist, this can rise to £26,000, while principal dancers can earn £36,000+.

Dance teachers are mainly self-employed and receive salaries dependent on the type and size of dance school they work in.

Related opportunities

- Choreographer p438
- Theatre Producer/Production Assistant p454
- Actor/Actress p436

Further information

Council for Dance Education and Training
Toynbee Hall, 28 Commercial Street, London E1 6LS
020 7247 4030; www.cdet.org.uk

Royal Academy of Dance
36 Battersea Square, London SW11 3RA
020 7223 0091; www.rad.org.uk

Royal Ballet School
White Lodge, Richmond Park, London TW10 5HR
020 8876 5547; www.royal-ballet-school.org.uk

Performing Arts

CRCI: Q
CLCI: B

DISC JOCKEY

What the work involves

- Working as a club DJ, you use a wide variety of equipment including multimedia and specialist lighting.

- You may entertain live audiences at events and parties and may act as the master of ceremonies.

- As a radio DJ, you work in a studio playing records and chatting to listeners – with some stations, this could include a phone-in option.

- VJing is a new way forward using a good PC and software to mix/inter-splice sounds with images from video clips and loops, in real time.

The type of person suited to this work

To succeed, you must have a passion for music and skills in music technology. The work requires excellent coordination, good communication and listening skills, and a lively outgoing personality.

DJs use the latest in turntables, amplifiers and multimedia – and practice techniques such as mixing, scratching, beat mixing and cross fading to make their live performance interesting.

Sheer hard work and persistence are keys to success. As most DJs are self-employed, basic business skills are an advantage. Initially, time will be spent promoting your skills in a search for work.

Working conditions

As a DJ, you may work in clubs, on radio, in hotels, in holiday camps or at festivals and gigs – even on boats.

Keeping up with the latest technology and music genres is time-consuming.

High noise levels are an occupational hazard for DJs; you need to take steps to protect your hearing.

Future prospects

Some DJs stay in the job only a short time before moving on. Many work part time alongside a daytime job.

You have to be a self-starter, looking for opportunities, as jobs are rarely advertised. Experienced DJs can get seasonal work in holiday camps. Some move into careers in music production or retail.

Increasingly, DJs are finding opportunities working with VJs who create pop videos, while some experienced DJs find work abroad.

Advantages/disadvantages

You will be working late nights and at weekends, and over public holidays.

There can be heavy equipment to move around, often in the early hours. You may travel considerable distances between venues.

Qualifications and courses

There is no specific entry route to this job, and no formal qualifications are required.

An Edexcel/BTEC National award in DJ Technology is offered at some colleges of further education, often combined with music technology. The normal entry requirements are 4 GCSEs/S grades (A–C/1–3). There are also BTEC qualifications in Popular Music, Music Technology and Performing Arts that can be useful.

NCFE and City & Guilds also award qualifications in DJ skills/DJ Technique/DJ – Mix, offered as short, full-time courses by a few colleges and specialist training centres.

There are many degrees, HNC/Ds and Foundation degrees available in related areas, e.g. creative music technology, music production, as well as NVQ Level 3 in Radio Production.

Training in radio skills is offered by CSV Media which runs Media Clubhouses around the UK.

Work experience is highly advisable. A technical career in radio is a good start to becoming a radio DJ and there are many college and hospital radio networks where you can practise.

Some top DJs offer masterclasses; some club DJs allow work-shadowing to gain technical skills.

Set-up equipment costs over £1000.

Money guide

Income varies with the event and venue; your reputation will determine your fee. Your charges/pay should reflect local DJ rates; when starting out, expect a little less!

Depending on the club size, DJs can charge between £50 and £300+ per session.

With your own record releases, fees rise to well over £1000 in superclubs, while a few top European DJs earn £100,000 per year.

Many DJs do other work to boost their income.

Related opportunities

- Sound Engineer/Technician p450
- Musician p446
- Nightclub Manager p394

Further information

SAE Institute
United House, North Road, Islington, London N7 9DP
020 7609 2653; www.sae.edu

Access to Music
Lionel House, 35 Millstone Lane, Leicester LE1 5JN
0800 281 842; www.accesstomusic.co.uk

ENTERTAINER

What the work involves

- Entertainers perform amusing or amazing acts in front of audiences. They include comedians, circus performers, street artists, cabaret performers, dancers, musicians, and magicians.

- You could specialise in one area or skill such as magic, dance or comedy, or you may have several skills that you can combine into one act.

- You will have to source your own props and costumes, attend regular auditions, book venues, rehearse your routine, and also carry out your own promotional work.

The type of person suited to this work

You will need natural confidence and a very outgoing nature in order to present a lively and entertaining act to your audience.

You will need to be extremely talented in your chosen field, be it comedy, music, dance or magic.

You should be good with a wide range of people, as your audience could include members of all ages and backgrounds.

You should have good business awareness and a creative approach to marketing yourself in order to attract interest in your act and increase your bookings.

You must be extremely punctual and reliable so as not to disappoint or annoy a venue or your audience.

Working conditions

Working hours vary. Most performances take place during evenings and weekends, and you may also work morning matinees. You can choose to work full time if you have a number of bookings, or part time in order to supplement your income with that from another job.

You could have regular weekly, fortnightly or monthly jobs, but a great deal of work is on a one-off basis.

You may work across numerous venues throughout the UK (and abroad), so a driving licence would be useful.

Future prospects

The majority of entertainers are self-employed, although there are employment opportunities with circuses, theme park operators and cruise ship companies.

Some may also work with one or more agents, who help with promotion and finding bookings in return for a small fee or commission from earnings.

Overseas work is possible, especially if you work for a cruise ship company or if you have an act that is appreciated across a variety of cultures.

Advantages/disadvantages

You will travel across the UK, and even the world, showcasing your talent to a variety of people to entertain and amaze them.

Qualifications and courses

Entertainers do not need to hold any academic qualifications, although they may be beneficial in honing your skills and proving your ability and commitment to potential employers.

Entry routes are numerous and varied, ranging from entering talent competitions, to working in holiday centres, to performing in local clubs and bars, through to undertaking professional training courses.

Courses that will lead to useful qualifications include: BTEC National Certificates in live entertainment; HND in performance, entertainment and media, foundation degrees and degrees in entertainment or similar. BTEC entry requirements are usually 4 GCSEs (A-C) or equivalent. All degree courses require at least 2 A-levels or equivalent, 1 in a related subject.

If you are intending to work with children and/or vulnerable adults, you will also be required to undergo a Criminal Bureau Records check prior to starting.

Apprenticeships and Creative Apprenticeships are also available to entrants aged 16–24.

If you are self-employed, you have the opportunity to choose your hours and bookings to fit in around other commitments.

The industry is competitive, and few entertainers are able to pursue their career on a full time basis.

Money guide

Salaries for entertainers vary depending on your genre and level of success. New entrants who have regular work can expect around £10,000.

With experience, you should be paid more per booking and could earn between £12,000 and £20,000.

Well established entertainers, such as those with regular bookings at reputable venues, or regular TV appearances, can earn £30,000+.

Related opportunities

- Singer p449
- Musician p446
- Actor/Actress p436
- Dancer p441

Further information

Spotlight
7 Leicester Place, London WC2H 7RJ
020 7437 7631; www.spotlight.com

The Circus Space
Coronet Street, London N1 6HD
020 7729 9522; www.thecircusspace.co.uk

Performing Arts

CRCI: Q
CLCI: G

LIGHTING TECHNICIAN

What the work involves

- Lighting technicians are responsible for creating stage lighting effects, working closely with the set designer and producer.

- You will do lighting for advertising sets, in video production, animation and broadcasting work.

- Making sure the power system is suitable for amplifiers and sound equipment will be a part of your job.

- It is important to visit venues before productions start, watching rehearsals to get the lighting effects right for live performances.

The type of person suited to this work

Anyone entering this career must have an interest in electrical work and electronics, have a strong interest in theatre and performance, or live concerts. You will also need to be physically fit and work well in a team.

Lighting technicians need to have a creative flair as the main aim of this job is to create the atmosphere required by the producer.

In some situations, for example changing or operating spotlights, the tasks could involve working at heights, and would not suit a person who suffers from vertigo.

Many lighting technicians have to travel long distances to do their work.

Working conditions

Most of your work will be indoors, usually working afternoons, evenings and weekends. You will work with lots of heavy equipment and you may sometimes need to wear protective steel toe-capped boots.

You may have to work in cramped spaces with computerised control systems.

You will often be away from home for weeks and months if you are travelling with a roadshow.

Future prospects

Theatre lighting is being covered by specialist companies who employ technicians on a short-term contract basis. However, once you are experienced and known in the trade, your opportunity to join the backstage crew of a particular theatre group is increased.

Progression as a lighting technician relies on skills and dedication. When in demand, you can become a senior or chief lighting technician and, in some cases, technical manager.

Advantages/disadvantages

You will have irregular working hours, including evening and weekend work – usually, away from home.

Qualifications and courses

All lighting technicians must be fully qualified electricians. Relevant qualifications include the City & Guilds Certificate in Electrotechnical Technology (2330), or SVQs Levels 2 and 3 in Lighting (Live Performance). Full-time or part-time college courses are available or you may find a traineeship with a specialist lighting company.

Colleges and universities offer courses in subjects such as technical theatre, theatre design and theatre production, which include the study of lighting.

Specialist degrees in lighting design are offered by Rose Bruford College and Central School of Speech and Drama. Drama schools offer degrees and vocational training courses in technical theatre or stage management which include lighting. Many of these are accredited by the National Council for Drama Training.

The BBC offers a central work experience scheme, but places are limited. The Association of British Theatre Technicians and Skillset offer professional qualifications in Lighting and Lighting Direction. Apprenticeships/ Skillseekers may be available to those aged 16–24.

Seeing your skills and experience light up a set or production will be a great confidence booster.

Money guide

Trainee technicians start at around £10,000 per year. With experience, this rises to around £16,000 for full-time techinicians in established theatres. A qualified lighting technician working in television could earn up to £30,000. A number of experienced theatre lighting technicians work freelance earning £300+ per week.

Related opportunities

- Special Effects Technician p451
- Stage Manager p452

Further information

Association of British Theatre Technicians
47 Bermondsey Street, London SE1 3XT
020 7403 3778; www.abtt.org.uk

National Electrotechnical Training
34 Palace Court, London W2 4HY
020 7313 4846; www.net-works.org.uk

**City&
Guilds**

www.cityandguilds.com/myperfectjob

MAKE-UP ARTIST

What the work involves

- Your work will involve applying make-up and arranging hair for male and female artists and performers in films, TV and stage productions.

- You will need to listen to the director in order to create the desired finished look for the individual characters or troupe.

- Most of your work will be done off stage in a make-up or dressing room.

- You could be employed in TV, by a video production company or by a theatre or film company, or be self-employed, perhaps as part of a backstage team.

The type of person suited to this work

Anyone who considers doing make-up work needs to be creative, with the imagination to visualise the finished effect. You will have to pay great attention to detail. The job requires excellent communication as advising colleagues or clients on their image will need a sense of tact and clarity.

At times, there will be many people needing to be made up for a particular scene, and you could be working under intense pressure. Self-confidence, an outgoing personality are positive factors in building relationships and succeeding at work.

Working conditions

Most of your work will be indoors in theatres, in studios and, at first, possibly in retail outlets. Try to get work experience as a make-up artist with local amateur dramatic or operatic groups. Doing make-up involves many busy hours spent standing and bending over customers and you will need to be physically fit.

If you are self-employed, you will probably need to provide your own cosmetics.

Future prospects

Although this is not a huge area for employment there will always be a demand for make-up artists. The larger towns and cities present the best opportunities. Although limited, some work could be available in the larger hotels or on cruise ships.

Securing full-time work in TV or video, on a cruise ship, in a hotel, a retail store or with a theatre company are all possible, once you have gained experience.

It will be possible to set up your own beauty salon.

Advantages/disadvantages

Handling some cosmetics could cause skin irritations.

Working hours may be irregular and unsociable, especially if you do make-up both before and during performances.

Make-up is a highly satisfying job when you see your work on stage or set.

Money guide

Self-employed make-up artists can earn around £15,000

Qualifications and courses

Make-up artists in theatre/TV/film are usually trained in beauty therapy, and may have an NVQ/SVQ or a Diploma of the Vocational Training Charitable Trust (VTCT) or equivalent qualification.

There are a range of specialist further education courses in theatrical and/or media make-up. VTCT offers a Diploma course, and BTEC National awards and Certificates and SQA modules are also available. These courses can be studied at college on a full- or part-time basis.

Greasepaint offers short courses in make-up for TV, film, fashion and theatre.

A number of universities and colleges run HND courses in theatrical and/or media make-up or make-up artistry. A degree course in costume, technical effects and make-up for performing arts is offered at London College of Fashion, and allows students to specialise in make-up. The usual entry requirements for HND and degree courses are 2 A levels or equivalent (for example an Edexcel National Diploma). Their 2-year full-time Foundation degree course in specialist make-up design has lower entry requirements.

Apprenticeships/Skillseekers may be available to those aged 16–24.

per year. With experience this can rise to £25,000. The highest paid earn up to £45,000. Employed by a company, you can start on £15,000–£16,000, earning more with specialist skills.

Artists employed full-time by television or film companies to create and apply make-up and style hair and wigs for actors can earn over £28,000 per year.

Related opportunities

- Beauty Therapist p459
- Beauty Consultant p458
- Hairdresser/Barber p469

Further information

British Association of Beauty Therapy and Cosmetology Ltd
Ambrose House, Meteor Court, Barnett Way, Barnwood, Gloucester GL4 3GG
0845 065 9000; www.babtac.com

Make Up Artist magazine
www.makeupmag.com

Greasepaint
Greasepaint Studio, 143 Northfield Avenue, Ealing W13 9QT
www.greasepaint.co.uk

www.cityandguilds.com/myperfectjob

Performing Arts

CRCI: Q
CLCI: G

MUSICIAN

What the work involves

- Whether you work as a classical, popular or armed forces musician, your main responsibility will be to perform to and entertain an audience.

- You will spend the majority of your time practising in order to develop and strengthen your ability on the instrument/s you play.

- You could compose your own material, or play that of other people from a variety of genres.

The type of person suited to this work

You will need to be extremely musical, particularly if you are looking to work as a classical musician.

Throughout the music industry, there is intense competition for jobs. You will need determination, tenacity and resilience in order to cope with knock-backs and persevere.

You will need to be very confident in yourself and your abilities, as well as having considerable stage presence and hold the attention of an audience.

Working conditions

You must be prepared to work long, unsociable hours in a variety of environments, including clubs and bars.

Classical musicians tend to work in locations such as concert halls, theatres, parks and recording studios. Musicians employed by the Armed Forces usually perform for military parades, regimental dinners, state occasions, sporting events and other special occasions.

All musicians could find themselves having to work away from home for long periods of time.

Future prospects

Classical musicians may rise to enjoy success as solo artists, or may work in group ensembles such as orchestras in which there are chances for promotion. Diversifying into teaching is also common.

Prospects for popular musicians are varied, and depend a great deal on how successful you become. Many decide to move into a business role such as that of a manager or representative for a recording company.

Armed Forces musicians usually move across various bands throughout their career, whilst also progressing up through the standard ranks as they gain relevant management, leadership and military skills.

Advantages/disadvantages

As a musician, you could work in a variety of disciplines and with a range of different people, so the work will be stimulating and interesting.

Competition is intense in the music industry, so you will have to work extremely hard.

Qualifications and courses

Classical musicians undertake extensive musical training and academic qualifications. Most take graded examinations in their chosen instrument/s, as well as further related courses. These include GCSE/A-level music, BTEC National Diploma in music practice, music degrees at university, specialist courses at music colleges (conservatoires), and relevant postgraduate qualifications.

Popular musicians do not need to hold any qualifications for entry to the industry, but they may help as proof of your ability and dedication. Relevant courses include: GCSEs/ A-levels in music or similar; BTEC National Diploma in music, music technology and music practice; HND/HNC courses; degrees in popular music or a related subject.

BTEC entry requirements are usually 4 GCSEs (A-C) or equivalent. All degree courses require at least 2 A-levels or equivalent, 1 in a related subject. Postgraduate programmes require entrants to hold a relevant first degree.

Armed Forces musicians do not need to hold any formal qualifications for entrance, but aptitude in your chosen instrument/s is expected. You will be assessed by audition at the Royal Military School of Music.

Money guide

Classical musicians employed by an orchestra usually earn between £22,000 and £40,000. Solo artists can command anything from £80 and £600 per concert.

Session musicians could earn between £120 and £350 for a three hour job, and solo musicians can earn anywhere from £500-£2000+ a week depending on their popularity.

Armed forces musicians start on a trainee salary of about £14,000, and this can rise to £70,000+ as they are promoted in the course of their military service.

Related opportunities

- Singer p449
- Entertainer p443
- Composer/Songwriter p439

Further information

Arts Council England
14 Great Peter Street, London SW1P 3NQ
0845 300 6200; www.artscouncil.org.uk

Associated Board of the Royal Schools of Music (ABRSM)
24 Portland Place, London W1B 1LU
020 7636 5400; www.abrsm.org

Royal Military School of Music
Kneller Hall, Kneller Hall Road, Twickenham TW2 7DU
www.army.mod.uk/music/; nco2crt@hq.dcamus.mod.uk

PROPS MAKER/ASSISTANT

What the work involves

- Props makers and their assistants are responsible for designing, changing, making and finishing the props used in theatre, video, film, television or circus work.

- You will be working with a range of materials, including wood, fibreglass, fabric and metal, and will use a range of practical skills including carpentry, modelling and good painting ability.

- You will spend a good amount of your time researching the historical and cultural background of the props to ensure they fit the era they represent.

The type of person suited to this work

You will need to have a mixture of practical and artistic skills in order to have the vision to design props and the ability to make them yourself.

You will be taking direction from theatre/TV producers, so must be able to listen carefully to their briefs and ideas so that you can translate them into actual props.

You will need good problem solving skills so that you can think round issues such as meeting both expectations and budget with your props.

The ability to use a variety of ICT packages, including CAD, is useful.

Working conditions

Working hours vary, but you can expect to work long hours over evenings and weekends in order to meet deadlines now and again. You will be working in small studios and prop rooms and such conditions can often be cramped.

You may also spend a good amount of time visiting suppliers for equipment, and also libraries and museums to carry out research.

You will have to wear relevant safety equipment when dealing with materials such as wood, metal, fibreglass and any chemical products.

Future prospects

The majority of props makers are freelance, so you will be employed on short-term projects most of the time. These could be for film studios, theatres, television companies, or museums.

Career progression is dependent upon building a good reputation and excellent portfolio of work. With experience, you could move into set design or take a more general role in stage management.

Advantages/disadvantages

Working in a creative industry such as theatre or film provides challenging, exciting work opportunities.

Qualifications and courses

It is possible to enter the profession without any academic qualifications, but even if you start as an assistant most employers look for at least GCSEs (A-C) or equivalent, in English, maths and art. You will also need a good history of relevant work experience, and a lot of talent and dedication.

Most props makers have relevant qualifications, including HNDs, degrees and postgraduate diplomas, in subjects such as stage management or art. Most HND courses require that you hold at least 1 relevant A-level, whereas degree courses require at least 2 A-levels including art or similar. Postgraduate courses always ask for a related first degree as an entry requirement.

Most course providers also ask candidates to present a portfolio of work for entrance assessment, as well as holding the qualifications specified above.

The Diploma in creative and media could be a relevant course for entrants looking to start in the industry as a props maker's assistant, from where you can build on-the-job experience and a strong portfolio.

You will be using a mixture of artistic, practical and intellectual skills which will be tiring but rewarding.

Working freelance can bring a feeling of instability and can be hard when work dries up for a month or two.

Money guide

As a props maker's assistant, you can expect to earn about £12,000. Props makers who are just starting in the industry usually earn around £15,000.

If you gain a good reputation and start to work on large productions with big budgets, you could earn in excess of £40,000.

Related opportunities

- Wardrobe Assistant p455
- Make-up Artist p445
- Stage Manager p452

Further information

The Stage Management Association (SMA)
55 Farringdon Road, London EC1M 3JB
020 7242 9250; www.stagemanagementassociation.co.uk

Creative & Cultural Skills
4th Floor Lafone House, The Leathermarket, Weston Street, London SE1 3HN
020 7015 1800; www.creative-choices.co.uk; info@creative-choices.co.uk

Royal Academy of Dramatic Art (RADA)
62–64 Gower Street, London WC1E 6ED
020 7636 7076; www.rada.org; enquiries@rada.org

Performing Arts

CRCI: Q
CLCI: G

ROADIE

What the work involves

- Roadies have to lift, move and set up heavy equipment, load and unload vans and trailers and do lots of driving around.

- You will be responsible for setting up a range of equipment including amplifications systems, electric cabling, stage and special effects lighting, videos and other media.

- You will need to maintain and fine-tune your equipment on a regular basis.

- Your work could include handling pyrotechnics, laser displays, computers – as well as videos.

The type of person suited to this work

You will need to have a strong interest in music, technology and electrics. It is essential for anyone working in this career to have good communication skills and an interest in people, and to be creative and practical.

Physical fitness and stamina will be essential, and a sense of humour is a bonus in this work. You should be able to work whilst under pressure. Because many roadies are self-employed, a well-organised person with some business skills will do well with maintaining their accounts, keeping records and dates of bookings.

Working conditions

You will have exceptionally long working hours, mainly evenings, nights and weekends, and if you are on a tour, you might be working 7 days a week.

The work is very physical and there is lots of heavy lifting involved, and sometimes you could be working at heights on electrical cabling.

Future prospects

There are more roadies looking for work than there are jobs. The work is unpredictable and you may need another job to boost your income. Work can be seasonal, with more roadies needed for summer festivals and gigs.

Marketing your services will be essential for getting gigs; many roadies now use websites to advertise.

Expanding your areas of expertise to include technical skills such as sound or lighting will certainly improve your chances of employment.

Advantages/disadvantages

Roadies work long unsociable hours and there is lots of travelling.

You will stay throughout the concert or gig, as equipment may need moving onto/off stage.

Very loud sounds will damage your hearing if your ears are unprotected.

Qualifications and courses

ENTRY LEVEL 1

There are no formal entry qualifications for becoming a roadie. Most people enter this career through experience of working with a friend or other contacts. If you are under 18 you may not be able to work in some licensed premises.

If you are planning to do the more technical work you may need qualifications. Suitable courses would be in lighting, pyrotechnics, video work and sound production. Details of suitable courses are available from the Production Services Association and British Phonographic Industry and many of these do not require formal entry qualifications.

The majority of roadies will learn the trade from working with other more experienced people. Although the job has no specific training route, courses such as electrics and video, and music technician courses, would be a useful addition to help expand job prospects.

Useful skills and qualifications include a health and safety certificate, a First Aid certificate, a Light Goods Vehicle or Passenger Service Vehicle driving licence and the ability to speak one or more foreign languages.

Money guide

There is no set earning scale.

Most roadies work freelance and your pay will depend on the gig, your experience and general availability of roadies.

As a starter, with regular work, you could earn around £12,000–£13,000 per year.

A roadie with electrical, audio or video skills can earn £20,000+. With excellent technical skills, pay can rise to £32,000.

On contract to a big touring band, you could earn £35,000+.

Related opportunities

- Sound Engineer/Technician p450
- Lighting Technician p444
- Stage Manager p452
- Large Goods Vehicle Driver p606

Further information

Production Services Association
Centre Court, 1301 Stratford Road, Hall Green, Birmingham B28 9HH
0121 639 7127; www.psa.org.uk

British Phonographic Industry
25 Savile Row, London W1S 2ES
020 7534 5300; www.bpi.co.uk

The Stage Management Association
55 Farringdon Road, London EC1M 3JB
020 7242 9250; www.stagemanagementassociation.co.uk;
admin@stagemanagementassociation.co.uk

SINGER

What the work involves

■ Singers perform in front of an audience in clubs, at gigs, on television or radio, in a recording studio, or in an opera house. They work as solo artists, or as part of a backing group, choir or chorus.

■ You will spend many hours practising in order to develop and strengthen your breathing and vocal ability.

■ You will need to have good diction, and be able to pronounce songs written in a variety of languages including Latin and French.

■ You will work with a variety of musicians and music industry professionals, including orchestras, bands, session musicians, sound engineers, and maybe a manager.

The type of person suited to this work

You will need to have an exceptional talent for singing in order to get noticed in the music industry.

Because of the intense competition in this area, you will also need determination, self-discipline and resilience in order to cope with knock-backs and to persevere in order to achieve your goals.

You will need to be very confident in yourself and your abilities. It is difficult to hold an audience without stage presence and charisma.

Working conditions

As a singer, you can expect to work long and unsociable hours over evenings and weekends, as this is when the majority of your audience will be free.

You may have to travel long distances for gigs and rehearsals.

You could work in a variety of locations, from small clubs and theatres, to large concert halls and even outdoor venues.

Future prospects

Singing is a highly competitive industry, and opportunities for full time work are extremely limited. Because of this, most professionals supplement their income with another job, so you could look into teaching or writing songs and jingles for other artists.

Most successful singers move to London to pursue their careers, as this is where the majority of opportunities lie.

You may well work with an agent or manager at some point in your career. Their purpose is to offer you career advice and to find you singing opportunities.

Advantages/disadvantages

You will be fulfilling a passion whilst also doing your job, which is rare and satisfying.

You will be bringing pleasure to the people in your audience, no matter how big or small.

Qualifications and courses

Academic qualifications are not strictly required in order to become a singer, but they quite often demonstrate talent, commitment, and the necessary expertise to succeed in the music industry to potential employers or clients.

Relevant qualifications include GCSEs and A-levels in music, BTEC courses in music, performing arts, music performance, music practice and music technology, HNC/HND courses in music-related subjects, and a degree in popular music or similar. Entry requirements for these courses vary; BTECs usually require 4 GCSEs (A-C) or equivalent, whilst HNC/HND programmes require an additional A-level, degree programmes require at least 2 A-levels (often including music).

Classical singers will need to undergo far more extensive formal training, often to postgraduate level, in order to achieve the depth of specialist knowledge and technical ability required to perform in public.

Building up singing experience, through performing with choirs, in amateur productions or in talent contests, is also important in order to help you develop as a rounded performer who can hold the attention of an audience.

You will have to work long and unsociable hours.

You will have to be resilient in order to persevere despite negative feedback on occasion.

Money guide

As a solo singer, you could earn between £150 and £450 per concert. Chorus singers usually earn £70-£100. Backing singers on albums are paid £110+ for a 3 hour recording session.

If you go on to perform in the theatre, there are set rates of pay that employers must adhere to. For example, chorus members command £650 per week for performances onstage in London's West End.

Related opportunities

■ Composer/Songwriter p439
■ Musician p446
■ Entertainer p443

Further information

The BRIT School for Performing Arts and Technology
60 The Crescent, Croydon CR0 2HN
020 8665 5242; www.brit.croydon.sch.uk;
admin@brit.croydon.sch.uk

Creative & Cultural Skills
4th Floor Lafone House, The Leathermarket, Weston Street, London SE1 3HN
020 7015 1800; www.creative-choices.co.uk;
info@creative-choices.co.uk

Performing Arts

CRCI: Q
CLCI: GAD

SOUND ENGINEER AND TECHNICIAN

What the work involves

- Sound engineers and technicians set up, operate and maintain a range of technical equipment that is designed to capture, magnify and manipulate words and music.

- Theatrical sound engineers create 'sound plots', choose equipment and insert sound effects according to the instructions of the director of the production.

- Sound engineers working in the recording industry capture speech, music and other sound effects and modify them using sophisticated electronic equipment for a number of purposes including creating pop songs, adverts, computer game soundtracks, film and TV.

The type of person suited to this work

You will need a good musical ear and excellent sense of timing in order to put together pleasing and appropriate soundtracks/ background audio to a range of productions.

You should also have knowledge of both electronics and ICT systems.

Recording industry sound engineers must also have a good knowledge of both recording and post-production processes.

Working conditions

Sound engineers working in both theatre and the recording industry should expect to work varied hours that will encompass day, evening and weekend commitments.

Theatre sound engineers will spend the majority of their working day confined to a small control box which may be cramped and often is plunged into semi-darkness.

Recording sound engineers work in studios, some of which are large and air-conditioned, whilst others can be small and cramped. You will usually be working in artificial light and the atmosphere can be stressful when working against deadlines.

Future prospects

Competition for jobs is intense, and you may spend a long while proving your credentials as a runner or gofer.

You could work for a variety of employers, including theatres, opera and ballet houses, commercial recording studios or media post-production departments.

Theatre sound engineers may go on to become sound designers with greater creative input in productions, whereas many recording sound engineers move into roles as producers.

Advantages/disadvantages

You will work with a variety of people on diverse projects, so each day will bring new challenges and rewards.

Qualifications and courses

It is possible to become a sound engineer without gaining any relevant qualifications, as many companies take on trainees as runners or assistants, and you can build your knowledge whilst you work.

Larger studios and companies do prefer candidates to hold relevant qualifications. These could include: BTEC National Certificates in live sound, stage sound, or light and sound; HNDs in sound technology or sound engineering and electronics; foundation degrees and degrees in music production or audio technology. BTEC entry requirements are usually 4 GCSEs (A-C) or equivalent.

Postgraduate qualifications are also offered by a limited number of providers. The University of Westminster runs an MA course in audio production, and the National Film and Television School offers a Diploma in sound recording or an MA in sound design for film and television.

For theatre sound engineers, many drama schools offer courses in theatre lighting and sound which may be useful. All good programmes are accredited by the National Council for Drama Training.

Theatre and media are exciting industries to work in as there is constant cultural and technical development.

You will have to work long hours that will often fall over evenings and weekends.

Money guide

Starting salaries for sound engineers, whether they work in theatre or the recording industry, range from £13,000-£15,000. With experience, this should rise to £30,000. Sound engineers working on large productions, with big companies or well-known artists, can earn £40,000+.

Related opportunities

- Special Effects Technician p451
- Lighting Technician p444

Further information

Professional Lighting and Sound Association (PLASA)
Redoubt House, 1 Edward Road, Eastbourne BN23 8AS
01323 524 120; www.plasa.org; info@plasa.org

National Film and Television School
The Registry, Beaconsfield Studios, Station Road, Beaconsfield HP9 1LG
01494 731 425; www.nftsfilm-tv.ac.uk

SPECIAL EFFECTS TECHNICIAN (TV, FILM AND THEATRE)

What the work involves

- As a technician you'd work to create special effects in the television and film industry.

- You might work with either physical effects, pyrotechnic, or visual. The first involves robotics, the second explosions, and the third superimposes images after filming.

- You'll work with colleagues to plan effects, create them, test them, and oversee their staging during filming.

- You may superimpose effects post filming, and will work to strict health and safety regulations, travelling to shooting locations and working long and flexible hours.

The type of person suited to this work

An interest in films and television is useful for this profession.

You need to be creative and imaginative, but at the same time practical and logical.

A visual mind is important, as you'll need to imagine how things will look on screen, and you should also be resourceful as you'll be working to a budget.

You'll be working under pressure, both with people and on your own, so need to be good at coping with all of these scenarios.

You should be adaptable and capable of coping with criticism.

Working conditions

Hours are flexible, and you should be prepared to fit around filming schedules. This may mean late nights, early mornings, and weekends.

You could work freelance, which may well mean you are very busy for a while, then unemployed for a long period of time.

When you're working, you could be travelling anywhere, sometimes for quite a while. Be prepared to stay away from home often.

Work takes place wherever filming takes place - in a studio or workshop, outdoors in the sunshine, outdoors in the rain, on location etc.

Future prospects

Once you've been working for about ten years, you can advance to a senior technician position.

With five years more experience, you can move into a supervisor role.

Progression is much easier when you've built a list of contacts, and vacancies in this industry are often only advertised internally.

Advantages/disadvantages

This is a really exciting job, and seeing your hard work on the big screen can be really rewarding.

Qualifications and courses

There is no specific entry route into this profession, but employers like to see degrees and diplomas in art subjects, especially stage crafts and animation.

Courses are available in areas such as technical arts and special effects. Most applicants take a Foundation Art and Design course prior to entry. In order to do this, you'll probably need at least five good GCSEs and two A Levels.

Relevant work experience is essential, and can be in any aspect of special effects, from theatre stage crafts to pyrotechnics and working with explosives.

When you gain employment, you will be trained whilst shadowing an experienced technician. During this time, you will also create a 'showreel' of your work to present at interviews with prospective employers.

You'll probably be a trainee for about five years, unless you're going into visual effects, in which case it will be two years due to the less dangerous environment. If you do choose to work in pyrotechnics, you'll need to take additional courses.

It's a fiercely competitive profession, and you may have to face periods of unemployment.

Money guide

As a trainee, you can expect to earn between £200 and £500 a week, depending on how advanced your skills are.

Once you're a technician this can rise to about £1,250 for a week of work.

If you make it to a senior technician role, this might rise to between £3,000 and £4,000 a week.

Related opportunities

- Animator p176
- Lighting Technician p444
- Props Maker/Assistant p447
- Sound Technician p450

Further information

The Association of British Theatre Technicians (ABTT)
55 Farringdon Road, London EC1M 3JB
020 7242 9200; www.abtt.org.uk

BBC Recruitment
PO Box 48305, London W12 6YE
www.bbc.co.uk

Broadcasting Entertainment Cinematographic and Theatre Union (BECTU), and the BECTU Special Effects Branch
373–377 Clapham Road, London SW9 9BT
020 7346 0900; www.bectu.org.uk

ENTRY LEVEL 2

Performing Arts

CRCI: PA
CLCI: GAB

STAGE MANAGER

What the work involves

- Stage managers work with designers, directors and producers, assessing and discussing what props, lighting and other stage support are needed for the production.

- You are the link between the artistic and technical aspects of all productions, as you are in charge of everything that happens on stage including calling actors, giving technical cues and moving scenery.

- You could work on numerous types of production, including theatrical performances, opera, ballet, and even music festivals.

The type of person suited to this work

You will need to have artistic flair, be practical, communicate instructions clearly and manage others confidently, working as part of a team with artists, directors, the production team and technical and backstage staff. Good time management skills are crucial.

The work is demanding and stressful as the successful running of the backstage support for the performance rests with you. A cool head and a sense of humour – while still being assertive – will make the work easier for you. An excellent stage manager can help create a good team atmosphere backstage between artists, props manager and stagehands.

Working conditions

You will spend long hours in theatres and studios, sometimes working into the night to meet deadlines. In addition, you will have to travel to different venues.

The atmosphere backstage during rehearsals and performances can be very enclosed, hot and dusty.

Finding work is not easy and can take up a huge amount of your time, so be prepared for rejection and periods without work.

Future prospects

The employment demand for stage managers has remained stable for some years. This is a competitive area of work and the opportunities for employment are not extensive. Opportunities exist in theatre companies, opera, theatre in education and touring companies.

Experience in amateur theatre – with student productions and drama clubs – shows commitment and gives you valuable experience.

Advantages/disadvantages

You will work long, unpredictable hours to meet production deadlines.

Permanent contracts are difficult to find.

Qualifications and courses

Usually, entrants to this job have undertaken professional training. Also, it may be possible to enter with relevant practical experience.

Stage managers have usually taken a stage management course at drama school. The National Council for Drama Training accredits some vocational stage management courses. Diplomas and degrees are studied over 2 or 3 years full time, and entry is by interview and portfolio of practical work.

Some universities offer degrees and HNDs in technical theatre or theatre production which include study of stage management. Candidates should also aim to gain practical experience in student productions or fringe theatre as a degree is not recognised as vocational training.

You could be employed as a stagehand and work your way up.

The Stage Management Association runs a variety of short courses for people already working as stage managers or assistant stage managers.

NVQs/SVQs are available in Stage Management, and there are BTEC/SQA qualifications in relevant subjects. Some drama schools offer short, part-time courses in stage management.

The work is both creative and practical.

There is a great sense of achievement at the end of a successful run when everything has operated smoothly.

Money guide

Starting out as a trainee stage manager you will earn about £14,500 per year. With experience, your annual salary can rise to £20,000+. With lengthy experience, you will be in demand, earning up to £40,000 annually.

Related opportunities

- Entertainments Manager p388
- Props Maker/Assistant p447
- Wardrobe Assistant p455
- Lighting Technician p444

Further information

EQ
Suite E229, Dean Clough, Halifax, West Yorkshire HX3 5AX
01422 381618; www.thinkeq.org.uk

Stage Management Association
47 Bermondsey Street, London SE1 3XT
020 7403 6655; www.stagemanagementassociation.co.uk;
admin@stagemanagementassociation.co.uk

STUNT PERFORMER

What the work involves

- Stunt performers plan, design, practise and perform stunts in areas such as motorbike riding, car driving, diving, flying, paragliding, bungee jumping, skiing and horse riding.

- Standing in for actors in TV, film or video productions, you will enter flaming buildings, crash vehicles, drive at speed or do dangerous stunts at sea. Sometimes, performances are in front of live audiences.

- You may advise other performers on health and safety issues.

The type of person suited to this work

Being skilled in a range of sports, including gymnastics, trampolining, parachuting, wrestling, fencing and some of the well-known martial arts, is often useful.

Stunt performers are dedicated to their art, and committed to ensuring that their skills are highly developed.

You will be happy to practise every aspect of your stunts over and again until they are reproducible in all details, so, you must be a perfectionist. You must always be aware of the dangers you face, practising long hours to make the performance appear easy!

Working conditions

Part of your working day could be spent within a studio, on location or on a film set.

You could be working indoors or out, in cramped spaces, at heights, or sometimes in bad weather conditions.

The hours could be very long, often up to 16 hours per day depending on the production, with weekend work and travelling to distant places being the norm.

Future prospects

Opportunities for live stunt work are decreasing, as digital graphics and new media can simulate stunts, so competition for work is growing increasingly fierce.

Stunt artists work anywhere in the world, with main employers being film, TV and video production companies. You will need a high level of stamina and fitness; this is a young person's career.

Some stunt performers progress into advisory work, helping film directors or advising and training other stunt artists.

Advantages/disadvantages

This is difficult, dangerous work, involving many risks.

You will be out in all weathers, working in blazing buildings, enclosed spaces or at great heights.

Long hours will be spent practising or away on location.

This is a very competitive area of work with poor prospects.

Qualifications and courses

There are no academic entry requirements for this work. Stunt performers may have trained as actors.

Stunt performers should have skills in areas such as martial arts, fencing, horse riding, boxing, diving and climbing. Qualifications should not be more than 5 years old.

Stage combat is taught on professional acting courses at drama schools.

Organisations such as the British Academy of Dramatic Combat, the British Academy of Stage and Screen Combat, and YoungBlood Ltd run year-long courses, workshops and classes in stage combat for practising actors.

Most stunt performers are self-employed and look for contract work with film or TV companies, but to work as a stunt artist in the UK, you need to be accepted on the Joint Industry Stunt Committee (JISC) register, and should be aged 18 or over. To register, you must present your skills qualifications to the JISC, together with evidence that you have spent a minimum of 60 days in front of a camera. Equity recommends that film and TV producers only draw up contracts with stunt performers who are on the JISC register.

Money guide

There is no formal pay scale for stunt performers, and income varies greatly. Equity sets fees for stunt work with television companies and independent producers.

Recommended daily rates are £250 to £370 for TV work, and £425 a day for film work.

Although the majority of stunt artists are freelance, you might enter full-time employment at around £11,000 per year. A very experienced performer may earn £25,000+ per year.

Related opportunities

- Actor/Actress p436
- Entertainer p443
- Special Effects Technician p451
- Choreographer p438

Further information

EQ
Suite E229, Dean Clough, Halifax, West Yorkshire HX3 5AX
01422 381618; www.thinkeq.org.uk

YoungBlood Ltd
16 Gunnersbury Close, Chiswick High Road, London W4 4AH
0845 644 9418; www.youngblood.co.uk

British Academy of Stage and Screen Combat
Suite 280, 14 Tottenham Court Road, London W1T 1JY
020 8352 0605; www.bassc.org

Performing Arts

CRCI: Q
CLCI: G

THEATRE PRODUCER/ PRODUCTION ASSISTANT

What the work involves
Producer

- Producers lead theatrical productions. You will select the performers, choose a suitable director, adapt scripts, coordinate and supervise the work of different departments as well as the artists. You will also be responsible for raising interest in future programmes to get financial backing.

Production assistant

- Assisting the producer, you will have a coordinating role on the production team distributing scripts, keeping the team up-dated, and arranging rehearsing schedules. You will need to be very well organised with good administrative skills.

The type of person suited to this work
Producer

You will need to be highly organised, creative and a good communicator. As part of the role is securing funds for the production, a background in finance or business could be helpful.

Production assistant

Production assistants must be efficient, pay attention to detail and able to work under pressure. You will need to be good at problem-solving and have excellent communication skills, be methodical and have the ability to prioritise your work.

Working conditions
Producer

This job requires negotiating and communication skills – you will be a link between the company's management structure, their backers, the artists and technical staff.

Production assistant

You need to be patient and calm to work with team members who may be under pressure.

Future prospects
Producer

This is a competitive area of work at all stages of your career. Most producers are self-employed working on a contract basis. It is important to keep up to date with developing areas of work such as cable and satellite television, and the growth and development of interactive media.

Production assistant

This is a popular and competitive area to work in. With experience, there may be opportunities for promotion to a senior production assistant, and then producer.

Advantages/disadvantages
Producer

The stress of overseeing a production, while continually

Qualifications and courses
Producer

They may have progressed from roles such as production assistant, or even runner. A number will have obtained degrees or HNDs.

Production assistant

There are no specific entry requirements for this job. However, it is highly competitive and most entrants have relevant academic qualifications and/or experience. Administrative skills, high levels of computer literacy, even shorthand – are required. Production assistants may be promoted from secretarial or administrative roles.

A levels and BTEC National qualifications are available in media production. There are HNDs and degrees in broadcasting or media production. Film and Television Freelance Training (FT2) offers training for technical and production careers.

People already employed within the industry can work towards the Skillset qualifications at Levels 2, 3 and 4. Most training is done on the job. Apprenticeships/ Skillseekers may be available to those aged 16–24.

exploring future work, can play a big part in a producer's life.

Production assistant

You will work irregular hours – possibly, away from home on location for days or weeks at a time.

Money guide
Producer

Established producers can earn salaries of around £50,000, but earnings will depend on experience, talent, regular work and the type of production.

Production assistant

£16,000–£22,000 per year is a typical salary as a trainee production assistant, but wages are lower for radio productions. You could earn up to £26,000, with some experience. £27,000–£40,000 is possible at senior levels with lots of experience.

Related opportunities

- TV, Film and Radio Producer p433
- Artistic Director p437
- Stage Manager p452

Further information

Skillset (Sector Skills Council for the audiovisual industries)
Prospect House, 80–110 New Oxford Street, London WC1A 1HB
08080 300900; www.skillset.org

WARDROBE ASSISTANT

What the work involves

- Wardrobe assistants work within the production team, making sure actors/actresses are dressed authentically for the performance.

- You may have to help artists dress for performances, making sure they are wearing their costumes and props correctly.

- In charge of the dress of several performers, you will have to clean, iron and repair costumes, look after accessories and keep the stockroom clean and tidy between performances.

- You have to keep records and catalogue all the items in stock.

The type of person suited to this work

Wardrobe assistants should have a strong interest in the theatre. You will need to be creative, with an eye for detail and have strong practical skills, including sewing. Much of the work will involve dressing and communicating with artists who may be under stress just before, or during, a performance when quick costume changes are demanded.

It will be important to have good communication skills, know how to be tactful and diplomatic, and have the ability to stay calm in a crisis.

Working conditions

You will spend most of your time backstage, often in dusty conditions. You will be using sewing or cleaning equipment to clean, iron or repair costumes. Costumes need to be taken to artists for quick changes mid-performance. You may help artists dress/undress.

Your working hours will be daytime for rehearsals and evening for performances – working public holidays and weekends. Some wardrobe assistants are attached to touring companies and work away for several weeks a year.

Future prospects

This area of employment remains as it has been for the past few years, with just a few opportunities in theatre, film or in TV. However, a young person starting out can get experience of costume work in local amateur operatic, drama or opera groups, or with a school/college productions.

With good training and experience in dressmaking and theatrical work, you may become wardrobe assistant with a company, or work in a costume museum or National Trust venues.

Advantages/disadvantages

You will receive low pay for skilled work that has big responsibilities associated with the work.

Evening work is a regular part of this job.

Working with a touring company, you will live in rented accommodation for many weeks.

Qualifications and courses

ENTRY LEVEL 1

There are no formal entry qualifications for this work. Wardrobe assistants should have skills/experience or a qualification in areas such as dressmaking, hand- and machine-sewing and pattern cutting.

Many colleges offer part-time courses such as City & Guilds Certificates in fashion, pattern cutting, theatre costume, dressmaking, etc.

It could be an advantage to have an HND, degree or postgraduate qualification in a relevant subject. Wardrobe skills are taught on most drama school technical theatre courses. The National Council for Drama Training accredits full-time vocational training courses.

Universities, colleges and art schools offer HNDs and degrees in theatre costume and related areas. You would need 5 GCSEs/S grades (A–C/1–3) for entry.

Other qualifications available include: City & Guilds Certificates/Diplomas in Design and Craft, BTEC National Certificates/Diplomas in Production Arts, BTEC Certificates/Diplomas in Fashion and Clothing (Levels 1–2), and the BTEC Level 5 Professional Diploma in Costume Management.

You will work in an exciting environment – perhaps, with famous dancers, singers and actors.

Money guide

Salaries are initially low; a wardrobe assistant with good sewing skills could expect a starting salary of around £10,500–£15,000 in the theatre, but rather more in film and TV.

An experienced wardrobe assistant could earn between £18,000–£20,000.

Large commercial theatres employ experienced wardrobe mistresses/masters who earn £25,000+ per year.

Related opportunities

- Costume Designer p178
- Knitting/Sewing Machinist p232
- Museum/Art Gallery Curator p359

Further information

CAPITB Trust
80 Richardshaw Lane, Pudsey, Leeds LS28 6BN
0113 227 3345; www.careers-in-clothing.co.uk

Film and Television Freelance Training (FT2)
4th Floor, Warwick House, 9 Warwick Street, London W1B 5LY
020 7734 5141; www.ft2.org.uk

City&
Guilds

www.cityandguilds.com/myperfectjob

Performing Arts

CRCI: Q
CLCI: G

Personal and Other Services including Hair and Beauty

This is a very wide job family and covers everything from hairdressing and beauty to cleaning to wedding consulting. You can enter this career sector with a host of different skills and qualifications. What all of the jobs have in common is that they provide a particular service that a customer has asked for so you need to be good at listening to others and giving customers exactly what they want – people in this sector have a brilliant way with people. You should also demonstrate creativity and strong practical and technical skill as many of the jobs in this family require you to use specialist equipment, and a have knowledge of health and safety.

In this section we look at the following jobs:

For similar jobs to the ones in this section turn to *Catering and Hospitality* on page 139.

BEAUTY CONSULTANT

What the work involves

- You will work in department stores and other public locations promoting and selling beauty products on behalf of cosmetics companies.

- You will provide product demonstrations to individual customers or groups, including facials, make-up applications and manicures. You will give advice and information on cosmetic products.

- Your work may involve selling items and taking payments, managing stock levels and keeping the demonstration area attractive and presentable.

- If you are self-employed you will have to control every aspect of your business including sales, finances and marketing.

The type of person suited to this work

A sociable and professional approach is important because you will meet many customers. Working on a store counter can be fast-paced so you should be able to stay calm in busy situations. You will use your communication skills to encourage customers to find out more about your products. You should also have a strong interest in helping people make the best of themselves. For applying make-up and other products you will need an eye for design and good practical skills. Numeracy skills will help you manage stock and take payments. You should enjoy the challenge of working towards sales targets.

Working conditions

You could work between 37 and 40 hours a week, with some weekend and evening hours. If you are self-employed a lot of your hours will be in the evening.

You may have to do some lifting and carrying from the stockroom. Depending on where you work, you may wear a uniform and you will normally be expected to wear the cosmetics that you are selling.

Future prospects

Beauty consultancy offers a flexible career to people who want to combine their interest in beauty with working in sales. As well as employment within department stores, there are opportunities to work in airports and hotels. You may choose to promote and sell products from your own home. With experience, you could progress to working as a team manager and then move on to an area management role. Progression might involve changing employers and moving to a larger company.

Advantages/disadvantages

This type of work is often available on a part-time or flexible basis which may suit people with other commitments.

You might spend a lot of time on your feet which may prove tiring.

You may receive a product allowance of either discounted or free cosmetic products.

Qualifications and courses

Although formal qualifications are not generally required, GCSEs may prove useful, particularly in maths and English.

The VTCT offers Level 2 Certificates in Cosmetic Make-up and Beauty Consultancy, and NVQ/SVQs are available in Retail Skills, Customer Services, and Beauty Therapy (Make-Up). There is also a diploma available in hair and beauty studies. These qualifications may be taken prior to employment as a beauty consultant or whilst working. Although these qualifications are not essential, they may be extremely valuable.

The Hairdressing and Beauty Industry Authority (HABIA) validates various beauty, hairdressing and barbering courses. There is also the possibility of completing an apprenticeship which would enable you to train on the job, whilst receiving a small salary.

If you plan on being self-employed, you must be over 18 years old. A car and driving licence would also be useful.

Training is generally a combination of in house training from more experienced colleagues and company training courses which might cover topics such as sales techniques, skincare and make-up techniques and stock recording and ordering.

Money guide

Starting salaries range from between £11,000 and £13,000 a year. With experience you could earn £16,000 per year. At senior/management levels you could earn between £20,000 and £30,000 a year.

There are usually opportunities to earn extra income through sales of beauty products. If you are a self-employed beauty consultant you will be paid on a commission and rewards scheme only.

Related opportunities

- Beauty Therapist p459
- Hairdresser/Barber p469
- Make-up Artist p445
- Nail Technician p471

Further information

Skillsmart Retail
93 Newman Street, London W1T 3EZ
020 7462 5060; www.skillsmartretail.com

Hairdressing and Beauty Industry Authority (HABIA)
Oxford House, Sixth Avenue, Sky Business Park, Robin Hood Airport, Doncaster DN9 3GG
08452 306 080; info@habia.org; www.habia.org

www.cityandguilds.com/myperfectjob

BEAUTY THERAPIST

What the work involves

- You will provide a range of face and body treatments. This could include facials, massages, electrolysis and waxing treatments.

- Your work will involve cleaning and tidying the treatment room before and after each client.

- Beauty therapists provide services in beauty salons, health clubs and hotels. They also work on a self-employed basis in rented treatment rooms or from their homes.

- You may also have to complete some administrative duties and keep client records.

The type of person suited to this work

People often choose to have a beauty therapy treatment to help them relax, so you will need a calm, confident approach. An interest in helping people with a range of therapies is essential. You will need good communication skills when advising clients about the treatments they can have. A well-presented appearance and a good level of physical fitness are also important. You will work to a high standard of health and hygiene.

Working conditions

Beauty therapists work in salons, health clubs or hotels. You will generally work between 37 and 40 hours a week, including some weekends and evenings. Therapy rooms or cubicles are private, clean and warm. You could visit clients in their homes. Beauty therapists usually wear a uniform. People with allergies to beauty products may not be suitable for this role.

Future prospects

With the increase in public awareness of the benefits of holistic therapies, people are seeking more beauty treatments. You could be based in a beauty salon or hotel, working as part of a team. With experience you could progress into a management role. You may choose to set up your own beauty therapy business or, with further experience, move into training and lecturing in beauty therapy. There are opportunities to work on cruise ships and in resorts overseas.

Advantages/disadvantages

Therapists working in health and beauty companies or clubs may be provided with free club membership and reduced cost treatments. If based in a hotel, you could get free accommodation (but with a reduction in pay) as well as meals on and off duty.

You may find the amount of standing and bending physically demanding.

Money guide

These figures are only approximate as salaries will vary depending on location and employer.

Once qualified as a beauty therapist you could earn a starting salary of around £11,000 per year. With experience you could earn between £16,000 and £19,000 a year. At senior/management levels or if you set up your own salon you could earn over £20,000 per year.

Qualifications and courses

ENTRY 3 LEVEL

Courses include NVQ/SVQs, Vocational Training Charitable Trust (VTCT) awards, BTEC Certificate/Diploma in Retail Beauty Consultancy, International Therapy Examination Council (ITEC) awards, and C&G qualifications in a range of therapies and salon management. The Diploma in hair and beauty studies may also be relevant.

Universities and higher education colleges offer HNCs/Ds, Foundation degrees and degrees in beauty therapy, cosmetic science and beauty combined with hospitality or travel and tourism. Degree programmes usually require applicants to have at least two A levels and five GCSEs grades A*-C. A BTEC National Diploma in applied science (beauty therapy) or an NVQ Level 3 will usually be accepted.

Trainee beauty therapists work towards NVQs/SVQs at Levels 2 and 3. Candidates are usually required to have some GCSEs/S grades A*–C/1–3. Level 3 is the usual qualification for a professional beauty therapist.

Apprenticeships/Skillseekers are available for candidates aged 16–24.

Beauty therapists often extend their knowledge into holistic or alternative treatments such as massage and aromatherapy. The International Federation of Professional Aromatherapists (IFPA) accredits courses at private schools and colleges in the UK.

Related opportunities

- Beauty Consultant p458
- Hairdresser/Barber p469
- Make-up Artist p445
- Nail Technician p471
- Spa Therapist p474

Further information

Hairdressing And Beauty Industry Authority
Oxford House, Sixth Avenue, Sky Business Park, Robin Hood Airport, Doncaster DN9 3GG
08452 306080; www.habia.org.uk

British Association of Beauty Therapy and Cosmetology Ltd
Ambrose House, Meteor Court, Barnett Way, Barnwood, Gloucester GL4 3GG
0845 065 9000; www.babtac.com

City& Guilds

www.cityandguilds.com/myperfectjob

CAR VALET

What the work involves

- Car valets clean and finish car exteriors and interiors using specialist equipment.

- You may clean every part of a vehicle or the exterior only. You may also clean the engine and help prepare cars for bodywork repairs.

- You will clear the interior of rubbish and polish the surfaces and windows. You will also clean the seats. For exteriors you will clean the bodywork and wheels.

- Car valets work for vehicle service centres, new and used car centres, crash repair centres and valeting companies.

The type of person suited to this work

You should be physically fit, as jobs can take between 1 and 4 hours.

You should be able to use different types of cleaning equipment and apply your knowledge of health and safety to your work.

As you will be providing a service to customers, you must work to a consistently high standard. You will also need to be a quick but thorough worker with an eye for detail.

You will be reliable and a good team player.

As with all cleaning and maintenance jobs, you should be able to cope with messy or dirty working conditions.

Working conditions

The work is very hands on and can be tiring because it involves reaching into and across vehicles. Car valets also spend a lot of time on their feet.

You may be based outside, cleaning cars on a forecourt, sometimes in poor weather conditions.

This job requires regular contact with cleaning chemicals, so it may not suit people with allergies or skin conditions.

Future prospects

Car valeting is a key part of the sales and services end of the motor vehicle industry. You could work for a large vehicle repair company or service centre as part of a valeting team.

You may choose to set up your own valeting company. Some professional car valets offer a mobile service, going out to visit customers at their premises. With experience and further training, you could progress into a technical or sales role.

Advantages/disadvantages

Car valeting jobs may include some regular travel, either when providing services to customers on their premises, or when returning vehicles to customers.

Qualifications and courses

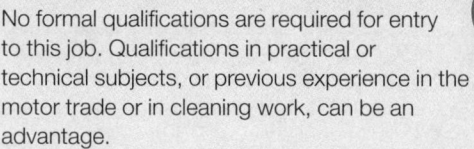

No formal qualifications are required for entry to this job. Qualifications in practical or technical subjects, or previous experience in the motor trade or in cleaning work, can be an advantage.

Entrants are usually aged 17, as a full driving licence is almost always required.

Training is done on the job. In addition to practical training, car valets may be sent on short courses run by the manufacturers of cleaning products. The British Institute of Cleaning Science offers a Car Valeting Certificate.

NVQs/SVQs Level 1 in Vehicle Maintenance and related areas include modules on valeting.

This type of job offers the chance to work in close contact with a range of cars and other vehicles.

Money guide

Starting salaries begin at £10,400 per year.

With experience you could earn £14,560.

Working overtime could possibly increase your salary to around £17,000.

Related opportunities

- Cleaner p463
- Vehicle Parts Operative p501
- Motor Vehicle Technician p241
- Butler p154

Further information

British Institute of Cleaning Science
9 Premier Court, Boarden Close, Northampton NN3 6LF
01604 678710; www.bics.org.uk

Automotive Skills
93 Newman Street, London W1T 3DT
020 7436 6373; www.automotiveskills.org.uk

Asset Skills
2 The Courtyard, 48 New North Road, Exeter, Devon EX4 4EP
01329 423399; www.assetskills.org; enquiries@assetskills.org

**City&
Guilds**

www.cityandguilds.com/myperfectjob

CARETAKER

What the work involves

- Caretakers manage the security, cleaning and general maintenance of sites such as schools, colleges and office blocks.

- In some jobs, you would combine caretaking with other roles such as cleaner, gardener, porter or security attendant.

- You will be responsible for opening and locking the premises and checking building security. You will repair broken equipment and reorder supplies.

- Your work may also involve some gardening. You may also clean parts of the site or manage the work of the site cleaners.

The type of person suited to this work

Caretakers need good communication skills, because they have a lot of contact with the people based on their premises. You may be responsible for the security of an entire site and all its contents, so it's important to have a mature, honest attitude. The ability to work independently is essential, for example when repairing broken equipment or dealing with emergencies. You should also be able to work as part of a team.

Physical fitness is essential for lifting and moving equipment, gardening work and other activities. You will work to a high standard of health and safety at all times.

Working conditions

Whilst some caretakers work full time, many work on a split-shift basis with some evening and weekend work.

Caretaking work is physically demanding. Some of your work will be based outside using ladders and other tools.

Caretakers work with cleaning chemicals and wear protective clothing such as gloves and overalls. The job may not suit people with allergies or skin conditions.

Future prospects

Caretaking is an essential part of premises management. Being the only person on a whole site early in the morning with responsibility for security can be challenging.

Many locations, such as schools, only employ one caretaker, so you may need to change employers and locations to progress. Larger employers may employ a small team of caretakers. With experience you could work up to senior caretaker level.

Advantages/disadvantages

As the premises keyholder, you may be on call for emergencies.

This job can be sociable and caretakers often build up a good working relationship with the people based on their premises.

It is possible to do this kind of work on a part-time basis.

Qualifications and courses

No formal qualifications are required for entry to this job. Some GCSEs/S grades (A–E/1–5), particularly English, maths and practical subjects, may be an advantage. However, hands-on skills and experience in basic DIY, carpentry, painting and decorating or glazing are more important.

Experience in maintenance or security work is useful, as is a driving licence. Within some areas, for example schools and colleges, you will need to pass a police check.

Maturity is an advantage and employers often prefer older applicants with relevant experience.

Caretakers are trained on the job. It may be possible for entrants to work towards an NVQ/SVQ Level 3 in Property and Caretaking Supervision. Caretakers can also work towards the Chartered Institute of Housing's Level 3 Certificate in Housing, specialist pathway in Caretaking and Concierge Services. This can be achieved in 1 year through part-time study, distance learning, or in-house training with an employer.

Money guide

Starting salaries range from £12,480 to £14,500 per year.

With experience it is possible to earn between £16,000 and £24,000.

You could earn a higher salary as a senior or mobile caretaker.

In some work areas, such as education, caretakers are offered on-site subsidised housing as part of their contract.

Related opportunities

- Cleaner p463
- Refuse and Recycling Operative p473
- Hotel Porter p150
- Labourer/Construction Operative p86

Further information

Chartered Institute of Housing
Octavia House, Westwood Way, Coventry CV4 8JP
024 7685 1700; www.cih.org

Chartered Institute of Housing – Scotland
6 Palmerston Place, Edinburgh EH12 5AA
0131 225 4544; www.cih.org/home_scotland

The Caretakers' website
www.thecaretakers.net

www.cityandguilds.com/myperfectjob

Personal and Other Services including Hair and Beauty

CRCI: RB
CLCI: IJ

CHIMNEY SWEEP

What the work involves

- Chimney sweeps help prevent chimney fires and dangerous fuel emissions by inspecting and cleaning chimney and flue systems, heating appliances and vents.

- Your work will involve using brush and vacuum equipment to clear chimneys and vents of blockages.

- You will provide information and advice to customers on the repair and maintenance of their chimneys.

The type of person suited to this work

Chimney sweeps combine their professional knowledge with practical skills to protect public safety. You will need a good knowledge of different types of chimney and flue systems. Operating brush and vacuum chimney cleaning equipment requires good manual skills.

You will visit customers in their homes, so you should have a friendly, professional attitude. Your communication skills will help you to provide advice on correctly maintaining chimney systems. In a job that involves travelling and working alone, a good level of physical fitness is essential.

Working conditions

When clearing chimneys, you will wear protective clothing, such as overalls, gloves, helmet, eye guard and respiratory protection.

Travel to different locations is a regular part of the work, so holding a driving licence is essential.

You may work unsocial hours, at weekends or evenings, to suit customers.

Future prospects

Chimney sweeping is a specialist but essential service. After gaining the relevant experience and professional qualifications, you could set up your own business, providing services within your local area. Most chimney sweeps build up a network of loyal and regular customers.

You could also offer additional roofing or ventilation services. There may be opportunities to work with another professional or to join a small specialist company.

Advantages/disadvantages

Whilst the job involves meeting different people, the actual work is usually undertaken alone.

Most chimney sweeps work on a self-employed basis, which can lead to some job insecurity, particularly at the start of their careers.

Money guide

Most chimney sweeps are self-employed and are paid on a job-by-job basis.

Qualifications and courses

There are no formal entry requirements, but basic qualifications in English and maths are useful. Previous experience of practical/manual work is an advantage. You would normally be trained on the job by an experienced chimney sweep.

Trainee chimney sweeps can work towards membership of the National Association of Chimney Sweeps (NACS). NACS provides an induction course accredited by CITB and City & Guilds, covering basic chimney sweeping techniques and health and safety. On completion of the training, sweeps become probationary members of NACS until they have gained sufficient experience and on-site training to work as professional sweeps.

NACS also provides an NVQ Level 2 in Chimney Engineering based on assessments in the workplace and at the NACS centre.

The other professional body for chimney sweeps is the Guild of Master Sweeps. To become a member, you must hold a City & Guilds 7641 qualification in Chimney Cleaning and successfully complete the Guild entrance exam.

NACS also provides short courses in particular areas of the world. To be qualified to carry out inspections and work on gas appliances you need to gain a certificate of competence through the Accredited Certification Scheme (ACS), leading to registration with CORGI (Council of Registered Gas Engineers).

A driving licence is required for driving and transporting equipment to customers' homes.

Earnings will depend on a sweep's speed at the task and the hours worked. If working full time you could expect to earn between £16,000 and £25,000 per year.

Related opportunities

- Heating and Ventilating Engineer p104
- Roofer p122
- Steeplejack p127
- Cleaner p463

Further information

National Association of Chimney Sweeps
Unit 15, Emerald Way, Stone Business Park, Stone, Staffordshire ST15 0SR
01785 811732; www.chimneyworks.co.uk

Guild of Master Sweeps
www.guild-of-master-sweeps.co.uk

City&
Guilds

www.cityandguilds.com/myperfectjob

CLEANER

What the work involves

Carpet/upholstery

- You will use specialist equipment to clean carpets, curtains and furniture in private homes, offices and other locations.

- You may specialise in cleaning specific types of carpets or offer additional carpet and upholstery repair services.

Domestic

- You will clean, dust and tidy the floors and surfaces of private homes.

- To undertake your job you will work with a vacuum cleaner, mop and other equipment.

Industrial

- You will use specialist equipment to clean and clear the surfaces and interiors of industrial systems in factories and other sites.

- Industrial cleaners usually work in a team for cleaning companies that provide services for businesses such as chemical manufacturers and engineering companies.

Street

- Working as part of a team you will maintain the clean appearance of streets, car parks and other large areas. This will involve sweeping away rubbish and emptying council bins.

- Street cleaners work as part of street-cleansing teams employed by local councils or for the companies that provide these services to councils.

Window

- You will clean the exterior windows of private homes, offices, shops and other buildings.

- You will use a ladder and other equipment to reach and clean windows.

Hospital

- Your job will be to make sure all areas of the hospital are kept clean, free of germs and safe for patients, staff and visitors.

- You will use special cleaning equipment and chemicals and you may work in theatres and wards.

The type of person suited to this work

Cleaners provide an important public service, so you should enjoy working to a high standard. You will also need a down-to-earth, practical attitude to your work. You should be able to cope with dirty or messy conditions. Practical skills are very important when using your hands to clean or to operate cleaning equipment. A good knowledge of health and safety is essential. If you are self-employed, you will need good financial management skills.

You should enjoy meeting a wide range of people and providing a public service. You will also be a good team player. A well-motivated, reliable and highly trustworthy approach is essential.

Working conditions

Cleaning is physically demanding work which involves carrying equipment and working on your feet.

Because the job often involves the use of specialist cleaning chemicals it may not suit people with skin conditions or allergies.

You will have to deal with messy or dirty conditions on a regular basis.

Window

As a window cleaner, you will need a head for heights.

Hospital

You might have to clean theatres and wards. Some of this can be distressing. Your work will fit around the needs of the nurses and doctors, and could include speaking to patients and their families.

Future prospects

Cleaning is a growing industry and there is currently a shortage of skilled cleaners in a range of areas. There are opportunities to work on a temporary basis, to suit other commitments. Increasingly, there are routes to develop a career as a professional cleaner on a permanent basis. You could work for a large cleaning company as an industrial cleaner, carpet cleaner or domestic cleaner. Or you could choose to set up your own domestic or window-cleaning business.

There has been interest in keeping hospitals clean due to the recent problems with MRSA. The role that cleaners and all hospital staff play in reducing this are now recognised and additional training is being offered to hospital cleaners.

Advantages/disadvantages

This type of work is often available on a shift basis, which may suit people with other commitments.

The work can be physically tiring, with the risk of injury from the equipment or environment you are in contact with. However, most employers provide health and safety training.

You may have to work in poor weather conditions, if based outdoors, for example as a window or street cleaner.

Money guide

Salaries vary according to the type of work you do.

Personal and Other Services including Hair and Beauty

CRCI: RB
CLCI: IJ

Carpet/upholstery

With experience – and if employed by a large company – you could earn £16,000–£20,000 per year. Top rates are unlikely in the present economic recession when carpet sales have slumped.

Domestic

Domestic cleaners are often employed on an hourly basis, and may work for a number of employers. Working full time you could get £11,000–£13,000 (more in London).

Industrial

Salaries vary starting at £11,000. With experience and supervisory responsibilities, you could earn up to £16,000. Shift allowances are possible.

Street

Salaries vary from £11,000 to £14,500. With experience, this can increase to £16,000.

Window

Self-employed window cleaners can earn £11,000–£16,000.

Hospital

Average salaries for hospital cleaners are between £11,000 and £14,560.

Related opportunities

- Caretaker p461
- Car Valet p460
- Care Assistant p576
- Pest Control Technician p472

Further information

Asset Skills
2 The Courtyard, 48 New North Road, Exeter, Devon EX4 4EP
01392 423399; www.assetskills.org

Qualifications and courses

No formal qualifications are required for these jobs although basic numeracy is useful for measuring cleaning fluids.

Certain types of cleaning may have specific practical requirements, for example the ability to work at heights, physical fitness and (usually) a driving licence for window cleaners.

Cleaners are trained on the job, and usually receive training from their employer in areas such as health and safety and use of equipment.

Cleaners can work towards NVQ/SVQ Levels 1 and 2 in Cleaning and Support Services. Specialist options are available at Level 2 in Cleaning Building Interiors, Cleaning Carpets and Soft Furnishings, Cleaning Food Premises and Cleaning Windows, Glass and Facade Surfaces. City & Guilds offer Level 2 and 3 awards in Cleaning Science and Supervision. Cleaners can also work towards the British Institute of Cleaning Science (BICS) Cleaning Operators Proficiency Certificate and other specialist certified courses.

Apprenticeships/Skillseekers may be available for people aged 16–24.

British Institute of Cleaning Science
9 Premier Court, Boarden Close, Northampton NN3 6LF
01604 678710; www.bics.org.uk

National Carpet Cleaners Association
62c London Road, Oadby, Leicester LE2 5DH
0116 271 9550; www.ncca.co.uk

Federation for Window Cleaners
Summerfield House, Harrogate Road, Stockport, Cheshire SK5 6HQ
0161 432 8754; www.nfmwgc.com

City&Guilds

www.cityandguilds.com/myperfectjob

CREMATORIUM TECHNICIAN

What the work involves

- Crematorium technicians assist with the running of the crematorium and cemetery premises.

- Your work will involve operating cremation equipment to a high standard of health and safety. You will ensure that the cremated remains are stored and disposed of correctly.

- You will help manage the chapel and cemetery and attend cremation ceremonies.

- Crematorium technicians often combine their work with assisting with cemetery duties, such as excavating graves and grounds maintenance. However, grave digging work is mostly undertaken by contractors working for local authorities.

The type of person suited to this work

Meeting and working with bereaved people requires a mature, sympathetic attitude. You will use your communication skills to liaise with people in the process of cremation ceremonies. A good level of physical fitness is helpful in a role that covers a wide range of activities. You should also have good manual handling skills to operate cremation equipment.

It's important that cremations are undertaken to a high standard of health and safety, so you should be able to follow strict working guidelines. Office and ICT skills can be helpful in this job. The ability to work as part of a team is also useful.

Working conditions

This can be a tiring job due to the range of activities involved and the physical requirements of operating cremation machinery.

Crematorium technicians need good practical handling skills to operate cremation equipment correctly.

You will normally work 37–40 hours a week, with some overtime.

Future prospects

Due to changing public attitudes, the number of cremations is increasing, as is the demand for skilled professionals.

Crematorium technicians are usually employed by local councils. Most are trained by more experienced colleagues whilst working. With experience, you could progress to working as a senior crematorium technician and manage a team of technicians.

Advantages/disadvantages

This role provides the opportunity to provide support to people at an important and challenging time.

The nature of the job means this work will be distressing at times.

Qualifications and courses

There are no formal entry requirements for this type of work, and training is done on the job.

Trainees follow the Crematorium Technicians' Training Scheme (CTTS) provided by the Institute of Cemetery and Crematorium Management (ICCM). The scheme consists of a BTEC Intermediate Certificate and a BTEC Advanced Certificate. Employees may also work towards NVQ/SVQ Level 2 in Amenity Horticulture (Cemeteries and Graveyards).

Another work-based training route is provided by the Federation of British Cremation Authority's (FBCA) TEST scheme.

Experienced crematorium technicians can progress to management roles. The ICCM Diploma in Cemetery and Crematorium Management can be studied by correspondence. The ICCM also operates a Continuing Professional Development scheme for crematorium staff at all levels.

A driving licence is useful.

Money guide

Starting salaries are around £11,000 per year.

With experience you could earn £17,500.

At senior/management level you could earn £20,000+.

Related opportunities

- Embalmer p467
- Funeral Worker p468
- Cleaner p463
- Pest Control Technician p472

Further information

Institute of Cemetery and Crematorium Management
City of London Cemetery, Aldersbrook Road,
London E12 5DQ
020 8989 4661; www.iccm-uk.com

The Cremation Society of Great Britain
2nd Floor, Brecon House, 16/16a Albion Place,
Maidstone ME14 5DZ
01622 688292; www.crematorium.org.uk

The Federation of Burial and Cremation Authorities (FBCA)
41 Salisbury Road, Carshalton SM5 3HA
020 8669 4521; www.fbca.org.uk

www.cityandguilds.com/myperfectjob

DRY CLEANING/ LAUNDRY ASSISTANT/MANAGER

What the work involves

Assistant

- You will greet and serve customers, take and return their dry cleaning and laundry orders, and process payments. Your work will involve operating machinery, putting clothes through laundry and dry-cleaning processes, and folding and preparing the clothes and other items for collection.

Manager

- You will take customer orders and deal with queries. You will manage budgets, staff rotas and stock levels for your shop or premises. You will also be involved in maintaining the security and health and safety of the premises and buildings. You will manage the dry cleaning and laundry machinery.

The type of person suited to this work

Customer care and communication skills are essential. You will need a good knowledge of how to clean and process different types of materials as well as a good level of physical fitness.

You will be handling cash and managing budgets so you will need good money management skills and a well-organised approach to your work. You should also be reliable and self-motivated.

Working conditions

You may have to wear a uniform whilst working. It is likely that you will have to work some weekend or evening hours. In some jobs you will have close contact with potentially hazardous chemicals and cleaning processes, which may be unsuitable for people with allergies or skin conditions.

Future prospects

There is a growing demand for efficient, reliable laundry and dry-cleaning services. As an assistant, you could move into supervisory or management roles by gaining further experience and qualifications. You could also progress to running your own laundry or dry-cleaning business.

Advantages/disadvantages

This type of work is often available part time which may suit people with other commitments.

Some employers pay overtime for bank holiday and holiday period working.

Money guide

Earnings vary widely throughout the industry and will depend on the location and size of your employer.

Qualifications and courses

Assistant

There are no formal minimum qualifications for this type of work. Communication and numeracy skills are useful. Training normally takes place on the job.

You could gain Practical Laundry Certificates through the Guild of Cleaners and Launderers. You could also work towards examinations through the Guild's Qualification Star Scheme. NVQs/SVQs are available too.

If aged 16–24, you could undertake an Apprenticeship/ Skillseekers opportunity.

Manager

A good level of general education is usually required. With experience, laundry assistants can become supervisors and managers.

It can be helpful to have gained Practical Laundry Certificates through the Guild of Cleaners and Launderers. NVQ/SVQ Level 2 in Team Leading and Level 3 and 4 in Management may be useful. You could go on to achieve a supervisory certificate and intermediate qualifications through the Guild of Cleaners and Launderers. Additional training courses are available through organisations such as the SATRA Technology Centre and the Textile Services Association.

As a dry cleaning assistant you could expect a salary of £11,500 per year. Salaries for managers range between £16,500 and £18,000. Senior managers in larger companies can receive £25,000+.

Related opportunities

- Cleaner p463
- Car Valet p460
- Textile Operative p252

Further information

Textile Services Association
7 Churchill Court, 58 Station Road, North Harrow, Middlesex HA2 7SA
020 8863 7755; www.tsa-uk.org

Guild of Cleaners and Launderers
1 Wellfield Road, Offerton, Stockport, Cheshire SK2 6AS
0845 600 1838; www.gcl.org.uk

City& Guilds

www.cityandguilds.com/myperfectjob

EMBALMER

What the work involves

- Embalmers prepare the bodies of deceased people for funerals and for viewing by their relatives. Embalming also helps to reduce the spread of infection.

- You will use specialist equipment to remove all blood and gases from the deceased person's body and replace these with disinfecting fluid.

- Your work will involve preparing and cleaning the embalming equipment and treatment area.

- Embalmers work in operating rooms within funeral parlours.

The type of person suited to this work

You must be able to cope with working with the bodies of deceased people. A respectful approach to your work is essential. You may have to deal with distressing sights so a mature, detached and down-to-earth attitude is very important.

You should be able to work to a high standard of health and hygiene. You will need good manual handling skills for undertaking embalming work because you will be using a range of equipment.

Embalming work involves presenting a deceased person in the most positive way for grieving relatives. A creative flair and attention to detail will help you to achieve this.

Working conditions

Embalmers work in operating rooms within funeral parlours. These are maintained to a very high standard of hygiene and kept at a low temperature.

Whilst embalming you will wear protective clothing such as latex gloves. The regular contact with chemicals means that this job may not suit people with skin conditions or allergies.

Embalming is physically demanding work and you should expect to work irregular hours and be on call.

Future prospects

Embalming is often an integral part of the funeral care process, so there is constant demand for embalmers. You could gain employment with a funeral care company or you may choose to work on a self-employed basis, providing services for a number of funeral companies.

There are opportunities to work abroad. With extensive experience, you could go into teaching or training.

There are around 1300 qualified embalmers in the UK, but the industry has a slow turnover of staff and getting in may be difficult.

Advantages/disadvantages

There are opportunities for self-employment, working for a number of employers at the same time.

There are also opportunities to work overseas.

Qualifications and courses

There are no formal entry requirements for working as an embalmer, but GCSEs/S grades including English, maths, chemistry, biology and religious studies may be useful.

Training is mainly on the job, with part-time tuition from a registered tutor at weekends or evenings, or through distance learning. Most embalmers work for qualifications awarded by the International Examinations Board of Embalmers (IEBE).

The BIE training is modular, and trainees must pass the foundation module and test before proceeding with the rest of the training. Once you have passed the foundation module, you can register with the BIE as a student member.

The main BIE training involves modules in anatomy, physiology, bacteriology and practical embalming, including examinations and practical work. Once you have passed these you can apply for full membership of the BIE.

Some embalmers train to work in specialist areas, such as with disaster teams, embalming the bodies of victims.

This can be distressing work, so you will need to be able to stay detached and professional.

Money guide

Starting salaries begin at around £12,480 per year.

With experience you could earn £17,800.

At senior levels or, with a good reputation professionally, it is possible to earn £20,000+.

Related opportunities

- Crematorium Technician p465
- Funeral Work p468

Further information

British Institute of Embalmers
21c Station Road, Knowle, Solihull B93 0HL
01564 778991; www.bioe.co.uk

The Federation of Burial and Cremation Authorities (FBCA)
41 Salisbury Road, Carshalton SM5 3HA
020 8669 4521; www.fbca.org.uk

City&Guilds

www.cityandguilds.com/myperfectjob

Personal and Other Services including Hair and Beauty

CRCI: RA
CLCI: IP

FUNERAL WORKER

What the work involves

- Funeral workers coordinate funeral and cremation arrangements.

- You will liaise with the family of the deceased, offering advice and taking note of the details they would like included in the funeral ceremony.

- By providing practical arrangements for the funeral you will assist in matters such as organising the funeral location. You will also attend at the funeral.

- Some funeral directors assist with preparing the deceased person's body for viewing by relatives or for the funeral itself. You might also undertake embalming work.

The type of person suited to this work

You need to have a sensitive and mature attitude to your work.

You must have excellent communication skills for providing advice to bereaved relatives. You will need to be able to work to a high standard of health and safety at all times.

For liaising with local authorities and completing paperwork you will need a good knowledge of the relevant legal issues, and to be able to manage a business you will need good office and budgetary skills. A good knowledge of different cultures and religions is helpful.

Working conditions

Funeral directors work in funeral homes or centres based within high-street outlets or other areas.

This job can be physically demanding.

You may work on call at weekends and in the evenings. You may also be required to work extra hours during busy times.

Funeral directors must dress smartly and usually wear suits.

Future prospects

Most people start a career in this area by gaining experience as a funeral operative or assistant. They learn the varied aspects of the job from more experienced colleagues and work towards professional qualifications.

You could work for one of the large funeral services companies or for a smaller company. With experience, you could work as a funeral director in the UK or abroad. With additional experience, you could set up your own funeral services company.

Advantages/disadvantages

Depending on the size of funeral company you work for, you may be on call on a regular basis, which can affect your personal life.

Providing a professional sympathetic service to people experiencing a very difficult time can be rewarding.

Money guide

Starting salaries are around £12,500 per year.

With experience as a funeral director's assistant, you could earn £16,000–£24,000.

Qualifications and courses

There are no minimum academic qualifications to work as a funeral director. You will normally start as funeral operative or assistant and learn whilst working. Your choice of qualifications and training will depend on the company you work for. For funeral operatives/assistants with driving duties, a driving licence is essential.

BTEC and SQA offer vocational qualifications for people working as funeral operatives/assistants and directors. The Certificate in Funeral Services is for operatives/assistants, and the Advanced Diploma in Funeral Directing is for funeral directors.

NVQs/SVQs are available in Funeral Services at Levels 2 and 3, and there is a Level 4 qualification in Funeral Services Management.

Another route is to gain the National Association of Funeral Directors' (NAFD) Foundation Certificate in Funeral Directing. This is an introductory course which candidates must have completed before they can start the NAFD Diploma in Funeral Directing (DipFD). In order to work towards this professional qualification you must have a minimum of 2 years' employment in funeral services. This includes experience of personally arranging at least 25 funerals.

Once working in funeral services you could choose to go on to gain the NAFD and Institute of Leadership and Management's Diploma in Funeral Service Management, or the Higher Certificate in Funeral Service Management of the British Institute of Funeral Directors (BIFD). To be eligible to do these you must have the NAFD Diploma in Funeral Directing or be a full member of the BIFD.

At senior/management level, you could earn £32,000+.

Additional benefits may include a car.

Related opportunities

- Crematorium Technician p465
- Embalmer p467
- Cleaner p463
- Pest Control Technician p472

Further information

National Association of Funeral Directors
618 Warwick Road, Solihull B91 1AA
0845 230 1343; www.nafd.org.uk

British Institute of Funeral Directors
41 Bridge Street, Tranent, East Lothian EH33 1AH
0800 032 2733; www.bifd.org.uk

City&
Guilds

www.cityandguilds.com/myperfectjob

HAIRDRESSER/BARBER

What the work involves

- Hairdressers shampoo, cut and style clients' hair to a range of modern or classic looks. You may also provide dry or wet shaves and haircuts to male clients.

- You will discuss hair treatments with clients and may carry out colouring, tinting, perming and fixing hair extensions. You will also give advice on general haircare and hair products.

- At senior levels, you may provide training to junior hairdressers.

- Most hairdressers/barbers are based in salons in high streets and other areas. Some work as mobile hairdressers, providing services to clients in their own homes.

The type of person suited to this work

Cutting and styling hair involves close personal contact with clients so hairdressers need to be able to make people feel relaxed. Good communication skills and a friendly manner are essential.

You should have an interest in fashion, a creative flair and an eye for detail. You will need manual dexterity when using specialist chemicals and equipment required to style, perm and colour customers' hair.

In smaller salons you may work on the reception desk booking appointments and taking cash, so you will have to be efficient, confident and numerate.

Some salons require staff to be able to offer a wider choice of services, such as nail and beauty treatments.

Working conditions

Most of your work will be indoors in salons or clients' homes.

Hairdressing involves standing and bending over customers for long periods of the day, so you will need to be physically fit.

Future prospects

The demand for high quality hairdressing/barbering services is growing, with most areas likely to have a salon. You could work in a salon or set up your own business. If working as a mobile hairdresser, you could provide services to people in hospitals, care homes or prisons as well as private clients.

There are opportunities to work on cruise ships. With further beauty therapy training you could work in film, television or the theatre.

Advantages/disadvantages

Hairdressers/barbers have regular contact with beauty products and chemicals, which means that this type of work may not suit people with skin conditions or allergies.

The demand for qualified and experienced hairdressers is increasing.

Qualifications and courses

ENTRY LEVEL 1

There are no minimum entry requirements for this job. Some people start as unqualified assistants/trainees and progress with experience.

Hairdressing can be studied full time at college by taking an NVQ/SVQ (Levels 1–3 in hairdressing, Levels 2 and 3 in barbering). Some NVQs combine hairdressing with beauty therapy, and it is possible to specialise in ladies' or gentlemen's hairdressing.

The Freelance Hair and Beauty Federation (FHBF) runs courses for hairdressers on planning, setting up and managing their business, and ongoing continuing personal development courses.

NVQ/SVQs validated by the Hairdressing and Beauty Industry Authority (HABIA) can be taken part time whilst working in a hairdressing salon or barber's, or you can undertake an Apprenticeship/Skillseekers if aged 16–24.

Qualified hairdressers can take more specialised courses through part-time study, for example City & Guilds certificates, NVQ units, VTCT/ITEC beauty therapy qualifications. It is possible to take an NVQ/SVQ Level 4 or HNC in Salon Management.

A few Foundation degrees in Hairdressing and Salon Management are also available.

Money guide

As a trainee at entry level you could earn the national minimum wage of £9210 or £10,400 per year, aged 17 or 18.

With experience and full training you could earn £12,480–£16,500.

Top national hairdressers earn £20,000–£30,000+, even £40,000 for famous stylists.

Tips from customers will increase salaries at all levels.

Related opportunities

- Beauty Therapist p459
- Image Consultant p470
- Make-up Artist p445
- Nail Technician p471

Further information

Hairdressing And Beauty Industry Authority
Oxford House, Sixth Avenue, Sky Business Park, Robin Hood Airport, Doncaster DN9 3GG
08452 306080; www.habia.org.uk

The Hairdressing Council
30 Sydenham Road, Croydon CR0 2EF
020 8760 7010; www.haircouncil.org.uk

City & Guilds

www.cityandguilds.com/myperfectjob

Personal and Other Services including Hair and Beauty

CRCI: RC
CLCI: IL

IMAGE CONSULTANT/ PERSONAL SHOPPER

Personal and Other Services including Hair and Beauty

CRCI: RC
CLCI: IK

What the work involves

Image consultant

- You will advise people on how to make the most of their appearance using clothes, accessories and make-up. You will help them improve their confidence, body language and communication skills. You will undertake consultations with clients to help them choose clothes and accessories that match their lifestyle and desired image.

Personal shopper

- You will provide customers with advice in all aspects of fashion from clothes to beauty products. Using information on their body shape, skin tone, budget and taste you will select items for them and provide them with honest opinions.

The type of person suited to this work

Image is as much about confidence as it is about looks, so a strong interest in helping people make the best of themselves is essential. Excellent communication skills are required for working in consultation with individual clients or large groups. As you will be working around clients' ideas and interests, you should be flexible. You will have an eye for design, a good sense of colour coordination and a strong interest in clothes.

Working conditions

Freelance image consultants usually have some flexibility in their working hours, but some evening or weekend work is likely. Travelling to different locations is often a part of this job.

Some meet and work with clients in their homes or workplaces.

Personal shoppers may see their clients in a lounge area which incorporates a fitting room and refreshments. Your hours will also be varied, including some evening and weekend hours.

Future prospects

With experience, an image consultant could develop their own image consultancy or work for a specialist company or salon. Many freelance image consultants offer classes to companies as well as working with individual clients.

High-profile image consultants provide advice and support to celebrities, company managers and even politicians.

Personal shoppers do not have a set route of progression. Within larger companies they could be promoted into a managerial role. They could also move into image consultancy.

Advantages/disadvantages

This type of work provides the satisfaction of helping to build people's confidence and communication skills in the workplace and in their personal lives.

There is no set progression route and so promotion may prove difficult.

There is the possibility of self-employment.

Qualifications and courses

Image consultant

There are no set entry requirements for this career, but experience in a related field is usual.

Entrants may hold a degree or HND in a related area, such as beauty therapy, marketing or media. Candidates need at least four GCSEs/S grades (A–C/1–3) for HNC/D courses; for degrees, two A levels/H grades and five GCSEs/S grades (A–C/1–3) are required. Candidates coming from a background in hairdressing have usually attained NVQ Level 4.

The professional qualification for image consultants is The Federation of Image Consultants (TFIC)/City & Guilds joint award in Image Consultancy. It is available at private training colleges. TFIC also offers seminars and workshops for the professional development of its members.

Personal shopper

Although there are no specific requirements you should have had experience within the beauty or fashion industry; either on the shop floor or within a fashion house. Most personal shoppers have worked within a successful retail environment.

Money guide

Image consultants usually charge for individual sessions. This can vary from £35 to £80+ per session. Charges vary according to a consultant's experience and expertise. Very experienced image consultants can earn up to £30,000–£40,000, depending on location.

Personal shoppers might have a starting salary of between £16,000 and £22,000 per year; this could increase to over £30,000 a year with experience.

Related opportunities

- Beauty Consultant p458
- Make-up Artist p445
- Fashion Designer p181

Further information

Hairdressing And Beauty Industry Authority
Oxford House, Sixth Avenue, Sky Business Park,
Robin Hood Airport, Doncaster DN9 3GG
08452 306080; www.habia.org.uk

Federation of Image Consultants
The Gables, Lammas, Norwich NR10 5AF
07010 701018; www.tfic.org.uk

City& Guilds

www.cityandguilds.com/myperfectjob

NAIL TECHNICIAN

What the work involves

- Nail technicians provide a range of nail treatments to clients, including manicures, nail extensions, nail art and nail jewellery.

- You will prepare clients' hands and nails for treatments. You may also provide advice on nail care and maintenance.

- Depending on the treatment you are providing, you will work with a range of beauty products and equipment such as brushes, stencils and airbrushes.

- You will clean and tidy the treatment area before and after each client.

The type of person suited to this work

Nail technicians work with many people so you should have good communication skills and a friendly manner. A professional appearance is also important. You will need excellent manual handling skills to undertake nail design work. In addition, a good knowledge of nail and beauty products is important. An eye for design and an interest in fashion are essential.

It will also be important that you are able to maintain a high standard of health and hygiene at all times.

If you work as a freelance technician you will need good financial management and business skills. You should also be able to cope with travelling to different work locations.

Working conditions

Nail technicians work in nail or beauty salons and other locations. Mobile nail technicians provide treatments to clients in their own homes.

Salon-based technicians usually work between 30 and 40 hours a week with some evening/weekend work.

Nail technicians come into regular contact with chemicals, so the job might not suit people with skin conditions or allergies. You may wear a uniform and face mask whilst working.

Future prospects

With nail salons opening in high streets throughout the country, nail technology is a popular area of beauty therapy. Beauty and hairdressing salons are increasingly offering nail treatments as a service.

You could work as a freelance nail technician, providing services to care homes and hotels as well as private clients. If you gain additional professional qualifications you could offer other therapies.

There are opportunities to work abroad or on cruise ships.

Advantages/disadvantages

Working on a freelance basis can allow you to work flexible hours but unsocial hours are likely.

Some salons provide bonus schemes and commission

Qualifications and courses

There are no formal entry requirements for this career. However, in many areas nail technicians must be licensed by their local environmental health department. A nationally recognised qualification is required to become licensed, and some local authorities insist on an NVQ/SVQ.

Relevant courses include the Vocational Training Charitable Trust (VTCT) Certificate in Nail Treatments with the option to specialise in Nail Technology or Nail Art and NVQ/SVQ in Nail Services at Levels 2 and 3. A nail services unit is included in NVQ/SVQ Beauty Therapy at Levels 2 and 3. The BTEC National Award, Certificate or Diploma in Beauty Therapy Sciences includes a specialist unit in nail technology.

The qualification recommended by the Association of Nail Technicians (ANT) is the nail unit of NVQ/SVQ Level 3 in Beauty Therapy.

Apprenticeships/Skillseekers are available to those aged 16–24.

payments for product sales. Additional perks include free or reduced cost beauty treatments.

Money guide

Freelance nail technicians usually charge per job. This varies according to the nature of the treatment, from £12 to £50+.

Starting salaries are around £10,600- £11,500 per year.

With experience, and fully trained, you could earn £15,000–£20,000.

At senior/management level you could earn £25,000+.

Related opportunities

- Beauty Therapist p459
- Hairdresser/Barber p469
- Make-up Artist p445
- Image Consultant p470

Further information

British Association of Beauty Therapy and Cosmetology (BABTAC)
Ambrose House, Meteor Court, Barnett Way, Barnwood, Gloucester GL4 3GG
0845 069 900; www.babtac.com

International Therapy Examination Council (ITEC)
2nd Floor, Chiswick Gate, 598–608 Chiswick High Road, London W4 5RT
020 8994 4141; www.itecworld.co.uk

Confederation of International Beauty Therapy and Cosmetology (CIBTAC)
CIBTAC Administration Office, Meteor Court, Barnett Way, Barnwood, Gloucester GL4 3GG
0845 069 900; www.cibtac.com

PEST CONTROL TECHNICIAN

What the work involves

- Pest control technicians protect public health by treating and eradicating infestations of insects and vermin such as cockroaches and rats.

- Pest control technicians work in private homes, offices, shops and other sites.

- Your job may involve investigating or monitoring a site to check for pests.

- You will use a range of specialist chemicals and equipment. Your work may involve fitting traps or spraying areas with chemicals.

- In some situations you will provide advice to customers on the prevention of pest problems.

The type of person suited to this work

This job is all about protecting public health so you should be able to work to a high standard of health and safety. Working with chemical treatments and specialist equipment demands a professional approach. You will need to be calm when dealing with large numbers of insects, rodents and other pests. A strong stomach will also help you cope with working in unpleasant conditions.

Physical fitness and good manual handling skills are essential. You will need to be able to communicate and have a tactful approach when providing advice to customers. You will use your writing skills to keep records and write reports.

Working conditions

Whilst not all pest control work is unpleasant, dealing with dirty or unhygienic situations is a likely part of the job.

You will travel to different locations on a regular basis.

Pest control technicians must wear protective clothing, such as overalls and eye goggles. They work with a range of chemicals, so the job may not suit people with skin conditions or allergies.

Future prospects

Pest control technicians provide an important service to domestic homes, factories, offices and other locations in cities and rural areas. Many pest control technicians run their own businesses. Others gain work with local councils or with specialist companies.

With experience you could progress to supervising teams of staff, managing a large pest control company or working in a management role for local councils.

Advantages/disadvantages

Some employers provide extra pay for overtime.

This type of work is sometimes available on a flexible basis.

Qualifications and courses

ENTRY LEVEL 2

A good standard of education is required, with GCSEs/S grades (A–E/1–5) in English, maths and science being useful. Because the job involves using specialist equipment and dangerous substances, some employers prefer candidates to be over 18.

A driving licence is usually required.

Training is undertaken on the job, supervised by an experienced technician. There may also be opportunities to attend training courses.

The entry-level qualification for the industry is the British Pest Control Association/Royal Society for the Promotion of Health Certificate in Pest Control, which equates to NVQ Level 2.

NVQs/SVQs are available in Pest Control Supervision at Level 3. The British Pest Control Association also offers a Pest Control Diploma and specialist short courses in fumigation, rodents, insects, bird management and field biology, and a Technical Inspector Certificate.

The British Wood Preserving and Damp-Proofing Association offer short courses covering insect infestation. The National Proficiency Training Council (NPTC) offers Certificates in Competence in the use of pesticides in rural areas.

Money guide

As a trainee you could start at around £12,000 per year.

With experience and qualifications, this rises to £16,500–£23,500.

At senior levels you could earn £30,000+.

Related opportunities

- Environmental Health Practitioner/Officer p35
- Refuse and Recycling Operative p473
- Cleaner p463
- Toxicologist p535

Further information

British Pest Control Association
Ground Floor, Gleneagles House, Vernongate, Derby DE1 1UP
0870 6092687; www.bpca.org.uk

National Pest Technicians Association
NPTA House, Hall Lane, Kinoulton,
Nottinghamshire NG12 3EF
01949 81133; www.npta.org.uk

City&
Guilds

www.cityandguilds.com/myperfectjob

REFUSE & RECYCLING OPERATIVE

What the work involves

- You will collect rubbish and unwanted items and take them to an official rubbish tip or recycling depot.

- Working as part of a team you will travel round your area, emptying bins, removing plastic sacks of waste or picking up recyclable waste.

- Recycling operatives may have additional duties, such as sorting rubbish or collecting hazardous waste. Recycling technicians also work in recycling facilities, sorting through recycled materials in preparation for re-use.

The type of person suited to this work

A good level of physical fitness is essential for this type of work. A strong stomach is useful when dealing with rubbish. You should also be able to cope with getting your hands dirty.

Team-working skills are essential in this job. Most companies are required to complete their rounds to deadlines, so you should be able to work under pressure.

You may also need manual handling skills to lift and move recycling collections. For work in a recycling sorting facility, you will need good eyesight and attention to detail.

Working conditions

You will wear protective clothing, such as gloves and overalls, and you will come into contact with dirt and rubbish on a regular basis. The work will involve nasty smells and some unpleasant sights.

The hours are generally around 6am to 3pm, except for busy holiday periods when the amount of rubbish increases.

This type of work may not suit people with skin conditions or allergies.

Future prospects

Loaders will always be in demand as even recyclable rubbish has to be collected.

You could work for a contracting company providing services for a local authority and there are some jobs with specialist companies who collect paper or food waste.

It is likely that there will be a growth in the number of recycling jobs in local councils, contracting companies providing services to councils and recycling companies.

With experience, you could progress to supervisory or management work.

Advantages/disadvantages

For most jobs, you will have to start very early in the morning. However, this means that you will be able to finish your working day quite early.

Qualifications and courses

You should be at least 18 and drivers must be over 21 to get a Large Goods Vehicle Licence (LGV licence).

Apprenticeships/Skillseekers may be available for people aged 16–24.

On starting, you will have to take a short course on health and safety and then be trained on the job by an experienced colleague.

You can work towards NVQs/SVQs at Levels 1 and 2 in Waste Management Operations with specialist options in waste collection or recycling and Level 3 in Waste Management Supervision. You could also complete NVQs/SVQs in Recycling Operations at Levels 1 and 2. An NVQ/SVQ in Community Recycling is also available.

People working in supervisory roles can gain an NVQ/SVQ Level 3 in Management of Recycling Operations. It is also possible to work towards Level 3 and 4 qualifications in Environmental Conservation and Conservation Control.

The work is physically demanding and potentially unsafe.

Money guide

Salaries start at about £11,000 per year. With experience you could earn between £15,000 and £17,000 a year. At senior levels it is possible to earn between £18,000 and £25,000 per year.

Drivers can earn between £17,000 and £20,000 a year.

There are usually opportunities to earn extra by working overtime or in holiday periods.

Related opportunities

- Large Goods Vehicle Driver/Driver's Mate p606
- Loader p608
- Removals Operative p621
- Van Driver p628

Further information

Waste Management Industry Training and Advisery Board (WAMITAB)
Peterbridge House, 3 The Lakes, Northampton NN4 7HE
01604 231950; www.wamitab.org.uk

www.cityandguilds.com/myperfectjob

Personal and Other Services including Hair and Beauty

CRCI: RB
CLCI: IJ

SPA THERAPIST/ TECHNICIAN

What the work involves

- Spa Therapists provide various treatments which are designed to enhance appearance, reduce stress or improve well-being.

- You will offer an assortment of treatments which may include facials, manicures and pedicures, massage, body treatments like wraps and exfoliation and specialist treatments such as light therapy and lymphatic drainage.

- You will be required to talk to your clients in order to discover their specific health needs and personal expectations. You will ensure they are comfortable at all times and provide them with any necessary aftercare advice.

- You will be expected to maintain the various areas of the salon.

The type of person suited to this work

You will need a caring manner and the ability to make people feel at ease. You should be discreet and understand the role of confidentiality within the industry. It is important that you are able to work effectively as part of a team. You should have excellent dexterity, outstanding attention to detail and good time management skills. You will need to have strong personal hygiene and a smart appearance. A solid understanding of health and safety requirements would also prove beneficial.

Working conditions

Most of the work will be based in private treatment rooms which will be warm and clean, however you may be required to complete some treatments in wet rooms. A great deal of time will be spent standing and bending. Some products may irritate your skin, particularly if you are prone to such reactions.

Most spa therapists wear a uniform. Full-time hours are usually between 37 and 40 hours a week and may often include evening and weekend work.

Future prospects

You will have the possibility of working in various beauty related professions. You may choose to progress to a supervisory or management post. You could decide to combine the more practical aspects with administrative work. There is also the option of becoming a trainer or lecturer. There are numerous options available for overseas work.

Advantages/disadvantages

The unusual working hours may prove inconvenient.

Opportunities within this industry are varied and so you will have many options regarding which environment you wish to work in.

Being on your feet all day might be tiring.

You may receive bonuses, discounted/free products and the use of facilities.

Qualifications and courses

Beauty Therapists/Technicians need qualifications in the areas of treatment or therapy they wish to offer. There are a wide range of colleges and training providers available in the UK. Alternatively, it is possible to gain experience by working in a salon and building on the treatments you are qualified to offer. Apprenticeships and Advanced Apprenticeships are also offered in this industry.

Relevant qualifications include an NVQ Level 3 in spa therapy, a BTEC National Diploma in beauty therapy sciences or equivalent. These courses generally expect candidates to have attained three or four GCSEs grade A*-C (English, maths and science are valuable here) or an NVQ Level 2 in beauty therapy.

If you wish to progress into management then Higher Level courses may prove useful. Higher Level qualifications include a foundation degree in beauty and spa services and a foundation degree/degree in spa management. Foundation degrees generally require candidates to have one A level, a BTEC National Diploma in beauty therapy sciences or NVQ Level 3 along with three GCSEs grade A*-C, including a science subject. Degree courses generally require two A levels and five GCSEs grade A*-C or equivalent.

Money guide

Salaries range depending on location and employer.

Starting salaries for newly qualified spa therapists are usually in the area of £12,000–£14,000 a year.

After a few years that may increase to between £15,000 and £19,000.

Upon progression to management level that might swell to somewhere between £20,000 and £40,000.

These amounts may vary depending on the number of hours worked.

Related opportunities

- Aromatherapist p295
- Beauty Consultant p458
- Nail Technician p471

Further information

The Guild of Professional Beauty Therapists
Guild House, 320 Burton Road, Derby DE23 6AF
0845 21 77 383; www.beautyguild.com

City& Guilds

www.cityandguilds.com/myperfectjob

WEDDING CONSULTANT

What the work involves

- Wedding consultants organise wedding ceremonies, parties and other events to suit your clients' plans and budgets.

- Working closely with clients, you will help them decide on the type of wedding they want.

- Your work will also involve liaising with catering professionals, venue managers and suppliers.

- Depending on individual projects, you may be responsible for creating a whole look or style for a wedding. You could be responsible for all the practical arrangements such as catering, flowers, booking venues and guest transport.

The type of person suited to this work

Helping to create and plan the big day for clients requires excellent communication skills. A strong interest in helping people organise the wedding they want is important. To do this, you will need a combination of creative and practical skills to develop ideas and make them a reality.

You will have to have strong attention to detail and be a perfectionist to ensure that the weddings you plan run smoothly.

You should be able to negotiate agreements with suppliers on behalf of your clients, keep calm under pressure and be reliable with an outgoing, confident personality. Financial skills are useful.

Working conditions

Working hours can be long, especially in the period leading up to a wedding. You may also have to attend meetings with clients at evenings and weekends.

This type of work can be very highly pressured due to limited deadlines and the level of responsibility.

You will attend meetings at a variety of locations and your working day is likely to include some travel.

Future prospects

Professional wedding planning is a growing area. You could work on a freelance basis, offering planning services through your own company, or could work for a larger wedding planning company.

There are also opportunities to work within large hotels combining wedding consultancy and planning with other events-related work.

Advantages/disadvantages

This is a sociable job which provides the opportunity to help clients have the kind of wedding they want.

Having responsibility for ensuring that wedding days run smoothly means that there is little room for mistakes.

When everything turns out well, it can be very rewarding!

Qualifications and courses

There are no set entry requirements for this career.

Wedding consultants/planners/organisers may have a background in hospitality, design or business. The skills you bring to work are more important than the qualifications you might hold.

Larger employers may require people with events planning experience.

Degrees, Foundation degrees and HNDs are available in events management.

Those with proof of more than 3 years' business trading, three client references and a satisfactory quality inspection can become members of the National Association of Professional Wedding Services. The Association can also provide details about the Advanced Certification in Wedding Design and Management, which is an intensive, in-depth course covering all aspects of wedding organisation.

Money guide

You could earn £16,000+ working for a specialist wedding and events planning company.

With a good level of experience, you could earn £25,000+.

Company managers can earn £40,000+ , in this expanding business area.

Freelance planners usually charge a percentage of the total cost of the wedding.

Related opportunities

- Civil Service/Local Government Administrator p29
- Image Consultant/Personal Shopper p470
- Entertainment Manager p388
- Tour Guide/Manager p401
- Costume Designer p178

Further information

National Association of Professional Wedding Services
Shelley Way, Wimbledon, London SW19 1TH
020 8090 1921; www.theweddingassociation.co.uk

Eventia, the Events Industry Association
5th Floor, Galbraith House, 141 Great Charles Street, Birmingham B3 3LG
0121 212 1400; www.eventia.org.uk

www.cityandguilds.com/myperfectjob

Personal and Other Services including Hair and Beauty

CRCI: R
CLCI: IZ

WIGMAKER

What the work involves

- Wigmakers design and create a range of wigs and hairpieces using human hair or synthetic fibres.

- You may create or design wigs to suit individual customers.

- Your work could involve meeting with customers and helping them decide on the styles of wig to suit them. You may also provide advice to customers on caring for and maintaining their wigs.

- Wigmakers provide services for the entertainment industry, hospitals, wig supply companies, theatrical costume companies and private customers.

The type of person suited to this work

Wigmaking requires a combination of creative flair, practicality and people skills. You may work closely with customers requiring wigs due to illness or medical treatment, so a tactful approach is essential. You should also be able to understand the type of look an individual client wants. Your eye for design will help you create a variety of styles of wigs.

Wigmaking is a slow, detailed process so you will need excellent practical skills, attention to detail and a lot of patience! You must work to a very high standard at all times. As wigs are often made to order, you should be able to work to deadlines.

Working conditions

You may be based in a studio or workshop. Your work may also involve visiting private homes and hospital departments for customer fittings and consultations.

You will work with a range of equipment and chemicals and you will need manual handling skills and good eyesight.

This type of work may be unsuitable for people with skin conditions and allergies.

Future prospects

There are very limited employment opportunities in this area.

Wigmakers in entertainment and media usually provide additional make-up and hair services. They may run their own companies working for television, media and theatre companies or be employed in-house. Wigmakers also provide specialist care and services for clients experiencing hair loss due to a medical condition.

With experience, you could set up your own business or work for a wig supplier.

Advantages/disadvantages

By creating and fitting attractive wigs for customers, you can help build their confidence.

Qualifications and courses

There are no set entry requirements for this work.

It is possible to study wigmaking part time at college. A City & Guilds Certificate (3013) is available in Wigmaking. The VTCT Diploma in Theatrical and Media Make-up includes study of wigmaking. NVQs/SVQs in Hairdressing may include units in wigmaking.

Wigmaking can also be studied at higher education level, as part of an HND in media make-up or theatrical and media make-up.

The level of contact you have with customers depends on your employer. In some jobs you may have minimum contact with clients and work solely in a studio.

Money guide

Salaries vary according to sector and employer; you could start on £12,000 per year and rise to over £20,000, with lots of experience.

Wigmakers working in large theatres, for film or TV companies, usually earn more than those working for companies supplying hospitals.

Most wigmakers set a rate per job - depending on the requirements of the client.

Related opportunities

- Hairdresser/Barber p469
- Make-up Artist p445
- Nail Technician p471
- Beauty Consultant p458

Further information

Wigmakers' Association c/o The Hairdressing and Beauty Suppliers Association
Greenleaf House, 128 Darkes Lane, Potters Bar, Herfordshire EN6 1AE
01707 649499; www.hbsa.uk.com

The Institute of Trichologists
Ground Floor Office, 24 Langroyd Road, London SW17 7PL
0870 607 6062; www.trichologists.org.uk

www.cityandguilds.com/myperfectjob

Retail, Sales and Customer Services

Jobs in this sector are suited to those of you who are very good at communicating with others and are interested in making your customers happy. Maybe you're interested in working with food and want to give your customers high quality, fresh produce. Your interest may lie in fashion retail and you could spend your time providing style advice. You should also be commercially minded and think about how your work relates to the success of the company you work for. Jobs in this sector also involve maintaining standards such as safety and quality to ensure guidelines are met, so a practical outlook can be useful.

In this section we look at the following jobs:

For similar jobs to the ones covered in this section turn to *Administration, Business, Office Work and Financial Services* on page 15.

ANTIQUES DEALER

What the work involves

- You will be buying and selling things such as furniture, clocks, jewellery and pictures, which are either old or which people collect.

- You will go to auctions and fairs to buy things to sell in shops, markets or antique salerooms.

- You will need to develop specialist knowledge so that you can assess an object's age and value and whether it will sell at a profit.

- You will advise customers on the value of their antiques.

The type of person suited to this work

You should be fascinated by antiques and working out where they come from and what they are worth.

You will need to be interested in history and dedicated enough to travel and visit fairs and auctions all over the country and possibly abroad, searching out bargains and objects to sell. You will need to develop good specialist knowledge, know what is likely to be popular and then sell quickly at a profit.

Antiques do not have fixed prices so you will need to be able to make quick decisions, and cope with the stress of buying things at auction. You will need to have good all round business skills.

Working conditions

You will work in a shop, in an antiques saleroom or on a market stall. You could be outside in all weathers and will probably have to travel to different markets.

You could be dealing with heavy objects like furniture or dusty and dirty things such as clothes and books.

Your working hours will vary a lot. Shops and stalls will be open at fixed times and on public holidays, and you could be visiting auctions or customers at any time.

Future prospects

Most antique dealers are self-employed or work in a family business, but you could start in an auction house or as a sales assistant in a larger shop.

Once you have developed contacts and a knowledge of antiques and their value, you could work for yourself, perhaps starting with a market stall and expanding your business from there.

Most dealers specialise in a particular period of history or type of antique.

Advantages/disadvantages

You will be working with things that you love and have the thrill of finding bargains or rare items.

It can be a very uncertain business and prices will rise and fall as things go in and out of fashion. You can make a lot of money but you can also lose a lot.

Qualifications and courses

There are no formal qualifications needed for this work, but enthusiasm and sales skills are useful. GCSEs/S grades (A–C/1–3) in art, design and history are an advantage.

Apprenticeship/Skillseekers may be available for those aged 16–24.

Entry is normally through work experience or as a trainee. Many auction houses will employ people as general workers or assistants. An NVQ/SVQ in Retail Operations can be an advantage.

The University of Central Lancashire offers a 3-year degree in Antiques and Design Studies and a Master's by distance learning in Antiques. There are also some privately-run courses available. Information about careers in antiques dealing and current vacancies with dealers may be available from the British Antique Dealers Association (BADA) or the Association of Art and Antique Dealers (LAPADA).

The British Antique Dealers Association (BADA) may offer advice about current vacancies with dealers. The Association of Art and Antique Dealers (LAPADA) also offers basic guidance on careers in antique dealing.

Money guide

You can expect around £12,000 per year as an assistant.

£20,000–£30,000 is usual for a dealer with a flair for the trade and considerable experience.

£50,000+ is possible for successful dealers or people with a high level of specialist knowledge.

Related opportunities

- Archivist p350
- Market Trader p490
- Museum/Art Gallery Curator p359
- Sales/Retail Assistant p495

Further information

British Antique Dealers Association
20 Rutland Gate, London SW7 1BD
020 7589 4128; www.bada.org

Sotheby's
34–35 New Bond Street, London W1S 2RT
020 7293 5000; www.sothebys.com

City&
Guilds

www.cityandguilds.com/myperfectjob

BOOKSELLER

What the work involves

- You will be serving customers, taking money and answering queries, giving advice and ordering books.

- You will keep the shelves tidy, putting new books out and arranging displays. You will be keeping records of books and sometimes adding a classification system.

- You will be ordering books from publishers and wholesalers and keeping stock information up to date.

- You might be working with local colleges or universities to make sure you have got the books needed for their courses.

The type of person suited to this work

You will need to be genuinely interested in books and in keeping up to date with new publications so that you can help and advise customers.

You will need good communication skills for dealing with customers and sales reps and will work as part of a team, but should also be able to use your own initiative. You should be polite and helpful and able to stay calm when you are busy.

You will need to keep up to date with when new books by popular authors are due out.

You will be taking cash and using tills and computers to check and order stock.

Working conditions

You will be working in a shop and most jobs are likely to be in large book chain stores. You will be dealing with customers, working in a team and you will have responsibility for a particular section.

You will be on your feet all day and could be carrying heavy books.

You will work 39–40 hours a week, and will probably have to work weekends on a rota basis and also do late and early shifts as large stores can be open long hours.

Future prospects

A lot of smaller book shops have closed due to competition from larger stores and the internet, so most opportunities are with the big chains.

You can get responsibility quite quickly as a supervisor or the person in charge of a section. You can go on to management level or to work for head office.

There is not much chance of promotion in smaller shops but you could use your knowledge and experience to open your own store, possibly specialising in antique or second-hand books.

Advantages/disadvantages

You could be using your knowledge and love of books to help other people and keep up to date with new publications.

You could develop specialist knowledge, for example in children's books.

Qualifications and courses

There are no formal qualifications to enter this work, but most employers look for GCSEs/S grades (A–3/1–C) in English and maths. You can enter and train for this career with qualifications at Levels 2–3 or go in with higher qualifications at Level 3 and above.

A degree in English or a degree/HND/Foundation degree in retail, business management or retail marketing can be an advantage.

Relevant courses at FE level include the Retail and Distributive Services, NVQs/SVQs in Retail Operations at Levels 2 and 3, Distributive Operations at Level 1, Customer Service at Levels 2, 3 and 4, Visual Merchandising at Level 2 and BTEC First and National qualifications in Retail/SQA National qualifications in Retail and Distribution.

Apprenticeships/Skillseekers may be available to those aged 16–24.

Membership of the Booksellers Association of the United Kingdom and Ireland may be useful.

You will be dealing with the public, which can be rewarding but also stressful!

Money guide

Salaries vary a lot depending on the size of the shop. With large chains, you may get bonuses for high levels of sales or for meeting targets.

You can expect £11,000–£12,000 per year when you start.

With experience this can rise to £14,300.

£40,000+ a year is possible as a manager of a large bookshop with specialist departments.

Related opportunities

- Librarian p358
- Archivist p350
- Publisher/Commissioning Editor p426
- Sales/Retail Assistant p495

Further information

Booksellers Association
Minster House, 272–274 Vauxhall Bridge Road, London SW1V 1BA
020 7802 0802; www.booksellers.org.uk

British Shops and Stores Association Limited
Middleton House, 2 Main Road, Middleton Cheney, Banbury, Oxfordshire OX17 2TN
01295 712277; www.british-shops.co.uk

City& Guilds

www.cityandguilds.com/myperfectjob

Retail, Sales and Customer Services

CRCI: SB
CLCI: OFM

BUILDERS' MERCHANT/ ASSISTANT

What the work involves

Builders' merchant

- You will be dealing with building materials and bathroom fittings. You will keep track of stock using computer or paper systems, order new stock and take deliveries.

- You will supply goods to building firms and individual builders – plumbers, electricians, plasterers – and members of the public, taking payments and using tills.

Builders' merchant's assistant

- You will work in a builders' merchants looking after the stock.

- You will handle a range of building materials, take deliveries, store deliveries properly, and keep the yard clean and deal with customers.

The type of person suited to this work

You will need to have a certain level of physical fitness for both of these positions as there will be heavy lifting and carrying involved. Asthma and allergies to dust and chemicals may be a problem.

You will need solid communication skills for dealing with customers and suppliers. You should have good numeracy and computer skills and the ability to handle money and paperwork efficiently.

Builders' merchant's assistant

You will be able to carry out instructions effectively. You should also be able to check invoices, deal with customers and possibly handle payments.

Working conditions

You will work about 40 hours a week, usually on Saturdays and sometimes Sundays. You may start at about 7.30am so that builders can buy their materials on the way to their work.

You may also need to use a forklift truck and climb ladders, which could be dangerous. You will be wearing overalls and protective boots or shoes.

You could be working outside in all weathers.

Future prospects

There are job opportunities in all areas of the country, but these vary depending on the strength of the building trade, and at present there are good opportunities.

The number of builders' merchants has increased with a lot of stores on out-of-town retail sites.

You can work part time and if you work for large merchants, or a chain, you could become a supervisor or manager. You could also work for a supplier or as a sales representative.

Qualifications and courses

ENTRY 1 LEVEL

You can enter and train in this career with qualifications at Levels 1 or 2. Most employers prefer applicants to have English and maths GCSEs/S grades.

Previous experience within the construction industry or retailing is beneficial, as many employers view experience and personality as being more important than academic qualifications. A qualification in retail or construction may however also be useful. Relevant courses include BTEC Introductory Diploma in Construction, Retail and Administration, BTEC First Certificate/Diploma in Retail, and Vocational GCSE in Construction and Built Environment.

Apprenticeships/Skillseekers may be available for those aged 16–24. The Builders' Merchants Federation (BMF) offers an Apprenticeship scheme leading to NVQs/SVQs at Levels 2 and 3. The BMF also offers other qualifications; see their website for more information. Builders' merchants can work towards NVQs/SVQs in relevant subjects such as Distribution and Warehousing, Customer Service and Retail Operations.

Advantages/disadvantages

The work can be a great way of using your interest in building and knowledge of materials, tools and equipment.

There's a lot of paperwork involved in keeping track of the stock.

You could be starting early in the morning and working outside.

Money guide

Builders' merchant's assistants can start on around £12,000 a year. Once you have built on your experience and responsibilities you can expect to earn up to £20,000 per year. Delivery van drivers can earn around £16,500 a year.

You could earn more as the manager of a department or store and managers of large companies could earn £50,000+.

Related opportunities

- Builder p72
- Sales/Retail Assistant p495
- Warehouse Manager/Worker p629

Further information

Builders' Merchants Federation
15 Soho Square, London W1D 3HL
0870 901 3380; www.bmf.org.uk

City& Guilds

www.cityandguilds.com/myperfectjob

BUTCHER

What the work involves

- You might prepare an assortment of meat and poultry products. This could involve cutting, de-boning, trimming and slicing.

- You could offer advice to customers about varieties of meat available and preparation techniques involved with them. Some butchers offer a delivery service.

- You will take part in the everyday running of the business, visiting markets, ordering stock, taking deliveries from suppliers, organising displays and selling the products.

- Butchers can also work in the wholesale area of the industry, receiving the meat from the abattoir, then preparing and storing it for sale to the retailers or wholesale customers.

The type of person suited to this work

You will have to be meticulous and practical. You will need to have a strong understanding of and a professional approach to health and hygiene. Due to the fact you will be using sharp tools and machinery you need to be safety conscious. You should be personable, maintaining a high level of customer service. You need to have an outstanding knowledge of the various products and cuts of meat. You should have cash handling skills.

Working conditions

A retail butcher works in a shop environment with a chilled storage area. You will be expected to prepare meat in front of customers, using knives, cleavers and saws and will therefore be required to wear protective clothing, such as disposable gloves and an apron. This profession involves a great deal of standing, lifting and carrying as butchers are required to transport joints of meat. Average working hours are between 39 and 40 a week, including Saturdays and sometimes evenings and Sundays. Work starts as early as 7am.

Future prospects

With a great deal of local butchers having closed down and the ones left being small businesses, prospects are becoming somewhat limited. Supermarkets have however resurrected the idea of the meat counter over simply selling packaged meats and promotion opportunities within these chains are plentiful.

Once you have gained experience there is the option of setting up your own retail outlet. Other options include making the move into meat catering, meat wholesale or meat manufacture.

Advantages/disadvantages

You will have a great deal of customer contact and the opportunity to share your knowledge.

The amount of time spent on your feet, heavy lifting and cold temperatures may cause discomfort.

Qualifications and courses

ENTRY LEVEL 2

There are no formal qualifications required to become a butcher, most people train on the job. Many employers will however want proof of a certain level of literacy and numeracy. They may require employees to have acquired English, maths and a science GCSE at grade A*-E or even set aptitude tests.

Work experience in the food and drink industry is beneficial.

A good way to begin in this career is through an Apprenticeship scheme. These may include Young Apprenticeships, Apprenticeships, Pre-Apprenticeships and Advanced Apprenticeships in England. The Apprenticeships available in the rest of the UK may vary. The pay for these schemes may differ depending on location and industry sector.

Many employers provide employees with the opportunity to work towards qualifications including food safety qualifications and NVQs/SVQs in Meat and Poultry Processing at Levels 1 and 2.

The MTC (Meat Training Council) offers a range of qualifications which include the Intermediate Certificate in Meat and Poultry, the Intermediate Certificate in Meat and Poultry Management and the Intermediate Certificate in Hazard Analysis Critical Control Points (HACCP).

Money guide

On average, a trainee butcher will earn a starting salary of around £7,176 a year.

That will increase to £11,107 once the individual has become skilled in their trade.

A butchery manager could make up to £14,650 per year.

If an individual chose to open their own shop this may increase further.

Related opportunities

- Food Processing Operative p229
- Kitchen Supervisor p153
- Meat Process Worker p239

Further information

Meat Hygiene Service
MHS Headquarters, Kings Pool, Peasholme Green, York YO1 7PR
01904 455501; www.food.gov.uk/foodindustry/meat/mhservice/

City& Guilds

www.cityandguilds.com/myperfectjob

BUYER

What the work involves

- Buyers work in all sorts of industries and organisations, but in retail you would probably work in the merchandising and marketing team.

- You will probably work for a large retail company and be looking for products which fit the company image and will appeal to their customers.

- You will visit manufacturers and suppliers to negotiate prices and decide on quantities and colours. You will also check on the quality of the products.

- You will help to predict and set trends, using computers to analyse sales figures.

The type of person suited to this work

You will need to be confident and decisive because you will be dealing with large budgets.

You will need to be assertive with good communication skills to negotiate prices and make presentations to managers and staff.

You will need to be able to analyse figures and use them to set prices and targets and check stock levels.

You should be creative, well organised and good at planning ahead, and have an eye for detail.

Working conditions

You will be office-based but spend a lot of time visiting suppliers and manufacturers in this country and abroad, so will probably have to spend time away from home.

You will work office hours but probably need to work longer at busy times and to meet deadlines.

Future prospects

There are job opportunities all over the country but most will be in larger towns and cities.

In a small company there may not be much chance of promotion, but in a larger company prospects are good.

You could use your skills to work as a buyer in other areas, including manufacturing, the civil service and local government.

Advantages/disadvantages

This can be an exciting job and the decisions you make will affect what the public can buy and the image of the stores.

You will have a lot of responsibility which can be exciting, but also very stressful.

Money guide

You can expect on average around £15,000 per year when you start as a trainee buyer. The variation in pay is wide because it depends on the company you work for and the location. Pay will rise to around £20,000 as you gain experience.

You can earn £22,000–£35,000 in the responsible position of buyer.

Qualifications and courses

There are no set qualifications for entry to a buyer job. However, entry is usually by degree, though an HND or equivalent can also be acceptable. Useful subjects include business, management, purchasing, logistics and marketing. Some specialist degrees are available in fashion buying. The minimum entry requirements for a degree course are normally 2 A levels/3 H grades or equivalent.

Buyers are often required to study for the professional qualifications of the Chartered Institute of Purchasing and Supply (CIPS). CIPS offers a Certificate and Advanced Certificate for people employed in purchasing at a clerical level.

Entrants with an HND or degree study towards the CIPS Graduate Diploma. CIPS-accredited degrees in purchasing or business are available at some institutions, and give exemption from part or all of the Graduate Diploma.

People employed in buying can work towards NVQs/SVQs at Levels 2–4 in Procurement. The British Shops and Stores Association offers a Buying and Merchandising Foundation Course by distance learning, aimed at trainee or assistant buyers.

Some companies offer their own training schemes, but only take on a few candidates each year.

Employers often like you to be a member of the Chartered Institute of Purchasing and Supply (CIPS). CIPS runs qualifications from Level 2 (Introductory Certificate) to Level 7 (Executive Diploma).

£50,000+ is possible as a successful, senior buyer for a large company or multiple retail chain.

You may earn large bonuses if you do well.

Related opportunities

- Marketing Manager Assistant/Executive p417
- Merchandiser p492
- Purchasing/Procurement Manager p617
- Store Manager p499

Further information

British Shops and Stores Association Limited
Middleton House, 2 Main Road, Middleton Cheney, Banbury, Oxfordshire OX17 2TN
01295 712277; www.british-shops.co.uk

Chartered Institute of Marketing
Moor Hall, Cookham, Maidenhead, Berkshire SL6 9QH
01628 427500; www.cim.co.uk

Chartered Institute of Purchasing & Supply
Easton House, Easton on the Hill, Stamford, Lincolnshire PE9 3NZ
01780 756777; www.cips.org

CAR SALESPERSON

What the work involves

- You will be selling new or used cars, motorbikes or vans; greeting customers, advising them and explaining different models, features and prices, and demonstrating cars by going out on test drives.

- Your job will include arranging finance for customers and doing paperwork for the sale and the finance.

- Garages promote their cars through advertising, special events and direct contact with customers, which may also be part of your work.

- Sales staff help keep the forecourt, salesroom and cars clean and tidy.

The type of person suited to this work

You will need to be smart, confident and outgoing with a polite, friendly manner and an ability to deal with all types of people and be persuasive without being pushy. You will need good negotiation and numeracy skills.

You should be interested in cars, know a lot about the ones you are selling and be able to explain technical features clearly and simply.

Your wages will depend on how much you sell so you will need to be motivated and determined and able to deal with stress and pressure.

Your job will also involve working out prices and deals and completing forms and paperwork accurately.

You will need to be able to work without supervision.

Working conditions

You could be working in a small, local garage selling used cars or for a large main dealership.

You will be based in a showroom but will also be outside on the forecourt and going on test drives.

You will spend most of your time dealing with customers but will also do paperwork.

Future prospects

There are currently good opportunities in all parts of the country but it is a popular industry, so jobs can be competitive, especially with the large main dealers.

Prospects are good and you can earn a lot if you do well.

In larger dealerships you can progress to senior salesperson, sales manager or dealer principal.

At management level you will probably earn bonuses linked to the sales of the whole team.

Advantages/disadvantages

You will be using your knowledge of cars to interest customers and persuade them to buy.

You can do very well and earn a high salary.

Qualifications and courses

You do not need formal qualifications to enter and train in this career, but employers will expect GCSEs (A-C)/S in maths and English.

Much of the training is done on the job, and trainees may be expected to attend short courses and training about the cars they are selling.

Apprenticeships/Skillseekers may be available to those aged 16–24.

Car salespeople receive on-the-job training, and may also work towards NVQs/SVQs at Levels 2 and 3 in Vehicle Sales, or the Institute of the Motor Industry (IMI) Certificate and Diploma in Vehicle sales. The Level 2 Certificate leads to Licentiate Membership of the IMI and the Level 3 Diploma provides Associate Membership.

Other suitable courses include the ISMM Level 2 course in Sales and Marketing and Level 3 course in Advanced Sales Skills.

Sales people may also attend short courses run by vehicle manufacturers.

It can be very stressful working on commission and having to meet targets and you will probably work long hours.

Money guide

Wages vary a lot. You may be on a fairly small basic salary plus commission and bonuses related to your sales.

As a starting salary you could expect £10,000–£13,500 per year. With experience this can rise to £14,000–£17,000, up to £25,000 with bonuses.

In an improving economic climate, top sales people will expect to earn £30,000–£35,000.

Related opportunities

- Customer Services Assistant/Executive p486
- Motor Vehicle Technician p241
- Sales/Retail Assistant p495
- Store Manager p499

Further information

Retail Motor Industry Federation
201 Great Portland Street, London W1W 5AB
020 7580 9122; www.rmif.co.uk

Institute of the Motor Industry
Fanshaws, Brickendon, Hertford SG13 8PQ
01992 511521; www.motor.org.uk

www.cityandguilds.com/myperfectjob

Retail, Sales and Customer Services

CRCI: SB
CLCI: OE

CHECKOUT OPERATOR

What the work involves

- You will work on a till, probably in a supermarket or large store receiving payments for goods.

- You will pass goods over a scanner or enter the price onto the till using a keypad. You might weigh and price items such as fruit and vegetables.

- Working on a till involves taking payments using cash, cheques and credit/debit cards, and often giving cashback to customers.

- As part of serving the customers, you may help them pack their purchases into bags, and you will have to keep your area clean and tidy.

The type of person suited to this work

You will need to enjoy meeting people and working with the public to provide a good service, being polite, efficient and helpful. You will need to have good listening and speaking skills.

You should be able to work accurately and quickly and handle cash and other payments, making sure you give the right change or checking details such as signatures or expiry dates on credit cards.

Checkout operators have to sit for quite long periods and do fairly routine, repetitive work. They also work under pressure and must stay calm when the queues get long and the customers impatient.

You should be well presented and be happy to wear an overall or uniform.

Working conditions

Shops are usually light, airy and warm but can be crowded and stressful.

Checkout operators usually work around 39–40 hours a week, often doing shifts.

A lot of the opportunities are part time. You will probably get staff discount and have a uniform provided.

Future prospects

Retail is a big industry employing around 3 million people in the UK and large stores are opening in out-of-town developments all over the country. There are opportunities in all areas but many of these are for part-time workers.

Most checkout operators work for large companies which usually offer good prospects for promotion and staff training. You could go on to become a supervisor with responsibility for a particular section, for example the bakery, and even become a trainee manager.

Advantages/disadvantages

There are lots of job opportunities and you can work flexible and part-time hours and go on to work in other types of shops.

You do not need qualifications and you could go on to become a supervisor and even move into management.

Qualifications and courses

There are no formal qualification needed to enter and train in this career, although many employers are increasingly asking for good GCSEs/S grades in English and maths.

You may need to pass a maths test at interview.

Most training is done on the job working with experienced staff.

A number of relevant qualifications are available in Retail and Distributive Services including NVQs/SVQs in Retail Operations at Levels 2 and 3, Distributive Operations at Level 1, Retail Sales Delivery at Level 2, Sales at Level 2 and Customer Service at Levels 2 and 3, or BTEC First and National qualifications in Retail/SQA National qualifications in Retail and Distribution.

Apprenticeships are available for those under 24 years of age.

The work can be routine and repetitive.

Money guide

You can expect around £11,000, rising to £12,200 per year when you first start work. Pay can increase to £14,500 when you have been working a while and have got some experience.

£16,000–£19,000 is possible if you are working as a supervisor.

Managerial positions are rewarded at a considerably higher level – up to £40,000 – for those with qualifications and experience.

Related opportunities

- Contact Centre Operative p485
- Customer Services Assistant/Manager p486
- Sales/Retail Assistant p495
- Builders' Merchant/Assistant p480

Further information

British Shops and Stores Association Limited
Middleton House, 2 Main Road, Middleton Cheney, Banbury, Oxfordshire OX17 2TN
01295 712277; www.british-shops.co.uk

Skillsmart Retail Ltd
The Sector Skills Council for Retail
4th Floor, 93 Newman Street, London W1T 3EZ
020 7462 5060; www.skillsmartretail.com

City&
Guilds

www.cityandguilds.com/myperfectjob

CONTACT CENTRE OPERATIVE

What the work involves

- You will be dealing with customers over the phone and using a computer to log details or find information.

- You may do telesales or telemarketing, selling, mail ordering, banking, or promoting goods and services, which could involve 'cold calling'.

- You could be doing market research, asking about people's buying habits or what services they would like from a company.

- You may be providing a service – receiving calls from customers who could be ordering goods, complaining about a service, or accessing their bank accounts.

The type of person suited to this work

You should have good spoken English, with a clear voice and good hearing. You will need excellent customer-service skills and must be able to be polite and calm when dealing with angry or impatient callers.

For telesales or telemarketing, you will need to be motivated and persistent as well as persuasive, but polite.

Good ICT skills are important so that you can input information quickly but accurately, whilst talking to the customer.

You will probably work to targets and could be very busy so should be able to stay calm under pressure and work on your own initiative, but also as part of a team.

Working conditions

You will be office-based, usually working 38–40 hours a week. You may work shifts which could include nights, weekends and evenings.

Call centre staff have their own workstations with a headset and computer and work as part of a team.

The work is usually based on targets and can be busy and stressful; calls are often monitored by supervisors and staff turnover can be fairly high.

Future prospects

There has been a huge growth in call centres recently as more services are available over the phone – such as mail order, banking and insurance – and more companies are using telesales and marketing to sell their goods and services.

You could become a team leader or supervisor, training staff to improve their skills and checking their work and targets.

Advantages/disadvantages

Job opportunities are increasing and you can work flexible hours.

You could use the customer-service and sales skills you will develop to move into other jobs.

The work can be repetitive; you will probably work to targets and be under pressure to make sales.

Qualifications and courses

There are no formal entry qualifications for this work, but some employers prefer English and maths GCSEs (A-C)/S grades You can enter and train in this career with qualifications at Levels 1 or 2.

Call centre staff can work towards NVQ/SVQ Levels 2 and 3 in Telesales, NVQ/SVQ Levels 2 and 3 in Customer Service, NVQs Levels 2 & 3 in Call Handling Operations, Level 3 in Supervising Call Handling and Level 4 in Managing Call Handling, or SVQ Level 2 in Contact Centre Operations and Levels 3 and 4 in Contact Centre Professionals.

BTEC offers a course in Contact Centre Skills and City & Guilds offers a certificate course in Contact Centre Techniques. Some colleges offer introductory courses in Contact Centre Skills. Call centre training and qualifications are also offered by e-skills UK.

The Call Centre Association offers a Professional Certificate, achieved through completion of a call centre induction programme, and a Professional Diploma, which requires further CPD activities. A Higher Diploma, university Diploma and postgraduate qualification are available for team leaders and managers. The Chartered Institute of Marketing offers courses on telephone selling techniques.

Money guide

You can expect £13,000–£15,000 per year when you start.

This can rise to £16,000–£17,500 when you have experience and depending on where you work. Financial services call centres tend to pay best.

As a supervisor you could get £18,500–£22,500. Managerial roles pay over £25,000 per year.

You may get commission on sales or bonuses if you meet targets.

Related opportunities

- Customer Services Assistant/Manager p486
- Marketing Manager/Assistant/Executive p417
- Sales/Retail Assistant p495
- Public Relations Executive p425

Further information

Institute of Direct Marketing
1 Park Road, Teddington, Middlesex TW11 0AR
020 8614 0277; www.theidm.com

Institute of Customer Service
2 Castle Court, St Peter's Street, Colchester, Essex CO1 1EW
01206 571716; www.instituteofcustomerservice.com

www.cityandguilds.com/myperfectjob

CUSTOMER SERVICES ASSISTANT/MANAGER

What the work involves

Assistant

- You could be selling products or services or providing a service or information about the company. You will work with people face to face or over the telephone and will need a good knowledge of the company and its products.

Manager

- As a manager you will be responsible for recruiting and training a team of customer service assistants, motivating them to meet their targets and helping them to develop their skills.

The type of person suited to this work

You should be friendly, helpful and polite, and enjoy meeting people. You will need to have a genuine interest in helping people. You could be dealing with difficult customers, so will need to be patient and able to stay calm under pressure.

Manager

As a manager, you will also need to be able to take responsibility, motivate people and have good organisational and planning skills. You will need to be good with figures and computers, and be decisive.

Working conditions

You could be based in an office, mainly on the telephone, using a headset and computer. You will probably be sitting or standing in one place a lot. You could work normal office hours but may do shifts, including evenings, weekends and even nights.

Future prospects

There are many opportunities in all types of organisations throughout the country, but especially in towns and cities. You might work for shops, banks, call centres, airports or tourist information centres.

Assistant

You could go on to become a supervisor and then a manager.

Manager

Most opportunities for customer service managers are in larger companies. You might be able to move into high-level jobs in the company's head office.

Advantages/disadvantages

The work can be repetitive and dealing with difficult people or problems may be stressful.

You can earn a good salary if you continually provide an excellent service.

Qualifications and courses

Assistant

You can enter and train in this career with qualifications at Level 2, possibly Level 1. You will usually need 3–4 GCSEs/S grades (A–C/1–3), including maths and English. Some organisations may require higher qualifications such as NVQs/SVQs at Levels 3 and 4, HNCs/HNDs, A levels. NVQ/SVQ Levels 2 or 3 in Customer Service would be an advantage. Training is often done on the job.

Manager

You can enter and train in this career with qualifications at Levels 2 or 3 but will need relevant experience. You will usually need 3–4 GCSEs/3–5 S grades (A–C/1–3), including maths and English. NVQ/SVQ Levels 2 or 3 in Customer Service or Management would be an advantage. Some employers ask for qualifications at a higher level, such as A levels/H grades or other Level 3 courses.

Large organisations may have management training schemes, including fast-track schemes for graduates.

Money guide

Assistant

You could earn £11,000–£12,000 a year when you start work. This may rise to £13,000–£18,000 when you have got some experience. £21,000+ is possible with experience and working in a large organisation.

Manager

You could earn £16,000–£21,500 as a trainee manager. £22,000–£27,000 is possible with experience and working in a large organisation. Experienced managers can earn £30,000+. Senior managers in large organisations could earn in excess of £40,000–£55,000.

Related opportunities

- Sales/Retail Assistant p495
- Store Manager p499
- Receptionist p54

Further information

Institute of Customer Service
2 Castle Court, St Peter's Street, Colchester, Essex CO1 1EW
01206 571716; www.instituteofcustomerservice.com

www.cityandguilds.com/myperfectjob

FISHMONGER

What the work involves

- Fishmongers prepare and sell fish, offering advice to customers on how to store and cook it. They can work in various environments including shops, supermarkets and market stalls.

- You will be required to provide customers with information such as how the fish was caught, the sustainability of its stock and whether it has been previously frozen.

- You will buy fish from the wholesaler and prepare it for retail sales. This preparation includes removing bones, skin and scales then gutting the fish and maybe cutting it into portions.

- You may also complete tasks like preparing crab.

The type of person suited to this work

You will require good hand eye coordination as you will be using small knives to complete detailed jobs such as filleting and taking out little bones. It is important that you can cope with messy jobs as you will be both cleaning and gutting fish. You should be able to stand for long periods of time. You should have a strong level of personal hygiene. You will need to be personable, as customer service is extremely important for this role. People with skin allergies may not be suitable for this job.

Working conditions

The conditions in this industry can be cold and wet. You will be expected to spend a great deal of time on your feet, moving between the counter and storage areas. Most fishmongers will work for approximately 40 hours a week; these hours may include Saturdays with a day and a half off a week. There are often early mornings as this is when stock deliveries arrive. Protective clothing and footwear are required.

Future prospects

Fishmongers work in many different environments including supermarkets, small local stores and mobile fish units and so individuals who choose this career can move between them. The mobile fish trade incorporates travel and would provide more variety in the working day. Other possibilities might involve supplying fishmonger stores with fresh fish or moving into other industries which require food preparation for example working with meat. There may also be management opportunities and the possibility of opening your own shop.

Advantages/disadvantages

The early mornings may prove inconvenient.

You will have the opportunity to be creative, both in the preparation of the fish and in providing customers with advice on how best to prepare or cook it.

The amount of time spent on your feet and cold temperatures may cause discomfort.

Qualifications and courses

You do not require any formal qualifications to enter into this industry; most employers will however expect a good basic level of education including English and maths. Apprenticeships are also available, competition is fierce and so good grades at GCSE will be beneficial.

People normally begin at counter assistant level and gain on the job training either through direct entry or training schemes. Whilst working you will need to attain your basic food hygiene certification, followed by Hazard Analysis and Critical Control Point (HACCP) training.

It could also be beneficial to work towards NVQs in Retail Skills at level 2 or Retail (Sales Professional) at level 3, both of which contain a fish-specific unit.

There are short courses available including a one-day introductory course, knife skills and training and the two day City & Guilds Seafood Retail Certificate at the Seafood Training School in Billingsgate. These courses are designed for people who have never had contact with the industry and will provide valuable practical experience.

Money guide

Pay rates vary depending on location and employer.

Fishmongers usually receive around £11,500–£13,500 a year, this figure can rise to about £19,500 per year, depending on experience. There is also the possibility of self-employment; this could be a great deal better paid, however with the decline of the independent fishmongers this may be a risk.

Related opportunities

- Butcher p481
- Chef p143
- Kitchen Assistant p152
- Shopkeeper p497

Further information

Billingsgate Seafood Training School
Office 30, Billingsgate Market, Trafalgar Way, London E14 5ST
020 7517 3548; info@seafoodtraining.org; www.seafoodtraining.org

Sea Fish Industry Authority
Origin Way, Europarc, Grimsby DN37 9TZ
01472 252300 ; training@seafish.co.uk ; www.seafish.org

City& Guilds

www.cityandguilds.com/myperfectjob

Retail, Sales and Customer Services

CRCI: SB
CLCI: OFM

FLORIST

What the work involves

- Florists combine creativity with knowledge of plants and flowers to design and create floral displays. These are sold via shops and market stalls.

- You will be responsible for ordering and caring for the plants and flowers, aiding customers in choosing flowers suitable for specific occasions and creating floral displays.

- You may also be required to deliver to customers and set up displays at events.

- You will be expected to handle money, complete regular stock takes and help with the day to day running of the business.

The type of person suited to this work

You will need to be extremely creative, with an understanding of shape, colour and design. As a great deal of this job is hands-on you will need to be dexterous. A strong knowledge of plants and flowers and the care required for them is essential, along with a desire to expand that information. You will need to be patient, with good customer service skills and sensitivity to the needs of the client. You should have brilliant telephone communication skills and the ability to work within tight deadlines. Administration and sales skills are also important.

Working conditions

Florists usually work inside in a shop environment. Some travel may be required when making deliveries and so a driving licence might be needed. Those who work on a floristry stall will spend most of their time outdoors. This job involves a great deal of standing at the work bench/counter. Some shops provide uniforms or aprons. Working hours usually vary between 35 and 40 hours per week, shop opening hours are normally 9am to 5pm. This job may not be suitable for people who suffer from pollen allergies.

Future prospects

Those with a certain amount of experience and the desire to may progress to a managerial role. There is also the possibility of becoming self-employed by opening your own business once you have the required business skills. Another progression option is working as a freelance worker for a variety of businesses where you work on a contract basis, arranging flowers. Other choices include teaching floristry and becoming a professional demonstrator.

Advantages/disadvantages

You can combine creativity, skill and knowledge to create floral displays.

You will be on your feet for a great deal of time and those who work on florist market stalls will be outdoors in all weathers.

Every day will be different as you will be working with a wide range of customers towards a variety of events.

Qualifications and courses

There are no specific academic qualifications required to become a florist, however any formal qualifications in floristry would be advantageous.

Qualifications that are available include NVQs in floristry Levels 2 & 3, Level 2 National Certificate in floristry, Level 3 Advanced National Certificate in floristry, BTEC National Award in floristry, BTEC National Certificate/Diploma in floristry and BTEC First Diploma in floristry. The Diploma in environmental and land-based studies available at Levels 1, 2 and 3 would also be of benefit.

The requirements for entry into these courses will vary, however GCSEs grades A*-E in subjects such as English, maths and arts and crafts would be beneficial. Any other relevant experience and skills including numeracy and literacy skills might be taken into account. Work experience in a florists shop would also be valuable.

Apprenticeships and Advanced Apprenticeships may also be available. These allow participants to gain paid, on the job training. Young Apprenticeships are available for those aged 14–16 years old.

Money guide

These figures may vary depending on location and employer.

The starting salary for a florist is the national minimum wage (visit the HM Revenue and Customs website for more information).

Once experience is gained this figure may rise to around £18,000 per year and might increase again to approximately £25,000 a year once management status is reached.

Related opportunities

- Display Designer/Window Dresser p180
- Gardener/Garden Designer p272
- Landscape Architect/Designer p277
- Landscaper/Landscape Manager p278

Further information

British Florist Association (BFA)
PO Box 5161, Dudley DY1 9FX
01384 213263; www.britishfloristassociation.org

Flowers and Plants Association
266–270 Flower Market, New Covent Garden Market, London SW8 5NB
020 7738 8044; www.flowers.org.uk

City&
Guilds

www.cityandguilds.com/myperfectjob

JEWELLER

What the work involves

- Retail jewellers sell jewellery and sometimes watches, clocks and silverware in shops to customers. Other services they offer might include valuation, alteration and repair. Customer service and sales are particularly important in this industry.

- You may work for a company which specialises in selling a particular gemstone such as diamonds.

- Manufacturing jewellers create rings, necklaces, earrings, bracelets and cufflinks using metals and other materials. The items constructed might be mass-produced or individually designed and hand crafted.

- You could specialise in one area such as casting or enamelling or learn a variety of techniques.

The type of person suited to this work

A retail jeweller needs to be extremely trustworthy and security minded. You should be well turned out with good communication skills and friendly manner. You should also be capable of handling money and have any practical repair skills required.

A manufacturing jeweller needs to have an artistic flair and be highly creative. You should have good hand-to-eye co-ordination, be dexterous, patient and accurate. You should have solid problem solving skills, the ability to concentrate for long periods of time.

Working conditions

Retail jewellers work in shops, varying from small stores to larger chains. They usually work 37 to 40 hours per week, these hours may include weekends, evenings and bank holidays.

Manufacturing jewellers work in small factories, studios or workshops which are normally warm and bright. However, depending on the techniques being used working conditions could be hot, dusty, wet or noisy.

Future prospects

A retail jeweller might continue on to become a sales assistant, assistant manager or even a manager. Specialist skills can improve prospects and so learning valuation or alteration may lead to higher paid roles.

Manufacturing jewellers' prospects also improve with training and experience as they will be able to complete more challenging work. Due to the small nature of manufacturing companies progression may involve a change of employers.

Advantages/disadvantages

As a retail jeweller being on your feet all day may cause discomfort.

As a manufacturing jeweller you can be creative, putting the skills you learn to use.

Qualifications and courses

Retail Jeweller: Although there are no set qualifications required to enter into this industry many employers will expect GCSEs grades A*-C (or equivalent).

Manufacturing Jeweller: Again there are no formal entry requirements; however qualifications in art, craft or design would be highly beneficial.

There are two ways to begin your career as a manufacturing jeweller. The first of these is studying for a national certificate/diploma, HNC/HND, foundation degree or a degree. The second is to train on the job, working for a jewellery company.

HNC/HND courses will probably require one A level/two or three H grades (or equivalent). Degree courses might request candidates have attained at least two A levels/three H grades and five GCSEs (or equivalent). It is always best to check with the institution as entry requirements do vary.

Many of these courses are available on a part time basis.

The Jewellery and Allied Industries Training Council has a list of relevant courses.

Apprenticeships are available from The Goldsmiths' Company for people aged between 16 and 21.

Money guide

Salaries vary depending on location and employer.

Retail jewellers have a starting salary of around £11,000 and usually earn commission.

This may increase to about £25,000 if they reach managerial level. Senior sales consultants can earn up to £60,000.

Manufacturing jewellers usually start on a salary of around £10,500 per year, with experience this can rise to around £25,000 a year. Top salaries can be as high as £50,000 a year.

Related opportunities

- Gold/Silversmith/Engraver p185
- Sales/Retail Assistant p495

Further information

The Goldsmiths' Company
Goldsmiths' Hall, Foster Lane, London EC2V 6BN
020 7606 7010; www.thegoldsmiths.co.uk

British Jewellers' Association
Federation House, 10 Vyse Street, Birmingham B18 6LT
0121 237 1112; www.bja.org.uk

www.cityandguilds.com/myperfectjob

Retail, Sales and Customer Services

CRCI: SB
CLCI: OM

MARKET TRADER

What the work involves

- Market traders buy goods from a wholesaler or manufacturer, and then sell them from a market stall which they rent in an open-air or covered market.

- You might sell things you have made yourself at specialist craft markets.

- You will be dealing with customers, encouraging them to buy items on your stall, weighing and wrapping goods, and taking money and possibly cheques, credit and debit cards.

- As well as setting up the stall in the morning, arranging your things and keeping the stall clean and tidy, you will also pack up and clear away in the evenings.

The type of person suited to this work

You will need to be friendly and outgoing and enjoy working with the public in an informal way, persuading them to buy your goods.

Market traders have to be fit and active to transport their goods, be on their feet all day and then pack up when the market closes. You should be prepared to work outside in all weathers, and even covered markets can be cold.

When you are buying goods you will have to know what will sell and negotiate a good price. You will deal with money and will have to do your own accounts, if you are self-employed.

You should be self-motivated and hard-working and produce attractive, desirable products.

Working conditions

You will probably have a very early start and work from about 5am–6.00pm. You will probably have to work Saturdays and often Sundays.

You may have to travel to buy the goods you sell.

You could be working on your own or with one or two other people. You may work at the same market every day or move round to several different markets during the week.

Future prospects

It can be hard to do well with a market stall: there is a lot of competition and you will need good products.

On craft markets, it can be difficult to sell things at a competitive price.

For a while when you start, you may need to arrive very early in the morning to get a spare pitch, before an opportunity comes up to get your own, permanent stall.

Most market traders are self-employed and you could expand by taking on staff to run extra stalls or you could open a shop.

Advantages/disadvantages

You will be your own boss, working outside in an active, practical job with lots of contact with the public.

Qualifications and courses

There are no formal entry requirements but you will need to have basic maths and English skills.

Most of the training is done on the job, learning from the person you work for or from other traders.

There are some short courses you can take, usually run by the local authority, and the National Market Traders Federation (NMTF) can give advice.

You could also do short courses on running your own business, provided by small business advice services.

If you are selling things you have made, you will probably need to do a specialist course, for example jewellery making or a fashion course at university.

Many markets insist that traders have insurance for public liability. The National Market Traders' Federation can provide this.

Markets are often very lively, friendly places.

The hours can be long.

Money guide

You may earn around £7,000 per year if you have got a stall for 1 or 2 days a week (less than the minimum wage).

You could earn around £15,000–£22,000 a year if you are working 5+ days a week. If you are selling specialist goods you may earn more. This is around £500 profit per week.

A few market traders who are selling specialist goods can earn around £30,000–£40,000 a year.

Related opportunities

- Checkout Operator p484
- Customer Services Assistant/Manager p486
- Sales/Retail Assistant p495
- Shopkeeper p497

Further information

National Market Traders' Federation
Hampton House, Hawshaw Lane, Hoyland, Barnsley S74 0HA
01226 749021; www.nmtf.co.uk

British Shops and Stores Association Limited
Middleton House, 2 Main Road, Middleton Cheney, Banbury, Oxfordshire OX17 2TN
01295 712277; www.british-shops.co.uk

www.cityandguilds.com/myperfectjob

MEAT HYGIENE INSPECTOR

What the work involves

- Meat hygiene inspectors visit slaughterhouses and meat stores to check that meat is being processed and produced safely and hygienically by following relevant laws and regulations.

- You will work with live animals and poultry to check that they are healthy and disease free, and also do post mortems.

- You will check that animals are cared for and transported properly and that meat plants and deliveries are run safely and hygienically, and that unwanted meat or carcases are destroyed properly.

- You will write detailed reports and make sure that any action you have recommended is taken quickly and to the right standards.

The type of person suited to this work

Meat inspectors have usually have worked somewhere like an abattoir or meat-processing plant first to get experience.

You will be dealing with people in lots of different organisations and at all levels, so will need to be able to establish good working relationships and deal calmly with problems.

You will need to have good written and communication skills, understand and apply laws and regulations, and have a good eye for detail.

It is a fairly active job so you will need to be fit and healthy, practical and good with your hands and able to work to strict safety guidelines.

Working conditions

You will spend most of your time travelling to farms and processing plants. You will be wearing protective clothing, using tools and equipment and handling heavy meat carcasses.

Slaughterhouses can be cold and noisy and smell strongly, and on farms you will be working outdoors in all weathers.

Meat inspectors usually do normal office hours but may need to work evenings and weekends to work at short notice if there is a hygiene emergency.

Future prospects

Most meat inspectors work for the Meat Hygiene Service which is part of the government's Food Standards Agency. Others work for companies producing or selling food and meat products.

There are jobs in all parts of the UK but opportunities are limited with only around 2800 meat inspectors in the country.

You will need experience in the industry before you can become an inspector. You can then progress to be a supervisor or manager for the Meat Hygiene Service or go into management in a large food company.

Qualifications and courses

You can enter and train in this career with qualifications at Levels 2 or 3.

All meat inspectors must hold the Royal Society for the Promotion of Health's Certificate in Meat Inspection or Poultry Meat Inspection.

To get onto the course you will need to have at least 5 GCSEs/S grades (A–C/1–3), including English and maths or a science, or Associate membership of the Meat Training Council.

NVQs/SVQs are available in Meat and Poultry Plant Operations at Level 2 and Meat and Poultry Processing and Meat Processing at Level 2. RSPH offers a Level 2 Certificate in Wild Game Meat Hygiene to meet the food hygiene laws. RSPH also offer Level 3 and Level 4 Awards in Food Safety Supervision for Manufacturing.

Apprenticeships/Skillseekers may be available for people aged 16–24.

Advantages/disadvantages

You need to be flexible with your working hours as you may be asked to respond to an emergency at anytime.

Money guide

You can expect to earn £17,000 per year as a trainee inspector.

Up to £22,500 is the usual salary when you have got some experience.

You could earn £24,000–£33,000 as a Senior Meat Inspector with qualifications and experience.

Related opportunities

- Health and Safety Adviser p40
- Trading Standards Officer p500
- Butcher p481
- Meat Process Worker p239

Further information

Meat Hygiene Service
Kings Pool, Peasholme Green, York YO1 7PR
01904 455501; www.foodstandards.gov.uk

Royal Society for Public Health
3rd Floor Market Towers, 1 Nine Elms Lane,
London SW8 5NQ
020 3177 1600; www.rsph.org.uk/

www.cityandguilds.com/myperfectjob

MERCHANDISER

What the work involves

- You will probably work for a large chain of shops as part of their buying and marketing team, helping to create and maintain the brand image of the company, and to monitor how well their goods might sell.

- You will be involved in deciding what goods the stores will sell to get the best profits, and make sure they are displayed and presented in an attractive way that is consistent throughout the company.

- You will work closely with buyers, and help predict trends. You may also visit suppliers and manufacturers to find products which will appeal to your customers.

- You could work for a wide range of companies including fashion retailers, supermarkets or a chain of stores.

The type of person suited to this work

You will need to be interested in your product and in working out and predicting what will sell and how best to display it. You will need to understand what the customers want.

Merchandisers must be creative and self-motivated with initiative and confidence, because they make decisions involving large amounts of money and have to present their ideas to managers and staff.

You should be able to work well in a team and deal with people at all levels, including negotiating prices and arranging deliveries.

The job involves analysing statistics and sales figures and working under pressure to meet targets and deadlines. You will need excellent communication and negotiation skills.

Working conditions

You will mainly be based in an office in a large store, or in a head office and will probably visit other stores in your region.

You will also be visiting suppliers and manufacturers, so you may have to be away from home regularly.

As a senior merchandiser or with more experience, this will probably include going abroad.

You will probably work normal office hours, but might have to work much longer at busy times.

Future prospects

The retail industry employs a lot of people and is expanding and changing at quite a fast rate and so it is an exciting and challenging area.

In a large company, you could get promotion by specialising in a particular product or being responsible for all the stores in an area. Or you could move into related areas such as buying and marketing.

Advantages/disadvantages

You will be making decisions which will directly affect the image of your company and what the public can buy.

Qualifications and courses

Most entrants to this career have a degree, or a Higher National Diploma (HND) but you may be able to start with qualifications at Level 3, and receive further training from your employer.

Larger companies will accept degrees in any subjects, although retailing, marketing or business studies, economics or maths would be useful.

You may be able to get a trainee post with Level 3 qualifications but these would be very competitive and you would probably have to have retail experience as well.

You may be able to do an Apprenticeship/Skillseekers if you are aged 16–24. NVQs/SVQs are available in Supply Chain Management at Levels 2–5, Retail Operations at Levels 2 and 3, Sales at Levels 2 and 3 or Sales Management at Level 4/5.

Merchandisers are trained on the job, and may also work towards the professional qualifications of the Chartered Institute of Purchasing and Supply or the Chartered Institute of Marketing.

Some colleges and universities offer HNDs and Foundation degrees in relevant subjects.

Keeping your finger on the pulse of fashion, future trends and next year's 'must haves' can be exciting.

Money guide

As a starter you can expect £15,000–£18,000 per year.

This could rise to £22,000–£40,000 for an experienced merchandiser.

Senior merchandisers, with responsibilities for price-setting across large companies, can earn £50,000+.

Related opportunities

- Buyer p482
- Marketing Manager/Assistant/Executive p417
- Purchasing Manager p617
- Store Manager p499

Further information

British Shops and Stores Association Limited
Middleton House, 2 Main Road, Middleton Cheney, Banbury, Oxfordshire OX17 2TN
01295 712277; www.british-shops.co.uk

Chartered Institute of Marketing
Moor Hall, Cookham, Maidenhead, Berkshire SL6 9QH
01628 427500; www.cim.co.uk

City&
Guilds

www.cityandguilds.com/myperfectjob

METER READER

What the work involves

- You will be reading electric, gas or water meters at private homes or commercial buildings. You will be putting the information in to a portable computer or on to a form, to work out what the customer owes.

- You will visit houses and companies reading meters which are inside the building or outside in a box for which you will have a key.

- If the customer is out, you may need to estimate the reading or leave a card to say when you will be back.

- You will probably cover a particular area in a van, car or on foot, and have to work to targets, meet customers and answer questions about the service and the meters.

The type of person suited to this work

You will work mainly on your own and so will need to be able to use your initiative and be motivated and self-disciplined in order to meet your targets and get the work done.

Meter readers must work accurately with numbers and use computers and be happy to deal with the public.

You should be able to organise your own work and plan your routes to make sure you cover your whole area.

As you are out and about in all weathers and will do a lot of walking, you will need to be fit and healthy. You should also be polite, honest and trustworthy because you may be going into people's homes.

Working conditions

You will work alone and will spend most of your day driving or walking. You may need to crawl into small, dark places to find the meter.

The job involves meeting a lot of people and going into all sorts of homes and businesses.

Meter readers usually wear a uniform, always carry ID and may need safety clothing.

A normal week will be around 37–40 hours and you may be able to do overtime. You could have to work at evenings and weekends when people are at home to let you in.

Future prospects

There are job opportunities with companies which supply water, gas and electricity in all parts of the country.

The companies vary in size and some will pay bonuses if you meet or go over your targets.

You could get promotion and lead a team covering a particular area, become a supervisor or manager or become involved in training new staff.

Qualifications and courses

You can enter and train for this career with qualifications at Levels 1 or 2.

There are no minimum entry requirements but you will need a good general education and may need GCSEs/S grades (A–C/1–3), usually including English and maths.

You will probably need to be over 18 and have a clean driving licence, particularly in rural areas.

Your employer will train you on the job. You will learn about the different meters and how to read them and how to enter the readings accurately on a handheld computer terminal.

You will then spend time working with an experienced meter reader to learn how to do the job before you go out on your own.

It is possible to get a relevant NVQ such as Level 2 Utilities Metering Operations or NVQ Level 3 in Revenue Protection.

Advantages/disadvantages

You will be out and about, doing active, practical work and meeting lots of different people.

You will be working alone and will need to be motivated and self-disciplined to do the work and meet your targets.

Money guide

You can expect around £13,700 per year when you start. £14300–£16,500 is usual when you have got some experience, and you could earn up to £22,000 with a few years' experience and some additional responsibilities.

You may get bonuses for meeting targets.

Related opportunities

- Customer Service Assistant/Manager p486
- Postal worker p616
- Sales/Retail Assistant p495
- Courier p600

Further information

Office of Gas and Electricity Markets (Ofgem)
9 Millbank, London SW1P 3GE
020 7901 7000; www.ofgem.gov.uk

Office of Water Services (Ofwat)
Centre City Tower, 7 Hill Street, Birmingham B5 4UA
0121 625 1300; www.ofwat.gov.uk

City&
Guilds

www.cityandguilds.com/myperfectjob

Retail, Sales and Customer Services

CRCI: SA
CLCI: RAKA

POST OFFICE CLERK

What the work involves

- Post office clerks provide customers with a variety of postal services along with banking services, bill payment, lottery sales, passport applications and offering advice to customers on these services.

- Tasks you will complete on a daily basis include sending important and expensive mail, selling stamps, weighing, measuring and mailing letters and parcels and dispatching mail abroad.

- Other services you may offer include banking services, passport applications, bill payments, car tax renewal, currency exchange, insurance and lottery sales.

- You might also be required to complete administrative work such as keeping accounts.

The type of person suited to this work

A post office clerk should be able to work within a team and without supervision. You should have excellent communication skills, being both polite and helpful with the ability to adjust to the needs of each client. You should have a certain level of numeracy and be able to handle money with confidence and accuracy. You will be able to cope under pressure. You should have an interest in the numerous services you will be offering along with a willingness to learn about the various forms that clients may require information on. You should have a keen eye for detail and a high concentration span.

Working conditions

If you work for a sub post office you might be working in a newsagent, stationer or village shop. You will be working mainly at a counter but could also do some behind the scenes work in an office environment. You may be required to wear a uniform. The job will probably involve some lifting of heavy parcels. You will usually work between 35 and 36 hours per week, Monday to Friday and occasionally Saturday mornings. Part-time, temporary and flexible working hours may be arranged.

Future prospects

You could progress to the role of postmaster or training officer. Experienced post office clerks may have the opportunity to work on the post office helpline. Within this role you would answer any queries customers or sub-postmasters/mistresses had regarding the products and services that the Post Office Ltd offers.

The skills you acquire in this role stand you in good stead to move on to careers within other industries such as banking, for example you may wish to work as a bank cashier.

Advantages/disadvantages

You may, at times, find this role stressful particularly when the post office is especially busy.

The skills you acquire will be transferable to other industries and roles.

Qualifications and courses

There are no set requirements for this role. Most people enter directly into employment. Training is done on the job and involves two weeks in a training centre followed by two supervised weeks at the counter.

Despite the lack of formal academic entry requirements it would be preferable to have achieved some GCSEs at grade A*-C, particularly in English and maths. A Higher Diploma may also be a valid qualification, this offers a mixture of academic and work related study. An aptitude for languages would also be beneficial.

Any experience of working in a customer service industry would be advantageous, as would experience of handling money. This experience might involve working in a shop as a sales assistant, working in a restaurant as a waiter/waitress or maybe as an assistant in a launderette.

You might be able to work flexible hours which suit you.

There may be some lifting involved.

Money guide

The rate of pay will vary depending on the location and the employer.

Post office clerks generally start on a salary of around £12,500. After experience this may increase to an amount somewhere in the vicinity of £18,000 a year.

A promotion to the role of postmaster or training officer would result in a pay increase.

Related opportunities

- Bank Cashier/Customer Adviser p22
- Customer Service Assistant/Manager p486
- Finance Clerk p19
- Sales Assistant p495

Further information

Royal Mail Group Ltd
148 Old Street, London EC1V 9HQ
www.royalmailgroup.com/portal/rmg

Royal Mail Group Ltd Northern Ireland
Royal Mail House, 20 Donegall Quay, Belfast BT1 1AA

Irish Enquiries
028 9089 2116; press.office@royalmail.com;
www.royalmailgroup.com/portal/rmg

City&
Guilds

www.cityandguilds.com/myperfectjob

SALES/RETAIL ASSISTANT

What the work involves

- You will deal with customers, offering them a polite, helpful and speedy service to sell a range of goods.

- You will help keep the shop tidy and well stocked, answer questions, deal with complaints and give suggestions and advice.

- Shops range from small specialist outlets to huge department stores, so your duties will vary.

- When you are working on the till, you will take payments, give change, deal with refunds, wrap goods and arrange orders and deliveries.

The type of person suited to this work

You will need to be well presented, outgoing, friendly and polite, enjoy meeting people and be able to deal with awkward customers and stay calm when you are busy.

Sales assistants have to learn about the things they are selling, which could involve in-house training, and they must be able to help and advise customers to find what they want.

You could be working to targets and earning bonuses according to how much you sell, so will need to be persuasive but not pushy.

You should be responsible and trustworthy, and fit and active to cope with being on your feet all day.

You should be able to work within a team and on your own when required.

Working conditions

In small shops you could spend most of the time at the till/checkout. In large stores you could be working on the shop floor, helping and advising customers and fetching goods from stockrooms.

You may have to carry heavy items.

You will keep the shop clean and tidy and may wear a uniform.

You could work early or late shifts and at weekends and evenings.

Future prospects

There are shops in all areas of the country and opportunities are increasing as the retail industry is expanding. Large retail parks and shopping centres have meant that some smaller shops in town centres have closed.

Working in a small shop you may get to know your regulars well and be given responsibility quite quickly, but promotion prospects can be limited.

In large stores and chains you will probably get training and can quickly become a supervisor and then move into management jobs. Depending on your employer, you might have to move around from shop to shop gaining experience within different-sized shops and departments.

Qualifications and courses

You can enter and train for this career with qualifications at Levels 1 or 2.

If you have a relevant qualification at Level 3 or above, you may be able to go straight into trainee management jobs. There are specific retail management degree and HND courses available.

There are no minimum entry requirements for this work. However, larger companies may ask for 2–4 GCSEs/S grades (A–C/1–3).

You may have to pass tests in basic maths and English.

You could do an Apprenticeship/Skillseekers if aged 16–24. You would get NVQs/SVQs at Levels 2 and 3, probably in Customer Service.

Sales assistants can also work towards NVQs/SVQs in Retail Operations at Levels 2 and 3, or Distributive Operations at Levels 2 and 3, an OCR Certificate in Retail, or a C&G Certificate in Retailing.

Advantages/disadvantages

There are lots of opportunities and you will be meeting new people.

The hours can be long.

You will have very busy times and very quiet times.

Money guide

Wages vary a lot depending on the type and size of the shop and its location.

When you first start work you can expect a salary of around £11,000–£12,500 per year.

With experience, this rises to £19,000+ as a supervisor.

You will get discounts and may get bonuses and commission on what you sell, and may get more money for working shifts.

Related opportunities

- Checkout Operator p484
- Customer Services Assistant/Manager p486
- Receptionist p54
- Bank Cashier/Customer Adviser p22

Further information

British Shops and Stores Association Limited
Middleton House, 2 Main Road, Middleton Cheney, Banbury, Oxfordshire OX17 2TN
01295 712277; www.british-shops.co.uk

The British Retail Consortium
21 Dartmouth Street, London SW1H 9BP
020 7854 8900; www.brc.org.uk

www.cityandguilds.com/myperfectjob

Retail, Sales and Customer Services

CRCI: SB
CLCI: OE

SHOE REPAIRER

What the work involves

- Shoe repairers mend and repair shoes, boots and other footwear. They can also repair belts, bags and briefcases, using specialist tools and materials including nail and staple guns and stitching machines.

- You will replace soles and heels by stitching or gluing on new ones and finishing them off neatly.

- A lot of shoe repairers also use specialist machinery to cut keys and do metal engraving.

- You will be serving customers, labelling the shoes they leave, issuing customers with tickets, taking payments, using a till and probably selling things like shoe dyes and polishes, belts and handbags.

The type of person suited to this work

It is important to be practical, good at working with your hands and able to do quite small, detailed work quickly and neatly. As the machinery and tools can be dangerous, you will need to be responsible and work safely, be happy wearing overalls and getting your hands dirty.

You might be dyeing shoes, so good colour vision is essential. You will need to enjoy meeting people and be able to cope with being busy and working quickly whilst customers wait for their repairs. You should be happy to work on your own or in a small team, and be able to work out costs and deal with money and payments.

You will need to have good listening skills, and have business skills if you are self-employed.

Working conditions

You will be on your feet a lot, using a range of tools and equipment. You will be using dyes and glues and it can be noisy and dirty with strong smells, so you will wear an overall.

Shoe repairers usually work around 40 hours a week, including Saturdays.

You may work on your own or with one or two others and will be dealing with the public.

Some shoe repairers work in factories repairing goods which customers have returned.

Future prospects

There are around 8000 shoe repairers in all areas of the country but job opportunities can be limited as most are small shops only employing a few people.

Shoe repairers also work in small outlets in supermarkets or department stores.

You will learn a skill, probably including engraving, and could open your own business. You would need some money to start up, and business skills to plan your work and keep accounts.

In a large chain you could go on to management jobs.

Qualifications and courses

You can enter and train in this career with qualifications at Levels 1 or 2.

NVQs/SVQs are available in Retail Operations at Levels 2 and 3, and a City & Guilds certificate in Retail Principles. City & Guilds also offer a Higher Professional Diploma in Retail Management.

Training is done on the job, working alongside an experienced shoe repairer. It is possible to work towards an NVQ/SVQ Footwear Repair at Levels 2 and 3. Or a Vocationally Related Qualification (VRQ) in Footwear and Leather production.

Apprenticeship/Skillseekers may be available to those aged 16–24.

Advantages/disadvantages

You do not need qualifications and will be doing a practical, hands-on job and meeting lots of people.

You could work for yourself, running your own shoe repair outlet.

The work can be repetitive and fiddly.

Money guide

Wages can vary a lot. Many shoe repairers are self-employed, so wages may depend on how big the shop is, where it is and how well it is doing.

Working for someone else, you will probably earn around £10,500 per year when you start.

This could rise to £17,000 with experience and perhaps extra responsibility. Shop managers could get £21,000+.

You might get paid bonuses and will probably get discounts.

Related opportunities

- Locksmith p234
- Customer Services Assistant/Manager p486
- Sales/Retail Assistant p495
- Shopkeeper p497

Further information

MultiService Association (Shoe Repairs, Watch Repairs, Engraving and Key Cutting)
St Crispin's House, Station Road, Desborough, Northamptonshire NN14 2SA
01536 760374; www.msauk.biz/

www.cityandguilds.com/myperfectjob

SHOPKEEPER

What the work involves

- A shopkeeper owns or manages one or more shops, such as greengrocers, bakeries, newsagents, supermarkets, fishmongers, dry cleaners, fashion retailers, jewellers and florists.

- You will be finding manufacturers and suppliers. For shops that sell foodstuffs this may mean sourcing local produce and purchasing it for the best price.

- As well as keeping the shop tidy and well stocked, you will pay staff wages and keep books and accounts.

The type of person suited to this work

You need to be determined and motivated, with a real interest in what you are doing; you should also be prepared to work long hours and to travel in order to find stock and suppliers.

You will need to be able to sell and market your goods and be confident about finding products that people want to buy.

Excellent communication skills are essential. Also important is a good business sense and being able to plan your finances and keep your accounts. You should be well organised, have some marketing, business and sales skills to succeed in this area of work.

Working conditions

Your hours and conditions will depend on what you are selling and how well you do.

Shops usually open at weekends and often in the evenings, with newsagents and convenience stores opening early and late.

Being your own boss can be stressful but also extremely satisfying and rewarding. Shops vary in size and appearance and how pleasant the working environment is will depend on its staff and clientele. You might wear a uniform and do some heavy lifting.

Future prospects

One option is to operate a franchise, for example a local convenience store, paying a larger company to use their name and sell their products.

If you are successful, you could expand by opening more or larger stores.

The trend towards large shops has meant that lots of smaller shops have closed. It's a very competitive business so you will need to find the right product.

Advantages/disadvantages

There is a lot of freedom in being your own boss: you do not have to answer to anyone else and can make all your own decisions.

You will need to develop good business skills as success will depend on your abilities.

Qualifications and courses

There are no formal entry requirements although customer service and sales experience would be useful. Business experience is also important.

NVQs/SVQs are available in Retail Operations at Levels 2 and 3, and a City & Guilds certificate in Retail Principles. City & Guilds also offer a Higher Professional Diploma in Retail Management.

Other qualifications available include the University Certificate in SME Retail Management which is offered by Manchester Metropolitan University. And some local colleges may offer evening courses in Marketing and Sales skills.

Local training facilities provide courses in all aspects of owning and running a business including marketing, VAT and starting a business.

If you want to buy your own store, you will need funding, either from your own pocket or through a loan from the bank. There are organisations which provide advice on opening a business, such as the National Federation of Enterprise Agencies (NFEA) and Business Link.

Money guide

Earnings can vary enormously and will depend on how successful you are, the size of the business, where it is and what you are selling.

On average, shopkeepers earn £15,000–£30,000 a year but if you do well you could earn a lot more.

If you are highly successful you could make an annual turnover of between £60,000 and £70,000+ per year.

Related opportunities

- Buyer p482
- Market Trader p490
- Merchandiser p492
- Sales/Retail Assistant p495

Further information

British Franchise Association (BFA)
A2 Danebrook Court, Oxford Office Village, Langford Lane, Oxford OX5 1LQ
01865 379892; www.thebfa.org

National Federation of Enterprise Agencies (NFEA)
12 Stephenson Court, Fraser Road, Priory Business Park, Bedford MK44 3WJ
01234 831623; www.nfea.com

www.cityandguilds.com/myperfectjob

Retail, Sales and Customer Services

CRCI: SB
CLCI: OE

STOCK CONTROL/ REPLENISHMENT ASSISTANT

What the work involves

- You will work in a supermarket or retail environment, refilling the shelves.

- You must be aware of where each product is, both for when you need to restock it and for when a customer inquires about the whereabouts of an item.

- Your duties will include checking to see which goods need replacing, adding labels to products, tidying the display areas and shelves and transporting goods from the stockroom.

- You may be required to order stock, take deliveries and serve customers.

The type of person suited to this work

This role involves physical activity and so you will need to have a certain level of fitness. You will be expected to, at times, work alone and unsupervised and so you must be trustworthy. You will also spend some time working as part of a team so you will need to be comfortable working with others. You must have an approachable and friendly disposition as you may need to advise customers. You might use a BHT (battery-hand terminal) or HHT (hand-held terminal) in order to keep track of stock or print labels and so you should be comfortable working with computerised equipment.

Working conditions

You will be working in a retail environment; your surroundings will vary depending on which area you choose to work in. Supermarkets can sometimes be cold. You will be on your feet for most of the day; you will be lifting and transporting sometimes heavy stock. Average working hours are about 37 to 40 a week; you will probably be on a rota and so could be working at any time of the day (or night). Part time work and flexitime are available. You might wear a uniform.

Future prospects

Working in stock control/replenishment stands you in good stead to move into other retail positions such sales assistant or checkout operator. Your skills will be transferable to other retail environments. However, if you have not completed any qualifications progression may prove difficult.

You might be able to complete extra training whilst working which would enhance your chances of promotion. There is a possibility, with training and/or qualifications you could progress into a supervisory or managerial position.

Advantages/disadvantages

You may find the physical nature of this job tiring.

This job has a social element as it allows you to meet people from all walks of life everyday.

You might find this role repetitive.

Your job will allow you to be active.

Qualifications and courses

No formal requirements are necessary, however some employers might expect applicants to have GCSEs in maths and English grades A*-E or equivalent. Most employers will want candidates to have solid communication skills for dealing with customers, a basic level of numeracy as they will need to know how much of each item needs to be restocked and a can-do attitude.

Apprenticeships are available. This would allow you to gain valuable training whilst being paid a small salary. Many people within this industry begin on a part time basis, such as weekend or holiday work and are then offered a permanent position as and when one becomes available. Details of apprenticeships can be found on www.apprenticeships.org.uk. The salaries available for apprenticeships will vary depending on geographical location.

Previous experience dealing with the public within a relevant industry such as retail would prove beneficial when applying for a post in stock control/replenishment.

Training is done on the job and most retailers expect employees to complete an induction course and training programme

Money guide

These figures are only approximate and will vary depending on location and employer.

On average the starting salary for this role will be around £10,000 per year. This amount could increase to approximately £15,000 with experience. If you reach the role of supervisor you can expect to earn up to £18, 000 per year.

Related opportunities

- Checkout Operator p484
- Customer Service Assistant/Manager p486
- Sales/Retail Assistant p495
- Store Manager p499

Further information

The British Retail Consortium
2nd Floor, 21 Dartmouth Street, London SW1H 9BP
020 7854 8900; www.brc.org.uk

British Shops and Stores Association Limited (BSSA)
Middleton House, 2 Main Road, Middleton Cheney,
Banbury OX17 2TN
01295 712277; www.british-shops.co.uk

City&
Guilds

www.cityandguilds.com/myperfectjob

STORE MANAGER

What the work involves

- You will be running a shop, maybe a small or a large department store, overseeing a team of staff.

- Managers recruit, train and supervise staff, encouraging them to develop their skills and meet targets.

- You will monitor sales and look at ways of improving them and oversee supplies by checking stock, placing orders and making sure you do not run out or over-order.

- The store manager has overall responsibility for everything that happens in the shop and must deal with any problems or complaints.

The type of person suited to this work

As you could be dealing with customers and complaints you will need excellent negotiation skills. You will also need to motivate, train, and sometimes discipline staff. You should be energetic and able to take responsibility and make quick decisions.

You will need an understanding of business and of relevant laws. You should be able to analyse sales figures and have creative ideas for selling and promoting goods to improve profits. You will have to be organised and able to deal with paperwork whilst working to targets and deadlines.

Working conditions

Many stores are open long hours, at weekends and overnight, so you will probably have to work shifts, usually over 5 days.

You will be on your feet a lot as well as doing administration and paperwork.

You may be based in one store, or be visiting several that you have responsibility for.

Future prospects

There are lots of opportunities but trainee posts with large chains can be very competitive.

With a large retail chain your prospects can be good and you can quickly take on more responsibilities.

You could move into other areas of the company, for example marketing or buying, and may be able to work abroad.

You could work for yourself but will need money to start up your own store.

Advantages/disadvantages

Retail is an expanding, developing business and so can offer you an exciting career with good promotion prospects.

You will have a lot of responsibility quite early in your career.

Working with the public can be demanding and stressful.

Money guide

Wages vary with the company and the size of the store.

Qualifications and courses

You can enter and train in this career with qualifications at Levels 2, 3 or 4 and will probably need relevant experience as well. Some of the larger stores may require 5 GCSEs/S grades (A-C) including maths and English.

NVQs/SVQs are available in Retail Operations at Levels 2 and 3. Other qualifications include BTEC Retail qualifications at Levels 2 and 3 and the City & Guilds Higher Professional Diploma in Retail Management at Level 4.

You could join a management development scheme after gaining experience in the store. You could also consider a Diploma or Certificate Level 3 course in First Line Management offered by the Institute of Leadership and Management (ILM).

With A levels/H grades or equivalent you could go directly onto a management training scheme. These are available with most of the major retail companies and are usually available on an annual recruitment basis.

Fast-track training is usually available to graduates with a degree in any subject.

Management degrees are offered by universities across the country.

You could earn £14,300–£18,000 per year when you start as a non-graduate trainee with a large chain.

£11,000–£12,500 is likely as a trainee with a smaller company.

With experience this could rise to £21,000–£24,000.

£45,000+ is possible if you are working for a large company with a lot of responsibility. This could be £60,000 if you are a manager in a large superstore.

You will probably also get discounts, commission and bonuses related to sales.

Related opportunities

- Buyer p482
- Distribution Manager p602
- Merchandiser p492
- Shopkeeper p497

Further information

British Shops and Stores Association Limited
Middleton House, 2 Main Road, Middleton Cheney, Banbury, Oxfordshire OX17 2TN
01295 712277; www.british-shops.co.uk

Chartered Institute of Purchasing & Supply
Easton House, Easton on the Hill, Stamford, Lincolnshire PE9 3NZ
01780 756777; www.cips.org

City&
Guilds

www.cityandguilds.com/myperfectjob

Retail, Sales and Customer Services

CRCI: SB
CLCI: OE

TRADING STANDARDS OFFICER

What the work involves

- Trading Standards Officers work for local government to protect consumers. You will check that any individual or company selling products or services is keeping to the law and providing a fair service.

- You will be working with a range of people and organisations. You will travel to check premises, or to follow up on a complaint from the public.

- You will be enforcing the law, taking cases to court but also giving help and advice to companies and to consumers.

The type of person suited to this work

You will be enforcing laws and regulations so will need to be able to take in and apply a lot of complex information.

You must have an eye for detail and make sure the reports you write are accurate because they could be used in court.

Excellent communication skills are vital because you will be dealing with lots of different people, advising them and enforcing the law. You will need to be forceful but not aggressive.

You will need to be efficient at using computers and be good at maths as you will be dealing with lots of statistics.

Working conditions

You would probably work for local government but could work for private industry advising on relevant legislation.

You will be office-based but will spend time on your own, visiting places such as shops and factories, which could be dirty or cold. TSOs work normal office hours and possibly evenings and weekends when shops and factories are open.

Future prospects

There are jobs all over the country and the work varies: in rural areas you would spend a lot of time working with farm animals. If you work near a port or airport you could be checking imported goods.

There is a shortage of qualified staff but trainee jobs are competitive.

You can get promotion to the head of a section and could become the chief trading standards officer. As relevant laws and regulations are increasing, opportunities in private industry are growing.

Advantages/disadvantages

This can be an interesting and satisfying job where you are helping the public to get a fair deal.

You could be dealing with difficult or aggressive people.

Money guide

As a new enforcement officer or a trainee, you could expect

Qualifications and courses

To become a qualified trading standards officer, you need a Diploma in Consumer Affairs and Trading Standards (DCATS) awarded by the Trading Standards Institute, and you must be working for a local authority to achieve this. All applicants need to have 5 GCSEs/S grades (A–C) including English language, maths and a science, and 2 A levels or another Level 3 course.

Non graduates can join a Trading Standards authority as an enforcement officer or consumer adviser and follow the Accreditation of Prior Experience Learning route (APEL) to the DCATS. The Trading Standards Institute also offers a Diploma in Consumer Affairs for people employed in these positions.

Alternatively, you can follow a relevant degree course, such as a consumer protection degree. The normal entry requirements for a degree in trading standards or consumer protection are 2 A levels/3 H grades or equivalent. The degree provides exemption from certain parts of the DCATS.

The Training Standards Institute (TSI) has introduced a new series of qualifications, for details visit their website.

Apprenticeships/Skillseekers may be available in this area for people aged 16–24.

£16,000-£20,000 per year, although employed Apprentices earn less.

You would start on £25,000–£32,000 per year when newly qualified/graduated.

You could earn £35,000–£50,000 as a senior trading standards officer.

£70,000+ is possible for the head of a service, depending on the size of the local authority.

Related opportunities

- Environmental Health Practitioner/Officer p35
- Health and Safety Inspector p40
- Police Officer p551
- Quality Control Inspector p246

Further information

The Trading Standards Institute
1 Sylvan Court, Sylvan Way, Southfields Business Park, Basildon SS15 6TH
0870 8729000; www.tscareers.org.uk

www.cityandguilds.com/myperfectjob

VEHICLE PARTS OPERATIVE

What the work involves

- This job involves ordering and looking after vehicle parts and accessories and selling them to the public, garages and mechanics.

- You need specialist knowledge of stock, and when ordering or supplying parts have to know the exact make, model and year of the vehicle.

- You will do stock control using computerised systems or possibly keeping paper records, and reorder from warehouses or manufacturers when stocks are low. You will be checking off parts that arrive against delivery notes before placing them in a stock room.

- As well as taking deliveries and taking orders over the phone and in person, you will use tills, take payments and sometimes invoice customers.

The type of person suited to this work

You should be interested in cars and know about a wide range of parts and accessories and which makes of vehicles they are for. You will need to be well organised and able to research where to find more unusual parts.

You will also deal with mechanics and the public over the phone and in person and have to explain technical information clearly and simply.

You will need to have good communication skills, be good in a team situation or able to work on your own.

The job involves being on your feet a lot so you will need to be fit and active.

Working conditions

You could be working in a large shop open to the public or a warehouse used by the motor trade. You could be in a fairly small, local garage or work for a large dealership.

You may have to lift weights, move trolleys and climb ladders to reach high shelves. You will work with the public and staff from the motor trade and probably as part of a team.

Normal hours are Monday to Friday from 8.30am–5.00pm, and you may work evenings and weekends.

Future prospects

There will probably be a shortage of skilled staff in the future so job opportunities are good.

If you work for a smaller company your promotion prospects might be limited but in larger companies you could get additional responsibility more quickly.

You could become a trainee manager in other areas of the retail trade or move into car sales.

Advantages/disadvantages

It is a skilled job with training and you will be using your knowledge of, and interest in, cars and the motor trade.

Qualifications and courses

You can enter and train in this career with qualifications at Levels 1 or 2.

There are no formal entry requirements for this work, but GCSEs/S grades (A–C/1–3) in English, maths and ICT and science are useful.

You could do an Apprenticeship/Skillseekers if you are aged 16–24. You would then take NVQs/SVQs at Levels 2 and 3.

Trainee parts operatives can study for the Institute of the Motor Industry's Certificate (Level 2) and Diploma (Level 3) in Vehicle Parts Operations, or a City & Guilds award in Tyre Fitting. NVQs/SVQs at Levels 1–3 in Vehicle Parts Operations, Levels 1 and 2 in Vehicle Fitting, and Levels 2 and 3 in Vehicle Parts Distribution and Supply can be achieved in the workplace.

You might want to study for a Certificate in Customer Service for the Motor Industry at Levels 2 or 3 available from The Institute of Motor Industry (IMI).

There is a lot of information to remember and the work can be repetitive.

This is a good job for those wanting to work with vehicles who do not want to be mechanics.

Money guide

You can expect £9,200–£11,000 per year when you start as a trainee.

You might earn from £12,500 to £18,000 when you have got some experience.

£25,000+ is possible as a senior vehicle parts operative.

Some employers offer performance related bonuses.

Related opportunities

- Car Salesperson p483
- Motor Vehicle Mechanic p241
- Stock Control/Replenishment Assistant p498
- Warehouse Manager/Worker p629

Further information

Automotive Skills
93 Newman Street, London W1T 3DT
020 7436 6373; www.automotiveskills.org.uk

Retail Motor Industry Federation
201 Great Portland Street, London W1W 5AB
020 7580 9122; www.rmif.co.uk

www.cityandguilds.com/myperfectjob

Retail, Sales and Customer Services

CRCI: SB
CLCI: OFM

WINE MERCHANT

Retail, Sales and Customer Services

CRCI: SD
CLCI: OFM

What the work involves

- You will use your interest and knowledge of wine to buy from vineyards and suppliers and sell to the public or shops, pubs and restaurants.

- As a buyer you probably spend a lot of time abroad finding and tasting new wines, agreeing prices and checking quality.

- In a small, independent merchant, you will probably buy wine from companies who ship it in to the country and go to wine tastings to make selections.

- You could work in a shop or you might sell wine over the internet or by mail order and could be doing your own deliveries.

The type of person suited to this work

Wine merchants are keen to develop their knowledge and expertise, finding new wines and growers and keeping up to date with new developments and tastes.

You will need a good sense of taste and smell to be able to judge the quality of a wine. You should be able to advise people what goes well with what food.

The job involves dealing with the public and negotiating prices with growers and suppliers, and so requires excellent communication and good customer service skills.

Working conditions

Working for yourself you will have freedom and flexibility, but will probably work long hours.

Wine shops are often open all day until 10pm so you might work shifts including weekends. You will be on your feet a lot and could be lifting heavy boxes.

As a buyer you will travel a lot or you might be based in a head office.

You could be working with the public and will deal with people at all levels, sometimes even travelling to people's homes to sell wine.

Future prospects

The wine trade is a very competitive market with a lot of people buying wine from supermarkets, making it difficult for small shops to do well.

There are good prospects for promotion to store manager and above if you work for a chain.

To start your own business you will need experience, a good knowledge of wine, and money to buy stock and premises

Advantages/disadvantages

You will be using your knowledge and love of wine in your job and could get to travel and work abroad a lot.

Jobs as a buyer, travelling abroad to find new wines, are scarce.

Qualifications and courses

There are no formal entry requirements for this career but many new entrants have a degree or vocational qualification. Some employers prefer entrants to have 5 GCSEs/S grades (A–C/1–3) and experience in the retail industry.

Trainee wine merchants can study for the Wine and Spirit Education Trust (WSET) Exams which range from a Foundation Certificate in Wines at Level 1 to the Level 4 Diploma in Wines and Spirits. Once the Diploma has been completed, it is possible to progress to the Master of Wine qualification.

Other relevant qualifications include BTEC Higher National Diploma (HND) in Hospitality Management (Licensed Retail), Advanced Certificate in Wines and Spirits qualifications offered by WSET, or a Foundation degree in Wine Business.

If you want to become an independent wine merchant you will need a premises licence and a personal licence to sell alcohol, which can only be obtained with an accredited qualification. This is the Level 2 National Certificate for Personal Licence Holders (provided by the professional bodies, the BIIAB, GOAL and GQAL).

Money guide

You could expect £12,500 per year starting out. Pay will rise to £17,000, with some experience.

You might earn £18,500–£26,500 as an experienced merchant or manager.

£35,000 is possible if you are very successful, usually running your own business, or in a top job with one of the big wine merchants.

Related opportunities

- Publican/Bar Manager/Licensee p140
- Buyer p482
- Store Manager p499
- Importer/Exporter p605

Further information

Wine & Spirit Education Trust
International Wine & Spirit Centre, 39–45 Bermondsey Street, London SE1 3XF
020 7089 3800; www.wset.co.uk

British Shops and Stores Association Limited
Middleton House, 2 Main Road, Middleton Cheney, Banbury, Oxfordshire OX17 2TN
01295 712277; www.british-shops.co.uk

City&
Guilds

www.cityandguilds.com/myperfectjob

Science, Mathematics and Statistics

Do you have a very mathematical brain? Are you logical in how you approach tasks? Maybe you are fascinated by scientific advances and would like to be involved in future discoveries? People who work in this sector can spend long periods of time carrying out meticulous research. You may find yourself working for a variety of employers, from the health service to a cosmetics company or even a charity. You should be willing to work on your own but also be happy to present your findings in reports to others. People in this sector are very highly skilled individuals who have often been through a lot of training, and possess a questioning and inquisitive mind.

In this section we look at the following jobs:

ACOUSTICIAN

What the work involves

- As an acoustician you will manage, regulate and control sound and vibrations in various environments.

- You might work at researching material for defence, music, healthcare or telecommunications.

- Your work can include many kinds of noise, from building acoustics, architectural acoustics and aerodynamic noise to electroacoustics, environmental issues and even therapeutic uses of ultrasound, as well as diagnostic techniques.

- In your daily work you could be doing anything from advising on sound insulation to researching new ways to adapt the noise levels created by machinery.

The type of person suited to this work

If you want to be an acoustician, you should have an interest not only in how sound behaves, but in problem solving and environmental science too. You need to understand sound and acoustics, and be good at physics and maths.

You need to be creative and innovative in your approach to problem solving, and have good skills in technology for testing and planning any designs you or others create.

You should be organised, and design and plan projects methodically.

You need to be good at working with people, and have good communication and project management skills.

It's also important that you understand legislation and standards.

Working conditions

Working conditions vary depending exactly what job you do within acoustics. If you work in a laboratory doing research, this will probably be a 9–5 job.

It's rare that you'll stay in one place though: acousticians tend to move around and carry out jobs in recording and music studios, or on site. The work therefore involves standing and bending, and you may occasionally be required to lift and install heavy instruments.

You may spend time away from home and travel abroad.

Future prospects

Prospects are much better once you've registered with the IOA.

Possibilities for promotion include moving into management and supervision roles, or specialising in a particular area.

You could work freelance, or even consider setting up your own company.

Qualifications and courses

Most jobs in acoustics require degree-level qualifications. Occasionally opportunities arise at trainee level. Relevant degrees include acoustics, sciences (particularly physics), environmental science, and subjects related to construction. For entrance onto a degree course, you usually need five good GCSEs and at least two A Levels.

There are also specialist postgraduate courses available in e.g building acoustics or transport.

Apprenticeships are available for candidates aged 16–24. If you're between 14 and 16 years of age you may be able to do a Young Apprenticeship.

Once you have a job, most employers have training programmes or graduate schemes in place. If you're doing an apprenticeship you may well be encouraged to follow an NVQ in an engineering subject.

You can also become a member of the IOA and follow courses in acoustics with them. Membership comes at different levels, and following significant contributions to the industry you may be awarded the status of Fellow. This can only happen if you are over 35 and have been working in acoustics for a considerable length of time.

Advantages/disadvantages

If you're interested in science and sound, this could be a good career option.

You won't be stuck at a desk and might get to travel to some really interesting locations.

Money guide

When you start out, you can expect to earn between £18,000 and £22,000 a year. Once you qualify as an acoustics engineer, this could rise to about £34,000. If you become a senior acoustic consultant you might earn over £50,000 a year.

Related opportunities

- Aerospace Engineer p220
- Aerospace Engineering Technician p220
- Electronics Engineer p226

Further information

Engineering and Technology Board.
Websites: www.scenta.co.uk and www.enginuity.org.uk

Institute of Acoustics (IOA)
77a St Peter's Street, St Albans, Hertfordshire AL1 3BN
01727 848195; www.ioa.org.uk

SEMTA (Sector Skills Council for Science Engineering and Manufacturing Technologies)
14 Upton Road, Watford WD18 0JT
0800 282 167; www.semta.org.uk

ASTRONOMER

What the work involves

■ Astronomers investigate and study the universe. Astronomy covers a wide range of areas and astronomers usually focus on a specific subject, such as planets or stars.

■ You will plan and coordinate projects using specialist equipment, such as telescope systems to observe the skies and collect information.

■ You will analyse a wide range of information to identify specific characteristics of the natural world.

■ You may work on mathematical and physics problems using specialist computer software.

The type of person suited to this work

As a professional astronomer you should have a keen interest in the natural world. You will also need a good understanding of the sciences. Whether you are observing the skies or analysing detailed information, you should be able to take in a range of facts and figures. You will use your decision-making skills to make informed conclusions from the information you work with.

A patient and organised approach is essential. You should be confident in working with computers to complete a range of tasks. You will also need strong communication skills and enjoy working with numbers.

Working conditions

Late or antisocial working hours can often be a feature of this type of work, whether you are based in a university, observatory or research centre.

The job may involve spending time away from home as many of the major telescopes are in remote locations.

Close observation is often part of this job, so it may be unsuitable for people with visual impairments.

Future prospects

Employment as a professional astronomer is very competitive and demands a great deal of academic study.

Opportunities are starting to increase, particularly in industrial research and development.

If you followed the academic route you could undertake original research combined with a PhD-level degree and then progress to lecturing.

You may choose to work as part of a technical team providing support for astronomy research projects.

Advantages/disadvantages

This job provides the opportunity to increase public understanding of the natural world.

You may have to spend a lot of time undertaking observations, which requires patience and commitment.

Undertaking research on-site can be physically tiring.

Qualifications and courses

A degree in physics, maths, astrophysics, geophysics or a related science is required.

Specialist degrees are available in astronomy, astrophysics and space science, and in astronomy combined with maths, physics or another science.

Entry requirements for a relevant first degree are usually 3 A levels/4 H grades, including physics and mathematics, as well as 5 GCSEs/S grades (A–C/1–3), including English and possibly chemistry.

Some degrees courses include fieldwork in the UK or overseas in countries such as Italy and Germany.

Many institutions offer 1-year Foundation courses for candidates without the necessary scientific background. Foundation courses may be taught at the university or at a local partner college.

Taught postgraduate courses in astronomy are available at some universities for people who have a degree in physics, maths or a related area.

To work as a research astronomer, candidates should have a 1st or 2.1 MSci or MPhys degree, followed by further study for a PhD.

University physics departments may include astronomical research groups, and some universities offer MPhil/PhD programmes specifically in astronomy. Specialist research areas vary between institutions.

Money guide

Starting salaries for academic research posts begin at approximately £21,000–£27,000 per year.

As a senior scientist, you could earn £28,000–£37,000, rising to £45,000 with experience and responsibility.

At managerial level, you could earn £48,000–£60,000.

The Royal Astronomical Society's online joblist advertises worldwide vacancies.

Related opportunities

■ Geographer p520
■ Mathematician p527
■ Physicist p533
■ Geophysicist p522

Further information

Royal Astronomical Society
Burlington House, Piccadilly, London W1J 0BQ
020 7734 4582; www.ras.org.uk

British Astronomical Association
Burlington House, Piccadilly, London W1J 0DU
020 7734 4145; www.britastro.org

Institute of Physics
76 Portland Place, London W1B 1NT
020 7470 4800; www.iop.org

Science, Mathematics and Statistics

CRCI: TD
CLCI: QOF

BIOCHEMIST

What the work involves

- You will undertake scientific research into a range of living organisms and processes, using specialist equipment.

- Your work may involve collating detailed information and producing reports.

- Biochemists investigate the chemistry of a wide variety of living organisms. They use their investigations to plan experiments and undertake techniques to solve problems.

- Biochemists apply their knowledge and skills in many areas, including food and nutrition, agriculture, medicine, plant research and brewing.

The type of person suited to this work

You will need to be curious about biological organisms and interested in improving systems and products. You will constantly use your problem-solving skills in this job. Your excellent observational skills will also come in very useful. You should enjoy working as part of a team.

You will be confident in using a range of scientific equipment to gain information. You will need a patient and methodical approach for sometimes repetitive but important activities. Your strong communication skills will help you explain and record your work. Confidence in working with numbers and detailed information is also essential.

Working conditions

You would normally work in a laboratory as part of a team. You may also do some of your work in an office environment.

In some sectors, biochemists work on a shift system.

The job involves the regular use of specialist equipment which requires good manual handling skills.

As you become more senior, it is likely you will be involved with managing staff or projects.

Future prospects

Many of the products you use on a daily basis have been developed by biochemists. Biochemists have an important role in organisations ranging from research institutes to multinational companies.

If you go into research and development, you would start by working as part of a team. With experience, you would progress to planning and managing experimental work. You may choose to undertake academic research and go into lecturing or teaching.

Advantages/disadvantages

You may have to work very long hours in this job.

This type of work is often project-based which provides job variety.

Qualifications and courses

A degree in biochemistry or a related subject is required for entry to this profession. Many posts also require a postgraduate qualification. A levels/ H grades including chemistry and/or biology are required for entry to a biochemistry degree. Some universities offer Foundation or bridging years as pre-degree courses for applicants who do not have the required qualifications.

Biochemists with a degree and relevant work experience are eligible to join a professional body, the Biochemical Society or the Institute of Biology.

Biochemists continue their training in service. Those with a first degree are often encouraged to study part time for an MSc or PhD.

It is possible to enter as a technician with a minimum of 4 GCSEs/S grades (A–C/1–3), including English, maths and sciences.

NVQs/SVQs are available in Laboratory and Associated Technical Activities at Levels 2, 3 and 4. A levels/H grades, or a National Certificate/Diploma or HNC/D in a science subject may be required.

Biochemistry offers a wide range of areas in which to specialise.

Money guide

Starting salaries for graduate trainees start at around £23,000 per year.

Post registration and with experience, as a project leader you could earn £27,500 - £38,000.

At senior/management/consultancy level you can earn from £40,000 in the NHS, but pay can rise to £75,000–£100,000.

Salaries tend to be higher in industry compared with the NHS and universities, especially at junior levels.

Related opportunities

- Biotechnologist p508
- Chemist p510
- Biomedical Scientist/Medical Laboratory Assistant p507
- Clinical Scientist p512

Further information

Biochemical Society Membership Office
Portland Customer Services, Commerce Way, Whitehall Industrial Estate, Colchester, Essex CO2 8HP
01206 796351; www.biochemistry.org

Association of Clinical Biochemists
130–132 Tooley Street, London SE1 2TU
020 7403 8001; www.acb.org.uk

Institute of Biomedical Science
12 Coldbath Square, London EC1R 5HL
020 7713 0214; www.ibms.org/

BIOMEDICAL SCIENTIST/ MEDICAL LABORATORY ASSISTANT

What the work involves

- A Biomedical scientist carries out laboratory tests on bodily fluid and tissue in order to help doctors assess what is wrong with their patients. They use a range of equipment to carry out tests designed to discover abnormalities.

- Medical laboratory assistants support the work of biomedical scientists. As a medical laboratory assistant, you will carry out a variety of tasks including: sorting and labelling tissue samples, sterilising and disinfecting equipment, making up chemical solutions, separating blood serum and plasma from samples, recording and analysing information.

The type of person suited to this work

Biomedical scientist

You must be interested in science and medicine and have strong scientific skills. You must be practical, responsible, and have good IT skills. You should have the ability to supervise junior members of staff and to follow complex instructions.

Medical laboratory assistant

You need a careful, methodical approach to your work. You should be able to concentrate and pay attention to detail. You will work accurately under pressure to meet deadlines. Solid communication skills are essential.

Working conditions

Most medical laboratory assistants and biomedical scientists work in pathology laboratories within hospitals, but some work directly with patients.

Future prospects

Biomedical scientist

You will probably specialise in a specific area. In order to progress you might need a higher qualification. Within the NHS you may progress to a managerial role.

Work abroad is a possibility, especially within developing countries.

Medical laboratory assistant

Most employment is available in NHS hospitals. You may specialise or move to a related career such as pharmacy technician. To train as a clinical or biomedical scientist you will need to study for a relevant degree.

Advantages/disadvantages

The work can be repetitive and you will probably need more qualifications to progress.

You will be performing an important part of a hospital's medical

Qualifications and courses

Biomedical scientist entry level 6

Medical laboratory assistant entry level 1

Biomedical scientist

You cannot become a Biomedical Scientist without registering with the Health Professions Council (HPC). To do this you must have an honours degree, accredited by the Institute of Biomedical Science (IBS) and approved by the HPC. If you complete a degree which is not accredited, you can apply to the IBMS to have it assessed.

Alternatively, you can start as a Trainee Biomedical Scientist in the NHS, whilst studying part time for four years to acquire an accredited biomedical science degree.

Medical laboratory assistant

There are no formal entry requirements, but four or more GCSEs/S grades (A*–C/1–3) in English, maths and a science, or an equivalent qualification such as a BTEC First Diploma in Applied Science may be valuable. Laboratory assistants can work towards qualifications such as NVQs/ SVQs.

work, because you will be helping to diagnose patients' illnesses.

You may have to deal with angry doctors/patients who want results sooner than you can deliver them.

Money guide

The starting salary for an NHS biomedical scientist is between £20,225 and £26,123 a year. At an advanced level you might earn up to £38,352. A healthcare scientist at professional manager level might earn up to £64,118.

As a trainee medical laboratory assistant in the NHS you would start at around £12,177 per year. With experience this rises to around £15,107. At senior level you could earn up to £19,730 per year.

Related opportunities

- Laboratory Technician p524
- Phlebotomist p333
- Chemist p510
- Clinical Scientist p512

Further information

NHS Careers
0845 60 60 655; www.nhscareers.nhs.uk

Institute of Biomedical Science
12 Coldbath Square, London EC1R 5HL
020 7713 0214; www.ibms.org; mail@ibms.org

Science, Mathematics and Statistics

CRCI: TD
CLCI: QOD

BIOTECHNOLOGIST

What the work involves

- You will utilise biological organisms and processes to develop and adapt products. Biotechnologists work in a range of areas, many of which are very new, such as genetic engineering.

- You could work in research and development or in aspects of production such as quality control.

- Your work may involve enhancing existing products or developing new types of organisms.

- Biotechnology provides the scientific basis for agriculture, pharmaceuticals, waste management, food and medical care.

The type of person suited to this work

You will need a keen interest in science for working in any area of biotechnology. Strong observational skills and an organised approach are also essential. You will also be confident working with scientific equipment. You should be able to use computers to manage information and undertake research.

Most biotechnologists are employed as part of a group so the ability to work as part of a team is helpful. If you work as a technician, you should be able to cope with undertaking routine but required testing activities. Biochemists in industry also need to understand the commercial applications of their work.

Working conditions

Biotechnologists usually work in a laboratory or research centre in sterile conditions to undertake experimental and testing work.

Some jobs involve spending time in a noisy factory or manufacturing plant.

Your work is likely to involve using microscopes and electronic testing equipment, and spending time on a computer doing analysis work.

Future prospects

In this developing area of science, biotechnologists enable organisations to create and modify organisms for medical, environmental and commercial use.

They work within government research institutions whilst others play a central role in developing and enhancing products in commercial biotechnology companies.

There is also the option to develop an academic career – this may provide additional opportunities to undertake commercial research.

Advantages/disadvantages

Laboratory work, particularly at technician level, can be time-consuming and requires a lot of patience.

Biochemistry is a varied area of science which offers a variety of areas in which to work.

This role requires a good level of manual dexterity.

Qualifications and courses

A degree in biotechnology, bioscience or a related subject, such as microbiology, biochemistry or chemical engineering, is required for entry to this profession.

A levels/H grades in chemistry and/or biology are required for entry to these degree courses.

A postgraduate qualification is often required. For research posts, a PhD may be a requirement.

School-leavers may start work as trainee technicians. The usual minimum entry requirements are 4 GCSEs/S grades (A–C/1–3), including a science and maths.

Some posts require A levels/H grades, BTEC/SQA National qualifications, or an HNC/D.

Technicians are mainly trained on the job. It is possible to work towards further qualifications, such as a degree or HND, through part-time study or day- or block-release.

Graduates are also employed as technicians. In all cases, qualifications in science subjects are required.

NVQs/SVQs are available at Levels 2–4 in Laboratory and Associated Technical Activities.

Money guide

As a graduate working in a university you could start on a salary of £20,000–£27,000 per year.

With a specialist higher degree, your salary can range from £28,000 to £37,500.

Established senior lecturers can earn £38,000–£50,000.

Professors with a great deal of experience can expect to earn up to £60,000.

Biotechnologists earn higher salaries in industry.

Related opportunities

- Biochemist p506
- Biomedical Scientist/Medical Laboratory Assistant p507
- Chemist p510

Further information

BioIndustry Association
14–15 Belgrave Square, London SWIX 8PS
020 7565 7190; www.bioindustry.org

Institute of Biology
9 Red Lion Court, Londo EC4A 3EF
020 7936 5900; www.iob.org

Biotechnology and Biological Sciences Research Council
Polaris House, North Star Avenue, Swindon SN2 1UH
01793 413200; www.bbsrc.ac.uk

BOTANIST

What the work involves

- Botanists study all kinds of plant life and plant biology. They are increasingly employed within industry and research in areas such as plant-cell technology and genetic engineering.

- Your work could involve managing rare plant collections, environmental conservation, horticulture, agriculture and other areas.

- You will use specialist equipment such as electron microscopes and satellite imaging technology.

- You might look into how human activity affects plants in farming or you may try and discover useful chemicals produced by plants.

The type of person suited to this work

As a botanist you should have a real interest in science and plants. This interest should stretch to a particular field of work such as conservation. This profession will involve detailed analysis so you will need strong observational skills. You must also have a methodical approach to your work activities.

You should be comfortable working with a range of scientific equipment. However you will also need to be happy undertaking practical research work, sometimes in unpleasant weather conditions. You may also need to be a good leader as you might be in charge of junior staff, students and volunteers.

Working conditions

You could be working in one or more of the following environments; laboratories, classrooms, lecture theatres, offices and outdoors. Hours will vary, but within research and higher education you will work about 37 hours a week.

Field work takes place in all weather conditions and you may find it physically demanding. Whilst working in a laboratory you will be using specialist equipment and might be required to wear protective clothing. A driving licence may be required if you need to travel between locations.

Future prospects

Within conservation and field work, progression would entail taking on more responsibility and possibly managing others. Within the higher education sector there is a set career path leading from researcher to head of department or professor. Within industry there is the possibility of promotion. You also have the option of working as a freelance consultant and therefore being self-employed. There is the potential to work overseas in most areas of botany.

Advantages/disadvantages

There are opportunities to visit different types of outside locations on research trips.

Research jobs are often offered on a short-term basis, which can create job insecurity.

Qualifications and courses

Botanists may enter this career as laboratory technicians or technical assistants. Although you do not need a degree to enter these posts a scientific background is essential.

If you choose to enter by the degree route then relevant subjects include botany, plant biology, plant science, environmental science and ecology. A levels/H grades in biology and another science, often chemistry, are required for entry to botany degrees. You will also require five GCSEs grade A*-C.

It may also be a good idea to complete some voluntary work in relevant organisations and to acquire relevant skills such as plant identification.

Good GCSE/A level choices include sciences (especially biology), maths and English. You might also want to consider geography and geology as these are also looked upon favourably.

To work as a researcher, a postgraduate qualification is required. Candidates may enter with a PhD, or enter as a trainee researcher in a university department and work towards a PhD. In order to apply for a postgraduate qualification you will need to successfully complete a first degree.

You will have the opportunity to combine your love of plants with your passion for science.

Money guide

These figures will vary depending on location, sector and employer.

Starting salaries are around £16,000 a year. Technical assistants begin on about £18,000 per year. With experience this could increase to between £25,000 and £35,000 a year. In a senior role you could earn in excess of £45,000 per year.

Salaries within the private industry will vary considerably.

Related opportunities

- Microbiologist/Bacteriologist p530
- Ecologist p515
- Entomologist p516

Further information

Botanical Society of the British Isles (BSBI)
Botany Department, Natural History Museum, Cromwell Road, London SW7 5BD
www.bsbi.org.uk

British Trust for Conservation Volunteers (BTCV)
Sedum House, Mallard Way, Potteric Carr, Doncaster DN4 8DB
01302 388888; www.btcv.org.uk

CHEMIST

What the work involves

- Chemists work in many different sectors, undertaking the analysis and use of complex scientific processes and substances on a detailed molecular level.

- As well as research and development, chemists also check that products are developed to a safe standard.

- Professional chemists are employed in a wide range of sectors, including the oil industry, pharmaceuticals, medical research and academia.

The type of person suited to this work

Chemists need strong observational skills. They must also be able to think around complex scientific problems. You will have good manual handling abilities for undertaking research with a range of scientific equipment.

Working conditions

The average chemist works about 37 hours a week. Your job could involve working in a laboratory as part of a research centre, but you may also undertake research outdoors on-site. You may have to wear protective clothing such as lab coat, protective glasses and gloves. If you are employed by a private company you may be required to work shifts organised by a rota. At senior levels, you may be involved with business development and managerial activities.

Future prospects

Professional chemists play an important role in developing and updating products and systems. Public research institutes, academic institutions and private companies employ chemists. There are also opportunities in government research, health and education. Some chemists move into areas such as law, IT, science journalism and marketing. With experience you could enter a supervisory role. There are also opportunities to teach in schools and universities. Postgraduate qualifications may improve your chances for progression.

Advantages/disadvantages

Low numbers of entrants taking chemistry degrees means that there are many opportunities.

Laboratory tasks can sometimes be repetitive and time-consuming.

Many large companies employ chemists, so promotion can be possible without moving employers.

Money guide

These figures are only approximate and will vary depending on sector, employer and location. Salary levels should increase

Qualifications and courses

For entry to a chemistry degree, A level/H grade in chemistry and at least one other science or maths is required. Degree courses are available in chemistry, biological chemistry, environmental chemistry, medical chemistry, and in chemistry combined with other subjects. Many institutions offer 1-year Foundation courses for candidates without the necessary scientific background.

Many chemists also have a postgraduate qualification in chemistry or in a specialist area such as materials chemistry, medicinal chemistry or pharmaceutical chemistry. Chemists often study for postgraduate qualifications or work towards professional membership of the Royal Society of Chemistry.

Alternatively, it is possible to enter as a technician in a chemistry laboratory with a minimum of four GCSEs/S grades A*–C/1–3, including English, maths and sciences. A levels/H grades, a National Certificate/Diploma or HNC/D in a science subject may be required.

Some posts require A levels/H grades, BTEC/SQA National qualifications, or an HNC/D. Graduates are also employed as technicians. In all cases, qualifications in science subjects are required. NVQs/SVQs are available.

with the level of academic qualification. At graduate entry you can earn between £15,000 and £20,000 per year. With experience, and when established, you can expect £30,000 a year. With added responsibility, such as if you are in charge of a team or project you could expect to earn between £35,000 and £40,000 a year.

Related opportunities

- Biochemist p506
- Biotechnologist p508
- Cosmetic Scientist p514

Further information

Royal Society of Chemistry
Burlington House, Piccadilly, London W1J 0BA
020 7437 8656; Main website www.rsc.org;
Careers and jobs website: www.chemsoc.org

Association of the British Pharmaceutical Industry
12 Whitehall, London SW1A 2DY
0870 890 4333; Main website: www.abpi.org.uk;
Careers website: www.abpi-careers.org.uk

CLINICAL GENETICIST

What the work involves

■ Geneticists analyse and modify human, animal or plant DNA. If working as a human geneticist, you could be involved with medical genetics or human genetic research.

■ You could undertake genetic engineering in agricultural research

■ This profile focuses on clinical geneticists who are responsible for identifying and diagnosing genetic disorders. There are two main jobs in this field; cytogeneticists (studying chromosomes which contain genes) and molecular geneticists (studying DNA).

■ Clinical geneticists test samples from patients, record their findings and draw a conclusion from them. They also supervise the work of others.

The type of person suited to this work

You should be an excellent communicator, both verbally and on paper. You will need to be able to work accurately and meticulously, whilst keeping to deadlines. You must have a good understanding of computers. You will need to be discreet as you will be dealing with confidential medical information. You should be able to work effectively as part of a team and be able to take on the role of a supervisor when training junior staff. You must have strong problem-solving skills.

Working conditions

You will be based in a sterile laboratory. You will have to wear protective clothing such as overalls, laboratory glasses and gloves. You will also have to ensure that you reach all health and safety standards.

As a clinical geneticist within the NHS you will be working about 37.5 hours per week, from Monday to Friday. There may also be a rota in place which covers bank holidays and weekends.

Future prospects

Genetics is a fast-developing area of science that offers the chance to work directly with patients as a medical geneticist within the NHS or directly within research in research centres and universities. You could also go on to work in research and development in industry.

In order to be promoted you will need to gather experience, responsibility and training. Once you have worked for two or three years as a registered geneticist you can begin to apply for more senior positions.

Advantages/disadvantages

You may have to repeat procedures which could become tedious.

This job contains a great deal of responsibility.

You will be working with a wide range of samples and so every day will be different.

Qualifications and courses

ENTRY LEVEL 2

An Honours degree in genetics, biomedical or biological sciences is required. In order to become a clinical geneticist with the NHS you will need a 2:1 degree in genetics or another life science. Competition to become a clinical geneticist within the NHS is fierce as there are only two training posts a year.

Two or more science A levels/H grades are normally required for entry to relevant degree courses. Chemistry and/or biology may be specified. You will also need five GCSEs grades A*-C.

A postgraduate qualification is desirable. In order to complete postgraduate study, you will need to successfully complete a first degree.

Training is undertaken in an accredited genetics laboratory, and follows the clinical scientist training programme lasting two to three years.

It is also possible to enter the profession at technician or trainee level with GCSEs/S grades, A levels/H grades, or equivalent qualifications in subjects such as biology, maths, science and English.

Money guide

These figures will vary depending on sector, location and employer.

The average starting salary for a graduate clinical scientist trainee is about £24,000. Once registered, you can expect to earn between £29,000 and £38,352. If you reach the level of principal clinical scientist you could earn up to £44,527. As a consultant this can increase to as much as £77,179.

You may also receive an additional allowance if you work in London.

Related opportunities

■ Clinical Scientist p512
■ Forensic Scientist p519
■ Laboratory Technician p524
■ Pharmacologist p331

Further information

Genetics Society
Roslin BioCentre, Wallace Building, Roslin, Midlothian EH25 9PP
0131 200 6392; www.genetics.org.uk

British Society of Human Genetics
Clinical Genetics Unit, Birmingham Women's Hospital, Birmingham B15 2TG
0121 627 2634; www.bshg.org.uk; www.zsl.org

NHS Careers
PO Box 2311, Bristol BS2 2ZX
0845 606 0655; www.nhscareers.nhs.uk

Science, Mathematics and Statistics

CRCI: TD
CLCI: QOX

CLINICAL SCIENTIST

What the work involves

- Clinical scientists work mainly for the NHS but are also employed in the Health Protection Agency, research centres and industry.

- Your work may involve supporting doctors, suggesting suitable tests for diagnosing patients, reporting on results and recommending treatments.

- You may also research and test new methods of treatment and make recommendations on the best equipment or test materials.

- You might specialise in a particular area such as clinical embryology (the study of infertility) or clinical microbiology (identifying infections in patients caused by bacteria, fungus or parasites).

The type of person suited to this work

You should have a keen interest in medicine and science, and a desire to help others. You should have excellent observational skills. You need technical skills and be able to use scientific equipment to get results.

You will need an organised approach for undertaking practical work and the ability to work to set deadlines. You should be able to interact well as part of a team. As a scientist you will get results by combining a logical approach with a creative flair. You should have strong computer skills.

Working conditions

You might work around 37.5 hours a week, usually from Monday to Friday, although these hours could vary depending on your specialism. You may need to work some evenings and weekends if you are on-call. You will usually work in a laboratory or within a specialist department. You may have some contact with patients. You will be working in a sterile environment, which may demand that you wear protective clothing. You might need to use ionising radiation.

Future prospects

Progression is performance based, you will need to accept more responsibility and/or take part in research and development projects to reach a more senior level. As a consultant, you would be responsible for a large department and have the chance to make important contributions to your area of expertise. There is also the option of moving between departments to gain further training. You could move into lecturing or training. There is the possibility of working abroad.

Advantages/disadvantages

You will be helping to diagnose patients and suggest treatments, which will improve their quality of life.

Mistakes could lead to an incorrect diagnosis and so you will be working under a lot of pressure.

Qualifications and courses

ENTRY LEVEL 6

Entrants to this profession require a 1st or 2:1 class degree in a relevant subject, such as biochemistry, biology, chemistry, engineering, genetics, microbiology, physics or physiology. Entry to a degree typically requires a minimum of two A levels/three H grades, including appropriate science subjects. Equivalent qualifications, such as the International Baccalaureate, foundation degrees in science, BTEC National and BTEC Higher Nationals and science Access to Higher Education courses may also be relevant.

An MSc or PhD in your specialist area is an advantage. In order to apply for postgraduate study, you usually require a 1st or 2:1 in your first degree.

Clinical scientists start as Grade A trainees. The training lasts two–three years. On completion of the training, candidates are eligible for state registration, and can apply for Grade B posts. In-service training continues, and many clinical scientists work towards membership qualifications of professional bodies or a PhD. After a minimum of four years in a training post scientists can register with the Health Professional Council allowing them to use their correct title of Clinical Scientist and work unsupervised.

Money guide

These figures vary depending on employer and location. If you work in London you will be given an additional allowance.

As a trainee clinical scientist within the NHS you could earn between £24,100 and £27,191 per year. Once registered, you could earn between £29,091 and £38,352 a year. This could increase to £93,098 if you become an advanced practitioner clinical scientist or consultant clinical scientist.

Related opportunities

- Biochemist p506
- Doctor p315
- Medical Physicist p320
- Radiographer p339

Further information

Association of Clinical Scientists (ACS)
The Administrator, c/o The Association for Clinical Biochemistry, 130–132 Tooley Street, London SE1 2TU
020 7940 8960; www.assclinsci.org

Clinical Scientists Recruitment Centre
239 Thorpe Road, Thorpe Park, Peterborough PE3 6JU
0871 433 3070; www.nhsclinicalscientists.info

Federation of Clinical Scientists
c/o Association for Clinical Biochemistry, 130–132 Tooley Street, London SE1 2TU
020 7403 8001; www.acb.org.uk/federation

CONSUMER SCIENTIST

What the work involves

- Consumer scientists or home economists provide support, information and specialist services related to healthy living and eating.

- You will be the point of communication between consumers and manufacturers. You study what the consumer needs and provide advice on how to develop it.

- Your work could involve developing new food products, educating people about healthy eating or assessing new cookery equipment.

- This profession varies widely depending on the specific company. Jobs are available within quality assurance, marketing, media and journalism, food product development, education, government, product and service development and catering.

The type of person suited to this work

You will need to have strong communication skills, which allow you to talk to people of all ages and backgrounds. You should also have an interest in food and how people live their lives within the home environment. You should have solid computer skills and a knack for describing information in a clear way, both orally and in writing. You must be creative and have proficient design skills.

Working conditions

This role may involve travelling to meetings, conferences and other environments in the UK and abroad.

Your working environment will vary according to which industry you work within. You could be in an office, kitchen, classroom, laboratory or a selection of these.

You will be working about 35 to 40 hours per week, usually from Monday to Friday. There is however often the opportunity to work unusual hours in order to leave some of your week days free. You may also have to complete reports in your free time.

Future prospects

Consumer scientists can move between industries as their services are always required. Specific industries include retail chains, marketing bodies, local authorities, magazines, television and newspapers, health authorities, producers of food, advisory and consumer organisations, hotels and restaurants, consumer pressure groups, schools, colleges and universities and many others. In most areas there is the opportunity to progress to managerial level. Promotion may involve moving to a new location within the country.

Advantages/disadvantages

You may find it frustrating when asked to complete tests in the later stages of the factory process.

This profession will give you the opportunity to move into a vast number of industries, which will aid you career progression possibilities.

Qualifications and courses

HNDs and degrees are available in a variety of relevant subjects, for example consumer studies/science, food studies/science, food and nutrition, food and marketing, food technology. Degrees are also available in specialist areas of consumer science, such as consumer protection or consumer psychology. To gain acceptance to a HND course you will usually require at least one A level and four GCSES grade A*-C (or equivalent). Most degree courses expect candidates to have at least two A levels and five GCSEs, grade A*-C (or equivalent). These requirements may vary so be sure to check with the institution.

Relevant courses at further education level include NVQs/SVQs in Food Preparation or Food and Drink Manufacturing Operations and BTEC/SQA National qualifications in Hospitality. Employers may offer in-house training leading to NVQs/SVQs.

Candidates with a relevant degree or HNC/D and two years' relevant work experience are eligible for corporate membership of the Institute of Consumer Sciences. People with experience and a position of responsibility in the industry are also eligible for membership.

You may have to complete reports in your free time.

Money guide

Salary levels vary according to employer, sector and location and so the following figures are approximate.

Starting salaries range from £18,000 to £20,000 per year. With experience, you could earn between £25,000 and £30,000 a year. At senior level you could get up to £50,000 per year. Consumer scientists working on a consultancy basis can earn £150–£500 a day.

Related opportunities

- Chef p143
- Dietitian p306
- Environmental Health Practitioner p35
- Market Researcher p416
- School Teacher p212

Further information

Improve Ltd
Ground Floor, Providence House, 2 Innovation Close, Heslington, York YO10 5ZF
0845 644 0448; www.improveltd.co.uk

Institute of Food Research
Norwich Research Park, Colney, Norwich NR4 7UA
01603 255 000; www.ifr.ac.uk

Institute of Food Science and Technology
5 Cambridge Court, 210 Shepherds Bush Road, London W6 7NJ
020 7603 6316; www.foodtechcareers.org

Science, Mathematics and Statistics

CRCI: TA
CLCI: QON

COSMETIC SCIENTIST

What the work involves

- The cosmetics industry requires scientists to help develop, test and produce new and existing cosmetics and beauty products, such as make-up, perfumes and haircare products.

- There are various elements to this profession, including researching new ingredients, developing cosmetic products, developing the processes used to create the product, quality control, safety testing, packaging development and regulatory affairs which involves ensuring the product meets all legal requirements.

- Most work takes place in a sterile, laboratory environment.

The type of person suited to this work

You will have an interest in the science of cosmetics, along with knowledge and skill in chemistry and biology. You will need to be meticulous, but also able to work at speed. You will need to understand statistics and have the ability to use the relevant computer software. You should have an extremely methodical approach to your work and the ability to follow instructions effectively. You must have strong communication skills, which will be required to convey information to your colleagues and clients.

Working conditions

Most of your work will take place in a sterile, laboratory environment. Your job may involve handling potentially dangerous materials, so you would need to wear protective clothing. This job might involve repetitive analysis work in the laboratory, which can be physically demanding.

In addition to hands-on experimental work, your work may include using computers. Your job might involve travelling to meetings, conferences and other events in the UK and abroad.

Future prospects

Progression generally comes in the form of moving to a supervisory or managerial role, which could allow you to spend more time with the client. Alternatively, you might consider changing departments and moving into a sales or marketing position, where the scientific knowledge you have acquired would be extremely relevant.

There is also the option of self-employment, working as a consultant, providing specialist support to cosmetic companies. You might also consider lecturing on cosmetic science courses.

Advantages/disadvantages

You may find some elements of the job extremely repetitive and monotonous.

Your work will be directly influenced by the fashion industry; you will be working to predict the latest trends, which could be exciting.

Qualifications and courses

Career entry can be achieved at more than one level, including a relevant degree (cosmetic science, chemistry, chemical engineering, biology, microbiology, physics, medicine and pharmacy), Foundation degree or HNC/D. Most degree courses require applicants to have achieved a minimum of two A levels, which should include relevant sciences (particularly chemistry) and five GCSEs grade A*-C (including English and maths). Some universities may accept alternative qualifications and so you should check with the individual institution. Many colleges include a 1-year introductory (Access) course for students who have not studied the requisite science subjects at A level/H grade. Foundation degrees and HNC/HND qualifications normally expect applicants to have achieved at least one A level (or equivalent).

The Diploma in Cosmetic Science can be attained by distance learning, after approximately 300 hours of study. The Principles and Practice of Cosmetic Science course is a shorter course, which is particularly useful for those who have been in the industry for a while and are looking to move into supervisory or managerial roles and/or who are taking on a new field of expertise.

This profession can be fast paced and you may find it stressful.

Money guide

Salary levels will vary according to employer, sector and location. Starting salaries are roughly between £16,000 and £23,000 per year. With experience and training this will increase and you could earn from £25,000 to £45,000 a year.

At senior levels, such as within management, it is possible to earn over £50,000 a year.

Related opportunities

- Biochemist p506
- Laboratory Technician p524
- Pharmacologist p331

Further information

The Cosmetic Toiletry and Perfumery Association (CTPA) Ltd
Josaron House, 5–7 John Princes Street, London W1G 0JN
020 7491 8891; www.ctpa.org.uk

Society of Cosmetic Scientists
G.T. House, 24–26 Rothesay Road, Luton LU1 1QX
01582 726661; www.scs.org.uk and www.cosmeticlearning.com

Royal Society of Chemistry
Burlington House, Piccadilly, London W1J 0BA
020 7437 8656; www.rsc.org

ECOLOGIST

What the work involves

- Ecologists help to protect the natural world by investigating the relationship between living organisms and their environment.

- You will undertake ecological surveys of animals and plants and monitor the state of urban and rural environments.

- You may also write reports and analyse statistical information.

- Ecologists are employed by conservation charities, government departments, public bodies and environmental consultancies. A small number work in industry.

The type of person suited to this work

A keen interest in the natural world is essential for ecologists. You will collect detailed factual information about many aspects of the environment. Your observational skills and scientific knowledge will be an essential part of this. Your organised approach and ability to work to a high standard of accuracy will help you when collating statistics. You will use your manual handling skills to use scientific equipment.

You will need to be comfortable working outdoors in sometimes poor weather conditions. Your practical and hands-on approach will help you when undertaking this type of work. You will use your communication skills and your ability to complete complex calculations on a regular basis.

Working conditions

Ecologists work in laboratories or research centres when undertaking analysis activities.

You would work outside in all kinds of weather conditions when undertaking fieldwork such as surveys of plants or animals. For fieldwork you would need a good level of physical fitness and good observational skills. This may make the job unsuitable for people with visual impairments.

Future prospects

Ecology offers a wide range of opportunities and you could shape your career according to your interests. But there is a lot of competition for jobs. Some jobs are available only on a contract basis and it can take time to find a permanent role.

Many types of organisations employ ecologists. You could go into scientific research, environmental management, teaching or conservation for organisations such as environmental consultancies, research bodies and private companies.

Advantages/disadvantages

This job provides the satisfaction of having a positive impact on the natural environment.

It is likely that you will need to move around to develop your professional experience.

Qualifications and courses

Entrants require an Honours degree or above in the field of biological and earth sciences. Relevant subjects include ecology, environmental biology/management; conservation or marine biology. Additionally, many employers seek experience (as a research assistant or a conservation project volunteer), and postgraduate qualifications are increasingly an advantage.

A levels/H grades in sciences are required for entry to degrees in ecology or biological sciences. Biology A level or equivalent is a required or preferred subject for some degrees.

NVQs/SVQs are available in Environmental Conservation at Levels 2 and 3 and Environmental Management at Level 4.

A driving licence is useful.

Ecologists with relevant qualifications and experience can become members of the Institute of Ecology and Environmental Management (IEEM). Different levels of membership are available depending on qualifications and experience. The IEEM also provides short professional development courses for its members.

Opportunities in areas such as environmental consultancy and management are increasing.

Money guide

Salaries vary according to the type of organisation, but are low for technical assistants and recent graduates. Salaries can be higher in industry.

Starting salaries range from around £12,000 for non-graduates; from £18,000 to £24,000 per year for graduates. With experience you could earn £24,000–£45,000. Senior/management roles in larger organisations can pay in excess of £45,000+.

Related opportunities

- Environmental scientist p517
- Environmental Conservation Manager/Officer p265

Further information

British Ecological Society
26 Blades Court, Putney, London SW15 2NU
020 8871 9797; www.britishecologicalsociety.org

Institution of Environmental Sciences
Suite 1, 38 Ebury Street, London SW1 0LU
020 7730 5516; www.ies-uk.org.uk

Institute of Ecology and Environmental Management (IEEM)
43 Southgate Street, Winchester, Hants SO23 9EH
01962 868626; www.ieem.net

Science, Mathematics and Statistics

CRCI: TD
CLCI: QOD

ENTOMOLOGIST

What the work involves

- Entomology is the study of insects, including how they live and how they interact with their environment. Entomologists also observe the behaviour of insects to gain valuable information on the state of specific natural areas.

- As an entomologist, you could analyse and assess the effects of insect life on agriculture. Entomologists are also employed to undertake research in medicine or to support ecological and environmental conservation work.

- Work in the field might include searching for new species or studying insect ecology.

- Work in the laboratory could include developing insecticides or classifying insects.

The type of person suited to this work

An interest in insects, natural history and biological sciences are essential for this role, along with an understanding of the specific area you want to work in. You should have a methodical, logical and meticulous approach to your work and the ability to be patient and persevere when you encounter problems. You will need to be able to work effectively both alone and within a team. As you will need to remember a great deal of information such as insect names and classifications, you should have an excellent memory. You will also require good communication, computer and leadership skills.

Working conditions

Working hours and environments will depend upon the area of entomology you work in. Research entomologists spend the majority of their time in a laboratory and will generally work regular hours from Monday to Friday. Those working in higher education will also have office hours and will spend their time in classrooms and lecture theatres, offices and laboratories.

Future prospects

Entomologists work in a wide range of areas, including agricultural research and development, ecological protection and conservation, forensics and pest control. Others go on to develop their research interests as academic professionals after gaining postgraduate qualifications.

Progression within conservation and in the field will depend on merit and responsibilities such as managing others. Within universities there is a progression path from researcher to head of department. Within industry, promotion opportunities to senior positions are available. Self-employment is a possibility.

Advantages/disadvantages

It could get frustrating when an experiment or investigation does not go according to plan.

Your work could take you all over the world.

There is a wide variety of career options available to entomologists.

Qualifications and courses

An Honours degree in a relevant field is required. There are no entomology degree courses; however biology, zoology, environmental science and biological sciences would all be appropriate. A level/H grade biology is normally required for entry to relevant degree courses. Candidates usually need at least two A levels/3 H grades including biology and five GCSEs/S grades A*-C/1–3 for entry to relevant degree courses. You should check entry requirements with the individual university as they may vary.

Quite often a postgraduate qualification will be required. There are numerous entomology postgraduate qualifications offered in the UK. In order to apply for a postgraduate course you must have successfully completed a first degree.

Entry at technician level requires GCSEs/S grades and A levels/H grades. Relevant subjects include biology (and other sciences), maths, English, geography and geology.

Foreign language qualifications may also prove beneficial.

If you work in the field or within conservation, you might have to live and work in inhospitable environments.

Money guide

These figures are only approximate as salaries will vary depending on location, sector and employer.

Starting salaries for entomologists are usually about £16,000 per year. This could increase to around £35,000 a year once enough experience has been gathered. If you progress to the stage when you are one of the most highly regarded entomologists you could earn over £60,000 per year.

Related opportunities

- Agricultural Scientist p258
- Botanist p509
- Ecologist p515
- Environmental Scientist p517
- Zoologist p536

Further information

British Entomological and Natural History Society
The Pelham-Clinton Building, Dinton Pastures Country Park, Davis Street, Hurst, Reading RG10 0TH
www.benhs.org.uk

The Natural History Museum
Cromwell Road, London SW7 5BD
020 7942 5000; www.nhm.ac.uk

Royal Entomological Society
The Mansion House, Chiswell Green Lane, St Albans AL2 3NS
01727 899387; www.royensoc.co.uk

ENVIRONMENTAL SCIENTIST

What the work involves

- Environmental scientists apply scientific techniques to study and protect the natural environment.

- You might look for ways to ensure 'sustainable development' by discovering and experimenting with ways to reduce the damage caused to the world and our natural resources.

- You could work in pollution monitoring, conservation, energy, engineering, environmental consultancy and research or other areas.

- You will probably be advising colleagues and clients, some of whom may not have a scientific background, on the damage particular developments could cause to the environment.

The type of person suited to this work

To work in this industry you should have an interest in geography, science and environmental issues. You will need to be practical and methodical, as well as having the ability to think outside the box in order to problem solve. You will need to be meticulous in your approach to work, as the results you find could have an impact on whether developments go ahead.

Working conditions

How many hours you work and the environment you are in will depend on the specific role you take. Some environmental scientists work a 9–5 week but others, involved in fieldwork, will have to complete extra hours in order to meet deadlines.

When working in the field you will be outside in all weather conditions. Field roles are dependent on their geographical location and so the work field environmental scientists do varies greatly. You will also spend some time in an office and/or lab.

Future prospects

There is a growing demand for environmental scientists, mainly due to the increasing concern about climate change, global warming and other environmental issues.

You can progress to team manager or project manager, which will involve taking on more responsibilities. You could also become self-employed, working as a consultant and advising clients on a variety of environmental issues. You might also consider lecturing in environmental science.

Advantages/disadvantages

Your work will have a positive impact on the environment.

There could be opportunities to work abroad in unusual environments, such as rainforests and deserts.

You might face animosity if you refuse to approve a development.

Qualifications and courses

ENTRY LEVEL 6

Most employers expect candidates to have completed an environmental science degree. However, you do not have to take environmental science as your first degree; you can continue on to postgraduate study in environmental science. Examples of relevant environmental science degrees include sustainable development or environmental management.

Most universities require applicants to have achieved two relevant A levels and five GCSEs grades A*-C (or equivalent qualifications). Relevant subjects at A level include biology, chemistry, physics, geography, English, maths and geology. Some admissions tutors will also favour foreign languages.

You do not necessarily have to have completed a degree, it is possible to start as a technician and work your way up to environmental scientist. In order to do this you will have to have achieved at least four GCSEs grades A*-C which should include two sciences, English and maths or technology. Equivalent qualifications, for example a BTEC First Diploma in science, might be considered. Many technicians also complete A levels and so you might also want to consider this.

Relevant work experience would also be beneficial.

Money guide

These figures are approximate and may vary depending on sector, employer and location.

Starting salaries range from about £18,000 to £25,000 per year. With more experience and training you could earn up to £27,000 a year. As a senior environmental scientist, with managerial duties, it would be possible to earn over £55,000 per year.

Related opportunities

- Botanist p509
- Ecologist p515
- Environmental Health Practitioner/Officer p35
- Hydrologist p523
- Oceanographer p531

Further information

Institution of Environmental Sciences
Suite 1, 38 Ebury Street, London SW1 0LU
020 7730 5516; www.ies-uk.org.uk

The Environment Agency, National Recruitment Service
Richard Fairclough House, Knutsford Road, Latchford, Warrington WA4 1HT
01925 542050; www.environment-agency.gov.uk

StudentForce for Sustainability
Oakham Railway Station, Station Approach, Oakham LE15 6QT
01572 723419; www.studentforce.org.uk

Science, Mathematics and Statistics

CRCI: TD
CLCI: QOL

FOOD SCIENTIST/ TECHNOLOGIST

What the work involves

- Food scientists undertake research, production and quality assurance work in all areas of the food industry.

- You could apply your knowledge of food, chemistry, biology and nutrition to analyse food products, set up manufacturing processes and develop food labelling.

- Your research may involve ensuring that food is safe to eat by testing it under different conditions. Alternatively, you might decrease the risk of contamination by analysing the food safety systems in place.

- You will be using both laboratory and computer equipment to carry out your role.

The type of person suited to this work

You will need to have a high level of ability in biology and chemistry and an interest in food and its production. You must also possess a certain level of ability in maths and physics. You will require strong communication and teamwork skills. You should be meticulous, with a keen eye for detail. You will need to be organised, with the ability to prioritise. Good problem-solving skills are key and you will need to be extremely logical. You should be able to follow strict health and safety and hygiene rules.

Working conditions

You could be working in research units, laboratories or in a factory within the quality department. The working environment will always be clean to prevent the food being contaminated and you will be required to wear protective clothing.

You will probably work somewhere between 35 and 40 hours per week and if your employer operates a shift system you might need to work weekends. This role may include travel to warehouses, factories and distribution centres. A driving licence may be useful.

Future prospects

You might be offered the opportunity of promotion to team leader, technical director or project co-ordinator if you work within a larger organisation. If you work for a smaller employer you may need to change companies in order to progress.

Your skills would be transferable to several related areas such as production management, marketing and buying raw materials. You could also specialise.

Working abroad may also be a possibility, especially within larger organisations.

Advantages/disadvantages

You will be able to combine your love of food with your scientific background.

You may find some aspects of the job tedious, for example if you need to repeat the same tests over a period of time.

Qualifications and courses

Entrants to this profession usually have a degree, HNC/D or Foundation degree. Most of these degree courses require applicants to have three A levels and five GCSEs grades A*-C (A levels in chemistry and/or biology might be required). HNC/HND programmes usually require one A level and three GCSEs grades A*-C. Some people study for a postgraduate qualification in food science before entering work.

You can enter with lower qualifications as a laboratory or quality control technician. Typical entry requirements are four GCSEs/S grades A*–C/1–3, including English, mathematics, chemistry and biology, or an Applied A level in science, or a BTEC National qualification in food science and manufacturing technology. Technicians can work towards NVQs/SVQs at Levels 1–4 in Food and Drink Manufacturing Operations, and at Levels 2–4 in Laboratory and Associated Technical Activities. They can also study part time for an HNC to gain promotion to food scientist. Once qualified, you can apply for registration with the Institute of Food Science and Technology (IFST).

Apprenticeships may be available.

This career has the possibility of leading to a number of areas.

Money guide

These figures are approximate and will vary depending on sector, location and employer.

Starting salaries range from about £20,000 to £25,000 per year. This could then increase to around £30,000 to £45,000 a year, depending on experience and/or training.

At senior or management levels this could increase to over £50,000 a year.

Related opportunities

- Chef p143
- Dietitian p306
- Environmental Health Practitioner/Officer p35
- Microbiologist/Bacteriologist p530

Further information

Institute of Food Science & Technology
5 Cambridge Court, 210 Shepherd's Bush Road, London W6 7NJ
020 7603 6316; www.ifst.org or www.foodtechcareers.org

Food and Drink Federation
6 Catherine Street, London WC2B 5JJ
020 7836 2460; www.fdf.org.uk

Improve Limited
Ground Floor, Providence House, 2 Innovation Close, Heslington, York YO10 5ZF
0845 644 0448; www.improveltd.co.uk

FORENSIC SCIENTIST

What the work involves

- You will use your skills to provide important scientific information and help resolve legal and criminal cases.

- By analysing samples and assessing accident and crime scenes, you will support the work of police and lawyers.

- Your work will involve identifying anything that may be used as evidence from a crime scene, including organs, blood, bodily fluids, illegal drugs, fire arms and explosives, DNA and even paint or glass pieces. You will carry out the necessary tests to extract the information the police require.

- You will use techniques including photography, DNA profiling, chromatography and metallurgy.

The type of person suited to this work

You need strong scientific skills and the desire to help solve crime. You will need to be confident, as you might have to make court appearances. You should be able to handle distressing situations well. You will need to pay attention to detail whilst in the field, in the laboratory and when producing reports. You will have to be able to explain scientific findings to people without a scientific background. You should be able to use statistics to interpret your findings. You must be a great communicator.

Working conditions

You will spend the majority of your time in the laboratory; however you will also need to visit crime scenes. You might have to deal with unpleasant or upsetting sights. You may also be outdoors in all weathers. You could be standing or crouching for long periods of time to examine evidence. You might have to spend time away from home. The average forensic scientist works about 35 to 37 hours per week, you may also have to spend time on-call.

Future prospects

As an assistant forensic scientist with an appropriate degree, you can progress to become a forensic scientist.

As a forensic scientist in the FSS (Forensic Science Service) you could progress to reporting officer level, delivering reports in court.

Promotion to management is generally based on appraisal reports and levels of experience. You could become self-employed by working as a forensic consultant. You might also have the opportunity to work abroad.

Advantages/disadvantages

You will be using your scientific knowledge to help the police to catch criminals, which would be extremely rewarding.

This job comes with a lot of responsibility as your evidence may be the reason someone gets convicted.

This is a varied job; no two cases will be the same.

Qualifications and courses

You will need a good Honours degree (1st or upper 2:1) in biology, chemistry, forensic science or a related subject. Some employers may accept an equivalent professional qualification. You will usually require at least two A levels (often more) in relevant subjects and five GCSEs grades A*-C in order to apply for a degree course. Equivalent qualifications might be accepted.

An MSc in forensic science or a related subject is an advantage, as is laboratory experience.

To enter as an assistant or technician forensic scientist in England and Wales four GCSEs grades A*–C, including a science or maths subject along with at least one science A level or equivalent are required. In Scotland, a Higher National qualification in chemistry, biology or a related subject is normally required for technician/assistant entry. Assistant forensic scientists often have a degree or postgraduate qualification.

Forensic scientists are mainly trained on the job and through in-house courses. Once qualified, you can apply for registration with the Council for the Registration of Forensic Practitioners.

Money guide

Salary levels vary according to employer and location.

Starting salaries for trainee or assistant forensic scientists are around £14,000 to £18,000 per year. After two or three years this can increase to between £25,000 and £30,000 a year. As a head of department you could earn up to £50,000 a year.

Salaries in London will normally be higher.

Related opportunities

- Biomedical Scientist/Medical Laboratory Assistant p507
- Chemist p510
- Clinical Scientist p512
- Laboratory Technician p524
- Microbiologist/Bacteriologist p530

Further information

Forensic Science Society
18a Mount Parade, Harrogate, North Yorkshire HG1 1BX
01423 506 068; www.forensic-science-society.org.uk

The Forensic Science Service (FSS)
Trident Court, 2920 Solihull Parkway,
Birmingham Business Park, Birmingham B37 7YN
0121 329 8444; www.forensic.gov.uk

Skills for Justice
Centre Court, Atlas Way, Sheffield S4 7QQ
0114 261 1499; www.skillsforjustice.com

Science, Mathematics and Statistics

CRCI: TD
CLCI: QOT

GEOGRAPHER

What the work involves

- Geography combines the study of people and places, covering physical, environmental, human and economic issues.

- You will apply your specialist skills and knowledge in one or more of a variety of job areas, such as environmental management, planning, surveying, oceanography and travel and tourism.

- You could also teach and lecture on geography-related subjects.

- Your job could involve undertaking fieldwork and other types of research to increase public understanding of natural and human environments.

The type of person suited to this work

As a geographer you need to be curious about the world around you, whatever area you work in. You also need the skills and knowledge to support your research. It's essential to have a practical and logical approach to your work.

You will be able to apply your problem-solving skills to analyse the information that you collect.

It is essential that you are comfortable undertaking fieldwork outside in sometimes poor conditions.

You will need good written communication skills for producing detailed reports and other forms of information. Your ICT skills will help you organise and manage this information. The nature of the job makes team-working skills essential for geographers.

Working conditions

The nature of jobs vary widely so working conditions could range from an office, to a research centre, to a college.

For jobs involving a high level of research, you may spend periods of time outside, sometimes in poor weather conditions. For research activities, a good level of physical fitness is helpful. Fieldwork may involve spending periods of time away from home and working unsocial hours.

Future prospects

With a geography-based qualification, you could move into a wide range of areas. Because opportunities in geographical research are quite limited you may need a good level of voluntary experience before being taken on as a professional researcher.

Managing natural resources, protecting the environment or promoting places – these are some of the key areas you could choose to work in. You could also move into educating others about the varied aspects of geography.

Advantages/disadvantages

There are opportunities to work overseas whilst undertaking geographical research.

You may need to move around to gain professional experience in research.

Qualifications and courses

An Honours degree or above in geography or a related field is required. Geography degrees cover varied aspects of human, economic and physical geography, but it is also possible to gain a first degree in one particular aspect, such as human or physical geography.

Entry requirements for geography degrees vary, but often include an A level/H grade in geography. For science-based geography courses (BSc), science A levels/H grades may be required.

Geography degrees usually include fieldwork at varied kinds of sites whilst some courses offer the chance to study abroad.

For roles in environmental or conservation work, relevant voluntary experience can be useful. A driving licence can also be helpful.

The Royal Geographical Society offers a Chartership scheme to members at fellowship level with a first degree in geography or equivalent and the required level of experience. The status of Chartered Geographer (CGeog) may benefit job applications and further career development.

More specialised jobs may require a postgraduate degree in areas such as environmental management and applied geographic information systems.

Money guide

Salaries vary according to the type of job you do and the organisation you work for.

Environmental management professionals can earn from £24,500 to £36,000 per year.

An academic research assistant could earn £17,500–£24,500.

Salaries for geography teachers start at around £23,000 with qualified teacher status and go up to £36,000. Further education college lecturers' salaries start around £18,000 per annum.

Related opportunities

- Cartographer p79
- Planning and Development Surveyor p115
- Teacher p212
- Town Planner p133

Further information

Geographical Association
160 Solly Street, Sheffield S1 4BF
0114 296 0088; www.geography.org.uk

Royal Geographical Society (with the Institute of British Geographers)
1 Kensington Gore, London SW7 2AR
020 7591 3000; www.rgs.org

GEOLOGIST/GEOLOGICAL TECHNICIAN

What the work involves

Geologist

- Geologists analyse and study the planet earth, including its materials, structure and history.

- Your work may involve organising practical field and laboratory research to gain specific information. You may use your skills to support development work, for example mineral mining and the oil industry.

Geological technician

- You will work closely with geologists, undertaking practical research work in the field and laboratory. You will collect and examine samples and produce test results.

- You will work with other sources, for example surveys, to provide detailed information on specific geological features and aspects.

The type of person suited to this work

You should have the ability to pay close attention to detail. You will need to be meticulous, practical and logical in your approach to work. You will have to work with technical equipment and so you have high levels of dexterity. You must be able to uphold health and safety regulations. Geologists need to be able to make important decisions and communicate well, both in person and on paper. A geological technician needs good graphical skills including computer-aided-design if they are to help produce maps.

Working conditions

The hours and working conditions of a geologist will vary considerably depending on the sector they are working in.

Geological technicians normally work 9–5, Monday-Friday, with some exceptions when they have approaching deadlines.

Future prospects

Geologists could progress to a managerial role, although this may involve changing employers. There is also the possibility of becoming self employed if you work as a consultant. You could alternatively work as a university lecturer.

There are more promotion opportunities for Geological technicians within larger organisations. If you choose to work for a smaller company you may need to change employers to progress. Training to become a geologist is possible.

Advantages/disadvantages

You may have difficulty gaining enough money to fund your research or projects.

Qualifications and courses

Geologist entry level 5.
Geological technician entry level 2.

Geologist

You generally need a degree in a geosciences subject. A levels/H grades in science subjects and/or maths are usually required. The British Geological Survey recruits assistant scientific officers with A levels/H grades and scientific officers with a relevant degree.

Geological technician

The usual minimum entry requirements are four GCSEs/S grades A*–C/1–3, including a science and maths. It is possible to work towards further qualifications, such as a degree or HND, through part-time study, day- or block-release. Some posts require A levels/H grades, AVCEs/GSVQ Level 3 or an HNC/D. Qualifications in science subjects are required. NVQs/SVQs are available at Levels 2–4.

There are job opportunities within multinational corporations which would allow you access to the latest technology.

Employers generally prefer applicants who have completed postgraduate study.

There are opportunities for international travel.

Money guide

Geologist

Starting out as a graduate you can expect to get £25, 000 per year and this will increase with postgraduate qualifications. At senior levels this can increase to £40,000–£50,000.

Geological technician

Starting salaries begin at around £18,500–£24,000 per year. With experience you can expect £25,000–£35,000 a year. At senior levels this can increase to £40,000+.

Related opportunities

- Ecologist p515
- Geophysicist p522
- Oceanographer p531

Further information

British Geological Survey
Kingsley Dunham Centre, Keyworth, Nottingham NG12 5GG
0115 936 3143; www.bgs.ac.uk

Cogent Sector Skills Council Limited
Unit 5, Mandarin Court, Centre Park, Warrington, Cheshire WA1 1GG
01925 515200; www.cogent-ssc.com

Science, Mathematics and Statistics

CRCI: TB
CLCI: QOL

GEOPHYSICIST

What the work involves

- You will apply physics-based investigation techniques to explore and analyse the nature of the rocks, structures and minerals below the earth's surface. You would spend a lot of time undertaking practical work and writing up your results.

- Most geophysicists are involved with helping companies explore for oil and gas. You would help plan and organise exploration work and interpret detailed geological information.

- Geophysicists work in research in universities and research institutes and for companies involved in oil and mineral exploration.

- You will work as part of a team of geologists, engineers and/or engineering geologists.

The type of person suited to this work

You should have an interest in rock structures and a desire to travel. Your scientific and technical skills will be of a high quality. You should pay excellent attention to detail and have a methodical and meticulous approach to solving problems. You will need to have strong numeracy skills and the ability to use software packages which may be extremely complex. You should be able to communicate well, both in person and on paper.

Working conditions

You will spend some time in an office or laboratory and the rest in the field. If you are involved in data collection you will travel the world, operating from base camps.

You might also work offshore (at sea) on oil or gas platforms or ships. This work will involve being away from home for long periods of time in a confined space, living and working with the same people.

Future prospects

Construction, fuel and mineral exploration and development organisations within the public and private sectors need the skills of geophysics professionals. Developing a career in industry may mean having to move around to gain the relevant professional experience. For some jobs, this could involve spending time working overseas.

You also have the option of becoming self-employed or consultancy work.

Advantages/disadvantages

You can live and work abroad while you undertake research work.

The work can be physically demanding and may involve visiting potentially hazardous sites.

You may have the opportunity to study and observe the natural world in a variety of locations.

Qualifications and courses

An Honours degree in geoscience, geology, geotechnology or a related field is required. A typical offer for a geophysics degree would normally be three A levels including maths and physics. Geology courses usually expect applicants to have attained two A levels in subjects such as biology, chemistry, maths, physics, geography or geology.

A postgraduate qualification is usually also required. Alternatively you can complete a four years masters programme in geophysics. Relevant postgraduate courses include the MSc in petroleum, geoscience and exploration geophysics. It is also possible to achieve a PhD in particular areas of geophysics. Pre-entry experience is desirable.

For entry at technician level, A level/H grade in physics is normally required. It may be possible to enter with an Intermediate GNVQ, SQA National at Intermediate 2, or BTEC First Certificate/Diploma in Science, or to undertake an Apprenticeship/Skillseekers.

In order to apply for an engineering Apprenticeship you should have achieved four GCSEs grades A*-C or a BTEC First. Apprenticeships allow you to train whilst being paid a basic salary.

Some employment in this area is offered on a short-term contract basis only, which can lead to job insecurity.

Money guide

These figures are only approximate as salary levels vary widely depending on the company and sector.

Starting salaries are around £22,000 per year. With a few years of experience you could expect to be earning between £25,000 and £45,000 a year.

Once you reach a more senior level you could earn over £50,000 per year.

Related opportunities

- Environmental Scientist p517
- Geological Technician p521
- Hydrologist p523
- Oceanographer p531
- Oil and Gas Drilling Industry p243

Further information

British Geological Survey
Kingsley Dunham Centre, Keyworth, Nottingham G12 5GG
0115 936 3100; www.bgs.ac.uk

The Geological Society
Burlington House, Piccadilly, London W1J 0BG
020 7434 9944; www.geolsoc.org.uk

British Geophysical Association
www.ras.org.uk

HYDROLOGIST

What the work involves

- As an invaluable natural resource, water needs to be monitored and managed by hydrologists. You will help ensure that safe drinking water is available when and where it is needed.

- Your work could involve measuring river flows, rainfall, evaporation and ground water. You may assess water use in agriculture and forestry, or be involved with dealing with water-management emergencies, for example in droughts.

- Your research might involve working out potential flood risks, designing water supply systems or developing resources such as reservoirs.

- You will work with civil engineers, freshwater ecologists, chemists and other professionals.

The type of person suited to this work

You will need to have an interest in environmental protection and management and an understanding of how a water supply affects a society. You should have strong geographical, scientific, mathematical and technical capabilities.

The job calls for the ability to problem-solve and think creatively to resolve specific issues. You'll also need to be confident in using and creating maps and other ways of portraying and creating a record of a landscape.

The job demands excellent observational skills and attention to detail. You will need the ability to work with detailed factual information. You should be comfortable in communicating your work.

Working conditions

Most hydrologists work mainly within an office environment, with conventional office hours. If there is an emergency or a deadline approaching you might need to work some evenings and weekends.

You might also be required to complete time in the field. You will be outdoors, working in a variety of weather conditions and using heavy equipment, so you may need to have a certain level of physical stamina.

This job might involve travel within and outside of the UK.

Future prospects

The opportunities available for promotion will vary depending on the organisation and employer. Progression also depends a great deal on experience, skills, responsibility and merit. You may be able to increase your chances of promotion by moving to another team or geographical location in order to increase experience. To progress you should be able to manage people, projects and budgets.

Self-employment is possible if you become a consultant.

There are many opportunities to work overseas for international organisations.

Qualifications and courses

The minimum requirement for entry to the profession is usually an Honours degree in geography, environmental science, civil engineering or mathematics. For entry to a degree, students usually require a minimum of two A levels/three H grades and five GCSEs grades A*-C or equivalent.

A postgraduate qualification is usually also required, normally in a subject like engineering hydrology or water resources. In order to gain entry to a postgraduate course a successful first degree in a relevant subject is required.

The Chartered Institution of Water and Environmental Management (CIWEM) accredits a number of undergraduate and postgraduate courses in the field.

Pre-entry work experience is recommended, as this is such a competitive industry. You should consider completing placements during your holidays or as part of a sandwich degree. This will increase your industry understanding and hopefully improve your career prospects.

Advantages/disadvantages

You can live and work abroad while you undertake research work.

You may have to work outdoors in the wind and rain.

Some employment in this area is offered on a short-term contract basis only, which can lead to job insecurity.

If you work within consultancy, you will have a wide variety of work available to you.

Money guide

These figures are only approximate as salary levels vary widely according to sector, location and employer.

Starting salaries range from around £17,000 to £25,000 per year. Once you have gained five years' experience this can rise to between £28,000 and £35,000 a year.

If you reach senior level you could earn up to £45,000 a year.

Related opportunities

- Civil Engineering Technician p83
- Geophysicist p522
- Meteorologist p529
- Oceanographer p531

Further information

British Hydrological Society
1 Great George Street, London SW1P 3AA
020 222 7722; www.hydrology.org.uk

The Chartered Institution of Water and Environmental Management (CIWEM)
15 John Street, London WC1N 2EB
020 7831 3110; www.ciwem.org.uk

Science, Mathematics and Statistics

CRCI: TB
CLCI: QOL

LABORATORY TECHNICIAN

What the work involves

■ You will analyse samples of different types of substances and materials using specialist equipment.

■ You could specialise in a particular area, such as microbiology or clinical chemistry.

■ Your work may involve recording detailed information and developing and maintaining microbiological or other cultures.

■ Laboratory technicians apply their scientific analysis and measurement skills in organisations such as the military services, the National Health Service, industry and scientific research institutions.

The type of person suited to this work

You will provide important factual information, so must work to a high standard of accuracy. It is also essential that you pay attention to detail and are methodical. Your patient attitude will help you undertake sometimes repetitive but important laboratory activities.

The job involves organising and setting up laboratory equipment so you will need good manual handling skills. As well as practical skills, you will also need to be confident in communicating with others. Your ICT skills will help you record and analyse a range of information. Because your work may involve handling potentially dangerous materials you must work to a good standard of health and safety at all times.

Working conditions

You will spend most of your working day in a laboratory which has to be kept clean and sterile at all times.

You may work with specialist computer software in an office to complete some of your research and recording activities.

You will need to wear protective clothing when you are working in close contact with potentially harmful substances in the laboratory.

Future prospects

Scientific laboratory technicians play an important role in protecting public health. Their work also helps to make safe, high-quality products that many of us use every day.

Scientific laboratory technicians are employed within industry, health service organisations, public research and other areas.

With further experience, you could progress to supervising a team of technicians or managing a laboratory.

Advantages/disadvantages

Laboratory tasks can be repetitive and time-consuming and require patience.

Because of the transferable nature of lab skills, you could move from one organisation to another quite easily.

Qualifications and courses

ENTRY LEVEL 2

At least 4 GCSEs/S grades (A–C/1–3), including English, mathematics and a science, are required for entry into this career. Equivalent qualifications such as an Intermediate GNVQ/SQA National at Intermediate 2, BTEC First Certificate or Diploma in science may be accepted.

Qualifications at a higher level may be required. Entrants may have A levels/H grades, a BTEC/SQA National qualification, an HNC/D or a degree in science subjects.

Work experience in a laboratory can be helpful to applications.

Laboratory technicians are trained on the job, and may be able to study towards NVQs/SVQs at Levels 2–4 in Laboratory and Associated Technical Activities or Levels 2–3 in Laboratory Technician: Working in Education, or an HNC/D or degree in a science subject.

Apprenticeships/Skillseekers may be available to those aged 16–24.

In some organisations you would work on a shift basis.

Money guide

Salary levels vary between sectors. Organisations requiring more specialist skills – e.g. animal handling – may pay more.

Starting salaries begin at around £12,000–£13,000 per year.

With experience and qualifications, you could earn up to £30,000.

At senior level, as a team leader or laboratory manager, it is possible to earn £32,000–£40,000.

Related opportunities

■ Biochemist p506
■ Biomedical Scientist p507
■ Forensic Scientist p519
■ Pharmacy Technician p332

Further information

Biochemical Society Membership Office
Portland Customer Services, Commerce Way, Whitehall Industrial Estate, Colchester, Essex CO2 8HP
01206 796351; www.biochemistry.org

Science Council
210 Euston Road, London NW1 2BE
020 7611 8754; www.sciencecouncil.org

Semta
14 Upton Road, Watford WD18 0JT
01923 238441; www.semta.org.uk

MARINE BIOLOGIST

What the work involves

■ You will undertake practical research and analysis into animal and plant life in the world's seas and oceans. As well as academic research, you could apply your skills in fisheries, research or fish-farming development.

■ You may undertake practical research trips above or below the sea's surface and keep detailed research records.

■ By increasing understanding of the sea you will be able to make predictions about the effects man will have on the marine ecosystem and how it will cope with these changes.

■ You may provide specialist advice to organisations such as governments or environmental pressure groups.

The type of person suited to this work

You should have a strong interest in science and a particular interest in marine life. You will require both a scientific understanding and practical ability. You will need to be meticulous and extremely patient. You should have good numerical and computer based skills. You must be observant and have a questioning mind. You will need to be able to analyse and interpret data effectively. You should have a certain level of physical stamina. You will need a desire to travel and not mind being at sea. You should be highly organised and able to work autonomously and as part of a team.

Working conditions

You will spend time in an office environment, laboratory and researching in the field. Whilst in the laboratory or office you will usually work normal office hours, however some projects and deadlines may require overtime.

When working on projects at sea you will probably be working longer hours. Operating at sea might mean you are away for long periods of time, in cramped and possibly uncomfortable conditions. You will be living and working with the same people.

Future prospects

Due to high levels of interest, there can be a lot of competition for jobs. Gaining a good level of practical experience in addition to the relevant training shows commitment and provides useful skills.

Once you have gathered enough field experience you could go freelance or alternatively, set up your own consultancy.

You could alternatively lecture students which you could combine with completing your own research.

Working abroad is a distinct possibility.

Advantages/disadvantages

A lot of your research in the field will depend on the tides and weather conditions, which could slow down your progress.

You will use your skills and knowledge to increase public understanding of the natural environment.

Qualifications and courses

ENTRY LEVEL 6

Candidates can either take an Honours degree in marine biology, marine science, or oceanography, or a degree in chemistry or physics, followed by a specialised postgraduate qualification. At least two A levels/H grades in relevant science subjects are required for entry to degree courses along with five GCSEs grades A*-C (or equivalent). For degrees in marine biology, A level/H grade biology is normally required also, maths and another science subject would be enormously relevant. Other technological subjects or languages would also be beneficial.

A postgraduate qualification is an advantage and you will probably require a 1st or a 2:1 in your first degree in order to be accepted onto a Masters or PhD programme.

Entrants for research posts need a relevant degree and usually a postgraduate qualification.

If you want to apply for a technological support role you should have achieved A levels in biology, maths or geography and another science subject.

Finding funding for your research projects may prove problematic.

Money guide

Starting salaries tend to be at the higher end of the scale for people with a higher or postgraduate degree.

Once you are a qualified marine biologist you can expect a starting salary of somewhere between £17,000 and £20,000 per year.

With experience, salaries can increase to around £25,000 a year.

The highest earning marine biologists, who are at the top of their field can earn up to £60,000 a year.

Related opportunities

■ Ecologist p515
■ Environmental Scientist p517
■ Oceanographer p531
■ Zoologist p536

Further information

Marine Biological Association
The Laboratory, Citadel Hill, Plymouth PL1 2PB
01752 633207; www.mba.ac.uk

National Oceanography Centre
Southampton, University of Southampton Waterfront Campus, European Way, Southampton SO14 3ZH
02380 596666; www.noc.soton.ac.uk

The Centre for Environment, Fisheries and Aquaculture Science (CEFAS)
CEFAS Lowestoft Laboratory, Pakefield Road, Lowestoft, Suffolk NR33 OHT
01502 595106; www.cefas.co.uk

Science, Mathematics and Statistics

CRCI: TD
CLCI: QOD

MATERIALS SCIENTIST

What the work involves

- Materials scientists measure, define and process materials. They help decide the types of materials to use in engineering, construction and product processing work.

- You will use your knowledge of the properties of metals and alloys, glass, ceramics and other materials in many areas of industrial research, development and production.

- You will research how and why materials react to certain conditions and how they can be used in our everyday lives.

- You will use technology and computer equipment to carry out tests on different materials, keep records of your findings and draw conclusions from the results.

The type of person suited to this work

You will need to have creative flair and you should have an inquisitive and logical mind. You will need to be meticulous. You will be able to write coherent reports and be a good public speaker, as you may need to give presentations. You will need solid computer skills. You should work well in a team environment. You should have dexterity as you will be working with a selection of test equipment. You will need good eyesight (including colour vision for some projects).

Working conditions

Material scientists in industry work normal office hours or shifts, however the more senior your role is, the longer you will have to work.

You could be working in a sterile laboratory or an industrial environment. The most common working environments for material scientists are laboratories and offices. There is a possibility you will have to complete work in the field. You may have to wear protective clothing.

Future prospects

You will have the option to change industries and purchase raw materials, work in sales, management or marketing. You could progress to become a project manager or a technical director, meaning you would be leading people in developing new products.

Alternatively, you could move into a career in teaching.

Opportunities for self-employment are limited but you could work in NDT (non-destructive testing) or failure analysis. There may be the possibility to work abroad.

Advantages/disadvantages

You will have the opportunity to apply your skills and knowledge to develop new products and provide new scientific information.

Scientists are constantly in demand in most areas of industry.

This can be a highly lucrative career.

Qualifications and courses

ENTRY LEVEL 6

The usual entry qualification for a professional materials scientist or metallurgist is a degree. Degrees are available in metallurgy and in materials science, materials technology and materials engineering. It is also possible to enter with a degree in a general science subject. A Foundation year is available at some institutions for candidates without the required scientific background.

Most degree courses expect applicants to have achieved at least two A levels and five GCSEs grade A*-C (or equivalent). Most institutions require maths and English GCSEs. For entry to a relevant degree course, A level/H grade maths and a science are required.

To become a chartered materials engineer, you need to have studied a four year MEng degree or a three year BEng or BSc followed by a period of professional development.

Postgraduate courses are available, and may be studied prior to entry, or through company training schemes. In order to be accepted to a postgraduate qualification you must have successfully completed a first degree.

Technicians need at least four GCSEs grade A*-C which should include two sciences, English and maths (or equivalent).

Money guide

On entering this career you can expect to earn around £18,000 per year. Entry salaries tend to be higher with a postgraduate qualification. Once you have gained experience this figure can increase to £35,000 a year. Once you have reached a senior role you could earn in excess of £50,000 per year.

Related opportunities

- Biochemist p506
- Chemist p510
- Laboratory Technician p524

Further information

Institute of Materials, Minerals and Mining (IOM3)
1 Carlton House Terrace, London SW1Y 5DB
020 7451 7300; Main website: www.iom3.org;
Careers website: www.materials-careers.org.uk

UK Centre for Materials Education
Second Floor, Brodie Tower, University of Liverpool, Liverpool L69 3GQ
0151 794 5364; www.materials.ac.uk and
www.whystudymaterials.ac.uk

SEMTA (Sector Skills Council for Science Engineering and Manufacturing Technologies)
14 Upton Road, Watford WD18 0JT
0800 282 167; www.semta.org.uk

MATHEMATICIAN

What the work involves

- Mathematics is the study of measurements and quantities using numbers and symbols.

- Your work may involve undertaking research and analysis, planning and setting up research programmes and assessing research findings.

- You could work in job roles requiring mathematical skills and knowledge, for example actuary, operational researcher or statistician.

- As a mathematician you could work at all levels of industry, research and education and help to inform the work of different organisations.

The type of person suited to this work

As a mathematician it is essential that you have a strong interest in working with numerical information to solve complex problems. You will also need to have a logical and methodical approach to your work. But your flexible and innovative approach will help you analyse a range of problems.

Your work may help shape the activities of your company so you must have good attention to detail. You should also be able to record your work accurately. Strong communication skills will help you explain mathematical ideas to people without a background in maths. As maths-related research can take time to plan and set up, a patient attitude can be helpful.

Working conditions

For many maths-related roles, you would work in an office and use computers to manage and analyse information.

If you work in education, you will spend time teaching in classrooms and in lecture rooms. You may also spend time undertaking research.

Mathematicians who work in business, such as accountants and finance consultants, will spend time in meetings with their clients.

Future prospects

Right now there is a lot of demand for professional mathematicians in many areas. From academic research, to teaching to a statistical research role as an operational researcher or statistician, there is a range of available careers.

Other opportunities include working in business, finance or industry. There is a demand for professional mathematicians in companies that develop new products such as new computer software and pharmaceuticals.

Advantages/disadvantages

Mathematical skills apply to many different sectors, so you could move across a range of areas.

You may need to take a second degree to follow your chosen career.

A shortage of qualified mathematicians means that there are a variety of opportunities.

Qualifications and courses

A degree in maths is normally required to work as a professional mathematician in industry, business/finance, education or research. Degrees are available in general maths or in specific areas, for example, financial maths or business maths.

Entry onto maths degree courses usually requires at least 2 A levels/3H grades (A–C/1–3), including maths, and 5GCSEs/S grades (A–C/1–3), including English and maths. Science and or computing-related subjects are also viewed favourably.

Maths graduates are recruited directly by some companies and public sector organisations. Most mathematicians also have postgraduate qualifications, which require a first degree in mathematics, physics or another subject with a high mathematical content.

To teach maths in primary and secondary schools, maths graduates need to study for a PGCE.

It is possible to become a Chartered Mathematician with the Institute of Mathematics and its Applications. The requirements for chartered status are an Honours degree in maths or with more than two-thirds maths content, and 3 years in employment.

Money guide

Salary levels vary widely according to employer and sector, but maths graduates earn the highest salaries of all graduates.

Starting salaries for graduates range from £20,000–£25,000 per year.

A higher degree – a Masters degree or PhD – can raise pay awards to between £26,000 and £29,000.

With several years' experience you could earn £33,000–£40,000.

At senior level, possibly as a director, earnings can exceed £55,000.

Related opportunities

- Accountant p16
- Actuary p20
- Stockbroker p64
- Systems Analyst p171

Further information

Institute of Mathematics and its Applications
Catherine Richards House, 16 Nelson Street, Southend-on-Sea, Essex SS1 1EF
01702 354020; www.ima.org.uk

Mathematical Association
259 London Road, Leicester LE2 3BE
0116 221 0013; www.m-a.org.uk

Maths Careers
www.mathscareers.org.uk
Council of Mathematical Sciences Careers website

Science, Mathematics and Statistics

CRCI: TC
CLCI: QOJ

METALLURGIST

What the work involves

- Metallurgists apply their materials science and engineering knowledge to support product and process development in areas such as aerospace, rail, construction and oil and gas.

- You may be involved with the metal extraction process, managing projects or researching metals and materials.

- You may help develop practical solutions for production problems.

- Whatever job you do, it is likely that your role will involve aspects of quality control, project management and process/product development.

The type of person suited to this work

Metallurgists need an excellent knowledge of metals and related materials, whatever area they work in. They must also be able to understand the uses for different materials. You will need to have good communication and team-working skills. But you will also have to be confident in making decisions that could affect major industrial processes and understand the commercial impact of your work.

Your flexible approach and attention to detail will help you adapt to the changing demands of different projects. Your ICT and numeracy skills will also be important. Because you may work with potentially dangerous materials you must have a good knowledge of health and safety.

Working conditions

You may have to work in a noisy location if you are employed by a large manufacturing company. In other roles you could be based in a laboratory-style setting.

Hours vary from employer to employer, but they can be long, for example if you are working to complete a specific project to a set deadline.

In many roles, you will be part of a team and may also meet with clients on a regular basis.

In some roles you may be required to write detailed reports.

Future prospects

Many industries are quite literally built on metals and related materials! With a strong demand for high quality materials in a wide range of industries, there are all kinds of opportunities.

You could undertake project management for individual companies. You may choose to work for companies that develop materials for industries such as automotive and aerospace engineering. Or you could directly manage the process of mining and extracting materials.

Advantages/disadvantages

The role can provide the satisfaction of developing new products and materials.

Qualifications and courses

The usual entry qualification for a professional materials scientist or metallurgist is a degree. Degrees are available in metallurgy and in materials science, materials technology and materials engineering. It is also possible to enter with a degree in a general science subject, such as physics or chemistry.

Entry to a relevant degree course (such as physics, chemical engineering, metallurgy or materials science) usually requires a minmum of 2 A levels/3H grades and 5 GCSEs/S grades (A–C/1–3). BTEC/SQA National qualifications may be offered as alternatives. For those seeking entry to the profession with HNC/HNDs or Foundation degrees (in a subject such as metallurgy and materials, metals technology, manufacturing engineering or applied science) then at least 1 science A level/H grade will be required.

The role can provide the satisfaction of developing new products and materials.

There are opportunities to work and live abroad.

There are opportunities to work and live abroad.

Money guide

Starting salaries range from around £18,500 to reach £28,000 per year.

With experience and at a senior level it is possible to earn £30,000–£38,000.

With chartered engineer status and considerable experience, as a senior manager you could earn between £38,000 and £50,000.

Related opportunities

- Materials Scientist p526
- Aerospace Engineer p220
- Laboratory Technician p524
- Structural Engineer p129

Further information

Institute of Materials, Minerals and Mining (IOM3)
1 Carlton House Terrace, London SW1Y 5DB
020 7451 7300; Main website: www.iom3.org;
Careers website: www.materials-careers.org.uk

Engineering Council UK
246 High Holborn, London WC1V 7EX
020 7206 0500; www.engc.org.uk

Institute of Cast Metals Engineers
National Metalforming Centre, 47 Birmingham Road, West Bromwich, West Midlands B70 6PY
0121 601 6979; www.icme.org.uk

METEOROLOGIST

What the work involves

- Information gained from observing the sky, the atmosphere and natural phenomena gives a picture of everyday weather conditions.

- As well as providing weather forecast information that is used throughout the media and to inform industries such as fishing, meteorologists undertake research into the earth's atmosphere. You could be employed by the Royal Navy, the RAF, the Meteorological Office and other employers.

- You will be using specialist computer programmes and mathematical techniques to gather information, which you will combine in order to form a weather picture.

- Within meteorology you can work as a forecaster or a researcher.

The type of person suited to this work

You should have a strong interest in the environment, science, research and climate change. You will need to excel in maths and physics. The job calls for the ability to problem-solve and think creatively to resolve specific issues. You should be happy to work in various locations, however remote.

The job demands excellent observational skills and attention to detail. You should be able to comprehend and evaluate complex information. You must be able to communicate effectively, both in person and on paper. You will be computer literate, and work well as part of a team.

Working conditions

You will generally conduct your work from an office environment, using specialised computers. When you are working in the field you could be living and working in extremely isolated areas with basic living conditions.

Researchers generally work ordinary office hours. Forecasters and observers however will usually work in shifts. When working in the field will not usually have set hours.

Future prospects

There are three main areas that a meteorologist can work in; these are forecasting, research and teaching. You may wish to move between them in order to progress.

Once you have gained experience as a forecaster you might be able to move into broadcasting, research or consultancy work.

There are careers available at the Met office, within utility companies, shipping, insurance companies and in the armed forces. There could be the possibility of working abroad.

Advantages/disadvantages

You may have the opportunity to study and observe the natural world in a variety of locations.

Qualifications and courses

Entrants to this profession need a degree and often a postgraduate qualification. Degrees in meteorology are available, but other suitable subjects are physics, maths, computer science, oceanography and environmental science. Employers may also require A levels/H grades in maths and physics – these usually form part of the entry requirements for meteorology degrees.

Relevant taught postgraduate courses are available. Subject areas include meteorology, climatology and atmospheric science. There are also opportunities to do a research PhD at some institutions.

The Met Office provides initial training for new entrants without a postgraduate qualification. The training consists of an 18-week Initial Forecasting Course, followed by eight months' practical training at a weather station, and a three week Forecasting Consolidation Course. You will generally need a 1st or 2:1 to apply for a post at the Met Office.

You can also enter work at the Met Office in a support role, for which you will generally require at least two A levels at grade C or above, preferably including maths and physics.

Relevant work experience would be extremely valuable.

You might have to work inconvenient shifts.

There is a wide variety of work within this industry so you shouldn't get bored.

Employers increasingly require applicants to have a postgraduate qualification in a relevant subject.

Money guide

These figures are only approximate and may vary based on sector, employer and location. Starting salaries begin at around £18,000 to £21,000 per year. With experience this rises to somewhere between £25,000 and £35,000 a year. If you reach a more senior level, with managerial responsibilities you could earn up to between £50,000 and £60,000 per year.

Related opportunities

- Geophysicist p522
- Hydrologist p523
- Oceanographer p531
- Physicist p533

Further information

Royal Meteorological Society
104 Oxford Road, Reading, Berkshire RG1 7LL
020 7470 4800; www.royalmetsoc.org

Met Office
Fitzroy Road, Exeter, Devon EX1 3PB
01392 885680; www.metoffice.gov.uk

Science, Mathematics and Statistics

CRCI: TB
CLCI: QOL

MICROBIOLOGIST/ BACTERIOLOGIST

What the work involves

Microbiologist

- Microbiologists study microorganisms such as bacteria and viruses. They research and analyse different types of microscopic organisms to support work in medicine, agriculture, food and milk production and pollution control.

- Your specialist skills and knowledge could be used in government defence departments, environmental conservation and medicine.

Bacteriologist

- Bacteriologists study and analyse microscopic organisms, particularly ones that cause disease.

- Their research provides important information on protecting against illnesses and caring for people with specific kinds of diseases.

The type of person suited to this work

You will need to be scientifically capable. You will require a high level of dexterity and you will need to be meticulous, practical and logical in your approach to work. You should also be patient as you might find you have to repeat tests.

Working conditions

Both of these professions generally work normal office hours; however these may be extended for fieldwork or to meet approaching deadlines. You will be working in a laboratory, factory or in the field.

Future prospects

Microbiologist

Microbiologists work in a range of fields. There are opportunities within the NHS and government laboratories and research centres. Microbiologists also work for private companies developing food, drink, pharmaceuticals and other products. A smaller number undertake teaching and research in universities.

Bacteriologist

Bacteriology is a specialism that most people go into after gaining experience and professional skills in related areas such as microbiology. There are a small number of opportunities within the NHS, research institutes and industry.

Advantages/disadvantages

There are opportunities to visit different types of outside locations on research trips.

Experiments can take a long time to complete and some aspects might become tedious.

Employers such as the National Health Service can offer the

Qualifications and courses

Microbiologist

Most entrants have a degree, and sometimes a postgraduate qualification, in microbiology or a related science subject. Many institutions offer 1-year Foundation courses for candidates without the necessary scientific background.

It is possible to work as a technician or medical laboratory technician. You will need four GCSEs/S grades (A*–C/1–3) including two sciences, maths and English. NVQs/SVQs are available in Laboratory and Associated Technical Activities at Levels 2, 3 and 4.

Bacteriologist

To work as a clinical bacteriologist, a 1st or 2.1 degree in a relevant subject is required and an MSc or PhD is an advantage. For entry to an academic research post, a postgraduate qualification is required. Applicants without a PhD may start as a research assistant and work towards a PhD.

You could alternatively enter as a laboratory assistant; for this you will need a minimum of four GCSEs including two sciences, maths and English.

chance to gain experience in different departments and provide well-structured career paths.

You will be handling potentially dangerous substances.

Money guide

If you begin your career as a laboratory assistant you can expect to earn between £13,000 and £19,000 a year. Newly qualified microbiologists can earn between £20,000 and £35,000 per year. Newly qualified bacteriologists can expect between £20,000 and £38,000 a year. Top salaries for microbiologists can reach £60,000 and for bacteriologists this is a bit higher at about £65,000 a year.

Related opportunities

- Biochemist p506
- Biomedical Scientist p507
- Immunologist p317

Further information

NHS Careers
PO Box 2311, Bristol BS2 2ZX
0845 606 0655; www.nhscareers.nhs.uk and
www.nhsclinicalscientists.info

Society for General Microbiology
Marlborough House, Basingstoke Road, Spencers Wood, Reading RG7 1AG
0118 988 1800; Main website: www.socgenmicrobiol.org.uk;
Careers website: www.biocareers.org.uk

OCEANOGRAPHER

What the work involves

- Oceanographers investigate how ocean organisms and structures work together.

- Your work could involve undertaking fieldwork above and below the sea's surface. You may also interpret the information you find and write research reports.

- You could specialise as a marine geologist (studying the ocean floor), marine chemist (studying the chemical composition of water and/or sediment), marine physicist (measuring the properties of currents etc) or a marine biologist (studying the plants and animals in the sea).

- The information you produce could be used by government and/or industry.

The type of person suited to this work

You will require a passion for the environment and ocean life, along with an interest in maths, science and engineering. You will need to be prepared to travel and spend time working at sea. As you may be working in the field you will need to be physically fit. You should have strong verbal and written communication skills. You will be carrying out detailed research and so will need to be meticulous, logical and practical. You will also need to be able to present your findings in front of an audience and so should have a certain level of confidence. Good team work is essential.

Working conditions

Much of your time will be spent working in a laboratory or an office, with typical office hours from Monday to Friday. Fieldwork may be carried out at sea or along the coastline. When working at sea you might be required to spend six weeks or more away from home. You will be living and working with the same people.

Future prospects

Most oceanographic work is structured around, fixed, short-term contracts and so progression can prove tricky. You might find that you have to move between employers in order to achieve a promotion. Progression is based on merit and taking on more responsibilities, such as leading a team. It is possible to become self-employed and work as a consultant. Another option might be university lecturing, where progression opportunities are easier to come by.

Advantages/disadvantages

You will be able to combine your love of the environment with your scientific ability.

Most employers expect candidates to have a postgraduate qualification.

You will have the opportunity to travel.

Money guide

These figures are only approximate as salaries will vary depending on location, sector and employer.

Qualifications and courses

Entrants to this profession usually need a first degree. Degrees are available in oceanography and related areas, such as marine biology. Other relevant degree subjects include biology, chemistry, physics, mathematics and geology. A levels/H grades in sciences and maths are required.

In order to enter a relevant degree course, candidates usually require three relevant A levels such as maths and science subjects and five GCSEs grades A*-C, relevant subjects include sciences, English and maths along with foreign languages, IT and geography.

Most employers expect candidates to hold A level/H grade in maths. It is possible to join the Merchant or Royal Navy without a degree and take additional training to become an oceanographer.

A postgraduate qualification in oceanography is an advantage (and for most posts a requirement). Taught courses are available in oceanography and related/specialist areas. In order to be accepted onto a masters degree you will usually need a first degree in a science based subject. Some masters programmes will accept graduates without a scientific background. It is also possible to do research for an MPhil or PhD.

Starting salaries begin at around £18,000 to £22,000 per year; with a PhD you could start on £20,000 to £22,000 a year.

Once you have gained experience as an oceanographer you could get £30,000 a year.

As a senior oceanographer, with management responsibilities you could earn £60,000 per year.

Related opportunities

- Diver p543
- Ecologist p515
- Environmental Scientist p517
- Geophysicist p522
- Marine Biologist p525

Further information

Institute of Marine Engineering, Science and Technology (IMarEST)
80 Coleman Street, London EC2R 5BJ
020 7382 2600; www.imarest.org

National Oceanography Centre Southampton
University of Southampton Waterfront Campus,
European Way, Southampton SO14 3ZH
023 8059 6666; www.noc.soton.ac.uk

The Centre for Environment, Fisheries and Aquaculture Science (CEFAS)
CEFAS Lowestoft Laboratory, Pakefield Road, Lowestoft,
Suffolk NR33 0HT
01502 562244; www.cefas.co.uk

Science, Mathematics and Statistics

CRCI: TB
CLCI: QOL

OPERATIONAL RESEARCHER

What the work involves

■ Operational researchers use mathematical, scientific and other analytical methods to help improve the performance of organisations in business, industry and government.

■ You will work closely with managers and other staff to develop practical solutions to very varied kinds of management and organisational issues.

■ You will develop analytical models or strategies to improve a specific area or aspect of an organisation.

■ You may also be involved with putting your ideas into practice within companies.

The type of person suited to this work

Operational research (which is also known as operations research or management science) is all about getting practical results from in-depth analysis. So you should enjoy solving problems and applying your analytical and mathematical abilities to develop practical solutions.

You will have a strong interest in helping organisations develop - and put your understanding of each company to practical use. You will need excellent communication skills for working closely with managers and other staff. Your flexible approach will help you cope with the varied demands of each project. Whilst you will need strong ICT skills, a creative flair can also benefit you in this job.

Working conditions

You will undertake most of your work in an office setting with meetings with managers, technical specialists and staff likely to be a regular part of your job.

In the course of your work you may undertake visits to different sites in an organisation to undertake research into specific problems.

Future prospects

Operational researchers help many different organisations to develop successfully. There are increasing opportunities in manufacturing, finance and other sectors and you can build a varied career. You could move into managing an OR team or work in areas such as marketing. With more experience, you could develop a career as an OR consultant.

The Civil Service offers a well-structured career path and a range of opportunities in operational research.

Advantages/disadvantages

Strong demand in many sectors means you can develop your career in varied types of companies.

Operations research work is fast-moving and varied.

Qualifications and courses

The normal entry requirement for this profession is an Honours degree in a mathematical subject, for example maths, physics, chemistry, engineering, computer science, statistics or economics. Specialist degrees in operational research are available at some institutions, and operational research is also offered in combination with certain other degree subjects, such as maths or statistics.

For entry to a relevant degree course, applicants should expect to offer a minimum of 2 A levels/4 H grades, including mathematics. It may be possible to become an operational researcher with a degree in a non-mathematical subject if you have a good A level/H grade in maths.

Postgraduate courses are available in operational research.

The Fast Stream Development Programme offers opportunities for graduates in the Civil Service. The government's Operational Research Service scheme is open to graduates with a degree or MSc in a numerate discipline.

The Operational Research Society organises open days for undergraduates who may be interested in a career in this area. The society also offers a wide range of training courses and in-house training.

Resolving production, resource or staffing problems for a company can be confrontational and stressful.

Money guide

Salary levels vary between management consultancies, the Government Operational Research Service and other employers. Although there is strong competition for fewer jobs, generally, starting salaries range from £20,000 to £29,000 per year. With experience and some management responsibility, you could earn £32,000–£50,000. At operational research consultant level, you could earn £60,000–£80,000+.

Related opportunities

■ Mathematician p527
■ Statistician p534
■ Actuary p20

Further information

Operational Research Society
Seymour House, 12 Edward Street, Birmingham BH1 2RX
0121 233 9300; www.theorsociety.org.uk

Government Operational Research Service
www.operational-research.gov.uk

PHYSICIST

What the work involves

- Physicists apply their understanding of matter and energy and how they work together, in industry, government research, academia and medicine.

- You could apply your specialist skills and knowledge to investigate diverse subjects, including space, nuclear, thermal, atomic and materials physics.

- You may be involved with research and development work or with designing projects.

- Your role could involve developing products and systems in areas such as computing, aeronautics, electronics and medicine.

The type of person suited to this work

Physicists must combine their scientific knowledge with strong problem-solving skills to develop knowledge of a range of issues. For this job you will need the confidence to work with complex numerical information. You should also have excellent attention to detail for undertaking research.

ICT skills are also important. You should have good written and verbal communication skills to explain your work. A patient approach for completing detailed projects can be useful.

Working conditions

You would be based in a laboratory, using specialist equipment when undertaking research. This work can involve handling dangerous chemicals and wearing protective clothing.

Your work may also involve spending periods looking at and assessing information on a computer.

For some jobs you will have to do a certain amount of late or weekend working. Jobs in industry may involve working shifts.

Future prospects

Physicists work at the cutting edge of science and industry. They apply their skills in areas as varied as electronics, power, communications and defence. They are employed by research institutions, government bodies and private companies to improve and develop products and systems.

Advantages/disadvantages

Physics offers the chance to develop public understanding of important scientific questions.

The job can involve working with detailed information for long periods which can be very tiring.

There is a strong demand for qualified physicists.

Money guide

Salary levels vary according to employer and sector. You will earn more with a relevant postgraduate degree.

Qualifications and courses

A relevant degree and a postgraduate qualification are required to work as a research physicist.

Relevant work experience is an advantage, and may be required by employers.

Entry to a degree course usually requires a minimum of at least 2 A levels/3–4 H grades, including physics and maths or equivalent, together with 5 GCSEs/S grades (A–C/1–3) including English, maths and science.

Many institutions offer 1-year Foundation courses for candidates without the necessary scientific background. Foundation courses may be taught at the university or at a local partner college.

Physicists are trained on the job, and often study towards postgraduate qualifications, a PhD or the membership examinations of relevant professional bodies. For example, medical physicists must work towards the Clinical Science Diploma of the Institute of Physics and Engineering in Medicine (IPEM).

For entry at technician level, an A level/H grade in physics or an equivalent qualification such as a BTEC/SQA National in science is required. Some technicians may hold a science-based degree. Technicians can work towards NVQs/SVQs in Laboratory and Associated Technical Activities at Levels 2–4.

Starting salaries for graduates begin at £20,000, reaching £27,500 per year. Look for worldwide opportunities on http://tiptop.iop.org/

With further training and qualifications salaries increase from £28,000–£38,000.

At senior/management levels you could earn £40,000–£60,000.

Related opportunities

- Astronomer p505
- Medical Physicist p320
- Aerospace Engineer p220
- Meteorologist p529

Further information

Institute of Physics
76 Portland Place, London W1B 1NT
020 7470 4800; Main website: www.iop.org;
Careers website: www.careers.iop.org

Physics World
www.physicsworld.com

Institute of Physics and Engineering in Medicine
Fairmount House, 230 Tadcaster Road, York YO24 1ES
01904 610821; www.ipem.ac.uk

Science, Mathematics and Statistics

CRCI: TD
CLCI: QOF

STATISTICIAN

What the work involves

- Statistics involves the use of mathematical techniques to collect, analyse and present large quantities of factual information.

- You will plan and undertake surveys using a range of mathematical research methods. You could apply your skills to investigate a range of subjects such as population levels, patterns of illness or national shopping habits.

- Statistical research plays a vital role in informing the activities of many areas such as government, advertising, medicine and scientific research.

The type of person suited to this work

Strong mathematical skills are essential for producing and analysing a range of statistical information. But you will also need excellent problem-solving abilities to create practical solutions and collect information on specific issues.

You will need to have excellent ICT skills as it is likely you will use specialist computer software. Your work could help to shape the work of different organisations, so you must work to a high standard of accuracy and attention to detail at all times. The ability to communicate with managers, staff and clients is essential.

Working conditions

You will be based in an office environment and spend a lot of time using computers. For some jobs you may work in a laboratory or research centre.

The job involves working closely with other people on a consultancy basis or as part of a team.

Future prospects

There is a wide range of opportunities. Statisticians investigate and research issues within the environment, medicine, business, social science and many other areas.

You may choose to develop a career in the Government Statistical Service. There are many opportunities in scientific and medical research and pharmaceutical development. Or you could choose to research and lecture on statistics in academia.

Advantages/disadvantages

Working to a high level of accuracy at all times can be very demanding.

Roles in areas such as environmental or forensic statistics are more likely with a postgraduate qualification.

As the job is often project-based, it offers a lot of variety.

Money guide

Starting salaries for graduates begin around £22,000 per year.

Qualifications and courses

The usual entry qualification for this profession is a degree in statistics, or a combined degree in statistics and another subject such as maths, economics or computer science. It is possible to enter with degrees in other subjects, providing the degree has substantial statistics content. A level/H grade maths is required for entry to a statistics degree.

Those with degrees in other mathematical subjects might enter after gaining a postgraduate qualification in statistics.

The professional examinations of the Royal Statistical Society provide an alternative entry route for people already in relevant employment and for mature entrants.

The Royal Statistical Society offers courses at three levels. The Ordinary Certificate requires a GCSE/S grade in maths or the equivalent and relevant work experience. The Higher Certificate is modular and follows on from the Ordinary Certificate. The Graduate Diploma is equivalent to an Honours degree. The courses can be studied by day-release, at evening classes or by distance learning.

The Government Statistical Service has a fast-stream programme for assistant statistician recruitment. Candidates must have a 1st or 2nd class degree in a numerate subject.

Statistical officer posts are also available to people with a 1st or 2nd class degree or 2 years' relevant work experience.

The Government Statistical Service offers work experience placements for students.

After 4 or 5 years' professional experience, statisticians with an approved degree or Graduate Diploma can qualify for Chartered Statistician status.

With experience, you can earn £40,000, increasing to £50,000+ at senior levels.

Government Statistical Service (GSS) employs over 1000 statisticians. Starting salaries range from £22,000–£24,000.

Senior level GSS salaries are £40,000–£53,000.

Related opportunities

- Mathematician p527
- Actuary p20
- Economist p34
- Operational Researcher p532

Further information

Royal Statistical Society
12 Errol Street, London EC1Y 8LX
020 7638 8998; www.rss.org.uk/careers

Statisticians in Central government
www.statistics.gov.uk/recruitment/GSS

Science, Mathematics and Statistics

CRCI: TC
CLCI: QOJ

TOXICOLOGIST

What the work involves

- As a toxicologist, you'll study the effects of the chemicals on the environment and everything within it, from humans and animals to plants.

- Work is very varied. You may find yourself working on the development of products, on testing new drugs, or lecturing and carrying out your own research.

- You may deal with poisons and drugs, or study the effects of chemicals on the environment or on human health.

- Some toxicologists work for the government.

The type of person suited to this work

You should have a strong interest in the environment, science, and public health and safety. For forensic toxicology, an interest in law is also useful.

Your level of scientific and technical knowledge should be high, and you need an excellent eye for detail as well as the ability to work carefully and accurately.

You should be able to apply scientific knowledge to practical work, and have excellent communication skills in order to explain technical and scientific information to others both verbally and in written reports.

You will also need good ICT skills.

Working conditions

The hours worked by toxicologists tend to follow the standard 9–5, Monday-Friday working week pattern, and this doesn't tend to vary too much. However, if you're carrying out experimental work you might be expected to be more flexible, you might be on call on occasional weekends and evenings in case emergencies occur.

You'll spend most of your time working in a laboratory, but may sometimes have to visit scenes where incidents have taken place.

Expect to wear protective clothing most of the time, and be prepared to work occasionally with animals.

Future prospects

You can work towards being promoted to a more senior position such as project manager. This will involve spending less time with actual hands-on toxicology, and more carrying out tasks such as administration and supervision.

If you decide that this doesn't suit you, it's also possible to become self-employed and/or work on a freelance basis.

Advantages/disadvantages

Toxicology is an interesting and challenging profession, and you may be involved in exciting cases. You will constantly be learning and expanding your knowledge.

Qualifications and courses

ENTRY LEVEL 5

You'll need a science degree to become a toxicologist. Relevant subjects include pharmacology or biochemistry. For entrance onto a degree course, you will need science A-levels, including maths and chemistry.

Following your degree, it may be possible to take up a post that offers training as you work, but the usual route nowadays is to take a postgraduate qualification. Entry requirements are at least a 2.1 classification for your undergraduate degree.

After completing a Masters degree, students may choose to study for a PhD or MPhil by carrying out research into toxicology if you wish to do so. There are diplomas offered by many institutions across the UK in the subject, and you could even choose to go into Ecotoxicology and may wish to study pollution or pesticide science.

There are many examination boards that provide qualifications in toxicology, and these include the British Toxicology Society and Federation of European Toxicologists.

It can be difficult, and you may see some distressing things. You also need to be constantly alert and can't make mistakes.

Money guide

When you start out in toxicology, you may earn about £20,000 a year.

This can increase to around £40,000 with experience.

In clinical toxicology salaries can rise to up to £65,000 a year, and in other fields this can reach £100,000.

Related opportunities

- Chemist p510
- Biochemist p506
- Biomedical Scientist p507
- Clinical Scientist p512

Further information

Association of the British Pharmaceutical Industry (ABPI)
12 Whitehall, London SW1A 2DY
020 7930 3477; www.abpi-careers.org.uk

British Toxicology Society (BTS)
Administration Office, PO Box 249, Macclesfield SK11 6FT
01625 267881; www.thebts.org

Council for the Registration of Forensic Practitioners (CRFP)
Tavistock House, Tavistock Square, London WC1H 9HX
020 7383 2200; www.crfp.org.uk

Science, Mathematics and Statistics

CRCI: TD
CLCI: QOX

ZOOLOGIST

What the work involves

- Zoologists are involved with classifying, studying and researching all kinds of animal life. You could be involved with protecting endangered species through practical work and raising public awareness.

- Some zoologists work within industry, developing pharmaceuticals or enhancing agricultural products. Others are involved with research in their specific area of interest in academic or research institutions.

- You may choose to specialise in an area such as mammalogy (mammals), entomology (insects) or herpetology (amphibians and reptiles).

- You could work in a variety of environments including safari parks, wildlife centres and zoos.

The type of person suited to this work

You will need to have a passion for environmental issues and a love of science.

You should feel comfortable dissecting dead animals as part of your work for some roles in this area. You must be meticulous, logical, practical and patient. The ability to problem-solve is a key feature of this role. Communication skills are important as you may need to share your findings with people with little or no scientific knowledge. Leadership and computer skills are also essential.

Working conditions

If you are working in the field, you will have to base your hours upon the animals you are studying, for example if studying nocturnal animals you will have to work some nights. Your working environment will also vary depending on your area of interest. Many zoologists spend the majority of their time in laboratories or teaching in lecture theatres.

Future prospects

Whilst this is a specialist area, zoologists work for a variety of organisations such as environmental consultancies, conservation bodies, animal charities and local authorities. Others go into research and development in industry.

Many choose to work in universities which have a set progression path from researcher to head of department. Promotion within industry and government is also clearly defined. Within other areas such as conservation, progression is more limited; you made need to change employers in order to achieve promotion.

Advantages/disadvantages

There are opportunities to visit different types of outside locations on research trips.

You will use your skills and knowledge to increase public understanding of many aspects of the natural environment.

When working in the field you may find yourself in inhospitable environments.

Qualifications and courses

ENTRY LEVEL 6

A degree and, often, an MSc or PhD is required for entry to this profession. Your degree can be in zoology or a related subject, such as wildlife biology, marine biology, parasitology, animal behaviour or ecology. Most degree courses require candidates to have achieved two A levels and five GCSEs grades A*-C. An A level/H grade in biology is required for entry to these degree courses. Some courses ask for a second science, usually chemistry.

The usual entry route is a post as a trainee researcher in a university research department. Trainees work towards a PhD.

It is also possible to enter the profession at technician or trainee level with GCSEs/S grades, A levels/H grades, or equivalent qualifications including biology, maths, science and English.

Some people undertake a degree after gaining practical experience working as a zookeeper or laboratory technician. Often, admissions tutors will grant these candidates a placement, regardless of their formal qualifications.

Some institutions run one year Access courses for students without the necessary educational qualifications to catch up before they undertake their degree.

Money guide

These figures are only approximate and will vary depending on sector, location and employer. A PhD may increase your starting salary.

Your starting salary will probably be in the region of £17,000 to £20,000 per year. This may increase, with experience, to somewhere between £25,000 and £35,000 a year. As a senior zoologist you could be earning over £45,000 per year.

Related opportunities

- Ecologist p515
- Entomologist p516
- Veterinary Surgeon p288
- Zoo Keeper p290

Further information

British and Irish Association of Zoos and Aquariums (BIAZA)
Regents Park, London NW1 4RY
020 7449 6351; www.biaza.org.uk

Institute of Zoology
ZSL, Regent's Park, London NW1 4RY
020 7722 3333; www.zsl.org

Institute of Biology
9 Red Lion Court, London EC4A 3EF
020 7936 5900; www.iob.org

Security and the Armed Forces

Working in the security and armed forces may give you many incredible experiences and opportunities not open to most people. You need to be an excellent team player and in some instances you may find yourself in a potentially dangerous situation, therefore it's essential that you are a great communicator. Working in this sector you can expect to spend your day absolutely anywhere! Some roles involve a lot of office work whereas others can involve spending a lot of your time on the road, or even at sea. If you're looking for a job that will be exhilarating but are able to remain calm and professional under pressure this sector could offer you a lot of opportunities.

In the section we look at the following jobs:

For similar jobs to the ones in this section turn to *Legal and Political Services* on page 363 and *Healthcare* on page 291.

ARMY OFFICER

What the work involves

- The Army is responsible for defending the UK and its allies across the world, as well as taking part in peacekeeping and humanitarian operations in volatile countries.

- Army officers lead, command and train a team of soldiers on day-to-day activities, either on training exercises or on a range of combat, peacekeeping or disaster-relief missions.

- Your platoon's training, welfare and discipline will be entirely your responsibility.

- You will work within a specific professional or skill area such as medicine, dentistry, engineering, intelligence or combat.

The type of person suited to this work

You will need to have excellent self-discipline, confidence, and a natural ability to lead and motivate your team, which will consist of soldiers, non-commissioned officers and junior officers.

You must be able to keep a clear head and make sensible decisions under pressure in order to take responsibility for the safety of your team.

Initial training, with its physical and mental challenges, often comes as a shock. You will need to have determination, courage and resilience as well as a good level of physical fitness in order to get through.

Working conditions

Your hours will depend upon which specialism you have chosen to work in. Some officers work within a normal office timeframe, whilst others are required to work shifts. Hours may also be long and irregular when away on training or taking part in field-based operations.

You could be stationed anywhere in the world, and have to travel to destinations at short notice.

Officers must wear a uniform at all times.

Future prospects

Only around 1000 officer cadets are recruited each year for the training programme at Sandhurst, so entry is competitive.

Throughout your career, you will undertake further training and study for professionally recognised qualifications in order to be promoted through the ranks right up to a brigadier level after many years in service.

Army training provides a good grounding for numerous careers in civilian life.

Advantages/disadvantages

You will be working within a close-knit team of professionals, so will build strong personal and working relationships within the job.

Qualifications and courses

Entrants for officer training must have at least 2 A-levels or equivalent, as well as 7 GCSEs/ S grades (A-C/1–3) or equivalent, including English, maths, a science and a foreign language.

It is worth noting that over 80% of the 1000 cadets accepted each year are university graduates. Some regiments and corps, such as the medical corps, may specify a particular degree as an entry requirement.

The University Officers Training Corps (UOTC) can help with degree funding by offering paid experience with the Army during your years at university. Many members of the UOTC go on to become Army officers, but there is no requirement to do so.

You will need to pass a vigorous medical and fitness entrance test, as well as a range of interview and written tests during the selection process.

Once on the officer cadet programme, you will undertake intensive training in areas such as weapons handling, leadership, tactics and fitness.

You may be involved in implementing large-scale peace initiatives which would be rewarding.

You may be posted overseas for long periods of time, including over Christmas and other family events, which can be disruptive to your personal life.

Money guide

Officer cadets joining the programme straight after their A-levels can expect to earn £14,850, whilst graduate entrants start on £23,475.

Once you reach the rank of lieutenant, your salary will increase to £28,200-£31,000.

If you become a brigadier, after 15–20 years with the Army, you could earn up to £96,000.

Related opportunities

- Royal Air Force (RAF) Officer p557
- Royal Navy Officer p560
- Soldier p564
- Police Officer p551

Further information

Army
www.army.mod.uk

Welbeck College
The Defence Sixth Form College, Forest Road, Woodhouse, Loughborough LE12 8WD
0845 600 1483; www.welbeck.mod.uk

City&Guilds

www.cityandguilds.com/myperfectjob

BODYGUARD

What the work involves

- You will be guarding your client or group, keeping them safe from harm or unwanted attention. You may also be known as a Personal Protection Officer or a Close Protection Officer.

- Protecting an executive on a business trip to a dangerous region of the world, an overseas royal visiting the UK, or a celebrity during an autograph-signing session could all be part of your work.

- You will be planning how your client can go about their business without being at risk.

- It is possible to be a specialist in areas such as close protection, surveillance or defensive driving.

The type of person suited to this work

This is not a first job – most have related experience and the people who win the most lucrative contracts have backgrounds in the Special Forces or specialist close-protection police units. Also, most of the work is on a self-employed basis, so you need to have a flair for business because you will need to sell your services, network and keep your accounts.

You will have to have exceptional planning skills to make sure that your client is free from harm or unwanted attention.

You will also need to be confident, physically fit to cope with the demands of the work, and have good eyesight and hearing.

Your appearance, diplomacy and communication skills also need to be top level, because you will be with your client and need to blend into the background to observe at high profile events.

Working conditions

Your work will be wherever your client goes and so this could mean lots of travelling.

You may be at risk as you would protect your client if necessary with your own body – but this is more an issue when working in dangerous areas of the world.

You may work long and irregular hours during a contract as some clients may need 24 hour protection.

Future prospects

Most commercial officers work protecting high-profile business executives either in the UK or on projects overseas (especially in dangerous areas like parts of the former Soviet Union). Others work protecting celebrities and pop stars, usually from the constant media and public attention.

Very few officers are in long-term employment. The vast majority are self-employed. There is an increasing demand for good female officers.

Some progress into more mainstream security work, for example security guard or security manager. There may be opportunities to specialise in areas such as driving, and residential security.

Qualifications and courses

There are no formal entry requirements, but since 2006 there is a legal requirement for all Close Protection Officers (CPOs) to hold a Security Industry Authority Licence (SIA) which lasts for 3 years and covers some other security sectors which also require licences.

Training is through courses. They cover terrorist methods of operation, trauma management and vehicle anti-ambush drills as well as elements such as driving skills and conflict resolution. It leads to a BTEC Level 4 Diploma in close protection.

Buckinghamshire New University offers a Foundation degree in Protective Security Operations. Applicants need at least 2 A levels/H grades. Edexcel and City & Guilds also offer Level 3 certificates in Close Protection Operations and Close Protection.

Advantages/disadvantages

This job is often done on a self-employed basis so your earnings may be high but could have to cover periods of unemployment.

Training courses are residential and expensive.

Money guide

New entrants can earn over £18,000 per year, rising to £25,000-£30,000 with experience. Working in high risk areas, with considerable experience, you could earn up to £100,000.

Many close protection officers earn daily or hourly rates for specific contracts. These could be from about £180 to £275 a day, plus expenses for routine work, and up to £500 a day in a very hostile environment or for protecting a key principal.

Related opportunities

- Army Officer p538
- Police Officer p551
- Royal Air Force (RAF) Officer p557
- Royal Marine Officer p559
- Security Officer/Manager p562

Further information

Security Industry Authority
PO Box 9, Newcastle upon Tyne NE82 6YX
0870 243 0100; www.the-sia.org.uk

Professional Bodyguard Association
72 New Bond Street, Mayfair, London W1S 1RR
0800 585505; www.bodyguards-pba.com

City&
Guilds

www.cityandguilds.com/myperfectjob

Security and the Armed Forces

CRCI: UK
CLCI: MAG

COASTGUARD WATCH ASSISTANT/OFFICER

What the work involves

- You will work as part of a team responding to vessels and people in distress. You will be dealing with 999 coastguard calls and radio distress calls, and may also be using the services of the Royal National Lifeboat Institution (RNLI).

- You will keep records of all activity and weather conditions, giving information to vessels and reporting anything unusual.

Watch assistants

- Watch assistants work as administration support – keeping details of calls and rescues, and providing information to the general public.

Watch officers

- Watch officers are involved in all areas of the work and may lead coastal, sea or cliff searches and rescues.

The type of person suited to this work

You will need to enjoy working with computers, be able to concentrate for long periods and have a clear voice to make sure that you send rescuers to the right place.

If you are involved in active search and rescue work you will need a high level of physical fitness, because your work may include carrying heavy equipment, climbing and working out at sea. Watch officers also lead and train groups of auxiliary coastguards, so will need good management and teaching skills.

Working conditions

Most of your work will be in an operations centre, using a computer and talking to others using hands-free communications equipment. If actively involved in search and rescue work, you will be working outside in dangerous conditions. Coastguards operate 24/7 – you will be working 12-hour shifts and a 42-hour week.

Future prospects

There are about 1000 coastguards employed at centres around the UK coastline and a further 3000 auxiliary coastguards working as paid volunteers. This is a competitive job to enter.

It is possible to work up to officer or sector management level. However, there are a limited number of senior jobs in this fairly small service. It is also expected that numbers will continue to drop in some areas of the service in the next few years.

Advantages/disadvantages

Satellite technology means that you will be able to organise the successful rescue of someone in distress even if they are hundreds of miles away from your control centre.

Qualifications and courses

Most people join HM Coastguard as a coastguard watch assistant (CWA).

There are no minimum entry qualifications, but maths and English to GCSE/S grade and Key Skills in communication and numeracy are useful. Most CWAs start as volunteers and you will need to be aged over 16 to apply.

A few join at coastguard watch officer level (CWO). You will need a good standard of hearing and eyesight and a high level of fitness. Significant sea-going experience, preferably in a search and rescue capacity, and a driving licence are required.

You would initially train for 7 weeks at the Coastguard Training Centre in Dorset. Training is then on the job with a further short course after 9 months. You have to pass a series of exams to be retained.

Alternatively, you could become a CWA or CRO, which is a voluntary post. You will need to be over 16 and most volunteers work in a different career as well. You would be paid for the hours you work.

However, the sea is more dangerous than the average leisure-user understands and you may arrive too late, which is an upsetting event for the whole team.

Money guide

When starting out you could earn around £15,000 per year as a Coastguard Watch Assistant. Coastguard Watch Officers can earn up to £24,000. Shift and on-call allowances, plus overtime pay, can increase earnings at every level of experience.

Additional allowances are paid to those working in the Scottish Islands.

Related opportunities

- Air Traffic Controller p595
- Merchant Navy Deck Officer/Rating p609
- Police Officer p551
- Royal Navy officer p560

Further information

Maritime & Coastguard Agency, Human Resources Team
Bay 3/19 Spring Place, 105 Commercial Road,
Southampton SO15 1EG
023 8032 9308; www.mcga.gov.uk

Port Skills and Safety Ltd
Room 220, Africa House, 64–78 Kingsway,
London WC2B 6AH
020 2423538; www.portskillsandsafety.co.uk

Maritime Skills Alliance
1 Hillside, Beckingham, Lincoln, LN5 0RQ
www.maritimeskills.org/

Security and the Armed Forces

CRCI: UE
CLCI: MAZ

CRIME SCENE INVESTIGATOR

What the work involves

- You may also be known as a 'scenes of crime officer'. You will be collecting, storing and recording evidence such as fibres, hair and blood to help investigate crimes like burglary or offences against the person, accidents and suspicious deaths.

- You will use equipment and materials to lift, package and preserve evidence, such as biological samples, paint, tyre marks and fingerprints.

- Your job will involve taking photographic and video evidence of both crime scenes and victims of crime.

- You will also need to keep thorough records and attend court when required to give evidence.

The type of person suited to this work

Sifting through evidence in minute detail is the main aspect of this job so you will need to be the type of person who has good attention to detail. You will need to be methodical and patient while sifting through evidence.

This job can be very distressing. You will need to be able to distance yourself emotionally from the crime, and be able to record the scene and collect evidence in an analytical, scientific way. Good team working is essential as you may be working on a project with many others.

An interest in science and technology is essential. You will need to keep up to date with developments in forensic science and technology as they will affect how you do your job.

Working conditions

You will work both outside and inside at crime scenes and inside back at base.

You will do a 37-hour working week, including shifts, but hours may be longer at times. You may also be on a 24-hour call out.

Conditions at crime scenes can be very difficult and unpleasant but you will be provided with protective clothing. You will usually need a driving licence.

Future prospects

Crime scene investigators are recruited by all regional police forces. Some forces only recruit civilians to do this work but a few also recruit specialist police officers. There are currently about 1800 crime scene investigators in the UK. Competition for vacancies is great.

It is possible to move into more specialised areas of work, such as the investigation of suspicious fires, or scenes where firearms have been used. There may be opportunities for promotion to senior investigator with management responsibilities.

Advantages/disadvantages

This is a job with an exciting image but it can be frequently repetitive, unpleasant and dirty.

Qualifications and courses

There are no minimum entry requirements but some forces require 3–5 GCSEs/S grades (A–C/1–3), including maths, English and science. Some forces may require A levels/H grades or equivalent. Others may specify that you need a GSCE, A level or HNC/HND in photography.

The majority of investigators start this job in their 20s and often have degrees or HNDs.

Work experience is usually required, ideally in a related area such as photography or scientific work. Previous work dealing with the public would also be an advantage.

Once in the job you would have a 1-month induction with your force, followed by a residential course at the National Training Centre (CENTREX NTC) in Durham. This course covers photography, forensics and combined trace evidence, theory and practice. Specialist and refresher courses are also on offer. CENTREX organisation is now part of the National Policing Improvement Agency.

Refresher courses must be taken every 5 years.

You will have the satisfaction of working with a team of investigating officers, forensic scientists and colleagues to find the evidence needed to trace, arrest and convict offenders.

Money guide

£16,500–£18,300 per year is usual for starting salaries.

This rises to £28,000 for experienced officers.

£29,000–£35,000 is possible for senior officers, depending on area Police Force and responsibility level.

If you work in London you may get additional allowances.

Related opportunities

- Forensic Scientist p519
- Police Officer p551
- Forensic Computer Analyst p547
- Private Investigator p555

Further information

National Training Centre for Scientific Support to Crime Investigation
Harperley Hall, Fir Tree, Crook, Co Durham DL15 8DS
01388 762191; www.forensic-training.police.uk; Part of Centrex NTC; see www.centrex.police.uk

Police recruitment information
0845 608 3000; www.policecouldyou.co.uk

Forensic Science Service
Trident Court, 2920 Solihull Parkway,
Birmingham Business Park, Birmingham B37 7YN
www.forensic.gov.uk/html/

Security and the Armed Forces

CRCI: UG
CLCI: MAB

CUSTOMS AND EXCISE OFFICER

What the work involves

- You will be working as a civil servant for the Home Office, enforcing tax regulations on all goods entering and leaving the country and all goods bought and sold in the UK.

- You may specialise in customs or checking for anyone either not paying tax or smuggling in illegal items or substances.

- You may specialise in excise work: visiting traders, manufacturers and importers to check licences and accounts to make sure that the right duties are being paid on goods like petrol, alcohol and tobacco.

- You may specialise in VAT: visiting businesses to check their accounts and that the right amount of VAT is being collected.

The type of person suited to this work

If you are involved in front-line detection work, trying to detect illegal goods or entry into the UK, you will be involved in observing, questioning and challenging people. You will need top-notch communication skills plus a flair for observation, intuition and persistence. Knowledge of or a willingness to learn a foreign or minority language is useful.

If you work in VAT or excise, an aptitude for numbers and computers is a must, because you will be checking business accounts and watching out for sometimes quite sophisticated cover-ups.

Working conditions

Customs and immigration officers mainly work in airports, seaports and freight terminals but also may need to do some surveillance work outside. You will wear a uniform if working in front-line detection work.

Excise and VAT officers are based in offices but also travel around their local areas carrying out checks and interviews.

Customs and immigration officers work shifts. Excise and VAT officers generally work office hours, Monday to Friday.

Future prospects

There are about 23,000 staff based all over the country. Customs specialist staff are mainly located at air- and seaports and the Channel Tunnel. It is possible to move on to senior or management posts. There are also specialist areas within customs, for example the job of detection officer or work with the operations and intelligence unit or the dog unit.

Advantages/disadvantages

When dealing with front-line detection work you may have to question or detain angry or abusive people. It can be a high-pressure job as large volumes of people arrive or depart at peak times.

No two days are ever the same, especially in detection work.

Qualifications and courses

For an Officer grade you will need 5 GCSEs/S grades (A–C/1–3) including English and maths, and 2 A levels/H grades. Many entrants at this level have a degree. You could join at a lower level into an administration job with a minimum of 2 GCSEs/S grades (A–C/1–3). If you do not have the minimum grades you could still enter if you sit and pass a selection test.

For those with Honours degrees at 2.2 or above, fast-stream entry is possible. This is for entry into all Civil Service departments and although a preference can be expressed, entry into Customs and Excise is not guaranteed.

Your training would last up to 9 months and may include some residential training courses.

All fast-stream candidates must meet the requirements of Civil Service nationality. For all other entrants, you must be a British national, EU national or Commonwealth citizen.

It can be very rewarding to know that you have prevented dangerous items such as drugs and firearms getting into the country.

Money guide

All staff working shifts or unsocial hours are paid additional allowances.

Salaries for administration posts start around £13,000.

A Customs and Excise Officer can earn £19,500–£25,200.

Senior grades can earn up to £38,000.

Related opportunities

- Local Government/Civil Service Administrator p29
- Civil Service Officer p27
- Police Officer p551
- Army Officer p538

Further information

Civil Service Careers
Unit 2–4 Lescren Way, Avonmouth, Bristol BS11 8DG
0117 982 1171; www.civil-service.gov.uk/jobs

General Fast Stream Programme
Application Helpdesk: Civil Service Fast Stream, Pilgrims Well, 427 London Road, Camberley, Surrey GU15 3HZ
01276 400333; www.faststream.gov.uk

City&
Guilds

www.cityandguilds.com/myperfectjob

DIVER

What the work involves

■ As a diver you may do repair work on an oil rig, carry out an underwater survey or recover a body.

■ You may repair structures underwater, for example oil rigs, harbour walls or bridge supports.

■ You could be a professional camera operator or photographer recording underwater structures or marine life.

■ You may search rivers, canals and lakes for stolen property or missing people.

The type of person suited to this work

Commercial diving work is often done in difficult conditions and can be hazardous and exhausting.

You need to be an excellent swimmer and a good team player. When deep-water diving, you will need to spend time in a decompression chamber waiting for your body to readjust.

This work is so physically demanding that you will need very high levels of fitness and must accept that diving is a short career. You will need to be able to follow safety procedures carefully.

Working conditions

Most of your work will be in cold, wet, dark and possibly cramped conditions. You will wear protective clothing and breathing apparatus.

You could be based on a ship or an oil rig and may need to spend nights away from home. You may need to travel overseas for work.

This job is risky; decompression can be hazardous and there is also a risk of accidents when underwater.

Future prospects

Employers include construction or civil engineering companies, the police and the Navy.

Some qualify as diving instructors, teaching other people to dive for work or leisure.

There is lots of competition and remotely operated technology is replacing some of the tasks that divers have done in the past, so there may be fewer opportunities in the future.

Advantages/disadvantages

Experienced, fit divers are currently in demand, but it is often short-term contract work.

You may need to pay for your own training and equipment to become a commercial diver. These courses are expensive.

Money guide

Most divers are paid by the day or by the job. Civil engineering divers can earn £70–£175 per day. Very experienced divers working in the oil industry can earn up to £300 per day, while deep-sea divers can be paid around £1,000 per day.

Qualifications and courses

ENTRY LEVEL 1

There are no minimum requirements for diver training but you will need to pass a medical test. A qualification in recreational diving would be an advantage.

The Royal Navy train its divers at the Defence Diving School at Portsmouth on a 20-week course. The Army also train divers here although their course is in two parts: 6 weeks initial training and then a further 8 weeks advanced diving. Army divers are drawn from those serving in the Royal Engineers.

Many divers gain academic and/or technical qualifications before they train to dive.

Offshore industries often require divers. For this role, a science or engineering degree would be needed.

A construction diver would need a qualification like an NVQ/SVQ Level 3 in Welding and Fabrication.

A relevant qualification approved by the Health and Safety Executive (HSE) must be held by anyone who dives professionally.

Police officers must have been with the force for at least 2 years before applying to become a police diver. They must pass fitness and medical tests, as well as swimming skills tests. Police diver training lasts for 8 weeks.

Inland divers earn around £15,500 per year.

Divers in the UK offshore industry earn about £30,000. Very experienced divers can earn £46,000+.

Related opportunities

■ Civil/Construction Engineer p83
■ Marine Engineering/Marine Industry p238
■ Police Officer p551
■ Royal Navy Officer p560

Further information

Health and Safety Executive – Diving Operations
South Wing, Rose Court, 2 Southwark Bridge,
London SE1 9HS
0845 345 0055; www.hse.gov.uk

Underwater Centre
An Aird, Fort William, Inverness-shire PH33 6AN
01397 703786; www.theunderwatercentre.co.uk

International Marine Contractors Association
5 Lower Belgrave Street; London SW1W 0NR
020 7824 5520; www.imca-int.com/careers

City&
Guilds

www.cityandguilds.com/myperfectjob

Security and the Armed Forces

CRCI: U
CLCI: YAZ

DOOR SUPERVISOR/ BOUNCER

What the work involves

- You will be standing at the entrance to a building, for example a nightclub, and will help to control people entering and leaving. You will be judging whether a person should be allowed into the premises.

- You may search customers' bags and clothing and may collect tickets or entrance fees

- If trouble breaks out inside or outside the building, you will call the police if needed for assistance.

- When any incidents happen near to your club you will write short reports. You may need to use these in court if charges are made.

The type of person suited to this work

This is a high-profile job where you will be dealing with customers. You will need a smart appearance and excellent interpersonal skills as you will have to be firm enough to keep trouble-makers away from the venue but welcoming to most customers.

You will also need to have a calm, steady personality, not easily provoked in conflict situations which can be frequent when customers have been drinking and become argumentative.

You may be dealing with money or confiscating illegal items so you will need to be law abiding and trustworthy.

Working conditions

Most door supervisors work under cover outside the entrance but may be exposed to all weather conditions. You may need to wear a uniform or smart clothes.

Evening and night work is common in this job with shifts from early evening right into the early hours of the following day.

You may be at risk from aggressive customers.

Future prospects

There are opportunities throughout the UK but the majority are in large cities with thriving night-time economies. There are currently about 95,000 door supervisors employed in pubs, bars and clubs. This is a growth industry as the leisure industry continues to improve security.

Door supervisors can progress into related security work. Training and experience could be used to move into related areas such as security guard and security management.

Advantages/disadvantages

The introduction of licensing and qualifications is expected to improve the image of this job, so you will find it easier to progress into other areas of security management.

You will be mainly working when other people are out having fun so your social life could be affected.

Qualifications and courses

No academic qualifications are needed for this role. However, you will need to be over 18, be physically fit and have good knowledge of the licensing laws and customer service skills. You will also undergo a police check.

The Security Industry Authority (SIA) exists to manage the licensing of the private security industry. The SIA endorses training providers through whom you can gain a Door Supervision Licence. To receive a licence you must have a Level 2 National Certificate in Door Supervision. BTEC Award in Level 2 Door Supervision or NOCN Level 2 Award in Door Supervision. As part of the Door Supervision licence scheme, you will have to undergo a criminal record check.

The British Institute of Innkeeping, SITO and NCFE also run door supervision courses that may count towards qualifying for the SIA licence.

Some employers will take you on as a trainee and support you through the training and licensing processes.

Money guide

Wages are generally about £13,000 per year when starting out, rising to about £18,000 with experience.

Earnings for trained and licensed supervisors can reach £30,000 per year.

Some door supervisors are paid an hourly rate between £9 and £15, occasionally more, depending on the organisation you work for.

Related opportunities

- Publican/Bar Manager/Licensee p140
- Bodyguard p539
- Security Officer p562
- Police Officer p551
- Army Officer p538

Further information

Security Industry Authority
PO Box 9, Newcastle upon Tyne NE82 6YX
0870 243 0100; www.the-sia.org.uk

Door Superviser Training Organisation (DSTO)
Maurice House, 2 Iddesleigh Road, Bournemouth, Dorset BH3 7JR
01202 299969; www.dsto.co.uk

www.cityandguilds.com/myperfectjob

EMERGENCY PLANNING/ MANAGEMENT OFFICER

What the work involves

- Emergency planners and managers work as part of a larger team to help maintain public safety, especially at times when this is threatened by an external force.

- You will be required to respond quickly to and learn from emergency situations that have arisen from natural disasters, outbreaks of serious contagious diseases, industrial accidents and terrorism.

- You will compile reports from lengthy research and planning on the most efficient ways to protect the general public should an emergency situation arise.

- You will carry out risk assessments, write safety briefs to train emergency response services and help with the recovery process after an incident has occurred.

The type of person suited to this work

The type of person that would be suited to this role would enjoy working in a high pressure situation as part of a large team and should be enthusiastic about helping to provide better public safety.

You will also need to respond quickly and calmly in an emergency and keep a level head in what may be a dangerous situation.

The job requires someone willing to work long hours, sometimes at unsociable times as well as a neat and organised person who can take comprehensive notes and present their findings accurately.

Working conditions

You may often find yourself in a highly pressured situation especially in the aftermath of a major incident so you could find yourself in danger or not knowing when you will finish the job.

You can expect travel to feature heavily as part of your job with many trips away from home a distinct possibility.

Future prospects

If you enter the career as an assistant you can expect to progress, with experience, to a management or senior role if you show signs of willingness to go where the work takes you and put in long hours.

Once you reach a more senior role you will not be working in such a hands-on environment but would provide more managerial support to your team.

Advantages/disadvantages

Your future prospects could take you all over the world to work with individuals who enjoy working as part of a close knit team.

The work has the potential to be highly distressing especially as you could be one of the first people on the scene after a major natural disaster or a terrorist attack.

Qualifications and courses

All graduates are eligible to apply to work in this profession although some degree subjects are considered more desirable in candidates applying for their first job in the field.

Many of the courses that are more directly related to the industry will be sandwich courses to give students the chance to spend a year working in the sector and gain valuable experience.

There are also more specific courses available which are geared towards a job in emergency planning but these do not guarantee a job in the sector.

Candidates who have previous experience of working in this sector or a related career will be at an advantage when applying for their first role in the industry.

Individuals who enter the profession as an assistant will take part in a lot of training on the job as well as complete several external courses as they go along many of which are run by the Emergency Planning Society. The courses available allow individuals to specialise in certain areas of emergency planning as well as gain more broad professional skills.

Money guide

A typical starting salary in the profession as an assistant is likely to be £20,000 to £27,000.

You can expect this to progress to around £40,000 after 3 to 5 years of experience.

Senior roles come with a lot of responsibility but you could expect to earn £70,000 at this level.

Related opportunities

- Health and Safety Inspector p40
- Police Officer p551
- Firefighter p546
- Environmental Health Practitioner/Officer p35

Further information

Emergency Planning Society
The Media Centre, Culverhouse Cross, Cardiff CF5 6XJ
Tel: 0845 600 9587; Fax: 029 2059 0397; www.the-eps.org

The Emergency Planning College
The Hawkhills, Easingwold, York YO61 3EG
Tel: 01347 821 406; Fax: 01347 822 575;
epc.marketing@cabinet-office.x.gsi.gov.uk;
www.cabinetoffice.gov.uk

City& Guilds

www.cityandguilds.com/myperfectjob

Security and the Armed Forces

CRCI: UG
CLCI: MAZ

FIREFIGHTER

What the work involves

- You will be dealing with a range of emergencies, not only fires but also helping at incidents such as when people are trapped in lifts, handling chemical spillages and assisting at road, rail or air crash scenes.

- If your team arrives on the scene before the paramedics you will have to give First Aid.

- You may give advice to organisations on fire safety and check that buildings or public events meet fire regulations.

The type of person suited to this work

You will need to stay calm in dangerous situations. People in danger tend to react in extreme ways and you will need to be good at talking to them, giving instructions, reassuring them and leading them to safety.

You need to be an excellent team worker. You will be assigned to a 'watch' (a team) and need to work together to keep yourself and others safe.

You will need to be able to deal with very stressful and disturbing situations.

Working conditions

You will be based at a fire station but go out to attend incidents. Fire stations have good facilities for eating and resting.

Working conditions can often be unpleasant and dangerous. You will wear a uniform and, when needed, protective clothing and equipment.

You will work 2 day shifts then 2 night shifts followed by 4 days off and work a total of 42 hours per week.

Future prospects

The main employers are regional fire services who employ about 41,000 firefighters. Airports, the Ministry of Defence, the RAF and the Royal Navy also recruit firefighters. Some firefighters start their career as retained firefighters to gain experience. Entry is competitive.

You could move into driving by taking an LGV licence. Promotion to supervisory and management roles is by clear grades and given on ability, but exams must also be passed.

Advantages/disadvantages

This job can be very stressful and you cannot just leave an emergency situation if your shift has ended.

You will get to know your watch really well and firefighters say they really enjoy the team spirit at work.

There is demanding training but it will help to keep you safe.

Qualifications and courses

To be considered for selection as a firefighter you must be at least 18 years old.

A full UK driving licence is preferred.

You will be required to pass certain rigorous physical and job-related tests (such as working within confined spaces and at heights).

You will also be required to undergo stringent medical examinations to make sure you are fit enough to undertake arduous firefighting duties.

You must have good colour vision (as tested by Ishihara plates). Your eyesight will also be tested. At present, laser treatment is unacceptable to some forces and entry is barred. Glasses or contact lenses may occasionally be permitted.

Firefighters need a good general education. Some brigades may ask for specific GCSEs/S grades and some entrants have A levels/H grades or a degree. A numerical and written entrance test is required to ensure there is an understanding of problem solving and situation awareness. Apprenticeships/Skillseekers may be available.

Money guide

As a trainee you will earn around £21,000 per year.

With experience you can earn £22,000–£28,000.

A leading firefighter can earn £31,500.

A station officer can earn up to £36,000 and a senior divisional officer up to £45,000.

Retained firefighters earn a retainer fee of around £2,600 per year. They also receive additional payments for attending fires.

Related opportunities

- Ambulance Person p328
- Paramedic p328
- Police Officer p551
- Royal Air Force (RAF) Officer p557
- Royal Navy Officer p560

Further information

Fire Service recruitment information
www.fireservice.co.uk

Fire Brigade Union
www.fbu.org.uk

DFTDC
Manston, Ramsgate, Kent CT12 5BS
01843 823351; www.dftdc.org/

FORENSIC COMPUTER ANALYST

What the work involves

- You will be responsible for inspecting computers (and other technology such as mobile phones) for criminal activity.

- You might be looking for evidence of identity theft, child abuse, hacking, phishing and other illegal activity.

- Even if evidence of the crime has been deleted or corrupted you will need to retrieve it without altering it in any way.

- You might be using specialist software and working with the police to look through files, photographs, emails and phone conversations in order to discover evidence of criminal activity. You may need to appear in court to relay your findings.

The type of person suited to this work

You will need to have a certain level of skill using computers, as well as an interest in detecting and preventing crime. You should be a patient and determined person as some investigations may take place over a long period of time. You might come across unpleasant or even horrific material and you must be able to distance yourself and deal with it objectively. You will need to be able to record your findings in a clear, coherent and logical manner. You should be able to understand the law in relation to IT crime. Articulateness and strong communication skills are essential.

Working conditions

You will spend most of your time in an office using a computer. You will generally work standard office hours (9am-5pm from Monday to Friday). Although you might need to be on call over weekends and public holidays or work overtime to meet deadlines. You may also be required to go into other people's homes and offices to confiscate their computer equipment for analysis, which could lead to confrontation.

Future prospects

Postgraduate qualifications will enhance your chances of promotion (particularly if you work within the commercial world). You could progress to the level of supervisor or line manager.

The police force has its own progression route and you could eventually reach the level of chief inspector.

You may have to change employers in order to progress. Jobs are available with the police force, MI5, government, the Serious and Organised Crime Agency and IT firms who specialise in computer security.

Advantages/disadvantages

Your workload will be varied and opportunities are available in many different sectors.

You will spend a lot of time crouched over a computer.

Qualifications and courses

Most people who enter this career have completed a degree in IT (or equivalent computing subject). If your degree is not IT based you can take an IT conversion course. There are specific degrees in forensic computing and information security which would be highly valuable.

In order to gain a place on a degree course you will normally require at least two A levels and five GCSEs grade A*-C. Computing, mathematics and science subjects are all relevant A level subjects.

You could alternatively complete a foundation degree in an IT subject. These courses generally require applicants to have attained at least one A level and about four GCSEs grades A*-C (or equivalent).

There is also a diploma in information technology which might be of interest.

A postgraduate degree would be extremely valuable. Entry to postgraduate programmes is reliant on the successful completion of a first degree.

Members of police staff can complete specialist training from the National Policing Improvement Agency (NPICA).

If you work within a police or government sector you might help to send criminals to jail.

Money guide

These figures are only approximate and will vary depending on location, sector and employer. As a trainee you can expect to earn around £20,000 a year. After a year's experience, this can rise to somewhere between £25,000 and £35,000 per year. A senior forensic analyst might earn in the region of £40,000 to £60,000 a year.

Related opportunities

- Computer Engineer/Scientist p159
- Crime Scene Examiner p541
- Information Scientist p356
- Forensic Scientist p519

Further information

The British Computer Society (BCS)
1st Floor, Block D, North Star House, North Star Avenue, Swindon SN2 1FA
01793 417417; www.bcs.org

National Policing Improvement Agency
High Tech Crime Training, The Willows, Wyboston Lakes, Great North Road, Wyboston MK44 3AL
01480 401986; www.npia.police.uk

Skills for Justice
Centre Court, Atlas Way, Sheffield S4 7QQ
0114 261 1499; www.skillsforjustice.com

Security and the Armed Forces

CRCi: V
CLCI: MAB

IMMIGRATION OFFICER

What the work involves

- You will be working as a civil servant for the Home Office and you will be controlling the entry of people into the UK by checking the passports and visas of passengers arriving at ports, airports or via the Channel Tunnel.

- You may ask questions to find out more about them and if suspicious, conduct a more detailed interview.

- As an assistant officer you would refer to a more senior officer if they are concerned about documentation or answers to questions.

- You may work in an office processing immigration applications and dealing with appeals.

The type of person suited to this work

You will need to be confident, assertive and have the ability to work under pressure and to deadlines. You will need to be well organised, reliable and have good report-writing skills. You will need an ability to get on with people from across the world.

You should enjoy investigating and collecting information very quickly with the ability to write up and pass on your concerns to others in your team or colleagues from other professions.

Working conditions

You could work in a range of places such as ports and airports where you will have access to a desk, PC, phone and interviewing area.

Some security officers have to undertake surveillance duties and work with other intelligence officers, but normally you will check documents and interview individuals within your office or interviewing booth.

You will work shifts that will include out of office hours and weekends.

Future prospects

Half of all immigration staff are employed in the south-east of England at Heathrow, Gatwick and the Channel ports. The numbers of people entering the UK and asking for asylum has increased over recent years. This has impacted on the service, which has grown in numbers from 1800 to more than 2500 employees. Entry is competitive at officer level and the majority of entrants are graduates.

It is possible to enter at assistant grade and work up to officer grade. Placements are also possible, for example, to Immigration Visa sections at the British Deputy High Commissions overseas or to police forces around the UK.

Advantages/disadvantages

You will play an important role in helping protect national security.

This job is part of the civil service, so entry can be competitive.

The civil service offers excellent conditions of service and training.

Qualifications and courses

Assistant Immigration Officers have to sit a literacy and numeracy test and must attend interview.

Immigration Officers need no formal qualifications although most employers expect a minimum of an A level/ H grade or equivalent. Assistant Immigration Officers can apply for promotion to this level.

Applicants with a minimum of a 2.2 Honours degree can apply for fast-stream entry. This is for entry into all Civil Service departments and although a preference can be expressed, entry into Immigration is not guaranteed.

All fast-stream candidates must be UK nationals. For all other entrants, you must be a European Economic Area national, EU national or Commonwealth citizen. Swiss nationals, although Switzerland is not an EEA country, are also eligible to apply for non-reserved posts.

After a period of 10 weeks initial training, entrants are placed with more experienced officers, usually at Dover, Heathrow or Gatwick. Financial support may be available for officers wishing to learn a foreign language.

Money guide

All staff working shifts or unsocial hours are paid additional allowances.

Those working in and around London receive an additional allowance.

When starting out as an assistant officer, you earn around £15,000 per year. With experience, you can earn £17,500, rising to £25,000.

Salaries for immigration officers start at around £22,000 rising with experience to £38,000.

Related opportunities

- Civil Service Officer p27
- Coastguard p540
- Equal Opportunities Officer p36
- Police Officer p551

Further information

Civil Service Careers
Unit 2–4 Lescren Way, Avonmouth, Bristol BS11 8DG
0117 982 1171; www.civil-service.gov.uk/jobs

General Fast Stream Programme
Application Helpdesk: Civil Service Fast Stream, Pilgrims Well, 427 London Road, Camberley, Surrey GU15 3HZ
01276 400333; www.faststream.gov.uk

Immigration and Nationality Directorate
www.ind.homeoffice.gov.uk

Home Office
Direct Communications Unit, 2 Marsham Street, London SW1P 4DF
020 7035 4848; www.homeoffice.gov.uk

PARKING ATTENDANT/ CIVIL ENFORCEMENT OFFICER

What the work involves

- You will be enforcing parking regulations for a local authority or contractors working on their behalf: patrolling and checking for illegal parking and non-payment of parking fees.

- Using a hand-held computer you will regularly check details of vehicles parked in limited-stay parking areas and issue fixed penalty tickets. You may take pictures of any illegally parked vehicles.

- You may need to arrange for vehicles to be clamped or sent to the pound. You will attend court to give evidence if any prosecution results from your work. You will have to report any suspected abandoned vehicles to the police.

The type of person suited to this work

All employers look for a polite but firm manner as well as good communication skills. You will need to be very good at dealing with people, many of whom may be feeling irate about the ticket you have just given them.

You need to be a good observer and able to follow rules and instructions. You will have to watch out at all times for illegal parking and enforce the rules.

You will meet a lot of people but you will also be working unsupervised and independently so you need to be confident, self-disciplined and reliable.

Working conditions

Most of your work will be out on the streets in all weathers. You will need to wear a uniform and carry a hand-held computer.

You will work shifts to a total of 36 hours over a 5-day week. Shifts cover early morning until late evening Monday to Sunday.

Future prospects

Parking attendants now do most of the work that traffic wardens used to do. There are government proposals to extend powers by decriminalising some public highway offences such as stopping in a yellow box junction. Although many of these offences will be monitored by cameras they will lead to an expansion of work for parking contractors. More than 100 local authorities now work in partnership with parking contractors to enforce parking legislation. Jobs are on offer with many of the main contractors.

Parking attendants and traffic wardens can be promoted into supervisory or training roles initially and then on into management if suitable. There are NVQ/SVQs in parking supervision and administration. However, prospects may be more limited in more rural areas.

Advantages/disadvantages

You will keep fit, walking an average of 10 miles a day, 5 days a

Qualifications and courses

You do not need any particular qualifications to enter this work. However, English and maths GCSE/S grade or equivalent would be useful.

Some employers prefer you to have had experience of working with the public. You can work towards City & Guilds Level 2 Certificate for Parking Attendants or an NVQ Level 2 in Controlling Parking Areas. On completion you could work towards a Level 3 course in Parking Management/Supervision or an NVQ Level 3 in Parking Clerical work.

Training is always given on entry about parking legislation, to help you do your job well. Training covers on-street enforcement activity, car park patrolling and enforcement, clamping and towaway and CCTV operation.

week carrying a 5kg pack (including your computer, printer and radio).

There is no doubt that parking attendants are not always popular and there has been a rise in the number of attacks on them.

Illegal parking can cause real problems for most law-abiding motorists and many attendants feel a sense of satisfaction from keeping the roads clear.

Money guide

Starting pay is about £12,900 per year.

Supervisors earn about £16,500. Top salaries are around £20,700.

There may be additional payment for shift work.

Related opportunities

- Police Officer p551
- Police Community Support Officer p550
- Train Conductor p625
- Bailiff Enforcement Agent p364

Further information

British Parking Association
Stuart House, 41–43 Perrymount Road, Haywards Heath, West Sussex RH16 3BN
01444 447300; www.britishparking.co.uk

Security Industry Authority
PO Box 9, Newcastle upon Tyne NE82 6YX
0870 243 0100; www.the-sia.org.uk

The Institute of Parking Professionals
Stuart House, 41–43 Perrymount Road, Haywards Heath, West Sussex RH16 3BN
01444 447 300; www.theipp.co.uk

Security and the Armed Forces

CRCI: UK
CLCI: M

POLICE COMMUNITY SUPPORT OFFICER (PCSO)

What the work involves

- Police community support officers are uniformed members of the force whose role is to work within their local community, supporting the activities and initiatives of police officers.

- You will be part of the group of officers that provides visible police presence on the streets and in other public areas.

- You will be on the frontline, offering help and advice to members of the public, as well as tackling anti-social behaviour.

- Everyday duties could include crowd-control and traffic directing, dealing with minor offences, checking out abandoned vehicles, or imposing fines for acts such as littering or dog fouling.

The type of person suited to this work

You will need to be an excellent communicator, as you will encounter a range of people in your work. You must also be able to remain calm but authoritative when confronted with potentially difficult or violent members of the public.

You must be able to work effectively within a team. This means you should be able to take orders and act on your own initiative when necessary.

You should have good, accurate written skills, as you will need to produce reports on events and deal with complex paperwork at times.

Working conditions

You will work up to 40 hours on a shift basis, encompassing night and weekend work. Flexible or part time hours are available.

Although you will be based at a police station, you will work in a variety of locations including patrolling the streets, within people's homes, or in public places such as train stations.

You will be required to wear a uniform, which includes a high visibility jacket and protective hat. Additional protective equipment may need to be worn of carried on occasion.

Future prospects

Competition for entry to become a PCSO can be fierce, depending on the force you are applying to.

Experienced PCSOs are often responsible for teaching, training and guiding new recruits. There are also opportunities to move into supervisory or managerial roles within the PCSO contingent.

It is also a good role to start in if you would like to become a police officer.

Advantages/disadvantages

You will play a direct role in protecting your local community and finding solutions to problems and crime in the area.

Qualifications and courses

ENTRY LEVEL 1

There are no specific entry requirements to become a PCSO, and applicants from a diverse range of backgrounds are encouraged to apply in order to get a good representational mix across the force.

Some employers may view your application more favourably if it demonstrates some commitment to community service schemes, or if you have undertaken a relevant course such as an NVQ Level 2 in public services, BTEC National Diploma in uniformed public services, or a foundation degree in police studies or public services.

During the application progress, you will be required to sit written tests, as well as undergo medical and security checks.

Once accepted as a PCSO, you will undertake between 3 weeks and 3 months of training that will involve classroom-based learning, as well as hands-on experience in the community. Areas covered will include relevant areas of law, self-defence, first aid, interviewing skills, and using police communication equipment.

There are good opportunities for career development, including progression to become a police officer.

You may be confronted with difficult and dangerous situations, which can be both frightening and unnerving.

Money guide

As a new recruit to the force, you could expect to earn around £17,000. If you are working specifically on British Transport, your starting salary will be slightly higher at £18,500.

Once you have gained a few years' experience, you can expect to earn £21,500.

If you reach a supervisory or managerial role, you earnings will reach about £25,000.

Related opportunities

- Police Officer p551
- Army Soldier p564
- Security Officer/Manager p562
- Prison Officer p554

Further information

National Police Recruitment Team
www.policecouldyou.co.uk

City&
Guilds

www.cityandguilds.com/myperfectjob

POLICE OFFICER

What the work involves

- Police officers are responsible for safeguarding communities from crime by apprehending criminals and maintaining order.

- You will spend your time on patrol, responding to any situation that occurs whilst you are on shift.

- You will keep records, take statements, and write reports. You may need to give evidence in court on occasion, and may also give educational talks in community venues.

- Once trained, you could specialise in a department such as CID, Mounted Police, Child Protection, Drugs Squad or Traffic Police.

The type of person suited to this work

You must have excellent communication skills in order to deal with a variety of people on a daily basis whose position could range from that of a criminal who needs restraining, to a victim who needs careful treatment.

You will need to be non-judgemental, and have the ability to view situations from numerous situations.

You will need courage, initiative, and common sense in order to deal with many of the circumstances you will be presented with. You will also need to have good problem-solving skills.

Working conditions

You will be required to work 40 hours a week, covering early, late and night shifts 7 days a week. Part time or flexible working hours can usually be accommodated.

You will be based at a police station, but the majority of your time will be spent on patrol, either on foot or by car. This means you will be out in all weather conditions, and will travel to many different locations.

Future prospects

The police force operates throughout the length and breadth of the UK, so there are opportunities in regional forces throughout.

You can move upwards to the level of sergeant and inspector, and these promotions are subject to examination and interview. To progress further you must demonstrate your skills to a board of judges. You could opt to specialise in a department such as the CID, or Mounted Police.

Advantages/disadvantages

You will be meeting new challenges each day and adapting to unusual environments, which will keep you mentally and physically alert and ensures the work never gets dull.

You will be responsible for promoting safety and wellbeing in the local community, which is rewarding.

You will be required to work unsociable hours including nights and weekends.

Qualifications and courses

There are no specific academic requirements for entry to the police force, but you must be aged 18+, and be a UK or European Union national, or come from within the European Economic Area.

You could also take a relevant qualification to enhance your application. These include an NVQ Level 2 or BTEC First Diploma in public services, and the BTEC National Diploma in uniformed public service.

The police force operates an intensive selection process, in which you will need to pass medical, fitness, eyesight, literacy, and numeracy tests. You will also be assessed using a variety of scenario exercises by which your communication, decision making, and problem solving skills will be judged.

You will need to have a Criminal Records Bureau check, as you will be working with children and vulnerable adults.

Once you are a member of the force, you will undergo further officer training over 2 years through the Initial Police Learning and Development Programme (IPLDP). This consists of a combination of classroom-based study and on-the-job experience.

You will have to deal with difficult, distressed, and occasionally violent members of the public.

Money guide

The starting salary for a student police officer is about £21,500. This will rise to £24,000 on completion of the IPLDP training programme. Once you reach the rank of sergeant, you can earn £34,000+.

Very senior officers, especially those in the larger and more active police forces, can earn in excess of £57,000.

Related opportunities

- Police Community Support Officer p550
- Police Support Worker p552
- Road Safety Officer p622
- Security Officer/Manager p562

Further information

National Police Recruitment Team
www.policecouldyou.co.uk

Civil Nuclear Constabulary
Culham Science Centre, Abingdon, Oxfordshire OX14 3DB
01235 466 666; www.cnc.police.uk; jobs@cnc.police.uk

City&Guilds

www.cityandguilds.com/myperfectjob

POLICE SUPPORT WORKER

What the work involves

- Police support workers are the first point of contact for members of the public in a police station.

- You will be responsible for answering and directing calls, passing walk-ins to appropriate members of staff, and carrying out general administrative tasks within the station.

- You will be on the front desk, so will receive firearms, knives, driving licences, and any other paraphernalia seized by police whilst on patrol. You will also be the first point of contact for missing persons and lost property enquiries.

- You will need to look after victims and witnesses when they come into the station, which may require providing first aid on occasion.

The type of person suited to this work

You must have excellent communication skills in order to deal with a wide variety of people on a daily basis, ranging from victims to aggressive detainees. Assertiveness, confidence and sensitivity are all desirable personality traits.

You should be happy working within a team, supporting your colleagues, taking directions, and working on your own initiative when required.

You will also need to adhere to confidentiality, diversity and data protection issues.

Working conditions

You will usually work a 37 hour week based on a shift pattern, which will require early morning and weekend work. There are usually part time opportunities.

You will be based within a police station, and will spend most of your time on the front desk answering queries or updating information on a computer. It is unlikely that you will need to travel in the course of your working day.

Stations can get very busy at times, so you should expect to work in pressurised and potentially stressful conditions at times.

Future prospects

The police force operates throughout the length and breadth of the UK, so there are opportunities in all regional forces.

Opportunities for promotion within a station are limited to its size. Larger establishments may have room to move you to a more senior, supervisory role whereas the smaller one will not be able to.

You could move to a more specialised area of support work, such as manning the crime helpdesk, or working in an enquiry centre.

It is possible to train as a police officer from a support role.

Advantages/disadvantages

You will be working within a close knit team, so your support work will be essential to the successful running of the station.

Qualifications and courses

ENTRY LEVEL 1

There are no specific academic requirements for entry to the police force, but most employers prefer that you are educated to GCSE standard or equivalent. You must also be aged 18+, a UK or European Union national, or come from within the European Economic Area.

There are several qualifications that would be viewed favourably by employers. These include an NVQ Level 2 or BTEC First Diploma in public services, and the BTEC National Diploma in uniformed public services. Entry requirements for these courses are usually 5 GCSEs/S grades (A-C/1–3) or equivalent, including English and maths.

If you reach interview stage, you will need to have medical, criminal record, and other background checks to assess your suitability for the role. You must declare any previous convictions prior to this stage.

Once you have been accepted onto the force, your training will be provided by a more experienced support worker and you will learn on the job. Training usually lasts between 3 weeks and 3 months.

Part time and flexible working hours are commonly available.

You will have to deal with difficult, distressed, and occasionally violent members of the public.

Money guide

The starting salary for an entry level police support worker is about £15,500.

With a couple of years' experience, this should rise to around £19,000.

If you pursue promotion and attain a high level administrative role, or become a police officer, you could earn £40,000+.

Related opportunities

- Police Community Support Officer p550
- Police Officer p551
- Secretary p60
- Civil Service/Local Government Administrator p29

Further information

National Police Recruitment Team
www.policecouldyou.co.uk

Police Oracle
www.policeoracle.com

City&
Guilds

www.cityandguilds.com/myperfectjob

PRISON GOVERNOR/ OPERATIONAL MANAGER

What the work involves

- Prison governors/operational managers are responsible for the overall running and security of the establishment.

- You will supervise security measures, make inspections, carry out disciplinary procedures, and advise both staff and inmates on behavioural standards and guidelines.

- You will also be dealing with each prisoner's casework and administration. This will include processing parole applications and complaints, and require liaison with other social and healthcare professionals.

- You will be working within strict parameters set out by the government, and must ensure that you meet their targets on service, health and safety, and prisoner welfare and development.

The type of person suited to this work

You will need excellent communication skills, including confidence, assertiveness and a motivational ability, all of which will be essential when managing and inspiring staff, and also for building effective relationships with inmates.

You must have integrity and be committed to working with vulnerable people with various social issues. This should include respect for those in your care, and for the other professionals working around you.

Working conditions

You will be expected to work on a shift basis, including night and weekend hours, in order to meet the 24 hour needs of the prison. On average, you will work a 39 hour week.

You could work in a modern prison with excellent facilities, or an older, more austere establishment that will come with maintenance problems and perhaps a less comfortable working environment.

Future prospects

Prisons are located in large cities, towns, and very rural locations, so you have a good range of options of the working conditions that would most suit you.

Prison governors are at the top of their sector, so only sideways movements are possible. You could opt to work in a specialist institution, such as one dealing with inmates with specific medical needs. Extra qualifications may be required for this.

Advantages/disadvantages

You could be responsible for turning the lives of inmates around, both by providing them with opportunities whilst serving their sentence, and also by encouraging them to pursue better lives when they leave.

You may have to control difficult and violent situations at times.

Qualifications and courses

Most prisoner governors enter the profession as a prison officer.

Generally, expectations for candidates include good health and physical fitness, Commonwealth, British or European Union nationality, no current or historical association with racist or homophobic groups, and that you have Criminal Records Bureau clearance if you are going to work with inmates under 18 years of age.

If you meet all of the criteria above, you may be asked to attend an assessment day at which employers will observe how you react to the prison environment and work-related simulations, in order to see if you would be suitable for the role.

Once you have gained experience as a prison officer you will need to work your way through supervisory and senior positions, taking relevant work-related qualifications as you go, in order to become a prison governor.

A fast-track initiative, the Intensive Development Scheme (IDS), provides an alternative route into the profession for graduates only, and is designed to encourage rapid progression through the grades into a management position.

Money guide

Prison officers start on around £17,000. Once you have worked through the grades and become a junior governor, your salary will start at around £30,000.

With experience, and on gaining the full title and responsibilities of a prison governor, you could earn between £40,000 and £75,000.

Related opportunities

- Prison Officer/Instructor p554
- Police Officer p551
- Police Community Support Officer p550
- Security Officer/Manager p562

Further information

HM Prison Service
Cleland House, Page Street, London SW1P 4LN
www.hmprisonservice.gov.uk

Scottish Prison Service
Room 338 Carlton House, 5 Redheughs Rigg,
Edinburgh EH12 9HW
0131 244 8745; www.sps.gov.uk; gaolinfo@sps.pnn.gov.uk

www.cityandguilds.com/myperfectjob

Security and the Armed Forces

CRCI: UI
CLCI: MAD

PRISON OFFICER/ INSTRUCTOR

What the work involves

- Prison officers are responsible for supervising inmates within a secure institution.

- You will need to build positive relationships with the prisoners in your care in order to educate and encourage them to pursue a law-abiding life.

- You could work with a variety of inmates, ranging from high risk criminals in top security institutions, to those with minor offences in low security prisons.

- Prison instructors undertake the same duties as prison officers, but are also responsible for training prisoners in order to help them develop new skills and qualifications.

The type of person suited to this work

You should have excellent communication skills and be a confident person so that you can interact positively with inmates whilst also retaining your authority when necessary.

You must be non-judgemental and have respect for the prisoners in your care. The ability to remain calm in pressurised or uncomfortable situations is also an asset.

Prison instructors should be approachable and patient. You will need to be understanding and encouraging in order to help prisoners learn and progress.

Working conditions

You will usually work 39 hours a week. Prison officers will work on a shift basis including night and weekend shifts, but prison instructors usually only work during the week.

Most work is indoors and within a prison. Prison officers will also be responsible for supervising outdoor exercise and patrolling the prison grounds. Prison instructors will work in a setting suitable for their subject, for example a workshop within the prison, or in the grounds if they are teaching horticulture.

Some travel between prisons may be expected to provide extra staffing on occasion. Prison officers may also have to escort prisoners to and from court appearances.

Future prospects

Opportunities for promotion are good, and both prison officers and prison instructors can move into a position as a senior officer or principal officer of a prison. Promotion is based solely on merit, so the more you put in the more you can get out of this career.

Advantages/disadvantages

Helping to rehabilitate and educate prisoners can be rewarding, and you will be providing an important public service.

Working in a prison environment can be claustrophobic and stifling.

Qualifications and courses

Entry requirements for roles as a prison officer vary throughout the UK. Generally, expectations for candidates include good health and physical fitness, Commonwealth, British or European Union nationality, no current or historical association with racist or homophobic groups, and that you have Criminal Records Bureau clearance if you are going to work with inmates under 18 years of age.

You will also need to undergo a medical and physical fitness assessment, as well as a sight test.

If you meet all of the criteria above, you may be asked to attend an assessment day at which employers will observe how you react to the prison environment and work-related simulations, in order to see if you would be suitable for the role.

Candidates hoping to become a prison instructor must hold a relevant qualification in the subject they wish to teach, such as a degree, NVQ, or City and Guilds Advanced Certificate. You will also need to hold a qualification in health and safety, and be able to demonstrate teaching or supervisory experience.

You may be faced with difficult and occasionally violent prisoners, which can be both stressful and unpleasant.

Money guide

New officers and instructors typically earn around £17,500 in England and Wales. Wages in Scotland are slightly lower at £14,500.

If you become a senior prison officer, after gaining several years of experience, your salary should rise to about £28,500.

Principal officers in England and Wales earn up to £31,000. Wages in Scotland are slightly lower at about £28,000.

Related opportunities

- Prison Governor/Operational Manager p553
- Police Officer p551
- Police Support Worker p552
- Social Worker p585

Further information

HM Prison Service
Cleland House, Page Street, London SW1P 4LN
www.hmprisonservice.gov.uk

City&
Guilds

www.cityandguilds.com/myperfectjob

PRIVATE INVESTIGATOR

What the work involves

- You will be collecting information for a private client or a solicitor by asking questions, researching, obtaining evidence and making sense of what you find out.

- Private investigators (PIs) do a variety of different jobs such as surveillance, tracing people, serving legal documents or investigating road accidents, suspected fraud and employee backgrounds.

- You could be recording your findings using a computer, and you may be asked to present your findings in court or to a large company. You will probably take witness statements, attend court hearings and give evidence.

The type of person suited to this work

Much of the day-to-day work of this exciting-sounding job is actually routine, so you will need to be patient and persistent and be happy with your own company

You need to be interested in learning about the law.

You will need to have excellent communications skills, both spoken and written in order to write reports and take witness statements. You may need to calm down anxious or aggressive people when you serve legal papers or repossess their car to pay a debt.

Working conditions

Most of your working hours will be spent driving or walking around. You may be in your vehicle for hours or out in all weathers.

Hours are irregular and in some cases they could be long and include evening and weekend work.

You may be at risk of assault from aggressive individuals who you are serving with legal papers.

Future prospects

Opportunities for this type of work have increased.

There is work but also competition and many PIs do not stay in the business for long. With the introduction of licensing there may be more opportunities for those with licences. A lot of the work is for legal, insurance or financial companies.

Some PIs go on to specialise in areas such as commercial piracy or insurance fraud. A few set up their own agencies and others move into supervisory or security management work.

Advantages/disadvantages

Private investigators are usually self-employed and so need to buy their own equipment. Licences and training will also add to the expense.

A lot of the work is routine, but PIs say that there is a lot of satisfaction when after months of patient work you manage to find the evidence your client needs.

Qualifications and courses

There are no formal entry qualifications for this work. However, many entrants have degrees or advanced level qualifications. Some employers like you to have some experience of work in the police or other security firms.

You will need a driving licence and most successful PIs work in a related job such as the police, law, customs and excise or security work first.

Applicants new to the role would benefit from having a relevant qualification, which may include an NVQ Level 3 in Intelligence Analysis, C&G in Security (Investigation) or a degree in an appropriate subject.

Your training should be accepted by the Security Industry Authority (SIA), and include the topics of the law, investigative methods, equipment and legislation.

A scheme is being introduced where a government licence issued by the SIA will be required to practise. Check with the SIA for the latest developments.

Courses are available from a number of private companies and listed by the Association of British Investigators (ABI). Topics such as theft, court work, investigation and surveillance are offered. A City & Guilds Certificate in conflict management and communication skills is also available, offered through the National Investigations Group.

Money guide

Starting salaries are around £12,000 per year. Experienced investigators could earn £15,000–£22,000. Well-qualified specialists can get £60,000+.

If self-employed, you could expect to get £21,000–£27,000.

Top salaries for a corporate investigator can be £55,000–£100,000 yearly.

Related opportunities

- Bailiff/Enforcement Agent p364
- Insurance Loss Adjuster p45
- Police Officer p551
- Store Detective p565
- Forensic Computer Analyst p547

Further information

Academy of Professional Investigation
Clair House, 3–5 Clair Road, Haywards Heath, West Sussex RH16 3DP
01444 441111; www.becomeadetective.com

Association of British Investigators
27 Old Gloucester Street, London WC1N 3XX
0871 474 0006; www.theabi.org.uk

Institute of Professional Investigators
83 Guildford Street, Chertsey, Surrey KT16 9JL
0870 330 8622; www.ipi.org.uk

Security and the Armed Forces

CRCI: UK
CLCI: MAG

ROYAL AIR FORCE (RAF) AIRMAN/WOMAN

What the work involves

- The Royal Air Force (RAF) is responsible for protecting UK airspace, performing search and rescue missions offshore and on land, transporting aid to the victims of war and natural disaster, and pursuing military action in a war situation.

- Opportunities include positions in catering, aircrew, engineering, protection and medical support.

- You will work within a team of other RAF professionals, under the guidance of an officer.

- You will also be expected to undertake general military duties, such as guarding RAF bases, and taking part in training exercises and military initiatives.

The type of person suited to this work

You should be able to work well within a team. This includes being able to follow orders, work calmly under pressure, support colleagues, and use your own initiative when necessary.

You should be self-disciplined in order to maintain high levels of fitness, mental agility, and a positive attitude to your work.

You should be good at interpreting and analysing information, both verbal and written.

Working conditions

Airmen/women usually work regular office hours, but you are required to be available for duty at all times in case of an emergency. There are also occasional social functions or other duties that need to be fulfilled over weekends.

You will be stationed at an RAF base, many of which have all the amenities of a small town.

You should be prepared to be posted overseas at short notice, and to spend long periods of time away from friends and family.

Future prospects

On joining the RAF as an airman/woman, you sign up for a minimum length of service that ranges from 12 months for non-commissioned aircrew, up to 9 years for other specialisations.

After six months or on completion of specialist training, you should be promoted to leading aircraftman/woman, and from there you can work up the ranks to the position of corporal or higher. Promotion is based on merit, so you will be rewarded for the hard work that you put in.

Advantages/disadvantages

You will work on diverse assignments within a supportive team environment, so each day will be both diverse and interesting.

There are good training schemes and potential for promotion and career progression within the RAF.

You may have to enter war situations, which can be traumatic and stressful.

Qualifications and courses

Entry requirements to become an RAF airman/woman vary according to the specialist trade you are looking to work in. Most trades require entrants to be at least 16 years old, and others set a higher age limit. The maximum age of entry is 29.

To become an RAF Regiment gunner, you do not need any formal qualifications. Most other fields require between 2–5 GCSEs/S grades (A-C/1–3) or equivalent. If you are looking to enter as a student nurse or similar, then you will need 2 A-levels or equivalent.

You will need to pass a vigorous medical and fitness entrance test, as well as a range of interview and written tests during the selection process.

It is also essential that you have been registered as a citizen of the UK, Commonwealth or Republic of Ireland since birth.

Once accepted into the RAF, you will complete a 9 week training course at RAF Halton in Buckinghamshire which will cover fitness and weapons training, followed by a 10 week aircraft training course at RAF College Cranwell in Lincolnshire.

On completion of these general elements, you will then start on more specialised training for your chosen trade, and this can take between 3 weeks and 18 months.

Money guide

On completion of your initial 6 months of training, your salary will be £15,677. After 2 or 3 years you could earn between £16,110 and £26,660 depending on your trade.

If you work as a member of non-commissioned aircrew, your salary will be around £25,422 on completion of 6 months initial training. Your salary will rise to between £30,180 and £34,000 once all your training has been completed.

Related opportunities

- Royal Air Force (RAF) Officer p557
- Army Soldier p564
- Air Traffic Controller p595
- Engineering Technician p83

Further information

RAF Careers
0845 605 5555; www.raf.mod.uk

RAF Halton
Aylesbury HP22 5PG
www.raf.mod.uk/rafhalton/halstnadj@halton.raf.mod.uk

City& Guilds

www.cityandguilds.com/myperfectjob

ROYAL AIR FORCE (RAF) OFFICER

What the work involves

- The Royal Air Force (RAF) is responsible for protecting UK airspace, performing search and rescue missions offshore and on land, transporting aid to the victims of war and natural disaster, and pursuing military action in a war situation.

- Royal Air Force officers are responsible for managing, leading and inspiring a team of airmen.

- You will occupy a specialist post within the RAF, such as that of a pilot, engineer, catering manager, or medical officer.

- You will be involved in planning and implementing various procedures from rescues to humanitarian aid drops.

The type of person suited to this work

You must have excellent communication skills as you will be responsible for briefing, leading and motivating your team. This also includes being able to listen and get on with all team members.

You will be called upon to make difficult decisions in highly pressurised situations, so must be able to think on your feet in order to reach mature, responsible conclusions.

You must be physically fit and mentally alert.

Working conditions

Officers usually work regular office hours, but you are required to be available for duty at all times in case of an emergency. There are also occasional social functions or other duties that need to be fulfilled over weekends.

You will be stationed at an RAF base, many of which have all the amenities of a small town, including shops, banks, a gym and childcare facilities.

You should be prepared to be posted overseas at short notice, and to spend long periods of time away from friends and family.

Future prospects

On joining the RAF as an officer, you sign up to a minimum length of service. This can range from 6–12 years according to your specialisation.

There is defined career progression through the ranks from flying officer, to flight lieutenant, squadron leader, wing commander, group captain, and further if you wish.

The training, qualifications and personal skills that come with being an RAF officer are easily transferred to a number of civilian positions.

Advantages/disadvantages

You will be responsible for training and organising a team that will carry out essential defence and humanitarian functions for the UK and the world.

You may have to enter combat situations which can be distressing and unpleasant.

Qualifications and courses

You will need to be at least 17½ to apply for an officer position with the RAF. Some specialisations impose an older age limit.

Most specialisations require applicants to hold at least 2 A-levels/Highers or equivalent, and 5 GCSEs/S grades (A-C/1–3) or equivalent, including English and maths.

Some specialisations, including engineering, legal, and the medical divisions, require a relevant degree. For entrance onto related degree courses, you will need 3 A-levels/Highers or equivalent, as well as at least 5 GSCEs/S grades (A-C/1–3) or equivalent, including English, maths and science.

You must also be a UK, Commonwealth, or Republic of Ireland citizen since birth. For a role as an intelligence officer, you must have been a British Citizen from birth.

If you meet the entrance criteria, you may be invited to attend the four day selection event held at the RAF College Cranwell, in Lincolnshire. During this process, you will have to undertake interviews, fitness and health assessments, and various aptitude tests.

The RAF also offers sponsorship to sixth form and university students.

Money guide

If you enter the RAF without a degree, as a pilot officer, you can expect to earn £22,650 as a starting salary. If you hold a degree and therefore enter as a flying officer, this will increase your starting wages to £27,250.

As a flying officer, you can earn up to £30,000.

On promotion to lieutenant, your salary should rise to between £34,925 and £41,550.

If you become a squadron leader with experience, you could earn £50,000+.

Related opportunities

- Royal Air Force Airman/woman p556
- Air Traffic Controller p595
- Army Officer p538
- Royal Navy Officer p560

Further information

RAF College Cranwell
Sleaford, Lincolnshire NG34 8HB
01400 261201; www.raf.mod.uk/cranwell/

www.cityandguilds.com/myperfectjob

Security and the Armed Forces

CRCI: UA
CLCI: BAL

ROYAL MARINES COMMANDO

What the work involves

- The Royal Marines are a specialist, highly trained, amphibious division of the Royal Navy. They carry out operations on land, in the sea or in the air. They operate in combat, peacekeeping and humanitarian situations, and also as a law enforcement agency at sea.

- You will be a commando and rifleman, working within an operational commando unit.

- You will be ready to take immediate action in any emergency or threat to national security, and this means performing to a very high standard at all times whether on land or at sea.

- You will specialise either in general duties, or in one of 26 trades which include assault engineer, mountain leader or swimmer canoeist.

The type of person suited to this work

You will need high levels of fitness, discipline, commitment and self-confidence in order to get through one of the most demanding and gruelling training programmes in the armed forces prior to qualifying as a commando.

You must be able to work well within a team and also use your own initiative when required. The ability to lead and motivate others is also an asset.

You should be level-headed and be able to react quickly and logically when under pressure. Courage and determination are also necessary in order to head into combat situations.

Working conditions

You will usually work 37 hours a week, unless you are on an operation or in training. In these instances, you could expect to work long, unpredictable hours. Even if you are not at work, though, you will always be on call in case of emergency.

You could be stationed or deployed anywhere in the world at short notice, including undertaking operations in areas of desert, jungle, and even out in the Arctic.

You will be expected to wear a uniform.

Future prospects

Within the UK, you are most likely to be stationed within the south west of England or in Scotland, as that is where the majority of naval bases are located.

You will be expected to serve with the Royal Marines for 22 years, although you can leave at any point after completing the minimum 3 years of service and giving 12 months notice.

You will be promoted on merit, so hard work should be rewarded. You could move up the ranks from lance corporal right up to warrant officer 1.

Advantages/disadvantages

You will be operating at you optimum level of mental and

Qualifications and courses

There is a rigorous selection process. You will need to attend an interview and pass a medical examination.

You will also have to undertake the Potential Royal Marines Course. This lasts 2.5 days and is designed to test your fitness, determination, stamina and mental ability. This is a gruelling assessment designed to push you to your limits, so you will have to train and prepare for it for a number of months.

You must be between 17 and 32 years of age to apply to the Royal Marines. They also require candidates to be at least 151.5cm tall and 60kg in weight.

You will also have to prove that you have been a citizen of Britain, Ireland or the Commonwealth since birth, and will have to submit to a detailed security clearance before you can be considered for entry.

physical fitness, meeting new challenges each day and adapting to unusual and inhospitable situations.

You will be working within a close knit team, providing essential services such as delivering aid or maintaining order in areas across the globe.

You are continually on call, and could be sent anywhere in the world at a moment's notice.

Money guide

New entrants to the Royal Marines at commando level receive a starting salary of £13,000.

Once you have completed your training, this should rise to about £16,000. With increasing experience you could expect to earn up to £27,500.

If you move up the ranks and reach the level of warrant officer 1 you should earn £44,500.

Related opportunities

- Royal Marines Officer p559
- Army Officer p538
- Soldier p564
- Royal Air Force (RAF) Airman/Woman p556

Further information

The Royal Marines
0845 607 5555; www.royalnavy.mod.uk/royalmarines/

www.cityandguilds.com/myperfectjob

ROYAL MARINES OFFICER

What the work involves

- The Royal Marines carry out operations on land, in the sea or in the air. They operate in combat, peacekeeping and humanitarian situations, and also as a law enforcement agency at sea.

- You will be responsible for leading and managing a team both on training operations and on real missions including combat situations and peace-keeping tasks.

- You will be in charge of training your team, keeping them disciplined, and looking out for their welfare.

- You will be given the opportunity to specialise in one of 10 areas, including weapons training, signals, physical training, or as a pilot.

The type of person suited to this work

You will need high levels of fitness, discipline, commitment and self-confidence in order to get through the demanding and gruelling training programme prior to qualifying as an officer.

You must be able to lead and motivate your team, looking out for their welfare and making decisions for them in dangerous and stressful conditions.

You should be able to focus on the operations you undertake fully in order to function at your maximum level of mental and physical capacity.

Working conditions

You will usually work 37 hours a week, unless you are on an operation or in training. In these instances, you could expect to work long, unpredictable hours. Even if you are not at work, you are always on call in case of emergency.

You could be stationed or deployed anywhere in the world at short notice, including undertaking operations in areas of desert, jungle, and even out in the Arctic.

You will be expected to wear a uniform, and specialised clothing when required.

Future prospects

Competition for entry as a Royal Marines officer is fierce. You will be expected to join on a 12 year commission, and must serve at least 3–5 years of this. 12 months notice is required prior to departure.

You will normally move appointments every other year, so you will be able to experience numerous areas of work in various locations throughout your career.

Promotion is awarded on merit, and you could work through the ranks from 2nd lieutenant right up to major-general.

Advantages/disadvantages

You will be operating at your optimum level of mental and physical fitness, meeting new challenges each day and adapting to unusual and inhospitable situations.

Qualifications and courses

Although most applicants are graduates, the minimum entry criteria are at least 2 A-levels/Highers or equivalent, and 5 GCESs/S grades (A-C/1–3) including English language and maths.

Only men can serve as Royal Marines officers, and you must be between 17 and 26 to enter training. You must be at least 151.5cm tall and 60kg in weight, and meet strict medical, fitness and eyesight criteria. You must also have British or dual British nationality and have lived in the UK for a minimum of 5 years.

You will attend a 3 day Potential Officers Course, which is a gruelling assessment designed to push you to your limits.

If you successfully complete the 3 day assessment, you will be invited to attend a further 2 day interview process, during which you will sit further tests in maths, reasoning, accuracy, written communication, spatial orientation, leadership, and problem solving and undergo a series of interviews.

If you are selected to train as an officer, you will then have to complete a further 15 month programme prior to being given your own team to lead.

You will be working within a close knit team, leading them through essential operations such as delivering aid or maintaining order in areas across the globe.

Money guide

Entrants who do not have a degree can expect a starting salary of £14,800 at the start of their training, rising to £23,500 on completion. Graduates start on £28,200 and can progress to £31,200 on completion of their training.

If you become a captain, you can expect to earn between £36,100 and £43,000.

High ranking colonels can earn between £77,500 and £85,300.

Related opportunities

- Royal Marines Commando p558
- Army Officer p538
- Soldier p564
- Royal Air Force (RAF) Officer p557

Further information

The Royal Marines
0845 607 5555; www.royalnavy.mod.uk/royalmarines/

www.cityandguilds.com/myperfectjob

Security and the Armed Forces

CRCI: UA
CLCI: BAB

Security and the Armed Forces

CRCI: UA
CLCI: MAG

ROYAL NAVY OFFICER

What the work involves

- You will command and train ratings, looking after their welfare, development and discipline.

- Your day-to-day work will involve you in managing operations in one of four areas of duty: as a warfare officer, engineer officer, supply officer or specialist officer (for example chaplain, doctor or dentist).

- Your ship may be sent into a war zone, on peacekeeping duties.

- You may be tasked to do a specific job such as policing the North Sea fishing grounds or helping out in a disaster situation.

The type of person suited to this work

Officers especially need top-level leadership and communication skills as well as good judgement. You will be required to inspire ratings, be resourceful and have excellent communication skills. You should have good levels of physical fitness and stamina. You may need to work in combat zones.

You should also have a very strong sense of responsibility as your decisions may impact upon your colleagues' safety as well as your own. You should display a very high level of personal awareness and a keen sense of personal safety.

Working conditions

Most of your work will be on board a ship or submarine, or at land-based establishments in Britain or overseas. At sea, conditions can be cold, cramped and damp.

You will need to wear a uniform, and protective clothing when necessary.

Hours vary but you will usually work 8-hour turns of duty on a shift rota including weekends and holidays.

You may find yourself working in a dangerous or highly unpredictable situation.

Future prospects

There are about 7500+ officers in the Royal Navy. There are annual vacancies but some specialisms are more competitive than others. A naval college entrant usually starts out as midshipman rising to sub-lieutenant after 2 years. A graduate starts as sub-lieutenant rising to lieutenant commander by their early 30s. If you have got the right qualities you can progress on to the ranks of commander, captain and, for a few, admiral.

Advantages/disadvantages

You will be trained to a high level and will be offered a resettlement package to help you find work in civilian life when you leave.

You will be living in cramped conditions with lots of other people. However, most officers say that they enjoy the feeling of camaraderie on board and make life-long friendships.

Qualifications and courses

You will need to be at least 151.5cm tall and be of proportionate weight. A medical, with strict eyesight standards, must be passed, and you must meet the Royal Navy nationality and residence requirements. Women can still not enter the submarine or mine clearance diving branches of the Royal Navy.

There are several entry points for Officers: Non-Graduate Entry for those aged 17–26 who have at least 5 GCSEs/S grades and 2 A levels/H grades or 140 tariff points including English language and maths.

There are a limited number of scholarships for those with 5 GCSEs/S grades and no break before continuing further education available as well as the Defence Sixth Form College (Welbeck) which focuses on gaining entry to the Armed Forces.

There is also the Defence Technical Undergraduate Scheme (DTUS) for those under 23 with 5 GCSEs/S grades including English language and maths and 240 tariff points including grade C in maths and physics and graduate entry for those with a UK degree. All candidates undergo a selection interview and medical examination before the Admiralty Interview Board AIB. Training takes place at Britannia Royal Naval College, Dartmouth, Devon.

Money guide

Entering this career you can expect to start on £14,000 as a midshipman, but this will increase to between £20,000-£25,000 once you have completed basic training.

As a graduate sub-lieutenant you can earn £25,000-£30,000 a year. Rising through the ranks to the level of captain could see you earning £75,000 and more.

Related opportunities

- Army Officer p538
- Royal Air Force (RAF) Officer p557
- Royal Marines Officer p559
- Royal Navy Rating p561

Further information

Armed Forces Careers Navy
22 Unthank Road, Norwich NR2 1AH
01603 620033; www.royalnavy.mod.uk

Welbeck Defence 6th Form College
Garden Court, Lockington Hall, Main Street, Lockington, Derby DE74 2SJ
0150 967 8428; info@direct-ed.com

City&
Guilds

www.cityandguilds.com/myperfectjob

ROYAL NAVY RATING

What the work involves

■ The Royal Navy protects the UK's ports and coastline, and also undertakes international missions such as delivering humanitarian aid, entering combat, and enforcing the law on the seas.

■ Royal Navy ratings work on board a ship, submarine or onshore, and are responsible for operating, maintaining and repairing technical equipment.

■ You will specialise in one of the six main trades; medical, warfare, logistics, engineering, fleet air arm, or submarine.

■ You will take part in naval exercises and operations both in UK and overseas waters.

The type of person suited to this work

You should be able to work within a team, reacting quickly to orders, working on your own initiative where necessary, and supporting other team members both professionally and emotionally at times.

You must be responsible and decisive and find solutions to problems under difficult or pressurised circumstances. You should also have a methodical and logical approach to your work.

You will need to have a good level of fitness, including the ability to swim and tread water for a number of minutes.

Working conditions

You will usually work 37 hours a week, which can include weekends and public holidays. You will also be on call at all times, in case of an emergency.

You could be based at sea on a ship or submarine, or in a naval station onshore. Living conditions on ships and submarines tend to be basic, and men and women always sleep in separate accommodation.

You will have to spend long periods of time away from friends and family, and may be posted overseas at a moment's notice.

Future prospects

The career progression for a Royal Navy rating is clearly mapped out. Promotion is awarded on merit so the harder you work the faster you will progress. The grades that you will move upwards through are able rating, leading rating, petty officer, chief petty officer, and warrant officer.

If you have the necessary qualifications, you could apply to become an officer. This is a popular route of career progression amongst ratings.

Advantages/disadvantages

You will be meeting new challenges each day and adapting to unusual and inhospitable situations, which will keep you

Qualifications and courses

There are no formal qualifications for entry, but holding at least 2 GCSEs/S grades (A-C/1–3) or equivalent is helpful.

Selection takes place at local armed forces careers offices, where you will be required to fill in a questionnaire and take several tests including numeracy, English language, reasoning and mechanical comprehension. If you complete these successfully, you will be invited back for an interview. You will then have to pass a medical assessment and fitness test prior to being offered a place.

You will join the Royal Navy on a Full Career, which lasts 18 years. You can leave after completing 2.5 years training, though, but you must give 12 months notice.

Once you have become a rating, you will undertake 9 weeks basic training, followed by specialist training in your chosen trade.

mentally and physically alert and ensures the work never gets dull.

You will be working within a close knit team, supporting them both in practice and when out on real operations.

You are continually on call, and could be sent any where in the world at a moment's notice.

Money guide

You will enter the Royal Navy as a rating on a starting salary of £12,500.

Once you have completed your training and have qualified as an able rating, this will rise to £15,700 and, as you continue to learn and progress, could reach £26,600.

If you are promoted to the role of leading rating, your salary will increase to between £24,300 and £30,500.

Related opportunities

■ Royal Marines Commando p558
■ Royal Navy Officer p560
■ Soldier p564
■ Royal Air Force (RAF) Airman/woman p556

Further information

The Royal Navy
0845 607 5555; www.royalnavy.mod.uk

www.cityandguilds.com/myperfectjob

Security and the Armed Forces

CRCI: UA
CLCI: BAB

SECURITY OFFICER/ MANAGER

What the work involves

- Security work is about protecting organisations, people, places, valuable goods or money. You could be protecting people or valuable items on the move, for example in security vans or on planes.

Officer

- If you are working at a base you may have specific tasks. You may work at reception monitoring visitors and deliveries. Or you may patrol a building or site, checking for intruders or fire risks.

Manager

- You will be managing a team of security guards, and be responsible for their work, training and supervision. You will do security surveys, give advice on improvements and liaise with other organisations such as the emergency services.

The type of person suited to this work

You will need to be a mature, responsible and honest person. You should be keen on technology and keep up to date with new security systems. You will also have to keep records of all incidents, so you will also need to be happy to do paperwork. To become a manager you will need lots of experience in security work as well as a talent for motivating a team of staff.

Working conditions

You may be based at one place which could be inside, or outside in all weathers. Many security jobs involve driving and you will spend a lot of time in a security van.

You will probably be working shifts of up to 12 hours covering days, nights and weekends. Some guards work permanent nights. Many security guards work a 48-hour week.

Future prospects

Jobs are on offer throughout the UK and you could be employed by any type of organisation. This area is one of massive growth with rising levels of fraud, theft and security breaches in organisations as well as increasing terrorist threats.

This work will increasingly use sophisticated technology with the growing use of computer security systems and also biometrics (fingerprint recognition systems) to control access to buildings and other secure areas. Security staff with training and technical ability are likely to be in demand in this growing industry.

Advantages/disadvantages

As training becomes essential, and with the introduction of security licences, if you are willing to get qualified, your progression and earnings prospects are excellent.

Qualifications and courses

You will need to be numerate, literate, and aged over 18 (occasionally over 21) and may need a driving licence.

Officer

All security guards require by law an industry licence, approved by the Security Industry Authority (SIA) which you must pay for. The licence is awarded to candidates who pass the two-part assessment process, usually delivered over 4 days. Employers may offer additional training such as NVQ/SVQ Level 2 Providing Security Services. Other qualifications available include a degree in Security and Risk Management or a Postgraduate Certificate in Maritime and Supply Chain Security. Apprenticeships/Skillseekers may be available.

Manager

Specialist managers may need specific training and experience, for example in security systems, legislation and anti-terrorist or close protection work. Your employer may offer training. The International Institute of Security offers courses.

At high levels in large international organisations you may have the opportunity to travel or be based overseas.

Money guide
Officer

As a starting salary, guards can earn about £12,500–£15,300 per year. With experience this can rise to £22,500–£28,500.

Manager

On entry, managers earn £26,500–£28,500 per year, rising to £35,000+ with experience. Area managers can earn £40,000+ and international security managers can earn up to £70,000.

Related opportunities

- Bodyguard p539
- Door Supervisor/Bouncer p544
- Police Officer p551

Further information

Security Industry Authority
PO Box 9, Newcastle upon Tyne NE82 6YX
0870 243 0100; www.the-sia.org.uk

www.cityandguilds.com/myperfectjob

SECURITY SERVICE OFFICER

What the work involves

■ You will be a member of the Security Service, employed to protect the country from attack, terrorism and other forms of crime.

■ Working alongside other security forces such as the police and other international law enforcement agencies, you will help to protect UK citizens and businesses across the world.

■ You could be employed to undertake a number of roles depending on need and your skills. These include vetting investigation officers, surveillance officers, linguists and ICT specialists.

The type of person suited to this work

You will need an excellent range of skills across a range of areas. This job requires you to think on your feet and be aware of the full picture. You should be confident making decisions, be flexible and adaptable.

You will need good verbal and written communication skills with the ability to recall events accurately. You will also need commitment to your job and the ability to see everything through until it is finished. Some of your work will include informing and working alongside professionals from other national and international security services.

The skills you need will depend on your specialism, such as language or ICT ability.

Working conditions

Some of the posts operate shifts, which might include weekends. You could also be required to travel both nationally and internationally. It might be possible to work from home for some posts.

If you provide support services you will normally work in London and operate office hours.

This job can become more of a way of life than a career so you should be completely dedicated and be able to keep information totally confidential.

Future prospects

There are around 3,000 people working for the Service, many of whom are based in London. Although there are specialist jobs, 67% work within generalist roles. Applicants should refer to the Security Service website for details on current vacancies, which change regularly.

The Service has a promotion programme that is based on performance and potential.

Advantages/disadvantages

You will be helping to protect national security.

Some jobs involve lots of travelling for long periods at a time.

The current recruitment drive aims to attract people of all backgrounds.

Qualifications and courses

Applicants for any post within MI5 or the Secret Intelligence Service (SIS) must be British citizens and one or both of your parents must also be British or have substantial ties to the UK. You normally have to have been resident in the UK for 10 years prior to your application.

MI5 applicants must be aged 18 or over. SIS applicants must be aged 21 or over and A-levels/H grades or degrees may be required by some organisations.

Graduates from a wide range of disciplines are considered. Specialist areas may require more precise subject choices, for example linguistics or computer software development. Mature applicants and those with experience are also considered.

Each applicant is considered individually during the rigorous vetting procedure, known as Developed Vetting (DV) clearance. Some candidates who already have clearance from previous employment may be exempt from some sections of the vetting process. Some applicants may require additional vetting, for example medical assessments.

Specialist fields within MI5 include English Language Monitor, Intelligence Officer, Security Guard and Mobile Surveillance Officer.

Money guide

Salaries are based on your role and the information below should be used as a guide only.

Administrative assistants earn an average of £17,000 per year. Generalists, surveillance and linguist officers start at £25,000. Development vetting officers start at £34,500.

In addition to pay, there are excellent benefits including leisure and fitness facilities, childcare vouchers and travel assistance.

Related opportunities

■ Army Officer p538
■ Customs and Excise Officer p542
■ Police Officer p551
■ Private Investigator p555

Further information

MI5 Careers
www.mi5careers.co.uk

Secret Intelligence Service
www.sis.gov.uk

City&
Guilds

www.cityandguilds.com/myperfectjob

Security and the Armed Forces

CRCI: UK
CLCI: MAG

SOLDIER

What the work involves

- The Army is responsible for defending the UK and its allies across the world, as well as taking part in peacekeeping and humanitarian operations.

- You will be involved in regular training exercises to ensure you maintain a high level of fitness and military skills so that you are ready for combat at any time.

- You will also choose to train and work within one of more than 130 different trades.

- You may be posted to dangerous areas and inhospitable environments at any time, whether for peacekeeping and aid missions, or to engage in warfare.

The type of person suited to this work

You should be able to work within a team, reacting quickly to orders, working on your own initiative where necessary, and supporting other team members both professionally and emotionally at times.

You must be extremely disciplined and responsible, with the ability to think and act logically under pressure.

You must be physically fit with excellent stamina.

You should be practical, with good manual dexterity, so that you will be able to operate various machines and military equipment.

Working conditions

Your hours will depend upon which trade you choose to specialise in. Some soldiers work normal office hours, whilst others are expected to undertake shifts that encompass night and weekend work.

You could be stationed in the UK or overseas, and must be prepared for life in a number of environments including deserts, war torn cities, and mountains.

You will wear a uniform at all times.

Future prospects

There is a constant demand for new recruits, so career prospects are good if you meet the selection criteria.

You will sign up for an open engagement lasting 22 years, but you can leave after serving 4 years. You must give 12 months notice prior to leaving.

All soldiers start as a private, and are awarded promotion according to their increasing levels of skill and commitment.

Advantages/disadvantages

You will be meeting new challenges each day and adapting to unusual and inhospitable situations, which will ensure the work never gets dull.

You will be working within a close knit team, supporting their work both in practice and actually out on operations.

Qualifications and courses

There are no formal qualifications for entry, but holding at least 2 GCSEs/S grades (A-C/1–3) or equivalent is recommended.

You will need to complete the Army Entrance Test (known as BARB) and undergo an interview. Once these stages are done, you will take a physical assessment, medical, and a further interview.

Entrants aged 16 or 17 enter as a junior recruit and have to complete phase 1 and 2 training, which can take between 24 weeks and two years.

Entrants who are 18 or over will attend training programmes according to the regiment they wish to join. Adult infantry soldiers go to the Infantry Training Centre (ITC) to complete a 24 week Combat Infantryman's Course.

Those planning to join the Royal Engineers, Household Cavalry, Royal Armoured Corps or Royal Artillery attend an Army Training Regiment (ATR) where they undertake a 12 week course in weapon handling, navigation, fieldcraft, drill, health and safety, and personal administration. They then join their chosen regiment to undertake further, more specific training.

You are continually on call, and could be sent anywhere in the world at a moment's notice.

Money guide

New entrants to the Army can expect to earn £13,000. Once you have qualified as a private, this will increase to between £16,200 and £25,100. If you become a sergeant, you can expect to earn £28,600-£35,200.

In addition to a basic salary, you will receive subsidised accommodation and food, medical and dental care, discounted rail fares and subsidised nursery facilities.

Related opportunities

- Army Officer p538
- Royal Navy Rating p561
- Royal Marine Commando p558
- Royal Air Force (RAF) Airman/Woman p556

Further information

Army
www.army.mod.uk; www.armyjobs.mod.uk

Welbeck College
The Defence Sixth Form College, Forest Road, Woodhouse, Loughborough LE12 8WD
0845 600 1483; www.welbeck.mod.uk

www.cityandguilds.com/myperfectjob

STORE DETECTIVE

What the work involves

- You will be preventing and detecting theft or fraud in a retail outlet. You may need to chase the suspected offender and make arrests.

- Working undercover, wearing plain clothes, you will merge with shoppers, looking out for suspicious behaviour or theft.

- Using a radio you will call for assistance and listen for alerts from other staff about known offenders entering the store.

- You will make notes of any incidents and may need to use these if a decision is made to prosecute.

The type of person suited to this work

Your communication skills need to be excellent for this job. You will have to talk down customers who have become anxious or aggressive when challenged. Your written reports will be used in court if you prosecute and you will need to be fluent and precise to get a conviction.

Observation is also crucial: you need to be able to spot suspicious behaviour and also remember the faces of known shoplifters. You will need to be good at planning and thinking ahead so that when a situation happens you can act quickly.

You will need to be mature, responsible and be able to handle difficult situations sensitively.

Working conditions

Most of your work will be inside the store in pleasant, warm conditions.

A 40-hour week is common and you may work shifts to cover long opening hours and weekends. You will be on your feet most of your shift.

You may wear a uniform but the majority wear their own clothes to blend in.

Future prospects

Shoplifters cost stores more than £2 billion a year so most large stores in the UK employ store detectives to minimise their losses. Some retail chains employ their own detectives, while others use agencies on a contract basis.

You may be able to progress into supervisory work or move into more general security management.

Advantages/disadvantages

Store detectives say they feel a sense of achievement when they manage to successfully prosecute an offender.

This job can be a good stepping stone into jobs such as security management.

Qualifications and courses

There are no formal entry requirements, but you will need to be able to write clearly and accurately. A GCSE/S grade in English or a Key Skill in communication would be useful.

You will have to undergo a police check. Some employers may also do an employment history and credit check.

Previous relevant work experience is preferred, especially within the police, prison or security industry.

Training is through courses or on the job. Most companies run an induction course for new employees covering topics such as relevant criminal law and principles of investigation.

The International Institute of Security and the International Professional Security Association both offer courses by distance learning.

The Security Industry Authority (SIA) now has a requirement for you to be licensed to operate as a security guard.

Money guide

Starting wages are usually around £13,500 per year.

Experienced store detectives can earn up to £25,000.

£28,000+ is possible for top earners.

Related opportunities

- Door Supervisor/Bouncer p544
- Police Officer p551
- Private Investigator p555
- Security Officer/Manager p562

Further information

Security Industry Authority
PO Box 9, Newcastle upon Tyne NE82 6YX
0870 243 0100; www.the-sia.org.uk

British Security Industry Association
Kirkham House, John Comyn Drive, Worcester UK WR3 7NS
0845 389 3889; www.bsia.co.uk

City& Guilds

www.cityandguilds.com/myperfectjob

Security and the Armed Forces

CRCI: UK
CLCI: MAG

Social Work and Counselling Services

People who work in this sector are dedicated to caring and talking through people's problems and anxieties to improve their general well-being and their future prospects in life. The work requires a lot of patience, an open mind and a friendly and approachable personality. You could be helping people who are distressed and need help and guidance but equally you may be helping people who want to move on to the next stage in their careers or educational choices. Either way, you should be someone who enjoys helping people change their lives for the better. If you are interested in working in this field you need to show that you are compassionate and very good at communicating with people from all walks of life and of all ages. You should also be someone who can maintain a strong sense of professionalism as you could be in a position of trust and you must be very respectful of your clients' privacy.

In this section we look at the following jobs:

- Careers Adviser p568
- Childminder p569
- Clinical/Health Psychologist p570
- Counsellor p571
- Debt Counsellor/Money Advice Caseworker p572
- Educational Psychologist p573
- Forensic Pyschologist p574
- Fundraiser p575
- Healthcare Assistant p576
- Life Coach p577
- Occupational Psychologist p578

- Personal Adviser – Connexions p579
- Probation Officer p580
- Psychoanalyst/ Psychotherapist p581
- Recruitment Centre Consultant p582
- Rehabilitation Officer – Visually Impaired p583
- Religious Leader p584
- Social Worker p585
- Trade Union Official p587
- Volunteer Organiser p588

- Warden p589
- Welfare Benefits Adviser/ Welfare Rights Caseworker p590
- Youth and Community Worker p591

For similar jobs to the ones covered in this section turn to *Healthcare* on page 291 and *Education and Training* on page 199.

CAREERS ADVISER

What the work involves

- You will help people make realistic choices about education, training and work by listening to their ideas, discussing their interests and skills, and providing information on different jobs.

- Researching information about job opportunities in different sectors from newspapers, the internet or through visits to employers is all part of the role.

- Advisery work is one to one, but you may work with large groups.

- Careers advisers work with young people in schools/colleges, but also with higher education students or adults.

The type of person suited to this work

Since much of the work involves talking and listening to people, careers advisers need to have excellent speaking and listening skills. They need to be impartial, allowing people to come to their own decisions rather than making up their minds for them.

Careers information and guidance is largely ICT-based, so computer skills are essential, along with the ability to write reports and perform administrative tasks.

You will need to enjoy research, to keep up to date with changes in skills and opportunities across industrial sectors, with new qualifications and training routes.

Working conditions

Most of your work is office-based, either in a careers centre open to the public or an educational establishment.

You will travel between different educational establishments and visit employers and training organisations, which means that a driving licence is almost essential.

Some time will be spent in a careers centre or library, keeping up to date with job information.

Future prospects

Careers advisers will continue to work in schools, colleges, universities and adult guidance services – some will be based in one institution, others will work for several organisations. In England, Connexions provides a support service which includes careers advice and guidance for those aged 13–19. In Scotland, Wales and Northern Ireland, all-age guidance services are available.

In a careers service, you could move into managerial-level posts; you could become self-employed as a consultant or researcher. Ongoing professional development is essential.

Advantages/disadvantages

The work is varied and can be highly satisfying.

You will work some evenings or weekends to attend school/college parents' evenings and for careers conventions.

The job also includes a great deal of administrative work.

Qualifications and courses

There are two main routes into this profession: the Qualification in Careers Guidance (QCG) or the work-based route leading to NVQ/SVQ Level 4 in Advice and Guidance, Guidance and Advocacy. Most candidates are graduates and are aged 21 or over. The new Foundation degree in Working with Young People and Young People's Services provides useful background.

The QCG is a 1-year full-time or 2 years part-time course at university. Candidates must then achieve the NVQ/SVQ Level 4 in Advice, Guidance and Advocacy to become a qualified careers adviser.

People already working in a careers guidance organisation can follow a work-based route to the NVQ/SVQ Level 4. The qualification is a combination of practical experience and taught sessions at college.

You do not need a professional careers qualification to work as a careers adviser in higher education, although many candidates have qualified prior to working in HE. A specialist qualification for HE careers advisers, the Certificate/Diploma in Careers Education, Information and Guidance in Higher Education, is available.

Qualified careers advisers who join the Connexions service must complete further in-service training.

Money guide

Pay is around £18,500 when starting, rising to £20,500 per year with experience.

Salaries can reach £25,000–£27,500 per year when fully qualified and with some experience.

Salaries for middle management are around £35,000 and as a senior manager you can get £55,000.

Related opportunities

- Advice Centre/Benefits Adviser p590
- Counsellor p571
- Employment Agency Consultant/Interviewer p582
- Human Resources/Personnel Officer p41
- Personal Adviser – Connexions p579
- Probation Officer p580
- Teacher p212
- Youth and Community Worker p591

Further information

Institute of Careers Guidance
27a Lower High Street, Stourbridge DY8 1TA
01384 376464; www.icg-uk.org

Connexions Service National Unit
Department for Children, Schools and Families, Moorfoot, Sheffield S1 4PP
0114 259 1283; www.connexions.gov.uk

CRAC: The Career Development Organisation
2nd Floor, Sheraton House, Castle Park, Cambridge CB3 0AX
01223 460277;www.crac.org.uk

CHILDMINDER

What the work involves

■ As a childminder, you will care for children in your own home, ensuring they are comfortable and happy while with you.

■ You will plan the children's day so your charges know what to expect.

■ You may accompany children to and from playgroup, nursery or school.

■ You will need to keep parents informed about their children, for example if a child has been unwell or if you have noticed anything important.

The type of person suited to this work

Childminders must be patient and caring. You will need imagination to plan varied activities for children of different ages.

Childminders must share information with parents which means that good observation and communication skills are important. They must be prepared to make quick decisions if necessary.

Since childminders are self-employed, they need to be organised, with good administrative and numeracy skills to work out tax and invoices. ICT skills are useful for maintaining a database of relevant information about each child.

Working conditions

You will work in your own home which may have to be altered to meet childminding standards by fitting equipment such as gates on stairs and checking the security of garden fences and gates.

You may travel locally to take children to playgroup, so a driving licence is useful.

You will do a lot of bending, lifting and clearing up and will be on the go from very early morning into the evening.

Future prospects

Although the minimum age for entry is 18, most childminders are older, with experience of care work. The demand for childminders can vary regionally and at different times of the year. Your registration certificate will tell you how many children you can look after.

Childminders can move into jobs such as care assistant or home care assistant, or can go on to train for similar work as a nursery nurse or registered nurse.

Advantages/disadvantages

The work will be varied, fun and likely to be full of surprises.

Working from home often suits people who have young children themselves.

Some jobs can be messy and unpleasant.

The hours can be very long and it can sometimes be hard work for low pay.

Qualifications and courses

Qualifications in childcare are useful. Candidates must be 18 or over. They, and everyone in their households over 16, must be police-checked.

All childminders must hold a registered childminders' certificate. Registration and inspection of childminders is administered by Ofsted in England and the Care Commission in Scotland.

There are various childminding courses which can be studied part-time or by distance learning. The Council for Awards in Children's Care and Education (CACHE) awards the Certificate in Childminding Level 3. It is also possible to work towards the NVQ/SVQ Level 3 in Children's Care, Learning and Development. The National Childminding Association of England and Wales (NCMA), the Scottish Childminding Association (SCMA) and the Northern Ireland Childminding Association (NICMA) all provide advice on training and qualifications.

Money guide

Your earnings will depend on the number of children you look after, how many hours you work and where you live.

Most childminders charge an hourly rate of between £4.90 and £6.50 an hour plus expenses. Your income can vary at different times of the year: for example, your hours might go up or down during school holidays.

If you are working full-time, you can expect around £9,500 per year when starting out, rising to £13,000–£17,000 when experienced. Top hourly rates are charged in London where experienced, full-time childminders can earn up to £25,000.

Related opportunities

■ Healthcare Assistant p576
■ Children's Nurse p298
■ Early Years Specialist/Nursery Worker p202
■ Play Worker/Hospital Play Specialist p211
■ Teaching Assistant/Learning Support Assistant p217

Further information

National Childminding Association of England and Wales
8 Masons Hill, Bromley, Kent BR2 9EY
020 8464 6164; www.ncma.org.uk

Scottish Childminding Association
Suite 3, 7 Melville Terrace, Stirling FK8 2ND
01786 445377; www.childminding.org

Northern Ireland Childminding Association
16–18 Mill Street, Newtownards, Co Down BT23 4LU
028 9181 1015; www.nicma.org

www.cityandguilds.com/myperfectjob

Social Work and Counselling Services

CRCI: V
CLCI: KEB

CLINICAL/HEALTH PSYCHOLOGIST

Social Work and Counselling Services

CRCI: V
CLCI: KEL

What the work involves

Clinical psychologist

- You will work with people whose health problems affect their behaviour, to learn what they do and why they do it.

Health psychologist

- This is a new and rapidly growing field of applied psychology which promotes changes in people's attitudes, behaviour and thinking about health.

The type of person suited to this work

As the work is mostly about people and their behaviour, an interest in people, their personalities, abilities and interests is essential. The work involves contact with many different types of people which means you must be good at relating to others and have excellent communication skills.

Psychologists must think logically, analyse data and statistics, and work in an organised and methodical way. They need administrative and ICT skills for writing reports and analyses, and presenting information at case conferences or company meetings.

Working conditions

Clinical psychologist

Your work will take you to schools, colleges, hospitals and health centres. You may find yourself working with social services or with adolescent and child mental health services. Most clinical psychologists are employed by the NHS.

Health psychologist

You will be based in an office but you may also travel to different health centres such as hospitals.

Future prospects

Entry to psychology degrees is competitive and it takes a long time to become a chartered psychologist. The jobs available tend to be within government services, education and health, in the public and private sectors. Ongoing professional development will be important throughout your career.

Clinical psychologist

Clinical psychologists, a very large specialist area, work mainly in the Health Service but there are also opportunities in the Civil Service and private practice.

Health psychologist

Health psychology is a rapidly growing field with opportunities in many health-related areas.

Advantages/disadvantages

The work is varied, interesting and challenging. You will meet many different types of people.

Qualifications and courses

ENTRY LEVEL 4

Entrants must be graduates with Graduate Basis for Registration (GBR) with the British Psychological Society (BPS). GBR can be obtained by taking a BPS-accredited degree in psychology or a non-accredited degree plus a conversion course. Additional postgraduate training is usually required to qualify in a specialist area.

Clinical psychologist

To specialise, you need to follow a BPS-accredited 3-year postgraduate training course, which is mostly hospital-based. This is full-time only and will lead to a Doctorate in Clinical Psychology. To start training on this postgraduate course you will have to have lots of experience which can be in the form of working as a psychological assistant or volunteering with the NHS.

Health psychologist

A BPS-accredited MSc and 2 years of appropriate supervised experience are essential for professional recognition. If you want to achieve chartered status and your course is not BPS accredited it is still possible to do this if you sit the BPS qualifying examination which would give you GBR.

Some people may be aggressive or even violent and you may sometimes have difficulty remaining impartial.

Money guide

Clinical psychologist

Working for the NHS you can expect your salary to start at around £26,000 whilst working as a trainee clinical psychologist. Once you reach a very senior position your salary could increase to £70,000 and more.

Health psychologist

You can expect to start on around £17,000 if you start work as a university assistant. Pay rises with experience to between £27,500 and £40,000 and as a senior health psychologist with the NHS salaries can reach £55,000.

Related opportunities

- Educational Psychologist p573
- Occupational Psychologist p578

Further information

NHS Careers
0845 60 60 655; www.nhscareers.nhs.uk

The British Association for Counselling and Psychology
01455 883300; www.bacp.co.uk

COUNSELLOR

What the work involves

- Counsellors listen to what their patients say and ask questions in response, to help them explore, talk about and eventually resolve their problems.

- You will help your patients to see things more clearly, perhaps from a different point of view.

- You will not tell people what to do but will help them work out their next steps themselves.

- You might work with people with a range of problems or specialise in a particular area, such as bereavement, gambling, relationship difficulties or eating disorders.

The type of person suited to this work

As most of the work involves talking and listening to people, excellent communication skills are essential.

As clients come from a variety of backgrounds and have a wide range of problems, you must be able to work with people from different cultures and ethnic groups.

Counselling workers may not always agree with the views held by their clients, which means they have to be open-minded and tolerant. You must also be highly discreet as you will be given a lot of confidential information.

You need to be interested in how the mind works, and in people's welfare.

Working conditions

You will work indoors, usually sitting in a quiet, comfortable room in places such as advice centres, schools, colleges, outpatient clinics and health centres.

If you are self-employed, you might work from home, visit your clients at home, or both. Some counselling work is done exclusively over the phone.

You will work mainly with people on a one-to-one basis but also, on occasions, with couples, families or groups. Most counselling sessions last 50 minutes. You may work in the evenings and at weekends and many counsellors work part time.

Future prospects

Most people gain voluntary experience before moving into part time paid work. They usually have experience in a career such as social work, nursing or teaching.

While the demand is increasing, there is keen competition for full time posts and many people combine counselling work with another role.

You could work in education or health, or with a specialist agency. Experienced counselling workers can become self-employed or train for a specialist area.

Advantages/disadvantages

The work can be very rewarding but also highly stressful.

Qualifications and courses

Counselling is often a second career, and maturity and experience are beneficial. It is rare for someone to enter a full time position in this field before their mid 20s. Entrants may have worked as teachers/lecturers, personal tutors, careers advisers, social workers or nurses, or in other fields.

Many private, voluntary and charitable counselling organisations have their own training programmes which focus on a particular client group.

Certificate courses in counselling skills and theory take 1 year part time. A Diploma/Advanced Diploma course lasts 2–3 years, studying part time.

To obtain BACP accreditation, candidates need to have studied a course lasting 1 year full time or 2–3 years part time, and must have a certain number of hours in practice.

Degrees, HNDs and Foundation degrees in counselling are offered at a number of universities and colleges.

Starting salaries can be low, until you are fully trained and have gained some experience.

You must be able to take constructive criticism from an experienced counselling worker, therapist or psychoanalyst – both during and after completing training.

Some clients may become dependent on therapy or analysis sessions and will have to be carefully assisted to refocus.

Money guide

Expect £19,000–£25,000 per year when newly qualified.

Qualified and experienced counselling workers earn £35,000.

Earnings can reach £40,000–£50,000 with management responsibilities.

Counsellors are paid £30–£50 an hour when consulted within a private practice.

Related opportunities

- Careers Adviser p568
- Debt Counsellor p572
- Mental Health Nurse p321

Further information

British Association for Counselling and Psychotherapy
BACP House, 35–37 Albert Street, Rugby CV21 2SG
0870 443 5252; www.bacp.co.uk

Counselling and Psychotherapy Central Award Body (CPCAB)
PO Box 1768, Glastonbury, Somerset BA6 8XP
01458 850 350; www.cpcab.co.uk

COSCA
18 Viewfield Street, Stirling FK8 1UA
01786 475140; www.cosca.org.uk

Social Work and Counselling Services

CRCI: V
CLCI: KEK

DEBT COUNSELLOR/ MONEY ADVICE CASEWORKER

What the work involves

- You will help people in serious debt by giving them free, impartial and confidential advice.

- If your clients are being taken to court, you can guide them through the legal procedures and may represent them in court.

- To make sure clients are claiming available tax allowances and benefits, you will list clients' income and expenditure, then try to help them plan their spending by devising a budget.

- By liaising with creditors, you will try to arrange realistic repayments over a reasonable timescale.

The type of person suited to this work

People experience money problems for reasons such as unemployment, redundancy and bad money management; you will need to work with very different people and be non-judgemental about their circumstances. You will need good writing and speaking skills and a confident manner so that people trust you.

Much of the work involves figures, so you do need high-level numeracy skills. It is important to be a quick-thinking negotiator to get the best deal for your clients.

Good time management and work planning are essential, as are excellent ICT skills. This job suits people who have worked in financial services.

Working conditions

You will work with a computer in an office, usually in an advice centre, but may also spend time in court, at meetings or visiting clients in their own homes.

You could travel around locally, so a driving licence is useful. You will have to work some evenings, to visit your clients at home, perhaps doing shift work. Other agencies may contact you for advice on money matters.

Future prospects

You are unlikely to become a money adviser straight from school. Some entrants have degrees; others gain experience through paid or voluntary work. Although money advisers are in demand, there are more applicants than jobs. Most openings are town- or city-based, in advice centres, money advice units or with local authorities.

Prospects are very limited. You could move into other social care jobs or change to work in the financial sector.

Advantages/disadvantages

You will get satisfaction by helping people balance their affairs – some may be very distressed and frightened.

You may work some evenings and weekends.

Some people can be unpleasant, rude and difficult.

Qualifications and courses

There are no fixed minimum entry requirements for this kind of work but it is preferable to have a good standard of general education, including a minimum of 3 GCSEs/S grades (A–C/1–3).

Many applicants have training and/or experience in finance or accounting, consumer advice or volunteer work in an advice centre.

Many candidates apply for paid posts after voluntary work giving general advice, during which they undertake short training courses.

Money advisers need a clear understanding of the problems faced by people with low income and debt and also detailed knowledge of the relevant laws. Short courses in specialist areas such as court procedures, housing law or bankruptcy are available.

NVQs/SVQs Levels 2–4 in Advice and Guidance are available. The Money Advice Trust and the Citizens Advice Bureau also provide training courses for debt counsellors.

Additional skills such as advising/counselling, communication, information handling, ICT, managing money and general numeracy skills, problem solving and working with others are also highly valued.

Money guide

On entry, debt counsellors can expect to earn around £17,000–£18,000 per year.

Earnings can rise to £25,000 with experience of casework.

£28,500 is an average salary for senior posts. Some self-employed debt counsellors with lots of experience can earn up to £30,000.

Related opportunities

- Accountant p16
- Financial Adviser p39
- Counsellor p571
- Welfare Benefits Adviser/Welfare Rights Caseworker p590

Further information

Citizens Advice Bureau
Myddelton House, 115–123 Pentonville Road, London N1 9LZ
020 7833 2181; www.citizensadvice.org.uk

Advice UK
12th Floor, 2 London Bridge House, 25 London Bridge Street, London SE1 9ST
020 7407 4070; www.adviceuk.org.uk

Financial Services Skills Council
51 Gresham Street, London EC2V 7HQ
0845 257 3772; www.fssc.org.uk

Social Work and Counselling Services

CRCI: V
CLCI: KEZ

EDUCATIONAL PSYCHOLOGIST

What the work involves

- You will work with children with social, behavioural or learning difficulties to assess their progress and their academic and emotional needs.

- You will give help and guidance, and design activities which will help them to learn.

- Your work will also involve working closely with parents and teaching professionals to broaden their understanding of the psychological needs and difficulties that children face.

- You will carry out research and keep completely up to date with new government policies and measures that have been brought in with regard to assessing a child's psychological progression.

The type of person suited to this work

You should be someone who enjoys working closely with children and accept that your work is going to involve working with those who are finding school difficult and may not be very receptive to your help and efforts.

Working with children and adults alike, you should be very good at communicating on all levels. You should make sure that you are good at explaining procedures and assessment methods in a way that is easy to understand.

You need administrative and ICT skills for writing reports and analyses, and presenting information.

Working conditions

You will spend a lot of your time in schools and colleges but also around half your time will be spent writing reports and assessing your findings in an office.

You will run training sessions for parents and teachers as well as attend meetings in the evenings.

You will probably have to travel between different locations, so a driving licence is useful.

You are likely to be employed by the local authorities but there are also opportunities to work for private organisations and to do volunteer work.

Future prospects

Most educational psychologists work for local authorities but an increasing number are self-employed as independent consultants. You will be more restricted in the way you can progress whilst working for a local authority as there are only a certain number of positions you can work up to. However, being an independent consultant will give you a lot more opportunities to branch into different areas of psychology. One other area that is closely linked to educational psychology is occupational psychology so you may find this is a sector you would like to transfer into.

Advantages/disadvantages

The work is varied, interesting and challenging.

Qualifications and courses

Entrants must be graduates with Graduate Basis for Registration (GBR) with the British Psychological Society (BPS).

GBR can be obtained by taking a BPS-accredited degree in psychology or a non-accredited degree plus a conversion course.

For entry to a degree course, you will need 2 A levels/3 H grades (A–C) including mathematics.

Since 2006, additional postgraduate training is required to qualify as an educational psychologist. In order to be accepted onto this course you should demonstrate that you have a lot of work experience in the field of educational psychology. This may be in the form of working with children and young people in a variety of settings from schools to health centres. You will also have to have achieved a 2.1 at degree level or higher.

Working with difficult children can be stressful and hard work.

You will have a lot of recording and administrative follow-up work to do.

Parents may not be willing to accept that their child has a psychological problem so may be difficult to work with.

Money guide

As a graduate trainee in the NHS expect around £26,500 per year - depending on the kind of work you do.

£50,000+ is possible in a senior post.

You will be paid an additional allowance if you work in or around London and salaries throughout the country will vary.

Related opportunities

- Youth and Community Worker p591
- Personal Adviser – Connexions p579
- Health Psychologist/Clinical Psychologist p570
- Counsellor p571

Further information

Educational Psychology Postgraduate Grant Scheme
Local Government Employers, Local Government House (Formerly known as Transport House), Smith Square, London SW1P 3HZ
020 7187 7373; info@lge.gov.uk; www.lge.gov.uk

Children's Workforce Development Council (CWDC)
2nd Floor, City Exchange, 11 Albion Street, LEEDS LS1 5ES
0113 244 6311; www.cwdcouncil.org.uk

The British Psychological Society
St Andrews House, 48 Princess Road East, Leicester LE1 7DR
0116 254 9568; enquiries@bps.org.uk;www.bps.org.uk

FORENSIC PSYCHOLOGIST

What the work involves

- You will apply psychology to the criminal and civil justice systems.

- Your job will involve direct contact with offenders to carry out assessments and you may design programmes to help in their rehabilitation.

- You may be required to present your findings on a criminal case in court.

- Your work will also include carrying out detailed research on what provokes people to carry out crimes and analyse their behavioural patterns and personality traits.

The type of person suited to this work

You should have brilliant communication skills and be able to work with people from a wide variety of backgrounds.

You must be prepared to work with criminals and be enthusiastic about helping them during their rehabilitation process.

You should not be a judgmental person and hold no prejudice against the people you are working with even if they have committed an awful crime.

You should be very good at reading people's unconscious behaviour and take detailed notes of your findings to present in reports.

Working conditions

You will spend a lot of time working in prisons, secure hospitals, police stations and mental health rehabilitation units.

You may be employed by a variety of organisations; from the NHS to Her Majesty's Prison Service to the Police Service.

Work will typically be a 37 hour week from Monday to Friday but flexible work is available. You will also find that evening and weekend work is expected of you.

If you are working in a prison you will need to become adjusted to the conditions and regulations.

Future prospects

If you achieve chartered status as a forensic psychologist there may be the opportunity to progress to a senior role. In this position you may be in charge of a complete rehabilitation scheme for a certain type of offender. You will have the possibility to work for a consultancy once you have built up enough experience. As this is a fairly new and emerging sector, there are many new opportunities to progress and branch into different areas of psychology and forensics once you have some experience behind you.

Advantages/disadvantages

You may find yourself working with people who have committed very serious crimes which can be distressing.

Qualifications and courses

Entrants must be graduates with Graduate Basis for Registration (GBR) with the British Psychological Society (BPS).

GBR can be obtained by taking a BPS-accredited degree in psychology or a non-accredited degree plus a conversion course.

Additional postgraduate training is usually required to qualify in a specialist area.

For entry to a degree course, you will need 2 A levels/3 H grades (A–C) including mathematics.

A BPS-accredited MSc or diploma in Forensic Psychology, followed by at least 2 years' supervised practice, are prerequisites for qualified status.

Helping to rehabilitate offenders back into society can be immensely rewarding.

As this is a fairly new sector you will be learning new things all the time which will make the job exciting and fulfilling.

Money guide

As a psychological assistant you can expect to start on £14,000 and there is the opportunity to receive a local pay allowance (from £1,000 to £4,000) for prisons. As a trainee in this sector, you can expect to start on £17,000–£20,000 which will increase to around £25,000–£40,000 with experience as a chartered forensic psychologist.

Senior position salaries can reach over £60,000 after 10–15 years experience.

Related opportunities

- Clinical Psychologist/Health Psychologist p570
- Probation Officer p580
- Counsellor p571
- Forensic Computer Analyst p547

Further information

HM Prison Service
Parliamentary, Correspondence and Briefing Unit,
HM Prison Service Headquarters, Cleland House,
Page Street, London SW1P 4LN
www.hmprisonservice.gov.uk

Division of Forensic Psychologists
The British Psychological Society, St Andrews House,
48 Princess Road East, Leicester LE1 7DR
0116 254 9568; enquiries@bps.org.uk;
www.bps.org.uk/dfp

National Probation Service
1st Floor Abell House, John Islip Street, London SW1P 4LH
www.probation.homeoffice.gov.uk

FUNDRAISER

What the work involves

- Your job will be to initiate and organise fundraising activities for your charity – from publicly-sponsored events to membership schemes with various benefits, besides corporate sponsorship.

- You will represent your charity at public events, such as dinners, giving talks to possible sponsors.

- There is administration and report writing – possibly, managing other staff and volunteers.

- You will prepare publicity material and liaise with broadcasters, the press and other media, keeping your charity in the public eye.

The type of person suited to this work

As you will deal with people in every strata of society, it's important to get on with all types. Good spoken communication is essential to persuade people to support your charity; also, you will need confidence to speak engagingly in public.

People need to be persuaded to support your charity and it will require good negotiating skills and excellent writing skills to produce persuasive publicity material. You will have to be imaginative and creative to come up with novel fundraising ideas.

You will need to be able to organise your time and workload so you can keep running costs down to a minimum and save money for your charity.

Working conditions

You will normally be based in an office working on a computer, but you can be home-based, particularly if you work for a very small charity.

There may be pressure to hit deadlines for organising events and/or fundraising targets to meet.

You will travel fairly widely so a driving licence is useful.

You may spend time outdoors at fundraising activities.

Future prospects

It is not usual to become a charity fundraiser straight from school – most entrants have experience in sales or marketing and voluntary fundraising. Most jobs are with charities, pressure groups and non-profit-making organisations, including hospitals.

It may be necessary to move around – possibly to larger organisations – to progress your career. With experience you could move into management, become self-employed or offer consultancy advice.

Advantages/disadvantages

There is office work plus talking to individuals and groups – sometimes, answering tough questions.

Qualifications and courses

There are no specific entry requirements for this work although you will need a good all-round background education and an interest in politics and social affairs. Many entrants are graduates and/or people with experience in marketing, sales or in working for other charities. Voluntary fundraising experience is useful.

Large charities, such as Cancer Research UK, offer training schemes for entrants, while others, including Oxfam, run unpaid internships. Competition for places is fierce.

The Institute of Fundraising runs an introductory course for charity fundraisers and a Certificate in Fundraising Management, equivalent to NVQ/SVQ Level 4, for experienced fundraisers. Short courses for people working as fundraisers/fundraising managers are also available.

Skills in communication, information handling and ICT, money management and general numeracy, organising and supervision or leadership, plus an ability to work with others, are also required.

You will get satisfaction from seeing your charity flourish, delivering positive outcomes.

People who do not support your charity can be unpleasant.

You will work evenings and weekends.

Money guide

Your starting salary will be around £18,500, rising to £22,000 per year, depending on the charity.

With experience and managerial responsibilities, you could be earning £25,000–£30,000.

Senior managers in large charities can earn between £35,000 and £60,000.

Related opportunities

- Advertising Account Executive p406
- Public Relations Executive p425
- Marketing Manager/Assistant/Executive p417
- Events and Exhibition Organiser p389

Further information

Institute of Fundraising
Market Towers, 1 Nine Elms Lane, London SW8 9NQ
020 7627 3436; www.institute-of-fundraising.org.uk

Association of Chief Executives of Voluntary Organisations
83 Victoria Street, London SW1H 0HW
0845 345 8481; www.acevo.org.uk

Directory of Social Change
24 Stephenson Way, London NW1 2DP
020 7391 4800; www.dsc.org.uk

Social Work and Counselling Services

CRCI: V
CLCI: KEM

HEALTHCARE ASSISTANT

What the work involves

- Your clients could be children, elderly people or people with disabilities living in residential healthcare or in their own homes.

- Healthcare assistants help people who find it difficult to look after themselves with everyday tasks.

- You will help individuals to bath, perhaps changing dressings, and to use the toilet or commode, and help with eating, washing, ironing, cleaning and shopping.

- Part of your time will be spent talking to clients, helping them to write letters, budget their money or pay bills.

The type of person suited to this work

As the job involves working with people who need individual support, you will have to work out what help they need and provide it in a sympathetic and tactful way. Healthcare assistants need to be cheerful, outgoing and friendly, as their clients may be lonely or depressed.

The job usually involves domestic work so you need to be happy and skilled at doing housework and laundry.

Helping with handling money, and writing and reading personal and business letters, is work that must remain confidential, so healthcare assistants need to be very trustworthy and discreet, able to keep clients' personal information private.

Working conditions

Most of your work is indoors but you may go out with people, for example to hospital appointments or on outings. You may have to live in for some jobs.

You need to be physically fit to help people who are unable to move around for themselves, and there could be heavy lifting.

You will be expected to be very careful about health and safety issues, such as fire and hot water.

Future prospects

There are over a million healthcare assistants in the UK and demand is increasing. Many healthcare assistants work in residential homes and day-healthcare centres, but more people are being cared for in their own homes. The main employers are health authorities, social services, private homes and voluntary agencies.

Promotion depends on qualifications and experience. With experience in healthcare work, you could train for related jobs such as social work or nursing.

Advantages/disadvantages

The work can be very satisfying but, occasionally, you may find that people are very demanding and not always pleasant.

You may have to work shifts, evenings, weekends and public holidays, including Christmas Day.

Some jobs can be messy and unpleasant.

Qualifications and courses

There are no fixed entry qualifications for this job.

Previous experience, for example in voluntary work and/or an NVQ/SVQ in Healthcare at Level 2 is useful, and may be required by some employers.

You can study a range of relevant courses full-time at school or college, prior to entry. The First Diploma in Caring and Intermediate GNVQ in Health and Social Healthcare are 1-year courses that do not require particular qualifications, although institutions may ask for some GCSEs/S grades. The National Diploma in Healthcare and A level in Health and Social Healthcare are 2-year courses, and usually require 4 GCSEs/S grades (A–C/1–3) or a BTEC First Diploma.

Most training is work-based, and Healthcare assistants can work towards NVQs/SVQs in Healthcare at Levels 1–3.

Healthcare Assistants must have good interpersonal skills and have practical, physical and domestic abilities.

Healthcare assistants are required to be at least 18 years old.

Money guide

Salaries are around £11,500–£14,300 per year at entry. With experience and qualifications you could get up to £17,500.

You can earn £17,000+ in a residential post.

Salaries can rise to £22,000 in a senior post.

Managers can earn up to £30,000 in some locations.

You will be paid more for shift work and unsocial hours, i.e. for working late hours or providing overnight healthcare.

Related opportunities

- Childminder p569
- Adult Nurse p293
- Children's Nurse p298
- Early Years Specialist/Nursery Worker p202
- Social Worker p585

Further information

General Social Care Council
Goldings House, 2 Hays Lane, London SE1 2HB
020 7397 5100; www.gscc.org.uk

NHS Careers
0845 60 60 655; www.nhscareers.nhs.uk

www.cityandguilds.com/myperfectjob

CRCI: JI
CLCI: KEB

Social Work and Counselling Services

LIFE COACH

What the work involves

- You will help people – independent clients or employees – to recognise and develop their special attributes and skills.

- You will coach individuals to become more successful in career matters, financial affairs or personal relationships.

- Using empathy and exceptional listening skills, you will establish a warm, personal yet professional relationship with clients.

- With your client, you will enter cycles of agreement and commitment; later you will review and revise the action plans you have created.

The type of person suited to this work

Once a bond of trust is established – that you are non-judgemental and hold personal information in strictest confidence – individuals will reveal their present feelings and frustrations, their future ambitions and their perceived restrictions to progress.

Besides integrity and discretion, life coaches need excellent interpersonal skills, patience and perseverance to allow clients the time to set themselves goals for change.

You will get satisfaction from seeing people fulfil their potential. Life coaching takes clarity of thought and firmness of purpose. You may need to overcome an inherent inertia (lack of drive to change) in your clients to get them to make progress!

Working conditions

You will agree timetables with clients for coaching sessions and hold one-to-ones at their work-base or in a neutral location. Later sessions are often by phone or email. Many life coaches work with busy, highly successful chief executives, usually outside normal business hours.

Coaching sessions can be weekly, fortnightly or monthly; the frequency may change.

Future prospects

Life coaching is a relatively new field, but interest has increased as more attention is paid to developing the whole person – both within and outside the workplace. A life coach can help to refocus individuals' goals and aspirations, improving work–life balance and job satisfaction, boosting productivity and creating good teamwork. All these factors can help companies with staff retention.

Life coaches work as independent consultants or for business consultancy agencies.

Advantages/disadvantages

There is great satisfaction in observing changes in your clients.

Qualifications and courses

ENTRY LEVEL 3

Although there are no specific requirements to enter this area of work, you need to have gained a great deal of life experience and to have tasted many different approaches to conducting business and managing an organisation's workforce performance and delivery.

A degree in human resources work, organisations and structures, sociology or psychology would be helpful startpoints. For entry to a degree course, you need a minimum of 5 GCSEs/S grades at A–C/1–3, plus 2 or 3 A levels/H grades with an emphasis on the humanities.

There are a number of private agencies and academies offering training in life coaching, for example the Coaching Academy, where you can take a 2-day fast-track course by distance learning to focus on corporate or individual (personal performance) life coaching.

It is possible to take a longer diploma course in life coaching.

If clients fail to implement action plans, it can be dispiriting and frustrating.

You may have long-term coaching relationships with clients – who want to work on different aspects of their lives.

Money guide

Life coaches earn an agreed sessional rate.

Working for an agency, you can earn around £30 per session plus expenses. Hourly rates for private clients could be £40–£100+ for a coaching session lasting an hour.

It is possible to earn the full-time equivalent income of between £18,000 and £24,000.

Life coaches who become well-known and sought out can charge higher fees for periods of life coaching lasting 6 months or longer.

Related opportunities

- Careers Adviser p568
- Counsellor p571
- Personal Adviser – Connexions p579
- Social Worker p585

Further information

Coaching Academy
0800 783 4823; www.the-coaching-academy.com

New Insights
Brightwire House, 114a Church Road, Hove, East Sussex BN3 2EB
0845 094 0212; www.life-coach-training-uk.com

Social Work and Counselling Services

CRCI: V
CLCI: KEZ

OCCUPATIONAL PSYCHOLOGIST

What the work involves

- You will explore how organisations function and how people behave at work to improve an organisation's efficiency and employees' job satisfaction.

- You will help managers plan how they recruit and train staff, and advise on matters concerning communication between individuals in the workplace, the most effective working environment and coping with change.

- Part of your job may involve helping to recruit the right person for a particular role as well as offering support to those facing redundancy.

- You will also be working with bosses and managers to help them to understand the psychological needs of their staff so that they can maintain a stress-free environment for their staff as much as possible.

The type of person suited to this work

You should have a great interest in how organisations function and what makes people tick in the workplace. You should be comfortable working with adults and also be happy to help them progress professionally. You must be a brilliant communicator and it will also be very useful for you to have strong business skills because you will have been employed to improve the overall efficiency of a company. Your personal safety awareness should be very good as well.

Working conditions

Much of your work will take place in offices and businesses of the companies you are working for. This may involve working by yourself or as part of a team. You can expect to work around 37 hours a week from Monday to Friday but you may run or attend courses that require you to travel away and stay overnight in places. There is the opportunity to be self-employed but this is often after working for an organisation and building up your work experience.

Future prospects

Occupational psychologists work in large companies in the public and private sectors. They can work with government and public services as private consultants. Some specialise in a certain area, for example ergonomics (the interaction of people with where they work), or health and safety – studying the causes of accidents and how to prevent them.

Once you have progressed to a senior role you may set up your own consultancy.

Advantages/disadvantages

Your work will really make a difference to people's day to day lives at work which will be very rewarding.

You may be working with unmotivated or stressed individuals.

You may find that bosses are not willing to take on your advice for their staff.

Qualifications and courses

Entrants must be graduates with Graduate Basis for Registration (GBR) with the British Psychological Society (BPS).

GBR can be obtained by taking a BPS-accredited degree in psychology or a non-accredited degree plus a conversion course.

Additional postgraduate training is usually required to qualify in a specialist area.

For entry to a degree course, you will need 2 A levels/3 H grades (A–C) including mathematics.

Psychology graduates need to gain an accredited MSc followed by 2 years of supervised practice, or 3 years' supervised practice and the BPS Postgraduate Certificate in Occupational Psychology to become fully qualified.

If you want to achieve Chartered Occupational Psychologist status you will have to complete stage two of the Qualification in Occupational Psychology. One way to do this is with the BPS or alternatively you can keep a log book of your work carried out under the supervision of a qualified chartered occupational psychologist which demonstrates your progression and the knowledge that you have built up. This will then be assessed by the Division of Occupational Psychology who will decide whether to award you chartered status.

Money guide

As a trainee occupational psychologist you can earn around £18,000 as your starting salary. This can progress to around £55,000 with experience in a senior position. Salaries vary in the private sector but senior positions can carry a £70,000+ salary.

Related opportunities

- Personal Adviser – Connexions p579
- Educational Psychologist p573
- Health and Safety Inspector p40
- Recruitment/Employment Agency Consultant p582

Further information

Association of Business Psychologists
211/212 Piccadilly, London W1J 9HG
0207 917 1733; www.theabp.org.uk

The Health Professions Council
Park House, 184 Kennington Park Road, London SE11 4BU
020 7582 0866; www.hpc-uk.org

Occupational Psychology Services
Townsend Chambers, Riverhead, Sevenoaks, Kent TN13 2EL
0845 50 50 181; 01732 742 544; www.opsltd.com

PERSONAL ADVISER – CONNEXIONS

What the work involves

- You will provide information, advice and guidance to young people in England aged 13–19 on their options in learning, personal development and future careers.

- You will work with young people whose circumstances prevent them making the best of their opportunities.

- With schools/colleges, training providers and employers, you will help design programmes to meet individuals' learning needs.

- Being a personal adviser also involves interaction with parents/carers and a range of other support agency professionals.

The type of person suited to this work

It is important to be able to gain young people's trust and confidence. Excellent communication skills are needed to talk with them, listening carefully to what they say.

You need to have a flexible approach and an ability to adapt quickly to unexpected situations. The job involves dealing with many different types of people. Patience and tolerance are vital since people develop in different ways. You must be non-judgemental, as you may not always agree with your clients, yet need to forge close links of trust.

The work involves administration and negotiation with other agencies, so report writing, ICT and communication skills are required.

Working conditions

You could be based in a school, college, Connexions centre or Connexions information resource area. You may meet clients in their home or a neutral setting such as a café.

You will travel locally to visit employers, young people you work with and representatives from other agencies working with young people. A driving licence and car are useful.

Work could include some evenings and occasional weekends.

Future prospects

Most entrants are at least 21 and have previous experience working with young people, through either voluntary or paid work. The Connexions service only operates in England.

Some personal advisers specialise in supporting a small number of young people with severe problems over a long period of time, while others work with a larger group over shorter periods. There is a promotion structure within Connexions, based on qualifications and experience.

Advantages/disadvantages

The work will be interesting and varied and bring you into contact with many different people.

You will find it satisfying to see young people moving on.

Some people may be unpleasant and difficult.

You might have to work some evenings.

Qualifications and courses

Many entrants to this work already hold the NVQ/SVQ Level 4 in Advice and Guidance, the professional qualification for careers advisers. To qualify as a personal adviser, they must then complete the Diploma for Connexions Personal Advisers or the Understanding Connexions Training Programme. Usually, the training programmes can be attended by day release, followed up with recording information, research and data analysis, and short theses based on your job.

It is also possible to enter without the NVQ/SVQ Level 4 and work as a probationary personal adviser. You can become fully qualified by working towards the Diploma for Connexions Personal Advisers and the NVQ/SVQ.

Both the Diploma and the Understanding Connexions Training Programme are accredited by universities.

You need to be endorsed by a Connexions Partnership and vetted to work with young people.

Other Key Skills are advising and counselling, communication, information handling and working with others.

Money guide

Expect to earn between £18,000 and £20,000 per year while training.

When qualified you can get £22,500–£28,000.

Earnings can rise from £29,000–£35,000 with 5–10 years' experience, plus a specialism and team leader or managerial responsibility.

You may receive an additional cost of living allowance if you work in and around London.

Related opportunities

- Counsellor p571
- Recruitment/Employment Agency Consultant p582
- Welfare Benefits Adviser/Welfare Rights Caseworker p590
- Primary and Secondary Teacher p212
- Youth and Community Worker p591

Further information

Connexions Service National Unit
Department for Children, Schools and Families, Moorfoot, Sheffield S1 4PP
0114 259 1283; www.connexions.gov.uk

Institute of Careers Guidance (ICG)
Third Floor, Copthall House, 1 New Road, Stourbridge, West Midlands DY8 1PH
01384 376464; http://www.icg-uk.org/

Department for Children, Schools and Families
Sanctuary Buildings, Great Smith Street, London SW1P 3BT
0870 000 2288; http://www.dcsf.gov.uk/

Social Work and Counselling Services

CRCI: V
CLCI: KED/KEG

PROBATION OFFICER

What the work involves

- You will spend time interviewing offenders to provide courts with pre-sentence reports offering guidance on the kind of sentence the court should consider.

- Working on a regular basis with offenders, you will ensure court orders are carried out and try to help your clients not to re-offend.

- You will work closely with other agencies to solve practical problems that offenders have in obtaining work, benefits, housing, etc.

- You may also work with victims of crime, helping them recover from the experience.

The type of person suited to this work

As you may work with particular offenders over a period of time, it is important to gain their trust and confidence so that you can help them. You will need to be able to cope under pressure when dealing with offenders who are non-compliant or aggressive.

You will work with people of all ages and backgrounds, from colleagues to clients; this means you will need good speaking, listening and negotiating skills. It is important to be able to get on with all types of people.

A good knowledge of the criminal justice system is essential, as is the ability to research information and write clear, concise reports.

Working conditions

You will be based in an office but will move around to interview clients in prison or in their homes.

Much of your time will be spent in court, presenting pre-sentence reports and dealing with offenders once they are sentenced. Also, you will prepare reports and contribute to risk assessments for scrutiny by the Parole Board.

You may travel quite a bit locally, so a driving licence is useful.

Future prospects

In England and Wales, probation officers work for the National Probation Service. Crown Courts and some larger Magistrates' Courts have a probation team attached to them. There is a great need for new probation officers across England and Wales. In Scotland, the work is carried out by the Criminal Justice Team in local authority social work services. Court Teams are attached to the Sheriff and High Courts.

Promotion to senior grades is possible but management posts mean less contact with clients

Advantages/disadvantages

The work is varied, challenging and never dull.

You will get satisfaction from helping people stay out of trouble.

A considerable amount of time is spent preparing court reports.

You may find it hard to remain impartial.

Qualifications and courses

To qualify as a probation officer in England and Wales you will need a Diploma in Probation Studies (DipPS). Trainees are employed by individual probation services and follow a 2-year integrated course combining an NVQ Level 4 in Community Justice with a degree in Community Justice (Probation Studies). The minimum age to start the DipPS is 22.

As a general guideline, the following qualifications are needed: candidates under 21 – 2 A levels and 3 GCSEs (A–C) or 3 A levels and 1 GCSE (A–C); candidates aged 21–25 – 5 GCSEs (A–C); candidates over 25 – formal qualifications may not be required but the recruitment and selection process includes written exercises designed to test the applicant's ability to study at a higher education level.

In Scotland, trainees are required to be at least 22 and to hold a degree in social work.

Other useful attributes include skills in advising or counselling work, communication, ICT and information handling, supervision and management, plus experience in working with others.

You will be on call at weekends – on a rota basis.

Money guide

Expect around £17,000–£19,500 per year while training.

Your salary will rise to between £25,500–£30,000 when qualified and with experience.

Earnings can go up to around £38,000+ as a chief probation officer.

In Scotland, criminal justice social workers earn around £22,000–£27,500.

Related opportunities

- Careers Adviser p568
- Counsellor p571
- Education Welfare Officer p205
- Social Worker p585
- Solicitor/Notary Public p384

Further information

National Probation Directorate
Home Office, Horseferry House, Dean Ryle Street, London SW1 2AW
020 7217 0659, www.homeoffice.gsi.gov.uk

National Association of Probation Officers
4 Chivalry Road, London SW11 1HT
020 7223 4887; www.napo.org.uk

Scottish Social Services Council
Compass House, 11 Riverside Drive, Dundee DD1 4NY
01382 207101; www.sssc.uk.com

PSYCHOANALYST/ PSYCHOTHERAPIST

What the work involves

- Psychoanalysts and psychotherapists are concerned with helping patients to explore their unconscious feelings and emotions in order to remove conscious symptoms or problems.

- You will have to build strong relationships with your patients over long periods of time, guiding them through stressful and upsetting occurrences and emotions.

- You will work with patients on a one-to-one basis in order to begin to understand the effect these are having on their everyday life.

The type of person suited to this work

You will need excellent communication skills, in particular the ability to listen to and observe your patients closely.

You must be open-minded and professional at all times, especially when patients are describing and dealing with unpleasant and distressing experiences. Alongside compassion for your patients, you must also be able to detach yourself from work related issues at the end of each day.

Self-awareness is also essential, and you will be required to undergo analysis yourself prior to qualifying.

Working conditions

The majority of psychoanalysts and psychotherapists are self-employed and work in private practice. The number of hours they work depends on the number of patients they have or wish to see.

Because of the intense nature of the work, many psychoanalysts choose to work part time and may work in other areas, related or otherwise, for the rest of the week. You will usually work from an office, although it will be more comfortably equipped than most. Patients usually sit on a comfortable chair or couch, with the psychoanalyst sitting slightly behind them.

Future prospects

Psychoanalysts work mainly in London and the surrounding areas, although there should be demand for such a service throughout the UK.

With experience, you could specialise in a particular area such as child or criminal psychoanalysis. Other professionals choose to move into a teaching role within their discipline.

You will be required to do continuing professional development (CPD) throughout your career in order to extend your understanding of psychoanalysis and keep up-to-date with any new developments in theory or practice.

Qualifications and courses

Applicants who wish to train in psychoanalysis must have a first degree. Most degree courses expect applicants to hold at least 2 A-levels and 5 GCSEs (A-C) or equivalent, although alternative qualifications gained from BTEC Nationals and Access courses may also be accepted.

The training course undertaken by candidates wishing to qualify as a psychoanalyst or psychotherapist is part time and takes at least 4 years to complete. At the moment, the only courses in the UK approved by the International Psychoanalytical Association (IPA) are those offered by the British Psychoanalytic Association (BPA) and the Institute of Psychoanalysis.

The training programme consists of 3 elements: personal psychoanalysis; theoretical and clinical seminars; psychoanalysis of patients under supervision. On successful completion of these areas, you will become a member of the IPA, and be eligible to become an associate member of the British Psychoanalytical Society or the British Psychoanalytical Association.

Advantages/disadvantages

Working with a patient towards achieving an end to physical symptoms or emotional issues is demanding but rewarding work.

You may uncover extremely upsetting and unpleasant issues in your patients, which can be distressing and difficult to deal with in a professional manner.

Money guide

Salaries vary according to the number of hours worked and the location in which each professional operates. Generally, newly qualified psychoanalysts/psychotherapists can earn about £40,000. With further experience, this should rise to around £50,000. Experienced psychoanalysts, who have built up a good reputation and practice, can earn £60,000+.

Related opportunities

- Psychiatrist p338
- Counsellor p571

Further information

British Association of Psychotherapists (BAP)
020 8452 9823; www.bap-psychotherapy.org

International Psychoanalytical Association (IPA)
020 8446 8324; www.ipa.org.uk; ipa@ipa.org.uk

The British Psychoanalytical Society and the Institute of Psychoanalysis
020 7563 5000; www.psychoanalysis.org.uk

ENTRY **5** LEVEL

Social Work and Counselling Services

CRCI: V
CLCI: KEL

RECRUITMENT CENTRE CONSULTANT

What the work involves

- You will interview people looking for jobs to investigate their skills and interests, matching individuals with suitable vacancies.

- Part of the work could be giving aptitude tests to clients to explore their skills needs and to suggest suitable training.

- Working with employers, you will make contact to ask about their organisations' skills needs, encouraging them to use the agency's services.

- You will help employers draw up job descriptions and may also draft adverts for your agency.

The type of person suited to this work

To discuss individuals' job requirements and potential, you will need good speaking and listening skills. Also, you will have to gain people's confidence and put them at ease. There is administrative work and record-keeping, so good writing and ICT skills are useful.

You will need a sensitive, mature attitude to work with job seekers who are anxious about their prospects.

Some job vacancies placed with your agency may need to be filled quickly, so you will need to be flexible, adaptable and able to cope under pressure.

Working conditions

You will be based in an employment centre, usually in a town centre. You will work normal office hours, but expect to work evenings and weekends if there is an unusually large contract. Most agencies have 'shop front' premises open to job-seekers.

You may travel to visit employers, so a driving licence is useful.

You will need to be smartly dressed and well groomed at all times.

Future prospects

There are over 16,000 employment agencies in the UK, mainly in towns and cities. Many are around London. Most entrants have experience in areas such as retail and sales, personnel or administrative work. More agencies are specialising in particular sectors of employment.

You would normally start as a trainee consultant and progress with your existing employer. Larger agencies have more clearly defined promotion structures. Some people become self-employed or move into other areas such as personnel and sales.

Advantages/disadvantages

The work brings you into contact with a range of employers and jobseekers, which can be interesting.

Qualifications and courses

ENTRY LEVEL 3

There are no specific entry qualifications for this work, and entrants come from a variety of backgrounds.

Often, entrants to this job have previous experience in personnel, sales or administration.

Employers may recruit graduates to trainee recruitment consultant positions. No specific degree subject is required.

Trainee consultants receive training on the job, with larger agencies running their own internal training. The Recruitment and Employment Confederation (REC) offer courses which cover topics such as essential legislation, candidate management and recruitment processes. It may also be possible to study for an NVQ/SVQ at Level 3 in Recruitment.

You will get satisfaction from helping job-seekers and employers.

You could work awkward hours in an agency specialising in jobs such as transport and distribution or nursing.

Some people can be difficult to deal with.

Money guide

Expect around £16,500+ a year upon entry.

Pay rises to between £17,500 and £23,000 with 2–3 years' experience.

It is possible to reach a salary of £40,000 in large, prestigious agencies.

Many agencies will pay commission based on how many positions you succeed in filling and how many jobs/contracts you bring to the agency.

Related opportunities

- Careers Adviser p568
- Human Resources/Personnel Officer p41
- Personal Adviser – Connexions p579
- Business Adviser p24

Further information

Recruitment and Employment Confederation
36–38 Mortimer Street, London W1W 7RG
020 7462 3260; www.rec.uk.com

Chartered Institute of Personnel and Development
CIPD House, 151 The Broadway, London SW19 1JQ
020 8971 9000; www.cipd.co.uk

Employment National Training Organisation (ENTO)
4th Floor, Kimberley House, 47 Vaughan Way,
Leicester LE1 4SG
0116 251 7979; www.ento.co.uk

Social Work and Counselling Services

CRCI: AA
CLCI: KED

REHABILITATION OFFICER – VISUALLY IMPAIRED

What the work involves

- You will visit blind and partially sighted people to explore the help they need to keep their independence, and then organise that support.

- A major part of your job will be showing your clients how to perform day-to-day tasks, such as cooking, as well as help with paperwork, sorting out benefits and finance.

- In addition, you will provide training in mobility – walking with a white cane and making journeys by public transport.

- Your role will be to provide ongoing support, to involve them in social activities.

The type of person suited to this work

As the work often involves dealing with people coming to terms with sight loss, you will need to be sympathetic, patient and understanding. Also, you will need to be a good listener because people may unburden themselves on you. Tact is essential when dealing with carers and families who may be over-protective.

You will be in contact with many different people and agencies, so you will need to get on with all sorts of people. There is a lot of report writing which needs good writing and ICT skills.

Clear decision making is needed to determine the best way to help, plus good organisational skills to manage your time and workload.

Working conditions

You will be based in an office but will spend most of your time visiting clients in their own homes. You may have to travel widely in your area, so a driving licence is useful.

You may accompany clients on outings and to appointments.

Future prospects

Most jobs are with local authority social work departments, statutory and voluntary agencies and schools and colleges providing specialist services for people with visual impairment.

There are few jobs and you may have to move to work, and to broaden your experience later in your career.

Prospects for promotion are limited. It is possible to retrain for jobs such as careers adviser, personal adviser (Connexions) or social work.

Advantages/disadvantages

The work is challenging and each case requires individual consideration.

It is very satisfying seeing people keep their independence and adjust to sight loss.

Qualifications and courses

To work as a mobility/rehabilitation officer for the visually impaired within social services, you will need the Diploma of Higher Education (DipHE) in Rehabilitation (Visual Impairment). The course is a 2-year distance-learning programme via Birmingham City University and comprises specialist modules at certificate, diploma and degree level.

You will be required to undertake an 80-day placement with a statutory or voluntary agency in the second year of the course.

Candidates must be at least 18, preferably with some experience of care work. Entry requirements usually include GCSEs/S grades in English and maths (A–C/1–3) and A levels/H grades or BTEC National Diplomas. Entry for mature candidates is flexible but they must be able to demonstrate that they can already study at A level/H grade.

In addition, employers will look for skills in counselling, caring for people, communication, organisation and working with others.

The job may be emotionally demanding and you will need to remain impartial.

Some clients may be reluctant to accept help.

Money guide

Mobility officers are paid between £18,600–£24,200 per year on entry, depending on their experience.

You may earn rather less if you work for a voluntary organisation: around £12,500-£15,000 annually.

Salaries for trained rehabilitation officers can rise to £27,000, with qualifications and experience.

A disability adviser can expect to earn up to £35,000 a year with promotion to a team leader post, but these opportunities are limited.

Related opportunities

- Careers Adviser p568
- Counselling Work p571
- Personal Adviser - Connexions p579
- Social Worker p585
- Healthcare Assistant p576

Further information

Royal National Institute of the Blind (RNIB)
105 Judd Street, London WC1H 9NE
0845 702 3153; www.rnib.org.uk

Skills for Care and Development
2nd Floor, City Exchange, 11 Albion Street, Leeds LS1 5ER
0113 390 7666; www.skillsforcareanddevelopment.org.uk

Social Work and Counselling Services

CRCI: V
CLCI: KEB

RELIGIOUS LEADER

What the work involves

- Although exact duties vary across different religions, most leaders undertake the following tasks:

- Religious leaders conduct meetings/services/prayers, lead important ceremonies, and give people support, advice and guidance on numerous matters.

- You will play a key part in the local community, attending local events, focusing on the spiritual welfare of children, their parents/carers, the sick, the bereaved, etc, often paying home visits.

- You may also be consulted on points of faith or law, particularly if you are a Jewish rabbi, Anglican vicar, Muslim imam or Roman Catholic priest.

The type of person suited to this work

You will need to have dedication and strong belief, as well as a thorough understanding of your religion's values and traditions. If you are the leader for your faith in the community, you will be expected to discuss and defend your faith.

You will meet and deal with many different kinds of people so need excellent interpersonal skills. You must be sympathetic and discreet when dealing with personal confidences and sensitive issues.

You will also spend time researching information and preparing talks, and you may have to learn long passages by heart which requires a good memory.

Working conditions

Some of your work will be office-based, in your home or at your place of worship, but you may be expected to deliver or attend morning and evening worship.

You will travel locally a lot, so a driving licence may be useful.

You may spend time visiting people at home, in hospitals and in care homes, attending local meetings and events such as festivals and religious 'life cycle' events.

Many religions require particular forms of dress.

Future prospects

There are around 18 recognised religions in the UK. Each religion has a different structure and there is no set way of being promoted.

Most people become religious leaders after gaining substantial life experience. Young people of religious faith frequently do volunteering work, in this country or abroad, helping disadvantaged young and older people improve their lives through education, their own efforts and moral purpose.

You may travel to holy places or do missionary work, and work on an international level to promote peace and religious tolerance.

Advantages/disadvantages

This work provides variety and challenge.

Qualifications and courses

ENTRY LEVEL 4

There is no set route or standard entry requirements to become a religious worker, although a good general education is useful. The most important entry requirements are a strong belief in your faith and an active interest in its rules and traditions.

In a number of religions, there are restrictions on who can become a religious leader, particularly in terms of gender, although some barriers have come down.

Age is not a restriction to becoming a religious leader, and life experience, communicative ability and maturity can be the three most essential skills needed.

It is possible to study religion, divinity or theology at universities or colleges. Degree and diploma courses are available across the UK, but it is important to check carefully that the course is acceptable to your religion.

Each religion has a different way of training its religious leaders, and this will often involve attending a specialist school or college for several years.

You will meet many different types of people.

You will be on call 24 hours a day, seven days a week.

You may have to make lifestyle changes, for example not getting married or eating only certain foods.

Money guide

Religious leaders often work on a voluntary basis, with expenses to cover their costs.

Some faiths provide accommodation and use of a vehicle.

Stipends for those who are salaried start low at around £9,500 per year. When experienced, you may get £23,000.

Some people also have other paid employment.

Related opportunities

- Counsellor p571
- Education Welfare Officer p205
- Social Worker p585
- Primary and Secondary Teacher p212

Further information

INFORM (Information Network Focus on Religious Movements)
Houghton Street, London WC2A 2AE
020 7955 7654; www.inform.ac

Inter Faith Network
8A Lower Grosvenor Place, London SW1W 0EN
020 7931 7726; www.interfaith.org.uk

Churches Together in Britain and Ireland
3rd Floor, Bastille Court, 2 Paris Garden, London SE1 8ND
020 7654 7254; www.ctbi.org.uk

SOCIAL WORKER

What the work involves

Field social worker

- To help and support people at difficult times in their lives, you will assess people's needs, then plan and deliver a range of services to help them solve their problems.

- You will spend time listening to what they say, and may visit your clients at home to get a complete picture of their lives.

- Your work will be with health professionals, schools, the police, benefits agencies and the courts, depending on your clients, who could be of any stage of their lives and from any background.

- You will also attend meetings, conferences and perhaps court hearings, and prepare and write reports.

Residential social worker

- You will help people in residential care to be as independent as possible by caring for their physical needs and providing counselling, teaching and appropriate therapy.

- You will help clients to budget their money, you will probably have to sort out their benefits. This is all part of developing their personal and social skills.

- Your residents could be people of any age, many of whom may have physical disabilities, learning difficulties, or mental health or emotional problems.

- You will attend meetings and conferences, deal with administration and write reports.

The type of person suited to this work

Dealing with people and their problems requires being able to get on with a wide range of people and understand different attitudes and lifestyles. You need to have excellent communication skills to talk to people, listen to them and write reports.

You will have to have lots of patience as clients will not always be ready to accept your advice and support. You will need to be able to keep a clear head in very stressful situations.

Because social workers are bound by the law, you will have to be very thorough when checking and recording information to make sure you are completely up to date. This job requires people who are good time managers, to fit in all the administration work required by the courts, hospitals, etc.

Working conditions

Field social worker

Field social workers are office-based, but may move around between clients' homes, day centres, hospitals, health centres and the courts.

You could travel quite a lot, so a driving licence is useful.

Residential social worker

Residential social workers are based in residential establishments for children, the elderly or people with disabilities, but they do go out with their clients for outings and appointments, for example to a hospital.

The work can be physically tiring. Expect to work a basic 37-hour week, including weekend and evening shifts.

Future prospects

Field social worker

There are about 26,000 qualified field social workers in the UK and the demand is increasing. Main employers are local authority social services and the health service. Because social care covers so many areas, social workers are tending to specialise, for example in work with children, people with mental health problems or in criminal justice.

Residential social worker

Although recent trends are towards caring for people in their own homes, there is still a high demand for residential social workers. Main employers are local authorities, private nursing and residential homes, voluntary agencies and specialist employment agencies.

Social workers are generally at least in their twenties with social work qualifications and/or experience of care work. Social work offers many opportunities for training to achieve advanced qualifications. It is also possible to move into a range of caring careers with appropriate training, for example teaching, nursing or careers guidance. There is a clearly defined promotion path in the public sector and you will be able to widen your experience by transferring into different areas of work.

Advantages/disadvantages

The job is varied, interesting and challenging.

You will work with a wide range of people, one-to-one and in teams, and may work with a particular group of people over quite a long time.

You may be torn between what you would like to do to help and what you are allowed to do.

The job will often be very stressful and some people may be angry, difficult or even violent.

You may work evenings, weekends and public holidays.

Occasionally, as a field social worker, you have to be on call-out duty overnight.

Money guide

Field social worker

Pay is around £20,000 per year for a newly qualified field social worker. This rises to £29,500 with experience.

Social Work and Counselling Services

CRCI: V
CLCI: KEB

A yearly salary for a senior team leader post can be £33,000–£36,000. Senior social services managers can earn up to £50,000.

Residential social worker

There are no national pay scales for residential social workers; you could start at around £18,500 per year depending on the job, qualifications and experience.

You can progress to £28,000+, depending on qualifications, experience and responsibilities.

Related opportunities

- Counsellor p571
- Healthcare Assistant p576
- Youth and Community Worker p591

Further information

General Social Care Council
Goldings House, 2 Hays Lane, London SE1 2HB
020 7397 5100; www.gscc.org.uk

Northern Ireland Social Care Council
7th Floor, Millennium House, 19–25 Great Victoria Street, Belfast BT2 7AQ
028 9041 7600; www.niscc.info

Scottish Social Services Council
Compass House, 11 Riverside Drive, Dundee DD1 4NY
01382 207101; www.sssc.uk.com

Care Council for Wales/Cygnor Gofal Cymru
6th Floor, West Wing, Southgate House, Wood Street, Cardiff CF10 1EW
029 2022 6257; www.ccwales.org.uk

Qualifications and courses
Field social worker

ENTRY LEVEL 4

The 3-year social work Honours degree course has replaced the Diploma in Social Work (DipSW), and is required in order to become a social worker. For entry to a degree course you will need 2 A levels/4 H grades plus 5 GCSE/S grades (A–C/1–3) including English and maths. Other Level 3 qualifications may also be accepted.

There are also postgraduate programmes. For further information, graduates should contact one of the following: the General Social Care Council (GSCC), the Scottish Social Services Council (SSSC), the Northern Ireland Social Care Council (NISCC) or the Care Council for Wales (CCW).

There is no upper age limit for entry onto degree courses. Maturity and life and work experience are seen as an asset. Some universities are now offering a graduate-entry degree course that leads to a Master's qualification. Applications for these courses must be made through UCAS.

An employment-based route is also available. Here, the candidate works full time as an unqualified social worker for a social services organisation which funds their training. To become qualified, you attend short training courses and follow a distance learning programme.

Social workers are subject to a criminal record check and certain criminal convictions may prevent entry to this field.

Residential social worker

Many residential social workers, also known as care officers, gain experience through voluntary work in a caring role.

Residential social workers may be encouraged to undertake relevant NVQs/SVQs, which are available at Levels 2–4, in subjects such as Care, Caring for Children and Young People, and Promoting Independence.

For career progression, it may be necessary to become a qualified social worker (see above).

TRADE UNION OFFICIAL

What the work involves

- Trade union officials negotiate with employers over pay, working conditions, health and safety, dismissal and redundancy.

- Working in regional offices, you will recruit members, train shop stewards, support local officials and negotiate individual cases with employers.

- In head office, you will work on national policies and negotiate at national level.

- At all levels, your role will be to bring about the best deal for the workforce by finding common ground between employers and employees.

The type of person suited to this work

As the work is about obtaining good working conditions for your members, it is important to have a genuine interest in people's welfare and to believe in the aims of your union. You will need to see issues from different view points.

You will spend time dealing with individuals or groups, which requires good speaking, listening and negotiating skills – being able to calm people down at times. You may have to speak in public, which takes confidence.

Union matters involve problem-solving and negotiation which needs a patient, methodical approach and the ability to research and analyse information.

Working conditions

As a local shop steward you will have another job and attend to union business part time.

Paid officials at regional and national level are office-based.

You may travel quite extensively to meetings, tribunals and conferences so a driving licence is useful.

You will make maximum use of ICT and will probably have a lot of phone work – some after normal work hours.

Future prospects

Most people become paid union officials after voluntary experience.

Your prospects depend very much on the size of the union, ie they are greater with the large unions which are never out of the news.

In the case of some unions, there is no fixed pay and promotion structure. Most training is in house. Head-office posts are usually in London. Some people move from union work into politics by becoming councillors or Members of Parliament.

Advantages/disadvantages

The work is varied, but you may be working on one theme in preparation for a meeting.

You will work with a very wide range of people.

Qualifications and courses

The two main routes into trade union work are via a branch or regional office, or by joining the staff at head office.

Head-office staff are usually qualified in the area in which they specialise, for example law or economics. They may have qualified and worked in these areas beforehand or they may be direct entrants with either a relevant degree or the equivalent – such as NVQ/SVQ Levels 3 and 4. Workers at union headquarters may have worked their way up through the organisation from branch or regional office level.

Branch or regional office staff will have spent several years involved in union work in an unpaid capacity, either as a representative or as a shop steward.

Training for trade union officials is mainly on the job. The Trades Union Congress (TUC) runs regular short training programmes.

It may be possible to take NVQs/SVQs in administration or other relevant subjects.

Some people may be aggressive and unpleasant and sometimes you have to support people you do not agree with.

You may have to work long and unsocial hours.

Money guide

Local shop stewards/union representatives are generally unpaid.

If you are working as a paid official, expect around £16,000 per year on entry.

As a policy officer you can expect to start at around £19,500–£26,000.

As an experienced regional official you could earn £30,000–£60,000.

A general secretary could get as much as £100,000.

Related opportunities

- Equality and Diversity Officer p36
- Health and Safety Inspector p40
- Human Resources/Personnel Officer p41
- Social Worker p585

Further information

Trades Union Congress
Congress House, Great Russell Street, London WC1B 3LS
020 7636 4030; www.tuc.org.uk

Scottish Trades Union Congress
333 Woodlands Road, Glasgow G3 6DF
0141 337 8100; www.stuc.org.uk

Directgov
www.direct.gov.uk/en/Employment/TradeUnions/index.htm

Social Work and Counselling Services

CRCI: V
CLCI: CAS

VOLUNTEER ORGANISER

What the work involves

- Your job will be to organise volunteers to give additional help in hospitals, social service departments and volunteer organisations.

- After interviewing volunteers, you will match them to the kind of work that suits them, such as volunteer driving, hospital visiting or befriending.

- You will deal with administration, budgets, correspondence and report writing.

- Other tasks will be preparing publicity material, attending meetings, training volunteers and liaising with other agencies.

The type of person suited to this work

As volunteers come from many different backgrounds, it is important to be able to get on with all sorts of people and keep them motivated. You will need tact and patience, as not all volunteers are suited to the kind of volunteering they think they want to do.

It is essential to be confident when looking for volunteering opportunities and have good communication skills to sell placements to volunteers and volunteers to placements. You will need to be flexible to fit in with everyone's needs.

The job will demand a good deal of administration and record-keeping, which requires excellent organisational and time-management skills.

Working conditions

You will be based in an office or work from home, depending on the size of the organisation you work for.

You will travel locally to arrange placements and visit volunteers, so a driving licence is useful.

You will make a lot of use of ICT and the phone in your work.

Future prospects

You are unlikely to start this work straight from school. Opportunities are increasing, but there is keen competition for jobs and you may have to move to gain experience.

Promotion prospects are limited and many jobs may be part time. Volunteer organising is a good background for moving into careers such as social work or other management posts in the voluntary sector. You will have opportunities for further training, mainly through short courses.

Advantages/disadvantages

This work is varied and provides a challenge.

You will get satisfaction from helping volunteers get placements and from improving the lot of many people in need.

Qualifications and courses

No formal qualifications are needed to enter this career, but relevant work experience as a volunteer is valuable.

A degree or professional qualification can be an asset.

Professional courses vary. The National Association of Voluntary Service Managers offers a certificate for those working in the health and social care service.

The Directory of Social Change runs short courses.

The National Centre for Volunteering organises many 1- or 2-day courses which cover key areas of volunteer involvement.

Learndirect offers an online course entitled Managing Volunteers. This is primarily a distance learning course for those who are already volunteer leaders.

You may work some evenings and weekends.

Some people may be unpleasant and difficult to please.

Money guide

Starting salaries are around £18,000 per year. This rises to £26,500 with experience.

As a manager, you can expect up to £30,000.

Earnings can be up to £40,000 for senior staff in large organisations who have substantial supervisory experience.

Related opportunities

- Charity Fundraiser p575
- Social Worker p585
- Education Welfare Officer p205
- Youth and Community Worker p591

Further information

Association of Chief Executives of Voluntary Organisations
83 Victoria Street, London SW1H 0HW
0845 345 8481; www.acevo.org.uk

Directory of Social Change
24 Stephenson Way, London NW1 2DP
020 7391 4800; www.dsc.org.uk

Scottish Council for Voluntary Organisations (SCVO)
Mansfield Traquair Centre, 15 Mansfield Place, Edinburgh EH3 6BB
0131 556 3882; www.scvo.org.uk

WARDEN (ACCOMMODATION)

What the work involves

- Wardens look after the welfare of people living in supervised accommodation, including the elderly, people with disabilities, temporary hostel residents and students.

- You will make sure that meals are organised, cooked and served at set times, and that cleaning and maintenance are up to standard.

- It will be your responsibility to make sure health and safety standards are met, insurance is up to date and that security is effective.

- You will also collect rents and fees and organise social events, and sort out any disputes.

The type of person suited to this work

As you could be responsible for the accommodation of many different groups of people, it is important to be able to get on with all sorts of people and to have a friendly, outgoing personality. You will need to be understanding, patient and tolerant.

There are likely to be crises in the job so it is important to be able to cope under pressure and make decisions quickly. Problem solving is useful in these situations.

If you are dealing with rents and fees, being good with figures is helpful. There will be a lot of administration work which needs a well-organised and methodical approach.

Working conditions

Most of your work will be indoors, but you may handle maintenance and repair work, using tools and climbing ladders.

You will be on the go all day and evening so you will need lots of physical stamina.

You will use ICT for administration and record-keeping.

Many accommodation wardens live on-site or in the grounds, but you may travel locally, so a driving licence is useful.

Future prospects

Although there are opportunities throughout the UK, there are few vacancies for wardens. Most jobs are in cities and major towns. The main employers are local authorities, housing associations, private companies, voluntary organisations, universities and colleges.

Promotion is likely to be from assistant warden to warden. You may have to move jobs to progress your career. It is possible to move into other caring jobs such as social work.

Advantages/disadvantages

The work is varied and you will need to be able to multi-task.

You will get great job satisfaction from helping people.

Some residents may be difficult to deal with.

Qualifications and courses

There are no particular qualifications necessary to become a warden. However, it would be an advantage to have previous experience of caring for people, such as nursing or working with the disabled, elderly or homeless.

The minimum entry age is 20 due to the responsibilities involved.

It is possible to study for the Chartered Institute of Housing (CIH) National Certificate in Housing as well as NVQ/SVQ Levels 2, 3 and 4 in Housing.

Qualifications in care, including NVQs/SVQs, are also useful.

Wardens (managers) with the Youth Hostels Association (YHA, England and Wales) generally either start as seasonal assistants and work their way up, or are mature entrants with relevant work experience, for example as managers. A broad skills set can be useful as duties may include cooking, gardening, maintenance, housekeeping, acting as guide and marketing the youth hostel, as well as office work.

You will work long hours, evenings and weekends and may have to live in.

Money guide

Starting salaries are around £11,500 per year.

Wages can rise to £20,000, with experience.

Earnings range from £24,000-£32,000 for those with substantial experience - in some instances having individual responsibility for a group in supported accommodation.

Accommodation and food may also be provided.

Related opportunities

- Caretaker p461
- Hotel Manager p149
- Cleaner p463

Further information

Chartered Institute of Housing
Octavia House, Westwood Way, Coventry CV4 8JP
024 7685 1700; www.cih.org

General Social Care Council
Goldings House, 2 Hays Lane, London SE1 2HB
020 7397 5100; www.gscc.org.uk

Scottish Social Services Council
Compass House, 11 Riverside Drive, Dundee DD1 4NY
01382 207101; www.sssc.uk.com

Social Work and Counselling Services

CRCI: V
CLCI: IB

WELFARE BENEFITS ADVISER/ WELFARE RIGHTS CASEWORKER

What the work involves

- In this job you will help people cope with problems by listening, asking questions and giving impartial and confidential advice.

- You will explain people's rights on matters such as tenancy, employment, conflicts with neighbours, consumer law and finance, sometimes referring clients to other professionals.

- Helping people fill in forms to claim benefits and making phone calls on their behalf will be part of the job.

- Benefit advisers may represent their clients at tribunals, or act as advocates in a court of law.

The type of person suited to this work

As the work is mainly about dealing with people, it is essential to get on with all types of people and to remain impartial and non-judgemental. In order to explain issues very clearly to your clients, and help them to complete forms and documents, you will need excellent verbal and written communication skills.

You will be handling large amounts of information, often to find answers to queries, which means you must enjoy research and be able to grasp facts and analyse data quickly.

Clients may be upset and under stress. It is important to be sympathetic, tactful and discreet when handling these situations.

Working conditions

Benefit advisers are based in an open-access centre within a local community, town or city.

You will see clients on a one-to-one basis by appointment, but also liaise with colleagues and other professionals, such as social workers and solicitors.

You will do research using ICT to consult client records, access email and the internet. You might do shift work, including Saturdays and some evenings.

Future prospects

Advice centre work is not open to school-leavers; it suits mature people, experienced in other fields. Entry is competitive; you could gain experience in helping people through volunteering work.

Most jobs are with local authorities or charities. There are a few paid jobs with the Citizens Advice Bureau, but many posts are voluntary. Training will be given in counselling skills or benefits, for example.

Promotion prospects are limited, although every advice centre has a manager.

Advantages/disadvantages

You will work with many different people.

Qualifications and courses

There are no set minimum entry requirements for this job, but a good standard of education is desirable.

Although a degree is not specified, many applicants have degrees in a range of subjects and/or professional qualifications.

Life experience is essential, with applicants generally having a background of working with people.

It will help if you have experience in advising/counselling work, communication, information handling, ICT, money management, problem-solving or working with others.

Once in post, you will attend in-house training and updating courses.

Depending on your advisery area, you may work certain evenings and occasional weekends.

Some clients may be angry and difficult to deal with; a few will have mental health problems.

It is satisfying to help people sort out their difficulties and concerns.

Money guide

Pay varies, depending on where you work and who you work for.

Earnings are around £18,000 per year on entry.

Pay can rise to £26,000–£28,000+ with experience.

Salaries can exceed £33,000 for advisers with a lot of experience. London rates are higher.

Related opportunities

- Counsellor p571
- Debt Counsellor/Money Adviser p572
- Education Welfare Officer p205
- Equality and Diversity Officer p36
- Solicitor/Notary Public p384

Further information

Citizens Advice Bureau
Myddelton House, 115–123 Pentonville Road, London N1 9LZ
020 7833 2181; www.citizensadvice.org.uk

Citizens Advice Scotland
2 Powderhall Road, Edinburgh EH7 4GB
0131 550 1000; www.cas.org.uk

Advice UK
12th Floor, 2 London Bridge House, 25 London Bridge Street, London SE1 9ST
020 7407 4070; www.adviceuk.org.uk

YOUTH AND COMMUNITY WORKER

What the work involves

- You will work with people in their local community, encouraging them to take part in local learning opportunities and community activities.

- You could be in charge of a community centre, arranging activities for people of all ages, such as youth clubs, over-60s lunch clubs and playgroups.

- Youth workers are mainly involved with young people while community workers try to make sure that people of all ages in the local community have access to opportunities.

- The work is usually with groups of people.

The type of person suited to this work

As the work involves contact with all sorts of people, it is important to be able to get on with everyone and earn their trust. You also need to be genuinely interested in the local community and in equal opportunities.

Local people have a say in what they want in their area, so you must be a good listener, able to balance local groups' ideas with local and national government policies.

Working conditions

You might be based in a community centre or in an area office.

Depending on your job, you could also be based in a school, FE college or Connexions centre.

You work where young people go, including drop-in centres, cafés and youth clubs; this includes attending evening and weekend sessions.

Some workers travel around their local area, so a driving licence is useful.

Future prospects

Youth and community work is a growth area. As well as roles in youth club and community centre management, there are new strands to the work with developing rock music, drama, art or skateboarding groups. Local lifelong learning adult centres also require youth and community workers.

Local authorities have a defined promotion structure but in some jobs you may have to move around to widen your experience. You could progress to work for voluntary organisations or for a specific young people's services, for example Connexions.

Advantages/disadvantages

This work provides variety and challenge.

You will play a major part in developing your local community and/or the lives of young people.

You might have to work evenings, weekends and public holidays.

Qualifications and courses

A disclosure check with the Criminal Records Bureau will be made for everyone working in this area.

People in part-time or voluntary youth work can study for NVQs in Youth Work at Levels 2 and 3.

Professional training courses will usually require GCSEs/S grades (A–C/1–3) and A levels/H grades or equivalent for candidates under 21. Entry requirements may be waived for mature applicants with relevant experience.

In England, the National Youth Agency validates DipHE, degree and postgraduate courses, including the DipHE in community and youth work studies, the Foundation degree in Community Studies (Development and youth work), degrees in Youth and Community work and community development and youth work, as well as postgraduate courses in community and youth work. Some postgraduate courses require a first degree in a related subject to enter.

In Scotland, there are three routes: BA/BA Honours degree, postgraduate certificate/diploma and a work-based route.

Additional aptitudes which are needed include caring for people, and high-level skills in communication, managing and organising, and working with others.

Full-time youth and community workers normally need to do a professional training course.

Money guide

Once qualified you can earn between £19,000 and £25,500 per year. Salaries rise to around £28,500 with experience. For managers, pay ranges between £29,900–£35,000.

You may be paid an additional amount for working unsocial hours.

Related opportunities

- Education Welfare Officer p205
- FE Lecturer/HE Lecturer p206
- Social Worker p585
- Primary and Secondary Teacher p212

Further information

National Youth Agency
17–21 Albion Street, Leicester LE1 6GD
0116 285 3700; www.nya.org.uk

Wales Youth Agency
Leslie Court, Lôn y Llyn, Caerphilly CF83 1BQ
029 2085 5700; www.wya.org.uk

Youth Council for Northern Ireland
Forestview, Purdys Lane, Belfast BT8 7AR
028 9064 3882; www.youthcouncil-ni.org.uk

Social Work and Counselling Services

CRCI: V
CLCI: KEG

Transport and Logistics

The jobs in this sector are immensely varied because of the wide range of transport and communication links that exist today to keep our lives running. You could need a high level of technical knowledge in this sector especially for jobs such as a pilot or a train driver. But you could also be great at keeping attention to detail and maintaining schedules if logistics is more where your interest lies. Jobs in transport and logistics require very efficient and practical people to ensure that our infrastructure continues to run smoothly and safely. You may need to cope well under pressurised situations as well as be very good at communicating so that any problems can be sorted out quickly.

This section looks at the following jobs:

For similar jobs to the ones in this section see *Security and the Armed Forces* on page 537 and *Leisure, Sport and Tourism* on page 385.

AIR CABIN CREW

What the work involves

■ Once you have checked the cabin, you will welcome your passengers on board and make sure they are comfortable.

■ You will be responsible for safety and security on board – this will include making sure that customers are safely belted up and their bags are put away, and demonstrating safety procedures.

■ During the flight you will help to care for any young children and sick passengers, giving First Aid if needed.

■ You will also serve food and drinks and sell items such as jewellery, toys and alcohol and you will ensure passengers are ready for landing and will see them all safely off the plane.

The type of person suited to this work

You will need to be welcoming, friendly, well groomed, confident and caring, with a clear voice.

You should be happy working in a team with the rest of the crew, but also be able to be on your own as you will spend some nights alone away from home.

As you will serve refreshments and clean up, you will need to be prepared to get your hands dirty.

Your ability to stay calm under pressure will be vital if you need to deal with an emergency.

Working conditions

You will work in a cramped, noisy, warm cabin. In bad weather the cabin may be unstable.

Planes fly 24/7 which means long hours, shifts and regular work at weekends and bank holidays.

There is also a risk of security incidents or accidents and it can cause stress and delay.

You may have health problems, for example ear pain from cabin pressure or jet lag from long flights.

Future prospects

There is fierce competition for jobs, although there are growing opportunities, with a growth in numbers of smaller airlines and an increase in routes.

With experience, you could progress to working as a purser (looking after a particular cabin such as first class) and then to cabin service director.

You could go on to train new cabin crew.

Advantages/disadvantages

You will travel to dream destinations, but on short flights you will not always get off the plane!

No two working days will be the same.

Whilst working with people can be very rewarding, you may have to deal with difficult or demanding passengers.

Qualifications and courses

Entry requirements depend on the airline, many require 4–5 GCSEs (A–C)/S grades (1–3) or equivalent and fluency in English. You will need to be at least 18 and be physically fit, and there are height and weight restrictions. You will also need a valid passport allowing unrestricted world travel. Most airlines will expect you to be able to swim 25 metres. It is an advantage if you can speak another language.

Key Skills in communication and working with others are very useful.

You could study a related college or university course, for example a BTEC/SQA National Certificate/Diploma or HNC/D in travel and tourism, or a degree in travel and tourism or a modern language.

Nationally recognised qualifications for air cabin crew include the Edexcel Certificate in Preparation for Air Cabin Crew Service, EMTA Awards Ltd's Intermediate Certificate in Air Cabin Crewing, NCFE Level 2 Certificate in Airline Cabin Crew and Edexcel BTEC Level 3 National Award, Certificate or Diploma in Aviation Operations.

Once accepted by an airline you will take part in their 4 to 6 week training course followed by an opportunity to take NVQ/SVQ Levels 2 and 3 in Aviation Operations in the Air (Cabin Crew).

Money guide

£12,000–£14,000 per year is usual for starting salaries.

With experience this rises to £15,000–£21,000.

£25,000+ is usual for senior crew.

Companies offer free flights and meals and allowances may be paid for working away from home and unsocial hours.

Air cabin crew can boost earnings with commission on in-flight sales.

Related opportunities

■ Airport Baggage Handler p597
■ Holiday Representative p391
■ Tour Guide/Manager p401
■ Travel Agency Clerk p403

Further information

EMTA Awards Ltd (EAL)
SEMTA House, 14 Upton Road, Watford WD18 OJT
01923 652 400; www.eal.org.uk

NCFE national awarding body
Citygate, St James' Boulevard, Newcastle upon Tyne NE1 4JE
0191 239 8000; www.ncfe.org.uk

www.cityandguilds.com/myperfectjob

AIR TRAFFIC CONTROLLER

What the work involves

- You will be responsible for a specific section of airspace, keeping air traffic flying safely and quickly.

- Using computers, radar, radio equipment and weather reports you will check pilots' flight plans and current positions.

- You will use a radio to give pilots the instructions, advice and information they need to fly safely.

- Any difficult weather, security alerts or emergencies will mean that you would have to make quick but safe decisions.

The type of person suited to this work

To avoid disaster you will have to take quick, calm, logical action and stay alert at all times, even at the end of your shift.

You cannot afford to be unclear when you are sending instructions to pilots, so you need to be confident and able to speak clearly.

You should be keen on ICT and maths. When checking your pilots' flight plans you will use lots of new technology and calculate distances and angles.

The technology and software used is regularly upgraded to improve safety, so you will need to be willing to train throughout your working life.

Working conditions

You will work from 37 to 40 hours a week at a flight control centre, or in an airport traffic control tower.

As it's a 24/7 job, shift work is usual and includes nights, weekends and holidays.

You will use computers, radar displays and radio headphones.

The lighting in the control room is kept at the right level to help you read the radar screens.

Future prospects

Most of the 2,500 UK air traffic controllers are employed by the National Air Traffic Services (NATS) and work in one of three main area control centres: Swanwick in Southampton, West Drayton near London and Prestwick in Scotland. Others work at airports.

There are regular trainee vacancies as air traffic continues to increase. However, entry is competitive with about 150 people applying for each vacancy.

With experience, you could manage and train other air traffic controllers.

Advantages/disadvantages

No two working days are the same: you will work at different times.

You will be well paid for the level of responsibility you take on.

Excellent training is on offer including an exciting 15 hours' flying time, but you will have to pass all your assessments.

Qualifications and courses

The main route into this work is to apply to National Air Traffic Services (NATS). You will need a minimum of 5 GCSEs (A–C)/S grades (1–3), including English and maths. Post-GCSE qualifications are also usually required, such as 2 A levels, 3 H grades or equivalent. Many entrants are graduates. Applicants should be over 18 years of age.

You will also need a good standard of health, hearing, colour vision and a clear voice.

All Key Skills are useful for this job but especially communication, information technology and numeracy skills.

NATS entrants are trained at the College of Air Traffic Control, next to Bournemouth International Airport. You will start by doing a 9–15 month course, during which an allowance is paid. After graduation trainees go on to an operational unit for validation training. It takes 3–4 years to become fully qualified.

Some air traffic controllers are employed directly by airport operators. Private employers either recruit people with air traffic control experience or send trainees to the College of Air Traffic Control. Some also take on trainees with 5 GCSEs/S grades (A–C/1–3) including English and maths, or equivalent qualifications.

Money guide

Trainee air traffic controllers get a training allowance of just over £10,000 per year at college. This can rise to, £15,000–£20,000 during the validation period.

Fully qualified and with experience you can get up to £45,000.

Senior controllers in highly responsible positions earn £85,000.

Shift work payments can increase earnings.

Related opportunities

- Coastguard Watch Assistant/Officer p540
- Aircraft Baggage Handler p597
- Airline/Helicopter Pilot p596
- Royal Air Force (RAF) Officer p557

Further information

Civil Aviation Authority
Personnel Department, Room 216, CAA House, 45–59 Kingsway, London WC2B 6TE
020 7453 6040; www.caa.co.uk

National Air Traffic Services Ltd
Fifth Floor, Brettenham House South, Lancaster Place, London WC2E 7EN
020 7309 8666; www.nats.co.uk

City&
Guilds

www.cityandguilds.com/myperfectjob

Transport and Logistics

CRCI: WA
CLCI: YAB

AIRLINE/HELICOPTER PILOT

What the work involves

- You will be responsible for the safety of your passengers, crew and cargo and will need to carry out a range of safety, route and fuel checks before each flight.
- When flying you will keep in radio contact with air traffic controllers, inform and direct the crew, plan your route and use computer systems to control and monitor the aircraft.
- After each flight you will need to write a report and record any problems that took place.

The type of person suited to this work

You must have a strong sense of responsibility. You will need to be technical and confident enough to take charge of your aircraft and follow the instructions of air traffic control exactly. Good communication and team-work skills are essential.

Even when you have earned your wings, your health, plus your skills and competencies, will be regularly assessed, so you must be keen to keep on learning and be committed to keeping fit.

Working conditions

You will wear a uniform and sit for hours in a noisy, fairly cramped flight deck.

Planes fly 24/7 so you will have to work some unsocial hours and holidays.

Future prospects

Competition for vacancies is intense. Competition for pilot training in the forces is also intense and pilots must serve for a minimum of 12 years before they can take up employment with a commercial employer. You could pay for your own training through an approved training school, but this is a very expensive route.

Airline

As a newly qualified pilot you would begin as a second pilot working with a training captain, to give you maximum experience. Promotion to captain usually requires at least 5,000 flying hours, which takes up to ten years.

Helicopter

Employment prospects in the UK offshore sector are currently good. Some helicopter pilots take more advanced training as a pilot. There are some limited opportunities for self-employment.

Advantages/disadvantages

You will need to raise a lot of money if you can't get sponsorship. Helicopter training is even more expensive.

Qualifications and courses

In all cases you will need to be physically fit with good health, hearing and eyesight as well as normal colour vision.

All Key Skills are useful but especially numeracy, communication and ICT.

You will need to get a Commercial Pilot's Licence CPL (A) and at least the taught part of the higher level Airline Transport Pilot's Licence ATPL (A) to be a commercial pilot, or the CPL (H) or ATPL (H) to be a helicopter pilot.

You can pay for a full-time 15-month training course or if you have a Private Pilot's Licence (PPL) do a part-time modular course. Full-time training courses typically cost between £50,000 and £65,000.

You will usually need at least 5 GCSEs/S grades (A–C/1–3), including English, maths and science, and 2 A levels/3 H grades, preferably in maths and physics. You should be at least 18 and may find it easier to gain sponsorship if you have got a Private Pilot's Licence (PPL).

It is an exciting job that sometimes involves travelling to exotic locations, but you will need to rest and so may not be able to do much sight-seeing.

Money guide
Airline

Co-pilots start on around £25,000 per year, but their salary rises to £45,000 with experience. Captains can earn £50,000 to £85,000. Pay for experienced pilots can reach £100,000+. Perks include subsidised travel.

Helicopter

Newly qualified commercial helicopter pilots can earn £28,000.

Experienced pilots carrying passengers can earn £45,000–£70,000.

Related opportunities

- Air Traffic Controller p595
- Royal Air Force (RAF) Airman/woman p556

Further information

British Airline Pilots Association
81 New Road, Harlington, Hayes, Middlesex UB3 5BG
020 8476 4000; www.balpa.org.uk

British Helicopter Advisery Board
The Graham Suite, West Entrance, Fairoaks Airport, Chobham, Surrey GU24 8HX
01276 856100; www.bhab.org

AIRPORT BAGGAGE HANDLER

What the work involves

- You will be responsible for safely loading, unloading and transporting baggage, cases, and freight around an airport.

- By checking the baggage against flight lists, you will sort items to make sure you get the baggage to the right place on time.

- You will then lift the baggage onto the ramp or conveyor belt to move it onto the plane or into the baggage hall.

- If you spot any unusual or suspicious baggage, you will use a radio to get security back-up.

The type of person suited to this work

As you will be responsible both for making sure that all baggage goes to the right place by checking labels against flight lists, and for reporting suspicious baggage, you should be alert with an eye for detail. You will be the sort of person who likes to be active and busy as you will be expected to move at speed to get aircraft loaded and unloaded in a short timescale.

Flexibility and a willingness to get your hands dirty are also vital, as you may need to carry out jobs such as helping to clean the aircraft and keep runways free of hazards such as snow and birds. You should enjoy working as part of a team.

Working conditions

You will wear a uniform and work mainly outdoors in all weathers. You may need to work in cramped spaces such as cargo holds.

You will work around 39 hours per week on a shift system.

Working near aircraft can be noisy, but you will have ear protectors.

Your job will involve a lot of bending, lifting and carrying. This can make it an active, but physically tiring job.

Future prospects

Most of the 5000 UK baggage handlers work for large airlines, airports or handling agents at the biggest airports, such as Heathrow, Gatwick, Stansted and Manchester. There are usually vacancies and currently demand outstrips supply. Seasonal work is on offer at busy holiday periods.

Technological changes could make this job safer in the future: for example, the development of mechanised belt loaders is predicted to reduce the risk of injury.

Promotion is possible to a supervisory post or managing ground transport on the runways.

Advantages/disadvantages

You will have to move fast to get baggage transported, but this means that you will have a busy working day.

If you are working for an airline, one of the perks may be subsidised travel opportunities.

You may have to work outside in poor weather conditions.

Qualifications and courses

ENTRY LEVEL 1

There are no minimum entry requirements for this job. You will usually need to be at least 18, be physically fit with normal colour vision, pass medical and strict security checks and may need a clean driving licence.

Key Skills in communication and working with others are useful. You will also need some numeracy skills to identify the correct conveyor belt for each flight.

Given that you will be working a variety of shifts at various times, day or night, it is advisable to live near the airport and possess personal transport.

Once accepted you will be trained in all aspects of the job including barcode recognition equipment, lift equipment and operating vehicles safely and effectively.

NVQs/SVQs in Providing Aviation Operations on the Ground at Levels 2 and 3 may be available. Other qualifications available include BTEC Nationals or CandG at Levels 2 and 3 in Aviation Operations or Aviation Operations on the Ground.

Baggage handlers generally need to live within easy access of an airport, and have their own transport.

Money guide

Starting salaries are usually £11,000–£16,000 per year.

Experienced baggage handlers can earn £16,000+.

Team leaders can earn up £20,000.

Allowances are paid for shift work and this - plus overtime pay - can increase your earnings.

Related opportunities

- Hotel Porter p150
- Removals Operative p621
- Van Driver p628
- Warehouse Worker/Manager p629

Further information

Royal Aeronautical Society
4 Hamilton Place, London WCJ 7BQ, 020 7670 4326
www.aerosociety.com

International Air Transport Association
IATA UK, Spencer House, 23 Sheen Road, Richmond upon Thames TW9 1BN
020 7660 0068; www.iata.org

City&
Guilds

www.cityandguilds.com/myperfectjob

Transport and Logistics

CRCI: WA
CLCI: YAB

BUS/COACH DRIVER

What the work involves

- Bus/coach drivers are responsible for providing an acceptable transport service for passengers making short or long journeys.

- You will be responsible for the safety and comfort of your passengers throughout their journey, which includes ensuring that passengers are safely on or off your vehicle before pulling out, and that they are wearing seatbelts when applicable.

- You may have to work out passenger fares and issue tickets and passes if you do not have a conductor.

- You will also be responsible for checking your vehicle, coping with breakdowns and other emergencies, and driving safely at all times.

The type of person suited to this work

You will need to be an extremely competent driver.

You should have a polite and approachable manner when dealing with passengers, but have the confidence to handle disagreements or other situations which may arise on journeys.

You will need good eyesight and excellent concentration in order to remain alert for very long periods of time. Quick reactions are also useful in case you need to respond to an unforeseen event on the road.

You should be a punctual person, as you will have to adhere to a strict timetable.

Working conditions

You will work on a shift pattern, encompassing evening, overnight and weekend work. You cannot work more than 56 hours a week, or 90 hours over two weeks. You are also required, by law, to take a 45 minute break every 4.5 hours.

Coach drivers will be required to help passengers with luggage, and provide assistance to disabled travellers. You will have to wear a uniform.

Future prospects

There is a continuous shortage of bus/coach drivers, so job opportunities are good.

Over 80% of the workforce is employed by one of 6 companies; Stagecoach, First, National Express, Transdev, Arriva and Go-Ahead.

You could work anywhere in the UK, undertake long distance tour driving, or provide a transport service for specific groups such as the elderly or disabled.

You can progress to become a supervisor, service controller, or instructor within your company.

Advantages/disadvantages

You will be providing an essential public service.

Qualifications and courses

There are no specific academic requirements, but most employers prefer that you have 4 GCSEs/S grades (A-C/1–3) or equivalent, including English and maths.

You must hold a PCV licence, and obtain the PCV driver certificate of professional competence (Driver CPC). You cannot train for this licence until you are 18, and even then you will not be permitted to drive certain routes until you reach 21.

Most companies are willing to fund employees to take the PCV licence whilst paying them a trainee wage. Alternatively, you can arrange your own lessons and test via the Driving Standards Agency. Some areas also provide training courses for those who are registered unemployed; you will need to go to your local Jobcentre Plus for details.

PVC training lasts 4–5 weeks and includes both a theory and practical test, along with a medical. During this period, your company will also give you training in relevant areas such as customer care, disability awareness, defensive driving and health and safety.

Part time and flexible hours are available so you can fit work around other commitments.

You may have to deal with difficult or distressed passengers. Driving the same route or for long periods of time can become monotonous.

Money guide

As a trainee driver, whist working towards gaining your PCV licence, you could expect to earn £11,000.

Once you have gained your licence, your earnings should rise to about £16,000.

With a few years' experience, your wages could increase to £23,500.

Related opportunities

- Large Goods Vehicle Driver/Driver's Mate p606
- Taxi Driver p624
- Chauffeur p599
- Driving Examiner/Instructor p603

Further information

Driving Standards Agency
Stanley House, 56 Talbot Street, Nottingham NG1 5GU
0115 901 2500; www.dsa.gov.uk or for specific Driver CPC information www.drivercpc.org

City&
Guilds

www.cityandguilds.com/myperfectjob

CHAUFFEUR

What the work involves

- Chauffeurs are responsible for driving their client to and from appointments or events, as well as the maintenance of the vehicle.

- You will have to clean the vehicle regularly, inside and out, and also undertake any minor maintenance work when necessary, or book it in to see a mechanic.

- You will be providing a personal service to your passenger, including opening and closing doors for them, assisting them in and out of the vehicle, and carrying and loading their luggage or shopping.

- You may also be required to provide a low level of security protection to your client, as well as maintaining confidentiality at all times.

The type of person suited to this work

You must be an excellent driver who observes the law and keeps cool under pressure, even when faced with endless traffic jams or unpredictable clients. You will also need to have a good awareness of safety and security, both on the road and with regard to your client.

You should have excellent interpersonal skills. You must be punctual, respectful and polite.

Good map reading skills, knowledge of basic vehicle maintenance, and a reasonable level of fitness are also helpful.

Working conditions

It is unlikely that you will work regular hours as a chauffeur, as most clients will require your services during the evenings and at weekends. Split shifts are common, where you will find yourself with 2 or 3 free hours in between appointments.

You may be required to spend nights away from home on occasion.

You will need to wear a uniform in most instances.

Future prospects

Most chauffeurs are employed by limousine companies, but there are opportunities with hotel groups, car-hire companies, park and ride schemes, tour operators, businesses and private employers.

The British Chauffeurs Guild operates a specialist employment agency for their members, through which they can find suitable opportunities.

With experience, you can command a higher salary, or you could branch into a related career such as that of a taxi driver or driving instructor.

Advantages/disadvantages

You may work for some interesting, high profile clients.

The work offers some flexibility with hours.

There is a lot of waiting around for clients, which can get boring and frustrating.

Qualifications and courses

You do not need any specific academic qualifications to become a chauffeur. The only necessity is that you hold a full driving licence. Most employers will expect this to be clean, but some do consider candidates with penalty points.

You may benefit from holding an advanced driving certificate, details of which can be found through the Institute of Advanced Motorists. This demonstrates an enhanced driving ability and additional skills that may be valued by some employers.

It is beneficial to have several years' driving experience. Not only does this demonstrate a proven ability behind the wheel, but if you are over 21 you will cost your employer less to ensure.

There are professional courses that you could take to enhance your application and understanding of the job. These include NVQs in road passenger vehicle driving, and the ASET Level 2 Certificate in defensive driving. The British Chauffeurs Guild also offer a 2 day Security Chauffeur Training Course which covers the fundamental areas of chauffeuring; theory, practice, protocol, security and etiquette.

Some employers may also require you to pass a medical assessment, and a Criminal Records Bureau check, prior to taking you on.

Money guide

Salaries vary depending on your employer, but on average the starting wage for a chauffeur is usually around £18,000. With 3–5 years' experience, this could rise to £25,000.

An experienced chauffeur, especially one with advanced driving or additional security qualifications, could earn £30,000+.

Related opportunities

- Taxi Driver p624
- Driving Examiner/Instructor p603
- Bus/Coach Driver p598
- Motor Vehicle Technician p241

Further information

British Chauffeurs Guild
13 Stonecot Hill, Sutton, Surrey SM3 9HB
020 8641 1740; www.britishchauffeursguild.co.uk;
bcg.london@btconnect.com

Institute of Advanced Motorists
IAM House, 510 Chiswich High Road, London W4 5RG
020 8996 9600; www.iam.org.uk

City&
Guilds

www.cityandguilds.com/myperfectjob

Transport and Logistics

CRCI: WE
CLCI: YAD

COURIER

What the work involves

- You will collect fragile, valuable or urgent letters and packages and deliver them within an agreed time limit.

- Once you have been allocated your job, you will travel to a collection point for pick-up. You will load up the goods and then take them to the drop-off point where you will obtain a signature for delivery.

- Motorcycle couriers may travel long distances and van couriers carry larger parcels in a town or city.

- You will need to check the lights, brakes and tyres of your motorbike, van or bicycle regularly.

The type of person suited to this work

Map-reading skills are essential. You may only be paid for the number of deliveries you do so you need to be quick and know where you are going.

You will be in constant contact with customers, collecting items, asking for instructions and getting signatures for deliveries, so you need to be good with people. You should also be reliable – you may be dealing with high value or very urgent items.

Working conditions

You will spend a lot of time travelling but with regular stops to make deliveries. Long distance or overseas deliveries may mean time away from home.

Motorcycle and bicycle couriers will be out in the weather at all times.

Courier services operate 24/7 and many couriers work on overnight deliveries.

You may have to provide your own car or van. Motorcycle and bicycle couriers usually use their own bikes.

Future prospects

Work can be irregular but currently delivery is a growth area with a shortage of couriers especially in the South-East. The continued growth of online shopping and customer online tracking means that the demand for same and next day courier delivery, in particular, is on the increase.

Technology is starting to change this industry. Mobile phones have been the norm for communicating but the internet and email are now also used.

Promotion generally depends on the size of the courier company – large companies may have sales and management opportunities. It may be possible to become self-employed and start your own courier service. However, high operational costs (fuel, congestion charges, etc) are currently making it difficult for small companies.

Advantages/disadvantages

Pay rates are good but if you are using your own transport you will have running, insurance and maintenance costs.

Qualifications and courses

You will need to be at least 17 – many couriers are over 21 because of high insurance costs for young drivers. School leavers could start as bicycle couriers.

Employers ask for a full UK driving licence for driver couriers and motorcycle couriers will need the CBT qualification issued by the DVLA. Motorcycle and bicycle couriers usually use their own bikes.

Couriers driving light trucks will also need to have their C1 Category licence if they passed their driving test after 1 January 1997.

Key Skills in communication and working with others are useful.

Apprenticeships/Skillseekers are available for candidates aged 16–24

You may be able to do an NVQ/SVQ at Level 2 in Carry and Deliver Goods. An NVQ/SVQ Level 2 is also available in Transporting Goods by Road.

Making up to 20 journeys a day and possibly working 50-hour weeks make this a stressful job,

Most couriers take up the job because they are attracted to the freedom of travel. However most couriers do lots of repeat deliveries in a small, often congested, urban area.

Money guide

Couriers are often self-employed and paid for individual deliveries, so earnings vary.

Employed couriers can earn £14,000 per year (£18,000 in London).

Experienced couriers can earn up to £23,000 per year (£25,000+ in London).

Couriers travelling by air may be employed by airlines on a one-off basis, receiving reduced cost flights instead of wages.

Related opportunities

- Airport Baggage Handler p597
- Taxi Driver p624
- Van Driver p628
- Warehouse Worker/Manager p629

Further information

Driving Standards Agency
Stanley House, 56 Talbot Street, Nottingham NG1 5GU
0115 901 2500; www.dsa.gov.uk

www.cityandguilds.com/myperfectjob

CRUISE SHIP PURSER/ STEWARD

What the work involves

Purser

- Pursers provide the administrative support necessary to ensure the ship operates smoothly and that passengers have a good holiday. You might work in the reception area, do secretarial duties or order various items of stock.

- As well as providing passengers services you might also support crew members by paying their salaries or updating and maintaining records.

Steward

- You will be responsible for keeping the public and private areas that passengers use clean and serviced to a very high standard.

- You might do housekeeping duties in cabins or keep restaurants and passenger areas clean and tidy.

The type of person suited to this work

As you will probably have some contact with passengers, you should be happy meeting, talking with and helping people of all types with different backgrounds and nationalities. You should be polite and happy to help, and have good customer service skills. You will need to be a dedicated employee as the work can be hard at times.

Working conditions

You will be expected to work long shifts, which for some posts can last up to ten hours. Although cruise ships appear to be glamorous, you might work in cramped conditions including in rough weather. However, you will get to see other parts of the world and meet lots of new people.

You might have to share your accommodation with other members of staff.

Short-term, holiday and summer work is available.

Future prospects

In the last seven years the cruise ship industry has become the second fastest growing sector in the UK and USA, so prospects are good.

There is a clear process of career progression. You will start as a member of crew, then rise to officer as you gain skills and responsibilities.

The skills gained on board will also be useful on dry land in many areas of the business sector (purser) or hospitality and catering (steward).

Advantages/disadvantages

You might be away from home for months at a time.

You will be able visit lots of places around the world.

Qualifications and courses

Purser

A levels/H grades or equivalent are normally required, and many employers prefer a degree in a related subject such as hospitality or travel and tourism. The normal entry requirements for a degree in a travel or hospitality subject are 2 A levels/3 H grades, or equivalent. No specific A level subjects are required. The University of Plymouth offers a degree in Cruise Operations Management.

Related experience is normally required. For senior positions, managerial experience may be required.

Knowledge of a language other than English is an advantage.

Steward

There are no formal entry requirements for this work, but relevant experience in the leisure and hospitality industry is normally required.

Training is provided on the job, and covers subjects such as safety, health, environment, survival and rescue, fire, First Aid, etc, as well as company-specific training.

It may be possible to gain NVQs/SVQs in areas such as hospitality, catering and housekeeping.

Your accommodation could be cramped and you might have to share with other crew members.

Pay can be better than on shore.

Money guide

Salaries for all on-board positions are higher than for comparable jobs ashore. Salaries vary with company and liner, so contact companies directly for their earnings guide. Starting salaries normally start from £19,000, rising to around £25,000, with experience. A chief purser or steward can earn between £45,000 and £55,000.

Free accommodation and food, as well as tips from passengers, boost the value of earnings.

Related opportunities

- Tourist Information Centre Worker p402
- Holiday Representative p391

Further information

International Cruise Services
Cook & Co, Glasgow G2 6HJ
0141 649 8644; www.cruiseservices.co.uk

www.cityandguilds.com/myperfectjob

Transport and Logistics

CRCI: WE
CLCI: YAD

DISTRIBUTION MANAGER

What the work involves

- You will be responsible for planning and managing the control and movement of goods or raw materials held in stock.

- Using ICT, you will manage stock levels and monitor the ordering and storage of goods.

- Distribution managers work for distribution and manufacturing companies, wholesalers and major retail companies such as supermarkets.

The type of person suited to this work

Distribution is a fast-moving industry and ICT is at its centre, so your computer skills will need to be excellent. Like the computer programs you will use, you will need to be systematic and logical but you will also need brilliant communication skills to deal with people at different levels.

It may be that the goods you have to order come from far-flung places. This means that the supply chain you will be managing might be very complex. You will also need to able to deal with the stress of making sure that you get the goods at the best price and supply them in the right condition.

Working conditions

Most of your work will be in an office, working on a computer and using a phone. You will also travel to meetings with suppliers or customers and visit storage depots.

Your hours will be mainly office hours, Monday–Friday, but you may have to do shift work or work weekends and evenings on a rota system.

There may be travel away from home and, for some, travel overseas.

Future prospects

There are more than 83,000 distribution managers working for a wide range of companies, including warehouse and distribution firms but also manufacturers, major retail companies, the Armed Forces and central and local government. It is a growth industry because if it is done well organisations have less waste and bigger profit margins.

Advantages/disadvantages

As a key figure in your company, you will have the satisfaction of making sure your supply chain works and that your customers are happy.

The demands of coordinating vehicles, products and people, and tight deadlines, can make this a stressful role.

Money guide

Salaries start between £19,000–£20,000 per year, increasing to £25,000. Experienced managers earn from £20,000 to £40,000. Senior managers responsible for transport schedules can earn up to £60,000.

Qualifications and courses

There are no specific entry requirements; however, many employers recruit graduates. It is also possible to work your way up from a junior post by gaining NVQ/SVQ qualifications or professional qualifications.

Degrees and postgraduate courses are available in areas such as logistics, transport management and supply chain management. The usual minimum entry requirements for a degree course are 5 GCSEs/S grades and 2 A levels/3 H grades or equivalent. For postgraduate courses, a relevant degree or a professional qualification and relevant work experience are required.

People working in the industry can study for the CILT's professional qualifications at college or by distance learning. The Introductory Certificate is suitable for employees new to the profession. The Certificate is aimed at supervisors and first line managers. The Professional Diploma is intended for middle managers, including recent graduates, and fulfils the requirements for membership of the Institute.

Senior distribution managers can take the CILT Advanced Diploma or study for a Master's in Logistics. A distance learning MSc is offered by Aston University in partnership with CILT.

Distribution Managers may find it helpful to take the Certificate of Professional Competence of the Department of Transport (Department of the Environment in Northern Ireland).

There may be allowances for shiftwork and unsocial hours, as well as a company car.

Related opportunities

- Freight Forwarder p604
- Importer/Exporter p605
- Road Transport Manager p623
- Warehouse Worker/Manager p629

Further information

Freight Transport Association
Hermes House, St Johns Road, Tunbridge Wells TN4 9UZ
01892 526171; www.fta.co.uk

Careers in Logistics
www.careersinlogistics.co.uk

www.cityandguilds.com/myperfectjob

DRIVING EXAMINER/ INSTRUCTOR

What the work involves

- You will teach people how to drive safely, and well enough to pass their driving test.

- You will explain or assess basic motor and road skills as well as safe and courteous driving.

- You could be a specialist examiner or instructor, for example working with trainee LGV or PCV drivers, or motorbike riders.

The type of person suited to this work

Not only will you need to be a good, safe driver, you will also need teaching or assessing skills. Instructors need to plan lessons to cover individual weaknesses whilst examiners need to assess whether a trainee driver should be given a full driving licence.

People learning to drive or being examined are often stressed and anxious, so you will need to be calm, steady and patient.

Working conditions

Instructors can spend more than eight hours a day sitting in the car ready to operate the dual controls to avert problems. Early morning, evening and weekend work is common.

Driving examiners tend to work mainly 8.30 am–4.30 pm, taking up to seven tests per day.

Future prospects

Driving instructors may work for driving schools, operate under a franchise, or have their own businesses. Around 80% of instructors are self-employed. There are no restrictions on the numbers of instructors, so in some areas there is strong competition for pupils.

Driving examiners are trained and employed by the Driving Standards Agency (DSA). The 1600 driving examiners work from one of the 400 test centres throughout England, Scotland and Wales.

Advantages/disadvantages

It can be very rewarding to enable learners to become safe, qualified drivers.

If you run your own car to give lessons you will have to pay for your fuel, insurance and maintenance costs.

Examiners can face difficult situations when trainees react badly to being told they have failed.

Money guide

Instructors charge £20-£30 per hour for a driving lesson. Full time driving instructors could earn £15,000 as a starting

Qualifications and courses
Driving instructor

ENTRY LEVEL 1

To work as a driving instructor, you must be registered with the Driving Standards Agency as an Approved Driving Instructor (ADI). You will need to be over 21 and have held a full clean driving licence for four out of the last six years, with no criminal or motoring convictions. The ADI examination is in three parts: an IT-based theory test and a video-based hazard perceptions test; a practical driving test; and a practical teaching test. Applicants must pass the practical driving test within 3 attempts.

NVQ/SVQs at Level 3 in Driving Instructor and in Bus/ Coach Driving Instructor are available.

Driving examiner

To work as a driving examiner you should be at least 21, have held a UK or European Union driving licence continuously for four years, and have no more than three current penalty points on your driving licence. You will need to pass an exam, driving test and interview before being selected for training and further assessment by the Driving Standards Agency (DSA).

salary. With several years' experience this can rise to around £26,000-£30,000. Your income will be reduced by the costs of running and maintaining your vehicle or paying a franchise fee.

Full-time, experienced driving examiners can earn about £28,000. Supervising examiners may earn £30,000+. Salaries are higher in London.

Related opportunities

- Taxi Driver p624
- Work-based Training Instructor p218

Further information

Driving Instructors Association
Safety House, Beddington Farm Road, Croydon CR0 4XZ
0845 345 5151; www.driving.org

Motor Schools Association of Great Britain Ltd
101 Wellington Road North, Stockport, Cheshire SK4 2LP
0161 429 9669; www.msagb.co.uk

City& Guilds

www.cityandguilds.com/myperfectjob

Transport and Logistics

CRCI: WE
CLCI: YAD

FREIGHT FORWARDER

What the work involves

- You will organise the transport of goods across the world for importers and exporters.

- Your role will involve working out if the freight needs special handling and whether it should go by sea, road or air.

- Arranging the packing, carriage, collection and storage of the goods will be part of your job.

- You will be responsible for dealing with paperwork, applying for customs clearance and calculating insurance, transport and customs costs.

The type of person suited to this work

As you will deal with lots of different customers, some of whom may not speak fluent English, your communication skills must be excellent. You will need to communicate by telephone, fax, letter, email or face to face.

You must be determined and have excellent bargaining skills to get the best prices and terms. You will also be a good problem-solver. For example, you might have to work out how to transport a valuable racehorse from Hong Kong to the UK.

Your basic maths skills will need to be good as you will be asked to calculate exchange rates, or work out if a large piece of cargo will fit into the cargo hold of a small aircraft.

Working conditions

Most of your work will be in an office at a workstation using the telephone, computer and fax.

You will also need to travel to meet customers and contractors – this could mean being away from home.

You may need to work extra hours or shifts to cover urgent deliveries and world time zones.

Working to meet strict deadlines can make this a stressful job.

Future prospects

Freight forwarding agents are specialised companies that collect and deliver goods for importers/exporters. Freight forwarding offices are usually in cities and near airports and ports. Opportunities are growing but it is a competitive industry and it helps if you have related work experience.

As you progress, there are opportunities to specialise in specific countries and industries. You could work within the entertainment industry, shipping film and concert sets around the world, or with medical and pharmaceutical supplies.

Advantages/disadvantages

This work varies. You may be specialising in, for example, moving film and TV crews and their equipment or handling perishable goods such as fruit.

You may get a chance to travel or work overseas.

You will get a buzz from helping customers meet tight delivery deadlines.

Qualifications and courses

Qualifications vary from a minimum of 4 GCSEs, including English and maths, to A levels, BTEC National in logistics, or a degree. Language skills are useful.

You can enter with a degree, HND or Foundation degree in a related subject, for example logistics, supply chain management, international transport or transport management. Some companies have graduate training schemes.

Key Skills in communications, ICT, problem solving and working with others are useful.

Training after GCSE/S level or Advanced/Higher levels is usually an NVQ/SVQ in International Trade and Services, Traffic Office, or Distribution, Storage and Warehousing Operations.

The British International Freight Association provides specialist training and a professional qualification for freight forwarders.

Certificates and Diplomas in International Trade are also available from the Institute of Export.

Entry to specialist degree courses in such subjects as International transport, logistics, supply chain management and transport management will require a minimum of 2 A levels/3 H grades and 5 GCSEs/S grades (A–C/1–3) or equivalent. For HNC/HND courses, you will normally need at least 1 A level/2 H grades and 4 GCSEs/ S grades (A–C/1–3) or equivalent.

Money guide

Trainees usually earn around £11,000–£15,000 per year.

With experience you could earn around £16,000–£29,000.

£30,000–£50,000 is possible for senior freight forwarders, directors and managers.

Related opportunities

- Distribution Manager p602
- Importer/Exporter p605
- Warehouse Worker/Manager p629

Further information

Institute of Export
Export House, Minerva Business Park, Lynch Wood, Peterborough PE2 6FT
01733 404400; www.export.org.uk

Chartered Institute of Logistics and Transport
Logistics and Transport Centre, Earlstree Court, Earlstree Road, Corby NN17 4XQ
01536 740104; www.ciltuk.org.uk

City&
Guilds

www.cityandguilds.com/myperfectjob

IMPORTER/EXPORTER

What the work involves

- You will organise all aspects of exporting or importing goods for companies who source or sell them overseas.

- Liaising with shipping and forwarding companies, you will get the best prices, sources, quality and delivery services.

- You will deal with all the necessary financial paperwork, including invoicing and checking, and issuing Letters of Credit so that payment can be made.

- Working out accurate costings, including customs duties, insurance and forwarding charges will also be part of your job.

The type of person suited to this work

As you will be making arrangements with a wide range of customers by telephone and email, your communication skills and social confidence need to be good. Language skills are a real advantage.

Dealing with numbers will be one of your key strengths because you will be responsible for working out currency exchanges and import and export duties. In addition, ICT skills are vital. You must have a flair for negotiation as you will need to bargain with shipping and distribution companies, as well as your customers and suppliers.

Working conditions

Most of your work will be in an office using the telephone, computer and fax. You may need to work early mornings or late evenings if your customers or suppliers operate in a different time zone.

You may travel to meet suppliers or customers, which at higher levels could involve significant overseas travel.

Future prospects

As more products are bought and sold in a global market, the numbers of companies employing an import/export specialist have increased. Large freight-forwarding companies and import and export agencies also employ importers/exporters.

Vacancies are competitive and usually require work experience in a related area, for example freight forwarding.

Some import/export specialists move across into overseas sales management as progression can be limited in small export/import departments.

Advantages/disadvantages

This job allows you to use specialist skills to make the global supply chain work.

Tight deadlines and budgets mean that stress is very much part of the job.

Qualifications and courses

You can enter export or import at different levels. It is possible to enter following GCSEs/S grades or A levels/H grades, and work towards an NVQ/SVQ in International Trade and Services or a professional qualification. While there are no set minimum qualifications, most employers will expect: 4 GCSEs/S grades (A–C/1–3) including English and maths.

Apprenticeships/Skillseekers may be available for candidates aged 16–24.

You can enter with a degree, HND or Foundation degree in a related subject, for example logistics, supply chain management, international transport, business or languages. Some companies have graduate training schemes.

The Institute of Export offers professional qualifications for people working in the field of international trade. The Advanced Certificate in International Trade leads to Associate Membership of the Institute, and the Diploma in International Trade leads to Graduate Membership. These qualifications are offered at colleges of further and higher education and by distance learning. Candidates must be at least 18 with 4 GCSEs/S grades at A–C/1–3 and 1 A level/H grade or equivalent, or an NVQ/SVQ Level 2 in International Trade and Services, or an Introductory Certificate of International Trade (Institute of Export), or be 21 years old with three years' practical experience.

If you move into managerial level work you will travel overseas to meet suppliers and customers.

Money guide

Starting salaries at clerk level range from £13,000 to £16,000 per year. Experienced staff with more responsibility can earn up to £30,000. Import or export managers of companies with global interests can earn over £70,000.

Related opportunities

- Road Transport Manager p623
- Distribution Manager p602
- Freight Forwarder p604

Further information

Institute of Export
Export House, Minerva Business Park, Lynch Wood, Peterborough PE2 6FT
01733 404400; www.export.org.uk

www.cityandguilds.com/myperfectjob

LARGE GOODS VEHICLE DRIVER/DRIVER'S MATE

What the work involves

- Large goods vehicle (LGV) drivers move and distribute goods throughout the UK and Europe.

- You will be working with a transport manager to plan your delivery schedule, and they will also be on hand to advise you of alternative routes if there is congestion on the roads.

- You will be responsible for checking that your lorry is safe to drive by carrying out routine maintenance checks such as tyre pressure and oil levels. You will also have to ensure delivery paperwork is filled out correctly.

- The driver's mate works with a driver, helping to plan the route, and load and unload goods.

The type of person suited to this work

You will need to be an extremely competent driver.

You should have a polite manner in order to build good relationships with colleagues and customers.

You must enjoy working alone, as you will spend a great deal of your time on your own on the road.

Quick reactions are useful in case you need to respond to an unforeseen event on the road.

You should be a punctual person, as you will have to adhere to a strict timetable.

Working conditions

You will work on a shift pattern, encompassing evening, overnight and weekend work. You cannot work more than 60 hours a week, and are required by law to take regular rest breaks when driving for hours at a time.

You will spend most of your time on the road in your truck, and this regularly includes eating and sleeping in the cab compartment. Cabs are usually quite comfortable, and generally have both air conditioning and heating.

You should be fairly strong and physically fit, as you may well need to help load and unload heavy goods from your vehicle.

Future prospects

There is currently a shortage of LGV drivers in the UK, and the industry is growing. This means that demand is high and there are plenty of job opportunities.

You could work for a manufacturer, retailer, or specialist distribution company, or you could be self-employed.

Advantages/disadvantages

Part time and flexible hours are available so you can fit work around other commitments.

Qualifications and courses

No specific academic qualifications are required for LGV drivers or driver's mates, but some employers prefer candidates with some GSCEs (A-E) or equivalent, including English and maths.

There are other necessary criteria that you must meet to gain employment as a driver. You should be over 21 years of age, hold a full clean driving licence, and pass both medical and eyesight tests.

You will also need to hold an LGV licence. 2 kinds of licence are available; that classed as category C which will allow you to drive a truck ranging from 3.5 to 32 tonnes in weight, and the category C + E licence which allows you to drive vehicles up to 44 tonnes in weight. You will also need to pass the Driver Certificate of Professional Competence (CPC) in order to obtain your LGV licence.

Skills for Logistics offer a Young LGV Driver Training Scheme, open to entrants aged 16–21, which offers a fast-track route to obtaining your LGV licence as well as an NVQ Level 2 in a relevant subject such as transporting goods by road.

Apprenticeships/Skillseekers may also be available for entrants aged 10–24.

Driving alone for long periods of time can be lonely and monotonous. Absence from home overnight or longer is common.

Money guide

Newly qualified LGV drivers will start on about £14,000. With experience, this could rise to around £30,000. If you drive vehicles in a specialist industry you could earn about £35,000.

A driver's mate can expect to earn between £9,000 and £15,500, although those working in a specialist field can earn up to £24,000.

Related opportunities

- Bus/Coach Driver p598
- Taxi Driver p624
- Train Driver p626
- Driving Examiner/Instructor p603

Further information

Driving Standards Agency
Stanley House, 56 Talbot Street, Nottingham NG1 5GU
0115 901 2500; www.dsa.gov.uk or for specific Driver CPC information www.drivercpc.org

City&
Guilds

www.cityandguilds.com/myperfectjob

LIFT TRUCK OPERATOR

What the work involves

- You will use a lift truck, which has a special lifting and carrying platform, to load, unload, move and stack heavy goods.

- Once you have made sure your truck is working safely, you will drive it to collect the items you will be moving.

- You will operate the controls so that your fork or lifting gear is under the load to raise it safely.

- You will then deliver the goods, either to a vehicle for transportation or to a depot or warehouse for stacking.

The type of person suited to this work

An aptitude for driving is vital, because you will be manoeuvring your lift truck in very narrow awkward spots and watching out for hazards at all times. A responsible, mature outlook is required for working to strict safety rules. A good standard of physical fitness is helpful.

The ability to plan your work is also crucial so that when the transport arrives to deliver or collect your goods, you are in the right place at the right time.

You will be operating the truck on your own, but you will also need to be a team player as others will be working alongside you to do the job, for example warehouse operatives and LGV drivers.

Working conditions

Your work will be both inside a warehouse or factory and also outside in loading bays in all weather conditions.

Operating your equipment will mean sitting in a driving seat for long periods. There is also a risk of accidents.

Hours vary depending on your employer. You may work regular hours Monday to Friday, but many jobs include shift work covering evening, nights and weekends.

Future prospects

Lift truck operators work for any employer who uses lift truck equipment to move heavy goods. They can work for the manufacturing, transport, haulage, warehouse or retail industry. There are about 100,000 lift truck operators in the UK.

With experience, you can move on into supervisory or management jobs such as warehousing. You could go on to train new lift truck operators. Some large employers train lift truck operators up to become LGV drivers or Lift Truck Instructors.

Advantages/disadvantages

You may be based outside in poor weather conditions.

If you are keen on driving, large employers might give you the chance to move on to LGV driver training.

It can be stressful to get a load out quickly, but there's a buzz when transport leaves on time.

Qualifications and courses

ENTRY 1 LEVEL

There are no minimum entry qualifications for this job but basic maths is useful to work out safe loads and weights. You will need to be physically fit and may have to pass a medical. Entrants may have experience of warehouse work, but direct entry is also possible.

Key Skills in numeracy and working with others are useful.

You will need to be at least 18 to work without supervision. A driving licence is required if the truck is to be used on public roads.

You will receive basic training approved by the Health and Safety Commission, either in the workplace or in a training centre. A certificate of basic training is awarded on successful completion of theoretical and practical tests.

Lift truck operators can work towards the NPTC (National Proficiency Tests Council) Level 2 Certificate of Competence in Fork Lift Truck Operations or NVQ/SVQ Levels 1 and 2 in Specialised Plant and Machinery Operations.

Apprenticeships/Skillseekers may be available in such areas as Storage and Warehousing, Wholesale and Distribution, leading to NVQs/SVQs Levels 2 and 3.

Money guide

Starting wages are about £12,000–£13,000 per year.

With experience you could earn between £14,000 and £20,000.

Some specialist operators can earn up to £28,000.

Usually, there are shift allowances and the opportunity to do overtime.

Related opportunities

- Airport Baggage Handler p597
- Construction Plant Operator p87
- Van Driver p628
- Warehouse Worker/Manager p629

Further information

Association of Industrial Truck Trainers, United Kingdom Warehousing Association
Walter House, 418–422 The Strand,
London WC2R 0PT
020 7836 5522; www.ukwa.org.uk

National Plant Operators Registration Scheme (NPORS)
PO Box 204, Northwich, Cheshire CW9 7PL
01606 49909; www.npors.com

www.cityandguilds.com/myperfectjob

LOADER

What the work involves

- Loaders are operatives who load and unload goods into or out of a container or lorry.

- You will be responsible for moving goods, either by hand or using specialist lifting equipment.

- You may be operating a lift truck or a specialist lorry loader (crane) if you are loading or unloading heavy items.

- You may also have additional tasks such as cleaning the loading bay or working as a driver's mate.

The type of person suited to this work

If you like practical tasks and being outside in all weathers, this job is for you. You will also need to be prepared to learn about and follow safety rules because you will be working in a loading bay alongside a heavy goods operating plant. A good level of physical fitness is essential.

You will need to be good at working with others, for example drivers, and listening to any instructions you may be given to keep yourself and others safe.

You should also be good at working out how items can be fitted tightly into a space, as no employer is happy to pay high transportation costs for fresh air!

Working conditions

Most of your work will be outside in the loading depot. There may be some limited cover.

Hours vary. You may work regular hours, Monday to Friday, but it is often shift work and sometimes permanent night work.

There is a risk of accidents.

You may have to wear safety boots and gloves. Some employers require you to provide your own safety clothing.

Future prospects

A range of firms employ loaders, but usually expect you to do other duties. You could work for a manufacturing company moving goods from the factory floor onto wagons, or for a parcel company sorting and loading in delivery order, or a building materials supplier using a lorry loader to lift bricks onto a wagon.

It is possible to progress from this type of work, after additional training, into delivery, driving or warehouse management.

Advantages/disadvantages

If you are keen on going into LGV driving, your employer may be willing to train you.

It is stressful working at speed to get a delivery loaded or unloaded.

This job provides the satisfaction of working as part of a team to get deliveries out on time.

Qualifications and courses

ENTRY LEVEL 1

There are no minimum entry qualifications for this job. You will need to be physically fit and may have to pass a medical. Some employers prefer you to have a driving licence and be at least 18.

You may be able to take an NVQ/SVQ Level 2 in Transporting Goods by Road and NVQ/SVQ Level 3 in Road Haulage and Distribution Operations or an NVQ/SVQ Levels 1–3 in Distribution, Warehousing and Storage Operations.

If your employer expects you to operate a lift truck, they will give you basic training approved by the Health and Safety Commission. You may also be able to work towards NVQ/SVQs Levels 1 and 2 in Specialised Plant and Machinery Operations.

If your employer expects you to operate a hydraulic lorry loader you will need to take a 2-day Lorry Loader Operating Safety Course. Many employers also expect you to be a category C driver to train as a specialist lorry loader.

Money guide

Starting salaries are usually £10,500 per year.

Loaders working as specialist lift truck operators can earn up to £20,000. Hydraulic lorry loaders who also work as an LGV driver can earn up to £28,000.

Shift work or permanent nights can significantly increase your earnings.

Related opportunities

- Airport Baggage Handler p597
- Van Driver p628
- Lift Truck Operator p607
- Warehouse Worker/Manager p629

Further information

United Kingdom Warehousing Association
Walter house, 418–422 Strand, London WC2R 0PT
020 7836 5522; www.ukwa.org.uk

Association of Industrial Truck Trainers
The Spring Board Centre, Mantle Lane, Coalville, Leicestershire LE67 3DW
01530 277857; www.aitt.co.uk

National Plant Operators Registration Scheme (NPORS)
PO Box 204, Northwich, Cheshire CW9 7PL
01606 49909, www.npors.com

City&Guilds

www.cityandguilds.com/myperfectjob

MERCHANT NAVY DECK OFFICER/RATING

What the work involves

- The Merchant Navy consists of thousands of civilian ships, operated by individual shipping companies. They include fuel tankers and cargo ships, as well as ferries and cruise liners.

- Merchant navy deck officers are responsible for navigating ships, as well as being involved in communications and cargo handling.

- You will use satellite and radar systems in order to navigate the ship, maintain machinery and safety equipment, and train and support junior officers and ratings.

- Deck ratings are responsible for supporting the ship's officers by helping to navigate and steer the ship, as well as carrying out maintenance tasks and helping to load and unload cargo.

The type of person suited to this work

Both officers and ratings need to have good social skills in order to work successfully as part of a team. You will also need to be calm and logical in the face of emergency situations.

In addition, officers will need to have excellent numeracy skills and be able to use complex technology in order to successful make navigational calculations. Officers will also need to have good leadership qualities, so that they inspire respect and dedication from their crew members.

Working conditions

You will expect to work shifts, known as 'watches'. These can vary in length from 4 hours on and 4 hours off, to 6 hours on and 6 hours off, or even 12 hours on and 12 hours off at times. These shifts can take place at any time.

Ratings can expect to live in close proximity to their colleagues, often in fairly cramped accommodation. Officers have their own private, en-suite cabin. Generally, good leisure facilities are provided on-board so that crew can make the most of their time off.

Future prospects

With over 20 UK shipping companies in operation, and a predicted increase in shipping activity over the next few years, prospects for Merchant Navy officers and ratings are good.

As a rating, you could gain promotion to Seaman (Grade 2), or even take a conversion course in order to progress to a position as an officer.

Officers may move into related onshore work, including shipbuilding, maritime law and ship and fleet management.

Advantages/disadvantages

You will be working within a strong team environment, so will build excellent relationships with colleagues from a variety of backgrounds.

Shift work can be exhausting.

Qualifications and courses

To become a rating, you will need to have gained GCSEs (A-D) or equivalent, in both maths and English. You must also pass the Merchant Navy medical.

Entrants wishing to become officers can pursue 1 of 3 routes, each of which requires sponsorship by a shipping company.

You could choose to take an HND in nautical science, or alternatively a foundation degree/SQA professional diploma in nautical science or marine operations. The third option is undertaking a degree in nautical science or merchant ship operations, for which employers will require that you hold 2 A-levels (including maths or physics) or equivalent, in addition to your GCSE grades.

The HND and foundation degree/diploma courses usually last 3 years, whilst a full degree will take 4. All will encompass a mixture of classroom-based learning and practical experience gained whilst you work.

You will have to spend long periods of time away from your family. This could encompass months as well as weeks.

Money guide

Trainee merchant navy ratings usually start on between £13,000 and £16,000. This can increase up to £22,000 with experience.

Newly qualified deck officers may have a starting salary of £20,000-£25,000. With experience, this should increase to around £33,000.

Ship captains can earn £30,000-£65,000+.

Related opportunities

- Merchant Navy Engineering Officer p611
- Marine Engineer p238

Further information

The Merchant Navy Association
9 Saxon Way, Caistor, Market Rasen LN7 6SG
01472 851 130; www.mna.org.uk; enquiries@mna.org.uk

Merchant Navy Training Board
Carthusian Court, 12 Carthusian Street, London EC1M 6EZ
0800 085 0973; www.careersatsea.org.uk;
enquiry@careersatsea.org

The Marine Society & Sea Cadets
202 Lambeth Road, London SE1 7JW
020 7654 7000; www.ms-sc.org; info@ms-sc.org

www.cityandguilds.com/myperfectjob

Transport and Logistics

CRCI: WF
CLCI: YAL

MARINE ENGINEER

Marine engineer trainee Robert Kelsey

I have always wanted to be an Engineer but living in the North East with so much of the manufacturing industry in trouble, it seemed unlikely that I would be able to start training with a company that would still be there when I was due to finish!

Going to university was a possibility because I had the right 'A' Levels for a place – Maths, Physics and Technology – but I wasn't sure I would get a qualification that would be in demand and thus guarantee me a job. So I was running out of options! I am interested in sailing so finding out what the career prospects were in Merchant Shipping seemed like a good idea. The minimum entry was 4 GCSEs levels A-C in Maths, English, Science, and any other subject.

I completed an internet search and came up with several options. I contacted SSTG and they invited me for an interview. At the interview they explained everything, they made sure that I chose the right company to sponsor me and took care of all the arrangements. At the time there was only the HND route available, now I believe there are 4 routes, HNC, HND, Foundation Degree, and HONS.

It's hard to believe you can get somebody to pay for your degree especially when you hear of people running up debts of over £30,000. Some of my friends at university struggle to make ends meet, but I seem to manage very nicely even though I am only training. I run a good car and as I'm an engineer and interested in car maintenance, I can look after it myself

I am enjoying my training. It is only natural I suppose to prefer the time spent at sea to the time in College because that is where I will be when I finish training. The work of an engineer trainee officer is very hands on, particularly on smaller ships, but this builds up your self confidence. On one occasion I was able to help with major work on a cracked sump: I felt then that I was learning about real engineering and also gaining responsibility.

I have had two sessions in college with one more to complete. The work is demanding and more concentrated towards the end of the phases. Perhaps the workload could be more evenly spread. Phase 5 is going to be tough with deadlines to meet and exams every week, but I know it will all be worth while because I have a target: to get my first qualification and get back to sea as an officer. Then I will get some real savings in the bank! Later I can work toward further qualifications and hopefully progress in seniority.

'I know the skills I'm acquiring and the qualifications I'm studying for are in demand, so I feel very confident about my future'

If you are interested in a career in the Merchant Navy contact SSTG
www.sstg.org
recruitment@sstg.org
Phone: 01634 820820

MERCHANT NAVY ENGINEERING OFFICER

What the work involves

- The Merchant Navy consists of thousands of civilian ships, operated by individual shipping companies. They include fuel tankers and cargo ships, as well as ferries and cruise liners.

- Merchant navy engineering officers work with all the mechanical and electrical equipment onboard ships.

- You will work on areas of the ship such as the engines, the computer-controlled engine management systems, and the pumps and fuel systems.

- Engineering officers are based in the engine control room of a ship. They are responsible for assisting engineering officers in the repair and servicing of technical equipment.

The type of person suited to this work

You will need to be interested in working with very hi-tech machinery and enjoy learning about new, state-of-the-art technology. You will also need to be very practical and logical so that you can work quickly and efficiently to rectify problems that occur with the equipment. You should also enjoy working as part of a close-knit team and have a high level of self-discipline. Impeccable communication skills are essential for these roles.

Working conditions

You will expect to work shifts, known as 'watches'. These can vary in length from 4 hours on and 4 hours off, to 6 hours on and 6 hours off, or even 12 hours on and 12 hours off at times. These shifts can take place at any time, day or night.

You will spend the majority of your time in the engine control room or the engine room itself, where it will be hot and noisy. As an engineering officer you could be responsible for all of the ship's systems.

Generally, good leisure facilities are provided on-board so that crew can make the most of their time off.

Future prospects

There are fewer people applying to become trainee engineers now so your chances of success are good. The large shipping companies that recruit trainees are recruiting more people than they used to.

Officers may rise through the ranks to reach the level of chief engineer. Alternatively, there are also opportunities in related areas such as ship surveying or ship management.

Advantages/disadvantages

You will be working within a strong team environment, so will build excellent relationships with colleagues from a variety of backgrounds.

The relentless nature of shift work can be exhausting.

Qualifications and courses

You will need to gain five GCSEs (grade A*-C) which include science (physics or combined science awards) as well as maths and English.

To study for a foundation degree (the most common route to this profession) will require a minimum of 120 UCAS points from your A levels which should also be taken in engineering, science-related subjects, maths and English. You can enter the profession with a science-based degree but this is not obligatory.

Merchant Navy Ratings once in the Navy can apply to do a conversion course to become an engineer. This would involve either: studying for a BTEC in marine or mechanical engineering (taking 2–3 years to complete depending on if it is a HNC or HND course) or studying for a degree in some form of engineering (usually marine) which takes up to 4 years.

To enter as a trainee, you must have sponsorship from a training organisation or from a shipping company.

You will have to spend long periods of time away from your family. This could encompass months as well as weeks.

Money guide

Trainees start on between £13,000 and £16,000. This can increase up to £22,000 with experience.

Newly qualified junior engineering officers are usually paid a starting salary of around £25,000. With experience, this should increase to between £26,000 and £50,000 depending on rank.

Chief engineers can earn in excess of £60,000.

Related opportunities

- Merchant Navy Deck Officer/Rating p609
- Royal Marines Commando p558
- Royal Marines Officer p559
- Marine Engineer p238

Further information

The Merchant Navy Association
9 Saxon Way, Caistor, Market Rasen LN7 6SG
01472 851 130; www.mna.org.uk; enquiries@mna.org.uk

Merchant Navy Training Board
Carthusian Court, 12 Carthusian Street, London EC1M 6EZ
0800 085 0973; www.careersatsea.org.uk;
enquiry@careersatsea.org

www.cityandguilds.com/myperfectjob

Organisation Profile

MAERSK GROUP

MAERSK

The A.P. Moller - Maersk Group is a worldwide organisation with about 110,000 employees and offices in around 130 countries – with global headquarters in Copenhagen, Denmark. In addition to owning one of the world's largest shipping companies, we are also involved in a wide range of activities within the energy, shipbuilding, retail and manufacturing industries.

Maersk is a great example of a dynamic employer that recognises the many valuable skills that students can bring to the company. Part of the global A.P.Moller – Maersk Group, The Maersk Company was set up in the UK over 50 years ago, and has a strong history of investment in - and development of – people.

The Maersk Company established its Officer Training Scheme for people who are interested in developing a career at sea. The scheme offers many opportunities for development, whether a person wants to become a Marine Engineer Officer or a Deck Officer. In addition, later on in their career, qualified seafarers often move into careers ashore within The Maersk Company and the A.P.Moller – Maersk Group.

Officer Trainees will spend part of their training studying at nautical college, where they will combine academic work with basic practical training. Sea phases then give trainees the opportunity to gain invaluable practical skills onboard state of the art vessels.

For information on training opportunities please visit our website, www.seacareers.co.uk or contact the recruitment team at GBRMMSREC@maersk.com

MAERSK GROUP

Nicole Fiolet is a fine example of where dedication and hard work can take you;

My name is Nicole Fiolet and I am one of the few women engineers in the British Merchant Navy. I wanted to have a career at sea after sailing as a waitress for a few months while deciding what to do with my future; I decided that this life was for me as I hated the monotony of office life and I loved the banter and atmosphere on the ship.

I started doing a cadetship in marine engineering/electro-technical engineering and my course was sponsored by Maersk, meaning that during my sea phases I got to sail on a container ship, travelling to the Far East and seeing many different places and cultures. At first I thought that working in a male-dominated environment would be difficult and that I'd have to work harder to prove myself but I found that sailors were really friendly and helpful in my learning process. Everyone from the motormen to the Chief Engineers taught me something, whether it was safety or procedures, technical or theory related. I did, however, try harder to be the best during my college phases and that's maybe how I won the prize for Engineer cadet of the year (sponsored by IMAREST) and the prize for Engineering Portfolio (sponsored by the Marine Society) which I went and collected in London during the Marine Society Annual Court. I was amazed to receive both these prizes, as it showed that all the hard work during my 3 year cadetship hadn't gone unnoticed. It was a real achievement for me.

I now sail as an Electro-technical Officer on the Maersk Dunkerque, one of the ferries on the Dover-Dunkerque route, and I love the fact that not one day is the same. It is hard work, but everyday is a challenge and I like the sense of achievement that I get after a hard day's work. The only thing about sea life that I think is a shame is that there are so few women. We can all do the job and get great rewards for it but I think a lot of women are still scared of going away and spending time away from their loved ones. To them, I can say that we're never really away from a telephone call or an email, and it's great to be visiting far away places while earning a decent living. It makes the "coming home" times all the better...

PASSENGER CHECK IN OFFICER

What the work involves

- You will be responsible for making sure that passengers and their baggage board the right aircraft.

- You will greet passengers, provide information, ask security questions and check tickets and passport details.

- Once you have weighed and put luggage on the conveyor belt you will issue boarding passes and prepare paperwork for customs.

- You may also work at the flight gate, making announcements and checking boarding cards and passports.

The type of person suited to this work

As the public face of your airline, you will need a pleasant, confident and helpful manner with a well-groomed appearance.

You need to be confident with ICT. You will use a sophisticated computer system to allocate seats, print boarding cards and baggage labels and produce post-flight figures.

It is vital that you like people, as you may be helping people with disabilities and unaccompanied children from check-in, through security and customs and on to their flight. You will also need to be able to deal with difficult situations. Communication skills are essential for working with your colleagues and other airport staff.

Working conditions

You will wear a uniform and work indoors in an airport.

When you are working at the check-in desk you may sit behind a counter for long periods.

If you are escorting passengers or helping with boarding at a gate, you will spend periods of time on your feet, sometimes walking quite long distances.

Hours may include shifts covering evenings, weekends and holidays.

Future prospects

Employers are either airlines or the ground handling companies that work on behalf of airlines. About 70% of passenger handling work takes place at the four main airports – Heathrow, Gatwick, Stansted and Manchester – so there are more opportunities if you live within travelling distance of one of the big four. There is a lot of competition for jobs, many of which are seasonal.

Advantages/disadvantages

Working with people can be very rewarding.

If there is a delay to their flight, you may have to deal with difficult or demanding passengers.

If you are keen to work in an air cabin crew job then experience in this work will be a big advantage.

Qualifications and courses

Entry requirements vary, but many employers prefer applicants with 3–5 GCSEs (A–C)/S grades (1–3), including English and maths. Minimum age for entry varies from 16 to 20 years of age. There is no upper age for entry. You will need to be physically fit, and there may be height and weight restrictions. It's an advantage to be able to speak another language.

Key Skills in communication and information technology are useful but even more important is being able to demonstrate having put these skills into practice, by doing some work experience with the public in a caring, catering or travel agency job.

You could study a related college or university course, for example a BTEC/SQA National Certificate/Diploma or HNC/D in travel and tourism, an Edexcel BTEC Level 3 National Award, Certificate or Diploma in Aviation Operations or a degree in travel and tourism or a modern language.

Once accepted you will be trained for 4–8 weeks in all aspects of the job.

NVQs/SVQs in Handling Aircraft Passengers at Levels 2 and 0 may be available.

Money guide

Starting salaries are around £12,000 to £14,000 per year. Experienced customer service agents can earn £15,000–£20,000.

At supervisory or management level you could earn up to £25,000.

Shift allowances are usually paid. There may be opportunities to earn overtime pay.

Related opportunities

- Air Cabin Crew p594
- Airport Baggage Handler p597
- Holiday Representative p391
- Tour Guide/Manager p401

Further information

GoSkills (Sector Skills Council for passenger transport)
Concorde House, Trinity Park, Solihull B37 7UQ
0121 635 5520; www.goskills.org

Royal Aeronautical Society
4 Hamilton Place, London WCJ 7BQ
020 7670 4326; www.aerosociety.com

City& Guilds

www.cityandguilds.com/myperfectjob

PASSENGER TRANSPORT CLERK

What the work involves

- As a passenger transport clerk you will deal with customer enquiries regarding departure times, fares, routes, connections and disruptions on bus and rail services.

- You will use computerised systems to organise the purchase or refund of tickets and in order to issue travel cards.

- You will research the best rail or coach fares for a customer and ensure that their transport is as efficient and affordable as possible.

- You may specialise in either sales or customer enquiries but usually members of staff share these responsibilities amongst themselves.

The type of person suited to this work

You should be friendly and polite and have a genuine interest in working with the public.

Some maths and IT skills will be necessary as you will be dealing with fares and payments.

You must be able to work quickly and efficiently so that passengers are not delayed getting to their train/bus.

As you may have to deal with customers in busy times or times when there are unexpected delays you need to have patience and the ability to deal with frustrated or angry customers.

You should have an interest in travel and customer service.

Working conditions

You will work an average of 37–40 hours each week. This may include shift work, evenings, weekends and even public holidays.

You may have the opportunity to work part-time, overtime and flexible hours.

You will be based in stations or travel centres which will function essentially as an office but you will deal with customers on the phone or as they come to the ticket office or information desk you are based at.

Future prospects

You may gain NVQs as you work in order to progress to supervisory and managerial roles.

You may be employed by any bus or coach operator or private rail companies, Train Operating Companies throughout the UK, the London Underground or Eurostar.

Advantages/disadvantages

You will have the opportunity to work in an ever-changing

Qualifications and courses

There are no formal qualifications required to enter this profession. However GSCEs in English, maths or any relevant subjects (A-C) will be useful.

Customer service experience will also be an advantage.

You will learn largely on-the-job, although some training may be provided, depending on the organisation you work for.

Many companies will provide their own in-house training, or day-release training for clerical staff. If you are going into a position as a rail passenger transport clerk or a member of telephone enquiry bureau staff you will be trained in fare structures, customer care, railway geography and computerised ticket systems.

You may also be provided with training from bus and coach companies which may be provided in-house. This will involve learning how to use timetables, ticket systems, price structures and customer care information.

environment as bus and rail services are constantly updated and new customers use them each day.

At times your work may be repetitive.

Money guide

Your starting salary as a transport clerk may start around £14,500 a year.

With some experience this can increase to £17,000 a year.

With several years' experience and qualifications you can earn between £19,000 and £20,000 a year.

Related opportunities

- Customer Service Assistant/Manager p486
- Passenger Check In Officer p614
- Travel Agency Sales Consultant p403

Further information

Customer Contact Association
20 Newton Place, Glasgow G3 7PY
0141 564 9010; www.cca.org.uk

GoSkills
Concorde House, Trinity Park, Solihull,
West Midlands B37 7UQ
0121 635 5520; info@goskills.org; www.goskills.org

City&
Guilds

www.cityandguilds.com/myperfectjob

POSTMAN/POSTWOMAN

What the work involves

- You will have responsibility for the sorting and daily delivery of mail to homes, shops, factories and offices for your patch.

- Your day will start at the sorting office getting your mail ready for delivery, by sorting and packing your bag in the best order for your route.

- You will then deliver your mail by foot or bicycle or, in rural areas, by van.

- You may also be responsible for mail collections from post boxes and places of work.

The type of person suited to this work

Your round could include several hundred addresses and cover up to eight miles a day so you will need to be fit, especially if you are doing the job on foot or by bicycle. You will also have to like being outdoors as you will be expected to deliver the mail in all weathers.

Honesty and reliability are vital qualities in this job. You will be carrying lots of valuable and urgent mail around and you are responsible for delivering it to the right place.

Do not think of this job if you do not like meeting people, because you will be talking to and advising customers every day when you are out on your round.

Working conditions

Most of your work will be outside in all weathers. A uniform, footwear and protective clothing will be provided.

If on foot, you may have to carry your mail in bags, though there will be arrangements to transport you and your mail out to the start of your route.

Shift work with an early morning (5am) start or late evening (10pm) finish is usual.

You may have to walk up steep hills and deal with minor hazards.

Future prospects

Postal delivery workers mainly work for the Royal Mail. Despite the growth of email and texting, the amount of mail sent continues to grow.

Recruitment tends to be steady and there are opportunities in urban and rural areas throughout the UK. Some workers start out with temporary work over the Christmas period and are retained.

It is possible to move into parcel deliveries, supervisory or managerial work.

Advantages/disadvantages

With a regular round you will really get to know your customers.

There may be some hazards on your round; you will soon learn what to avoid. All the walking or cycling will keep you fit.

Qualifications and courses

No specific qualifications are required for this job. Candidates should be aged 18 or over, and selection is by an aptitude test, a fitness assesment and interview. You may have to have a medical examination.

The ability to ride a bicycle and/or a driving licence with no more than six penalty points may be required.

Postmen/women receive induction training. Further training is done on the job.

Apprenticeships/Skillseekers are available for candidates aged 16–24. However, most candidates need to be at least 18 years of age and are recruited following an aptitude test (to check your ability to read addresses properly), fitness assessment and a competency-based interview.

Training is chiefly on-the-job, lasting 18 months, and can include the chance to work towards an NVQ/SVQ in Mail Services at Level 2. With a minimum of one year's experience, you can seek advancement to supervisory or managerial levels.

Although you will have to start work by 5am if you are on the early shift, you will finish at around lunchtime.

Money guide

Starting pay for staff over 18 is between £13,000 and £15,200 (in London).

After one year's experience you would earn about £18,500–£22,000 (in London).

Supervisors with additional responsibilities can earn around £28,000.

There are additional payments for overtime and – once qualified – for driving duties.

Related opportunities

- Courier p600
- Van Driver p628
- Freight Forwarder p604
- Warehouse Worker/Manager p629

Further information

Royal Mail Group plc
148 Old Street, London EC1V 9HQ; www.royalmail.com

Skills for Logistics
14 Warren Yard, Warren Farm Office Village,
Milton Keynes MK12 5NW
01908 313360; www.skillsforlogistics.org

City & Guilds

www.cityandguilds.com/myperfectjob

PURCHASING/PROCUREMENT MANAGER

What the work involves

- You will be responsible for buying the goods or services needed by a business, and providing the best value for money.

- Your first job is to find out what your employer wants to buy and how much the budget is.

- An important aspect will be to find the best suppliers and negotiate with them to get products or services at the right conditions and price.

- You will then be responsible for quality checks to make sure that the goods or services provided are of the standard agreed.

The type of person suited to this work

You will need to have a flair for identifying good suppliers, negotiation, tact and persuasion to do well in this job. Your communication skills also need to be excellent.

You will also need to be keen on computers, as you will use them both to research and keep in touch with suppliers.

Having a head for figures is essential as you will be dealing with your employer's budget and calculating all the costs involved in procuring your goods or services.

Working conditions

Most of your work will be undertaken in a busy office, using a phone and computer (including software such as spreadsheets and databases).

You may travel to meet suppliers and customers, which can mean time away from home.

You will work mainly office hours Monday to Friday. If your suppliers are in a different time zone to the UK, this can mean early mornings or late nights.

Future prospects

This is a developing area with more employers using a qualified purchaser to obtain the best value goods and services. Purchasing administrator jobs are competitive, but there is a shortage of qualified applicants for purchasing manager jobs.

Some buyers move into specialist areas, for example construction or chemicals. ICT purchasing is a new specialism and is predicted to grow with the expansion of e-business.

Promotion prospects are good, especially in large organisations.

Advantages/disadvantages

If successful, you can reach high levels of responsibility, and even travel overseas, early in your career.

There is no doubt that this job is stressful. Businesses spend over half their money on the goods and services they need to buy, so mistakes could be expensive.

Qualifications and courses

Employers usually ask for a degree or HND qualification. It may be possible to enter at a lower level and progress with experience and on-the-job training.

The Chartered Institute of Purchasing and Supply (CIPS) accredits some degree courses in business (with purchasing options), logistics and supply chain management, and purchasing and supply chain management.

To progress you will need the CIPS professional qualifications. The Certificate and Advanced Certificate and the Graduate Diploma can be studied full time or part time at college, or by distance learning. The Certificate has no formal entry requirements. On completion of the Certificate, you can progress to the Advanced Certificate.

The Graduate Diploma is made up of the Foundation Stage (exemptions available to accredited graduates) and the Professional Stage. You will need 2 A levels/three H grades and 3 GCSEs/S grades (A–C/1–3), a National Certificate/Diploma or the CIPS Advanced Certificate, or to be over 21 with relevant work experience.

You can take NVQ/SVQs at Levels 2, 3 and 4 in Supply Chain Management as an alternative route.

Money guide

Starting pay for purchasing administrators is about £17,000 per year. For experienced purchasing administrators or new purchasing managers the salary range is £20,000–£29,000. £33,000 is usual for senior purchasing managers, rising to £45,000 for a few large retail chains. £60,000+ is possible for purchasing directors with a proven track record.

Related opportunities

- Importer/Exporter p605
- Distribution Manager p602
- Warehouse Worker/Manager p629

Further information

Chartered Institute of Purchasing & Supply
Easton House, Easton on the Hill, Stamford, Lincolnshire PE9 3NZ
01780 756777; www.cips.org

Skillsmart Retail
0800 093 5001; www.skillsmartretail.com

www.cityandguilds.com/myperfectjob

Transport and Logistics

CRCI: WC
CLCI: OP

RAIL SIGNALLING TECHNICIAN

What the work involves

- Rail signalling technicians are responsible for installing and repairing all of the signalling and telecommunications systems that are used to support the railways.

- Equipment that you will be working on will include signal boxes, warning systems, manual lever frame boxes, and coloured light signals.

- You will also install new signalling equipment, such as GSM-R communication masts, and update existing systems.

The type of person suited to this work

You should have good manual dexterity in order to operate a range of tools and machines.

A logical approach to your work will help when tracing faults, as will the ability to understand technical drawings and engineering instructions when repairing systems. You will need good eyesight and full colour vision.

You should have a reasonable level of numeracy, and good ICT skills so that you can operate computerised machinery.

You will also need to be physically fit, as the work can include lifting and carrying heavy equipment, as well as working up ladders or in awkward places.

Working conditions

You will work around 37 hours a week, most likely in a shift pattern that could include early morning, evening and weekend work. You may also be expected to work overtime fairly regularly.

Your time will be divided between working outside, carrying out repairs trackside, and undertaking maintenance near signal boxes or within stations. You should be prepared to work in any weather conditions. You may well have to travel to various different locations each day, and overnight absence from home is common.

Future prospects

You could be employed by Network Rail, working on the UK's commercial railway tracks, or by a number of underground, metro or light rail operators such as London Underground, Metronet, Translink and the Docklands Light Railway.

With experience, you can become a member of the Institution of Railway Signal Engineers, which offers a route into becoming a registered engineering technician.

Promotion opportunities are good, and you could end up as a team manager, or even move into a consultancy role when you have built up significant experience.

Advantages/disadvantages

You will be playing an essential role in maintaining and developing the infrastructure of the UK.

Qualifications and courses

ENTRY LEVEL 2

Network Rail operates a large Apprenticeship programme for those aged 16–24, as do many other employers of rail signalling technicians. Employers usually require candidates to have 3–5 GCSEs/S grades (A-C/1–3) or equivalent, including English, maths and science. A double GCSE in engineering or a related technical subject would also be helpful.

Apprentices work towards an NVQ Level 3 in railway engineering (signalling), undertaking a mixture of classroom-based and on-the-job learning.

Most employers operate their own selection process on top of these academic requirements. This usually consists of a medical test, which will assess your fitness, eyesight and hearing, as well as drug and alcohol screening. Occasionally, you may also have to sit an aptitude test.

You could undertake a full time or part time course prior to looking for work as a rail signalling technician. Relevant courses include the BTEC National Certificate in electronics and railway signals/telecommunications, and the BTEC National Certificate in signalling and communication.

Promotion opportunities are good, and there is also the chance to undertake extra training to drive forward your career.

Working in all weather conditions and cramped surroundings can be uncomfortable and extremely unpleasant at times.

Money guide

Your starting salary as a newly qualified rail signalling technician will be about £13,000. As you gain experience, this should increase to around £22,000. If you become a senior technician, or move into a consultancy role, your salary could reach £30,000+.

Related opportunities

- Telecommunications Engineer p251
- Electrician p94
- Electricity Distribution Worker p227

Further information

Railway-technology.com
c/o SPG Media Ltd, Brunel House, 55–57 North Wharf Road, London W2 1LA
01207 915 9957; www.railway-technology.com

City& Guilds

www.cityandguilds.com/myperfectjob

RAIL TRACK MAINTENANCE OPERATIVE

What the work involves

- Rail track maintenance workers are responsible for building, repairing and maintaining the rail track network across the UK.

- You will use a variety of manual and automated tools, including welding equipment, clamping machines, and cement mixers.

- You will also be responsible for inspecting the track in order to spot potential faults, which will involve walking along live tracks with trains passing nearby.

The type of person suited to this work

You will need to be fit and strong to undertake this work, as you will be lifting and moving heavy pieces of track, as well as operating powerful machinery at times. You should also have good manual skills in order to use tools effectively and safely.

You must be a good communicator so you can work effectively within a team. You should be able to listen to instructions and take direction, whilst also having the confidence to use your own initiative and help colleagues when necessary.

You should have a good awareness of onsite safety practice and a responsible attitude to your work.

Working conditions

You will work an average of 35 hours per week on a shift system. You will have to work nights and weekends regularly, as these are the times at which maintenance work causes least disruption to the train timetable.

Work usually takes place outdoors, in all weather conditions. You should be prepared to get cold and wet working in muddy conditions, and also extremely hot in the summer months.

You will have to wear protective clothing, including a hard hat, high visibility jacket and reinforced boots.

Future prospects

Network Rail employs almost all the rail track maintenance workers in the UK, and they continuously update track all around the country.

There are also opportunities with rail employment agencies, who recruit workers for specific projects managed by rail engineering contractors.

With experience, you could progress to a supervisory role, or become a specialist in a technical area such as line-laying or welding.

You could take further training in order to gain qualifications for managerial roles, or study to become an engineer.

Advantages/disadvantages

The work is physically tiring but rewarding, as you will be working towards maintaining the infrastructure of the UK.

You will be working in a team, so the job will be sociable and you will build strong relationships with your colleagues.

Qualifications and courses

Network Rail and most other employers look for candidates with a minimum of 4 GCSEs/S grades (A-C/1–3) or equivalent, including English and maths. A technical subject is also desirable.

Qualifications in related subjects such as a GCSE, A-level or a Diploma in engineering, or the City & Guilds NVQ Level 1 in rail engineering, may be helpful in demonstrating your enthusiasm for the role and securing you employment.

You will have to be fit, and most employers will ask you to take a medical assessment to measure your fitness, stamina, and also test your hearing and eyesight. You will also have to take tests for drugs and alcohol. Some employers also require candidates to go through a Criminal Records Bureau check, as the role of a maintenance operative is critical in ensuring railway safety.

Experience in a similar construction or engineering related role may be beneficial, but is not essential.

Network Rail operates a large Apprenticeship programme for those aged 16–24.

Working in all weather conditions can be uncomfortable and extremely unpleasant at times.

Money guide

Your starting salary as an inexperienced rail track worker will be about £14,000.

Once you have spent a few years in the role and built up your skills, you could be earning £18,000.

Rail track workers with additional supervisory responsibilities can earn up to £20,000.

Related opportunities

- Rail Signalling Technician p618
- Stonemason p128
- Bricklayer p72
- Labourer p86

Further information

Network Rail
Kings Place, 90 York Way, London N1 9AG
020 3356 9595; www.networkrail.co.uk

Institute of Mechanical Engineers (IMechE)
1 Birdcage Walk, Westminster, London SW1H 9JJ
020 7222 7899; www.imeche.org; enquiries@imeche.org

City&
Guilds

www.cityandguilds.com/myperfectjob

CRCI: WD
CLCI: YAF

Transport and Logistics

RAILWAY STATION ASSISTANT

What the work involves

- Railway station assistants work within train stations, assisting customers, dealing with queries, and ensuring that passengers are happy.

- You may work behind a ticket desk, on an information stand, or on the station platforms so that you are accessible to passengers.

- You will need to provide assistance to wheelchair users and other people who require help boarding or disembarking from a train.

- You will check tickets, and be on the look out for any security threats or other problems within the station.

The type of person suited to this work

You will need to be a confident communicator so that you can impart information to passengers, and also field any negative comments or occasional anger that may be directed towards you.

You should be polite and approachable, and maintain a clean, smart appearance.

You will need good hearing and eyesight, as well as a high level of fitness in order to physically assist customers and move around the station quickly when necessary.

You should be able to work well within a team, taking instructions and helping colleagues, but also enjoy working autonomously and using your initiative.

Working conditions

You will usually work 37 hours per week, and this will include early morning, late night and weekend shifts. There are usually opportunities to undertake paid overtime work.

You will also be working within ticket offices or passenger information areas in the station. You will have to wear a uniform so that you are easily recognisable to passengers.

Future prospects

You could either work for a train operating company (TOC) or for Network Rail, within large or small train stations across the UK. There are also opportunities to work for underground or metro operators in some cities.

Many future opportunities are open to railway station assistants. You could work on the trains as a conductor or driver, move upwards to become a customer services manager, or even reach the position of station manager.

Advantages/disadvantages

You will be working in a variety of roles each day so work should not get monotonous.

You will spend a lot of time on freezing station platforms in the winter.

Qualifications and courses

You must be at least 18 years of age. Good communication skills and numerical ability are viewed as extremely important by employers, so most TOCs require candidates to have 4 GCSEs/S grades (A-C/ 1–3) or equivalent, including English and maths.

You may also be required to pass medical assessments, which will include eyesight, colour vision and hearing tests, as well as those for drugs and alcohol use.

Employers favour candidates who have previous experience in customer relations roles, whether paid or voluntary.

Apprenticeships may be available for entrants aged 18–21.

Once employed as a railway station assistant, you will have to undergo a training period that will encompass classroom-based learning programmes including health and safety, customer care, railway operating systems and coping in emergency situations. This will be followed by practical training in the station.

Some TOCs also encourage employees to work towards an NVQ Level 2 in rail transport operations as part of their training.

You may have to deal with angry and aggressive passengers at times.

Money guide

Your starting salary as a railway station assistant is likely to be about £13,000. As you gain experience and knowledge, this should rise to £18,500. If you are promoted to team leader, your salary will increase to £21,000+.

Overtime is always available, so your wages can be increased if you are willing to work extra hours.

Related opportunities

- Train Conductor p625
- Train Driver p626
- Rail Track Maintenance Operative p619

Further information

Network Rail
Kings Place, 90 York Way, London N1 9AG
020 3356 9595; www.networkrail.co.uk

City&
Guilds

www.cityandguilds.com/myperfectjob

REMOVALS OPERATIVE

What the work involves

- Fragile items will need to be carefully packed and large items need to be taken apart to fit them into the removals van.

- You will have to pack the van in a planned way to make the most of the space and prevent damage in transit.

- Once you have driven the goods to their destination you will have to unload and unpack.

- You will also need to put large items of furniture back together again and put items where the customer wants them.

The type of person suited to this work

The removals business is a people business. Your customers will be stressed about moving and will need your help. They will also rely on you to keep calm and cheerful. Your careful nature and honesty are also vital as you will be dealing with valuable and fragile items on a regular basis.

As you will be working in a small team you will need to be good at working with others and listening to any instructions you may be given to keep yourself and others safe.

You should be fit and enjoy practical work. You will be lifting and carrying large items and sometimes removing door or window frames to get them out of or into a property.

Working conditions

Most of your work will be either in your van or in customers' homes or workplaces. Some trips can involve time away from home and quite long journeys.

Basic hours are 39–40 per week, but some days will be very long as you will have to work until the job is finished. A lot of moves take place at weekends.

You may be at risk of back injuries as there is a lot of lifting and carrying.

Future prospects

There are removals companies throughout the UK, though most are based in urban areas. There are about 30,000 removal operatives and it is a steady area of work as people and businesses are always on the move. The level of work may be affected by the housing market.

Promotion prospects are limited, but you may be able to progress on to driving, specialist packing, supervisory or managerial work.

Self-employment may be possible by buying or leasing a van and offering a removal service.

Advantages/disadvantages

The job may involve early starts and late finishes, especially during house removals when legal processes can cause delays.

Qualifications and courses

No particular educational qualifications are needed although GCSEs/S grades in English and maths are useful. You will need to be in good health and physically fit. Some firms will accept you at 16, whilst others specify a minimum age of 18, or even 21. A full driving licence is sometimes required.

Key Skills in communication and working with others are useful.

Most people are trained on the job by experienced staff. Some firms send staff on short courses run by the British Association of Removers. Courses include removals management and specialist packing.

You may be able to take an NVQ/SVQ Level 2 in Storage and Warehousing, or Carry and Deliver Goods and NVQs/SVQs Levels 2 and 3 in Driving Goods Vehicles, or other related areas.

You will get satisfaction from doing a really professional job when you complete the move. Plus, happy customers may give tips.

Money guide

Starting wages are about £11,500–£13,000 per year.

Experienced removal operatives earn from £15,000–£18,000.

Supervisory staff may earn up to £24,000.

Wages can sometimes be increased by overtime pay, shift allowances and tips.

Related opportunities

- Airport Baggage Handler p597
- Van Driver p628
- Loader p608
- Roadie p448

Further information

Skills for Logistics
14 Warren Yard, Warren Farm Office Village,
Milton Keynes MK12 5NW
01908 313360; www.skillsforlogistics.org

British Association of Removers
Tangent House, 62 Exchange Road, Watford,
Hertfordshire WD18 0TG
01923 699480; www.bar.co.uk

City&
Guilds

www.cityandguilds.com/myperfectjob

Transport and Logistics

CRCI: WG
CLCI: YAT

ROAD SAFETY OFFICER

What the work involves

- You will be working to reduce the number of motorists, cyclists and pedestrians injured or killed on the roads in your area.

- You will educate the public by giving presentations to groups such as children.

- Promoting national road safety campaigns by distributing leaflets and running exhibitions may also be part of your job.

- You will collect information about traffic accidents and make recommendations about how to prevent them.

The type of person suited to this work

As this job is all to do with marketing and persuading, you will need to be an excellent communicator. You will use these skills to develop publicity materials and encourage people to behave more responsibly on the roads.

Self-confidence is vital to build good working relationships with lots of other professionals, such as safety engineers, police officers and local councillors.

To persuade others, you will need teaching or training skills and to be able to work with all age groups. You could give advice on fitting child car seats outside supermarkets, or teach small groups of young children how to cross the road safely.

Working conditions

Most of your work will be office-based, but you will make visits to schools and other locations.

You will usually work 37 hours a week, Monday to Friday. Some evening work is required.

When working on-site with engineers, or investigating accidents, you will wear high visibility clothing.

Your office work will involve using a computer to collect and analyse information.

Future prospects

Road safety officers usually work for local authorities and work towards targets to lower the number of people killed and injured on the roads. Some jobs are temporary as they are paid for by short-term government funding.

Promotion can be to a specialist post, for example publicity, or working with schools, or into management. There are also some jobs coordinating national safety and environmental initiatives, for example the National Walk to School Campaign.

Advantages/disadvantages

You will have the satisfaction of seeing the results of your work in reduced death and injury figures in your area.

There may be delays or obstacles to putting in place the safety improvement work you have recommended, which can be frustrating.

Qualifications and courses

ENTRY LEVEL 3

Entrants to this job may have a degree or relevant experience. Experience and personal qualities are as important as academic qualifications. A driving licence is essential.

Key Skills in communication, working with others and ICT would be useful.

It is possible to work towards an NVQ/SVQ in Transportation at Levels 3–5 or a BTEC Professional Diploma in Accident and Safety Management.

The National Staff Training Group offers a training programme for road safety officers. Phase 1 of the programme provides training for newly appointed officers. Phase 2 consists of a residential short course, and Phase 3 involves a series of seminars. Completion of Phase 2 training can lead to Associate Membership of the Institute of Road Safety Officers (IRSO).

Requirements for becoming a member of IRSO are a relevant degree, a BTEC Professional Development Diploma in Accident and Safety Management, or NVQ/SVQ Levels 3/4 in Transportation.

Money guide

Newly qualified officers earn £18,000, rising to £23,000 per year.

Experienced officers, with inspection responsibilities, earn up to £32,000.

Officers with management responsibility can earn £36,000+.

Local authorities may offer essential car user allowances.

Some employers also offer performance related bonus schemes.

Related opportunities

- Health and Safety Adviser p40
- Police Officer p551
- Public Relations Officer p425
- Primary and Secondary Teacher p212

Further information

Employers' Organisation for Local Government
Layden House, 76–86 Turnmill Street, London EC1M 5LG
020 7296 6600; www.lgcareers.com

Institute of Road Safety Officers
www.irso.org.uk

MOL Enquiry Team D9
Moston Centre, Ashley Lane, Moston, Manchester M9 4WU
0161 203 2103; www.mol-openlearning.co.uk

City&
Guilds

www.cityandguilds.com/myperfectjob

ROAD TRANSPORT MANAGER

What the work involves

- You will work for a business that moves goods or passengers, planning the routes and work timetables of your drivers.

- You will oversee the day-to-day movement of your vehicles, checking that they are in the right places at the right times.

- Putting health and safety regulations into place, and monitoring compliance, will be part of your role.

- Your job will include checking costs to make sure that your company makes a profit.

The type of person suited to this work

Planning timetables, journeys and loads means that you will need to be organised. You should also be logical and enjoy using computers to manage and develop information.

You will cost up journeys, work out timetables and stick to a strict budget, so you must enjoy working with figures.

When you are out there in the depot, the job will be hands on. For example, you may be quality checking a vehicle repair, or chasing up drivers to get your vehicles out on time.

Working conditions

Most of your work will be based in an office. You will also spend time at vehicle depots, and may need to travel to carry out spot checks on your drivers. Transport is a 24/7 business, so you may need to work shifts and weekends.

Future prospects

Transport is on the move and it is a growing industry. You could work for a range of employers such as logistics and distribution companies, road haulage firms, manufacturers, retail chains or coach and bus operators.

It is possible to be promoted to area or general manager. Prospects are better if you are flexible about moving to a larger company or into other modes of transport.

Transport planning is currently a severe skill shortage area, and it is possible to move into it with management experience in the transport sector.

Advantages/disadvantages

No two days are the same – traffic levels, problems and weather conditions vary from day to day.

You will have the satisfaction of seeing an instant result when you make decisions. The way you manage a problem can mean happier customers.

Money guide

Starting salaries are usually £22,000–£23,000 per year. Experienced managers – depending on the company's size – can earn £25,000–£40,000.

Qualifications and courses

ENTRY LEVEL 3

It is possible to enter the transport industry with qualifications ranging from a few GCSEs/S grades (including English and maths) to a degree. Apprenticeships/Skillseekers are available. There are also NVQ/SVQ Levels 2 and 3 in Road Passenger Transport (passenger work) and Traffic Office (freight work).

Some companies recruit graduates to management positions. It is possible to enter with a degree in any subject. There are specialist degrees and postgraduate courses in transport management, transport planning and logistics.

Once working you can study for the Chartered Institute of Logistics and Transport's professional qualifications part time at college or by distance learning. The Certificate is aimed at supervisors and first line managers. The Professional Diploma is intended for middle managers, including recent graduates, and fulfils the requirements for membership of the Institute. New or aspiring senior transport managers can take the CILT Advanced Diploma or study for an MSc in Logistics or Passenger Transport Management. Master's courses are offered by Aston University in partnership with CILT, and take 3 years by distance learning.

The essential qualification to become a road transport senior manager is the Certificate of Professional Competence of the Department of Transport (Department of the Environment in Northern Ireland). This course is roughly equivalent to NVQ Level 3.

Senior managers earn up to £50,000, but the economic climate has reduced opportunities at this level. A small number employed by major companies may earn up to £80,000.

Allowances are usually paid for shift work and unsocial hours.

Related opportunities

- Distribution Manager p602
- Freight Forwarder p604
- Warehouse Worker/Manager p629

Further information

Chartered Institute of Logistics and Transport
Logistics and Transport Centre, Earlstree Court
Earlstree Road, Corby NN17 4XQ
01536 740104; www.ciltuk.org.uk

City& Guilds

www.cityandguilds.com/myperfectjob

Transport and Logistics

CRCI: WE
CLCI: YAD

TAXI DRIVER

Transport and Logistics

CRCI: WE
CLCI: YAD

What the work involves

- Taxi drivers pick up and transport passengers between destinations in a licensed vehicle for an agreed fee.

- You could either drive your own black cab (also known as a hackney carriage) or operate a private hire vehicle (more commonly called a minicab).

- If you drive a black cab, you will be able to pick up people who are waiting at a taxi rank, in the street, or those who have pre-booked. Minicabs are only allowed to carry pre-booked passengers.

- You will also need to assist passengers in and out of your vehicle, and help them with bags as necessary.

The type of person suited to this work

You will need to be personable and pleasant to passengers, but also have the confidence to handle difficult or aggressive fares should the need arise.

You should have a good local knowledge of the area in which you operate. Black cab drivers in London are required to pass a test in order to demonstrate their knowledge of the city prior to gaining a licence.

You will need a good level of numeracy, as you will be handling money regularly and need to ensure that you give passengers their correct change.

Working conditions

Your working hours will vary according to your employer. If you work for a company, you may undertake shifts that include night and weekend hours. Self-employed drivers can choose their own hours.

Most work is available in larger towns and cities, and taxi drivers are busiest on Friday and Saturday night when people are looking to go home after an evening out.

You will spend the majority of your time in your vehicle, either driving passengers to their destination, or waiting for a job to come up.

Future prospects

Taxi usage is growing at a rapid rate, so job opportunities in the industry are plentiful.

Although you can work anywhere in the UK, the majority of work is focused within the larger towns and cities.

Many taxi drivers are self-employed, and with experience and knowledge you could gain an operator's licence and build up your own company.

Advantages/disadvantages

You will be dealing with a variety of people on a daily basis, so the work is sociable and interesting from that point of view.

You will be confined to your vehicle for most of your working

Qualifications and courses

It is not necessary to have any formal qualifications in order to become a taxi driver, but you do have to fulfil the conditions set out by your local licensing authority prior to them granting you a licence to work.

Criteria vary across the licensing authorities, but all require applicants to pass an enhanced Criminal Records Bureau check to prove they are not a threat to members of the local community, to have held a full driving licence for at least 12 months (3 years in London). You must also pass a medical assessment, and to be over the age of 21 (18 in Northern Ireland.)

The strictest local licensing authority is that of London, which requires all registered taxi drivers to pass an extensive, knowledge-based test. It takes an average of 40 months to accumulate and learn all the necessary road information to pass.

day, and may spend long periods of time waiting around in between jobs.

You will occasionally have to deal with drunk, aggressive or distressed passengers.

Money guide

Taxi drivers who are just starting out usually earn about £12,000 for working full time hours. Figures will vary for those working part time, or undertaking significant overtime.

If you work around 40 hours a week and take a good amount of fares for the majority of the time, you could earn £18,000.

Taxi drivers in London and other very busy cities can earn £30,000+, but they work long and often unsociable hours.

Related opportunities

- Chauffeur p599
- Tour Guide p 401
- Driving Examiner/Driving Instructor p603
- Courier p600

Further information

Licensed Taxi Drivers Association (LTDA)
Taxi House, Woodfield Road, London W9 2BA
020 7286 1046; www.ltda.co.uk

Driving Standards Agency (DSA)
Stanley House, 56 Talbot Street, Nottingham NG1 5GU
0115 901 2618; www.dsa.gov.uk

City&
Guilds

www.cityandguilds.com/myperfectjob

TRAIN CONDUCTOR

What the work involves

- Train conductors work on passenger trains, checking and issuing tickets, and ensuring that passengers are enjoying a comfortable and pleasant journey.

- You will mainly focus on providing an excellent level of customer service to those riding the train. This will include fielding any queries or complaints, and handling rowdy passengers at times.

- You will be responsible for making announcements to notify passengers about approaching stations, times of arrival, and any delays in the journey.

- You may also need to look after passengers with special requirements, such as assisting the elderly and disabled, and keeping an eye on children travelling alone.

The type of person suited to this work

You must have excellent interpersonal skills in order to advise passengers about their journey, answer queries, deal with complaints calmly and professionally, and to maintain authority when dealing with aggressive or difficult passengers.

You should be very confident, as you will be working alone as the first point of contact for all train passengers.

You must be able to quickly and effectively deal with a number of unexpected situations.

It is also beneficial to be medically fit, and have good eyesight and hearing.

Working conditions

You will usually work 37 hours per week, according to a shift rota that will include early morning, night and weekend work. Overtime opportunities are regular.

If you work on long distance routes, you may be required to stay overnight at the destination on occasion.

Although most of your time is spent walking through the train, you will usually also have a small, private office onboard. This will have equipment for making announcements, CCTV and usually a computer terminal.

You will be expected to wear a uniform and maintain a clean, smart appearance at all times.

Future prospects

Job opportunities for conductors have decreased slightly in recent years with the introduction of driver-only trains on shorter routes. Nowadays, roles are concentrated on cross-country trains.

Most train conductors are employed by a TOC that specialises in passenger transportation. TOCs operate throughout the UK, so there are opportunities in most towns and cities.

Promotions can include titles such as senior conductor or train manager, and there may also be opportunities to move into general management within the rail sector.

Qualifications and courses

Although there are no set qualifications for entry to become a train conductor, almost all train operating companies (TOCs) look for candidates with 5 GCSEs/S grades (A-C/1–3) or equivalent, including English and maths.

You will need to be 18 years of age before you are legally allowed to work onboard a train. You can work within a railway station from the age of 16, which could help to build up the customer services skills that employers desire in candidates applying for conductor roles.

When you apply, you will need to pass a series of tests in order to assess your suitability. These include a full medical to gauge your level of fitness, eyesight, colour vision, and hearing.

You may also have to pass a drugs test, and may be asked to take these at random intervals in your career in compliance with the rigid safety policy that is in place regarding alcohol and drug abuse.

Apprenticeships may be available for those aged 16–24.

Advantages/disadvantages

You will be dealing with a variety of people on a daily basis, so work is rarely monotonous or boring.

You will be providing an important and valuable service to railway passengers.

You may have to deal with drunk, aggressive, or distressed passengers from time to time.

Money guide

The starting salary for a trainee conductor is about £13,000.

Once you have qualified, this will rise to £14,000.

With experience, and having gained extra supervisory responsibilities, this could increase to £21,000.

Related opportunities

- Train Driver p626
- Railway Station Assistant p620
- Signalling Technician p618
- Air Cabin Crew p594

Further information

The National Rail website provides details of individual TOCs

www.nationalrail.co.uk

City&
Guilds

www.cityandguilds.com/myperfectjob

Transport and Logistics

CRCI: WD
CLCI: YAF

TRAIN DRIVER

Transport and Logistics

CRCI: WD
CLCI: YAF

What the work involves

- Train drivers are responsible for safely operating trains that carry both passengers and goods around the UK.

- You will drive the train on set routes aiming to arrive punctually at your destination, as long as there are no interferences with signalling or other unforeseen problems.

- You must check your route carefully prior to setting off to ensure that it is still viable. You should also carry out safety-related checks on the train itself.

- You will provide a safe and efficient service by observing railway signs, signals and speed limits, and staying alert at all times.

The type of person suited to this work

You will need to have excellent concentration and good observational skills, coupled with a responsible attitude towards safety, so that you can effectively operate a train.

You will need good eyesight and hearing, as well as quick reactions in order to respond to unexpected situations. Being able to keep calm under pressure is also an asset as difficult circumstances can arise during journeys.

You should have some mechanical or engineering knowledge so that you can carry out the necessary safety checks on the train.

You must be happy working alone for long periods of time.

Working conditions

You will usually work 35–40 hours per week on a shift system, which will include early morning, late night, and weekend work. Overtime is commonly available, and part time work can be an option.

Occasionally you may need to stay overnight at a destination if it is a long way from home, although this is more common for freight train drivers than those providing passenger services.

You will usually work alone, operating the train from the driver's cab. You may occasionally have company in the form of a driver inspector or trainee driver.

Future prospects

Most train drivers are employed by a TOC, of which there are 24 in the UK. These consist of passenger operators, light rail companies that provide underground services, freight companies, and engineering supply organisations.

With experience, you could become a trainer or an inspector of other drivers. Your company would probably fund your studies towards gaining a professional qualification in this area.

It may also be possible to move into a management role within your company or the rail sector.

Advantages/disadvantages

It can be very peaceful and pleasant driving through the British countryside on journeys.

Qualifications and courses

Although there are no set qualifications for entry to train as a driver, almost all train operating companies (TOCs) look for candidates with 5 GCSEs/S grades (A-C/1–3) or equivalent, including English, maths and a science subject.

You will need to be 21 years of age before you are legally allowed to train as a driver, but you can build up rail-related experience from the age of 16 working within a station, and from 18 onboard trains. This way, you can gain beneficial experience of dealing with railway passengers and understand how the industry works prior to applying as a trainee driver.

When you apply, you will need to pass a series of tests in order to assess your suitability. These include operating hand and foot controls, concentration, basic mechanical knowledge, and staying calm under pressure. You will also need to pass a medical assessment that will encompass fitness, hearing, eyesight and colour vision.

Once you have gained a position as a trainee driver, you will undergo 9–18 months of training prior to becoming a qualified driver. This will take the form of both classroom-based learning, and practical experience of driving trains.

You may have to work nights and weekends on a fairly regular basis.

It can get quite lonely being on your own in the driver's cab for long periods of time.

Money guide

Starting salaries for trainee drivers are usually about £18,000.

Once you are fully qualified, this should rise to £25,000.

With 5–7 years' experience, you could earn £35,000. If you work on mainline/high-speed passenger services, this could increase to £40,000.

Related opportunities

- Train Conductor p625
- Signalling Technician p618
- Large Goods Vehicle Driver/Driver's Mate p606
- Van Driver p628

Further information

The National Rail website provides details of individual TOCs

www.nationalrail.co.uk

City & Guilds

www.cityandguilds.com/myperfectjob

Organisation Profile

Passenger transport provides a wide range of job opportunities. Below are just a few people's stories.

James – Aircraft Dispatcher at Birmingham Airport

James works as part of a team responsible for coordinating activities that make sure that flights are prepared ready for the next departure as quickly and efficiently as possible. He also has to make sure that all work is carried out safely and that the flight meets any required regulations and rules to take off.

"I have to make sure that we have correctly calculated the weights of aircraft, taking into account passengers and luggage, and help to work out how much fuel is required. It's a big pressure to make sure it's all right, but very exciting knowing that you are helping people make journeys all over the world."

Jacqueline – Train Driver in Scotland

Becoming a train driver isn't easy and requires a lot of training, which can be intense and challenging. Most people move into driving from another rail-related job, be it customer service (such as station staff or train crew) or engineering. Jacqui drives on several routes, including local services and high speed cross country routes.

"The work can be lonely, you can be in the cab of your train for very long periods on your own, but at the same time it's interesting as no one day is the same, you can face different challenges. You've got to be able to think fast, but if you do your job, and do it well, then you can really get on in the rail industry."

Dan – Bus Engineer in Bristol

Dan maintains a fleet of buses, making sure that they are road-worthy and safe. He carries out checks and fault finding and can work on areas of a bus from replacing lights and batteries to fixing brakes and exhausts and can also use high tech equipment to carry out diagnostic tests.

"I've always been interested in vehicles and grabbed at the chance to do an apprenticeship in engineering. I like the detail I have to work in, and also the feeling of making a bus engine run efficiently when it wasn't working well before. You get to learn off your mentors too, as most garages work in teams, and people can work their way up."

Alex – Transport Planner in Cardiff

Working as a transport planner provides opportunities to influence transport systems, their infrastructure and how they are used. Alex's job as a transport planner involves undertaking surveys, analysing data and drawing up designs. It is important that she understands a wide range of issues that can affect transport including the environment, health and safety and social inclusion.

"In my job you can influence how systems work – I get great satisfaction from seeing through projects to the end and making a positive impact with them. In this job you can get a variety of work; and this encourages you to develop yourself and your career."

For more information visit www.careersinpassengertransport.org

VAN DRIVER

What the work involves

- You could be responsible for the safe transportation and delivery of a variety of goods, including food and drink, parcels, furniture, and domestic appliances.

- You will be loading and unloading goods from your vehicle, and making sure that your load is secure prior to starting on your journey. You will also be responsible for ensuring that your van is well maintained and road worthy.

- You will need to organise your own delivery schedule in order to meet strict distribution times each day.

The type of person suited to this work

You will need to be an extremely competent driver, and hold a current driving licence.

You should have a polite manner in order to build good relationships with colleagues and customers.

Good map reading and navigational skills are helpful for finding your way round new and unfamiliar areas on a delivery.

You should be physically fit, as you may need to load and unload heavy items from your van.

You will need to be accurate and methodical in order to ensure that all paperwork involved in the delivery process is correctly completed and filed.

Working conditions

You will usually work 35–40 hours per week, and this may encompass shift work over evenings and weekends, or could be limited to deliveries within standard working hours. Part time work is often available.

You may work on your own or with another person who will help navigate and plan your route, and assist with loading and unloading goods.

You will spend the majority of your time in the van, and will have to drive and meet time-restricted schedules no matter what the weather. You may have to wear a uniform.

Future prospects

The rise of internet shopping has resulted in an increase in opportunities for van drivers, so job prospects are good.

There is demand for drivers all over the UK, so you could work anywhere although most opportunities are found in larger towns and cities.

You could work for a variety of companies, including retail, delivery and supermarkets, or you could opt for self-employment.

Advantages/disadvantages

Part time and flexible hours are available so you can fit work around other commitments. There are also good opportunities

Qualifications and courses

No specific academic qualifications are required for van drivers, but some employers prefer candidates with some GSCEs (A-E) or equivalent, including English and maths.

You will need to hold an appropriate driving licence to work as a van driver. Usually, a regular driving licence that entitles you to drive vehicles weighing up to 3.5 tonnes is all that is required. You may also find holding a licence for category C1 useful as it will allow you to drive vehicles that weigh between 3.5 and 7.5 tonnes.

If you plan to work for a company that transports large sums of money or valuable items, you will also need an SIA licence. This can be obtained on completion of the National Open College Network (NOCN) Level 2 Award in cash and valuables transit.

Apprenticeships may also be available for entrants aged 16–24.

for self-employed drivers, so you can plan your own work schedule.

You will be providing a valuable service to people, either delivering food or appliances to their homes, or transporting parcels or money safely around the UK.

Driving in traffic all day can be stressful and tiring.

Money guide

Starting salaries for full time van drivers are usually around £11,000. With experience, and a record of delivering items safely and on time, this could rise to between £15,000 and £18,000. Most van drivers peak at earnings of around £22,000.

Related opportunities

- LGV Driver p606
- Taxi Driver p624
- Train Driver p626
- Chauffeur p599

Further information

National Open College Network (NOCN)
The Quadrant, Parkway Business Park, 99 Parkway Avenue, Sheffield S9 4WG
0114 227 0500; www.nocn.org.uk; nocn@nocn.org.uk

Driving Standards Agency
Stanley House, 56 Talbot Street, Nottingham NG1 5GU
0115 901 2500; www.dsa.gov.uk or for specific Driver CPC information www.drivercpc.org

www.cityandguilds.com/myperfectjob

WAREHOUSE WORKER/ MANAGER

What the work involves

Manager

- You will be in overall charge of the warehouse, responsible for maintaining stock levels, storing the goods safely and in the right condition, and dispatching them onwards when needed.

- Managing a team of staff, and making sure that essential health and safety training is taking place, will be part of your role.

- You will use a computer to monitor stock levels and orders, and to check the times when deliveries are due in and dispatches due out of your warehouse.

Worker

- You will be responsible for checking a delivery or dispatch to make sure that the goods are in the right condition and quantity.

- Once you have approved the delivery or dispatch, you will input details into a hand-held computer terminal.

- If trained you may drive a lift truck, or if not you may help to move or pack the goods (for example, helping to load lorries to make the best use of space).

The type of person suited to this work

Warehouses often store valuable stock – such as medical supplies or audio-visual equipment – so you will need to be honest and security conscious.

You will also need to be a team player because getting the goods in and out of the warehouse quickly but safely is a team task. Warehouses can be dangerous places, because of the use of machinery to move and stack goods at heights, so you should be able to follow or put in place safety regulations.

You should enjoy working with computers. Deliveries and dispatches are recorded and monitored on the warehouse's computer tracking system – so your working day is likely to be planned by a computer.

Working conditions

Protective clothing may be needed when warehousing some goods.

You will work a 37–40-hour week but this could include shift work or overtime at busy periods.

Manager

You will work both at a computer in an office and out in the warehouse.

Worker

You will spend a lot of time on your feet; you may also need to lift heavy items and climb ladders.

Future prospects

Warehouses are owned and managed by companies who either store large quantities of goods for their own businesses, or charge customers to store goods for them. The biggest employers of warehouse staff are retail and manufacturing companies, logistics and distribution service providers and specialist freight and haulage companies. Opportunities are increasing for warehouse management work.

Some warehouses are small, for example the ones at the rear of supermarkets, and only employ a few warehouse workers.

Others can be the size of several football pitches and employ both management and workers.

Warehouses are becoming more computerised and some of the heavier work is being automated. This is likely to change the job in the future. Some warehouses will have fewer operatives and some are already 'lights out' warehouses with no human workers at operative level.

Manager

There are good opportunities for promotion either by moving to a larger warehousing operation or into general management.

Worker

With experience you can become a team leader or supervisor, or with additional qualifications move into warehouse management.

Advantages/disadvantages

Warehouse work can be stressful as goods often need to be shipped out quickly – they may only be stored for a few hours!

You can get a brilliant feeling of team spirit from working together to get a job done on time.

The work can peak at certain times of the year such as Christmas, but many workers appreciate overtime pay, especially at that time of year.

Money guide

Manager

Starting pay is £16,000–£18,500 per year. Experienced managers can earn up to £30,000 with experience (up to £40,000+ with large companies).

Worker

Starting pay is about £12,000, rising with experience to £17,500.

Team leaders can earn up to £24,500.

Some employers offer performance bonus schemes in addition to extra for night shifts.

Transport and Logistics

CRCI: WG
CLCI: YAT

Related opportunities

- Airport Baggage Handler p597
- Distribution Manager p602
- Freight Forwarder p604
- Lift Truck Operator p607

Further information

Skills for Logistics
14 Warren Yard, Warren Farm Office Village,
Milton Keynes MK12 5NW
01908 313360; www.skillsforlogistics.org

Chartered Institute of Logistics and Transport
Logistics and Transport Centre, Earlstree Court,
Earlstree Road, Corby NN17 4XQ
01536 740104; www.ciltuk.org.uk

United Kingdom Warehousing Association
Walter House, 418–422 Strand, London WC2R 0PT
020 7836 5522; www.ukwa.org.uk

www.cityandguilds.com/myperfectjob

Qualifications and courses

Manager

There are no specific entry qualifications for this job. It is possible to work as a warehouse worker, gain NVQ/SVQ qualifications or the professional qualifications of the Chartered Institute of Logistics and Transport (CILT), and progress to supervisory or management roles. Good management, ITC, literacy and numeracy skills can be an advantage.

Some employers may require qualifications such as A levels/H grades. Increasingly, companies recruit graduates. Degrees are on offer in related subjects such as logistics and supply chain management. The usual minimum entry requirements for a degree course are 2 A levels/3 H grades or equivalent.

People working in the industry can study for the CILT's professional qualifications part time at college or by distance learning. The Introductory Certificate in Logistics and Transport is aimed at new entrants and the standard Certificate is aimed at supervisors and first line managers. The Professional Diploma is intended for middle managers, including recent graduates, and fulfils the requirements for membership of the Institute. New or aspiring senior warehouse managers can take the CILT Advanced Diploma or study for an MSc in Logistics. The MSc is offered by Aston University in partnership with CILT, and takes 3 years by distance learning.

Worker

There are no minimum entry requirements for this job. You will need to be physically fit, and a medical may be required.

Apprenticeships/Skillseekers may be available for those aged 16–24. This leads to NVQ/SVQ Levels 2 and 3 in Distribution, Storage and Warehousing Operations. Three GCSEs/S grades may be required.

Most training takes place on the job. The National Proficiency Tests Council's Level 2 Certificate of Competence in Fork Lift Truck Operations may be offered by employers.

ENTRY
1
LEVEL

INDEX OF LEVELS

Level 1

Index

Level 2

Index

Index

Level 5

Level 6

Level 7

Index

INDEX

Index